Contemporary Political Philosophy

BLACKWELL PHILOSOPHY ANTHOLOGIES

Each volume in this outstanding series provides an authoritative and comprehensive collection of the essential primary readings from philosophy's main fields of study. Designed to complement the *Blackwell Companions to Philosophy* series, each volume represents an unparalleled resource in its own right, and will provide the ideal platform for course use.

Contemporary Political Philosophy
An Anthology

Second Edition

Edited by

Robert E. Goodin and Philip Pettit

Blackwell Publishing

Editorial material and organization © 1997, 2006 by Blackwell Publishing Ltd

BLACKWELL PUBLISHING
350 Main Street, Malden, MA 02148–5020, USA
9600 Garsington Road, Oxford OX4 2DQ, UK
550 Swanston Street, Carlton, Victoria 3053, Australia

First edition published 1997
Second edition published 2006 by Blackwell Publishing Ltd

5   2008

Library of Congress Cataloging-in-Publication Data

Contemporary political philosophy: an anthology /
edited by Robert E. Goodin and Philip Pettit.–2nd ed.
      p. cm. – (Blackwell philosophy anthologies)
   Includes bibliographical references and index.
   ISBN: 978-1-4051-3064-6 (hardback: alk. paper)
   ISBN: 978-1-4051-3065-3 (pbk.: alk.paper)
   1. Political science—Philosophy. I. Goodin, Robert E. II. Pettit, Philip, 1945-   III. Series.

JA71.C578 2006
320—dc22

                                                    2005001283

A catalogue record for this title is available from the British Library.

Set in 9 on 11pt Ehrhardt
by SPI Publisher Services, Pondicherry, India
Printed and bound in Singapore
by C.O.S. Printers Pte Ltd

For further information on
Blackwell Publishing, visit our website:
www.blackwellpublishing.com

Contents

Contents

Contents

Preface

The essays contained in this collection represent what seem to us to be canonical texts in contemporary political philosophy. But they only represent the contemporary canon, they do not exhaust it. Although this collection is two or perhaps three times the size of most, we nevertheless found that we had space for only a sample of the very many more texts and topics that we would like to have included.

The collection is deliberately designed as a companion to our earlier *Companion to Contemporary Political Philosophy* (Oxford: Blackwell, 1993). We attempted to retain something of the same flavour in this collection, much the same scope of substantive concerns and much the same diversity of analytic styles. Inevitably, though, there is so much more surveyed in the *Companion's* many chapters than can be reprinted here. Interested readers are referred back to the *Companion* not only to situate the texts in the present collection but also for further readings and whole other sets of concerns.

The *Companion* as a whole, and our own introduction to it, serves effectively as a preface to this collection. So we will not expound at length here upon our views as to the nature of the political philosophical enterprise. Let this one comment suffice. We have tried to select and organize the texts included here so as to show political philosophy as it truly is: as a set of ongoing conversations and disputations, arguments and debates.

Robert E. Goodin
Philip Pettit

Preface to the Second Edition

The feedback on the first edition of the *Anthology* has been very gratifying and we hope that this revised collection will prove equally appealing. We benefited greatly from the advice of a number of friends and colleagues in revising the collection but we should mention in particular those who provided detailed comments on our proposals: Peter Baumann, Graham Finlay, Mark Fielding, Colin Farrelly, Noelle McAfee, Christopher Morris, William Edmundson, Peter Lindsay, Benjamin Gregg, Michael Gorr, Avi Tucker, and Chuck Beitz.

Robert E. Goodin
Philip Pettit

Acknowledgments

We are grateful to many friends and colleagues, as well as Blackwell's formal referees, for advice as to what was useful in and what was lacking from the first edition of this anthology.

The editors and publisher gratefully acknowledge the permission granted to reproduce the copyright material in this book:

Quentin Skinner, "The State" from *Political Innovation and Conceptual Change*, edited by Terence Ball, James Farr, and Russell L. Hanson (Cambridge: Cambridge University Press, 1989), pp. 90–131. Copyright © 1989 by Cambridge University Press. Reprinted by permission of Cambridge University Press.

James C. Scott, "State Simplification" from *Journal of Political Philosophy* 3 (1995): 191–234. Reprinted by permission of Blackwell Publishing Ltd.

David Gauthier, "The Social Contract as Ideology" from *Philosophy and Public Affairs* 6 (1977): 130–64. Reprinted by permission of Blackwell Publishing Ltd.

Carole Pateman, "The Fraternal Social Contract" from *The Disorder of Women* (Cambridge: Polity Press, 1980), pp. 33–57. Copyright © 1980 by Carole Pateman. Reprinted by permission of Polity Press and also with the kind permission of the author.

Charles Taylor, "Invoking Civil Society" from *Philosophical Arguments* (Cambridge, MA: Harvard University Press, 1995), pp. 204–24, 303. Copyright © 1995 by Charles Taylor. Originally a working paper for Center for Psychological Studies, Chicago, 1990. Reprinted with permission of Harvard University Press and also with the kind permission of the author.

Jürgen Habermas, "The Public Sphere" from *Jürgen Habermas on Society and Politics: A Reader*, edited by Steven Seidman (Boston, MA: Beacon Press, 1989). Copyright © 1989 by Beacon Press. Reprinted by permission of Beacon Press, Boston.

Robert A. Dahl, "Procedural Democracy" from *Philosophy, Politics and Society*, 5th series, edited by Peter Laslett and James S. Fishkin (Oxford: Blackwell, 1979), pp. 97–133. Reprinted by permission of Blackwell Publishing Ltd.

Cass R. Sunstein, "Preferences and Politics" from *Philosophy and Public Affairs* 20 (1991): 3–34. Copyright © 1991. Reprinted by permission of Blackwell Publishing Ltd.

Jon Elster, "The Market and the Forum" from *Foundations of Social Choice Theory*, edited by Jon Elster and Aanund Hylland (Cambridge: Cambridge University Press, 1986), pp. 102–132. Copyright © Cambridge University Press. Reprinted by permission of Cambridge University Press.

Joshua Cohen, "Deliberation and Democratic Legitimacy" from *The Good Polity*, edited by Alan

Hamlin and Philip Pettit (Oxford: Blackwell, 1989), pp. 17–34. Reprinted by permission of Blackwell Publishing Ltd.

Anne Phillips, "Dealing with Difference: A Politics of Ideas or a Politics of Presence?" from *Constellations* 1 (1994): 74–91. Reprinted by permission of Blackwell Publishing Ltd.

John Rawls, "Justice as Fairness", originally published in *Philosophical Review* 67 (1958): 164–94.

Robert Nozick, "Distributive Justice" from *Anarchy, State and Utopia* (Oxford: Blackwell, 1974), pp. 149–82, 213–31. Copyright © 1974 by Basic Books Inc. Reprinted by permission of Blackwell Publishing Ltd.

Brian Barry, "Chance, Choice and Justice" from *Liberty and Justice* (Oxford: Oxford University Press, 1989), pp. 142–58 Reprinted by permission of Oxford University Press.

Michael J. Sandel, "The Procedural Republic and the Unencumbered Self" from *Political Theory* 12 (1984): 81–96. Copyright © 1984 by Sage Publications, Inc. Reprinted by permission of Sage Publications, Inc.

Iris Marion Young, "Polity and Group Difference: A Critique of the Ideal of Universal Citizenship" from *Ethics* 99 (1989): 250–74. Copyright © 1989 by the University of Chicago Press. Reprinted by permission of the University of Chicago Press.

Jeremy Waldron, "Superseding Historic Justice" from *Ethics* 103 (1992): 4–28. Copyright © 1992 by the University of Chicago Press. Reprinted by permission of the University of Chicago Press.

H. L. A. Hart, "Are There Any Natural Rights?" originally published in *Philosophical Review* 64 (1955): 175–91.

Ronald Dworkin, "Taking Rights Seriously," originally published in *New York Review of Books* (December 18, 1970), 184–205. Reprinted by the kind permission of the author.

Henry Shue, "Basic Rights" from *Basic Rights* (Princeton: Princeton University Press, 1980), pp. 35–46, 51–64. Copyright © 1980 by Princeton University Press. Reprinted by permission of Princeton University Press.

Judith Jarvis Thomson, "A Defense of Abortion" from *Philosophy and Public Affairs* 1 (1971): 47–66. Reprinted by permission of Blackwell Publishing Ltd.

Will Kymlicka, "Justice and Minority Rights" from *Multicultural Citizenship* (Oxford: Clarendon Press, 1995), pp. 26–33, 108–30. Copyright © 1995 by Will Kymlicka. Reprinted by permission of Oxford University Press.

Charles R. Beitz, "Human Rights as a Common Concern" from *American Political Science Review* 95 (2001): 269–82. Copyright © 2001 American Political Science Association. Published by Cambridge University Press. Reprinted by permission of Cambridge University Press.

Isaiah Berlin, "Two Concepts of Liberty," originally published in *Four Essays on Liberty* (Oxford: Clarendon Press, 1969), pp. 121–54, 169–72. Copyright © Isaiah Berlin 1958. Reproduced with permission of Curtis Brown Group Ltd, London, on behalf of the Isaiah Berlin Literary Trust.

Charles Taylor, "What's Wrong with Negative Liberty?" from *The Idea of Freedom*, edited by Alan Ryan (Oxford: Oxford University Press, 1979), pp. 175–93. Copyright © 1979 by Charles Taylor. Reprinted by the kind permission of the author.

Quentin Skinner, "A Third Concept of Liberty" from *Proceedings of the British Academy* 117 (2001): 237–68. Copyright © 2001 by Quentin Skinner. Reprinted by the kind permission of the author.

G. A. Cohen, "Are Freedom and Equality Compatible?" originally published as two articles: "Self-ownership, World Ownership and Equality," from *Justice and Equality Here and Now*, edited by Frank S. Lucash (Ithaca, NY: Cornell University Press, 1986), pp. 108–35. Copyright © 1986 by Cornell University. Used by permission of Cornell University Press; and "Self-ownership, World Ownership and Equality: Part II" from *Marxism and Liberalism*, edited by Ellen Frankel Paul, Fred D. Miller Jr, Jeffrey Paul, and John

Ahrens (Oxford: Basil Blackwell, 1986), pp. 77–96. Reprinted by permission of Blackwell Publishing Ltd.

William A. Galston, "Liberal Pluralism and Constitutional Democracy: The Case of Freedom of Conscience," from *Philosophy and Public Policy Quarterly* 24, no. 3 (Summer 2004): 21–7. Reprinted by the kind permission of the author.

Jeremy Waldron, "Homelessness and the Issue of Freedom," from *UCLA Law Review* 39 (1991): 295–324. Reprinted by the kind permission of the author.

Bernard Williams, "The Idea of Equality," from *Philosophy, Politics and Society*, Series 2, edited by Peter Laslett and W. G. Runciman (Oxford: Blackwell, 1979), pp. 110–31. Reprinted by permission of Blackwell Publishing Ltd.

Derek Parfit, "Equality and Priority," from *Ratio* 10 (1997): 202–21. Reprinted by permission of Blackwell Publishing Ltd.

Amartya Sen, "Equality of What?" from *The Tanner Lectures on Human Values*, edited by S. M. McMurrin (Cambridge: Cambridge University Press, 1980), pp. 195–220. Reprinted courtesy of Utah Press and the Trustees of the Tanner Lectures on Human Values.

Michael Walzer, "Complex Equality," from *Spheres of Justice* (Oxford: Martin Robertson, 1983), pp. 3–30. Reprinted by permission of Blackwell Publishing Ltd.

Martha Minow, "Justice Engendered," from *Harvard Law Review* 101 (1987): 10–95. Copyright © 1987 by Harvard Law Review Association. Reprinted by permission of Harvard Law Review and the author

Richard J. Arneson, "Egalitarianism and the Undeserving Poor," from *Journal of Political Philosophy* 5 (December 1997): 327–50. Reprinted by permission of Blackwell Publishing Ltd.

Michel Foucault, "Power, Right, Truth," from *Power/Knowledge*, edited by Colin Gordon (Brighton: Harvester, 1980), pp. 92–108. Copyright © 1972, 1975, 1976, 1977 by Michel Foucault. Reprinted by permission of Prentice Hall (part of Pearson Inc.).

Richard A. Wasserstrom, "Racism, Sexism, and Preferential Treatment," originally published in *UCLA Law Review* 24 (1977): 581–622. Copyright © 1977 by Richard Wasserstrom. Reprinted by the kind permission of the author

Susan Moller Okin, "Mistresses of Their Own Destiny: Group Rights, Gender, and Realistic Rights of Exit," from *Ethics* 112 (2002): 205–30. Reprinted by permission of University of Chicago Press.

Nancy Fraser and Linda Gordon, "Dependency Demystified: Inscriptions of Power in a Keyword of the Welfare State," from *Social Politics* 1 (1994): 4–31. Copyright © 1994 by Nancy Fraser and Linda Gordon. Reprinted by the kind permission of the authors.

Peter Jones, "Bearing the Consequences of Belief," from *Journal of Political Philosophy* 2 (March 1994): 24–43. Reprinted by permission of Blackwell Publishing Ltd.

G. E. M. Anscombe, "Just War: The Case of World War II," first published in *Ethics, Religion and Politics* (Minneapolis: University of Minnesota Press, 1981), pp. 62–81. Reprinted by permission of Mary Gormally.

Avishai Margalit and Joseph Raz, "National Self-determination," from *Journal of Philosophy* LXXXVII (September 9, 1990): 439–61. Reprinted by kind permission of the authors.

John Rawls, "The Law of Peoples," from *On Human Rights: Oxford Amnesty Lectures*, edited by Stephen Shute and Susan Hurley (New York: Basic Books, 1993), pp. 41–82. Copyright © 1993 by Basic Books Inc. Reprinted by permission of Basic Books, a member of Perseus Books, LLC.

David Luban, "The Romance of the Nation-State," from *Philosophy and Public Affairs* 9, no. 2 (1980): 160–81. Reprinted by permission of Blackwell Publishing Ltd.

Acknowledgments

David Held, "Democracy: From City-states to a Cosmopolitan Order?" from *Political Studies* 40 Special Issue (1992): 10–39. Copyright © 1992 by Political Studies Association. Reprinted by permission of Blackwell Publishing Ltd.

Robert O. Keohane, "Global Governance and Democratic Accountability," from *Taming Globalization*, edited by David Held and Mathias Koenig-Archibugi (Cambridge: Polity Press, 2003), pp. 130–59. Reprinted by permission of Polity Press.

Thomas Pogge, "Migration and Poverty," from *Citizenship and Exclusion*, edited by Veit Bader (London: Macmillan, 1997), pp. 12–27. Reprinted by permission of Palgrave Macmillan.

Brain Barry, "Humanity and Justice in Global Perspective," originally published in *Nomos XXIV: Ethics, Economics and the Law*, edited by J. R. Pennock and J. W. Chapman (New York: New York University Press, 1982), pp. 219–52. Reprinted with permission of New York University Press.

PART I

State and Society

1

The State

Quentin Skinner

I

In the Preface to *De cive*, his first published work on government, Hobbes describes his own project as that of undertaking "a more curious search into the rights of states and duties of subjects."[1] Since that time, the idea that the confrontation between individuals and states furnishes the central topic of political theory has come to be almost universally accepted. This makes it easy to overlook the fact that, when Hobbes issued his declaration, he was self-consciously setting a new agenda for the discipline he claimed to have invented, the discipline of political science. His suggestion that the duties of subjects are owed to the state, rather than to the person of a ruler, was still a relatively new and highly contentious one. So was his implied assumption that our duties are owed exclusively to the state, rather than to a multiplicity of jurisdictional authorities, local as well as national, ecclesiastical as well as civil in character. So, above all, was his use of the term "state" to denote this highest form of authority in matters of civil government.

Hobbes's declaration can thus be viewed as marking the end of one distinct phase in the history of political theory as well as the beginning of another and more familiar one. It announces the end of an era in which the concept of public power had been treated in far more personal and charismatic terms. It points to a simpler and altogether more abstract vision, one that has remained with us ever since and has come to be embodied in the use of such terms as *état, stato, staat*, and state.[2] My aim in what follows will be to sketch the historical circumstances out of which these linguistic and conceptual transformations first arose.

II

As early as the fourteenth century, the Latin term *status* – together with such vernacular equivalents as *estat, stato*, and state – can already be found in general use in a variety of political contexts. During this formative period these terms appear to have been employed predominantly to refer to the state or standing of rulers themselves.[3] One important source of this usage was undoubtedly the rubric *De statu hominum* from the opening of Justinian's *Digest*. There the authority of Hermogenianus had been adduced for the fundamental claim that, "since all law is established for the sake of human beings, we first need to consider the *status* of such persons, before we consider anything else."[4] Following the revival of Roman Law studies in twelfth-century Italy, the word *status* came

Originally published in *Political Innovation and Conceptual Change*, edited by Terence Ball, James Farr, and Russell L. Hanson (Cambridge: Cambridge University Press, 1989), pp. 90–131. Copyright © 1989 by Cambridge University Press. Reprinted by permission of Cambridge University Press. A revised and expanded version of this chapter appears as "From the State of Princes to the Person of the State," *Visions of Politics: Renaissance Virtues* (Cambridge: Cambridge University Press, 2002), vol. 2, pp. 368–413.

in consequence to designate the legal standing of all sorts and conditions of men, with rulers being described as enjoying a distinctive "estate royal," *estat du roi*, or *status regis*.[5]

When the question of a ruler's *status* was raised, this was generally in order to emphasize that it ought to be viewed as a state of majesty, a high estate, a condition of stateliness. Within the well-established monarchies of France and England, we encounter this formula in chronicles and official documents throughout the latter half of the fourteenth century. Froissart, for example, recalls in book I of his *Chroniques* that when the young king of England held court to entertain visiting dignitaries in 1327, "the queen was to be seen there in an *estat* of great nobility."[6] The same usage recurs poignantly in the speech made by William Thirnyng to Richard II in 1399, in which he reminds his former sovereign "in what presence you renounced and ceased of the state of King, and of lordship and of all the dignity and worship that [be]longed thereto" (Topham *et al.* 1783: 424, col. 1).

Underlying the suggestion that a distinctive quality of stateliness "belongs" to kings was the prevailing belief that sovereignty is intimately connected with display, that the presence of majesty serves in itself as an ordering force. This was to prove the most enduring of the many features of charismatic leadership eventually subverted by the emergence of the modern concept of an impersonal state.[7] As late as the end of the seventeenth century, it is still common to find political writers using the word "state" to point to a conceptual connection between the stateliness of rulers and the efficacy of their rule. As one might expect, exponents of divine-right monarchy such as Bossuet continue to speak of the *état* of *majesté* in just such terms (Bossuet 1967: 69, 72). But the same assumptions also survived even among the enemies of kingship. When Milton, for example, describes in his *History of Britain* the famous scene where Canute orders the ocean to "come no further upon my land," he observes that the king sought to give force to his extraordinary command by speaking "with all the state that royalty could put into his countenance" (Milton 1971: 365).

By the end of the fourteenth century, the term *status* had also come to be regularly used to refer to the state or condition of a realm or commonwealth.[8] This conception of the *status reipublicae* was of course classical in origin, appearing frequently in the histories of Livy and Sallust, as well as in Cicero's orations and political works.[9]

It can also be found in the *Digest*, most notably under the rubric *De institia et iure*, where the analysis opens with Ulpian's contention that law is concerned with two areas, the public and the private, and that "public law is that which pertains to the *status rei Romanae*."[10]

With the revival of Roman Law, this further piece of legal terminology also passed into general currency. It became common in the fourteenth century, both in France and England, to discuss "the state of the realm" or *estat du roilme* (Post 1964: 310–22). Speaking of the year 1389, for example, Froissart remarks that the king decided at that point "to reform the country *en bon état*, so that everyone would be contented."[11] The idea of linking the good state of a king and his kingdom soon became a commonplace. By the middle of the fifteenth century, petitioners to the English parliament regularly ended their pleas by promising the king that they would "tenderly pray God for the good estate and prosperity of your most noble person of this your noble realm."[12]

If we turn from northern Europe to the Italian city-states, we encounter the same terminology at an even earlier date. The first known advice-books addressed to *podestá* and other city-magistrates in the early years of the thirteenth century already indicate that their main concern is with the *status civitatum*, the state or condition of cities as independent political entities.[13] The anonymous *Oculus pastoralis*, perhaps written as early as the 1220s,[14] repeatedly employs the phrase,[15] as does Giovanni da Viterbo in his treatise *De regimine civitatum*,[16] completed around the year 1250.[17] By the early fourteenth century we find the same concept widely expressed in the vernacular, with writers of *Dictamina* such as Filippo Ceffi offering extensive instruction to magistrates, in the form of model speeches, on how to maintain the *stato* of the city given into their charge (Giannardi 1942: 27, 47, 48, etc.).

Discussing the state or standing of such communities, the point these writers generally wish to stress is that chief magistrates have a duty to maintain their cities in a good, happy, or prosperous state.[18] This ideal of aspiring to uphold the *bonus* or even the *optimus status reipublicae* was again Roman in origin, and was largely taken over from Cicero and Seneca by the thirteenth-century writers of advice-books.[19] The author of the *Oculus pastoralis* frequently speaks of the need to uphold the happy, advantageous, honorable and prosperous *status* of one's *civitas*.[20] Giovanni da

Viterbo likewise insists on the desirability of maintaining the *bonus status* of one's community,[21] while Filippo Ceffi writes with equal confidence in the vernacular of the obligation to preserve a city "in a good and peaceful *stato*," in a "good *stato* and complete peace" (Giannardi 1942: 28).

These writers also provide the first complete restatement of the classical view of what it means for a *civitas* or *respublica* to attain its best state.[22] This requires, they all agree, that our magistrates should follow the dictates of justice in all their public acts, as a result of which the common good will be promoted, the cause of peace upheld, and the general happiness of the people assured. This line of reasoning was later taken up by Aquinas and his numerous Italian disciples at the end of the thirteenth century. Aquinas himself presents the argument at several points in his *Summa*, as well as in his commentary on Aristotle's *Politics*. A judge or magistrate, he declares, "has charge of the common good, which is justice," and ought therefore to act in such a way "as to exhibit a good aspect from the point of view of the *status* of the community as a whole."[23] But the same line of reasoning can already be found a generation earlier in advice-books for city-magistrates. Giovanni da Viterbo, for example, develops precisely the same theory of the *optimus status* in his treatise *De regimine civitatum*, while Brunetto Latini reiterates and enlarges on Giovanni's arguments in his chapter "Dou gouvernement des cités" at the end of his encyclopedic *Livres dou trésor* of 1266.[24]

This vision of the *optimus status reipublicae* later became central to *quattrocento* humanist accounts of the well-ordered political life. When Giovanni Campano (1427–77)[25] analyzes the dangers of faction in his tract *De regendo magistratu*, he declares that "there is nothing I count more unfavourable than this to the *status* and safety of a *respublica*."[26] If the good *status* of a community is to be preserved, he goes on, all individual or factional advantage must be subordinated to the pursuit of justice and "the common good of the city as a whole" (Campano 1502, fo. xxxxvii^{r-v}). Filippo Beroaldo (1453–1505) endorses the same conclusions in a treatise to which he actually gave the title *De optimo statu*. The best state, he argues, can be attained only if our ruler or leading magistrate "remains oblivious of his own good, and ensures that he acts in everything he does in such a way as to promote the public benefit."[27]

Finally, the Erasmian humanists imported precisely the same values and vocabulary into north-ern Europe in the early years of the sixteenth century. Erasmus (1974:162) himself contrasts the *optimus* with the *pessimus reipublicae status* in his *Institutio* of 1516, and argues that "the happiest *status* is reached when there is a prince whom everyone obeys, when the prince obeys the laws and when the laws answer to our ideals of honesty and equity."[28] His younger contemporary Thomas Starkey (1948: 63; also 65, 66–7) offers a very similar account in his *Dialogue* of what constitutes "the most prosperous and perfect state that in any country, city or town, by policy and wisdom may be established and set." And in More's *Utopia* the figure of Hythloday, the traveller to "the new island of Utopia," likewise insists that because the Utopians live in a society where the laws embody the principles of justice, seriously aim at the common good, and in consequence enable the citizens to live "as happily as possible," we are justified in saying that the Utopians have in fact attained the *optimus status reipublicae* – which is of course the title of More's famous book (More 1965: 244).

III

I now turn to consider the process by which the above usages – all of them common throughout late-medieval Europe – eventually gave rise to recognizably modern discussions of the concept of the state. I shall argue that, if we wish to trace both the acquisition of this concept and at the same time its expression by means of such terms as *status*, *stato* or state, we ought not to focus our main attention – as medieval historians have commonly done – on the evolution of legal theories about the *status* of kings in the fourteenth and fifteenth centuries.[29] It was rare even among civil lawyers of that period to use the Latin word *status* without qualification,[30] and virtually unheard of for political writers to employ such a barbarism at all. Even when we find *status* being used in such contexts, moreover, it is almost always evident that what is at issue is simply the state or standing of the kind or his kingdom, not in the least the modern idea of the state as a separate apparatus of government.

I shall instead suggest that, in order to investigate the process by which the term *status* and its vernacular equivalents first came to acquire their modern range of reference, we need to keep our main attention fixed on the early histories and advice-books for magistrates I have already singled out, as well as on the later mirror-for-princes literature to which they eventually gave rise. It was within these traditions of practical political reasoning, I shall argue, that the terms *status* and *stato* were first consistently used in new and significantly extended ways.[31]

These genres of political literature were in turn a product of the new and distinctive forms of political organization that arose within late-medieval Italy. Beginning in the early years of the twelfth century, a growing number of cities throughout the *Regnum Italicum* succeeded in acquiring for themselves the status of autonomous and self-governing republics.[32] It is true that these communities later proved unstable, and were widely reorganized in the course of the next century under the stronger and more centralized regimes of hereditary princes (Waley 1978: 128–40). But even in this later period, the great city-republics of Florence and Venice managed to preserve their traditional hostility to the idea of hereditary monarchy, and thereby carried the ideals of participatory republican government into the era of the high Renaissance.[33]

The development of these new political formations posed a new series of questions about the concept of political authority. One of the most pressing concerned the type of regime best suited to ensuring that an independent *civitas* or *respublica* is able to remain in its *optimus status* or best state. Is it wisest to opt for the rule of an hereditary *signore*, or ought one to retain an elective system of government based on a *podestá* or other such magistrate?

Although this question remained in contention throughout the history of Renaissance Italy, it is possible to distinguish two main phases of the debate. The earliest treatises intended for city-magistrates invariably assumed – in line with their Roman authorities – that the best state of a *civitas* can be attained only under an elective form of republican government. After the widespread usurpation of these regimes, however, by the rise of hereditary *signori* in the fourteenth century, this commitment increasingly gave way to the claim that the best means of ensuring the good standing of any political community must be to institute the rule of a wise prince, a *pater patriae*, whose actions will be governed by a desire to foster the common good and hence the general happiness of all his subjects.[34]

Building on this assumption, the writers of mirror-for-princes treatises in the Renaissance gener-ally devoted themselves to considering two related points. Their loftiest aim was to explain how a good ruler can hope to reach the characteristically princely goals of honour and glory for himself while at the same time managing to promote the happiness of his subjects.[35] But their main concern was with a far more basic and urgent question of statecraft: how to advise the new *signori* of Italy, often in highly unsettled circumstances, on how to hold on to their *status principis* or *stato del principe*, their political state or standing as effectively governing rulers of their existing territories.

As a result, the use of the term *stato* to denote the political standing of rulers, together with the discussion of how such rulers should behave if they are to manage *mantenere lo stato*, began to resound through the chronicles and political literature of fourteenth-century Italy. When Giovanni Villani, for example, speaks in his *Istorie Fiorentine* of the civic dissensions that marked the city during the 1290s, he observes that they were largely directed against *il popolo in suo stato e signoria* – against the people in their positions of political power.[36] When Ranieri Sardo in his *Cronaca Pisana* describes the accession of Gherardo d'Appiano as leader of the city in 1399, he remarks that the new *capitano* continued to enjoy the same *stato e governo* – the same political standing and governmental authority – as his father had enjoyed before him (Sardo 1845: 240–1). By the time we reach such late contributions to the mirror-for-princes literature as Machiavelli's *Il principe* of 1513, the question of what a ruler must do if he wishes to maintain his political standing had become the chief topic of debate. Machiavelli's advice is almost entirely directed at new princes who wish *tenere* or *mantenere lo stato* – who wish to maintain their positions as rulers over whatever territories they may have managed to inherit or acquire.[37]

If such a ruler is to prevent the state in which he finds himself from being altered to his disadvantage, he must clearly be able to fulfil a number of preconditions of effective government. If we now turn to consider the ways in which these preconditions were formulated and discussed in the traditions of thought I am considering, we shall find the terms *status* and *stato* employed in an increasingly extended manner to refer to these various aspects of political power.[38] As an outcome of this process, we shall eventually find these writers deploying at least some elements of a recognizably modern conception of the state.

One precondition of maintaining one's standing as a ruler is obviously that one should be able to preserve the character of one's existing regime. We accordingly find the terms *status* and *stato* being used from an early period to refer not merely to the state or condition of princes, but also to the presence of particular regimes or systems of government.

This usage in turn appears to have arisen out of the habit of employing the term *status* to classify the various forms of rule described by Aristotle. Aquinas has sometimes been credited with popularizing this development, since there are versions of his *Expositio* of Aristotle's *Politics* in which oligarchies are described as *status paucorum* and the rule of the people is identified as the *status popularis*.[39] Such usages later became widespread in humanist political thought. Filippo Beroaldo begins his *De optimo statu* with a typology of legitimate regimes, speaking of the *status popularis*, the *status paucorum* and even the *status unius* when referring to monarchy (1508, fos. xi^r and xii^v). Francesco Patrizi (1412–94) opens his *De regno* with a similar typology, one in which monarchy, aristocracy, and democracy are all characterized as types of *civilium status* or states of civil society (Patrizi 1594b: 16–17, 19, and esp. 21). Writing in the vernacular at the same period, Vespasiano da Bisticci (1421–98) likewise contrasts the rule of *signori* with the *stato populare*, while Guicciardini later invokes the same distinction in his *Discorsi* on the government of Florence (Vespasiano 1970–6, vol. I: 406; Guicciardini 1932: 274). Finally, Machiavelli used *stato* in just this fashion at a number of places in *Il principe*,[40] most notably in the opening sentence of the entire work, in which he informs us that "All the *stati*, all the dominions that have had or now have power over men either have been or are republics or principalities."[41]

By this stage, the term *stato* was also in widespread use as a way of referring simply to prevailing regimes. When Giovanni Villani, for example, notes that in 1308 "it was the members of the *parte Nera* who held control" in Florence, he speaks of the government they established as *lo stato de'Neri*.[42] When Ranieri Sardo (1845: 125) writes about the fall of the Nove in Siena in 1355, he describes the change of regime as the loss of *lo stato de'Nove*. When Vespasiano (1970–6, vol. II: 171, 173) relates how the enemies of Cosimo de'Medici succeeded in setting up a new government in 1434, he expresses the point by saying that "they were able to change *lo stato*." By the time we

reach a theorist such as Machiavelli's friend Francesco Vettori, writing in the early part of the sixteenth century, both these usages of *stato* were firmly established. Vettori employs the term not only to refer to different forms of government, but also to describe the prevailing regime in Florence that he wished to see defended.[43]

A second precondition of maintaining one's existing state as a ruler is obviously that one should suffer no loss or alteration in the range of territories given into one's charge. As a result of this further preoccupation we find the terms *status* and *stato* pressed into early service as a way of referring to the general area over which a ruler or chief magistrate needs to exercise control. When the author of the *Oculus pastoralis*, for example, wishes to describe the duty of chief magistrates to look after their cities and localities, he already speaks of it as a duty to promote *suos status* (Franceschi 1966: 24). When the authors of the *Gratulatio* sent to the people of Padua in 1310 wish to express the hope that the entire province may be able to live in peace, they say that they are hoping for the *tranquillitas vestri status* (Muratori 1741: 131). Similarly, when Ambrogio Lorenzetti tells us, in the verses that accompany his celebrated frescoes of 1337–9 on the theme of good government, that a *signore* must cultivate the virtues if he is to succeed in levying taxes from the areas under his command, he expresses his point by saying that this is how he must act *per governare lo stato*.[44]

These early and isolated usages first begin to proliferate in the chronicles and political treatises of the high Renaissance. When Sardo (1845: 91), for example, wants to describe how the Pisans made peace throughout their territories in 1290, what he says is that the truce extended throughout *stato suo*. When Guicciardini (1933: 298) remarks in his *Ricordi* that the French revolutionized warfare in Italy after 1494, producing a situation in which the loss of a single campaign brought with it the forfeiture of all one's lands, he describes such defeats as bringing with them the loss of *lo stato*. So too with Machiavelli, who frequently uses the term *stato* in *Il principe* in order to denote the lands or territories of a prince. He clearly has this usage in mind when he talks at length in chapter 3 about the means a wise prince must adopt if he wishes to acquire new *stati*; and he evidently has in mind the same usage when he asks in chapter 24 why so many of the princes of Italy have lost their *stati* during his own lifetime (Machiavelli 1960: 18, 22, 24, 97).

Finally, due in large measure to these Italian influences, the same usage can be found in northern Europe by the early years of the sixteenth century. Guillaume Budé, for example, in his *L'Institution du prince* of 1519, equates the range of *les pays* commanded by Caesar after his victory over Antony with the extent of *son estat*.[45] Similarly, when Thomas Starkey (1948: 167) argues in his *Dialogue* of the early 1530s that everyone living in England should be represented by a Council, he remarks that such a body "should represent the whole state." And when Lawrence Humphrey warns in his tract *The Nobles* of 1563 that evil conduct on the part of a ruler can easily set a bad example throughout an entire community, he expresses his point by saying that the vices of a ruler can easily "spread the same into the whole state" (1973, sig. Q. 8^r).

As the writers of advice-books always emphasized, however, by far the most important precondition of maintaining one's state as a prince must be to keep one's hold over the existing power structure and institutions of government within one's *regnum* or *civitas*. This in turn gave rise to the most important linguistic innovation that can be traced to the chronicles and political writings of Renaissance Italy. This took the form of an extension of the term *stato* not merely to denote the idea of a prevailing regime, but also, and more specifically, to refer to the institutions of government and means of coercive control that serve to organize and preserve order within political communities.

Vespasiano speaks on several occasions in his *Vite* of *lo stato* as just such an apparatus of political authority. In his life of Alessandro Sforza, for example, he describes how Alessandro conducted himself "in his government of *lo stato*" (Vespasiano 1970–6, vol. I: 426). In his life of Cosimo de'Medici he speaks of "those who hold positions of power in *stati*," and praises Cosimo for recognizing the difficulties of holding on to power in *uno stato* when faced by opposition from influential citizens.[46] Guicciardini in his *Ricordi* similarly asks why the Medici "lost control of *lo stato* in 1527," and later observes that they found it much harder than Cosimo had done "to maintain their hold over *lo stato di Firenze*," the institutions of Florentine government.[47] Finally, Castiglione in *Il cortegiano* likewise makes it clear that he thinks of *lo stato* as a distinct power structure which a prince needs to be able to control and dominate. He begins by remarking that the Italians "have greatly contributed to discussions about the government of *stati*," and later advises courtiers that "when it comes to questions about *stati*, it is necessary to be prudent and wise" in order to counsel one's ruler about the best way to behave.[48]

Of all the writers of advice-books, however, it is Machiavelli in *Il principe* who shows the most consistent willingness to distinguish the institutions of *lo stato* from those who have charge of them. He thinks of *stati* as having their own foundations, and speaks in particular of each *stato* as having its own particular laws, customs, and ordinances (Machiavelli 1960: 53; 76, 84). He is willing in consequence to speak of *lo stato* as an agent, describing it as capable, among other things, of choosing particular courses of action and of calling in times of crisis upon the loyalty of its citizens (Machiavelli 1960: 48, 92). This means, as Machiavelli makes clear at several points, that what he takes himself to be discussing in *Il principe* is not simply how princes ought to behave; he also sees himself as writing more abstractly about statecraft (*dello stato*) and about *cose di stato* or affairs of state (Machiavelli 1960: 21, 25).

IV

It has often been argued that, by the time we reach the usages I have just been examining, we are already dealing with a recognizably modern conception of the state as an apparatus of power whose existence remains independent of those who may happen to have control of it at any given time. Gaines Post and others have even suggested that this conception is already present in a number of allusions to the *status regni* in the fourteenth century.[49] A similar claim has been advanced with even greater confidence about the employment of the term *stato* by Machiavelli and some of his contemporaries. As Chiappelli puts it, for example, "the word bears the meaning of 'State' in its full maturity" in a majority of the places where Machiavelli uses it.[50]

These claims, however, are I think greatly exaggerated. It is usually clear – except in the small number of deeply ambiguous cases I have cited[51] – that even when *status* and *stato* are employed by these writers to denote an apparatus of government, the power structure in question is not in fact viewed as independent of those who have charge of it. As Post himself concedes, the usual aim in early legal discussions of the *status regni* was to insist on a far more personal view of political power,[52] a view that was later to be revived by the proponents of absolute monarchy in the seventeenth century.[53] According to this argument, the ruler or chief magistrate, so far from being distinguishable from the institutions of the state, is said to possess and even embody those institutions himself. The same point can in most cases be made about Machiavelli's invocations of *lo stato* in *Il principe*. When he uses the term to refer to an apparatus of government, he is usually at pains to emphasize that it needs to remain in the hands of the prince: that *lo stato*, as he often puts it, remains equivalent to *il suo stato*, the prince's own state or condition of rulership.[54]

Even after the reception of humanist ideas about *lo stato* in northern Europe, the belief that the powers of government should be treated as essentially personal in character was to die hard. It is clearly this assumption, for example, which underlies many of the quarrels between kings and parliaments over the issue of taxation in the course of the sixteenth century. The basis of the parliamentary case was generally an assertion of the form that, except in times of dire necessity, kings should be able "to live of their own."[55] They should be able, that is, to ensure that their personal revenues remain sufficient to uphold both their own kingly state and the good state of their government.

I conclude that, for all the importance of the writers I have been considering, they cannot in general be said to articulate a recognizable concept of the state with anything like complete self-consciousness. It would not perhaps be too bold to assert, indeed, that in all the discussions about the state and government of princes in the first half of the sixteenth century, there will be found scarcely any instance in which the *état, staat* or state in question is unequivocally separated from the status or standing of the prince himself.[56]

This is not to deny, however, that the crystallizing of a recognizable concept of the state was one of the legacies of Renaissance political thought. It is merely to suggest that, if we wish to follow the process by which this development took place, we need to focus not merely on the mirror-for-princes literature on which I have so far concentrated, but also on the other strand of thought about the *optimus status reipublicae* that I began by singling out. We need, that is, to turn our attention to the rival tradition of Renaissance republicanism, the tradition centring on the claim that, if there is to be any prospect of attaining the

optimus status reipublicae, we must always institute a self-governing form of republican regime.

Among the republican theorists of Renaissance Italy, the main reason given for this basic commitment was that all power is liable to corrupt. All individuals or groups, once granted sovereignty over a community, will tend to promote their own interest at the expense of the community as a whole. It follows that the only way to ensure that the laws promote the common good must be to leave the whole body of citizens in charge of their own public affairs. If their government is instead controlled by an authority external to the community itself, that authority will be sure to subordinate the good of the community to its own purposes, thereby interfering with the liberty of individual citizens to attain their chosen goals. The same outcome will be no less likely under the rule of an hereditary prince. Since he will generally seek his own ends rather than the common good, the community will again forfeit its liberty to act in pursuit of whatever goals it may wish to set itself.

This basic insight was followed up within the republican tradition in two distinct ways. It was used in the first place to justify an assertion of civic autonomy and independence, and so to defend the *libertas* of the Italian cities against external interference. This demand was initially directed against the Empire and its claims of feudal suzerainty over the *Regnum Italicum*. It was first developed by such jurists as Azo, and later by Bartolus and his followers,[57] seeking to vindicate what Bartolus described as "the *de facto* refusal of the cities of Tuscany to recognize any superior in temporal affairs."[58] But the same demand for *libertas* was also directed against all potential rivals as sources of coercive jurisdiction within the cities themselves. It was claimed on the one hand against local feudatories, who continued to be viewed, as late as Machiavelli's *Discorsi*, as the most dangerous enemies of free government (Machiavelli 1960, 1.55: 254–8). And it was even more vehemently directed against the jurisdictional pretensions of the church. The most radical response, embodied for example in Marsilius's *Defensor pacis* of 1324, took the form of insisting that all coercive power is secular by definition, and thus that the church has no right to exercise civil jurisdictions at all (Marsilius 1956, esp. II.4: 113–26). But even in the more orthodox treatises on city government, such as that of Giovanni da Viterbo, the church is still refused any say in civic affairs. The reason, as Giovanni expresses it, is that the ends of temporal and ecclesiastical authority are completely distinct (Giovanni da Viterbo 1901: 266–7). The implication is that, if the church tries to insist on any jurisdiction in temporal matters, it will simply be "putting its sickle into another man's harvest."[59]

The other way in which the basic insight of the republican tradition was developed was in the form of a positive claim about the precise type of regime we need to institute if we are to retain our *libertas* to pursue our chosen goals. The essence of the republican case was that the only form of government under which a city can hope to remain "in a free state" will be a *res publica* in the strictest sense. The community as a whole must retain the ultimate sovereign authority, assigning its rulers or chief magistrates a status no higher than that of elected officials. Such magistrates must in turn be treated not as rulers in the full sense, but merely as agents of *ministri* of justice, charged with the duty of ensuring that the laws established by the community for the promotion of its own good are properly enforced.

This contrast between the freedom of republican regimes and the servitude implied by any form of monarchical government has often been viewed as a distinctive contribution of *quattrocento* Florentine thought.[60] But the underlying assumption that liberty can be guaranteed only within a republic can already be found in many Florentine writers of the previous century.[61] Dante speaks in the *Inferno* of the move from seigneurial to republican rule as a move from tyranny to a *stato franco*, a state or condition of civic liberty (1966, xxvii. 54: 459). Ceffi repeatedly emphasizes in his *Dicerie* that the only means of guaranteeing civic *libertá* is to ensure that one's city remains under the guidance of an elected magistrate (Giannardi 1942: 32, 35, 41, 44). And Villani in his *Istorie Florentine* likewise contrasts the free *stato* of the Florentine republic with the tyranny imposed by the Duke of Athens as *signore* in 1342 (1802–3, vol. VIII:11).

It is certainly true, however, that the equation between living in a republic and living "in a free state" was worked out with the greatest assurance by the leading republican theorists of Venice and Florence in the course of the high Renaissance. Among the Venetian writers, Gasparo Contarini furnished the classic statement of the argument in his *De republica Venetorum* of 1543. Owing to the city's elective system of government, he declares, in which "a mixture of the *status* of the nobility and of the people" is maintained, "there is nothing less to be feared in the city of Venice than that the head of the republic will interfere with the *libertas* or the activities of any of the citizens."[62] Among Florentine theorists, it was of course Machiavelli in his *Discorsi* who provided the most famous version of the same argument. "It is easy to understand," as he explains at the start of book II, "whence the love of living under a free constitution springs up in peoples. For experience shows that no cities have ever increased in dominion or in riches except when they have been established in liberty."[63] The reason, he goes on, "is easy to perceive, for it is not the pursuit of individual advantage but of the common good that makes cities great, and there is no doubt that it is only under republican regimes that this ideal of the common good is followed out."[64]

From the point of view of my present argument, these commitments can now be seen to be crucial in two different ways. It is within this tradition of thought that we encounter, for the first time, a vindication of the idea that there is a distinct form of "civil" or "political" authority which is wholly autonomous, which exists to regulate the public affairs of an independent community, and which brooks no rivals as a source of coercive power within its own *civitas* or *respublica*. It is here, in short, that we first encounter the familiar understanding of the state as a monopolist of legitimate force.

This view of "civil government" was of course taken up in France and England at an early stage in their constitutional development. It underlies their hostility to the jurisdictional power of the church, culminating in France in the "Gallican" Concordat of 1516, in England in the Marsiglian assumptions underpinning the Act of Appeals in 1533. It also underlies their repudiation of the Holy Roman Empire's claim to exercise any jurisdictions within their territories, a repudiation founded on a reworking of Azo's and later Bartolus's theories of *imperium* into the celebrated dictum that *Rex in regno suo est Imperator*.

For the origins of this view of civil government, however, we need to turn back to thirteenth-century Italy, and specifically to the political literature engendered by the self-governing city-republics of that period. Writing in the 1250s, Giovanni da Viterbo already takes his theme to be the analysis of civil power, that form of power which upholds the *civium libertas* or liberty of those who live together as citizens (Giovanni da Viterbo 1901: 218). Writing only a decade later,

Brunetto Latini goes on to add that those who study the use of such power in the government of cities are studying "politics," "the noblest and the highest of all the sciences."[65] It is this neoclassical tradition to which later theorists of popular sovereignty are ultimately alluding when they speak of an autonomous area of "civil" or "political" authority, and offer to explicate what Locke (1967: 283) was to call "the true original, extent and end of civil government."

The other way in which the republican tradition contributed to crystallizing a recognizable concept of the state is of even greater importance. According to the writers I have been considering, a city can never hope to remain in a free state unless it succeeds in imposing strict conditions on its rulers and magistrates. They must always be elected; they must always remain subject to the laws and institutions of the city which elects them; they must always act to promote the common good – and hence the peace and happiness – of the sovereign body of its citizens. As a result, the republican theorists no longer equate the idea of governmental authority with the powers of particular rulers or magistrates. Rather they think of the powers of civil government as embodied in a structure of laws and institutions which our rulers and magistrates are entrusted to administer in the name of the common good. They cease in consequence to speak of rulers "maintaining their state" in the sense of maintaining their personal ascendancy over the apparatus of government. Rather they begin to speak of the *status* or *stato* as the name of that apparatus of government which our rulers may be said to have a duty to maintain.

There are already some hints of this momentous transition in the earliest treatises and *dictamina* intended for chief magistrates of city-republics. Brunetto Latini insists in his *Trésor* of 1266 that cities must always be ruled by elected officials if the *bien commun* is to be promoted. He further insists that these *sires* must follow the laws and customs of the city in all their public acts (Latini 1948, esp. pp. 392, 408, 415; 402, 412). And he concludes that such a system is indispensable not merely to maintaining such officials in a good *estat*, but also to maintaining "the *estat* of the city itself."[66] A similar hint can be found in Giovanni da Vignano's *Flore de parlare* of the 1270s. In one of his model letters, designed for the use of city ambassadors when seeking military help, he describes the government of such communities as their *stato*, and accordingly appeals for support

"in order that our good *stato* can remain in wealth, honor, greatness and peace."[67] Finally, the same hint recurs soon afterwards in Matteo dei Libri's *Arringa* on the identical theme. He sets out a very similar model speech for ambassadors to deliver, advising them to appeal for help "in order that our good *stato* may be able to remain in peace."[68]

It is only with the final flowering of Renaissance republicanism, however, that we find such usages occurring with their unequivocally modern sense. Even here, moreover, this development is largely confined to the vernacular literature. Consider, by contrast, a work such as Alamanno Rinuccini's Latin dialogue of 1479, *De libertate* (1957). This includes a classic statement of the claim that individual as well as civic liberty is possible only under the laws and institutions of a republic. But Rinuccini never stoops to using the barbarous term *status* to describe the laws and institutions involved; he always prefers to speak of the *civitas* or *respublica* itself as the locus of political authority. So too with such classic Venetian writers as Contarini in his *De republica Venetorum*. Although Contarini has a clear conception of the apparatus of government as a set of institutions independent of those who control them, he never uses the term *status* to describe them, but always prefers in a similar way to speak of their authority as embodied in the *respublica* itself.[69]

If we turn, however, to the rather less pure latinity of Francesco Patrizi's *De institutione reipublicae*, we encounter a significant development in his chapter on the duties of magistrates. He lays it down that their basic duty is to act "in such a way as to promote the common good," and argues that this above all requires them to uphold "the established laws" of the community.[70] He then summarizes his advice by saying that this is how magistrates must act "if they are to prevent the *status* of their city from being overturned."[71]

It is in the vernacular writers on republicanism of the next generation, however, that we find the term *stato* being used with something approaching full self-consciousness to express a recognizable concept of the state. Guicciardini's *Discorso* on how the Medici should act to improve their control over Florence provides a suggestive example. He advises them to gather around themselves a group of advisers who are loyal to the *stato* and willing to act on its behalf. The reason is that "every *stato*, every form of sovereign power, needs dependents" who are willing "to serve the *stato* and benefit it in everything."[72] If the Medici can manage to base their regime on such a group, they can hope to establish "the most powerful foundation for the defence of the *stato*" that anyone could aspire to set up.[73]

Finally, if we turn to Machiavelli's *Discorsi*, we find the term *stato* being used with even greater confidence to denote the same apparatus of political authority. It is of course true that Machiavelli continues largely to employ the term in the most traditional way to refer to the state or condition of a city and its way of life (Machiavelli 1960: 135, 142, 153, 192, 194, etc.). And even when he mentions *stati* in the context of describing systems of government, these usages are again largely traditional: he is generally speaking either about a species of regime,[74] or about the general area or territory over which a prince or republic holds sway.[75]

There are several occasions, however, especially in the analysis of constitutions at the start of book I, where he appears to go further. The first is when he writes in chapter 2 about the founding of Sparta. He emphasizes that the system of laws promulgated by Lycurgus remained distinct from, and served to control, the kings and magistrates entrusted with upholding the laws themselves. And he characterizes Lycurgus's achievement in creating this system by saying that "he established *uno stato* which then endured for more than eight hundred years."[76] The next instance occurs in chapter 6, where he considers whether the institutions of government in republican Rome could have been set up in such a way as to avoid the "tumults" which marked that city's political life. He puts the question in the form of asking "whether it might have been possible to establish *uno stato* in Rome" without that distinctive weakness.[77] That last and most revealing case occurs in chapter 18, where he considers the difficulty of maintaining *uno stato libero* within a corrupt city. He not only makes an explicit distinction between the authority of the magistrates under the ancient Roman republic and the authority of the laws "by means of which, together with the magistrates, the citizens were kept under control."[78] He adds in the same passage that the latter set of institutions and practices can best be described as "the order of the government or, indeed, of *lo stato*."[79]

It has often been noted that, with the reception of Renaissance republicanism in northern Europe, we begin to encounter similar assumptions among Dutch and English protagonists of "free states" in the middle of the seventeenth century.[80] It has less often been recognized that the same assumptions, couched in the same vocabulary, can already be found more than a century earlier among the first writers who attempted to introduce the ideals of civic humanism into English political thought. Thomas Starkey, for example,[81] distinguishes at several points in his *Dialogue* between the state itself and "they which have authority and rule of the state" (Starkey 1948: 61; cf. also 57, 63). It is the "office and duty" of such rulers, he goes on, to "maintain the state established in the country" over which they hold sway, "ever looking to the profit of the whole body" rather than to their own good (Starkey 1948: 64). The only method, he concludes, of "setting forward the very and true commonweal" is for everyone to recognize, rulers and ruled alike, that they are "under the same governance and state" (Starkey 1948: 71).

The same assumptions can be found soon afterwards in John Ponet's *Short Treatise of Politic Power* of 1556. He too speaks of rulers simply as the holders of a particular kind of office, and describes the duty attaching to their office as that of upholding the state. He is thus prompted to contrast the case of "an evil person coming to the government of any state" with a good ruler who will recognize that he has been "to such office called for his virtue, to see the whole state well governed and the people defended from injuries" (Ponet 1942: 98).

Finally, and perhaps most significantly, we find the same phraseology in Tudor translations of the classic Italian treatises on republican government. When Lewes Lewkenor, for example, issued his English version of Contarini's *De republica Venetorum* in 1599, he found himself in need of an English term to render Contarini's basic assumption that the authority of the Venetian government remains inherent at all times in the *civitas* or *respublica* itself, with the Doge and Council serving merely as representatives of the citizen-body as a whole. Following standard humanist usage, he generally expresses this concept by the term "commonwealth." But in speaking of the relationship between a commonwealth and its own citizens, he sometimes prefers instead to render *respublica* as "state." When he mentions the possibility of enfranchising additional citizens in Venice, he explains that this can take place in special circumstances when someone can be shown to have been especially "dutiful towards the state." And when he discusses the Venetian ideal of citizenship, he feels able to allude in even more general terms to "the citizens, by whom the state of the city is maintained" (Lewkenor 1969: 18, 33).

V

For all the undoubted importance of these classical republican theorists, however, it would still be misleading to conclude that their use of the term *stato* and its equivalents may be said to express our modern concept of the state. That concept has come to embody a doubly impersonal character.[82] We distinguish the state's authority from that of the rulers or magistrates entrusted with the exercise of its powers for the time being. But we also distinguish its authority from that of the whole society or community over which its powers are exercised. As Burke (1910: 93) remarks in his *Reflections* – articulating a view already well entrenched by that time – "society is indeed a contract," but "the state ought not to be considered as nothing better than a partnership agreement" of a similar nature. Rather the state must be acknowledged to be an entity with a life of its own; an entity which is at once distinct from both rulers and ruled and is able in consequence to call upon the allegiances of both parties.

The republican theorists embrace only one half of this doubly abstract notion of the state. On the one hand there is, I think, no doubt that they constitute the earliest group of political writers who insist with full self-consciousness on a categorical distinction between the state and those who have control of it, and at the same time express that distinction as a claim about the *status*, *stato* or state. But on the other hand they make no comparable distinction between the powers of the state and those of its citizens. On the contrary, the whole thrust of classical republican theory is directed towards an ultimate equation between the two. Although this undoubtedly yields a recognizable concept of the state – one that many Marxists and exponents of direct democracy continue to espouse – it is far from being the concept we have inherited from the more conservative mainstream of early-modern political thought.

The differences can be traced most clearly in the literature in praise of "free states." Consider again, for example, one of the earliest English works of this character, John Ponet's *Short Treatise of Politic Power*. As we have seen, Ponet makes a firm distinction between the office and person of a ruler,

and even uses the term "state" to describe the form of civil authority our rulers have a duty to uphold. But he makes no analogous distinction between the powers of the state and those of the people. Not only does he maintain that "kings, princes and governors have their authority of the people"; he also insists that ultimate political authority continues to reside at all times in "the body or state of the realm or commonwealth" (Ponet 1942: 106, 105). If kings or princes are found to be "abusing their office," it is for the body of the people to remove them, since the ultimate powers of sovereignty must always remain lodged within "the body of every state" (Ponet 1942: 105; cf. also pp. 111, 124).

The same commitment is upheld even by the most sophisticated defenders of "free states" in the seventeenth century. A good example is furnished by Milton's *Ready and Easy Way to Establish a Free Commonwealth*. If we are to maintain "our freedom and flourishing condition," he argues, and establish a government "for preservation of the common peace and liberty," it is indispensable that the sovereignty of the people should never be "transferred." It should be "delegated only" to a governing Council of State (Milton 1980: 432–3, 456). The institutions of the state are thus conceived as nothing more than a means of expressing the powers of the people in an administratively more convenient form. As Milton had earlier emphasized in *The Tenure of Kings and Magistrates*, whatever authority our rulers may possess is merely "committed to them in trust from the people, to the common good of them all, in whom the power yet remains fundamentally" at all times (Milton 1962: 202). As a result, Milton, Harrington, and other defenders of "free states" hardly ever use the term "state" when speaking of the institutions of civil government. Believing as they do that such institutions must remain under the control of the whole community if its members are to preserve their birthright of liberty, they almost always prefer the term "commonwealth" as a means of referring not merely to bodies of citizens, but also to the forms of political authority by which they must be governed if they are to remain "in a free state."[83]

The same is no less true of the "monarchomachs" and other contractarian opponents of early-modern absolutism who first rose to prominence in the later sixteenth century, especially in Holland and France. Deriving their arguments mainly from scholastic rather than classical republican sources, these writers are not generally republican in the strict sense of believing that the common good of a community can never be satisfactorily assured under a monarchical form of government. Usually they are quite explicit in claiming that (to cite Marsilius of Padua's terminology) as long as the ultimate powers of a *legislator humanus* within a *civitas* or *respublica* remain in the hands of the *populus*, there is no reason to doubt that – as Aristotle had taught – a variety of different constitutional forms may be equally capable of promoting the common good, and hence the peace and happiness of the community as a whole. Some writers within this tradition, such as Marsilius himself, in consequence exhibit little interest in whether a republican or a monarchical regime is established, save only for insisting that if the latter type is chosen, the *pars principans* must always be elected.[84] Others, including François Hotman and other French monarchomachs who followed his lead in the 1570s, remain content to assume that the body of the commonwealth will normally have a monarchical head, and similarly concentrate on hedging the institution of monarchy in such a way as to make it compatible with the liberty and ultimate sovereignty of the people.[85] Still others, such as Locke in his attack on Filmer's absolutism in the *Two Treatises of Government*, suppose there to be good reasons for preferring a monarchical form of government with a liberal allowance of personal prerogative, if only to mitigate the rigours of an undiluted theory of distributive justice by allowing a "power to act according to discretion for the public good."[86]

In common with the defenders of "free states," however, these writers still assume that the apparatus of government in a *civitas* or *respublica* amounts to nothing more than a reflection of, and a device for upholding, the sovereignty of the people. Even in a theory such as Locke's, government is still viewed simply as a trust established by the members of a community for the more effective promotion of their own good, "the peace, safety and public good of the people" (Locke 1967: 371).

The effect of this commitment, in this tradition no less than in classical republicanism, is that no effective contrast is drawn between the power of the people and the powers of the state.[87] These writers do distinguish, of course, between the apparatus of government and the authority of those who may happen to have control of it at any one time. Just as strongly as the republican theorists,

they insist on a complete separation between a ruler's person and his office, and argue that – as Locke puts it – even a supreme magistrate is merely a "public person" who is "vested with the power of the law" and charged with directing the legislative toward the attainment of the common good.[88] They still assume, however, that the range of powers a community establishes over itself when its members consent to become subjects of a civil government must ultimately be identified with its own powers as a community. As Locke (1967: 369, 385) insists, we never "deliver up" our fundamental liberties in establishing a commonwealth, but merely depute or delegate a known and indifferent judge to safeguard them more effectively on our own behalf. Although this means that we commit ourselves to setting up a complex apparatus of government, it also means that the powers of such a government can never amount to anything more than "the joint power of every member of the society." This is how it comes about, as Locke concludes, that "the community perpetually retains a supreme power" over its prince or legislative, "and must, by having deputed him, have still a power to discard him when he fails in his trust" (Locke 1967: 375, 385, 445).

As a result, these writers never find themselves tempted to use the terms *status* or state when describing the powers of civil government. When they envisage the members of a *civitas* or community instituting what Locke (1967: 434) calls a form of umpirage for the settlement of their controversies, they conceive of them not as entering a new state, but simply as setting up a new form of society – a civil or political society within which the wealth or welfare of the community can be better secured. So they continue to invoke the terms *civitas* or *respublica* to refer to the apparatus of civil government, usually translating these terms as "city" or "commonwealth." As Locke (1967: 373) explicitly states, "by commonwealth I must be understood all along" to mean "any independent community which the Latins signified by the word *civitas*, to which the word which best answers in our language is commonwealth."

If we wish, therefore, to trace the process by which the powers of the state finally came to be described as such, and seen at the same time as distinct from both the powers of the people and of their magistrates, we need at this juncture to turn to a strongly contrasting tradition of early-modern political thought. We need to turn to those writers who addressed themselves critically to the thesis of popular sovereignty we have just been considering, whether in its republican guise as a claim about "free states," or in its neoscholastic form as a claim about the inalienable rights of communities. We need to turn, that is, to those theorists whose aspirations included a desire to legitimize the more absolutist forms of government that began to develop in western Europe in the early part of the seventeenth century. It was as a by-product of their arguments, and in particular of their efforts to insist that the powers of government must be something other than a mere expression of the powers of the governed, that the concept of the state as we have inherited it was first articulated with complete self-consciousness.

Some of these counter-revolutionary theorists were mainly concerned with the radical scholastic thesis – associated in particular with Marsilius and his successors – to the effect that the *populus* and the *legislator humanus* can be equated. The repudiation of this doctrine became one of the chief polemical aims of later sixteenth-century Thomism, with Suarez's *De legibus* of 1612 containing the fullest and most influential summary of the alleged counter arguments.[89] Others were more disturbed by the monarchomach theories of popular sovereignty thrown up by the religious wars in the latter part of the sixteenth century. Bodin in particular seeks in his *Six livres de la république* of 1576 to refute the arguments of those who were claiming that, as Knolles's translation of 1606 puts it, "princes sent by providence to the human race must be thrust out of their kingdoms under a pretence of tyranny."[90] Still others were no less perturbed by the implications of the republican allegation that, as Hobbes (1968: 369) scornfully paraphrases it in *Leviathan*, "the subjects in a popular commonwealth enjoy liberty," while "in a monarchy they are all slaves." Hobbes himself, like Grotius before him, engages with this as well as with the neoscholastic thesis of popular sovereignty, and undoubtedly offers the most systematic attempt to answer the question that preoccupies all these theorists: how to vindicate an account of civil government which at once concedes the original sovereignty of the people and is at the same time absolutist in its political allegiances.

If there is one thesis by which these writers are all especially agitated, it is the suggestion that the powers of civil government constitute nothing more than a reflection of the powers of the people.

They concede, of course, that coercive authority must be justified by its capacity to ensure the common good, and in consequence the peace and happiness of the citizen-body as a whole. Hobbes believes no less firmly than Marsilius that, as he repeatedly declares in *Leviathan*, all governments must be judged by their "aptitude to produce the peace and security of the people, for which end they were instituted."[91] What none of these writers can accept, however, is the idea that the form of authority required to produce such benefits can appropriately be envisaged as nothing more than a trustee, a type of official to whom the people delegate the exercise of their own authority purely as a matter of administrative convenience. Political power, they all admit, is originally instituted by the people, but never in the form of a trust. It is instituted by means of what Suarez calls "absolute transfer" of the people's sovereignty, one that takes the form of "a kind of alienation, not a delegation at all."[92] To set up a mere "depository" or "guardian" of sovereign power, as Bodin agrees, is not to set up a genuine "possessor" of sovereignty at all.[93] For the people to perform that particular act, as Hobbes similarly stresses at several points in *Leviathan*, it is essential for them to recognize that they are "renouncing and transferring" their own original sovereignty, with the implication that it is totally "abandoned or granted away" to someone else (Hobbes 1968: 190, 192).

Civil government, they insist, cannot therefore be seen as the powers of citizens under another guise. It must be seen as a distinct form of power, for reasons that Hobbes enunciates with complete assurance in *De cive* almost a decade before giving them classic expression in *Leviathan*. "Though a government," he declares, "be constituted by the contracts of particular men with particulars, yet its right depends not on that obligation only" (Hobbes 1983: 105). By constituting such a government, "that right which every man had before to use his faculties to his own advantages is now wholly translated on some certain man or council for the common benefit" (Hobbes 1983: 105). It follows that whatever power is thereby installed in authority must be recognized "as having its own rights and properties, insomuch as neither any one citizen, nor all of them together" can now be accounted its equivalent (Hobbes 1983: 89). This, as he was later to put it, "is the generation of that great Leviathan, or rather (to speak more reverently) of that mortal God, to which we owe, under the immortal God, our peace and defence. For by this authority, given him by every particular man in the commonwealth, he hath the use of so much power and strength conferred on him, that by terror thereof, he is enabled to form the wills of them all to peace at home and mutual aid against their enemies abroad" (Hobbes 1968: 227).

It is important, however, not to conflate this form of absolutism with that of the divine-right theorists who rose to such prominence during the same period. A writer like Bossuet, for example, deliberately sets out to obliterate the distinction between the office and person of a king. Echoing the celebrated remark attributed to Louis XIV, he insists that the figure of a ruler "embodies in himself the whole of the state": *tout l'état est en lui.*[94] By contrast, even Hobbes declares as unambiguously as possible that the powers of a ruler are never personal powers at all. They are owed entirely to his standing as holder of "the office of the sovereign," the principal duty of which, as Hobbes never tires of repeating, "consisteth in the end for which he was trusted with the sovereign power, namely the procuration of the safety of the people" (Hobbes 1968: 376).

With Hobbes no less than with Bodin, Suarez, Grotius, and the whole developing tradition of natural-law absolutism, we accordingly arrive at the view that the ends of civil or political association make it indispensable to establish a single and supreme sovereign authority whose power remains distinct not merely from the people who originally instituted it, but also from whatever office-holders may be said to have the right to wield its power at any particular time. What, then, is this form of political authority to be called?

Not surprisingly, these writers at first respond by reaching for traditional names. One suggestion, much canvassed by Bodin and later adopted by Hobbes in *De cive*, was that we should think of the authority in question as embodied in the *civitas*, the *ville* or the city as opposed to either its citizens or its magistrates.[95] But the most usual proposal was that we should think of it as that form of authority which inheres in the *respublica*, the *république* or the commonwealth. Suarez and Grotius, writing in Latin, both speak of the *respublica*.[96] Bodin, writing originally in French, speaks analogously of *la république*; translating his treatise into Latin in 1586, he rendered this as *respublica*; and when Knolles issued his English version in 1606, he in turn called the work *The Six Bookes of a Commonweale*.[97] Finally, Hobbes largely comes

round to this terminology in *Leviathan*, speaking far less frequently of the city, and instead describing his work on its title-page as an enquiry into "the matter, form and power of a commonwealth" (Hobbes 1968: 73).

As these writers increasingly recognized, however, none of these traditional terms really served to render their meaning adequately. One obvious difficulty with "commonwealth" was the fact that, as Raleigh (1661: 3,8) complains in his *Maxims of State*, it had come to be used "by an usurped nickname" to refer to "the government of the whole multitude." To invoke it was thus to risk confusion with one of the theories of popular sovereignty they were most anxious to repudiate. Nor was it altogether satisfactory to speak instead of the city or *civitas*. It is true that Hobbes (1983: 89) consistently does so in *De cive*, declaring that "a city therefore (that we may define it) is one person whose will, by the compact of many men, is to be received for the will of them all." But the obvious difficulty here – in the face of which even Hobbes's confidence seems to have evaporated – was the need to insist on such a purely stipulative definition so strangely at variance with the ordinary meaning of the term.

It was at this juncture, within this tradition of thought, that a number of these theorists began to resolve their difficulties by speaking instead of the *state*, while making it clear at the same time that they were consciously using the term to express their master concept of an impersonal form of political authority distinct from both rulers and ruled.

Bodin already hints at this final crystallizing of the concept at several points in his *République*.[98] Although he continues to write in traditional terms about rulers "who maintain their *estats*," he also uses the word *estat* on several occasions as a synonym for *république*.[99] Most significantly of all, he feels able to speak of "the state in itself" (*l'estat en soi*), describing it both as a form of authority independent of particular types of government, and as the locus of "indivisible and incommunicable sovereignty."[100] It is striking, moreover, that when Knolles came to translate these passages in 1606, he not only used the word "state" in all these instances, but also in a number of other places where Bodin himself had continued to speak in a more familiar vein of the authority of the *cité* or *république*.[101]

If we turn to English writers of the next generation, and above all to those "politic" humanists who were critical of classical republicanism, we find the same terminology used with increasing confidence. Raleigh, for example, not only speaks freely of the state in his *Maxims*, but makes it clear that he thinks of the state as an impersonal form of political authority, defining it as "the frame or set order of a commonwealth" (Raleigh 1661: 2). Bacon (1972: 89) writes in the final version of his *Essays* in a way that often suggests a similar understanding of political authority. He describes rulers as well as their councillors as having a duty to consider "the weal and advancement of the state which they serve." And he writes in a number of other passages about the state and its rulers, the state and its subjects, the "founders of states" and the "subversion of states and governments" (Bacon 1972: 11, 42, 160, 165).

It is above all in Hobbes, however, and in other theorists of *de facto* sovereignty in the English revolution, that we find this new understanding of the state being articulated with complete assurance. It is true, as we have seen, that if we turn to the body of Hobbes's texts, we still find him exhibiting a preference for the traditional terminology of "city" and "commonwealth." But if we turn instead to his Prefaces, in the course of which he stands back from his own arguments and reviews their structure, we find him self-consciously presenting himself as a theorist of the state.

This transition can already be observed in the Preface to *De cive*, in the course of which he describes his project as that of explaining "what the quality of human nature is, in what matters it is, in what not, fit to make up a civil government, and how men must be agreed among themselves, that intend to grow up into a well-grounded state" (Hobbes 1983: 22). But it is in the Introduction to *Leviathan* that he proclaims most unequivocally that the subject matter of his entire investigation has been "that great Leviathan, called a Commonwealth or State (in Latin Civitas)" (Hobbes 1968: 81). Hobbes's ambition as a political theorist had always been to demonstrate that, if there is to be any prospect of attaining civil peace, the fullest powers of sovereignty must be vested neither in the people nor in their rulers, but always in the figure of an "artificial man."[102] Surveying this final redaction of his political philosophy, he at last felt able to add that, in speaking about the need for such an impersonal form of sovereignty, what he had been speaking about all along could best be described as the state.

VI

As the above account suggests, the idea that the supreme authority within a body politic should be identified as the authority of the state was originally the outcome of one particular theory of politics, a theory at once absolutist and secular-minded in its ideological allegiances. That theory was in turn the product of the earliest major counter-revolutionary movement within modern European history, the movement of reaction against the ideologies of popular sovereignty developed in the course of the French religious wars, and, subsequently, in the English Revolution of the seventeenth century. It is perhaps not surprising, therefore, to find that both the ideology of state power and the new terminology employed to express it provoked a series of doubts and criticisms that have never been altogether stilled.

Some of the initial hostility derived from conservative theorists anxious to uphold the old ideal of *un roi, une foi, une loi*. They wished to repudiate any suggestion that the aims of public authority should be purely civil or political in character, and thereby to reinstate a closer relationship between allegiance in church and state. But much of the hostility stemmed from those who wished to uphold a more radical ideal of popular sovereignty in place of the sovereignty of the state. Contractarian writers sought in consequence to keep alive a preference for speaking about the government of civil or political society,[103] while the so-called commonwealthmen maintained their loyalty to the classical ideal of the self-governing republic throughout much of the eighteenth century.[104]

It is true that, at the end of the century, a renewed counter-revolutionary effort was made to neutralize these various populist doubts. Hegel and his followers in particular argued that the English contractarian theory of popular sovereignty merely reflected a failure to distinguish the powers of civil society from those of the state, and a consequent failure to recognize that the independent authority of the state is indispensable if the purposes of civil society are to be fulfilled. But this hardly proved an adequate reassurance. On the one hand, the anxiety of liberal theorists about the relationship between the powers of states and the sovereignty of their citizens generated confusions which have yet to be resolved. And on the other hand, a deeper criticism developed out of these Hegelian roots, insisting that the state's vaunted independence from its own agents as well as from the members of civil society amounts to nothing more than a fraud. As a result, sceptics in the tradition of Michels and Pareto, no less than socialists in the tradition of Marx, have never ceased to insist that modern states are in truth nothing more than the executive arms of their own ruling class.

Given the importance of these rival ideologies and their distinctive vocabularies, it is all the more remarkable to observe how quickly the term "state" and its equivalents nevertheless became established at the heart of political discourse throughout western Europe. By the middle of the eighteenth century the new terminology had become virtually inescapable for all schools of thought. Even so nostalgic an exponent of classical republicanism as Bolingbroke found himself constrained in his pamphleteering of the 1720s to talk about the authority of the state, and about the need for the state to be supported, protected, and above all reformed (1967a: 19, 43, 93, 131). By the time we come to Hume's essays of the 1750s,[105] or Rousseau's *Contrat social* of a decade later,[106] we find the concept of the state and the terms *état* and *state* being put to work in a consistent and completely familiar way.

The immediate outcome of this conceptual revolution was to set up a series of reverberations in the wider political vocabularies of the western European states. Once "state" came to be accepted as the master noun of political argument, a number of other concepts and assumptions bearing on the analysis of sovereignty had to be reorganized or in some cases given up. To complete this survey, we need finally to examine the process of displacement and redefinition that accompanied the entrenchment of the modern idea of the state.

One concept that underwent a process of redefinition was that of political allegiance. A subject or *subditus* had traditionally sworn allegiance to his sovereign as liege lord. But with the acceptance of the idea that sovereignty is lodged not with rulers but with the state, this was replaced by the familiar view that citizens owe their basic loyalty to the state itself.

This is not to say that those who originally advanced this argument had any desire to give up speaking of citizens as *subditi* or subjects. On the contrary, the earliest theorists of the state retained a strong preference for this traditional terminology, using it as a means of countering both the contractarian inclination to speak instead about the

sovereignty of the *populus* or people, and the classical republican contention that we ought to speak only of *civitates* and *cives*, of cities and their citizens. Hobbes, for example, with his usual cunning, maintains in the first published version of his political theory that he is writing specifically "about the citizen" – *de cive*. Yet he makes it one of his most important polemical claims that "each citizen, as also every subordinate civil person" ought properly to regard himself as "the subject of him who hath the chief command" (Hobbes 1983: 90).

Hobbes is in complete agreement with his radical opponents, however, when he goes on to argue that citizens ("that is to say, subjects") ought not to pay allegiance to those who exercise these rights of sovereignty, but rather to the sovereignty inherent in the state or commonwealth itself (Hobbes 1983: 151). Hotman and later "monarchomach" theorists had already insisted that even holders of offices under a monarchy must be viewed as councillors of the kingdom, not of the king, and as servants of the crown, not of the person wearing it.[107] Hobbes simply reiterates the same argument when he declares with so much emphasis in *De cive* that the "absolute and universal obedience" owed by each and every subject is due not to the person of their ruler, but rather "to the city, that is to say, to the sovereign power" (Hobbes 1983: 186).

A further and closely connected concept that was comparably transformed was that of treason. As long as the concept of allegiance was connected with that of doing homage, the crime of treason remained that of behaving treacherously towards a sovereign lord. By the end of the sixteenth century, however, this came to seem less and less satisfactory. Even in the case of England, still bound by the Statute of 1350 which defined treason as compassing or imagining the king's death, the judges began to place increasingly wide constructions upon the meaning of the original Act. The aim in almost every case was to establish a view of treason essentially as an offence against the king in virtue of his office as head of state.[108] Meanwhile the political writers of the same period, untrammeled by the need to wrestle with precedents, had already arrived by a more direct route at the familiar view of treason as a crime not against the king but against the state. As always, Hobbes states the new understanding of the concept most unequivocally. As he declares at the end of his analysis of dominion in *De cive*, those who are guilty of treason are those who refuse to perform the duties "without which the State cannot stand"; the crime of treason is the crime of those who act "as enemies to the Government" (Hobbes 1983: 181).

Finally, the acceptance of the state as both a supreme and an impersonal form of authority brought with it a displacement of the more charismatic elements of political leadership which, as I indicated at the outset, had earlier been of central importance to the theory and practice of government throughout western Europe.

Among the assumptions that suffered displacement, the most important was the claim I began by stressing: that sovereignty is conceptually connected with display, that majesty serves in itself as an ordering force. Machiavelli, for example, still assumes that a ruler can expect to derive protection from *la maestá dello stato*, from a connection between his own high state of stateliness and his capacity to maintain his state.[109] It proved impossible, however, for such beliefs about the charisma attaching to public authority to survive the transfer of that authority to the purely impersonal agency – the "purely moral person," in Rousseau's phrase[110] – of the modern state. By the start of the eighteenth century, we already find conservative writers lamenting that, as Bolingbroke (1967b: 333) puts it, "the state is become, under ancient and known forms, an undefinable monster," with the result that a monarchy like England finds itself left with "a king without monarchical splendour" as head of state.

It was of course possible to transfer these attributes of majesty to the state's agents, permitting them to conduct state openings of parliament, to be granted state funerals, to lie in state, and so forth. Once it became accepted, however, that even heads of state are simply holders of offices, the attribution of so much pomp and circumstance to mere functionaries came to be seen not merely as inappropriate but even absurd, a case not of genuine pomp but of sheer pomposity. This insight was first elaborated by the defenders of "free commonwealths" in their anxiety to insist that, in Milton's phrase, rulers should never be "elevated above their brethren" but should "walk the streets

as other men" (1980: 425). More's *Utopia*, for example, contains an early and devastating portrayal of public magnificence as nothing more than a form of childish vanity (1965: 152–6). Ponet's *Politic Power* includes a more minatory reminder of the punishments God visited upon the Israelites for demanding "a gallant and pompous king" (1942: 87). And Milton in *The Ready and Easy Way* condemns with deep disdain those rulers who aspire "to set a pompous face upon the superficial actings of state" (1980: 426).

One outcome of distinguishing the authority of the state from that of its agents was thus to sever a time-honoured connection between the presence of majesty and the exercise of majestic powers. Displays of stateliness eventually came to be seen as mere "shows" or "trappings" of power, not as features intrinsic to the workings of power itself.[111] When Contarini concedes, for example, that the Doge of Venice is permitted to uphold the dignity of his office with a certain magnificence, he emphasizes that this is just a matter of appearances, and uses a phrase that Lewkenor translates by saying that the Doge is allowed a "royal appearing show."[112] Speaking with much greater hostility, Milton (1980: 426, 429) agrees that a monarch "sits only like a great cypher," with all his "vanity and ostentation" being completely inessential to the ordering force of public authority.

Finally, for the most self-conscious rejection of the older images of power, as well as the most unambiguous view of the state as a purely impersonal authority, we need to turn once more to Hobbes. Discussing these concepts in chapter 10 of *Leviathan*, Hobbes deploys the idea of an effective power to command in such a way as to absorb every other element traditionally associated with the notions of public honor and dignity. To hold dignities, he declares, is simply to hold "offices of command"; to be held honorable is nothing more than "an argument and sign of power" (Hobbes 1968: 152, 155). Here, as throughout, it is Hobbes who first speaks, systematically and unapologetically, in the abstract and unmodulated tones of the modern theorist of the state.

Notes

1   Hobbes (1983: 32). *De cive* was first published in Latin in 1642, in English in 1651. See Warrender (1983: 1). Warrender argues that the translation is at least mainly Hobbes's own work (1983: 4–8). But this is disputed by Tuck (1985: 310–12). Note that, in this as in most other quotations from

primary sources, I have modernized spelling and punctuation.

2 On "the state as an abstract entity," and the political transformations that underlay the emergence of the concept, see further in Shennan (1974); and cf. Maravall (1961).

3 See Hexter (1973: 155) on "the first of its medieval political meanings."

4 Mommsen (1970, 1.5.2: 35): "Cum igitur hominum causa omne ius constitutum sit, primo de personarum statu ac post de ceteris . . . dicemus."

5 For example, see Post (1964: 333–67, 368–414).

6 Froissart (1972: 116): "La [sc. the queen] peut on veoir de l'estat grand noblece."

7 For a comparison between those systems of state power in which "the ordering force of display" is proclaimed, and those in which (as in the modern West) it is deliberately obscured, see Geertz (1980: 121–3), whose formulation I have adopted.

8 See Ercole (1926: 67–8). Hexter (1973: 115) similarly notes that *status* acquired this "second political meaning during the middle ages." Cf. Rubinstein (1971: 314–15), who begins his analysis by discussing this stage.

9 See for example Livy (1962, 30.2.8: 372; 1966, 23.24.2: 78); Sallust (1921, 40.2: 68); Cicero (1913, 2.1.3: 170).

10 Mommsen (1970, I.1.2: 29): "publicum ius est quod ad statum rei Romani spectat." Ercole (1926: 69) emphasizes the importance of this passage.

11 Froissart (1824–6, vol. XII: 93): "Le roi . . . réforma le pays en bon état tant que tous s'en contentèrent."

12 Petition from the abbey of Syon in Shadwell (1912, vol. I: 64). Cf. also vol. I: 66; I: 82, etc.

13 For a survey of this literature see Hertter (1910).

14 Sorbelli (1944) discusses this claim, originally put forward by Muratori; Sorbelli prefers a date in the 1240s.

15 See Franceschi (1966: 26, 27, 28, etc.).

16 Giovanni da Viterbo (1901: 230–2, etc.).

17 For a discussion of the date of composition see Sorbelli (1944).

18 See Ercole (1926: 67–8) and the similar discussions in Post (1964: 18–24, 310–32, 377–81), Rubinstein (1971: 314–16), and Mansfield (1983: 851–2).

19 There are references to the *optimus status reipublicae* in Cicero (1914, 5.4.11: 402 and 1927, 2.11.27: 174), and to the *optimus civitatis status* in Seneca (1964, 2.20.2: 92).

20 See Franceschi (1966: 26) on the need to act "ad . . . comodum ac felicem statum civitatis" and p. 28: "ad honorabilem et prosperum statum huius comunitatis."

21 See Giovanni da Viterbo (1901: 230) on the "bonus status totius communis huius civitatis."

22 Note that they begin to discuss this issue nearly a century earlier than such chroniclers as Giovanni Villani, one of the earliest sources usually cited in

this context. See Ercole (1926: 67–8), Hexter (1973: 155), and Rubinstein (1971: 314–16). For Villani on the "buono et pacifico stato" see Villani (1802–3, vol. III: 159; vol. IV: 3, etc.).

23 Aquinas (1963, I.II.19.10: 104): "Nam iudex habet curam boni communis, quod est iustitia, et ideo vult occisionem latronis, quae habet rationem boni secundum relationem ad statum commune."

24 See Giovanni da Viterbo (1901: 220–2) on the attributes and policies to be demanded of an elected *rector*, and cf. Latini (1948: 402–5), paraphrasing Giovanni's account.

25 Note that, in providing dates for the more obscure humanists, I have taken my information from consenza (1962).

26 Campano (1502, fo. xxxxvii^r): "nihil existimem a statu et salute reipublicae alienius."

27 Beroaldo (1508, fo. xv^v): "oblitis suorum ipsius commodorum ad utilitatem publicam quicquid agit debet referre."

28 Erasmus (1974: 194): "felicissimus est status, cum principi paretur ab omnibus atque ipse princeps paret legibus, leges autem ad archetypum aequi et honesti respondent."

29 Cf. Kantorowicz (1957, esp. pp. 207–32, 268–72), Post (1964, esp. pp. 247–53, 302–9), Strayer (1970, esp. pp. 57–9), and Wahl (1977: 80). By contrast, see Ullmann (1968–9, esp. pp. 43–4) on traditional legal concepts as an obstacle to the emergence of the concept of the state.

30 Note how loftily Hotman still speaks of such usages in his *Francogallia* as late as the 1570s. Writing about the Public Council, he observes that its powers extend "to all those matters which the common people in vulgar parlance nowadays call Affairs of State" ("de iis rebus omnibus, quae vulgus etiam nunc Negotia Statuum populari verbo appellat") (1972: 332).

31 For the thesis that "*stato*, meaning a State, derives in the main . . . from *lo stato del principe*, meaning the status or estate of an effectively sovereign prince," see Dowdall (1923: 102). Cf. also Skinner (1978, vol. II: 352–8).

32 On this development see Waley (1978: 83–330).

33 On this "moment" see Pocock (1975: 83–330). Cf. also Skinner (1978, vol. I: 139–89).

34 On the *pater patriae*, see for example Beroaldo (1508, fos. xiv^r and xv^r) and Scala (1940: 256–8, 273).

35 Petrarch already states these twin ideals (1554: 420–1, 428). They become standard during the *quattrocento*, even recurring in Machiavelli's *Il principe* (1960: 102).

36 Villani (1802–3, vol. IV: 24). Cf. also vol. IV: 190–4.

37 For these phrases see Machiavelli (1960: 16, 19, 22, 25–6, 27, 28, 35, etc.).

38 Rubinstein (1971) similarly analyzes some of these extended usages. While I have avoided duplicating his examples, I am much indebted to his account.

39 See Aquinas (1966: 136–7, 139–40, 310–11, 319–21, 328–30). Rubinstein (1971: 322) credits Aquinas with popularizing these usages. But they were largely the product of the humanist revision of his text issued in 1492. See Mansfield (1983: 851), and cf. Cranz (1978: 169–73) for a full account.

40 See for example Machiavelli (1960: 28 and 29) on the *stato di pochi*.

41 Machiavelli (1960: 15): "Tutti li stati, tutti e'dominii che hanno avuto et hanno imperio sopra li uomini sono stati e sono o repubbliche o principati."

42 Villani (1802–3, vol. IV: 190–1). Cf. also vol. IV: 25; vol. VIII: 186.

43 Vettori (1842: 432, 436). Rubinstein (1971: 318) notes that these were already standard usages in late *quattrocento* Florence.

44 The verses are reproduced in Rowley (1958, vol. I: 127).

45 Budé (1966: 140). Although Budé's *Institution* was not published until 1547, it was completed by the start of 1519. See Delaruelle (1907: 201).

46 Vespasiano (1970–6, vol. I: 177, 192). On the latter passage see also Rubinstein (1971: 318).

47 Guicciardini (1933: 287, 293). Note that Guicciardini – though not Machiavelli – also speaks explicitly of *ragione di stato*. See Maffei (1964, esp. pp. 712–20). For the subsequent history of that concept in *cinquecento* Italy, see Meinecke (1957, esp. pp. 65–145).

48 Castiglione (1960: 10, 117–18). For other *cinquecento* uses see Chabod (1962, esp. pp. 153–73).

49 See Post (1964, esp. pp. viii, 247–53, 302–9, 494–8 and pp. 269, 333) for alleged "anticipations" of Machiavelli's thought. Cf. also Kantorowicz (1957, esp. pp. 207–32) on "polity-centered kingship."

50 Chiappelli (1952: 68). Cf. also Cassirer (1946: 133–7), Chabod (1962: 146–55), D'Entrèves (1967: 30–2).

51 It is important to emphasize, however, that in the cases cited in nn. 46 to 48, as in the case of Machiavelli, it would arguably be no less of an overstatement to insist that these are all unequivocally traditional usages. In the retreat from the type of overstatements cited in n. 50, this point seems in danger of being lost. Hexter in particular irons out a number of ambiguities that ought to be admitted (1973, esp. pp. 164–7 and cf. the corrective in Gilbert [1965, 329–30]). Mansfield (1983: 853) similarly concludes that we do not find anywhere in Machiavelli's writings "an instance of the impersonal modern state among his uses of *stato*." If by this he means that Machiavelli cannot unambiguously be said to express that concept, this is undoubtedly correct. My only objection is that there are several ambiguous passages; the history of the acquisition of the concept cannot be divided into such watertight compartments.

52 See Post (1964: 334), on *status* being used to stress that the king "was not only the indispensable ruler but also the essence of the territorial State which he ruled."

53 For this revival, see below, n. 94. Post claims that the medieval sources he discusses "anticipated the idea" of "l'état, c'est moi" (1964: 269; and cf. also pp. 333–5). But when this remark was uttered in seventeenth-century France (if it ever was) it was by then blankly paradoxical, and this would have been the point of uttering it. On this point see Mansfield (1983: 849) and cf. Rowen (1961) on Louis XIV as "proprietor of the state."

54 See Machiavelli (1960: 16, 47, 87, 95). Cf. on this point Mansfield (1983: 852).

55 In England this demand (and this phrase) can be found as late as early-Stuart arguments over royal revenues. See for example the parliamentary debate of 1610 quoted in Tanner (1930: 359).

56 Even in France, the country in which, after Italy, traditional assumptions about the *status* of princes first changed, this arguably remains true until the 1570s. On this point see below, section V, and cf. Lloyd (1983: 146–53). In Spain the old assumptions appear to have survived until at least the middle of the seventeenth century, *pace* Maravall (1961). See Elliot (1984: 42–5, 121–2). In Germany a purely patrimonial concept of government appears to have survived even longer. See the comments in Shennan (1974: 113–14).

57 See Calasso (1957: 83–123), and Wahl (1977). For analogous reinterpretations of the Decretals, see Mochi Onory (1951). For a survey see Tierney (1982).

58 See Bartolus (1562, 47.22: 779) on the "civitates Tusciae, quae non recognoscunt de facto in temporalibus superiorem."

59 Giovanni da Viterbo (1901: 266): "in alterius messem falcem suam mittere."

60 This is, for example, the main thesis of Baron (1966).

61 For this assumption in *trecento* Florentine diplomacy, see Rubinstein (1952).

62 Contarini (1626: 22 and 56): "temperandam . . . ex optimatum et populari statu . . . nihil minus urbi Venetae timendum sit, quam principem reipublicae libertati ullum unquam negocium facessere posse." On Contarini see Pocock (1975: 320–8).

63 Machiavelli (1960, II.2: 280): "E facil cosa è conoscere donde nasca ne' popoli questa affezione del vivere libero: perché si vede per esperienza le cittadi non avere mai ampliato né di dominio né di ricchezza se non mentre sono state in libertà."

64 Machiavelli (1960, II.11: 280): "La ragione è facile a intendere: perché non il bene particulare ma il bene comune è quello che fa grandi le città. E sanza dubbio questo bene comune non è osservato se non nelle repubbliche."

65 See Latini (1948: 391) on "politique . . . la plus noble et la plus haute science."

66 Latini (1948: 403) on "l'estat de vous et de cette ville." Cf. p. 411 on the idea of remaining "en bon estat."

67 Giovanni da Vignano (1974: 247): "che il nostro bom stato porà remanere in largheça, honore, grandeça e reponso."

68 Matteo dei Libri (1974: 12): "ke 'l nostro bon stato potrà romanire in reposo."

69 See Contarini (1626, at pp. 28 and 46), two cases where, in Lewkenor (1969), *respublica* is rendered as "state." On Lewkenor's translation see Fink (1962: 41–2).

70 Patrizi (1594: 281) on the duty to uphold "veteres leges" and act "pro communi utilitate."

71 Patrizi (1594a: 292 and 279) on how to act "ne civitatis status evertatur" and "statum reipublicae everterunt."

72 Guicciardini (1932: 271–2): "ogni stato ed ogni potenzia eminente ha bisogno delle dependenzie . . . che tutti servirebbono a beneficio dello stato." Cf. also pp. 276, 279.

73 Guicciardini (1932: 273): "uno barbacane e fondamento potentissimo a difesa dello stato."

74 See for example Machiavelli (1960, I.2: 130–2, and also pp. 182, 272, 357, etc.).

75 See in particular Machiavelli (1960, II.24: 351–3).

76 Machiavelli (1960, I.2: 133): "Licurgo . . . fece uno stato che durò più che ottocento anni."

77 Machiavelli (1960, I.6: 141): "se in Roma is poteva ordinare uno stato . . ."

78 Machiavelli (1960, I.18: 180): "le leggi dipoi che con i magistrati frenavano i cittadini."

79 Ibid.: "l'ordine del governo o vero dello stato."

80 See Fink (1962: 10–20, 56–68); Raab (1964: 185–217); Pocock (1975: 333–422); Haitsma Mulier (1980: 26–76).

81 I see no justification for the claim that Starkey merely "dressed up" his *Dialogue* in civic humanist terms. See Mayer (1985: 25) and cf. Skinner (1978, vol. I: 213–42) for an attempt to place Starkey's ideas in a humanist context.

82 A point emphasized by Shennan (1974: 9, 113–14) and Mansfield (1983: 849–50).

83 See Harrington (1977: 173) for the claim that "the interest of the commonwealth is in the whole body of the people," and his invariable preference, in the "Preliminaries" to *Oceana* for speaking of "the city" or "commonwealth" as the locus of political authority. See also pp. 161, 170, 171–2, 182–3.

84 Marsilius of Padua (1956, I.8 and 9: 27–34). For the special significance of Marsilius within this tradition of thought see Condren (1985: 262–9).

85 See esp. Hotman (1972: 287–321), where he lays out his view of the French constitution as a mixed monarchy.

86 Locke (1967: 393). On Locke's *Two Treatises* essentially as an attack on Filmerian absolutism, see

Laslett (1967: 50–2, 67–78) and cf. Dunn (1969: 47–57, 58–76, 87–95). On the place of this concept in Locke's theory see Dunn (1969: 148–56).

87 Howell (1983: 155), while agreeing that this is true of Hotman, argues that two other "monarchomach" theorists – Beza and the author of the *Vindiciae contra tyrannos* – "implied the existence of the secular state as an entity distinct from ruler and people." I cannot see that either writer distinguished the powers of the state from those of the people. Cf. Skinner (1978, vol. II: 318–48).

88 Locke (1967: 386). Cf. also pp. 301, 360–1, 371, 381 for the idea of rulers as mere trustees. See also Hotman (1972: 154 and 402–4) on kings as magistrates "tied" by the duties of their office.

89 On this school of thought see Hamilton (1963) and Fernandez–Santamaria (1977). On the character of their natural-law (as opposed to divine-right) theories of absolutism see Sommerville (1982 and 1986: 59–80). For a contrast with later theories of popular sovereignty see Tully (1980: 64–8 and 111–16).

90 See Bodin (1962: A71). For Bodin's concern to refute the "monarchomachs" see Franklin (1973, esp. pp. vii. 50, 93) and Salmon (1973, esp. pp. 361, 364).

91 Hobbes (1968: 241). Cf. also pp. 192, 223, 237, etc.

92 Suarez (1612: 210): "Quocirca translatio huius potestatis a republica in principem non est delegatio, sed quasi alienatio . . . simpliciter illi conceditur."

93 Bodin (1576: 125) distinguishes between "possesseurs" of sovereignty and those who "ne sont que depositaires et gardes de cette puissance."

94 Bossuet (1967: 177). On this variety of absolutism see Keohane (1980: 241–61) and Sommerville (1986: 9–50).

95 See Bodin (1576: 9 *et passim*) on the "ville" and "cité." Cf. Hobbes (1983: 89–90 *et passim*) for the concept of "a city or civil society."

96 See Suarez (1612: 351–60) on the relations between the *princeps*, *leges* and *respublica*, and cf. Grotius (1625: 65) on *civitas* and *respublica* and p. 84 on the *romana respublica*.

97 Cf. the full titles of Bodin (1576), Bodin (1586), and Bodin (1962).

98 See Lloyd (1983: 156–62). Fell (1983, esp. pp. 92–107, 175–205) lays all his emphasis on Bodin's contemporary Corasius, though without investigating the extent to which he used the term *status* to express his concept of "the legislative state." But by the next generation the use of the vernacular term *état* (or *estat*) to express such a concept had become well entrenched in France. See Church (1972: 13–80) and Keohane (1980: 54–82, 119–82). Dowdall (1923: 118) singles out Loyseau's discussion in his *Traité des seigneuries* (1608) of the relationship between "seigneuries souveraines" and "estats" as being of particular importance, and this point has been much developed. See Church (1972: 33–4) and Lloyd (1981 and 1983: 162–8).

99 Bodin (1576, e.g. at pp. 219, 438).

100 Bodin (1576: 282–3): "Et combien que le gouverne-ment d'une Republique soit plus ou moins popu-laire, ou Aristocratique, ou Royale, si est-que l'estat en soi ne reçoit compairison de plus ni de moins: car toujours la souveraineté indivisible et incommunic-able est à un seul." Note also Bodin's use of the phrase "en matière d'estat" (1576: 281, 414).

101 See Bodin (1962: 184, 250, 451) and cf. pp. 10, 38, 409, 700 for some additional uses of "state."

102 Hobbes (1968: 82) states that the aim of *Leviathan* is "to describe the nature of this artificial man."

103 Benjamin Hoadly, for example, continues to speak about "the civil power," "civil government" and "the power of the civil magistrate" rather than about the state. See "The Original and Institution of Civil Government, Discussed" in Hoadly (1773, vol. II: 189, 191, 201, 203 *et passim*).

104 See the usages in Robbins (1959: 125, 283) and cf. Kramnick (1968, esp. pp. 236–60) and Pocock (1975, esp. pp. 423–505).

105 Hume's main discussions of state power occur in his essays "Of Commerce" and "That Politics may be Reduced to a Science." See Hume (1875, vol. I: 100, 105 and 289, 294–5).

106 See Rousseau (1966, "De l'état civil", pp. 55–6). On "état" in the political vocabulary of Rousseau and his contemporaries see Derathé (1950: 380–2) and Keohane (1980, esp. pp. 442–9).

107 See Hotman (1972, e.g. pp. 254, 298, 402).

108 On this process see Holdsworth (1925: 307–33).

109 Machiavelli (1960: 74, and cf. also pp. 76, 93). The same applies even more strongly to Machiavelli's contemporaries among "mirror-for-princes" writers. See for example Pontano (1952: 1054–6), Sacchi (1608: 68).

110 Rousseau (1966: 54) on "la personne morale qui constitue l'Etat."

111 On the distinctiveness of this conception of public power see Geertz (1980: 121–3).

112 See Lewkenor (1969: 42), translating "specie regia" from Contarini (1626: 56). For invaluable help with earlier drafts I am greatly indebted to John Dunn and Susan James.

References

Aquinas, St. Thomas. 1963. *Summa theologiae*, 3 vols., edited by P. Caramello. Turin: Marietti.

—— 1966. *In octo libros politicorum Aristotelis expositio*, edited by R. Spiazzi. Turin: Marietti.

Bacon, F. 1972. *Essays*, edited by M. Hawkins. London: Dent.

Baron, H. 1966. *The Crisis of the Early Italian Renaissance*, 2nd edn. Princeton, NJ: Princeton University Press.

Bartolus of Sassoferrato. 1562. *Digestum novum commentaria*. Basel.

Beroaldo, F. 1508. "Libellus de optimo statu." In *Opuscula*. Venice, fos. x–xxxiiii.

Bodin, J. 1576. *Les Six Livres de la république*. Paris.

—— 1586. *De republica libri sex*. Paris.

—— 1962. *The Six Books of a Commonweale*, translated by R. Knolles and edited by K. McRae. Cambridge, MA: Harvard University Press.

Bolingbroke, Lord. 1967a. "A Dissertation upon Parties." In *The Works*, 4 vols., vol II. London: F. Cass, pp. 5–172.

—— 1967b. "Letters on the Study and Use of History." In *The Works*, 4 vols., vol. II. London. F. Cass, pp. 173–334.

Bossuet, J.-B. 1967. *Politique tirée des propres paroles de l'Ecriture Sainte*, edited by J. Le Brun. Geneva: Droz.

Budé, G. 1966. *De l'institution du prince*. Farnborough: Gregg.

Burke, E. 1910. *Reflections on the Revolution in France*, Everyman edn. London: Dent.

Calasso, F. 1957. *I Glossatori e la teoria della sovranitá*. Milan: Giuffrè.

Campano, G. 1502. "De regendo magistratu." In *Opera omnia*. Venice, fos. xxxxiii–xxxxviii.

Cassirer, E. 1946. *The Myth of the State*. New Haven, CT: Yale University Press.

Castiglione, B. 1960. *Il libro del cortegiano*. In *Opere*, edited by C. Cordié. Milan: R. Ricciardi, pp. 5–361.

Chabod, F. 1962. *L'idea di nazione*, 2nd edn. Bari: G. Laterza.

Chiappelli, F. 1952. *Studi sul linguaggio del Machiavelli*. Florence: F. Le Monnier.

Church, W. 1972. *Richelieu and Reason of State*. Princeton, NJ: Princeton University Press.

Cicero, 1913. *De officiis*, translated by W. Miller. London: Heinemann.

—— 1914. *De Finibus*, translated by H. Rackham. London: Heinemann.

—— 1927. *Tusculanae Disputationes*, translated by J. King. London: Heinemann.

Condren, C. 1985. *The Status and Appraisal of Classical Texts*. Princeton, NJ: Princeton University Press.

Contarini, G. 1626. *De republica Venetorum*. Lyons.

Cosenza, M. 1926. *Biographical and Bibliographical Dictionary of the Italian Humanists*, vol. V: *Synopsis and Bibliography*. Boston, MA: G.K. Hall.

Cranz, F. 1978. "The Publishing History of the Aristotle Commentaries of Thomas Aquinas." *Traditio* 34: 157–92.

Dante Alighieri. 1966. *Inferno*, edited by G. Petrocchi. Milan: A. Mondadori.

Delaruelle, L. 1907. *Guillaume Budé*. Paris: H. Champion.

D'Entrèves, A. 1967. *The Notion of the State*. Oxford: Oxford University Press.

Derathé, R. 1950. *Jean-Jacques Rousseau et la science politique de son temps*. Paris: Presses Universitaires de France.

Dowdall, H. 1923. "The Word 'State.' " *The Law Quarterly Review* 39: 98–125.

Dunn, J. 1969. *The Political Thought of John Locke*. Cambridge: Cambridge University Press.

Elliott, J. 1984. *Richelieu and Olivares*. Cambridge: Cambridge University Press.

Erasmus, D. 1974. *Institutio christiani principis*, edited by O. Herding. In *Opera omnia*, part IV, vol. I. Amsterdam: North-Holland, pp. 95–219.

Ercole, F. 1926. *La politica di Machiavelli*. Rome: Anonima Romana Editoriale.

Fell, A. 1983. *Origins of Legislative Sovereignty and the Legislative State*, vol. I. Cambridge, MA: Atheneum.

Fernandez–Santamaria, J.A. 1977. *The State, War and Peace*. Cambridge: Cambridge University Press.

Fink, Z. 1962. *The Classical Republicans*, 2nd edn. Evanston, IL: Northwestern University Press.

Franceschi, E. 1966. "Oculus pastoralis." *Memorie dell' accademia delle scienze di Torino* 11: 19–70.

Franklin, J. 1973. *Jean Bodin and the Rise of Absolutist Theory*. Cambridge: Cambridge University Press.

Froissart, J. 1824–6. *Chroniques*, 14 vols., edited by J. Buchon. Paris: Vordière, J. Carez.

—— 1972. *Chroniques: début du premier libre*, edited by G. Diller. Geneva: Droz.

Geertz, C. 1980. *Negara*. Princeton, NJ: Princeton University Press.

Giannardi, G. 1942. "Le 'Dicerie' di Filippo Ceffi." *Studi di filologia italiana* 6: 27–63.

Gilbert, F. 1965. *Machiavelli and Guicciardini*. Princeton, NJ: Princeton University Press.

Giovanni da Vignano. 1974. *Flore de parlare*. In Matteo dei Libri, *Arringhe*, edited by E. Vincenti. Milan: R. Ricciardi, pp. 229–325.

Giovanni da Viterbo. 1901. *Liber de regimine civitatum*, edited by C. Salvemini. In *Bibliotheca iuridica medii aevi*, 3 vols., edited by A. Gaudenzi, vol. III. Bologna: Società Azzoguidiana, pp. 215–80.

Grotius, H. 1625. *De iure belli ac pacis*. Paris.

Guicciardini, F. 1932. *Dialogo e discorsi del reggimento di Firenze*, edited by R. Palmarocchi. Bari: G. Laterza.

—— 1933. *Scritti politici e ricordi*, edited by R. Palmarocchi. Bari: G. Laterza.

Haitsma Mulier, E. 1980. *The Myth of Venice and Dutch Republican Thought in the Seventeenth Century*, translated by G. T. Moran. Assen: Van Gorcum.

Hamilton, B. 1963. *Political Thought in Sixteenth-century Spain*. Oxford: Clarendon.

Harrington, J. 1977. *The Political Works of James Harrington*, edited by J. Pocock. Cambridge: Cambridge University Press.

Hertter, F. 1910. *Die Podestalitteratur Italiens im 12. und 13. Jahrhundert*. Leipzig: B.G. Teubner.

Hexter, J. 1973. *The Vision of Politics on the Eve of the Reformation*. New York: Allen Lane.

Hoadly, B. 1772. *The Works*, 3 vols. London: W. Bowyer and J. Nichols.

Hobbes, T. 1968. *Leviathan*, edited by C. Macpherson. Harmondsworth: Penguin.

—— 1983. *De cive: The English Version*, edited by H. Warrender. Oxford: Clarendon.

Holdsworth, W. 1925. *A History of English Law*, vol. VIII. London: Methuen.

Hotman, F. 1972. *Francogallia*, edited by R. Giesey and J. Salmon. Cambridge: Cambridge University Press.

Hume, D. 1875. *Essays*, 2 vols., edited by T. Green and T. Grose. London: Longmans Green.

Humphrey, L. 1973. *The Nobles, or Of Nobility*. In *The English Experience*, no. 534. New York: Da Capo Press.

Kantorowicz, E. 1957. *The King's Two Bodies*. Princeton, NJ: Princeton University Press.

Keohane, N. 1980. *Philosophy and the State in France*. Princeton, NJ: Princeton University Press.

Kramnick, I. 1968. *Bolingbroke and his Circle*. Cambridge, MA: Harvard University Press.

Laslett, P. 1967. "Introduction." In Locke 1967: 1–120.

Latini, B. 1948. *Li Livres dou trésor*, edited by F. Carmody. Berkeley, CA: University of California Press.

Lewkenor, L. 1969. *The Commonwealth and Government of Venice*. In *The English Experience*, vol. 101. New York: Da Capo Press.

Livy. 1962. *Ab urbe condita*, vol. VIII, translated by F. Moore. London: Heinemann.

—— 1966. *Ab urbe condita*, vol. VI, translated by F. Moore, London: Heinemann.

Lloyd, H. 1981. "The Political Thought of Charles Loyseau (1564–1610)." *European Studies Review* 11: 53–82.

—— 1983. *The State, France and the Sixteenth Century*. London: George Allen and Unwin.

Locke, J. 1967. *Two Treatises of Government*, edited by P. Laslett, 2nd edn. Cambridge: Cambridge University Press.

Machiavelli, N. 1960. *Il principe e discorsi*, edited by S. Bertelli. Milan: Feltrinelli.

Maffei, R. de. 1964. "Il problema della 'Ragion di Stato' nei suoi primi affioramenti." *Rivista internazionale di filosofia del diritto* 41: 712–32.

Mansfield, H. 1983. "On the Impersonality of the Modern State: A Comment on Machiavelli's Use of *Stato*." *The American Political Science Review* 77: 849–57.

Maravall, J. 1961. "The Origins of the Modern State." *Journal of World History* 6: 789–808.

Marsilius of Padua. 1956. *The Defender of Peace*, translated by A. Gewirth. New York: Columbia University Press.

Matteo dei Libri. 1974. *Arringhe*, edited by E. Vincenti. Milan: R. Ricciardi.

Mayer, T. 1985. "Faction and Ideology: Thomas Starkey's *Dialogue*." *Historical Journal* 28:1–25.

Meinecke, F. 1957. *Machiavellism*, translated by D. Scott. London: Routledge & Kegan Paul.

Milton, J. 1962. *The Tenure of Kings and Magistrates*. In *Complete Prose Works*, vol. III, edited by M. Hughes. New Haven, CT: Yale University Press, pp. 190–258.

—— 1971. *History of Britain*. In *Complete Prose Works*, vol. V, edited by F. Fogle. New Haven, CT: Yale University Press.

—— 1980. *The Ready and Easy Way to Establish a Free Commonwealth*. In *Complete Prose Works*, vol. VII, edited by R. Ayers, revised edn. New Haven, CT: Yale University Press, pp. 407–63.

Mochi Onory, S. 1951. *Fonti canonistiche dell' idea moderna dello stato*. Milan: Società Editrice "Vita e pensiero."

Mommsen, T. (ed.). 1970. *Digesta*, 21st edn. Zurich: Weidmannes.

More, St. Thomas. 1965. *Utopia*. In *The Complete Works of St. Thomas More*, vol. IV, edited by E. Surtz and J. Hexter. New Haven, CT: Yale University Press.

Muratori, L. (ed.). 1741. "Gratulatio." In *Antiquitates Italicae*, vol. IV. Milan: Arretti, pp. 131–2.

Patrizi, F. 1594a. *De institutione reipublicae*. Strassburg.

—— 1594b. *De regno et regis institutione*. Strassburg.

Petrarch, F. 1554. *Opera quae extant omnia*. Basel.

Pocock, J. 1975. *The Machiavellian Moment*. Princeton, NJ: Princeton University Press.

Ponet, J. 1942. *A Short Treatise of Politic Power*. Reprinted in W. Hudson, *John Ponet*. Chicago, IL: University of Chicago Press, pp. 131–62.

Pontano, G. 1952. "De principe." In *Prosatori Latini del quattrocento*, edited by E. Garin. Milan: R. Ricciardi, pp. 1023–63.

Post, G. 1964. *Studies in Medieval Legal Thought*. Princeton, NJ: Princeton University Press.

Raab, F. 1964. *The English Face of Machiavelli*. London: Routledge & Kegan Paul.

Raleigh, W. 1661. "Maxims of State." In *Remains of Sir Walter Raleigh*. London: W. Sheares, pp. 1–65.

Rinuccini, A. 1957. *Dialogus de libertate*, edited by F. Adorno. In *Atti e memorie dell' accademia toscana di scienze e lettere La Colombaria* 22: 265–303.

Robbins, C. 1959. *The Eighteenth-century Commonwealthman*. Cambridge, MA: Harvard University Press.

Rousseau, J.-J. 1966. *Du contrat social*, edited by P. Burgelin. Paris: Garnier-Flammarion.

Rowen, H. 1961. " 'L'état, c'est à moi.' Louis XIV and the State." *French Historical Studies* 2: 83–98.

Rowley, G. 1958. *Ambrogio Lorenzetti*, 2 vols. Princeton, NJ: Princeton University Press.

Rubinstein, N. 1952. "Florence and the Despots. Some Aspects of Florentine Diplomacy in the Fourteenth Century." *Transactions of the Royal Historical Society*, 2: 21–45.

—— 1971. "Notes on the word *stato* in Florence before Machiavelli." In *Florilegium historiale*, edited by J. Rowe and W. Stockdale. Toronto: University of Toronto Press, pp. 313–26.

Sacchi, B. 1608. *De principe viro*. Frankfurt.

Sallust. 1921. *Bellum Catilinae* translated by J. Rolfe. London: Macmillan.

Salmon, J. 1973. "Bodin and the Monarchomachs." In H. Denzer (ed.), *Bodin*. Munich: Beck, pp. 359–78.

Sardo, R. 1845. *Cronaca Pisana*. In *Archivio storico italiano* 6, part II: 73–244.

Scala, B. 1940. *De legibus et iudiciis dialogus*, edited by L. Borghi. In *La Bibliofilia* 42: 256–82.

Seneca. 1964. *De beneficiis*, translated by J. Basore. London: Heinemann.

Shadwell, L. (ed.). 1912. *Enactments in Parliament Specially Concerning the Universities of Oxford and Cambridge*, 4 vols. London: Clarendon.

Shennan, J. 1974. *The Origins of the Modern European State, 1450–1725*. London: Hutchinson.

Skinner, Q. 1978. *The Foundations of Modern Political Thought*, 2 vols. Cambridge: Cambridge University Press.

Sommerville, J. 1982. "From Suarez to Filmer: A Reappraisal." *The Historical Journal* 25: 525–40.

—— 1986. *Politics and Ideology in England, 1603–1640*. London: Longman.

Sorbelli, A. 1944. "I teorici del reggimento comunale." *Bullettino dell' istituto storico italiano per il medio evo* 59: 31–136.

Starkey, T. 1948. *A Dialogue between Reginald Pole and Thomas Lupset*, edited by K. Burton. London: Chatto and Windus.

Strayer, J. 1970. *On the Medieval Origins of the Modern State*. Princeton, NJ: Princeton University Press.

Suarez, F. 1612. *Tractatus de legibus, ac Deo legislatore*. Coimbra.

Tanner, J. 1930. *Constitutional Documents of the Reign of James I*. Cambridge: Cambridge University Press.

Tierney, B. 1982. *Religion, Law and the Growth of Constitutional Thought, 1150–1650*. Cambridge: Cambridge University Press.

Topham, J. *et al.* (eds.). 1783. *Rotuli Parliamentorum*, vol. III. London.

Tuck, R. 1985. "Warrender's *De cive.*" *Political Studies* 33: 308–15.

Tully, J. 1980. *A Discourse on Property*. Cambridge: Cambridge University Press.

Ullmann, W. 1968–9. "Juristic Obstacles to the Emergence of the Concept of the State in the Middle Ages." *Annali di storia del diritto* 12–13: 43–64.

Vespasiano da Bisticci. 1970–6. *Le vite*, 2 vols., edited by A. Greco. Florence: Nella sede dell' istituto nazionale di studi sul rinascimento.

Vettori, F. 1842. *Parero* [On the Government of Florence, 1531–2]. In *Archivio storico italiano* 1: 433–6.

Villani, G. 1802–3. *Istorie fiorentine*, 8 vols. Milan: Società tipografica dei classici italiani.

Wahl, J. 1977. "Baldus de Ubaldis and the Foundations of the Nation-State." *Manuscripta* 21: 80–96.

Waley, D. 1978. *The Italian City-republics*, 2nd edn. London: Longman.

Warrender, H. 1983. "Editor's Introduction." In Hobbes 1983.

2

State Simplification

James C. Scott

Certain forms of knowledge and control require a narrowing of vision. The great advantage of such tunnel vision is that it brings into very sharp focus certain limited aspects of an otherwise far more complex and unwieldy reality. This very simplification, in turn, makes the phenomenon at the center of the field of vision far more legible and, hence, far more susceptible to careful measurement, calculation, and manipulation.

The invention of scientific forestry in late eighteenth century Prussia and Saxony serves as something of a model of this process.[1] While the history of scientific forestry is important in its own right, I plan to use it here as a metaphor for the forms of knowledge and manipulation characteristic of large institutions with sharply defined interests, of which the state is perhaps the outstanding example. Once we have seen how simplification, legibility and manipulation operate in forest management, we can then explore how a similar optic is applied by the modern state to urban planning, rural settlement, land administration, and agriculture.

I The State and Scientific Forestry: A Parable

The early modern European state, even prior to the development of scientific forestry, viewed its forests primarily through the fiscal lens of revenue needs. To be sure, other concerns such as timber for masts, shipbuilding, state construction, and sufficient fuel wood for the economic security of its subjects were not entirely absent from official management. These concerns, too, had heavy implications for state revenue and security.[2] Exaggerating only slightly, one might say that the crown's interest in forests was resolved through its fiscal lens into a single number: that number being the revenue yield of the timber which might be extracted annually.

The best way to appreciate exactly how heroic this constriction of vision is, is to notice what was left out of its field of vision. Lurking behind the number indicating revenue yield were not so much trees as "commercial wood," representing so many thousands of board feet of saleable timber and so many cords of firewood fetching a certain price. Missing, of course, were all those trees, bushes and plants holding little or no potential for state revenue. Missing as well, were all those parts of trees – even "revenue-bearing" trees – which might have been useful to the population but whose value could not be converted into fiscal receipts. Here I have in mind the uses of foliage as fodder and thatch, fruits as food for domestic animals and people, twigs and branches as bedding, fencing, hop poles and kindling, bark and roots for medicine and tanning, sap for resins, and so forth. The actual tree with its vast number of possible uses was replaced by an "abstract" tree representing a volume of lumber or firewood. If the princely conception of the forest was utilitarian, it

Originally published in *Journal of Political Philosophy* 3 (1995): 191–234. Reprinted by permission of Blackwell Publishing Ltd.

was surely a utilitarianism confined to the direct needs of the state.

From a naturalist's perspective, nearly everything was missing from the state's picture. Gone were the vast majority of flora, the grasses, flowers, lichen, ferns, mosses, shrubs, and vines. Gone, too, were reptiles, birds, amphibians, and innumerable species of insects. Gone was the vast majority of fauna except, perhaps, those of interest to the crown's gamekeepers.

From an anthropologist's perspective, nearly everything touching on human interaction with the forest was also missing from the state's tunnel vision. Except for poaching, which did impinge on either the state's claim to revenue in wood or to royal game, the state typically ignored the vast and complex negotiated social uses of the forest for hunting and gathering, pasturage, digging valuable minerals, fishing, charcoal-making, trapping and food collection as well as its significance for magic, worship, refuge, etc.[3]

If the utilitarian state could not see the real existing forest for the (commercial) trees, if its view of its forests was abstract and partial, it was hardly unique in this respect. A certain level of abstraction is necessary for certain forms of analysis and it is not at all surprising that the abstractions of state officials should have reflected the paramount fiscal interests of their employer. The vocabulary used to organize nature typically betrays the overriding interests of its human users. In fact, the term "nature" is, in utilitarian discourse, replaced by the term "natural resources" in which the focus is on those aspects of nature that can be appropriated for human use. A comparable logic extracts from a more generalized natural world those flora or fauna that are of utilitarian value (usually marketable commodities) and, in turn, reclassifies those species which compete with, prey on, or otherwise diminish the yields of the valued species. Thus, *plants* which are valued become *crops*; the species which compete with them are reclassified as *weeds*, and the insects which ingest them are reclassified as *pests*. Thus, *trees* which are valued become *timber* while species which compete with them become "trash" trees or underbrush. The same logic applies to fauna. Those *animals* which are highly valued become *game* or *livestock*, while those animals which compete with or prey upon them become *predators* or "*varmints.*"

The kind of abstracting, utilitarian logic which the state, through its officials, applied to the forest is thus not entirely distinctive. What is distinctive about it, however, is the narrowness of its field of vision, the degree of elaboration to which it can be subjected, and above all, as we shall see, the unique capacity of the state to impose (in part) its optic on the very reality it is observing.[4]

Scientific forestry was developed from about 1765 to 1800, largely in Prussia and Saxony. Eventually, it would become the basis of forest management techniques in France, England, the US, and throughout the Third World. Its emergence can hardly be understood outside the larger context of centralized state-making initiatives of the period. In fact, the new forestry science was a sub-discipline of so-called "cameral science" – an effort to reduce the fiscal management of a kingdom to scientific principles that would allow systematic planning.[5] Traditional domainal forestry had hitherto simply divided the forest into roughly equal plots – the number of plots coinciding with the number of years in the assumed growth cycle.[6] One plot was cut each year on the assumption of equal yields (and value) from plots of equal size. Owing to poor maps, the uneven distribution of the most valuable large trees (*Hochwald*) and very approximate cordwood (*Bruststaerke*) measures, the results were unsatisfactory for fiscal planning.

The first attempt at more precise measurement was made by Johann Gottlieb Beckmann on a carefully surveyed sample plot. Walking abreast, several assistants carried compartmentalized boxes with color-coded nails corresponding to five size-categories of trees which they had been trained to identify. Each tree was "tagged" with the appropriate nail until the whole sample plot was covered. Having begun with a specified number of nails, it was a simple matter to subtract those remaining from the initial total and arrive at an inventory of trees by size-class for the entire plot. The sample plot had been carefully chosen for its representativeness, allowing the foresters then to calculate the timber and, given certain price assumptions, the revenue yield of the whole forest. For the forest scientists (*Forstwissenschaftler*) the goal was always to "deliver the greatest possible *constant* volume of wood."[7]

The effort at precision was pushed further as mathematicians worked from the cone/volume principle to specify the volume of saleable wood contained by a standardized tree (*Normalbaum*). Their calculations were checked empirically against the actual volume of wood in sample trees.[8] The final result of such calculations was the development of elaborate tables with data organized by classes of trees by size and age under specified conditions of normal growth and maturation. References to these tables coupled with field tests allowed the forester to estimate closely the inventory, growth and yield of a given forest. In the regulated, abstract forest of the *Forstwissenschaftler*, calculation and measurement prevailed and the three watchwords were "minimum diversity," "the balance sheet," and "sustained yield."

The achievement of German forestry science in standardizing techniques to calculate the sustainable yield of commercial timber and, hence, revenue, was impressive enough. What is decisive for our purposes, however, is the next logical step in forest management. That step was to attempt to create, through careful seeding, planting and cutting, a forest that was easier for state foresters to count, manipulate, measure and assess. The fact is that forest science and geometry, backed by state power, had the capacity to transform the real, disorderly, chaotic forest so that it more closely resembled the administrative grid of its techniques. To this end the underbrush was cleared, the number of species was reduced (often to monoculture), planting was done simultaneously and in straight rows for large tracts. These management practices, as Lowood observes,

> ... produced the monocultural, even-age forests that eventually transformed the *Normalbaum* from abstraction to reality. The German forest became the archetype for imposing on disorderly nature the neatly arranged constructs of science. Practical goals had encouraged mathematical utilitarianism, which seemed, in turn, to promote geometric perfection as the outward sign of the well-managed forest; in turn the rationally ordered arrangements of trees offered new possibilities for controlling nature.[9]

The tendency was toward "regimentation" in the strict sense of the word. The forest trees were drawn up into serried ranks, as it were, to be measured, counted off, felled and replaced by a new rank-and-file of lookalike conscripts. At the limit, the forest itself would not have to be seen; it could be "read" accurately from the tables and maps in the foresters' office.

This utopian dream of scientific forestry was, of course, only the *immanent* logic of its techniques. It was not, and could not, ever be realized in practice.

Both nature and "the human factor" intervened. The existing topography of the landscape and the vagaries of fire, storms, blights, climatic changes, insect populations and disease conspired to thwart foresters and to shape the actual forest. Given the insurmountable difficulties of policing large forests, the adjacent human populations also typically continued to graze animals, poach firewood and kindling, make charcoal, and generally make use of the forest in ways that prevented the foresters' management plan from being fully realized.[10] Though, like all utopian schemes, it fell well short of attaining its goal, the critical fact is that it did partly succeed in stamping the actual forest with the imprint of its designs.

II   Social Facts, Raw and Cooked

The administrators' forest cannot be the naturalists' forest. Even if the ecological interactions at play in the forest were known, they would constitute a reality so complex and variegated as to defy easy shorthand description. The intellectual filter necessary to reduce the complexity to manageable dimensions was provided by the state's interest in commercial timber and revenue.

If the natural world, however shaped by human use, is too unwieldy in its "raw" form for administrative manipulation, so too are the actual social patterns of human interaction with nature bureaucratically indigestible in their raw form. No administration system is capable of representing *any* existing social community except through a heroic and greatly schematized process of abstraction and simplification. It is not simply a question of capacity, though, like the forest, a human community is surely far too complicated and variable to yield its secrets easily to bureaucratic formulae. It is also a question of purpose. State agents have no interest – nor should they – in describing an entire social reality any more than the scientific forester has an interest in describing the ecology of a forest in detail. Their abstractions and simplifications are disciplined by a small number of objectives, the most prominent of which were, until the nineteenth century, typically: taxation, political control, and conscription. They needed only the techniques and understanding adequate to these tasks. Here, as we shall see, there are some instructive parallels between the development of modern "fiscal forestry" and modern forms of taxable property in land. Pre-modern states were no less concerned with tax receipts than modern states. But, like pre-modern state forestry, the techniques and reach of the state left much to be desired.

Absolutist France in the seventeenth century is a case in point.[11] Indirect taxes – for example, excise levies on salt, tobacco, tolls, licenses and the sale of offices and titles – were favored forms of taxation inasmuch as they were easier to administer and required little or nothing in the way of information about landholding and income. The tax-exempt status of the nobility and clergy meant that a good deal of the landed property was not taxed at all, transferring much of the burden to wealthy commoner farmers and the peasantry. Common land, though it was a vitally important subsistence resource for the rural poor, yielded no revenue either. In the eighteenth century, the physiocrats would condemn all common property on two presumptive grounds: that it was inefficiently exploited and that it was fiscally barren.[12]

What must strike any observer of absolutist taxation is how wildly variable and unsystematic it was. Collins found that the major direct land tax, the *taille*, was frequently not paid at all and that no community paid more than one-third of what they were assessed.[13] The result was *routine* state reliance on exceptional measures to make good shortfalls in revenue or to pay for new expenses, particularly military campaigns. The crown exacted "forced loans" (*rentes, droits aliénés*) in return for annuities which it might or might not honor; it sold offices and titles (*vénalités d'office*); it levied exceptional hearth taxes (*fouages extraordinaires*); and, above all, it billeted troops directly on communities, often ruining them in the process.[14]

The billeting of troops, a common form of fiscal punishment, was to modern forms of systematic taxation as the drawing-and-quartering of would-be regicides (so strikingly described by Michel Foucault at the beginning of *Discipline and Punish*) was to modern forms of systematic criminal incarceration. Not that there was a great deal of choice involved. The state simply lacked both the information and administrative grid that would have allowed it to exact a reliable revenue from its subjects that was more closely tied to their actual capacity to pay. As with forest revenue, there was no alternative to rough and ready calculations with a corresponding fluctuation in yields. Fiscally, the pre-modern state was, to use Charles Lindblom's felicitous term, "all thumbs and no fingers"; it was incapable of fine tuning.

Here is where the rough analogy between forest management and taxation breaks down. In the absence of reliable information about sustainable timber yield, the state might either inadvertently overexploit its resources and threaten future supply, or else fail to realize the level of proceeds it might sustain.[15] The trees themselves, however, were not political actors while the taxable subjects of the crown most certainly were. They signaled their dissatisfaction by flight, by various forms of quiet resistance and evasion and, *in extremis*, by open revolt. A reliable format for taxation of subjects thus depended not just on discovering what their economic condition was, but also on trying to judge what exactions they would vigorously resist.

How were the agents of the state to begin measuring and codifying, throughout each region of an entire kingdom, its population, their land-holdings, their harvests, their wealth, the volume of commerce, and so on? The obstacles in the path of even the most rudimentary knowledge of these matters were simply enormous. The struggle to establish uniform weights and measures and to carry out a cadastral mapping of land-holdings can serve as diagnostic examples. Each required a large, costly, long run campaign against determined resistance.

Each undertaking also exemplified a pattern of relationships between local knowledge and practices on the one hand, and state administrative routines on the other that will find echoes throughout our subsequent analysis. In each case, local practices of measurement and land-holding were *illegible* to the state in their "raw" form. They exhibited a diversity and intricacy that reflected a great variety of purely local, not state, interests. That is to say, they could not be assimilated directly into an administrative grid without either being transformed or else reduced to a convenient, if partly fictional, shorthand. The logic behind the required shorthand was provided, as in scientific forestry, by the pressing material interests of rulers: fiscal receipts, military manpower, and state security. Finally, this shorthand functioned, in turn, like Beckmann's *Normalbaume*, not just as an (inadequate) description. Backed by state power through records, courts, and ultimately coercion, these state fictions transformed the reality they presumed to observe, though never so thoroughly as to precisely fit the grid.

III   Popular Measures, State Measures

Non-state forms of measurement grew from the logic of local practice. As such, they shared some generic features despite their bewildering variety – features which made them an impediment to administrative uniformity. Thanks to the synthesis of the medievalist Witold Kula, the reasoning that animated local practices of measurement may be set out fairly succinctly.[16]

Most early measures were anthropomorphic. One sees this logic at work in surviving expressions such as "a stone's throw" or "within earshot" for distances and in expressions such as "a cartload," "a basketful," "a handful" for volume. Given that the local cart or basket might vary from place to place and that local notions of "a stone's throw" might not be precisely uniform, these units of measurement varied geographically and temporally. Even measures which were apparently fixed might be deceptive.[17] The *pinte* in eighteenth century Paris, for example, was equivalent to 0.93 liters, whereas in Seine-en-Montagne it was 1.99 liters and in Precy-sous-Thil, an astounding 3.33 liters. The *aune*, a measure of length used especially for cloth, varied depending on the material (for example, the unit for silk being smaller than that for linen) and in France as a whole there were at least 17 different *aunes*.

Local measures were also relational or "commensurable."[18] Virtually any request for a judgment of measure allows a range of responses depending on the context of the request. A common response to the question, "How far is it to the next village?" in that part of Malaysia with which I am most familiar is, literally, "three rice-cookings." The answer assumes that the questioner is interested in how long it will take him to get there, not how many miles away it is. In varied terrain, of course, distance in miles is an utterly unreliable guide to travel time, especially when the traveller is on foot or bicycle. The answer also expresses time not in minutes – until recently wristwatches were rare – but in units that were locally meaningful. Everyone knows how long it takes to cook the local rice. Thus an Ethiopian response to a query about how much salt is required for a dish might be: "Half as much as to cook a chicken." The reply refers back to a standard which everyone is expected to know. Such measurement practices are irreducibly local inasmuch as regional differences in, say, the rice eaten

or in the preferred way of cooking chicken will give different results.

Many local units of measurement are tied very practically to a particular activity. Maharashtran peasants, as Appadurai notes, express the desired distance between the onion sets they plant in terms of hand-spans. Moving along a row, the hand is, well, the most "handy," as a gauge. In similar fashion, a common measure for twine or rope is the distance between the thumb and elbow because this corresponds with how it is wrapped and stored. As with onion-sets the process of measuring is embedded in the activity itself and requires no separate operation. Such measurements are, moreover, often approximate; they are only as exact as the task at hand requires.[19] Rainfall may be said to be abundant or inadequate if the context of the query implies an interest in a particular crop. A reply in terms of inches of rainfall, however accurate, would fail to convey the desired information, inasmuch as it ignores vital matters like the timing of the rain. For many purposes, as well, an apparently vague measurement may communicate more valuable information than a statistically exact average. The cultivator who reports that his rice yield from a plot is anywhere between four and seven baskets is conveying more accurate information, if the focus of attention is on the variability of the yield, than if he reported a ten-year statistical average of 5.6 baskets.

There is, then, no single, all-purpose, correct answer to a question implying measurement unless we specify the relevant local concerns that give rise to the question. Particular customs of measurement are thus situationally, temporally, and geographically bound.

Nowhere is the particularity of customary measurement more evident then when it comes to cultivated land. Modern measures of land by abstract surface area – so many hectares or acres – are singularly uninformative figures to a family which proposes to make its living from these acres. Telling a farmer only that he is leasing 20 acres is about as helpful as telling a scholar that he has bought 6 kilos of books! Customary measures of land have, therefore, taken a variety of forms corresponding to those aspects of the land that are of greatest practical interest. Where land was abundant and manpower and/or draftpower scarce, the most meaningful gauge of land was often the number of days required to plough it or to weed it. A plot of land in nineteenth century France, for example, would be described as representing so many *morgen* or *journal(s)* (days of work), and the kind of work (*homée, bechée, fauchée*) required would be specified. How many *morgen* a field of, say, ten acres represented could vary greatly; if the land was rocky and steeply pitched it might require twice as much labor to work than if it were rich bottom land. The *morgen* would, moreover, differ from place to place depending on, say, the strength of local draftpower and the crops sown, and it would differ from time to time as technology (plough tips, yokes, harnesses) affected the work a man could accomplish in a day.

Land might also be evaluated according to the amount of seed required to sow it. If the soil was very good, a field would be densely sown, while poor land would be more lightly seeded. The amount of seed sown to a field is, in fact, a relatively good proxy for average yield, as the sowing is done in anticipation of average growing conditions, while the actual seasonal yield would be more variable. Given a particular crop regimen, the amount of seed sown would indicate roughly how productive a field had been, though it would indicate nothing directly about how arduous it was to cultivate or how variable the harvests were. The average yield from a plot of land is itself, however, a rather abstract figure. What most farmers near the subsistence margin want, above all, to know is whether a particular farm will meet their basic needs reliably. Thus, small farms in Ireland were described as "a farm of one cow" or "a farm of two cows" to indicate their grazing capacity to those who lived largely by milk products (and potatoes). The physical area a farm might represent was of little interest compared to whether it would feed a particular family.[20]

To grasp the prodigious variety of customary ways of "measuring" land, we would have to imagine literally scores of "maps" constructed along very different lines than mere surface area. I have in mind the sorts of maps devised to capture our attention in which, say, the size of a country is made proportional to its population rather than its geographical size – a "fun house" effect for most viewers, in which China and India loom menacingly over Russia, Brazil and the USA, while Libya, Australia and Greenland virtually disappear. These customary maps (for there would be a great many) would construct the landscape according to units of work, yield, soil, accessibility and subsistence, none of which would necessarily accord with surface area. These measurements are decidedly *local, interested, contextual* and *historic-*

ally specific. What meets the subsistence needs of one family may not meet the subsistence needs of another. Factors such as local crop regimens, labor supply, agricultural technology, weather, etc. ensure that the standards of evaluation vary from place to place and over time. Directly apprehended by the state, they would represent a hopelessly bewildering welter of local standards. They decidedly would not lend themselves to aggregation into a single statistical series that would allow state officials to make meaningful comparisons.

(a) Statecraft and the hieroglyphics of measurement

Because local standards of measurement were tied to practical needs, because they reflected particular cropping patterns and agricultural technology, because they varied with climate and ecology, because they were "an attribute of power and an instrument of asserting class privilege" and because they were "at the center of bitter class struggle,"[21] they represented a mind-boggling problem for statecraft. Efforts to simplify or standardize measures recur like a leitmotif throughout French history – their reappearance a sure sign of previous failure. Even more modest attempts to simply codify local practices and create conversion tables were quickly overtaken and rendered obsolete by changes on the ground. The King's ministers were confronted, in effect, with a patchwork of local measurement codes, each of which had to be "cracked" separately. It was as if each district spoke its own local dialect: one that was unintelligible to outsiders and, at the same time, liable to change without notice. The central state either risked making large and potentially damaging miscalculations about local conditions or else it relied heavily on the advice of "local trackers" – the nobles and clergy in the crown's confidence – who, in turn, were not slow to take full advantage of their power.

The *illegibility* of local measurement practice was more than an administrative headache for the monarchy. It compromised the most vital and sensitive aspects of state security. Food supply was the Achilles heel of the early modern state; nothing short of religious war so menaced the state as food shortages and the resulting social upheaval. Without comparable units of measurement, it was difficult, if not impossible, to monitor markets, to compare regional prices for basic commodities, or to regulate food supplies effectively.[22] Obliged to grope its way on the basis of sketchy information, rumor and self-interested local reports, the state often responded late and inappropriately. Equity in taxation, another very sensitive political issue, was beyond the reach of a state which found it difficult to know the basic *comparative* facts about harvests and prices. A vigorous effort to collect taxes, to requisition for military garrisons or to relieve urban shortages, or any number of other measures might, given the crudeness of state intelligence, actually provoke a political crisis. Short of jeopardizing state security, the Babel of measurement produced gross inefficiencies and a pattern of either "undershooting" or "overshooting" fiscal targets.[23] No effective central monitoring or controlled comparisons were possible without standard, fixed units of measurement.

(b) *Simplification and standardization of measurement*

If scientific forestry's project of creating a simplified and legible forest encountered opposition from villagers whose use of such rights was being challenged, the political opposition to standard and legible units of measurement was even more refractory. The power to establish and impose local measures was an important feudal prerogative with material consequence which the aristocracy and clergy would not willingly surrender. Testimony to their capacity to thwart standardization is evident in the long series of abortive initiatives by "absolutist" rulers to insist on some degree of uniformity. The very particularity of local feudal practices and their impenetrability to would-be centralizers helped to underwrite the autonomy of local spheres of power.

Three factors, in the end, conspired to make what Kula calls the "metrical revolution" possible. First, the growth of market exchange encouraged uniformity in measures. Second, both popular sentiment and Enlightenment philosophy favored a single standard throughout France. And, finally, it was only the Revolution itself and, most especially, Napoleonic state-building that actually enforced the metric system in France and the Empire.

Large-scale commercial exchange and long distance trade tend to promote common standards of measurement. For relatively small-scale trade, grain dealers could trade with several suppliers so long as they knew the measure each was using. They might actually profit from their superior

grasp of the profusion of units, much as smugglers take advantage of small differences in taxes and tariffs. Beyond a certain point, however, much of commerce is composed of long chains of transactions – often over great distances – between anonymous buyers and sellers. Such trade is greatly simplified and made legible by standard weights and measures. Whereas artisinal products were typically made by a single producer according to the desires of a particular customer and carried a price specific to that object, the mass produced commodity is made by no one in particular and is intended for any purchaser at all. The virtue, in a sense, of the mass commodity is its reliable uniformity. In proportion, then, as the volume of commerce grew and the goods exchanged became increasingly standardized (for example, a ton of wheat, a dozen plough tips, twenty cartwheels), there was a growing tendency to widely agreed upon units of measurement.

The perennial state project of unifying measures throughout the Kingdom received a large degree of popular support in the eighteenth century, thanks to the "reaction feodale." Owners of feudal domains – many of them bourgeois *arrivistes* – were under pressure to maximize the return on their estates and did so, in part, by manipulating units of measurement. This sense of victimization was evident in the *cahiers* of grievances prepared for the meeting of the Estates General just before the Revolution. Although it was hardly the major grievance of members of the Third Estate, they consistently called for equal measures whereas the *cahiers* of the clergy and nobility were silent, and presumably satisfied with the status quo, on this issue. The following petition from Brittany is typical of the way in which an appeal for unitary measures could be assimilated to devotion to the Crown.

> We beg them [i.e. the King, his "noble family" and his "esteemed" chief minister Necker] to join with us in checking the abuses being perpetrated by tyrants against that class of citizens which is kind and considerate and which, until this day has been unable to present its very grievances to the very foot of the throne, and now we call on the King to mete out justice, and *we express our most sincere desire for but one king, one law, one weight, and one measure.*[24]

The simplification of measures depended, however, on the other great and revolutionary political simplification of the modern era: the concept of a uniform, homogeneous citizenship. So long as each estate operated within a separate legal sphere, so long as different categories of people were unequal in law, it followed that they might have unequal rights with respect to measures as well.[25] Equal citizenship as an idea can be traced to Enlightenment ideas and is evident in the writings of the Encyclopedists. For the Encyclopedists, the cacophony of measurement, of institutions, of inheritance laws, of taxation, of market regulations was the great obstacle to France becoming a single people. They envisioned a series of centralizing and rationalizing reforms that would transform France into a national community where, everywhere, the same codified laws, measures, customs and beliefs would prevail. It is worth noting that this project forcibly implies the concept of *national* citizenship – a national French citizen perambulating the kingdom and encountering exactly the same fair, equal conditions as the rest of his compatriots. In place of a welter of incommensurable small communities, familiar to its inhabitants but mystifying to outsiders, there would rise a single national society perfectly legible from the center. The proponent of this vision well understood that it was not mere administrative convenience that was at stake, but rather the transformation of a people: "The uniformity of customs, viewpoints, and principles of action will, inevitably, lead to a greater community of habits and predispositions."[26] The abstract grid of equal citizenship would create a new reality: the French citizen.

The homogenization of measures was, then, part and parcel of a larger, emancipatory simplification. At one stroke the equality of all Frenchmen before the law was guaranteed by the state. All of the previous "natural" distinctions were now "denaturalized" and nullified, at least in law. In an unprecedented revolutionary context where an entirely new political system was being created from first principles, it was surely no great matter to legislate uniform weights and measures. As the revolutionary decree read: "The centuries old dream of the masses of only one just measure has come true! The Revolution has given the people the meter."[27]

Proclaiming the meter officially was far simpler than ensuring that it became the daily practice of French citizens. The state could insist on the exclusive use of its units in property deeds, legal contracts, tax codes, in the courts and in the state school system. Outside these official spheres the metric system made its way only very slowly.

Despite a decree confiscating the use of the older "toise" sticks in shops and replacing them with meter sticks, the populace continued to use the older system, marking, for example, their meter sticks with the old measures. Even as late as 1828 the new measures were more a part of *le pays légal* than of *le pays réel*. As Chateaubriand remarked, "Whenever you meet a fellow who, instead of talking *arpents*, *toises*, and *pieds*, refers to hectares, meters, and centimeters, rest assured, the man is a prefect."[28]

IV Land Tenure: Local Practice and Fiscal Shorthand

The revenue of the early modern state came mainly from levies on commerce and land, the major sources of wealth. For commerce, this implied an array of excise taxes, tolls and market duties, licensing fees and tariffs. For landed wealth, this meant somehow attaching every parcel of taxable property to an individual or an institution responsible for paying the tax on it. As straightforward as this procedure seems in the context of the modern state, its achievement was enormously difficult for at least two reasons. First, the actual social facts of customary land tenure were frequently so varied and intricate as to virtually defy any simple one-to-one equation of taxpayer and taxable property. Second, there were, as in the case of units of measurement, social forces whose interests could only be damaged by the unified and transparent set of property relations desired by the state's fiscal agents. The centralizing state succeeded, in the end, in imposing a novel and legible (from the center) property system which, like the work of scientific foresters, not only radically abridged the actual tenure practices they described but, at the same time, transformed those practices to align them more closely with their shorthand, schematic reading.

(a) *An illustration*

A hypothetical case of customary land tenure practices may help demonstrate how difficult it is to assimilate such practices to the bare-bones schema of a modern cadastral map. The patterns I describe below are an amalgam of practices I have encountered in the literature or in the course of field work in Southeast Asia. While the case is hypothetical, it is not unrealistic.

Let us imagine a community in which families have usufruct rights to parcels of cropland during the main growing season. Only certain crops, however, may be planted and every seven years the usufruct land is redistributed among resident families according to each family's size and number of able-bodied adults it comprises. After the harvest of the main season crop, all cropland reverts to common land where any family may glean, graze their fowl and livestock, and even plant quickly-maturing, dry-season crops. Rights to graze fowl and livestock on pasture land held in common by the village is extended to all local families. The number of animals grazed, however, is restricted according to size of family, especially in dry years when forage is scarce. Families not using their grazing rights can give them to other villagers but not to outsiders. Everyone has the right to gather firewood for normal family needs of heat and fuel, except for the village blacksmith and baker who have larger allotments. No commercial sale from village woodlands is permitted.

Trees which are known to have been planted are, together with their fruit, the property of the family which planted them, no matter where they are now growing. Fruit fallen from such trees, however, is the property of anyone who gathers it. When a family fells one of its trees or it is felled by wind, the trunk of the tree belongs to the family, branches to the immediate neighbors, and the "tops" (leaves, twigs, fronds) to any poorer villager who carries them off. Land is set aside, exceptionally, for use or leasing out by widows with children or dependents of conscripted males. Usufruct rights to land and trees may be "let" to anyone within the village but not to anyone outside the village unless no one in the community wishes to use it.

After a crop failure leading to severe food shortage, many of these arrangements are readjusted. Better off villagers are expected to assume some responsibility for poorer relatives – by sharing their land, by hiring them or by simply feeding them. Should the shortage persist, the council of lineage heads may inventory food supply and begin daily rationing. In case of an outright famine, the women who have married into the village but have not yet borne children will not be fed and are expected to return to their natal village.

This description could be further elaborated. It is itself a simplification, but it does convey some of the actual complexity of property relations in contexts where customary local arrangements have tended to prevail. To describe the usual practices in this fashion, as if they were laws, is itself a serious distortion. They are better understood as a living, negotiated tissue of practices which are continually being adopted to new ecological and social circumstances – including, of course, power relations. Their very plasticity is the source of micro-adjustments which may or may not lead to shifts in prevailing practice.

Imagine a "law-giver" whose only concern was to respect land practices. Imagine, in other words, a written system of positive law that attempted to represent this complex skein of property relations and land tenure. The mind fairly boggles at the clauses, sub-clauses, and sub-sub-clauses that would be required to reduce these practices to a set of regulations which an administrator might understand, let alone enforce. If, in principle, they could nevertheless be codified, the resulting code would necessarily sacrifice much of the plasticity and subtle adaptability of practice. The circumstances that might provoke a new wrinkle in practices are too numerous to foresee, let alone to specify in a regulatory code. That code would, in effect, freeze a living process. Changes in the positive code designed to reflect evolving practice would, at best, represent a jerky and mechanical adaptation.

And what of the *next* village, and the village after that? Our hypothetical code giver, however devilishly clever and conscientious, would find that the code devised to fit one set of local practices would not travel well. Each village, with its own particular history, its own ecology, its particular cropping patterns, kinship alignments and economic activity would require a substantially new set of regulations. At the limit, there would be at least as many legal codes as there were communities.

Administratively, of course, such a cacophony of local property regulations would be a nightmare. Notice, especially, that the nightmare in question is not a nightmare experienced by those whose particular practices are being represented but rather by those – that is, state officials – who aspire to a uniform homogeneous, national administrative code. Local land tenure practice is, as were the "exotic" units of weights and measures discussed earlier, perfectly legible to all those inhabitants who "live" it on a day-to-day basis. Its details may often be contested and far from satisfactory to all of its local practitioners, but there is no doubting its familiarity; local residents have no difficulty in grasping its subtleties and using its flexible provisions for their own purposes. State officials, on the other hand, cannot be expected to decipher and then apply a new set of property hieroglyphs for each jurisdiction. The very concept of the modern state is inconceivable without a vastly simplified and uniform property regime that is legible, and hence manipulable from the center.

Use of the term "simple" to describe modern property law, whose intricacies provide employment to armies of legal professionals, will seem grossly misplaced. It is surely the case that property law has in any respects become an impenetrable thicket for ordinary citizens. The use of the term "simple" in this context is thus both *relative* and *perspectival*. Modern freehold tenure is tenure that is mediated through the state and therefore readily legible only to those who have sufficient training and grasp of the state statutes to allow them to decipher it. Its relative simplicity is lost on those who cannot break the code, just as the relative clarity of customary tenure to the villagers who live it is lost on the mystified outsider.

The fiscal/administrative goal toward which all modern states aspire is to measure, codify and simplify land tenure in much the same way as scientific forestry reconceived the forest. In no way could the state begin to incorporate the luxuriant variety of customary land tenure. The historical solution, at least for the liberal state, has typically been the heroic simplification of individual, freehold tenure. Land is owned by a legal individual who disposes of wide powers of use, inheritance or sale and whose ownership is represented by a uniform title deed enforced through the judicial and police institutions of the state. Just as the flora of the forest were reduced to *Normalbaum*, so were the complex tenure arrangements of customary practice reduced to freehold, transferrable title. In an agrarian setting, the administrative landscape was blanketed with a uniform grid of homogeneous land, each parcel of which has a legal person as owner and, hence, taxpayer. How much easier it then becomes to assess such property and its owner on the basis of its acreage, its soil class, the crops it *normally* bears and its assumed yield than to untangle the thicket of common property and mixed forms of tenure.

The crowning artifact of this mighty simplification is the *cadastral map*: a more or less complete and accurate survey of land-holdings conducted by trained surveyors and mapped to a given scale. Since the driving logic behind the map is to create a manageable and reliable format for taxation, the map is associated with a property register in which each specified (usually numbered) lot on the map is linked to an "owner" who is responsible for paying its taxes. The cadastral map and property register is to the taxation of land as the maps and tables of the scientific forester were to the fiscal exploitation of the forest.

(b) *The* Code Rural *that "almost" was*

The rulers of post-Revolutionary France confronted a rural society that was a nearly impenetrable web of feudal *and* revolutionary practices. It was inconceivable that they could catalogue its complexities let alone effectively eliminate them in the short run. Ideologically, their commitment to equality and liberty was contradicted by customary rural contracts that, as in craft guilds, still employed the terms "master" (*maître*) and "servant" (*serviteur*). As rulers of a new nation – not a kingdom – they were likewise offended by the utter absence of any overall legal framework for social relations. For some, a new civil code covering all Frenchmen would be sufficient.[29] But for bourgeois owners of rural property who had, like their noble neighbors, been threatened by the local uprisings of the Revolution and La Grand Peur and, more generally, by the aggressiveness of an emboldened and autonomous peasantry, an explicit Code Rural seemed necessary to underwrite their security.

In the end, no post-Revolutionary rural code attracted a winning coalition, even amidst a flurry of Napoleonic codes in nearly all other realms. The history of the stalemate is, for our purposes, very instructive. The first proposal for a code, drafted between 1803 and 1807, swept away most traditional rights (for example, common pasturage and free passage through others' property) and essentially recast rural property relations in the light of bourgeois property rights and freedom of contract.[30] Although it pre-figured modern French practice, many revolutionaries blocked it because, at the time, they feared that its hands-off liberalism would allow large landholders to recreate the subordination of feudalism in a new guise.

A re-examination of the entire issue was then ordered by Napoleon and presided over by Joseph Verneilh Puyrasseau. Concurrently, the Deputé Lalouette proposed to do precisely what I supposed, in the hypothetical example, was impossible. That is, he undertook to systematically gather information about all local practices, to classify and codify them, and then to sanction them by decree. The decree in question would become the *Code Rural*. Two problems undid this charming scheme to present the rural populace with a rural code that simply reflected its own practices. The first difficulty was to specify which aspects of the literally "infinite diversity"[31] of rural production relations to represent and codify. Even in a particular locality, practices varied greatly from farm to farm and over time; any codification would be quasi-arbitrary and artificially static. To codify local practices was, thus, a profoundly political act. Local notables would be able to sanction their preferences with the mantle of law while others would fear the loss of practices they depended on. Second, of course, Lalouette's plan was mortal threat to all those state-centralizers and economic modernizers for whom legible, national property regime was the precondition of progress. As Aberdam notes, "the Lalouette project would have brought about exactly what Merlin de Douai and the bourgeois, revolutionary jurists always sought to avoid."[32] Lalouette's proposal code was never passed, nor was the "official" proposal by Verneilh because it, like its predecessor in 1807, seemed to be designed exclusively to strengthen the hand of landowners.

(c)   *The illegibility of communal tenure*

The pre-modern and early modern state, as we have noted, dealt fiscally more with communities than with individuals. Some apparently individual taxes, such as the notorious Russian "soul tax" collected from all subjects, were actually paid by the community directly or through the nobles whose subjects they were. Failure to deliver the required sum would usually lead to collective punishment.[33] The only agents of taxation who regularly reached to the level of the household and its cultivated fields were the local nobility and clergy in the course of collecting feudal dues and the religious tithe. For its part, the state had neither the administrative tools nor the information to penetrate to this level.

The limitations on state knowledge were partly due to the complexity and variability of local production. This was not the most important reason, however. The collective form of taxation meant that it was generally in the interest of local officials to misrepresent their situation so as to minimize the local tax and conscription burden. To this end,

they might minimize the local population, systematically understate the acreage under cultivation, hide new commercial profits, exaggerate crop losses after storms, droughts, etc.[34] The whole point of the cadastral map and land register was precisely to eliminate this fiscal feudalism and rationalize the fiscal take of the state. As the scientific forester needed an inventory of trees to realize the commercial potential of the forest, so the fiscal reformer needed a detailed inventory of landownership to realize the maximum, sustainable revenue yield.[35]

Assuming that the state had the will to challenge the resistance of the local nobles and elites and the financial resources to undertake a full cadastral survey, which was very time-consuming and expensive, it faced other obstacles as well. There were, in particular, communal forms of tenure that could just not be adequately represented in cadastral form. Rural living in seventeenth and early eighteenth century Denmark, for example, was organized by *ejerlav*, whose members had certain specified rights to use local arable, waste and forest land. It would have been impossible in such a community to associate a household or individual with a particular holding on a cadastral map. The Norwegian large farm (*gard*) posed similar problems. Households held rights to a given proportion of the value (*skyld*) of the farm, not to plots of land. "Normally the joint owners could not point to any part of the farm which was their own."[36] Although it was possible to estimate the arable land of a community and, making some assumptions about crop yields and subsistence needs, arrive at a plausible tax burden, these were villages which derived a substantial part of their livelihood from the "commons" – for example, fishing, forestry, resin collection, hunting, charcoal making, etc. Monitoring this kind of income was almost impossible. Nor would crude estimates of the value of the commons solve this problem, inasmuch as inter-commoning between several villages was (though outlawed) widely practiced. The mode of production in such communities was simply incompatible with the assumption of individual freehold tenure implicit in a cadastral map. It was claimed, though the evidence is not convincing, that common property was less productive than freehold property.[37] The state's case against communal forms of land tenure, however, was based on the correct observation that it is fiscally illegible and, hence, fiscally less productive. Rather than trying, like the hapless.

Lalouette, to bring the map into line with reality, the historical resolution has generally been for the state to impose a property system in line with its fiscal grid.

Pre-revolutionary Russia provides a nearly textbook example of state attempts to create individual tenure in keeping with its convictions about agricultural growth and administrative order. Most of rural Russia, even after the emancipation of 1861, was a model of fiscal illegibility. Communal farms of tenure prevailed and the state had little or no knowledge of who cultivated which strips of land or what their yields and income were.

Maps of two villages *before* the consolidation of individual farms serve to illustrate the fiscal complexity of "open-field" land tenure.

Novoselok village had a varied economy of cultivation, grazing, and forestry while Khotynitsa village was limited to arable and some grazing. The complex welter of strips is designed to ensure that every village household receives a strip of land in each and every ecological zone. An individual household might have as many as ten to fifteen different plots constituting something of a representative sample of the village's ecological zones and micro-climates. The logic of distribution spread a family's risks prudently and, from time to time, the land was reshuffled as families grew or shrank.[38] It was enough to make the head of a cadastral surveyor swim. At first glance it would seem as if the village itself would need a staff of professional surveyors to get things right. In practice, the system was quite simple to those who lived it. The strips of land were generally straight and parallel so that a readjustment could be made by moving small stakes along just one side of a field without ever having to think of areal dimensions. Where the other end of the field was not parallel, the stakes would be shifted to compensation for the fact that the strip lay toward the narrower or wider end of the larger field. Irregular fields were divided, not according to area, but according to yield. Visually – and especially as a problem in cadastral mapping – the pattern seemed convoluted and irrational. But to those familiar with it, it was simple enough and worked admirably for their purposes.

The dream of state officials and agrarian reformers, at least since emancipation, was to transform the open field system into a series of consolidated, independent farmsteads on what they took to be the western European model. They were driven by the desire to break the

hold of the community over the individual household and to move from collective taxation of the whole community to a tax on individual landholders. Fiscal goals were very much connected to reigning ideas of agricultural progress. Under Count Witte and Stolypin, plans for reform shared common premises which Yaney describes as follows:

> *First tableau*: poor peasants, crowded together in villages, suffering from hunger, running into each other with their plows on their tiny strips.
> *Second tableau*: agriculture specialist agent leads a few progressive peasants off to new lands, leaving those remaining more room.
> *Third tableau*: departing peasants, freed from restraints of strips, set up khutors [integral farmstead with dwelling] on new fields and adapt latest methods. Those who remain, freed of village and family restraints, plunge into a demand economy – all are richer, more productive, the cities get fed, and the peasants are not proletarianized.[39]

It was abundantly clear that the prejudicial attitude toward inter-stripping was based as much on the autonomy of the Russian village, its illegibility to outsiders and prevailing dogma about scientific agriculture as it was on hard evidence.[40] Once given a consolidated private plot, they reasoned, the peasant would suddenly want to get rich, would organize his household into an efficient workforce and take up scientific agriculture. The maps below (Figs. 1 and 2) illustrate the cadastral order brought to both villages in the wake of the Stolypin Reform.

In Novoselok village, seventeen independent farmsteads (*khutor*) were created in a way that aimed at giving each household a share of meadow, arable and forest. In Khotynitsa village, ten *khutor* were created as well as 78 farms (*otrub*) whose owners continued to dwell in the village center. As a cadastral matter, the new farms were mappable, easily legible from above and outside, and, since each was owned by an identifiable person, assessable.

These two maps, taken alone, are very misleading. Such model villages suggest an efficient cadastral machinery working its way diligently through the countryside turning open-field chaos into tidy little farms. Reality was something else. In fact, the dream of orderly, rectangular fields was only approximated on newly settled land,

Figure 1. Novoselok village, before (above) and after (see p. 39) the Reform. *Source*: Reproduced with permission from Yaney 1982, © 1992 Board of Trustees of the University of Illinois. Used with permission of the University of Illinois Press

where the surveyor faced little geographical or social resistance.[41] Elsewhere, the reformers were generally thwarted despite tremendous pressure to produce integral farms. There were unauthorized consolidations, though they were forbidden; there were "paper" consolidations in which the new farmers continued to farm their strips as before.

Inadvertently, the Peasant Bank, under great pressure to loan money to poor peasants, encouraged the older allotment system. The bank needed collateral it could seize in the event of a default, but poorer peasants farming village allotment land had no fixed land that could serve as security.[42] Faced with this quandary, the bank found itself loaning

Khutor boundaries

Consolidated plot belonging to one household

Cultivated land

Meadow land

Forest

Swamp

Road

Abinetovo Lake

| feet | | | |
| 0 | 1000 | 2000 | 3000 |

| meters | | | |
| 0 | 300 | 600 | 900 |

to whole villages or to groups of peasants farming adjacent, identifiable plots. The best evidence that the agricultural property system had *not* become legible to central tax officials was the immensely damaging procurement policies pursued by the Tsarist government during World War I. No one knew what a reasonable levy of grain or draft animals might be; as a result, some districts were ruined and others managed to hoard grain and livestock.[43] The same experience of forced procurement without any adequate knowledge of land-holdings and wealth was repeated again after the October Revolution during the period of "War Communism."[44]

Figure 2. Khotynitsa village, before (above) and after (see p. 41) the Reform. *Source*: Reproduced with permission from Yaney 1982, © 1992 Board of Trustees of the University of Illinois. Used with permission of the University of Illinois Press.

(d) *The cadastral map as objective information for outsiders*

The value of the cadastral map to the state lies in its abstraction and universality. In principle, at least, the same objective standard can be applied throughout the kingdom, regardless of local context, to produce a complete and unambiguous map of all landed property. The completeness of the cadastral map depends, in a curious way, on its very thinness. For, taken alone, it is essentially a geometric representation of the borders or frontiers between parcels of land. What lies inside the parcel is left blank – unspecified – since it is not germane to the map plotting itself.

There are surely many other things far more important to know about a parcel of land than its surface area and the location of its boundaries. What kind of soil it has, what crops can be grown on it, how hard it is to work and how close it is to a market are the first kinds of questions a potential purchaser might ask. These are also questions a tax assessor would want to ask as well. From a capitalist perspective, the physical dimensions of land are beside the point. But these other qualities only become relevant (especially to the state) once the terrain to which they apply has been located and measured. They also, unlike location and dimension, involve judgments that are complex (hence more open to fraud) and easily overtaken by events. Crop rotations and yields may change, new tools or machines may transform cultivation and markets may shift. The cadastral survey, by contrast, is precise, schematic,

Khutor boundaries — — —
Otrub boundaries ———
Village dwellings
Arable land
Alluvial meadow

Meadow
Sands
Clay
Quarry
Road ———

Consolidated plot
belonging to one
household (see p. 40)

general and uniform. Whatever its other defects, it is the precondition of a tax regimen that comprehensively links every patch of land with its owner – and taxpayer.[45] In this spirit, the survey for a 1807 Dutch land tax (inspired by Napoleonic France) stresses that all surveyors were to use the same measurements, their instruments were to be periodically inspected to ensure conformity, and all maps were to be drawn up on a uniform scale of 1:2,880.[46]

Land maps in general and cadastral maps in particular are designed to make the local situation legible to an *outsider*. For purely local purposes, a cadastral map was redundant. Everyone knew who held, say, the meadow by the river and the feudal dues it carried; there was no need to know its precise dimensions. A substantial domain might

have the kind of prose map, or *terrier*, one finds in old deeds ("from the large oak tree, north 120 feet to the river bank, thence...") with a notation about the holder's obligations to the domain. But a proper map seems to have come into use especially when a brisk market in land developed. The Netherlands was thus a leader in land mapping because of its early commercialization and the unique fact that the draining of new land by windmills was often a speculative enterprise in which the land was surveyed so each investor would know his holding. The map was especially crucial to the new bourgeois owners of landed estates as it allowed them to survey a large territory at a glance. Its miniaturization served as an *aide-mémoire* when the property consisted of many small parcels and/ or the owner was not intimately familiar with the terrain. As early as 1607, an English surveyor, John Norden, sold his services to the aristocracy on the premise that the map was a substitute for the tour of inspection.

> A plot rightly drawne by true information, discribeth so the lively image of a mannor, and every branch and member of the same, as the lord sitting in his chayre, may see what he hath, and where and how he lyeth, and in whole use and occupation of every particular is upon suddaine view.[47]

A national tax administration requires the same logic: a legible bureaucratic formula which a new official can quickly grasp and administer from the documents in his office.

(e) *What's missing in this picture?*

Isaiah Berlin, in his study of Tolstoy, compared the hedgehog who knew "one big thing" to the fox who knew "many things." The sharply focused interest of the scientific foresters in commercial lumber and that of cadastral officials in land revenue constrain them, like the hedgehog, to find clear-cut answers to one question. The naturalist and the farmer are like the fox; they know many things about forests and cultivable land respectively. Although the *range* of knowledge of the forester and cadastral official is far narrower, we should not forget that they know what they do know in a systematic and comprehensive way – a way that allows them to see and understand things a fox would not grasp. What we want to emphasize here, however, is how this knowledge is gained at the expense of rather static and myopic view of land tenure.

The cadastral map is very much like a *still* photograph of the current in a river. It represents the parcels of land as they were arranged and owned at the moment the survey was conducted. But the current is always moving and, in periods of major social upheaval and growth, a cadastral survey may freeze a scene of great turbulence. Changes are taking place on field boundaries; land is being sub-divided or consolidated by inheritance or purchase, new canals, roads and railways are being cut; land use is changing, and so forth. Inasmuch as these particular changes directly affect tax assessments, there are provisions for recording them on the map or in a title register. The annotations and marginalia at some point, render the map illegible, whereupon a more up-to-date, but still static, map must be drawn up and the process is repeated.

No operating land revenue system can, however, stop at the mere identification of parcel and ownership. Other schematic facts, themselves static, must be created to arrive at some judgment of a sustainable tax burden. Land may be graded by "soil class," how well watered it is, what crops are grown on it, and its presumed "average yield" – this last often checked by sample "crop-cuttings." These facts are themselves changing or they are averages that may mask great variation. Like the still photo of the cadastral map, they grow more unrealistic with time and must be re-examined.

These state simplifications, like all state simplifications, are always far more static and schematic than the actual social phenomena they presume to typify. The farmer very rarely experiences an average crop, an average rainfall, or average price for his crops. Much of the long history of rural "tax revolts" in early modern Europe and elsewhere can be illuminated by the lack of fit between an unyielding fiscal claim on the one hand and the often wildly fluctuating capacity of the rural population to meet that claim, on the other.[48] And yet, even the most equitable, well-intentioned cadastral system cannot be uniformly administered except on the basis of stable units of measurement and calculation. It can no more reflect the actual complexity of a farmer's experience than the scientific forester schemes can reflect the complexity of the naturalist's forest.[49]

Governed by a practical, concrete objective, the cadastral lens also ignored anything lying outside its sharply etched field of vision. This was reflected in a loss of detail in the survey itself. Surveyors, one recent Swedish study found, made the fields more "regular" geometrically than they in fact were. Ignoring small "jogs" and "squiggles" made their job easier and did not materially affect the outcome.[50] Just as the commercial forester found it convenient to overlook minor forest products, so the cadastral official tended to ignore all but the major commercial use of a field (for example, wheat, hay). That the field might also be a significant source of bedding straw, gleaning, rabbits, birds, frogs, mushrooms, etc., was not so much unknown as ignored lest it needlessly complicate a straightforward administrative formula.[51] The most significant myopia, of course, was that the cadastral map and assessment system considered only the dimensions of the land and its value as a productive asset or as a commodity for sale. Any value land might have for subsistence purposes or for the local ecology were bracketed as, of course, were aesthetic, ritual or sentimental values.

(f) *Transformation and resistance*

The cadastral map is an instrument of control which both reflects and consolidates the power of those who commission it ... The cadastral map is partisan: where knowledge is power, it provides comprehensive information to be used to the advantage of some and the detriment of others, as rulers and ruled were well aware in the tax struggles of the 18th and 19th centuries. Finally, the cadastral map is active: in portraying one reality, as in the settlement of the new world or in India, it helps obliterate the old.[52]

The shorthand formulas through which tax officials must apprehend reality are not mere tools of observation. By a kind of "fiscal Heisenberg principle," they frequently have the power to transform the facts they take note of.

The "door and window tax" established in France under the Directory and abolished only in 1917 is a striking case in point.[53] Its originator must have reasoned that the number of windows and doors in a dwelling was proportional to its size. Thus a tax assessor need not enter the house or measure it but merely count the doors and windows. As a simple, workable formula, it was a brilliant stroke, but it was not without consequences. Peasant dwellings were subsequently designed or renovated with the formula in mind so as to have as few openings as possible. While the fiscal losses could be recouped by raising the tax *per* opening, the long run effects on the health of the rural population lasted more than a century.

Novel state-imposed forms of land tenure were far more revolutionary than a door and window tax. It was a whole new institutional nexus. However simple and uniform the new tenure system was to an administrator, it flung villagers willy-nilly into a world of title deeds, land offices, fees, assessments and applications. They faced powerful new specialists in the form of land clerks surveyors, judges and lawyers whose rules of procedure and decisions were unfamiliar.

Where the new tenure system was a colonial imposition – that is, where it was totally unfamiliar, where it was imposed by alien conquerors using an unintelligible language and institutional

context, and where local practices bore no resemblance to freehold tenure – the consequences were far-reaching. The permanent settlement in India, for example, literally created a new class who, because they paid the revenue, became full owners with rights of inheritance and sale where none had existed earlier.[54] At the same time, literally millions of cultivators, tenants and laborers lost their customary rights of access to the land and its products. Those in the colonies who first plumbed the mysteries of the new tenure administration enjoyed unique opportunities. Thus the Vietnamese *secrétaires* and *interprètes* who served as intermediaries between the French officials in the Mekong Delta and their Vietnamese subjects were in a position to make great fortunes. By concentrating on getting the paperwork in order – the title deeds and appropriate fees – they occasionally became, overnight, landlords to whole villages of cultivators who had imagined they had opened common land free for the taking. They might, of course, occasionally use their knowledge to see their compatriots safely through the new legal thicket. Whatever their conduct their fluency in a language of tenure specifically designed to be legible and transparent to administrators, coupled with the illiteracy of the rural population under them to whom the new tenure was indecipherable, was a momentous shift in power relations.[55]

Freehold title and standard land measurement were to central taxation and the market in real estate what central bank currency was to the marketplace. By the same token, they threatened to destroy a great deal of local power and autonomy. No wonder then, that they should have been so vigorously resisted. In the eighteenth century European context, any general cadastral survey was, by definition, a gambit of centralization; the local clergy and nobility were bound to see both their own taxing powers and the exemptions they enjoyed menaced. Commoners were likely to see it as a pretext for an additional local tax. Colbert proposed to conduct a national cadastral survey of France but was thwarted in 1679 by the combined opposition of the aristocracy and clergy. More than a century later, after the Revolution, Babeuf, in his "Projet de cadastre perpetuel," dreamed of a perfectly egalitarian land reform in which everyone would get an equal parcel.[56] He too was thwarted.

We must keep in mind not only the capacity of state simplifications to transform the world, but also the capacity of the society to modify, subvert, block and even overturn the categories imposed upon them. Here it is useful to distinguish what might be called "facts-on-paper" from "facts-on-the-ground." As Sally Falk Moore and many others have emphasized, the land office records may serve as the basis for taxation, but they may have little to do with the actual rights to the land. Paper owners may not be the effective owners.[57] Russian peasants, as we saw, might register a "paper" consolidation while continuing to inter-strip. Land invasions, squatting and poaching, if successful, represent the exercise of de facto property rights which are not represented on paper. Certain land taxes and tithes have been evaded or defied to the point where they have become a dead letter.[58] The gulf between land tenure "facts-on-paper" and facts-on-the-ground is probably greatest at moments of social turmoil and revolt. But even in more tranquil times there will always be a "shadow land tenure system" lurking beside and beneath the official account in the land records office. We must never assume that local practice conforms with state "theory."

All central states recognized the value of a uniform, comprehensive cadastral map. Carrying it out, however, was another matter. As a rule of thumb, cadastral mapping was earlier and more comprehensive where a powerful central state could impose itself on a relatively weak civil society. Where, by contrast, civil society was well organized and the state relatively weak, cadastral mapping was late, often voluntary, and fragmentary. Thus, Napoleonic France was mapped much earlier than England where the legal profession managed for a long time to stymie this threat to their local, income-earning function. It followed from the same logic that conquered colonies ruled by fiat would often be cadastrally mapped before the metropolitan nation which ordered it. Ireland may have been the very first. After the Cromwellian conquest, as Ian Hacking notes, "Ireland was completely surveyed for land, buildings, people, and cattle under the directorship of William Petty, in order to facilitate the rape of that nation by the English in 1679."[59]

Where the colony was a thinly populated settler-colony, as in North America or Australia, the obstacles to a thoroughgoing, uniform cadastral grid were minimal. It was a question, in this context, less of mapping pre-existing patterns of land use than of surveying parcels of land that would be given or sold to new arrivals from Europe and ignoring, of course, indigenous practices. Thomas Jefferson, with his rational Enlightenment eye, imagined dividing the United States west of the Ohio River into "hundreds" – squares ten miles on a side – with settlers required to take an already designated parcel. The geometrical clarity of Jefferson's proposal was not merely an aesthetic choice; he "argued that irregular lots inspired fraud, and could point to the experience of Massachusetts which discovered that holdings in the country typically yielded 10% more land, and often 100% more land, than had been granted."[60] Not only did the regularity of the grid create legibility for the taxing authority but it was a convenient and cheap way to package land and market it in homogeneous units. Jefferson's plan was modified by Congress to provide for rectangular lots and townships that were 36 square miles and, in practice, land titling did not always follow the prescribed pattern.

The Torrens system of land titling, developed in Australia and New Zealand in the 1860s, provided a lithographed, pre-surveyed grid of allotments which had only to be registered by settlers on a first-come, first-served basis. It was the quickest and most economical means yet devised to sell land and it was later adopted in many British colonies. The more homogeneous and rigid the geometric grid, however, the more likely it was to run afoul of the actual natural features of the non-conforming landscape. The possibility for surprises was nicely captured in this satirical verse from New Zealand.[61]

Now the road through Michael's section
    though it looked well on the map
For the use it was intended
    wasn't really worth a rap
And at night was not unlikely
    to occasion some mishap.

It was nicely planned on paper
    and was ruled without remorse
Over cliffs, and spurs and gullies
    with a straight and even course
Which precluded locomotion
    on part of man or horse.

(g) *Cadastral surveys and the utilitarian state*

The cadastral survey was but one technique in the growing armory of the modern, utilitarian state. Where the pre-modern state was content with a level of intelligence sufficient to allow it to keep order, extract taxes and raise armies, the utilitarian state increasingly aspired to "take in charge" the physical and human resources of the nation and make them more productive. These more positive ends of statecraft required a much greater knowledge of the society. An inventory of land, people, incomes, occupations, resources and deviance was the logical place to begin. "The need for the increasingly bureaucratic state to organize itself and control its resources gave an impulse to the collection of vital and other statistics; to forestry and rational agriculture; to surveying and exact cartography; and to public hygiene and climatology."[62]

Although the purposes of the state were broadening, what the state wanted to know was still directly related to those purposes. The nineteenth century Prussian state was, for example, very much interested in the ages and sexes of immigrants and emigrants, but it was *not* interested in their religion or "race." What mattered to the state was keeping track of possible draft-dodgers and maintaining a supply of men of military age.[63] The increasing concern of the state with productivity, health, sanitation, education, transportation, mineral resources, grain production and investment was less an abandonment of the older objectives of statecraft than a broadening and deepening of what those objectives entailed in the modern world.

V   Legibility and Centralization

(a)   *Surnames*

Some of the most taken-for-granted categories with which we now routinely apprehend the social world around us had their origin in state projects of standardization and legibility. Consider something as fundamental as permanent surnames.

A vignette from the popular film *The Witness* illustrates how, among strangers, we rely on surnames as key navigational aids.[64] The police detective in the story is attempting to locate a young Amish boy who may have witnessed a murder in a bus station. Although he has a surname to go on, he is thwarted by several aspects of Amish traditionalism, including their antique dialect of German. His first instinct is, of course, to reach for the telephone book – a list of proper names and addresses – but the Amish don't have telephones! Furthermore, he learns that the Amish have a very small number of very common last names. His

quandary reminds us that a great variety of surnames and "given-names" allow us to identify unambiguously a large number of individuals whom we may never have met. A world without such names is bewildering; the detective finds Amish society, for his purposes, so opaque that he needs a "native-tracker" to find his way.

Customary naming practices throughout much of the world are enormously rich. Among some peoples, it is not uncommon to have different infant names, childhood names, adult names and, in some cases, death names, joking names, ritual names, names to use with same-sex friends, names one is called by in-laws, sorrow names and so forth. Each name is specific to a stage of life, a social setting, or a particular interlocutor. Two people will frequently, in this context, use different names for the same individual. To the question, "What is your name?" – which has an unambiguous answer in the contemporary West – the only plausible answer is, "it depends."[65]

For the insider who grows up using these naming practices they are both legible and clarifying. Each name and the contexts of its use conveys important social knowledge. Like the network of alleys in Bruges, the assortment of local weights and measures and the intricacies of customary land tenure, its complexity has some very direct and often quite practical relationship to local purposes. For an outsider, however, the Byzantine complexity of local names is a formidable obstacle to understanding the local society. Finding someone, let alone situating him or her in a kinship network or tracing the inheritance of property, becomes a major production. If, in addition, the population in question has reason to conceal its identity and its activities from external authority, the camouflage value of such naming practices is considerable.

Until at least the fourteenth century, the great majority of Europeans did not have permanent patronymic. An individual's name was typically an amalgam of his (if male) given name and his father's given name. Thus, in the English case, William *Robertson's* male son might be called Thomas Williamson (son of William) while Thomas's son, in turn might be called Henry Thompson (Thomas's son). Note that the grandson's name, by itself, bears no evidence of his grandfather's identity, complicating the tracing of descent through names alone. The adoption of a *permanent* patronym – largely a state project connected to taxation and inheritance – greatly improved the legibility of kinship and property. At the time of their establishment, last names often had a kind of local logic to them: John who owned a mill became John Miller; John who made cart-wheels became John Wheelwright; John who was physically very small became John Short, etc. As their male descendants retained the patronym, whatever their subsequent occupations or stature, the names later assumed an arbitrary cast.

The development of fixed surnames (literally, a name *added* to another) went hand-in-hand with the development of written official documents such as tithe records, marriage entries, censuses, tax records, land records, etc.[66] One source suggests that last names were established by statute in the fourteenth century under Edward II.[67] A brief anecdote by the same source illustrates the kinds of official situations that might create a fixed patronymism where none existed before. A Welsh-man appearing in an English court in the early sixteenth century was asked to identify himself. He replied in Welsh – and in Old Testament style, "Thomas Ap [son of] William, Ap Thomas, Ap Richard, Ap Hoel, Ap Evan Vaghan" and was admonished by the judge. "Whereupon he after called himself Moston, according to the name of his principal house, and left that surname to his posteritie."[68] For this newly-minted Thomas Moston, it is entirely plausible that the official surname remained on the official court records but was never known or used by his own local contemporaries. Colonial situations and religious conversions routinely produce new names that are specific to the new context. Thus in many British colonies with a substantial Chinese population, all school pupils were assigned an English given-name at school which served both to make the class more legible to an English-speaking in-structor and to emphasize that the colonists' school required a new identity. Those who came most frequently into contact with officials and docu-ments were, one suspects, the most likely to take permanent surnames first.[69] In the West, women, domestic servants and tied laborers were typically the last to adopt surnames (and to be given the vote) precisely because they were legally subsumed as minors in the charge of the head-of-family.

Universal last names are a fairly recent historical phenomenon. They were a great step forward in the legibility of the entire population. The tracking of property ownership and inheritance, the collec-tion of the title and other taxes, police work, con-scription, court records, and the control of epidemics were all made immeasurably easier by the clarity of full names and, increasingly, fixed addresses. While the utilitarian state was commit-ted to a complete inventory of its population, liberal ideas of citizenship, which implied voting rights and conscription, also contributed greatly to the standardization of naming practices. The le-gislative imposition of permanent surnames is par-ticularly clear in the case of Jews in Western Europe who had no tradition of last names. A Napoleonic decree "concernant les Juifs qui n'ont pas de nom de famille et de prénoms fixes," in 1808, mandated last names. Austrian legislation of 1787, as part of the emancipation process, re-quired Jews to choose last names or, if they refused, to have fixed last names chosen for them. In Prussia the emancipation of the Jews was contingent upon the adoption of surnames.[70] Many of the immi-grants (Jewish and non-Jewish) to the United States had no permanent surnames when they set sail. Very few, however, made it through the initial paperwork without an official last name that they and their descendants continued to carry.

The process of creating fixed last names con-tinues today in much of the Third World and on the "tribal frontiers" of more developed coun-tries.[71] Reze Shah, the father of the deposed Shah, ordered all Iranians to take the last name of their town of residence in order to "rationalize the country's family names." Ali Akbar Rafsanjani thus means Ali Akbar from Rafsanjan.[72] Today, of course, there are now many other state-impelled standard designations which have vastly improved the capacity of the state to identify an individual. The creation of birth and death certificates, spe-cific addresses (for example, not John-on-the-hill), identity cards, internal passports, social security numbers, photographs, fingerprints and, finally, DNA profiles, have superseded the rather crude instrument of the permanent surname. That sur-name was, however, a first and crucial step in making individual citizens officially legible and it is, along with the photograph, the first fact on documents of identity.

(b) *The creation of a standard official language*

The great cultural barrier posed by a separate and unintelligible language is perhaps the most effect-ive guarantee that a social world, easily accessible to insiders, will remain opaque to outsiders.[73] Just as the stranger or state official might need a local guide to find his way around sixteenth century

Bruges, he would need a local interpreter to understand or be understood in an unfamiliar linguistic environment. A real language barrier is, however, a far more powerful basis for autonomy than a complex residence pattern. It is also the bearer of a distinct history, a cultural sensibility, a literature, a mythology, a musical past, etc. In this respect, a unique language represents a formidable obstacle to state knowledge, let alone colonization, control, manipulation, instruction and propaganda.

Of all state simplifications, then, the imposition of a single, official language may be the most powerful and the precondition of many other simplifications. This process should probably be viewed, as Eugen Weber suggests in the case of France, as a process of domestic colonization in which various foreign provinces (for example, Brittany, Occitanie) were to be linguistically subdued and culturally incorporated.[74] The first efforts to insist on the use of French make it very clear that the objective of the state was the legibility of local practice. Officials insisted, above all, that every legal document, will, inquest, document of sale, debt, contract, annuity, and property deed be drawn up in French. So long as these documents remained in local vernaculars they were daunting to an official sent from Paris and virtually impossible to bring into conformity with central schemes of legal and administrative standardization. The campaign of linguistic centralization was virtually assured some success since it went hand-in-hand with an expansion of state power. By the late nineteenth century, dealing with the state was all but unavoidable for any but a small minority of the population. Petitions, court cases, school documents, applications, correspondence with officials were all necessarily in French. One can hardly imagine a more effective formula for immediately devaluing local knowledge and privileging all those who had mastered the official linguistic code. It was a gigantic shift in power. Those at the periphery lacking competence in French were rendered mute and marginal. They were now in need of a local guide to the new "state-culture" which appeared in the form of lawyers, *notaires*, schoolteachers, clerks, soldiers, etc.

A cultural project, as one might suspect, lurked behind linguistic centralization. French was seen as the bearer of a national civilization; the purpose of imposing it was not merely to have provincials digest the Code Napoleon but also to bring them Voltaire, Racine, Parisian newspapers and a na-

tional education. As Weber provocatively puts it, "There can be no clearer expression of imperialist sentiment, a white man's burden of Francophony, whose first conquests were to be right at home."[75] Where the command of Latin had once defined participation in a wider culture for a small elite, the command of French now defined full participation in French culture. The implicit cultural logic of the move was to define a hierarchy of cultures, relegating local languages and their regional cultures to, at best, a quaint provincialism. At the apex of this implicit pyramid was Paris and its institutions: ministries, schools, academies (including the guardian of the language, the Académie Française). The relative success of this cultural project hinged on both coercion and inducements. "It was centralization," said Alexandre Sanguinetti, "which permitted the making of France despite the French, or in the midst of their indifference . . . France is a deliberate political construction for whose creation the central power has never ceased to fight." Standard (Parisian) French and Paris were not only focal points of power; they were also magnets. The growth of markets, physical mobility, new careers, political patronage, public service, and a national educational system all meant that facility in French and connections to Paris were the paths of social advancement and material success. It was a state simplification that promised to reward those who complied with its logic and penalize those who ignored it.

(c) *The centralization of traffic patterns*

The linguistic centralization impelled by the imposition of Parisian French as the official standard was replicated in a centralization of traffic. Just as the new dispensation in language made Paris the hub of communication, so the new road and rail systems increasingly favored movement to and from Paris over interregional or local traffic. State policy resembled, in computer parlance, a "hardwiring" pattern which made the provinces far more accessible – far more legible – to central authorities than even the absolutist kings had imagined.

Let us contrast, in an ideal-typical fashion, a relatively uncentralized network of communication on the one hand, with a relatively centralized network on the other. The uncentralized pattern, if mapped, would be the physical image of the actual movements of goods and people along routes not created by administrative fiat. Such movements would not be random; they would necessarily reflect the ease of movement along valleys, by watercourses and defiles, and the location of important resources and ritual sites. Eugen Weber captures the wealth of human activities that animate these movements across the landscape:

> ...not that traffic was lacking. On the contrary, much traffic and a poor communication network were characteristic of the old society. Trails, packs, tracks, lanes, and causeways covered the countryside...They served private needs going from village to village, from farm or hamlet to field, orchard, pasture, or bourg: They served professional pursuits, like the special trails followed by glassmakers, carriers or sellers of salt, potters, or those that led to forges, mines, quarries and hemp fields, or those along which flax, hemp, linen and yarn were taken to market. There were pilgrimage routes and procession trails...[77]

If we can imagine, for the sake of argument, physical resources being evenly distributed and their being no great physical barrier to movement (for example, mountains, swamps), then the map of paths in use might come to approximate a dense capillary network. The tracing would, of course, never be entirely random. Market towns based on location and resources would constitute small hubs and so would religious shrines, quarries, mines, etc.[78] In the French case, as well, the network of roads would long have reflected the centralizing ambitions of local lords and national monarchs. The point of this simplification is merely to indicate a landscape of communication routes that is only lightly marked by state centralization. It would resemble, in many ways, the complex urbanscape of a late medieval city like Bruges.

The modernizers of nineteenth century France, most notably Napoleon, superimposed on this pattern a carefully planned grid of administrative centralization. This grid of road and rail lines (for example, Gare du Nord, Gare de l'Est) radiated from the capital city like the spokes of a wheel.

The similarity between such a grid and the grids cleared in "well-managed" state forests are not accidental. They were both built to maximize access and to facilitate central control. The kind of "simplification" involved is, again, entirely relative to location. For an official at the hub, it is now

vastly easier to go to "A" or to "B" along the new routes. The layout was designed "to serve the government and the cities and lacking a network of supporting thoroughfares had little to do with popular habit or need. Administrative highways, a historian of the center called them, made for troops to march on and for tax revenues to reach the treasury."[79] For anyone wanting to travel or move goods between A and B on the periphery, however, things were not so simple. Just as all documents had to "pass through" the official French legal language, so did much of the commercial traffic have to pass through the capital. This "retrofitting" of traffic patterns had enormous consequences. It further empowered and privileged Paris and the state at the expense of the provinces; it greatly affected the economics of location; it facilitated central fiscal and military control; and it severed or weakened lateral cultural and economic ties while favoring hierarchical links. At a stroke it marginalized some areas the way that official French marginalized local dialects.

VI Conclusion

Officials of the modern state are, of necessity, at least one step – and often several steps – removed from the society they are charged with governing. They observe and assess the life of their society by a series of typifications that are always some distance from the full reality these abstractions are meant to capture. Thus the foresters' charts and tables, despite their power to distill many individual facts into a larger pattern, do not quite capture (nor are they meant to) the real forest in its full diversity. Thus the cadastral survey and the title deed are a very rough, and sometimes misleading, representation of actual existing rights to land use and disposal. The functionary of any large organization actually "sees" the human activity of interest to him largely through the simplified approximations of documents and statistics: for example, tax proceeds, lists of taxpayers, land records, average income, unemployment numbers, mortality rates, trade and productivity figures, the cases of cholera in a certain district.

These typifications are indispensable to statecraft as well as being potentially valuable. State simplifications such as maps, censuses, cadastral-lists, and standard units of measurement represent techniques for grasping a large and complex reality that *must be reduced to schematic categories* of some kind to allow officials to comprehend aspects of the ensemble. There is no other way of accomplishing this end than to reduce an infinite array of detail to a set of categories that will facilitate summary descriptions, comparisons, and aggregation. Such is the power of these techniques that they discover social truths as well as merely summarizing known facts. The Center for Disease Control in Atlanta is a striking case in point. Its structure of sample reporting hospitals allowed it to first "discover" – in the epidemiological sense – such hitherto unknown diseases as toxic shock syndrome, legionnaire's disease, and AIDS. Stylized facts of this kind are a very powerful form of state knowledge, making it possible for officials to intervene early in epidemics, to understand economic trends that greatly affect public welfare, to gauge whether their policies are having the desired effect, and to make policy with many of the crucial facts at hand.[80]

The techniques devised to enhance the legibility of a society to its rulers have become vastly more sophisticated, but the political motives driving them are little changed. Appropriation, control, and manipulation remain the most prominent. If we imagine a state that has no reliable means of enumerating its population, gauging its wealth, mapping its land, resources and settlements, and locating specific individuals, we are imagining a state whose interventions in that society are necessarily crude and ineffective. A society which is relatively opaque to the state is thereby insulated from some forms of finely tuned state interventions (both benign – for example, universal vaccinations – and resented – for example, personal income taxes). The interventions it does experience will typically be mediated by "local trackers" who know the society from inside and who are likely to interpose their own particular interests. Without this mediation – and often with it – state action is liable to be inept, greatly overshooting or undershooting its objective.

An illegible society is, then, a hindrance to *any* effective intervention by the state, whether the purpose of that intervention is plunder or public welfare. So long as the state's interest was largely confined to grabbing a few tons of grain and rounding up a few conscripts, the state's ignorance might not be fatal. When, however, the state's interest required changing the daily habits (for example, sanitation practices) or work performance (for example, quality labor and machine maintenance), then such ignorance was frequently fatal.

Legibility implies a *viewer* whose place is central. State simplifications of the kind we have examined are designed to provide authorities with a schematic view of their society: a view not afforded to those without authority. Rather like the intimidating one-way mirrored glasses of some US highway police, the authorities enjoy a quasi-monopolistic picture of selected aspects of the whole society. This privileged vantage point is typical of all institutional settings where command and control of complex human activities is paramount. The monastery, the barracks, the factory floor, the administrative bureaucracy (private or public) exercise many state-like functions and often mimic its information structure as well.

State simplifications can be considered part of an on-going "project of legibility": a project that is never fully realized. The actual data from which such simplifications arise are, to a varying degree, riddled with inaccuracies, missing data, faulty aggregation, fraud, negligence, political distortion, etc. A project of legibility is thus "immanent" in any statecraft that aims at manipulating society. But it is undermined by intra-state rivalries, technical obstacles, and, above all, the active resistance of its subjects.

State simplifications, by their very nature, have a particular character. Most obviously, they are observations of those aspects, and only those aspects, of social life that are of official interest. They are *interested*, utilitarian facts. They are also, of course, nearly always written or numerical facts recorded in documents. Third, they are typically static facts. Even when they appear dynamic, they are typically the result of multiple static observations through time. Observation of, say, land records or income figures over two or more points in time may reveal a greater inequality in landownership or an increase in income, but it will not reveal how this new state-of-affairs came about or whether it will persist. Finally, most stylized state facts are *aggregate* facts. Aggregate facts may be impersonal (for example, the density of transportation networks) or simply a collection of facts about individuals – for example, employment rates, literacy rates, residence patterns. For most purposes, state officials need to group citizens in a way that permits them to make a collective assessment.

Facts that can be aggregated and presented as averages or distributions *must* forcibly be *standardized* facts. However unique the actual circumstances of the various individuals who make up the aggregate, it is their sameness or, more precisely, their differences along a standardized scale or continuum that are of interest. Take, for example, simplifications about employment. The working lives of many people are exceptionally complex and may change from day to day. For the purposes of official statistics, however, "gainfully employed" is a stylized fact; one is or is not gainfully employed. The problems of how to categorize many rather exotic working lives are, in the final analysis, obscured by the categories reflected in the aggregate statistics.[81] Those who gather and interpret such aggregate data understand that there is a certain fictional and arbitrary quality to each of the categories they must employ – that they hide a wealth of problematic variation. Once set, however, these thin categories operate unavoidably *as if all* cases similarly classified are in fact, homogeneous and uniform. All *Normalbaum* in a given size range are the same; all the soil in a defined soil-class is statistically identical, all autoworkers (if we are classifying by industry) are the same, all Catholics (if we are classifying by religious faith) are the same.

To this point, I have been making a rather straightforward, even banal, point about the simplifications, abstractions and standardizations which are necessary for the observation by state officials of the circumstances of some or all of the population. I want, however, to make a further claim, analogous to that made for scientific forestry, that *the modern state, through its officials, attempts – with varying success – to create a population with precisely those standardized characteristics which will be easier to monitor, count, assess, and manage.* The utopian (immanent) tendency of the modern state, continually frustrated, is to reduce the chaotic, disorderly, constantly changing social reality beneath it to something more closely resembling the administrative grid of its observations. As the scientific forester may have dreamed of a perfectly legible

forest[82] planted with same age, single species, uniform trees growing in straight lines in a rectangular flat space cleared of all underbrush and poachers, so one might conjure up an exacting state official aspiring to a perfectly legible population with registered, unique names and addresses, living in grid settlements, pursuing single occupations, owning rectangular lots and planting a single crop, all of whose transactions are documented according to the designated formula and in the official language. This caricature of society as a military parade ground is overdrawn, but the grain of truth it embodies may help us understand grandiose development plans.[83]

This tendency is perhaps one shared by many large hierarchical organizations. As Chisholm, reviewing the literature on administrative coordination, concludes, "Central coordinating schemes do work effectively under conditions where the task environment is known and unchanging, where it can be treated as a closed system."[84] The more static, standardized and uniform a population or social space is, the more legible it is to the techniques of state officials. I am suggesting that many state activities aim at transforming the population, space and nature under their jurisdiction into the closed system without surprises that can best be observed and controlled. The reason that state officials can, to some considerable degree, make their categories stick and impose their simplifications, is because the state, of all institutions, is best equipped to insist on treating people according to its schema. If you want to defend your claim to real property you are normally obliged to defend it with a document called a property deed, and in the courts and tribunals created for that purpose. If you wish any standing in law, you must have the documents (for example, birth certificate, passport, identity card) that officials accept as a claim of citizenship. The categories used by state agents are not merely a means to make their environment legible; they are an authoritative tune to which much of the population must dance.

Notes

1 The following account is largely drawn from Lowood's (1991) fine analysis.
2 The most striking exception was the royal attention to the supply of "noble game" (e.g., deer, boar, fox) for the hunt and hence to the protection of its habitat. Lest one imagine this to be a quaint pre-modern affectation, it is worth recalling the enormous social importance of the hunt to such recent "monarchs" as Erich Honneker and Tito.
3 For an evocative and wide-ranging attempt to explore the changing cultural meaning of the forest in the West, see Harrison 1992.

4   This last is a kind of reverse Heisenberg principle. Instead of altering the phenomenon observed through the act of observation, so that the pre-observation state of the phenomenon is unknowable in principle, the effect of (interested) observation in this case is to alter the phenomenon in question over time so that it, in fact, more closely resembles the stripped down, abstract image the lens had revealed.

5   The more general process of codifying the principles of state administration in seventeenth and eighteenth century Europe is examined by Michel Foucault under the (misleading) heading of "police state" (from *Polizeiwissenschaft*) in his lectures on "governmentality" at the Collège de France. See the collection by Bucchell et al. 1991, esp. ch. 4.

6   In the late seventeenth century Colbert had extensive plans to "rationalize" forest administration both to prevent poaching and to generate a more reliable revenue yield. To this end, Etienne Dralet's *Traité du Régime Forestier* proposed regulated plots (*tire-aire*) "so that the growth is regular and easy to guard." Despite these initiatives, nothing much came of it in France until 1820 when the new German techniques were imported. See Sahlins 1992.

7   Lowood 1991, p. 338.

8   Various techniques were tried: cutting an actual tree into very tiny bits and then compressing it to find its volume; putting wood in a barrel of known volume and adding measured amounts of water to calculate the volume of the barrel *not* occupied by the wood, etc. Lowood 1991, p. 328.

9   Lowood 1991, p. 341; see also Harrison 1992, pp. 122–3.

10 See for example: Balzac 1949; Thompson 1975; Hay 1975; and Hahn 1982. For a directly apposite German case, see one of Karl Marx's first published articles linking the theft of wood to the business cycle and unemployment in the Rhineland: reported in Linebaugh 1976.

11 This brief description is drawn largely from Collins 1988.

12 Jones 1988, p. 17.

13 Collins 1988, pp. 201, 204. It was precisely this capacity to evade taxes that gave the fiscal regime a degree of unintended (from the top at least) flexibility and avoided even more open rebellion in the troubled seventeenth century.

14 Heilbron (1991a, p. 13) notes that in 1791 an English colonel of the militia obliged the Scottish clergy to send him inventories of their population by threatening to quarter troops upon their parish.

15 This assumes that the crown wants to maximize its long run proceeds. It was and is common, of course, for regimes in political or military crises to mortgage their future by squeezing as much as possible from their forests and/or their subjects.

16 Kula 1986.

17 Heilbron 1991b, pp. 207–8.

18 For an illuminating discussion along these lines see Appadurai (forthcoming).

19 Appadurai forthcoming.

20 The same motive was at work in the folk-categories of stratification used by Javanese villagers: the *Kekurangons* (those-who-have-less-than-enough) and the *Kecukupans* (those-who-have-enough). See Geertz 1963.

21 Geertz 1963, pp. 98–9.

22 Geertz 1963, p. 173.

23 It was, in fact, the active evasion of regions that were fiscally hard-pressed that provided the "drag" or gyroscope that often prevented an ill-considered tax claim from provoking an actual resistance.

24 Quoted in Kula 1986, p. 203–4.

25 Kula 1986, p. 122–3.

26 Kula 1986, p. 211.

27 For all the advance in human rights that equal citizenship carried with it, it is worth recalling that this momentous step also undercut the intermediary structures between the state and the citizen and gave the state, for the first time, direct access to its subjects. Equal citizenship not only implied legal equality and universal suffrage, it also implied universal conscription, as those mobilized into Napoleon's armies were shortly to discover. From the heights of the state the society increasingly appeared as an endless series of nationally equal "*particuliers*" with whom it dealt in their capacity as subjects, taxpayers, and potential military draftees. See Poggi 1978, p. 78

28 Kula 1986, p. 286.

29 The *Code Civil* did not deal with agriculture explicitly, with the single exception of specifying guidelines for tenant farming (*fermage*), in recognition of the wealthy and influential large tenants in the Paris Basin and to the north. I am grateful to Peter Jones for bringing to my attention the study on which this brief discussion is based: Aberdam 1979.

30 "En résumé, la ligne générale du projet de 1807 est de refuser toute specificité ou droiten rural ramenant, autant que possible, les rapports sociaux à la campagne à la forme d'authorité legale que la bourgeoisie projette sur l'ensemble de la population" (Aberdam 1979, p. 19).

31 Aberdam 1979, p. 18.

32 Aberdam 1979, p. 22.

33 In colonial Vietnam, the head tax or "capitation" was levied on whole communities on the basis of their presumed population. If the sum was not remitted, the police came and held an auction of whatever they could seize (e.g., water buffalos, furniture, jewelry) until the required sum was reached. This system gave the village notables, who owned most of the goals worth seizing, an incentive to make sure the taxes were remitted on time.

34 The same generalization has considerable validity for modern socialist forms of collective farming as well. Thus a considerable amount of farm land "disappeared" from the books when Hungary's collective farms were created. (See Rev 1987). In China, after the deadly Great Leap Forward, many collective farms systematically hid production from central authorities in the interest of local survival. (See Kelliher 1992.)

35 Cadastral surveys might also be undertaken by *large* (i.e., state-like) aristocratic fief-holders who were convinced that they could thereby uncover taxable land and subjects which had hitherto eluded them.

36 Both the Danish and Norwegian examples are from the valuable historical analysis in Kain and Baigent (1992, p. 116).

37 The great efficiency of the Hutterite communal grain farmers in the Northern plain states and Canada is but one of many pieces of conflicting evidence. For some other evidence, see Yaney (1982, pp. 165–9).

38 Here I am guilty of conveying a false sense of uniformity: there were, in fact, a host of land arrangements, even in "black earth" Russia and many villages did not redistribute land at all (Yaney, 1982, p. 169).

39 Yaney 1982, p. 212.

40 Yaney (1982, p. 160) points out that Mennonite land was interstripped and was just as productive as Mennonite land organized into consolidated farms.

41 And not always here inasmuch as *group* land settlement, against the government's wishes, was also common.

42 Yaney 1982, chs. 7 and 8. It is worth noting in this context that the modern credit system, as the modern state tax system, requires a legible property regime for its functioning.

43 Yaney 1982, pp. 412 ff.

44 Figes 1989, ch. 6 ("The Rural Economy under War Communism").

45 There were, before comprehensive cadastral surveys, land that was open to all and belonged to no one, though social arrangements might regulate its use. By and large, such land was designated state land with the first cadastral map. All the land was "accounted for"; everything not owned privately became the property of the state.

46 Kain and Baigent 1992, p. 33. Seas, rivers and wastes were to be omitted since they did not bear revenue. The whole operation was guided by a manual entitled, "Mode d'arpentage pour l'impot foncier."

47 Quoted in Kain and Baigent 1992, p. 5.

48 In an earlier work I have examined this problem in some detail in its Southeast Asian context. See Scott, 1976, ch. 4.

49 In 1785 Austria's Franz Joseph had to choose between using net income or gross income as a basis or land taxation. Gross income was chosen because it was far simpler (e.g. average crop per unit of land x units of land x average grain price = gross income). It was necessary to sacrifice accuracy and fairness to create a procedure that was administratively feasible. Kain and Baigent 1992, p. 193.

50 Kain and Baigent 1992, p. 59.

51 Issue of mineral rights and mineral income from sub-soil deposits was a significant exception to this generalization.

52 Kain and Baigent 1992, p. 344.

53 Weber 1976, p. 156.

54 See Guha 1976.

55 For a remarkably thoughtful and thorough examination of how the colonial legal code transformed land dispute settlement, land tenure and social structure, see Moore 1986.

56 The equality was, of course, purely areal! See Kain and Baigent 1992, p. 225.

57 In Malaysia Chinese are legally barred from owning certain kinds of agricultural land. To get around this they register land in the name of a Malay confederate. To ensure that the confederate does not attempt to exercise his formal property rights, they have him sign, simultaneously, loan papers worth far more than the property, with the Chinese as creditor.

58 Revolutionary legislation in France, rather than abolishing the tithe outright, attempted to phase them out with temporary "tithe redemption payments"! Popular defiance was so massive and intractable that they were, finally, abandoned altogether. See Scott 1987.

59 Hacking 1990, p. 17.

60 Heilbron 1991a, p. 17.

61 Quoted in Kain and Baigent 1992, p. 320.

62 Heilbron 1991a, p. 22–3.

63 Hacking 1990, p. 145. Napoleon avoided conducting a census after 1806 for fear that its results would show the catastrophic demographic impact of his wars.

64 I owe this astute observation about *The Witness* to Ben Anderson.

65 See, for example, Wormsley 1980.

66 I am indebted to Kate Stanton, an astute research assistant, for her background research on this issue.

67 Camden 1605/1984. If Camden's supposition is correct it is nonetheless true that the statute was only episodically enforced for some time.

68 Camden 1605/1984, p. 122.

69 Readers of colonial documents come across many names followed by one or more "aka" or "alias." While viewed suspiciously as a means of escaping detection, many of these aliases were undoubtedly acquired innocently in the course of a complex social life.

70 Chazon 1972.

71 The exception which proves the rule appears to be China. Having the oldest elaborate state system it

has mandated designated family names for more than two millennia. "Laobaixing," meaning literally "the old hundred (many) surnames" and now designating more generally "the common people", may well have been the official list. Personal Communication from Bill (W. J. F.) Jenner and Ian Wilson.

72 Although this system has the advantage of designating "home town" for the generation that takes it, it certainly does not clarify much locally in Rafsanjan. It may well be that the state is particularly concerned with monitoring those who are mobile or "out of place."

73 Dietary laws that all but preclude commensality are also very powerful social exclusionary devices. If one were designating a set of cultural rules to wall off a group from surrounding groups, making sure its members cannot easily speak to or eat with other groups is a splendid beginning!

74 Weber (1976, ch. 6) points out that in the last 25 years of the nineteenth century, fully half of the Frenchmen reaching adulthood had a native tongue other than French.

75 Weber 1976, p. 73.

76 Weber 1976, p. 113.

77 Weber 1976, p. 197.

78 For a careful depiction of the geography of standard marketing areas, see Skinner 1975.

79 Weber 1976, p. 195.

80 See Hacking 1975.

81 There are at least three problems here. The first is the hegemony of the categories. How does one classify someone who works largely for relatives who may sometimes feed him, let him use some land as his own, and sometimes pay him in crops or cash? The decisions, sometimes quite arbitrary, about how to classify such cases are obscured by the final result in which only the prevailing categories appear. The second problem, and one to which we shall return, is how the categories – more particularly, the state power behind the categories – shape the data. For example, during the recession of the 1970s in the US there was some concern that the official unemployment rate which had reached 13% was greatly exaggerated. A major reason, it was claimed, was that many nominally unemployed were working in the informal economy "off-the-books" and would not report their income or employment for fear of being taxed. One could say then and today that the fiscal system had provoked an "off-stage" reality that was designed to stay out of the data bank. The third problem is that those who collect and assemble the information may have very special interests in what the data show. During the Vietnam War the importance of "body-counts" and "pacified villages" as a measure of counter-insurgency success led commanders to produce inflated figures which pleased their superiors – in the short run – but increasingly bore little relation to the facts-on-the-ground.

82 Indicative of this tendency is the substantial literature on "optimum control theory" imported from management science into scientific forestry. For an application and bibliography, see Donnelly and Betters 1991.

83 The caricature is not so far-fetched that it does not capture the lyrical utopianism of early advocates of state-sciences. I quote the "father" of Prussian statistics, Ernst Engel: "in order to obtain an accurate representation, statistical research accompanies the individual through his entire earthly existence. It takes account of his birth, his baptism, his vaccination, his schooling and the success thereof, his diligence, his leave of school, his subsequent education and development; and, once he becomes a man, his physique and his ability to bear arms. It also accompanies the subsequent steps of his walk through life; it takes note of his chosen occupation, where he sets up his household and his management of the same; if he saved from the abundances of his youth for his old age, if and when and at what age he marries and whom he chooses as his wife – statistics look after him when things go well for him and when they go awry. Should he suffer shipwreck in his life, undergo material moral or spiritual ruin, statistics takes note of the same. Statistics leaves a man only after his death – after it has ascertained the precise age of his death and noted the causes that brought about his end" (quoted in Hacking 1990, p. 34). One could hardly ask for a more complete list for the early nineteenth century, of state interests in its population and the paper trail it generated.

84 Chisholm 1989, p. 10.

References

Aberdam, Serge (ca. 1979) Aux origines du code rural 1789–1900: Un Siècle de débat, mimeo.

Appadurai, Arjun (forthcoming) Measurement discourse in rural Maharashtra. *Agriculture, Language, and Knowledge in South Asia: Perspectives from History and Anthropology*, ed. Arjun Appadurai *et al.*, Berkeley: University of California Press.

Balzac, Honoré de (1949) *Les Paysans*, Paris: Pléiades.

Bucchell, Graham, Colin Gordon and Peter Miller, eds. (1991) *The Foucault Effect: Studies in Governmentality*, London: Harvester Wheatsheaf.

Camden, William (1605) *Remains Concerning Britain*, ed. R. D. Dunn, Toronto: University of Toronto Press, 1984.

Chazon, Robert (1972) Names: medieval period and establishment of surnames, vol. 12, pp. 809–13 in *Encyclopedia Judaica*, New York: Macmillan.

Chisholm, Donald (1989) *Coordination Without Hierarchy: Informal Structures in Multiorganizational Systems*, Berkeley: University of California Press.

Collins, James B (1988) *Fiscal Limits of Absolutism: Direct Taxation in Early 17th Century France*, Berkeley: University of California Press.

Donnelly, D. M. and D. R. Betters (1991) Optimum control for scheduling final harvest in even-aged forest stands, *Forest Ecology and Management*, 46: 135–49.

Figes, Orlando (1989) *Peasant Russia, Civil War: The Volga Countryside in the Revolution 1917–1921*, Oxford: Clarendon Press.

Frangsmyr, Tore, J. L. Heinbron and Robin E. Rider, eds. (1991) *The Quantifying Spirit in the 18th Century*, Berkeley: University of California Press.

Geertz, Clifford (1963) *Agricultural Involution*, Berkeley: University of California Press.

Guha, Ranajit (1963) *A Rule of Land in Bengal*, Property for Paris: Mouton.

Hacking, Ian (1975) *The Emergence of Probability: A Philosophical Study of Early Ideas About Probability, Induction, and Statistical Inference*, Cambridge: Cambridge University Press.

Hacking, Ian (1990) *The Taming of Chance*, Cambridge: Cambridge University Press.

Hahn, Steven (1982) Hunting, fishing, and foraging: common rights and class relations in the postbellum South, *Radical History Review*, 26: 37–64.

Harrison, William Pogue (1992) *Forests: The Shadow of Civilization*, Chicago: University of Chicago Press.

Hay, Douglas (1975) Poaching on Cannock Chase, *Albion's Fatal Tree*, ed. Douglas Hay et al., New York: Pantheon.

Heilbron, J. L. (1991a) Introductory essay. In Frangsmyr *et al.* 1991.

Heilbron, J. L. (1991b) The measure of Enlightenment, pp. 207–8 in Frangsmyr *et al.*

Jones, P. M. (1988) *The Peasantry in the French Revolution*, Cambridge: Cambridge University Press.

Kain, Roger J. P. and Elizabeth Baigent (1992) *The Cadastral Map in the Service of the State: A History of Property Mapping*, Chicago: University of Chicago Press.

Kelliher, Daniel (1992) *Peasant Power in China*, New Haven, CT: Yale University Press.

Kula, Witold (1986) *Measures and Men*, trans. R. Szreter, Princeton, NJ: Princeton University Press.

Linebaugh, Peter (1976) Karl Marx, the theft of wood, and working-class composition: a contribution to the current debate, *Crime and Social Justice*, vol. 6 (Fall–Winter): 5–16.

Lowood, Henry E. (1991) The calculating forester: quantification, cameral science, and the emergence of scientific forestry management in Germany, pp. 315–42, in Frangsmyr et al., 1991.

Moore, Sally Falk (1986) *Social Facts and Fabrications: "Customary" Law on Mt. Kilimanjaro, 1880–1980*, Cambridge: Cambridge University Press.

Poggi, Gianfranco (1978) *The Development of the Modern State: A Sociological Introduction*, Stanford, CA: Stanford University Press.

Rev, Istvan (1987) The advantages of being atomized: how Hungarian peasants coped with collectivization, *Dissent*, vol. 34 (Summer): pp. 335–49.

Sahlins, Peter (1992) Forest rites: the war of the 'Demoiselles' in Ariège, France (1829–1831). Unpublished paper presented to the Program in Agrarian Studies, Yale University, January 1992.

Scott, James C. (1976) *The Moral Economy of the Peasant: Subsistence and Rebellion in Southeast Asia*, New Haven, CT: Yale University Press.

Scott, James C. (1987) Resistance without protest and without organization: peasant opposition to the Islamic *Zakat* and the Christian tithe, *Comparative Studies in Society and History*, 29 (3): pp 417–52.

Skinner, G. William (1975) *Marketing and Social Structure in Rural China*, Tucson, AZ: Association of Asian Studies.

Thompson, E. P. (1975) *Whigs and Hunters: The Origin of the Black Act*, New York: Pantheon.

Weber, Eugen J. (1976) *Peasants into Frenchmen: The Modernization of Rural France, 1870–1914*, Stanford, CA: Stanford University Press.

Wormsley, William E. (1980) Traditional change in Imbonggu names and naming practices, *Names*, 28: 183–94.

Yaney, George (1982) *The Urge to Mobilize: Agrarian Reform in Russia*, Urbana: University of Illinois Press.

3

The Social Contract as Ideology

David Gauthier

Author's Note (1996)

Reprinting this essay makes me somewhat uneasy, because it now seems to me that in it, I fail to distinguish clearly the underlying rationale for society and for social relationships from the character of those relationships. And so I treat contractarian thought as coming to conceive all social relationships as contractual. But this is a mistake. We may appeal to a social contract – a hypothetical rational agreement on mutually beneficial terms of interaction – without supposing that what we agree to is itself contractual in character. We benefit, all of us, from the capacity to form and sustain friendships, but friendship is not a relationship conceived in terms of mutual benefit and its norms are not contractual ones. This essay should then be read as an exposition and critique of understanding social relationships as if they were contractual, and not as a discussion of the justificatory role of hypothetical rational agreement. It should not be read as impugning the view (which I hold) that the norms of friendship (but not, say, the norms of enmity) are morally binding on us because, were we in a position to agree on the terms of our interaction, we should accept the norms of friendship (but not those of enmity) among those terms.

The conception of social relationships as contractual lies at the core of our ideology. Indeed, that core is constituted by the intersection of this conception with the correlative conceptions of human activity as appropriative and of rationality as utility-maximizing. My concern is to clarify this thesis and to enhance its descriptive plausibility as a characterization of our ideology, but to undermine its normative plausibility as ideologically effective.

I

The thesis refers to our ideology. There are two terms here which require immediate clarification; the first is "our." Philosophers habitually use the first-person plural pronoun; its use demands specification. Who are "we"? In this essay, first-person plural references are intended to denote those persons who have inhabited Western Europe, who are descended from such inhabitants, or who live or have lived in social structures developed from those of Western Europe during the past three to four hundred years. I am supposing, without further defense, that these persons share certain ideas and certain ways of thinking and behaving that permit the attribution to them of an ideology.

"Ideology" is the second term which requires clarification. It has not been employed with great consistency or clarity by social thinkers.[1] It picks out some aspect of our consciousness, frequently pejoratively, whether because of its allegedly derivative character (superstructure) or its allegedly misleading character (false consciousness).

Originally published in *Philosophy and Public Affairs* 6 (1977): pp. 130–64. Reprinted by permission of Blackwell Publishing Ltd.

David Gauthier

Although the demise of ideology as a determinant of social values and practices has been widely celebrated, more recent reports suggest that the celebrations may themselves be ideological in character. My use of the term is intended to retain the place of ideology in consciousness, and indeed perhaps to ensure the permanence of that place, without pejorative commitment.

Ideology is part of the deep structure of self-consciousness.[2] By self-consciousness I understand that capacity of human beings to conceive themselves in relation to other humans, to human structures and institutions, and to the nonhuman or natural environment, and to act in the light of these conceived relationships. Exhibited in these thoughts and activities is a conception of the self-as-human. This conception need not be, and typically is not, actually expressed in self-consciousness. Rather, it must be inferred from a person's actual thoughts and activities, insofar as they concern himself, his fellows, his society, and his world, as that underlying structure of ideas which affords their most economical foundation. This conception of self-as-human is thus a theoretical construct that we attribute to the ground of self-consciousness to explain its content, the surface of overt thought and action. This theoretical construct is what I refer to as ideology.

A conception of oneself as a person may be part of the content of consciousness. But this conception is not what I refer to as ideology, for it need not be identical with that conception which is exhibited in one's other thoughts and activities. Of course, ideology must afford the foundation for one's conscious self-awareness, but this does not preclude a difference, and even a contradiction, between the content of the ideological substructure, and the content of overt self-awareness. As with language, deep structure and surface structure must be distinguished, and their characteristics may be found to be opposed.

This similarity of language and consciousness is not accidental; in my view, self-consciousness depends on the actualization of linguistic capacity. Both language and consciousness have the deceptive appearance of transparency; both conceal a deep structure which unconsciously affects conscious activity. Ideology is not, or at least need not be, false consciousness, but it is necessarily prereflective consciousness. It can be the subject of reflection; it can be brought to the surface of our thought, as indeed this essay is intended to exhibit. But its role does not require this reflection

or an assessment of its validity or truth. Whether its role can be affected by reflection – whether the deep structure of self-consciousness can be affected by surfacing it – is a matter to which I shall allude in the course of this essay, although it may be exhibited more fully by the response to an enquiry into ideology rather than by the enquiry itself.

The structure of the ideas that comprise an ideology is not idiosyncratic. Persons who differ fundamentally in the ideological grounds of their activities would find interaction and communication difficult, if not frequently impossible. Whatever their supposed purpose, one of the main functions of social institutions is, and must be, to maintain and transmit a common ideology among those who compose a society. Without the effective functioning of such institutions, a society would rapidly disintegrate as its members ceased to be able to interact.

However, I do not suppose that a single, invariant structure of ideas holds for all persons in all times and places. My basic thesis presupposes only the existence of a common structure for us, that is, for modern Western Europeans and their descendants and offshoots.

The articulation of an ideology, like the articulation of any deep structure, cannot be expected to be an easy task. Many recent studies, especially in moral philosophy but also in political philosophy, have tended to ignore it. They have focused on the language or the logic of morals and politics and on practical, moral, and political reasoning, but frequently they have examined only the surface structure, the ideas we consciously express about ourselves. John Rawls' *A Theory of Justice* is a pioneering work in many respects, but in none more important than in its awareness of the significance of deep structure, although Rawls seems to suggest that this structure is invariant for human beings and not relative only to our own society.[3] And it is most noteworthy that in articulating this deep structure, he is led to develop, once again in the history of our political thought, the theory of the social contract.

II

The theory of the social contract has been advanced in more and less embracing forms. Thomas Hobbes and John Locke are classic exponents of these contrasting approaches. Since my concern is primarily with the Hobbist variant, I shall begin with a brief sketch of its alternative.

Locke supposes that a certain group of men, namely landed proprietors, those who have successfully appropriated or inherited real property or estate, contract together for mutual protection and wellbeing.[4] Their contract brings civil government into existence, but civil government is not, in Locke's view, the only or the primary ground for social relationships among human beings. Locke's landed proprietors are heads of households, and their household relationships – of man with wife, father with child, and master with servant – are prior to and indeed fall outside of the contractual relationship which gives rise to political society. Furthermore, although here Locke is less explicit, it seems evident that landed proprietors enter into relationships of sociability, one with another, which are neither conditions nor consequences of the contract among them. And their relations one with another, and with other human beings, explicitly fall under the divine law of nature, which regulates conduct outside political society, in the state of nature, as well as conduct within it.

Hobbes' theory affords an altogether larger scope to contractual relations.[5] Indeed, for Hobbes, relations among human beings are of two kinds only: relations of hostility, which obtain in and constitute the state of nature, and relations of contract, which obtain in and constitute the state of society. In the state of nature, every man has the right to do whatever he will in order to preserve and benefit himself; the result is the state of war "where every man is Enemy to every man." To bring this self-defeating condition to an end, every man is supposed to contract with his fellows to establish a commonwealth under a single and all-powerful sovereign. Only within a commonwealth is any sociability possible. The family is itself a miniature commonwealth; the father, or sometimes the mother, is sovereign, and the children are supposed to contract with their parent to obey in return for being allowed to live, in the way in which the vanquished in war contracts with the victor. And this latter contract, of vanquished with victor, which establishes sovereignty by acquisition, is explicitly stated by Hobbes to constitute the relation between servant and master. The contractual relationship among men, in establishing political society, is thus the model on which all other human relationships are interpreted.

It is Hobbes' radical contractarianism which I am attributing to our ideology. To make this attribution is to hold that our thoughts and activities, insofar as they concern ourselves and our relationships, are best understood by supposing that we treat all of these relationships as if they were contractual. Only the relation of hostility is excluded from the scope of contract, and only it is natural to man. All other human relationships are treated as essentially similar in character, and all are conventional, the product of human agreement.

The theory of the social contract, as part of our ideology, is not concerned with the objective character of social institutions and relationships. It is not a piece of speculative, but purportedly actual, history or sociology. Contractarians do not suppose, either explicitly or implicitly, that human society originated in a contract, or is now maintained by contract. They do not suppose that children contract with their parents. To suppose that the theory of the social contract must be intended to explain the origin of actual societies is to confuse deep structure with surface structure; our contractual conception of human relationships may ground an explanation which makes no appeal to contract.

The theory itself concerns the rationale of relationships among persons, and between society and its members, rather than the cause of those relationships. The justification of rights and duties, institutions and practices, is to be found by regarding them as if they were contractual, and showing the rationality of this hypothetical contractual base. Of course, a theory of rationale does have an explanatory function. Were the theory true, then fully self-conscious beings whose social environment was entirely the product of their deliberate choice would only relate contractually one to another. For such beings the theory of the social contract, and indeed our entire ideology, would not be a theoretical construct, but rather the conscious basis of their social thought and practice. As part of our ideology, then, the contract theory rationalizes social relationships by providing an ideal, nonactual explanation of their existence.

In attributing this ideology to us, I am not defending it. I am not claiming that society is to be understood, or ought to be understood, as if it were contractual. It may well be absurd so to understand society. What I am doing is claiming that our thoughts and actions are to be understood as if we supposed that all social relationships were to be rationalized in contractual terms. Note that "as if" plays a dual role in my account: our conscious thoughts, and overt actions, are to be explained *as if* we held the theory of the social contract, that is, the theory that all social relationships are to be understood *as if* they were contractual.

I should not want to argue that radical contractarianism of a Hobbist kind has unequivocally dominated our thoughts and practices. Rather, I believe this to be the final form of the contractarian conception of society, the form towards which it develops as an ideology, gradually increasing its influence on our thoughts, and leading us to abandon earlier ideas of human relationships as natural or supernatural rather than as conventional. I believe, although I cannot fully defend this belief here, that our society is moving towards a more Hobbist position. Evidence for this may be found in political life, for example in the "social contract" proposals of the British government under former Prime Minister Harold Wilson. But the most significant recent evidence is found in the extension of contractarian thought to family and domestic life. We may cite the arguments and practices of those who seek to divest the marriage contract of its religious and moral overtones, to treat it as the ordinary contract which, they argue, it really is. We may cite those who suppose that housework should be paid for, or that childraising is but one occupation among many possible vocations, and that those who do it, too, should be remunerated. And we may cite the words of a Montreal girl on the "jock circuit" (the circuit of those who offer non-professional diversion to professional athletes): "In a way, it's a sort of business arrangement – but then, aren't all man-woman relationships?"[6]

On reflection, we may disavow contractarianism. We may insist that there is more to human relationships than the conventions which result from agreement. The contractarian can admit this, as long as he holds that these other features of human relationships are nonessential, a sentimental residue from the past, or an emotional patina which affords a more pleasing aura to an otherwise bare artifice. But the contractarian can also maintain that we delude ourselves, and that indeed our ideology induces us to preach what we do not practice. The practice of contractarianism may indeed be most effective if it is explicitly denied. The surface structure induced by the ideology may have a content incompatible with it.

This suggests a different linkage between ideology and false consciousness than the Marxian identification. Ideology, deep structure, may give rise to false consciousness, as surface structure. If

so, then presumably bringing the ideology to consciousness, surfacing it, will undermine its effectiveness, for the contradiction between the ideology and our conscious conceptions will become patent.

In appraising contractarianism in this essay, I shall not go beyond questions of logical coherence and practical effectiveness. The further question of truth or validity is a difficult one for any ideology. The problem, at least in part, is that social institutions, practices, and relationships do not exist independently of human activity and human thought. Hence the view of these relationships presented by an ideology may be confirmed, for its adherents, because they act to constitute their relationships in accordance with it, while it may be disconfirmed, for its opponents, because they act to constitute their relationships on a quite different basis. No doubt many social theorists would insist that institutions and practices have an objective character quite independent of the thought and intent of those persons involved in them, and that ideology may falsify this objective character. But it will not do simply to insist that human relationships are not, in fact, to be explained as they are ideologically conceived, since ideology concerns rationale rather than literal explanation. To say that an ideology is false or invalid must, then, be to say that the rationale it provides for society is *incompatible* with the literal truth about that society. But how are we to determine incompatibility between the "as-if" and the "is"? This question I raise only to put aside.

III

To conceive all social relationships as contractual is to suppose that men, with their particular human characteristics, are prior to society. The contract theory expresses this priority in temporal terms, giving us the picture of men in a state of nature entering society on the basis of a contract. But, as I have pointed out, the language of the theory is the language of ideal explanation; the men in the state of nature are not ourselves. The theory does not require that actual human individuals are temporally prior to their society; here, as elsewhere, temporal priority is a metaphor for conceptual priority.

What contractarianism does require is, first of all, that individual human beings not only can, but must, be understood apart from society. The fundamental characteristics of men are not products of their social existence. Rather, in affording the motivations that underlie human activity in the state of nature and that are expressed in natural hostility, they constitute the conditions of man's social existence. Thus man is social because he is human, and not human because he is social. In particular, self-consciousness and language must be taken as conditions, not products, of society.

But more than this is implicit in contractarianism. It would be compatible with the claim that the individual is prior to society, to suppose nonetheless that human sociability is itself a natural and fundamental characteristic of individuals, which expresses itself directly in social relations among human beings. And this is denied by contract theory in its insistence upon the essentially conventional character of society. Men who were naturally sociable would not need to contract together in order to form society, and would not rationalize society in contractarian terms. Although contract might be the foundation of government, as in Locke, society would not be a purely artificial creation. Contract as the foundation of all society is required only by men who are not inherently sociable.

Furthermore, radical contractarianism is incompatible with the view that men undergo fundamental change in becoming members of society. Men's reasons for contracting one with another are supposed to arise out of their presocial needs in the state of nature. If contractarian ideology is to be effective in rationalizing social relationships, then these needs must be represented, not as only presocial, but as permanent, so that the reasons for entering the contract will also be reasons for maintaining the society created thereby. Society is thus conceived as a mere instrument for men whose fundamental motivation is presocial, nonsocial, and fixed. If men are, in fact, socialized beings, so that human nature is in part a social product, then contractarian ideology must conceal this, representing social needs as if they were the product of presocial nature. Rousseau may use the device, and even the title, of the social contract, but the theory which he formulates tends to subvert contractarian ideology, in its overt distinction of social man from natural man.[7]

Although the contractarian cannot represent man as a social being, he need not deny, as Hobbes may seem to, that human beings as we know them, within society, do display sociable characteristics.[8] The contractarian need but insist that

man is sociable only because he creates society; human sociability is the product, and not the condition, of social existence. And as the product of what is itself conventional, this sociability is but an accidental attribute of human nature, an overlay on a fundamentally and permanently nonsocial character, possessing a merely conventional existence.

The correlate of the claim that man is nonsocial by nature is, of course, the claim that society is not, and cannot be, an end in itself. Man's social existence is not self-justifying. In offering an effective rationale for society, the contractarian must face the charge that because society is conventional, it is therefore arbitrary. Thrasymachus argued this against Socrates;[9] today there is a strong tendency to extrapolate from the contractarian, conventionalist view of such fundamental human relationships as male and female, or parent and child, to the contention that such relationships are arbitrary. The debate about the relation between *physis* and *nomos* has not advanced greatly in the past twenty-four hundred years. But to suppose that what is conventional must therefore be arbitrary is entirely contrary to the spirit of contractarianism, which finds only in convention a sufficient rationale for society.

To consider society arbitrary is to suppose that it affords no sufficient fulfilment or meets no fundamental need of most or all of its members. To avoid the charge of arbitrariness, then, the contractarian must relate the conventional character of society to a natural base in human nature. He must show society to be the indirect, rationalized expression of natural and essential human characteristics. In this way, by showing that society has, and must have, instrumental value to the naturally nonsocial human being, the contractarian justifies society to the individual, and thus resolves what has been the central problem in our political philosophy.

But how does the contractarian show that society must have instrumental value to human beings? I shall argue that he relies on the view that human activity is basically appropriative, thus establishing one of the links set out in my original thesis. Before I can make this argument convincing, however, I must first sketch part of the outline of a general formal theory of human interaction. By attending to the requirements of this theory, I shall seek to develop a conception of human good which will assure to society a sufficient instrumental value.

David Gauthier

IV

Consider any situation in which there are several persons, each with several possible actions, and in which the outcome, as it affects each person, depends on the particular combination of actions performed. I shall define the *state of nature* as that relation holding between any two persons in the situation if and only if each acts on an independently selected principle of action, and *society* as that relation holding between any two persons in the situation if and only if both act on a mutually selected principle of action.[10] Note that, so defined, the state of nature and society are exclusive, but not exhaustive, alternatives. Both exclude fundamentally unequal relationships, in which there is a one-way dependence in the selection of principles of action. (It is perhaps worth mentioning that thinkers like Thrasymachus assume such a one-way dependence in arguing for the arbitrariness of society.)

Suppose that in a given situation, every person is in the state of nature with respect to every other person. I shall call the outcome of the actions performed in this full state of nature, the *natural outcome*. That is, the natural outcome results if each person acts on a principle of action which he selects for himself independently of the others. It is evident that a society will be considered arbitrary by those persons for whom the outcome of social action is worse than the natural outcome. Hence, a nonarbitrary society must improve on the natural outcome for everyone.

The outcome of a situation is *optimal* (in the Pareto sense) if and only if any alternative outcome which would be better for some person would be worse for some other person. If the natural outcome is optimal, then every alternative must make someone worse off, and so it is not possible for society to improve on the full state of nature for everyone. A society embracing all of the persons in the situation would either bring about the natural outcome, which would make the existence of the society pointless, or some outcome worse for some persons than the natural outcome, which would make the society arbitrary from their standpoint.

A nonarbitrary society embracing all of the persons in a situation is therefore possible only if the natural outcome of the situation is not optimal. Of course, not every society conceivable in such a situation will be nonarbitrary. The mutually selected principle of action must be such that the outcome is better for some persons, and at least as good for all persons, as the outcome in the full state of nature. It is reasonable to require further that the outcome of society be itself optimal, for otherwise some persons will consider it arbitrary, not because it is worse for them than the natural outcome, but because it is worse for them than some alternative which would leave everyone else at least as well off.

In addition to optimality, the stability of an outcome is of importance in analyzing nonarbitrary societies. An outcome is *stable*, or in equilibrium, if and only if no one person can bring about an alternative outcome which is better for himself, by unilaterally changing his way of acting. If an outcome is not stable, then it is evident that some person or persons will be tempted to defect from an agreement to accept a principle of action which brings it about.

Situations in which the natural outcome is not optimal may be divided into three types, using the concept of stability. Note that in all such situations, there must be some outcome which is both optimal and no worse for anyone than the natural outcome.

A situation is of *type I* if and only if (1) there are some outcomes which are (a) stable, (b) optimal, (c) no worse for anyone than the natural outcome, and (2) there is a nonempty set of outcomes, each satisfying (1), such that no member of the set is strongly dispreferred to any outcome satisfying (1) by any person. I shall suppose that the persons in a type I situation will be prepared to act on any principle of action which has as its outcome a member of the set of outcomes specified in (2). For such an outcome will be stable and optimal, worse for no one than the state of nature, and no one will strongly disprefer it to any other outcome satisfying these conditions.

A situation is of *type II* if and only if (1) there are some outcomes which are (a) stable, (b) optimal, (c) no worse for anyone than the natural outcome, and (2) any outcome which satisfies (1) is strongly dispreferred by some person to some other outcome satisfying (1). I shall suppose that the persons in a type II situation will be prepared all to act on some member of the set of principles of mutual action each of which has, as its outcome, a state of affairs satisfying (1). But these persons will not be prepared, without further ado, to act on any member of the set, since the outcome of each will be strongly dispreferred, by some person or persons, to the outcome of some other member.

Hence they will bargain with each other to select a principle of mutual action from the set.

A situation is of *type III* if and only if (1) there are some outcomes which are (a) optimal, (b) no worse for anyone than the natural outcome, but (2) no outcome satisfying (1) is stable. In such a situation, some persons will be tempted to defect from any principle of mutual action which has, as its outcome, a state of affairs satisfying (1), since these persons can bring about an outcome better for themselves by such unilateral defection. Hence I shall suppose that the persons in a type III situation will be prepared all to act on some member of the set of principles of mutual action each of which has as its outcome a state of affairs satisfying (1), *provided* these persons have some guarantee that their agreement will be effective, that is, that no person will unilaterally violate it.

The persons in a type I situation require some procedure for *coordination*, to ensure that all adhere to the same principle of action. The persons in a type II situation require some procedure for *bargaining*, to enable them to agree on a principle of action (and possibly a coordination procedure, if bargaining results in a set of principles, each of which is about equally acceptable to each member of society). The persons in a type III situation require, in addition to bargaining and perhaps coordination procedures, some *constraining* devices, both internal ("conscience") and external ("authority"), to afford them the guarantee that each will act to bring about the agreed outcome. The rationale for society, and hence for the social contract on which it is based, is thus provided by these three desiderata: coordination, bargaining, and constraint.

Following Hobbes, I shall suppose that what characterizes political society is the existence of some form of external constraint, that is, coercive authority.[11] Coercive authority induces men to conform to principles of mutual action not in themselves maximally beneficial for all persons, by imposing costs, penalties, or punishments on failure or refusal to conform. Coercive authority will appear arbitrary from the standpoint of those subjected to it if the outcome of the coerced actions is not better than the outcome these persons would achieve in the state of nature, when they are not subject to such coercion. Were it not for type III situations, coercion would be arbitrary, and anarchism might be the only defensible form of human society. Hence it is necessary to consider further the nature of human beings and the goods which they seek, if type III situations are essential to the human condition.

V

All members of society must regard coercion as both beneficial and necessary. This imposes a severe constraint on the goods which these persons seek. Were these goods strictly competitive in nature, so that no increase in joint supply was possible and any increase in one person's good entailed a corresponding decrease in the good available to some other person, then there could be no basis for mutual improvement from the outcome of the state of nature, and coercion could not be beneficial for all. Some might better their position by coercing others, but such coercion would be totally arbitrary from the standpoint of those whose position was worsened by it.

However, were the goods sought by the members of society essentially noncompetitive, so that an increase in one person's good was generally compatible with an increase in the goods available to others, then there would be little reason for anyone to prefer one optimal outcome to another, and some optimal outcomes would be stable, so that men would face only a problem of coordination. If coercion is necessary, then there must be considerable competition for the goods sought, so that despite the possibility of mutual improvement, frequently an increase in the good of one person must entail a decrease in the good of another. Each person's good must therefore be sharply distinct from, and in some respects opposed to, the good of others. The resources available to the members of society must be insufficient to permit the full or almost full satisfaction of everyone simultaneously, so that they face extensive conflict over the distribution of goods.

What goods satisfy these conditions? Goods such as companionship may be left aside, since only those goods which nonsocial creatures might seek can be involved. These must be goods whose supply can be increased by cooperative action, so that mutual improvement is possible. But they must be goods which are possessed or used individually, so that distributive problems can arise. And they must be goods for which the demand is unlimited, or at least always in excess of the supply, however much that supply is augmented by cooperation, so that potential distribution problems become actual.

In classifying goods, a simple Platonic schematism will serve present purposes.[12] I shall distinguish the goods of intellect, of spirit, and of desire. Men may cooperate in the pursuit of all three, but whereas the supply of such goods as knowledge and food may be increased by concerted action, only the distribution of such a good as honor is affected. Men may possess all three, but whereas the possession of food or honor is exclusive, the possession of knowledge by one person does not affect its possession by another. Hence of the three types, only goods of desire satisfy the two requirements that cooperation increase supply and that possession create distributive problems.

But are goods of desire the object of unlimited demand? Need they be in short supply? If these goods are related to physical need, to the natural appetites for food and drink, warmth, comfort, and sex, then surely they are not – as Rousseau pointed out, in criticizing Hobbes' account of the state of nature as one in which men were in constant conflict, making a coercive society the necessary instrument of peace.[13] Only a population explosion would make the goods of desire in necessarily short supply, and there is no reason to attribute that to the state of nature. Thus if man is motivated by his natural, nonsocial appetites, and material goods are considered in relation to these appetites, the demand for these goods will not usually exceed the supply, and no distribution problem will arise which only coercive authority could resolve.

Rousseau's own argument for the necessity of coercion is not available to the radical contractarian, since it depends on the introduction of competitive motivation in the process of socialization. There are, it would seem, two possible arguments consistent with contractarian premises: either the threat of scarcity inherent in the state of nature must be the basis for a necessarily competitive endeavor to assure oneself against its actualization or further appetites, of a kind such that scarcity of the goods satisfying them is assured, must be attributed to men in the state of nature.

Hobbes adopts the first alternative.[14] He argues that in the absence of coercive authority, the threat of scarcity among the goods of desire leads to competition for the goods of spirit. He characterizes men as seeking endless power, not because they always lack sufficient means to preserve and gratify themselves, but because they always lack the assurance that their means are sufficient.

The emergence of the desire for power turns a situation in which there is potential for cooperation into one which is actually increasingly competitive. Since the goods which preserve us are largely the same, I increase the assurance of my survival and well-being only by decreasing your assurance. Power is thus relative, so that men who seek only power must be engaged in a zero-sum conflict – one gains only at the expense of the other. This is the pure war of every man against every man. However, its outcome is to lessen every man's ability to assure his own preservation, so that the state of nature is far worse for everyone than what would result, were there a coercive force sufficient to deter each from the active pursuit of unlimited power, while enabling all to cooperate in increasing the supply of those goods necessary to preservation and wellbeing.

Hobbes' argument for the competitive drive for power is not fully convincing. For if goods of desire are in sufficient supply in the state of nature, so that the real threat of scarcity is slight, then the cost each person incurs in embarking on the search for ever greater power – the cost of being a party to the war of every man against every man – will be greater than the risk each runs in being satisfied with his present means to preserve himself. Hence some political theorists, such as C.B. Macpherson, have argued with considerable plausibility that Hobbes' real answer to the type of criticism advanced by Rousseau is to be found, not in his explicit account of the desire for power, but in his implicit acceptance of an appetite for material goods different in kind from the limited appetites for food, drink, sex, and the like, an appetite for unlimited appropriation.[15] This appetite, peculiarly characteristic of men in Hobbes' – and in our – society, is what turns the state of nature into an arena of unlimited combat. The view which explains the need for coercion is that man is by nature and necessity an appropriator.

To appropriate is to make one's own. The most complete and literal appropriation is of course appropriation into oneself – the conversion of an external object into one's body. But not all goods can be appropriated in such a way that they lose their own bodily identity; what is one's own thus extends beyond one's body to the physically distinct objects which constitute property. To appropriate is then to acquire property; the very object of appropriation is individual possession. Now there can be property in both the goods of intellect and the goods of appetite, but primarily it is the goods of desire which are appropriated and constitute property. Since the supply of these goods can be increased by cooperative action, the goods of appropriation clearly satisfy the first two conditions requisite if coercion is to be both beneficial and necessary. But do the goods of appropriation necessarily give rise to distributive problems? Are they in short supply? Why is the appetite for appropriation characteristically *unlimited*?

The natural appetites for food, drink, and sex are *satis*fiable; one eats, drinks, copulates enough, *satis*. The appetites are constantly renewed, but so are their objects, so that a balance can be achieved between supply and demand. The desire to appropriate is not similarly satisfiable; there is no natural level of satiation for appropriate activity. If one is an appropriator *by nature*, then one must continue to appropriate, or to seek to appropriate, but the objects for appropriation are not continually renewed; what one appropriates is removed from the stock of goods available for appropriation, so that, even with the increased supply of some goods made possible by cooperation, the supply is limited by the finitude of the earth, if by no previous limit of accessibility. Hence the demand for property always exceeds the supply of goods to be appropriated. The goods of desire are always scarce from the standpoint of the appropriator, and this scarcity is increased by the presence of other appropriators. Men therefore find themselves necessarily in conflict with respect to their desire for property.

The competitive search for power is easily derived from the insatiable desire for appropriation. Hence, men find themselves in an increasingly competitive situation, in which the security of their property is continually decreasing. Thus, simply in terms of the desire to appropriate and without reference to man's other natural appetites, the state of nature leads to an outcome far worse for everyone than what would result were there a coercive force sufficient to curb each man's appetite for power and to channel his desire to appropriate into an arena which is competitive yet peaceful – the marketplace rather than the battlefield.

The market is the primary social forum for the members of a society of appropriators. Their social concern for their fellows derives from their interest in appropriation, and is expressed in the relationship of exchange, whereby they transfer the possession of appropriated objects. Exchange of property is the primary function of the market; its efficient organization enables the appropriators to contract one with another to maximize the production and determine the allocation of their goods. Hence within society, the primary relationships of appropriators are contractual.

One might suppose that much of the argument I have developed, in seeking to link the contractarian conception of social relationships with the appropriate conception of human activity, could have been avoided quite simply by noting that the desire to appropriate necessarily manifests itself socially as the desire to exchange. Appropriators think of their fellows as partners in exchange, and so they think of social relations as contractual. But this, although true, would not show that appropriators conceive of society itself as contractual. The radical contractarian supposes that the marketplace, the locus of contract, is itself the product of a social contract, and is embedded in a coercive order which is also the product of that contract. From the claim that man is by nature an appropriator, it does not follow *directly* that he finds a coercive order beneficial and necessary. My concern has been to establish this further connection, and to introduce appropriative activity as that which naturally leads to hostility among men, yet which also affords scope for mutually beneficial cooperation, thus affording sufficient rationale for coercive society.

I have not shown that conceiving human activity as essentially appropriative requires one to accept a contractarian view of society. Locke's men are primarily appropriators, but they exist within a divinely ordained framework of natural law which relates them nonconventionally to their fellows.[16] Nor have I shown that conceiving all social relationships as contractual requires one to hold that human activity is primarily appropriative, for I have not shown that no alternative account of human activity would afford nonsocial individuals with a rationale for a social contract. What I have shown is that the contractarian conception of social relationships and the appropriative conception of human activity are mutually supporting. Given the undoubted historical importance of appropriative activity in our society, I conclude that within our ideology, the ideology of Western Europeans, the conceptions of appropriation and contract intersect in the person of the individual property-owner, related only by convention to his fellows. I shall therefore take the first connection in my initial thesis to be sufficiently defended.

VI

To conceive all social relationships as contractual is to deny that reason either determines or presupposes an order, a rational order, within which men are related prior to any agreement among themselves. This severely constrains the contractarian conception of rationality; I shall argue that it requires that rationality be conceived as related instrumentally to the satisfaction of individual interests.

Hobbes offers a useful way of formulating the problem of relating rationality to the theory of the social contract. "That is done by *right*, which is not done against reason," Hobbes claims, so that "we ought to judge those actions only *wrong*, which are repugnant to right reason . . . But that *wrong* which is done, we say it is done against some law. Therefore *true reason* is a certain *law*."[17] Reason, in other words, determines a framework of rights and laws, within which all men find themselves. But surely these rights and laws must determine relationships among men, which, being grounded in reason alone, are natural rather than conventional. If this were so, then radical contractarianism would have to be abandoned in favor of the Lockean theory that contract supplements and completes man's natural social relationships. Hobbes does not accept any such relationships; how then does he accommodate reason?

Hobbes keeps his conception of rationality consistent with his contractarianism by treating reason as both individualistic and instrumental. He speaks of "that Reason, which dictateth to every man his own good," and says that "all the voluntary actions of men tend to the benefit of themselves; and those actions are most Reasonable, that conduce most to their ends."[18] Given this conception of rationality, he is able to argue that every man has an unlimited, permissive right or liberty to do all things, so that each may do as he sees fit in order to preserve and benefit himself. The laws, to which every man is naturally subject, are but "Theorems concerning what conduceth to the conservation and defence of themselves." Hence reason does not in itself determine a system of rights and laws which relate men one to another in any way other than the natural relation of hostility. The "rational" order corresponding to the unlimited right of nature is the condition of war of every man with every man.

Contrast Hobbes' conception of reason with views which suppose rational standards transcending individual interests.[19] The Stoic holds that all men, as rational, are capable of apprehending the laws of nature, in terms of which all are related as members of a cosmopolis transcending more limited, conventional societies. The medieval Christian supposes that all men, as rational, are capable of apprehending the divinely ordained laws of nature, in terms of which all are related directly to God, and indirectly to their fellows. The Kantian supposes that all men, as rational, are directly related one to another as members of a Kingdom of Ends in which each must treat his fellows, not merely as means, but as ends in themselves. In each case there is an order – the Stoic cosmopolis, the Christian Kingdom of God, the Kantian Kingdom of Ends – which is constituted either by or in accordance with reason, to which all men belong, and within which all are related. This relationship is prior to human agreement, depending solely on man's rationality. It may of course be the basis of further, contractual relationships, but these are only of secondary importance.

Each of these positions may be brought into verbal agreement with Hobbes' claim that "those actions are most Reasonable, that conduce most to their ends," but only by equivocating on "ends." Where Hobbes speaks of the ends subjectively given by men's passions, the Stoic, Christian, or Kantian speaks of the ends objectively given by Nature, God, or Reason itself. Such objective ends constitute a natural order within which all men are related, and so each of these views is incompatible with radical contractarianism.

To specify the contractarian conception of rationality more precisely I shall relate it to the view of human activity developed in the preceding section. A person is a rational agent if and only if he acts to fulfill his (subjective) ends as far as possible. If it be agreed, as I have argued, that the contractarian ideology involves the conception of human activity as appropriative, then a person is a rational agent if and only if he acts to appropriate as much as possible. As much what? Here, our ideology exhibits a historical development. What is to be appropriated is first thought of as real property, land or estate. The distinction between land and other forms of property is then denied, and what is to be appropriated becomes the universal measure of property, money. Finally, in a triumph of abstraction, money as a particular object is replaced by the purely formal notion of utility, an object conveniently divested of all content. The rational man is, as Samuel Gompers succinctly recognized, simply the man who seeks *more*.

Thus it follows that not only the individualistic instrumental conception of rationality, but more precisely the individualistic utility-maximizing conception, is part of the ideology of the social contract, derived by means of the appropriate conception of human activity which is historically central to our ideology. But more than this may be said about reason, for it is not a merely derivative conception in contractarian thought.

I have argued that the appropriative conception of human activity, although consonant with contractarian thought, does not in itself require a contractarian interpretation of all human relationships, for it is at least possible to view man as belonging to a natural order, perhaps divinely ordained, within which he is noncontractually related to his fellows. But the instrumental conception of rationality rules out any ultimate natural or supernatural ground for human relationships. By itself, instrumental rationality does not imply any form of order or any type of relationship among human beings; it is compatible with the supposition that human existence is entirely solitary. But conjoined with the conception of human activity as appropriative, instrumental, maximizing rationality determines the hostile order of the state of nature, and this in turn makes it necessary for men to establish a conventional order among themselves by agreement or contract. Hence instrumental rationality conjoined with appropriative human nature entails contractarian society.

This concludes my exposition of the initial thesis of this essay. Radical contractarianism entails the instrumental conception of rationality; radical contractarianism together with the conception of human nature as appropriative entail more precisely the individualistic utility-maximizing conception of rationality. Conversely, instrumental rationality, together with the appropriative conception of human nature, entails the radical contractarian view that coercive society, and all social relationships, are the product of human convention. Thus society as conventional, human nature as appropriative, and rationality as maximizing cohere together at the core of our ideology.

VII

The maximizing conception of rationality is entailed by contractarianism, but it also undercuts the very possibility of rational agreement among men, and thus the very possibility of contractually based society. There is an apparent incoherence in contractarian ideology to which I now turn.

Individual appropriators find themselves naturally and necessarily in conflict one with another. But individual utility-maximizers have no direct rational means for resolving their conflicts. Hobbes expresses this point clearly: "And therefore, as when there is a controversy in an account, the parties must by their own accord, set up for right Reason, the Reason of some Arbitrator, or Judge, to whose sentence they will both stand, or their controversie must either come to blowes, or be undecided, for want of a right Reason constituted by Nature; so is it also in all debates of what kind soever..."[20] The Stoic, the Christian, or the Kantian may appeal to a right reason constituted by nature, as the basis of conflict resolution among human beings. But for the contractarian there is no such appeal.

Why is this important? Consider once again the functions which society must perform – coordination, bargaining, and constraint. Each of these requires procedures for decision and action which are not strictly contained in the principle of individual utility-maximization. Each then involves at least an extension in the contractarian conception of rationality. I have argued elsewhere that coordination and bargaining are fully compatible with utility-maximization.[21] These raise no problem. But constraint is not so compatible. The necessity for constraint arises when the outcome of bargaining is not stable, so that if each person acts to maximize his own utility, some persons will not act to bring about the agreed outcome. Voluntarily to act in a constrained manner is contrary to the dictates of individual utility-maximization.

Individual appropriators must enter into contractual relationships to resolve their conflicts and to bring about an optimal state of affairs, better for each than the natural outcome. But their conception of rationality leads them to violate their contracts whenever, as must often be the case, adherence would require them to abstain from directly maximizing behavior. In section IV, I insisted that agreement in a type III situation – a situation in which no acceptable optimal outcome is stable – is possible only given some assurance that the agreement will be honored. This assurance requires external constraints, and thus I introduced the need for coercion. But it also needs internal constraints, the constraints of conscience, and these contradict the requirements of reason. The contractarian principle of rational action undercuts the internal constraints necessary to maintain contractual relationships.

This problem can be resolved only if it is possible to remedy the want of a right reason established by nature. The remedy can only be conventional. Natural reason, the reason of the individual maximizer, leads only to the natural relationship of hostility among men. A conventional rationality which upholds adherence to one's agreements even against the dictates of individual utility-maximization must therefore be accepted as the basis of the social contract, and so of social relationships among men.

Hobbes recognizes this need for a conventional standard of right reason, for he continues the passage quoted above: "And when men that think themselves wiser than all others, clamor and demand right Reason for judge; yet seek no more, but that things should be determined, by no other mens reason but their own, it is as intolerable in the society of men, as it is in play after trump is turned, to use for trump on every occasion, that suite whereof they have most in their hand." This passage contains the heart of the matter. Trump is established by the social contract, as that convention required to achieve an optimal state of affairs, better for each than the natural outcome. But each man, guided by his own reason, uses for trump his own interest. And this is intolerable, for it undercuts the contract and makes society impossible. However, Hobbes fails to establish a conventional standard of right reason, adhering to his individualist view that "those actions are most Reasonable, that conduce most to their ends." In the state of nature this is true, but as Hobbes himself recognizes, this is exactly what is intolerable in society or, indeed, intolerable if there is to be any society.

This is the point at which the theory of the social contract seems to collapse into incoherence. As I have noted, contract – the generic relationship of which the social contract is but the focal expression – is the fundamental relationship among appropriators. Their prime concern one with another is to exchange objects of appropriation, and contracts are their necessary means. But contracts are not fully self-sustaining. The society established by the social contract, market society, is from one point of view simply the network of contracts among individual men. But this network is maintained by a legal order which enforces the contracts. The contractual relationships of appropriators must be embedded within a political framework which coerces them into remaining within the market in their actions and relationships. Contractarian ideology represents this framework as itself contractual. But the condition of the market – the condition of the network of contracts – cannot itself be the product of a contract, which would be only part of that network. If the market is not self-sustaining, then it cannot be sustained by a part of itself.

The charge of incoherence operates at two levels. The argument which I have sketched suggests that radical contractarianism is incoherent as a *theory*, in providing an account of human relationships which presupposes a noncontractual base. I shall suggest that it can answer this charge. But there is a further argument which suggests that contractarianism is incoherent as an *ideology* in providing an account of human relationships which, in practice, undermines their base. I shall suggest in section IX that this charge succeeds, that the price contractarianism must pay for theoretical coherence is too great to allow it to maintain ideological effectiveness, once its adherents come to be aware of that price.

This last clause is important. Questions about the theoretical coherence of contractarianism need not affect its ideological coherence, except insofar as they become questions in the minds of its adherents. Suppose it were true that contractual relationships, to be effectively maintained, must be embedded within a coercive order which itself were not contractually grounded. This would not prevent persons from conceiving of this coercive order as contractual, or from conceiving of all of their social relationships as contractual without attending to their framework. As long as the question of the coercive basis of contractual relationships did not arise in thought, the incoherence of the ideology would not be recognized, and its effectiveness would be unimpaired.

But now I want to defend contractarianism against the criticism that the instrumental conception of rationality, which it requires, must undermine the theory of the contractual rationale for society. What is essential, as Hobbes recognized, is a conventional standard of rational action, which will enjoin adherence to the social contract even when strict individual maximization calls for nonadherence, yet which itself is grounded in the individualistic utility-maximizing conception of rationality.

This may seem impossible. Surely any standard of rational action which is grounded in individual utility-maximization must have its same corrosive effect on adherence to agreements which require persons to refrain from maximizing behavior. But, I have argued elsewhere, this is not so.[22] A person who begins as an individual utility-maximizer will find it rational, on individualistic maximizing grounds, to change his very *conception* of rationality, and come to adopt a conventional standard of right reason, which I have termed *constrained maximization*.

The principle of constrained maximization corresponds to straightforward individual utility-maximization in its application to state-of-nature situations, but it enjoins each person to agree with his fellows on actions leading to outcomes which are optimal and better for all than the corresponding natural outcomes, and to perform such actions within society. The rationale for the adoption of this new conception of rationality by utility-maximizers is quite simple; constrained maximizers are able to make agreements which straightforward maximizers cannot, because constrained maximizers will, and straightforward maximizers will not, adhere to these agreements, and the benefits of making such agreements are greater than the costs of adhering to them. Persons who adopt the standard of constrained maximization will find that, under widely prevailing, albeit not universal, conditions, it is rational for them to enter into and to adhere to a social contract with at least some of their fellow human beings, thereby replacing the natural relationship of hostility with the conventional relationship of sociability.

Reason itself neither determines nor presupposes any relationships among men, so that the contractarian requirement that all social relationships be conventional is not violated. But reason does lead men to enter by agreement into social relationships, and to adopt a standard of rationality which sustains these relationships rather than undermining them. Contractarian theory takes the individualistic utility-maximizing conception of rationality as the natural standard, but provides for its rational replacement by a constrained maximizing conception which grounds those mutually optimizing actions to which men agree as the basis of their society.

VIII

I have distinguished two aspects of contractarian society: the market, the locus of the particular contracts which relate men as producers and distributors of goods, and the coercive order, or state, which ensures that the market does not revert to the battlefield of the state of nature. This distinction corresponds, in an interesting and important way, to the distinction which I have introduced between straightforward utility-maximization and constrained maximization.

Straightforward maximization corresponds to the rule of self-interest. Throughout most of human history the rule of self-interest has been considered a primary threat to society, as indeed my analysis of the problem posed to contractarianism by straightforward maximization would suggest that it is. Religion, law, morality, and tradition have combined to repress the force of self-interest. The great discovery of our society is, of course, the discovery of the social value of self-interest. The triumph of the science of economics was to demonstrate that under appropriate conditions, those of perfect competition in a free market, if each person acted purely self-interestedly, to maximize his own utilities, then the outcome would necessarily be optimal, the particular optimum depending solely on the initial positions of the persons in the market. Instead of repressing self-interest, our society has harnessed it. The benefits have been striking; critics of our society would hold that the costs have been overlooked.

Within the perfectly competitive market, straightforward individual utility-maximization is an adequate rule of reason. However, the market may fail to be perfectly competitive because of the presence of externalities – free goods or uncompensated costs, and the market is never fully self-sustaining, since force and fraud always threaten it. Hence it requires to be regulated and controlled by the power of the state, and here straightforward maximization must be supplanted by constrained maximization. The distinction which I have drawn between these two conceptions of rationality parallels the distinction between the two primary sectors of contractarian society.

This may be indicated by a suitable relabeling of the two conceptions of rationality. Straightforward individual utility-maximization, the natural standard of reason, is effective in maintaining optimal productive and distributive activities for men in the market, and so may be termed the standard of *economic* rationality. Constrained individual utility-maximization, the conventional standard of reason for contractarians, is effective in maintaining the beneficial and necessary coercive order of the state against those directly maximizing actions which would restore the hostility of the state of nature, and so may be termed the standard of *political* rationality.

Since contractarian ideology is at the basis of our social thinking, it should not be surprising that the conception of society which is consonant with it proves familiar to us, in focusing on the economic, bargaining order of the market and viewing the political, coercive order of the state as sustaining the market. It should also not be surprising that contractarian society is of limited extent, and is not a single society of the human race.

Not all persons need find it mutually advantageous to leave the state of nature to establish a market and a state. Only if all can improve on their original situation can all have sufficient reason to enter the social contract. If, however, the relations among some persons, or among some groups previously established by contract, are such that a gain for one must be a loss for another, then not everyone will have reason to agree to a departure from the existing state of affairs.

The implication of this for the present world situation is worth noting. On the contractarian view, it is evident that people should enter into contractual relations only with those with whom cooperation will prove profitable. Now we – Western Europeans and offshoots whose thinking is shaped by contractarian ideology – have no reason to expect it to be profitable or beneficial to us to cooperate with the overpopulated and underdeveloped peoples of much of the rest of the world. Given the finitude of the earth's resources, their gains are our losses.

To the question, Who is my neighbor? the radical contractarian has a simple answer. My neighbor, according to our ideology, is the man with whom I can make a mutually profitable agreement. Everyone else is my enemy – to be exploited if I can, to exploit me if he can. One might take as one measure of the hold of contractarian ideology upon us the extent to which this answer determines our practice, whatever we may preach.

IX

Radical contractarianism has come more and more to dominate our thoughts and actions, or so I would contend. Correlatively, contractarianism has passed increasingly from covert to overt manifestation in our self-awareness. Institutions and practices which derive their rationale from non-contractarian considerations are being discarded or rejected. The effect of this is to throw into sharp relief the contractarian conception of rationality, and its relationship to man's appropriative desires.

Insofar as the two are mutually supportive, all is well. The supposition that all human relationships other than hostility are conventional, the product of mutually beneficial agreement, will sustain bargaining activity within the market, for here economic rationality and the desire to appropriate reinforce each other. But the coercive order of the state is a quite different matter, for here political rationality imposes a constraint on the unlimited appetite of the contractarian. However rational it may be to stand to one's advantageous agreements even against direct interest, yet reason is insufficient in practice to overcome the motivations which, on the contractarian view, direct our actions. Awareness of oneself as an appropriator undercuts one's willingness to accept the constraints of the political order.

Historically the political order, which is necessary to the maintenance of peace and security within society, has been supported by motivations quite different from those that enter the contractarian conception of human nature. As this conception comes to be both more overt and more pervasive, these other factors lose their hold on us, and the political order loses its motivational base.

To the extent to which it has not been self-enforcing, political society has rested on *patriotism* – the love of country which binds men to the coercive order because it is surrounded with the emotional trappings of fatherland or motherland (trappings which themselves are corroded as the contractarian conception of the family comes to the fore!). It is, I suggest, this attachment of individuals to their society which has generated sufficient voluntary support to enable coercion to be effective. To be sure, not all members of society have felt this attachment, but enough have been moved by it to permit the remainder to be constrained through the further motive of *fear* – fear of the coercive order itself.

In addition to patriotic feeling, familial feeling has been a fundamental motive supporting the political order. The effect of familial feeling has been primarily to strengthen society as an entity enduring in time. Since future generations have little to contribute to the wellbeing of those now alive, a contract between us and our descendants seems a tenuous basis for an enduring society.

However, the transgenerational affective ties which bind together members of a family supply the motivation needed for each generation to seek the continuation of society. I shall term this motive *love*, and suggest that it operates primarily at a prerational level. By this I mean that membership in the family, and the ties of love, precede, causally if not logically, the emergence of that individual self who engages in the appropriate and contractual activities of the market, and aligns with others to create and maintain the state.

Patriotism and love thus maintain the enduring political basis of contractual market society. Because our ideology is part of the deep structure of our thought about ourselves, it has been possible for us to think in contractarian ways while acting on these quite uncontractarian motives. We may suppose that our ties to our fellows and our society are strictly contractual, and yet act on ties which are not contractual. However, as the ideology of contract comes increasingly to manifest itself at the level of conscious thought, so that we come consciously to disavow nonappropriative motivation, patriotism and love must seem more and more irrelevant and even unintelligible. The rejection by the young of America's role in the Vietnam War and the emergence of radical feminism are manifestations of this increasingly overt contractarian consciousness.

Patriotism and love have had a further effect on the development of our society. Historically they have served, together with the fear engendered by the coercive order which they sustain, to exclude most human beings from effective membership in market society, and thus from what, to the contractarian, are the essentially human activities of appropriation and exchange. Neither workers, who have lacked control over the means of production, nor women, who have engaged in reproduction rather than production, have conceived themselves, or been in a position to conceive themselves, as full human beings in the sense implicit in radical contractarian ideology.[23] Marx, mistakenly, thought religion to be the opium of the people;[24] the real opiates, in contractarian society, have been love and patriotism. By removing wide areas of human activity, and even more important, most people, from the effective scope of the ideology, love and patriotism have enabled those remaining within its scope to conduct their appropriative activities more successfully.

Indeed, this restriction of appropriation to, largely, the male bourgeoisie has been essential to the development of our society. If every person had considered himself, or herself, to be an appropriator, in competition with every other person, then, as Hobbes insisted, only an all-powerful sovereign could have prevented endless conflict. The mode of rationality which would have led every person to make and carry out an agreement to check competition and ensure mutual advantage would have been insufficient to overcome the competitive desire to appropriate.

C.B. Macpherson, in his introduction to *Leviathan*, emphasizes this when he says: "Given the postulate that the power of every man necessarily opposed and hindered the power of other men, so that every man in society necessarily sought more power over others, *and provided* that this centrifugal force was not offset by any centripetal force, it would follow that any slackening or temporary absence of a sovereign power would tend to lead to internecine strife. What Hobbes overlooked and failed to put into his model was the centripetal force of a cohesive bourgeois class within the society."[25] The male bourgeoisie have acted as a cohesive, centripetal force because they have recognized, implicitly, that they must retain appropriative activity exclusively in their hands to prevent the strife which would result from the competition of every person with every other person. But they have been able to retain appropriative activity for themselves alone, not just because of their cohesion, but because neither workers nor women have conceived of themselves as appropriators. Acceptance by workers and women of the contractarian view of human beings would lead to their refusal to remain excluded from truly human, appropriative activity.

I have suggested that the ideology of radical contractarianism is manifesting itself increasingly in our overt consciousness. And this consciousness is spreading more and more widely. In itself, the ideology embraces everyone, so that, as more and more people attain self-awareness, they do so in the terms provided by the deep structure of our thought – in the terms, then, of contractarianism.

The likely end of the current fad for liberation movements, whatever the ostensible aim of these movements, will be to extend contractarian self-awareness to new areas of human activity and new groups of human beings. Radical feminists will go the way of radical trades unionists; women will join the system rather than overthrow it. But as all persons come to consider all human relationships to be contractual, they will not achieve the happy state of ideally rational appropriators, or even the cohesive unity of the male bourgeoisie. The absorptive capacity of the system is being overstrained, so that the effect of extending contractarian ideology is and will continue to be to corrode all of those bonds which in the real world have been the underpinning of the market. Bereft of its framework, the bargaining order will collapse into competitive chaos.

Love and patriotism are myths to the contractarian. But these myths, and not reason, have been the real support for the enduring coercive order, enabling it to enlist fear and thus assure the survival of the state. And the contractarian state, rational to the constrained maximizer but effective only because of its basis in these myths, has maintained the bargaining order of the market. Remove this basis by bringing all human beings to awareness of themselves as appropriators, and the practical incoherence of contractarian ideology manifests itself in the inability of conscious contractarians to maintain the coercive basis of their social relationships. Thus the triumph of radical contractarianism leads to the destruction, rather than the rationalization, of our society, for what real men and women who believe the ideology need to keep them from the war of all against all is not reason, but the Hobbist sovereign, and he is not available.

The ideology of radical contractarianism is, of course, but one among many possible ways of structuring our thought about man, society, and reason. We may see that this way of thinking is, from a practical point of view, bankrupt, and indeed that it will destroy us if we remain its adherents. But other ways of thinking, however possible they may be, are not produced to order. Faced with the falling of the dusk, the owl of Minerva spreads its wings – and takes flight.[26]

Notes

1   For some brief characterizations of ideology, see Chaim I. Waxman, ed., *The End of Ideology Debate* (New York: Simon & Schuster, 1968), pp. 3–4. Superstructure and false consciousness are, of course, part of the Marxian account of ideology. The demise of ideology was celebrated in Daniel Bell, *The End of Ideology* (New York: The Free Press, 1960), and discussed in Waxman. Note such titles as "The End of Ideology as Ideology" by Robert A. Haber, "The Anti-Ideology Ideologues" by Michael Harrington, "The End of 'The End of Ideology' " by Donald Clark Hodges.

2   My sketchy characterization of ideology needs to be amplified and embedded in a theory of consciousness. There is, of course, no space for that here. What I have to say owes much to my reading of D.C. Dennett, *Content and Consciousness* (London: Routledge & Kegan Paul, 1969), especially chap. VI. But I should not want to suggest that Dennett would accept parenthood for my ideas.

3   "Now one may think of moral philosophy ... as the attempt to describe our moral capacity; ... This enterprise is very difficult. For by such a description is not meant simply a list of the judgments on institutions and actions that we are prepared to render, accompanied with supporting reasons when these are offered. Rather, what is required is a formulation of a set of principles which, when conjoined to our beliefs and knowledge of the circumstances, would lead us to make these judgments with their supporting reasons were we to apply these principles conscientiously and intelligently.... The principles which describe them [our moral capacities] must be presumed to have a complex structure, and the concepts involved will require serious study.

"A useful comparison here is with the problem of describing the sense of grammaticalness that we have for the sentences of our native language.... This is a difficult undertaking which ... is known to require theoretical constructions that far outrun the ad hoc precepts of our explicit grammatical knowledge. A similar situation presumably holds in moral philosophy.... A correct account of moral capacities will certainly involve principles and theoretical constructions which go much beyond the norms and standards cited in everyday life; ... " John Rawls, *A Theory of Justice* (Cambridge, Mass.: Harvard University Press, 1971), pp. 46–7. Other relevant passages are on pp. 126–8, 137–8, 143–145.

4   John Locke, *Two Treatises of Government*, especially Second Treatise, chaps. VII–IX. See also chap. II for discussion of the law of nature.

5   Thomas Hobbes, *Leviathan*, especially chaps. 13, 17, and 20.

6   The source for this is one of the magazines distributed in Canada with the Saturday newspaper. The magazine has found its way from my desk into a bundle of old newspapers, leaving behind only the quote.

7   "This passage from the state of nature to civil society produces in man a very remarkable change, in substituting justice for instinct in his conduct, and giving his actions the morality which previously they lacked.... If the abuses of this new condition did not

often degrade him below that from which he has come, he should bless unceasingly the happy moment... which, from a stupid and limited animal, made an intelligent being and a man." Jean-Jacques Rousseau, *Du contrat social*, book I, chap. VIII, my translation. Also, "He who dares undertake to create a people ought to feel himself capable of changing, so to speak, human nature, of transforming each individual, who by himself is complete and solitary, into part of a larger whole from which he receives almost his very life and being, of changing his constitution to strengthen it, of substituting an interdependent and moral existence for the physical and independent existence which we all have received from nature. It is necessary, in a word, that he remove man's own powers, in order to give him ones which are foreign to him and which he can not use without the help of others." Book II. chapter VII, also my translation.

It should be noted here that Rawls subverts contractarianism in a way very similar to Rousseau. Having determined one's fundamental legitimating principle for society (for Rousseau, that social relationships respect liberty in avoiding the dependence of one man on another; for Rawls, that social relationships embody mutual respect), one then introduces a "most favored" initial situation, in which persons would rationally choose a society based on the legitimating principle. One then supposes that in society, human beings are so socialized that their self-conception comes to center on that legitimating principle; hence they will consider their social relationships to be those they would have chosen. Thus the principle acquires a contractarian rationale.

But the rationale is spurious; since the initial situation is selected to ensure the "correct" choice, the act of choice is evidently neither necessary nor sufficient to justify the legitimating principle. The real character of the theory then emerges when one asks for the grounds of the legitimating principle.

8 *Leviathan*, chap. 13, "men have no pleasure, (but on the contrary a great deal of griefe) in keeping company, where there is no power able to overawe them all."

9 Plato, *Republic*, 338d–339a.

10 To act on a mutually selected principle of action is to act on the basis of a choice, made by each person, of a single set of actions, one for each person in the situation; until all choose the same set, no one acts.

11 *Leviathan*, chap. 17, especially "the agreement... of men, is by Covenant only, which is Artificiall: and therefore it is no wonder if there be somewhat else required (besides Covenant) to make their Agreement constant and lasting; which is a Common Power, to keep them in awe, and to direct their actions to the Common Benefit."

12 The classification of goods obviously corresponds to the tripartite division of the soul in *Republic*, 436a–441c.

13 Hobbes "ought to say that, the state of nature being where the care of our own conservation is the least prejudicial to that of others, it was consequently the most conducive to peace and the most appropriate for mankind. He says precisely the opposite, having inopportunely introduced into the savage's care for his own conservation the need to satisfy a multitude of passions which are the work of society..." Jean-Jacques Rousseau, *Discours sur l'origine et les fondements de l'inégalité parmi les hommes*, première partie. Translation mine.

14 *Leviathan*, chaps. 13 and 11.

15 "Hobbes... came nearest to postulating man as an infinite appropriator (though he did not quite do so),..." C.B. Macpherson, *Democratic Theory: Essays in Retrieval* (Oxford: At the Clarendon Press, 1973), p. 29n.

16 *Two Treatises of Government*, Second Treatise, chap. V (on appropriation), and chap. II (on the law of nature).

17 *De Cive*, chap. II, para. I.

18 *Leviathan*, chap. 15.

19 The comparisons in this paragraph are intended to be commonplace; I have not tied them to particular references to Stoics, medieval Christians, and Kant.

20 *Leviathan*, chap. 5.

21 The argument on pp. 205–6 of "Coordination," *Dialogue* 14, no. 2 (June 1975), may be transferred from the case of act-utilitarianism to that of individual utility-maximization, to show that coordination is a natural extension of maximization. Bargaining is discussed in "Rational Cooperation," *Nous* 8, no. 1 (March 1974), pp. 53–65.

22 See "Reason and Maximization," *Canadian Journal of Philosophy* 4, no. 3 (March 1975), especially pp. 427–30.

23 Lacking control over the means of production, workers have been required to sell their labor, and thus their claim to own their products, in order to survive. Thus they have been excluded from appropriative activity, an exclusion which continued even after they combined in trade unions, until those unions abandoned the goal of replacing the appropriative, competitive economy with a noncompetitive order, and adopted instead the aim of exercising power within the existing system. Reproduction, the activity of women, has been considered inferior and instrumental to true production. Being unable to engage in production, women have been required to sell *their* labor in order to survive; the husband has thus appropriated the children as products.

24 Karl Marx, *Contribution to the Critique of Hegel's Philosophy of Right*, Introduction.

25 Thomas Hobbes, *Leviathan*, edited and introduced by C. B. Macpherson (Harmondsworth, Middlesex: Penguin Books, 1968), pp. 55–6. See also pp. 61–3.

26 "One word more about giving instruction as to what the world ought to be. Philosophy in any case always comes on the scene too late to give it. As the thought of the world, it appears only when actuality is already there cut and dried after its process of formation has been completed. . . . When philosophy paints its grey in grey, then has a shape of life grown old. By philosophy's grey in grey it cannot be rejuvenated but only understood. The owl of Minerva spreads its wings only with the falling of the dusk." *Hegel's Philosophy of Right*, tr. T.M. Knox (Oxford: Clarendon Press, 1942), pp. 12–13.

Hegel played a larger role in earlier drafts of this essay. The discussion of property and contract in the first part of the *Philosophy of Right* is a fundamental source for any articulation of contractarian ideology, however much Hegel rejects the view that all social relationships are contractual. But the exposition of Hegel is a problem in itself, and this essay faces enough problems, so Hegel has been unfairly relegated to a footnote.

4

The Fraternal Social Contract

Carole Pateman

The sons form a conspiracy to overthrow the despot, and in the end substitute a social contract with equal rights for all...Liberty means equality among the brothers (sons)...Locke suggests that the fraternity is formed not by birth but by election, by contract...Rousseau would say it is based on will.

Norman O. Brown, *Love's Body*

The stories of the origins of civil society found in the classic social contract theories of the seventeenth and eighteenth centuries have been repeated many times. More recently, John Rawls and his followers have given new lease of life to the story of the contract that generates political right. But in all the telling of the tales, and in the discussion and argument about the social contract, we are told only half the story. Political theorists present the familiar account of the creation of civil society as a universal realm that (at least potentially) includes everyone and of the origins of political right in the sense of the authority of government in the liberal state, or Rousseau's participatory polity. But this is not the 'original' political right. There is silence about the part of the story which reveals that the social contract is a fraternal pact that constitutes civil society as a patriarchal or masculine order. To uncover the latter, it is necessary to begin to tell the repressed story of the genesis of patriarchal political right which men exercise over women.

Most discussions of contract theory accept uncritically the claim that the stories successfully show why the authority of the state is legitimate; but the critical failure to recognize the social contract as fraternal pact is of a different kind. Only half the story appears in commentaries on the classic texts or in contemporary Rawlsian arguments, because modern political theory is so thoroughly patriarchal that one aspect of its origins lies outside the analytical reach of most theorists. Political theorists argue about the individual, and take it for granted that their subject matter concerns the public world, without investigating the way in which the 'individual', 'civil society' and 'the public' have been constituted as patriarchal categories in opposition to womanly nature and the 'private' sphere. The civil body politic created through the fraternal social contract is fashioned after only one of the two bodies of humankind.

The patriarchal character of civil society is quite explicit in the classic texts – if they are read from a feminist perspective. In this chapter, I can draw attention to only a few of the implications of such a reading and to some of the most obvious omissions in standard discussions of contract theory.[1] For instance, civil society is public society, but it is not usually appreciated that feminist arguments refer to a different sense of the separation of 'public' and 'private' from that typically found in discussions of civil society.

The meaning of 'civil society' in the contract stories, and as I am using it here, is constituted through the 'original' separation and opposition between the modern, public – civil – world and the modern, private or conjugal and familial sphere: that is, in the new social world created through contract, everything that lies beyond the domestic (private) sphere is public, or 'civil', society. Feminists are concerned with *this* division. In contrast, most discussions of civil society and such formulations as 'public' regulation versus 'private' enterprise presuppose that the politically relevant separation between public and private is drawn *within* 'civil society' as constructed in the social contract stories. That is to say, 'civil society' has come to be used in a meaning closer to that of Hegel, the social contract theorists' greatest critic, who contrasts the universal, public state with the market, classes and corporations of private, civil society.

Hegel, of course, presents a threefold division between family, civil society, state – but the separation between the family and the rest of social life is invariably 'forgotten' in arguments about civil society. The shift in meaning of 'civil', 'public' and 'private' goes unnoticed because the 'original' creation of civil society through the social contract is a patriarchal construction which is also a separation of the sexes. Political theorists have repressed this part of the story from their theoretical consciousness – though it is implicit in the assumption that civil life requires a natural foundation – and thus liberals and (non-feminist) radicals alike deal only with the liberal understanding of civil society, in which 'civil' life becomes private in opposition to the public state.

Perhaps the most striking feature of accounts of the contract story is the lack of attention paid to fraternity, when liberty and equality are so much discussed. One reason for the neglect is that most discussions pass over the insights about fraternity found in Freud's versions of the contract story. Fraternity is central to socialism, and nineteenth- and twentieth-century liberalism, as a recent study has shown, relies heavily on fraternity as a crucial bond integrating individual and community. However, discussions of fraternity do not touch upon the constitution of the 'individual' through the patriarchal separation of private and public, nor upon how the division within the (masculine) 'individual' includes an opposition between fraternity and reason. Fraternity comes to the fore in liberals' attempts to formulate a more sociologically adequate account of the individual than is found in the abstract conceptions of classic liberal contract

theory. But for feminists explicit recourse to liberal or socialist fraternal bonds merely exposes the patriarchal character of ostensibly universal categories and calls attention to the fundamental problem of whether and how women could be fully incorporated into a patriarchal civil world.

A feminist reading of the contract stories is also important for another reason. The contemporary feminist movement has brought the idea of patriarchy into popular and academic currency, but confusion abounds about its meaning and implications and recently some feminists have argued that the term is best avoided. 'Patriarchy' is, to my knowledge, the only term with which to capture the specificities of the subjection and oppression of *women* and to distinguish this from other forms of domination. If we abandon the concept of patriarchy, the problem of the subjection of women and sexual domination will again vanish from view within individualist and class theories. The crucial question, therefore, is the sense in which it can be said that our own society is patriarchal.

Two popular feminist claims about patriarchy add to the confusion. The first is that the literal meaning of 'patriarchy', rule by fathers, is still relevant. To insist that patriarchy is nothing more than paternal rule is itself a patriarchal interpretation, as an examination of the classic texts reveals. The second claim is that patriarchy is a timeless, human universal, which obviously rules out the possibility that men's domination of women takes different forms in different historical periods and cultures. More precisely, neither claim about patriarchy can acknowledge that our own momentous transition from the traditional to the modern world – a transition which the contract stories encapsulate theoretically – involved a change from a traditional (paternal) form of patriarchy to a new *specifically modern* (or fraternal) form: patriarchal civil society.

Few of the participants in recent feminist debates about patriarchy seem aware of the significance of patriarchal political theory in the classic sense: that is, the patriarchalism of Sir Robert Filmer and other less well-known writers of three centuries ago. Nor have they taken account of the theoretical and practical significance of the battle waged between the patriarchalists and the social contract theorists. Zillah Eisenstein has done so, but on the other hand Jean Elshtain's references to patriarchal theory merely reiterate the standard view in political theory that patriarchalism had suffered a fatal defeat by the end of the seventeenth century.[2] This is far from the case, and an understanding of the exact sense in which, and the limits within which, the contract theorists emerged victorious over the patriarchalists is central to an appreciation of how a specifically modern form of patriarchy was brought into being.

Patriarchal political theory had little in common with the ancient tradition of patriarchalism that took the family as the general model for social order and made claims about the emergence of political society from the family, or the coming together of many families. In *Patriarchalism in Political Thought*, Schochet emphasizes that patriarchal theory was formulated explicitly as a justification for political authority and political obedience, and – as he also stresses – it was systematized in opposition to the social contract theories that were developing at the same time and challenging (one half of) the patriarchalists' most fundamental assumptions.[3] Patriarchalism developed, and was 'defeated', in a specific historical and theoretical context.

The standard interpretation of the conflict between the patriarchalists and the contract theorists treats it as a battle over paternal rule and focuses on the irreconcilable differences between, the two doctrines over the political right of fathers and the natural liberty of sons. The patriarchalists claimed that kings and fathers ruled in exactly the same way (kings were fathers and vice versa); that family and polity were homologous; that sons were born naturally subject to their fathers; and that political authority and obedience and a hierarchy of inequality were natural. The contract theorists rejected all these claims: they argued that paternal and political rule were distinct; that family and polity were two different and separate forms of association; that sons were born free and equal and, as adults, were as free as their fathers before them; that political authority and obligation were conventional and political subjects were civil equals.[4] It is true that in this particular controversy the patriarchalists were defeated. The theoretical assumptions of the contract theorists were an essential part of the transformation of the traditional order and the world of father-kings into capitalist society, liberal representative government and the modern family.

However, this familiar version of the story in which the sons gain their natural liberty, make the contract and create liberal civil society, or Rousseau's participatory civil order, is only half the tale.

It is a patriarchal reading of the texts which identifies patriarchy with paternal rule; it therefore omits the story of the real origin of political right. Patriarchalism has two dimensions: the paternal (father/son) and the masculine (husband/wife). Political theorists can represent the outcome of the theoretical battle as a victory for contract theory because they are silent about the sexual or conjugal aspect of patriarchy, which appears as non-political or natural and so of no theoretical consequence. But a feminist reading of the texts shows that patriarchalism was far from defeated. The contract theorists rejected paternal right, but they absorbed and simultaneously transformed conjugal, masculine patriarchal right.

To see how this came about – and hence to take a necessary first step towards elucidating some of the characteristics of modern patriarchy – it is necessary to begin with the patriarchal story of monarchical fatherhood exemplified in the writings of Sir Robert Filmer. Although Filmer's father is overthrown in the story of the social contract, his sons receive a vital inheritance that is, paradoxically, obscured by the doctrine of paternal right.

Filmer's aim was to show the awful error of the contract theorists' claim that men were by nature free and equal, a claim he saw as the 'main foundation of popular sedition'.[5] Filmer argued that all law was of necessity the product of the will of one man. All titles to rule devolved from the original divine grant of kingly right to Adam, the first father. The ground was immediately swept from under the feet of the proponents of the doctrine of the natural freedom of mankind once it was recognized that 'the natural and private dominion of Adam [is] the fountain of all government and propriety'.[6] Filmer writes that 'the title comes from the fatherhood';[7] Adam's sons, and hence all succeeding generations of sons, were born into political subjection by virtue of Adam's 'right of fatherhood', his 'fatherly power' or the 'power of the fatherhood'.[8]

At the birth of his first son, Adam became the first monarch, and his political right passed to all subsequent fathers and kings. For Filmer, fathers and kings ruled by virtue of their fatherhood and all fathers were monarchs in their families: 'the Father of a family governs by no other law than by his own will.'[9] Filmer argued that no government could be a tyranny because the king's will was law; similarly, the will of the father was the absolute, arbitrary will of the *patria potestas* who, under Roman law, had the power of life and death over his children. Laslett comments that Filmer 'did not adopt the capital punishment of children by their fathers, but he quoted examples of it from Bodin with approval.'[10]

Filmer's view of the origin of political right seems, therefore, to be unmistakable: it derives from fatherhood. But patriarchy, even in its classical formulation, is more complex than its literal meaning suggests. Fatherly power is only one dimension of patriarchy, as Filmer himself reveals. Filmer's apparently straightforward statements obscure the foundation of patriarchal right. Paternal power is not the origin of political right. The genesis of political power lies in Adam's conjugal or sex right, not in his fatherhood. Adam's political title is granted *before* he becomes a father. Sons, as Filmer caustically reminds Hobbes, do not spring up like mushrooms. If Adam was to be a father, Eve had to become a mother and if Eve was to be a mother, then Adam must have sexual access to her body. In other words, sexual or conjugal right must *necessarily precede* the right of fatherhood.

Filmer makes it clear that Adam's political right is originally established in his right as a husband over Eve: 'God gave to Adam . . . the dominion over the woman', and 'God ordained Adam to rule over his wife, and her desires were to be subject to his'.[11] However, sexual or conjugal right then fades from view in Filmer's writings. After proclaiming that Adam's first dominion or political right is over a woman, not another man (son), Filmer then subsumes conjugal right under the power of fatherhood. Eve and her desires are subject to Adam but, Filmer continues, 'here we have the original grant of government, and the fountain of all power placed in the Father of all mankind'. Recall that in the Bible story in the Book of Genesis, Eve is created only after Adam and the animals have been placed on earth. Moreover, she is not created *ab initio* but *from* Adam, who is thus in a sense her parent. Filmer is able to treat all political right as the right of a father because the patriarchal father has the creative powers of both a mother and a father. He is not just one of two parents; he is *the* parent.

The patriarchal image of political fathers (here in Locke's words) is that of 'nursing Fathers tender and careful of the publick weale'.[12] The patriarchal story is about the procreative power of a father who is complete in himself. His procreative power both gives and nurtures physical life and creates and maintains political right. Filmer is able

to dismiss Adam's power over Eve so easily because, in the story, women are procreatively and politically irrelevant. The reason Adam has dominion over 'the woman' is, according to Filmer (here following a very ancient notion), that 'the man . . . is the nobler and principal agent in generation'.[13] Women are merely empty vessels for the exercise of the father's sexual and procreative power. The original political right which God gives to Adam is, so to speak, the right to fill the empty vessel.

There is therefore no question to be asked, or error to be corrected, about women's natural freedom. Filmer invokes women merely to highlight the folly of the doctrine of the natural liberty of sons. The contract theorists' argument about natural freedom entails that 'there can be no superior power'. The full absurdity of that conclusion is revealed for Filmer in its corollary that 'women, especially virgins, [would] by birth have as much natural freedom as any other, and therefore ought not to lose their liberty without their own consent.'[14]

Filmer could present the natural freedom of women as the *reductio ad absurdum* of the contract argument because there was no controversy between the patriarchalists and contract theorists about women's subjection. The contract theorists' aim was theoretical parricide, not the overthrow of the sexual right of men and husbands. Both sides agreed, first, that women (wives), unlike sons, were born and remained naturally subject to men (husbands); and, second, that the right of men over women was *not political*. Locke, for example, concurred with Filmer's view that a wife's subjection has a 'Foundation in Nature'. The husband is naturally 'the abler and the stronger', so he must rule over his wife.[15] Rousseau, the vehement critic of the fraudulent liberal social contract that brings into being a corrupt civil society of inequality and domination, is no less insistent that women must be 'subjected either to a man or to the judgements of men and they are never permitted to put themselves above these judgements'. When a woman becomes a wife, she acknowledges her husband as 'a master for the whole of life'.[16]

The contract theorists' 'victory' hinged on the separation of paternal from political power, so they could not, like Filmer, subsume sexual under paternal – that is, political – rule. Instead, the social contract story hides original political right by proclaiming sexual or conjugal right as *natural*. Men's dominion over women is held to follow from the respective natures of the sexes, and Rousseau spells out this claim in detail in Book V of *Emile*. Locke has no quarrel with Filmer about the *legitimacy* of sexual, patriarchal right; rather, he insists that it is not political. Eve's subordination:

> can be no other Subjection than what every Wife owes her Husband, . . . Adam ['s] . . . can only be a Conjugal Power, not Political, the Power that every Husband hath to order the things of private Concernment in his Family, as Proprietor of the Goods and Land there, and to have his Will take place before that of his wife in all things of their common Concernment.[17]

Both sides in the seventeenth-century controversy – unlike contemporary political theorists – were well aware that the new doctrine of natural freedom and equality had subversive implications for *all* relationships of power and subordination. The patriarchalists claimed that the doctrine was so absurd that the problems it raised of justifying, say, the power of a husband over his wife were immediately shown to be figments of the contract theorists' disordered imaginations. But if the contract theorists were content with conjugal patriarchy, the individualist language of their attack on paternal right meant that they had (as Sir Robert Filmer argued) opened the thin ends of numerous revolutionary wedges, including a feminist wedge. Women almost at once seized on the contradiction of an 'individualism' and a 'universalism' which insisted that women were born into subjection and that their subjection was natural and politically irrelevant. By the end of the seventeenth century, for example, Mary Astell was asking: 'If all Men are born Free, how is it that all Women are born Slaves?'[18]

The difficulty for the contract theorists was that given their premises, an answer to the question was impossible. Logically, there is no reason why a free and equal female individual should always (contract to) subordinate herself to another free and equal (male) individual upon marriage. The difficulty, however, was easily overcome. Political theorists, whether liberal or socialist, absorbed masculine right into their theories and 'forgot' the story of the origin of patriarchal power. Natural subjection was seen in terms of paternal power and three centuries of feminist criticism – whether written by women whose names never appear in political theory textbooks, by the cooperative or utopian socialists, or by the otherwise acceptable philosopher, John Stuart Mill – was suppressed and ignored.

The standard view that the rise of social contract theory and the development of civil society was also a defeat for patriarchalism has meant that some vital questions about the construction of the civil body politic have never been asked. One problem about the social contract that has received some attention is the question of exactly who makes the agreement. Many commentators talk uncritically of 'individuals' sealing the pact, but Schochet, for example, points out that in the seventeenth century it was taken for granted that fathers of families entered the social contract.

When I first began to think about these matters from a feminist perspective, I assumed that the social contract was a patriarchal contract because it was made by fathers whose agreement was taken to bind their families. Certainly, 'individuals', in the universal sense in which the category is usually used to mean anyone and everyone, do not make the social contract. Women have no part in it: as natural subjects they lack the requisite capacities and abilities. The 'individuals' of the stories are *men*, but they do not act as fathers. After all, the stories tell of the defeat of the father's political power. Men no longer have a political place as fathers. But fathers are also husbands – Locke's friend Tyrrell wrote that wives were 'concluded by their Husbands'[19] – and, from yet another viewpoint, the participants in the social contract are sons or brothers. The contract is made by brothers, or a *fraternity*. It is no accident that fraternity appears historically hand in hand with liberty and equality, nor that it means exactly what it says: brotherhood.

If 'patriarchy' is all too often interpreted literally, 'fraternity' is usually treated as if its literal meaning had no relevance today and as if the terms in the revolutionary slogan, 'Liberty, Equality, Fraternity', unquestionably applied to us all, not only to men joined by fraternal bonds. Bernard Crick has recently pointed out that fraternity has been relatively little analysed, even though, he says, 'fraternity with liberty is humanity's greatest dream'.[20] When it is mentioned, fraternity is usually presented as an expression of community; it is seen as 'at bottom, a certain type of social cooperation . . . a relation between a group of equals for the utmost mutual help and aid'.[21] Or as Crick argues, addressing his fellow socialists, fraternity is an ethic and social practice that 'goes with simplicity, lack of ostentation, friendliness, helpfulness, kindliness, openness, lack of restraint between individuals in everyday life and a willingness to work together in common tasks.'[22] The general acceptance that 'fraternity' is no more than a way of talking about the bonds of community illustrates how deeply patriarchal conceptions structure our political theory and practice. Feminists have long appreciated the extent to which socialist solidarity and community has meant that women are little more than auxiliaries to the comrades and that women's political demands must wait until after the revolution. But the problems women have in finding a language in which to make their demands is illustrated by the final words of Simone de Beauvoir's *The Second Sex*, where she states that 'men and women [must] unequivocally affirm their brotherhood.'[23]

The fact that the social contract is not an agreement between individuals, fathers or husbands, but a fraternal pact, becomes particularly clear in Freud's versions of the social contract story. Freud's account of the murder of the primal father by his sons is not usually considered in discussions of the social contract. Yet, as Brown states, 'the battle of books re-enacts Freud's primal crime.'[24] And Rieff treats Freud's myth of the parricide as a version of the social contract, to be considered as part of the same tradition as the theories of Hobbes, Locke or Rousseau.[25] The best warrant of all is available for this interpretation. In *Moses and Monotheism* Freud refers to the pact made by the brothers after their dreadful deed as 'a sort of social contract'.[26]

But, it could be objected, Freud's myth is about the origins of society itself. Freud claims – and this is taken at face value by Juliet Mitchell's *Psychoanalysis and Feminism*, which has been very influential among feminists – that the parricide ushers in 'civilization': that is, human society. However, the classic social contract theorists are also sometimes read in the same way; the passage from 'the state of nature' can be seen as the transition from nature or savagery to the first human social order. In neither case is there good reason to accept a universal reading that identifies 'civilization' or 'civil society' with society itself. When the form of the laws instituted by the brothers is examined, it is clear that the stories are about the origin of a culturally and historically specific form of social life. The close connection between 'civil society' and 'civilization' is suggested too by the fact that the term 'civilization' came into general use only

towards the end of the eighteenth century, 'to express a particular stage of European history, sometimes the final or ultimate stage.'[27] 'Civilization' expressed the 'sense of modernity: an achieved condition of refinement and order.'[28]

In her interpretation of Freud, Mitchell claims that the 'law of the father' is established after the parricide. On the contrary: the law of the father, the absolute rule of one father-king, holds sway before his murder. The crucial point about the contract is that it takes place after the death of the father and abolishes his arbitrary right. Instead, the brothers (sons), prompted by remorse for their dreadful deed, by love and hatred and by a desire to prevent parricide in future, establish their *own* law. They establish justice, 'the first "right" or "law" '[29] – or civil society. The law, or arbitrary will, of the father is overthrown by the combined action of the brothers, who then place mutual restrictions on themselves, establishing an equality which, Freud states, 'saved the organization which had made them strong'.[30] A contract between free and equal brothers replaces the 'law of the father' with public rules which bind all equally. As Locke makes clear, the rule of one man (father) is incompatible with civil society, which requires an impartial, impersonal set of rules promulgated by a collective body of men who stand to the law and each other as free equals, as a fraternity.

At this point the objection might be raised that even if brothers enter the contract, they cease to be brothers once the pact is concluded. In the act of contracting they constitute themselves as equal, civil 'individuals' and thus cast off familial and, hence, fraternal ties. The fundamental distinction between the traditional patriarchy of the father and modern patriarchy is precisely that the latter is created in separation from, and opposition to, the familial sphere.

However, it does not follow that all ascriptive ties are therefore abandoned and that the term 'fraternal' ceases to be appropriate. Brown claims that there is an 'inner contradiction' in the trilogy of liberty, equality, fraternity: 'without a father there can be no sons or brothers.'[31] However, as recent accounts of fraternity make clear, the concept covers much more than bonds of kinship. 'Individuals' can be part of a fraternity or a brotherhood – a "community" – even though they are not brothers (sons of a father or kin). The father is dead and the participants in civil society have left kinship behind them, but as civil individuals they still share an ascriptive bond – a bond *as men*.

Freud's story of the parricide is important because he makes explicit what the classic tales of theoretical murder leave obscure: the motive for the brothers' collective act is not merely to claim their natural liberty and right of self-government, but *to gain access to women*. In the classic theorists' state of nature the 'family' already exists and men's conjugal right is deemed a natural right.[32] Freud's primal father, his *patria potestas*, keeps all the women of the horde for himself. The parricide eliminates the father's political right, and also his *exclusive* sexual right. The brothers inherit his patriarchal, masculine right and share the women among themselves. No man can be a primal father ever again, but by setting up rules that give all men equal access to women (compare their equality before the laws of the state) they exercise the 'original' political right of dominion over women that was once the prerogative of the father.

Freud writes of the brothers' 'renunciation of the passionately desired mothers and sisters of the horde.'[33] This is misleading. The fraternity do not renounce the women, but each gives up the desire to put himself in the place of the father. As part of the fraternal social contract the brothers institute what Freud calls the law of exogamy or kinship. In historically specific terms, the brothers create the modern system of marriage law and family and establish the modern order of conjugal or sexual right. The 'natural foundation' of civil society has been brought into being through the fraternal social contract.

The separation of 'paternal' from political rule, or the family from the public sphere, is also the separation of women from men through the subjection of women to men. The brothers establish their own law and their own form of sexual or conjugal dominion. The fraternal social contract creates a new, modern patriarchal order that is presented as divided into two spheres: civil society or the universal sphere of freedom, equality, individualism, reason, contract and impartial law – the realm of men or 'individuals'; and the private world of particularity, natural subjection, ties of blood, emotion, love and sexual passion – the world of women, in which men also rule.

In short, the contract constitutes patriarchal civil society and the modern, ascriptive rule of men over women. Ascription and contract are usually seen as standing at opposite poles, but the social contract is sexually ascriptive in both form (it is made by brothers) and content (the patriarchal right of a fraternity is established). Civil individuals have a fraternal bond because, *as men*, they share a common interest in upholding the contract which legitimizes their masculine patriarchal right and allows them to gain material and psychological benefit from women's subjection.

One important question raised by the contract stories is exactly how the 'foundation in nature', which upholds the subjection of women, should be characterized. Locke tells us that the strength and ability of the man (husband) is the natural basis of the wife's subordination: a view which becomes absorbed into patriarchal liberalism, but also opens the way for liberal feminism. Feminists began to criticize the argument from strength long ago,[34] and although the claim is still heard today, historically it has become less and less plausible to rely on strength as the criterion for masculine political right. Contemporary liberal feminists, following the lead of much earlier writers like Mary Astell and Mary Wollstonecraft, have attacked the alleged lesser ability and capacity of women as an artifact of defective education, as a matter of deliberate social contrivance, not a fact of nature.

The difficulty for the liberal feminist argument is that education cannot be equal while men and women remain differentially positioned within their 'separate spheres', but the patriarchal division between the private family and public, civil society is a central structural principle of liberalism. Moreover, the problem runs deeper than a liberal perspective suggests. Liberal feminism assumes that the relevant political problem is to show that women possess the capacities men possess and can do what men can do. However, this also assumes that there is no political significance to the fact that women have one natural ability which men lack: women, but not men, are able to give birth.

Now, it may be claimed that this provides no 'foundation in nature' for women's subjection because birth (unlike child-rearing) is ultimately irrelevant to the development of the capacities of civil beings. The difficulty with this argument is that it, too, ignores the story of the 'origin' of patriarchal political right, and thus the importance of birth for patriarchal civil society. The ability to give birth, both actually and metaphorically, is central to patriarchal theory.

Filmer's argument shows that Adam's right of domination over Eve is the right to become a father: a right to demand sexual access to Eve's body and to insist that she give birth. Eve's procreative, creative capacity is then denied and appropriated by *men* as the ability to give *political birth*, to be the 'originators' of a new form of political order. Adam and the participants in the fraternal social contract gain an amazing patriarchal ability and become the 'principal agents' in political generation. Moreover, in patriarchal argument birth also symbolizes and encapsulates all the reasons why it has been claimed that women must be bodily removed from civil society.[35]

Some of the murky depths become clearer in the stories told by Rousseau and Freud. Women, they insist, are unable to transcend their bodily natures in the manner required of 'individuals' who are to participate in civil life and uphold the universal laws of civil society. The female body, subject to uncontrollable natural processes and passions, deprives women of the reason and moral character which can be educated for civil society.[36]

Rousseau's solution is that the sexes must be segregated to the greatest possible extent, even in domestic life. Significantly, in *Emile* Rousseau allows the tutor to give only one direct command, in which he sends Emile away from Sophie for an extended period to learn about politics and citizenship before he is permitted to claim her body as a husband. Freud offers no solution but states explicitly that from the 'beginning' – from the original parricide in which women are at stake, and which is endlessly reproduced through the Oedipus complex – women continue to have 'a hostile attitude towards' civil society.[37] Or, as Mitchell interprets Freud, a woman 'cannot receive the "touch" of the law, her submission to it must be in establishing herself as its opposite.'[38]

Women are 'opposite' to and outside the fraternal social contract and its civil law in two senses. First, they are 'originally', necessarily, excluded from an agreement through which the brothers inherit their legacy of patriarchal sex right and legitimize their claim over women's bodies and ability to give birth. Second, the civil law encapsulates all that women lack. The civil law stems from a reasoned agreement that it is to the rational mutual advantage of the participants to the contract to constrain their interactions and desires through a law equally applicable to all. Women's passions render them incapable of making such a reasoned agreement or of upholding it if made. In other words, the patriarchal claim that there is a 'foundation in nature' for women's subjection to

men is a claim that women's bodies must be governed by men's reason. The separation of civil society from the familial sphere is also a division between men's reason and women's bodies.

Feminist scholars are now showing how, from ancient times, political life has been conceptualized in opposition to the mundane world of necessity, the body, the sexual passions and birth: in short, in opposition to women and the disorders and creativity they symbolize.[39] In Filmer's classic patriarchalism the father is both mother and father and creates political right through his fatherhood, but Filmer's account is only one version of a long Western tradition in which the creation of political life has been seen as a masculine act of birth: as a male replica of the ability which only women possess.

The fraternal social contract is a specifically modern reformulation of this patriarchal tradition. The father is dead, but the brothers appropriate the ability specific to women; they, too, can generate new political life and political right. The social contract is the point of origin, or birth, of civil society, and simultaneously its separation from the (private) sphere of real birth and the disorder of women. The brothers give birth to an artificial body, the body politic of civil society; they create Hobbes's 'Artificial Man, we call a Commonwealth,' or Rousseau's 'artificial and collective body', or the 'one Body' of Locke's 'Body Politick'.

The 'birth' of the civil body politic, however, is an act of reason; there is no analogue to a bodily act of procreation. The social contract, as we are all taught, is not an actual event. The natural paternal body of Filmer's patriarchy is metaphorically put to death by the contract theorists, but the 'artificial' body that replaces it is a construct of the mind, not the creation of a political community by real people. Whereas the birth of a human child can produce a new male or female, the creation of civil society produces a social body fashioned after the image of only one of the two bodies of humankind. Or, more exactly, the civil body politic is fashioned after the image of the male 'individual' who is constituted through the separation of civil society from women. This individual has some singular – and largely unrecognized – aspects precisely because his defining characteristics are thrown into relief only through the contrast with the womanly nature that has been excluded from civil society.

The abstract character of the individual in liberal contract theory has been criticized from the left ever since Rousseau's initial attack. But because the critiques invariably pass silently over the separation of male reason from female body in the original creation of the civil individual, one of his most notable features has also silently been incorporated by the critics. The 'individual' is disembodied. For three centuries the figure of the individual has been presented as universal, as the embodiment of all, but it is only because he is disembodied that the 'individual' can appear universal. Like the new body politic he, too, is 'artificial': he is nothing more than a 'man of reason'.[40]

In the most recent rewriting of the liberal contract story, *A Theory of Justice*, Rawls claims that his parties in their original position know none of the essential facts about themselves. Thus it might seem that Rawls's parties are truly universal and that the original choices include a choice between the two bodies (sexes) of humankind. The fact that Rawls ignores this possibility, and writes that the parties can be seen as heads of families,[41] shows how deeply entrenched are patriarchal assumptions about the proper characteristics of the 'individual'. Moreover, the attributes of the parties and their original position illustrate the fact that Rawls stands at the logical conclusion of the fraternal contract tradition. The original position and its choices are explicitly hypothetical (logical) and the parties are nothing more than disembodied entities of reason; otherwise they could not help but know the natural facts about themselves, inseparable from their bodies, such as the facts of sex, age and colour.[42]

Ironically, the disembodiment necessary to maintain the political fiction of the universal civil individual poses profound problems for fraternity. For individualist liberals the problems are part of their wider difficulties over the self, and involve an opposition within the individual between fraternity and reason. The opposition between reason and fraternity is an opposition between the public and the private. But this is not the patriarchal opposition between 'private' and 'public', between family (women) and civil society (men); instead, the relevant division between public and private is the other opposition to which I referred earlier: the opposition located within 'civil society' as I am using the term.[43] For liberals relying on a social view of the self or for socialist critics of liberalism the problems arise because in the 1980s an emphasis on fraternity begins to reveal the patriarchal character of their theories. To preserve universality, '*the* individual' must be abstracted even from

his masculinity and fraternity, so that the individual has no body and, hence, no sex.

The creation of the 'individual' presupposes the division of rational civil order from the disorder of womanly nature. It might thus seem that the civil individual and the body politic made in his image would be unified. Indeed, they are so presented in liberal theory, but its critics from Rousseau onward argue that the individual and civil society are inherently divided, one from the other and within themselves. The individual is torn between *bourgeois* and *citoyen*, or between *Homo economicus* and *Homo civicus*, and civil society is divided between private interest and the public universal interest, or between 'civil' society and state. The point about such critiques, however, is exactly that they are concerned with extrafamilial social life and with the individual as an inhabitant of the public world.

The liberal opposition between private and public (like the patriarchal opposition between the sexes) appears in a variety of guises: for example, society, economy and freedom stand against state, public and coercion. Liberals see these dualities as posing important problems of freedom, since the private sphere of civil society must be protected from the coercive intrusions of the state, and they now spend a good deal of time and effort trying to sort out where the dividing line plausibly can be drawn. Their critics, on the other hand, argue that the opposition between private and public poses an insoluble problem; that it is an unbridgeable structural fissure at the centre of liberalism. I agree with the critics; but the criticism does not go far enough because it takes no account of the 'original' patriarchal division and thus leaves the critics' own conception of the 'individual' and 'civil society' untouched.

In *Knowledge and Politics*, Robert Unger presents a comprehensive discussion and critique of the liberal dichotomies, but even his analysis of the division between fact and theory, values and rules, desire and reason, ignores the fact that it also represents the opposition between the sexes. The 'self' is implicitly taken to be masculine. The reference to 'men' must be taken literally when he writes: 'The dichotomy of the public and private life is still another corollary of the separation of understanding and desire... When reasoning [men] belong to a public world.... When desiring, however, men are private beings.'[44] In Unger's account, the 'desire' and associated disorder represented by women and their private world has been 'forgotten'. The 'self' has become that of the male individual in civil society, an individual torn between the claims of public interest ('reason') and private or subjective interest ('desire'). The opposition between women, bodies, passion, and men, reason, rational advantage, is repressed and replaced by the dichotomy between the individual's private interest and the claims of the public interest or universal law.

In this form, the dichotomy is also expressed as an opposition between the fraternity and reason of civil individuals. The only ties between the individuals of liberal contract theory are those of self-interest. The individual is, as it were, a collection of pieces of property that can, through rational calculation of the mind, be made the subject of contract. The individual thus enters into only certain kinds of relationship and this limitation gives rise to another familiar difficulty within liberal theory: that of presenting a coherent conception of citizenship or the political. The liberal individual's political bonds with other citizens are merely another expression of the pursuit of self-interest; *Homo civicus* is absorbed into, or is nothing more than one face of, the 'private' *Homo economicus*. However, this view of the individual as citizen – as public or civil individual – systematically undermines one of the most significant expressions of fraternity.

Liberal individuals interact in a benign public world. They compete one with the other, but the competition is regulated and the rules are fair; the only coercion required is to enforce the rules. Hence the division between private and public as an opposition between society and state is often presented as between freedom and coercion. Currently this position is associated with the New Right, but in the past *le doux commerce* could be offered as the antithesis of violence and the idealist liberals, claiming to have reconciled the oppositions, could assert that will, not force, is the basis of the state.

On the other hand, it is also clear that the individual can be required to protect his protection (as Hobbes put it) by something more than mere obedience to the law. He may have to surrender his body in defence of the state. Indeed, this has always been seen as the ultimate act of loyalty and allegiance, the truly exemplary act of citizenship. However, it is also an act which will never be to the rational advantage of a liberal individual, as Hobbes's logical working out of radical individualism reveals. In the clash between private and

public interest, the private claim always has the rational advantage. It is not in the individual's self-interest to be a soldier; thus reason is torn apart from the fraternity on which citizenship, in the last analysis, depends. Of all the male clubs and associations, it is in the military and on the battlefield that fraternity finds its most complete expression.

The opposition between the figure of the soldier and the figure of the individual, or between fraternity and reason, is unique to liberal civil society. In many respects the fraternal contract story transforms ancient patriarchal themes into a specifically modern theory, but the conception of a liberal individual breaks with older traditions in which citizenship has involved a distinctive form of activity and has also been closely tied to the bearing of arms. Feminist scholars are now showing that from ancient times there has been an integral connection between the warrior and conceptions of self-identity, sexuality and masculinity, which have all been bound up with citizenship. The peculiarity of the liberal individual is that although he is male he is also defined – unlike either his predecessors in the traditional world or the 'individuals' that appear in social-liberal and socialist theory – in opposition to the political and the masculine passions that underlie the defence of the state by arms.

Although our consciousness is informed by the liberal individual's image, and many of our social practices and institutions presuppose that we are motivated by self-interest (the contemporary preoccupation with freeriders is no accident), the state has never relied on rational self-interest as the basis for socio-political order. Nor did most classic theorists, except Hobbes, have the courage of their theoretical convictions on this point. Hobbes's conclusion that Leviathan's sword was the only alternative to an inherently insecure 'artificial' ground for order was rejected in favour of such devices as natural law, sympathy, benevolence or hidden hands – and socialists have appealed to solidarity, comradeship and community or, in a word, to *fraternity*. Historically, obedience and loyalty to the state have been fostered by appeals not to individual rational advantage but to ascriptive, psychological bonds, especially to nationalism, patriotism and fraternity. These are ties of a much more full-blooded character than, for example, Rawls's sense of justice and, most importantly, they appeal directly to the masculine self's sense of identity. However, the real and ideological basis for the motivating force of self-interest means that it is hard to eliminate the opposition between fraternity and reason.

When some liberals over the past century attempted to develop an adequately social and developmental conception of individuality, one that restored the affective ties of community that had been stripped away in liberal contract theory, they also turned to the idea of fraternity. In the eyes of these liberals, Gaus states, fraternity is the 'most powerful of communal bonds'.[45] The ideal of fraternity provides the 'pre-eminent conception of communal bonds in modern liberal theory', so that Dewey, for example, wrote of a 'fraternally associated public', and Rawls sees his difference principle as a 'natural meaning of fraternity'.[46]

The explicit use of 'fraternity' in both social-liberal and socialist attempts to reintegrate the civil individual and the community (or to reintegrate the liberal division between private and public) means that the patriarchal character of civil society begins to come to the surface. Moreover, the masculine attributes of the individual begin to be exposed. The universalism of the category of the 'individual' can be maintained only as long as the abstraction from the body is maintained. 'The individual' is a fiction: individuals have one of two bodies, masculine or feminine. But how can the feminine body become part of a (liberal or socialist) fraternal body politic?

Citizenship has now been extended formally to women, raising the substantive problem of how we can become civil 'individuals' made in the masculine image. The importance, in practice, of the intimate connection between masculinity, citizenship and bearing arms became explicit when women, taking the universalism of the principles of civil society at face value, demanded to be enfranchised. The 'jewel' in the armoury of the anti-suffragists was the argument from physical force.[47] Women, it was claimed, were naturally unable and unwilling to bear arms or use violence, so that if they became citizens, the state would inevitably be fatally weakened.

Now that women are enfranchised (and are even prime ministers) the same patriarchal view of citizenship is still found. In the British House of Commons in 1981, in a debate on the Nationality Bill, Enoch Powell argued that a woman should not pass on her citizenship to her child because 'nationality, in the last resort, is tested by fighting. A man's nation is the nation for which he will fight.' The difference between men and women, which must be expressed in citizen-

ship, is that between 'fighting on the one hand and the creation and preservation of life on the other'.[48] It is true that women are now included as members of the armed forces but they are still excluded from combat units, which exemplify fraternities in action.[49]

'Men are born free': the rejection of (masculine) natural subjection generated the revolutionary claim that will, not force, is the basis of the state. One of the major successes of the fraternal contract story is the way it has helped to obscure coercion and violence in civil society and the manner in which 'will' is determined within relations of domination and subjection. Critics of contract theory have said a good deal about the inequality of parties to contracts and exploitation, but less about the consequences of contract and subordination. Only rarely have they discussed how contract gives the appearance of freedom to sexually ascriptive domination and subjection. Contract also hides the figure of the armed man in the shadows behind the civil individual. Foucault has counterposed a 'military dream' of a society against the original contract (what is presented as the original pact in the familiar stories), but the two are not so far apart as they may seem.

Foucault writes that the military dream looked, 'not to the state of nature, but to the meticulously subordinated cogs of a machine, not to the primal social contract, but to permanent coercions, not to fundamental rights, but to indefinitely progressive forms of training, not to the general will but to automatic docility.'[50] Automatic docility and the disciplines of the body portrayed by Foucault are part of the consequences of the fraternal social contract. Foucault states that 'the development and generalization of disciplinary mechanisms constituted the other, dark side' of the development of a 'formally egalitarian juridical framework'. However, it is less that the disciplines 'distort the contractual link systematically'[51] than that discipline in civil society, *which is also patriarchal discipline*, is typically established through contract. The forms of subjection specific to civil society are, as Foucault emphasizes, developed by the complicity of subordinates as well as by force – complicity made all the easier (as, importantly, is resistance) when consciousness is informed by patriarchal forms of liberty and equality. For example, when 'individuals' have a free choice of marriage partner, publicly recognized by a free contract, it is made harder to acknowledge that the marriage contract is a political fiction which ceremonially recognizes the patriarchal subjection of a wife and the masculine privileges of a husband.[52]

The modern discipline of the body is aided by political theory that has already separated reason from the body and the reason of men from the bodies of women. Foucault ignores the significant fact that the 'military dream' is a dream of men, whereas the fraternal social contract is also a dream of women. But the women's dream cannot be fulfilled, although the ostensibly universal categories of the contract make it always enticing. The history of liberal feminism is the history of attempts to generalize liberal liberties and rights to the whole adult population; but liberal feminism does not, and cannot, come to grips with the deeper problems of *how* women are to take an equal place in the patriarchal civil order.

Now that the feminist struggle has reached the point where women are almost formal civil equals, the opposition is highlighted between equality made after a male image and the real social position of women *as women*. Women have never, of course, been excluded entirely from civil life – the two spheres of the modern civil order are not separate in reality – but our inclusion has been singular. In a world presented as conventional, contractual and universal, women's civil position is ascriptive, defined by the natural particularity of being women; patriarchal subordination is socially and legally upheld throughout civil life, in production and citizenship as well as in the family. Thus to explore the subjection of women is also to explore the fraternity of men. Recent feminist research has begun to uncover – despite the important divisions between men of different classes and races (and associations and clubs where fraternity is given explicit expression are usually so divided) – how men, *as men*, maintain the power and privileges of their patriarchal right throughout the whole of socio-political life.

The fraternal social contract story shows that the categories and practices of civil society cannot simply be universalized to women. The social contract is a modern patriarchal pact that establishes men's sex right over women, and the civil individual has been constructed in opposition to women and all that our bodies symbolize, so how can we become full members of civil society or parties to the fraternal contract?

The contradictory answer is that women in civil society must disavow our bodies and act as part of the brotherhood – but since we are never regarded as other than women, we must simultaneously continue to affirm the patriarchal conception of femininity, or patriarchal subjection.[53] The peculiar relation between civil society and women and our bodies is illustrated by the fact that few legal jurisdictions have abolished the right of a husband to use his wife's body against her will, that coercive sexual relations ('sexual harassment') are part of everyday working life; that women's bodies are sold in the capitalist market,[54] that women, until 1934 in the USA and 1948 in Britain, lost their citizenship if they married foreigners; that only in 1983 did all British women citizens win the right to pass on their citizenship to their husbands and so enable them to live in Britain,[55] and that welfare policies still do not fully recognize women's status as individuals.

The theoretical and social transformation required if women and men are to be full members of a free, properly democratic (or properly 'civilized') society is as far-reaching as can be imagined. The meaning of 'civil society' (in both senses discussed here) has been constructed through the exclusion of women and all that we symbolize. To 'rediscover' a patriarchal conception of civil society will do little to challenge men's patriarchal right. To create a properly democratic society, which includes women as full citizens, it is necessary to deconstruct and reassemble our understanding of the body politic. This task extends from the dismantling of the patriarchal separation of private and public, to a transformation of our individuality and sexual identities as feminine and masculine beings. These identities now stand opposed, part of the multi-faceted expression of the patriarchal dichotomy between reason and desire. The most profound and complex problem for political theory and practice is how the two bodies of humankind and feminine and masculine individuality can be fully incorporated into political life. How can the present of patriarchal domination, opposition and duality be transformed into a future of autonomous, democratic differentiation?

The traditional patriarchy of the fathers was long ago transformed into the fraternal, modern patriarchy of civil society. Perhaps there is hope, since these observations could be written only under the shadow of the owl of Minerva's wings. Alternatively, perhaps the time for optimism is past; feminism may have re-emerged at a point in the crisis of patriarchy in which the figure of the armed man – now armed not with the sword but with plastic bullets, cluster bombs, chemical, biological and nuclear weapons – has totally obliterated the figure of the civil individual.

Perhaps, as Mary O'Brien suggests, 'the brotherhood have gone quite mad and lost control of their creations in some cosmic sorcerers' apprenticeship.'[56]

Notes

1 A more extensive and detailed feminist reading of the contract stories and of their significance for the marriage contract and other contracts, such as that between prostitute and client, is presented in my book, *The Sexual Contract* (Polity Press, Cambridge, 1988: Stanford University Press, Stanford, 1988).

2 Z. Eisenstein, *The Radical Future of Liberal Feminism* (Longman, New York, 1981), chap. 3, but Eisenstein develops her argument in a different direction from my own; J. Elshtain, *Public Man, Private Woman: Women in Social and Political Thought* (Princeton University Press, Princeton, 1981), chap. 3. More recently, see L. Nicholson, *Gender and History: The Limits of Social Theory in the Age of the Family* (Columbia University Press, New York, 1986).

3 G. Schochet, *Patriarchalism in Political Thought: The Authoritarian Family and Political Speculation and Attitudes Especially in Seventeenth Century England* (Basil Blackwell, Oxford, 1975).

4 This brief summary highlights the essential points of conflict between the protagonists, and thus glosses over the differences among theorists on both sides. Hobbes, for instance, saw paternal and political rule as homologous, but rejected patriarchal claims about paternity.

5 Sir R. Filmer, *Patriarchia and Other Political Works*, ed. P. Laslett (Basil Blackwell, Oxford, 1949), p. 54.

6 Ibid., p. 71.

7 Ibid., p. 188.

8 Ibid., pp. 71, 57, 194.

9 Ibid., p. 96.

10 Laslett, 'Introduction', *Patriarchia*, p. 28. Filmer writes (p. 256): 'where there are only Father and sons, no sons can question the Father for the death of their brother.'

11 Filmer, *Patriarchia*, pp. 241, 283.

12 J. Locke, *Two Treatises of Government*, ed. P. Laslett, 2nd edn (Cambridge University Press, Cambridge, 1967), II, §110.

13 Filmer, *Patriarchia*, p. 245.

14 Ibid., p. 287.

15 Locke, *Two Treatises*, I, §47; II, §82.

16 J.-J. Rousseau, *Emile, or On Education*, tr. A. Bloom (Basic Books, New York, 1979), pp. 370, 404.

17 Locke, *Two Treatises*, I, §48.

18 M. Astell, *Some Reflections Upon Marriage* (Source Book Press, New York, 1970), p. 107 (from the 1730 ed., first published 1700). On analogies drawn between the marriage contract and social contract and powers of husbands and kings, see M. Shanley, 'Marriage Contract and Social Contract in Seventeenth Century English Political Thought', *Western Political Quarterly*, 32(1), 1979, pp. 79–91.

19 Cited by Schochet, *Patriarchalism in Political Thought*, p. 202. I have discussed liberty, equality and the social contract in *The Problem of Political Obligation*, 2nd edn (Polity Press, Cambridge, 1985; University of California Press, Berkeley, CA, 1985).

20 B. Crick, *In Defence of Politics*, 2nd edn (Penguin Books, Harmondsworth, Middlesex, 1982), p. 228.

21 E. Hobsbawm, 'The Idea of Fraternity', *New Society*, November 1975, cited in M. Taylor, *Community, Anarchy and Liberty* (Cambridge University Press, Cambridge, 1982) p. 31.

22 Crick, *In Defence of Politics*, p. 233. Crick (p. 230) suggests that 'sisterhood' is 'in some ways truly a less ambiguous image of what I am trying to convey by "fraternity".' Although he notes the relation between fraternity, the 'aggressive brothers' band' and 'stereotypes' of manliness, he argues that it is better to 'try to desex, even to feminize, old "fraternity", rather than to pause to rewrite most languages'; which exactly misses the point that language expresses and forms part of the patriarchal structure of our society ('language is a form of life').

23 S. de Beauvoir, *The Second Sex*, tr. H. M. Parshley (Penguin Books, New York, 1953), p. 732. But of course we must remember that de Beauvoir was writing without the support of the organized feminist movement. Today, feminists have devoted a good deal of attention to language – and have provided some fascinating accounts of how, in practice, fraternity has shaped the working class and the labour movement, so that the 'worker' is a man and a member of the 'men's movement'; see especially C. Cockburn, *Brothers: Male Dominance and Technological Change* (Pluto Press, London, 1983), also B. Campbell, *The Road to Wigan Pier Revisited: Poverty and Politics in the 80s* (Virago Books, London, 1984). (The term 'men's movement' is Beatrix Campbell's.)

24 N. O. Brown, *Love's Body* (Vintage Books, New York, 1966), p. 4. I am grateful to Peter Breiner for drawing my attention to Brown's interpretation in *Love's Body*. A similar point is made, though its implications for patriarchy are not pursued, by M. Hulliung, 'Patriarchalism and Its Early Enemies', *Political Theory*, 2(1974), pp. 410–19. Hulliung (p. 416) notes that there is no reason why

the parricide 'cannot just as well be turned into a morality play on behalf of... democratic ideals' and that 'the assassins are "brothers" towards each other, and brothers are equal.'

25 P. Rieff, *Freud: The Mind of the Moralist* (Methuen, London, n.d.), chap. VII.

26 S. Freud, *Moses and Monotheism*, tr. K. Jones (Vintage Books, New York, 1939), p. 104.

27 S. Rothblatt, *Tradition and Change in English Liberal Education* (Faber & Faber, London, 1976), p. 18.

28 R. Williams, *Keywords: A Vocabulary of Culture and Society*, revised edn (Oxford University Press, New York, 1985), p. 58. I am grateful to Ross Poole for drawing my attention to the emergence of 'civilization'.

29 S. Freud, *Civilization and its Discontents* (W. W. Norton & Co., New York, n.d.), p. 53.

30 S. Freud, *Totem and Taboo*, tr. A. Brill (Vintage Books, New York, n.d.), p. 186.

31 Brown, *Love's Body*, p. 5.

32 Again, Hobbes is an exception. There are no families in his radically individualist state of nature; women are as strong as men. However, he merely assumes that in civil society women will always enter a marriage contract that places them in subjection to their husbands.

33 S. Freud, *Moses and Monotheism*, p. 153.

34 For example, Mary Astell sarcastically remarks (*Reflections Upon Marriage*, p. 86) that if 'Strength of Mind goes along with Strength of Body, [then] 'tis only for some odd Accidents which Philosophers have not yet thought worthwhile to enquire into, that the Sturdiest Porter is not the wisest Man!' Or consider William Thompson, *Appeal of One Half of the Human Race, Women, Against the Pretensions of the Other Half, Men, to Retain them in Political, and Thence in Civil and Domestic, Slavery* (Source Book Press, New York, 1970; originally published 1825), p. 120: 'If strength be the superior title to happiness, let the knowledge and skill of man be employed in adding to the pleasurable sensations of horses, elephants, and all stronger animals. If strength be the title to happiness, let all such qualifications for voters as the capacity to read and write, or any *indirect* means to insure intellectual aptitude be abolished; and let the simple test for the exercise of political rights, both by men and women, be the capacity of carrying 300lbs weight.'

35 This helps to explain why we do not have 'a philosophy of birth'; see M. O'Brien, *The Politics of Reproduction* (Routledge & Kegan Paul, London, 1981), especially chap. 1.

36 In another chapter I began to explore one aspect of this perception of women and its corollary, that we pose a permanent threat to civil life; see Carole Pateman, *The Disorder of Women* (Oxford, Polity, 1980), chapter 1.

37 S. Freud, *Civilization and Its Discontents*, p. 56.

38 J. Mitchell, *Psychoanalysis and Feminism* (Penguin Books, Harmondsworth, Middlesex, 1975), p. 405.

39 See for example N. Hartsock, *Money, Sex and Power: Towards a Feminist Historical Materialism* (Northeastern University Press, Boston, MA, 1983), chap. 8; O'Brien, *The Politics of Reproduction*, chaps. 3, 4; Elshtain, *Public Man, Private Woman*, chap. 1; H. Pitkin, *Fortune Is A Woman: Gender and Politics in the Thoughts of Niccolo Machiavelli* (University of California Press, Berkeley, CA, 1984).

40 For his history, see G. Lloyd, *The Man of Reason; 'Male' and 'Female' in Western Philosophy* (Methuen, London, 1984). On the Cartesian 'drama of parturition', see S. Bordo. 'The Cartesian Masculinization of Thought', *Signs*, 11(3), (1986), pp. 439–56.

41 J. Rawls, *A Theory of Justice* (Harvard University Press, Cambridge, MA, 1971), p. 128.

42 It will probably be objected that one can look younger or older than one's real age, or be convinced that one is in the 'wrong' body, or 'pass' as white. However, these examples all depend on the knowledge of age, sexual and colour differences and the specific meaning given to them in different cultures. One cannot, say, be a transsexual without already being fully aware of what 'masculine' and 'feminine' involve and how these are integrally connected to bodies. That Rawls's arguments, despite his apparently sexually undifferentiated 'parties', presuppose a sexually differentiated morality is shown in D. Kearns, '*A Theory of Justice* and Love: Rawls on the Family', *Politics*, 18(2), (1983), pp. 36–42.

43 This division between private and public is constituted in the second stage of the familiar story of the social contract (Locke's theory shows this clearly); see my books, *The Problem of Political Obligation*, chap. 4 and *The Disorder of Women*, chap. 6.

44 R.M. Unger, *Knowledge and Politics* (Free Press, New York, 1976), p. 45. Unger has little to say about women or the family, but his comments (like those on the division of labour) illustrate that his critique is not the 'total critique' at which he aims. He notes, for example, that the family 'draws men back into an association that competes with loyalties to all other groups' (p. 264) – but it 'draws back' only those who go into civil society.

45 G.F. Gaus, *The Modern Liberal Theory of Man* (Croom Helm, London, 1983), p. 90.

46 Gaus, *Modern Liberal Theory*, p. 94; he cites Dewey and Rawls on pp. 91 and 94.

47 The description comes from B. Harrison, *Separate Spheres: The Opposition to Women's Suffrage in Britain* (Holmes & Meier, New York, 1978), chap. 4. Women were once an essential part of armies, but by the First World War 'the once integral place of women in Western armies had faded from memory' (like so much else about women!); see B.C. Hacker, 'Women and Military Institutions in Early Modern

Europe: A Reconnaissance', *Signs*, 6(4), (1981), pp. 643–71 (the quotation is from p. 671).

48 Cited in *Rights*, 4(5), (1981), p. 4.

49 On women, the military and combat, see J. Stiehm, 'The Protected, The Protector, The Defender', *Women's Studies International Forum*, 5(1982), pp. 367–76; and 'Reflections on Women and Combat', Postscript to *Bring Me Men and Women: Mandated Change at the US Air Force Academy* (University of California Press, Berkeley, CA, 1981).

50 M. Foucault, *Discipline and Punish: The Birth of the Prison*, tr. A. Sheridan (Vintage Books, New York, 1979), p. 169.

51 Foucault, *Discipline and Punish*, pp. 222–3.

52 See C. Pateman, 'The Shame of the Marriage Contract', in J. Stiehm, ed., *Women's View of the Political World of Men* (Transnational Publishers, Dobbs Ferry, NY, 1984).

53 Mrs Thatcher provides a fascinating illustration. On the one hand she is 'the best man in the Cabinet', the victor of the Falklands War, accomplice of Reagan's state terrorism against Libya, and is photographed with weapons. On the other hand she talks to the press about 'feminine' matters (such as having her hair tinted), draws headlines like 'Four Years on and looking Ten Years Younger', and uses the language of good house-keeping to talk about cuts in social welfare spending (see A. Carter, 'Masochism for the Masses', *New Statesman*, 3 June 1983, pp. 8–10).

54 For a critique of a contractarian defence of prostitution, see my 'Defending Prostitution: Charges Against Ericsson', *Ethics*, 93 (1983), pp. 561–5, and *The Sexual Contract*, chap. 7.

55 The right is still hedged with immigration restrictions that make it hard for black British women to exercise it; for an account of the interaction of sex and race in British law, see Women, Immigration and Nationality Group, *Worlds Apart: Women Under Immigration and Nationality Law* (Pluto Press, London, 1985). For the USA, see V. Sapiro, 'Women, Citizenship and Nationality: Immigration and Naturalization Policies in the United States', *Politics and Society*, 13(1) (1984), pp. 1–26.

56 O'Brien, *The Politics of Reproduction*, p. 205.

5

Invoking Civil Society

Charles Taylor

In recent years the notion of civil society has come back into circulation. The intention is to invoke something like the concept that developed at the turn of the nineteenth century, which stands in contrast to "the state." But in fact those who introduced it were trying to articulate features of the development of western civilization which go back much further.

One of the first fields of application of the revived term was to the polities of Eastern Europe. "Civil society" defined what they had been deprived of and were struggling to recreate: a web of autonomous associations, independent of the state, which bound citizens together in matters of common concern, and by their mere existence or action could have an effect on public policy. In this sense, western liberal democracies were thought to have functioning civil societies.

"Civil society" in this sense refers to what the Leninist model of rule had essentially negated. That model arose first in the Soviet Union, then was reproduced in other "Marxist–Leninist" regimes, finally was imitated more or less completely, and sometimes caricaturally, by a number of newly independent third-world countries. The essential virtue of the model for its protagonists was that it offered a kind of total mobilization of society toward what were seen as revolutionary goals. The central instrument was a vanguard party dominated by a revolutionary elite. And a crucial feature of this

system was the satellitization of all aspects of social life to this party. Trade unions, leisure clubs, even churches, all had to be permeated and made into "transmission belts" of the party's purposes. Leninism in its heyday was one of the principal sources of modern totalitarianism.

This system has been in decay for a number of decades – since the death of Stalin in its original homeland, and somewhat later in countries that followed the Russian example with an indigenous revolutionary elite, such as China and Cuba. In fact there was a long period of retreat, where the drive to total mobilization flagged more and more visibly, but without any of the fundamental principles of the system being renounced. Future generations will probably describe this period of slow inner decay as the Age of Brezhnev. With Gorbachev, we entered a new phase, in which some of the tenets of total mobilization were themselves challenged. Unanimity was no longer an unambiguously good thing. They began to have real, if restricted, elections in Moscow. But under Brezhnev the goal was to keep the facade of unanimity unbroken. In principle no dissident opinions should be expressed, everyone should turn out for Leninist holidays, people should pass spontaneous resolutions on critical occasions denouncing US imperialism; at the same time, the demands of the regime on private life were lessening. Governments like Czechoslovakia's even encouraged a

Originally published in *Philosophical Arguments* (Cambridge, MA: Harvard University Press, 1995), pp. 204–24, 303. Copyright © 1995 by Charles Taylor. Originally a working paper for Center for Psychological Studies, Chicago, 1990. Reprinted with permission of Harvard University Press and also the author.

kind of privatization of life. Let everyone cultivate their gardens, provided they turned out for May Day parades and otherwise kept their mouths shut. It was a Leninism of fatigue.

In these circumstances, as the furious terror of Stalinism receded, the pressure rose in certain East European societies for reform. A total change of regime seemed, for obvious geopolitical reasons, utopian. The goal was rather to undo Leninism partially from below, to open a margin of free association out of party control but enjoying legal recognition. It is understandable that an aspiration of this kind should find expression in a distinction between civil society and the state. For on this model, the state – understood in flatly Weberian terms as the agency with the monopoly of physical force – would have an entirely different basis than society would. Its ultimate foundation would be external, in the threat of Soviet intervention, whereas the different components of the newly freed "civil society" would express indigenous social forces.

But in using this term, thinkers in both East and West wanted to express something more than the mutual independence of state and society. They wanted also to invoke something of the history and practice of the western democracies as a model. The notion was, first, that in the West there already is a civil society and, second, that this contemporary reality is heir to a centuries-long development of the distinction between society and state. There is truth in both claims, but to get at it we have to modulate the meaning of "civil society". This turns out to be a more complex and many-faceted idea than one might have thought at first. The nuances are worth exploring because they color the models of the political process we want to steer our lives by in coming decades.

To take the first claim: civil society already exists in the West. Yes, there is in western societies a web of autonomous associations, independent of the state, and these have an effect on public policy. But there has also been a tendency for these to become integrated into the state, the tendency toward what has been called (often in a slightly sneering tone, because of the origins of the term in fascist Italy) "corporatism." States like Sweden, Holland, and Germany, but also many others, have gone some way to integrating trade unions, employers' associations, and the like into government planning. To speak of integration "into the state" may be tendentious here; some people see it as a loss of government independence to special inter-

ests. But in fact what occurs is an interweaving of society and government to the point where the distinction no longer expresses an important difference in the basis of power or the dynamics of policymaking. Both government and associations draw on and are responsive to the same public. For instance, issues of national income policy, debated between management and labor unions in tripartite negotiations with the government as third party, can also be debated in parliament, where the same social forces are represented in the form of the social-democratic and conservative parties. In fact, these two loci of negotiation and debate are generally complementary; the issue about corporatism could be phrased as a question – how much of the crucial negotiation takes place outside parliament?

Of course, there are many associations in western societies which are not involved in corporatist negotiations. Some of these are capable of having an impact on policy through lobbying or public campaigns, while others are marginal and easy to ignore. But the drift toward corporatism in modern industrial democracies consists in the first category, with strong associations being more and more integrated into the process of decision-making. It makes sense for a democratic government to consult before deciding, not only to determine the most popular policy, but also to soften the edges of confrontation with the losers, who will at least have the sense that they have been listened to and will be listened to again.

This style of government is roundly condemned, on the right and the left. But it is not clear that either has come up with a viable alternative. The attack from the right is mainly in evidence in the English-speaking countries. Margaret Thatcher was its best-known protagonist. She certainly upset the rules of the game as they were understood under her predecessors of both parties. She introduced a politics of conflict into what formerly had been negotiation. It has been argued by her supporters that this was necessary in order to challenge the position that the labor unions had won in British society. She had to fight a war, ending in the bruising battle of a miners' strike. But the outcome of war is generally peace restored on a new basis. Confrontation as a style of government is not sustainable in the long run in democratic countries.

Of course, right-wing politicians like Thatcher don't subscribe theoretically to endless conflict. They envisage a new dispensation after the special interests have been dealt with, and various enter-prises and functions privatized. Many things that the government now orchestrates will run them-selves without state interference. State and society will do their own thing without getting in each other's way. This is especially espoused by the right because of their belief in the efficacy of unadulterated market forces.

Now I believe that this hope is utopian – or dystopian, if you don't share the moral outlook of the right. Too much is at stake to allow govern-ment and society to coexist without coordination. The really successful economies in the late twen-tieth century were resolutely corporatist, for in-stance, Germany and Japan. The idea that there is another path to competitive success on world mar-kets seems to be a nostalgic illusion of the English-speaking countries, remembering an earlier, braver era of economic purity. But those days are gone forever. The obvious failure of the Marxist policy of suppressing the market altogether can be taken only by the simple-minded as proof that total reliance on the market is the best policy. Obviously we are all going to have to live with some mix of market and state orchestration. The difficult ques-tion is what mix suits each society. In fact, right-wing governments go on orchestrating far more than they admit. And to the extent that they re-frain from doing so – that, say, Britain and the United States turn their backs on industrial policy – they will probably live to rue the day.

What is the relevance of all this to the idea of civil society? It is that the anti-corporatist aspir-ation can very well be, and often is, expressed in this society/state distinction. So the idea that civil society is something we *have* in the West needs to be nuanced. In one sense we do; in another sense it is a goal that has to be striven for against the grain of modern democratic government.

Let's look more closely at these different senses. (1) In a minimal sense, civil society exists where there are free associations that are not under tutel-age of state power. (2) In a stronger sense, civil society exists where society as a whole can structure itself and coordinate its actions through such free associations. (3) As an alternative or supplement to the second sense, we can speak of civil society wher-ever the ensemble of associations can significantly determine or inflect the course of state policy.

No one can deny that civil society exists in sense (1) in the West; or that it was lacking under Len-inism and was a crucial aspiration of those living under Leninist regimes. But civil society as con-trasted with the state in western political theory incorporated more than this; it involved (2) and sometimes (3). It was in virtue of this that it could be referred to in the singular as civil *society*. We might say that (2) and (3) introduce a public di-mension that has been crucial to the concept in the western tradition.

One aspect of the right-wing indictment of cor-poratism could be formulated in the charge that it has suppressed civil society in sense (2). Sense (3) might be thought to be integrally fulfilled by cor-poratist mechanisms of negotiation. But this will not be easily accepted by one who suspects that the associations are in fact being integrated into the state apparatus, rather than bringing to bear their independent weight on it.

This brings us to the left-wing criticism of corporatism, which also can be and sometimes is expressed in terms of civil society. Here too it is the enriched concept involving senses (2) and (3) which is in play. I'm thinking of the criticism that comes from what are sometimes called the "new social movements," and which has found expres-sion, for instance, in Germany's green party.

On this outlook, the state and the large powerful associations it consults form a unity. They tend equally toward elite control and growing distance from the constituencies they claim to speak for. In addition, they are equally committed to increasing bureaucratic control in the name of technological efficacy over more and more aspects of human life. Even such seemingly benign features of modern society as the welfare state, originally introduced on the initiative of the left, become suspect as mechanisms of control and "normalization." To be a beneficiary of the welfare state is to submit to bureaucratic regulation, to have your life shaped by categories that may cut across those in which you want to live your life.

One response to this has been to try to open a sphere of independent self-regulation by spontan-eously associating groups. Another has been to try to win for the new social movements themselves greater impact on the formation of policy. These correspond to senses (2) and (3) respectively, and so it is not surprising that this New Left has also been tempted to bring the term "civil society" into play. The sense, justified or not, of an analogy between their situation and that of dissidents in the eastern European bloc has strengthened this temptation.[1]

So the first claim mentioned above, that civil so-ciety already exists in the West, is more problematic than it appeared. But the second claim is also not simply true, and it would be worth exploring at even greater length.

The relative freedom we enjoy is seen as having sources deep in the history of the West, and in particular in conceptions of society going back to medieval Christendom. These sources can be articulated with something like the conception of civil society. In the context of contemporary Eastern Europe, the obvious pole of comparison is Russia. At successive stages, Russia took a different political path from western polities. The development of an independent noble class, of free cities, and hence of a regime of "estates" was cut short at crucial moments by the state building of Ivan the Terrible and later by Peter the Great. Subsequent initiatives aimed at joining the West were repressed by Nicholas I and then by Lenin. A mainstay of western development, that is, a church independent of political authority, never existed in the Russian Orthodox tradition.

So runs the story, and it obviously has a great deal of truth to it, and particular relevance to the situation of Eastern Europe; at least to Hungary, Poland, Czechoslovakia, East Germany. These societies developed in close cultural contact and symbiosis with western Europe. They share analogous institutional developments and some of the same ideals. For instance, republican ideals of self-rule were present in Poland and enshrined even in the name of the pre-partition state, Rzeczpospolita Polska (the Commonwealth of Poland). The poignant fate of these societies was to have been forced to accept an alien political system, in fact of Russian origin, which ran against the grain of those societies and was the cause of endless conflict. The aspiration to greater freedom is in effect synonymous with an aspiration to rejoin Europe. That is why it finds natural expression in a view of the European political tradition and in the notion of civil society.[2]

Perhaps this contrast between Russia and the West has been overdrawn. Sometimes it is put in such a way as to imply that the tragic political plight of Russia has been virtually inevitable from the Mongol conquest on. And western freedom is described in a symmetrically self-congratulatory way as flowing inevitably out of a more remote past. In fact, there were moments when things could have been reversed. Arguably, the Bolshevik takeover was a contingent political disaster for Russia, which interrupted the slow development of civil society that had been gathering

pace in the last decades of tsarism. Arguably, Peter's was not the only road to modernization open to Russia. At the same time, when Peter did try to imitate Europe, he took what was seen as the latest, most effective model, the so-called absolute monarchies. Those were in fact constrained by a context of law and independent associations. But no one would then have predicted confidently that they wouldn't grow stronger, that they would give way before a totally different governing formula, then effective only in England and Holland. Western democracy was never written in the genes. At the same time, the chauvinistic idea that representative institutions can't take root outside their home culture is refuted by the existence of such societies as India and Japan (and, dare we hope, post-Gorbachev Russia and post-Deng China).

But when all this is said, it remains true that western liberal democracy has deep roots in its past, that certain socially entrenched self-conceptions greatly facilitated its rise, and that many of these were absent in Russia or were ruthlessly rooted out by earlier rulers. What were these roots, and how do they relate to the term "civil society"?

There are a number of factors worth talking about in this connection; some of them are ideas, some are institutions, but most often they are both at once: institutions and practices that incorporate their own self-interpretation. In one form or another, they seem to be part of the background of western democratic society. But the relation is sometimes more complex and ambiguous than at first appears, mainly because modern democracy itself is a more complex and tension-ridden reality than is generally acknowledged. Some of these tensions will emerge from looking at how the society/state distinction arose.

(A) The medieval notion of society is one of those which has turned out to be important in the development of the West. What is important is in a sense a negative fact: that society is not defined in terms of its political organization. The underlying issue is this: what gives a society its identity? What are the features without which it would cease to be a society, or would become a wholly different one? In many civilizations and eras, these questions are answered in terms of political structure. For both the Greeks and the Romans, the identity of society was defined by its *politeia*, its political constitution. Under the Empire unity came from a common subjection to authority, although a fiction was maintained that this authority came from an act of the people. Now to the extent that a society is defined by its political organization, to that degree it is permeable by political power. It lacks a principle of resistance to the invasive force of sovereign political authority. Just being politically defined is hardly a sufficient condition for this kind of takeover by despotic power, as the Greek polis attests. It is rather that the basis for a certain kind of limitation on this power is lacking, whenever the conditions ripen for its advance.

Now unlike the ancient conceptions, the notion that developed in the early Middle Ages was of a society where political authority was one organ among others. Royal authority, for instance, was *singulis major* but *universis minor*. This idea, that society is not identical with its political organization, can be seen as a crucial differentiation, one of the origins of the later notion of civil society and one of the roots of western liberalism.

(B) This differentiation was carried further by one of the most important features of Latin Christendom: the development of an idea of the church as an independent society. In principle, the inhabitants of Christendom were Christian. But these same people were organized in two societies, one temporal and one spiritual, of which neither could be simply subordinated to the other. This was, of course, a formula for perpetual struggle, and extravagant claims were made for one side or the other, including an arrogation of *plenitudo potestatis* by Pope Innocent III. But the underlying common understanding remained within the Gelasian definition of "two swords." There were two sources of authority, both granted for different purposes by God. Each was subordinate to the other for some purposes and supreme for others. Western Christendom was in its essence bifocal.

Alongside these two pervasive features, there were particular facets of medieval political arrangements which with hindsight appear important. (C) One is the development of a legal notion of subjective rights. This was linked to the peculiar nature of feudal relations of authority. The relations of vassalage were seen in a quasi-contractual light. The superior had obligations as well as the inferior. To repudiate these obligations was a felony, as much as for the vassal. So inferiors were seen as the beneficiaries of obligations, privileges enjoyed as a kind of property. This is the origin of the western notion of subjective rights. It starts off as a notion of purely positive law, before being transposed by the natural-rights doctrines of the

seventeenth and eighteenth centuries. But it meant that medieval sovereigns faced a society that was partly defined as a skein of rights and duties, which imposed on them the necessity of winning consent for important changes. This, along with the existence of relatively independent, self-governing cities (D), brought about the standard political structures of medieval polities (E), in which a monarch ruled with the intermittent and uncertain support of a body of estates, which had to be called together from time to time to raise the resources he needed to govern and wage war. This dyarchy constituted another, purely secular dualism, linking the political structure to society at large.

We can recognize our roots in all of this. But it didn't ensure trouble-free progress for modern liberal democracy. Between us and that time lies the great early-modern attempt over most of Europe to set up absolute monarchies. Kings won the power to raise taxes without calling the estates, built standing armies on these resources, which in turn made their power harder to challenge. Around 1680 this looked like the wave of the future; it must have seemed to many that only this kind of state could be militarily effective. Moreover, influential theories justified the new model of political society. On one hand, the concepts of Roman law, favoring monarchical power, become dominant. On the other hand, Bodin and later Hobbes develop a notion of sovereignty which quite undermines or supersedes the medieval understanding of society. The notion comes to be accredited that a society, in order to exist at all, must be held together by sovereign power, that is, by a power unlimited by any other. In other words, the identification of society with its political organization returns, and in a form that is unambiguously favorable to despotism. Important vestiges of feature A emerge in social-contract doctrines, where society is accorded existence prior to government, as it is with the jurists Grotius and Pufendorf. This is the feature of contract theory that Hobbes wanted to suppress. But even with Grotius and Pufendorf in the seventeenth century, the "contract of subjection" is seen as setting up absolute power, against which society henceforth has no legal recourse.

Meanwhile, throughout this period, a satellitization of the church is taking place in a number of Protestant countries, and the very division of Christendom undermines the idea at the heart of B, that everyone belongs to a single alternative society.

As I said above, absolute monarchies were really rather limited exercises in despotism, seen in the light of twentieth-century dictatorships. They did away with D and E, but remained limited by C, the entrenched traditions of rights. Of course, nothing assured that C in turn would not be eroded if absolutism pursued its course. The important stream of reform thinking in the eighteenth century that looked to "enlightened despotism" to reorder society on rational lines was hostile to traditional rights, wanted them swept aside in the name of reason. But absolutism couldn't run its course. What undermined it was the military, and behind that the economic success of the at-first relatively minor powers who operated on another, more consensual model, especially England and the Low Countries. In that sense, the end of the eighteenth century may have parallels with the end of the twentieth.

Around this alternative model, there crystallized a number of anti-absolutist doctrines. The most celebrated and influential was that of Locke. In a sense he transposed and renewed both A and B and brought them back into political theory. Feature A returns in the unprecedentedly strong form that defines government as a trust.[3] Society exists before government; it issues from a first contract that takes individuals out of the state of nature. The newly formed body then sets up government. This may be defined as supreme, but it is in fact in a fiduciary relation to society. Should it violate its trust, society recovers its freedom of action.

But Locke also reintroduces a version of B. Prior to all political society, mankind forms a kind of community. We are constituted as such by being under natural law, which is enjoined on us by God.[4] We are made a community, in other words, by our enjoyment of natural rights. This community is in fact defined as a transform of C, now written into the order of things rather than simply inscribed in positive law. Any particular political society has to respect this higher law, since those who set it up were bound by it, and they couldn't pass on powers they didn't have.

Locke is, of course, still using the term "civil society" in its traditional sense, where it is synonymous with "political society." But he is preparing the ground for the emergence of the new, contrastive sense a century later. This contrast arises out of the anti-absolutist doctrines of the eighteenth century, but in two rather different ways. One develops out of Locke's embryonic notion of mankind as a prepolitical community.

Locke's state of nature is not the scene of devastation portrayed by Hobbes. It lacks security, which is why humans are driven to set up governments. But otherwise it is the possible scene of great progress in what was later called civilization, of economic development, the division of labor, the development of money, and the accumulation of property. This idea was developed in the eighteenth century into a picture of human social life in which much that is valuable is seen as coming about in a pre- or nonpolitical realm, at best under the protection of political authority, but by no means under its direction.

There was another source of the contrast, which we can perhaps most handily identify with Montesquieu. His portrait of monarchy in De l'esprit des lois offers an alternative anti-absolutist doctrine to Locke's. Unlike Locke, he assumes a strong monarchical government that is unremovable. The important issue turns on whether this government is unchecked, and veering toward despotism, or whether it is limited by law. But limitation by law is ineffective unless independent bodies exist which have a standing in this law and are there to defend it. The rule of law and the corps intermédiaires stand and fall together. Without law, bodies like parliament and estates like the nobility have no standing; without such bodies and estates, the law has no effective defenders. The free monarchy (a pleonasm for Montesquieu, since the unfree one is despotism) is in equilibrium between a powerful central authority and an interlocking mass of agencies and associations it has to work with.

Montesquieu's theory draws on different elements of the tradition from Locke's. It is based on elements C, D, and E of the medieval constitution. Indeed, the long debate in France over the rise of absolutism was seen as one that pitted the ancient constitution, inherited originally from the Frankish conquerors, against models drawn from Roman law. Montesquieu saw himself as reformulating the "German" case. Speaking of the English constitution, which he admired, Montesquieu says that it was derived from the ancient Germans. "Ce beau système a été trouvé dans les bois."[5] What he doesn't need to draw on at all is A and B. Society is not defined independently of its political constitution. On the contrary, the free society is identified with a certain such constitution.

For all the importance of the medieval constitution to him, in this respect Montesquieu thinks more like an ancient. The polis too was defined politically. The very terms we use show this to be a tautology. This vision of things allowed no place for a distinction between civil society and the state. This would have been incomprehensible to a Greek or Roman. Montesquieu, along with many anti-absolutists of his era, was an admirer of ancient freedom. But he didn't make it an alternative model to absolute rule. His genius was rather to articulate a third standard, in some ways antithetical to the polis, which was nevertheless one of freedom and dignity for the participant. Monarchy was antithetical to the republic because the latter supposed "vertu", a dedication to the public good as well as austere mores and equality; but monarchy required a lively sense of one's own rights and privileges, and thrived on differences of status and displays of wealth and power, which were bound up with honor. Patriotic virtue was what kept society free in the ancient republic, because it led people to defend laws to the death against internal and external threats. The lively sense of one's own rights and status protected freedom in the modern monarchy, because it made the privileged resist royal encroachment and feel shame in obeying any order that derogated their code.

So while retaining a thoroughly political definition of society, like the ancients, Montesquieu laid the ground for a society/state distinction that was alien to the ancients. He did this with a view of society as poised between central power and a skein of entrenched rights.

Both anti-absolutist doctrines are reflected in the distinction eventually drawn around the turn of the century, which found its most celebrated statement in Hegel's *Philosophy of Right*. But in fact they sit uneasily together in this new concept of civil society. There is a tension between them, and between the different models for a free society which can be articulated with this new concept.

Thus two streams come together into "civil society." Let's call them the L-stream and the M-stream, after the figures I have somewhat arbitrarily chosen to represent them. What I want to do here is map the convergence and highlight some of the tensions.

The central feature of the L-stream is the elaboration of a richer view of society as an extrapolitical reality. One facet of this elaboration has dominated the discussion of civil society until quite recently: the development of a picture of society as an "economy," that is, as an entity of interrelated acts of production, exchange, and consumption which has its own internal dynamic, its own autonomous laws. This crystallizes in the eighteenth century with the work of the physiocrats and, more definitively, with Adam Smith. Just how great an intellectual revolution is involved here can be measured in the transformation of the word's meaning. "Economics" is etymologically the art of household management; it designated a particular field of prudent administration. The *nomos* was that imposed by the manager, the head of household or *oikos*. It already involved one revolution in thinking to begin to consider whole kingdoms as like households, needing to have their production and consumption "managed" in this way. This gives us the jump to "political economy." But the important change is to a view of this domain as in a sense organizing itself, following its own laws of equilibrium and change. The *nomos* in the word now comes to resemble its use in a term like "astronomy," referring us to an "autonomous" domain of causal laws. The modern "economy" is born, as a domain with its own organization.

This gives a new twist and a new force to the idea of society as enjoying an extrapolitical identity. The "economy" now defines a dimension of social life in which we function as a society potentially outside the ambit of politics. Of course, there are differences among the practitioners of the new science as to how autonomous it should be. Even Adam Smith was in favor of much more state regulation than his popular reputation allows. But this intellectual revolution allows us to raise the issue of economic autonomy; without the notion of the economic as governed by its own laws, the issue couldn't even be framed. Now everyone thinks in these terms, interventionist and free-enterpriser alike. They differ only in their assessment of the likely outcome of unregulated flow, and hence of the need or lack of it for remedial action of a more or less radical kind. Even Marx, especially Marx, has a theory of unimpeded flow. It is the disaster scenario laid out in *Capital*.

This provided an important part of the content of the new concept of civil society, at least of its L-facet. It figures in Hegel's formulation, where the self-regulating, entrepreneurial economy is given a central place on this level of society. Marx took over Hegel's concept and reduced it almost exclusively to this, and it is partly due to Marx's influence that "civil society" was for so long defined in economic terms. But this represents an impoverishment of Hegel's concept. It also owed something to the M-stream, so that his civil society incorporated bodies engaged in conscious self-management – the corporations – which were also integrated in their own way into the state.

But I want to return to this later, when we look at the tension between the two streams. Right now it is important to see that, even in what I call the L-stream, the economy is not the only component. What is also of great importance is the development in the eighteenth century of an autonomous public with its own "opinion."

This involves a quite new use of the notion of "public." The term designates what is of common concern, and not just objectively or from an outsider's perspective, but what is commonly recognized as of common concern. So public is what matters to the whole society, or belongs to this whole society, or pertains to the instruments, institutions, or loci by which the society comes together as a body and acts. So plainly the political structure of a society is public – its executive organs, the loci of its legislative power, and whatever spaces of assembly these require – from the agora in which the citizen assembly meets to the court where a king exercises his rule. These are loci of what one might call public space.

The new notion of opinion in the eighteenth century defines a quite different model of public space. Through the circulation of newspapers, reviews, and books among the educated classes, and scattered, small-scale personal exchanges in salons, coffeehouses, and (in some cases) political assemblies, there emerges a sense of nation, or its literate segment, an opinion that deserves to be called "public." Public opinion, as originally conceived, is not just the sum of our private individual opinions, even where we spontaneously agree. It is something that has been elaborated in debate and discussion, and is recognized by everyone as something held in common. This element of common recognition is what makes it public, in the strong sense.

This is also what gives it its force, a new force in history. The novel aspect is that public opinion is elaborated entirely outside the channels and public spaces of the political structure. More radically, it is developed outside the channels and public spaces of any authority whatever, since it is also independent of that second focus of European societies, the church. Governments were used to facing the independent power of religious opinion, articulated by churches. What was new was opinion, presented as that of society, which was elaborated through no official, established, hierarchical organs of definition.[6]

Like the economy, public opinion was here to stay. And though some thinkers envisaged a kind of absolute rule which would align itself on enlightened opinion, in fact free opinion and absolute power don't consort too well. But it can't be simply forgotten, and so contemporary despotisms are forced not only to suppress public opinion, but also to counterfeit it. Official newspapers write editorials and report meetings and resolutions, all of which purportedly come spontaneously from individual authors and initiators. The orchestrated character of all this has to be hidden from view. Such is the prestige of public opinion.

The self-regulating economy and public opinion – these are two ways in which society can come to some unity or coordination outside the political structures. They give body to the Lockean idea, which in turn has medieval roots, that society has its own identity beyond the political dimension. It seems to follow from this that political authority ought to respect the autonomy of society in the spheres where it is manifest. This involves a new kind of limitation of authority. It was always understood as limited in Christendom by the church, to some degree or other; and also by rights ascribed to individuals or corporations. But the political used to be the only domain in which secular social purpose could be articulated and carried out. To the extent that these new spheres of nonpolitical social identity become recognized, this is no longer the case.

Indeed, the new space of public opinion, mediated by printed materials, can be the source of a more radical challenge, questioning the primacy of political structures on their own ground. Previously it was axiomatic that societies found their political identities and defined their political direction through the traditionally established political structures, and only there – whether these were royal courts or parliaments or some combination of the two. Unofficial pressure might be exercised through agitation and pamphleteering, but this didn't challenge the principle that the authoritative locus for defining political ends lay in the established bodies. With the development of the new space of public opinion, more far-reaching claims had to be made. It has been argued, for instance, that in early eighteenth-century America a new form of discourse emerges in newspapers and pamphlets.[7] It is a discourse that implicitly arrogates to this print-sustained space the power and duty to define the goals of the people and to call the established bodies to book for their deviations from these goals. The discourse is cast in the traditional rhetoric of republicanism, but under this familiar cover a radically new formula is being advanced. In republican societies, the people did indeed criticize and control their officers, but assembled in the *ekklesia* or general meeting. This was itself a governing body, the foundational one. Now the powers of the assembled people are being arrogated to a new print-mediated public space, unembodied in any traditional structure or, indeed, in face-to-face meetings of any kind. The political identity of society shifts to an unprecedented locus. Whether or not this analysis holds for the eighteenth-century British colonies, something like this shift plainly became central to modern democratic self-understanding.

This congeries of ideas about the economy and public space constituted one of the strands in the new notion of "civil society" as distinguished from the state. It comprised a public, but not a politically structured domain. The first feature was essential: civil society was not the private sphere. Where Aristotle distinguishes *polis* from *oikos*, and only the first is a public domain, Hegel distinguishes three terms in *Sittlichkeit*: family, civil society, and the state. Civil society is not identical with the third term, the polis, and not with the first term either. That is why I argue that any definition of civil society in sense (1), which identifies it simply with the existence of autonomous associations free from state tutelage, fails to do justice to the historical concept. This defines a pattern of public social life, and not just a collection of private enclaves.

This notion of civil society, the L-variant, can inspire radical political hopes, sometimes of an anti-political kind. Even Locke saw the political structure as an emanation of a society that in one sense was already political, because people had put in common their power to enforce the Law of Nature, but had as yet no political structure. With the enriching of the concept, we can formulate the idea that society has its own prepolitical life and unity which the political structure must serve. Society has the right and power to make and unmake political authority, according as it does so serve or fail to serve.

This is the radical doctrine of Thomas Paine. In a somewhat less radical variant, something like this was acted on by the American colonists in their war of independence. It was less radical because the decision to rebel was taken by political authorities in the thirteen colonies. The early-modern idea, that a rebellion against a supreme authority in violation of its trust could be carried out by duly constituted subordinate authority (the central notion of *vindiciae contra tyrannos*), would also have served to justify the rebellion. Americans saw themselves as fighting for established right as against usurpation. But in fact the language they adopted, that of "We, the People," had a more radical impact. It seemed to draw the revolutionary conclusion from the L-variant: the people have an identity, they have purposes, even a will, outside any political structure. In the name of this identity, following this will, they have the right to make and unmake these structures. The duality of focus in the western concept of society, which goes back in different forms to the Middle Ages, finally takes on its most revolutionary formulation.

This has become a commonplace of modern thought. Between 1776 and now, the notion of a people's prepolitical identity has taken a new and much more powerful form, that of the nation. We now speak of this right to make and unmake structures as the right of self-determination. No one today dares deny this in principle, however suppressed it may be in practice.

But radical hopes can also take an antipolitical form. One could dream of the nonpolitical spheres of society becoming more and more autonomous, more and more self-sufficient. Taken to the extreme, this offers a vision of a society without politics, where the government of men gives way to the administration of things, as Saint-Simon articulated it, followed by Engels. In less extreme fashion, one could hope for a society in which the development of industry and commerce would serve to tie people together in peace, and thus drastically reduce the role of government, lessening its policing function and doing away with war altogether.

The eighteenth-century developments described above, which gave us the notions of economy and public opinion, also provided a notion of "civilization." A civilized society was partly so in virtue of its political constitution – indeed, the term in some respects replaces the earlier French expression *état policé*. But "civilization" included a lot more – pacification, enlightenment, technical development, arts and sciences, polished mores. Within the self-definition of modern Europe as civilized, in contrast to other societies and to its own past, the virtues of peaceful production bulked large, and the older warrior virtues were seen in an unfavorable light. European society gained in polish as it turned its back on these and on the honor ethic behind them. But it was also the honor ethic that gave the political life intrinsic value. For the new social ethic of peaceful productivity, as we see for instance with the utilitarians, political structures had purely instrumental significance. The less we needed them, the better.

So two rather different kinds of political hopes arise from this notion of society as having a pre- or nonpolitical identity. The one moves toward the norm of self-determination; the other toward the goal of marginalizing the political. So we can see why the L-stream was not the only one to feed the new concept of civil society. It was not just that these hopes each in their own way undermine the very distinction between society and state. This they did, of course. Radical self-determination swallows up the state in society, in a supposed common will; while the goal of marginalization tries to approach as closely as possible to anarchy.

But also, much more importantly, both hopes pose a threat to freedom, and the distinction was introduced in the first place in the context of counter-absolutist thought. One recurring threat to freedom has come from the politics of what would later be called the general will. This *idée force*, as elaborated by Rousseau, fuses the idea of a people's will independent of all political structure with the ethic of ancient republicanism, drawing its power from both. Rousseau invokes the prepolitical in the very unancient idea of a social contract, of society as constituted by will, as well as in his understanding of nature as inner voice. He invokes the ancient ethic of virtue in the ideal of a transparent face-to-face political society. The latter, of course, drops out of the picture as unrealizable in the modern world. What remains is the notion of popular will as the ultimate justification for all political structures and authority.

The most thoroughgoing destruction of civil society has been carried out in the name of some variants and successors of this idea in the twentieth century, notably the nation and the proletariat. A strange and horrifying reversal has taken place, whereby an idea whose roots lie in a prepolitical concept of society can now justify the total subjection of life to an enterprise of political transformation. And in less spectacular form, the power of the state has often been enhanced by its self-definition as an instrument of the national will.

But in a more subtle way, the politics of marginalizing politics has also been seen as posing a threat to freedom. This is particularly so when the sphere of society in the name of which the political is being marginalized is that of the self-regulating economy. For in this domain the disposition of things in society as a whole is seen as arising not out of any collective will or common decision, but by way of an "invisible hand." To leave our collective fate to blind economic forces can be portrayed as a kind of alienation. On top of this, all those whose allegiance is to an ideal of the political life as good in itself will see the marginalization of politics as an abandonment of what is most valuable in life, a flight from the public into the narrower and less significant sphere of private satisfactions, the "petty and paltry pleasures" of which Tocqueville speaks in *Democracy in America*.

Marx, who developed a theory of alienation, himself subscribed to his own version of a world without politics. But Tocqueville spelled out the dangers implicit in the kinds of hopes generated by the L-theory. The modern democracy of the general will can degenerate, he argues, into a kind of mild despotism (*despotisme doux*) in which citizens fall prey to a tutelary power that dwarfs them; and this is both cause and effect of a turn away from the public to the private which, although tempting, represents a diminution of their human stature.

Those who are thus dissatisfied with the L-variant of the notion of civil society are induced to turn to Montesquieu. Tocqueville can be seen as the greatest disciple of Montesquieu in the nineteenth century. But Hegel, in his dissatisfaction with the L-variant, had already drawn on Montesquieu. Like Marx after him, Hegel couldn't believe in the benign effects of an autonomous, unregulated economic sphere. And he produced his own variant of the civic-humanist doctrine that the life of the citizen had value in itself. At the same time, his theory of modern life, in distinction from the ancients, turned on the differentiated development of this nonpolitical public sphere, which related individuals in their separate identities. The result was the Hegelian concept of civil society – a separate sphere, but not self-sufficient. Not only did its constituent economic processes need regulation, which was undertaken partly within civil society, but this society could only escape destruction by being incorporated in the higher unity of the state, that is, society as politically organized.

Hegel combines both the L- and the M-streams in his concept of civil society. If the L-concept, to repeat, turns on the idea of a nonpolitical dimension to society, Montesquieu's contribution is the picture of a society defined by its political organization, but where this is constitutionally diverse, distributing power among many independent agencies. It is important here too that there be independent associations for nonpolitical purposes. But their significance is not that they form a nonpolitical social sphere, but rather that they form the basis for the fragmentation and diversity of power *within* the political system. What is relevant is not their life outside, but the way they are integrated into the political system and the weight they have in it.

Thus the different elements of Hegel's political society take up their role in the state, make up the different estates, and form the basis for a differentiated constitution, whose formula was partly inspired by Montesquieu. In this way, we avoid both the undifferentiated homogeneity of the general-will state, which Hegel thought must lead inevitably to tyranny and terror, and also the unregulated and ultimately self-destructive play of blind economic forces, which then seemed to be menacing England.

With Tocqueville, the heritage of Montesquieu is even clearer. The only bulwark against mild despotism is free associations. Voluntary associations for all purposes are valuable. But their significance is that they give us the taste and habit of self-rule, and so they are essential for political purposes. But if they are to be real loci of self-rule, they have to be nongigantic and numerous, and exist at many levels of the polity. This itself should be decentralized, so that self-government can be practiced also at the local and not just the national level. If it dies out at the former, it is in danger at the latter. "In democratic countries the science of association is the mother of science," according to Tocqueville.

So our notion of civil society is complex. It is an amalgam of two rather different influences, which I have called the L-stream and the M-stream. It clearly goes beyond the minimal definition (1) above. But it hovers between the other two because of its dual origin. For the purposes of deconstructing a Leninist dictatorship, any one of these definitions will do. But when we come to ask how the concept of civil society relates to the freedom of western liberal democracies, we find a more complex story.

We can see now why the question discussed at the outset, whether we in fact have a functioning independent civil society in the West, was not so easy to answer. Among the other reasons is the fact that there are different definitions of what this independence involves, which have equally strong warrant in our two-streamed tradition. No easier to answer is the question of what role a concept of civil society has to play in the future defense of freedom.

It is tempting to think that it is almost guaranteed a role, just because of its place in the complex intellectual and institutional background of western liberty. The distinction between civil society and the state is indeed important to the western tradition, not just because of all the roots of the idea in earlier epochs, but more especially because it has been central to the different forms of counter-absolutist thinking. Indeed, it owes its existence and relevance to the development in the West of reforming absolutism, of "the well-ordered police state" in the seventeenth and eighteenth centuries.[8] It made no sense in the context of the polis, or in the medieval polity, no more than it did in a host of traditional nonwestern polities. It arose, one might say, as a necessary instrument of defense in face of the specific *threats* to freedom implicit in the western tradition. But precisely to the extent that the modern state is still drawn to a vocation of mobilizing and reorganizing its subjects' lives, the distinction would seem to be guaranteed a continuing relevance.

So one can argue that the distinction is essential to our conception of what it is to preserve freedom. But it has also been shouldered aside by supposedly simpler and more arresting definitions of a free society, which turn on the idea of a general will or a politics-free sphere. To make the notion of civil society central to our political discourse ought to involve a rejection of these seductively limpid formulas.

But those who find these simpler definitions unsatisfactory (as I do), and want to recur to "civil society," will find that it is not a unified idea. Both its sources are deeply woven into our political traditions and way of life. Which definition we accept of civil society will have important consequences for our picture of the free society and hence our political practice.

In fact, our choice today lies not simply between the two variants. The force of the L-idea is too great and too obtrusive to be altogether denied. The choice seems to lie between a view of civil society almost exclusively concerned with the

L-stream and one that tries to balance both. In the first category fall those critics of corporatist politics on the right who aim to roll back the power of the state. In the second are found the contemporary followers of Tocqueville, some of whom along with a bewilderingly diverse variety of utopians end up on the ecological left, but who are also found near the center of many western societies.

I hope an impression has emerged that the second view, which balances both streams, is greatly superior to the first; more, that the first is in constant danger of falling victim to the simpler formulas of a prepolitical freedom that end up subverting the distinction or neutralizing its force as a counterthrust to bureaucratic power. In any case, this is what I propose.

Notes

1 For a work in which both predicaments are discussed together in a very illuminating way, see John Keane, ed., *Civil Society and the State* (London, 1988). The civil-society tradition has been mediated to thinkers on the left partly through the work of Antonio Gramsci, who had a much richer concept than Marx, one more indebted to Hegel. It should also be said that the concern on the left with the "colonization of the life-world" by bureaucracies dedicated to technological efficacy is not confined to ecological green parties. A well-known theorist who has addressed this issue, and who is in no sense a "green," is Jürgen Habermas. See his *Theorie des kommunikativen Handelns* (Frankfurt, 1981); *The Theory of Communicative Action*, 2 vols. (Boston, 1985, 1989).

2 For a discussion of Eastern Europe in this context, see Jenö Szücs, "Three Historical Regions of Europe," and Mihaly Vajda, "East-Central European Perspectives," in Keane, *Civil Society*.

3 See *Second Treatise of Civil Government*, paras. 221–2, in Peter Laslett, ed., *Locke's Two Treatises of Government*, 2nd edn (Cambridge, 1967), p. 430.

4 Ibid., para. 172. Locke speaks of "the common bond whereby humane kind is united into one fellowship and societie" (Laslett, p. 401).

5 Montesquieu, *De l'esprit des lois*, 11.6, in *Oeuvres complètes* (Paris, 1964), p. 590.

6 This whole development has been interestingly discussed by Jürgen Habermas in his *Strukturwandel der Öffentlichkeit* (Berlin, 1962); *Structural Transformation* (Cambridge, Mass., 1989).

7 I have drawn here on the interesting discussion in Michael Warner, *The Letters of the Republic* (Cambridge, Mass., 1989).

8 See Marc Raeff, *The Well-Ordered Police State* (New Haven, 1983). Of course the term is used not in its present-day sense. "Police" translates the eighteenth-century German "Polizei," which covered the state's action in ordering the lives of its subjects rather than in suppressing violence.

PART II

Democracy

6

The Public Sphere

Jürgen Habermas

Concept

By "public sphere" we mean first of all a domain of our social life in which such a thing as public opinion can be formed. Access to the public sphere is open in principle to all citizens. A portion of the public sphere is constituted in every conversation in which private persons come together to form a public. They are then acting neither as business nor professional people conducting their private affairs, nor as legal consociates subject to the legal regulations of a state bureaucracy and obligated to obedience. Citizens act as a public when they deal with matters of general interest without being subject to coercion; thus with the guarantee that they may assemble and unite freely, and express and publicize their opinions freely. When the public is large, this kind of communication requires certain means of dissemination and influence: today, newspapers and periodicals, radio and television are the media of the public sphere. We speak of a political public sphere (as distinguished from a literary one, for instance) when the public discussions concern objects connected with the practice of the state. The coercive power of the state is the counterpart, as it were, of the political public sphere, but it is not a part of it. State power is, to be sure, considered "public" power, but it owes the attribute of publicness to its task of caring for the public, that is, providing for the common good of all legal consociates. Only when the exercise of public authority has actually been subordinated to the requirement of democratic publicness does the political public sphere acquire an institutionalized influence on the government, by way of the legislative body. The term "public opinion" refers to the functions of criticism and control of organized state authority that the public exercises informally, as well as formally during periodic elections. Regulations concerning the publicness (or publicity [*Publizität*] in its original meaning) of state-related activities, as, for instance, the public accessibility required of legal proceedings, are also connected with this function of public opinion. To the public sphere as a sphere mediating between state and society, a sphere in which the public as the vehicle of public opinion is formed, there corresponds the principle of publicness – the publicness that once had to win out against the secret politics of monarchs and that since then has permitted democratic control of state activity.

It is no accident that these concepts of the public sphere and public opinion were not formed until the eighteenth century. They derive their specific meaning from a concrete historical situation. It was then that one learned to distinguish between opinion and public opinion, or *opinion publique*. Whereas mere opinions (things taken for granted as part of a culture, normative convictions, collective prejudices and judgments) seem to persist unchanged in their quasi-natural structure as a kind of sediment of history, public opinion, in terms of its very idea, can be formed only if a public that engages in rational discussion exists. Public discussions that are institutionally protected and that take, with critical intent, the exercise of political authority as their theme have not existed since time immemorial – they developed only in a specific phase of bourgeois society, and only by virtue of a specific constellation of interests could they be incorporated into the order of the bourgeois constitutional state.

History

It is not possible to demonstrate the existence of a public sphere in its own right, separate from the private sphere, in the European society of the High Middle Ages. At the same time, however, it is not a coincidence that the attributes of authority at that time were called "public." For a public representation of authority existed at that time. At all levels of the pyramid established by feudal law, the status of the feudal lord is neutral with respect to the categories "public" and "private"; but the person possessing that status represents it publicly; he displays himself, represents himself as the embodiment of a "higher" power, in whatever degree. This concept of representation has survived into recent constitutional history. Even today the power of political authority on its highest level, however much it has become detached from its former basis, requires representation through the head of state. But such elements derive from a pre-bourgeois social structure. Representation in the sense of the bourgeois public sphere, as in "representing" the nation or specific clients, has nothing to do with *representative publicness*, which inheres in the concrete existence of a lord. As long as the prince and the estates of his realm "are" the land, rather than merely "representing" it, they are capable of this kind of representation; they represent their authority "before" the people rather than for the people.

The feudal powers (the church, the prince, and the nobility) to which this representative publicness adheres disintegrated in the course of a long process of polarization; by the end of the eighteenth century they had decomposed into private elements on the one side and public on the other. The position of the church changed in connection with the Reformation; the tie to divine authority that the church represented, that is, religion, became a private matter. Historically, what is called

the freedom of religion safeguarded the first domain of private autonomy; the church itself continued its existence as one corporate body under public law among others. The corresponding polarization of princely power acquired visible form in the separation of the public budget from the private household property of the feudal lord. In the bureaucracy and the military (and in part also in the administration of justice), institutions of public power became autonomous vis-à-vis the privatized sphere of the princely court. In terms of the estates, finally, elements from the ruling groups developed into organs of public power, into parliament (and in part also into judicial organs); elements from the occupational status groups, insofar as they had become established in urban corporations and in certain differentiations within the estates of the land, developed into the sphere of bourgeois society, which would confront the state as a genuine domain of private autonomy.

Representative publicness gave way to the new sphere of "public power" that came into being with the national and territorial states. Ongoing state activity (permanent administration, a standing army) had its counterpart in the permanence of relationships that had developed in the meantime with the stock market and the press, through traffic in goods and news. Public power became consolidated as something tangible confronting those who were subject to it and who at first found themselves only negatively defined by it. These are the "private persons" who are excluded from public power because they hold no office. "Public" no longer refers to the representative court of a person vested with authority; instead, it now refers to the competence-regulated activity of an apparatus furnished with a monopoly on the legitimate use of force. As those to whom this public power is addressed, private persons subsumed under the state form the public.

As a private domain, society, which has come to confront the state, as it were, is on the one hand clearly differentiated from public power; on the other hand, society becomes a matter of public interest insofar as with the rise of a market economy the reproduction of life extends beyond the confines of private domestic power. The *bourgeois public sphere* can be understood as the sphere of private persons assembled to form a public. They soon began to make use of the public sphere of informational newspapers, which was officially regulated, against the public power itself, using those papers, along with the morally and critically oriented weeklies, to engage in debate about the general rules governing relations in their own essentially privatized but publicly relevant sphere of commodity exchange and labor.

The Liberal Model of the Public Sphere

The medium in which this debate takes place – public discussion – is unique and without historical prototype. Previously the estates had negotiated contracts with their princes in which claims to power were defined on a case-by-case basis. As we know, this development followed a different course in England, where princely power was relativized through parliament, than on the Continent, where the estates were mediatized by the monarch. The "third estate" then broke with this mode of equalizing power, for it could no longer establish itself as a ruling estate. Given a commercial economy, a division of authority accomplished through differentiation of the rights of those possessing feudal authority (liberties belonging to the estates) was no longer possible – the power under private law of disposition of capitalist property is nonpolitical. The bourgeois are private persons; as such, they do not "rule." Thus their claims to power in opposition to public power are directed not against a concentration of authority that should be "divided" but rather against the principle of established authority. The principle of control, namely publicness, that the bourgeois public opposes to the principle of established authority aims at a transformation of authority as such, not merely the exchange of one basis of legitimation for another.

In the first modern constitutions the sections listing basic rights provide an image of the liberal model of the public sphere: they guarantee society as a sphere of private autonomy; opposite it stands a public power limited to a few functions; between the two spheres, as it were, stands the domain of private persons who have come together to form a public and who, as citizens of the state, mediate the state with the needs of bourgeois society, in order, as the idea goes, to thus convert political authority to "rational" authority in the medium of this public sphere. Under the presuppositions of a society based on the free exchange of commodities, it seemed that the general interest, which served as the criterion by which this kind of rationality was to be evaluated, would be assured if the dealings of private persons in the marketplace were emancipated from social forces and their dealings

in the public sphere were emancipated from political coercion.

The political daily press came to have an important role during this same period. In the second half of the eighteenth century, serious competition to the older form of news writing as the compiling of items of information arose in the form of literary journalism. Karl Bücher describes the main outlines of this development: "From mere institutions for the publication of news, newspapers became the vehicles and guides of public opinion as well, weapons of party politics. The consequence of this for the internal organization of the newspaper enterprise was the insertion of a new function between the gathering of news and its publication: the editorial function. For the newspaper publisher, however, the significance of this development was that from a seller of new information he became a dealer in public opinion." Publishers provided the commercial basis for the newspaper without, however, commercializing it as such. The press remained an institution of the public itself, operating to provide and intensify public discussion, no longer a mere organ for the conveyance of information, but not yet a medium of consumer culture.

This type of press can be observed especially in revolutionary periods, when papers associated with the tiniest political coalitions and groups spring up, as in Paris in 1789. In the Paris of 1848 every halfway prominent politician still formed his own club, and every other one founded his own *journal*: over 450 clubs and more than 200 papers came into being there between February and May alone. Until the permanent legalization of a public sphere that functioned politically, the appearance of a political newspaper was equivalent to engagement in the struggle for a zone of freedom for public opinion, for publicness as a principle. Not until the establishment of the bourgeois constitutional state was a press engaged in the public use of reason relieved of the pressure of ideological viewpoints. Since then it has been able to abandon its polemical stance and take advantage of the earning potential of commercial activity. The ground was cleared for this development from a press of viewpoints to a commercial press at about the same time in England, France, and the United States, during the 1830s. In the course of this transformation from the journalism of writers who were private persons to the consumer services of the mass media, the sphere of publicness was changed by an influx of private interests that achieved privileged representation within it.

The Public Sphere in Mass Welfare-State Democracies

The liberal model of the public sphere remains instructive in regard to the normative claim embodied in institutionalized requirements of publicness; but it is not applicable to actual relationships within a mass democracy that is industrially advanced and constituted as a social-welfare state. In part, the liberal model had always contained ideological aspects; in part, the social presuppositions to which those aspects were linked have undergone fundamental changes. Even the forms in which the public sphere was manifested, forms which made its idea seem to a certain extent obvious, began to change with the Chartist movement in England and the February Revolution in France. With the spread of the press and propaganda, the public expanded beyond the confines of the bourgeoisie. Along with its social exclusivity the public lost the cohesion given it by institutions of convivial social intercourse and by a relatively high standard of education. Accordingly, conflicts which in the past were pushed off into the private sphere now enter the public sphere. Group needs, which cannot expect satisfaction from a self-regulating market, tend toward state regulation. The public sphere, which must now mediate these demands, becomes a field for competition among interests in the cruder form of forcible confrontation. Laws that have obviously originated under the "pressure of the streets" can scarcely continue to be understood in terms of a consensus achieved by private persons in public discussion; they correspond, in more or less undisguised form, to compromises between conflicting private interests. Today it is social organizations that act in relation to the state in the political public sphere, whether through the mediation of political parties or directly, in interplay with public administration. With the interlocking of the public and private domains, not only do political agencies take over certain functions in the sphere of commodity exchange and social labor; societal powers also take over political functions. This leads to a kind of "refeudalization" of the public sphere. Large-scale organizations strive for political compromises with the state and with one another, behind closed doors if possible; but at the same time they have to secure at least plebiscitarian approval from the mass of the population through the deployment of a staged form of publicity.

The political public sphere in the welfare state is characterized by a singular weakening of its critical functions. Whereas at one time publicness was intended to subject persons or things to the public use of reason and to make political decisions susceptible to revision before the tribunal of public opinion, today it has often enough already been enlisted in the aid of the secret policies of interest groups; in the form of "publicity" it now acquires public prestige for persons or things and renders them capable of acclamation in a climate of nonpublic opinion. The term "public relations" itself indicates how a public sphere that formerly emerged from the structure of society must now be produced circumstantially on a case-by-case basis. The central relationship of the public, political parties, and parliament is also affected by this change in function.

This existing trend towards the weakening of the public sphere, as a principle, is opposed, however, by a welfare-state transformation of the functioning of basic rights: the requirement of publicness is extended by state organs to all organizations acting in relation to the state. To the extent to which this becomes a reality, a no longer intact public of private persons acting as individuals would be replaced by a public of organized private persons. Under current circumstances, only the latter could participate effectively in a process of public communication using the channels of intra-party and intra-organizational public spheres, on the basis of a publicness enforced for the dealings of organizations with the state. It is in this process of public communication that the formation of political compromises would have to achieve legitimation. The idea of the public sphere itself, which signified a rationalization of authority in the medium of public discussions among private persons, and which has been preserved in mass welfare-state democracy, threatens to disintegrate with the structural transformation of the public sphere. Today it could be realized only on a different basis, as a rationalization of the exercise of social and political power under the mutual control of rival organizations committed to publicness in their internal structure as well as in their dealings with the state and with one another.

7

Procedural Democracy

Robert A. Dahl

If one makes certain minimal assumptions about a human association, I shall argue here, then one must also accept the reasonableness of certain criteria for evaluating how that association governs itself. These criteria specify democratic procedures, and an association that satisfied all of the criteria would be fully democratic in its procedures.

However, since their origins in classical Greece, democratic ideas have been plagued by the problem of inclusion: what persons have a rightful claim to be included as citizens with full and equal rights to participate in governing the association? My strategy will be to leave this problem initially unsolved in order to set out the assumptions and the criteria of procedural democracy. I shall then examine several well known solutions to the problem – those advanced by Schumpeter, Locke, Rousseau and Mill – and show that they are defective. I shall conclude by offering what seems to me a more satisfactory solution to the problem of inclusion.

I   Assumptions

Let me start by assuming that each of a number of persons has in mind the idea of forming an association for certain purposes, or changing an already existing association in order to adapt to conditions as they now understand them. Among other things, the association will have rules, or will make decisions about rules, that are to be binding on the members. Anyone to whom the rules apply is defined as a member. Thus being subject to the rules and decisions of the association is an essential characteristic of membership; it is sufficient to distinguish members from non-members.

Suppose one believes that the following assumptions are valid:

(A1)   There is a need among the members or putative members[1] for *binding decisions* on at least some matters, and so for a process that will eventuate in binding decisions on these matters.

This condition has two aspects. First, at least some of the purposes the members have in mind can be satisfactorily attained if and only if at least some members are influenced to act, or not to act, in certain ways.[2] Second, the actions necessary to these purposes can be brought about if, and only if, there exists a procedure by means of which the members, or some of them, can decide on a rule, policy, purpose, principle, act, or pattern of conduct with which members will be obliged to act consistently. The obligation to act consistently with the rule is imposed on *all* members in the sense that even when acts by particular members or offices are specified, all members are required not to act in such a way as to impede or prevent that particular act.

In order to bring about the acts they seek, rule makers might create an expectation that violators of the rule will be punished by officials. Conceiv-

Originally published in *Philosophy, Politics and Society*, 5th series, edited by P. Laslett and J. S. Fishkin (Oxford: Blackwell, 1979), pp. 97–133. Reprinted by permission of Blackwell Publishing Ltd.

ably, however, decisions might be binding without punishments by officials or other members. It might be enough to evoke an expectation of divine or magical sanctions. Or the mere process of enacting and announcing a rule might cause enough members to adopt it as a principle of conduct so as to produce a quite satisfactory level of compliance. In short, the need for binding decisions, and for procedures to bring them about, does not imply that the association is necessarily coercive, employs the threat of violent sanctions to bring about compliance, or possesses other characteristics that are often used to distinguish a state from other sorts of associations.

(A2) A process for making binding decisions ought to include at least two stages: setting the agenda and deciding the outcome.

Setting the agenda is the part of the process during which the matters are selected on which decisions are to be made (including a decision not to decide the matter). Deciding the outcome, or the *decisive stage*, is the time during which the process culminates in an outcome, signifying that a rule has definitely been adopted or rejected. If setting the agenda is, so to speak, the first say, the decisive stage is the last say, the final word, the controlling decision, the moment of sovereignty with respect to the matter at hand. Until the decisive stage is completed, the process of decision-making is tentative; it may lead to discussion, agreements, even outcomes of votes; but these are all preliminary, may be over-ruled at the decisive stage and are not binding on the members. Decisions are binding only at the conclusion of the decisive stage.

(A3) Binding decisions should be made only by members.

That is, no person who is not a member is properly qualified, in the broadest sense, to make, or participate in making, decisions that will be binding on members. I say nothing about the possible grounds for such a belief, which are many. It may be, for example, that the founders of the association have managed to include among the members everyone who is considered to be fully qualified, or everyone who must be included if the rule is to be useful, or everyone whose interests are affected. But other reasons would also suffice.

(A4) Equally valid claims justify equal shares.

That is, if the claims made on behalf of A,B,C...to an object of value, X, are judged to be equally valid, then any procedure for allocating X to A,B,C... must give equal regard to the claims of each.

Because this principle seems to have well-nigh universal acceptability, one might suspect that it is tautological. I think it falls just short of a tautology, but it is close enough to being so as to make its contradiction seem quite fundamentally arbitrary. Thus suppose that Christopher, Ann and Jane each claims the last piece of pie; they agree (or I hold) that their claims are equally valid; that is, there are no grounds for asserting that, say, Christopher's claims are superior to Ann's or Jane's; or that either Ann's or Jane's are better. Then they must also agree (or I must insist) that any procedure for allocating the piece of pie must give equal regard to the claims of each. The principle does not specify a particular procedure. Several procedures might therefore be thought to satisfy the principle equally well: The piece of pie might be divided equally among them, or awarded according to a random process, etc.

Even with the addition of this elementary principle of fairness, the conditions set out so far do not constitute grounds for asserting that an association ought to be governed by democratic procedures. If a single member were judged by all the others to be definitely more qualified than they to make decisions on all the matters which the association is to deal with, or if there were a graded hierarchy of competencies, then to say that the association ought to be governed by the one person, or by a graded hierarchy, would not be inconsistent with the judgement that all the preceding conditions also hold.

In order for democratic procedures to be required, it is sufficient to add one additional and highly crucial assumption:

(A5) The claims of a significant number of members as to the rules, policies, etc., to be adopted by binding decisions are valid and equally valid, taken all around, and no member's claims are, taken all around, superior or overriding in relation to the claims of this set of members.

This set of members I am going to call the demos. Members of the demos are citizens, though this usage is not meant to imply that they are necessarily citizens of a state.

A 'significant number' must, of course, be more than one member; otherwise democratic procedures would not be required nor could the procedures be democratic. What constitutes a sufficiently large number or proportion, however, has been an issue of great theoretical and practical importance. It is directly bound up with the question of whose claims are valid and equally valid. These issues are central to the problem of inclusion: what persons have a rightful claim to be included in the demos? Since this question is too important to be closed off merely by stipulation, I want to defer it for the time being. Meanwhile, the grounds that would properly justify having one's claims accepted as equally valid are not at issue here. I shall simply assume that one arrives at such a judgement somehow; whether the grounds are reasonable or unreasonable is not at this point a matter of concern. In this way a controversial issue in the history of democratic ideas and practices can be set aside for consideration later on.

II Criteria

Suppose, then, some collection of persons wish to form an association, and one believes that the five assumptions described above are valid with respect to this group. Then it is reasonable to hold that the procedures by which the demos is to arrive at its decisions ought to meet certain criteria, which I am going to call the criteria of procedural democracy.

When I say that the procedures ought to meet certain criteria, I mean that if one believes in the assumptions, then one must reasonably affirm the desirability of the criteria; conversely, to reject the criteria is in effect to deny that the assumptions apply.

One additional point. The criteria do not specify any *particular* procedure, such as majority rule. Specific procedures cannot be extracted from the criteria. The criteria are standards against which proposed procedures are to be evaluated. They do not eliminate all elements of judgement in evaluation. I think it should not be surprising that democratic theory, like most other normative theories, cannot furnish completely unambiguous answers in all concrete situations in which a choice has to be made between alternative proposals.

Political equality

First, all proposed procedures for making binding decisions must be evaluated according to *the criterion of political equality*. That is, the decision rule for determining outcomes at the decisive stage must take into account, and take equally into account, the expressed preferences of each member of the demos as to the outcome. The expression of preferences as to the outcome at the decisive stage is, of course, what we usually mean by 'voting' and 'a vote'; thus the criterion of political equality specifies that at the decisive stage each citizen has an equal vote.

To reject this criterion would be to deny at least one of two premises discussed earlier. Either equally valid claims do not justify equal shares, or it is not true that the claims of a significant number of members are valid and equally valid.

However, the criterion does not explicitly embody a particular method of voting or elections. It is not reducible solely to the principle of one man one vote, or to the principle that each citizen should have an equal vote in districts of equal numbers of voters, potential voters, or residents, or to a system of proportional representation based on equal votes. To adopt the criterion implies that specific procedures like these ought to be evaluated according to the extent to which they satisfy the conclusions. How preferences may best be expressed and what the specific rules should be for taking preferences into account, and equally into account, are questions requiring additional judgements; but procedures judged to meet the criterion better ought to be preferred over those that meet it worse. Obviously the requirement that the better be preferred to the worse holds even if all the procedures proposed are in some respects defective.

Nor does the criterion explicitly specify the majority principle. It requires only that the majority principle and alternatives to it be evaluated according to the criterion, and the solution that best meets the criterion of political equality be adopted. Whether majority voting is the best, or always the best, is thus left open.

Effective participation

The second criterion according to which all proposed procedures must be evaluated is the criterion of *effective participation*. According to this criterion, throughout the process of making binding decisions, one must have an adequate opportunity, and an equal opportunity, for expressing his or her preferences as to the final outcome. Thus citizens must have adequate and equal opportunities for placing questions on the agenda, and for expressing reasons for endorsing one outcome rather than another. For to deny any citizen adequate opportunities for effective participation means that their preferences cannot be known, or cannot be correctly known, and hence cannot be taken into account. And if some citizens have less opportunity than others, then their preferences as to the final outcome are less likely to be taken equally into account. But not to take their preferences as to the final outcome equally into account is to reject the criterion of political equality, and thus to deny the condition of roughly equal qualification, taken all around.

Any specific procedures, then, must be evaluated according to the adequacy of the opportunities they provide for, and the relative costs they impose on, expression and participation by the demos in making binding decisions. Other things being equal, procedures that meet the criteria better are to be preferred over those that meet it less well. Once again, the requirement that the better be chosen over the worse clearly applies even if all the options are thought to be imperfect in some respect. Thus having the agenda for the assembly determined by a council of 500, chosen by lot, as in classical Athens, would meet the criterion better than having the agenda set single-handedly by Pericles or Creon, even if the system of selection by lot involved some minor departures from a strictly random selection in which every citizen had an exactly equal chance of being selected.

I think it is consistent with historic usage to say that any association satisfying these two criteria is, at least to that extent, *procedurally democratic*. To put it somewhat formally, in order to leave room for some important distinctions to come, I want to call such an association *procedurally democratic* (or a *procedural democracy*) in a *narrow sense*. The criteria enable one to evaluate a large number of possible procedures. They are not decisive in cases where a procedure is better according to one criterion and worse by the other. Moreover, any evaluation would ordinarily require additional judgements about the facts of the particular situation, or about general tendencies and regularities of human behaviour and action. Nonetheless, the criteria are far from vacuous. Although I will not introduce a rigorous argument here, it would be hard to deny that procedures providing for decisions by a randomly selected sample of citizens would satisfy the criteria better than a procedure by which one citizen makes binding decisions for

all the rest, or that a voting scheme allocating one vote to each citizen would be better than a scheme in which some citizens had ten votes and others none. I do not mean to imply that judgements about alternatives like these could invariably result from a perfectly rigorous argument ending in a completely unassailable conclusion.

Enlightened understanding

As I have already suggested, judgements about the existence, composition, and boundaries of a demos are highly contestable. Thus one might simply challenge such judgements outright by asserting that some citizens are more qualified than the rest to make the decisions required. This objection of course raises a fundamental challenge to procedural democracy and is generally a premise in a counter-argument for aristocracy, meritocracy, or rule by a qualified elite. It is not this fundamental objection that I wish to consider at the moment, but rather a second kind of objection which might run rather like this:

> I agree – the objector might say – that the citizens are equally well qualified, taken all around. I agree also that none among them, or among the other members, or among non-members are so definitely better qualified as to warrant their making the decisions instead of the demos. Yet for all that, I think the citizens are not as well qualified as they might be. They make mistakes about the means to the ends they want; they also choose ends they would reject if they were more enlightened. I agree then that they ought to govern themselves by procedures that are satisfactory according to the criteria of procedural democracy, narrowly defined. Yet a number of different procedures will satisfy the criteria about equally well; among these, however, some are more likely to lead to a more enlightened demos – and thus to better decisions – than others. Surely these are better procedures, and ought to be chosen over the others.

One might object, I suppose, that enlightenment has nothing to do with democracy. But I think this would be a foolish and historically false assertion. It is foolish because democracy has usually been conceived as a system in which 'rule by the people' makes it more likely that 'the people' will get what it wants, or what it believes is best, than alternative systems, like aristocracy, in which an elite determines what is best. But to know what it wants, or what is best, the people must be enlightened, at least to some degree. And because advocates of democracy have invariably recognized this, and placed great stress on the means to an informed and enlightened demos, such as education and public discussion, the objection is also historically false.

I propose therefore to amplify the doctrine of procedural democracy by adding a third criterion. Unfortunately, I do not know how to formulate the criterion except in words that are rich in meaning and correspondingly ambiguous. Let me, however, offer this formulation for *the criterion of enlightened understanding*:

> In order to express his or her preferences accurately, each citizen ought to have adequate and equal opportunities for discovering and validating, in the time permitted by the need for a decision, what his or her preferences are on the matter to be decided.

This criterion implies, then, that alternative procedures for making decisions ought to be evaluated according to the opportunities they furnish citizens for acquiring an understanding of means and ends, and of oneself and other relevant selves. Yet if the criterion is accepted, ambiguous as it may be, I think it would be hard to justify procedures that cut off or suppressed information which, were it available, might well cause citizens to arrive at a different decision; or gave some citizens much easier access than others to information of crucial importance; or presented citizens with an agenda of decisions that had to be decided without discussion, though time was available; and so on. To be sure, these may look like easy cases; but a great many political systems – perhaps most – operate according to the worse not the better procedures.

Control of the agenda

If an association were to satisfy all three criteria, it could properly be regarded as a *full procedural democracy with respect to its agenda* and *in relation to its demos*. The criteria are to be understood as aspects of the best possible political system, from a democratic point of view; while no actual system could be expected to satisfy the criteria perfectly, systems could be judged more democratic or less,

and to that extent better or worse, according to how nearly they meet the criteria.

Yet to say that a system is governed by fully democratic procedures 'with respect to an agenda' and 'in relation to a demos' suggests the possibility that the three criteria are incomplete. The two qualifying clauses imply the possibility of restrictions – of democratic decision-making processes limited to a narrow agenda, or responsive to a highly exclusive demos, or both. To judge whether a demos is appropriately inclusive and exercises control over an appropriate agenda evidently requires additional standards. The catch is that the condition of equal qualification is of indefinite range: it need apply only to certain matters or to some members of an association. Obviously, to say that some persons are sufficiently well qualified to govern themselves on some matters is not to say that all persons are sufficiently competent to govern themselves on all matters.

Thus the conditions set out earlier are no longer sufficient for generating the additional criteria we need. To remedy this defect in the conditions, I now propose a change of strategy. I shall propose a fourth criterion, and show what sort of judgement as to equality would impose this criterion.

In order to see more clearly why a fourth criterion is needed, let us suppose that Philip of Macedon, having defeated the Athenians at Chaeronea, deprives the Athenian assembly of the authority to make any decisions on matters of foreign and military policy. The citizens continue to assemble some forty times a year and decide on many matters; but on some of the most important questions they must remain silent. With respect to 'local' matters, the Athenian polis is no less democratic than before; but with respect to foreign and military affairs, the Athenians are now governed hierarchically by Philip or his minions.

Again: let us imagine that during the Nazi occupation of Norway, Hitler had allowed the Norwegians to use their democratic political institutions for one or two matters – driving speeds for civilian traffic, let us say – but nothing else. If the Norwegians had gone along with this arrangement, we might conclude that while they had retained some nominal degree of 'democracy', in a broad sense they had lost it. Save for one subject of minor importance, Norwegians would be denied the opportunity to make binding decisions on the matters they felt important and fully qualified to decide for themselves. If we were to take as valid their own judgement as to their competence, then we must also hold that the criteria of procedural democracy ought to apply to all the questions they feel are important and not merely to trivial matters. For to say that some persons outside the demos should be able to prevent the demos from deciding for itself which questions it wishes to put on the agenda of things to be decided according to the criteria of procedural democracy is to deny at least one of the original premises: binding decisions ought to be made only by members, equally valid claims justify equal shares, and no member's claims are, taken all around, superior or overriding in relation to the claims of the demos.

These considerations suggest an additional criterion, *final control of the agenda by the demos*:

> The demos must have the exclusive opportunity to make decisions that determine what matters are and are not to be decided by means of procedural democracy.

The criterion of final control is perhaps what is also meant when we say that in a democracy the people must have the final say, or must be sovereign. A system that satisfies this criterion as well as the other three could be regarded as *a full procedural democracy in relation to its demos*.

According to this criterion, a political system would be procedurally democratic even if the demos decided that it would not make every decision on every matter, but instead chose to have some decisions on some matters made, say, in a hierarchical fashion by judges or administrators. As long as the demos could effectively retrieve any matter for decision by itself, the criterion would be met. In this respect, then, the doctrine of procedural democracy allows more latitude for delegation of decision-making than would be permissible by Rousseau's eccentric definition of democracy in the *Social Contract*. By defining democracy so as to make delegation impermissible, Rousseau could hardly avoid concluding, as he did, that democracy (in his sense) would be impossible among human beings, though perhaps satisfactory for gods.

Thus the criterion of final control does not presuppose a judgement that the demos is qualified to decide *every* question requiring a binding decision. It does presuppose a judgement that the demos is qualified to decide (1) which matters do or do not require binding decisions, (2) of those that do, which matters the demos is qualified to decide for itself, and (3) the terms on which the

demos delegates authority. To accept the criterion as appropriate is therefore to imply that the demos is the best judge of its own competence and limits. Consequently, to say that certain matters ought to be placed beyond the final reach of the demos – in the sense that the demos ought to be prohibited from dealing with them at all – is to say that on these matters the demos is not qualified to judge its own competence and limits.

Let me now phrase our revised assumption as follows:

> **(A5.1)** *The Full Condition of Equal Qualification*. With respect to all matters, citizens are qualified, and equally well qualified, taken all around, to decide which matters do or do not require binding decisions; of those that do, which matters the demos is qualified to decide for itself; and the terms on which the demos delegates authority.

By *delegation* I mean a revocable grant of authority, subject to recovery by the demos. Empirically, of course, the boundaries between delegation and alienation are not always sharp, and what begins as delegation might end as alienation. But the theoretical distinction is nonetheless crucial.

In a system of full procedural democracy decisions about delegation would be made according to democratic procedures. But alienation would clearly violate the criterion of final control, and would be inconsistent with the judgement that the full condition of equal qualification existed among a demos.[3]

The criterion of final control completes the requirements for full procedural democracy in relation to a demos. If all the members of some set of persons are judged equally qualified, in the full sense, and if the other conditions set out earlier are held to exist among them, then the procedures according to which these persons, the demos, make binding decisions ought to be evaluated according to the four criteria. If citizens were reasonable, they would select the procedures that best meet the criteria.

III The Problem of Inclusion

The criteria of procedural democracy assume the existence of a demos of qualified citizens. However, neither the existence of a demos nor the scope of its competence can be settled satisfactorily merely by assumption. Any specific claim of either kind would surely be highly contestable. Thus the assumptions have allowed me to by-pass two interrelated problems:

1. The problem of inclusion: What persons have a rightful claim to be included in the demos?
2. The scope of its authority. What rightful limits are there on the control of a demos? Is alienation ever permissible?

Finding solutions is particularly difficult for two reasons. First, not only is it hard to find much direct confrontation with these problems by democratic theorists, but political and moral theory is typically expressed in universalistic terms – 'all men', 'all persons' – that belie the need for boundaries even as the theory prescribes limits on conduct. Second, the two problems are interdependent; a solution to one seems to depend on a solution to the other.

Thus the extent to which a particular demos ought to have final control over the agenda evidently depends on a prior judgement as to the scope of matters which the demos is qualified to decide. In this sense, judgements as to the scope of the agenda and the composition of the demos are interdependent. A judgement as to the competence of the demos bears on the scope of its agenda; and the nature of an agenda bears on a judgement as to the composition of the demos. The demos being given, the scope of its agenda can be determined. The scope of an agenda being given, the composition of an appropriate demos to make decisions on those matters can be determined. But in principle the one cannot be determined independently of the other.

In this essay, however, I intend to explore only the first problem. I shall argue that we cannot successfully deal with it without directly meeting the question of competence and openly confronting the view that a meritorious elite of exceptional knowledge and virtue ought to govern. This rival idea, which the Greeks called aristocracy and I shall call meritocracy, seems to me to constitute the greatest challenge to democracy, both historically and in the present world. I shall show that insofar as democratic theorists like Locke and Rousseau evaded taking direct and explicit issue with the challenge of meritocracy, they allowed a lethal defect to remain in the foundations of democratic ideas.

What properly constitutes a demos? Who must be included in a properly constituted demos, and who may or must be excluded from it?

The question of inclusion in (or exclusion from) the demos would scarcely present a serious challenge if a demos could enact rules that were binding only on itself. In that case, an outsider might still argue that a demos was acting unwisely or unjustly toward itself; but this would hardly give the outsider a justifiable claim to be included. Some associations do escape the problem in this way. The rules of an association might be binding only on its demos, either because all members of the association are also citizens, in which case the association is fully inclusive, or because every member is free to leave the association at any time with no great difficulty, in which case a member who objects to a rule can simply escape the application of the rule by withdrawing from the association.

It is by no means true of every association, however, that its demos can enact rules that are binding only on itself. A trade union might enforce a rule preventing non-members from working at a particular trade or workplace. An even more obvious and certainly more important exception is of course the state. Even if a state met all four of the criteria for procedural democracy and thus were a full procedural democracy in relation to its citizens, it could enact laws that were enforceable against persons who were not citizens, did not have the right to participate in making the laws, and had not given their consent either explicitly or implicitly to the laws they were forced to obey. Indeed every state has done so in the past, and there are grounds for thinking that all states will continue to do so in the future.

If some persons are excluded from the demos of a state, and yet are compelled to obey its laws, do they have a justifiable claim to be included in the demos or else to be excluded from the domain of enforcement? How inclusive should the demos be? Are there criteria for judging when, if ever, exclusion is rightful or inclusion is obligatory?

Citizenship as wholly contingent

One response is that the grounds for deciding who ought to be included in a demos are inherently particularistic and historical, often indeed primordial, and cannot be set forth as general principles. Thus citizenship is wholly contingent on circumstances that cannot be specified in advance. This is Schumpeter's solution.

Although democratic ideas often yield rather ambiguous answers to the question of inclusion,

Schumpeter was an exception. It is an 'inescapable conclusion', he asserted, that we must 'leave it to every populus to define himself' [sic]. He rested his argument on an incontestable historical fact: what had been thought and legally held to constitute a 'people' has varied enormously, even among 'democratic' countries. What is more, there are no grounds for rejecting any exclusion whatsoever as improper: 'it is not relevant whether we, the observers, admit the validity of those reasons or of the practical rules by which they are made to exclude portions of the population; all that matters is that the society in question admits it.' He pressed his argument relentlessly. The exclusion of Blacks in the American South does not allow us to say that the South was undemocratic. The rule of the 'Bolshevik party' in the Soviet Union 'would not *per se* entitle us to call the Soviet Republic undemocratic. We are entitled to call it so only if the Bolshevik party itself is managed in an undemocratic manner – as obviously it is.'[4]

The last two examples beautifully illustrate the absurdities to which we may be led by the absence of any criterion for defining the *demos*. It is undeniable that in the United States, southern Blacks were excluded from the *demos*. But surely *to that extent* the South was undemocratic: *undemocratic in relation to its Black population*. Suppose that in the South, as in Rhodesia or South Africa, Blacks had been a preponderant majority of the population. Would Schumpeter still have said that the Southern states were 'democratic'? Is there not some number or proportion of a population below which a 'people' is not a demos but rather an aristocracy, oligarchy, or despotism? If the rulers numbered 100 in a population of 100 million, would we call the rulers a demos and the system a democracy? On Schumpeter's argument, Britain was already a 'democracy' by the end of the eighteenth century – even though only one adult in twenty could vote.

Consider the monumental implications of the second example, in which Schumpeter asserts that 'the Soviet Republic' would be a democracy if only the ruling party itself were internally democratic. Schumpeter imposes no minimum limits on the relative size of the party. Suppose it were one per cent of the population? Or suppose that the Politburo were internally democratic, and ruled the party, which ruled over the State, which ruled over the people. Then the members of the Politburo would constitute the Soviet *populus*, and the Soviet State would be, on Schumpeter's interpretation, a democracy.

His definition thus leaves us with no particular reason for wanting to know whether a system is 'democratic' or not. Indeed, if a demos can be a tiny group that exercises a brutal despotism over a vast subject population, then 'democracy' is conceptually, morally, and empirically indistinguishable from autocracy. Thus Schumpeter's solution is truly no solution at all, for its upshot is that there are simply no principles for judging whether anyone is unjustly excluded from citizenship. But the argument leads, as we have seen, to absurdities.

These consequences follow because Schumpeter failed to distinguish, indeed insisted on conflating, two different kinds of propositions:

System X is democratic in relation to its own demos.

System Y is democratic in relation to everyone subject to its rules.

Perhaps because he was convinced by historical experience that no state like Y had ever existed or was likely to, he felt that any 'realistic' theory of democracy, such as he proposed, could scarcely require that a 'democracy' be a system like Y. For if this requirement were imposed, then no democratic state would, or probably ever could, exist. But by carrying historicism and moral relativism to their limits, he obliterated the possibility of any useful distinction between democracy, aristocracy, oligarchy and one-party dictatorship.

Citizenship as a categorical right

Schumpeter's solution, or rather non-solution, was to allow a demos to draw any line it chooses between itself and other members. Suppose instead that one were to insist that no one subject to the rules of the demos should be excluded from the demos. Then the demos and the members (in the language used here) would be identical.

It is possible to interpret Locke, Rousseau, and a long succession of writers they influenced as advancing a solution along these lines.[5] The argument is grounded on the moral axiom that no person ought to be governed without his consent, or, with Rousseau, required to obey laws that are not of his own making in some genuine sense. In developing the argument writers have found it useful to distinguish between the initial act of forming the polity, (society, association, community, city, or state) and the subsequent process of making and enforcing the rules of the polity. Thus both Locke and Rousseau held that the initial formation required the agreement of everyone who has to be subject to it; thereafter, however, laws could be enacted and enforced if they were endorsed by a majority. Both sought to explain why, even though unanimity is required in the first instance, thereafter a majority is sufficient. I wish to ignore this question, for my concern here is a different one: in speaking of agreement by 'all' or a 'majority', what is the collection of persons to which they refer? Does 'the consent of every individual' and 'the determination of the *majority*' of such individuals[6] literally refer to *every* member, in the sense that a majority must be *a majority of every person subject to the laws?*

Clearly, neither Locke nor Rousseau meant to imply this conclusion. To begin with, children are of course to be excluded from the demos. The exclusion of children from the demos is so often taken as unproblematical that one hardly notices how much the claim to citizenship based on categorical right is embarrassed by this simple exclusion: for it is made on the grounds that children are not competent to govern themselves or the community. Yet if we permit the exclusion of children from the demos (and who seriously does not?) then we allow a contingent element, based on qualifications for governing, to limit the universality of the claim based on categorical right. Never mind; let us momentarily ignore this embarrassment, though I intend to return to it.

Suppose, then, that the claim based on a categorical right is revised to read: all *adults* subject to the laws of a state should be members of the demos of that state. Citizenship is no longer fully coextensive with membership; but all adult members are citizens by categorical right. Did Rousseau and Locke mean to justify such a claim?

Certainly Rousseau did not, though it is easy to see why the *Social Contract* is sometimes understood as saying so. There Rousseau occasionally appears to be asserting an unqualified right to membership in the demos.[7] But Rousseau makes it clear that he means no such thing. Thus he lauds Geneva, even though its demos consisted of only a small minority of the population. Children were, of course, excluded. But so too were women. What is more, a majority of adult males were also excluded from the Genevan demos. Rousseau was well aware of these exclusions. Yet he neither condemned them as inconsistent with his principles, nor provided grounds on which they might be justified. Rather, he seems simply to have taken them for granted.

Rousseau may, in fact, have anticipated Schumpeter's solution. In arguing that it is wrong to take the government of Venice as an instance of true aristocracy, he remarks that although the ordinary people in Venice have no part in the government, there the nobility takes the place of the people. This is Schumpeter's populus defining itself. Rousseau then goes on to show that Venice and Geneva are truly alike. Thus the government of Venice is actually no more aristocratic than that of Geneva! (Book IV, Chapter 3).

What Rousseau does not feel it important to say is that in both cities the great bulk of the people subject to the laws were not only excluded from the execution and administration of the laws (the *government*, in Rousseau's terminology) but also from any participation in *making* the laws. In neither republic were the people – that is, most people – entitled to assemble in order to vote on the laws, or even to vote for representatives who would make the laws. In both cities, most people were thus subject to laws which they had no part in making.[8] One might conclude that neither republic could be legitimate in Rousseau's eyes. But this was not his conclusion, nor did he even hint at such an inference.

What Rousseau seems to have assumed, as other advocates of democracy had done since the Greek city states of antiquity, is that a large number of persons in any republic – children, women, foreigners and many male adult residents – will be subjects but are not qualified to be citizens. In this way, Rousseau himself undermined the categorical principle of inclusion that he appeared to set forth in the *Social Contract*.

Locke's language in *The Second Treatise* is as categorical and universalistic as Rousseau's, if not more so.[9] Yet his apparent assertion of an unqualified and categorical claim was limited both explicitly and implicitly by a requirement as to competence. Naturally, children were excluded; I shall return later to Locke's argument on 'paternal power'. It is highly doubtful that he meant women to be included as a matter of right.[10] As to adult males, he explicitly excluded 'lunatics and idiots [who] are never set free from the government of their parents.'[11] In addition, 'slaves, . . . being captives taken in a just war, are by the right of nature subjected to the absolute dominion and arbitrary power of their masters.' He probably intended to exclude servants as well.[12] Thus a claim to citizenship was not categorical but, as it turns out, contingent on a judgement as to the relative qualifications of a person for participating in the government of the commonwealth. Like Rousseau, Locke torpedoed his own view (if indeed it was his view) that every person subject to the laws made by the demos possesses a categorical and unqualified right to membership in the demos.

Citizenship as contingent on competence

Locke and Rousseau appear to have advanced two different principles on which a claim to citizenship might be grounded. One is explicit, categorical and universal; the other is implicit, contingent and limiting:

- *Categorical Principle*: Every person subject to a government and its laws has an unqualified right to be a member of the demos (i.e., a citizen).
- *Contingent Principle*: Only persons who are qualified to govern, but all such persons, should be members of the demos (i.e., citizens).

If some persons subject to the laws are not qualified to govern, then obviously the two principles lead to contradictory conclusions. Which principle should take precedence? As we have seen, Locke and Rousseau held, at least implicitly, that the second principle takes precedence over the first.

What was only or mainly implicit in the arguments of Locke and Rousseau was made explicit by John Stuart Mill. Mill openly confronted the conflict he believed to exist between the two principles. Like his predecessors he also insisted that in case of conflict the first must give way to the second.

To be sure, on a careless reading Mill could be interpreted as favouring the categorical principle.[13] Yet although on casual inspection his language has a universalistic tone, in fact Mill does not endorse a categorical principle of general inclusion. It is hardly surprising that he argues, not from principles of right, but rather from considerations of social utility. His judgements are meant to reflect a balancing of social utilities and disutilities. And while his argument is powerful, it does not lead him to a categorical principle but to a contingent and contestable judgement about social utility. If the question is one of social utility, however, then relative competence is also a factor to be weighed.

As every reader of *Representative Government* soon discovers, it was Mill himself who undermined his own argument for universal inclusion by posing a counterargument based on considerations of competence. In the course of his discussion, he gave explicit and careful recognition that the criterion of competence must take priority over any principle, whether categorical or utilitarian, that makes inclusion in the demos a matter of general right among all adults subject to the laws. At a minimum, he argued, to demonstrate that persons are qualified to engage in governing requires a showing that they have 'acquired the commonest and most essential requisites for taking care of themselves, for pursuing intelligently their own interests and those of the persons most nearly allied to them.' It was Mill's judgement that in the England of his day, many categories of adults could not meet this standard and ought therefore to be denied the suffrage until they acquired the competence they at that time lacked.[14]

By giving priority to the criterion of competence, recognizing the contingent and socially specific nature of judgements about competence, and accepting a restricted demos as the consequence of his own judgement as to the qualifications of fellow Englishmen, Mill brought into the open a problem that has been glossed over by some of his most illustrious predecessors. Yet in justifying an exclusionary demos Mill did no more than to make explicit what had generally been implicit in all previous democratic theory and practice.

The formal opportunities for participation available to citizens in the democratic city-states of Greece, the universalistic language in which democratic beliefs are often presented, and the emphasis on participation by Rousseau and Mill have induced some writers to interpret 'classical' democratic ideas as much less 'elitist' than they actually were.[15]

In classical Athens itself, the demos could hardly have consisted of more than a third of the free adults, a sixth of all free persons, and a seventh – or less – of the total population. In relation to its own demos, the Athenians may have come about as close as any people to procedural democracy, and possibly a good deal closer than any modern state. But the fact is that the Athenian demos, as a modern admirer rather nonchalantly admits, was 'a minority elite'.[16]

One might choose to dismiss these limits as transitory deficiencies in a revolutionary new political idea which transcended the historical limits of actual practice. But as we have seen, Locke and Rousseau accepted, and Mill defended, the principle that a demos might properly exclude large numbers of adults who are subject to laws made by the demos. Thus the attempt to ground 'participatory democracy' on Mill and his predecessors is fatally flawed. Participation indeed. But only for the qualified! And in principle the qualified might be a tiny minority. Thus it is not only Schumpeter's solution that would permit the demos to shrink into a ruling elite. Rousseau himself, as we saw, regarded Geneva and Venice both as true republics, governed 'by the people', even though in both cities the demos constituted a minority of the adults: in Venice about one-tenth of one per cent of the population!

Modern admirers of 'classical' democratic ideas seem to have reversed the relation between citizenship and competence as it was generally understood from the Greeks to Mill. In the 'classical' perspective not every adult, much less every person, was necessarily qualified to govern and thus to enter into the demos. Rather, the demos consisted of all those who *were* qualified to govern. It was precisely because citizens were a qualified minority of the whole people that they were entitled to govern and could on the whole be counted on to govern well.

As a consequence, 'classical' ideas leave the intellectual defence of procedural democracy lethally vulnerable. Consider the standing of the case for procedural democracy if the criterion of competence is given priority over a categorical and universal principle of right.

If everyone subject to law has a categorical right to participate in the process of making laws, if the requirement of consent is universal and uncontestable, then the case for democracy is very powerful and the case against exclusionary alternatives – aristocracy, meritocracy, rule by a qualified elite, monarchy, dictatorship, and so on – is correspondingly weakened. If the claim to citizenship is a categorical and universal right of all human beings, then among any human group a demos always exists and that demos must always be inclusive. To put it in another way, among any body of persons who wish to establish or maintain an association having a government capable of making binding decisions, the conditions of equal qualification, the most crucial of the conditions for procedural democracy set forth earlier, must necessarily exist.

But if the criterion of competence overrides a claim based on rights, then the argument for dem-

ocracy rests on mushy grounds. Citizenship depends on contingent judgements, not categorical rights. And the contingent judgements need not lead to universal inclusion. Indeed, as we have seen, the boundaries between democracy on the one side and meritocracy on the other become fuzzy and indeterminate. The arguments for the one or the other become indistinguishable except for a crucial judgement as to the relative magnitude of the competent members, the citizenry or ruling group.

IV   Towards a Criterion of Inclusiveness

Three questions arise: First, is it possible to get around the principle of competence in deciding on the inclusiveness of the demos? Second, if not, is it possible to avoid the contingent and contestable nature of a judgement as to competence? Third, if again not, can we develop strong criteria that such a judgement ought to satisfy?

That we cannot get round the principle of competence in deciding on the inclusiveness of the demos is decisively demonstrated by the exclusion of children. It is virtually never argued, no doubt because it would be so obviously untenable to do so, that children either must be members of the state's demos, or else ought not to be subject to laws made by the demos. So far as I am aware, no one seriously contends that children should be full members of the state's demos. An eight-year-old child can hardly be enlightened enough to participate equally with adults in deciding on laws to be enforced by the government of the state. Yet these laws are enforced on children – without their explicit or implied consent. It is often held – and legal systems tend to reflect the force of the argument – that because of their limited competence children should not be subject to exactly the same laws as adults; they cannot, for example, enter into legally enforceable contracts. Yet they are not wholly exempt from the enforcement of all laws.

Children therefore furnish us with a clear instance of violation of the principle that a government must rest on the consent of the governed, or that no one should be subject to a law not of one's own choosing, or subject to a law made by an association not of one's own choosing. Yet this violation is nearly always taken for granted; or else it is interpreted as not actually a violation. One way of interpreting it is to say that the principle of consent applies only to adults. But this is to admit that some persons who are subject to the rules of a state can nevertheless be properly excluded from the demos of the state.

On what grounds? The only defensible ground on which to exclude children from the demos is that they are not yet fully capable of the 'exercise of reason', to use the common phrase. The need to exclude children on this ground was of course perfectly obvious to early democratic theorists. Locke devotes a whole chapter to Paternal Power. After reminding us of 'that equal right that every man hath to his natural freedom, without being subject to the will or authority of any other man', he immediately turns to the exceptions, of which children are the most numerous, obvious and important.[17]

The example of children is sufficient to show that the criterion of competence cannot reasonably be evaded, that any reasonable bounding of a demos must, by excluding children, necessarily exclude a large body of persons subject to the laws, and that any assertion of a universal right of *all* persons to membership in a demos cannot be sustained. It might be argued, however, that children constitute a comparatively well-defined and unique exception.[18] Thus once a distinction is allowed between children and adults, all *adults* subject to the laws must be included. The categorical principle might then be re-stated as follows:

> *Modified Categorical Principle*: Every adult subject to a government and its laws must be presumed to be qualified as, and has an unqualified right to be, a member of the demos.

There are, however, at least two sources of difficulty with the modified categorical principle. First, the boundary between childhood and adulthood is itself something of a difficulty. There is the well known arbitrariness of imposing a dichotomy – child/adult – on what is clearly a continuous process of development; we may reasonably disagree about whether one becomes qualified at 21, or 18, or whatever. There are also the troublesome cases for which experience, even when joined with compassion, points to no clear solution. As Locke put it:

> ... if, through defects that may happen out of ordinary course of nature, any one comes not to such a degree of Reason wherein he might be supposed capable of knowing the Law, and so

living within the rules of it, he is never capable of being a Free Man, ... but is continued under the Tuition and Government of others all the time his own understanding is incapable of that charge. And so Lunatics and Idiots are never set free from the government of their Parents...[19]

Thus the modified categorical principle runs the risk of circularity by defining 'adult' as persons who are presumed to be qualified to govern.

A second source of difficulty with the modified principle is caused by the presence in a country of foreigners who might be adult by any reasonable standards, who are subject to the laws of the country in which they temporarily reside, but who are not thereby qualified to participate in governing.

Suppose that France is holding an election on Sunday and I, an American, arrive in Paris on Saturday as a tourist. Would anyone argue that I should be entitled to participate in the election – much less acquire all the other political rights of French citizenship? I think not. On what grounds could I properly be excluded? On the ground that I am unqualified.[20]

To sum up:

1. Schumpeter's solution to the problem of the composition of the demos is unacceptable because it effectively erases the distinction between democracy and a non-democratic order dominated by a collegial elite.

2. A categorical principle of inclusion that overrides the need for a judgement as to competence is also unacceptable, for it is rendered untenable by such cases as children, feeble-minded persons and foreigners of temporary residence. In so far as Locke and Rousseau advanced a categorical principle, their defence of it is unconvincing. However, evidence suggests that they recognized these objections and never intended their argument to be taken as a rejection of the priority of a criterion of competence.

3. Because a judgement as to competence is contingent on weighing evidence and making inferences as to the intellectual and moral qualifications of specific categories of persons, a decision based on competence is inherently open to question. To be sure, a reasonable argument may be presented on behalf of a particular judgement as to the proper boundaries of inclusion and exclusion. But the exact location of any boundary is necessarily a highly debatable judgement. Thus Mill presented persuasive reasons to justify the particu-

lar exclusions he advocated; yet probably few contemporary democrats would accept his exclusions as reasonable.

In short, if Schumpeter's solution leads to absurdities, those found in earlier democratic ideas, whether in classical antiquity or in the works of early modern theorists like Locke, Rousseau and Mill, provide all too fragile a foundation for the doctrine of procedural democracy. Even though we must accept the need for, and the contingent and contestable nature of a judgement as to competence, we are in need of further criteria that will help to reduce the arbitrariness of such a judgement.

Further requirements

I now want to argue that a reasonable criterion of inclusion in a system of procedural democracy in relation to its demos must pass three tests. At the outset, a criterion of inclusion must satisfy the general principle of fairness that constitutes one of the conditions of procedural democracy: equally valid claims justify equal shares. Consequently if C_a is a citizen, and if another member, M, is about as well qualified as C_a, then either M must be included in the demos or C_a must be excluded from it. If C_a is excluded, then the same test must be applied in comparing the claims of C_a with any other citizen, C_i. And so on, until a fair boundary can be staked out.

Assuming that a boundary of inclusion and exclusion meets the general principle of fairness, several additional tests may reasonably be required. The reasonableness of these tests rests, however, on two additional principles, which I shall refer to as *equal consideration* and *burden of proof*. I do not propose to consider whether or how these principles might be derived from antecedent considerations. Although the burden of proof principle reflects a judgement as to human experience, I doubt whether it is wholly verifiable, at least as a practical matter. And the principle of equal consideration is a moral orientation so fundamental that it is hard to see how one might go about the task of demonstrating its validity to an adversary. Fortunately, the principle itself is widely accepted. I want to introduce it initially as a principle of universal application and then narrow it to include only the members of the association.

Equal consideration (universal inclusion). No distribution of socially allocated entities,

whether actions, forebearances, or objects, is acceptable if it violates the principle that the good or interest of each human being is entitled to equal consideration.[21]

The principle does not depend on an assumption as to whether one's good is distinguished from one's interests, or whether 'good' or 'interest' refer to want-regarding or ideal-regarding principles.[22] It simply asserts that the good or interest of each person, whatever they may be, ought to be given equal consideration in social allocations. If A and B are human beings, if some entity X is socially allocated, if X is equally beneficial to A and to B and if no benefits to others need to be taken into account, then the principle holds that there are no grounds for upholding a claim that X ought to go to A rather than B, or B rather than A. Whatever principle of distribution is adopted, it must not incorporate a bias toward either A or B. Thus if X is indivisible, the most appropriate solution might be to toss a coin. But to claim that because A is stronger than B or A has discovered X first, then A ought to have X, would not be acceptable.

To universalize the principle of equal consideration, however, poses a host of theoretical and practical problems that I do not wish to deal with here. Moreover, universality is not necessary in order to arrive at a reasonable solution to the problem of the composition of the demos. A much less inclusive version applying only to the *members* will prove satisfactory.

Equal Consideration for all members: No distribution of socially allocated entities, whether actions, forbearances, or objects, is acceptable if it violates the principle that the good or interest of each member is entitled to equal consideration.

If one accepts the principle of equal consideration of all members, then of course one must also hold that a criterion of inclusion is unacceptable if it violates this principle. However, the import of the principle is further amplified by an additional assumption that also reflects a widely held though not strictly universal judgement:

Burden of Proof: In the absence of a compelling showing to the contrary everyone is assumed to be the best judge of his or her own good or interests. Thus if A holds that her good consists of X, not Y, and B insists that A's good consists of Y, not X, then A's judgement is to be accepted unless the validity of B's judgement can be satisfactorily demonstrated.[23]

For any given member, M, an association that meets the criteria of procedural democracy in relation to its demos can satisfy the principle of equal consideration in one of two ways. M may be a citizen; that is, M is already included in the demos, in which case equal consideration is insured by procedural democracy. Alternatively, if M is excluded from the demos the principle of equal consideration can be satisfied if, but only if, the citizens give as much consideration to M's good or interest as to their own. However, the demos cannot reasonably be expected to give equal consideration to M unless (1) it *knows* at least as much about M's good as about its own, and (2) it will in fact *act* on this knowledge in such a way as to give equal consideration to M's good or interests. But the burden of proof principle requires a compelling showing that the demos definitely is a better judge than M as to M's own interests. The second test that M's exclusion must meet is precisely such a showing.

If the second test is met satisfactorily, M's exclusion will still violate the principle of equal consideration if the demos cannot reasonably be expected to *act* so as to give equal consideration to M. Thus, given the burden of proof, a positive showing is necessary that the demos has in fact given equal consideration to M's interests in the past and will continue to do so in the future; or, though it has neglected M's good in the past, there are nevertheless compelling reasons for believing that the demos has recently changed in this respect, or is about to change and will care equally for M's good in the future.

The arguments used in the past to justify the exclusions from full citizenship in the state of various categories of adults – the unpropertied, women, racial minorities, for example – would, I think, fail to meet these three tests. Experience has shown that any group of adults excluded from the demos will be lethally weakened in its own defence; and an exclusive demos will fail to protect the interests of those who are excluded.

We need not suppose that when power resides in an exclusive class, that class will knowingly and deliberately sacrifice the other classes to themselves; it suffices that, in the absence of its

natural defenders, the interest of the excluded is always in danger of being over-looked, and, when looked at, is seen with very different eyes from those of the persons whom it directly concerns.[24]

Mill was surely right. In rejecting the conclusion his own premises pointed to – the enfranchisement of the working classes – Mill's justification failed all three tests. 'Universal teaching must precede universal enfranchisement', he wrote. But it was not until *after* the extension of the suffrage in 1868 that Parliament passed the first act establishing public elementary schools. The historical record since then demonstrates even more fully that when a large class of adults is excluded from citizenship their interests will almost certainly not be given equal consideration. Perhaps the most convincing evidence is provided by the exclusion of Southern Blacks from political life in the United States until the late 1960s.

Though one might argue from numerous cases of child neglect that all too many children fall under III.2, there are reasonable grounds for holding that in general the exclusion of children meets the tests. The bonds between children and adults are unique in the human species. For one thing, while most citizens may not understand from their own direct experiences what it is like to be a member of an excluded class, race, or sex, every adult has once been a child. Moreover, many adults are closely tied to children by bonds of love, nurturance, pity, joy, compassion and hope. Among adults these bonds are far too weak to ensure enough mutuality of interests and understanding to ensure that members of a demos will protect the interests of other adults who are excluded. Consequently, as children approach 'the age of reason' the justification for their guardianship by parents, community, and state weakens and finally fails to meet the two tests.

What then of III.2? For example, what of the child in a community of uncaring adults? In this case, it is not possible for a procedural democracy to arrive at a satisfactory solution. Yet since the existing state of affairs violates the principle of equal consideration, an obligation arises for all who accept that principle to search for and bring about changes that will remedy the situation. There is an obligation to raise the level of M's competence or the enlightenment and compassion of the demos or both. Meanwhile III.2 ought to be viewed as a morally intolerable state of affairs.

A criterion of inclusion

These considerations provide reasonable grounds for adopting a criterion that approaches universality among adults. It is not only very much less arbitrary than Schumpeter's solution but far more inclusive than the restricted demos that was accepted, implicitly or explicitly, by Mill, Rousseau, Locke and the Greek *polis*.

> **(C.5)** *Inclusiveness*: The demos must include all adult members of the association except transients.

Admittedly the definition of adults and transients is a potential source of ambiguity. Probably no definition of the term adult can be completely watertight. In general, however, every member ought to be considered an adult who does not suffer from a severe mental disability or whose punishment for disobeying the rules is not reduced because he or she is younger than a given age. The meaning of the criterion seems to me to be clear enough: A demos that permitted the concept of adulthood to be manipulated in order to deprive certain persons of their rights – dissenters, for example – to that degree would simply fail to meet the criterion of inclusiveness. Obviously this criterion, like others, can never be self-enforcing.

Taken with the other four criteria, inclusiveness completes the requirements for procedural democracy. To the extent that a system approaches all five criteria, it is fully democratic in a procedural sense. The argument is summarized in Table 1.

V Comments

The argument for procedural democracy holds that if one believes in the half dozen assumptions in Table 1, then reason requires one to hold that an association should adopt procedures for making binding decisions that will satisfy the five criteria of procedural democracy.

I take it for granted that in the real world no system will fully meet these criteria. At best any actual polity is likely to be something of an approximation to procedural democracy. My guess is that any approximation will invariably fall pretty far short of meeting the criteria. However, I have not tried to specify thresholds of attainment above which a system may properly be called a procedural democracy, for that exercise promises to be rather sterile. Instead, the criteria serve as standards against which one may compare alternative procedures in order to judge their relative merits according to the criteria of procedural democracy: to compare different systems in order to judge their relative approximations to procedural democracy; and to compare a given system over time in order to judge whether its trend, if any, is toward or away from procedural democracy. I do not hold that the criteria of procedural democracy fully define the notion of a good polity or good society.

Test I   Is every citizen, C_i, definitely more qualified than the member M excluded by the criterion?

Test II   Is the judgement of the demos as to M's good demonstrably superior to M's judgement?

Test III   If M is excluded, will the demos act so as to care equally for M's good?

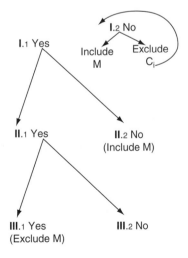

Figure 1. Three tests for a criterion of inclusion

Table 1. The argument for procedural democracy in schematic outline

If one belives that:	Then procedures for making binding decisions must satisfy the following criteria:	To the extent that procedures satisfy the criteria, then the system approaches:
A.1. A specific collection of people has a need for binding decisions.	C.1. Political equality	Procedural democracy in a narrow sense
A.2. Binding decisions involve two stages: Setting the agenda The decisive stage	C.2. Effective participation	Full procedural democracy with respect to an agenda and in relation to a demos
A.3. Binding decisions ought to be made only by persons who are subject to the decisions (i.e., by *members*)	C.3. Enlightened understanding	
A.4. Equally valid claims justify equal shares.		
A.5. The preferences of a significant number of members as to the decision are equally valid and no member's preferences are of overriding validity.	C.4. Final control of the agenda	Full procedural democracy in relation to its demos
A.5.1. The full condition of equal qualification exists.		
A.6. The good of each member is entitled to equal consideration, *and* each member is assumed to be the best judge of his or her own interasts in the absence of a compelling showing to the contrary.	C.5. Inclusiveness	Full procedural democracy

But to the extent that procedural democracy is worthwhile, then judgements of the sort I just mentioned bear directly on the relative worth or goodness of political arrangements.

The doctrine thus serves the task of clarification and prescription, of appraising and choosing among alternatives. For an example, suppose that I am a member of an association, and I believe that the conditions of procedural democracy exist among us but that my fellow members have not understood why the criteria of procedural democracy ought to apply to our processes of decision-making. My task is clarification: if we believe these things to be true, I would say to them, then we must reasonably adopt the criteria of procedural democracy. Or clarification might go in the other direction. Since you deny the validity of the criteria, I would say, then it must be that you reject one or more of these assumptions as valid among us. Which of the assumptions do you reject, and on what grounds?

Nor need I be a member of an association in order to arrive at judgements and recommendations as to the procedures the association ought to employ. If I judge that the conditions exist, then I must also conclude that the association should be procedurally democratic, whether or not I am a member.

As I have already said, I think that objections to procedural democracy will most often come to rest on a denial of the condition of equal qualification. This is why I have dealt at such length with that assumption. Sooner or later, to advocate procedural democracy requires a direct confrontation with its main alternative, which historically, today, and doubtless far into the future, is the doctrine of meritocracy. This enduring rival to democratic ideas is the view that adults in general are not qualified to govern, that the task of governing ought properly to be lodged with a meritorious minority, an elite possessing superior knowledge and virtue.

Many defences of democracy imply that democracy is always better than meritocracy. Yet even the most committed adherents of democracy have usually shrunk from insisting that every kind of human association must always follow democratic procedures.

In setting out the doctrine of procedural democracy I have not assumed that the condition of equal qualification always holds. Yet I would have to believe the doctrine irrelevant if I did not believe that the condition exists in at least some important associations.

Whether or not the state is the most important of all human associations, it is surely highly crucial. It is crucial because of its extraordinary influence, power, and authority, and thus the capacity of those who govern the state to control the resources, structures, agendas, and decisions of all other associations within the boundaries of the state. A people that alienates its final control over the agenda and decisions of the government of the state runs a very high risk of alienating its final control over other important associations as well.

I have not tried to show here what kinds of institutional arrangements procedural democracy would require for governing the state. Partly, though not wholly, in response to democratic ideas, a set of institutions for the government of the state has evolved during the last two centuries. The common features of these institutions have been called polyarchy. The institutions of polyarchy provide a much better approximation to procedural democracy among a numerous people, I believe, than the more exclusionary and authoritarian systems they replaced or serve as existing alternatives to polyarchy in the present world. Yet it seems clear to me that the institutions of polyarchy are not sufficient for a close approximation to procedural democracy.

However, I refrain here from arguing whether they are necessary, or how polyarchies might be further democratized, or whether radically different kinds of political institutions could provide a closer fit to procedural democracy.

A people that adhered to the doctrine of procedural democracy in the government of the state would also want to employ that doctrine in determining how other associations ought to be governed. For reasons I have already indicated, the doctrine bars a universalistic and *a priori* judgement that procedural democracy is best for all associations. But every system for governing any association ought to be tested against the doctrine, to determine whether the conditions are present; and, if they are, the relative merits of existing and alternative arrangements for satisfying the criteria.

As with the state, the question of what government is best for other associations will turn most frequently on a contestable and contingent judgement as to the relative competence of the members to govern. If, as I believe, a wise and humane people that sought to govern the state according to the criteria of procedural democracy would also employ the principles of equal consideration and burden of proof in making judgements about the relative qualifications of members to govern other associations, then it appears to me that many hier-

archic or meritocratic arrangements would have to give way to procedural democracy.

Notes

1 Hereafter, in the case of an association not yet formed, member means putative member.

2 Hereafter expressions like 'acting' are meant to include not acting in certain ways.

3 In this respect the criterion comes closer to meeting Rousseau's restrictions in the *Social Contract* than might first appear. Rousseau would allow a sovereign people to grant executive power to (1) itself or a majority ('democracy'), (2) a minority ('aristocracy'), or (3) a single person ('monarchy'). What the people may not do is alienate its sovereignty, the power to make laws. Although 'democracy' in sense (1) is impractical, all three forms of delegating executive power are equally legitimate because, and as long as, the people does not alienate any of its sovereignty. Cf. particularly Book 2, Chapters 1 and 6, and Book 3, Chapter 6.

4 The whole discussion occurs in less than three pages (243–5) in Joseph A. Schumpeter, *Capitalism, Socialism, and Democracy* (New York: Harper and Bros., 1942, 1947).

5 I do not mean to suggest that Locke and Rousseau (or later writers) presented similar views on democracy, for they were of course very different. Thus Locke permitted the delegation and even the indefinite alienation by the demos of the power to make laws. (*Second Treatise*, Ch. X and Ch. XIX, par. 243.) Rousseau, as we saw above, did not. However, because their differences are not directly relevant to the argument of this section, I ignore them here.

6 The phrases are from Locke's *Second Treatise of Government*, Chapter VIII, 'Of the Beginning of Political Societies', par. 95–7, and *passim*, in John Locke, *Two Treatises of Government*, ed. by Peter Laslett, 2nd edn (Cambridge: Cambridge University Press, 1967).

7 For example, in Book I, Chapters 4 and 6.

8 In Venice, the number of noblemen, who alone had rights to participate in the government, were from one to two per cent of the population of the city, and, if the mainland population is included, around one-tenth of one per cent. In 1797, there were 1,090 noblemen, 137,000 residents of the city, and 2.2 million people on the mainland. The number of noblemen was never larger than about 2,000. James C. Davis, *The Decline of the Venetian Nobility as a Ruling Class* (Baltimore: The Johns Hopkins Press, 1962), Table 1, p. 58.

In Geneva the percentage, though not as tiny, was small. Of the five orders subject to the laws, only males in the top two orders participated in making

laws: 'at the top, the "citizens", who had the legal right to hold office, and of whom Rousseau was one; next, the "burghers", who had the right to vote but not to hold office.' Together, the citizens and burghers were 'some 1,500 in number' in a population of 25,000. Moreover, the top offices were monopolized by a few families. R. R. Palmer, *The Age of the Democratic Revolution: A Political History of Europe and America, 1760–1800* (Princeton: Princeton University Press, 1959), p. 36. Palmer remarks that 'Rousseau himself, in all the study he made of Geneva politics at Neuchatel, showed no interest in the Natives. The Natives, however, (were) three-quarters of the population who were not Burghers' (p. 137).

9 For example, *Second Treatise*, Ch. VIII, §93.

10 See his discussion on the status of women in 'conjugal society', Ch. VIII, §§78–84. '…it seems highly improbable that Locke was thinking in terms of extending those rights to women.' Willmoore Kendall, *John Locke and the Doctrine of Majority Rule* (Urbana: Univ. of Illinois Press, 1941, p. 121, fn. vi.).

11 Ch. VI, §60.

12 Ch. VII, §85.

13 For example, *Considerations on Representative Government*, 3rd edn (1865), ed. by Currin V. Shields (New York: The Liberal Arts Press, 1958), pp. 42, 55, 131. A much fuller exposition of Mill's ideas about the conflict between 'the principle of participation' and 'the principle of competence', which draws on a wide variety of Mill's work, is Dennis F. Thompson, *John Stuart Mill and Representative Government* (Princeton: Princeton University Press, 1976).

14 Ibid., pp. 131–8.

15 For examples, see Peter Bachrach's comments on 'classical democratic theory' and its contrasts with 'elitist theory' in *The Theory of Democratic Elitism* (Boston: Little, Brown, 1967), pp. 2–9. And Carole Pateman, *Participation and Democratic Theory* (Cambridge: Cambridge University Press, 1970), who presents Rousseau and John Stuart Mill as 'two examples of "classical" democratic theorists, whose theories provide us with the basic postulates of a theory of participatory democracy' (p. 21).

16 M. I. Finley, *Democracy, Ancient and Modern* (New Brunswick: Rutgers University Press, 1973). The remark is made in the context of slavery; he does not mention that the exclusion of women and resi-

dent foreigners made the demos an even more restrictive 'minority elite'. All the conjectures about the relative size of the citizen body and the level of their participation in public affairs look very fragile to me. I have taken the estimates above from A.H.M. Jones, *Athenian Democracy* (Oxford: Basil Blackwell, 1969), pp. 78–9. As to actual participation, scholarly guess work looks even shakier. Though sympathetic to the Athenian democracy, Jones concludes that 'contrary to general belief, the average assembly was attended mainly by the relatively well-to-do citizens...' (ibid., p. 36; see also pp. 50, 55, and the discussion 104–7). However, unlike the Assembly and the Council, the magistracies chosen by lot 'were filled by quite humble citizens' (p. 104). I cannot help suspecting that an Athenian Survey Research Centre would have turned up a good deal of evidence of citizen apathy and non-participation.

17 *The Second Treatise*, op. cit., par. 55 and 63 (pp. 28, 31). In the *Social Contract*, Rousseau also recognizes, though merely in passing, the authority of the father over children 'before they reach the age of reason'; op. cit., p. 239.

18 Douglas Rae has commented that children may be thought of as having a life-time bundle of rights, some of which they become eligible for as they mature. Locke seems to make a similar point in the paragraphs cited above. By contrast, for excluded adults 'the bonds of... subjection' never 'quite drop off, and leave a man at his own free disposal'.

19 *Second Treatise*, par. 60, op. cit., p. 30.

20 Suppose I were able to demonstrate that I had carefully studied the issues, parties, candidates, and the like. My exclusion would seem rather less justified. Still, a French citizen might say, 'you will hardly be in France long enough to justify your inclusion. Your coming here is voluntary; you acknowledge by coming your willingness to obey our laws; you will have left the country before the election will effect any changes in existing laws; consequently you will not bear any responsibility for your choices. Therefore you are, in that respect, *morally* unqualified to participate in this election.' This seems to me a powerful rebuttal to my claim. However, the force of the objection derives mainly from the fact that I may not be subject to the laws my participation might have helped to bring about. To this extent, I am not a member in the sense defined earlier, and consequently I *ought* to be excluded under the assumption (No. 3) that binding decisions should be made only by members.

21 This assumption is, I think, roughly equivalent to, though not necessarily identical with, a widespread if contestable judgement that forms a fundamental ground for a good deal of moral theory. For instance, Hugo Adam Bedau specifies a not dissimilar notion that he calls 'the doctrine of metaphysical egalitarianism' in J. Roland Pennock and John W. Chapman, *Equality* (New York: Atherton Press, 1976), p. 17. Stanley I. Benn asserts the 'principle of equal consideration of interests' (ibid., p. 67). It is probably at least a second cousin to Rawls's assumption of human equality based on the capacity for moral personality (op. cit., p. 506).

22 Brian Barry, *Political Argument* (London: Routledge & Kegan Paul, 1965), pp. 38–9 and 173ff.

23 The principle is analogous to, though not identical with, the first of the two principles that according to Mill are, 'of as universal truth and applicability as any general propositions which can be laid down respecting human affairs. The first is that the rights and interests of every and any person are only secure from being disregarded when the person interested is himself able, and habitually disposed, to stand up for them... Human beings are only secure from evil at the hands of others in proportion as they have the power of being, and are, *self-protecting*...' (op. cit., p. 43).

24 Mill, op. cit., pp. 44–5.

8

Preferences and Politics

Cass R. Sunstein

The drafting of the United States Constitution, it is often said, signaled a rejection of conceptions of politics founded on classical ideals in favor of a quite different modern view.[1] The precise terms of the alleged shift are not altogether clear, but it is possible to identify the most prominent strands. The classical conception assumes a relatively homogeneous people and prizes active participation by the polity's citizenry. In the classical conception, the polity is self-consciously concerned with the character of the citizens; it seeks to inculcate in them and to profit from a commitment to the public good. Plato said that politics is the "art whose business it is to care for souls";[2] and under the classical conception, civic virtue, not private interest, is the wellspring of political behavior. Whether or not the state imposes a "comprehensive view"[3] on the nation, it relies relatively little on private rights to constrain government. The underlying vision of "republican" politics is one of frequent participation and deliberation in the service of decision, by the citizenry, about the sorts of values according to which the nation will operate.

In the modern account, by contrast, government is above all respectful of the divergent conceptions of the good held by its many constituents. People are taken as they are, not as they might be. Modern government has no concern with souls. Although electoral processes are ensured, no special premium is placed on citizen participation. Self-interest, not virtue, is understood to be the usual motivating force of political behavior. Politics is typically, if not always, an effort to aggregate private interests. It is surrounded by checks, in the form of rights, protecting private liberty and private property from public intrusion.

In this system, the goal of the polity is quite modest: the creation of the basic ground rules under which people can satisfy their desires and go about their private affairs. Much of this is famously captured in *The Federalist* No. 10, in which Madison redescribed the so-called republican problem of the corruption of virtue as the so-called liberal problem of the control of factions, which, as Madison had it, were inevitable if freedom was to be preserved.

In fact, the conventional division between the American founders and their classical predecessors is far too crude. The founders attempted to create a deliberative democracy, one in which the institutions of representation, checks and balances, and federalism would ensure a deliberative process among political equals rather than an aggregation of interests.[4] But respect for private preferences, rather than collective deliberation about public values or the good life, does seem to be a distinguishing feature of American constitutionalism. Indeed, the view that government should refuse to evaluate privately held beliefs about individual welfare, which are said to be irreducibly "subjective," links a wide range of views about both governmental structure and individual rights.

Originally published in *Philosophy and Public Affairs* 20 (1991): 3–34. Copyright © 1991. Reprinted by permission of Blackwell Publishing Ltd.

In this article I want to explore the question whether a contemporary democracy might not sometimes override the private preferences and beliefs of its citizens, not in spite of its salutary liberalism but because of it. It is one thing to affirm competing conceptions of the good; it is quite another to suggest that political outcomes must generally be justified by, or even should always respect, private preferences. A large part of my focus here is on the phenomenon of endogenous preferences. By this term I mean to indicate that preferences are not fixed and stable, but are instead adaptive to a wide range of factors – including the context in which the preference is expressed, the existing legal rules, past consumption choices, and culture in general. The phenomenon of endogenous preferences casts doubt on the notion that a democratic government ought to respect private desires and beliefs in all or almost all contexts.[5] It bears on a number of particular problems as well, including the rationale for and extent of the constitutional protection accorded to speech; proportional representation and checks and balances; and the reasons for and limits of governmental regulation of the arts, broadcasting, and the environment. I take up these issues at several points in this article.

The argument proceeds in several stages. In Section I, I set forth some fairly conventional ideas about welfare and autonomy, in conjunction with the endogeneity of desires, in order to argue against the idea that government ought never or rarely to override private preferences. In Section II, I contend that in three categories of cases, private preferences, as expressed in consumption choices, should be overridden. The first category involves what I call collective judgments, including considered beliefs, aspirations for social justice, and altruistic goals; the second involves preferences that have adapted to undue limitations in available opportunities or to unjust background conditions; the third points to intrapersonal collective action problems that, over a lifetime, impair personal welfare. In all of these cases, I suggest, a democracy should be free and is perhaps obliged to override private preferences. In Section III, I make some remarks about the relevance of these claims to several current issues of constitutional controversy. These include proportional representation in politics and governmental regulation of the speech "market," including rights of access to the media, democratic controls on the electoral process, hate speech, and pornography.

I Against Subjective Welfarism

Should a constitutional democracy take preferences as the basis for political choice? In contemporary politics, law, and economics, the usual answer is affirmative. Modern economics, for example, is dominated by a conception of welfare based on the satisfaction of existing preferences, as measured by willingness to pay; in politics and law, something called "paternalism" is disfavored in both the public and private realms.[6] But the idea that government ought to take preferences as the basis for political decisions is a quite modern one. This is not to say that the idea is without foundations. Partly a function of the perceived (though greatly overstated) difficulty of making interpersonal comparisons of utility, the idea is also a product of the epistemological difficulties of assessing preferences in terms of their true connection with individual welfare, and, perhaps most of all, the genuine political dangers of allowing government to engage in such inquiries.

The constellation of ideas that emerges from these considerations has been exceptionally influential. It embodies a conception of political justification that might be described as "subjective welfarism."[7] On this view, the government, even or perhaps especially in a democracy, should attend exclusively to conceptions of welfare as subjectively held by its citizens. A wide range of prominent approaches to politics turn out to be versions of subjective welfarism. These include, for example, certain forms of utilitarianism; the view that some version of Paretian efficiency ought to be treated as the foundational norm for political life; opposition to paternalism in public and private life; approaches to politics modeled on bargaining theory (rational or otherwise); and conceptions of politics that see the democratic process as an effort to aggregate individual preferences.

It is important to understand that subjective welfarism, thus defined, may or may not be accompanied by a broader notion that ethical and moral questions should generally be treated in welfarism or subjectivist terms. It is as a political conception, rather than an ethical one, that subjective welfarism underlies a wide range of approaches to public life, including ideas about institutional arrangements and individual or collective rights. What I want to argue here is that subjective welfarism, even as a political conception, is unsupportable by reference to principles of autonomy or welfare, the very ideas that are said to give rise to it.

The initial objection to the view that government should take preferences "as they are," or as the basis for political choice, is one of impossibility. Whether people have a preference for a commodity, a right, or anything else is in part a function of whether the government has allocated it to them in the first instance. There is no way to avoid the task of initially allocating an entitlement, and the decision to grant an entitlement to one person frequently makes that person value that entitlement more than if the right had been allocated to someone else. (It also makes other people value it less than they would otherwise.) Government must not only allocate rights to one person or another; it must also decide whether or not to make the right alienable through markets or otherwise. The initial allocation serves to reflect, to legitimate, and to reinforce social understandings about presumptive rights of ownership, and that allocation has an important causal connection to individual perceptions of the good or right in question.

For example, a decision to give employees a right to organize, farmers a right to be free from water pollution, or women a right not to be subjected to sexual harassment will have an impact on social attitudes toward labor organization, clean water, and sexual harassment. The allocation therefore has an effect on social attitudes toward the relevant rights and on their valuation by both current owners and would-be purchasers. And when preferences are a function of legal rules, the rules cannot be justified by reference to the preferences.[8] Moreover, the initial assignment creates the basic "reference state" from which values and judgments of fairness are subsequently made, and those judgments affect preferences and private willingness to pay.[9] Of course, a decision to make an entitlement alienable or inalienable (consider the right to vote or reproductive capacities) will have preference-shaping effects. Because of the preference-shaping effects of the rules of allocation, it is difficult to see how a government might even attempt to take preferences "as given" or as the basis for decisions in any global sense.

To some degree this concern might be put to one side. Surely there is a difference between a government that concerns itself self-consciously and on an ongoing basis with private preferences and a government that sets up the basic rules of property, contract, and tort, and then lets things turn out however they may. If this distinction can be sustained, disagreements about the relationship between politics and preferences turn on competing notions of autonomy or freedom on the one hand and welfare on the other. Subjective welfarism is founded on the claim that an approach that treats preferences as sovereign is most likely to promote both individual freedom, rightly conceived, and individual or social welfare.

It will be useful to begin with welfare. Even if one accepted a purely welfarist view, one might think that the process of promoting welfare should take place not by satisfying current preferences but by promoting those preferences and satisfying them to such an extent as is consonant with the best or highest conception of human happiness. This view is connected with older (and some current) forms of utilitarianism; it also has roots in Aristotle.[10] Here one does not take existing preferences as given, and one does not put all preferences on the same plane. A criterion of welfare remains the ultimate one, but the system is not focused solely on preference satisfaction, since it insists that welfare and preference satisfaction are entirely different things.[11]

A central point here is that preferences are shifting and endogenous rather than exogenous, and as a result are a function of current information, consumption patterns, legal rules, and general social pressures. An effort to identify welfare with preference satisfaction would be easier to understand if preferences were rigidly fixed at some early age, or if learning were impossible; if this were so, democratic efforts to reflect on, change, or select preferences would breed only frustration. But because preferences are shifting and endogenous, and because the satisfaction of existing preferences might lead to unhappy or deprived lives, a democracy that treats all preferences as fixed will lose important opportunities for welfare gains.

With respect to welfare, then, the problem posed by the endogeneity of preferences is not the origin of desires but their malleability. At least if the relevant cases can be confidently identified in advance, and if collective action can be justified by reference to particular good reasons, the argument for democratic interference will be quite powerful. Respect for preferences that have resulted from unjust background conditions and that will lead to human deprivation or misery hardly appears the proper course for a liberal democracy.[12]

For example, legal rules prohibiting or discouraging addictive behavior may have significant advantages in terms of welfare. Regulation of heroin or cigarettes (at least if the regulation can be made effective) might well increase aggregate social welfare, by decreasing harmful behavior, removing the secondary effects of those harms, and producing more healthful and satisfying lives. Similarly, governmental action relating to the environment, broadcasting, or culture – encouraging or requiring, for example, protection of beautiful areas, broadcasting about public issues, high-quality programs, or public support of artistic achievement – may in the end generate (or, better, prevent obstacles to the generation of) new preferences, providing increased satisfaction and in the end producing considerable welfare gains. The same may well be true of antidiscrimination measures, which affect the desires and attitudes of discriminators and victims alike. A system that takes existing private preferences as the basis for political choice will sacrifice important opportunities for social improvement on welfarist criteria. This point was a crucial one in the early stages of utilitarian thought; it has been lost more recently with the shift from older forms of welfarism to the idea of "revealed preferences."

Moreover, the satisfaction of private preferences, whatever their content and origins, does not respond to a persuasive conception of liberty or autonomy. The notion of autonomy should refer instead to decisions reached with a full and vivid awareness of available opportunities, with reference to all relevant information, and without illegitimate or excessive constraints on the process of preference formation. When these conditions are not met, decisions should be described as unfree or nonautonomous; for this reason it is most difficult to identify autonomy with preference satisfaction. If preferences are a product of available information, existing consumption patterns, social pressures, and governmental rules, it seems odd to suggest that individual freedom lies exclusively or by definition in preference satisfaction, or that current preferences should, on grounds of autonomy, be treated as the basis for settling political issues. It seems even odder to suggest that all preferences should be treated equally, independently of their basis and consequences, or of the reasons offered in their support.

For purposes of autonomy, then, governmental interference with existing desires may be justified because of problems in the origins of those desires. Welfare-based arguments that invoke endogeneity tend to emphasize the malleability of preferences after they are formed; arguments based on autonomy stress what happens before the preferences have been created, that is, the conditions that gave rise to them. Because of this difference, the two arguments will operate along different tracks; and in some cases autonomy-based arguments will lead to conclusions different from those that would emerge from arguments based on welfare. In many cases, however, considerations of autonomy will argue powerfully against taking preferences as the basis for social choice.

Consider, for example, a decision to purchase dangerous foods, consumer products, or cigarettes by someone unaware of the (serious) health risks; an employer's decision not to hire blacks because of a background of public and private segregation or racial hostility in his community; a person who disparages or has no interest in art and literature because the culture in which he has been reared centers mainly around television; a decision of a woman to adopt a traditional gender role because of the social stigma attached to refusing to do so; a decision not to purchase cars equipped with seat belts or not to wear a motorcycle helmet produced by the social pressures imposed by one's peer group; a lack of interest in environmental diversity resulting from limitation of one's personal experiences to industrialized urban areas; a decision not to employ blacks at a restaurant because of fear of violence from whites.

These examples are different from one another. The source of the problem varies in each. But in all of them, the interest in liberty or autonomy does not call for governmental inaction, even if that were an intelligible category. Indeed, in many or perhaps all of these cases, regulation removes a kind of coercion.

One goal of a democracy, in short, is to ensure autonomy not merely in the satisfaction of preferences, but also, and more fundamentally, in the processes of preference formation. John Stuart Mill himself was emphatic on this point, going so far as to suggest that government itself should be evaluated in large measure by its effects on the character of the citizenry.[13] The view that freedom requires an opportunity to choose among alternatives finds a natural supplement in the view that people should not face unjustifiable constraints on the free development of their preferences and beliefs. It is not altogether clear what such a view would require – a point to which I will return. At the very least, however, it would see a failure of autonomy, and a reason for collective response, in beliefs and preferences based on insufficient information or opportunities.

Governmental action might also be justified on grounds of autonomy when the public seeks to implement, through democratic processes culminating in law, widely held social aspirations or collective desires. Individual consumption choices often diverge from collective considered judgments: people may seek, through law, to implement a democratic decision about what courses to pursue. If so, it is ordinarily no violation of autonomy to allow those considered judgments to be vindicated by governmental action. Collective aspirations or considered judgments, produced by a process of deliberation on which competing perspectives are brought to bear, reflect a conception of political freedom having deep roots in the American constitutional tradition. On this view, political autonomy can be found in collective self-determination, as citizens decide, not what they "want," but instead who they are, what their values are, and what those values require. What they "want" must be supported by reasons.

To summarize: On the thinnest version of the account offered thus far, the mere fact that preferences are what they are is at least sometimes and perhaps generally an insufficient justification for political action. Government decisions need not be and in some cases should not be justified by reference to preferences alone. More broadly, a democratic government should sometimes take private preferences as an object of regulation and control – an inevitable task in light of the need to define initial entitlements – and precisely in the interest of welfare and autonomy. Of course, there are serious risks of overreaching here, and there must be some constraints (usually denominated "rights") on this process. Checks laid down in advance are an indispensable part of constitutional government. Those checks will include, at a minimum, basic guarantees of political liberty and personal security, and such guarantees may not be comprised by processes of collective self-determination. I return to this point below.

II Democratic Rejection of Revealed Preferences: a Catalogue

In this section I attempt to particularize the claims made thus far by cataloguing cases in which considerations of autonomy and welfare justify governmental action that subjective welfarism would condemn. In all of these cases, I claim that participants in a liberal government ought to be concerned with whether its citizens are experiencing satisfying lives and that the salutary liberal commitment to divergent conceptions of the good ought not to be taken to disable government from expressing that concern through law. The cases fall into three basic categories.

(a) *Collective judgments and aspirations*

Citizens in a democratic polity might act to embody in law not the preferences that they hold as private consumers, but instead what might be described as collective judgments, including aspirations or considered reflections. Measures of this sort are a product of deliberative processes on the part of citizens and representatives. In that process, people do not simply determine what they "want." The resulting measures cannot be understood as an attempt to aggregate or trade off private preferences.

Politics, markets, and the dependence of preferences on context Frequently political choices cannot easily be understood as a process of aggregating prepolitical desires. Some people may, for example, support nonentertainment broadcasting on television, even though their own consumption patterns favor situation comedies; they may seek stringent laws protecting the environment or endangered species, even though they do not use the public parks or derive material benefits from protection of such species; they may approve of laws calling for social security and welfare even though they do not save or give to the poor; they may support antidiscrimination laws even though their own behavior is hardly race- or gender-neutral. The choices people make as political participants are different from those they make as consumers. Democracy thus calls for an intrusion on markets.

The widespread disjunction between political and consumption choices presents something of a puzzle. Indeed, it sometimes leads to the view that market ordering is undemocratic and that choices made through the political process are a preferable basis for social ordering.

A generalization of this sort is far too broad in light of the multiple breakdowns of the political process and the advantages of market ordering in many arenas. Respect for private markets is an important way of respecting divergent conceptions of the good and is thus properly associated with individual liberty. Respect for markets is also an engine of economic productivity, an important individual and collective goal. But it would be a mistake to suggest, as some do, that markets always reflect individual choice more reliably than politics; or that democratic choices differ from consumption outcomes only because of confusion, as voters fail to realize that they must ultimately bear the costs of the programs they favor; or that voting patterns merely reflect a willingness to seek certain goods so long as other people are footing the bill.

Undoubtedly, consumer behavior is sometimes a better or more realistic reflection of actual preferences than is political behavior. But in light of the fact that preferences depend on context, the very notion of a "better reflection" of "actual" preferences is a confusing one; there is no such thing as an "actual" (in the sense of unitary or acontextual) preference in these settings. Moreover, the difference might be explained by the fact that political behavior reflects a variety of influences that are distinctive to the context of politics, and that justify according additional weight to what emerges through the political setting.

These influences include four closely related phenomena. First, citizens may seek to implement individual and collective aspirations in political behavior but not in private consumption. As citizens, people may seek the aid of the law to bring about a social state that they consider to be in some sense higher than what emerges from market ordering. Second, people may, in their capacity as political actors, attempt to satisfy altruistic or other-regarding desires, which diverge from the self-interested preferences sometimes characteristic of markets.[14] Third, political decisions might vindicate what might be called metapreferences or second-order preferences. People have wishes about their wishes, and sometimes they try to vindicate those second-order wishes, including considered judgments about what is best, through law. Fourth, people may precommit themselves, in democratic processes, to a course of action that they consider to be in the general interest. The

adoption of a constitution is itself an example of a precommitment strategy.

Three qualifications are necessary here. First, some of these objections might be translated into the terms of subjective welfarism. Some preferences, after all, are most effectively expressed in democratic arenas, and that expression can be supported precisely on the grounds that they are subjectively held and connected to a certain form of individual and collective welfare. My broader point, however, is that political choices will reflect a kind of deliberation and reasoning, transforming values and perceptions of interests, that is often inadequately captured in the marketplace. It is this point that amounts to a rejection or at least a renovation of subjective welfarism as a political conception. It is here that democracy becomes something other than an aggregative mechanism, that politics is seen to be irreducible to bargaining, and that prepolitical "preferences" are not taken as the bedrock of political justification.

Second, to point to these various possibilities is not at all to deny that market or private behavior frequently reflects considered judgments, altruism, aspirations, or far more complex attitudes toward diverse goods than are captured in conventional accounts of preference structures. There are countless counterexamples to any such claim. All I mean to suggest is that divergences between market and political behavior will sometimes be attributable to phenomena of the sort I have described.

Third, a democratic system must be built on various safeguards to ensure that its decisions are in fact a reflection of deliberative processes of the sort described here. Often, of course, such processes are distorted by the fact that some groups are more organized than others, by disparities in wealth and influence, and by public and private coercion of various kinds. I am assuming here that these problems have been sufficiently overcome to allow for a favorable characterization of the process.

Explanations Thus far I have suggested that people may seek, through law, to implement collective desires that diverge from market choices. Is it possible to come up with concrete explanations for the differences? There are a number of possibilities.

First, the collective character of politics, which permits a response to collective action problems, is critical here. People may not want to implement their considered judgments, or to be altruistic, unless there is assurance that others will be bound to do so as well. More simply, people may prefer not to contribute to a collective benefit if donations are made individually, with no guarantee that others will participate; but their most favored system, obtainable only or best through democratic forms, might be one in which they contribute if (but only if) there is assurance that others will do so as well. Perhaps people feel ashamed if others are contributing and they are not. Perhaps they feel victimized if they are contributing and others are not. In any case, the satisfaction of aspirations or altruistic goals will sometimes have the characteristics of the provision of public goods or the solution of a prisoner's dilemma.

Second, the collective character of politics might overcome the problem, discussed below, of preferences and beliefs that have adapted, at least to some extent, to an unjust status quo or to limits in available opportunities.[15] Without the possibility of collective action, the status quo may seem intractable, and private behavior, and even desires, will adapt accordingly. But if people can act in concert, preferences might take on a quite different form. Consider social movements involving the environment, labor, and race and sex discrimination. The collective action problem thus interacts with aspirations, altruistic desires, second-order preferences, and precommitment strategies. All of these are most likely to be enacted into law if an apparatus such as democratic rule is available to overcome collective action problems.

Third, social and cultural norms might incline people to express aspirational or altruistic goals more often in political behavior than in markets. Such norms may press people, in their capacity as citizens, in the direction of a concern for others or for the public interest.

Fourth, the deliberative aspects of politics, bringing additional information and perspectives to bear, may affect preferences as expressed through governmental processes. A principal function of a democratic system is to ensure that through representative or participatory processes, new or submerged voices, or novel depictions of where interests lie and what they in fact are, are heard and understood. If representatives or citizens are able to participate in a collective discussion of (for example) broadcasting or levels of risk in the workplace, they might well generate a far fuller and richer picture of diverse social goods, and of how they might be served, than can be provided through individual decisions as regis-

tered in the market. It should hardly be surprising if preferences, values, and perceptions of both individual and collective welfare are changed as a result of that process.

Fifth, and finally, consumption decisions are a product of the criterion of private willingness to pay, which creates distortions of its own. Willingness to pay is a function of ability to pay, and it is an extremely crude proxy for utility or welfare. Political behavior removes this distortion – which is not to say that it does not introduce distortions of new kinds.

Qualifications Arguments from collective desires are irresistible if the measure at issue is adopted unanimously. But more serious difficulties are produced if (as is usual) the law imposes on a minority what it regards as a burden rather than a benefit. Suppose, for example, that a majority wants to require high-quality television and to ban violent and dehumanizing shows, but that a significant minority wants to see the latter. (I put the First Amendment questions to one side.) It might be thought that those who perceive a need to bind themselves, or to express an aspiration, should not be permitted to do so if the consequence is to deprive others of an opportunity to satisfy their preferences.

The foreclosure of the preferences of the minority is unfortunate, but in general it is difficult to see what argument there might be for an across-the-board rule against collective action of this sort. If the majority is prohibited from vindicating its considered judgments through legislation, an important arena for democratic self-government will be eliminated. The choice is between the considered judgments of the majority and the preferences (and perhaps judgments as well) of the minority. On the other hand, the foreclosure of the minority should probably be permitted only when less restrictive alternatives, including private arrangements, are unavailable to serve the same end.

Of course, the argument for democratic outcomes embodying collective judgments is not always decisive. It is easy to imagine cases in which that argument is weak. Consider a law forbidding atheism or agnosticism, or barring the expression of unpatriotic political displays. And while I cannot provide in this space a full discussion of the contexts in which the case for democratic outcomes is overcome, it might be useful to describe, in a preliminary way, three categories of cases in which constraints on collective judgments seem especially appropriate.

First, if the particular choice foreclosed has some special character, and especially if it is a part of deliberative democracy itself, it is appropriately considered a right, and the majority has no authority to intervene. Political expression and participation are prime examples. The equal political rights of members of the minority, as citizens, should be respected even if a general aspiration, held by the majority, argues for selective exclusions. So, too, other rights fundamental to autonomy or welfare – consider consensual sexual activity – ought generally to be off-limits to government.

Second, some collective desires might be objectionable or a product of unjust background conditions. A collective judgment that racial intermarriage is intolerable could not plausibly be justified even if it is said to reflect a collective social aspiration. To explain why, it is of course necessary to offer an argument challenging that judgment and invoking principles of justice. Such an argument might itself involve notions of autonomy or welfare. However that may be, the example suggests that the collective judgment must not be objectionable on moral grounds.

Third, some collective desires might reflect a special weakness on the part of the majority: consider a curfew law, or perhaps prohibition. In such circumstances, a legal remedy might remove desirable incentives for private self-control, have unintended side effects resulting from the "bottling-up" of desires, or prove unnecessary in light of the existence of alternative remedies. When any one of these three concerns arises, the case for protection of collective judgments is implausible. But in many contexts, these concerns are absent, and democratic controls initiated on these grounds are justified.

(b) *Excessive limitations in opportunities or unjust background conditions*

Citizens in a democracy might override existing preferences in order to foster and promote diverse experiences, with a view to providing broad opportunities for the formation of preferences and beliefs and for distance on and critical scrutiny of current desires. This goal usually supports private ordering and freedom of contract as well. But it calls for collective safeguards when those forces push toward homogeneity and uniformity, as they often do in industrialized nations. Here the argument for governmental controls finds a perhaps ironic origin in Mill. Such controls are necessary to cultivate divergent conceptions of the good and to ensure a degree of reflection on those conceptions.

A system that took this goal seriously could start from a range of different foundations. It might find its roots in the principles that underlie a deliberative democracy itself.[16] Here the notions of autonomy and welfare would be defined by reference to the idea of free and equal persons acting as citizens in setting up the terms of democratic life. That idea will impose constraints on the sorts of preferences and beliefs that a political system would be permitted to inculcate. Perhaps more controversially, the system could be regarded as embodying a mild form of liberal perfectionism. Such a system would see the inculcation of critical and disparate attitudes toward prevailing conceptions of the good as part of the framework of a liberal democracy. Liberal education is of course the principal locus of this concern, but the principles embodied in liberal education need not be confined to the school system. Still another foundation would be Aristotelian. Here the governing goal would be to ensure that individual capacities and capabilities are promoted and not thwarted by governmental arrangements.[17] And this set of ideas, a different kind of perfectionism, is not so dramatically different from Mill's version of utilitarianism.

If government can properly respond to preferences that are based on limitations in available opportunities, it might well undertake aggressive initiatives with respect to the arts and broadcasting: subsidizing public broadcasting, ensuring a range of disparate programming, or calling for high-quality programming not sufficiently provided by the marketplace. Indeed, the need to provide diverse opportunities for preference formation suggests reasons to be quite skeptical of unrestricted markets in communication and broadcasting. There is a firm theoretical justification for governmental regulation here, including the much-criticized, and now largely abandoned, "fairness doctrine," which required broadcasters to cover controversial issues and to give equal time to competing views. In view of the inevitable effects of programming on character, beliefs, and even conduct, it is hardly clear that governmental "inaction" is always appropriate in a constitutional democracy. Indeed, the contrary seems true. I take up this issue in more detail below.

Market behavior is sometimes based on an effort to reduce cognitive dissonance by adjusting to undue limitations in current practices and opportunities. When this is so, respect for preferences seems unjustified on grounds of autonomy and under certain conditions welfare as well. Preferences might be regarded as nonautonomous insofar as they are reflexively adaptive to unjust background conditions, and collective responses to such preferences might yield welfare gains.[18] The point has significant implications. For example, workers appear to underestimate the risks of hazardous activity partly in order to reduce the dissonance that would be produced by an accurate understanding of the dangers of the workplace.[19] Democratic controls might produce gains in terms of both welfare and autonomy.

Similar ideas help account for principles of antidiscrimination. In general, the beliefs of both beneficiaries and victims of existing injustice are affected by dissonance-reducing strategies.[20] The phenomenon of blaming the victim has distinct cognitive and motivational foundations: the strategy of blaming the victim, or assuming that an injury or an inequality was deserved or inevitable, permits nonvictims or members of advantaged groups to reduce dissonance by enabling them to maintain that the world is just – a pervasively, insistently, and sometimes irrationally held belief.[21] The reduction of cognitive dissonance is a powerful motivational force, and it operates as a significant obstacle to the recognition of social injustice or irrationality.

Victims also participate in dissonance-reducing strategies, including the lowering of their own self-esteem to accommodate both the fact of victimization and the belief that the world is essentially just. Sometimes it is easier to assume that one's suffering is warranted than that it has been imposed cruelly or by chance. Consider here the astonishing fact that after a draft lottery, participants decided that the results of the purely random process, whether favorable or not, were deserved.[22] The phenomenon of blaming the victim also reflects the "hindsight effect," through which people unjustifiably perceive events as having been more predictable than they in fact were, and therefore suggest that victims or disadvantaged groups should have been able to prevent the negative outcome. All of these phenomena make reliance on existing or revealed preferences highly problematic in certain contexts.

There is suggestive evidence to this effect in the psychological literature in this area. Some work here reveals that people who engage in cruel behavior begin to devalue the objects of their cruelty; observers tend to do the same.[23] Such evidence bears on antidiscrimination law in general. Certain aspects of American labor and race discrimination law can be understood as a response to the basic problem of distorted beliefs and preferences. For example, the Supreme Court has emphatically rejected freedom-of-choice plans as a remedy for school segregation.[24] Such plans would simply permit whites and blacks to send their children to whichever school they wished. The Court's rejection of such plans might well be puzzling to proponents of subjective welfarism, but the outcome becomes more reasonable if it is seen as based in part on the fact that, in this area, preferences and beliefs have conspicuously grown up around and adapted to the segregative status quo. Under these circumstances, freedom of choice is no solution at all; indeed, in view of the background and context the term seems an oxymoron.

In labor law as well, American law rejects freedom of contract and freedom of choice in order to protect collective bargaining. Some of this legislation must stand on a belief that private preferences have been adaptive to a status quo skewed against unionization. Special steps are therefore necessary in order to encourage collective bargaining, which also, of course, overcomes the prisoner's dilemma faced by individual workers, and therefore facilitates collective deliberation on the conditions of the workplace.

Poverty itself is perhaps the most severe obstacle to the free development of preferences and beliefs. Programs that attempt to respond to the deprivations faced by poor people – most obviously by eliminating poverty, but also through broad public education and regulatory efforts designed to make cultural resources generally available regardless of wealth – are fully justified in this light. They should hardly be seen as objectionable paternalism or as unsupportable redistribution. Indeed, antipoverty efforts are tightly linked with republican efforts to promote security and independence in the interest of creating the conditions for full and equal citizenship.

Sometimes, of course, preferences are only imperfectly adapted. At some level there is a perception of injury, but a fear of social sanctions or a belief that the cause is intractable prevents people from seeking redress. Here the collective character of politics, permitting the organization of numerous people, can be exceedingly helpful.

Standing by itself, the fact that preferences are shifting and endogenous is hardly a sufficient reason for the imposition of democratic controls. All preferences are to some degree dependent on existing law and current opportunities, and that fact cannot be a reason for governmental action without creating a license for tyranny. The argument for democratic controls in the face of endogenous preferences must rely on a belief that welfare or autonomy will thereby be promoted. Usually governmental interference should be avoided. But far too often, the salutary belief in respect for divergent conceptions of the good is transformed into an unwillingness to protect people from either unjust background conditions or a sheer lack of options.

The actual content of democratic controls here will of course be controversial, and it probably should begin and usually end with efforts to provide information and to increase opportunities. Thus, for example, governmentally required disclosure of risks in the workplace is a highly laudable strategy. In a few cases, however, these milder initiatives are inadequate, and other measures are necessary. A moderately intrusive strategy could involve economic incentives, which might take the form of tax advantages or cash payments. For example, the government might give financial inducements to day-care centers as a way of relieving child-care burdens. Such a system might well be preferable to direct transfers of money to families, a policy that will predictably lead many more women to stay at home. In view of the sources and consequences of the differential distribution of child-care burdens, it is fully legitimate for the government to take steps in the direction of equalization. The most intrusive option, to be used rarely, is direct coercion, as in the case of governmentally mandated use of safety equipment.

The category of democratic responses to endogenous preferences of this sort overlaps with that of measures that attempt to protect collective aspirations. Frequently, aspirations form the basis for laws that attempt to influence processes of preference formation.

(c) *Intrapersonal collective action problems*

There is also a case for democratic controls on existing preferences when such preferences are a function of past acts of consumption and when such acts alter desires or beliefs in such a way as to cause long-term harm. In such cases, the two key facts are that preferences are endogenous to past consumption decisions and that the effect of those decisions on current preferences is pernicious. For government to act in this context, it is important that it be confident of its conclusions; in the face of uncertainty, freedom of choice is appropriate here. An absence of information on the part of the private actors is usually a necessary condition for collective controls.

Regulations of addictive substances, myopic behavior, and habits are familiar examples. In the case of an addiction, the problem is that the costs of nonconsumption increase dramatically over time as the benefits of consumption remain constant or fall sharply. The result is that the aggregate costs, over time or over a life, of consumption exceed the aggregate benefits, even though the initial consumption choice provides benefits that exceed costs. Individual behavior that is rational for each individual consumption choice ultimately leads people into severely inferior social states. In such cases, people, if fully informed, would in all likelihood not want to choose the good in the first place. Governmental action is a possible response.

Menahem Yaari offers the example of a group of traders attempting to induce alcoholism in an Indian tribe.[25] At the outset, alcoholic beverages are not extremely valuable to consumers. The consumers are willing to buy only for a low price, which the traders accept. But as a result of consumption, the value of the beverages to the consumers steadily increases to the point where they are willing to pay enormous sums to obtain them. Thus the traders are able "to manoeuvre the Indian into a position where rationality conflicts with Pareto-efficiency, i.e., into a position where to be efficient is to be irrational and to be rational is to be inefficient ... [T]he disadvantage, for an economic unit, of having endogenously changing tastes is that, even with perfect information and perfect foresight, the unit may find itself forced to follow an action which, by the unit's own standards, is Pareto-dominated."

Because of the effect over time of consumption on preferences, someone who is addicted to heroin is much worse off than he would have been had he never started, even though the original decision to consume was not irrational in terms of immediate costs and benefits. Statutes that regulate addictive substances respond to a social belief, grounded on this consideration, that the relevant preferences should not be formed in the first place.

We might describe this situation as involving an intrapersonal collective action problem, in which the costs and benefits, for a particular person, of engaging in an activity change dramatically over time.[26] A central point here is that consumption patterns induce a significant change in preferences, and in a way that makes people worse off in the long run.[27] In the case of addictions, there will also be interconnections between intrapersonal collective action problems and preferences and beliefs that are adaptive to unjust background conditions, at least as a general rule. (Yaari's own example, involving whites trading alcohol with native Americans, is a prime example.) The problem of drug addiction is hardly distributed evenly throughout the population, and the process of addiction is in large part a response to social institutions that severely limit and condition the range of options.

While addiction is the most obvious case, it is part of a far broader category. Consider, for example, myopic behavior, defined as a refusal, because the short-term costs exceed the short-term benefits, to engage in activity having long-term benefits that dwarf long-term costs. Another kind of intrapersonal collective action problem is produced by habits, in which people engage in behavior because of the subjectively high short-term costs of changing their behavior, regardless of the fact that the long-term benefits exceed the long-term costs. *Akrasia*, or weakness of the will, has a related structure, and some laws respond to its individual or collective forms.

For the most part, problems of this sort are best addressed at the individual level or through private associations, which minimize coercion; but social regulation is a possible response. Statutes that subsidize the arts or public broadcasting, or that discourage the formation of some habits and encourage the formation of others, are illustrations. There are similar arguments for compulsory recycling programs (the costs of participation in which decrease substantially over time, and often turn into benefits) and for democratic restrictions on smoking cigarettes.[28]

The problem with collective controls in this context is that they are unlikely to be fine-tuned. They will often sweep up so many people and circumstances as to create serious risks of abuse. In some settings, however, citizens will be able to say with confidence that the effect of consumption on preferences will lead to severe welfare or autonomy losses. In such cases democratic controls are justified.

III Examples

(a) The frontiers of free speech law: the fairness doctrine, campaign speech, hate speech, and pornography

The most important issues in the contemporary law of free expression have produced cleavages between groups and ideas that were previously closely allied. Thus the First Amendment has been invoked, with considerable vigor and passion, on behalf of cigarette companies seeking to advertise their products; corporations attempting to influence electoral outcomes; people engaged in racial hate speech; pornographers; and large networks objecting to a private right of access to broadcasting or to other efforts to promote quality and diversity in the media. The effort to invoke the First Amendment is increasingly resisted – often, ironically, on the theory that it runs counter to the goals of deliberative democracy and free expression itself – by individuals and groups formerly associated with an absolutist or near-absolutist position against governmental regulation of speech.

These debates raise exceedingly complex issues, and I can only touch on them briefly here. The complexities are increased by the fact that a system dedicated to freedom of expression ought to be highly sensitive to the idea that speech alters preferences and beliefs. It should also find that process to be one to which a democracy is generally quite receptive. As Justice Louis D. Brandeis wrote in what is probably the most distinguished judicial opinion in the entire history of free expression, "the fitting remedy for evil counsels is good ones ...If there be time to expose through discussion the falsehood and fallacies, to avert the evil by the processes of education, the remedy to be applied is more speech, not enforced silence."[29]

Justice Brandeis's statement notwithstanding, I want to suggest that attention to the endogenous character of preferences and to the considerations traced thus far provides some basis for receptivity to democratic controls in this context.

The fairness doctrine　There is a growing consensus that the government should not concern itself with the airwaves and that total reliance on private markets and consumer preferences is the appropriate strategy for government. On this view, broadcasting should be treated like soap, cereal, or any other commodity. Indeed, there is a growing consensus that this result is ordained by the First Amendment. But if the claims made here are persuasive, the consensus is misguided. The meaning of the First Amendment is a function of competing views about what sort of relation between government and markets will best promote democratic deliberation. Lawyers (and not a few nonlawyers) have an unfortunate habit of thinking that the meaning of the First Amendment precedes rather than postdates that inquiry.

The consequence of market-based strategies in broadcasting is a system in which most viewers see shows that rarely deal with serious problems; are frequently sensationalistic, prurient, dehumanizing, or banal; reflect and perpetuate a bland, watered-down version of the most conventional views about politics and morality; are influenced excessively by the concerns of advertisers; produce an accelerating "race to the bottom" in terms of the quality and quantity of attention that they require and encourage; and are often riddled with violence, sexism, and racism. It simply defies belief to suggest that such shows do not affect the preferences and even the character of the citizenry. Is it so clear that a constitutional democracy ought to consider itself unable to respond to this situation? Is it so clear that a First Amendment enacted in order to ensure democratic self-determination bars a democratic corrective here?

In my view, the considerations marshaled thus far suggest that citizens in a constitutional democracy ought to be conceded, and ought to exercise, the power to engage in a wide range of controls. If welfare and autonomy provide the governing criteria, large gains might be expected from such controls. All three of the categories I have described argue in favor of some form of regulation. Democratic controls would probably reflect collective desires, which deserve respect. They would respond to the fact that in spite of the large number of channels, the current regulatory regime diminishes genuine options, to the detriment of both welfare and autonomy; they would also counteract a kind of intrapersonal collective action problem faced by many of those habituated to the broadcasting status quo.

Such controls might permit the government to regulate advertising on television, certainly for children, but for others as well; to require broadcasters to pay attention to public affairs, as in, for example, an hour of compulsory programming per night; to ban gratuitous or prurient violence on television, especially when it is sexualized; to require, as a condition for licensing, a subsidy to public television; and to impose a broad fairness doctrine, in the form not only of an obligation of attention to important issues but also a chance to speak for divergent sides. The evident dangers notwithstanding, there would be a wide range of collective and external benefits from such controls, which would thus carry forward a strand of the liberal tradition that calls for governmental action in such cases.[30]

At least in principle, rights of private access to the media for differing positions and associated kinds of controls ought to be considered congenial to the free speech guarantee. Surely this is so if that guarantee is understood as a protection of a deliberative process centered on public values rather than of a "marketplace." The First Amendment need not be seen as an obstacle to such efforts. If anything, the existing system might be thought to raise serious constitutional questions. A system in which access to the media, with its inevitable consequences for the shaping of preferences and beliefs, is made dependent on private willingness to pay raises genuine problems for free expression.[31]

Campaign regulation It would not be difficult to argue that a variety of regulations on the electoral process are necessary both to promote a deliberative process among political equals and to ensure that the deliberative process is a genuine one. Properly conceived, such efforts would be highly congenial to the purposes of the free speech guarantee. Both restrictions on campaign contributions – to eliminate the distorting effects of wealth[32] – and qualitative measures to reduce the "soundbite" phenomenon and to promote more in the way of reflective discussion hold considerable promise.

Currently, however, there is a large if ironic obstacle to such efforts: the First Amendment. The Supreme Court has generally been unreceptive to governmental efforts to regulate electoral campaigns.[33] In the key passage in *Buckley v. Valeo*, the Court said that "the concept that government may restrict the speech of some elements of our society in order to enhance the relative voice of others is wholly foreign to the first amendment."[34] It is crucial to note here that the Court did not say that the effort to promote deliberation among political equals was insufficiently weighty or inadequately promoted by the legislation at hand. Instead the Court said, far more broadly, that the effort was constitutionally illegitimate.

Under the approach suggested here, campaign regulation would be treated more hospitably. In view of the effects of wealth on the formation of political beliefs, and the corrosive consequences of some forms of electioneering, democratic controls on the process might be welcomed. The First Amendment might be understood not as a guarantor of unrestricted speech "markets," and much less as a vehicle for the translation of economic inequalities into political ones, but instead as an effort to ensure a process of deliberation that would, under current conditions, be promoted rather than undermined through regulatory measures. This is so especially if citizens in a democratic polity support regulation of the electoral process in order to pursue their desire for a well-functioning deliberative process.

Of course, there are great risks here, and any regulatory efforts must be carefully monitored to ensure that they do not act as incumbent protection bills or as serious constraints on speech that should instead be encouraged. But the issue is far more complex, from the standpoint of the First Amendment itself, than existing law allows.

Violent pornography and hate speech   Many Western democracies, including those firmly committed to freedom of speech, regulate speech that casts contempt on identifiable social groups (hate speech). Some such democracies also control sexually explicit speech, especially when it associates sex and violence. These controls have been justified on mixed grounds of human dignity, community morality, and sexual equality. In the United States, the precise status of such restrictions remains unclear. Probably the best account of current law is that hate speech is protected, as is most speech that associates sex and violence, even if that speech is not conceivably part of a serious exchange of ideas but instead qualifies as pornography.[35]

The cases of hate speech and pornography raise somewhat different problems. Hate speech is self-consciously directed toward an issue of public concern; it is conspicuously and intentionally political in nature. Violent pornography is of course political too, in the sense that it has political origins and consequences. But it cannot be thought to be a self-conscious contribution to democratic deliberation about public issues. In this way it differs from misogynist speech of a more straightforward sort, where the political content is explicit. In terms of its connection to the First Amendment, pornography should probably be thought to fall in the same category as commercial speech, libel of private persons, bribes, and conspiracies. The rea-

son is that most pornography does not amount to an effort to contribute to deliberation on matters of public interest, even if that category is broadly conceived, as it should be. Expression that is not central to the free speech principle counts as speech, but it is entitled to a lesser degree of protection. It may be regulated, not on a whim, but on a basis of demonstration of harm that is weaker than that required for political speech.

Should the First Amendment be taken to disable government from regulating hate speech and pornography? The affirmative answer of current law may well be unsound. Both of these forms of speech have serious and corrosive effects on beliefs and desires. Both have the additional and unusual characteristic of denying victimized groups the right to participate in the community as free and equal persons. With respect to certain kinds of violent pornography, there are especially severe consequences in terms of how men and women perceive sexuality, how men perceive women, and how women perceive themselves. One need not believe that the regulation of violent pornography would eliminate sexual violence or even do a great deal to produce sexual equality in order to recognize that the pervasiveness of material that associates sex with violence has a variety of harmful social consequences.

The case for regulation of these forms of speech is strongest when the relevant speech is pervasive, when it causes tangible harm, and when it falls outside the category of speech that is guaranteed First Amendment protection unless there is a demonstration of unavoidable, imminent, and serious danger. The considerations marshaled here suggest that at least certain forms of violent pornography ought to be regulated, and that perhaps in certain restricted settings, hate speech may be an appropriate subject of democratic controls as well.

(b)   *Proportional representation*

In recent years, there has been a revival of interest in systems of proportional or group representation, both for disadvantaged groups and perhaps generally as well. There is a solid constitutional pedigree for such systems, notwithstanding the constant and emphatic rejections, by the Supreme Court, of constitutionally based arguments for representation of members of racial minority groups. Despite the rigidity of the one person-one vote formula, with its majoritarian and individualistic overtones, group representation has always been a feature of American constitutionalism.[36]

Moreover, the basic constitutional institutions of federalism, bicameralism, and checks and balances share some of the appeal of proportional representation, and owe their origins in part to notions of group representation. These institutions proliferate the points of access to government, increasing the ability of diverse groups to influence policy, multiplying perspectives in government, and improving deliberative capacities. In this respect, they ensure something in the way of group representation, at least when compared with unitary systems. Of course both the separation of powers and bicameralism grew in part out of efforts to promote representation of diverse groups: bicameralism allowed representation of both the wealthy and the masses, while the notion of separation derived from (though it also repudiated) notions of mixed government, which was designed to ensure a measure of representation of groups defined in social and economic terms.

Proportional representation might be designed, as in its Western European forms, to ensure representation in the legislature of all those groups that are able to attain more than a minimal share of the vote. In another form, the system might be an effort to ensure that members of disadvantaged groups are given the power to exert influence on political outcomes. In America, the Voting Rights Act goes far in this direction for blacks.

There are serious problems with both of these efforts, and I do not mean to evaluate them in detail here. I do suggest that efforts to ensure proportional representation become much more acceptable if they are justified on grounds that do not take existing preferences as the basis for governmental decisions and if they emphasize the preference-shaping effects of discussion and disagreement in politics.[37] The argument here is that deliberative processes will be improved, not undermined, if mechanisms are instituted to ensure that multiple groups have access to the process and are actually present when decisions are made. Proportional or group representation, precisely by having this effect, would ensure that diverse views are expressed on an ongoing basis in the representative process, where they might otherwise be excluded.

In this respect, proportional or group representation could be regarded as a kind of second-best solution for the real-world failures of Madisonian deliberation. And the primary purpose of access is not to allow each group to have its "piece of the action" – though that is not entirely irrelevant – but instead to ensure that the process of deliberation is not distorted by the mistaken appearance of a common set of interests on the part of all concerned. In this incarnation, proportional representation is designed to increase the likelihood that political outcomes will incorporate some understanding of all perspectives. That process should facilitate the healthy expression of collective values or aspirations and the scrutiny of preferences adaptive to unjust background conditions or limited opportunities.

For this reason, proportional representation may be the functional analogue of the institutions of checks and balances and federalism, recognizing the creative functions of disagreement and multiple perspectives for the governmental process. In this sense there is continuity between recent proposals for proportional representation and some of the attractive features of the original constitutional regime. Indeed, Hamilton himself emphasized that in a system of checks and balances, the "jarring of parties...will promote deliberation."[38] If this is so, proportional representation is most understandable in a democracy that does not take existing preferences as the basis for social choice but instead sees the broadest form of deliberation, covering ends as well as means, as a central ingredient in democratic politics.

IV   Conclusion

A constitutional democracy should not be self-consciously concerned, in a general and comprehensive way, with the souls of its citizens. Under modern conditions, liberal constraints on the operation of the public sphere and a general respect for divergent conceptions of the good are indispensable. At the same time, it would be a grave mistake to characterize liberal democracy as a system that requires existing preferences to be taken as the basis for governmental decisions and that forbids citizens, operating through democratic channels, from enacting their considered judgments into law, or from counteracting, through the provision of opportunities and information, preferences and beliefs that have adjusted to an unjust status quo. Ironically, a system that forecloses these routes – and that claims to do so in the name of liberalism or democracy – will defeat many of the aspirations that gave both liberalism and democracy their original appeal, and that continue to fuel them in so many parts of the world.

Notes

Some of this essay develops arguments set forth in chaps. 1 and 2 of my *After the Rights Revolution: Reconceiving the Regulatory State* (Cambridge, Mass.: Harvard University Press, 1990).

1 See Gordon Wood, *The Creation of the American Republic, 1776–1787* (New York: W.W. Norton, 1972); Thomas Pangle, *The Spirit of Modern Republicanism: The Moral Vision of the American Founders and the Philosophy of Locke* (Chicago: University of Chicago Press, 1988); and Martin Diamond, "Ethics and Politics: The American Way," in *The Moral Foundations of the American Republic*, ed. Robert Horwitz (Charlottesville: University Press of Virginia, 1986), pp. 75–106.

2 *The Laws* 650b.

3 See John Rawls, "The Idea of an Overlapping Consensus," *Oxford Journal of Legal Studies* 7 (1987): 1–25.

4 Indeed, participants in the liberal tradition, in its classical forms, emphasized the need for deliberation in government and placed a high value on political virtue. Many liberals do not take private preferences as the basis for social choice, without regard to their sources and consequences, or to the reasons that might be offered in their support. See my "Beyond the Republican Revival," *Yale Law Journal* 97 (1988): 1539–89.

5 On the limits of preference-based theories, see Amartya Sen, "Rational Fools: A Critique of the Behavioral Foundations of Economic Theory," *Philosophy & Public Affairs* 6, no. 4 (Summer 1977): 317–44; Jon Elster, *Sour Grapes* (New York: Cambridge University Press. 1983); and John Roemer, " 'Rational Choice' Marxism," in *Analytical Marxism*, ed. John Roemer (New York: Cambridge University Press, 1986), pp. 191–201. Of course, the satisfaction of private preferences in markets or elsewhere may create prisoners' dilemmas or collective action problems, and here governmental controls (or social norms) are a natural solution. I will not, however, deal with this narrower problem here.

It might well be that literature, in addition to economics and political theory, is a fruitful place to explore this subject. See Martha Nussbaum, *Love's Knowledge* (New York: Oxford University Press, 1990), and "Shame, Separateness, and Political Unity: Aristotle's Criticism of Plato," in *Essays on Aristotle's Ethics*, ed. Amelie Rorty (Berkeley: University of California Press, 1980), pp. 395–435. It is thus no accident that writers in politics and economics sometimes draw on literature. See, e.g., Elster, *Sour Grapes*.

6 David Gauthier, *Morals by Agreement* (New York: Oxford University Press, 1986), contains arguments in this direction; for a representative example at the intersection of economics and law, see Richard Posner,

Economics of Justice (Cambridge, Mass.: Harvard University Press, 1983), p. 53. There are, of course, criticisms within all of these fields. In economics, see Sen, "Rational Fools"; in politics, see Elster, *Sour Grapes*.

It is notable that the great expositors of liberalism in the nineteenth and twentieth centuries are emphatic in their rejection of the view that satisfaction of existing preferences is adequate for purposes of ethics or politics. See John Stuart Mill, *Considerations on Representative Government*, ed. C. V. Shields (1861; New York: Liberal Arts Press, 1958), and *The Subjection of Women*, ed. Susan Moller Okin (1869; Indianapolis: Hackett, 1988); and John Rawls, *A Theory of Justice* (Cambridge, Mass.: Harvard University Press, 1971). Mill's rejection of that view is especially emphatic in his essay on Bentham, where he criticizes Bentham for the view that "[t]o say either that man should, or that he should not, take pleasure in one thing, displeasure in another, appeared to him as much an act of despotism in the moralist as in the political ruler." Mill, by contrast, emphasized the need to explore the influences "on the regulation of . . . affections and desires," and pointed to "the deficiencies of a system of ethics which does not pretend to aid individuals in the formation of their own character" (*Mill on Bentham and Coleridge*, ed. F.R. Leavis [London: Chatto & Windus, 1950], pp. 68, 71, 70). Of course, there is a difference between what a system of ethics and what a system of politics should say about that question, as Mill clearly believed.

Dewey spoke in similar terms, invoking the need for critical reflection on the "conditions under which objects are enjoyed" and "the consequences of esteeming and liking them," and arguing that "judgments about values are judgments about that which should regulate the formation of our desires, affections and enjoyments" (John Dewey, *The Quest for Certainty: A Study of the Relation of Knowledge and Action* [New York: Putnam, 1960], pp. 259, 265, 272–3; emphasis in original).

7 I am grateful to Joshua Cohen for this formulation. I will not explore the complexities of the notion of "preference" here. I mean to refer simply to choices, mostly as these are observed in market behavior. This understanding of course captures the economic notion of "revealed preference" and also is a foundational part of subjective welfarism as I understand it. For a recent and interestingly offhand, example, see Ingemar Hansson and Charles Stuart, "Malthusian Selection of Preferences," *American Economic Review* 90 (1990): 529, 542: "We use natural selection to explain behavior, or equivalently, preferences," I do not explore the view, much broader than the claims defended here, that the existence of even widely held preferences, thus defined, furnishes no argument at all for governmental action.

If the notion of preference is intended to refer to an internal psychological force, or to a supposed wellspring of action, difficulties of course abound: people have first-, second-, and *n*th-order preferences, and their desires can be organized into many different categories, ranging from whimsy to considered judgments.

8   See Elster, *Sour Grapes*, and Rawls, *A Theory of Justice*. The problem here is not the simple fact of endogeneity, but that social rules and practices cannot be justified by reference to preferences that they have produced.

The point in the text receives empirical confirmation in the "endowment effect" frequently observed in social psychology and economics. See, e.g., David Brookshire and Don Coursey, "Measuring the Value of a Public Good: An Empirical Comparison of Elicitation Procedures," *American Economic Review* 77 (1987): 554–65; David Harless, "More Laboratory Evidence on the Disparity Between Willingness to Pay and Compensation Demanded," *Journal of Economic Behavior & Organization* 11 (1989): 359–70; Richard Thaler, "Toward a Positive Theory of Consumer Choice," *Journal of Economic Behavior & Organization* 1 (1980): 39–60; and Jack Knetsch and J. A. Sinden, "Willingness to Pay and Compensation Demanded: Experimental Evidence of an Unexpected Disparity in Measures of Value," *Quarterly Journal of Economics* 99 (1984): 507–21. The endowment effect is the consequence, for preferences and willingness to pay, of the initial allocation of an entitlement. Cf. Martha Nussbaum, "Shame, Separateness, and Political Unity," and "Aristotelian Social Democracy," in *Liberalism and the Good*, ed. R. Bruce Douglas, Gerald Mara, and Henry Richardson (New York: Routledge, 1990), pp. 203–52. A similar problem occurs when preferences are produced through an effort to counter the status quo, as in the "grass is always greener" phenomenon, in which people prefer things simply because they are unavailable. There is much less, however, in the way of empirical confirmation of this phenomenon.

9   See Daniel Kahneman, Jack Knetsch, and Richard Thaler, "Fairness and the Assumptions of Economics," in *Rational Choice: The Contrast Between Economics and Psychology*, ed. Robin Hogarth and Melvin Reder (Chicago: University of Chicago Press, 1987), pp. 101–16, esp. pp. 113–14. A related phenomenon is "loss aversion," which refers to the fact that a negative change from the status quo is usually seen as more harmful than a positive change is seen as beneficial. See Daniel Kahneman and Amos Tversky, "Prospect Theory: An Analysis of Decision under Risk," *Econometrica* 47 (1979): 263, 286–08. Loss aversion, together with the "reference state" phenomenon, may help to explain the endowment effect described in note 8 above.

10 For a modern utilitarian account along these lines, see Richard Brandt, *A Theory of the Good and the Right* (New York: Oxford University Press, 1979). For Aristotelian accounts, see Nussbaum, "Aristotelian Social Democracy," and Amartya Sen, "Well-Being, Agency, and Freedom," *Journal of Philosophy* 82 (1985): 169–221.

11 See Amartya Sen, *The Standard of Living*, The Tanner Lectures on Human Values, ed. Geoffrey Hawthorne (Cambridge: Cambridge University Press, 1987). On various conceptions of welfare, see James Griffin, *Well-Being: Its Meaning, Measurement and Moral Significance* (Oxford: Clarendon Press, 1986).

12 The objection here is not solely that preferences are endogenous to state action of some sort. As discussed in more detail below, the fact of endogeneity is not in itself an argument for democratic control of preferences. The argument is instead that misery that is a product of unjust background conditions calls for collective change. A subjectively satisfactory status quo produced by unjust background conditions will also call for change in some settings, for reasons taken up below. I do not deal with the possibility that subjective unhappiness that is a product of just background conditions also calls for governmental action, except insofar as an intrapersonal collective action problem is involved.

Moreover, to say that a preference is endogenous is not to say that it is a mere whim or fancy, or highly malleable. Some preferences are in fact relatively stable, even if they are a function of legal rules, social pressures, or existing institutions. A high degree of stability, and great resistance to change, will counsel against efforts at changing preferences, certainly on welfare grounds, and perhaps on grounds of autonomy as well (though even stable preferences may be nonautonomous, as in the case of rigid adaptations to an unjust status quo). In the face of extremely stable preferences, democratic efforts at change will merely breed resentment and frustration on the part of the objects of those efforts.

13 See Mill, *Considerations on Representative Government*.

14 See Howard Margolis, *Selfishness, Altruism, and Rationality: A Theory of Social Choice* (New York: Cambridge University Press, 1982). Of course the work by Kenneth Arrow and his followers in social choice theory creates serious problems for all preference-based theories of politics.

15 Cf. Mill's discussion of the ability of regimes to create active or passive characters, in *Considerations on Representative Government*.

16 See Joshua Cohen, "Deliberation and Democratic Legitimacy," in *The Good Polity: Normative Analysis of the State*, ed. Alan Hamlin and Philip Pettit (Oxford: Basil Blackwell, 1989), pp. 17–34. [Reprinted as chapter 10 of this volume.]

17 See Nussbaum, "Aristotelian Social Democracy."
    Here, as above, I do not attempt to choose among
    foundations but instead suggest that those adopting
    a wide range of starting points should reject
    subjective welfarism. To say this is not of course
    to deny the need to rely ultimately on some concep-
    tion of the good. For these purposes a wide variety
    of possibilities should do, including a form of liberal
    perfectionism, or a thin but relatively precise con-
    ception, as in Rawls's *A Theory of Justice*, or a thick
    but vague one, as in "Aristotelian Social Democ-
    racy."

18 There is a difference between self-conscious adapta-
    tion to an intractable status quo and the sorts of
    processes I am describing. If a person without musical
    talent decides to counteract and revise a desire to be a
    world-famous pianist, it would be odd to find that
    (healthy) decision to be inconsistent with personal
    autonomy. The cases under discussion involve a re-
    flexive process based on a socially produced absence
    of sufficient opportunities. Of course, the notion of
    sufficient opportunities itself requires a baseline;
    every system contains limited opportunities.

19 See George Akerlof and William Dickens, "The
    Economic Consequences of Cognitive Dissonance,"
    American Economic Review 72 (1982): 307–18.

20 On cognitive dissonance, see Leon Festinger, *A
    Theory of Cognitive Dissonance* (Stanford, Calif.:
    Stanford University Press, 1957); on some of its
    implications for social theory, welfare, and auton-
    omy, see Elster, *Sour Grapes*. See also the discussion
    of endowment effects and reference states in notes 8
    and 9 (above) and the accompanying text.
        Consider also Mary Wollstonecraft, *A Vindication
    of the Rights of Women*, ed. Carol Poston (1792; New
    York: W. W. Norton, 1975), which can be seen as an
    extended discussion of the social formation of prefer-
    ences and the phenomenon of the adaptation of pref-
    erences, beliefs, and desires to an unjust status quo.
    Thus Wollstonecraft writes, "I will venture to affirm,
    that a girl, whose spirits have not been damped by
    inactivity, or innocence tainted by false shame, will
    always be a romp, and the doll will never excite
    attention unless confinement allows her no alterna-
    tive" (p. 43). Similar points are made in Mill, *The
    Subjection of Women*, as against the claim that the
    existing desires of women are a product of consent.
        Consider finally the discussion of women's illiter-
    acy in Bangladesh in Nussbaum, "Aristotelian Social
    Democracy." Drawing on Martha Chen, *A Quiet
    Revolution: Women in Transition in Rural Bangladesh*
    (Cambridge, Mass.: Schenkman, 1983), Nussbaum
    explores the fact that many women in Bangladesh
    did not demand or even want greater education or
    literacy, and indeed expressed satisfaction with their
    current educational status. Of course, desires of this
    sort were a product of a lack of available opportunities
    and of social and cultural pressures.

21 See Melvin Lerner, *The Belief in a Just World: A
    Fundamental Delusion* (New York: Plenum Press,
    1980).

22 Zick Rubin and Anne Peplau, "Belief in a Just
    World and Reaction to Another's Lot," *Journal of
    Social Issues* 29 (1973): 73–93.

23 See Lerner, *The Belief in a Just World*.

24 See Green v. County School Bd., 391 US 430
    (1968), and Paul Gewirtz, "Choice in the Transi-
    tion," *Columbia Law Review* 86 (1986): 728–98.

25 Menahem Yaari, "Endogenous Changes in Tastes:
    A Philosophical Discussion," in *Decision Theory and
    Social Ethics: Issues in Social Choice*, ed. Hans Got-
    tinger and Werner Leinfellner (Boston: D. Reidel,
    1978), pp. 59–98.

26 Thomas Schelling, "Egonomics, or the Art of Self-
    Management," *American Economic Review* 68
    (1978): 290–4; Jon Elster, "Weakness of Will and
    the Free-Rider Problem," *Economics and Philosophy* 1
    (1985): 231–65.

27 Of course, all consumption has an effect on prefer-
    ences. For example, exposure to classical music
    usually increases appreciation. But the pattern
    under discussion is a rare one: it is that pattern,
    producing miserable lives, to which a democracy
    might respond. To be sure, in practice the response
    might make things worse rather than better.

28 See Robert Goodin, *No Smoking: The Ethical Issues*
    (Chicago: University of Chicago Press, 1989).

29 Whitney v. California, 274 US 357, 377 (1927).

30 See, e.g., John Stuart Mill, *Principles of Political
    Economy*, ed. W.J. Ashley (1871; London and New
    York: Longmans, Green, 1929). See also Owen Fiss,
    "Free Speech and Social Structure," *Iowa Law
    Review* 71 (1986): 1405–25; this essay carries the
    argument considerably further than I do here.

31 The Supreme Court seemed to recognize this point
    in Red Lion Broadcasting Co. v. FCC, 395 US 367
    (1969), but the point has dropped out of the current
    debate. If this analysis is correct, moreover, it is by
    no means clear that the print media should be more
    immunized from regulation than broadcasting, es-
    pecially now that the original scarcity rationale
    seems weak.

32 See John Rawls, "The Basic Liberties and Their
    Priority," in *The Tanner Lectures on Human Values*,
    ed. Sterling McMurrin (Salt Lake City: University
    of Utah Press, 1982), 3:76.

33 See Buckley v. Valeo, 424 US 1 (1976), and First
    National Bank of Boston v. Bellotti, 435 US 765
    (1978).

34 424 US at pp. 48–9.

35 I collapse some complex issues here. See Miller v.
    California, 413 US 15 (1973), and my "Pornography
    and the First Amendment," *Duke Law Journal*
    (September 1986): 589–627.

36 At the time of the framing, for example, geography
    was thought to define distinct communities with

distinct interests; representation of the states as such seemed only natural. It would not be impossible to argue that racial and ethnic groups (among others) are the contemporary analogues to groups that were defined in geographical terms during the founding period.

37 In part this is Mill's defense of such efforts. See *Considerations on Representative Government*. For valuable discussions, see Charles Beitz, *Political Equality: An Essay in Democratic Theory* (Princeton, NJ: Princeton University Press, 1989), pp. 123–40; and Iris Young, "Polity and Group Difference: A Critique of the Ideal of Universal Citizenship," *Ethics* 99 (1989): 250–84 [reprinted as chapter 16 of this volume]. Beitz's argument that proportional representation is not a requirement of political fairness is not inconsistent with the more prudential considerations invoked here; Young's claims about the need for discussion among the differently situated are highly compatible with my account.

38 *The Federalist*, no. 70.

9

The Market and the Forum: Three Varieties of Political Theory

Jon Elster

I want to compare three views of politics generally, and of the democratic system more specifically. I shall first look at social choice theory, as an instance of a wider class of theories with certain common features. In particular, they share the conception that the political process is instrumental rather than an end in itself, and the view that the decisive political act is a private rather than a public action, viz. the individual and secret vote. With these usually goes the idea that the goal of politics is the optimal compromise between given, and irreducibly opposed, private interests. The other two views arise when one denies, first, the private character of political behaviour and then, secondly, goes on also to deny the instrumental nature of politics. According to the theory of Jürgen Habermas, the goal of politics should be rational agreement rather than compromise, and the decisive political act is that of engaging in public debate with a view to the emergence of a consensus. According to the theorists of participatory democracy, from John Stuart Mill to Carole Pateman, the goal of politics is the transformation and education of the participants. Politics, on this view, is an end in itself – indeed many have argued that it represents the good life for man. I shall discuss these views in the order indicated. I shall present them in a somewhat stylized form, but my critical comments will not I hope, be directed to strawmen.

I

Politics, it is usually agreed, is concerned with the common good, and notably with the cases in which it cannot be realized as the aggregate outcome of individuals pursuing their private interests. In particular, uncoordinated private choices may lead to outcomes that are worse for all than some other outcome that could have been attained by coordination. Political institutions are set up to remedy such *market failures*, a phrase that can be taken either in the static sense of an inability to provide public goods or in the more dynamic sense of a breakdown of the self-regulating properties usually ascribed to the market mechanism.[1] In addition there is the redistributive task of politics – moving along the Pareto-optimal frontier once it has been reached.[2] According to the first view of politics, this task is inherently one of interest struggle and compromise. The obstacle to agreement is not only that most individuals want redistribution to be in their favour, or at least not in their disfavour.[3] More basically consensus is blocked because there is no reason to expect that individuals will converge in their views on what constitutes a just redistribution.

I shall consider social choice theory as representative of the private-instrumental view of politics, because it brings out supremely well the logic as well as the limits of that approach. Other varieties,

Originally published in *Foundations of Social Choice Theory*, edited by Jon Elster and Aanund Hylland (Cambridge University Press, 1986), pp. 103–32. Copyright © 1986 by Cambridge University Press. Reprinted by permission of Cambridge University Press.

such as the Schumpeterian or neo-Schumpeterian theories, are closer to the actual political process, but for that reason also less suited to my purpose. For instance, Schumpeter's insistence that voter preferences are shaped and manipulated by politicians[4] tends to blur the distinction, central to my analysis, between politics as the aggregation of given preferences and politics as the transformation of preferences through rational discussion. And although the neo-Schumpeterians are right in emphasizing the role of the political parties in the preference-aggregation process,[5] I am not here concerned with such mediating mechanisms. In any case, political problems also arise within the political parties, and so my discussion may be taken to apply to such lower-level political processes. In fact, much of what I shall say makes better sense for politics on a rather small scale – within the firm, the organization or the local community – than for nationwide political systems.

In very broad outline, the structure of social choice theory is as follows.[6] (1) We begin with a *given* set of agents, so that the issue of a normative justification of political boundaries does not arise. (2) We assume that the agents confront a *given* set of alternatives, so that for instance the issue of agenda manipulation does not arise. (3) The agents are supposed to be endowed with preferences that are similarly *given* and not subject to change in the course of the political process. They are, moreover, assumed to be causally independent of the set of alternatives. (4) In the standard version, which is so far the only operational version of the theory, preferences are assumed to be purely ordinal, so that it is not possible for an individual to express the intensity of his preferences, nor for an outside observer to compare preference intensities across individuals. (5) The individual preferences are assumed to be defined over all pairs of individuals, i.e. to be complete, and to have the formal property of transitivity, so that preference for *A* over *B* and for *B* over *C* implies preference for *A* over *C*.

Given this setting, the task of social choice theory is to arrive at a social preference ordering of the alternatives. This might appear to require more than is needed: why not define the goal as one of arriving at the choice of one alternative? There is, however, usually some uncertainty as to which alternatives are really feasible, and so it is useful to have an ordering if the top-ranked alternative proves unavailable. The ordering should satisfy the following criteria. (6) Like the individual preferences, it should be complete and transitive. (7) It should be Pareto-optimal, in the sense of never having one option socially preferred to another which is individually preferred by everybody. (8) The social choice between two given options should depend only on how the individuals rank these two options, and thus not be sensitive to changes in their preferences concerning other options. (9) The social preference ordering should respect and reflect individual preferences, over and above the condition of Pareto-optimality. This idea covers a variety of notions, the most important of which are *anonymity* (all individuals should count equally), *non-dictatorship* (*a fortiori* no single individual should dictate the social choice), *liberalism* (all individuals should have some private domain within which their preferences are decisive), and *strategy-proofness* (it should not pay to express false preferences).

The substance of social choice theory is given in a series of impossibility and uniqueness theorems, stating either that a given subset of these conditions is incapable of simultaneous satisfaction or that they uniquely describe a specific method for aggregating preferences. Much attention has been given to the impossibility theorems, yet from the present point of view these are not of decisive importance. They stem largely from the paucity of allowable information about the preferences, i.e. the exclusive focus on ordinal preferences.[7] True, at present we do not quite know how to go beyond ordinality. Log-rolling and vote-trading may capture some of the cardinal aspects of the preferences, but at some cost.[8] Yet even should the conceptual and technical obstacles to intra- and inter-individual comparison of preference intensity be overcome,[9] many objections to the social choice approach would remain. I shall discuss two sets of objections, both related to the assumption of given preferences. I shall argue, first, that the preferences people choose to express may not be a good guide to what they really prefer; and secondly that what they really prefer may in any case be a fragile foundation for social choice.

In actual fact, preferences are never 'given', in the sense of being directly observable. If they are to serve as inputs to the social choice process, they must somehow be *expressed* by the individuals. The expression of preferences is an action, which presumably is guided by these very same preferences.[10] It is then far from obvious that the individually rational action is to express these preferences as they are. Some methods for aggregating preferences are such that it may pay the individual to express false preferences, i.e. the outcome may in some cases be better according to his real preferences if he chooses not to express them truthfully. The condition for strategy-proofness for social choice mechanisms was designed expressly to exclude this possibility. It turns out, however, that the systems in which honesty always pays are rather unattractive in other respects.[11] We then have to face the possibility that even if we require that the social preferences be Pareto-optimal with respect to the expressed preferences, they might not be so with respect to the real ones. Strategy-proofness and collective rationality, therefore, stand and fall together. Since it appears that the first must fall, so must the second. It then becomes very difficult indeed to defend the idea that the outcome of the social choice mechanism represents the common good, since there is a chance that everybody might prefer some other outcome.

Amos Tversky has pointed to another reason why choices – or expressed preferences – cannot be assumed to represent the real preferences in all cases.[12] According to his 'concealed preference hypothesis', choices often conceal rather than reveal underlying preferences. This is especially so in two sorts of cases. First, there are the cases of anticipated regret associated with a risky decision. Consider the following example (from Tversky):

> On her twelfth birthday, Judy was offered a choice between spending the weekend with her aunt in the city (C), or having a party for all her friends. The party could take place either in the garden (GP) or inside the house (HP). A garden party would be much more enjoyable, but there is always the possibility of rain, in which case an inside party would be more sensible. In evaluating the consequences of the three options, Judy notes that the weather condition does not have a significant effect on C. If she chooses the party, however, the situation is different. A garden party will be a lot of fun if the weather is good, but quite disastrous if it rains, in which case an inside party will be acceptable. The trouble is that Judy expects to have a lot of regret if the party is to be held inside and the weather is very nice.

Now, let us suppose that for some reason it is no longer possible to have an outside party. In this situation, there is no longer any regret associated with holding an inside party in good weather because (in this case) Judy has no other place for holding the party. Hence, the elimin-ation of an available course of action (holding the party outside) removes the regret associated with an inside party, and increases its overall utility. It stands to reason, in this case, that if Judy was indifferent between C and HP, in the presence of GP, she will prefer HP to C when GP is eliminated.

What we observe here is the violation of condition (8) above, the so-called 'independence of irrelevant alternatives'. The expressed preferences depend causally on the set of alternatives. We may assume that the real preferences, defined over the set of possible outcomes, remain constant, contrary to the case to be discussed below. Yet the preferences over the *pairs* (choice, outcome) depend on the set of available choices, because the 'costs of responsibility' differentially associated with various such pairs depend on what else one 'could have done'. Although Judy could not have escaped her predicament by deliberately making it physically impossible to have an outside party,[13] she might well have welcomed an event outside her control with the same consequence.

The second class of cases in which Tversky would want to distinguish the expressed preferences from the real preferences concerns decisions that are unpleasant rather than risky. For instance, 'society may prefer to save the life of one person rather than another, and yet be unable to make this choice'. In fact, losing both lives through inaction may be preferred to losing only one life by deliberate action. Such examples are closely related to the problems involved in act utilitarianism versus outcome utilitarianism.[14] One may well judge that it would be a good thing if state A came about, and yet not want to be the person by whose agency it comes about. The reasons for not wanting to be that person may be quite respectable, or they may not. The latter would be the case if one were afraid of being blamed by the relatives of the person who was deliberately allowed to die, or if one simply confused the causal and the moral notions of responsibility. In such cases the expressed preferences might lead to a choice that in a clear sense goes against the real preferences of the people concerned.

A second, perhaps more basic, difficulty is that the real preferences themselves might well depend causally on the feasible set. One instance is graphically provided by the fable of the fox and the sour grapes.[15] For the 'ordinal utilitarian', as Arrow for instance calls himself,[16] there would be no welfare loss if the fox were excluded from consumption of the grapes, since he thought them sour anyway. But of course the cause of his holding them to be sour was his conviction that he would in any case be excluded from consuming them, and then it is difficult to justify the allocation by invoking his preferences. Conversely, the phenomenon of 'counter-adaptive preferences' – the grass is always greener on the other side of the fence, and the forbidden fruit always sweeter – is also baffling for the social choice theorist, since it implies that such preferences, if respected, would not be satisfied – and yet the whole point of respecting them would be to give them a chance of satisfaction.

Adaptive and counter-adaptive preferences are only special cases of a more general class of desires, those which fail to satisfy some substantive criterion for acceptable preferences, as opposed to the purely formal criterion of transitivity. I shall discuss these under two headings: autonomy and morality.

Autonomy characterizes the way in which preferences are shaped rather than their actual content. Unfortunately I find myself unable to give a positive characterization of autonomous preferences, so I shall have to rely on two indirect approaches. First, autonomy is for desires what judgment is for belief. The notion of judgment is also difficult to define formally, but at least we know that there are persons who have this quality to a higher degree than others: people who are able to take account of vast and diffuse evidence that more or less clearly bears on the problem at hand, in such a way that no element is given undue importance. In such people the process of belief formation is not disturbed by defective cognitive processing, nor distorted by wishful thinking and the like. Similarly, autonomous preferences are those that have not been shaped by irrelevant causal processes – a singularly unhelpful explanation. To improve somewhat on it, consider, secondly, a short list of such irrelevant causal processes. They include adaptive and counter-adaptive preferences, conformity and anti-conformity, the obsession with novelty and the equally unreasonable resistance to novelty. In other words, preferences may be shaped by adaptation to what is possible, to what other people do or to what one has been doing in the past – or they may be shaped by the desire to differ as much as possible from these. In all of these cases the source of preference change is not in the person, but outside him – detracting from his autonomy.

Morality, it goes without saying, is if anything even more controversial. (Within the Kantian tradition it would also be questioned whether it can be distinguished at all from autonomy.) Preferences are moral or immoral by virtue of their content, not by virtue of the way in which they have been shaped. Fairly uncontroversial examples of unethical preferences are spiteful and sadistic desires, and arguably also the desire for positional goods, i.e. goods such that it is logically impossible for more than a few to possess them.[17] The desire for an income twice the average can lead to less welfare for everybody, so that such preferences fail to pass the Kantian generalization test.[18] Also they are closely linked to spite, since one way of getting more than others is to take care that they get less – indeed this may often be a more efficient method than trying to excel.[19]

To see how the lack of autonomy may be distinguished from the lack of moral worth, let me use *conformity* as a technical term for a desire caused by a drive to be like other people, and *conformism* for a desire to be like other people, with anti-conformity and anti-conformism similarly defined. Conformity implies that other people's desires enter into the causation of my own, conformism that they enter irreducibly into the description of the object of my desires. Conformity may bring about conformism, but it may also lead to anti-conformism, as in Theodore Zeldin's comment that among the French peasantry 'prestige is to a great extent obtained from conformity with traditions, so that the son of a nonconformist might be expected to be one too'.[20] Clearly, conformity may bring about desires that are morally laudable, yet lacking in autonomy. Conversely, I do not see how one could rule out on *a priori* grounds the possibility of autonomous spite, although I would welcome a proof that autonomy is incompatible not only with anti-conformity, but also with anti-conformism.

We can now state the objection to the political view underlying social choice theory. It is, basically, that it embodies a confusion between the kind of behaviour that is appropriate in the market place and that which is appropriate in the forum. The notion of consumer sovereignty is acceptable because, and to the extent that, the consumer chooses between courses of action that differ only in the way they affect him. In political choice situations, however, the citizen is asked to express his preference over states that also differ in the way in which they affect other people. This means that there is no similar justification for the corresponding notion of the citizen's sovereignty, since other people may legitimately object to social choice governed by preferences that are defective in some of the ways I have mentioned. A social choice mechanism is capable of resolving the market failures that would result from unbridled consumer sovereignty, but as a way of redistributing welfare it is hopelessly inadequate. If people affected each other only by tripping over each other's feet, or by dumping their garbage into one another's backyards, a social choice mechanism might cope. But the task of politics is not only to eliminate inefficiency, but also to create justice – a goal to which the aggregation of pre-political preferences is a quite incongruous means.

This suggests that the principles of the forum must differ from those of the market. A long-standing tradition from the Greek *polis* onwards suggests that politics must be an open and public activity, as distinct from the isolated and private expression of preferences that occurs in buying and selling. In the following sections I look at two different conceptions of public politics, increasingly removed from the market theory of politics. Before I go on to this, however, I should briefly consider an objection that the social choice theorist might well make to what has just been said. He could argue that the only alternative to the aggregation of given preferences is some kind of censorship or paternalism. He might agree that spiteful and adaptive preferences are undesirable, but he would add that any institutional mechanism for eliminating them would be misused and harnessed to the private purposes of power-seeking individuals. Any remedy, in fact, would be worse than the disease. This objection assumes (i) that the only alternative to aggregation of given preferences is censorship, and (ii) that censorship is always objectionable. Robert Goodin, in his paper 'Laundering preferences', challenges the second assumption, by arguing that laundering or filtering of preferences by self-censorship is an acceptable alternative to aggregation. I shall now discuss a challenge to the first assumption, viz. the idea of a *transformation* of preferences through public and rational discussion.

II

Today this view is especially associated with the writings of Jürgen Habermas on 'the ethics of

discourse' and 'the ideal speech situation'. As mentioned above, I shall present a somewhat stylized version of his views, although I hope they bear some resemblance to the original.[21] The core of the theory, then, is that rather than aggregating or filtering preferences, the political system should be set up with a view to changing them by public debate and confrontation. The input to the social choice mechanism would then not be the raw, quite possibly selfish or irrational, preferences that operate in the market, but informed and other-regarding preferences. Or rather, there would not be any need for an aggregating mechanism, since a rational discussion would tend to produce unanimous preferences. When the private and idiosyncratic wants have been shaped and purged in public discussion about the public good, uniquely determined rational desires would emerge. Not optimal compromise, but unanimous agreement is the goal of politics on this view.

There appear to be two main premises underlying this theory. The first is that there are certain arguments that simply cannot be stated publicly. In a political debate it is pragmatically impossible to argue that a given solution should be chosen just because it is good for oneself. By the very act of engaging in a public debate – by arguing rather than bargaining – one has ruled out the possibility of invoking such reasons.[22] To engage in discussion can in fact be seen as one kind of self-censorship, a pre-commitment to the idea of rational decision. Now, it might well be thought that this conclusion is too strong. The first argument only shows that in public debate one has to pay some lip-service to the common good. An additional premise states that over time one will in fact come to be swayed by considerations about the common good. One cannot indefinitely praise the common good 'du bout des lèvres', for – as argued by Pascal in the context of the wager – one will end up having the preferences that initially one was faking.[23] This is a psychological, not a conceptual premise. To explain why going through the motions of rational discussion should tend to bring about the real thing, one might argue that people tend to bring what they mean into line with what they say in order to reduce dissonance, but this is a dangerous argument to employ in the present context. Dissonance reduction does not tend to generate autonomous preferences. Rather one would have to invoke the power of reason to break down prejudice and selfishness. By speaking with the voice of reason, one is also exposing oneself to reason.

To sum up, the conceptual impossibility of expressing selfish arguments in a debate about the public good, and the psychological difficulty of expressing other-regarding preferences without ultimately coming to acquire them, jointly bring it about that public discussion tends to promote the common good. The *volonté générale*, then, will not simply be the Pareto-optimal realization of given (or expressed) preferences,[24] but the outcome of preferences that are themselves shaped by a concern for the common good. For instance, by mere aggregation of given preferences one would be able to take account of some negative externalities, but not of those affecting future generations. A social choice mechanism might prevent persons now living from dumping their garbage into one another's backyards, but not from dumping it in the future. Moreover, considerations of distributive justice within the Pareto constraint would now have a more solid foundation, especially as one would also be able to avoid the problem of strategy-proofness. By one stroke one would achieve more rational preferences, as well as the guarantee that they will in fact be expressed.

I now want to set out a series of objections – seven altogether – to the view stated above. I should explain that the goal of this criticism is not to demolish the theory, but to locate some points that need to be fortified. I am, in fact, largely in sympathy with the fundamental tenets of the view, yet fear that it might be dismissed as Utopian, both in the sense of ignoring the problem of getting from here to there, and in the sense of neglecting some elementary facts of human psychology.

The *first objection* involves a reconsideration of the issues of paternalism. Would it not, in fact, be unwarranted interference to impose on the citizens the obligation to participate in political discussion? One might answer that there is a link between the right to vote and the obligation to participate in discussion, just as rights and duties are correlative in other cases. To acquire the right to vote, one has to perform certain civic duties that go beyond pushing the voting button on the television set. There would appear to be two different ideas underlying this answer. First, only those should have the right to vote who are sufficiently *concerned* about politics to be willing to devote some of their resources – time in particular – to it. Secondly, one should try to favour *informed* preferences as inputs to the voting process. The first argument favours participation and discussion as a sign of interest, but does not give it an instrumental value in itself. It would do just as well, for the purpose of this argument, to demand that people should pay for the right to vote. The second argument favours discussion as a means to improvement – it will not only select the right people, but actually make them more qualified to participate.

These arguments might have some validity in a near-ideal world, in which the concern for politics was evenly distributed across all relevant dimensions, but in the context of contemporary politics they miss the point. The people who survive a high threshold for participation are disproportionately found in a privileged part of the population. At best this could lead to paternalism, at worst the high ideals of rational discussion could create a self-elected elite whose members spend time on politics because they want power, not out of concern for the issues. As in other cases, to be discussed later, the best can be the enemy of the good. I am not saying that it is impossible to modify the ideal in a way that allows both for rational discussion and for low-profile participation, only that any institutional design must respect the trade-off between the two.

My *second objection* is that even assuming unlimited time for discussion, unanimous and rational agreement might not necessarily ensue. Could there not be legitimate and unresolvable differences of opinions over the nature of the common good? Could there not even be a plurality of ultimate values?

I am not going to discuss this objection, since it is in any case preempted by the *third objection*. Since there are in fact always time constraints on discussions – often the stronger the more important the issues – unanimity will rarely emerge. For any constellation of preferences short of unanimity, however, one would need a social choice mechanism to aggregate them. One can discuss only for so long, and then one has to make a decision, even if strong differences of opinion should remain. This objection, then, goes to show that the transformation of preferences can never do more than supplement the aggregation of preferences, never replace it altogether.

This much would no doubt be granted by most proponents of the theory. True, they would say, even if the ideal speech situation can never be fully realized, it will nevertheless improve the outcome of the political process if one goes some way towards it. The *fourth objection* questions the validity of this reply. In some cases a little discussion can be a dangerous thing, worse in fact than no discussion at all, viz. if it makes some but not all persons align themselves on the common good. The following story provides an illustration:

> Once upon a time two boys found a cake. One of them said, 'Splendid! I will eat the cake.' The other one said, 'No, that is not fair! We found the cake together, and we should share and share alike, half for you and half for me.' The first boy said, 'No, I should have the whole cake!' Along came an adult who said, 'Gentlemen, you shouldn't fight about this: you should *compromise*. Give him three quarters of the cake.'[25]

What creates the difficulty here is that the first boy's preferences are allowed to count twice in the social choice mechanism suggested by the adult: once in his expression of them and then again in the other boy's internalized ethic of sharing. And one can argue that the outcome is socially inferior to that which would have emerged had they both stuck to their selfish preferences. When Adam Smith wrote that he had never known much good done by those who affected to trade for the public good, he may only have had in mind the harm that can be done by *unilateral* attempts to act morally. The categorical imperative itself may be badly served by people acting unilaterally on it.[26] Also, an inferior outcome may result if discussion brings about partial adherence to morality in all participants rather than full adherence in some and none in others, as in the story of the two boys. Thus Serge Kolm argues that economies with moderately altruistic agents tend to work less well than economies where either everybody is selfish or everybody is altruistic.[27]

A *fifth objection* is to question the implicit assumption that the body politic as a whole is better or wiser than the sum of its parts. Could it not rather be the case that people are made more, not less, selfish and irrational by interacting politically? The cognitive analogy suggests that the rationality of beliefs may be positively as well as negatively affected by interaction. On the one hand there is what Irving Janis has called 'groupthink', i.e. mutually reinforcing bias.[28] On the other hand there certainly are many ways in which people can, and do, pool their opinions and supplement each other to arrive at a better estimate.[29] Similarly autonomy and morality could be enhanced as well as undermined by interaction.

Against the pessimistic view of Reinhold Niebuhr that individuals in a group show more unrestrained egoism than in their personal relationships,[30] we may set Hannah Arendt's optimistic view:

> American faith was not all based on a semireligious faith in human nature, but on the contrary, on the possibility of checking human nature in its singularity, by virtue of human bonds and mutual promises. The hope for man in his singularity lay in the fact that not man but men inhabit the earth and form a world between them. It is human worldliness that will save men from the pitfalls of human nature.[31]

Niebuhr's argument suggests an aristocratic disdain of the *mass*, which transforms individually decent people – to use a characteristically condescending phrase – into an unthinking horde. While rejecting this as a general view, one should equally avoid the other extreme, suggested by Arendt. Neither the Greek nor the American assemblies were the paradigms of discursive reason that she makes them out to be. The Greeks were well aware that they might be tempted by demagogues, and in fact took extensive precautions against this tendency.[32] The American town surely has not always been the incarnation of collective freedom, since on occasion it could also serve as the springboard for witch hunts. The mere decision to engage in rational discussion does not ensure that the transactions will in fact be conducted rationally, since much depends on the structure and the framework of the proceedings. The random errors of selfish and private preferences may to some extent cancel each other out and thus be less to be feared than the massive and coordinated errors that may arise through group-think. On the other hand, it would be excessively stupid to rely on mutually compensating vices to bring about public benefits as a general rule. I am not arguing against the need for public discussion, only for the need to take the question of institutional and constitutional design very seriously.

A *sixth objection* is that unanimity, were it to be realized, might easily be due to conformity rather than to rational agreement. I would in fact tend to have more confidence in the outcome of a democratic decision if there was a minority that voted against it, than if it was unanimous. I am not here referring to people expressing the majority preferences against their real ones, since I am assuming that something like the secret ballot would prevent this. I have in mind that people may come to change their real preferences, as a result of seeing which way the majority goes. Social psychology has amply shown the strength of this bandwagon effect,[33] which in political theory is also known as the 'chameleon' problem.[34] It will not do to argue that the majority to which the conformist adapts his view is likely to pass the test of rationality even if his adherence to it does not, since the majority could well be made up of conformists each of whom would have broken out had there been a minority he could have espoused.

To bring the point home, consider a parallel case of non-autonomous preference formation. We are tempted to say that a man is free if he can get or do whatever it is that he wants to get or do. But then we are immediately faced with the objection that perhaps he only wants what he can get, as the result of some such mechanism as 'sour grapes'.[35] We may then add that, other things being equal, the person is freer the more things he wants to do which he is not free to do, since these show that his wants are not in general shaped by adaptation to his possibilities. Clearly, there is an air of paradox over the statement that a man's freedom is greater the more of his desires he is not free to realize, but on reflection the paradox embodies a valid argument. Similarly, it is possible to dissolve the air of paradox attached to the view that a collective decision is more trust-worthy if it is less than unanimous.

My *seventh objection* amounts to a denial of the view that the need to couch one's argument in terms of the common good will purge the desires of all selfish arguments. There are in general many ways of realizing the common good, if by that phrase we now only mean some arrangement that is Pareto-superior to uncoordinated individual decisions. Each such arrangement will, in addition to promoting the general interest, bring an extra premium to some specific group, which will then have a strong interest in that particular arrangement.[36] The group may then come to prefer the arrangement because of that premium, although it will argue for it in terms of the common good. Typically the arrangement will be justified by a causal theory – an account, say, of how the economy works – that shows it to be not only *a* way, but the only way of promoting the common good. The economic theories underlying the early Reagan administration provide an example. I am not imputing insincerity to the proponents of these views, but there may well be an element of wishful thinking. Since social scientists disagree so strongly among themselves as to how societies work, what could be more human than to pick on a theory that uniquely justifies the arrangement from which one stands to profit? The opposition between general interest and special interests is too simplistic, since the private benefits may causally determine the way in which one conceives of the common good.

These objections have been concerned to bring out two main ideas. First, one cannot assume that one will in fact approach the good society by acting as if one had already arrived there. The fallacy inherent in this 'approximation assumption'[37] was exposed a long time ago in the economic 'theory of the second best':

> It is *not* true that a situation in which more, but not all, of the optimum conditions are fulfilled is necessarily, or is even likely to be, superior to a situation in which fewer are fulfilled. It follows, therefore, that in a situation in which there exist many constraints which prevent the fulfilment of the Paretian optimum conditions, the removal of any one constraint may affect welfare or efficiency either by raising it, by lowering it or by leaving it unchanged.[38]

The ethical analogue is not the familiar idea that some moral obligations may be suspended when other people act non-morally.[39] Rather it is that the nature of the moral obligation is changed in a non-moral environment. When others act non-morally, there may be an obligation to deviate not only from what they do, but also from the behaviour that would have been optimal if adopted by everybody.[40] In particular, a little discussion, like a little rationality or a little socialism, may be a dangerous thing.[41] If, as suggested by Habermas, free and rational discussion will only be possible in a society that has abolished political and economic domination, it is by no means obvious that abolition can be brought about by rational argumentation. I do not want to suggest that it could occur by force – since the use of force to end the use of force is open to obvious objections. Yet something like irony, eloquence or propaganda might be needed, involving less respect for the interlocutor than what would prevail in the ideal speech situation.

As will be clear from these remarks, there is a strong tension between two ways of looking at the relation between political ends and means. On the one hand, the means should partake of the nature of the ends, since otherwise the use of unsuitable means might tend to corrupt the end. On the other hand, there are dangers involved in choosing means immediately derived from the goal to be realized, since in a non-ideal situation these might take us away from the end rather than towards it. A delicate balance will have to be struck between these two, opposing considerations. It is in fact an open question whether there exists a ridge along which we can move to the good society, and if so whether it is like a knife-edge or more like a plateau.

The second general idea that emerges from the discussion is that even in the good society, should we hit upon it, the process of rational discussion could be fragile, and vulnerable to adaptive preferences, conformity, wishful thinking and the like. To ensure stability and robustness there is a need for structures – political institutions or constitutions – that could easily reintroduce an element of domination. We would in fact be confronted, at the political level, with a perennial dilemma of individual behaviour. How is it possible to ensure at the same time that one is bound by rules that protect one from irrational or unethical behaviour – and that these rules do not turn into prisons from which it is not possible to break out even when it would be rational to do so?[42]

III

It is clear from Habermas's theory, I believe, that rational political discussion has an *object* in terms of which it makes sense.[43] Politics is concerned with substantive decision-making, and is to that extent instrumental. True, the idea of instrumental politics might also be taken in a more narrow sense, as implying that the political process is one in which individuals pursue their selfish interests, but more broadly understood it implies only that political action is primarily a means to a non-political end, only secondarily, if at all, an end in itself. In this section I shall consider theories that suggest a reversal of this priority, and that find the main point of politics in the educative or otherwise beneficial effects on the participants. And I shall try to show that this view tends to be internally incoherent, or self-defeating. The benefits of participation are by-products of political activity. Moreover, they are *essentially* by-products, in the sense that any attempt to turn them into the main

purpose of such activity would make them evaporate.[44] It can indeed be highly satisfactory to engage in political work, but only on the condition that the work is defined by a serious purpose which goes beyond that of achieving this satisfaction. If that condition is not fulfilled, we get a narcissistic view of politics – corresponding to various consciousness-raising activities familiar from the last decade or so.

My concern, however, is with political theory rather than with political activism. I shall argue that certain types of arguments for political institutions and constitutions are self-defeating, since they justify the arrangement in question by effects that are essentially by-products. Here an initial and important distinction must be drawn between the task of justifying a constitution *ex ante* and that of evaluating it *ex post* and at a distance. I argue below that Tocqueville, when assessing the American democracy, praised it for consequences that are indeed by-products. In his case, this made perfectly good sense as an analytical attitude adopted after the fact and at some distance from the system he was examining. The incoherence arises when one invokes the same arguments before the fact, in public discussion. Although the constitution-makers may secretly have such side effects in mind, they cannot coherently invoke them in public.

Kant proposed a *transcendental formula of public right*: 'All actions affecting the rights of other human beings are wrong if their maxim is not compatible with their being made public.'[45] Since Kant's illustrations of the principle are obscure, let me turn instead to John Rawls, who imposes a similar condition of publicity as a constraint on what the parties can choose in the original position.[46] He argues, moreover, that this condition tends to favour his own conception of justice, as compared to that of the utilitarians.[47] If utilitarian principles of justice were openly adopted, they would entail some loss of self-esteem, since people would feel that they were not fully being treated as ends in themselves. Other things being equal, this would also lead to a loss in average utility. It is then conceivable that public adoption of Rawls's two principles of justice would bring about a higher average utility than public adoption of utilitarianism, although a lower average than under a secret utilitarian constitution introduced from above. The latter possibility, however, is ruled out by the publicity constraint. A utilitarian could not then advocate Rawls's two principles on utilitarian grounds, although he might well applaud them on such grounds. The fact that the two principles maximize utility would essentially be a by-product, and if chosen on the grounds that they are utility-maximizing they would no longer be so. Utilitarianism, therefore, is self-defeating in Kant's sense: 'it essentially lacks openness'.[48]

Derek Parfit has raised a similar objection to act consequentialism (AC) and suggested how it could be met:

This gives to all one common aim: the best possible outcome. If we try to achieve this, we may often fail. Even when we succeed, the fact that we are disposed to try might make the outcome worse. AC might thus be indirectly self-defeating. What does this show? A consequentialist might say: 'It shows that AC should be only one part of our moral theory. It should be the part that covers successful acts. When we are certain to succeed, we should aim for the best possible outcome. Our wider theory should be this: we should have the aim and dispositions having which would make the outcome best. This wider theory would not be self-defeating. So the objection has been met.'[49]

Yet there is an ambiguity in the word 'should' in the penultimate sentence, since it is not clear whether we are told that it is good to have certain aims and dispositions, or that we should aim at having them. The latter answer immediately raises the problem that having certain aims and dispositions – i.e. being a certain kind of person – is essentially a by-product. When instrumental rationality is self-defeating, we cannot decide on instrumentalist grounds to take leave of it – no more than we can fall asleep by deciding not to try to fall asleep. Although spontaneity may be highly valuable on utilitarian grounds, 'you cannot both genuinely possess this kind of quality and also reassure yourself that while it is free and creative and uncalculative, it is also acting for the best'.[50]

Tocqueville, in a seeming paradox, suggested that democracies are less suited than aristocracies to deal with long-term planning, and yet are superior in the long-run to the latter. The paradox dissolves once it is seen that the first statement involves time at the level of the actors, the second at the level of the observer. On the one hand, 'a democracy finds it difficult to coordinate the details of a great undertaking and to fix on some plan and carry it through with determination in spite of obstacles. It has little capacity for combining measures in secret and waiting patiently for the result'.[51] On the other hand, 'in the long run government by democracy should increase the real forces of society, but it cannot immediately assemble at one point and at a given time, forces as great as those at the disposal of an aristocratic government'.[52] The latter view is further elaborated in a passage from the chapter on 'The Real Advantages Derived by American Society from Democratic Government':

That constantly renewed agitation introduced by democratic government into political life passes, then, into civil society. Perhaps, taking everything into consideration, that is the greatest advantage of democratic government, and I praise it much more on account of what it causes to be done than for what it does. It is incontestable that the people often manage public affairs very badly, but their concern therewith is bound to extend their mental horizon and to shake them out of the rut of ordinary routine...Democracy does not provide a people with the most skillful of governments, but it does that which the most skillful government often cannot do: it spreads throughout the body social a restless activity, superabundant force, and energy never found elsewhere, which, however little favoured by circumstances, can do wonders. Those are its true advantages.[53]

The advantages of democracies, in other words, are mainly and essentially by-products. The avowed aim of democracy is to be a good system of government, but Tocqueville argues that it is inferior in this respect to aristocracy, viewed purely as a decision-making apparatus. Yet the very activity of governing democratically has as a by-product a certain energy and restlessness that benefits industry and generates prosperity. Assuming the soundness of this observation, could it ever serve as a public justification for introducing democracy in a nation that had not yet acquired it? The question is somewhat more complex than one might be led to think from what I have said so far, since the quality of the decisions is not the only consideration that is relevant for the choice of a political system. The argument from *justice* could also be decisive. Yet the following conclusion seems inescapable: if the system has no inherent advantage in terms of justice or efficiency, one cannot coherently and publicly advocate its introduction because of the side effects that would follow in its wake. There must be a *point* in democracy as such. If people are motivated by such inherent advantages to throw themselves into the system, other benefits may ensue – but the latter cannot by themselves be the motivating force. If the democratic method is introduced in a society solely because of the side effects on economic prosperity, and no one believes in it on any other ground, it will not produce them.

Tocqueville, however, did not argue that political activity is an end in itself. The justification for democracy is found in its effects, although not in the intended ones, as the strictly instrumental view would have it. More to the point is Tocqueville's argument for the jury system: 'I do not know whether a jury is useful to the litigants, but I am sure that it is very good for those who have to decide the case. I regard it as one of the most effective means of popular education at society's disposal.'[54] This is still an instrumental view, but the gap between the means and the end is smaller. Tocqueville never argued that the effect of democracy was to make politicians prosperous, only that it was conducive to general prosperity. By contrast, the justification of the jury system is found in the effect on the jurors themselves. And, as above, that effect would be spoilt if they believed that the impact on their own civic spirit was the main point of the proceedings.

John Stuart Mill not only applauded but advocated democracy on the ground of such educative effects on the participants. In current discussion he stands out both as an opponent of the purely instrumental view of politics, that of his father James Mill,[55] and as a forerunner of the theory of participatory democracy.[56] In his theory the gap between means and ends in politics is even narrower, since he saw political activity not only as a means to self-improvement, but also as a source of satisfaction and thus a good in itself. As noted by Albert Hirschman, this implies that 'the benefit of collective action for an individual is not the difference between the hoped-for result and the effort furnished by him or her, but the *sum* of these two magnitudes'.[57] Yet this very way of paraphrasing Mill's view also points to a difficulty. Could it really be the case that participation would yield a benefit even when the hoped-for results are nil, as suggested by Hirschman's formula? Is it not rather

true that the effort is itself a function of the hoped-for result, so that in the end the latter is the only independent variable? When Mill refers, critically, to the limitations of Bentham, whose philosophy 'can teach the means of organising and regulating the merely *business* part of the social arrangement',[58] he seems to be putting the cart before the horse. The non-business part of politics may be the more valuable, but the value is contingent on the importance of the business part.

For a fully developed version of the non-instrumental theory of politics, we may go to the work of Hannah Arendt. Writing about the distinction between the private and the public realm in ancient Greece, she argues that:

> Without mastering the necessities of life in the household, neither life nor the 'good life' is possible, but politics is never for the sake of life. As far as the members of the *polis* are concerned, household life exists for the sake of the 'good life' in the *polis*.[59]
>
> The public realm . . . was reserved for individuality; it was the only place where men could show who they really and inexchangeably were. It was for the sake of this chance, and out of love for a body politic that it made it possible to them all, that each was more or less willing to share in the burden of jurisdiction, defence and administration of public affairs.[60]

Against this we may set the view of Greek politics found in the work of M.I. Finley. Asking why the Athenian people claimed the right of every citizen to speak and make proposals in the Assembly, yet left its exercise to a few, he finds that 'one part of the answer is that the *demos* recognised the instrumental role of political rights and were more concerned in the end with the substantive decisions, were content with their power to select, dismiss and punish their political leaders'.[61] Elsewhere he writes, even more explicitly: 'Then, as now, politics was instrumental for most people, not an interest or an end in itself.'[62] Contrary to what Arendt suggests, the possession or the possibility of exercising a political right may be more important than the actual exercise. Moreover, even the exercise derives its value from the decisions to be taken. Writing about the American town assemblies, Arendt argues that the citizens participated 'neither exclusively because of duty nor, and even less, to serve their own interests but most of all because they enjoyed the discussions, the deliberations, and the making of decisions'.[63] This, while not putting the cart before the horse, at least places them alongside each other. Although discussion and deliberation in other contexts may be independent sources of enjoyment, the satisfaction one derives from *political* discussion is parasitic on decision-making. Political debate is about what to *do* – not about what ought to be the case. It is defined by this practical purpose, not by its subject-matter.

Politics in this respect is on a par with other activities such as art, science, athletics or chess. To engage in them may be deeply satisfactory, if you have an independently defined goal such as 'getting it right' or 'beating the opposition'. A chess player who asserted that he played not to win, but for the sheer elegance of the game, would be in narcissistic bad faith – since there is no such thing as an elegant way of losing, only elegant and inelegant ways of winning. When the artist comes to believe that the process and not the end result is his real purpose, and that defects and irregularities are valuable as reminders of the struggle of creation, he similarly forfeits any claim to our interest. The same holds for E.P. Thompson, who, when asked whether he really believed that a certain rally in Trafalgar Square would have any impact at all, answered: 'That's not really the point, is it? The point is, it shows that democracy's alive...A rally like that gives us self-respect. Chartism was terribly good for the Chartists, although they never got the Charter.'[64] Surely, the Chartists, if asked whether they thought they would ever get the Charter, would not have answered: 'That's not really the point, is it?' It was because they believed they might get the Charter that they engaged in the struggle for it with the seriousness of purpose that also brought them self-respect as a side effect.[65]

IV

I have been discussing three views concerning the relation between economics and politics, between the market and the forum. One extreme is 'the economic theory of democracy', most outrageously stated by Schumpeter, but in essence also underlying social choice theory. It is a market theory of politics, in the sense that the act of voting is a private act similar to that of buying and selling. I cannot accept, therefore, Alan Ryan's argument that 'On any possible view of the distinction between private and public life, voting is an element in one's public life.'[66] The very distinction between the secret and the open ballot shows that there is room for a private-public distinction within politics. The economic theory of democracy, therefore, rests on the idea that the forum should be like the market, in its purpose as well as in its mode of functioning. The purpose is defined in economic terms, and the mode of functioning is that of aggregating individual decisions.

At the other extreme there is the view that the forum should be completely divorced from the market, in purpose as well as in institutional arrangement. The forum should be more than the distributive totality of individuals queuing up for the election booth. Citizenship is a quality that can only be realized in public, i.e. in a collective joined for a common purpose. This purpose, moreover, is not to facilitate life in the material sense. The political process is an end in itself, a good or even the supreme good for those who participate in it. It may be applauded because of the educative effects on the participants, but the benefits do not cease once the education has been completed. On the contrary, the education of the citizen leads to a preference for public life as an end in itself. Politics on this view is not *about* anything. It is the agonistic display of excellence,[67] or the collective display of solidarity, divorced from decision-making and the exercise of influence on events.

In between these extremes is the view I find most attractive. One can argue that the forum should differ from the market in its mode of functioning, yet be concerned with decisions that ultimately deal with economic matters. Even higher-order political decisions concern lower-level rules that are directly related to economic matters. Hence constitutional arguments about how laws can be made and changed, constantly invoke the impact of legal stability and change on economic affairs. It is the concern with substantive decisions that lends the urgency to political debates. The ever-present constraint of *time* creates a need for focus and concentration that cannot be assimilated to the leisurely style of philosophical argument in which it may be better to travel hopefully than to arrive. Yet within these constraints arguments form the core of the political process. If thus defined as public in nature, and instrumental in purpose, politics assumes what I believe to be its proper place in society.

Notes

1 Elster (1978, Ch. 5) refers to these two varieties of market failure as *suboptimality* and *counterfinality* respectively, linking them both to collective action.

2 This is a simplification. First, as argued in Samuelson (1950), there may be political constraints that prevent one from attaining the Pareto-efficient frontier. Secondly, the very existence of several points that are Pareto-superior to the *status quo*, yet involve differential benefits to the participants, may block the realization of any of them.

3 Hammond (1976) offers a useful analysis of the consequences of selfish preferences over income distributions, showing that 'without interpersonal comparisons of some kind, any social preference ordering over the space of possible income distributions must be dictatorial'.

4 Schumpeter (1961, p. 263): 'the will of the people is the product and not the motive power of the political process'. One should not, however, conclude (as does Lively 1975, p. 38) that Schumpeter thereby abandons the market analogy, since on his view (Schumpeter 1939, p. 73) consumer preferences are no less manipulable (with some qualifications stated in Elster 1983a, Ch. 5).

5 See in particular Downs (1957).

6 For fuller statements, see Arrow (1963), Sen (1970), and Kelly (1978), as well as the contribution of Aanund Hylland to Elster and Hylland (1986).

7 Cf. d'Aspremont and Gevers (1977).

8 Riker and Ordeshook (1973, pp. 112–13).

9 Cf. the contributions of Donald Davidson and Allan Gibbard to Elster and Hylland (1986).

10 Presumably, but not obviously, since the agent might have several preference orderings and rely on higher-order preferences to determine which of the first-order preferences to express, as suggested for instance by Sen (1976).

11 Pattanaik (1978) offers a survey of the known results. The only strategy-proof mechanisms for social choice turn out to be the dictatorial one (the dictator has no incentive to misrepresent his preferences) and the randomizing one of getting the probability that a given option will be chosen equal to the proportion of voters that have it as their first choice.

12 Tversky (1981).

13 Cf. Elster (1979, Ch. II) or Schelling (1980) for the idea of deliberately restricting one's feasible set to make certain undesirable behaviour impossible at a later time. The reason this does not work here is that the regret would not be eliminated.

14 Cf. for instance Williams (1973) or Sen (1979).

15 Cf. Elster (1983b, Ch. III) for a discussion of this notion.

16 Arrow (1973).

17 Hirsch (1976)

18 Haavelmo (1970) offers a model in which everybody may suffer a loss of welfare by trying to keep up with the neighbours.

19 One may take the achievements of others as a parameter and one's own as the control variable, or conversely try to manipulate the achievements of others so that they fall short of one's own. The first of these ways of realizing positional goods is clearly less objectionable than the second, but still less pure than the non-comparative desire for a certain standard of excellence.

20 Zeldin (1973, p. 134).

21 I rely mainly on Habermas (1982). I also thank Helge Høibraaten, Rune Slagstad, and Gunnar Skirbekk for having patiently explained to me various aspects of Habermas's work.

22 Midgaard (1980).

23 For Pascal's argument, cf. Elster (1979, Ch. II. 3).

24 As suggested by Runciman and Sen (1965).

25 Smullyan (1980, p. 56).

26 Sobel (1967).

27 Kolm (1981a, b).

28 Janis (1972).

29 Cf. Hogarth (1977) and Lehrer (1978).

30 Niebuhr (1932, p. 11).

31 Arendt (1973, p. 174).

32 Finley (1973); see also Elster (1979, Ch. II.8).

33 Asch (1956) is a classic study.

34 See Goldman (1972) for discussion and further references.

35 Berlin (1969, p. xxxviii); cf. also Elster (1983b, Ch. III.3).

36 Schotter (1981, pp. 26 ff., pp. 43 ff.) has a good discussion of this predicament.

37 Margalit (1983).

38 Lipsey and Lancaster (1956–7, p. 12).

39 This is the point emphasized in Lyons (1965).

40 Cf. Hansson (1970) as well as Føllesdal and Hilpinen (1971) for discussions of 'conditional obligations' within the framework of deontic logic. It does not appear, however, that the framework can easily accommodate the kind of dilemma I am concerned with here.

41 Cf. for instance Kolm (1977) concerning the dangers of a piecemeal introduction of socialism – also mentioned by Margalit (1983) as an objection to Popper's strategy for piecemeal social engineering.

42 Cf. Ainslie (1982) and Elster (1979, Ch. II.9).

43 Indeed, Habermas (1982) is largely concerned with maxims for *action*, not with the evaluation of states of affairs.

44 Cf. Elster (1983b, Ch. III) for a discussion of the notion that some psychological or social states are essentially by-products of actions undertaken for some other purpose.

45 Kant (1795, p. 126).
46 Rawls (1971, p. 133).
47 Rawls (1971, pp. 177 ff., esp. p. 181).
48 Williams (1973, p. 123).
49 Parfit (1981, p. 554).
50 Williams (1973, p. 131); also Elster (1983b, Ch. II. 3).
51 Tocqueville (1969, p. 229).
52 Tocqueville (1969, p. 224).
53 Tocqueville (1969, pp. 243–4).
54 Tocqueville (1969, p. 275).
55 Cf. Ryan (1972). His contrast between 'two concepts of democracy' corresponds in part to the distinction between the first and the second of the theories discussed here, in part to the distinction between the first and the third, as he does not clearly separate

the public conception of politics from the non-instrumental one.
56 Pateman (1970, p. 29).
57 Hirschman (1982, p. 82).
58 Mill (1859, p. 105).
59 Arendt (1958, p. 37).
60 Arendt (1958, p. 41).
61 Finley (1976, p. 83).
62 Finley (1981, p. 31).
63 Arendt (1973, p. 119).
64 *Sunday Times*, 2 November 1980.
65 Cf. also Barry (1978, p. 47).
66 Ryan (1972, p. 105).
67 Veyne (1976) makes a brilliant statement of this non-instrumental attitude among the elite of the Ancient World.

References

Ainslie, G. (1982) 'A behavioral economic approach to the defense mechanisms', *Social Science Information* 21, 735–80.

Arendt, H. (1958) *The Human Condition*, Chicago: University of Chicago Press.

—— (1973) *On Revolution*, Harmondsworth: Pelican Books.

Arrow, K. (1963) *Social Choice and Individual Values*, New York: Wiley.

—— (1973) 'Some ordinal-utilitarian notes on Rawls's theory of justice', *Journal of Philosophy* 70, 245–63.

Asch, S. (1956) 'Studies of independence and conformity: I. A minority of one against a unanimous majority', *Psychology Monographs* 70.

Barry, B. (1978) 'Comment', in S. Benn et al (eds.), *Political Participation*, Canberra: Australian National University Press, pp. 37–48.

Berlin, I. (1969) *Two Concepts of Liberty*, Oxford: Oxford University Press.

d'Aspremont, C. and Gevers, L. (1977) 'Equity and the informational basis of collective choice', *Review of Economic Studies* 44, 199–210.

Downs, A. (1957) *An Economic Theory of Democracy*, New York: Harper.

Elster, J. (1978) *Logic and Society*, Chichester: Wiley.

—— (1979) *Ulysses and the Sirens*, Cambridge: Cambridge University Press.

—— (1983a) *Explaining Technical Change*, Cambridge: Cambridge University Press; Oslo: Universitets-forlaget.

—— (1983b) *Sour Grapes*, Cambridge: Cambridge University Press.

Elster, J. and Hylland, A. (eds.) (1986) *Foundations of Social Choice Theory*, Cambridge: Cambridge University Press.

Finley, M.I. (1973) *Democracy: Ancient and Modern*, London: Chatto & Windus.

—— (1976) 'The freedom of the citizen in the Greek world', reprinted as Ch. 5 in M.I. Finley, *Economy and Society in Ancient Greece*, London: Chatto & Windus 1981.

—— (1981) 'Politics', in M.I. Finley (ed.), *The Legacy of Greece*, Oxford: Oxford University Press, pp. 22–36.

Føllesdal, D. and Hilpinen, R. (1971) 'Deontic logic: an introduction', in R. Hilpinen (ed.), *Deontic Logic: Introductory and Systematic Readings*, Dordrecht: Reidel, pp. 1–35.

Goldman, A. (1972) 'Toward a theory of social power', *Philosophical Studies* 23, 221–68.

Goodin, R.E. (1986) 'Laundering preferences', in Elster and Hylland (eds, 1986), pp. 75–101.

Haavelmo, T. (1970) 'Some observations on welfare and economic growth', in W.A. Eltis, M. Scott and N. Wolfe (eds.), *Induction, Growth and Trade: Essays in Honour of Sir Roy Harrod*, Oxford: Oxford University Press, pp. 65–75.

Habermas, J. (1982) Diskursethik – notizen zu einem Begründingsprogram. Mimeographed.

Hammond, P. (1976) 'Why ethical measures need interpersonal comparisons', *Theory and Decision* 7, 263–74.

Hansson, B. (1970) 'An analysis of some deontic logics', *Nous* 3, 373–98.

Hirsch, F. (1976) *Social Limits to Growth*, Cambridge, Mass.: Harvard University Press.

Hirschman, A. (1982) *Shifting Involvements*, Princeton: Princeton University Press.

Hogarth, R.M. (1977) 'Methods for aggregating opinions', in H. Jungermann and G. de Zeeuw (eds.), *Decision Making and Change in Human Affairs*, Dordrecht: Reidel, pp. 231–56.

Janis, I. (1972) *Victims of Group-Think*, Boston: Houghton Mifflin.

Kant, I. (1795) *Perpetual Peace*, in H. Reiss (ed.), *Kant's Political Writings*, Cambridge: Cambridge University Press.

Kelly, J. (1978) *Arrow Impossibility Theorems*, New York: Academic Press.

Kolm, S.-C. (1977) *La transition socialiste*, Paris: Editions du Cerf.

—— (1981a) 'Altruismes et efficacités', *Social Science Information* 20, 293–354.

—— (1981b) 'Efficacité et altruisme', *Revue Economique* 32, 5–31.

Lehrer, K. (1978) 'Consensus and comparison. A theory of social rationality', in C.A. Hooker, J.J. Leach and E.F. McClennen (eds.), *Foundations and Applications of Decision Theory*. Vol. 1: *Theoretical Foundations*, Dordrecht: Reidel, pp. 283–310.

Lipsey, R.G. and Lancaster, K. (1956–7) 'The general theory of the second-best', *Review of Economic Studies* 24, 11–32.

Lively, J. (1975) *Democracy*. Oxford: Blackwell.

Lyons, D. (1965) *Forms and Limits of Utilitarianism*, Oxford, Oxford University Press.

Margalit, A. (1983) 'Ideals and second bests', in S. Fox (ed.), *Philosophy for Education*, Jerusalem: Van Leer Foundation, pp. 77–90.

Midgaard, K. (1980) 'On the significance of language and a richer concept of rationality', in L. Lewin and E. Vedung (eds.), *Politics as Rational Action*, Dordrecht: Reidel, pp. 83–97.

Mill, J.S. (1859) 'Bentham', in J.S. Mill, *Utilitarianism*, London: Fontana Books (1962), pp. 78–125.

Niebuhr, R. (1932) *Moral Man and Immoral Society*, New York: Scribner's.

Parfit, D. (1981) 'Prudence, morality and the prisoner's dilemma', *Proceedings of the British Academy*, Oxford: Oxford University Press.

Pateman, C. (1970) *Participation and Democratic Theory*, Cambridge: Cambridge University Press.

Pattanaik, P. (1978) *Strategy and Group Choice*, Amsterdam: North-Holland.

Rawls, J. (1971) *A Theory of Justice*, Cambridge, Mass.: Harvard University Press.

Riker, W. and Ordeshook, P.C. (1973) *An Introduction to Positive Political Theory*, Englewood Cliffs, NJ: Prentice Hall.

Runciman, W.G. and Sen, A. (1965) 'Games, justice and the general will', *Mind* 74, 554–62.

Ryan, A. (1972) 'Two concepts of politics and democracy: James and John Stuart Mill', in M. Fleisher (ed.), *Machiavelli and the Nature of Political Thought*, London: Croom Helm, pp. 76–113.

Samuelson, P. (1950) 'The evaluation of real national income', *Oxford Economic Papers* 2, 1–29.

Schelling, T.C. (1980) 'The intimate contest for self-command', *The Public Interest* 60, 94–118.

Schotter, A. (1981) *The Economic Theory of Social Institutions*, Cambridge: Cambridge University Press.

Schumpeter, J. (1939) *Business Cycles*, New York: McGraw-Hill.

—— (1961) *Capitalism, Socialism and Democracy*, London: Allen & Unwin.

Sen, A.K. (1970) *Collective Choice and Social Welfare*, San Francisco: Holden-Day.

—— (1976) 'Liberty, unanimity and rights', *Economica* 43, 217–45.

—— (1979) 'Utilitarianism and welfarism', *Journal of Philosophy* 76, 463–88.

Sobel, J.H. (1967) ' "Everyone", consequences and generalization arguments', *Inquiry* 10, 373–404.

Smullyan, R. (1980) *This Book Needs No Title*, Englewood Cliffs, NJ: Prentice Hall.

Tocqueville, A. de (1969) *Democracy in America*, New York: Anchor Books.

Tversky, A. (1981) 'Choice, preference and welfare: some psychological observations', paper presented at a colloquium on 'Foundations of social choice theory', Ustaoset (Norway).

Veyne, P. (1976) *Le pain et le cirque*, Paris: Seuil.

Williams, B.A.O. (1973) 'A critique of utilitarianism', in J.J.C. Smart and B.A.O. Williams, *Utilitarianism: For and Against*, Cambridge: Cambridge University Press, pp. 77–150.

Zeldin, T. (1973) *France 1848–1945*, vol. 1, Oxford: Oxford University Press.

10

Deliberation and Democratic Legitimacy

Joshua Cohen

In this essay I explore the ideal of a 'deliberative democracy'.[1] By a deliberative democracy I shall mean, roughly, an association whose affairs are governed by the public deliberation of its members. I propose an account of the value of such an association that treats democracy itself as a fundamental political ideal and not simply as a derivative ideal that can be explained in terms of the values of fairness or equality of respect.

The essay is in three sections. In section I, I focus on Rawls's discussion of democracy and use that discussion both to introduce certain features of a deliberative democracy, and to raise some doubts about whether their importance is naturally explained in terms of the notion of a fair system of social cooperation. In section II, I develop an account of deliberative democracy in terms of the notion of an *ideal deliberative procedure*. The characterization of that procedure provides an abstract model of deliberation which links the intuitive ideal of democratic association to a more substantive view of deliberative democracy. Three features of the ideal deliberative procedure figure prominently in the essay. First, it helps to account for some familiar judgements about collective decision-making, in particular about the ways that collective decision-making ought to be different from bargaining, contracting and other mar-

ket-type interactions, both in its explicit attention to considerations of the common advantage and in the ways that that attention helps to form the aims of the participants. Second, it accounts for the common view that the notion of democratic association is tied to notions of autonomy and the common good. Third, the ideal deliberative procedure provides a distinctive structure for addressing institutional questions. And in section III of the paper I rely on that distinctive structure in responding to four objections to the account of deliberative democracy.

I

The ideal of deliberative democracy is a familiar ideal. Aspects of it have been highlighted in recent discussion of the role of republican conceptions of self-government in shaping the American constitutional tradition and contemporary public law.[2] It is represented as well in radical democratic and socialist criticisms of the politics of advanced industrial societies.[3] And some of its central features are highlighted in Rawls's account of democratic politics in a just society, particularly in those parts of his account that seek to incorporate the 'liberty of the ancients' and to respond to radical demo-

Originally published in *The Good Polity*, edited by Alan Hamlin and Philip Pettit (Oxford: Blackwell, 1989), pp. 17–34. Reprinted by permission of Blackwell Publishing Ltd.

For joint treatment of the issues that I discuss here, see Cohen and Rogers (1983), ch. 6. The main differences between the treatment of issues here and the treatment in the book lies in the explicit account of the ideal deliberative procedure, the fuller treatment of the notions of autonomy and the common good, and the account of the connection of those notions with the ideal procedure.

Joshua Cohen

crats and socialists who argue that 'the basic liberties may prove to be merely formal'. In the discussion that follows I shall first say something about Rawls's remarks on three such features, and then consider his explanation of them.[4]

First, in a well-ordered democracy, political debate is organized around alternative conceptions of the public good. So an ideal pluralist scheme, in which democratic politics consists of fair bargaining among groups each of which pursues its particular or sectional interest, is unsuited to a just society (Rawls 1971, pp. 360–1).[5] Citizens and parties operating in the political arena ought not to 'take a narrow or group-interested standpoint' (p. 360). And parties should only be responsive to demands that are 'argued for openly by reference to a conception of the public good' (pp. 226, 472). Public explanations and justifications of laws and policies are to be cast in terms of conceptions of the common good (conceptions that, on Rawls's view, must be consistent with the two principles of justice), and public deliberation should aim to work out the details of such conceptions and to apply them to particular issues of public policy (p. 362).

Second, the ideal of democratic order has egalitarian implications that must be satisfied in ways that are manifest to citizens. The reason is that in a just society political opportunities and powers must be independent of economic or social position – the political liberties must have a fair value[6] – and the fact that they are independent must be more or less evident to citizens. Ensuring this manifestly fair value might, for example, require public funding of political parties and restrictions on private political spending, as well as progressive tax measures that serve to limit inequalities of wealth and to ensure that the political agenda is not controlled by the interests of economically and socially dominant groups (Rawls 1971, pp. 225–6, 277–8; 1982, pp. 42–3). In principle, these distributional requirements might be more stringently egalitarian than those fixed by the difference principle (1982, p. 43).[7] This is so in part because the main point of these measures is not simply to ensure that democratic politics proceeds under fair conditions, nor only to encourage just legislation, but also to ensure that the equality of citizens is manifest and to declare a commitment to that equality 'as the public intention' (1971, p. 233).

Third, democratic politics should be ordered in ways that provide a basis for self-respect, that encourage the development of a sense of political competence, and that contribute to the formation of a sense of justice;[8] it should fix 'the foundations for civic friendship and [shape] the ethos of political culture' (Rawls 1971, p. 234). Thus the importance of democratic order is not confined to its role in obstructing the class legislation that can be expected from systems in which groups are effectively excluded from the channels of political representation and bargaining. In addition, democratic politics should also shape the ways in which the members of the society understand themselves and their own legitimate interests.

When properly conducted, then, democratic politics involves *public deliberation focused on the common good*, requires some form of *manifest equality* among citizens, and *shapes the identity and interests* of citizens in ways that contribute to the formation of a public conception of common good. How does the ideal of a fair system of social cooperation provide a way to account for the attractiveness and importance of these three features of the deliberative democratic ideal? Rawls suggests a formal and an informal line of argument. The formal argument is that parties in the original position would choose the principle of participation[9] with the proviso that the political liberties have their fair value. The three conditions are important because they must be satisfied if constitutional arrangements are to ensure participation rights, guarantee a fair value to those rights, and plausibly produce legislation that encourages a fair distribution according to the difference principle.

Rawls also suggests an informal argument for the ordering of political institutions, and I shall focus on this informal argument here:

Justice as fairness begins with the idea that where common principles are necessary and to everyone's advantage, they are to be worked out from the viewpoint of a suitably defined initial situation of equality in which each person is fairly represented. The principle of participation transfers this notion from the original position to the constitution... [thus] preserv[ing] the equal representation of the original position to the degree that this is feasible. (Rawls 1971, pp. 221–2)[10]

Or, as he puts it elsewhere: 'The idea [of the fair value of political liberty] is to incorporate into the basic structure of society an effective political procedure which *mirrors* in that structure the fair representation of persons achieved by the original position' (1982, p. 45; emphasis added). The suggestion is that, since we accept the intuitive ideal of a fair system of co-operation, we should want our political institutions themselves to conform, in so far as it is feasible, to the requirement that terms of association be worked out under fair conditions. And so we arrive directly at the requirement of equal liberties with fair value, rather than arriving at it indirectly, through a hypothetical choice of that requirement under fair conditions. In this informal argument, the original position serves as an *abstract model* of what fair conditions are, and of what we should strive to mirror in our political institutions, rather than as an initial-choice situation in which regulative principles for those institutions are selected.

I think that Rawls is right in wanting to accommodate the three conditions. What I find less plausible is that the three conditions are natural consequences of the ideal of fairness. Taking the notion of fairness as fundamental, and aiming (as in the informal argument) to model political arrangements on the original position, it is not clear why, for example, political debate ought to be focused on the common good, or why the manifest equality of citizens is an important feature of a democratic association. The pluralist conception of democratic politics as a system of bargaining with fair representation for all groups seems an equally good mirror of the ideal of fairness.

The response to this objection is clear enough: the connection between the ideal of fairness and the three features of democratic politics depends on psychological and sociological assumptions. Those features do not follow directly from the ideal of a fair system of co-operation, or from that ideal as it is modelled in the original position. Rather, we arrive at them when we consider what is required to preserve fair arrangements and to achieve fair outcomes. For example, public political debate should be conducted in terms of considerations of the common good because we cannot expect outcomes that advance the common good unless people are looking for them. Even an ideal pluralist scheme, with equal bargaining power and no barriers to entry, cannot reasonably be expected to advance the common good as defined by the difference principle (1971, p. 360).

But this is, I think, too indirect and instrumental an argument for the three conditions. Like utilitarian defences of liberty, it rests on a series of highly speculative sociological and psychological judgements. I want to suggest that the reason why the three are attractive is not that an

order with, for example, no explicit deliberation about the common good and no manifest equality would be unfair (though of course it might be). Instead it is that they comprise elements of an independent and expressly political ideal that is focused in the first instance[11] on the appropriate conduct of public affairs – on, that is, the appropriate ways of arriving at collective decisions. And to understand that ideal we ought not to proceed by seeking to 'mirror' ideal fairness in the fairness of political arrangements, but instead to proceed by seeking to mirror a system of ideal deliberation in social and political institutions. I want now to turn to this alternative.

II[12]

The notion of a deliberative democracy is rooted in the intuitive ideal of a democratic association in which the justification of the terms and conditions of association proceeds through public argument and reasoning among equal citizens. Citizens in such an order share a commitment to the resolution of problems of collective choice through public reasoning, and regard their basic institutions as legitimate in so far as they establish the framework for free public deliberation. To elaborate this ideal, I begin with a more explicit account of the ideal itself, presenting what I shall call the 'formal conception' of deliberative democracy. Proceeding from this formal conception, I pursue a more substantive account of deliberative democracy by presenting an account of an *ideal deliberative procedure* that captures the notion of justification through public argument and reasoning among equal citizens, and serves in turn as a model for deliberative institutions.

The formal conception of a deliberative democracy has five main features:

D1 A deliberative democracy is an ongoing and independent association, whose members expect it to continue into the indefinite future.

D2 The members of the association share (and it is common knowledge that they share) the view that the appropriate terms of association provide a framework for or are the results of their deliberation. They share, that is, a commitment to co-ordinating their activities within institutions that make deliberation possible and according to norms that they arrive at through their deliberation. For them, free deliberation among equals is the basis of legitimacy.

D3 A deliberative democracy is a pluralistic association. The members have diverse preferences, convictions and ideals concerning the conduct of their own lives. While sharing a commitment to the deliberative resolution of problems of collective choice (D2), they also have divergent aims, and do not think that some particular set of preferences, convictions or ideals is mandatory.

D4 Because the members of a democratic association regard deliberative procedures as the source of *legitimacy*, it is important to them that the terms of their association not merely *be* the results of their deliberation, but also be *manifest* to them as such.[13] They prefer institutions in which the connections between deliberation and outcomes are evident to ones in which the connections are less clear.

D5 The members recognize one another as having deliberative capacities, i.e. the capacities required for entering into a public exchange of reasons and for acting on the result of such public reasoning.

A theory of deliberative democracy aims to give substance to this formal ideal by characterizing the conditions that should obtain if the social order is to be manifestly regulated by deliberative forms of collective choice. I propose to sketch a view of this sort by considering an ideal scheme of deliberation, which I shall call the 'ideal deliberative procedure'. The aim in sketching this procedure is to give an explicit statement of the conditions for deliberative decision-making that are suited to the formal conception, and thereby to highlight the properties that democratic institutions should embody, so far as possible. I should emphasize that the ideal deliberative procedure is meant to provide a model for institutions to mirror – in the first instance for the institutions in which collective choices are made and social outcomes publicly justified – and not to characterize an initial situation in which the terms of association themselves are chosen.[14]

Turning then to the ideal procedure, there are three general aspects of deliberation. There is a need to decide on an agenda, to propose alternative solutions to the problems on the agenda, supporting those solutions with reasons, and to conclude by settling on an alternative. A democratic con-

ception can be represented in terms of the requirements that it sets on such a procedure. In particular, outcomes are democratically legitimate if and only if they could be the object of a free and reasoned agreement among equals. The ideal deliberative procedure is a procedure that captures this principle.[15]

I1 Ideal deliberation is *free* in that it satisfies two conditions. First, the participants regard themselves as bound only by the results of their deliberation and by the preconditions for that deliberation. Their consideration of proposals is not constrained by the authority of prior norms or requirements. Second, the participants suppose that they can act from the results, taking the fact that a certain decision is arrived at through their deliberation as a sufficient reason for complying with it.

I2 Deliberation is *reasoned* in that the parties to it are required to state their reasons for advancing proposals, supporting them or criticizing them. They give reasons with the expectation that those reasons (and not, for example, their power) will settle the fate of their proposal. In ideal deliberation, as Habermas puts it, 'no force except that of the better argument is exercised' (1975, p. 108). Reasons are offered with the aim of bringing others to accept the proposal, given their disparate ends (D3) and their commitment (D2) to settling the conditions of their association through free deliberation among equals. Proposals may be rejected because they are not defended with acceptable reasons, even if they could be so defended. The deliberative conception emphasizes that collective choices should be *made in a deliberative way*, and not only that those choices should have a desirable fit with the preferences of citizens.

I3 In ideal deliberation parties are both formally and substantively *equal*. They are formally equal in that the rules regulating the procedure do not single out individuals. Everyone with the deliberative capacities has equal standing at each stage of the deliberative process. Each can put issues on the agenda, propose solutions, and offer reasons in support of or in criticism of proposals. And each has an equal voice in the decision. The participants are substantively equal in that the existing distribution of power and resources does not shape their chances to contribute to deliberation, nor does that distribution play an authoritative role in their deliberation. The participants in the deliberative procedure do not regard themselves as bound by the existing system of rights, except in so far as that system establishes the framework of free deliberation among equals. Instead they regard that system as a potential object of their deliberative judgement.

I4 Finally, ideal deliberation aims to arrive at a rationally motivated *consensus* – to find reasons that are persuasive to all who are committed to acting on the results of a free and reasoned assessment of alternatives by equals. Even under ideal conditions there is no promise that consensual reasons will be forthcoming. If they are not, then deliberation concludes with voting, subject to some form of majority rule.[16] The fact that it may so conclude does not, however, eliminate the distinction between deliberative forms of collective choice and forms that aggregate nondeliberative preferences. The institutional consequences are likely to be different in the two cases, and the results of voting among those who are committed to finding reasons that are persuasive to all are likely to differ from the results of an aggregation that proceeds in the absence of this commitment.

Drawing on this characterization of ideal deliberation, can we say anything more substantive about a deliberative democracy? What are the implications of a commitment to deliberative decisions for the terms of social association? In the remarks that follow I shall indicate the ways that this commitment carries with it a commitment to advance the common good and to respect individual autonomy.

Common good and autonomy

Consider first the notion of the common good. Since the aim of ideal deliberation is to secure agreement among all who are committed to free deliberation among equals, and the condition of pluralism obtains (D3), the focus of deliberation is on ways of advancing the aims of each party to it. While no one is indifferent to his/her own good, everyone also seeks to arrive at decisions that are acceptable to all who share the commitment to deliberation (D2). (As we shall see just below, taking that commitment seriously is likely to require a willingness to revise one's understanding of

one's own preferences and convictions.) Thus the characterization of an ideal deliberative procedure links the formal notion of deliberative democracy with the more substantive ideal of a democratic association in which public debate is focused on the common good of the members.

Of course, talk about the common good is one thing; sincere efforts to advance it are another. While public deliberation may be organized around appeals to the common good, is there any reason to think that even ideal deliberation would not consist in efforts to disguise personal or class advantage as the common advantage? There are two responses to this question. The first is that in my account of the formal idea of a deliberative democracy, I stipulated (D2) that the members of the association are committed to resolving their differences through deliberation, and thus to providing reasons that they sincerely expect to be persuasive to others who share that commitment. In short, this stipulation rules out the problem. Presumably, however, the objection is best understood as directed against the plausibility of realizing a deliberative procedure that conforms to the ideal, and thus is not answerable through stipulation.

The second response, then, rests on a claim about the effects of deliberation on the motivations of deliberators.[17] A consequence of the reasonableness of the deliberative procedure (I2) together with the condition of pluralism (D3) is that the mere fact of having a preference, conviction or ideal does not by itself provide a reason in support of a proposal. While I may take my preferences as a sufficient reason for advancing a proposal, deliberation under conditions of pluralism requires that I find reasons that make the proposal acceptable to others who cannot be expected to regard my preferences as sufficient reasons for agreeing. The motivational thesis is that the need to advance reasons that persuade others will help to shape the motivations that people bring to the deliberative procedure in two ways. First, the practice of presenting reasons will contribute to the formation of a commitment to the deliberative resolution of political questions (D2). Given that commitment, the likelihood of a sincere representation of preferences and convictions should increase, while the likelihood of their strategic misrepresentation declines. Second, it will shape the content of preferences and convictions as well. Assuming a commitment to deliberative justification, the discovery that I can offer no persuasive reasons on behalf of a proposal of mine may transform the preferences that motivate the proposal. Aims that I recognize to be inconsistent with the requirements of deliberative agreement may tend to lose their force, at least when I expect others to be proceeding in reasonable ways and expect the outcome of deliberation to regulate subsequent action.

Consider, for example, the desire to be wealthier come what may. I cannot appeal to this desire itself in defending policies. The motivational claim is the need to find an independent justification that does not appeal to this desire and will tend to shape it into, for example, a desire to have a level of wealth that is consistent with a level that others (i.e. equal citizens) find acceptable. I am of course assuming that the deliberation is known to be regulative, and that the wealth cannot be protected through wholly non-deliberative means.

Deliberation, then, focuses debate on the common good. And the relevant conceptions of the common good are not comprised simply of interests and preferences that are antecedent to deliberation. Instead, the interests, aims and ideals that comprise the common good are those that survive deliberation, interests that, on public reflection, we think it legitimate to appeal to in making claims on social resources. Thus the first and third of the features of deliberative democracy that I mentioned in the discussion of Rawls (p. 160 above) comprise central elements in the deliberative conception.

The ideal deliberative scheme also indicates the importance of autonomy in a deliberative democracy. In particular, it is responsive to two main threats to autonomy. As a general matter, actions fail to be autonomous if the preferences on which an agent acts are, roughly; given by the circumstances, and not determined by the agent. There are two paradigm cases of 'external' determination. The first is what Elster (1982) has called 'adaptive preferences'.[18] These are preferences that shift with changes in the circumstances of the agent without any deliberate contribution by the agent to that shift. This is true, for example, of the political preferences of instinctive centrists who move to the median position in the political distribution, wherever it happens to be. The second I shall call 'accommodationist preferences'. While they are deliberately formed, accommodationist preferences represent psychological adjustments to conditions of subordination in which individuals are not recognized as having the capacity for self-government. Consider Stoic slaves, who deliberately shape their desires to match their powers, with a view to minimizing frustration.

Since the existing relations of power make slavery the only possibility, they cultivate desires to be slaves, and then act on those desires. While their motives are deliberately formed, and they act on their desires, the Stoic slaves do not act autonomously when they seek to be good slaves. The absence of alternatives and consequent denial of scope for the deliberative capacities that defines the condition of slaves supports the conclusion that their desires result from their circumstances, even though those circumstances shape the desires of the Stoic slaves through their deliberation.

There are then at least two dimensions of autonomy. The phenomenon of adaptive preferences underlines the importance of conditions that permit and encourage the deliberative formation of preferences; the phenomenon of accommodationist preferences indicates the need for favourable conditions for the exercise of the deliberative capacities. Both concerns are met when institutions for collective decision-making are modelled on the ideal deliberative procedure. Relations of power and subordination are neutralized (I1, I3, I4), and each is recognized as having the deliberative capacities (D5), thus addressing the problem of accommodationist preferences. Further, the requirement of reasonableness discourages adaptive preferences (I2). While preferences are 'formed' by the deliberative procedure, this type of preference formation is consistent with autonomy since preferences that are shaped by public deliberation are not simply given by external circumstances. Instead they are the result of 'the power of reason as applied through public discussion'.[19]

Beginning, then, from the formal ideal of a deliberative democracy, we arrive at the more substantive ideal of an association that is regulated by deliberation aimed at the common good and that respects the autonomy of the members. And so, in seeking to embody the ideal deliberative procedure in institutions, we seek, *inter alia*, to design institutions that focus political debate on the common good, that shape the identity and interests of citizens in ways that contribute to an attachment to the common good, and that provide the favourable conditions for the exercise of deliberative powers that are required for autonomy.

III

I want now to shift the focus. While I shall continue to pursue the relationship between the ideal deliberative procedure and more substantive issues about deliberative democratic association, I want to do so by considering four natural objections to the conception I have been discussing, objections to that conception for being sectarian, incoherent, unjust and irrelevant. My aim is not to provide a detailed response to the objections, but to clarify the conception of deliberative democracy by sketching the lines along which a response should proceed. Before turning to the objections, I enter two remarks about what follows.

First, as I indicated earlier, a central aim in the deliberative conception is to specify the institutional preconditions for deliberative decision-making. The role of the ideal deliberative procedure is to provide an abstract characterization of the important properties of deliberative institutions. The role of the ideal deliberative procedure is thus different from the role of an ideal social contract. The ideal deliberative procedure provides a model for institutions, a model that they should mirror, so far as possible. It is not a choice situation in which institutional principles are selected. The key point about the institutional reflection is that it should *make deliberation possible*. Institutions in a deliberative democracy do not serve simply to implement the results of deliberation, as though free deliberation could proceed in the absence of appropriate institutions. Neither the commitment to nor the capacity for arriving at deliberative decisions is something that we can simply assume to obtain independent from the proper ordering of institutions. The institutions themselves must provide the framework for the formation of the will; they determine whether there is equality, whether deliberation is free and reasoned, whether there is autonomy, and so on.

Second, I shall be focusing here on some requirements on 'public' institutions that reflect the ideal of deliberative resolution. But there is of course no reason to expect as a general matter that the preconditions for deliberation will respect familiar institutional boundaries between 'private' and 'public' and will all pertain to the public arena. For example, inequalities of wealth, or the absence of institutional measures designed to redress the consequences of those inequalities, can serve to undermine the equality required in deliberative arenas themselves. And so a more complete treatment would need to address a wider range of institutional issues (see Cohen and Rogers 1983, chs 3, 6; Cohen 1988).

Sectarianism

The first objection is that the ideal of deliberative democracy is objectionably sectarian because it depends on a particular view of the good life – an ideal of active citizenship. What makes it sectarian is not the specific ideal on which it depends, but the (alleged) fact that it depends on some specific conception at all. I do not think that the conception of deliberative democracy suffers from the alleged difficulty. In explaining why not, I shall put to the side current controversy about the thesis that sectarianism is avoidable and objectionable, and assume that it is both.[20]

Views of the good figure in political conceptions in at least two ways. First, the *justification* of some conceptions appeals to a notion of the human good. Aristotelian views, for example, endorse the claim that the exercise of the deliberative capacities is a fundamental component of a good human life, and conclude that a political association ought to be organized to encourage the realization of those capacities by its members. A second way in which conceptions of the good enter is that the *stability* of a society may require widespread allegiance to a specific conception of the good, even though its institutions can be justified without appeal to that conception. For example, a social order that can be justified without reference to ideals of national allegiance may none the less require widespread endorsement of the ideal of patriotic devotion for its stability.

A political conception is objectionably sectarian only if its *justification* depends on a particular view of the human good, and not simply because its stability is contingent on widespread agreement on the value of certain activities and aspirations. For this reason the democratic conception is not sectarian. It is organized around a view of political justification – that justification proceeds through free deliberation among equal citizens – and not a conception of the proper conduct of life. So, while it is plausible that the stability of a deliberative democracy depends on encouraging the ideal of active citizenship, this dependence does not suffice to show that it is objectionably sectarian.

Incoherence

Consider next the putative incoherence of the ideal. We find this charge in an important tradition of argument, including Schumpeter's *Capitalism,*

Joshua Cohen

Socialism, and Democracy and, more recently, William Riker's work on social choice and democracy. I want here to say a word about the latter, focusing on just one reason that Riker gives for thinking that the ideal of popular self-government is incoherent.[21]

Institutionalizing a deliberative procedure requires a decision rule short of consensus – for example, majority rule. But majority rule is globally unstable: as a general matter, there exists a majority-rule path leading from any element in the set of alternatives to any other element in the set. The majority, standing in for the people, wills everything and therefore wills nothing. Of course, while anything can be the result of majority decision, it is not true that everything will be the result. But, because majority rule is so unstable, the actual decision of the majority will not be determined by preferences themselves, since they do not constrain the outcome. Instead decisions will reflect the particular institutional constraints under which they are made. But these constraints are 'exogenous to the world of tastes and values' (Riker 1982, p. 190). So the ideal of popular self-government is incoherent because we are, so to speak, governed by the institutions, and not by ourselves.

I want to suggest one difficulty with this argument that highlights the structure of the deliberative conception. According to the argument I just sketched, outcomes in majority-rule institutions reflect 'exogenous' institutional constraints, and not underlying preferences. This suggests that we can identify the preferences and convictions that are relevant to collective choices apart from the institutions through which they are formed and expressed. But that is just what the deliberative conception denies. On this conception, the relevant preferences and convictions are those that could be expressed in free deliberation, and not those that are prior to it. For this reason, popular self-government *premises* the existence of institutions that provide a framework for deliberation; these arrangements are not 'exogenous constraints' on the aggregation of preferences, but instead help to shape their content and the way that citizens choose to advance them. And, once the deliberative institutions are in place, and preferences, convictions and political actions are shaped by them, it is not clear that instability problems remain so severe as to support the conclusion that self-government is an empty and incoherent ideal.

Injustice

The third problem concerns injustice. I have been treating the ideal of democracy as the basic ideal for a political conception. But it might be argued that the ideal of democracy is not suited to the role of fundamental political ideal because its treatment of basic liberties is manifestly unacceptable. It makes those liberties dependent on judgements of majorities and thus endorses the democratic legitimacy of decisions that restrict the basic liberties of individuals. In responding to this objection I shall focus on the liberty of expression,[22] and shall begin by filling out a version of the objection which I put in the words of an imagined critic.[23]

'You embrace the ideal of a democratic order. The aim of a democratic order is to maximize the *power of the people* to secure its wants. To defend the liberty of expression you will argue that that power is diminished if the people lack the information required for exercising their will. Since expression provides information, you will conclude that abridgements of expression ought to be barred. The problem with your argument is that preventing restrictions on expression also restricts the power of the people, since the citizens may collectively prefer such restrictions. And so it is not at all clear as a general matter that the protection of expression will maximize popular power. So while you will, of course, not want to prevent everyone from speaking all the time, you cannot defend the claim that there is even a presumption in favour of the protection of expression. And this disregard for fundamental liberties is unacceptable.'

This objection has force against some conceptions on which democracy is a fundamental ideal, particularly those in which the value of expression turns exclusively on its role as a source of information about how best to advance popular ends. But it does not have any force against the deliberative conception, since the latter does not make the case for expression turn on its role in maximizing the power of the people to secure its wants. That case rests instead on a conception of collective choice, in particular on a view about how the 'wants' that are relevant to collective choice are formed and defined in the first place. The relevant preferences and convictions are those that arise from or are confirmed through deliberation. And a framework of free expression is required for the reasoned consideration of alternatives that comprises deliberation. The deliberative conception holds that free expression is required for *determining* what advances the common good, because what is good is fixed by public deliberation, and not prior to it. It is fixed by informed and autonomous judgements, involving the exercise of the deliberative capacities. So the ideal of deliberative democracy is not hostile to free expression; it rather presupposes such freedom.

But what about expression with no direct bearing on issues of public policy? Is the conception of deliberative democracy committed to treating all 'non-political expression' as second-class, and as meriting lesser protection? I do not think so. The deliberative conception construes politics as aiming in part at the formation of preferences and convictions, not just at their articulation and aggregation. Because of this emphasis on reasoning about preferences and convictions, and the bearing of expression with no political focus on such reasoning, the deliberative view draws no bright line between political speech and other sorts of expression. Forms of expression that do not address issues of policy may well bear on the formation of the interests, aims, and ideals that citizens bring to public deliberation. For this reason the deliberative conception supports protection for the full range of expression, regardless of the content of that expression.[24] It would violate the core of the ideal of free deliberation among equals to fix preferences and convictions in advance by restricting the content of expression, or by barring access to expression, or by preventing the expression that is essential to having convictions at all. Thus the injustice objection fails because the liberties are not simply among the topics for deliberation; they help to comprise the framework that makes it possible.[25]

Irrelevance

The irrelevance objection is that the notion of public deliberation is irrelevant to modern political conditions.[26] This is the most important objection, but also the one about which it is hardest to say anything at the level of generality required by the present context. Here again I shall confine myself to one version of the objection, though one that I take to be representative.

The version that I want to consider starts from the assumption that a direct democracy with citizens gathering in legislative assemblies is the only way to institutionalize a deliberative procedure. Premising that, and recognizing that direct democracy is impossible under modern conditions, the objection concludes that we ought to be led to reject the ideal because it is not relevant to our circumstances.

The claim about the impossibility of direct democracy is plainly correct. But I see no merit in the claim that direct democracy is the uniquely suitable way to institutionalize the ideal procedure.[27] In fact, in the absence of a theory about the operations of democratic assemblies – a theory which cannot simply stipulate that ideal conditions obtain – there is no reason to be confident that a direct democracy would subject political questions to deliberative resolution, even if a direct democracy were a genuine institutional possibility.[28] In the absence of a realistic account of the functioning of citizen assemblies, we cannot simply assume that large gatherings with open-ended agendas will yield any deliberation at all, or that they will encourage participants to regard one another as equals in a free deliberative procedure. The appropriate ordering of deliberative institutions depends on issues of political psychology and political behaviour; it is not an immediate consequence of the deliberative ideal. So, far from being the only deliberative scheme, direct democracy may not even be a particularly good arrangement for deliberation. But, once we reject the idea that a direct democracy is the natural or necessary form of expression of the deliberative ideal, the straightforward argument for irrelevance no longer works. In saying how the ideal might be relevant, however, we come up against the problem I mentioned earlier. Lacking a good understanding of the workings of institutions, we are inevitably thrown back on more or less speculative judgements. What follows is some sketchy remarks on one issue that should be taken in this spirit.

At the heart of the institutionalization of the deliberative procedure is the existence of arenas in which citizens can propose issues for the political agenda and participate in debate about those issues. The existence of such arenas is a public good, and ought to be supported with public money. This is not because public support is the only way, or even the most efficient way, of ensuring the provision of such arenas. Instead, public provision expresses the basic commitment of a democratic order to the resolution of political questions through free deliberation among equals. The problem is to figure out how arenas might be organized to encourage such deliberation.

In considering that organization, there are two key points that I want to underscore. The first is that material inequalities are an important source of political inequalities. The second point – which is more speculative – is that deliberative arenas which are organized exclusively on local, sectional or issue-specific lines are unlikely to produce the open-ended deliberation required to institutionalize a deliberative procedure. Since these arenas bring together only a narrow range of interests, deliberation in them can be expected at best to produce coherent sectional interests, but no more comprehensive conception of the common good.

These two considerations together provide support for the view that political parties supported by public funds play an important role in making a deliberative democracy possible.[29] There are two reasons for this, corresponding to the two considerations I have just mentioned. In the first place, an important feature of organizations generally, and parties in particular, is that they provide a means through which individuals and groups who lack the 'natural' advantage of wealth can overcome the political disadvantages that follow on that lack. Thus they can help to overcome the inequalities in deliberative arenas that result from material inequality. Of course, to play this role, political organizations must themselves be freed from the dominance of private resources, and that independence must be manifest. Thus the need for public funding. Here we arrive back at the second point that I mentioned in the discussion of Rawls's view – that measures are needed to ensure manifest equality – though now as a way of displaying a shared commitment to deliberative decisions, and not simply as an expression of the commitment to fairness. Second, because parties are required to address a comprehensive range of political issues, they provide arenas in which debate is not restricted in the ways that it is in local, sectional or issue-specific organizations. They can provide the more open-ended arenas needed to form and articulate the conceptions of the common good that provide the focus of political debate in a deliberative democracy.

There is certainly no guarantee that parties will operate as I have just described. But this is not especially troubling, since there are no guarantees of anything in politics. The question is how we can best approximate the deliberative conception. And it is difficult to see how that is possible in the absence of strong parties, supported with public resources (though, of course, a wide range of other conditions are required as well).

IV

I have suggested that we take the notion of democratic association as a fundamental political ideal, and have elaborated that ideal by reference to an ideal deliberative procedure and the requirements for institutionalizing such a procedure. I have sketched a few of those requirements here. To show that the democratic ideal can play the role of fundamental organizing ideal, I should need to pursue the account of fundamental liberties and political organization in much greater detail and to address a wide range of other issues as well. Of course, the richer the requirements are for institutionalizing free public deliberation, the larger the range of issues that may need to be removed from the political agenda; that is, the larger the range of issues that form the background framework of public deliberation rather than its subject matter. And, the larger that range, the less there is to deliberate about. Whether that is good news or bad news, it is in any case a suitable place to conclude.

Notes

1 I originally came across the term 'deliberative democracy' in Sunstein (1985). He cites (n. 26) an article by Bessette, which I have not consulted.

2 For some representative examples, see Sunstein (1984, 1985, 1986), Michelman (1986), Ackerman (1984, 1986).

3 I have in mind, in particular, criticisms which focus on the ways in which material inequalities and weak political parties restrict democracy by constraining public political debate or undermining the equality of the participants in that debate. For discussion of these criticisms, and of their connections with the ideal of democratic order, see Cohen and Rogers (1983), chs. 3, 6; Unger (1987), ch. 5.

4 In the discussion that follows, I draw on Rawls (1971, esp. sections 36, 37, 43, 54; 1982).

5 This rejection is not particularly idiosyncratic. Sunstein, for example, argues (1984, 1985) that ideal pluralism has never been embraced as a political ideal in American public law.

6 Officially, the requirement of fair value is that 'everyone has a fair opportunity to hold public office and to influence the outcome of political decisions' (Rawls 1982, p. 42).

7 Whatever their stringency, these distributional requirements take priority over the difference principle, since the requirement of fair value is part of the principle of liberty; that is, the first principle of justice (Rawls 1982, pp. 41–2).

8 The importance of democratic politics in the account of the acquisition of the sense of justice is underscored in Rawls (1971), pp. 473–4.

9 The principle of participation states that 'all citizens are to have an equal right to take part in, and to determine the outcome of, the constitutional process that establishes the laws with which they are to comply' (Rawls 1971, p. 221).

10 I assume that the principle of participation should be understood here to include the requirement of the fair value of political liberty.

11 The reasons for the phrase 'in the first instance' are clarified below at pp. 162–3.

12 Since writing the first draft of this section of the paper, I have read Elster (1986a) and Manin (1987), which both present parallel conceptions. This is especially so with Elster's treatment of the psychology of public deliberation (pp. 112–13). I am indebted to Alan Hamlin for bringing the Elster article to my attention. The overlap is explained by the fact that Elster, Manin and I all draw on Habermas. See Habermas (1975, 1979, 1984). I have also found the discussion of the contractualist account of motivation in Scanlon (1982) very helpful.

13 For philosophical discussions of the importance of manifestness or publicity, see Kant (1983), pp. 135–9; Rawls (1971), p. 133 and section 29; Williams (1985), pp. 101–2, 200.

14 The distinction between the ideal procedure and an initial-choice situation will be important in the later discussion of motivation formation (see pp. 163–4) and institutions (p. 164–5).

15 There are of course norms and requirements on individuals that do not have deliberative justification. The conception of deliberative democracy is, in Rawls's term, a 'political conception', and not a comprehensive moral theory. On the distinction between political and comprehensive theories, see Rawls (1987), pp. 1–25.

16 For criticism of the reliance on an assumption of unanimity in deliberative views, see Manin (1987), pp. 359–61.

17 Note the parallel with Elster (1986a) indicated in note 12. See also the discussion in Habermas (1975), p. 108, about 'needs that can be communicatively shared', and Habermas (1979), ch. 2.

18 For an interesting discussion of autonomous preferences and political processes, see Sunstein (1986, pp. 1145–58; 1984, pp. 1699–700).

19 Whitney *vs*. California, 274 US 357 (1927).

20 For contrasting views on sectarianism, see Rawls (1987); Dworkin (1985), pt 3; MacIntyre (1981); Sandel (1982).

21 See Riker (1982); for discussion of Riker's view see Coleman and Ferejohn (1986); Cohen (1986).

22 For discussion of the connection between ideals of democracy and freedom of expression, see Meiklejohn (1948), Tribe (1978; 1985, ch. 2) and Ely (1980, pp. 93–4, 105–16). Freedom of expression is a special case that can perhaps be more straightforwardly accommodated by the democratic conception than liberties of conscience, or the liberties associated with privacy and personhood. I do think, however, that these other liberties can be given satisfactory treatment by the democratic conception, and would reject it if I did not think so. The general idea would be to argue that other fundamental liberties must be protected if citizens are to be able to engage in and have equal standing in political deliberation without fear that such engagement puts them at risk for their convictions or personal choices. Whether this line of argument will work out on the details is a matter for treatment elsewhere.

23 This objection is suggested in Dworkin (1985), pp. 61–3. He cites the following passage from a letter of Madison's: 'And a people who mean to be their own Governors, must arm themselves with *the power which knowledge gives*' (emphasis added).

24 On the distinction between content-based and content-neutral abridgements, the complexities of drawing the distinction in particular cases, and the special reasons for hostility to content-based abridgements, see Tribe (1978), pp. 584–682; Stone (1987), pp. 46–118.

25 I am not suggesting that the deliberative view provides the only sound justification for the liberty of expression. My concern here is rather to show that the deliberative view is capable of accommodating it.

26 For an especially sharp statement of the irrelevance objection, see Schmitt (1985).

27 This view is sometimes associated with Rousseau, who is said to have conflated the notion of democratic legitimacy with the institutional expression of that ideal in a direct democracy. For criticism of this interpretation, see Cohen (1986a).

28 Madison urges this point in the *Federalist Papers*. Objecting to a proposal advanced by Jefferson which would have regularly referred constitutional questions 'to the decision of the whole of society', Madison argues that this would increase 'the danger of disturbing the public tranquillity by interesting too strongly the public passions'. And 'it is the reason, alone, of the public that ought to control and regulate the government . . . [while] the passions ought to be controlled and regulated by the government'. I endorse the form of the objection, not its content (*Federalist Papers* 1961, pp. 315–17).

Joshua Cohen

29   Here I draw on Cohen and Rogers (1983), pp. 154–7. The idea that parties are required to organize political choice and to provide a focus for public deliberation is one strand of arguments about 'responsible parties' in American political-science literature. My under-standing of this view has been greatly aided by Perl-man (1987), and, more generally, by the work of my colleague Walter Dean Burnham on the implications of party decline for democratic politics. See, for ex-ample, Burnham (1982).

References

Ackerman, B.A. 1984: The Storrs Lectures: Discovering the constitution. *Yale Law Journal*, 93: 1013–72.

—— 1986: Discovering the constitution. Unpublished manuscript.

Burnham, W.D. 1982: *The Current Crisis in American Politics*. Oxford: Oxford University Press.

Cohen, J. 1986a: Autonomy and democracy: reflections on Rousseau. *Philosophy and Public Affairs*, 15: 275–97.

—— 1986b: An epistemic conception of democracy. *Ethics*, 97: 26–38.

—— 1988: The material basis of deliberative democracy. *Social Philosophy and Policy*.

Cohen, J. and Rogers, J. 1983: *On Democracy*. Harmondsworth: Penguin.

Coleman, J. and Ferejohn, J. 1986: Democracy and social choice. *Ethics*, 97 (October): 6–25.

Dworkin, R. 1985: *A Matter of Principle*. Cambridge, Mass.: Harvard University Press.

Elster, J. 1982: Sour grapes. In A. Sen and B. Williams (eds), *Utilitarianism and Beyond*, Cambridge: Cambridge University Press, 219–38.

—— 1986: The market and the forum: three varieties of political theory. In J. Elster and A. Hylland (eds), *The Foundations of Social Choice Theory*. Cambridge: Cambridge University Press, 103–32.

Ely, J.H. 1980: *Democracy and Distrust: a theory of judicial review*. Cambridge, Mass.: Harvard University Press.

Federalist Papers 1961: ed. C. Rossiter. New York: New American Library.

Habermas, J. 1975: *The Legitimation Crisis of Late Capitalism*, tr. T. McCarthy. Boston, Mass.: Beacon Press; London: Heinemann.

—— 1979: *Communication and the Evolution of Society*, tr. T. McCarthy. Boston, Mass.: Beacon Press.

—— 1984: *The Theory of Communicative Action*, vol. I, tr. T. McCarthy. Boston, Mass.: Beacon Press.

Kant, I., tr. T. Humphrey 1983: To perpetual peace: a philosophical sketch. In *Perpetual Peace and other Essays*, Indianapolis: Hackett.

MacIntyre, A. 1981: *After Virtue*. Notre Dame, Ind.: University of Notre Dame Press.

Manin, B. 1987: On legitimacy and political deliberation. *Political Theory*, 15: 338–68.

Meiklejohn, A. 1948: *Free Speech and its Relation of Self-Government*. New York: Harper and Row.

Michelman, F.I. 1986: The Supreme Court, 1985 Term – Foreword: Traces of Self-Government. *Harvard Law Review*, 100: 4–77.

Perlman, L. 1987: Parties, democracy and consent. Unpublished.

Rawls, J. 1971: *A Theory of Justice*. Cambridge, Mass.: Harvard University Press; also Oxford: Clarendon Press (1972).

—— 1982: The basic liberties and their priority. *Tanner Lectures on Human Values*, Salt Lake City: University of Utah Press, vol. III.

—— 1987: The idea of an overlapping consensus. *Oxford Journal of Legal Studies*, 7: 1–25.

Riker, W. 1982: *Liberalism against Populism: a confrontation between the theory of democracy and the theory of social choice*. San Francisco: W.H. Freeman.

Sandel, M. 1982: *Liberalism and the Limits of Justice*. Cambridge: Cambridge University Press.

Scanlon, T.M. 1982: Contractualism and utilitarianism. In A.K. Sen and B. Williams (eds), *Utilitarianism and Beyond*, Cambridge: Cambridge University Press, 103–28.

Schmitt, C. 1985: *The Crisis of Parliamentary Democracy*, tr. E. Kennedy. Cambridge, Mass.: MIT Press.

Schumpeter, J.A. 1954: *Capitalism, Socialism and Democracy*, London: Unwin.

Stone, G. 1987: Content-neutral restrictions. *University of Chicago Law Review*, 54: 46–118.

Sunstein, C. 1984: Naked preferences and the constitution. *Columbia Law Review*, 84: 1689–732.

—— 1985: Interest groups in American public law. *Stanford Law Review*, 38: 29–87.

—— 1986: Legal interference with private preferences. *University of Chicago Law Review*, 53: 1129–84.

Tribe, L. 1978: *American Constitutional Law*. Mineola NY: Foundation Press.

—— 1985: *Constitutional Choices*. Cambridge, Mass.: Harvard University Press.

Unger, R. 1987: *False Necessity*. Cambridge: Cambridge University Press.

Williams, B. 1985: *Ethics and the Limits of Philosophy*. London: Fontana, Collins; Cambridge, Mass.: Harvard University Press.

11

Dealing with Difference: A Politics of Ideas or a Politics of Presence?

Anne Phillips

In the post-communist world of the 1980s and 1990s, liberalism and liberal democracy have achieved an impressive ascendancy, and can more plausibly present themselves as the only legitimate bases for equality, justice or democracy. Critics, of course, remain, but the grounds of complaint have shifted considerably. For many years, the central arguments against liberalism fell into three broad categories: that the liberal emphasis on individual freedoms and rights reflected a self-protective and competitive egotism that refused any wider community; that the liberal focus on "merely" political equalities ignored or even encouraged gross inequalities in social and economic life; and that the liberal consolidation of representative democracy reduced the importance of more active citizen participation. None of these complaints has disappeared, but each has been reformulated in terms of diversity and difference. Feminist theorists, in particular, have identified liberalism with an abstract individualism that ignores its own gendered content, and many have criticized the homogenizing ideals of equality that require us to be or become the same.[1] Accusations of gender-blindness and race- or ethnicity-blindness have added weight to older complaints that liberalism is blind to class. At a moment when most political theorists have situated themselves more firmly in the liberal tradition, liberalism is extensively criticized for erasing diversity and difference.

From the standpoint of that much maligned visitor from Mars (whose technical brilliance in negotiating the journey always combines with an astonishing ignorance of political ideas) it might well appear that liberals never thought about difference. Left at such a level of generality, the accusation is distinctly odd, for notions of diversity and difference have been central to liberalism from its inception and to liberal democracy throughout its formation. What gave the original impetus to liberalism was the perception that neither nature nor tradition guaranteed political order, and that the very equality of what we now see as male subjects increased the potential diversity and conflict. Hence the search for a contractual basis for political authority that would bind these different individuals into a coherent whole; hence the concern with rights and autonomies that would allow them to pursue part of their lives under their own steam. In these and subsequent developments, difference remained politically significant and theoretically important: a driving force, indeed, in the separation between public and private affairs.

The defining characteristics of liberal democracy, as Robert Dahl among others has clarified,[2] are also grounded in the heterogeneity of the societies that gave it birth. It was the diversity of the citizenry, as much as its absolute size, that made the earlier (more consensual) practices of Athenian democracy so inappropriate to the modern world. Lacking any half-credible basis for seeing citizens as united in their goals, theorists of liberal democracy took issue with the homogenizing presumptions

Originally published in *Constellations* 1 (1994): 74–91. Reprinted by permission of Blackwell Publishing Ltd.

of a common good or common purpose, and made diversity a central organizing theme. John Stuart Mill's famous vacillations over democracy derived from a double sense of democracy as both impetus and threat to diversity: something that breaks the hold of any single notion of the good life, but can also encourage a deadening conformity. In more straightforwardly confident vein, George Kateb has presented constitutional and representative democracy as that system *par excellence* that encourages and disseminates diversity. The procedures of electoral competition do not merely chasten and circumscribe the powers of government. By promoting a more skeptical attitude towards the basis on which competing claims are resolved, they also cultivate "a general tolerance of, and even affection for diversity: diversity in itself, and diversity as the source of regulated contest and competition."[3]

Difference is not something we have only just noticed. What we can more usefully say is that difference has been perceived in an overly cerebral fashion as differences in opinions and beliefs, and that the resulting emphasis on what I will call a politics of ideas has proved inadequate to the problems of political exclusion. The diversity most liberals have in mind is a diversity of beliefs, opinions, preferences and goals, all of which may stem from the variety of experience, but are considered as in principle detachable from this. Even the notion of interests, which seems most thoroughly grounded in differential material conditions, lends itself to at least semi-detachment. The preference for higher taxes on those with higher incomes may be stronger among those with little money, especially if they believe the proceeds will finance public provision of educational or health services that would be otherwise beyond their reach. But support for higher taxation and better public provision is not restricted to those who most directly benefit: political preferences are influenced by material circumstances without being reducible to these. The interests of pensioners or the long-term unemployed can then be championed by those who are neither retired nor out of work; the interests of geographical localities can be represented by people who no longer live in the area; the interests of mothers with young children can be represented by childless men.

One consequence for democracy is that what is to be represented then takes priority over who does the representation. Issues of political pres-

ence are largely discounted, for when difference is considered in terms of intellectual diversity, it does not much matter who represents the range of ideas. One person may easily stand in for another; there is no additional requirement for the representatives to "mirror" the characteristics of the person or people represented. What concerns us in the choice of representative is a congruity of political beliefs and ideals, combined perhaps with a superior ability to articulate and register opinions. The quality of the democracy is guaranteed by the extension of suffrage to all adults, each of whom contributes his or her vote to the opinions that gain public weight. Stripped of any predemocratic authority, the role of the politician is to carry a message. The messages will vary, but it hardly matters if the messengers are the same. (Those who believe that men have a monopoly on the political skills of articulating policies and ideas will not be surprised that most messengers are men.)

The notion of representation as primarily a matter of ideas has not, of course, gone unchallenged. In 1789, a group of Frenchwomen laid claim to a place in the Estates General in the following terms:

> Just as a nobleman cannot represent a plebeian and the latter cannot represent a nobleman, so a man, no matter how honest he may be, cannot represent a woman. Between the representatives and the represented there must be an absolute identity of interests.[4]

Shared experience here takes precedence over shared ideas; more precisely, no amount of thought or sympathy, no matter how careful or honest, can jump the barriers of experience. This assertion came, however, at a very particular point in the development of democracy, when the challenge to privilege momentarily centered around questioning which "estates" were entitled to representation. Subsequent notions of citizenship seemed to make this an anachronism, the last gasp of a feudal tradition. Hard fought extensions of suffrage combined with the evolution of political parties as the basic medium of representation to encourage an alternative notion of politics as a battleground for contested ideas.

The socialist tradition is of interest here, not only because it threw up a politics of pressing for the "representation of labour" (which seems to echo the earlier idea of representing different estates) but because it has been persistently troubled by tensions between a politics of ideas and an alternative politics of presence. Those involved in socialist parties often argued fiercely over the relationship between intellectuals and the "authentically" working class, some feeling that a socialist politics should privilege the voices and presence of workers, others that class identities should signify less than adherence to socialist ideas. In *What Is To Be Done*, Lenin offered one classic refutation of the politics of presence. Stressing the multiplicity of arenas within which the power of capital was exerted, he argued the limits of an experience confined to any one of these, and the overriding importance of strategic links between one set of struggles and another. This privileged the all-seeing intellectual (who might in principle originate from any class position or faction), the political activist who could look beyond each specific struggle or campaign to its wider connections and ramifications, and fit the various pieces of the jigsaw together. When socialist feminists challenged such views in the 1970s, one of the things they pointed out was that they denied legitimacy to women's self-understandings; another was that they presumed an objectivity on the part of these activists that raised them to a God-like level. As Sheila Rowbotham remarked in her critique of Leninist conceptions of the vanguard party, "(t)he Party is presented as soaring above all sectional concerns without providing any guarantees that this soaring will not be in fact an expression of the particular preoccupations of the group or groups with power within it."[5] Part of what was at issue in the development of an autonomous women's movement was the arrogance of those who thought that ideas could be separated from presence.

In Hannah Pitkin's influential discussion of representation, she criticizes the mirror view as beginning and ending with who is present, setting to one side the far more important question of what the representatives actually do. "Think of the legislature as a pictorial representation or a representative sample of the nation," she argues, "and you will almost inevitably concentrate on its composition rather than its activities."[6] But looking back at her discussion from a distance of twenty-five years, what is notable is how she elides the mapping of ideas with the mapping of people, not really distinguishing between a representative sample that captures the range of ideas, the range of interests, or the range of socially significant

groups. Her emphasis throughout is on the distinction between being and doing, and her arguments are as much directed against versions of proportional representation that would more adequately reflect the multiplicity of parties and opinion as against later preoccupations with representing excluded or marginalized groups. Questions of power and inequality do not figure largely in Pitkin's account. Such questions have become central to democratic debate today.

It is no part of my intention to disparage politics as a battleground for ideas. Much of the radicalizing impetus to democracy has centered around initiatives to make ideas more rather than less important, as in efforts to bind representatives more closely to the opinions they profess to hold, or in measures to reduce the backstage manipulations of pressure groups that disrupt the higher politics of ideas. But when the politics of ideas is taken in isolation from the politics of presence, it does not deal adequately with the experiences of those social groups who by virtue of their race or ethnicity or religion or gender have felt themselves excluded from the democratic process. Political exclusion is increasingly – I believe rightly – viewed in terms that can only be met by political presence, and much of this development has depended on a more complex understanding of the relationship between ideas and experience. The separation between who and what is to be represented, and the subordination of one to the other, relies on an understanding of ideas and interests as relatively unproblematic. It is as if the field of politics is already clearly demarcated, containing with it various clusters of preferences or ideas or concerns that exist independently of any process of formation. This is in stark contrast with the preoccupations that ran through the early years of the contemporary women's movement, when women talked of the difficulties in finding a voice, the way that dominant definitions of politics blocked out alternatives, or hegemonic culture controlled what could or could not be said. The emphasis then shifted from an objectively defined set of interests (that just needed more vigorous pursuit) to a more exploratory notion of possibilities so far silenced and ideas one had to struggle to express. In this later understanding of the processes that generate needs and concerns and ideas, it is harder to sustain the primacy of ideas over political presence. If it is simply a question of representing a given range of ideas and interests, it may not much matter who does the work of representation. But if

(173)

the range of ideas has been curtailed by orthodoxies that rendered alternatives invisible, there will be no satisfactory solution short of changing the people who represent and develop the ideas.

The renewed concern over the relationship between ideas and experience also figures in recent arguments over the limits of tolerance in dealing with difference. The classically liberal treatment of difference allows for private spaces within which people can get on with their own chosen affairs and a public realm ordered around a set of minimum shared presumptions. But the relegation of difference to a private world of private variation has been experienced as an injunction to keep peculiarities a secret, and the shared presumptions that control the public world have proved less than even-handed in their treatment of different groups. The separation of church from state has long been considered the solution to the problems of religious difference, but it achieves this by requiring all religions to adopt a similarly self-denying ordinance that will limit the relevance of religious precepts to practices in the private sphere. This resolution is more amenable to some religions than to others; in particular, it is more acceptable to the heavily secularized forms of Christianity that became the norm in contemporary Europe. In similar vein, we might say that the relegation of homosexuality to a private affair between consenting adults helps reduce more overt forms of discrimination, but it achieves this at the expense of any more public disruption of a heterosexual norm. Private deviation is permitted, but not equal public worth.

Part of the dissatisfaction with liberalism's treatment of difference is the feeling that toleration is a poor substitute for recognition.[7] We only tolerate what we do not like or approve of (otherwise there is no need for toleration[8]), and yet where difference is bound up with identity, this is hard for the tolerated to accept. You can put up with people thinking you a harmless freak for your membership in the flat earth society. You may even revel in people thinking you a dangerous lunatic for your belief in communist revolution. It is not so easy to live with mere tolerance of your perverted sexuality or your denial of femininity or your irrationally fundamentalist religion. Tolerance is perceived as non-egalitarian, resting in some way on a distinction between majority norms and minority deviance, and incorporating some implied preference for a particular way of life.[9] It is perhaps one of the tributes to democracy

that people do not find tolerance satisfactory for long, and that the imperatives of democratic equality seem to press on further towards the recognition of equal worth. One reflection of this pressure has been the emerging school of thought that looks to "democratic" rather than "liberal" ways of dealing with diversity[10]: instead of treating difference as something that can flourish in the private domain, it turns to public manifestations in which differences can be confronted and (hopefully) resolved. Here, too, presence becomes crucial, for any public domain marked by the systematic absence of significant groups cannot even approach this resolution.

Once raised, the issues of presence are unlikely to go away: these are questions that must be addressed if democracies are to deliver on political equality. My concern in the rest of this paper is with what happens next, and in particular, with the tensions that arise between ideas and political presence. In the caricatures of those most resistant to a politics of presence, it is frequently misrepresented as a kind of "group-think": something that is necessarily separatist, necessarily corrosive of any wider community, and falsely presuming not only that one has to be a member of a particular group in order to understand or represent that group's interests, but that all members of the group in question will think along similar lines.[11] The caricature misses its mark. Faced, for example, with that 1789 claim that "between the representatives and the represented there must be an absolute identity of interests," most contemporary theorists will shy away from the implications of an essential female subject, or an authentic black subject, that can be represented by any one of its kind. Far more dominant today is the notion of multiple identities or multiple "subject positions," each of which is subject to political transformation and change. An attention to difference does not entail an essentialist understanding of identity; nor does it demand any wholesale rejection of the politics of competing ideas. But then the very sophistication of contemporary theories of identity can paralyze development; the very distance people have traveled from the caricatures of their position can remove them from democracy as it currently exists. In both the theoretical and the movement-centered literature which I now go on to discuss, issues of difference have been construed within a robustly democratic future that bears little relationship to contemporary political life. One of the challenges of democracy is how to combine the insights from such discussion with prescriptions that can be made relevant to representative democracy as practiced today.

Democracy as Public Contestation

Much of the contemporary literature on democracy and difference operates with notions of a more active and vigorous democracy that depends crucially on public debate. Rejecting both the false harmony that stamps out difference, and the equally false essentialism that defines people through some single, authentic identity, many theorists look to a democracy which maximizes citizen participation, and requires us to engage and contest with one another. In a recent essay on feminism and democracy, Susan Mendus suggests that difference is the rationale for democracy, and that "whereas traditional democratic theory tends to construe difference as an obstacle to the attainment of a truly democratic state, feminist theory should alert us to the possibility that difference is rather what necessitates the pursuit of democracy."[12] In his work on multiculturalism, Charles Taylor calls for a politics of democratic empowerment as the way of dealing with demands for equal recognition without thereby entrenching people in fragmented identities.[13] In his discussion of the republican revival, Cass Sunstein argues for a deliberative democracy to which all citizens will have equal access, and where all perspectives can be equally addressed.[14]

All such arguments assume equality of access (without necessarily exploring the conditions that would deliver this result), and all differentiate themselves from merely majoritarian decision-making by anticipating some process of transformation and change. Where the classically liberal resolution of difference relies on a combination of private spaces and majority norms (these in turn established by majority vote), the democratic resolution of difference expects us to engage more directly with each other. We bring our differences to the public stage; we revise them through public debate. Major disagreements then surface between those who anticipate a full "resolution" in some newly achieved public consensus, and those who see differences as contingent but never as "difference" going away. The first position looks more utopian than the second, but both operate at a level of generality that barely touches on democracy as practiced today.

Consider William Connolly's arguments in *Identity/Difference*,[15] which are particularly interesting in that they both say what should happen and why it almost certainly won't. Here, a "robust" politics of democratic engagement is presented as something that neither evades nor confirms difference: a politics that enables people to disturb settled conventions and expose settled identities. All identities are formed through difference – you know who you are through your difference from some other – and all identities are simultaneously threatened by the difference(s) of the other. There is always a danger that identities will be dogmatized into some naturalistic or unchanging essence, and always a danger that difference will generate destructive resentments and fears. What keeps these at bay is a politics of mutual challenge and disruption in which we are constantly reminded of the contingent nature of our identities. This politics depends in turn on the successful permeation of a "culture of genealogy" which helps us to see our identities as ambiguous and contestable and contested. Democracy then appears as an exciting engagement with difference: the challenge of "the other"; the disruption of certainties; the recognition of ambiguities within one's self as well as one's differences with others.

All this is tremendously refreshing, and in no way relies on a future transcendence of difference. But just at the point where he has achieved the philosophical resolution, Connolly backs off from claiming any immediate relevance for today. The confidence that enables people to dispense with settled identities or to accept the contingencies of fate may not be available to those suffering from economic inequality and political exclusion. Indeed, in an environment characterized by systematic inequality, the appeals to a robust democracy in which no one shelters behind accusations of the other could "too readily be received as yet another attack on those already excluded from democratic politics."[16]

> One compelling attraction of democracy is that it enables anyone to engage in fundamental riddles of existence through participation in a public politics that periodically disturbs and denaturalizes elements governing the cultural unconscious. But these same characteristics can intensify the reactive demand to redogmatize conventional identities if a large minority of the society is already suffering under severe burden of material deprivation and effective exclusion from the good life offered to a majority.[17]

Robust democracy then becomes possible only when economic inequalities are substantially reduced. My problem with this is not that it begs the question of how we might achieve such a precondition (we all have difficulties answering this), but that so much of what currently drives a politics of identity and difference is precisely the sense of deprivation and exclusion that Connolly sees as making such a politics so dangerous. Again, this is a point Connolly himself makes, noting that against the background of US neo-conservatism, any politics of identity and difference tends to fuel "the energies of *ressentiment* and the dogmatization of identity."[18] The philosophical resolution of democracy and difference remains largely that.[19]

Democracy Inside Social Movements

The second context in which these discussions take place is as interventions into specific movements that have formed around the politics of race, gender, sexuality, and ethnicity. All these movements have involved a critique of the phony essentialisms that disguised systematic difference and inequality; nearly all of them, however, have also generated their own essentialisms that at some point or other claimed a unified female or lesbian or black or some other experience. Thus feminists took issue with the gender amnesia that transformed man "into a paradigm of humankind as such"[20] but, in the further explorations of sexual difference, they often insisted on a primary distinction between men and women that obscured further differences between women. Lesbian feminists took issue with the hegemonic controls of a heterosexual norm but, in the search for an affirming identity, they often constructed "the" authentic lesbian who would not tolerate differences of sexual practice or political attitudes within the lesbian community.[21] Anti-racists took issue with the mythologies of nation that had rendered black people invisible but, in the subsequent racial dualism that focused so exclusively on differences between "black" and "white" they tended to obscure the cultural and religious pluralism that characterizes the many non-white minorities.[22]

The problems of essentialism have, as a consequence, figured largely in the internal politics and debates of these movements. Much contemporary attention is focused on the conditions that can articulate group difference without thereby "disciplining" group members into a single authentic identity; in the process, many have suggested limits to the very notion of "a" group. As Shane Phelan puts it in her discussion of lesbian feminism in the United States: "Politics that ignores our identities, that makes them 'private', is useless; but nonnegotiable identities will enslave us whether they are imposed from within or without."[23] Speaking from the British context, Stuart Hall has suggested that we should pay more attention to the ways in which black experience is a diaspora experience, one in which the constructions of history and politics and culture are therefore fundamental, and not to be captured through notions of an essential black subject.[24] He talks here of "the end of innocence," "the recognition of the extraordinary diversity of subject positions, social experiences and cultural identities which compose the category 'black',"[25] and the impossibility of grounding the black subject or black experience in the essentialisms of nature or any other such guarantee.

These arguments cut across the balder distinction between ideas and presence, for what is being identified are differences in experiences and identities within what has hitherto been seen as an all-embracing category or group. It is not simply that "black" people or women or lesbians will disagree among themselves as to the appropriate policies and ideas and goals (they will vote for different parties, for example), but that their very senses of what it means to be black or female or lesbian will necessarily vary. In the context of the political movements with which these arguments engage, there seem to be two important implications. One is that the diversity of "subject positions" should be reflected within the organizational structures that define who does or doesn't get into the conversation. There should be no privileging of some voices as more authentic than others, and no coercive imposition of a supposedly unified point of view. The other implication, however, is that there is no way of knowing in advance whether this diversity has been successfully acknowledged. Any prior setting of the boundaries risks restoring some version of the authentic subject, for even if the boundaries are significantly pluralized, they still define in advance what are the appropriate or relevant differences. Thus Stuart Hall argues that it is no longer possible to represent "the black subject" without reference to class, gender, sexuality, ethnicity. But if this were taken as a series of guidelines about the different characteristics that must be covered within the membership of some campaigning organization, that would hardly be doing justice to his critique.

This is a problem that in some way or another besets every radical initiative, whether it is a matter of deciding whom to invite to address a meeting, who is to join an editorial board, or which groups are to participate in a campaign. We have become sufficiently attuned to the politics of presence to distrust the notion that anyone can "stand in" for anyone else, and sufficiently alert to the coercive powers of homogeneity to want to reflect diversity. But the critiques of essentialism deprive us of any simple mechanism for achieving the appropriate balance, and remind us that diversity is too great to be captured in any categorical list.

In the context of political movements, this is not such a serious difficulty. At their best, such movements already enjoy the kind of robust democracy that is proposed as an ideal for the polity as a whole: allowing for, indeed incapable of containing, the kind of contestation and mutual challenge that acknowledges difference and simultaneously disrupts it. The vehemence of debate indicates both a recurrent tendency towards essentialism and a continuous challenge to this: people are tough enough to resist prior classification and far too argumentative to accept someone else's definition of their selves. It is also worth noting that the fluidity of this politics lends itself more easily to a kind of learning through trial and error, for none of the consequences that people may derive from their current understandings of identity or difference is likely to be set in stone. The larger difficulties arise where we seek out more compromised intervention into democracies that are still pretty feeble.

Political Prescriptions for the Polity as a Whole

When we turn to the political prescriptions that might flow from a new understanding of democracy and difference, we are not dealing in far-off utopias: There is a range of policies already proposed or implemented; and change is neither distant nor unlikely. The problem, rather, is that because such prescriptions operate in a half-way house of remedial reform, they are less able to resolve the contradictory pressures between the politics of ideas and the politics of presence. The kinds of mechanisms I have in mind include the quota systems adopted by a number of European political parties to achieve gender parity in elected assemblies, the redrawing of boundaries around black-majority constituencies to raise the number of black politicians elected in the United States, and the longer established power-sharing practices of those European consociational democracies that have distributed executive power and economic resources between different religious and linguistic groups. In each of these instances, the initiatives operate within the framework of an existing (not very robust) democracy. Tensions that might more readily resolve themselves in a future ferment of activity and deliberation become more acute in what everyone knows is a compromised situation.

All the more immediate proposals for reform insist on deliberate intervention as necessary to break the link between social structures of inequality or exclusion and the political reflection of these in levels of participation and influence. All of them also agree in looking to specifically *political* mechanisms – rather than, or sometimes as well as, longer term social transformation. They take issue therefore with the complacencies of a free market in politics, which sees political equality as sufficiently guaranteed by the procedures of one person one vote; they also challenge the more standard radical alternative, which has focused attention on prior economic or social change. Whatever their differences on other issues, the traditions of revolutionary Marxism and welfare state social reform have tended to agree on a broadly materialist analysis of the problems of political equality, seeing equal political access as something that depends on more fundamental changes in social, economic, and sometimes educational, conditions. The current interest in achieving equal or proportionate presence reverses this, focusing instead on institutional mechanisms – its critics would say "political fixes" – that can achieve more immediate change.

The roots of this reversal lie partly in frustration with what has proved an unbelievably slow process of structural transformation (*first* eliminate the sexual division of labor... the racial ordering of income and education and employment... the class patterning that decides children's futures – is it any wonder we search for short cuts?) But political frustration is not new, and people do not normally change direction just because things take so long. The additional impetus comes from the kind of arguments already outlined, which suggest that the range of political ideas and preferences is seriously constrained by the characteristics of the people who convey them. In a more traditional base-superstructure model, we were advised to concentrate first on generating the social conditions for equal citizenship, then to enjoy the political equalization that flows from this. Such an approach, however, treats policy choices as more straightforward than they are, and fails to observe the way that strategies devised for equality reflect the limits of those currently in power.[26] Where policy initiatives are worked out *for* rather than *with* a politically excluded constituency, they rarely engage all relevant concerns. Again, it is only if we consider the field of politics as already clearly demarcated, with all possible options already in play, that we can put much confidence in such an approach.

I do not discount the criticism that regards institutional mechanisms for achieving equal or proportionate presence as a species of diversionary "political fixing," but we should not be required to choose between these and other urgent tasks of social and economic transformation. When political exclusion is such a marked feature of contemporary democratic life, it seems inappropriate to rely on distant prospects of a more robustly participatory democracy and/or structural changes in social and economic conditions. The very distance of such prospects puts a premium on political prescriptions that can be made relevant to representative democracy as currently practiced, and most of these will involve some form of affirmative action that can guarantee more equal representation in existing decision-making assemblies. Any specifically political mechanism, however, risks imposing a rigid definition of the identities that have to be included or the interests so far left out. The more complex understanding of multiple identities that change both over time and according to context is a potential casualty here, as is the continuing importance we would all want to attach to political disagreement and debate.

If we consider, for example, the mechanisms that might be appropriate in contemporary Britain to redress racial exclusions, one immediate problem is the diversity of non-white experience, and the major disagreements that have surfaced between taking race or ethnicity or religion as the basis of social identity and political exclusion. When we take race as the central indicator, this encourages a dualism of "black" or "white," a division of the universe which is often said to be closer to the political perceptions of Afro-Caribbeans than to the self-definitions of the significantly more numerous Asians. Tariq

Modood, indeed, has argued that "the concept of Black is harmful to Asians and is a form of political identity that most Asians do not accept as their primary public identity."[27] But if we take ethnicity or religion instead, these are felt to be too closely associated with a politics of multiculturalism that has looked to the greater dissemination of knowledge about ethnic and religious minorities as the way of breaking down racial stereotypes, and has been thought insufficiently vigorous in its challenges to racism *per se*. Alternative ways of defining group identities or redressing group exclusions have become loaded with political significance, with an attention to cultural diversity being variously perceived as something that depoliticizes the anti-racist struggle or is a crucial corrective to the simplicities of racial dualism.[28]

What, in this context, is an appropriate mechanism for dealing with political exclusion? Can Asians be represented by Afro-Caribbeans, Hindus by Muslims, black women by black men? Or do these groups have nothing more in common than their joint experience of being excluded from power? In their recent book on *Racialized Boundaries*, Floya Anthias and Nira Yuval-Davies conclude that "the form of political representation which has grown out of identity politics and equal opportunities and which has attempted to represent social difference more genuinely, has created an impossible mission for itself,"[29] and that what is a positive diversity of overlapping identities becomes dangerously constrained in efforts towards proportional representation. But does this mean that nothing can be done: that given the risks, on the one hand, of an imposed and misleading uniformity, and the absurdities, on the other, of an endless search for sufficiently pluralized categories, we have to abandon the quest for specifically political mechanisms? Caucuses and quotas are the most obvious political mechanisms for dealing with political exclusion, yet both of these depend on a prior categorization of the basis on which people have been excluded. Neither seems adequate to the complexity of political identities.

The politics that has developed in the United States around the strategy of black-majority, single-member constituencies might seem more straightforward, for it seems clear enough that it is race rather than ethnicity that has been at issue in the political exclusion of African-Americans, and racial bloc voting is plausibly described as "the single most salient feature of contemporary political life."[30] But even so, a political resolution that privileges race as the prime consideration can make it more difficult for people to articulate what are complex and multiple identities: can obscure tensions, for example, around gender and class, can block out major disagreements over policy preferences and political ideas. The implication that black representatives are representative merely by virtue of being black is inevitably problematic, even where "blackness" is a less contested category.

Those who consider the problems of political equality as adequately dealt with by provision for the equal right to vote will be happy to rest their case there, but criticism of the strategy of black electoral success has not been confined to these quarters. Equally powerful criticism comes from those who regard proportionate presence as a necessary but insufficient condition, and are concerned that the focus on numbers alone can reduce political accountability, limit prospects for multi-racial coalition, and undermine the urgency of policy debate.[31] There is, in other words, a strong sense of the tensions that can develop between a politics of presence and a politics of ideas. But instead of resolving this by opting for the second over the first, critics have looked to alternative patterns of representation that can make it possible to combine the two. Some of the most innovative work in this area comes from those pressing for a return to the more competitive politics of multi-member constituencies but based on forms of proportional representation and cumulative voting that would maintain the scope for electing representatives from minority groups.[32] It is felt, in other words, that mechanisms *can* be devised which continue the gains in black political presence without forcing an either/or choice between the politics of presence and the politics of ideas.

European initiatives on gender parity can also be seen as successfully negotiating the competing demands of ideas and presence – and here we enter the realm of policies already in position rather than proposals in contested debate. The favored strategy involves pressuring existing political parties to introduce a more balanced ticket of both women and men in their candidates for winnable seats, thus maintaining accountability through party policies and programs while changing the gender composition of elected assemblies. Often enough, the mechanism has been a straightforward quota, which has contributed to a remarkable increase in the numbers of women elected in the Nordic countries. Critics of such strategies usually rest their case on the paucity of "experienced" women, the potential loss of "good" men to politics, and the risk that the overall caliber of politicians (not too high in my opinion) will fall. They do not dwell particularly on the essentialist presumptions of "a" women's perspective, or the dangerous potential for women pressing only narrowly sectional concerns. There are just too many women for them to be considered as a unified or sectional group, and they are spread across every class or ethnic or religious dimension and every conceivable political persuasion. When it is applied to women, the politics of presence does not seriously disrupt the politics of competing ideas; it is relatively easy to pursue both of these together.

Outside the more established democracies of Europe and the United States, the arguments often start from the opposite direction, a feeling that *who* is to be represented has so far taken precedence over *what*, and that what is missing is the higher politics of ideas. One might think, for example, of the abuse of kinship networks and ethnic solidarities by political elites in postcolonial Africa, many of whom evacuated the terrain of contested policies and ideals to cultivate a power base around exclusionary identities. When the colonial powers retreated from Africa, they left behind societies in which the state had become the main avenue for economic and social advancement, and where the politics of patronage was almost doomed to flourish. In this context, people lived under what seemed an absence of politics, with the contrast between a civilian or military regime seeming of far less consequence than whether you had access to any of the rulers. As ethnic connections emerged as one of the main routes of access, ethnic rivalries became literally deadly, even when the ethnicities in question were relatively recent creations.[33] It is against this background that African radicals and writers have so eloquently called for a politics based on vision and ideals.[34]

Through all these examples, the biggest mistake is to set up ideas as the opposite of political presence: to treat ideas as totally separate from the people who carry them; or worry exclusively about the people without giving a thought to their policies and ideas. It should be said, however, that this is not such a frequent mistake as the caricatures suggest, and that those exploring equal or proportionate presence rarely regard it as a substitute for the politics of competing ideas. If anything, the most acute criticisms of the politics of presence have come from those most committed to challenging political exclusions, and the debate has long shifted beyond its either/or axis. What is, perhaps, emerging is that the more satisfactory ways of redressing group exclusion are those which are the less group-specific. This seems to be the case in relation to gender quotas, if only because the category of "woman" is so inclusive of other kinds of difference and division that it leaves open the necessary space for a multiplicity of political identities. It also seems to be the case in the proposals that have developed around the implementation of the Voting Rights Act in the United States, which have moved away from the more tightly drawn voting districts that provide a "safe seat" for minority representatives towards a larger geographical constituency that can no longer pretend to contain only one voice.

Such developments acknowledge the danger in preemptive classifications of people's political identities, and are well aware that essentialist definitions of the groups that have been excluded can work to reduce political accountability and debate. They nonetheless take issue with the more traditional treatment of diversity and difference as simply a matter of contested ideas. The overly cerebral understanding of difference has not engaged sufficiently with the problems of political presence, for it has encouraged an unacceptable level of complacency over the homogeneity of political elites. We can no longer pretend that the full range of ideas and preferences and alternatives has been adequately represented when those charged with the job of representation are all white or all male or all middle class; or that democracies complete their task of political equality when they establish a free market in political ideas. One would not want to take up permanent residence in the half-way house of remedial reform, but mechanisms should be – and can be – devised that address the problems of group exclusion without fixing the boundaries or character of each group.

Notes

1 I summarize and discuss many of these arguments in *Engendering Democracy* (Pennsylvania: University of Pennsylvania State Press, 1991). See also Jane Flax. "Beyond equality: gender, justice and difference," in G. Bock and S. James, eds., *Beyond Equality and Difference* (London: Routledge, 1992).

2 Robert A. Dahl, *Democracy and Its Critics* (New Haven: Yale University Press, 1989).

3 George Kateb, "The Moral Distinctiveness of Representative Democracy," *Ethics* 91:3 (1981): 361.

4 Cited by Silvia Vegetti Finzi, "Female identity between sexuality and maternity," in Bock and James, eds., *Beyond Equality and Difference*, 128.

5 Sheila Rowbotham, "The women's movement and organising for socialism," in S. Rowbotham, L. Segal and H. Wainwright, *Beyond the Fragments: Feminism and the making of socialism* (London: Newcastle Socialist Centre and Islington Community Press, 1979), 61.

6 Hannah F. Pitkin, *The Concept of Representation* (Berkeley: University of California Press, 1967), 226.

7 See Shane Phelan's discussion of the way that lesbian feminists in the United States came to reject liberalism. *Identity Politics: Lesbian Feminism and the Limits of Community* (Philadelphia: Temple University Press, 1989).

8 See Susan Mendus, *Toleration and the Limits of Liberalism* (London: Macmillan, 1989).

9 I do not know if this is intrinsic to tolerance, but I suspect it is. If we could imagine a world in which difference was genuinely detached from power – in which there really were multiple differences and none carried more weight than any other – then I am not sure we would be talking of the need for toleration. See also Kirstie McClure, "Difference, Diversity and the Limits of Toleration," *Political Theory* 18:3 (1990).

10 I owe this formulation to Peter Jones's paper "Groups, Beliefs and Identities," presented at the European Consortium for Political Research, Leiden, April 1993.

11 All these points can be found in Cynthia V. Ward, "The Limits of 'Liberal Republicanism': Why Group-Based Remedies and Republican Citizenship Don't Mix," *Columbia Law Review* 91:3 (1991). In querying the notion that *only* the members of particular disadvantaged groups can understand or represent their interests, she might usefully turn this question round to ask whether such understanding or representation is possible without the presence of *any* members of the disadvantaged groups.

12 Susan Mendus, "Losing the Faith: Feminism and Democracy" in John Dunn, ed., *Democracy: The Unfinished Journey 508BC to AD1993* (Oxford: Oxford University Press, 1992), 216.

13 Charles Taylor, *The Ethics of Authenticity* (Cambridge, Mass.: Harvard University Press, 1992); Charles Taylor and Amy Gutmann, *Multicultural-*

ism and The Politics of Recognition (Cambridge, MA: Harvard University Press, 1992).

14 Cass Sunstein, "Beyond the Republican Revival," *Yale Law Journal* 97:8 (1988).

15 William Connolly, *Identity/Difference: Democratic Negotiations of Political Paradox* (Ithaca: Cornell University Press, 1991).

16 Connolly, 197.

17 Connolly, 211.

18 Connolly, 213.

19 In a review of Connolly's book, Iris Young describes his prescriptions as "therapies." *Political Theory* 20:3 (1992): 514.

20 Adriana Cavarero, "Equality and sexual difference: amnesia in political thought," in Bock and James, eds., *Beyond Equality and Difference*, 36.

21 Phelan, *Identity Politics*. Phelan notes in particular the rows that broke out over sado-masochism, and whether this was an "acceptable" part of lesbian identity.

22 See the essays in Tariq Modood, *Not Easy Being British: colour, culture and citizenship* (Stoke on Trent: Runnymede Trust and Trentham Books, 1992). The largest non-white group in Britain is Asians of Indian origin, many of whom have felt the racial dualism of anti-racist politics rendered them invisible.

23 Phelan, *Identity Politics*, 170.

24 Stuart Hall, "New Ethnicities," in J. Donald and A. Rattansi, eds., *"Race", Culture and Difference* (London: Sage and Open University Press, 1992).

25 Hall, 254.

26 Obvious examples include the post-war preoccupation with full employment as a condition for equal citizenship, where full employment was either unthinkingly equated with full employment for men, or else extended formally to include women without any serious consideration of the structural changes that would then become necessary to re-order the relationship between paid and unpaid work. Will Kymlicka provides a different example in his discussion of the Trudeau reforms which set out to promote more equal citizenship in Canada, but equated full and equal participation for the native Indian population with a color-blind constitution that would dismantle the system of segregated reserves. Though widely applauded by the country's media and even opposition parties, the proposals had to be withdrawn in the face of almost unanimous opposition from the Indians themselves. Kymlicka, *Liberalism, Community and Culture* (Oxford: Clarendon Press, 1989).

27 Modood, *Not Easy Being British*, 29.

28 For an excellent overview of these debates, and an attempt to push beyond them, see the essays in Donald and Rattansi, eds., *"Race", Culture and Difference*.

29 Floya Anthias and Nira Yuval-Davies, *Racialized Boundaries: Race, Nation, Gender, Colour and Class and the Anti-Racist Struggle* (London: Routledge, 1992), 192.

30 S. Issacharoff, "Polarized Voting and the Political Process: the Transformation of Voting Rights Jurisprudence," *Michigan Law Review* 90:7 (1992): 1855.

31 Bernard Grofman and Chandler Davidson, eds., *Controversies in Minority Voting: The Voting Rights Act in Perspective* (Washington, DC: The Brookings Institution, 1992) provides a comprehensive range of the arguments that have developed around minority representation.

32 Lani Guinier, "The Triumph of Tokenism: The Voting Rights Act and The Theory of Black Electoral Success," *Michigan Law Review* 89:5 (1991); "No Two Seats: The Elusive Quest for Political Equality," *Virginia Law Review* 77:8 (1991). I discuss this material at greater length in "Political Inclusion and Political Presence. Or, Why Does It Matter Who Our Representatives Are?" (Paper presented at the Joint Sessions of the European Consortium on Political Research, Leiden, 2–7 April, 1993).

33 Think here of the Nigerian civil war and the attempted secession of Biafra. The Ibo people who provided the ethnic basis for Biafra only came into substantial existence as a unified "people" through this war.

34 See especially Chinua Achebe's novels and essays, especially *The Anthills of the Savannah* and *The Trouble with Nigeria*.

PART III

Justice

12

Justice as Fairness

John Rawls

1. It might seem at first sight that the concepts of justice and fairness are the same, and that there is no reason to distinguish them, or to say that one is more fundamental than the other.[1] I think that this impression is mistaken. In this paper I wish to show that the fundamental idea in the concept of justice is fairness; and I wish to offer an analysis of the concept of justice from this point of view. To bring out the force of this claim, and the analysis based upon it, I shall then argue that it is this aspect of justice for which utilitarianism, in its classical form, is unable to account, but which is expressed, even if misleadingly, by the idea of the social contract.

To start with I shall develop a particular conception of justice by stating and commenting upon two principles which specify it, and by considering the circumstances and conditions under which they may be thought to arise. The principles defining this conception, and the conception itself, are, of course, familiar. It may be possible, however, by using the notion of fairness as a framework, to assemble and to look at them in a new way. Before stating this conception, however, the following preliminary matters should be kept in mind.

Throughout I consider justice only as a virtue of social institutions, or what I shall call practices.[2] The principles of justice are regarded as formulating restrictions as to how practices may define positions and offices, and assign thereto powers and liabilities, rights and duties. Justice as a virtue of particular actions or of persons I do not take up

at all. It is important to distinguish these various subjects of justice, since the meaning of the concept varies according to whether it is applied to practices, particular actions, or persons. These meanings are, indeed, connected, but they are not identical. I shall confine my discussion to the sense of justice as applied to practices, since this sense is the basic one. Once it is understood, the other senses should go quite easily.

Justice is to be understood in its customary sense as representing but *one* of the many virtues of social institutions, for these may be antiquated, inefficient, degrading, or any number of other things, without being unjust. Justice is not to be confused with an all-inclusive vision of a good society; it is only one part of any such conception. It is important, for example, to distinguish that sense of equality which is an aspect of the concept of justice from that sense of equality which belongs to a more comprehensive social ideal. There may well be inequalities which one concedes are just, or at least not unjust, but which, nevertheless, one wishes, on other grounds, to do away with. I shall focus attention, then, on the usual sense of justice in which it is essentially the elimination of arbitrary distinctions and the establishment, within the structure of a practice, of a proper balance between competing claims.

Finally, there is no need to consider the principles discussed below as *the* principles of justice. For the moment it is sufficient that they are typical of a family of principles normally associated with

Originally published in *Philosophical Review* 67 (1958): 164–94.

the concept of justice. The way in which the principles of this family resemble one another, as shown by the background against which they may be thought to arise, will be made clear by the whole of the subsequent argument.

2. The conception of justice which I want to develop may be stated in the form of two principles as follows: first, each person participating in a practice, or affected by it, has an equal right to the most extensive liberty compatible with a like liberty for all; and second, inequalities are arbitrary unless it is reasonable to expect that they will work out for everyone's advantage, and provided the positions and offices to which they attach, or from which they may be gained, are open to all. These principles express justice as a complex of three ideas: liberty, equality, and reward for services contributing to the common good.[3]

The term "person" is to be construed variously depending on the circumstances. On some occasions it will mean human individuals, but in others it may refer to nations, provinces, business firms, churches, teams, and so on. The principles of justice apply in all these instances, although there is a certain logical priority to the case of human individuals. As I shall use the term "person," it will be ambiguous in the manner indicated.

The first principle holds, of course, only if other things are equal: that is, while there must always be a justification for departing from the initial position of equal liberty (which is defined by the pattern of rights and duties, powers and liabilities, established by a practice), and the burden of proof is placed on him who would depart from it, nevertheless, there can be, and often there is, a justification for doing so. Now, that similar particular cases, as defined by a practice, should be treated similarly as they arise, is part of the very concept of a practice; it is involved in the notion of an activity in accordance with rules.[4] The first principle expresses an analogous conception, but as applied to the structure of practices themselves. It holds, for example, that there is a presumption against the distinctions and classifications made by legal systems and other practices to the extent that they infringe on the original and equal liberty of the persons participating in them. The second principle defines how this presumption may be rebutted.

It might be argued at this point that justice requires only an equal liberty. If, however, a greater liberty were possible for all without loss or conflict, then it would be irrational to settle on a lesser liberty. There is no reason for circumscribing rights unless their exercise would be incompatible, or would render the practice defining them less effective. Therefore no serious distortion of the concept of justice is likely to follow from including within it the concept of the greatest equal liberty.

The second principle defines what sorts of inequalities are permissible; it specifies how the presumption laid down by the first principle may be put aside. Now by inequalities it is best to understand not *any* differences between offices and positions, but differences in the benefits and burdens attached to them either directly or indirectly, such as prestige and wealth, or liability to taxation and compulsory services. Players in a game do not protest against there being different positions, such as batter, pitcher, catcher, and the like, nor to there being various privileges and powers as specified by the rules; nor do the citizens of a country object to there being the different offices of government such as president, senator, governor, judge, and so on, each with their special rights and duties. It is not differences of this kind that are normally thought of as inequalities, but differences in the resulting distribution established by a practice, or made possible by it, of the things men strive to attain or avoid. Thus they may complain about the pattern of honors and rewards set up by a practice (e.g., the privileges and salaries of government officials) or they may object to the distribution of power and wealth which results from the various ways in which men avail themselves of the opportunities allowed by it (e.g., the concentration of wealth which may develop in a free price system allowing large entrepreneurial or speculative gains).

It should be noted that the second principle holds that an inequality is allowed only if there is reason to believe that the practice with the inequality, or resulting in it, will work for the advantage of *every* party engaging in it. Here it is important to stress that *every* party must gain from the inequality. Since the principle applies to practices, it implies that the representative man in every office or position defined by a practice, when he views it as a going concern, must find it reasonable to prefer his condition and prospects with the inequality to what they would be under the practice without it. The principle excludes, therefore, the justification of inequalities on the grounds that the disadvantages of those in one position are outweighed by the greater advantages of those in another position. This rather simple restriction is the main modification I wish to make in the utilitarian principle as usually understood. When coupled with the notion of a practice, it is a restriction of consequence,[5] and one which some utilitarians, e.g., Hume and Mill, have used in their discussions of justice without realizing apparently its significance, or at least without calling attention to it.[6] Why it is a significant modification of principle, changing one's conception of justice entirely, the whole of my argument will show.

Further, it is also necessary that the various offices to which special benefits or burdens attach are open to all. It may be, for example, to the common advantage, as just defined, to attach special benefits to certain offices. Perhaps by doing so the requisite talent can be attracted to them and encouraged to give its best efforts. But any offices having special benefits must be won in a fair competition in which contestants are judged on their merits. If some offices were not open, those excluded would normally be justified in feeling unjustly treated, even if they benefited from the greater efforts of those who were allowed to compete for them. Now if one can assume that offices are open, it is necessary only to consider the design of practices themselves and how they jointly, as a system, work together. It will be a mistake to focus attention on the varying relative positions of particular persons, who may be known to us by their proper names, and to require that each such change, as a once for all transaction viewed in isolation, must be in itself just. It is the system of practices which is to be judged, and judged from a general point of view: unless one is prepared to criticize it from the standpoint of a representative man holding some particular office, one has no complaint against it.

3. Given these principles one might try to derive them from a priori principles of reason, or claim that they were known by intuition. These are familiar enough steps and, at least in the case of the first principle, might be made with some success. Usually, however, such arguments, made at this point, are unconvincing. They are not likely to lead to an understanding of the basis of the principles of justice, not at least as principles of justice. I wish, therefore, to look at the principles in a different way.

Imagine a society of persons amongst whom a certain system of practices is *already* well estab-

lished. Now suppose that by and large they are mutually self-interested; their allegiance to their established practices is normally founded on the prospect of self-advantage. One need not assume that, in all senses of the term "person," the persons in this society are mutually self-interested. If the characterization as mutually self-interested applies when the line of division is the family, it may still be true that members of families are bound by ties of sentiment and affection and willingly acknowledge duties in contradiction to self-interest. Mutual self-interestedness in the relations between families, nations, churches, and the like, is commonly associated with intense loyalty and devotion on the part of individual members. Therefore, one can form a more realistic conception of this society if one thinks of it as consisting of mutually self-interested families, or some other association. Further, it is not necessary to suppose that these persons are mutually self-interested under all circumstances, but only in the usual situations in which they participate in their common practices.

Now suppose also that these persons are rational: they know their own interests more or less accurately; they are capable of tracing out the likely consequences of adopting one practice rather than another; they are capable of adhering to a course of action once they have decided upon it; they can resist present temptations and the enticements of immediate gain; and the bare knowledge or perception of the difference between their condition and that of others is not, within certain limits and in itself, a source of great dissatisfaction. Only the last point adds anything to the usual definition of rationality. This definition should allow, I think, for the idea that a rational man would not be greatly downcast from knowing, or seeing, that others are in a better position than himself, unless he thought their being so was the result of injustice, or the consequence of letting chance work itself out for no useful common purpose, and so on. So if these persons strike us as unpleasantly egoistic, they are at least free in some degree from the fault of envy.[7]

Finally, assume that these persons have roughly similar needs and interests, or needs and interests in various ways complementary, so that fruitful cooperation amongst them is possible; and suppose that they are sufficiently equal in power and ability to guarantee that in normal circumstances none is able to dominate the others. This condition (as well as the others) may seem excessively vague; but in view of the conception of justice to which the argument leads, there seems no reason for making it more exact here.

Since these persons are conceived as engaging in their common practices, which are already established, there is no question of our supposing them to come together to deliberate as to how they will set these practices up for the first time. Yet we can imagine that from time to time they discuss with one another whether any of them has a legitimate complaint against their established institutions. Such discussions are perfectly natural in any normal society. Now suppose that they have settled on doing this in the following way. They first try to arrive at the principles by which complaints, and so practices themselves, are to be judged. Their procedure for this is to let each person propose the principles upon which he wishes his complaints to be tried with the understanding that, if acknowledged, the complaints of others will be similarly tried, and that no complaints will be heard at all until everyone is roughly of one mind as to how complaints are to be judged. They each understand further that the principles proposed and acknowledged on this occasion are binding on future occasions. Thus each will be wary of proposing a principle which would give him a peculiar advantage, in his present circumstances, supposing it to be accepted. Each person knows that he will be bound by it in future circumstances the peculiarities of which cannot be known, and which might well be such that the principle is then to his disadvantage. The idea is that everyone should be required to make *in advance* a firm commitment, which others also may reasonably be expected to make, and that no one be given the opportunity to tailor the canons of a legitimate complaint to fit his own special conditions, and then to discard them when they no longer suit his purpose. Hence each person will propose principles of a general kind which will, to a large degree, gain their sense from the various applications to be made of them, the particular circumstances of which being as yet unknown. These principles will express the conditions in accordance with which each is the least unwilling to have his interests limited in the design of practices, given the competing interests of the others, on the supposition that the interests of others will be limited likewise. The restrictions which would so arise might be thought of as those a person would keep in mind if he were designing a practice in which his enemy were to assign him his place.

The two main parts of this conjectural account have a definite significance. The character and respective situations of the parties reflect the typical circumstances in which questions of justice arise. The procedure whereby principles are proposed and acknowledged represents constraints, analogous to those of having a morality, whereby rational and mutually self-interested persons are brought to act reasonably. Thus the first part reflects the fact that questions of justice arise when conflicting claims are made upon the design of a practice and where it is taken for granted that each person will insist, as far as possible, on what he considers his rights. It is typical of cases of justice to involve persons who are pressing on one another their claims, between which a fair balance or equilibrium must be found. On the other hand, as expressed by the second part, having a morality must at least imply the acknowledgment of principles as impartially applying to one's own conduct as well as to another's, and moreover principles which may constitute a constraint, or limitation, upon the pursuit of one's own interests. There are, of course, other aspects of having a morality: the acknowledgment of moral principles must show itself in accepting a reference to them as reasons for limiting one's claims, in acknowledging the burden of providing a special explanation, or excuse, when one acts contrary to them, or else in showing shame and remorse and a desire to make amends, and so on. It is sufficient to remark here that having a morality is analogous to having made a firm commitment in advance; for one must acknowledge the principles of morality even when to one's disadvantage.[8] A man whose moral judgments always coincided with his interests could be suspected of having no morality at all.

Thus the two parts of the foregoing account are intended to mirror the kinds of circumstances in which questions of justice arise and the constraints which having a morality would impose upon persons so situated. In this way one can see how the acceptance of the principles of justice might come about, for given all these conditions as described, it would be natural if the two principles of justice were to be acknowledged. Since there is no way for anyone to win special advantages for himself, each might consider it reasonable to acknowledge equality as an initial principle. There is, however, no reason why they should regard this position as final; for if there are inequalities which satisfy the second principle, the immediate gain which equality would allow can be considered as intelligently invested in view of its future return. If, as is quite likely, these inequalities work as incentives to draw out better efforts, the members of this society may look upon them as concessions to human nature: they, like us, may think that people ideally should want to serve one another. But as they are mutually self-interested, their acceptance of these inequalities is merely the acceptance of the relations in which they actually stand, and a recognition of the motives which lead them to engage in their common practices. *They* have no title to complain of one another. And so provided that the conditions of the principle are met, there is no reason why they should not allow such inequalities. Indeed, it would be short-sighted of them to do so, and could result, in most cases, only from their being dejected by the bare knowledge, or perception, that others are better situated. Each person will, however, insist on an advantage to himself, and so on a common advantage, for none is willing to sacrifice anything for the others.

These remarks are not offered as a proof that persons so conceived and circumstanced would settle on the two principles, but only to show that these principles could have such a background, and so can be viewed as those principles which mutually self-interested and rational persons, when similarly situated and required to make in advance a firm commitment, could acknowledge as restrictions governing the assignment of rights and duties in their common practices, and thereby accept as limiting their rights against one another. The principles of justice may, then, be regarded as those principles which arise when the constraints of having a morality are imposed upon parties in the typical circumstances of justice.

4. These ideas are, of course, connected with a familiar way of thinking about justice which goes back at least to the Greek Sophists, and which regards the acceptance of the principles of justice as a compromise between persons of roughly equal power who would enforce their will on each other if they could, but who, in view of the equality of forces amongst them and for the sake of their own peace and security, acknowledge certain forms of conduct insofar as prudence seems to require. Justice is thought of as a pact between rational egoists the stability of which is dependent on a balance of power and a similarity of circumstances.[9] While the previous account is connected with

this tradition, and with its most recent variant, the theory of games,[10] it differs from it in several important respects which, to forestall misinterpretations, I will set out here.

First, I wish to use the previous conjectural account of the background of justice as a way of analyzing the concept. I do not want, therefore, to be interpreted as assuming a general theory of human motivation: when I suppose that the parties are mutually self-interested, and are not willing to have their (substantial) interests sacrificed to others, I am referring to their conduct and motives as they are taken for granted in cases where questions of justice ordinarily arise. Justice is the virtue of practices where there are assumed to be competing interests and conflicting claims, and where it is supposed that persons will press their rights on each other. That persons are mutually self-interested in certain situations and for certain purposes is what gives rise to the question of justice in practices covering those circumstances. Amongst an association of saints, if such a community could really exist, the disputes about justice could hardly occur; for they would all work selflessly together for one end, the glory of God as defined by their common religion, and reference to this end would settle every question of right. The justice of practices does not come up until there are several different parties (whether we think of these as individuals, associations, or nations and so on, is irrelevant) who do press their claims on one another, and who do regard themselves as representatives of interests which deserve to be considered. Thus the previous account involves no general theory of human motivation. Its intent is simply to incorporate into the conception of justice the relations of men to one another which set the stage for questions of justice. It makes no difference how wide or general these relations are, as this matter does not bear on the analysis of the concept.

Again, in contrast to the various conceptions of the social contract, the several parties do not establish any particular society or practice; they do not covenant to obey a particular sovereign body or to accept a given constitution.[11] Nor do they, as in the theory of games (in certain respects a marvelously sophisticated development of this tradition), decide on individual strategies adjusted to their respective circumstances in the game. What the parties do is to *jointly* acknowledge certain *principles* of appraisal relating to their common *practices* either as already established or merely proposed. They accede to standards of judgment, not to a given practice; they do not make any specific agreement, or bargain, or adopt a particular strategy. The subject of their acknowledgment is, therefore, very general indeed; it is simply the acknowledgment of certain principles of judgment, fulfilling certain general conditions, to be used in criticizing the arrangement of their common affairs. The relations of mutual self-interest between the parties who are similarly circumstanced mirror the conditions under which questions of justice arise, and the procedure by which the principles of judgment are proposed and acknowledged reflects the constraints of having a morality. Each aspect, then, of the preceding hypothetical account serves the purpose of bringing out a feature of the notion of justice. One could, if one liked, view the principles of justice as the "solution" of this highest order "game" of adopting, subject to the procedure described, principles of argument for all coming particular "games" whose peculiarities one can in no way foresee. But this comparison, while no doubt helpful, must not obscure the fact that this highest order "game" is of a special sort.[12] Its significance is that its various pieces represent aspects of the concept of justice.

Finally, I do not, of course, conceive the several parties as necessarily coming together to establish their common practices for the first time. Some institutions may, indeed, be set up *de novo*; but I have framed the preceding account so that it will apply when the full complement of social institutions already exists and represents the result of a long period of development. Nor is the account in any way fictitious. In any society where people reflect on their institutions they will have an idea of what principles of justice would be acknowledged under the conditions described, and there will be occasions when questions of justice are actually discussed in this way. Therefore if their practices do not accord with these principles, this will affect the quality of their social relations. For in this case there will be some recognized situations wherein the parties are mutually aware that one of them is being forced to accept what the other would concede is unjust. The foregoing analysis may then be thought of as representing the actual quality of relations between persons as defined by practices accepted as just. In such practices the parties will acknowledge the principles on which it is constructed, and the general recognition of this fact shows itself in the absence of resentment and in the sense of being justly treated. Thus one common objection to the theory

of the social contract, its apparently historical and fictitious character, is avoided.

5. That the principles of justice may be regarded as arising in the manner described illustrates an important fact about them. Not only does it bring out the idea that justice is a primitive moral notion in that it arises once the concept of morality is imposed on mutually self-interested agents similarly circumstanced, but it emphasizes that, fundamental to justice, is the concept of fairness which relates to right dealing between persons who are cooperating with or competing against one another, as when one speaks of fair games, fair competition, and fair bargains. The question of fairness arises when free persons, who have no authority over one another, are engaging in a joint activity and amongst themselves settling or acknowledging the rules which define it and which determine the respective shares in its benefits and burdens. A practice will strike the parties as fair if none feels that, by participating in it, they or any of the others are taken advantage of, or forced to give in to claims which they do not regard as legitimate. This implies that each has a conception of legitimate claims which he thinks it reasonable for others as well as himself to acknowledge. If one thinks of the principles of justice as arising in the manner described, then they do define this sort of conception. A practice is just or fair, then, when it satisfies the principles which those who participate in it could propose to one another for mutual acceptance under the aforementioned circumstances. Persons engaged in a just, or fair, practice can face one another openly and support their respective positions, should they appear questionable, by reference to principles which it is reasonable to expect each to accept.

It is this notion of the possibility of mutual acknowledgment of principles by free persons who have no authority over one another which makes the concept of fairness fundamental to justice. Only if such acknowledgment is possible can there be true community between persons in their common practices; otherwise their relations will appear to them as founded to some extent on force. If, in ordinary speech, fairness applies more particularly to practices in which there is a choice whether to engage or not (e.g., in games, business competition), and justice to practices in which there is no choice (e.g., in slavery), the element of necessity does not render the conception of mutual acknowledgment inapplicable, although it may make it much more urgent to change unjust than unfair institutions. For one activity in which one can always engage is that of proposing and acknowledging principles to one another supposing each to be similarly circumstanced; and to judge practices by the principles so arrived at is to apply the standard of fairness to them.

Now if the participants in a practice accept its rules as fair, and so have no complaint to lodge against it, there arises a prima facie duty (and a corresponding prima facie right) of the parties to each other to act in accordance with the practice when it falls upon them to comply. When any number of persons engage in a practice, or conduct a joint undertaking according to rules, and thus restrict their liberty, those who have submitted to these restrictions when required have the right to a similar acquiescence on the part of those who have benefited by their submission. These conditions will obtain if a practice is correctly acknowledged to be fair, for in this case all who participate in it will benefit from it. The rights and duties so arising are special rights and duties in that they depend on previous actions voluntarily undertaken, in this case on the parties having engaged in a common practice and knowingly accepted its benefits.[13] It is not, however, an obligation which presupposes a deliberate performative act in the sense of a promise, or contract, and the like.[14] An unfortunate mistake of proponents of the idea of the social contract was to suppose that political obligation does require some such act, or at least to use language which suggests it. It is sufficient that one has knowingly participated in and accepted the benefits of a practice acknowledged to be fair. This prima facie obligation may, of course, be overridden: it may happen, when it comes one's turn to follow a rule, that other considerations will justify not doing so. But one cannot, in general, be released from this obligation by denying the justice of the practice only when it falls on one to obey. If a person rejects a practice, he should, so far as possible, declare his intention in advance, and avoid participating in it or enjoying its benefits.

This duty I have called that of fair play, but it should be admitted that to refer to it in this way is, perhaps, to extend the ordinary notion of fairness. Usually acting unfairly is not so much the breaking of any particular rule, even if the infraction is difficult to detect (cheating), but taking advantage of loop-holes or ambiguities in rules, availing oneself of unexpected or special circumstances which make it impossible to enforce them, insisting that rules be enforced to one's advantage when they should be suspended, and more generally, acting contrary to the intention of a practice. It is for this reason that one speaks of the sense of fair play: acting fairly requires more than simply being able to follow rules; what is fair must often be felt, or perceived, one wants to say. It is not, however, an unnatural extension of the duty of fair play to have it include the obligation which participants who have knowingly accepted the benefits of their common practice owe to each other to act in accordance with it when their performance falls due; for it is usually considered unfair if someone accepts the benefits of a practice but refuses to do his part in maintaining it. Thus one might say of the tax-dodger that he violates the duty of fair play: he accepts the benefits of government but will not do his part in releasing resources to it; and members of labor unions often say that fellow workers who refuse to join are being unfair: they refer to them as "free riders," as persons who enjoy what are the supposed benefits of unionism, higher wages, shorter hours, job security, and the like, but who refuse to share in its burdens in the form of paying dues, and so on.

The duty of fair play stands beside other prima facie duties such as fidelity and gratitude as a basic moral notion; yet it is not to be confused with them.[15] These duties are all clearly distinct, as would be obvious from their definitions. As with any moral duty, that of fair play implies a constraint on self-interest in particular cases; on occasion it enjoins conduct which a rational egoist strictly defined would not decide upon. So while justice does not require of anyone that he sacrifice his interests in that *general position* and procedure whereby the principles of justice are proposed and acknowledged, it may happen that in particular situations, arising in the context of engaging in a practice, the duty of fair play will often cross his interests in the sense that he will be required to forego particular advantages which the peculiarities of his circumstances might permit him to take. There is, of course, nothing surprising in this. It is simply the consequence of the firm commitment which the parties may be supposed to have made, or which they would make, in the general position, together with the fact that they have participated in and accepted the benefits of a practice which they regard as fair.

Now the acknowledgment of this constraint in particular cases, which is manifested in acting fairly or wishing to make amends, feeling ashamed, and the like, when one has evaded it, is one of the forms of conduct by which participants in a common practice exhibit their recognition of each other as persons with similar interests and capacities. In the same way that, failing a special explanation, the criterion for the recognition of suffering is helping one who suffers, acknowledging the duty of fair play is a necessary part of the criterion for recognizing another as a person with similar interests and feelings as oneself.[16] A person who never under any circumstances showed a wish to help others in pain would show, at the same time, that he did not recognize that they were in pain; nor could he have any feelings of affection or friendship for anyone; for having these feelings implies, failing special circumstances, that he comes to their aid when they are suffering. Recognition that another is a person in pain shows itself in sympathetic action; this primitive natural response of compassion is one of those responses upon which the various forms of moral conduct are built.

Similarly, the acceptance of the duty of fair play by participants in a common practice is a reflection in each person of the recognition of the aspirations and interests of the others to be realized by their joint activity. Failing a special explanation, their acceptance of it is a necessary part of the criterion for their recognizing one another as persons with similar interests and capacities, as the conception of their relations in the general position supposes them to be. Otherwise they would show no recognition of one another as persons with similar capacities and interests, and indeed, in some cases perhaps hypothetical, they would not recognize one another as persons at all, but as complicated objects involved in a complicated activity. To recognize another as a person one must respond to him and act towards him in certain ways; and these ways are intimately connected with the various prima facie duties. Acknowledging these duties in *some* degree, and so having the elements of morality, is not a matter of choice, or of intuiting moral qualities, or a matter of the expression of feelings or attitudes (the three interpretations between which philosophical opinion frequently oscillates); it is simply the possession of one of the forms of conduct in which the recognition of others as persons is manifested.

These remarks are unhappily obscure. Their main purpose here, however, is to forestall, together with the remarks in Section 4, the misin-

terpretation that, on the view presented, the acceptance of justice and the acknowledgment of the duty of fair play depends in everyday life solely on there being a *de facto* balance of forces between the parties. It would indeed be foolish to underestimate the importance of such a balance in securing justice; but it is not the only basis thereof. The recognition of one another as persons with similar interests and capacities engaged in a common practice must, failing a special explanation, show itself in the acceptance of the principles of justice and the acknowledgment of the duty of fair play.

The conception at which we have arrived, then, is that the principles of justice may be thought of as arising once the constraints of having a morality are imposed upon rational and mutually self-interested parties who are related and situated in a special way. A practice is just if it is in accordance with the principles which all who participate in it might reasonably be expected to propose or to acknowledge before one another when they are similarly circumstanced and required to make a firm commitment in advance without knowledge of what will be their peculiar condition, and thus when it meets standards which the parties could accept as fair should occasion arise for them to debate its merits. Regarding the participants themselves, once persons knowingly engage in a practice which they acknowledge to be fair and accept the benefits of doing so, they are bound by the duty of fair play to follow the rules when it comes their turn to do so, and this implies a limitation on their pursuit of self-interest in particular cases.

Now one consequence of this conception is that, where it applies, there is no moral value in the satisfaction of a claim incompatible with it. Such a claim violates the conditions of reciprocity and community amongst persons, and he who presses it, not being willing to acknowledge it when pressed by another, has no grounds for complaint when it is denied; whereas he against whom it is pressed can complain. As it cannot be mutually acknowledged it is a resort to coercion; granting the claim is possible only if one party can compel acceptance of what the other will not admit. But it makes no sense to concede claims the denial of which cannot be complained of in preference to claims the denial of which can be objected to. Thus in deciding on the justice of a practice it is not enough to ascertain that it answers to wants and interests in the fullest and most effective manner. For if any of these conflict with justice, they should not be counted, as their satisfaction is no reason at all for having a practice. It would be irrelevant to say, even if true, that it resulted in the greatest satisfaction of desire. In tallying up the merits of a practice one must toss out the satisfaction of interests the claims of which are incompatible with the principles of justice.

6. The discussion so far has been excessively abstract. While this is perhaps unavoidable, I should now like to bring out some of the features of the conception of justice as fairness by comparing it with the conception of justice in classical utilitarianism as represented by Bentham and Sidgwick, and its counterpart in welfare economics. This conception assimilates justice to benevolence and the latter in turn to the most efficient design of institutions to promote the general welfare. Justice is a kind of efficiency.[17]

Now it is said occasionally that this form of utilitarianism puts no restrictions on what might be a just assignment of rights and duties in that there might be circumstances which, on utilitarian grounds, would justify institutions highly offensive to our ordinary sense of justice. But the classical utilitarian conception is not totally unprepared for this objection. Beginning with the notion that the general happiness can be represented by a social utility function consisting of a sum of individual utility functions with identical weights (this being the meaning of the maxim that each counts for one and no more than one),[18] it is commonly assumed that the utility functions of individuals are similar in all essential respects. Differences between individuals are ascribed to accidents of education and upbringing, and they should not be taken into account. This assumption, coupled with that of diminishing marginal utility, results in a prima facie case for equality, e.g., of equality in the distribution of income during any given period of time, laying aside indirect effects on the future. But even if utilitarianism is interpreted as having such restrictions built into the utility function, and even if it is supposed that these restrictions have in practice much the same result as the application of the principles of justice (and appear, perhaps, to be ways of expressing these principles in the language of mathematics and psychology), the fundamental idea is very different from the conception of justice as fairness. For one thing, that the principles of justice should be accepted is interpreted as the contingent result of a higher order administrative decision. The form of this decision is regarded as being similar to that of an entrepreneur deciding how much to produce of this or that commodity in view of its marginal revenue, or to that of someone distributing goods to needy persons according to the relative urgency of their wants. The choice between practices is thought of as being made on the basis of the allocation of benefits and burdens to individuals (these being measured by the present capitalized value of their utility over the full period of the practice's existence), which results from the distribution of rights and duties established by a practice.

Moreover, the individuals receiving these benefits are not conceived as being related in any way: they represent so many different directions in which limited resources may be allocated. The value of assigning resources to one direction rather than another depends solely on the preferences and interests of individuals as individuals. The satisfaction of desire has its value irrespective of the moral relations between persons, say as members of a joint undertaking, and of the claims which, in the name of these interests, they are prepared to make on one another;[19] and it is this value which is to be taken into account by the (ideal) legislator who is conceived as adjusting the rules of the system from the center so as to maximize the value of the social utility function.

It is thought that the principles of justice will not be violated by a legal system so conceived provided these executive decisions are correctly made. In this fact the principles of justice are said to have their derivation and explanation; they simply express the most important general features of social institutions in which the administrative problem is solved in the best way. These principles have, indeed, a special urgency because, given the facts of human nature, so much depends on them; and this explains the peculiar quality of the moral feelings associated with justice.[20] This assimilation of justice to a higher order executive decision, certainly a striking conception, is central to classical utilitarianism; and it also brings out its profound individualism, in one sense of this ambiguous word. It regards persons as so many *separate* directions in which benefits and burdens may be assigned; and the value of the satisfaction or dissatisfaction of desire is not thought to depend in any way on the moral relations in which individuals stand, or on the kinds of claims which they are willing, in the pursuit of their interests, to press on each other.

7. Many social decisions are, of course, of an administrative nature. Certainly this is so when it is a matter of social utility in what one may call its ordinary sense: that is, when it is a question of the efficient design of social institutions for the use of common means to achieve common ends. In this case either the benefits and burdens may be assumed to be impartially distributed, or the question of distribution is misplaced, as in the instance of maintaining public order and security or national defense. But as an interpretation of the basis of the principles of justice, classical utilitarianism is mistaken. It *permits* one to argue, for example, that slavery is unjust on the grounds that the advantages to the slaveholder as slaveholder do not counterbalance the disadvantages to the slave and to society at large burdened by a comparatively inefficient system of labor. Now the conception of justice as fairness, when applied to the practice of slavery with its offices of slaveholder and slave, would not allow one to consider the advantages of the slaveholder in the first place. As that office is not in accordance with principles which could be mutually acknowledged, the gains accruing to the slaveholder, assuming them to exist, cannot be counted as in *any* way mitigating the injustice of the practice. The question whether these gains outweigh the disadvantages to the slave and to society cannot arise, since in considering the justice of slavery these gains have no weight at all which requires that they be overridden. Where the conception of justice as fairness applies, slavery is *always* unjust.

I am not, of course, suggesting the absurdity that the classical utilitarians approved of slavery. I am only rejecting a type of argument which their view allows them to use in support of their disapproval of it. The conception of justice as derivative from efficiency implies that judging the justice of a practice is always, in principle at least, a matter of weighing up advantages and disadvantages, each having an intrinsic value or disvalue as the satisfaction of interests, irrespective of whether or not these interests necessarily involve acquiescence in principles which could not be mutually acknowledged. Utilitarianism cannot account for the fact that slavery is always unjust, nor for the fact that it would be recognized as irrelevant in defeating the accusation of injustice for one person to say to another, engaged with him in a common practice and debating its merits, that nevertheless it allowed of the greatest satisfaction of desire. The charge of injustice cannot be rebutted in this way.

If justice were derivative from a higher order executive efficiency, this would not be so.

But now, even if it is taken as established that, so far as the ordinary conception of justice goes, slavery is always unjust (that is, slavery by definition violates commonly recognized principles of justice), the classical utilitarian would surely reply that these principles, as other moral principles subordinate to that of utility, are only generally correct. It is simply for the most part true that slavery is less efficient than other institutions; and while common sense may define the concept of justice so that slavery is unjust, nevertheless, where slavery would lead to the greatest satisfaction of desire, it is not wrong. Indeed, it is then right, and for the very same reason that justice, as ordinarily understood, is usually right. If, as ordinarily understood, slavery is always unjust, to this extent the utilitarian conception of justice might be admitted to differ from that of common moral opinion. Still the utilitarian would want to hold that, as a matter of moral principle, his view is correct in giving no special weight to considerations of justice beyond that allowed for by the general presumption of effectiveness. And this, he claims, is as it should be. The every day opinion is morally in error, although, indeed, it is a useful error, since it protects rules of generally high utility.

The question, then, relates not simply to the analysis of the concept of justice as common sense defines it, but the analysis of it in the wider sense as to how much weight considerations of justice, as defined, are to have when laid against other kinds of moral considerations. Here again I wish to argue that reasons of justice have a *special* weight for which only the conception of justice as fairness can account. Moreover, it belongs to the concept of justice that they do have this special weight. While Mill recognized that this was so, he thought that it could be accounted for by the special urgency of the moral feelings which naturally support principles of such high utility. But it is a mistake to resort to the urgency of feeling; as with the appeal to intuition, it manifests a failure to pursue the question far enough. The special weight of considerations of justice can be explained from the conception of justice as fairness. It is only necessary to elaborate a bit what has already been said as follows.

If one examines the circumstances in which a certain tolerance of slavery is justified, or perhaps better, excused, it turns out that these are of a rather special sort. Perhaps slavery exists as an inheritance from the past and it proves necessary to dismantle it piece by piece; at times slavery may conceivably be an advance on previous institutions. Now while there may be some excuse for slavery in special conditions, it is never an excuse for it that it is sufficiently advantageous to the slaveholder to outweigh the disadvantages to the slave and to society. A person who argues in this way is not perhaps making a wildly irrelevant remark; but he is guilty of a moral fallacy. There is disorder in his conception of the ranking of moral principles. For the slaveholder, by his own admission, has no moral title to the advantages which he receives as a slaveholder. He is no more prepared than the slave to acknowledge the principle upon which is founded the respective positions in which they both stand. Since slavery does not accord with principles which they could mutually acknowledge, they each may be supposed to agree that it is unjust: it grants claims which it ought not to grant and in doing so denies claims which it ought not to deny. Amongst persons in a general position who are debating the form of their common practices, it cannot, therefore, be offered as a reason for a practice that, in conceding these very claims that ought to be denied, it nevertheless meets existing interests more effectively. By their very nature the satisfaction of these claims is without weight and cannot enter into any tabulation of advantages and disadvantages.

Furthermore, it follows from the concept of morality that, to the extent that the slaveholder recognizes his position vis-à-vis the slave to be unjust, he would not choose to press his claims. His not wanting to receive his special advantages is one of the ways in which he shows that he thinks slavery is unjust. It would be fallacious for the legislator to suppose, then, that it is a ground for having a practice that it brings advantages greater than disadvantages, if those for whom the practice is designed, and to whom the advantages flow, acknowledge that they have no moral title to them and do not wish to receive them.

For these reasons the principles of justice have a special weight; and with respect to the principle of the greatest satisfaction of desire, as cited in the general position amongst those discussing the merits of their common practices, the principles of justice have an absolute weight. In this sense they are not contingent; and this is why their force is greater than can be accounted for by the general presumption (assuming that there is one) of the effectiveness, in the utilitarian sense, of practices which in fact satisfy them.

If one wants to continue using the concepts of classical utilitarianism, one will have to say, to meet this criticism, that at least the individual or social utility functions must be so defined that no value is given to the satisfaction of interests the representative claims of which violate the principles of justice. In this way it is no doubt possible to include these principles within the form of the utilitarian conception; but to do so is, of course, to change its inspiration altogether as a moral conception. For it is to incorporate within it principles which cannot be understood on the basis of a higher order executive decision aiming at the greatest satisfaction of desire.

It is worth remarking, perhaps, that this criticism of utilitarianism does not depend on whether or not the two assumptions, that of individuals having similar utility functions and that of diminishing marginal utility, are interpreted as psychological propositions to be supported or refuted by experience, or as moral and political principles expressed in a somewhat technical language. There are, certainly, several advantages in taking them in the latter fashion.[21] For one thing, one might say that this is what Bentham and others really meant by them, at least as shown by how they were used in arguments for social reform. More importantly, one could hold that the best way to defend the classical utilitarian view is to interpret these assumptions as moral and political principles. It is doubtful whether, taken as psychological propositions, they are true of men in general as we know them under normal conditions. On the other hand, utilitarians would not have wanted to propose them merely as practical working principles of legislation, or as expedient maxims to guide reform, given the egalitarian sentiments of modern society.[22] When pressed they might well have invoked the idea of a more or less equal capacity of men in relevant respects if given an equal chance in a just society. But if the argument above regarding slavery is correct, then granting these assumptions as moral and political principles makes no difference. To view individuals as equally fruitful lines for the allocation of benefits, even as a matter of moral principle, still leaves the mistaken notion that the satisfaction of desire has value in itself irrespective of the relations between persons as members of a common practice, and irrespective of the claims upon one another which the satisfaction of interests represents. To see the error of this idea one must give up the conception of justice as an executive decision altogether and refer to the notion of justice as fairness: that participants in a common practice be regarded as having an original and equal liberty and that their common practices be considered unjust unless they accord with principles which persons so circumstanced and related could freely acknowledge before one another, and so could accept as fair. Once the emphasis is put upon the concept of the mutual recognition of principles by participants in a common practice the rules of which are to define their several relations and give form to their claims on one another, then it is clear that the granting of a claim the principle of which could not be acknowledged by each in the general position (that is, in the position in which the parties propose and acknowledge principles before one another) is not a reason for adopting a practice. Viewed in this way, the background of the claim is seen to exclude it from consideration; that it can represent a value in itself arises from the conception of individuals as separate lines for the assignment of benefits, as isolated persons who stand as claimants on an administrative or benevolent largesse. Occasionally persons do so stand to one another; but this is not the general case, nor, more importantly, is it the case when it is a matter of the justice of practices themselves in which participants stand in various relations to be appraised in accordance with standards which they may be expected to acknowledge before one another. Thus however mistaken the notion of the social contract may be as history, and however far it may overreach itself as a general theory of social and political obligation, it does express, suitably interpreted, an essential part of the concept of justice.[23]

8. By way of conclusion I should like to make two remarks: first, the original modification of the utilitarian principle (that it require of practices that the offices and positions defined by them be equal unless it is reasonable to suppose that the representative man in *every* office would find the inequality to his advantage), slight as it may appear at first sight, actually has a different conception of justice standing behind it. I have tried to show how

this is so by developing the concept of justice as fairness and by indicating how this notion involves the mutual acceptance, from a general position, of the principles on which a practice is founded, and how this in turn requires the exclusion from consideration of claims violating the principles of justice. Thus the slight alteration of principle reveals another family of notions, another way of looking at the concept of justice.

Second, I should like to remark also that I have been dealing with the *concept* of justice. I have tried to set out the kinds of principles upon which judgments concerning the justice of practices may be said to stand. The analysis will be successful to the degree that it expresses the principles involved in these judgments when made by competent persons upon deliberation and reflection.[24] Now every people may be supposed to have the concept of justice, since in the life of every society there must be at least some relations in which the parties consider themselves to be circumstanced and related as the concept of justice as fairness requires. Societies will differ from one another not in having or in failing to have this notion but in the range of cases to which they apply it and in the emphasis which they give to it as compared with other moral concepts.

A firm grasp of the concept of justice itself is necessary if these variations, and the reasons for them, are to be understood. No study of the development of moral ideas and of the differences between them is more sound than the analysis of the fundamental moral concepts upon which it must depend. I have tried, therefore, to give an analysis of the concept of justice which should apply generally, however large a part the concept may have in a given morality, and which can be used in explaining the course of men's thoughts about justice and its relations to other moral concepts. How it is to be used for this purpose is a large topic which I cannot, of course, take up here. I mention it only to emphasize that I have been dealing with the concept of justice itself and to indicate what use I consider such an analysis to have.

Notes

1 An abbreviated version of this paper (less than one-half the length) was presented in a symposium with the same title at the American Philosophical Association, Eastern Division, December 28, 1957, and appeared in the *Journal of Philosophy*, LIV, 653–62.

2 I use the word "practice" throughout as a sort of technical term meaning any form of activity specified by a system of rules which defines offices, roles, moves, penalties, defenses, and so on, and which gives the activity its structure. As examples one may

think of games and rituals, trials and parliaments, markets and systems of property. I have attempted a partial analysis of the notion of a practice in a paper "Two Concepts of Rules," *Philosophical Review*, LXIV (1955), 3–32.

3 These principles are, of course, well-known in one form or another and appear in many analyses of justice even where the writers differ widely on other matters. Thus if the principle of equal liberty is commonly associated with Kant (see *The Philosophy of Law*, tr. by W. Hastie, Edinburgh, 1887, pp. 56 f.), it may be claimed that it can also be found in J.S. Mill's *On Liberty* and elsewhere, and in many other liberal writers. Recently H.L.A. Hart has argued for something like it in his paper "Are There Any Natural Rights?," *Philosophical Review*, LXIV (1955), 175–91 [reprinted as chapter 18 of this volume]. The injustice of inequalities which are not won in return for a contribution to the common advantage is, of course, widespread in political writings of all sorts. The conception of justice here discussed is distinctive, if at all, only in selecting these two principles in this form; but for another similar analysis, see the discussion by W.D. Lamont, *The Principles of Moral Judgment* (Oxford, 1946), ch. v.

4 This point was made by Sidgwick, *Methods of Ethics*, 6th ed. (London, 1901), Bk. III, ch. v, sec. 1. It has recently been emphasized by Sir Isaiah Berlin in a symposium, "Equality," *Proceedings of the Aristotelian Society*, n.s. LVI (1955–6), 305 f.

5 In the paper referred to above, note 2, I have tried to show the importance of taking practices as the proper subject of the utilitarian principle. The criticisms of so-called "restricted utilitarianism" by J.J.C. Smart, "Extreme and Restricted Utilitarianism," *Philosophical Quarterly*, VI (1956), 344–54, and by H.J. McCloskey, "An Examination of Restricted Utilitarianism," *Philosophical Review*, LXVI (1957), 466–85, do not affect my argument. These papers are concerned with the very general proposition, which is attributed (with what justice I shall not consider) to S.E. Toulmin and P.H. Nowell-Smith (and in the case of the latter paper, also, apparently, to me); namely, the proposition that particular moral actions are justified by appealing to moral rules, and moral rules in turn by reference to utility. But clearly I meant to defend no such view. My discussion of the concept of rules as maxims is an explicit rejection of it. What I did argue was that, in the *logically special* case of practices (although actually quite a common case) where the rules have special features and are not moral rules at all but legal rules or rules of games and the like (except, perhaps, in the case of promises), there is a peculiar force to the distinction between justifying particular actions and justifying the system of rules themselves. Even then I claimed only that restricting the utilitarian principle to practices as defined strengthened it. I did not argue for the pos-

ition that this amendment alone is sufficient for a complete defense of utilitarianism as a general theory of morals. In this paper I take up the question as to how the utilitarian principle itself must be modified, but here, too, the subject of inquiry is not all of morality at once, but a limited topic, the concept of justice.

6 It might seem as if J.S. Mill, in paragraph 36 of Chapter v of *Utilitarianism*, expressed the utilitarian principle in this modified form, but in the remaining two paragraphs of the chapter, and elsewhere, he would appear not to grasp the significance of the change. Hume often emphasizes that *every* man must benefit. For example, in discussing the utility of general rules, he holds that they are requisite to the "well-being of every individual"; from a stable system of property "every individual person must find himself a gainer in balancing the account . . ." "Every member of society is sensible of this interest; everyone expresses this sense to his fellows along with the resolution he has taken of squaring his actions by it, on the conditions that others will do the same." *A Treatise of Human Nature*, Bk. III, Pt. II, sec. II, par. 22.

7 It is not possible to discuss here this addition to the usual conception of rationality. If it seems peculiar, it may be worth remarking that it is analogous to the modification of the utilitarian principle which the argument as a whole is designed to explain and justify. In the same way that the satisfaction of interests, the representative claims of which violate the principles of justice, is not a reason for having a practice (see Section 7), unfounded envy, within limits, need not be taken into account.

8 The idea that accepting a principle as a moral principle implies that one generally acts on it, failing a special explanation, has been stressed by R.M. Hare, *The Language of Morals* (Oxford, 1952). His formulation of it needs to be modified, however, along the lines suggested by P.L. Gardiner, "On Assenting to a Moral Principle," *Proceedings of the Aristotelian Society*, n.s. LV (1955), 23–44. See also C.K. Grant, "Akrasia and the Criteria of Assent to Practical Principles," *Mind*, LXV (1956), 400–7, where the complexity of the criteria for assent is discussed.

9 Perhaps the best known statement of this conception is that given by Glaucon at the beginning of Book II of Plato's *Republic*. Presumably it was, in various forms, a common view among the Sophists; but that Plato gives a fair representation of it is doubtful. See K.R. Popper, *The Open Society and Its Enemies*, rev. ed. (Princeton, 1950), pp. 112–8. Certainly Plato usually attributes to it a quality of manic egoism which one feels must be an exaggeration; on the other hand, see the Melian Debate in Thucydides, *The Peloponnesian War*, Book V, ch. VII, although it is impossible to say to what extent the views expressed there reveal any current philosophical opinion. Also in this tradition are the remarks of Epicurus

John Rawls

on justice in *Principal Doctrines*, XXXI–XXXVIII. In modern times elements of the conception appear in a more sophisticated form in Hobbes *The Leviathan* and in Hume *A Treatise of Human Nature*, Bk. III, Pt. II, as well as in the writings of the school of natural law such as Pufendorf's *De jure naturae et gentium*. Hobbes and Hume are especially instructive. For Hobbes's argument see Howard Warrender's *The Political Philosophy of Hobbes* (Oxford, 1957). W. J. Baumol's *Welfare Economics and the Theory of the State* (London, 1952), is valuable in showing the wide applicability of Hobbes's fundamental idea (interpreting his natural law as principles of prudence), although in this book it is traced back only to Hume's *Treatise*.

10   See J. von Neumann and O. Morgenstern, *The Theory of Games and Economic Behavior*, 2nd ed. (Princeton, 1947). For a comprehensive and not too technical discussion of the developments since, see R. Duncan Luce and Howard Raiffa, *Games and Decisions: Introduction and Critical Survey* (New York, 1957). Chs. VI and XIV discuss the developments most obviously related to the analysis of justice.

11   For a general survey see J.W. Gough, *The Social Contract*, 2nd ed. (Oxford, 1957), and Otto von Gierke, *The Development of Political Theory*, tr. by B. Freyd (London, 1939), Pt. II, ch. II.

12   The difficulty one gets into by a mechanical application of the theory of games to moral philosophy can be brought out by considering among several possible examples, R.B. Braithwaite's study, *Theory of Games as a Tool for the Moral Philosopher* (Cambridge, 1955). On the analysis there given, it turns out that the fair division of playing time between Matthew and Luke depends on their preferences, and these in turn are connected with the instruments they wish to play. Since Matthew has a threat advantage over Luke, arising purely from the fact that Matthew, the trumpeter, prefers both of them playing at once to neither of them playing, whereas Luke, the pianist, prefers silence to cacophony, Matthew is allotted 26 evenings of play to Luke's 17. If the situation were reversed, the threat advantage would be with Luke. See pp. 36 f. But now we have only to suppose that Matthew is a jazz enthusiast who plays the drums, and Luke a violinist who plays sonatas, in which case it will be fair, on this analysis, for Matthew to play whenever and as often as he likes, assuming, of course, as it is plausible to assume, that he does not care whether Luke plays or not. Certainly something has gone wrong. To each according to his threat advantage is hardly the principle of fairness. What is lacking is the concept of morality, and it must be brought into the conjectural account in some way or other. In the text this is done by the form of the procedure whereby principles are proposed and acknowledged (Section 3). If one starts directly with the particular case as known,

and if one accepts as given and definitive the preferences and relative positions of the parties, whatever they are, it is impossible to give an analysis of the moral concept of fairness. Braithwaite's use of the theory of games, insofar as it is intended to analyze the concept of fairness, is, I think, mistaken. This is not, of course, to criticize in any way the theory of games as a mathematical theory, to which Braithwaite's book certainly contributes, nor as an analysis of how rational (and amoral) egoists might behave (and so as an analysis of how people sometimes actually do behave). But it is to say that if the theory of games is to be used to analyze moral concepts, its formal structure must be interpreted in a special and general manner as indicated in the text. Once we do this, though, we are in touch again with a much older tradition.

13   For the definition of this prima facie duty, and the idea that it is a special duty, I am indebted to H.L.A. Hart. See his paper "Are There Any Natural Rights?," *Philosophical Review*, LXIV (1955), 185 f. [reprinted as chapter 18 of this volume].

14   The sense of "performative" here is to be derived from J.L. Austin's paper in the symposium, "Other Minds," *Proceedings of the Aristotelian Society*. Supplementary Volume (1946), pp. 170–4.

15   This, however, commonly happens. Hobbes, for example, when invoking the notion of a "tacit covenant," appeals not to the natural law that promises should be kept but to his fourth law of nature, that of gratitude. On Hobbes's shift from fidelity to gratitude, see Warrender, *The Political Philosophy of Hobbes*, (Oxford, 1957) pp. 51–2, 233–7. While it is not a serious criticism of Hobbes, it would have improved his argument had he appealed to the duty of fair play. On his premises he is perfectly entitled to do so. Similarly Sidgwick thought that a principle of justice, such as every man ought to receive adequate requital for his labor, is like gratitude universalized. See *Methods of Ethics*, Bk. III, ch. v, sec. 5. There is a gap in the stock of moral concepts used by philosophers into which the concept of the duty of fair play fits quite naturally.

16   I am using the concept of criterion here in what I take to be Wittgenstein's sense. See *Philosophical Investigations* (Oxford, 1953); and Norman Malcolm's review, "Wittgenstein's *Philosophical Investigations*," *Philosophical Review*, LXIII (1954), 543–7. That the response of compassion, under appropriate circumstances, is part of the criterion for whether or not a person understands what "pain" means, is, I think, in the *Philosophical Investigations*. The view in the text is simply an extension of this idea. I cannot, however, attempt to justify it here. Similar thoughts are to be found, I think, in Max Scheler, *The Nature of Sympathy*, tr. by Peter Heath (New Haven, 1954). His way of writing is often so obscure that I cannot be certain.

17 While this assimilation is implicit in Bentham's and Sidgwick's moral theory, explicit statements of it as applied to justice are relatively rare. One clear instance in *The Principles of Morals and Legislation* occurs in ch. x, footnote 2 to sec XL: "... justice, in the only sense in which it has a meaning, is an imaginary personage, feigned for the convenience of discourse, whose dictates are the dictates of utility, applied to certain particular cases. Justice, then, is nothing more than an imaginary instrument, employed to forward on certain occasions, and by certain means, the purposes of benevolence. The dictates of justice are nothing more than a part of the dictates of benevolence, which, on certain occasions, are applied to certain subjects...." Likewise in *The Limits of Jurisprudence Defined*, ed. by C.W. Everett (New York, 1945), pp. 117 f., Bentham criticizes Grotius for denying that justice derives from utility; and in *The Theory of Legislation*, ed. by C. K. Ogden (London, 1931), p. 3, he says that he uses the words "just" and "unjust" along with other words "simply as collective terms including the ideas of certain pains or pleasures." That Sidgwick's conception of justice is similar to Bentham's is admittedly not evident from his discussion of justice in Bk. III, ch. v of *Methods of Ethics*. But it follows, I think, from the moral theory he accepts. Hence C. D. Broad's criticisms of Sidgwick in the matter of distributive justice in *Five Types of Ethical Theory* (London, 1930), pp. 249–53, do not rest on a misinterpretation.

18 This maxim is attributed to Bentham by J.S. Mill in *Utilitarianism*, ch. v, par. 36. I have not found it in Bentham's writings, nor seen such a reference. Similarly James Bonar, *Philosophy and Political Economy* (London, 1893), p. 234 n. But it accords perfectly with Bentham's ideas. See the hitherto unpublished manuscript in David Baumgardt, *Bentham and the Ethics of Today* (Princeton, 1952), App. IV. For example, "the total value of the stock of pleasure belonging to the whole community is to be obtained by multiplying the number expressing the value of it as respecting any one person, by the number expressing the multitude of such individuals" (p. 556).

19 An idea essential to the classical utilitarian conception of justice. Bentham is firm in his statement of it: "It is only upon that principle [the principle of asceticism], and not from the principle of utility, that the most abominable pleasure which the vilest of malefactors ever reaped from his crime would be reprobated, if it stood alone. The case is, that it never does stand alone; but is necessarily followed by such a quantity of pain (or, what comes to the same thing, such a chance for a certain quantity of pain) that the pleasure in comparison of it, is as nothing: and this is the true and sole, but perfectly sufficient, reason for making it a ground for pun-

ishment" (*The Principles of Morals and Legislation*, ch. II, sec. iv. See also ch. x, sec. x, footnote 1). The same point is made in *The Limits of Jurisprudence Defined*, pp. 115 f. Although much recent welfare economics, as found in such important works as I.M.D. Little, *A Critique of Welfare Economics*, 2nd ed. (Oxford, 1957) and K.J. Arrow, *Social Choice and Individual Values* (New York, 1951), dispenses with the idea of cardinal utility, and uses instead the theory of ordinal utility as stated by J.R. Hicks, *Value and Capital*, 2nd ed. (Oxford, 1946), Pt. I, it assumes with utilitarianism that individual preferences have value as such, and so accepts the idea being criticized here. I hasten to add, however, that this is no objection to it as a means of analyzing economic policy, and for that purpose it may, indeed, be a necessary simplifying assumption. Nevertheless it is an assumption which cannot be made in so far as one is trying to analyze moral concepts, especially the concept of justice, as economists would, I think, agree. Justice is usually regarded as a separate and distinct part of any comprehensive criterion of economic policy. See, for example, Tibor Scitovsky, *Welfare and Competition* (London, 1952), pp. 59–69, and Little, *A Critique of Welfare Economics*, 2nd ed., ch. VII.

20 See J.S. Mill's argument in *Utilitarianism*, ch. v, pars. 16–25.

21 See D.G. Ritchie, *Natural Rights* (London, 1894), pp. 95 ff., 249 ff. Lionel Robbins has insisted on this point on several occasions. See *An Essay on the Nature and Significance of Economic Science*, 2nd ed. (London, 1935), pp. 134–43, "Interpersonal Comparisons of Utility: A Comment," *Economic Journal*, XLVIII (1938), 635–41, and more recently, "Robertson on Utility and Scope," *Economica*, n.s. XX (1953), 108f.

22 As Sir Henry Maine suggested Bentham may have regarded them. See *The Early History of Institutions* (London, 1875), pp. 398 ff.

23 Thus Kant was not far wrong when he interpreted the original contract merely as an "Idea of Reason"; yet he still thought of it as a *general* criterion of right and as providing a general theory of political obligation. See the second part of the essay, "On the Saying 'That may be right in theory but has no value in practice'" (1793), in *Kant's Principles of Politics*, tr. by W. Hastie (Edinburgh, 1891). I have drawn on the contractarian tradition not for a general theory of political obligation but to clarify the concept of justice.

24 For a further discussion of the idea expressed here, see my paper, "Outline of a Decision Procedure for Ethics," in the *Philosophical Review*, LX (1951), 177–97. For an analysis, similar in many respects but using the notion of the ideal observer instead of that of the considered judgment of a competent person, see Roderick Firth, "Ethical Absolutism

John Rawls

and the Ideal Observer," *Philosophy and Phenomeno-logical Research*, XII (1952), 317–45. While the similarities between these two discussions are more important than the differences, an analysis based on the notion of a considered judgment of a competent person, as it is based on a kind of judgment, may prove more helpful in understanding the features of moral judgment than an analysis based on the notion of an ideal observer, although this remains to be shown. A man who rejects the conditions imposed on a considered judgment of a competent person could no longer profess to *judge* at all. This seems more fundamental than his rejecting the conditions of observation, for these do not seem to apply, in an ordinary sense, to making a moral judgment.

13

Distributive Justice

Robert Nozick

The minimal state is the most extensive state that can be justified. Any state more extensive violates people's rights. Yet many persons have put forth reasons purporting to justify a more extensive state. It is impossible within the compass of this book to examine all the reasons that have been put forth. Therefore, I shall focus upon those generally acknowledged to be most weighty and influential, to see precisely wherein they fail. In this chapter we consider the claim that a more extensive state is justified, because necessary (or the best instrument) to achieve distributive justice.

The term "distributive justice" is not a neutral one. Hearing the term "distribution," most people presume that some thing or mechanism uses some principle or criterion to give out a supply of things. Into this process of distributing shares some error may have crept. So it is an open question, at least, whether *re*distribution should take place; whether we should do again what has already been done once, though poorly. However, we are not in the position of children who have been given portions of pie by someone who now makes last minute adjustments to rectify careless cutting. There is no *central* distribution, no person or group entitled to control all the resources, jointly deciding how they are to be doled out. What each person gets, he gets from others who give to him in exchange for something, or as a gift. In a free society, diverse persons control different resources, and new holdings arise out of the voluntary exchanges and actions of persons. There is no more a distributing or distribution of shares than there is a distributing of mates in a society in which persons choose whom they shall marry. The total result is the product of many individual decisions which the different individuals involved are entitled to make. Some uses of the term "distribution," it is true, do not imply a previous distributing appropriately judged by some criterion (for example, "probability distribution"); nevertheless, despite the title of this chapter, it would be best to use a terminology that clearly is neutral. We shall speak of people's holdings; a principle of justice in holdings describes (part of) what justice tells us (requires) about holdings. I shall state first what I take to be the correct view about justice in holdings, and then turn to the discussion of alternate views.[1]

The Entitlement Theory

The subject of justice in holdings consists of three major topics. The first is the *original acquisition of holdings*, the appropriation of unheld things. This includes the issues of how unheld things may come to be held, the process, or processes, by which unheld things may come to be held, the things that may come to be held by these processes, the extent of what comes to be held by a particular process, and so on. We shall refer to the complicated truth about this topic, which we shall not formulate here, as the principle of justice in acquisition. The second topic concerns the *transfer of holdings* from one person to another. By what processes may a person transfer holdings to another? How may a person acquire a holding from another who holds it? Under this topic come general descriptions of voluntary exchange, and gift and (on the other hand) fraud, as well as reference to particular conventional details fixed upon in a given society. The complicated truth about this subject (with placeholders for conventional details) we shall call the principle of justice in transfer. (And we shall suppose it also includes principles governing how a person may divest himself of a holding, passing it into an unheld state.)

If the world were wholly just, the following inductive definition would exhaustively cover the subject of justice in holdings.

1   A person who acquires a holding in accordance with the principle of justice in acquisition is entitled to that holding.
2   A person who acquires a holding in accordance with the principle of justice in transfer, from someone else entitled to the holding, is entitled to the holding.
3   No one is entitled to a holding except by (repeated) applications of 1 and 2.

The complete principle of distributive justice would say simply that a distribution is just if everyone is entitled to the holdings they possess under the distribution.

A distribution is just if it arises from another just distribution by legitimate means. The legitimate means of moving from one distribution to another are specified by the principle of justice in transfer. The legitimate first "moves" are specified by the principle of justice in acquisition.[2] Whatever arises from a just situation by just steps is itself just. The means of change specified by the principle of justice in transfer preserve justice. As correct rules of inference are truth-preserving, and any conclusion deduced via repeated application of such rules from only true premises is itself true, so the means of transition from one situation to another specified by the principle of justice in transfer are justice-preserving, and any situation actually arising from repeated transitions in accordance with the principle from a just situation is itself just. The parallel between justice-preserving transformations and truth-preserving transformations illuminates

where it fails as well as where it holds. That a conclusion could have been deduced by truth-preserving means from premises that are true suffices to show its truth. That from a just situation a situation *could* have arisen via justice-preserving means does *not* suffice to show its justice. The fact that a thief's victims voluntarily *could* have presented him with gifts does not entitle the thief to his ill-gotten gains. Justice in holdings is historical; it depends upon what actually has happened. We shall return to this point later.

Not all actual situations are generated in accordance with the two principles of justice in holdings: the principle of justice in acquisition and the principle of justice in transfer. Some people steal from others, or defraud them, or enslave them, seizing their product and preventing them from living as they choose, or forcibly exclude others from competing in exchanges. None of these are permissible modes of transition from one situation to another. And some persons acquire holdings by means not sanctioned by the principle of justice in acquisition. The existence of past injustice (previous violations of the first two principles of justice in holdings) raises the third major topic under justice in holdings: the rectification of injustice in holdings. If past injustice has shaped present holdings in various ways, some identifiable and some not, what now, if anything, ought to be done to rectify these injustices? What obligations do the performers of injustice have toward those whose position is worse than it would have been had the injustice not been done? Or, than it would have been had compensation been paid promptly? How, if at all, do things change if the beneficiaries and those made worse off are not the direct parties in the act of injustice, but, for example, their descendants? Is an injustice done to someone whose holding was itself based upon an unrectified injustice? How far back must one go in wiping clean the historical slate of injustices? What may victims of injustice permissibly do in order to rectify the injustices being done to them, including the many injustices done by persons acting through their government? I do not know of a thorough or theoretically sophisticated treatment of such issues.[3] Idealizing greatly, let us suppose theoretical investigation will produce a principle of rectification. This principle uses historical information about previous situations and injustices done in them (as defined by the first two principles of justice and rights against interference), and information about the actual course of events that flowed from these injustices, until the present, and it yields a description (or descriptions) of holdings in the society. The principle of rectification presumably will make use of its best estimate of subjunctive information about what would have occurred (or a probability distribution over what might have occurred, using the expected value) if the injustice had not taken place. If the actual description of holdings turns out not to be one of the descriptions yielded by the principle, then one of the descriptions yielded must be realized.[4]

The general outlines of the theory of justice in holdings are that the holdings of a person are just if he is entitled to them by the principles of justice in acquisition and transfer, or by the principle of rectification of injustice (as specified by the first two principles). If each person's holdings are just, then the total set (distribution) of holdings is just. To turn these general outlines into a specific theory we would have to specify the details of each of the three principles of justice in holdings: the principle of acquisition of holdings, the principle of transfer of holdings, and the principle of rectification of violations of the first two principles. I shall not attempt that task here. (Locke's principle of justice in acquisition is discussed below.)

Historical Principles and End-result Principles

The general outlines of the entitlement theory illuminate the nature and defects of other conceptions of distributive justice. The entitlement theory of justice in distribution is *historical*; whether a distribution is just depends upon how it came about. In contrast, *current time-slice principles* of justice hold that the justice of a distribution is determined by how things are distributed (who has what) as judged by some *structural* principle(s) of just distribution. A utilitarian who judges between any two distributions by seeing which has the greater sum of utility and, if the sums tie, applies some fixed equality criterion to choose the more equal distribution, would hold a current time-slice principle of justice. As would someone who had a fixed schedule of trade-offs between the sum of happiness and equality. According to a current time-slice principle, all that needs to be looked at, in judging the justice of a distribution, is who ends up with what; in comparing any two distributions one need look only at the matrix presenting the distributions. No further informa-

tion need be fed into a principle of justice. It is a consequence of such principles of justice that any two structurally identical distributions are equally just. (Two distributions are structurally identical if they present the same profile, but perhaps have different persons occupying the particular slots. My having ten and your having five, and my having five and your having ten are structurally identical distributions.) Welfare economics is the theory of current time-slice principles of justice. The subject is conceived as operating on matrices representing only current information about distribution. This, as well as some of the usual conditions (for example, the choice of distribution is invariant under relabeling of columns), guarantees that welfare economics will be a current time-slice theory, with all of its inadequacies.

Most persons do not accept current time-slice principles as constituting the whole story about distributive shares. They think it relevant in assessing the justice of a situation to consider not only the distribution it embodies, but also how that distribution came about. If some persons are in prison for murder or war crimes, we do not say that to assess the justice of the distribution in the society we must look only at what this person has, and that person has, and that person has, . . . at the current time. We think it relevant to ask whether someone did something so that he *deserved* to be punished, deserved to have a lower share. Most will agree to the relevance of further information with regard to punishments and penalties. Consider also desired things. One traditional socialist view is that workers are entitled to the product and full fruits of their labor; they have earned it; a distribution is unjust if it does not give the workers what they are entitled to. Such entitlements are based upon some past history. No socialist holding this view would find it comforting to be told that because the actual distribution *A* happens to coincide structurally with the one he desires *D*, *A* therefore is no less just than *D*; it differs only in that the "parasitic" owners of capital receive under *A* what the workers are entitled to under *D*, and the workers receive under *A* what the owners are entitled to under *D*, namely very little. This socialist rightly, in my view, holds onto the notions of earning, producing, entitlement, desert, and so forth, and he rejects current time-slice principles that look only to the structure of the resulting set of holdings. (The set of holdings resulting from what? Isn't it implausible that how holdings are produced and come to exist has no effect at all on who should hold what?) His mistake lies in his view of what entitlements arise out of what sorts of productive processes.

We construe the position we discuss too narrowly by speaking of *current* time-slice principles. Nothing is changed if structural principles operate upon a time sequence of current time-slice profiles and, for example, give someone more now to counterbalance the less he has had earlier. A utilitarian or an egalitarian or any mixture of the two over time will inherit the difficulties of his more myopic comrades. He is not helped by the fact that *some* of the information others consider relevant in assessing a distribution is reflected, unrecoverably, in past matrices. Henceforth, we shall refer to such unhistorical principles of distributive justice, including the current time-slice principles, as *end-result principles* or *end-state principles*.

In contrast to end-result principles of justice, *historical principles* of justice hold that past circumstances or actions of people can create differential entitlements or differential deserts to things. An injustice can be worked by moving from one distribution to another structurally identical one, for the second, in profile the same, may violate people's entitlements or deserts; it may not fit the actual history.

Patterning

The entitlement principles of justice in holdings that we have sketched are historical principles of justice. To better understand their precise character, we shall distinguish them from another subclass of the historical principles. Consider, as an example, the principle of distribution according to moral merit. This principle requires that total distributive shares vary directly with moral merit; no person should have a greater share than anyone whose moral merit is greater. (If moral merit could be not merely ordered but measured on an interval or ratio scale, stronger principles could be formulated.) Or consider the principle that results by substituting "usefulness to society" for "moral merit" in the previous principle. Or instead of "distribute according to moral merit," or "distribute according to usefulness to society," we might consider "distribute according to the weighted sum of moral merit, usefulness to society, and need," with the weights of the different dimensions equal. Let us call a principle of distribution *patterned* if it specifies that a distribution is to vary

along with some natural dimension, weighted sum of natural dimensions, or lexicographic ordering of natural dimensions. And let us say a distribution is patterned if it accords with some patterned principle. (I speak of natural dimensions, admittedly without a general criterion for them, because for any set of holdings some artificial dimensions can be gimmicked up to vary along with the distribution of the set.) The principle of distribution in accordance with moral merit is a patterned historical principle, which specifies a patterned distribution. "Distribute according to I.Q." is a patterned principle that looks to information not contained in distributional matrices. It is not historical, however, in that it does not look to any past actions creating differential entitlements to evaluate a distribution; it requires only distributional matrices whose columns are labeled by I.Q. scores. The distribution in a society, however, may be composed of such simple patterned distributions, without itself being simply patterned. Different sectors may operate different patterns, or some combination of patterns may operate in different proportions across a society. A distribution composed in this manner, from a small number of patterned distributions, we also shall term "patterned." And we extend the use of "pattern" to include the overall designs put forth by combinations of end-state principles.

Almost every suggested principle of distributive justice is patterned: to each according to his moral merit, or needs, or marginal product, or how hard he tries, or the weighted sum of the foregoing, and so on. The principle of entitlement we have sketched is *not* patterned.[5] There is no one natural dimension or weighted sum or combination of a small number of natural dimensions that yields the distributions generated in accordance with the principle of entitlement. The set of holdings that results when some persons receive their marginal products, others win at gambling, others receive a share of their mate's income, others receive gifts from foundations, others receive interest on loans, others receive gifts from admirers, others receive returns on investment, others make for themselves much of what they have, others find things, and so on, will not be patterned. Heavy strands of patterns will run through it; significant portions of the variance in holdings will be accounted for by pattern-variables. If most people most of the time choose to transfer some of their entitlements to others only in exchange for something from them, then a large part of what many people hold will vary with what they held that others wanted. More details are provided by the theory of marginal productivity. But gifts to relatives, charitable donations, bequests to children, and the like, are not best conceived, in the first instance, in this manner. Ignoring the strands of pattern, let us suppose for the moment that a distribution actually arrived at by the operation of the principle of entitlement is random with respect to any pattern. Though the resulting set of holdings will be unpatterned, it will not be incomprehensible, for it can be seen as arising from the operation of a small number of principles. These principles specify how an initial distribution may arise (the principle of acquisition of holdings) and how distributions may be transformed into others (the principle of transfer of holdings). The process whereby the set of holdings is generated will be intelligible, though the set of holdings itself that results from this process will be unpatterned.

The writings of F. A. Hayek focus less than is usually done upon what patterning distributive justice requires. Hayek argues that we cannot know enough about each person's situation to distribute to each according to his moral merit (but would justice demand we do so if we did have this knowledge?); and he goes on to say, "our objection is against all attempts to impress upon society a deliberately chosen pattern of distribution, whether it be an order of equality or of inequality."[6] However, Hayek concludes that in a free society there will be distribution in accordance with value rather than moral merit; that is, in accordance with the perceived value of a person's actions and services to others. Despite his rejection of a patterned conception of distributive justice, Hayek himself suggests a pattern he thinks justifiable: distribution in accordance with the perceived benefits given to others, leaving room for the complaint that a free society does not realize exactly this pattern. Stating this patterned strand of a free capitalist society more precisely, we get "To each according to how much he benefits others who have the resources for benefiting those who benefit them." This will seem arbitrary unless some acceptable initial set of holdings is specified, or unless it is held that the operation of the system over time washes out any significant effects from the initial set of holdings. As an example of the latter, if almost anyone would have bought a car from Henry Ford, the supposition that it was an arbitrary matter who held the money then (and so bought) would not place Henry Ford's earnings

under a cloud. In any event, *his* coming to hold it is not arbitrary. Distribution according to benefits to others *is* a major patterned strand in a free capitalist society, as Hayek correctly points out, but it is only a strand and does not constitute the whole pattern of a system of entitlements (namely, inheritance, gifts for arbitrary reasons, charity, and so on) or a standard that one should insist a society fit. Will people tolerate for long a system yielding distributions that they believe are unpatterned?[7] No doubt people will not long accept a distribution they believe is *unjust*. People want their society to be and to look just. But must the look of justice reside in a resulting pattern rather than in the underlying generating principles? We are in no position to conclude that the inhabitants of a society embodying an entitlement conception of justice in holdings will find it unacceptable. Still, it must be granted that were people's reasons for transferring some of their holdings to others always irrational or arbitrary, we would find this disturbing. (Suppose people always determined what holdings they would transfer, and to whom, by using a random device.) We feel more comfortable upholding the justice of an entitlement system if most of the transfers under it are done for reasons. This does not mean necessarily that all deserve what holdings they receive. It means only that there is a purpose or point to someone's transferring a holding to one person rather than to another; that usually we can see what the transferrer thinks he's gaining, what cause he thinks he's serving, what goals he thinks he's helping to achieve, and so forth. Since in a capitalist society people often transfer holdings to others in accordance with how much they perceive these others benefiting them, the fabric constituted by the individual transactions and transfers is largely reasonable and intelligible.[8] (Gifts to loved ones, bequests to children, charity to the needy also are nonarbitrary components of the fabric.) In stressing the large strand of distribution in accordance with benefit to others, Hayek shows the point of many transfers, and so shows that the system of transfer of entitlements is not just spinning its gears aimlessly. The system of entitlements is defensible when constituted by the individual aims of individual transactions. No overarching aim is needed, no distributional pattern is required.

To think that the task of a theory of distributive justice is to fill in the blank in "to each according to his——" is to be predisposed to search for a pattern; and the separate treatment of "from each according to his——" treats production and distribution as two separate and independent issues. On an entitlement view these are *not* two separate questions. Whoever makes something, having bought or contracted for all other held resources used in the process (transferring some of his holdings for these cooperating factors), is entitled to it. The situation is *not* one of something's getting made, and there being an open question of who is to get it. Things come into the world already attached to people having entitlements over them. From the point of view of the historical entitlement conception of justice in holdings, those who start afresh to complete "to each according to his——" treat objects as if they appeared from nowhere, out of nothing. A complete theory of justice might cover this limit case as well; perhaps here is a use for the usual conceptions of distributive justice.[9]

So entrenched are maxims of the usual form that perhaps we should present the entitlement conception as a competitor. Ignoring acquisition and rectification, we might say:

From each according to what he chooses to do, to each according to what he makes for himself (perhaps with the contracted aid of others) and what others choose to do for him and choose to give him of what they've been given previously (under this maxim) and haven't yet expended or transferred.

This, the discerning reader will have noticed, has its defects as a slogan. So as a summary and great simplification (and not as a maxim with any independent meaning) we have:

From each as they choose, to each as they are chosen.

How Liberty Upsets Patterns

It is not clear how those holding alternative conceptions of distributive justice can reject the entitlement conception of justice in holdings. For suppose a distribution favored by one of these non-entitlement conceptions is realized. Let us suppose it is your favorite one and let us call this distribution D_1; perhaps everyone has an equal share, perhaps shares vary in accordance with some dimension you treasure. Now suppose that Wilt Chamberlain is greatly in demand by basketball teams, being a great gate attraction. (Also suppose contracts run only for a year, with players being free agents.) He signs the following sort of contract with a team: In each home game, twenty-five cents from the price of each ticket of admission goes to him. (We ignore the question of whether he is "gouging" the owners, letting them look out for themselves.) The season starts, and people cheerfully attend his team's games; they buy their tickets, each time dropping a separate twenty-five cents of their admission price into a special box with Chamberlain's name on it. They are excited about seeing him play; it is worth the total admission price to them. Let us suppose that in one season one million persons attend his home games, and Wilt Chamberlain winds up with $250,000, a much larger sum than the average income and larger even than anyone else has. Is he entitled to this income? Is this new distribution D_2, unjust? If so, why? There is *no* question about whether each of the people was entitled to the control over the resources they held in D_1; because that was the distribution (your favorite) that (for the purposes of argument) we assumed was acceptable. Each of these persons *chose* to give twenty-five cents of their money to Chamberlain. They could have spent it on going to the movies, or on candy bars, or on copies of *Dissent* magazine, or of *Monthly Review*. But they all, at least one million of them, converged on giving it to Wilt Chamberlain in exchange for watching him play basketball. If D_1 was a just distribution, and people voluntarily moved from it to D_2, transferring parts of their shares they were given under D_1 (what was it for if not to do something with?), isn't D_2 also just? If the people were entitled to dispose of the resources to which they were entitled (under D_1), didn't this include their being entitled to give it to, or exchange it with, Wilt Chamberlain? Can anyone else complain on grounds of justice? Each other person already has his legitimate share under D_1. Under D_1, there is nothing that anyone has that anyone else has a claim of justice against. After someone transfers something to Wilt Chamberlain, third parties *still* have their legitimate shares; *their* shares are not changed. By what process could such a transfer among two persons give rise to a legitimate claim of distributive justice on a portion of what was transferred, by a third party who had no claim of justice on any holding of the others *before* the transfer?[10] To cut off objections irrelevant here, we might imagine the exchanges occurring in a socialist society, after hours. After playing whatever basketball he does in his daily work, or doing whatever other daily work he does, Wilt Chamberlain decides to put in *overtime* to earn additional money. (First his work quota is set; he works time over that.) Or imagine it is a skilled juggler people like to see, who puts on shows after hours.

Why might someone work overtime in a society in which it is assumed their needs are satisfied? Perhaps because they care about things other than needs. I like to write in books that I read, and to have easy access to books for browsing at odd hours. It would be very pleasant and convenient to have the resources of Widener Library in my back yard. No society, I assume, will provide such resources close to each person who would like them as part of his regular allotment (under D_1). Thus, persons either must do without some extra things that they want, or be allowed to do something extra to get some of these things. On what basis could the inequalities that would eventuate be forbidden? Notice also that small factories would spring up in a socialist society, unless forbidden. I melt down some of my personal possessions (under D_1) and build a machine out of the material. I offer you, and others, a philosophy lecture once a week in exchange for your cranking the handle on my machine, whose products I exchange for yet other things, and so on. (The raw materials used by the machine are given to me by others who possess them under D_1, in exchange for hearing lectures.) Each person might participate to gain things over and above their allotment under D_1. Some persons even might want to leave their job in socialist industry and work full time in this private sector. I shall say something more about these issues in the next chapter. Here I wish merely to note how private property even in means of production would occur in a socialist society that did not forbid people to use as they wished some of the resources they are given under the socialist distribution D_1.[11] The socialist society would have to forbid capitalist acts between consenting adults.

The general point illustrated by the Wilt Chamberlain example and the example of the entrepreneur in a socialist society is that no end-state principle or distributional patterned principle of justice can be continuously realized without continuous interference with people's lives. Any favored pattern would be transformed into one unfavored by the principle, by people choosing to act in various ways; for example, by people exchanging goods and services with other people, or giving things to other people, things the transferrers are entitled to under the favored distributional pattern. To maintain a pattern one must either continually interfere to stop people from transferring resources as they wish to, or continually (or periodically) interfere to take from some persons resources that others for some reason chose to transfer to them. (But if some time limit is to be set on how long people may keep resources others voluntarily transfer to them, why let them keep these resources for *any* period of time? Why not have immediate confiscation?) It might be objected that all persons voluntarily will choose to refrain from actions which would upset the pattern. This presupposes unrealistically (1) that all will most want to maintain the pattern (are those who don't, to be "reeducated" or forced to undergo "self-criticism"?), (2) that each can gather enough information about his own actions and the ongoing activities of others to discover which of his actions will upset the pattern, and (3) that diverse and far-flung persons can coordinate their actions to dovetail into the pattern. Compare the manner in which the market is neutral among persons' desires, as it reflects and transmits widely scattered information via prices, and coordinates persons' activities.

It puts things perhaps a bit too strongly to say that every patterned (or end-state) principle is liable to be thwarted by the voluntary actions of the individual parties transferring some of their shares they receive under the principle. For perhaps some *very* weak patterns are not so thwarted.[12] Any distributional pattern with any egalitarian component is overturnable by the voluntary actions of individual persons over time; as is every patterned condition with sufficient content so as actually to have been proposed as presenting the central core of distributive justice. Still, given the possibility that some weak conditions or patterns may not be unstable in this way, it would be better to formulate an explicit description of the kind of interesting and contentful patterns under discussion, and to prove a theorem about their instability. Since the weaker the patterning, the more likely it is that the entitlement system itself satisfies it, a plausible conjecture is that any patterning either is unstable or is satisfied by the entitlement system.

Sen's Argument

Our conclusions are reinforced by considering a recent general argument of Amartya K. Sen.[13] Suppose individual rights are interpreted as the right to choose which of two alternatives is to be more highly ranked in a social ordering of the alternatives. Add the weak condition that if one alternative unanimously is preferred to another then it is ranked higher by the social ordering. If there are two different individuals each with individual rights, interpreted as above, over different pairs of alternatives (having no members in common), then for some possible preference rankings of the alternatives by the individuals, there is no linear social ordering. For suppose that person A has the right to decide among (X, Y) and person B has the right to decide among (Z, W); and suppose their individual preferences are as follows (and that there are no other individuals). Person A prefers W to X to Y to Z, and person B prefers Y to Z to W to X. By the unanimity condition, in the social ordering W is preferred to X (since each individual prefers it to X), and Y is preferred to Z (since each individual prefers it to Z). Also in the social ordering, X is preferred to Y, by person A's right of choice among these two alternatives. Combining these three binary rankings, we get W preferred to X preferred to Y preferred to Z, in the social ordering. However, by person B's right of choice, Z must be preferred to W in the social ordering. There is no transitive social ordering satisfying all these conditions, and the social ordering, therefore, is nonlinear. Thus far, Sen.

The trouble stems from treating an individual's right to choose among alternatives as the right to determine the relative ordering of these alternatives within a social ordering. The alternative which has individuals rank *pairs* of alternatives, and separately rank the individual alternatives is no better; their ranking of pairs feeds into some method of amalgamating preferences to yield a social ordering of pairs; and the choice among the alternatives in the highest ranked pair in the social ordering is made by the individual with the right to decide between this pair. This system also has the result that an alternative may be selected although *everyone* prefers some other alternative; for example, A selects X over Y, where (X, Y) somehow is the highest ranked *pair* in the social ordering of pairs, although everyone, including A, prefers W to X. (But the choice person A was given, however, was only between X and Y.)

A more appropriate view of individual rights is as follows. Individual rights are co-possible; each person may exercise his rights as he chooses. The exercise of these rights fixes some features of the world. Within the constraints of these fixed features, a choice may be made by a social choice

mechanism based upon a social ordering; if there are any choices left to make! Rights do not determine a social ordering but instead set the constraints within which a social choice is to be made, by excluding certain alternatives, fixing others, and so on. (If I have a right to choose to live in New York or in Massachusetts, and I choose Massachusetts, then alternatives involving my living in New York are not appropriate objects to be entered in a social ordering.) Even if all possible alternatives are ordered first, apart from anyone's rights, the situation is not changed: for then the highest ranked alternative *that is not excluded by anyone's exercise of his rights* is instituted. Rights do not determine the position of an alternative or the relative position of two alternatives in a social ordering; they *operate upon* a social ordering to constrain the choice it can yield.

If entitlements to holdings are rights to dispose of them, then social choice must take place *within* the constraints of how people choose to exercise these rights. If any patterning is legitimate, it falls within the domain of social choice, and hence is constrained by people's rights. *How else can one cope with Sen's result?* The alternative of first having a social ranking with rights exercised within *its* constraints is no alternative at all. Why not just select the top-ranked alternative and forget about rights? If that top-ranked alternative itself leaves some room for individual choice (and here is where "rights" of choice is supposed to enter in) there must be something to stop these choices from transforming it into another alternative. Thus Sen's argument leads us again to the result that patterning requires continuous interference with individuals' actions and choices.[14]

Redistribution and Property Rights

Apparently, patterned principles allow people to choose to expend upon themselves, but not upon others, those resources they are entitled to (or rather, receive) under some favored distributional pattern D_1. For if each of several persons chooses to expend some of his D_1 resources upon one other person, then that other person will receive more than his D_1 share, disturbing the favored distributional pattern. Maintaining a distributional pattern is individualism with a vengeance! Patterned distributional principles do not give people what entitlement principles do, only better distributed. For they do not give the right to choose what to do with what one has; they do not give the right to choose to pursue an end involving (intrinsically, or as a means) the enhancement of another's position. To such views, families are disturbing; for within a family occur transfers that upset the favored distributional pattern. Either families themselves become units to which distribution takes place, the column occupiers (on what rationale?), or loving behavior is forbidden. We should note in passing the ambivalent position of radicals toward the family. Its loving relationships are seen as a model to be emulated and extended across the whole society, at the same time that it is denounced as a suffocating institution to be broken and condemned as a focus of parochial concerns that interfere with achieving radical goals. Need we say that it is not appropriate to enforce across the wider society the relationships of love and care appropriate within a family, relationships which are voluntarily undertaken?[15] Incidentally, love is an interesting instance of another relationship that is historical, in that (like justice) it depends upon what actually occurred. An adult may come to love another because of the other's characteristics; but it is the other person, and not the characteristics, that is loved.[16] The love is not transferable to someone else with the same characteristics, even to one who "scores" higher for these characteristics. And the love endures through changes of the characteristics that gave rise to it. One loves the particular person one actually encountered. Why love is historical, attaching to persons in this way and not to characteristics, is an interesting and puzzling question.

Proponents of patterned principles of distributive justice focus upon criteria for determining who is to receive holdings; they consider the reasons for which someone should have something, and also the total picture of holdings. Whether or not it is better to give than to receive, proponents of patterned principles ignore giving altogether. In considering the distribution of goods, income, and so forth, their theories are theories of recipient justice; they completely ignore any right a person might have to give something to someone. Even in exchanges where each party is simultaneously giver and recipient, patterned principles of justice focus only upon the recipient role and its supposed rights. Thus discussions tend to focus on whether people (should) have a right to inherit, rather than on whether people (should) have a right to bequeath or on whether persons who have a right to hold also

have a right to choose that others hold in their place. I lack a good explanation of why the usual theories of distributive justice are so recipient oriented; ignoring givers and transferrers and their rights is of a piece with ignoring producers and their entitlements. But why is it *all* ignored?

Patterned principles of distributive justice necessitate *re*distributive activities. The likelihood is small that any actual freely-arrived-at set of holdings fits a given pattern; and the likelihood is nil that it will continue to fit the pattern as people exchange and give. From the point of view of an entitlement theory, redistribution is a serious matter indeed, involving, as it does, the violation of people's rights. (An exception is those takings that fall under the principle of the rectification of injustices.) From other points of view, also, it is serious.

Taxation of earnings from labor is on a par with forced labor.[17] Some persons find this claim obviously true: taking the earnings of *n* hours labor is like taking *n* hours from the person; it is like forcing the person to work *n* hours for another's purpose. Others find the claim absurd. But even these, *if* they object to forced labor, would oppose forcing unemployed hippies to work for the benefit of the needy.[18] And they would also object to forcing each person to work five extra hours each week for the benefit of the needy. But a system that takes five hours' wages in taxes does not seem to them like one that forces someone to work five hours, since it offers the person forced a wider range of choice in activities than does taxation in kind with the particular labor specified. (But we can imagine a gradation of systems of forced labor, from one that specifies a particular activity, to one that gives a choice among two activities, to . . . ; and so on up.) Furthermore, people envisage a system with something like a proportional tax on everything above the amount necessary for basic needs. Some think this does not force someone to work extra hours, since there is no fixed number of extra hours he is forced to work, and since he can avoid the tax entirely by earning only enough to cover his basic needs. This is a very uncharacteristic view of forcing for those who *also* think people are forced to do something *whenever* the alternatives they face are considerably worse. However, *neither* view is correct. The fact that others intentionally intervene, in violation of a side constraint against aggression, to threaten force to limit the alternatives, in this case to paying taxes or (presumably the worse alternative) bare subsistence, makes the taxation system one of forced labor and distinguishes it from other cases of limited choices which are not forcings.[19]

The man who chooses to work longer to gain an income more than sufficient for his basic needs prefers some extra goods or services to the leisure and activities he could perform during the possible nonworking hours; whereas the man who chooses not to work the extra time prefers the leisure activities to the extra goods or services he could acquire by working more. Given this, if it would be illegitimate for a tax system to seize some of a man's leisure (forced labor) for the purpose of serving the needy, how can it be legitimate for a tax system to seize some of a man's goods for that purpose? Why should we treat the man whose happiness requires certain material goods or services differently from the man whose preferences and desires make such goods unnecessary for his happiness? Why should the man who prefers seeing a movie (and who has to earn money for a ticket) be open to the required call to aid the needy, while the person who prefers looking at a sunset (and hence need earn no extra money) is not? Indeed, isn't it surprising that redistributionists choose to ignore the man whose pleasures are so easily attainable without extra labor, while adding yet another burden to the poor unfortunate who must work for his pleasures? If anything, one would have expected the reverse. Why is the person with the nonmaterial or nonconsumption desire allowed to proceed unimpeded to his most favored feasible alternative, whereas the man whose pleasures or desires involve material things and who must work for extra money (thereby serving whomever considers his activities valuable enough to pay him) is constrained in what he can realize? Perhaps there is no difference in principle. And perhaps some think the answer concerns merely administrative convenience. (These questions and issues will not disturb those who think that forced labor to serve the needy or to realize some favored end-state pattern is acceptable.) In a fuller discussion we would have (and want) to extend our argument to include interest, entrepreneurial profits, and so on. Those who doubt that this extension can be carried through, and who draw the line here at taxation of income from labor, will have to state rather complicated patterned *historical* principles of distributive justice, since end-state principles would not distinguish *sources* of income in any way. It is enough for now to get away from end-state principles and to

make clear how various patterned principles are dependent upon particular views about the sources or the illegitimacy or the lesser legitimacy of profits, interest, and so on; which particular views may well be mistaken.

What sort of right over others does a legally institutionalized end-state pattern give one? The central core of the notion of a property right in X, relative to which other parts of the notion are to be explained, is the right to determine what shall be done with X; the right to choose which of the constrained set of options concerning X shall be realized or attempted.[20] The constraints are set by other principles or laws operating in the society; in our theory, by the Lockean rights people possess (under the minimal state). My property rights in my knife allow me to leave it where I will, but not in your chest. I may choose which of the acceptable options involving the knife is to be realized. This notion of property helps us to understand why earlier theorists spoke of people as having property in themselves and their labor. They viewed each person as having a right to decide what would become of himself and what he would do, and as having a right to reap the benefits of what he did.

This right of selecting the alternative to be realized from the constrained set of alternatives may be held by an *individual* or by a *group* with some procedure for reaching a joint decision; or the right may be passed back and forth, so that one year I decide what's to become of X, and the next year you do (with the alternative of destruction, perhaps, being excluded). Or, during the same time period, some types of decisions about X may be made by me, and others by you. And so on. We lack an adequate, fruitful, analytical apparatus for classifying the *types* of constraints on the set of options among which choices are to be made, and the *types* of ways decision powers can be held, divided, and amalgamated. A *theory* of property would, among other things, contain such a classification of constraints and decision modes, and from a small number of principles would follow a host of interesting statements about the *consequences* and effects of certain combinations of constraints and modes of decision.

When end-result principles of distributive justice are built into the legal structure of a society, they (as do most patterned principles) give each citizen an enforceable claim to some portion of the total social product; that is, to some portion of the sum total of the individually and jointly made products. This total product is produced by individuals laboring, using means of production others have saved to bring into existence, by people organizing production or creating means to produce new things or things in a new way. It is on this batch of individual activities that patterned distributional principles give each individual an enforceable claim. Each person has a claim to the activities and the products of other persons, independently of whether the other persons enter into particular relationships that give rise to these claims, and independently of whether they voluntarily take these claims upon themselves, in charity or in exchange for something.

Whether it is done through taxation on wages or on wages over a certain amount, or through seizure of profits, or through there being a big *social pot* so that it's not clear what's coming from where and what's going where, patterned principles of distributive justice involve appropriating the actions of other persons. Seizing the results of someone's labor is equivalent to seizing hours from him and directing him to carry on various activities. If people force you to do certain work, or unrewarded work, for a certain period of time, they decide what you are to do and what purposes your work is to serve apart from your decisions. This process whereby they take this decision from you makes them a *part-owner* of you; it gives them a property right in you. Just as having such partial control and power of decision, by right, over an animal or inanimate object would be to have a property right in it.

End-state and most patterned principles of distributive justice institute (partial) ownership by others of people and their actions and labor. These principles involve a shift from the classical liberals' notion of self-ownership to a notion of (partial) property rights in *other* people.

Considerations such as these confront end-state and other patterned conceptions of justice with the question of whether the actions necessary to achieve the selected pattern don't themselves violate moral side constraints. Any view holding that there are moral side constraints on actions, that not all moral considerations can be built into end states that are to be achieved, must face the possibility that some of its goals are not achievable by any morally permissible available means. An entitlement theorist will face such conflicts in a society that deviates from the principles of justice for the generation of holdings, if and only if the only actions available to realize the principles themselves violate some moral constraints. Since deviation from the first two principles of justice (in acquisition and transfer) will involve other persons' direct and aggressive intervention to violate rights, and since moral constraints will not exclude defensive or retributive action in such cases, the entitlement theorist's problem rarely will be pressing. And whatever difficulties he has in applying the principle of rectification to persons who did not themselves violate the first two principles are difficulties in balancing the conflicting considerations so as correctly to formulate the complex principle of rectification itself; he will not violate moral side constraints by applying the principle. Proponents of patterned conceptions of justice, however, often will face head-on clashes (and poignant ones if they cherish each party to the clash) between moral side constraints on how individuals may be treated and their patterned conception of justice that presents an end state or other pattern that *must* be realized.

May a person emigrate from a nation that has institutionalized some end-state or patterned distributional principle? For some principles (for example, Hayek's) emigration presents no theoretical problem. But for others it is a tricky matter. Consider a nation having a compulsory scheme of minimal social provision to aid the neediest (or one organized so as to maximize the position of the worst-off group); no one may opt out of participating in it. (None may say, "Don't compel me to contribute to others and don't provide for me via this compulsory mechanism if I am in need.") Everyone above a certain level is forced to contribute to aid the needy. But if emigration from the country were allowed, anyone could choose to move to another country that did not have compulsory social provision but otherwise was (as much as possible) identical. In such a case, the person's *only* motive for leaving would be to avoid participating in the compulsory scheme of social provision. And if he does leave, the needy in his initial country will receive no (compelled) help from him. What rationale yields the result that the person be permitted to emigrate, yet forbidden to stay and opt out of the compulsory scheme of social provision? If providing for the needy is of overriding importance, this does militate against allowing internal opting out; but it also speaks against allowing external emigration. (Would it also support, to some extent, the kidnapping of persons living in a place without compulsory social provision, who could be forced to make a contribution to the needy in your community?) Perhaps the crucial component of the position that allows emigration solely to avoid certain arrangements, while not allowing anyone internally to opt out of them, is a concern for fraternal feelings within the country. "We don't want anyone here who doesn't contribute, who doesn't care enough about the others to contribute." That concern, in this case, would have to be tied to the view that forced aiding tends to produce fraternal feelings between the aided and the aider (or perhaps merely to the view that the knowledge that someone or other voluntarily is not aiding produces unfraternal feelings).

Locke's Theory of Acquisition

Before we turn to consider other theories of justice in detail, we must introduce an additional bit of complexity into the structure of the entitlement theory. This is best approached by considering Locke's attempt to specify a principle of justice in acquisition. Locke views property rights in an unowned object as originating through someone's mixing his labor with it. This gives rise to many questions. What are the boundaries of what labor is mixed with? If a private astronaut clears a place on Mars, has he mixed his labor with (so that he comes to own) the whole planet, the whole uninhabited universe, or just a particular plot? Which plot does an act bring under ownership? The minimal (possibly disconnected) area such that an act decreases entropy in that area, and not elsewhere? Can virgin land (for the purposes of ecological investigation by high-flying airplane) come under ownership by a Lockean process? Building a fence around a territory presumably would make one the owner of only the fence (and the land immediately underneath it).

Why does mixing one's labor with something make one the owner of it? Perhaps because one owns one's labor, and so one comes to own a previously unowned thing that becomes permeated with what one owns. Ownership seeps over into the rest. But why isn't mixing what I own with what I don't own a way of losing what I own rather than a way of gaining what I don't? If I own a can of tomato juice and spill it in the sea so that its molecules (made radioactive, so I can check this) mingle evenly throughout the sea, do I thereby come to own the sea, or have I foolishly dissipated my tomato juice? Perhaps the idea, instead, is that laboring on something improves it

and makes it more valuable; and anyone is entitled to own a thing whose value he has created. (Reinforcing this, perhaps, is the view that laboring is unpleasant. If some people made things effortlessly, as the cartoon characters in *The Yellow Submarine* trail flowers in their wake, would they have lesser claim to their own products whose making didn't *cost* them anything?) Ignore the fact that laboring on something may make it less valuable (spraying pink enamel paint on a piece of driftwood that you have found). Why should one's entitlement extend to the whole object rather than just to the *added value* one's labor has produced? (Such reference to value might also serve to delimit the extent of ownership; for example, substitute "increases the value of" for "decreases entropy in" in the above entropy criterion.) No workable or coherent value-added property scheme has yet been devised, and any such scheme presumably would fall to objections (similar to those) that fell the theory of Henry George.

It will be implausible to view improving an objects as giving full ownership to it, if the stock of unowned objects that might be improved is limited. For an object's coming under one person's ownership changes the situation of all others. Whereas previously they were at liberty (in Hohfeld's sense) to use the object, they now no longer are. This change in the situation of others (by removing their liberty to act on a previously unowned object) need not worsen their situation. If I appropriate a grain of sand from Coney Island, no one else may now do as they will with *that* grain of sand. But there are plenty of other grains of sand left for them to do the same with. Or if not grains of sand, then other things. Alternatively, the things I do with the grain of sand I appropriate might improve the position of others, counterbalancing their loss of the liberty to use that grain. The crucial point is whether appropriation of an unowned object worsens the situation of others.

Locke's proviso that there be "enough and as good left in common for others" (sect. 27) is meant to ensure that the situation of others is not worsened. (If this proviso is met is there any motivation for his further condition of nonwaste?) It is often said that this proviso once held but now no longer does. But there appears to be an argument for the conclusion that if the proviso no longer holds, then it cannot ever have held so as to yield permanent and inheritable property rights. Consider the first person Z for whom there is not enough and as good left to appropriate. The last person Y to appropriate left Z without his previous liberty to act on an object, and so worsened Z's situation. So Y's appropriation is not allowed under Locke's proviso. Therefore the next to last person X to appropriate left Y in a worse position, for X's act ended permissible appropriation. Therefore X's appropriation wasn't permissible. But then the appropriator two from last, W, ended permissible appropriation and so, since it worsened X's position, W's appropriation wasn't permissible. And so on back to the first person A to appropriate a permanent property right.

This argument, however, proceeds too quickly. Someone may be made worse off by another's appropriation in two ways: first, by losing the opportunity to improve his situation by a particular appropriation or any one; and second, by no longer being able to use freely (without appropriation) what he previously could. A *stringent* requirement that another not be made worse off by an appropriation would exclude the first way if nothing else counterbalances the diminution in opportunity, as well as the second. A *weaker* requirement would exclude the second way, though not the first. With the weaker requirement, we cannot zip back so quickly from Z to A, as in the above argument; for though person Z can no longer *appropriate*, there may remain some for him to *use* as before. In this case Y's appropriation would not violate the weaker Lockean condition. (With less remaining that people are at liberty to use, users might face more inconvenience, crowding, and so on; in that way the situation of others might be worsened, unless appropriation stopped far short of such a point.) It is arguable that no one legitimately can complain if the weaker provision is satisfied. However, since this is less clear than in the case of the more stringent proviso, Locke may have intended this stringent proviso by "enough and as good" remaining, and perhaps he meant the nonwaste condition to delay the end point from which the argument zips back.

Is the situation of persons who are unable to appropriate (there being no more accessible and useful unowned objects) worsened by a system allowing appropriation and permanent property? Here enter the various familiar social considerations favoring private property: it increases the social product by putting means of production in the hands of those who can use them most efficiently (profitably); experimentation is encouraged, because with separate persons controlling resources, there is no one person or small group whom someone with a new idea must convince to try it out; private property enables people to decide on the pattern and types of risks they wish to bear, leading to specialized types of risk bearing; private property protects future persons by leading some to hold back resources from current consumption for future markets; it provides alternate sources of employment for unpopular persons who don't have to convince any one person or small group to hire them, and so on. These considerations enter a Lockean theory to support the claim that appropriation of private property satisfies the intent behind the "enough and as good left over" proviso, *not* as a utilitarian justification of property. They enter to rebut the claim that because the proviso is violated no natural right to private property can arise by a Lockean process. The difficulty in working such an argument to show that the proviso is satisfied is in fixing the appropriate base line for comparison. Lockean appropriation makes people no worse off than they would be *how*?[21] This question of fixing the baseline needs more detailed investigation than we are able to give it here. It would be desirable to have an estimate of the general economic importance of original appropriation in order to see how much leeway there is for differing theories of appropriation and of the location of the baseline. Perhaps this importance can be measured by the percentage of all income that is based upon untransformed raw materials and given resources (rather than upon human actions), mainly rental income representing the unimproved value of land, and the price of raw material *in situ*, and by the percentage of current wealth which represents such income in the past.[22]

We should note that it is not only persons favoring *private* property who need a theory of how property rights legitimately originate. Those believing in collective property, for example those believing that a group of persons living in an area jointly own the territory, or its mineral resources, also must provide a theory of how such property rights arise; they must show why the persons living there have rights to determine what is done with the land and resources there that persons living elsewhere don't have (with regard to the same land and resources).

The Proviso

Whether or not Locke's particular theory of appropriation can be spelled out so as to handle various difficulties, I assume that any adequate theory of justice in acquisition will contain a proviso similar to the weaker of the ones we have attributed to Locke. A process normally giving rise to a permanent bequeathable property right in a previously unowned thing will not do so if the position of others no longer at liberty to use the thing is thereby worsened. It is important to specify *this* particular mode of worsening the situation of others, for the proviso does not encompass other modes. It does not include the worsening due to more limited opportunities to appropriate (the first way above, corresponding to the more stringent condition), and it does not include how I "worsen" a seller's position if I appropriate materials to make some of what he is selling, and then enter into competition with him. Someone whose appropriation otherwise would violate the proviso still may appropriate provided he compensates the others so that their situation is not thereby worsened; unless he does compensate these others, his appropriation will violate the proviso of the principle of justice in acquisition and will be an illegitimate one.[23] A theory of appropriation incorporating this Lockean proviso will handle correctly the cases (objections to the theory lacking the proviso) where someone appropriates the total supply of something necessary for life.[24]

A theory which includes this proviso in its principle of justice in acquisition must also contain a more complex principle of justice in transfer. Some reflection of the proviso about appropriation constrains later actions. If my appropriating all of a certain substance violates the Lockean proviso, then so does my appropriating some and purchasing all the rest from others who obtained it without otherwise violating the Lockean proviso. If the proviso excludes someone's appropriating all the drinkable water in the world, it also excludes his purchasing it all. (More weakly, and messily, it may exclude his charging certain prices for some of his supply.) This proviso (almost?) never will come into effect; the more someone acquires of a scarce substance which others want, the higher the price of the rest will go, and the more difficult it will become for him to acquire it all. But still, we can imagine, at least, that something like this occurs: someone makes simultaneous secret bids to the separate owners of a substance, each of whom sells assuming he can easily purchase more from the other owners; or some natural catastrophe destroys all of the supply of something except that in one person's possession. The total supply could not be permissibly appropriated by one person at the beginning. His later acquisition of it all does not show that the original appropriation violated the proviso (even by a reverse argument similar to the one above that tried to zip back from Z to A). Rather, it is the combination of the original appropriation *plus* all the later transfers and actions that violates the Lockean proviso.

Each owner's title to his holding includes the historical shadow of the Lockean proviso on appropriation. This excludes his transferring it into an agglomeration that does violate the Lockean proviso and excludes his using it in a way, in coordination with others or independently of them, so as to violate the proviso by making the situation of others worse than their baseline situation. Once it is known that someone's ownership runs afoul of the Lockean proviso, there are stringent limits on what he may do with (what it is difficult any longer unreservedly to call) "his property." Thus a person may not appropriate the only water hole in a desert and charge what he will. Nor may he charge what he will if he possesses one, and unfortunately it happens that all the water holes in the desert dry up, except for his. This unfortunate circumstance, admittedly no fault of his, brings into operation the Lockean proviso and limits his property rights.[25] Similarly, an owner's property right in the only island in an area does not allow him to order a castaway from a shipwreck off his island as a trespasser, for this would violate the Lockean proviso.

Notice that the theory does not say that owners do have these rights, but that the rights are overridden to avoid some catastrophe. (Overridden rights do not disappear; they leave a trace of a sort absent in the cases under discussion.)[26] There is no such external (and *ad hoc*?) overriding. Considerations internal to the theory of property itself, to its theory of acquisition and appropriation, provide the means for handling such cases. The results, however, may be coextensive with some condition about catastrophe, since the baseline for comparison is so low as compared to the productiveness of a society with private appropriation that the question of the Lockean proviso being violated arises only in the case of catastrophe (or a desert-island situation).

The fact that someone owns the total supply of something necessary for others to stay alive does *not* entail that his (or anyone's) appropriation of anything left some people (immediately or later) in a situation worse than the baseline one. A medical researcher who synthesizes a new substance that effectively treats a certain disease and who refuses to sell except on his terms does not worsen the situation of others by depriving them of whatever he has appropriated. The others easily can possess the same materials he appropriated; the researcher's appropriation or purchase of chemicals didn't make those chemicals scarce in a way so as to violate the Lockean proviso. Nor would someone else's purchasing the total supply of the synthesized substance from the medical researcher. The fact that the medical researcher uses easily available chemicals to synthesize the drug no more violates the Lockean proviso than does the fact that the only surgeon able to perform a particular operation eats easily obtainable food in order to stay alive and to have the energy to work. This shows that the Lockean proviso is not an "end-state principle"; it focuses on a particular way that appropriative actions affect others, and not on the structure of the situation that results.[27]

Intermediate between someone who takes all of the public supply and someone who makes the total supply out of easily obtainable substances is someone who appropriates the total supply of something in a way that does not deprive the others of it. For example, someone finds a new substance in an out-of-the-way place. He discovers that it effectively treats a certain disease and appropriates the total supply. He does not worsen the situation of others; if he did not stumble upon the substance no one else would have, and the others would remain without it. However, as time passes, the likelihood increases that others would have come across the substance; upon this fact might be based a limit to his property right in the substance so that others are not below their baseline position; for example, its bequest might be limited. The theme of someone worsening another's situation by depriving him of something he otherwise would possess may also illuminate the example of patents. An inventor's patent does not deprive others of an object which would not exist if not for the inventor. Yet patents would have this effect on others who independently invent the object. Therefore, these independent inventors, upon whom the burden of proving independent discovery may rest, should not be excluded from utilizing their own invention as they wish (including selling it to others). Furthermore, a known inventor drastically lessens the chances of actual independent invention. For persons who know of an invention usually will not try to reinvent it, and the notion of independent discovery here would be

murky at best. Yet we may assume that in the absence of the original invention, sometime later someone else would have come up with it. This suggests placing a time limit on patents, as a rough rule of thumb to approximate how long it would have taken, in the absence of knowledge of the invention, for independent discovery.

I believe that the free operation of a market system will not acutally run afoul of the Lockean proviso. (Recall that crucial to our story in Part I of *Anarchy, State and Utopia* of how a protective agency becomes dominant and a *de facto* monopoly is the fact that it wields force in situations of conflict, and is not merely in competition, with other agencies. A similar tale cannot be told about other businesses.) If this is correct, the proviso will not play a very important role in the activities of protective agencies and will not provide a significant opportunity for future state action. Indeed, were it not for the effects of previous *illegitimate* state action, people would not think the possibility of the proviso's being violated as of more interest than any other logical possibility. (Here I make an empirical historical claim; as does someone who disagrees with this). This completes our indication of the complication in the entitlement theory introduced by the Lockean proviso.

. . .

Natural Assets and Arbitrariness

Rawls comes closest to considering the entitlement system in his discussion of what he terms the system of natural liberty:

> The system of natural liberty selects an efficient distribution roughly as follows. Let us suppose that we know from economic theory that under the standard assumptions defining a competitive market economy, income and wealth will be distributed in an efficient way, and that the particular efficient distribution which results in any period of time is determined by the initial distribution of assets, that is, by the initial distribution of income and wealth, and of natural talents and abilities. With each initial distribution, a definite efficient outcome is arrived at. Thus it turns out that if we are to accept the outcome as just, and not merely as efficient, we must accept the

basis upon which over time the initial distribution of assets is determined.

In the system of natural liberty the initial distribution is regulated by the arrangements implicit in the conception of careers open to talents. These arrangements presuppose a background of equal liberty (as specified by the first principle) and a free market economy. They require a formal equality of opportunity in that all have at least the same legal rights of access to all advantaged social positions. But since there is no effort to preserve an equality or similarity, of social conditions, except insofar as this is necessary to preserve the requisite background institutions, the initial distribution of assets for any period of time is strongly influenced by natural and social contingencies. The existing distribution of income and wealth, say, is the cumulative effect of prior distributions of natural assets – that is, natural talents and abilities – as these have been developed or left unrealized, and their use favored or disfavored over time by social circumstances and such chance contingencies as accident and good fortune. Intuitively, the most obvious injustice of the system of natural liberty is that it permits distributive shares to be improperly influenced by these factors so arbitrary from a moral point of view.[28]

Here we have *Rawls'* reason for rejecting a system of natural liberty: it "permits" distributive shares to be improperly influenced by factors that are so arbitrary from a moral point of view. These factors are: "prior distribution ... of natural talents and abilities as these have been developed over time by social circumstances and such chance contingencies as accident and good fortune." Notice that there is no mention *at all* of how persons have chosen to develop their own natural assets. Why is that simply left out? Perhaps because such choices also are viewed as being the products of factors outside the person's control, and hence as "arbitrary from a moral point of view." "The assertion that a man deserves the superior character that enables him to make the effort to cultivate his abilities is equally problematic; for his character depends in large part upon fortunate family and social circumstances for which he can claim no credit."[29] (What view is presupposed here of character and its relation to action?) "The initial endowment of natural assets and the contingencies of their growth and nurture in early life are arbitrary

from a moral point of view ... the effort a person is willing to make is influenced by his natural abilities and skills and the alternatives open to him. The better endowed are more likely, other things equal, to strive conscientiously...."[30] This line of argument can succeed in blocking the introduction of a person's autonomous choices and actions (and their results) only by attributing *everything* noteworthy about the person completely to certain sorts of "external" factors. So denigrating a person's autonomy and prime responsibility for his actions is a risky line to take for a theory that otherwise wishes to buttress the dignity and self-respect of autonomous beings; especially for a theory that founds so much (including a theory of the good) upon persons' choices. One doubts that the unexalted picture of human beings Rawls' theory presupposes and rests upon can be made to fit together with the view of human dignity it is designed to lead to and embody.

Before we investigate Rawls' reasons for rejecting the system of natural liberty, we should note the situation of those in the original position. The system of natural liberty is *one* interpretation of a principle that (according to Rawls) they *do* accept: social and economic inequalities are to be arranged so that they both are reasonably expected to be to everyone's advantage, and are attached to positions and offices open to all. It is left unclear whether the persons in the original position explicitly consider and choose among *all* the various interpretations of this principle, though this would seem to be the most reasonable construal. Certainly they explicitly consider one interpretation, the difference principle. Rawls does not state why persons in the original position who considered the system of natural liberty would reject it. Their reason cannot be that it makes the resulting distribution depend upon a *morally* arbitrary distribution of natural assets. What we must suppose, as we have seen before, is that the self-interested calculation of persons in the original position does not (and cannot) lead them to adopt the entitlement principle. We, however, and Rawls, base our evaluations on different considerations.

Rawls has explicitly *designed* the original position and its choice situation so as to embody and realize his negative reflective evaluation of allowing shares in holdings to be affected by natural assets: "Once we decide to look for a conception of justice that nullifies the accidents of natural endowment and the contingencies of social circumstance...."[31] (Rawls makes many scattered references to this theme of nullifying the accidents of natural endowment and the contingencies of social circumstance.) This quest crucially shapes Rawls' theory, and it underlies his delineation of the original position. It is not that persons who *did* deserve their natural endowments would choose differently if placed in Rawls' original position, but rather that, presumably, for such persons, Rawls would not hold that the principles of justice to govern *their* mutual relations were fixed by what they would choose in the original position. It is useful to remember how much of Rawls' construction rests upon this foundation. For example, Rawls argues that certain egalitarian demands are not motivated by envy but rather, because they are in accord with his two principles of justice, by resentment of injustice.[32] This argument can be undercut, as Rawls realizes,[33] if the very considerations which underlie the original position (yielding Rawls' two principles of justice) themselves embody or are based upon envy. So in addition to wanting to understand Rawls' rejection of alternative conceptions and to assess how powerful a criticism he makes of the entitlement conception, reasons internal to his theory provide motivation to explore the basis of the requirement that a conception of justice be geared to nullify differences in social circumstances and in natural assets (and any differences in social circumstances they result in).

Why shouldn't holdings partially depend upon natural endowments? (They will also depend on how these are developed and on the uses to which they are put.) Rawls' reply is that these natural endowments and assets, being undeserved, are "arbitrary from a moral point of view." There are two ways to understand the relevance of this reply: It might be part of an argument to establish that the distributive effects of natural differences ought to be nullified, which I shall call the positive argument; or it might be part of an argument to rebut a possible counterargument holding that the distributive effects of natural differences oughtn't to be nullified, which I shall call the negative argument. Whereas the positive argument attempts to establish that the distributive effects of natural differences ought to be nullified, the negative one, by merely rebutting *one* argument that the differences oughtn't to be nullified, leaves open the possibility that (for other reasons) the differences oughtn't to be nullified. (The negative argument also leaves it possibly a matter of moral *indifference* whether the distributive effects of nat-

ural differences are to be nullified; note the difference between saying that something ought to be the case and saying that it's not that it oughtn't to be the case.)

The Positive Argument

We shall begin with the positive argument. How might the point that differences in natural endowments are arbitrary from a moral point of view function in an argument meant to establish that differences in holdings stemming from differences in natural assets ought to be nullified? We shall consider four possible arguments; the first, the following argument A:

1   Any person should morally deserve the holdings he has; it shouldn't be that persons have holdings they don't deserve.
2   People do not morally deserve their natural assets.
3   If a person's X partially determines his Y, and his X is undeserved then so is his Y.

Therefore,

4   People's holding shouldn't be partially determined by their natural assets.

This argument will serve as a surrogate for other similar, more complicated ones.[34] But Rawls explicitly and emphatically *rejects* distribution according to moral desert.

> There is a tendency for common sense to suppose that income and wealth, and the good things in life generally, should be distributed according to moral desert. Justice is happiness according to virtue. While it is recognized that this ideal can never be fully carried out, it is the appropriate conception [according to common sense] of distributive justice, at least as a *prima facie* principle, and society should try to realize it as circumstances permit. Now justice as fairness rejects this conception. Such a principle would not be chosen in the original position.[35]

Rawls could not, therefore, accept any premiss like the first premiss in argument A, and so no variant of this argument underlies his rejection of differences in distributive shares stemming from undeserved differences in natural assets. Not only does Rawls reject premiss 1, his theory is not coextensive with it. He favors giving incentives to persons if this most improves the lot of the least well off, and it often will be because of their natural assets that these persons will receive incentives and have larger shares. We noted earlier that the entitlement conception of justice in holdings, not being a patterned conception of justice, does not accept distribution in accordance with moral desert either. Any person may give to anyone else any holding he is entitled to, independently of whether the recipient morally deserves to be the recipient. To each according to the legitimate entitlements that legitimately have been transferred to him, is not a patterned principle.

If argument A and its first premiss are rejected, it is not obvious how to construct the positive argument. Consider next argument B:

1 Holdings ought to be distributed according to some pattern that is not arbitrary from a moral point of view.
2 That persons have different natural assets *is* arbitrary from a moral point of view.

Therefore,

3 Holdings ought not to be distributed according to natural assets.

But differences in natural assets might be *correlated* with other differences that are not arbitrary from a moral point of view and that are clearly of some possible moral relevance to distributional questions. For example, Hayek argued that under capitalism distribution generally is in accordance with perceived service to others. Since differences in natural assets will produce differences in ability to serve others, there will be some correlation of differences in distribution with differences in natural assets. The principle of the system is *not* distribution in accordance with natural assets; but differences in natural assets will lead to differences in holdings under a system whose principle is distribution according to perceived service to others. If conclusion 3 above is to be interpreted in extension so as to exclude this, it should be made explicit. But to add the premiss that any pattern that has some roughly coextensive description that is arbitrary from a moral point of view is itself arbitrary from a moral point of view would be far too strong, because it would yield the result

that *every* pattern is arbitrary from a moral point of view. Perhaps the crucial thing to be avoided is not mere coextensiveness, but rather some morally arbitrary feature's *giving rise to* differences in distributive shares. Thus consider argument C:

1 Holdings ought to be distributed according to some pattern that is not arbitrary from a moral point of view.
2 That persons have different natural assets is arbitrary from a moral point of view.
3 If part of the explanation of why a pattern contains differences in holdings is that other differences in persons give rise to these differences in holdings, and if these other differences are arbitrary from a moral point of view, then the pattern also is arbitrary from a moral point of view.

Therefore,

4 Differences in natural assets should not give rise to differences in holdings among persons.

Premiss 3 of this argument holds that any moral arbitrariness that underlies a pattern infects the pattern and makes it too morally arbitrary. But any pattern will have some morally arbitrary facts as part of the explanation of how it arises, including the pattern proposed by Rawls. The difference principle operates to give some persons larger distributive shares than others; which persons receive these larger shares will depend, at least partially, on differences between these persons and others, differences that are arbitrary from a moral point of view, for some persons with special natural assets will be offered larger shares as an incentive to use these assets in certain ways. Perhaps some premiss similar to 3 can be formulated so as to exclude what Rawls wishes to exclude while not excluding his *own* view. Still, the resulting argument would *assume* that the set of holdings should realize some pattern.

Why should the set of holdings be patterned? Patterning is *not* intrinsic to a theory of justice, as we have seen in our presentation of the entitlement theory: a theory that focuses upon the underlying principles that generate sets of holdings rather than upon the pattern a set of holdings realizes. If it be denied that the theory of these underlying principles *is* a separate theory of distributive justice, rather than merely a collection of diverse considerations from other areas, then the question becomes one of whether there *is* any separate subject of distributive justice which requires a separate theory.

On the manna-from-heaven model given earlier, there might be a more compelling reason to search for a pattern. But since things come into being already held (or with agreements already made about how they are to be held), there is no need to search for some pattern for unheld holdings to fit; and since the process whereby holdings actually come into being or are shaped, itself needn't realize any particular pattern, there is no reason to expect any pattern to result. The situation is not an appropriate one for wondering, "After all, what is to become of these things; what are we to do with them." In the non-manna-from-heaven world in which things have to be made or produced or transformed by people, there is no separate process of distribution for a theory of distribution to be a theory of. The reader will recall our earlier argument that (roughly) any set of holdings realizing a particular pattern may be transformed by the voluntary exchanges, gifts, and so forth, of the persons having the holdings under the pattern into *another* set of holdings that does not fit the pattern. The view that holdings *must* be patterned perhaps will seem less plausible when it is seen to have the consequence that people may not choose to do acts that upset the patterning, even with things they legitimately hold.

There is another route to a patterned conception of justice that, perhaps, should be mentioned. Suppose that each morally legitimate fact has a "unified" explanation that shows it is morally legitimate, and that *conjunctions* fall into the domain of facts to be explained as morally legitimate. If p and q are each morally legitimate facts, with their respective explanations as morally legitimate being P, and Q then if $p \wedge q$ is also to be explained as morally legitimate, and if $P \wedge Q$ does not constitute a "unified" explanation (but is a mere conjunction of different explanations), then some further explanation will be needed. Applying this to holdings, suppose there are separate entitlement explanations showing the legitimacy of my having my holdings, and of your having yours, and the following question is asked: "Why is it legitimate that I hold what I do *and* you hold what you do; why is that joint fact *and all the relations contained within it* legitimate?" If the conjunction of the two separate explanations will not be held to explain in a unified manner the legitimacy of the joint fact (whose legitimacy is not viewed as being constituted by the legitimacy of its constituent parts),

then some patterned principles of distribution would appear to be necessary to show its legitimacy, and to legitimate any nonunit set of holdings.

With scientific explanation of particular facts, the usual practice is to consider some conjunctions of explained facts as not requiring separate explanation, but as being explained by the conjunctions of the explanations of the conjuncts. (If E_1 explains e_1 and E_2 explains e_2 then $E_1 \wedge E_2$ explains $e_1 \wedge e_2$.) If we required that any two conjuncts and any n-place conjunction had to be explained in some unified fashion, and not merely by the conjunction of separate and disparate explanations, then we would be driven to reject most of the usual explanations and to search for an underlying pattern to explain what appear to be separate facts. (Scientists, of course, often do offer a unified explanation of apparently separate facts.) It would be well worth exploring the interesting consequences of refusing to treat, even in the first instance, any two facts as legitimately separable, as having separate explanations whose conjunction is all there is to the explanation of them. What would our theories of the world look like if we required unified explanations of *all* conjunctions? Perhaps an extrapolation of how the world looks to paranoid persons. Or, to put it undisparagingly, the way it appears to persons having certain sorts of dope experiences. (For example, the way it sometimes appears to me after smoking marijuana.) Such a vision of the world differs fundamentally from the way we normally look at it; it is surprising at first that a simple condition on the adequacy of explanations of conjunctions leads to it, until we realize that such a condition of adequacy must lead to a view of the world as deeply and wholly patterned.

A similar condition of adequacy on explanations of the moral legitimacy of conjunctions of separate morally legitimate facts would lead to a view that requires sets of holdings to exhibit an overall patterning. It seems unlikely that there will be compelling arguments for imposing such a principle of adequacy. Some may find such a unified vision plausible for only one realm; for example, in the moral realm concerning sets of holdings, but not in the realm of ordinary nonmoral explanation, or vice versa. For the case of explaining nonmoral facts, the challenge would be to produce such a unified theory. Were one produced that introduced novel considerations and explained no *new* facts (other than conjunctions of old ones) the decision as to its acceptability might be a difficult one and would depend largely on how explanatorily satisfying was the new way we saw the old facts. In the case of moral explanations and accounts which show the moral legitimacy of various facts, the situation is somewhat different. First, there is even less reason (I believe) to suppose a unified explanation appropriate and necessary. There is less need for a *greater* degree of explanatory unity than that provided when the same underlying principles for generating holdings appear in different explanations. (Rawls' theory, which contains elements of what he calls pure procedural justice, does not satisfy a strong condition of adequacy for explaining conjunctions and entails that such a condition cannot be satisfied.) Secondly, there is more danger than in the scientific case that the demand for a unified explanation will shape the "moral facts" to be explained. ("It can't be that both of those *are* facts for there's no unified patterned explanation that would yield them both.") Hence success in finding a unified explanation of such seriously primed facts will leave it unclear how well supported the explanatory theory is.

I turn now to our final positive argument which purports to derive the conclusion that distributive shares shouldn't depend upon natural assets from the statement that the distribution of natural assets is morally arbitrary. This argument focuses on the notion of equality. Since a large part of Rawls' argument serves to justify or show acceptable a particular deviation from equal shares (some may have more if this serves to improve the position of those worst off), perhaps a reconstruction of his underlying argument that places equality at its center will be illuminating. Differences between persons (the argument runs) are arbitrary from a moral point of view if there is no moral argument for the conclusion that there ought to be the differences. Not all such differences will be morally objectionable. That there is no such moral argument will seem important only in the case of those differences we believe oughtn't to obtain unless there is a moral reason establishing that they ought to obtain. There is, so to speak, a presumption against certain differences that can be overridden (can it merely be neutralized?) by moral reasons; in the absence of any such moral reasons of sufficient weight, there ought to be equality. Thus we have argument D:

1 Holdings ought to be equal, unless there is a (weighty) moral reason why they ought to be unequal.

2 People do not deserve the ways in which they differ from other persons in natural assets; there is no moral reason why people ought to differ in natural assets.

3 If there is no moral reason why people differ in certain traits, then their actually differing in these traits does not provide, and cannot give rise to, a moral reason why they should differ in other traits (for example, in holdings).

Therefore,

4 People's differing in natural assets is not a reason why holdings ought to be unequal.

5 People's holdings ought to be equal unless there is some other moral reason (such as, for example, raising the position of those worst off) why their holdings ought to be unequal.

Statements similar to the third premiss will occupy us shortly. Here let us focus on the first premiss, the equality premiss. Why ought people's holdings to be equal, in the absence of special moral reason to deviate from equality? (Why think there *ought* to be *any* particular pattern in holdings?) Why is equality the rest (or rectilinear motion) position of the system, deviation from which may be caused only by moral forces? Many "arguments" for equality merely *assert* that differences between persons are arbitrary and must be justified. Often writers state a presumption in favor of equality in a form such as the following: "Differences in treatment of persons need to be justified."[36] The most favored situation for this sort of assumption is one in which there is one person (or group) treating everyone, a person (or group) having *no* right or entitlement to bestow the particular treatment as they wish or even whim. But if I go to one movie theater rather than to another adjacent to it, need I justify my different treatment of the two theater owners? Isn't it enough that I felt like going to one of them? That differences in treatment need to be justified *does* fit contemporary *governments*. Here there is a centralized process treating all, with no entitlement to bestow treatment according to whim. The major portion of distribution in a free society does not, however, come through the actions of the government, nor does failure to overturn the results of the localized individual exchanges constitute "state action." When there is no *one* doing the treating, and all are entitled to bestow their holdings as they wish, it is not clear why the maxim that differences in treatment must be justified should be thought to have extensive application. Why must differences between persons be justified? Why think that we must change, or remedy, or compensate for any inequality which can be changed, remedied, or compensated for? Perhaps here is where social cooperation enters in: though there is no presumption of equality (in, say, primary goods, or things people care about) among all persons, perhaps there is one among persons cooperating together. But it is difficult to see an argument for this; surely not all persons who cooperate together explicitly agree to this presumption as one of the terms of their mutual cooperation. And its acceptance would provide an unfortunate incentive for well-off persons to refuse to cooperate with, or to allow any of their number to cooperate with, some distant people who are less well off than any among them. For entering into such social cooperation, beneficial to those less well off, would seriously worsen the position of the well-off group by creating relations of presumptive equality between themselves and the worse-off group. In the next chapter I shall consider the major recent argument for equality, one which turns out to be unsuccessful. Here we need only note that the connection argument D forges between not deserving natural assets and some conclusion about distributive shares *assumes* equality as a norm (that can be deviated from with, and only with, moral reason); and hence argument D itself cannot be used to establish any such conclusion about equality.

The Negative Argument

Unsuccessful in our quest for a convincing positive argument to connect the claim that people don't deserve their natural assets with the conclusion that differences in holdings ought not to be based upon differences in natural assets, we now turn to what we called the negative argument: the use of the claim that people don't deserve their natural assets to rebut a possible counter-argument to Rawls' view. (If the equality argument D were acceptable, the negative task of rebutting possible counterconsiderations would form part of the positive task of showing that a presumption for equality holds unoverridden in a particular case.) Consider the following possible counter-argument E to Rawls:

1 People deserve their natural assets.
2 If people deserve X, they deserve any Y that flows from X.
3 People's holdings flow from their natural assets.

Therefore,

4 People deserve their holdings.
5 If people deserve something, then they ought to have it (and this overrides any presumption of equality there may be about that thing).

Rawls would rebut this counterargument to his position by denying its first premiss. And so we see *some* connection between the claim that the distribution of natural assets is arbitrary and the statement that distributive shares should not depend upon natural assets. However, no great weight can be placed upon *this* connection. For there are other counterarguments, in a similar vein; for example the argument F that begins:

1 If people have X, and their having X (whether or not they deserve to have it) does *not* violate anyone else's (Lockean) right or entitlement to X, and Y flows from (arises out of, and so on) X by a process that does not itself violate anyone's (Lockean) rights or entitlements,[37] then the person is entitled to Y.
2 People's having the natural assets they do does not violate anyone else's (Lockean) entitlements or rights.

and goes on to argue that people are entitled to what they make, to the products of their labor, to what others give them or exchange. It is not true, for example, that a person earns Y (a right to keep a painting he's made, praise for writing *A Theory of Justice*, and so on) only if he's earned (or otherwise *deserves*) whatever he used (including natural assets) in the process of earning Y. Some of the things he uses he just may *have*, not illegitimately. It needn't be that the foundations underlying desert are themselves deserved, *all the way down*.

At the very least, we can parallel these statements about desert with ones about entitlements. And if, correctly, we describe people as entitled to their natural assets even if it's not the case that they can be said to deserve them, then the argument parallel to E above, with "are entitled to" replacing "deserve" throughout, *will* go through. This gives us the acceptable argument G:

1 People are entitled to their natural assets.
2 If people are entitled to something, they are entitled to whatever flows from it (via specified types of processes).

3 People's holdings flow from their natural assets.

Therefore,

4 People are entitled to their holdings.
5 If people are entitled to something, then they ought to have it (and this overrides any presumption of equality there may be about holdings).

Whether or not people's natural assets are arbitrary from a moral point of view, they are entitled to them, and to what flows from them.[38]

A recognition of people's entitlements to their natural assets (the first premiss of argument G) might be necessary to avoid the stringent application of the difference principle which would lead, we already have seen, to even stronger property rights in other persons than redistributive theories usually yield. Rawls feels that he avoids this[39] because people in his original position rank the principle of liberty as lexicographically prior to the difference principle, applied not only to economic well-being but to health, length of life, and so on.

We have found no cogent argument to (help) establish that differences in holding arising from differences in natural assets should be eliminated or minimized. Can the theme that people's natural assets are arbitrary from a moral point of view be used differently, for example, to justify a certain *shaping* of the original position? Clearly if the shaping is designed to nullify differences in holdings due to differences in natural assets, we need an argument for this goal, and we are back to our unsuccessful quest for the route to the conclusion that such differences in holdings ought to be nullified. Instead, the shaping might take place by excluding the participants in the original position from knowing of their own natural endowments. In this way the fact that natural endowments are arbitrary from a moral point of view would help to impose and to justify the veil of ignorance. But how does it do this; why should knowledge of natural endowments be excluded from the original position? Presumably the underlying principle would be that if any particular features are arbitrary from a moral point of view, then persons in the original position should not know they possess them. But this would exclude their knowing *anything* about themselves, for each of their features (including rationality, the ability to make choices, having a life span of more than three days, having a memory, being able to communicate with other organisms like themselves) will be based upon the fact that the sperm and ovum which produced them contained particular genetic material. The physical fact that those particular gametes contained particular organized chemicals (the genes for people rather than for muskrats or trees) is arbitrary *from a moral point of view*; it is, from a moral point of view, an accident. Yet the persons in the original position are to know some of their attributes.

Perhaps we are too quick when we suggest excluding knowledge of rationality, and so forth, merely because these features *arise from* morally arbitrary facts. For these features also have moral significance; that is, moral facts depend upon or arise from them. Here we see an ambiguity in saying that a fact is arbitrary from a moral point of view. It might mean that there is no moral reason why the fact ought to be that way, or it might mean that the fact's being that way is of no moral significance and has no moral consequences. Rationality, the ability to make choices, and so on, are not morally arbitrary in this second sense. But if they escape exclusion on this ground, now the problem is that the natural assets, knowledge of which Rawls wishes to exclude from the original position, are not morally arbitrary in this sense either. At any rate, the entitlement theory's claim that moral entitlements may arise from or be partially based upon such facts is what is now at issue. Thus, in the absence of an argument to the effect that differences in holdings due to differences in natural assets ought to be nullified, it is not clear how anything about the original position can be based upon the (ambiguous) claim that differences in natural assets are arbitrary from a moral point of view.

Collective Assets

Rawls' view seems to be that everyone has some entitlement or claim on the totality of natural assets (viewed as a pool), with no one having differential claims. The distribution of natural abilities is viewed as a "collective asset."[40]

We see then that the difference principle represents, in effect, an agreement to regard the distribution of natural talents as a common asset and to share in the benefits of this distribution whatever it turns out to be. Those who have been favored by nature, whoever they are, may gain from their good fortune only on terms that improve the situation of those who have lost out. . . . No one deserves his greater natural capacity nor merits a more favorable starting place in society. But it does not follow that one should eliminate these distinctions. There is another way to deal with them. The basic structure can be arranged so that these contingencies work for the good of the least fortunate.[41]

People will differ in how they view regarding natural talents as a common asset. Some will complain, echoing Rawls against utilitarianism,[42] that this "does not take seriously the distinction between persons"; and they will wonder whether any reconstruction of Kant that treats people's abilities and talents as resources for others can be adequate. "The two principles of justice . . . rule out even the tendency to regard men as means to one another's welfare."[43] Only if one presses *very* hard on the distinction between men and their talents, assets, abilities, and special traits. Whether any coherent conception of a person remains when the distinction is so pressed is an open question. Why we, thick with particular traits, should be cheered that (only) the thus purified men within us are not regarded as means is also unclear.

People's talents and abilities *are* an asset to a free community; others in the community benefit from their presence and are better off because they are there rather than elsewhere or nowhere. (Otherwise they wouldn't choose to deal with them.) Life, over time, is not a constant-sum game, wherein if greater ability or effort leads to some getting more, that means that others must lose. In a free society, people's talents do benefit others, and not only themselves. Is it the extraction of even more benefit to others that is supposed to justify treating people's natural assets as a collective resource? What justifies this extraction?

No one deserves his greater natural capacity nor merits a more favorable starting place in society. But it does not follow that one should eliminate these distinctions. There is another way to deal with them. The basic structure can be arranged so that these contingencies work for the good of the least fortunate.[44]

And if there weren't "another way to deal with them"? Would it then follow that one should

eliminate these distinctions? What exactly would be contemplated in the case of natural assets? If people's assets and talents *couldn't* be harnessed to serve others, would something be done to remove these exceptional assets and talents, or to forbid them from being exercised for the person's own benefit or that of someone else he chose, even though this limitation wouldn't improve the absolute position of those somehow unable to harness the talents and abilities of others for their own benefit? Is it so implausible to claim that envy underlies this conception of justice, forming part of its root notion?[45]

We have used our entitlement conception of justice in holdings to probe Rawls' theory, sharpening our understanding of what the entitlement conception involves by bringing it to bear upon an alternative conception of distributive justice, one that is deep and elegant. Also, I believe, we have probed deep-lying inadequacies in Rawls' theory. I am mindful of Rawls' reiterated point that a theory cannot be evaluated by focusing upon a single feature or part of it; instead the whole theory must be assessed (the reader will not know how whole a theory can be until he has read all of Rawls' book), and a perfect theory is not to be expected. However, we have examined an important part of Rawls' theory, and its crucial underlying assumptions. I am as well aware as anyone of how sketchy my discussion of the entitlement conception of justice in holdings has been. But I no more believe we need to have formulated a complete alternative theory in order to reject Rawls' undeniably great advance over utilitarianism, than Rawls needed a complete alternative theory before he could reject utilitarianism. What more does one need or can one have, in order to begin progressing toward a better theory, than a sketch of a plausible alternative view, which from its very different perspective highlights the inadequacies of the best existing well-worked-out theory? Here, as in so many things, we learn from Rawls.

We began this chapter's investigation of distributive justice in order to consider the claim that a state more extensive than the minimal state could be justified on the grounds that it was necessary, or the most appropriate instrument, to achieve distributive justice. According to the entitlement conception of justice in holdings that we have presented, there is no argument based upon the first two principles of distributive justice, the principles of acquisition and of transfer, for such a more extensive state. If the set of holdings is properly generated, there is no argument for a more extensive state based upon distributive justice.[46] (Nor, we have claimed, will the Lockean proviso actually provide occasion for a more extensive state.) If, however, these principles are violated, the principle of rectification comes into play. Perhaps it is best to view some patterned principles of distributive justice as rough rules of thumb meant to approximate the general results of applying the principle of rectification of injustice. For example lacking much historical information, and assuming (1) that victims of injustice generally do worse than they otherwise would and (2) that those from the least well-off group in the society have the highest probabilities of being the (descendants of) victims of the most serious injustice who are owed compensation by those who benefited from the injustices (assumed to be those better off, though sometimes the perpetrators will be others in the worst-off group), then a *rough* rule of thumb for rectifying injustices might seem to be

the following: organize society so as to maximize the position of whatever group ends up least well-off in the society. This particular example may well be implausible, but an important question for each society will be the following: given *its* particular history, what operable rule of thumb best approximates the results of a detailed application in that society of the principle of rectification? These issues are very complex and are best left to a full treatment of the principle of rectification. In the absence of such a treatment applied to a particular society, one *cannot* use the analysis and theory presented here to condemn any particular scheme of transfer payments, unless it is clear that no considerations of rectification of injustice could apply to justify it. Although to introduce socialism as the punishment for our sins would be to go too far, past injustices might be so great as to make necessary in the short run a more extensive state in order to rectify them.

Notes

1   The reader who has looked ahead and seen that the second part of this chapter discusses Rawls' theory mistakenly may think that every remark or argument in the first part against alternative theories of justice is meant to apply to, or anticipate, a criticism of Rawls' theory. This is not so; there are other theories also worth criticizing.

2   Applications of the principle of justice in acquisition may also occur as part of the move from one distribution to another. You may find an unheld thing now and appropriate it. Acquisitions also are to be understood as included when, to simplify, I speak only of transitions by transfers.

3   See, however, the useful book by Boris Bittker, *The Case for Black Reparations* (New York: Random House, 1973).

4   If the principle of rectification of violations of the first two principles yields more than one description of holdings, then some choice must be made as to which of these is to be realized. Perhaps the sort of considerations about distributive justice and equality that I argue against play a legitimate role in *this* subsidiary choice. Similarly, there may be room for such considerations in deciding which otherwise arbitrary features a statute will embody, when such features are unavoidable because other considerations do not specify a precise line; yet a line must be drawn.

5   One might try to squeeze a patterned conception of distributive justice into the framework of the entitlement conception, by formulating a gimmicky obligatory "principle of transfer" that would lead to the

pattern. For example, the principle that if one has more than the mean income one must transfer everything one holds above the mean to persons below the mean so as to bring them up to (but not over) the mean. We can formulate a criterion for a "principle of transfer" to rule out such obligatory transfers, or we can say that no correct principle of transfer, no principle of transfer in a free society will be like this. The former is probably the better course, though the latter also is true.

Alternatively, one might think to make the entitlement conception instantiate a pattern, by using matrix entries that express the relative strength of a person's entitlements as measured by some real-valued function. But even if the limitation to natural dimensions failed to exclude this function, the resulting edifice would *not* capture our system of entitlements to *particular* things.

6   F. A. Hayek, *The Constitution of Liberty* (Chicago: University of Chicago Press, 1960), p. 87.

7   This question does not imply that they will tolerate any and every patterned distribution. In discussing Hayek's views, Irving Kristol has recently speculated that people will not long tolerate a system that yields distributions patterned in accordance with value rather than merit. (" 'When Virtue Loses All Her Loveliness' – Some Reflections on Capitalism and 'The Free Society,' " *The Public Interest*, Fall 1970, pp. 3–15.) Kristol, following some remarks of Hayek's, equates the merit system with justice. Since some case can be made for the external

standard of distribution in accordance with benefit to others, we ask about a weaker (and therefore, more plausible) hypothesis.

8 We certainly benefit because great economic incentives operate to get others to spend much time and energy to figure out how to serve us by providing things we will want to pay for. It is not mere paradox mongering to wonder whether capitalism should be criticized for most rewarding and hence encouraging, not individualists like Thoreau who go about their own lives, but people who are occupied with serving others and winning them as customers. But to defend capitalism one need not think businessmen are the finest human types. (I do not mean to join here the general maligning of businessmen, either.) Those who think the finest should acquire the most can try to convince their fellows to transfer resources in accordance with *that* principle.

9 Varying situations continuously from that limit situation to our own would force us to make explicit the underlying rationale of entitlements and to consider whether entitlement considerations lexicographically precede the considerations of the usual theories of distributive justice, so that the *slightest* strand of entitlement outweighs the considerations of the usual theories of distributive justice.

10 Might not a transfer have instrumental effects on a third party, changing his feasible options? (But what if the two parties to the transfer independently had used their holdings in this fashion?) I discuss this question below, but note here that this question concedes the point for distributions of ultimate intrinsic noninstrumental goods (pure utility experiences, so to speak) that are transferable. It also might be objected that the transfer might make a third party more envious because it worsens his position relative to someone else. I find it incomprehensible how this can be thought to involve a claim of justice. On envy, see Chapter 8 of *Anarchy, State and Utopia*.

Here and elsewhere in this chapter, a theory which incorporates elements of pure procedural justice might find what I say acceptable, *if* kept in its proper place; that is, if background institutions exist to ensure the satisfaction of certain conditions on distributive shares. But if these institutions are not themselves the sum or invisible-hand result of people's voluntary (nonaggressive) actions, the constraints they impose require justification. At no point does *our* argument assume any background institutions more extensive than those of the minimal nightwatchman state, a state limited to protecting persons against murder, assault, theft, fraud, and so forth.

11 See the selection from John Henry MacKay's novel, *The Anarchists*, reprinted in Leonard Krimmerman and Lewis Perry, eds., *Patterns of Anarchy* (New York: Doubleday Anchor Books, 1966), in which an individualist anarchist presses upon a communist anarchist the following question: "Would you, in the system of society which you call 'free Communism' prevent individuals from exchanging their labor among themselves by means of their own medium of exchange? And further: Would you prevent them from occupying land for the purpose of personal use?" The novel continues: "[the] question was not to be escaped. If he answered 'Yes!' he admitted that society had the right of control over the individual and threw overboard the autonomy of the individual which he had always zealously defended; if on the other hand, he answered 'No!' he admitted the right of private property which he had just denied so emphatically.... Then he answered 'In Anarchy any number of men must have the right of forming a voluntary association, and so realizing their ideas in practice. Nor can I understand how any one could justly be driven from the land and house which he uses and occupies . . . every serious man must declare himself: for Socialism, and thereby for force and against liberty, or for Anarchism, and thereby for liberty and against force.' " In contrast, we find Noam Chomsky writing, "Any consistent anarchist must oppose private ownership of the means of production," "the consistent anarchist then . . . will be a socialist . . . of a particular sort." Introduction to Daniel Guerin, *Anarchism: From Theory to Practice* (New York: Monthly Review Press, 1970), pages xiii, xv.

12 Is the patterned principle stable that requires merely that a distribution be Pareto-optimal? One person might give another a gift or bequest that the second could exchange with a third to their mutual benefit. Before the second makes this exchange, there is not Pareto-optimality. Is a stable pattern presented by a principle choosing that among the Pareto-optimal positions that satisfies some further condition *C*? It may seem that there cannot be a counterexample, for won't any voluntary exchange made away from a situation show that the first situation wasn't Pareto-optimal? (Ignore the implausibility of this last claim for the case of bequests.) But principles are to be satisfied over time, during which new possibilities arise. A distribution that at one time satisfies the criterion of Pareto-optimality might not do so when some new possibilities arise (Wilt Chamberlain grows up and starts playing basketball); and though people's activities will tend to move then to a new Pareto-optimal position, *this* new one need not satisfy the contentful condition *C*. Continual interference will be needed to insure the continual satisfaction of *C*. (The theoretical possibility of a pattern's being maintained by some invisible-hand process that brings it back to an equilibrium that fits the pattern when deviations occur should be investigated.)

13 *Collective Choice and Social Welfare*, Holden-Day, Inc., 1970, chaps. 6 and 6*.

14   Oppression will be less noticeable if the background institutions do not prohibit certain actions that upset the patterning (various exchanges or transfers of entitlement), but rather prevent them from being done, by nullifying them.

15   One indication of the stringency of Rawls' difference principle, which we attend to in the second part of this chapter, is its inappropriateness as a governing principle even within a family of individuals who love one another. Should a family devote its resources to maximizing the position of its least well off and least talented child, holding back the other children or using resources for their education and development only if they will follow a policy through their lifetimes of maximizing the position of their least fortunate sibling? Surely not. How then can this even be considered as the appropriate policy for enforcement in the wider society? (I discuss below what I think would be Rawls' reply: that some principles apply at the macro level which do not apply to microsituations.)

16   See Gregory Vlastos, "The Individual as an Object of Love in Plato" in his *Platonic Studies* (Princeton: Princeton University Press, 1973), pp. 3–34.

17   I am unsure as to whether the arguments I present below show that such taxation merely *is* forced labor; so that "is on a par with" means "is one kind of." Or alternatively, whether the arguments emphasize the great similarities between such taxation and forced labor, to show it is plausible and illuminating to view such taxation in the light of forced labor. This latter approach would remind one of how John Wisdom conceives of the claims of metaphysicians.

18   Nothing hangs on the fact that here and elsewhere I speak loosely of *needs*, since I go on, each time, to reject the criterion of justice which includes it. If, however, something did depend upon the notion, one would want to examine it more carefully. For a skeptical view, see Kenneth Minogue, *The Liberal Mind*, (New York: Random House, 1963), pp. 103–12.

19   Further details which this statement should include are contained in my essay "Coercion," in *Philosophy, Science, and Method*, ed. S. Morgenbesser, P. Suppes, and M. White (New York: St. Martin, 1969).

20   On the themes in this and the next paragraph, see the writings of Armen Alchian.

21   Compare this with Robert Paul Wolff's "A Refutation of Rawls' Theorem on Justice," *Journal of Philosophy*, March 31, 1966, sect. 2. Wolff's criticism does not apply to Rawls' conception under which the baseline is fixed by the difference principle.

22   I have not seen a precise estimate David Friedman, *The Machinery of Freedom* (New York: Harper & Row, 1973), pp. xiv, xv, discusses this issue and suggests 5 percent of US national income as an upper limit for the first two factors mentioned. However he does not attempt to estimate the percentage of current wealth which is based upon such income in the past. (The vague notion of "based upon" merely indicates a topic needing investigation.)

23   Fourier held that since the process of civilization had deprived the members of society of certain liberties (to gather, pasture, engage in the chase), a socially guaranteed minimum provision for persons was justified as compensation for the loss (Alexander Gray, *The Socialist Tradition* (New York: Harper & Row, 1968), p. 188). But this puts the point too strongly. This compensation would be due those persons, if any, for whom the process of civilization was a *net loss*, for whom the benefits of civilization did not counterbalance being deprived of these particular liberties.

24   For example, Rashdall's case of someone who comes upon the only water in the desert several miles ahead of others who also will come to it and appropriates it all. Hastings Rashdall, "The Philosophical Theory of Property," in *Property, its Duties and Rights* (London: Macmillan, 1915).

We should note Ayn Rand's theory of property rights ("Man's Rights" in *The Virtue of Selfishness* (New York: New American Library, 1964), p. 94), wherein these follow from the right to life, since people need physical things to live. But a right to life is not a right to whatever one needs to live; other people may have rights over these other things. At most, a right to life would be a right to have or strive for whatever one needs to live, provided that having it does not violate anyone else's rights. With regard to material things, the question is whether having it does violate any right of others. (Would appropriation of all unowned things do so? Would appropriating the water hole in Rashdall's example?) Since special considerations (such as the Lockean proviso) may enter with regard to material property, one *first* needs a theory of property rights before one can apply any supposed right to life (as amended above). Therefore the right to life cannot provide the foundation for a theory of property rights.

25   The situation would be different if his water hole didn't dry up, due to special precautions he took to prevent this. Compare our discussion of the case in the text with Hayek, *The Constitution of Liberty*, p. 136; and also with Ronald Hamowy, "Hayek's Concept of Freedom; A Critique," *New Individualist Review*, April 1961, pp. 28–31.

26   I discuss overriding and its moral traces in "Moral Complications and Moral Structures," *Natural Law Forum*, 1968, pp. 1–50.

27   Does the principle of compensation introduce patterning considerations? Though it requires compensation for the disadvantages imposed by those

seeking security from risks, it is not a patterned principle. For it seeks to remove only those disadvantages which prohibitions inflict on those who might present risks to others, not all disadvantages. It specifies an obligation on those who impose the prohibition, which stems from their own particular acts, to remove a particular complaint those prohibited may make against them.

28 Rawls, *Theory of Justice*, p. 72. Rawls goes on to discuss what he calls a liberal interpretation of his two principles of justice, which is designed to eliminate the influence of social contingencies, but which "intuitively, still appears defective ... [for] it still permits the distribution of wealth and income to be determined by the natural distribution of abilities and talents ... distributive shares are decided by the outcome of the natural lottery; and this outcome is arbitrary from a moral perspective. There is no more reason to permit the distribution of income and wealth to be settled by the distribution of natural assets than by historical and social fortune" (pp. 73–4).

29 Rawls, *Theory of Justice*, p. 104.

30 Rawls, *Theory of Justice*, pp. 311–12.

31 Rawls, *Theory of Justice*, p. 15.

32 Rawls, *Theory of Justice*, pp. 538–41.

33 "In order to show that the principles of justice are based in part on envy it would have to be established that one or more of the conditions of the original position arose from this propensity." *Theory of Justice*, p. 538.

34 For example:

1 Differences between any two persons' holdings should be morally deserved; morally undeserved differences should not exist.

2 Differences between persons in natural assets are morally undeserved.

3 Differences between persons partially determined by other differences that are undeserved are themselves undeserved.

Therefore,

4 Differences between persons' holdings shouldn't be partially determined by differences in their natural assets.

35 Rawls, *Theory of Justice*, p. 310. In the remainder of this section, Rawls goes on to criticize the conception of distribution according to moral desert.

36 "No reason need be given for ... an equal distribution of benefits – for that is 'natural' – self-evidently right and just, and needs no justification, since it is in some sense conceived as being self-justified.... The assumption is that equality needs no reasons, only inequality does so; that uniformity, regularity, similarity, symmetry, ... need not be specially accounted for, whereas differences, unsystematic behavior, changes in conduct, need explanation and, as a rule, justification. If I have a cake and there are ten persons among whom I wish to divide it, then if I give exactly one-tenth to each, this will not, at any rate automatically, call for justification; whereas if I depart from this principle of equal division I am expected to produce a special reason. It is some sense of this, however latent, that makes equality an idea which has never seemed intrinsically eccentric...." [Isaiah Berlin, "Equality," reprinted in Frederick A. Olafson, ed. *Justice and Social Policy* (Englewood Cliffs, NJ: Prentice-Hall, 1961), p. 131]. To pursue the analogy with mechanics further, note that it is a substantive theoretical position which specifies a particular state or situation as one which requires no explanation whereas deviations from it are to be explained in terms of external forces. See Ernest Nagel's discussion of D'Alembert's attempt to provide an *a priori* argument for Newton's first law of motion. [*The Structure of Science* (New York: Harcourt, Brace, and World, 1961), pp. 175–7.]

37 A process, we might strengthen the antecedent by adding, of the sort that would create an entitlement to *Y* if the person were entitled to *X*. I use "Lockean" rights and entitlements to refer to those (discussed earlier) against force, fraud, and so on, which are to be recognized in the minimal state. Since I believe these are the only rights and entitlements people possess (apart from those they specially acquire), I needn't have included the specification to Lockean rights. One who believes some have a right to the fruits of others' labor will deny the truth of the first premiss as stated. If the Lockean specification were not included, he might grant the truth of 1, while denying that of 2 or of later steps.

38 If nothing of moral significance could flow from what was arbitrary, then no particular person's existence could be of moral significance, since which of the many sperm cells succeeds in fertilizing the egg cell is (so far as we know) arbitrary from a moral point of view. This suggests another, more vague, remark directed to the spirit of Rawls' position rather than to its letter. Each existing person is the product of a process wherein the one sperm cell which succeeds is no more deserving than the millions that fail. Should we wish that process had been "fairer" as judged by Rawls' standards, that all "inequities" in it had been rectified? We should be apprehensive about any principle that would condemn morally the very sort of process that brought us to be, a principle that therefore would undercut the legitimacy of our very existing.

39 But see also our discussion below of Rawls' view of natural abilities as a collective asset.

40 Rawls, *Theory of Justice*, p. 179.

41 Rawls, *Theory of Justice*, p. 102.

42 Rawls, *Theory of Justice*, p. 27.

43 Rawls, *Theory of Justice*, p. 183.

44 Rawls, *Theory of Justice*, p. 102.

45 Will the lexicographic priority that Rawls claims for liberty in the original position prevent the difference principle from requiring a head tax on assets and abilities? The legitimacy of a head tax is *suggested* by Rawls' speaking of "collective assets" and "common assets." Those underutilizing their assets and abilities are misusing a public asset. (Squandering public property?) Rawls may intend no such strong inferences from his terminology, but we need to hear more about why those in the original position wouldn't accept the strong interpretation. The notion of liberty needs elaboration which is to exclude a head tax and yet allow the other taxation schemes. Assets and abilities can be harnessed without a head tax; and "harnessing" is an appropriate term – as it would be for a horse harnessed to a wagon which doesn't *have* to move ever, but if it does, it must draw the wagon along.

With regard to envy, the difference principle, applied to the choice between either *A* having ten and *B* having five or A having eight and B having five, would favor the latter. Thus, despite Rawls' view (pp. 79–80), the difference principle is inefficient in that it sometimes will favor a status quo against a Pareto-better but more unequal distribution. The inefficiency could be removed by shifting from the simple difference principle to a staggered difference principle, which recommends the maximization of the position of the least well-off group, and *subject to that constraint*, the maximization of the position of the next least well-off group, and this point also is made by A.K. Sen (*Collective Choice and Social Welfare*, p. 138, note) and is acknowledged by Rawls (p. 83). But such a staggered principle does not embody a presumption in favor of equality of the sort used by Rawls. How then could Rawls justify an inequality *special* to the staggered principle to someone in the least well-off group? Perhaps these issues underlie the unclarity (see p. 83) as to whether Rawls accepts the staggered principle.

46 "But isn't justice to be tempered with compassion?" Not by the guns of the state. When private persons choose to transfer resources to help others, this fits within the entitlement conception of justice.

14

Chance, Choice and Justice

Brian Barry

I   Two Principles of Justice

The proposition that I want to examine in this chapter can be stated quite simply as follows. A just society is one whose institutions honour two principles of distribution. One is a principle of compensation. It says that the institutions of a society should operate in such a way as to counteract the effects of good and bad fortune. In particular, it says that the victims of ill luck should as far as possible be made as well off as those who are similarly placed in all respects other than having suffered this piece of bad luck. The other principle is one of personal responsibility. It says that social arrangements should be such that people finish up with the outcomes of their voluntary acts.

Let me say this at once. There is no suggestion that these two principles constitute a complete specification of principles relevant to the distribution of benefits and burdens within a society. In fact, it is fairly evident that these principles could not get going at all without other principles to lay the groundwork. The first principle depends for its application on our having as a benchmark for the compensation of victims of bad luck some idea of the welfare level appropriate to those similarly placed except for having suffered the bad luck. And the second principle presupposes an assignment of rights to act (e.g. a principle of equal civil and political rights) so as to provide a legitimate sphere of choice. I should also say that the applica-

tion of these two principles of justice would always have to be modified by the operation of a principle of expediency, which is I believe accepted in every society. According to this, which I shall call the principle of common advantage, an inequality is justified if it works to the benefit of everybody. It is perhaps worth noting here that utilitarianism consists of offering a particular interpretation of what it means to say that something is to everybody's advantage and then dumping all other principles. In putting forward these two principles of justice I am therefore rejecting utilitarianism.

The problem that I want to concentrate on is this. Let us suppose that we find ourselves initially attracted by both the principle of compensation and the principle of responsibility. How do we fit them together? On the face of it, they fit together very nicely. Indeed, they can be seen as two aspects of a single principle: that it is 'inequitable if an individual is in a worse situation than another because of factors beyond his control'.[1] If something is a matter of luck, that means it is beyond your control; if it is a matter of choice, that means it is within your control.

Unfortunately, however, this verbal resolution of the problem falls apart as soon as we press on it. I can illustrate the difficulties most dramatically by showing that it is possible to extend the scope of choice so that it leaves very little room for chance and conversely that it is possible to extend the scope of chance so that it threatens to engulf choice completely.

Originally published in *Liberty and Justice* (Oxford: Oxford University Press, 1989), pp. 142–58. Reprinted by permission of Oxford University Press.

II Choicism

Let us begin with the first case. I am not concerned here with the possibility that someone might simply accept the relevance of choice and deny that of chance, as a matter of principle. This is a possible position, and indeed it is in general terms that taken by Robert Nozick in *Anarchy, State, and Utopia*.[2] Nozick postulates a framework of rights and then says that just outcomes are those arising from the choices made by people in the exercise of those rights. You might have the bad luck to starve to death under these arrangements because you have not been so fortunate as to inherit or be given enough to live on, and for reasons beyond your control (e.g. disability or inability to find work) cannot earn enough to live on. But Nozick simply has no provision for modifying the outcomes arising from choice so as to deal with bad luck. I am not going to argue with that sort of view, whose unattractiveness seems to me patent. What I am interested in here is the way in which somewhat less extreme versions of Nozick's conclusions can be reached even if both choice and chance are recognized as being in principle relevant.

The best way of approaching this is to consider a simple lottery where people buy one or more tickets for some modest sum like fifty pence, the counterfoils are put into a hat and the winner, who gets everybody's stakes, is the person whose number is pulled out. Nothing could be a better example of an outcome determined by chance. The principle of compensation would appear to imply that the winner's prize should be redistributed among the participants in the lottery so as to restore the status quo ante. Yet there seems something odd in the suggestion that justice requires this. Why? Fairly obviously the answer lies in the presumptively voluntary nature of participation in the lottery. If people deliberately put themselves in a situation where they have a large chance of losing a small amount and a small chance of gaining a greater amount, isn't it fair that the outcome should stand?

Since a good deal hangs on our returning a positive answer, it will be advisable for us to test the ground carefully before going further. Thus, we should bear in mind that the principle of personal responsibility relates to voluntary actions and that choices may fail to be voluntary in a variety of ways. Conditions undermining voluntariness include coercion, internal compulsion, addiction, provocation and necessity (the lack of acceptable alternatives). It has to be said that the interpretation of these is itself open to controversy, and hardboiled choicists are liable to construe most of these phenomena as very strong preferences while denying the relevance of necessity altogether. However, even the softboiled might well be satisfied that in some instances the participants in a lottery such as I described were not suffering from such things as social pressure, compulsion, or desperation. So it could still be held that the winner could justly hang on to the prize.

Notice that this answer does not require us to make the claim that any just society must permit gambling. We might accept that a society could justly prohibit gambling either on paternalistic grounds (that some people will become compulsive gamblers and blanket prohibition is the only effective form of protection) or on the Puritanical ground that anything which divorces rewards from efforts is morally enervating. Notice, however, that these grounds do not themselves invoke justice. So long as we accept that a society may justly permit gambling, we can still arrive at the conclusion that, where it is permitted, the winner of a lottery has a just claim on the prize.

This might seem at first glance to be a quite small concession to the idea that choice can trump chance, but it can be used as the thin end of a very thick wedge. I shall invent the word 'choicist' to refer to someone who wants to show that it is consistent with justice to give the principle of personal responsibility a lot of scope at the expense of the principle of compensation, while acknowledging the validity of both principles. I shall now set out what seems to me the best case for choicism. I shall not go as far as some actual choicists but I shall push the case to the limits of intellectual respectability, and perhaps a bit beyond.

A very important weapon in the armoury of the choicist is the institution of insurance. By invoking the possibility of insuring oneself against various misfortunes it is possible to construct an argument that marginalizes the principle of compensation over a wide range of cases. We can connect this to the previous discussion by observing that insurance is simply a form of gambling, where a small loss in the form of a premium is voluntarily accepted in return for the prospect of a large gain in the form of a payout by the insurer. The peculiarity of insurance is simply that what triggers the payment is a piece of specified bad luck. (To the extent that the contingency triggering the payout is not solely due to luck, insurers start talking about 'moral hazard' and getting uncomfortable. Let us leave that complication on one side for now and think of insurance as being against bad luck.) Suppose, then, that your house burns down due to causes completely beyond your control. That is bad luck, straightforwardly enough, as even the most rabid choicist will admit. But, it may be said, whether you suffer financial loss from the destruction of your house depends on your prior decision to insure it fully, inadequately, or not at all. Thus, we can conclude that someone who loses everything in a fire can justly be left destitute because the option of insuring against the loss was available and not taken.

Let us go back to the Nozickian vision of a society in which market-derived outcomes are modified only by private arrangements. How far can it be reinstated by someone who admits the validity of the principle of compensation but wants to minimize its impact? We shall certainly be able to find, consistently with justice, people starving to death. All we need to show is that they had the option of avoiding that fate through insurance and didn't take it. For example, anyone now unable to work owing to sickness or accident but previously in good health could have taken out insurance against loss of earnings. Involuntary unemployment presents more of a problem, unless our choicist has the gall to claim that there is no such thing; but there could be a state-run system of insurance to which individuals could subscribe or not. An honest and intelligent choicist would also have to admit that a purely private system of medical insurance would fail to cover people against the bad luck of being bad medical risks. But again, subscription to the insurance scheme could be made voluntary, so that we could justly have people dying because they couldn't afford treatment. Destitution in old age could obviously be treated as voluntary, in almost all cases.

What about earned income? I think that any serious choicist would have to admit that some people are congenitally unemployable or employable only in jobs whose market value is very low. The principle of compensation would therefore mandate that the results of such bad luck should be modified by transfers, and here we have a clear departure from the Nozickian world. But this still leaves us with most of the enormous disparities in earnings that market systems produce. How far can a choicist defend these against the claim that

unequal earnings are largely a matter of good and bad luck – in genes, social background, schooling, or simply being in the right place at the right time?

To some degree the lottery example can be invoked to save the day. Thus, suppose that with given abilities you might acquire the qualifications to go into a high-variance occupation or a low-variance one – become a barrister or a solicitor – then it might be argued that if you do very badly in the high-variance occupation (get very few briefs as a barrister) you have no legitimate cause for complaint. This is a good point for the choicist as far as it goes, but it does not go very far, since the terms of comparison are confined to barristers and solicitors.

An across-the-board justification would require the claim that everybody initially faced the same choice set, and all subsequent differentiation of earnings prospects arises from different choices made along the way. This is on the face of it highly implausible, if we take it that for something to count as a choice it must be a real possibility that it be chosen. (A paraplegic does not have a choice of running or not.) But then everything turns on what has to be true for something to constitute a real possibility.

The classic choicist move here is to distinguish sharply between possibility and probability. For example, it might be conceded that a bright child with well-educated supportive parents will find it easier to do well in school and is, as a statistical matter, more likely to. (It is hard to see how anybody could deny that.) But it may be said that so long as a few children of average brightness and with disadvantageous home circumstances succeed that shows it is possible for all to do so. (This is the sense of 'equal opportunity' in which every private in Napoleon's armies carried a marshall's baton in his knapsack.)

Of course, for even these minimal claims about equal opportunities to be valid, we would already have to be some distance from a Nozickian world, since there would have to be an educational system accessible to all children, whatever their family circumstances, including financial support to enable all children to stay at school through the full term of full-time education, and this school system would have to be set up in such a way as to ensure that all children did actually have the means available to do well if they took advantage of them. This would fairly plainly not be true of contemporary Britain, for example.

Even after all these conditions were met, however, I believe that a sincere choicist would have to admit that not everything is possible to everybody, and concede the case for a somewhat progressive income tax system to deal in a rough and ready way with good and bad luck in relation to the job market. But it would be possible, I take it, to resist the suggestion that an ideally just system of earnings would be one providing everyone with equal final pay after compensating for the disutility of work.

In concluding my exposition of the choicist case, I want to come back to a point I made in connection with lotteries. I said that a just society does not have to allow lotteries to occur. The conclusion favourable to choicism is a purely hypothetical one: that if there are to be lotteries, it is just for the winner to hang on the prize. The decision whether or not to permit lotteries has to be taken on grounds other than those of justice: protection of the vulnerable or the maintenance of desirable dispositions on one side, and on the other presumably the value of individual liberty to do what one wishes in the absence of compelling reasons to the contrary.

The point can be generalized. Thus, if there are two occupations with the same mean income and different dispersions (as solicitors and barristers might be) then someone who does badly in the high-dispersion occupation cannot complain of injustice, even if failure is attributable wholly to bad luck (including perhaps the bad luck of not having influential connections). But it is not unjust for a society to get rid of high-variance occupations and make barristers part of a salaried legal service. The case for and against will have to be argued on other grounds.

In the same way, the most a choicist can claim on the basis of the principle of personal responsibility is this: *if* a society's institutions make insurance against a whole variety of misfortunes voluntary, and actually provide the insurance (supplementing or superseding privately offered insurance where necessary), then it is not unjust to leave uncompensated the losses suffered by those who have failed to avail themselves of the opportunity of taking out insurance. Considerations of justice will not, however, tell us whether to have a system like that or to have compulsory social insurance and a national health service. That decision will, again, have to be made on other grounds, presumably security and efficiency (since private insurance has high overhead costs) on one side and personal liberty – the opportunity of shaping one's life by one's choices – on the other.

Similarly, a choicist can say that it is consistent with justice for educational outcomes to be heavily dependent on choice, so that pupils who choose not to study are left by the wayside. But it would also be consistent with justice to charge schools with the duty of trying to motivate all their students and require all children to complete their secondary education.

III   Qualified Choicism

I have tried to give an idea of the way in which choicism works to produce policy implications. Before going further, let me pause for a few general remarks about the presuppositions of the choicist position. Choicism, then, builds upon some simple ideas about choice that appeal to the common sense of a basically liberal society such as ours. Thus, it is assumed that you have a free choice among kinds of fruit if all you have to do is to stretch out your hand and take one from a bowl containing a selection. Similarly, it is assumed that you have the option of acquiring a qualification if you could get it by enrolling in a course you can afford and doing some work that is within your capability. It would be regarded as paradoxical to claim that such choices do not generate responsibility for the outcomes because they flow from preferences that are not themselves chosen.

It is also assumed that if two people have the same choice set they are treated equally, so that two people are equally well treated as consumers if they have the same income, and members of two religious bodies have equal treatment if a uniform, non-discriminatory set of rules applies to both of the bodies. And again it would be thought of as paradoxical to deny this in the first case by pointing out that one person may be able to get more satisfaction from spending the income than the other and in the second case by pointing out that a rule of universal toleration suits a religion that favours toleration more than one that seeks to make everybody conform to it. Yet a case can certainly be made out for these paradoxical claims, which extend the scope of the principle of compensation at the expense of the principle of responsibility.

My main business in the rest of this chapter will be coming to grips with the kind of large-scale anti-choicism that I have just introduced. Before that, however, I should like to show that choicism, as I have expounded it so far, is vulnerable to attack without disputing the common sense premises about choice and personal responsibility on which it depends. Qualified choicism, as I shall call it for convenience, is the view that the significance (or potential significance) of choice in justifying unequal outcomes has been overstated.

In any attempt to cut choicism down to size, the weakest point in it must surely be the claim that a large proportion of all earnings differentials can be defended as arising from voluntary choice. To maintain this, the choicist claim about equality of opportunity has to be the strong one that at any rate most differences in final educational attainment come about as a result of children making different choices out of steadily divergent choice sets that were at some early stage identical. But if only a few children of average native ability from disadvantaged backgrounds do well educationally, this must cast doubt on the claim that doing well formed a real option for all the rest. It seems more plausible to suppose that we would find some special factors accounting for the exceptions, and that they could not therefore be used to show that the other children could have done the same if they had chosen to.

I deliberately built up the choicist position starting from its strongest case and working down from there. I do not therefore believe that there is any sound objection from the qualified choicist viewpoint to the lottery example. The extension to insurance, however, seems more open to challenge. Much, I suggest, turns on the answer to questions like these: under what conditions would it be rational for someone dependent on employment for an income to decline insurance, if available on reasonable terms, against loss of earnings? If the answer is (as I think it indeed is) that there are almost no circumstances in which this would be rational, the conclusion will have to be that those who do not take the insurance are lacking in foresight, suffer from weakness of will, or are simply too ill-organized to act appropriately. Any of these would be enough to at any rate call into question personal responsibility to the extent of suggesting that destitution is too high a penalty for failure to insure. Where almost all rational choices would go the same way, leaving people the choice is rather like leaving a stretch of dangerous cliff unfenced so as to leave people the option of plunging into the sea.

IV Anti-choicism

I now want to turn, as promised, to a more radical critique of the choicist position, which I shall call anti-choicism. It may be recalled that when defining choicism I excluded from consideration those people who simply do not recognize the validity of the principle of compensation. My choicists are people who recognize it but seek to minimize its role in determining just outcomes. I shall define anti-choicism so that it is the converse of choicism. I shall therefore leave on one side those who hold a normative theory that has no room for the principle of personal responsibility from the outset. Examples of such theories would be: that average utility should be maximized, that minimum utility should be maximized, or that some function with equal distribution and average level of utility as arguments should be maximized. Of course, in working out the implications of such theories it will no doubt be found necessary to attach consequences to actions so as to encourage socially beneficial actions and discourage anti-social ones. But this is purely instrumental, justified by its tendency to increase the maximand.

The position I am interested in is one which accepts in principle that choice and chance are both relevant to justice but goes on to claim that when we look carefully we shall find that chance will largely or wholly swallow up choice. To make it plain that I am focusing on only one way of not being a choicist, I might perhaps have done better to call anti-choicism 'chancism', but sufficient unto the day is the neologism thereof.

The issue between choicism and anti-choicism turns on the relevance of tastes, aspirations and beliefs to personal responsibility for the outcomes of choices made in accordance with them. Choicism, as I am defining it, adopts a robust line on this: naturally people's choices flow from their tastes, aspirations and beliefs; but this is precisely what endows the choices made on the basis of them with authenticity. (If someone suddenly did something totally 'out of character', that would be more liable to lead us to accept a plea of 'diminished responsibility' for the outcome.)

The anti-choicist position, in contrast, holds that people cannot be held personally responsible for their tastes, aspirations, or beliefs, and this entails that they also cannot be held responsible for the outcomes of actions that flow from them. To save repetition (though at the cost of some violation to the language) let us talk about 'preferences' to refer to tastes, aspirations and beliefs. Then the anti-choicist view can be explained in this way. Although the principle of personal responsibility is valid as a principle, it does not have any application in the world we actually live in, which is one of universal causality. Personal responsibility depends upon choice, but we do not in general choose our preferences. It is true that it is sometimes possible for us to change our preferences by working on them. But presumably the decision to try to change some existing preference derives from a second-order preference which is not itself chosen. And even if we admitted yet higher-order preferences, we would never get to a radical choice, a choice unconditioned by a preference that was not itself subject to choice.

A more moderate version of anti-choicism embraces the basic anti-choicist premiss by saying that the only preferences to generate personal responsibility are those that were deliberately created by the agent, whether or not they could now be changed, and those that could now be changed by the agent, whether or not they were deliberately created in the first place. The distinctive feature of moderate anti-choicism is that it abandons the dogma that no preferences can ever pass the test and instead settles for a case-by-case approach. Some preferences, it is supposed, will give rise to personal responsibility but many others will not.[3]

Rather than engage in any more preliminaries, let me exhibit anti-choicism, in both of its forms, in operation. I shall take up two questions which, I will note in passing, are usually discussed by quite different sets of people, even though the underlying theoretical issue is the same. For my first example, I shall return to the idea of equal educational opportunity.

In my discussion of qualified choicism, I pointed out that the size of the choice set facing an individual is always problematic. That some alternative is formally open to a certain person – to take an advanced course in physics, say – does not mean that it is a real possibility for that person: it may require capacities he or she simply has not got. Nevertheless, I still assumed that there are real choices open – to take one subject or another, to study hard or not, to stay on at school or not, and so on – and that these at any rate give rise to responsibility for their outcomes. On the extreme anti-choicist view, this is invariably a delusion. For the choice must flow from a preference which is, immediately or at some remove, not the result of choice. In case it seems hard to take this seriously, let me observe that much of the literature on the subject presupposes that choices are a source of unequal opportunity on all fours with home environment and quality of school. It is assumed, as an

unargued ideal of social justice, that if we factor out differences in native endowment we ought to be able to slice through the population of a society along any dimension – gender, religion, ethnic group, race, social class, region, and so on – and find on each side of the division a perfect microcosm of the society as a whole, as far as levels and perhaps even types of educational attainment are concerned. Since it seems evident that part of the explanation of systematic differences in group achievement is the existence of different patterns of preference among their members, it must be that these are to be regarded as sources of socially unjust inequalities in educational outcome.

The moderate version of anti-choicism would leave it open that some choices were genuine and could properly act as an acceptable basis for differences in outcome. But to just the extent that these choices were patterned, so that girls systematically tended to make different choices from boys, or WASPs from white 'ethnics', this very fact would suggest that the sources of the underlying preferences should be sought in cultural attitudes and thus seen as a matter of chance rather than choice.

It should perhaps be added that the choicist criterion accepts non-culpable ignorance as an excusing condition. (If I put white powder in your coffee, sincerely and reasonably believing it to be artificial sweetener, I am not responsible for your being poisoned when it turns out to have been strychnine.) No doubt some ill-advised educational choices can be brought within the range of that limitation on the scope of the principle of personal responsibility. But it is hard to see how it could be made to cover, say, the tendency for a smaller proportion of girls than boys to study science subjects, or the smaller appetite for a college education among white 'ethnics' as compared with WASPs. The gap between the implications of choicism and the implications of anti-choicism thus remains wide.

The best way into my second example is via a reconsideration of the choicist idea that can be expressed in the words: 'Equal choice sets constitute equal treatment.' It is fairly easy to see that as it stands this must be an incomplete specification. Confronting two people with the same set of options cannot be a sufficient condition of equal treatment. If I like apples and you like oranges, a bowl containing both gives us equal treatment; but one containing only oranges would just as well satisfy the condition of confronting us with an identical choice set. Similarly, a law permitting the practice of all varieties of Christianity but prohibiting all others is equal treatment among Christians but not between Christians and others; yet all of them face the same choice set.

It looks as if to the condition that the choice sets should be the same we need to add something about their having the same value. But how do we tell when two choice sets have the same value? Choicists are in the embarrassing position of having no general answer to this question. In the case of consumer goods, for example, it can be said that people are treated equally when they have equal amounts of money, because this means that they have an entitlement to the same share of the society's resources: the equality of value is established by the equal cost to the rest of the society. With members of religious faiths, a criterion of this kind gives no help. Equal treatment will have to mean that they all get the same tax treatment, the same treatment with regard to schooling, the same treatment under the blasphemy laws and so on. The legal framework has equal value for all religious faiths only in this sense: that it does not give special favours to one that it does not give to others.

Anti-choicists, in contrast, offer a simple and comprehensive criterion of equal value: a certain choice set has the same value for two people if the option in it that each most prefers produces the same level of welfare, understood subjectively as 'utility'. (This option may, of course, be a different one for the two people.) Since the same criterion applies in all areas, we can aggregate across them and arrive at the general conclusion that social justice requires equal welfare for all the members of a society. For whatever it is about them that results in their actions yielding more or less utility is a matter of good or bad luck. The principle of compensation demands, therefore, that the effects of this good or bad luck should be cancelled out by an appropriate redistribution of resources.

It may be objected immediately that, if all actions produce the same amount of welfare for the agent as everybody else has, nobody will have any incentive to behave prudently, or to do things that benefit others rather than things that harm them. The average level of welfare of the population, which everyone share in, will be lowered only infinitesimally over a large population. Everyone therefore stands to gain from a move away from guaranteed equal welfare to a set-up that attaches reward and penalties to beneficial and antisocial actions respectively.

Is this simply, then, a return to the principle of personal responsibility? No. It is true that the institutions called for by common advantage will at a number of points be similar to those implied by the principle of personal responsibility. But the rationale will be quite different. Some criminologists, for example, have taken a strong anti-choicist line and argued that all or almost all criminal behaviour is the result of some combination of unfavourable heredity and crime-inducing environment. It is quite consistent with this to say that crime should be punished in order to reduce its incidence. But at the same time it has to be admitted that the deliberately lowered welfare levels of convicted criminals are a matter of bad luck on their part, and thus unjust. It is simply that the common advantage requires that they suffer in order to provide an example to others (and themselves in future). Thus, if things could somehow be arranged so that prisoners enjoyed the average level of welfare, while everyone (including them when they left) could be induced to believe they were suffering, that would be an ideally just state of affairs. Actual punishment is a concession by justice to expediency.

By invoking the principle of common advantage, then, we can fend off the more disastrous implications of the anti-choice position. But we may still feel that there is something mildly crazy about the idea that an ideally just situation would be one where people who needed champagne and caviar to get to the average level of consumer satisfaction would get more money or where the adherents of some killjoy religion would have to be allowed to bring everybody else down to their own level by stopping others from enjoying themselves.

Let's suppose that we accept the basic anti-choicist premise that the outcomes of unchosen preferences are a matter of good or bad luck. We could move away from the implication that justice mandated equal welfare if we adopted what I called the moderate anti-choicist position. This, it will be recalled, made room for personal responsibility for preferences provided they had either come about as a result of choice or could now be changed as a result of choice. The claims of a person with below-average welfare for compensation could therefore be resisted if the preferences causing the trouble were subject to choice in either of these ways. It does not seem to me, however, that this move would do much to get rid of implications of the kind I outlined a moment ago. The whole idea of choosing to change one's beliefs is fishy, while tastes for luxuries are notoriously hard to extinguish once established. Religious beliefs are less often deliberately cultivated than acquired in the course of one's upbringing; and although expensive tastes *may* have been cultivated, we certainly cannot assume that all are.

A heroic solution, which has been adopted by John Rawls, is to say that people's tastes, aspirations and beliefs are always open to modification, so people can properly be held responsible for them. This enables him to adhere to what I have called the basic anti-choicist premiss and yet finish up with the classical choicist conclusion that people are treated equally if they have equal rights and equal incomes – in Rawls's terminology, equal shares of primary goods.

On the face of it, Rawls's claim about the malleability of preferences is an empirical one, and a hopelessly implausible one to boot. He has made it clear, however, that this is a part of a 'model conception of the person' which is presupposed by the theory.[4] An unkind, but I fear accurate, way of putting this would be to say that Rawls wants to salvage liberal conclusions about primary goods as the currency of distributive justice, and can do so without repudiating the anti-choicist premiss only by inserting between them a postulate ensuring personal responsibility for preferences. The justification of this postulate – that all preferences are subject to choice – is not that it is true (or even credible) but that it is needed to get the answer to come out in the right place.

It is easy enough to dismiss Rawls's proposed solution, and I have no doubt that we should not waste time on it. Unfortunately, however, Rawls's ill-fated venture in dogmatic psychology has provided a golden opportunity for theorists antipathetic to liberal conclusions to suggest that they depend on something of the sort. It is clear, however, that this is not so, because these conclusions can be derived quite straightforwardly so long as the anti-choicist premiss is repudiated. The most that Rawls's contortions show is that it is hard to get from anti-choicist premisses to choicist conclusions, and this should not surprise anybody.

V Responsibility for Preferences: an Alternative Approach

We come back, then, to the anti-choicist premiss. If it were to be generally accepted, it looks as if we would have to make fairly drastic changes in our ideas about what justice ideally entails, though problems of implementation would perhaps mean that we should see little change in actual social arrangements. But should we accept it? It seems to me to have appealed to too many people of undeniable intelligence to be simply dismissed in favour of the bluff choicist position that the status of preferences is irrelevant to personal responsibility. What I should like to propose instead is that we should divide the spoils between choicism and anti-choicism, accepting the more intuitively appealing part of the anti-choicist premiss but dropping the part that leads to the more unappetizing conclusions.

Let us agree, then, that it is legitimate to look behind choices to preferences before establishing personal responsibility for outcomes. People are, indeed, responsible for the outcomes of actions only if they are also responsible for the preferences from which those actions flow. But the error in the anti-choicist position lies, I suggest, in the next step which makes responsibility for preferences depend upon their being subject to choice. The alternative I propose is that people are responsible for their preferences whenever they are content with them. How these preferences originated is irrelevant, and the ease with which they could be changed is relevant only in this way: that we would have to question the sincerity of your claim not to want to have the preferences you actually do have if it were easy for you to change them.

I shall call this view 'semi-choicism', since it abandons the choicist resistance to any inquiry into responsibility for preferences, but rejects the anti-choicist criterion for responsibility for preferences. I wish to maintain that semi-choicism has two virtues: it has a certain intrinsic plausibility, and it also gets the right answers (or what seem to me the right answers) on particular problems.

Consider again the case of religious belief. Suppose you were raised in some strict, puritanical sect according to whose tenets most pleasures are sinful, and you continue to believe in those tenets. Now you could, obviously, wish that the truth about the will of God was more accommodating, but so long as you really believe that that is how things are, you cannot regret believing it, even if you recognize that some other set of beliefs would be compatible with choices having more enjoyable outcomes. The difficulty in changing your beliefs is not so much empirical as logical. Let us imagine your saying, 'Of course, it would be hard for me to change my beliefs now, after such a long process of indoctrination, but I wish I had been brought up in some less restrictive faith so that I would now have more congenial beliefs.' In saying that you would, it seems to me, be saying that you no longer did believe in what you had been brought up to believe. Once you thought it through, you would be more honest with yourself to say, 'Of course, I no longer believe that all those pleasures are really sinful, but I still experience powerful guilt feelings about them.' It would be quite reasonable, I suggest, for someone in this position to be offered psychotherapy on the National Health Service in order to be relieved of these irrational feelings of guilt. And this, it may be observed, is precisely what is mandated by semi-choicism. For in this case you have preferences left over from your religious upbringing that you do not identify with and would like to be rid of. So long as you continued to believe, however, you could hardly complain that it was bad luck to have the preferences you had, since you would not have wished things to be any different.

Beliefs raise special issues because it is hard to give any sense to the idea of wanting to believe something other than what you do believe (as against wanting it to be the case that something else is true). However, the semi-choicist approach works equally well on preferences which are not conditioned upon belief in the way that religiously derived preferences are. Consider, for example, sexual preference. Now at present homosexuals are not given equal treatment according to the choicist criterion of having rights with equal value to those of heterosexuals. For example, a homosexual couple is less favourably treated than a heterosexual one by the laws dealing with income tax and estate duty. Suppose, however, that homosexuals and heterosexuals were treated equally according to the choicist criterion of equality, but that for some reason homosexuals tended to be less satisfied with life than heterosexuals. This would not be properly regarded as bad luck in as far as people feel that their sexuality is a central aspect of their personality and do not wish to be changed into some other kind of person.

That such a change is, as an empirical matter, difficult or impossible to accomplish, is not important. If a pill were invented tomorrow that switched people's sexual orientation painlessly and without side-effects, it would (I assume) have few takers, even if it were generally believed that one kind of sexual orientation tended to create more satisfaction with life than the other. To see

this, I ask you to engage in another thought experiment. Imagine you were told that somebody who had been and could again be happier than you had suffered a ghastly accident, but that by killing you and attaching his head to your body he could, by a miracle of surgery, be restored to his old self. If you were a dedicated utilitarian, you might reluctantly agree that this was, impersonally considered, the best course of action. But you would surely not regard it as being in your interest. You would not, therefore, go around saying what bad luck it is that such an operation is not actually available. But if you wouldn't do that, why should you feel inclined to say what bad luck it is that you have your character rather than a quite different one?

As before, we can add that the semi-choicist position would call for the National Health Service to provide counselling and then assistance to anyone who genuinely, after careful consideration of all the implications, wanted to try to change sexual orientation – in either direction. But that seems to me perfectly reasonable. Once again, therefore, I suggest that the semi-choicist approach seems to come out in the right place.

What, finally, about tastes? Let us concede (though I doubt if it is invariably true) that a connoisseur gets less pleasure from a bottle of plonk than does somebody who wouldn't notice if it was Château Lafitte, and so on. Does that mean that a connoisseur reduced to drinking plonk wishes he were unable to tell that it is plonk and imagine how much better Château Lafitte would be? I doubt it. The ability to make fine discriminations is, after all, not something to be lightly wished away. But we should notice that where we do find tastes which many people wish they could change, it is considered quite appropriate for the National Health Service to offer help, examples being smoking, drinking, drug abuse, and eating disorders. To the extent that people want to change their preferences and cannot, the semi-choicist agrees with the anti-choicist that this is bad luck, and quite rightly so, it seems to me.

VI Conclusion

The issues that have been raised here about the roles of chance and choice are central to so many aspects of public policy that it is hardly surprising to find them surfacing constantly in everyday political arguments. The task of political philosophers in all this is to clarify the terms of debate. My experience in presenting the ideas contained here has been that some of my examples elicit unanimous responses where others give rise to mixed reactions. The conclusion I am inclined to draw from this is that there is more going on in some of these cases than I have yet identified. More work needs to be done to refine the analysis and to apply it.[5] I feel convinced, however, that any adequate theory of distributive justice will have to give a central position to chance and choice.

Notes

1 Julian Le Grand, 'Equity as an Economic Objective', *Journal of Applied Philosophy*, 1 (1984): 39–51, quotation from p. 46, italics suppressed.
2 Robert Nozick, *Anarchy, State, and Utopia* (New York: Basic Books, 1974).
3 See G. A. Cohen, 'On the Currency of Egalitarian Justice', *Ethics* 99 (1989): 906–44.
4 See especially the Dewey Lectures on 'Kantian Constructivism', *Journal of Philosophy*, 77 (1980): 515–72.
5 I contribute to this process myself by presenting a greatly extended analysis of chance and choice in *Justice as Impartiality* (Oxford: Clarendon Press, 1995).

15

The Procedural Republic and the Unencumbered Self

Michael J. Sandel

Political philosophy seems often to reside at a distance from the world. Principles are one thing, politics another, and even our best efforts to "live up" to our ideals typically founder on the gap between theory and practice.[1]

But if political philosophy is unrealizable in one sense, it is unavoidable in another. This is the sense in which philosophy inhabits the world from the start; our practices and institutions are embodiments of theory. To engage in a political practice is already to stand in relation to theory.[2] For all our uncertainties about ultimate questions of political philosophy – of justice and value and the nature of the good life – the one thing we know is that we live *some* answer all the time.

In this essay I will try to explore the answer we live now, in contemporary America. What is the political philosophy implicit in our practices and institutions? How does it stand, as philosophy? And how do tensions in the philosophy find expression in our present political condition?

It may be objected that it is a mistake to look for a single philosophy, that we live no "answer," only answers. But a plurality of answers is itself a kind of answer. And the political theory that affirms this plurality is the theory I propose to explore.

The Right and the Good

We might begin by considering a certain moral and political vision. It is a liberal vision, and like most liberal visions gives pride of place to justice, fairness, and individual rights. Its core thesis is this: a just society seeks not to promote any particular ends, but enables its citizens to pursue their own ends, consistent with a similar liberty for all; it therefore must govern by principles that do not presuppose any particular conception of the good. What justifies these regulative principles above all is not that they maximize the general welfare, or cultivate virtue, or otherwise promote the good, but rather that they conform to the concept of *right*, a moral category given prior to the good, and independent of it.

This liberalism says, in other words, that what makes the just society just is not the *telos* or purpose or end at which it aims, but precisely its refusal to choose in advance among competing purposes and ends. In its constitution and its laws, the just society seeks to provide a framework within which its citizens can pursue their own values and ends, consistent with a similar liberty for others.

The ideal I've described might be summed up in the claim that the right is prior to the good, and in two senses: The priority of the right means first, that individual rights cannot be sacrificed for the sake of the general good (in this it opposes utilitarianism), and second, that the principles of justice that specify these rights cannot be premised on any particular vision of the good life. (In this it opposes teleological conceptions in general.)

This is the liberalism of much contemporary moral and political philosophy, most fully elaborated by Rawls, and indebted to Kant for its philosophical foundations.[3] But I am concerned here less with the lineage of this vision than with what seem to me three striking facts about it.

First, it has a deep and powerful philosophical appeal. Second, despite its philosophical force, the claim for the priority of the right over the good ultimately fails. And third, despite its philosophical failure, this liberal vision is the one by which we live. For us in late twentieth century America, it is our vision, the theory most thoroughly embodied in the practices and institutions most central to our public life. And seeing how it goes wrong as philosophy may help us to diagnose our present political condition. So first, its philosophical power; second, its philosophical failure; and third, however briefly, its uneasy embodiment in the world.

But before taking up these three claims, it is worth pointing out a central theme that connects them. And that is a certain conception of the person, of what it is to be a moral agent. Like all political theories, the liberal theory I have described is something more than a set of regulative principles. It is also a view about the way the world is, and the way we move within it. At the heart of this ethic lies a vision of the person that both inspires and undoes it. As I will try to argue now, what make this ethic so compelling, but also, finally, vulnerable, are the promise and the failure of the unencumbered self.

Kantian Foundations

The liberal ethic asserts the priority of right, and seeks principles of justice that do not presuppose any particular conception of the good.[4] This is what Kant means by the supremacy of the moral law, and what Rawls means when he writes that "justice is the first virtue of social institutions."[5] Justice is more than just another value. It provides the framework that *regulates* the play of competing values and ends; it must therefore have a sanction independent of those ends. But it is not obvious where such a sanction could be found.

Theories of justice, and for that matter, ethics, have typically founded their claims on one or another conception of human purposes and ends. Thus Aristotle said the measure of a *polis* is the good at which it aims, and even J.S. Mill, who in the nineteenth century called "justice the chief part, and incomparably the most binding part of all morality," made justice an instrument of utilitarian ends.[6]

This is the solution Kant's ethic rejects. Different persons typically have different desires and ends, and so any principle derived from them can only be contingent. But the moral law needs a *categorical* foundation, not a contingent one. Even so universal a desire as happiness will not do. People still differ in what happiness consists of, and to install any particular conception as regulative would impose on some the conceptions of others, and so deny at least to some the freedom to choose their *own* conceptions. In any case, to govern ourselves in conformity with desires and inclinations, given as they are by nature or circumstance, is not really to be *self*-governing at all. It is rather a refusal of freedom, a capitulation to determinations given outside us.

According to Kant, the right is "derived entirely from the concept of freedom in the external relationships of human beings, and has nothing to do with the end which all men have by nature [i.e., the aim of achieving happiness] or with the recognized means of attaining this end."[7] As such, it must have a basis prior to all empirical ends. Only when I am governed by principles that do not presuppose any particular ends am I free to pursue my own ends consistent with a similar freedom for all.

But this still leaves the question of what the basis of the right could possibly be. If it must be a basis prior to all purposes and ends, unconditioned even by what Kant calls "the special circumstances of human nature,"[8] where could such a basis conceivably be found? Given the stringent demands of the Kantian ethic, the moral law would seem almost to require a foundation in nothing, for any empirical precondition would undermine its priority. "Duty!" asks Kant at his most lyrical, "What origin is there worthy of thee, and where is to be found the root of thy noble descent which proudly rejects all kinship with the inclinations?"[9]

His answer is that the basis of the moral law is to be found in the *subject*, not the object of practical reason, a subject capable of an autonomous will. No empirical end, but rather "a subject of ends, namely a rational being himself, must be made the ground for all maxims of action."[10] Nothing other than what Kant calls "the subject of all possible ends himself" can give rise to the right, for only this subject is also the subject of an autonomous will. Only this subject could be that "something which elevates man above himself as part of the world of sense" and enables him to participate in an ideal, unconditioned realm wholly independent of our social and psychological inclinations. And only this thoroughgoing independence can afford us the detachment we need if we are ever freely to choose for ourselves, unconditioned by the vagaries of circumstance.[11]

Who or what exactly *is* this subject? It is, in a certain sense, *us*. The moral law, after all, is a law we give *ourselves*; we don't *find* it, we *will* it. That is how it (and we) escape the reign of nature and circumstance and merely empirical ends. But what is important to see is that the "we" who do the willing are not "we" qua particular persons, you and me, each for ourselves – the moral law is not up to us as individuals – but "we" qua participants in what Kant calls "pure practical reason," "we" qua participants in a transcendental subject.

Now what is to guarantee that I *am* a subject of this kind, capable of exercising pure practical reason? Well, strictly speaking, there *is* no guarantee; the transcendental subject is only a possibility. But it is a possibility I must *presuppose* if I am to think of myself as a free moral agent. Were I wholly an empirical being, I would not be capable of freedom, for every exercise of will would be conditioned by the desire for some object. All choice would be heteronomous choice, governed by the pursuit of some end. My will could never be a first cause, only the effect of some prior cause, the instrument of one or another impulse or inclination. "When we think of ourselves as free," writes Kant, "we transfer ourselves into the intelligible world as members and recognize the autonomy of the will."[12] And so the notion of a subject prior to and independent of experience, such as the Kantian ethic requires, appears not only possible but indispensable, a necessary presupposition of the possibility of freedom.

How does all of this come back to politics? As the subject is prior to its ends, so the right is prior to the good. Society is best arranged when it is governed by principles that do not presuppose any particular conception of the good, for any other arrangement would fail to respect persons as being capable of choice; it would treat them as objects rather than subjects, as means rather than ends in themselves.

We can see in this way how Kant's notion of the subject is bound up with the claim for the priority of right. But for those in the Anglo-American tradition, the transcendental subject will seem a strange foundation for a familiar ethic. Surely, one may think, we can take rights seriously and affirm the primacy of justice without embracing the *Critique of Pure Reason*. This, in any case, is the project of Rawls.

He wants to save the priority of right from the obscurity of the transcendental subject. Kant's idealist metaphysic, for all its moral and political advantage, cedes too much to the transcendent, and wins for justice its primacy only by denying it its human situation. "To develop a viable Kantian conception of justice," Rawls writes, "the force and content of Kant's doctrine must be detached from its background in transcendental idealism" and recast within the "canons of a reasonable empiricism."[13] And so Rawls' project is to preserve Kant's moral and political teaching by replacing Germanic obscurities with a domesticated metaphysic more congenial to the Anglo-American temper. This is the role of the original position.

From Transcendental Subject to Unencumbered Self

The original position tries to provide what Kant's transcendental argument cannot – a foundation for the right that is prior to the good, but still situated in the world. Sparing all but essentials, the original position works like this: It invites us to imagine the principles we would choose to govern our society if we were to choose them in advance, before we knew the particular persons we would be – whether rich or poor, strong or weak, lucky or unlucky – before we knew even our interests or aims or conceptions of the good. These principles – the ones we would choose in that imaginary situation – are the principles of justice. What is more, if it works, they are principles that do not presuppose any particular ends.

What they *do* presuppose is a certain picture of the person, of the way we must be if we are beings for whom justice is the first virtue. This is the picture of the unencumbered self, a self understood as prior to and independent of purposes and ends.

Now the unencumbered self describes first of all the way we stand toward the things we have, or want, or seek. It means there is always a distinction between the values I *have* and the person I *am*. To identify any characteristics as *my* aims, ambitions, desires, and so on, is always to imply some subject "me" standing behind them, at a certain distance, and the shape of this "me" must be given prior to any of the aims or attributes I bear. One consequence of this distance is to put the self *itself* beyond the reach of its experience, to secure its identity once and for all. Or to put the point another way, it rules out the possibility of what we might call *constitutive* ends. No role or commitment could define me so completely that I could not understand myself without it. No project could be so essential that turning away from it would call into question the person I am.

For the unencumbered self, what matters above all, what is most essential to our personhood, are not the ends we choose but our capacity to choose them. The original position sums up this central claim about us. "It is not our aims that primarily reveal our nature," writes Rawls, "but rather the principles that we would acknowledge to govern the background conditions under which these aims are to be formed... We should therefore reverse the relation between the right and the good proposed by teleological doctrines and view the right as prior."[14]

Only if the self is prior to its ends can the right be prior to the good. Only if my identity is never tied to the aims and interests I may have at any moment can I think of myself as a free and independent agent, capable of choice.

This notion of independence carries consequences for the kind of community of which we are capable. Understood as unencumbered selves, we are of course free to join in voluntary association with others, and so are capable of community in the cooperative sense. What is denied to the unencumbered self is the possibility of membership in any community bound by moral ties antecedent to choice; he cannot belong to any community where the self *itself* could be at stake. Such a community – call it constitutive as against merely cooperative – would engage the identity as well as the interests of the participants, and so implicate its members in a citizenship more thoroughgoing than the unencumbered self can know.

For justice to be primary, then, we must be creatures of a certain kind, related to human circumstance in a certain way. We must stand to our circumstance always at a certain distance, whether as transcendental subject in the case of Kant, or as unencumbered selves in the case of Rawls. Only in this way can we view ourselves as subjects as well as objects of experience, as agents and not just instruments of the purposes we pursue.

The unencumbered self and the ethic it inspires, taken together, hold out a liberating vision. Freed from the dictates of nature and the sanction of social roles, the human subject is installed as sovereign, cast as the author of the only moral meanings there are. As participants in pure practical reason, or as parties to the original position, we are free to construct principles of justice unconstrained by an order of value antecedently given. And as actual, individual selves, we are free to choose our purposes and ends unbound by such an order, or by custom or tradition or inherited status. So long as they are not unjust, our conceptions of the good carry weight, whatever they are, simply in virtue of our having chosen them. We are, in Rawls' words, "self-originating sources of valid claims."[15]

This is an exhilarating promise, and the liberalism it animates is perhaps the fullest expression of the Enlightenment's quest for the self-defining subject. But is it true? Can we make sense of our moral and political life by the light of the self-image it requires? I do not think we can, and I will try to show why not by arguing first within the liberal project, then beyond it.

Justice and Community

We have focused so far on the foundations of the liberal vision, on the way it derives the principles it defends. Let us turn briefly now to the substance of those principles, using Rawls as our example. Sparing all but essentials once again, Rawls' two principles of justice are these: first, equal basic liberties for all, and second, only those social and economic inequalities that benefit the least-advantaged members of society (the difference principle).

In arguing for these principles, Rawls argues against two familiar alternatives – utilitarianism and libertarianism. He argues against utilitarianism that it fails to take seriously the distinction between persons. In seeking to maximize the general welfare, the utilitarian treats society as a whole as if it were a single person; it conflates our many, diverse desires into a single system of desires, and tries to maximize. It is indifferent to the distribution of satisfactions among persons, except insofar as this may affect the overall sum. But this fails to respect our plurality and distinctness. It uses some as means to the happiness of all, and so fails to respect each as an end in himself. While utilitarians may sometimes defend individual rights, their defense must rest on the calculation that respecting those rights will serve utility in the long run. But this calculation is contingent and uncertain. So long as utility is what Mill said it is, "the ultimate appeal on all ethical questions,"[16] individual rights can never be secure. To avoid the danger that their life prospects might one day be sacrificed for the greater good of others, the parties to the original position therefore insist on certain basic liberties for all, and make those liberties prior.

If utilitarians fail to take seriously the distinctness of persons, libertarians go wrong by failing to acknowledge the arbitrariness of fortune. They define as just whatever distribution results from an efficient market economy, and oppose all redistribution on the grounds that people are entitled to whatever they get, so long as they do not cheat or steal or otherwise violate someone's rights in getting it. Rawls opposes this principle on the ground that the distribution of talents and assets and even efforts by which some get more and others get less is arbitrary from a moral point of view, a matter of good luck. To distribute the good things in life on the basis of these differences is not to do justice, but simply to carry over into human arrangements the arbitrariness of social and natural contingency. We deserve, as individuals, neither the talents our good fortune may have brought, nor the benefits that flow from them. We should therefore regard these talents as common assets, and regard one another as common beneficiaries of the rewards they bring. "Those who have been favored by nature, whoever they are, may gain from their good fortune only on terms that improve the situation of those who have lost out ... In justice as fairness, men agree to share one another's fate."[17]

This is the reasoning that leads to the difference principle. Notice how it reveals, in yet another guise, the logic of the unencumbered self. I cannot be said to deserve the benefits that flow from, say, my fine physique and good looks, because they are only accidental, not essential facts about me. They describe attributes I *have*, not the person I *am*, and so cannot give rise to a claim of desert. Being an unencumbered self, this is true of *everything* about me. And so I cannot, as an individual, deserve anything at all.

However jarring to our ordinary understandings this argument may be, the picture so far remains intact; the priority of right, the denial of desert, and the unencumbered self all hang impressively together.

But the difference principle requires more, and it is here that the argument comes undone. The difference principle begins with the thought, congenial to the unencumbered self, that the assets I have are only accidentally mine. But it ends by assuming that these assets are therefore *common* assets and that society has a prior claim on the fruits of their exercise. But this assumption is without warrant. Simply because I, as an individual, do not have a privileged claim on the assets accidentally residing "here," it does not follow that everyone in the world collectively does. For there is no reason to think that their location in society's province or, for that matter, within the province of humankind, is any *less* arbitrary from a moral point of view. And if their arbitrariness within *me* makes them ineligible to serve *my* ends, there seems no obvious reason why their arbitrariness within any particular society should not make them ineligible to serve that society's ends as well.

To put the point another way, the difference principle, like utilitarianism, is a principle of sharing. As such, it must presuppose some prior moral tie among those whose assets it would deploy and whose efforts it would enlist in a common endeavor. Otherwise, it is simply a formula for using some as means to others' ends, a formula this liberalism is committed to reject.

But on the cooperative vision of community alone, it is unclear what the moral basis for this sharing could be. Short of the constitutive conception, deploying an individual's assets for the sake of the common good would seem an offense against the "plurality and distinctness" of individuals this liberalism seeks above all to secure.

If those whose fate I am required to share really are, morally speaking, *others*, rather than fellow participants in a way of life with which my identity is bound, the difference principle falls prey to the same objections as utilitarianism. Its claim on me is not the claim of a constitutive community whose attachments I acknowledge, but rather the claim of a concatenated collectivity whose entanglements I confront.

What the difference principle requires, but cannot provide, is some way of identifying those *among* whom the assets I bear are properly regarded as common, some way of seeing ourselves as mutually indebted and morally engaged to begin with. But as we have seen, the constitutive aims and attachments that would save and situate the difference principle are precisely the ones denied to the liberal self; the moral encumbrances and antecedent obligations they imply would undercut the priority of right.

What, then, of those encumbrances? The point so far is that we cannot be persons for whom justice is primary, and also be persons for whom the difference principle is a principle of justice. But which must give way? Can we view ourselves as independent selves, independent in the sense that our identity is never tied to our aims and attachments?

I do not think we can, at least not without cost to those loyalties and convictions whose moral force consists partly in the fact that living by them is inseparable from understanding ourselves as the particular persons we are – as members of this family or community or nation or people, as bearers of that history, as citizens of this republic. Allegiances such as these are more than values I happen to have, and to hold, at a certain distance. They go beyond the obligations I voluntarily incur and the "natural duties" I owe to human beings as such. They allow that to some I owe more than justice requires or even permits, not by reason of agreements I have made but instead in virtue of those more or less enduring attachments and commitments that, taken together, partly define the person I am.

To imagine a person incapable of constitutive attachments such as these is not to conceive an ideally free and rational agent, but to imagine a person wholly without character, without moral depth. For to have character is to know that I move in a history I neither summon nor command, which carries consequences nonetheless for my choices and conduct. It draws me closer to some and more distant from others; it makes some aims more appropriate, others less so. As a self-interpreting being, I am able to reflect on my history and in this sense to distance myself from it, but the distance is always precarious and provisional, the point of reflection never finally secured outside the history itself. But the liberal ethic puts the self beyond the reach of its experience, beyond deliberation and reflection. Denied the expansive self-understandings that could shape a common life, the liberal self is left to lurch between detachment on the one hand, and entanglement on the other. Such is the fate of the unencumbered self, and its liberating promise.

The Procedural Republic

But before my case can be complete, I need to consider one powerful reply. While it comes from a liberal direction, its spirit is more practical than philosophical. It says, in short, that I am asking too much. It is one thing to seek constitutive attachments in our private lives; among families and friends, and certain tightly knit groups, there may be found a common good that makes justice and rights less pressing. But with public life – at least today, and probably always – it is different. So long as the nation-state is the primary form of political association, talk of constitutive community too easily suggests a darker politics rather than a brighter one; amid echoes of the moral majority, the priority of right, for all its philosophical faults, still seems the safer hope.

This is a challenging rejoinder, and no account of political community in the twentieth century can fail to take it seriously. It is challenging not least because it calls into question the status of political philosophy and its relation to the world. For if my argument is correct, if the liberal vision we have considered is not morally self-sufficient but parasitic on a notion of community it officially rejects, then we should expect to find that the political practice that embodies this vision is not *practically* self-sufficient either – that it must draw on a sense of community it cannot supply and may even undermine. But is that so far from the circumstance we face today? Could it be that through the original position darkly, on the far side of the veil of ignorance, we may glimpse an intimation of our predicament, a refracted vision of ourselves?

How does the liberal vision – and its failure – help us make sense of our public life and its predicament? Consider, to begin, the following paradox in the citizen's relation to the modern welfare state. In many ways, we in the 1980s stand near the completion of a liberal project that has run its course from the New Deal through the Great Society and into the present. But notwithstanding the extension of the franchise and the expansion of individual rights and entitlements in recent decades, there is a widespread sense that, individually and collectively, our control over the forces that govern our lives is receding rather than increasing. This sense is deepened by what appear simultaneously as the power and the powerlessness of the nation-state. On the one hand, increasing numbers of citizens view the state as an overly intrusive presence, more likely to frustrate their purposes than advance them. And yet, despite its unprecedented role in the economy and society, the modern state seems itself disempowered, unable effectively to control the domestic economy, to respond to persisting social ills, or to work America's will in the world.

This is a paradox that has fed the appeals of recent politicians (including Carter and Reagan), even as it has frustrated their attempts to govern. To sort it out, we need to identify the public philosophy implicit in our political practice, and to reconstruct its arrival. We need to trace the advent of the procedural republic, by which I mean a public life animated by the liberal vision and self-image we've considered.

The story of the procedural republic goes back in some ways to the founding of the republic, but its central drama begins to unfold around the turn of the century. As national markets and large-scale enterprise displaced a decentralized economy, the decentralized political forms of the early republic became outmoded as well. If democracy was to survive, the concentration of economic power would have to be met by a similar concentration of political power. But the Progressives understood, or some of them did, that the success of democracy required more than the centralization of government; it also required the nationalization of politics. The primary form of political community had to be a recast on a national scale. For Herbert Croly, writing in 1909, the "nationalizing of American political, economic, and social life" was "an essentially formative and enlightening political transformation." We would become more of a democracy only as we became "more of a nation . . . in ideas, in institutions, and in spirit."[18]

This nationalizing project would be consummated in the New Deal, but for the democratic tradition in America, the embrace of the nation was a decisive departure. From Jefferson to the populists, the party of democracy in American political debate had been, roughly speaking, the party of the provinces, of decentralized power, of small-town and small-scale America. And against them had stood the party of the nation – first Federalists, then Whigs, then the Republicans of Lincoln – a party that spoke for the consolidation of the union. It was thus the historic achievement of the New Deal to unite, in a single party and political program, what Samuel Beer has called "liberalism and the national idea."[19]

What matters for our purpose is that, in the twentieth century, liberalism made its peace with concentrated power. But it was understood at the start that the terms of this peace required a strong sense of national community, morally and politically to underwrite the extended involvements of a modern industrial order. If a virtuous republic of small-scale, democratic communities was no longer a possibility, a national republic seemed democracy's next best hope. This was still, in principle at least, a politics of the common good. It looked to the nation, not as a neutral framework for the play of competing interests, but rather as a formative community, concerned to shape a common life suited to the scale of modern social and economic forms.

But this project failed. By the mid- or late twentieth century, the national republic had run its course. Except for extraordinary moments, such as war, the nation proved too vast a scale across which to cultivate the shared self-understandings necessary to community in the formative, or constitutive sense. And so the gradual shift, in our practices and institutions, from a public philosophy of common purposes to one of fair procedures, from a politics of good to a politics of right, from the national republic to the procedural republic.

Our Present Predicament

A full account of this transition would take a detailed look at the changing shape of political institutions, constitutional interpretation, and the terms of political discourse in the broadest sense. But I suspect we would find in the *practice* of the procedural republic two broad tendencies foreshadowed by its philosophy: first, a tendency to crowd out democratic possibilities; second, a tendency to undercut the kind of community on which it nonetheless depends.

Where liberty in the early republic was understood as a function of democratic institutions and dispersed power,[20] liberty in the procedural republic is defined in opposition to democracy, as an individual's guarantee against what the majority might will. I am free insofar as I am the bearer of rights, where rights are trumps.[21] Unlike the liberty of the early republic, the modern version permits – in fact even requires – concentrated power. This has to do with the universalizing logic of rights. Insofar as I have a right, whether to free speech or a minimum income, its provision cannot be left to the vagaries of local preferences but must be assured at the most comprehensive level of political association. It cannot be one thing in New York and another in Alabama. As rights and entitlements expand, politics is therefore displaced from smaller forms of association and relocated at the most universal form – in our case, the nation. And even as politics flows to the nation, power shifts away from democratic institutions (such as legislatures and political parties) and toward institutions designed to be insulated from democratic pressures, and hence better equipped to dispense and defend individual rights (notably the judiciary and bureaucracy).

These institutional developments may begin to account for the sense of powerlessness that the welfare state fails to address and in some ways doubtless deepens. But it seems to me a further clue to our condition that recalls even more directly the predicament of the unencumbered self – lurching, as we left it, between detachment on the one hand, the entanglement on the other. For it is a striking feature of the welfare state that it offers a powerful promise of individual rights, and also demands of its citizens a high measure of mutual engagement. But the self-image that attends the rights cannot sustain the engagement.

As bearers of rights, where rights are trumps, we think of ourselves as freely choosing, individual selves, unbound by obligations antecedent to rights, or to the agreements we make. And yet, as citizens of the procedural republic that secures these rights, we find ourselves implicated willy-nilly in a formidable array of dependencies and expectations we did not choose and increasingly reject.

In our public life, we are more entangled, but less attached, than ever before. It is as though the unencumbered self presupposed by the liberal ethic had begun to come true – less liberated than disempowered, entangled in a network of obligations and involvements unassociated with any act of will, and yet unmediated by those common identifications or expansive self-definitions that would make them tolerable. As the scale of social and political organization has become more comprehensive, the terms of our collective identity have become more fragmented, and the forms of political life have outrun the common purpose needed to sustain them.

Something like this, it seems to me, has been unfolding in America for the past half-century or so. I hope I have said at least enough to suggest the shape a fuller story might take. And I hope in any case to have conveyed a certain view about politics and philosophy and the relation between them – that our practices and institutions are themselves embodiments of theory, and to unravel their predicament is, at least in part, to seek after the self-image of the age.

Notes

1 An excellent example of this view can be found in Samuel Huntington, *American Politics: The Promise of Disharmony* (Cambridge: Harvard University Press, 1981). See especially his discussion of the "ideals versus institutions" gap, pp. 10–12, 39–41, 61–84, 221–62.

2 See, for example, the conceptions of a "practice" advanced by Alasdair MacIntyre and Charles Taylor. MacIntyre, *After Virtue* (Notre Dame: University of Notre Dame Press, 1981), pp. 175–209. Taylor, "Interpretation and the Sciences of Man," *Review of Metaphysics* 25, (1971): 3–51.

3 John Rawls, *A Theory of Justice* (Oxford: Oxford University Press, 1972). Immanuel Kant, *Groundwork of the Metaphysics of Morals*, trans. H. J. Paton. (1785; New York: Harper & Row, 1956). Kant, *Critique of Pure Reason*, trans. Norman Kemp Smith (1781, 1787; London: Macmillan, 1929). Kant, *Critique of Practical Reason*, trans. L. W. Beck (1788; Indianapolis: Bobbs-Merrill, 1956). Kant, "On the Common Saying: 'This May Be True in Theory, But It Does Not Apply in Practice,'" in Hans Reiss, ed., *Kant's Political Writings* (1793; Cambridge: Cambridge University Press, 1970). Other recent versions of the claim for the priority of the right over good can be found in Robert Nozick, *Anarchy, State and Utopia* (New York: Basic Books, 1974); Ronald Dworkin, *Taking Rights Seriously* (London: Duckworth, 1977); Bruce Ackerman, *Social Justice in the Liberal State* (New Haven: Yale University Press, 1980).

4 This section, and the two that follow, summarize arguments developed more fully in Michael Sandel, *Liberalism and the Limits of Justice* (Cambridge: Cambridge University Press, 1982).

5 Rawls (1971), p. 3.

6 John Stuart Mill, *Utilitarianism*, in *The Utilitarians* (1893; Garden City: Doubleday, 1973), p. 465. Mill, *On Liberty*, in *The Utilitarians*, p. 485 (originally published 1849).

7 Kant (1793), p. 73.

8 Kant (1785), p. 92.

9 Kant (1788), p. 89.

10 Kant (1785), p. 105.

11 Kant (1788), p. 89.

12 Kant (1785), p. 121.

13 Rawls, "The Basic Structure as Subject," *American Philosophical Quarterly* (1977): 165.

14 Rawls (1971), p. 560.

15 Rawls, "Kantian Constructivism in Moral Theory," *Journal of Philosophy* 77 (1980): 543.

16 Mill (1849), p. 485.

17 Rawls (1971), pp. 101–2.

18 Croly, *The Promise of American Life* (Indianapolis: Bobbs-Merrill, 1965), pp. 270–3.

19 Beer, "Liberalism and the National Idea," *The Public Interest*, Fall (1966): 70–82.

20 See, for example, Laurence Tribe, *American Constitutional Law* (Mineola: The Foundation Press, 1978), pp. 2–3.

21 See Ronald Dworkin, "Liberalism," in Stuart Hampshire, ed., *Public and Private Morality* (Cambridge: Cambridge University Press, 1978), p. 136.

16

Polity and Group Difference: A Critique of the Ideal of Universal Citizenship

Iris Marion Young

An ideal of universal citizenship has driven the emancipatory momentum of modern political life. Ever since the bourgeoisie challenged aristocratic privileges by claiming equal political rights for citizens as such, women, workers, Jews, blacks, and others have pressed for inclusion in that citizenship status. Modern political theory asserted the equal moral worth of all persons, and social movements of the oppressed took this seriously as implying the inclusion of all persons in full citizenship status under the equal protection of the law.

Citizenship for everyone, and everyone the same qua citizen. Modern political thought generally assumed that the universality of citizenship in the sense of citizenship for all implies a universality of citizenship in the sense that citizenship status transcends particularity and difference. Whatever the social or group differences among citizens, whatever their inequalities of wealth, status, and power in the everyday activities of civil society, citizenship gives everyone the same status as peers in the political public. With equality conceived as sameness, the ideal of universal citizenship carries at least two meanings in addition to the extension of citizenship to everyone: (*a*) universality defined as general in opposition to particular; what citizens have in common as opposed to how they differ, and (*b*) universality in the sense of laws and rules that say the same for all and apply to all in the same way; laws and rules that are blind to individual and group differences.

During this angry, sometimes bloody, political struggle in the nineteenth and twentieth centuries, many among the excluded and disadvantaged thought that winning full citizenship status, that is, equal political and civil rights, would lead to their freedom and equality. Now in the late twentieth century, however, when citizenship rights have been formally extended to all groups in liberal capitalist societies, some groups still find themselves treated as second-class citizens. Social movements of oppressed and excluded groups have recently asked why extension of equal citizenship rights has not led to social justice and equality. Part of the answer is straightforwardly Marxist: those social activities that most determine the status of individuals and groups are anarchic and oligarchic; economic life is not sufficiently under the control of citizens to affect the unequal status and treatment of groups. I think this is an important and correct diagnosis of why equal citizenship has not eliminated oppression, but in this article I reflect on another reason more intrinsic to the meaning of politics and citizenship as expressed in much modern thought.

The assumed link between citizenship for everyone, on the one hand, and the two other senses of citizenship – having a common life with and being treated in the same way as the other citizens – on the other, is itself a problem. Contemporary social movements of the oppressed have weakened the link. They assert a positivity and pride in group specificity against ideals of assimilation. They have

Originally published in *Ethics* 99 (1989): 250–74. Copyright © 1989 by the University of Chicago Press. Reprinted by permission of the University of Chicago Press.

also questioned whether justice always means that law and policy should enforce equal treatment for all groups. Embryonic in these challenges lies a concept of *differentiated* citizenship as the best way to realize the inclusion and participation of everyone in full citizenship.

In this article I argue that far from implying one another, the universality of citizenship, in the sense of the inclusion and participation of everyone, stands in tension with the other two meanings of universality embedded in modern political ideas: universality as generality, and universality as equal treatment. First, the ideal that the activities of citizenship express or create a general will that transcends the particular differences of group affiliation, situation, and interest has in practice excluded groups judged not capable of adopting that general point of view; the idea of citizenship as expressing a general will has tended to enforce a homogeneity of citizens. To the degree that contemporary proponents of revitalized citizenship retain that idea of a general will and common life, they implicitly support the same exclusions and homogeneity. Thus I argue that the inclusion and participation of everyone in public discussion and decision making requires mechanisms for group representation. Second, where differences in capacities, culture, values, and behavioral styles exist among groups, but some of these groups are privileged, strict adherence to a principle of equal treatment tends to perpetuate oppression or disadvantage. The inclusion and participation of everyone in social and political institutions therefore sometimes requires the articulation of special rights that attend to group differences in order to undermine oppression and disadvantage.

I Citizenship as Generality

Many contemporary political theorists regard capitalist welfare society as depoliticized. Its interest group pluralism privatizes policy-making, consigning it to back-room deals and autonomous regulatory agencies and groups. Interest group pluralism fragments both policy and the interests of the individual, making it difficult to assess issues in relation to one another and set priorities. The fragmented and privatized nature of the political process, moreover, facilitates the dominance of the more powerful interests.[1]

In response to this privatization of the political process, many writers call for a renewed public life

and a renewed commitment to the virtues of citizenship. Democracy requires that citizens of welfare corporate society awake from their privatized consumerist slumbers, challenge the experts who claim the sole right to rule, and collectively take control of their lives and institutions through processes of active discussion that aim at reaching collective decisions.[2] In participatory democratic institutions citizens develop and exercise capacities of reasoning, discussion, and socializing that otherwise lie dormant, and they move out of their private existence to address others and face them with respect and concern for justice. Many who invoke the virtues of citizenship in opposition to the privatization of politics in welfare capitalist society assume as models for contemporary public life the civic humanism of thinkers such as Machiavelli or, more often, Rousseau.[3]

With these social critics I agree that interest group pluralism, because it is privatized and fragmented, facilitates the domination of corporate, military, and other powerful interests. With them I think democratic processes require the institutionalization of genuinely public discussion. There are serious problems, however, with uncritically assuming as a model the ideals of the civic public that come to us from the tradition of modern political thought.[4] The ideal of the public realm of citizenship as expressing a general will, a point of view and interest that citizens have in common which transcends their differences, has operated in fact as a demand for homogeneity among citizens. The exclusion of groups defined as different was explicitly acknowledged before this century. In our time, the excluding consequences of the universalist ideal of a public that embodies a common will are more subtle, but they still obtain.

The tradition of civic republicanism stands in critical tension with the individualist contract theory of Hobbes or Locke. Where liberal individualism regards the state as a necessary instrument to mediate conflict and regulate action so that individuals can have the freedom to pursue their private ends, the republican tradition locates freedom and autonomy in the actual public activities of citizenship. By participating in public discussion and collective decision making, citizens transcend their particular self-interested lives and the pursuit of private interests to adopt a general point of view from which they agree on the common good. Citizenship is an expression of the universality of human life; it is a realm of rationality and freedom as opposed to the heteronomous realm of particular need, interest, and desire.

Nothing in this understanding of citizenship as universal as opposed to particular, common as opposed to differentiated, implies extending full citizenship status to all groups. Indeed, at least some modern republicans thought just the contrary. While they extolled the virtues of citizenship as expressing the universality of humanity, they consciously excluded some people from citizenship on the grounds that they could not adopt the general point of view, or that their inclusion would disperse and divide the public. The ideal of a common good, a general will, a shared public life leads to pressures for a homogeneous citizenry.

Feminists in particular have analyzed how the discourse that links the civic public with fraternity is not merely metaphorical. Founded by men, the modern state and its public realm of citizenship paraded as universal values and norms which were derived from specifically masculine experience: militarist norms of honor and homoerotic camaraderie; respectful competition and bargaining among independent agents; discourse framed in unemotional tones of dispassionate reason.

Several commentators have argued that in extolling the virtues of citizenship as participation in a universal public realm, modern men expressed a flight from sexual difference, from having to recognize another kind of existence that they could not entirely understand, and from the embodiment, dependency on nature, and morality that women represent.[5] Thus the opposition between the universality of the public realm of citizenship and the particularity of private interest became conflated with oppositions between reason and passion, masculine and feminine.

The bourgeois world instituted a moral division of labor between reason and sentiment, identifying masculinity with reason and femininity with sentiment, desire, and the needs of the body. Extolling a public realm of manly virtue and citizenship as independence, generality, and dispassionate reason entailed creating the private sphere of the family as the place to which emotion, sentiment, and bodily needs must be confined.[6] The generality of the public thus depends on excluding women, who are responsible for tending to that private realm, and who lack the dispassionate rationality and independence required of good citizens.

In his social scheme, for example, Rousseau excluded women from the public realm of citizenship because they are the caretakers of affectivity, desire, and the body. If we allowed appeals to

desires and bodily needs to move public debates, we would undermine public deliberation by fragmenting its unity. Even within the domestic realm, moreover, women must be dominated. Their dangerous, heterogeneous sexuality must be kept chaste and confined to marriage. Enforcing chastity on women will keep each family a separated unity, preventing the chaos and blood mingling that would be produced by illegitimate children. Chaste, enclosed women in turn oversee men's desire by tempering its potentially disruptive impulses through moral education. Men's desire for women itself threatens to shatter and disperse the universal, rational realm of the public, as well as to disrupt the neat distinction between the public and private. As guardians of the private realm of need, desire, and affectivity, women must ensure that men's impulses do not subvert the universality of reason. The moral neatness of the female-tended hearth, moreover, will temper the possessively individualistic impulses of the particularistic realm of business and commerce, since competition, like sexuality, constantly threatens to explode the unity of the polity.[7]

It is important to recall that universality of citizenship conceived as generality operated to exclude not only women, but other groups as well. European and American republicans found little contradiction in promoting a universality of citizenship that excluded some groups, because the idea that citizenship is the same for all translated in practice to the requirement that all citizens be the same. The white male bourgeoisie conceived republican virtue as rational, restrained, and chaste, not yielding to passion or desire for luxury, and thus able to rise above desire and need to a concern for the common good. This implied excluding poor people and wage workers from citizenship on the grounds that they were too motivated by need to adopt a general perspective. The designers of the American constitution were no more egalitarian than their European brethren in this respect; they specifically intended to restrict the access of the laboring class to the public, because they feared disruption of commitment to the general interests.

These early American republicans were also quite explicit about the need for the homogeneity of citizens, fearing that group differences would tend to undermine commitment to the general interest. This meant that the presence of blacks and Indians, and later Mexicans and Chinese, in the territories of the republic posed a threat that only assimilation, extermination, or dehumanization could thwart. Various combinations of these three were used, of course, but recognition of these groups as peers in the public was never an option. Even such republican fathers as Jefferson identified the red and black people in their territories with wild nature and passion, just as they feared that women outside the domestic realm were wanton and avaricious. They defined moral, civilized republican life in opposition to this backward-looking, uncultivated desire that they identified with women and nonwhites.[8] A similar logic of exclusion operated in Europe, where Jews were particular targets.[9]

These republican exclusions were not accidental, nor were they inconsistent with the ideal of universal citizenship as understood by these theorists. They were a direct consequence of a dichotomy between public and private that defined the public as a realm of generality in which all particularities are left behind, and defined the private as the particular, the realm of affectivity, affiliation, need, and the body. As long as that dichotomy is in place, the inclusion of the formerly excluded in the definition of citizenship – women, workers, Jews, blacks, Asians, Indians, Mexicans – imposes a homogeneity that suppresses group differences in the public and in practice forces the formerly excluded groups to be measured according to norms derived from and defined by privileged groups.

Contemporary critics of interest group liberalism who call for a renewed public life certainly do not intend to exclude any adult persons or groups from citizenship. They are democrats, convinced that only the inclusion and participation of all citizens in political life will make for wise and fair decisions and a polity that enhances rather than inhibits the capacities of its citizens and their relations with one another. The emphasis by such participatory democrats on generality and commonness, however, still threatens to suppress differences among citizens.

I shall focus on the text of Benjamin Barber, who, in his book *Strong Democracy*, produces a compelling and concrete vision of participatory democratic processes. Barber recognizes the need to safeguard a democratic public from intended or inadvertent group exclusions, though he offers no proposals for safeguarding the inclusion and participation of everyone. He also argues fiercely against contemporary political theorists who construct a model of political discourse purified of

affective dimensions. Thus Barber does not fear the disruption of the generality and rationality of the public by desire and the body in the way that nineteenth-century republican theorists did. He retains, however, a conception of the civic public as defined by generality, as opposed to group affinity and particular need and interest. He makes a clear distinction between the public realm of citizenship and civic activity, on the one hand, and a private realm of particular identities, roles, affiliations, and interests on the other. Citizenship by no means exhausts people's social identities, but it takes moral priority over all social activities in a strong democracy. The pursuit of particular interests, the pressing of the claims of particular groups, all must take place within a framework of community and common vision established by the public realm. Thus Barber's vision of participatory democracy continues to rely on an opposition between the public sphere of a general interest and a private sphere of particular interest and affiliation.[10]

While recognizing the need for majority rule procedures and means of safeguarding minority rights, Barber asserts that "the strong democrat regrets every division and regards the existence of majorities as a sign that mutualism has failed" (p. 207). A community of citizens, he says, "owes the character of its existence to what its constituent members have in common" (p. 232), and this entails transcending the order of individual needs and wants to recognize that "we are a moral body whose existence depends on the common ordering of individual needs and wants into a single vision of the future in which all can share" (p. 224). This common vision is not imposed on individuals from above, however, but is forged by them in talking and working together. Barber's models of such common projects, however, reveal his latent biases: "Like players on a team or soldiers at war, those who practice a common politics may come to feel ties that they never felt before they commenced their common activity. This sort of bonding, which emphasizes common procedures, common work, and a shared sense of what a community needs to succeed, rather than monolithic purposes and ends, serves strong democracy most successfully" (p. 244).

The attempt to realize an ideal of universal citizenship that finds the public embodying generality as opposed to particularity, commonness versus difference, will tend to exclude or to put at a disadvantage some groups, even when they have formally equal citizenship status. The idea of the public as universal and the concomitant identification of particularity with privacy makes homogeneity a requirement of public participation. In exercising their citizenship, all citizens should assume the same impartial, general point of view transcending all particular interests, perspectives, and experiences.

But such an impartial general perspective is a myth.[11] People necessarily and properly consider public issues in terms influenced by their situated experience and perception of social relations. Different social groups have different needs, cultures, histories, experiences, and perceptions of social relations which influence their interpretation of the meaning and consequences of policy proposals and influence the form of their political reasoning. These differences in political interpretation are not merely or even primarily a result of differing or conflicting interests, for groups have differing interpretations even when they seek to promote justice and not merely their own self-regarding ends. In a society where some groups are privileged while others are oppressed, insisting that as citizens persons should leave behind their particular affiliations and experiences to adopt a general point of view serves only to reinforce that privilege; for the perspectives and interests of the privileged will tend to dominate this unified public, marginalizing or silencing those of other groups.

Barber asserts that responsible citizenship requires transcending particular affiliations, commitments, and needs, because a public cannot function if its members are concerned only with their private interests. Here he makes an important confusion between plurality and privatization. The interest group pluralism that he and others criticize indeed institutionalizes and encourages an egoistic, self-regarding view of the political process, one that sees parties entering the political competition for scarce goods and privileges only in order to maximize their own gain, and therefore they need not listen to or respond to the claims of others who have their own point of view. The processes and often the outcomes of interest group bargaining, moreover, take place largely in private; they are neither revealed nor discussed in a forum that genuinely involves all those potentially affected by decisions.

Privacy in this sense of private bargaining for the sake of private gain is quite different from plurality, in the sense of the differing group experiences, affiliations, and commitments that operate in any large society. It is possible for persons to maintain their group identity and to be influenced by their perceptions of social events derived from their group-specific experience, and at the same time to be public spirited, in the sense of being open to listening to the claims of others and not being concerned for their own gain alone. It is possible and necessary for people to take a critical distance from their own immediate desires and gut reactions in order to discuss public proposals. Doing so, however, cannot require that citizens abandon their particular affiliations, experiences, and social location. As I will discuss in the next section, having the voices of particular group perspectives other than one's own explicitly represented in public discussion best fosters the maintenance of such critical distance without the pretense of impartiality.

A repoliticization of public life should not require the creation of a unified public realm in which citizens leave behind their particular group affiliations, histories, and needs to discuss a general interest or common good. Such a desire for unity suppresses but does not eliminate differences and tends to exclude some perspectives from the public.[12] Instead of a universal citizenship in the sense of this generality, we need a group differentiated citizenship and a heterogeneous public. In a heterogeneous public, differences are publicly recognized and acknowledged as irreducible, by which I mean that persons from one perspective or history can never completely understand and adopt the point of view of those with other group-based perspectives and histories. Yet commitment to the need and desire to decide together the society's policies fosters communication across those differences.

II Differentiated Citizenship as Group Representation

In her study of the functioning of a New England Town Meeting government, Jane Mansbridge discusses how women, blacks, working-class people, and poor people tend to participate less and have their interests represented less than whites, middle-class professionals, and men. Even though all citizens have the right to participate in the decision-making process, the experience and perspectives of some groups tend to be silenced for many reasons. White middle-class men assume authority more than others and they are more practiced at speaking persuasively; mothers and old people often find it more difficult than others to get to meetings.[13] Amy Gutmann also discusses how participatory democratic structures tend to silence disadvantaged groups. She offers the example of community control of schools, where increased democracy led to increased segregation in many cities because the more privileged and articulate whites were able to promote their perceived interests against blacks' just demand for equal treatment in an integrated system.[14] Such cases indicate that when participatory democratic structures define citizenship in universalistic and unified terms, they tend to reproduce existing group oppression.

Gutmann argues that such oppressive consequences of democratization imply that social and economic equality must be achieved before political equality can be instituted. I cannot quarrel with the value of social and economic equality, but I think its achievement depends on increasing political equality as much as the achievement of political equality depends on increasing social and economic equality. If we are not to be forced to trace a utopian circle, we need to solve now the "paradox of democracy" by which social power makes some citizens more equal than others, and equality of citizenship makes some people more powerful citizens. That solution lies at least in part in providing institutionalized means for the explicit recognition and representation of oppressed groups. Before discussing principles and practices involved in such a solution, however, it is necessary to say something about what a group is and when a group is oppressed.

The concept of a social group has become politically important because recent emancipatory and leftist social movements have mobilized around group identity rather than exclusively class or economic interests. In many cases such mobilization has consisted in embracing and positively defining a despised or devalued ethnic or racial identity. In the women's movement, gay rights movement, or elders' movements, differential social status based on age, sexuality, physical capacity, or the division of labor has been taken up as a positive group identity for political mobilization.

I shall not attempt to define a social group here, but I shall point to several marks which distinguish a social group from other collectivities of people. A social group involves first of all an affinity with other persons by which they identify with one another, and by which other people identify them. A person's particular sense of history,

understanding of social relations and personal possibilities, her or his mode of reasoning, values, and expressive styles are constituted at least partly by her or his group identity. Many group definitions come from the outside, from other groups that label and stereotype certain people. In such circumstances the despised group members often find their affinity in their oppression. The concept of social group must be distinguished from two concepts with which it might be confused: aggregate and association.

An aggregate is any classification of persons according to some attribute. Persons can be aggregated according to any number of attributes, all of them equally arbitrary – eye color, the make of car we drive, the street we live on. At times the groups that have emotional and social salience in our society are interpreted as aggregates, as arbitrary classifications of persons according to attributes of skin color, genitals, or years lived. A social group, however, is not defined primarily by a set of shared attributes, but by the sense of identity that people have. What defines black Americans as a social group is not primarily their skin color; this is exemplified by the fact that some persons whose skin color is fairly light, for example, identify as black. Though sometimes objective attributes are a necessary condition for classifying oneself or others as a member of a certain social group, it is the identification of certain persons with a social status, a common history that social status produces, and a self-identification that defines the group as a group.

Political and social theorists tend more often to elide social groups with associations rather than aggregates. By an association I mean a collectivity of persons who come together voluntarily – such as a club, corporation, political party, church, college, union, lobbying organization, or interest group. An individualist contract model of society applies to associations but not to groups. Individuals constitute associations; they come together as already formed persons and set them up, establishing rules, positions, and offices.

Since one joins an association, even if membership in it fundamentally affects one's life, one does not take that association membership to define one's very identity in the way, for example, being Navajo might. Group affinity, on the other hand, has the character of what Heidegger calls "thrownness": one finds oneself as a member of a group, whose existence and relations one experiences as always already having been. For a person's identity is defined in relation to how others identify him or her, and others do so in terms of groups which always already have specific attributes, stereotypes, and norms associated with them, in reference to which a person's identity will be formed. From the thrownness of group affinity it does not follow that one cannot leave groups and enter new ones. Many women become lesbian after identifying as heterosexual, and anyone who lives long enough becomes old. These cases illustrate thrownness precisely in that such changes in group affinity are experienced as a transformation in one's identity.

A social group should not be understood as an essence or nature with a specific set of common attributes. Instead, group identity should be understood in relational terms. Social processes generate groups by creating relational differentiations, situations of clustering and affective bonding in which people feel affinity for other people. Sometimes groups define themselves by despising or excluding others whom they define as other, and whom they dominate and oppress. Although social processes of affinity and separation define groups, they do not give groups a substantive identity. There is no common nature that members of a group have.

As products of social relations, groups are fluid; they come into being and may fade away. Homosexual practices have existed in many societies and historical periods, for example, but gay male group identification has existed only in the West since the twentieth century. Group identity may become salient only under specific circumstances, when in interaction with other groups. Most people in modern societies have multiple group identifications, moreover, and therefore groups themselves are not discrete unities. Every group has group differences cutting across it.

I think that group differentiation is an inevitable and desirable process in modern societies. We need not settle that question, however. I merely assume that ours is now a group differentiated society, and that it will continue to be so for some time to come. Our political problem is that some of our groups are privileged and others are oppressed.

But what is oppression? In another place I give a fuller account of the concept of oppression.[15] Briefly, a group is oppressed when one or more of the following conditions occurs to all or a large portion of its members: (1) the benefits of their work or energy go to others without those others

reciprocally benefiting them (exploitation); (2) they are excluded from participation in major social activities, which in our society means primarily a workplace (marginalization); (3) they live and work under the authority of others, and have little work autonomy and authority over others themselves (powerlessness); (4) as a group they are stereotyped at the same time that their experience and situation is invisible in the society in general, and they have little opportunity and little audience for the expression of their experience and perspective on social events (cultural imperialism); (5) group members suffer random violence and harassment motivated by group hatred or fear. In the United States today at least the following groups are oppressed in one or more of these ways: women, blacks, Native Americans, Chicanos, Puerto Ricans and other Spanish-speaking Americans, Asian Americans, gay men, lesbians, working-class people, poor people, old people, and mentally and physically disabled people.

Perhaps in some utopian future there will be a society without group oppression and disadvantage. We cannot develop political principles by starting with the assumption of a completely just society, however, but must begin from within the general historical and social conditions in which we exist. This means that we must develop participatory democratic theory not on the assumption of an undifferentiated humanity, but rather on the assumption that there are group differences and that some groups are actually or potentially oppressed or disadvantaged.

I assert, then, the following principle: a democratic public, however that is constituted, should provide mechanisms for the effective representation and recognition of the distinct voices and perspectives of those of its constituent groups that are oppressed or disadvantaged within it. Such group representation implies institutional mechanisms and public resources supporting three activities: (1) self-organization of group members so that they gain a sense of collective empowerment and a reflective understanding of their collective experience and interests in the context of the society; (2) voicing a group's analysis of how social policy proposals affect them, and generating policy proposals themselves, in institutionalized contexts where decision makers are obliged to show that they have taken these perspectives into consideration; (3) having veto power regarding specific policies that affect a group directly, for example, reproductive rights for women, or use of reservation lands for Native Americans.

The principles call for specific representation only for oppressed or disadvantaged groups, because privileged groups already are represented. Thus the principle would not apply in a society entirely without oppression. I do not regard the principle as merely provisional, or instrumental, however, because I believe that group difference in modern complex societies is both inevitable and desirable, and that wherever there is group difference, disadvantage or oppression always looms as a possibility. Thus a society should always be committed to representation for oppressed or disadvantaged groups and ready to implement such representation when it appears. These considerations are rather academic in our own context, however, since we live in a society with deep group oppressions the complete elimination of which is only a remote possibility.

Social and economic privilege means, among other things, that the groups which have it behave as though they have a right to speak and be heard, that others treat them as though they have that right, and that they have the material, personal, and organizational resources that enable them to speak and be heard in public. The privileged are usually not inclined to protect and further the interests of the oppressed partly because their social position prevents them from understanding those interests, and partly because to some degree their privilege depends on the continued oppression of others. So a major reason for explicit representation of oppressed groups in discussion and decision making is to undermine oppression. Such group representation also exposes in public the specificity of the assumptions and experience of the privileged. For unless confronted with different perspectives on social relations and events, different values and language, most people tend to assert their own perspective as universal.

Theorists and politicians extol the virtues of citizenship because through public participation persons are called on to transcend merely self-centered motivation and acknowledge their dependence on and responsibility to others. The responsible citizen is concerned not merely with interests but with justice, with acknowledging that each other person's interest and point of view is as good as his or her own, and that the needs and interests of everyone must be voiced and be heard by the others, who must acknowledge, respect, and address those needs and interests. The problem of universality has occurred when this responsibility has been interpreted as transcendence into a general perspective.

I have argued that defining citizenship as generality avoids and obscures this requirement that all experiences, needs, and perspectives on social events have a voice and are respected. A general perspective does not exist which all persons can adopt and from which all experiences and perspectives can be understood and taken into account. The existence of social groups implies different, though not necessarily exclusive, histories, experiences, and perspectives on social life that people have, and it implies that they do not entirely understand the experience of other groups. No one can claim to speak in the general interest, because no one of the groups can speak for another, and certainly no one can speak for them all. Thus the only way to have all group experience and social perspectives voiced, heard, and taken account of is to have them specifically represented in the public.

Group representation is the best means to promote just outcomes to democratic decision-making processes. The argument for this claim relies on Habermas's conception of communicative ethics. In the absence of a Philosopher King who reads transcendent normative verities, the only ground for a claim that a policy or decision is just is that it has been arrived at by a public which has truly promoted free expression of all needs and points of view. In his formulation of a communicative ethic, Habermas retains inappropriately an appeal to a universal or impartial point of view from which claims in a public should be addressed. A communicative ethic that does not merely articulate a hypothetical public that would justify decisions, but proposes actual conditions tending to promote just outcomes of decision-making processes, should promote conditions for the expression of the concrete needs of all individuals in their particularity.[16] The concreteness of individual lives, their needs and interests, and their perception of the needs and interests of others, I have argued, are structured partly through group-based experience and identity. Thus full and free expression of concrete needs and interests under social circumstances where some groups are silenced or marginalized requires that they have a specific voice in deliberation and decision making.

The introduction of such differentiation and particularity into democratic procedures does not encourage the expression of narrow self-interest;

indeed, group representation is the best antidote to self-deceiving self-interest masked as an impartial or general interest. In a democratically structured public where social inequality is mitigated through group representation, individuals or groups cannot simply assert that they want something; they must say that justice requires or allows that they have it. Group representation provides the opportunity for some to express their needs or interests who would not likely be heard without that representation. At the same time, the test of whether a claim on the public is just, or a mere expression of self-interest, is best made when persons making it must confront the opinion of others who have explicitly different, though not necessarily conflicting, experiences, priorities, and needs. As a person of social privilege, I am not likely to go outside of myself and have a regard for social justice unless I am forced to listen to the voice of those my privilege tends to silence.

Group representation best institutionalizes fairness under circumstances of social oppression and domination. But group representation also maximizes knowledge expressed in discussion, and thus promotes practical wisdom. Group differences not only involve different needs, interests, and goals, but probably more important different social locations and experiences from which social facts and policies are understood. Members of different social groups are likely to know different things about the structure of social relations and the potential and actual effects of social policies. Because of their history, their group-specific values or modes of expression, their relationship to other groups, the kind of work they do, and so on, different groups have different ways of understanding the meaning of social events, which can contribute to the others' understanding if expressed and heard.

Emancipatory social movements in recent years have developed some political practices committed to the idea of a heterogeneous public, and they have at least partly or temporarily instituted such publics. Some political organizations, unions, and feminist groups have formal caucuses for groups (such as blacks, Latinos, women, gay men and lesbians, and disabled or old people) whose perspectives might be silenced without them. Frequently these organizations have procedures for caucus voice in organization discussion and caucus representation in decision making, and some organizations also require representation of members of specific groups in leadership bodies. Under the influence of these social movements asserting group difference, during some years even the Democratic party, at both national and state levels, has instituted delegate rules that include provisions for group representation.

Though its realization is far from assured, the ideal of a "rainbow coalition" expresses such a heterogeneous public with forms of group representation. The traditional form of coalition corresponds to the idea of a unified public that transcends particular differences of experience and concern. In traditional coalitions, diverse groups work together for ends which they agree interest or affect them all in a similar way, and they generally agree that the differences of perspective, interests, or opinion among them will not surface in the public statements and actions of the coalition. In a rainbow coalition, by contrast, each of the constituent groups affirms the presence of the others and affirms the specificity of its experience and perspective on social issues.[17] In the rainbow public, blacks do not simply tolerate the participation of gays, labor activists do not grudgingly work alongside peace movement veterans, and none of these paternalistically allow feminist participation. Ideally, a rainbow coalition affirms the presence and supports the claims of each of the oppressed groups or political movements constituting it, and it arrives at a political program not by voicing some "principles of unity" that hide differences but rather by allowing each constituency to analyze economic and social issues from the perspective of its experience. This implies that each group maintains autonomy in relating to its constituency, and that decision-making bodies and procedures provide for group representation.

To the degree that there are heterogeneous publics operating according to the principles of group representation in contemporary politics, they exist only in organizations and movements resisting the majority politics. Nevertheless, in principle participatory democracy entails commitment to institutions of a heterogeneous public in all spheres of democratic decision making. Until and unless group oppression or disadvantages are eliminated, political publics, including democratized workplaces and government decision-making bodies, should include the specific representation of those oppressed groups, through which those groups express their specific understanding of the issues before the public and register a group-based vote. Such structures of group representation should not replace structures of regional or party representation but should exist alongside them.

Implementing principles of group representation in national politics in the United States, or in restructured democratic publics within particular institutions such as factories, offices, universities, churches, and social service agencies, would require creative thinking and flexibility. There are no models to follow. European models of consociational democratic institutions, for example, cannot be taken outside of the contexts in which they have evolved, and even within them they do not operate in a very democratic fashion. Reports of experiments with publicly institutionalized self-organization among women, indigenous peoples, workers, peasants, and students in contemporary Nicaragua offer an example closer to the conception I am advocating.[18]

The principle of group representation calls for such structures of representation for oppressed or disadvantaged groups. But what groups deserve representation? Clear candidates for group representation in policy making in the United States are women, blacks, Native Americans, old people, poor people, disabled people, gay men and lesbians, Spanish-speaking Americans, young people, and nonprofessional workers. But it may not be necessary to ensure specific representation of all these groups in all public contexts and in all policy discussions. Representation should be designated whenever the group's history and social situation provide a particular perspective on the issues, when the interests of its members are specifically affected, and when its perceptions and interests are not likely to receive expression without that representation.

An origin problem emerges in proposing a principle such as this, which no philosophical argument can solve. To implement this principle a public must be constituted to decide which groups deserve specific representation in decision-making procedures. What are the principles guiding the composition of such a "constitutional convention"? Who should decide what groups should receive representation, and by what procedures should this decision take place? No program or set of principles can found a politics, because politics is always a process in which we are already engaged; principles can be appealed to in the course of political discussion, they can be accepted by a public as guiding their action. I propose a principle of group representation as a part of such potential discussion, but it cannot replace that discussion or determine its outcome.

What should be the mechanisms of group representation? Earlier I stated that the self-organiza-

tion of the group is one of the aspects of a principle of group representation. Members of the group must meet together in democratic forums to discuss issues and formulate group positions and proposals. This principle of group representation should be understood as part of a larger program for democratized decision-making processes. Public life and decision-making processes should be transformed so that all citizens have significantly greater opportunities for participation in discussion and decision making. All citizens should have access to neighborhood or district assemblies where they participate in discussion and decision making. In such a more participatory democratic scheme, members of oppressed groups would also have group assemblies, which would delegate group representatives.

One might well ask how the idea of a heterogeneous public which encourages self-organization of groups and structures of group representation in decision making is different from the interest group pluralism criticism which I endorsed earlier in this article. First, in the heterogeneous public not any collectivity of persons that chooses to form an association counts as a candidate for group representation. Only those groups that describe the major identities and major status relationships constituting the society or particular institution, and which are oppressed or disadvantaged, deserve specific representation in a heterogeneous public. In the structures of interest group pluralism, Friends of the Whales, the National Association for the Advancement of Colored People, the National Rifle Association, and the National Freeze Campaign all have the same status, and each influences decision making to the degree that their resources and ingenuity can win out in the competition for policymakers' ears. While democratic politics must maximize freedom of the expression of opinion and interest, that is a different issue from ensuring that the perspective of all groups has a voice.

Second, in the heterogeneous public the groups represented are not defined by some particular interest or goal, or some particular political position. Social groups are comprehensive identities and ways of life. Because of their experiences their members may have some common interests that they seek to press in the public. Their social location, however, tends to give them distinctive understandings of all aspects of the society and unique perspectives on social issues. For example, many Native Americans argue that their traditional religion and relation to land gives them a unique and important understanding of environmental problems.

Finally, interest group pluralism operates precisely to forestall the emergence of public discussion and decision making. Each interest group promotes only its specific interest as thoroughly and forcefully as it can, and it need not consider the other interests competing in the political market-place except strategically, as potential allies or adversaries in the pursuit of its own. The rules of interest group pluralism do not require justifying one's interest as right or as compatible with social justice. A heterogeneous public, however, is a *public*, where participants discuss together the issues before them and are supposed to come to a decision that they determine as best or most just.

III Universal Rights and Special Rights

A second aspect of the universality of citizenship is today in tension with the goal of full inclusion and participation of all groups in political and social institutions: universality in the formulation of law and policies. Modern and contemporary liberalism hold as basic the principle that the rules and policies of the state, and in contemporary liberalism also the rules of private institutions, ought to be blind to race, gender, and other group differences. The public realm of the state and law properly should express its rules in general terms that abstract from the particularities of individual and group histories, needs, and situations to recognize all persons equally and treat all citizens in the same way.

As long as political ideology and practice persisted in defining some groups as unworthy of equal citizenship status because of supposedly natural differences from white male citizens, it was important for emancipatory movements to insist that all people are the same in respect of their moral worth and deserve equal citizenship. In this context, demands for equal rights that are blind to group differences were the only sensible way to combat exclusion and degradation.

Today, however, the social consensus is that all persons are of equal moral worth and deserve equal citizenship. With the near achievement of equal rights for all groups, with the important exception of gay men and lesbians, group inequalities nevertheless remain. Under these circumstances many feminists, black liberation activists, and others struggling for the full inclusion and participation of all groups in this society's institutions and positions of power, reward, and satisfaction, argue that rights and rules that are universally formulated and thus blind to differences of race, culture, gender, age, or disability, perpetuate rather than undermine oppression.

Contemporary social movements seeking full inclusion and participation of oppressed and disadvantaged groups now find themselves faced with a dilemma of difference.[19] On the one hand, they must continue to deny that there are any essential differences between men and women, whites and blacks, able-bodied and disabled people, which justify denying women, blacks, or disabled people the opportunity to do anything that others are free to do or to be included in any institution or position. On the other hand, they have found it necessary to affirm that there are often group-based differences between men and women, whites and blacks, able-bodied and disabled people that make application of a strict principle of equal treatment, especially in competition for positions, unfair because these differences put those groups at a disadvantage. For example, white middle-class men as a group are socialized into the behavioral styles of a particular kind of articulateness, coolness, and competent authoritativeness that are most rewarded in professional and managerial life. To the degree that there are group differences that disadvantage, fairness seems to call for acknowledging rather than being blind to them.

Though in many respects the law is now blind to group differences, the society is not, and some groups continue to be marked as deviant and as the other. In everyday interactions, images, and decision making, assumptions continue to be made about women, blacks, Latinos, gay men, lesbians, old people, and other marked groups, which continue to justify exclusions, avoidances, paternalism, and authoritarian treatment. Continued racist, sexist, homophobic, ageist, and ableist behaviors and institutions create particular circumstances for these groups, usually disadvantaging them in their opportunity to develop their capacities and giving them particular experiences and knowledge. Finally, in part because they have been segregated and excluded from one another, and in part because they have particular histories and traditions, there are cultural differences among social groups – differences in language, style of living, body comportment and gesture, values, and perspectives on society.

Acknowledging group difference in capacities, needs, culture, and cognitive styles poses a problem for those seeking to eliminate oppression only if difference is understood as deviance or deficiency. Such understanding presumes that some capacities, needs, culture, or cognitive styles are normal. I suggested earlier that their privilege allows dominant groups to assert their experience of and perspective on social events as impartial and objective. In a similar fashion, their privilege allows some groups to project their group-based capacities, values, and cognitive and behavioral styles as the norm to which all persons should be expected to conform. Feminists in particular have argued that most contemporary workplaces, especially the most desirable, presume a life rhythm and behavioral style typical of men, and that women are expected to accommodate to the workplace expectations that assume those norms.

Where group differences in capacities, values, and behavioral or cognitive styles exist, equal treatment in the allocation of reward according to rules of merit composition will reinforce and perpetuate disadvantage. Equal treatment requires everyone to be measured according to the same norms, but in fact there are no "neutral" norms of behavior and performance. Where some groups are privileged and others oppressed, the formulation of law, policy, and the rules of private institutions tend to be biased in favor of the privileged groups, because their particular experience implicitly sets the norm. Thus where there are group differences in capacities, socialization, values, and cognitive and cultural styles, only attending to such differences can enable the inclusion and participation of all groups in political and economic institutions. This implies that instead of always formulating rights and rules in universal terms that are blind to difference, some groups sometimes deserve special rights.[20] In what follows, I shall review several contexts of contemporary policy debate where I argue such special rights for oppressed or disadvantaged groups are appropriate.

The issue of a right to pregnancy and maternity leave, and the right to special treatment for nursing mothers, is highly controversial among feminists today. I do not intend here to wind through the intricacies of what has become a conceptually challenging and interesting debate in legal theory. As Linda Krieger argues, the issue of rights for pregnant and birthing mothers in relation to the workplace has created a paradigm crisis for our

understanding of sexual equality, because the application of a principle of equal treatment on this issue has yielded results whose effects on women are at best ambiguous and at worst detrimental.[21]

In my view an equal treatment approach on this issue is inadequate because it either implies that women do not receive any right to leave and job security when having babies, or it assimilates such guarantees under a supposedly gender neutral category of "disability." Such assimilation is unacceptable because pregnancy and childbirth are normal conditions of normal women, they themselves count as socially necessary work, and they have unique and variable characteristics and needs.[22] Assimilating pregnancy into disability gives a negative meaning to these processes as "unhealthy." It suggests, moreover, that the primary or only reason that a woman has a right to leave and job security is that she is physically unable to work at her job, or that doing so would be more difficult than when she is not pregnant and recovering from childbirth. While these are important reasons, depending on the individual woman, another reason is that she ought to have the time to establish breastfeeding and develop a relationship and routine with her child, if she chooses.

The pregnancy leave debate has been heated and extensive because both feminists and nonfeminists tend to think of biological sex difference as the most fundamental and ineradicable difference. When difference slides into deviance, stigma, and disadvantage, this impression can engender the fear that sexual equality is not attainable. I think it is important to emphasize that reproduction is by no means the only context in which issues of same versus different treatment arise. It is not even the only context where it arises for issues involving bodily difference. The last twenty years have seen significant success in winning special rights for persons with physical and mental disabilities. Here is a clear case where promoting equality in participation and inclusion requires attending to the particular needs of different groups.

Another bodily difference which has not been as widely discussed in law and policy literature, but should be, is age. With increasing numbers of willing and able old people marginalized in our society, the issue of mandatory retirement has been increasingly discussed. This discussion has been muted because serious consideration of working rights for all people able and willing to work implies major restructuring of the allocation of labor in an economy with already socially volatile levels of unemployment. Forcing people out of their workplaces solely on account of their age is arbitrary and unjust. Yet I think it is also unjust to require old people to work on the same terms as younger people. Old people should have different working rights. When they reach a certain age they should be allowed to retire and receive income benefits. If they wish to continue working, they should be allowed more flexible and part-time schedules than most workers currently have.

Each of these cases of special rights in the workplace – pregnancy and birthing, physical disability, and being old – has its own purposes and structures. They all challenge, however, the same paradigm of the "normal, healthy" worker and "typical work situation." In each case the circumstance that calls for different treatment should not be understood as lodged in the differently treated workers, per se, but in their interaction with the structure and norms of the workplace. Even in cases such as these, that is, difference does not have its source in natural, unalterable, biological attributes, but in the relationship of bodies to conventional rules and practices. In each case the political claim for special rights emerges not from a need to compensate for an inferiority, as some would interpret it, but from a positive assertion of specificity in different forms of life.[23]

Issues of difference arise for law and policy not only regarding bodily being, but just as importantly for cultural integrity and invisibility. By culture I mean group-specific phenomena of behavior, temperament, or meaning. Cultural differences include phenomena of language, speaking style or dialect, body comportment, gesture, social practices, values, group-specific socialization, and so on. To the degree that groups are culturally different, however, equal treatment in many issues of social policy is unjust because it denies these cultural differences or makes them a liability. There are a vast number of issues where fairness involves attention to cultural differences and their effects, but I shall briefly discuss three: affirmative action, comparable worth, and bilingual, bicultural education and service.

Whether they involve quotas or not, affirmative action programs violate a principle of equal treatment because they are race or gender conscious in setting criteria for school admissions, jobs, or promotions. These policies are usually defended in one of two ways. Giving preference to race or gender is understood either as just compensation for groups that have suffered discrimination in the past, or as compensation for the present disadvantage these groups suffer because of that history of discrimination and exclusion.[24] I do not wish to quarrel with either of these justifications for the differential treatment based on race or gender implied by affirmative action policies. I want to suggest that in addition we can understand affirmative action policies as compensating for the cultural biases of standards and evaluators used by the schools or employers. These standards and evaluators reflect at least to some degree the specific life and cultural experience of dominant groups – whites, Anglos, or men. In a group-differentiated society, moreover, the development of truly neutral standards and evaluations is difficult or impossible, because female, black, or Latino cultural experience and the dominant cultures are in many respects not reducible to a common measure. Thus affirmative action policies compensate for the dominance of one set of cultural attributes. Such an interpretation of affirmative action locates the "problem" that affirmative action solves partly in the understandable biases of evaluators and their standards, rather than only in specific differences of the disadvantaged group.

Although they are not a matter of different treatment as such, comparable worth policies similarly claim to challenge cultural biases in traditional evaluation in the worth of female-dominated occupations, and in doing so require attending to differences. Schemes of equal pay for work of comparable worth require that predominantly male and predominantly female jobs have similar wage structures if they involve similar degrees of skill, difficulty, stress, and so on. The problem in implementing these policies, of course, lies in designing methods of comparing the jobs, which often are very different. Most schemes of comparison choose to minimize sex differences by using supposedly gender-neutral criteria, such as educational attainment, speed of work, whether it involves manipulation of symbols, decision making, and so on. Some writers have suggested, however, that standard classifications of job traits may be systematically biased to keep specific kinds of tasks involved in many female-dominated occupations hidden.[25] Many female-dominated occupations involve gender-specific kinds of labor – such as nurturing, smoothing over social relations, or the exhibition of sexuality – which most task observation ignores.[26] A fair assessment of the skills and complexity of many female-dominated jobs may therefore involve paying explicit attention to gender differences in kinds of jobs rather than applying gender-blind categories of comparison.

Finally, linguistic and cultural minorities ought to have the right to maintain their language and culture and at the same time be entitled to all the benefits of citizenship, as well as valuable education and career opportunities. This right implies a positive obligation on the part of governments and other public bodies to print documents and to provide services in the native language of recognized linguistic minorities, and to provide bilingual instruction in schools. Cultural assimilation should not be a condition of full social participation, because it requires a person to transform his or her sense of identity, and when it is realized on a group level it means altering or annihilating the group's identity. This principle does not apply to any persons who do not identify with majority language or culture within a society, but only to sizeable linguistic or cultural minorities living in distinct though not necessarily segregated communities. In the United States, then, special rights for cultural minorities applies at least to Spanish-speaking Americans and Native Americans.

The universalist finds a contradiction in asserting both that formerly segregated groups have a right to inclusion and that these groups have a right to different treatment. There is no contradiction here, however, if attending to difference is necessary in order to make participation and inclusion possible. Groups with different circumstances or forms of life should be able to participate together in public institutions without shedding their distinct identities or suffering disadvantage because of them. The goal is not to give special compensation to the deviant until they achieve normality, but rather to denormalize the way institutions formulate their rules by revealing the plural circumstances and needs that exist, or ought to exist, within them.

Many opponents of oppression and privilege are wary of claims for special rights because they fear a restoration of special classifications that can justify exclusion and stigmatization of the specially marked groups. Such fear has been particularly pronounced among feminists who oppose affirming sexual and gender difference in law and policy. It would be foolish for me to deny that this fear has some significant basis.

Such fear is founded, however, on accession to traditional identification of group difference with deviance, stigma, and inequality. Contemporary movements of oppressed groups, however, assert a positive meaning to group difference, by which a group claims its identity as a group and rejects the stereotypes and labeling by which others mark it as inferior or inhuman. These social movements engage the meaning of difference itself as a terrain of political struggle, rather than leave difference to be used to justify exclusion and subordination. Supporting policies and rules that attend to group difference in order to undermine oppression and disadvantage is, in my opinion, a part of that struggle.

Fear of claims to special rights points to a connection of the principle of group representation with the principle of attending to difference in policy. The primary means of defense from the use of special rights to oppress or exclude groups is the self-organization and representation of those groups. If oppressed and disadvantaged groups are able to discuss among themselves what procedures and policies they judge will best further their social and political equality, and have access to mechanisms to make their judgments known to the larger public, then policies that attend to difference are less likely to be used against them than for them. If they have the institutionalized right to veto policy proposals that directly affect them, and them primarily, moreover, such danger is further reduced.

In this article I have distinguished three meanings of universality that have usually been collapsed in discussions of the universality of citizenship and the public realm. Modern politics properly promotes the universality of citizenship in the sense of the inclusion and participation of everyone in public life and democratic processes. The realization of genuinely universal citizenship in this sense today is impeded rather than furthered by the commonly held conviction that when they exercise their citizenship, persons should adopt a universal point of view and leave behind the perceptions they derive from their particular experience and social position. The full inclusion and participation of all in law and public life is also sometimes impeded by formulating laws and rules in universal terms that apply to all citizens in the same way.

In response to these arguments, some people have suggested to me that such challenges to the ideal of universal citizenship threaten to leave no basis for rational normative appeals. Normative reason, it is suggested, entails universality in a Kantian sense: when a person claims that something is good or right he or she is claiming that everyone in principle could consistently make that claim, and that everyone should accept it. This refers to a fourth meaning of universality, more epistemological than political. There may indeed be grounds for questioning a Kantian-based theory of the universality of normative reason, but this is a different issue from the substantive political issues I have addressed here, and the arguments in this paper neither imply nor exclude such a possibility. In any case, I do not believe that challenging the ideal of a unified public or the claim that rules should always be formally universal subverts the possibility of making rational normative claims.

Notes

1 Theodore Lowi's classic analysis of the privatized operations of interest group liberalism remains descriptive of American politics; see *The End of Liberalism* (New York: Norton, 1969). For more recent analyses, see Jürgen Habermas, *Legitimation Crisis* (Boston: Beacon, 1973); Claus Offe, *Contradictions of the Welfare State* (Cambridge, Mass.: MIT Press, 1984); John Keane, *Public Life in Late Capitalism* (Cambridge, Mass.: MIT Press, 1984); Benjamin Barber, *Strong Democracy* (Berkeley: University of California Press, 1984).

2 For an outstanding recent account of the virtues of and conditions for such democracy, see Philip Green, *Retrieving Democracy* (Totowa, NJ: Rowman & Allanheld, 1985).

3 Barber and Keane both appeal to Rousseau's understanding of civic activity as a model for contemporary participatory democracy, as does Carole Pateman in her classic work, *Participation and Democratic Theory* (Cambridge: Cambridge University Press, 1970). (Pateman's position has, of course, changed.) See also James Miller, *Rousseau: Dreamer of Democracy* (New Haven, Conn.: Yale University Press, 1984).

4 Many who extol the virtues of the civic public, of course, appeal also to a model of the ancient polis. For a recent example, see Murray Bookchin, *The Rise of Urbanization and the Decline of Citizenship* (San Francisco: Sierra Club Books, 1987). In this article, however, I choose to restrict my claims to modern political thought. The idea of the ancient Greek polis often functions in both modern and contemporary discussion as a myth of lost origins, the paradise from which we have fallen and to which we desire to return; in this way, appeals to the ancient Greek polis are often contained within appeals to modern ideas of civic humanism.

5 Hannah Pitkin performs a most detailed and sophisticated analysis of the virtues of the civic public as a flight from sexual difference through a reading of the texts of Machiavelli; see *Fortune Is a Woman* (Berkeley: University of California Press, 1984). Carole Pateman's recent writing also focuses on such analysis. See, e.g., Carole Pateman, *The Social Contract* (Stanford, Calif.: Stanford University Press, 1988). See also Nancy Hartsock, *Money, Sex and Power* (New York: Longman, 1983), chaps. 7 and 8.

6 See Susan Okin, "Women and the Making of the Sentimental Family," *Philosophy and Public Affairs* 11 (1982): 65–88; see also Linda Nicholson, *Gender and History: The Limits of Social Theory in the Age of the Family* (New York: Columbia University Press, 1986).

7 For analyses of Rousseau's treatment of women, see Susan Okin, *Women in Western Political Thought* (Princeton, NJ: Princeton University Press, 1978); Lynda Lange, "Rousseau: Women and the General Will," in *The Sexism of Social and Political Theory*, ed. Lorenne M. G. Clark and Lynda Lange (Toronto: University of Toronto Press, 1979); Jean Bethke Elshtain, *Public Man, Private Woman* (Princeton, NJ: Princeton University Press, 1981), chap. 4. Mary Dietz develops an astute critique of Elshtain's "maternalist" perspective on political theory; in so doing, however, she also seems to appeal to a universalist ideal of the civic public in which women will transcend their particular concerns and become general; see "Citizenship with a Feminist Face: The Problem with Maternal Thinking," *Political Theory* 13 (1985): 19–37. On Rousseau on women, see also Joel Schwartz, *The Sexual Politics of Jean-Jacques Rousseau* (Chicago: University of Chicago Press, 1984).

8 See Ronald Takaki, *Iron Cages: Race and Culture in 19th Century America* (New York: Knopf, 1979). Don Herzog discusses the exclusionary prejudices of some other early American republicans; see "Some Questions for Republicans," *Political Theory* 14 (1986): 473–93.

9 George Mosse, *Nationalism and Sexuality* (New York: Fertig, 1985).

10 Barber, chaps. 8 and 9. Future page references in parentheses are to this book.

11 I have developed this account more thoroughly in my paper, Iris Marion Young, "Impartiality and the Civic Public: Some Implications of Feminist Critiques of Moral and Political Theory," in *Feminism as Critique*, ed. S. Benhabib and D. Cornell (Oxford: Polity Press, 1987), pp. 56–76.

12 On feminism and participatory democracy, see Pateman.

13 Jane Mansbridge, *Beyond Adversarial Democracy* (New York: Basic Books, 1980).

14 Amy Gutmann, *Liberal Equality* (Cambridge: Cambridge University Press, 1980), pp. 191–202.

15 See Iris Marion Young, "Five Faces of Oppression," *Philosophical Forum* (1988).

16 Jürgen Habermas, *Reason and the Rationalization of Society* (Boston: Beacon, 1983), pt. 3. For criticism of Habermas as retaining too universalist a conception of communicative action, see Seyla Benhabib, *Critique, Norm and Utopia* (New York: Columbia University Press, 1986); and Young, "Impartiality and the Civic Public."

17 The Mel King for mayor campaign organization exhibited the promise of such group representation in practice, which was only partially and haltingly realized; see special double issue of *Radical America* 17, no. 6, and 18, no. 1 (1984). Sheila Collins discusses how the idea of a rainbow coalition challenges traditional American political assumptions of a "melting pot," and she shows how lack of coordination between the national level rainbow departments and the grassroots campaign committees prevented the 1984 Jackson campaign from realizing the promise of group representation; see *The Rainbow Challenge: The Jackson Campaign and the Future of US Politics* (New York: Monthly Review Press, 1986).

18 See Gary Ruchwarger, *People in Power: Forging a Grassroots Democracy in Nicaragua* (Hadley, Mass.: Bergin & Garvey, 1985).

19 Martha Minow, "Learning to Live with the Dilemma of Difference: Bilingual and Special Education," *Law and Contemporary Problems*, no. 48 (1985): 157–211.

20 I use the term "special rights" in much the same way as Elizabeth Wolgast, in *Equality and the Rights of Women* (Ithaca, NY: Cornell University Press, 1980). Like Wolgast, I wish to distinguish a class of rights that all persons should have, general rights, and a class of rights that categories of persons should have by virtue of particular circumstances. That is, the distinction should refer only to different levels of generality, where "special" means only "specific." Unfortunately, "special rights" tends to carry a connotation of *exceptional*, that is, specially marked and deviating from the norm. As I assert below, however, the goal is not to compensate for deficiencies in order to help people be "normal," but to denormalize, so that in certain contexts and at certain levels of abstraction everyone has "special" rights.

21 Linda J. Krieger, "Through a Glass Darkly: Paradigms of Equality and the Search for a Women's Jurisprudence," *Hypatia: A Journal of Feminist Philosophy* 2 (1987): 45–62. Deborah Rhode provides an excellent synopsis of the dilemmas involved in this pregnancy debate in feminist legal theory in "Justice and Gender" (typescript), chap. 9.

22 See Ann Scales, "Towards a Feminist Jurisprudence," *Indiana Law Journal* 56 (1980): 375–444. Christine Littleton provides a very good analysis of the feminist debate about equal vs. different treatment regarding pregnancy and childbirth, among other legal issues for women, in "Reconstructing Sexual Equality," *California Law Review* 25 (1987): 1279–1337. Littleton suggests, as I have stated above, that only the dominant male conception of work keeps pregnancy and birthing from being conceived of as work.

23 Littleton suggests that difference should be understood not as a characteristic of particular sorts of people, but of the interaction of particular sorts of people with specific institutional structures. Minow expresses a similar point by saying that difference should be understood as a function of the relationship among groups, rather than located in attributes of a particular group.

24 For one among many discussions of such "backward looking" and "forward looking" arguments, see Bernard Boxill, *Blacks and Social Justice* (Totowa, NJ: Rowman & Allanheld, 1984), chap. 7.

25 See R.W. Beatty and J.R. Beatty, "Some Problems with Contemporary Job Evaluation Systems," and Ronnie Steinberg, "A Want of Harmony: Perspectives on Wage Discrimination and Comparable Worth," both in *Comparable Worth and Wage Discrimination: Technical Possibilities and Political Realities*, ed. Helen Remick (Philadelphia: Temple University Press, 1981); D.J. Treiman and H.I. Hartmann, eds., *Women, Work and Wages* (Washington, DC: National Academy Press, 1981), p. 81.

26 David Alexander, "Gendered Job Traits and Women's Occupations" (PhD dissertation, University of Massachusetts, Department of Economics, 1987).

17

Superseding Historic Injustice

Jeremy Waldron

1   Injustice and History

The history of white settlers' dealings with the aboriginal peoples of Australia, New Zealand, and North America is largely a history of injustice. People, or whole peoples, were attacked, defrauded, and expropriated; their lands were stolen and their lives were ruined. What are we to do about these injustices? We know what we should think about them: they are to be studied and condemned, remembered and lamented. But morality is a practical matter, and judgments of "just" and "unjust" like all moral judgments have implications for action. To say that a future act open to us now would be unjust is to commit ourselves to avoiding it. But what of past injustice? What is the practical importance now of a judgment that injustice occurred in the past?

In the first instance the question is one of metaethics. Moral judgments are prescriptive in their illocutionary force; they purport to guide choices.[1] But since the only choices we can guide are choices in front of us, judgments about the past must look beyond the particular events that are their ostensible subject matter. The best explanation of this relies on universalizability. When I make a moral judgment about an event E, I do so not in terms of the irreducible particularity of E but on the basis of some feature of E that other events might share. In saying, for example, "E was unjust," I am saying, "There is something about E and the circumstances

in which it is performed, such that any act of that kind performed in such circumstances would be unjust." I am not so much prescribing the avoidance of E itself (a prescription that makes no sense if E is in the past), but prescribing the avoidance of E-type events. If E involved breaking a promise, or taking advantage of someone's credulity, then our condemnation of it commits us to a similar condemnation of breaches of faith or exploitation in the present. Though E occurred 150 years ago, to condemn it is to express a determination now that in the choices we face, we will avoid actions of this kind.[2]

The point of doing this is not that we learn new and better standards for our lives from the judgments we make about the past. Unless we had those standards already, we would not make those judgments. But our moral understanding of the past is often a way of bringing to imaginative life the full implications of principles to which we are already in theory committed. To be disposed to act morally, it is not enough to be equipped with a list of appropriate principles. One also needs a sense of the type of situation in which these things may suddenly be at stake, the temptations that might lead one to betray them, and the circumstances and entanglements that make otherwise virtuous people start acting viciously. That is what history provides: a lesson about what it is like for people just like us – human, all too human – to face real moral danger.

Beyond that, there is an importance to the historical recollection of injustice that has to do with

Originally published in *Ethics* 103 (1992): 4–28. Copyright © 1992 by the University of Chicago Press. Reprinted by permission of the University of Chicago Press.

identity and contingency. It is a well-known characteristic of great injustice that those who suffer it go to their deaths with the conviction that these things must not be forgotten. It is easy to misread that as vain desire for vindication, a futile threat of infamy upon the perpetrators of an atrocity. But perhaps the determination to remember is bound up with the desire to sustain a specific character as a person or community against a background of infinite possibility. That *this* happened rather that *that* – that people were massacred (though they need not have been), that lands were taken (though they might have been bought fairly), that promises were broken (though they might have been kept) – the historic record has a fragility that consists, for large part, in the sheer contingency of what happened in the past. What happened might have been otherwise, and, just because of that, it is not something one can reason back to if what actually took place has been forgotten or concealed.[3]

Each person establishes a sense of herself in terms of her ability to identify the subject or agency of her present thinking with that of certain acts and events that took place in the past, and in terms of her ability to hold fast to a distinction between memory so understood and wishes, fantasies, or various other ideas of things that might have happened but did not.[4] But remembrance in this sense is equally important to communities – families, tribes, nations, parties – that is, to human entities that exist often for much longer than individual men and women. To neglect the historical record is to do violence to this identity and thus to the community that it sustains. And since communities help generate a deeper sense of identity for the individuals they comprise, neglecting or expunging the historical record is a way of undermining and insulting individuals as well.

When we are told to let bygones be bygones, we need to bear in mind also that the forgetfulness being urged on us is seldom the blank slate of historical oblivion. Thinking quickly fills up the vacuum with plausible tales of self-satisfaction, on the one side, and self-deprecation on the other. Those who as a matter of fact benefited from their ancestors' injustice will persuade themselves readily enough that their good fortune is due to the virtue of their race, while the descendants of their victims may too easily accept the story that they and their kind were always good for nothing. In the face of all this, only the deliberate enterprise of recollection (the enterprise we call "history"), coupled with the most determined sense that there is a difference between what happened and what we would like to think happened, can sustain the moral and cultural reality of self and community.

The topic of this article is reparation. But before I embark on my main discussion, I want to mention the role that the payment of money (or the return of lands or artifacts) may play in the embodiment of communal remembrance. Quite apart from any attempt genuinely to compensate victims or offset their losses, reparations may symbolize a society's undertaking not to forget or deny that a particular injustice took place, and to respect and help sustain a dignified sense of identity-in-memory for the people affected. A prominent recent example of this is the payment of token sums of compensation by the American government to the survivors of Japanese-American families uprooted, interned, and concentrated in 1942. The point of these payments was not to make up for the loss of home, business, opportunity, and standing in the community which these people suffered at the hands of their fellow citizens, nor was it to make up for the discomfort and degradation of their internment. If that were the aim, much more would be necessary. The point was to mark – with something that counts in the United States – a clear public recognition that this injustice did happen, that it was the American people and their government that inflicted it, and that these people were among its victims. The payments give an earnest of good faith and sincerity to that acknowledgment. Like the gift I buy for someone I have stood up, the payment is a method of putting oneself out, or going out of one's way, to apologize. It is no objection to this that the payments are purely symbolic. Since identity is bound up with symbolism, a symbolic gesture may be as important to people as any material compensation.

II   The Counterfactual Approach to Reparation

I turn now to the view that a judgment about past injustice generates a demand for full and not merely symbolic reparation – a demand not just for remembrance but for substantial transfers of land, wealth, and resources in an effort actually to rectify past wrongs. I want to examine the difficulties that these demands give rise to, particularly when they conflict with other claims that may be made in the name of justice on the land, wealth, and resources in question.

It may seem as though the demand is hopeless from the start. What is it to correct an injustice? How can we reverse the past? If we are talking about injustice that took place several generations ago, surely there is nothing we can do now to heal the lives of the actual victims, to make them less miserable or to reduce their suffering. The only experiences we can affect are those of people living now and those who will live in the future.

But though these are obvious truths, we may miss something if we repeat them too often. To stand on the premise that the past cannot be changed is to ignore the fact that people and communities live whole lives, not just series of momentary events, and that an injustice may blight, not just hurt, such a life. Individuals make plans and they see themselves as living partly for the sake of their posterity; they build not only for themselves but for future generations. Whole communities may subsist for periods much longer than individual lifetimes. How they fare at a given stage and what they can offer in the way of culture, aspiration, and morale may depend very much on the present effect of events that took place several generations earlier. Thus, part of the moral significance of a past event has to do with the difference it makes to the present.

But then there is a sense in which we can affect the moral significance of past action. Even if we cannot alter the action itself we may be able to interfere with the normal course of its consequences. The present surely looks different now from the way the present would look if a given injustice of the past had not occurred. Why not therefore change the present so that it looks more like the present that would have obtained in the absence of the injustice? Why not make it now as though the injustice had not happened, for all that its occurrence in the past is immutable and undeniable?

This is the approach taken by Robert Nozick in his account of the role played by a principle of rectification in a theory of historic entitlement:

This principle uses historical information about previous situations and injustices done in them (as defined by the first two principles of justice [namely, justice in acquisition and justice in transfer] and rights against interference), and information about the actual course of events that flowed from these injustices, until the present, and it yields a description (or descriptions) of holdings in the society.

The principle of rectification presumably will make use of its best estimate of subjunctive information about what would have occurred (or a probability distribution over what might have occurred, using the expected value) if the injustice had not taken place. If the actual description of holdings turns out to be one of the descriptions yielded by the principle, then one of the descriptions yielded must be realized.[5]

The trouble with this approach is the difficulty we have in saying what would have happened if some event (which did occur) had not taken place. To a certain extent we can appeal to causal laws or, more crudely, the normal course of events. We take a description of the actual world, with its history and natural laws intact, up until the problematic event of injustice (which we shall call event "E"). In the actual course of events, what followed E (events F, G, and H) is simply what results from applying natural laws to E as an initial condition. For example, if E was your seizure of the only water hole in the desert just as I was about to slake my thirst, then F – the event that follows E – would be what happens normally when one person is deprived of water and another is not: you live and I die. So, in our counterfactual reasoning, we replace E with its closest just counterpart, $E+$ (say, we share the water hole), and we apply the laws of nature to that to see what would have happened next. Presumably what would have happened next is that we both slake our thirst and both survive. The same laws of nature that yield F given E, yield a different sequel $F+$ given the just alternative $E+$ and further sequels $G+$ and $H+$ on the basis of that.[6] The task of rectification then is to take some present event or situation over which we do have control (e.g., H, a distribution of resources obtaining now) and alter it so that it conforms as closely as possible to its counterpart $H+$ – the situation that would obtain now if $E+$ rather than E had occurred.

But what if some of the events in the sequel to $E+$ are exercises of human choice rather than the inexorable working out of natural laws? Is it possible to say counterfactually how choices subsequent to $E+$ would have been made, so that we can determine what state of affairs ($H+$) would obtain now in a society of autonomous choosers, but for the problematic injustice? Suppose that if E had not occurred, you would have made me a fair offer to form a partnership to cultivate land near the oasis? How are we to know whether I would have accepted the offer? Had I accepted it, I might have acquired wealth that I would not otherwise have had and with it the opportunity to engage in other transactions. How are we to know which transactions I would have chosen to engage in? The problem quickly becomes intractable particularly where the counterfactual sequence $\{E+, F+, G+, H+\}$ is imagined to extend over several generations, and where the range of choices available at a given stage depends on the choices that would have been taken at some earlier stage.

This is not a mere academic difficulty. Suppose (counterfactually) that a certain piece of land had not been wrongfully appropriated from some Maori group in New Zealand in 1865. Then we must ask ourselves: What would the tribal owners of that land have done with it, if wrongful appropriation had not taken place? To ask this question is to ask how people would have exercised their freedom if they had had a real choice. Would they have hung on to the land and passed it on to future generations of the tribe? Or would they have sold it – but this time for a fair price – to the first honest settler who came along?[7] And, if the latter, what would he have done with it? Sold it again? Passed it on to his children? Lost it in a poker game?

Part of our difficulty in answering these questions is our uncertainty about what we are doing when we try to make guesses about the way in which free will would have been exercised. The status of counterfactual reasoning about the exercise of human freedom is unclear. I do not mean that the exercise of human choice is necessarily unpredictable. We make predictions all the time about how people will exercise their freedom. But it is not clear why our best prediction on such a matter should have moral authority in the sort of speculations we are considering.

Suppose that I am attempting to predict how my aunt will dispose of her estate. My best guess, based on all the evidence, is that having no dependents she will leave it to Amnesty International, well known as her one cherished cause. In fact, my aunt surprises everyone by leaving everything to an obscure home for stray dogs that she has only just heard of. My prediction is confounded. But the important point is the following. Even though my prediction was reasonable, even though it was based on the best available evidence, it is her whimsical decision that carries

the day. My guess has no normative authority whatever with regard to the disposition of her estate. All that matters is what she eventually chooses.

If this is true of decision making in the real world, then I think it plays havoc with the idea that, normatively, the appropriate thing to do in the rectification of injustice is to make rational and informed guesses about how people would have exercised their freedom in a hypothetical world. For if such guesses carry no moral weight in the real world, why should any moral weight be associated with their use in counterfactual speculation?

This is not an epistemic difficulty. It is not that there is some fact of the matter (what this person would have chosen to do with her goods if things had been different) and our difficulty lies in discovering what that is. The thing about freedom is that there is no fact of the matter anywhere until the choice has been made. It is the act of choosing that has authority, not the existence as such of the chosen option.

Of course there are situations in which we do think it acceptable to substitute our best guess about what a person would have done for that person's actual choice. If my aunt's investments have been entrusted to me, and there is a crisis in the stock market while she is abroad and incommunicado, I must do what I figure she would have done: hold the stocks in the companies to which she has a sentimental attachment and sell the rest. Maybe she would have acted whimsically and done the opposite, but as her trustee this is morally the best I can do. By doing this I adopt in effect a rational choice approach to the decision: given what I know about her preferences, I act in a way that will maximize her utility. She might have acted perversely or she might not. But given that her hypothetical consent is my only warrant to act in this matter at all, I can do nothing except choose rationally to give content to the hypothesis.

Now we are unlikely to be able to reach conclusions this determinate in applying the rational choice approach to aboriginal land claims. We will probably not be in a position to say that selling to Q rather than to R would have been the rational thing for P to do if he had not been forcibly dispossessed, and that selling to S rather than T would have been the rational thing for Q to do if P had sold the land to him rather than to R, and so on down a reconstructed chain of entitlement. But broader conclusions may be available. Suppose P enjoyed a certain level of utility derived from his holdings, U_E, just before the events complained of took place. Then any rational choice reconstruction about what would have happened but for the injustice will maintain P's utility at that level at least. No rational chooser enters a voluntary transaction to make himself worse off. So any account of what would have happened had all transactions been voluntary will require P to emerge at least as well off as he was at the beginning of the story. If in actual reality he is worse off, the counterfactual approach will require that he be restored to a level at or above U_E. By making our rational choice assumptions airy enough, we can reach similar conclusions about the well-being of P's descendants and the well-being of the person who dispossessed P and of his descendants as well. And these conclusions are likely to match our intuitions: if the injustice had not taken place, the descendants of those who suffered it would be better off than they are and descendants of those who perpetrated it would be somewhat worse off than they are. So a transfer from the latter to the former seems justified.

However, several difficulties remain. One concerns what might be called the contagion of injustice. Suppose I possess a piece of land which I inherited from my father who bought it from his sister-in-law who bought it from a settler who obtained it in the mid-nineteenth century from a fraudulent transaction with a member of the Maori tribe. The counterfactual approach to reparation suggests that some transfer from me to the surviving members of the tribe may be required in order to bring the present state of affairs closer to the state of affairs that would have obtained if the fraud had not been perpetrated. Unfortunately we cannot leave the matter there. My neighbor may be in possession of a similar piece of land whose pedigree, considered in itself, is impeccable: there is no fraud, no coercion, no expropriation in the history of her holding. Still the price my neighbor (and her predecessors in title) paid for her land is likely to have been affected by the low price that was paid for my land (on account of the original fraud). Thus, rectification of the injustice will involve an adjustment of her holding as well. We cannot assume that rectificatory transfers will be confined to those who have had dealings with tainted holdings. All present holdings are called in question by this business of winding the film back to the injustice, changing that frame (from E to $E+$), and then winding the film forward to see what results. If one person behaves unjustly, particu-

larly in the context of a market, the injustice will have an effect not only on her immediate victim, but – via the price mechanism – on all those who trade in the market in question. Some will gain and some will lose as a result of the injustice, and any attempt at rectification – any attempt to implement the state of affairs that would have obtained but for the injustice – will involve interfering with those holdings as well.

Worse still, the events of justice and injustice may make a considerable difference in who exists at a later time. We cannot simply hold the dramatis personae constant in our speculations. Children may be conceived and born, and leave descendants, who would not have existed if the injustice had not occurred. Short of putting them to death for their repugnancy to our counterfactuals, the present approach offers no guidance at all as to how their claims are to be dealt with.

A more general difficulty has to do with our application of rational choice in counterfactual reconstruction. People can and often do act freely to their own disadvantage, and usually when they do, they are held to the result. A man who actually loses his land in a reckless though voluntary wager and who accepts the justice of the outcome may be entitled to wonder why, in the attention we pay to aboriginal reparations, we insulate people from the possibility of similar vicissitudes. He may say, "If we are going to reconstruct a history of rational choice, let us do so for all holdings, giving everyone what they would have had if they had never acted voluntarily to their own disadvantage. Maybe that will lead to a more just world. But if we are not prepared to do that, if we insist that it is alright, from the point of view of justice, to leave a person like me stuck with the results of his actual choices, it may be more consistent to admit that we simply can't say what (by the same token) justice now requires in the case of those whose ancestors were wrongfully dispossessed."

The dilemma is a difficult one. On the one hand, there is nothing normatively conclusive about rational choice predictions. Why should the exaction of specific reparation in the real world be oriented to what the idealized agents of rational choice would have secured for themselves in a hypothetical world? On the other hand, hypothetical rational choice is essential to our normative thinking about justice. Modern contractarian theories consist almost entirely of asking what the people of a society would have agreed to in the way of institutions governing the distribution of resources, had they been consulted.[8] But it is characteristic of such approaches that they are holistic, systemic, and structural rather than local and specific in their conclusions and recommendations. We deploy the counterfactuals of modern contractarianism to evaluate the entire basic structure of a society, not to evaluate some particular distribution among a subset of its members.[9]

The issue is particularly acute because the reparations that these counterfactuals support are likely to have a wide effect on holdings across the board. The case is quite different from the simple situation of my aunt's investments, where I ask only what she would have done with her capital and do not attempt to redistribute a whole array of different people's holdings. Reparation of historic injustice really is redistributive: it moves resources from one person to another. It seems unfair to do this on a basis that reconstructs a profile of holdings by attributing rational choice motivations to only some, and not all, of the parties who are affected.

Ultimately, what is raised here is the question of whether it is possible to rectify particular injustices without undertaking a comprehensive redistribution that addresses all claims of justice that may be made. The counterfactual approach aims to bring the present state of affairs as close as possible to the state of affairs that would have obtained if some specifically identified injustice had not occurred. But why stop there? Why be content merely to bring about the state of affairs that would have ensued if this injustice had not occurred? Why not try to make things even better than they would have been if that particular unjust transaction, or any unjust transaction, had not taken place? Are we so sure that a smooth transition, untainted by particular injustice, from some early nineteenth-century status quo ante would leave us now where we actually want to be? Quite apart from particular frauds and expropriations, things were not marvelous in the nineteenth century. Many people lacked access to any significant resources, and many people had much more than what one might regard as a fair share. Why take all that as the baseline for our present reconstruction?

III The Perpetuation and Remission of Injustice

So far we have focused on the effects of isolated acts of injustice like event E, events that took place firmly in the past. But we are seldom so fortunate

as to confront injustice in discrete doses. The world we know is characterized by patterns of injustice, by standing arrangements – rules, laws, regimes, and other institutions – that operate unjustly day after day. Though the establishment of such an arrangement was an unjust event when it took place in the past, its injustice then consisted primarily in the injustice it promised for the future. To judge that establishment unjust is to commit oneself to putting a stop to the ongoing situation; it is a commitment to prevent the perpetuation of the injustice that the law or the institution embodies; it is to commit oneself to its remission.

Suppose someone stole my car yesterday. That is an unjust act that took place at a certain place and at a certain time: at 9:30 a.m. on September 5, my car was stolen from the parking lot. Clearly anyone committed to the prevention of injustice should have tried to stop the theft taking place. But once the car has been driven nefariously out of the parking lot, the matter does not end there. For now there is a continuing injustice: I lack possession of an automobile to which I am entitled, and the thief possesses an automobile to which she is not entitled. Taking the car away from the thief and returning it to me, the rightful owner, is not a way of compensating me for an injustice that took place in the past; it is a way of remitting an injustice that is ongoing into the present. Phrases like "Let bygones be bygones" are inappropriate here. The loss of my car is not a bygone: it is a continuing state of affairs.

The implications of this example are clear for the historic cases we are considering. Instead of regarding the expropriation of aboriginal lands as an isolated act of injustice that took place at a certain time now relegated firmly to the past, we may think of it as a persisting injustice. The injustice persists, and it is perpetuated by the legal system as long as the land that was expropriated is not returned to those from whom it was taken. On this model, the rectification of injustice is a much simpler matter than the approach we discussed in the previous section. We do not have to engage in any counterfactual speculation. We simply give the property back to the person or group from whom it was taken and thus put an end to what would otherwise be its continued expropriation.

Difficulties arise of course if the original owner has died, for then there is no one to whom the property can be restored. We could give it to her heirs and successors, but in doing so we are already setting off down the counterfactual road, reckoning that this is what the proprietor's wish would have been had she had control of her property. Fortunately, that difficulty is obviated in the case of many aboriginal claims: usually the property is owned by a tribe, a nation, or a community – some entity that endures over time in spite of mortality of its individual members. It is this enduring entity that has been dispossessed, and the same entity is on hand now more than a hundred years later to claim its heritage.

What, if any, are the difficulties with this approach? It does not involve any of the problems of counterfactual reasoning that we identified earlier, but does it face any other problems? As I see it, the main difficulty is the following. Are we sure that the entitlement that was originally violated all those years ago is an entitlement that survives into the present? The approach we are considering depends on the claim that the right that was violated when white settlers first seized the land can be identified as a right that is still being violated today by settlers' successors in title. Their possession of the land today is said to be as wrongful vis-à-vis the present tribal owners as the original expropriation. Can this view be justified?

It is widely believed that some rights are capable of "fading" in their moral importance by virtue of the passage of time and by the sheer persistence of what was originally a wrongful infringement. In the law of property, we recognize doctrines of prescription and adverse possession. In criminal procedure and in torts, we think it important to have statutes of limitations. The familiarity of these doctrines no doubt contributes to the widespread belief that, after several generations have passed, certain wrongs are simply not worth correcting. Think of the earlier example of the theft of my automobile. Certainly, the car should be returned if the thief is discovered within weeks or months of the incident. But what if she is never caught? What if the stolen car remains in her family for decades and is eventually passed down as an heirloom to her children and grandchildren? Are we so sure that when the circumstances of its acquisition eventually come to light, it should be returned without further ado to me or my estate?

The view that a violated entitlement can "fade" with time may seem unfair. The injustice complained of is precisely that the rightful owner has been dispossessed. It seems harsh if the fact of her dispossession is used as a way of weakening her claim. It may also seem to involve some moral hazard by providing an incentive for wrongdoers to cling to their ill-gotten gains, in the hope that the entitlement they violated will fade away because of their adverse possession.

Still, the view that certain rights are prescriptable has a number of things to be said in its favor. Some are simply pragmatic. Statutes of limitations are inspired as much by procedural difficulties about evidence and memory, as by any doctrine about rights. It is hard to establish what happened if we are enquiring into the events that occurred decades or generations ago. There are nonprocedural pragmatic arguments also. For better or worse, people build up structures of expectation around the resources that are actually under their control. If a person controls a resource over a long enough period, then she and others may organize their lives and their economic activity around the premise that that resource is "hers," without much regard to the distant provenance of her entitlement. Upsetting these expectations in the name of restitutive justice is bound to be costly and disruptive.[10]

There may be reasons of principle as well. One set of reasons has to do with changes in background social and economic circumstances. If the requirements of justice are sensitive to circumstances such as the size of the population or the incidence of scarcity, then there is no guarantee that those requirements (and the rights that they constitute) will remain constant in relation to a given resource or piece of land as the decades and generations go by. I shall deal with this in detail in the next section of this article.

The other reason entitlements may fade has to do with the basis of the rights themselves. Theories of historic entitlement, like the theory of John Locke or the theory sketched more recently by Robert Nozick, focus on the establishment of an intimate relation between a person and a resource as the basis of property rights.[11] A person works with an object, shaping and modifying it, so that it becomes imbued with part of her personality; it comes to contain a part of herself. But if the right is taken out of her hands for a long period, the intimacy of that relation may evaporate.

Whether this happens depends partly on what we take to be the morally important relation between the person and the thing. In John Locke's theory, the relation is described as mixing one's labor.[12] A person mixes her labor her labor with a piece of land, and the land comes to embody her efforts; that labor is now like a jewel embedded in the land for all time. So anyone who takes hold of the land is necessarily taking hold of the jewel. And no one can doubt that the jewel – the labor – continues to belong to the original person who invested it. So even if a hundred years of adverse possession go by, the land still contains the labor – and thus part of the personality – of that individual. The labor is intrinsically and essentially hers, though embedded in an object that has been out of her possession for all that time. As long as the personality of this individual commands our moral respect, she is always entitled to demand this part of it back.[13]

Unfortunately, as I have argued elsewhere, the Lockean image of labor (whether it is individual or cooperative) being literally embedded or mixed in an object is incoherent.[14] Even if it did make sense, the idea would be far too strong to do the work its proponents want it to do. For it would it be impossible to explain how property rights thus acquired could be alienable – how they could be transferred, through sale or gift, from one person to another – without offense to the personality of the original acquirer. If a resource, once labored on, contains for all time a fragment of the laborer's personality, how can that same resource be held legitimately by someone to whom that laborer has chosen to transfer it? Not only that, but how can that second entitlement (the entitlement of the transferee) have anything like the moral force of the original entitlement?[15] Does a fragment of the transferee's personality replace the original nugget of labor in the object? If it does (and if we can make sense of the idea that this is possible), then surely we cannot dismiss out of hand the possibility that an expropriator may also in time replace the original embedded labor of the person she expropriated with something of her own.

In recent years, historical entitlement has been found its most able and consistent defender in Robert Nozick, and some reliance on Nozick's approach is almost inevitable for any defender of historic reparations.[16] But Nozick also dismissed the conundrums of Locke's theory about the "mixing of labor." He retained the form of a Lockean approach – insisting that an adequate theory of justice must be founded on some principle of unilateral acquisition – without telling us much about the content of that principle or how it might be justified.[17] However, the task of filling in the content cannot be indefinitely postponed because the substance and justification of a principle of acquisition will partly determine what we can do with it. Do entitlements based on acquisition fade over time, or can we appeal to them generations later as a basis for reparation? We cannot answer this question until we know what the entitlement theorist proposes to put in the place of the incoherent Lockean idea.

If we abandon Locke's image of the mixing of labor, the most plausible account of initial acquisition goes like this. An individual, P, who takes possession of an object or a piece of land and who works on it, alters it, and uses it, makes it in effect a part of her life, a pivotal point in her thinking, planning, and action. She shapes it in a certain way – ploughing it, for example, or practicing good husbandry in her hunting over it – so as to allow it to perform a certain role in her life and activity not only now but in the future. If someone else, Q, comes along and seizes the land, taking it from P without her consent, then the whole structure of action is disrupted. P's planning and the structure of P's action are destroyed and replaced by that of Q. Moreover, P did not have to do anything equivalent to this disruption in order to establish the resource as the center of her life. Before P took it, shaped it, and soon, the resource was the center of nobody's life. But when Q took it, it was already the center of P's. This asymmetry between the first and subsequent appropriator is the basis of P's historical entitlement and the basis of its moral priority. It is the reason why we say that Q's taking is wrong in a way that P's original appropriation was not, despite the fact that both parties are seeking to realize their autonomous purposes in the resource.

If any defense of historical entitlement is possible, it is going to be something along those lines. But – unfortunately – if this sort of line is taken, then we have a justification for historical entitlement that is vulnerable to prescription, a justification that is weakened by the historic persistence of dispossession, a justification that does fade over time. If something was taken from me decades ago, the claim that it now forms the center of my life and that it is still indispensable to the exercise of my autonomy is much less credible. For I must have developed some structure of subsistence. And that will be where my efforts have gone and where my planning and my practical thinking have been focused. I may of course yearn for the lost resource and spend a lot of time wishing that I had it back. I may even organize my life around the campaign for its restoration. But that is not the same thing as the basis of the original claim. The original entitlement is based on the idea that I have organized my life around the use of this object, not that I have organized my life around the specific project of hanging on to it or getting it back.

It may be objected that this argument furnishes an incentive to anyone who is inclined to violate another's rights. She knows that if she steals resources and hangs on to the proceeds, her victim will have to reorder his life and, once he does, he will no longer be in a position to claim that the stolen resources should be restored because of their centrality to his plans. But I do not see how this difficulty can be avoided, unless we introduce a different theory of the basis of property entitlements. We cannot pretend that a long-stolen resource continues to play a part in the original owner's life when in fact it does not, merely in order to avoid the moral hazard of this incentive effect. What the objection shows, I think, is that the normal line of argument for property entitlements based on autonomy is simply insufficient to establish imprescriptible rights. And what the failure of Locke's argument shows is that any case for making property rights fully imprescriptible is likely to run into other serious difficulties.

Historical entitlement theories are most impressive when moral entitlement is conjoined with present possession. Then it seems plausible to suggest that continued possession of the object might be indispensable to the possessor's autonomy and that an attack on possession is an attack on autonomy. But when the conjunction is disrupted, particularly when, as in the cases we are considering, it is disrupted for a considerable period of time, the claim looks much shakier.

I think this argument is important, by the way, but not always conclusive. It may not apply so clearly to cases where the dispossessed subject is a tribe or community, rather than an individual, and where the holding of which it has been dispossessed is particularly important for its sense of identity as a community. Many of the aboriginal claims, in New Zealand, Australia, and North America, have to do with burial grounds or lands which have some other symbolic or religious significance. Religions and cultural traditions we know are very resilient, and the claim that the lost lands form the center of a present way of life – and remain sacred objects despite their loss – may be as credible a hundred years on as it was at the time of the dispossession. In this regard, claims that land of religious significance should be returned to its original owners may have an edge over claims for the return of lands whose significance for them is mainly material or economic. Over the decades people are likely to have developed new modes of subsistence, making the claim that the land is crucial to their present way of life less credible in the economic case than in the religious case.

IV Circumstances and Supersession

I mentioned two ways in which an entitlement might be vulnerable to the passage of time. As well as the one we have just considered, there is also an important point to be made about changes in background circumstances that occur in the period after the original violation. I have in mind changes in population, changes in resource availability, occurrence of famine or ecological disaster, and so on. To assess these cases we have to ask questions about the relation between justice and background circumstances. Is justice relative to circumstances? Do entitlements change as circumstances change? If so, does the significance of past injustice change also? Or should we simply say that once something becomes mine it remains mine (and so it remains wrong for you to keep it), no matter what else happens in the world?

It is difficult to resist the conclusion that entitlements are sensitive to circumstances. Certainly, the level of our concern for various human predicaments is sensitive to the circumstances that constitute those predicaments. One's concern about poverty, for example, varies depending on the extent of the opportunities available to the poor: to be poor but to have some opportunity for amelioration is to be in a better predicament than to be poor with no opportunities at all. Similarly, our concern for the homeless may vary with the season of the year or the climate of the state in which they live. And these are not just fluctuations in subjective response: they are circumstantially sensitive variations in what we would take to be the appropriate level of concern. Now, the (appropriate) level of our concern about such predicaments is directly related to the burden of justification that must be shouldered by those who defend property rights. If an individual makes a claim to the exclusive use or possession of some resources in our territory, then the difficulty of sustaining that claim will clearly have some relation to the level of our concern about the plight of other persons who will have to be excluded from the resources if the claim is recognized. The only theory of property entitlement that would be totally immune to variations in background circumstances would be one that did not accept any burden of justification in relation to our real concerns.

We can express this claim about sensitivity to circumstances as follows. In the case of almost every putative entitlement, it is possible to imagine a pair of different circumstances, C_1 and C_2, such that the entitlement can only barely be justified in C_1 and cannot be justified at all in C_2. The shift from C_1 to C_2 represents a tipping point so far as the justification of the entitlement is concerned.

If this is accepted it clearly makes a difference to the original acquisition of property rights. A scale of acquisition that might be appropriate in a plentiful environment with a small population may be quite inappropriate in the same environment with a large population, or with the same population once natural resources have become depleted. In a plentiful environment with a small population, an individual appropriation of land makes no one worse off. As John Locke put it, "He that leaves as much as another can make use of, does as good as take nothing at all. No Body could think himself injur'd by the drinking of another Man, though he took a good Draught, who had a whole River of the same Water left him to quench his thirst. And the case of Land and Water, where there is enough of both, is perfectly the same."[18] But as Locke also recognized, the picture changed once the population increased to the point where scarcity was felt. If one person's appropriation cast a shadow on the survival prospects of others, then it evidently raised questions of a moral character that were not raised when resources were as plentiful as water in a river.[19] One does not need the exact formulation of a "Lockean proviso" to see this. It is simply that there are real and felt moral concerns in the one case that have to be addressed which are not present in the other.

The same point is recognized by Robert Nozick. The principle of acquisition that forms the linchpin of his theory depends for its acceptability on the claim that individual appropriations of previously unowned goods do not worsen anybody's situation.[20] (Nozick wishes, as far as possible, to present initial acquisition in the same light of Pareto improvement as consensual transfer.) We need not worry about the exact details of this proviso or of the various Lockean and Nozickian

formulations of it.[21] What is clear is that in any plausible theory of historic entitlement, there is some spectrum of social circumstances, relating to the effect a putative acquisition would have on the prospects and life chances of other people, such that the further one goes along this spectrum the less inclined we are to say that the acquisition in question generates legitimate rights.

So far I have talked about one acquisitive act, A_1, taking place in one set of circumstances, C_1, and another acquisitive act, A_2, taking place in different circumstances, C_2. I have said that circumstances may make a difference so that the conditions for the moral legitimacy of A_2 may be different from the conditions for the moral legitimacy of A_1 (even though, considered in themselves, A_1 and A_2 are the same type of act). However, we know that acquisition is not an isolated act. By laboring on a resource, the would-be acquirer not only takes it now but also purports to appropriate it permanently. The effect of her acquisition continues to be felt long after the acquisitive action has taken place. What happens, then, if circumstances change after the moment of the acquisitive act but during the time that the act has effect, that is, during the period of ownership to which the acquisitive action gives rise? A person performs acquisitive act A_1, in circumstances C_1 that make it legitimate. She establishes a title for herself (and her successors) that endures through time. During that time circumstances change, so that conditions C_2 now obtain, and conditions C_2 are such that an equivalent act of appropriation would not be legitimate. What effect does this change have on the legitimacy of the title founded by action A_1?

The answer has to be that it calls the legitimacy of that title into question. We can reach this conclusion by two routes.

The first and most straightforward argument is that property entitlements constrain us over a period of time, and they do so continually in the sense that they constantly call for action in support of them or they constantly involve action undertaken in their exercise. Day after day, an owner performs acts whose legitimacy is based on her entitlement; if she did not have the entitlement, she would have no right to perform these acts. Also, day after day, the owner faces explicit or implicit challenges from others, wanting to use her resource; if she did not have the entitlement to rely on she would not be in a moral position to rebut or resist these challenges. So each time she exercises her right and each time she resists an encroachment, she relies on the entitlement founded by A_1. At each of those times, the legitimacy of what she does depends on the appropriateness of her entitlement as a moral right at that time. So long as circumstances remain unchanged or so long as any changes are broadly consonant with the necessary conditions for the legitimacy of her entitlement, the fact that her claim is, so to speak, renewed day after day is not a worry. Its renewal is automatic. But if circumstances change radically in the way we have been envisaging, the continued application of her entitlement cannot be taken for granted.

The second line of argument is a response to an objection that might be made. Someone might object as follows:

> Surely if the original appropriation were legitimate, the conditions of its legitimacy would take into account the normal vicissitudes of human life including the prospect that things might change, goods become scarce, etc. To say that P acquires an entitlement by A_1 is surely to say that she acquires an entitlement that endures even in the face of changing circumstances. That is why we subject A_1 to such strict scrutiny, for its purports to found an enduring entitlement, not a temporary and circumstantially vulnerable one. The test for initial appropriation should be severe and morally rigorous, but if A_1 passes this test, it should not have to face further scrutiny later simply because conditions are not the same.

Here is the response to this objection. Maybe it is a good thing for the test of the initial acquisition, A_1, to take into account the possibility that conditions may change and therefore only to certify entitlements that survive that consideration. But it surely cannot be the upshot of this that, in circumstances C_1, only those acquisitions are certified that would be valid in all circumstances including C_2. That would be wasteful and pointless: why shouldn't people act as though goods are plentiful, at least when they are plentiful?

No. If a rigorous test of initial acquisition does take future vicissitudes into account, it will do so in a more subtle way. What it will do is provide ab initio, in the terms of the entitlement, that the exact array of rights, liberties, and powers is to be circumstantially sensitive. Thus, what P acquires through A_1, are rights that entitle her to

do one set of things in C_1, and another, perhaps more restricted, set of things in C_2. So, as before, the net effect of P's entitlement does vary, depending on the circumstances. If, for example, P acquires an oasis in conditions of plenty, she acquires (i) a right to use it freely and exclude others from its use so long as water remains plentiful in the territory, and (ii) a duty to share it with others on some fair basis if ever water becomes scarce. The right that is (permanently) acquired through A_1 is thus circumstantially sensitive in the actions it licenses.

If all this is accepted so far as justice in acquisition is concerned, it must also apply to issues and allegations of injustice. Suppose a person has legitimately acquired an object in circumstances of plenty, C_1, and another person comes along and snatches it from her. That act of snatching, we may say, is an injustice. But the very same action of snatching an already appropriated object may not be wrong in a different set of circumstances, C_2, where desperate scarcity has set in and the snatcher has no other means of staying alive. One and the same type of action may be injustice in one set of circumstances and not injustice in another.[22]

I hope it is clear where the argument is going. I said that the burden of justifying an exclusive entitlement depends (in part) on the impact of others' interests of being excluded from the resources in question and that that impact is likely to vary as circumstances change. Similarly an acquisition which is legitimate in one set of circumstances may not be legitimate in another set of circumstances. From this I inferred that an initially legitimate acquisition may become illegitimate or have its legitimacy restricted (as the basis of an ongoing entitlement) at a later time on account of a change in circumstances. By exactly similar reasoning, it seems possible that an act which counted as an injustice when it was committed in circumstances C_1 may be transformed, so far as its ongoing effect is concerned, into a just situation if circumstances change in the meantime from C_1 to C_2. When this happens, I shall say the injustice has been *superseded*.

Consider the following example.[23] On the savanna, a number of groups appropriate water holes, in conditions where it is known that there are enough water holes for each group. So long as these conditions obtain, it seems reasonable for the members of given group, P, to use the water hole they have appropriated without asking permission of other groups with whom they share the plains;

and it may even seem reasonable for them to exclude members of other groups from the casual use of their water holes, saying to them, "You have your own water hole. Go off and use that, and leave ours alone." But suppose there is an ecological disaster, and all the water holes dry up except the one that the members of P are using. Then in these changed circumstances, notwithstanding the legitimacy of their original appropriation, it is no longer in order for P to exclude others from their water hole. Indeed it may no longer be in order for members of P to casually use "their own" water hole in the way they did before. In the new circumstances, it may be incumbent on them to draw up a rationing scheme that allows for the needs of everyone in the territory to be satisfied from this one resource. Changing circumstances can have an effect on ownership rights notwithstanding the moral legitimacy of the original appropriation.

Next, suppose as before that in circumstances of plenty various groups on the savanna are legitimately in possession of their respective water holes. One day, motivated purely by greed, members of group Q descend on the water hole possessed by group P and insist on sharing that with them. (What's more they do not allow reciprocity; they do not allow members of P to share any water hole that was legitimately in the possession of Q.) That is an injustice. But then circumstances change, and all the water holes of the territory dry up except the one that originally belonged to P. The members of group Q are already sharing that water hole on the basis of their earlier incursion. But now that circumstances have changed, they are entitled to share that water hole; it no longer counts as an injustice. It is in fact part of what justice now requires. The initial injustice by Q against P has been superseded by circumstances.

Once again, it may be objected that this reasoning generates a moral hazard – an incentive for wrongdoers to seize others' lands confident in the knowledge that if they hang on to them wrongfully for long enough their possession may eventually become rightful.[24] But the argument of this section is not that the passage of time per se supersedes all claims of injustice. Rather, the argument is that claims about justice and injustice must be responsive to changes in circumstances. Suppose there had been no injustice: still, a change in circumstances (such as a great increase in world population) might justify our forcing the aboriginal inhabitants of some territory to share their

land with others. If this is so, then the same change in circumstances in the real world can justify our saying that the others' occupation of some of their lands, which was previously wrongful, may become morally permissible. There is no moral hazard in this supersession because the aboriginal inhabitants would have had to share their lands, whether the original injustice had taken place or not.

I do not think this possibility – of the supersession of past injustice – can be denied, except at the cost of making one's theory of historical entitlement utterly impervious to variations in the circumstance in which holdings are acquired and withheld from others. If circumstances make a difference to what counts as a just acquisition, then they must make a difference also to what counts as an unjust incursion. And if they make a difference to that, then in principle we must concede that a change in circumstances can affect whether a particular continuation if adverse possession remains an injustice or not.

Of course, from the fact that supersession is a possibility, it does not follow that it always happens. Everything depends on which circumstances are taken to be morally significant and how as matter of fact circumstances have changed. It may be that some of the historic injustices that concern us have not been superseded and that, even under modern circumstances, the possession of certain aboriginal lands by the descendants of those who expropriated their original owners remains a crying injustice. My argument is not intended to rule that out. But there have been huge changes since North America and Australasia were settled by white colonists. The population has increased manyfold, and most of the descendants of the colonists, unlike their ancestors, have nowhere else to go. We cannot be sure that these changes in circumstances supersede the injustice of their continued possession of aboriginal lands, but it would not be surprising if they did. The facts that have changed are exactly the sort of facts one would expect to make a difference to the justice of a set of entitlements over resources.

V Conclusion

It is important that defenders of aboriginal claims face up to the possibility of the supersession of historic injustice. Even if this particular thesis about supersession is mistaken, some account has to be given of the impact on aboriginal claims and on the reparation of generations-old injustices of the demographic and ecological changes that have taken place.

Apart from anything else, the changes that have taken place over the past two hundred years mean that the costs of respecting primeval entitlements are much greater now than they were in 1800. Two hundred years ago, a small aboriginal group could have exclusive domination of "a large and fruitful Territory"[25] without much prejudice to the needs and interests of very many other human beings. Today, such exclusive rights would mean many people going hungry who might otherwise be fed and many people living in poverty who might otherwise have an opportunity to make a decent life. Irrespective of the occurrence of past injustice, this imbalance would have to be rectified sooner or later. That is the basis for my argument that claims about historic injustice predicated on the status quo ante may be superseded by our determination to distribute the resources of the world in a way that is fair to all of its existing inhabitants.

Behind the thesis of supersession lies a determination to focus upon present and prospective costs – the suffering and the deprivation over which we still have some control. The idea is that any conception of justice which is to be made practically relevant for the way we act now must be a scheme that takes into account modern circumstances and the way those affect the conditions under which people presently live their lives. Arguments for reparation take as conclusive claims of entitlement oriented toward circumstances that are radically different from those we actually face: claims of entitlement based on the habitation of a territory by a small fraction of its present population, and claims of entitlement based on the determination to ignore the present dispersal of persons and peoples on the face of the earth, simply because the historic mechanisms of such dispersal were savagely implicated in injustice. And yet, here we all are. The present circumstances are the ones that are real: it is in the actual world that people starve or are hurt or degraded if the demands of justice in relation to their circumstances are not met. Justice, we say, is a matter of the greatest importance. But the importance to be accorded it is relative to what may actually happen if justice is not done, not to what might have happened if injustice in the past had been avoided.

I want to end by emphasizing two points that qualify or clarify this thesis of the supersession of historic injustice. First, what I have said applies only if an honest attempt is being made to arrange things justly for the future. If no such attempt is being made, there is nothing to overwhelm or supersede the enterprise of reparation. My thesis is not intended as a defense of complacency or inactivity, and to the extent that opponents of reparation are complacent about the injustice of the status quo, their resistance is rightly condemned. Repairing historic injustice is, as we have seen, a difficult business and, as a matter of fact, it is almost always undertaken by people of good will. The only thing that can trump that enterprise is an honest and committed resolve to do justice for the future, a resolve to address present circumstances in a way that respects the claims and needs of everyone.

Second, my thesis is not that such resolve has priority over all rectificatory actions. I claim only that it has priority over reparation which might carry us in a direction contrary to that which is indicated by a prospective theory of justice. Often and understandably, claims based on reparation and claims based on forward-looking principles will coincide, for, as we saw in Section III above, past injustice is not without its present effects. It is a fact that many of the descendants of those who were defrauded and expropriated live demoralized in lives of relative poverty – relative, that is, to the descendants of those who defrauded them. If the relief of poverty and the more equal distribution of resources is the aim of a prospective theory of justice, it is likely that the effect of rectifying past wrongs will carry us some distance in this direction. All the same, it is worth stressing that it is the impulse to justice now that should lead the way in this process, not the reparation of something whose wrongness is understood primarily in relation to conditions that no longer obtain.

Entitlements that fade with time, counterfactuals that are impossible to verify, injustices that are overtaken by circumstances – all this is a bit distant, I am afraid, from the simple conviction that, if something was wrongly taken, it must be right to give it back. The arguments I have made may seem to deflate a lot of the honest enthusiasm that surrounds aboriginal claims and the hope that now for the first time in centuries we may be ready to do justice to people and peoples whom we have perennially maltreated. The arguments may also seem to compromise justice unnecessarily, as they shift from the straightforward logic of compensation to an arcane and calculative casuistry that tries to balance incommensurable claims.

But societies are not simple circumstances, and it does not detract one bit from the importance of justice nor from the force of the duties it generates to insist that its requirements are complex and that they may be sensitive to differences in circumstance. Even the members of a modern society not afflicted by a history like ours would find the demands of justice difficult to discern and hard to weigh: the modern discussion of the subject, with the utopian cast of its "perfect compliance" assumptions, has made that at least clear.[26] It is true that in many cases the complexity of these issues does not diminish our ability to recognize acts of injustice – stark and awful – like direct expropri-

ation and genocide. The fallacy lies in thinking that the directness of such perception and the outrage that attends it translate into simple and straightforward certainty about what is to be done once such injustices have occurred.

"First come, first served." "We were here first." These simplicities have always been unpleasant ways of denying present aspirations or resisting current claims of need. They become no more pleasant, and in the end no more persuasive, by being associated with respect for aboriginal peoples or revulsion from the violence and expropriation that have disfigured our history.

Notes

1 Opinions differ in metaethics about whether this illocutionary function provides a complete explanation of the distinctively moral meaning of the words "right," "wrong," "unjust," etc. For the view that it does, see R.M. Hare, *The Language of Morals* (Oxford: Clarendon, 1952). But most moral philosophers concede that even if it is not the whole story, still it is an essential part of the explanation of the meaning of such words that they have this prescriptive function. The few philosophers who deny this do so purely because of the embarrassment it poses for their realist claims that moral judgments are nothing but judgments about matters of fact. For examples, see Michael Moore, "Moral Reality" (*Wisconsin Law Review* [1982], pp. 1061–1156); and David Brink, *Moral Realism and the Foundations of Ethics* (Cambridge: Cambridge University Press, 1989), ch. 3.

2 For this understanding of moral judgments made about the past, and for the assumed interaction between prescriptivity and universalizability, see R.M. Hare, *Freedom and Reason* (Oxford: Clarendon, 1963).

3 For a moving discussion, see Hannah Arendt, "Truth and Politics," in her collection *Between Past and Future: Six Exercises in Political Thought* (New York: Viking, 1968).

4 John Locke, *An Essay Concerning Human Understanding*, bk. 2, ch. 27, secs. 9–10, ed. John Yolton (London: Everyman's Library, 1965), vol. 1, pp. 280 ff.; see also Stuart Hampshire, *Thought and Action* (London: Chatto & Windus, 1970).

5 Robert Nozick, *Anarchy, State, and Utopia* (Oxford: Blackwell, 1974), pp. 152–3. To this passage, Nozick appends the following footnote: "If the principle of recodification of violations of the first two principles yields more than one description of holdings, then some choice must be made as to which of these is to

be realized. Perhaps the sort of considerations about distributive justice and equality that I argue against play a legimate role in this subsidiary choice" (p. 153n.).

6 We could of course imagine a world in which not only $E+$ occurs instead of E but also in which the laws of nature are different (e.g., living beings can survive and flourish without water). But those worlds are of limited practical interest. The reason why we choose (in David Lewis's terminology) the closest possible world in which $E+$ occurs, and why "closest" includes "same laws of nature" is that that is the world which ought to have been in the contemplation of the agent who faced the choice between E and $E+$. See David Lewis, *Counterfactuals* (Cambridge, Mass.: Harvard University Press, 1973).

7 Often the injustice complained of is that some renegade member of the tribe disposed of tribal land as though it were his own private property. So if a piece of land is indeed tribally owned and its alienation prohibited by tribal custom, is there any point in asking how it would have been disposed of if the injustice of this individual's alienation of it had not occurred? Surely we ought to assume that, if the land had not been wrongfully disposed of, it would have remained the property of the tribe. So, it might be thought, there should be no difficulty in showing that the counterfactual approach requires its present restoration to the tribe. Unfortunately, things are more complicated than that. There are two other things that might have happened if the injustice had not taken place. The members of the tribe might have decided, in the exercise of their powers as communal owners, to sell some of the land. Or the members of the tribe might have decided, in an exercise of sovereignty over their own laws and customs, to abrogate the system of communal property. Both possibilities need to be taken into account in any

realistic reconstruction of what would have happened if the injustice had not taken place. The second is particularly important. All societies change their customs and laws, including their property laws, from time to time, and there is every reason to imagine such change as a probable and reasonable response to new circumstances and conditions on the part of such flexible and resourceful polities as Maori tribes, for example. If we are honestly inquiring into what would have happened in a just world, we have to take at least the possibility of such adaptive exercises of sovereignty into account.

8 See John Rawls, *A Theory of Justice* (Oxford: Oxford University Press, 1971); and T.M. Scanlon, "Contractualism and Utilitarianism" in *Utilitarianism and Beyond*, eds. Amartya Sen and Bernard Williams (Cambridge: Cambridge University Press, 1986).

9 See Rawls, p. 7. For the distinction between holistic and piecemeal uses of contractarian models, see Kim Scheppele and Jeremy Waldron, "Contractarian Methods in Political and Legal Evaluation," *Yale Journal of Law and Humanities* 3 (1991): 206–10.

10 Hence the insistence of Jeremy Bentham on absolute security of expectations as the proper basis of a utilitarian theory of property. See the extract from Jeremy Bentham, *Principles of the Civil Code*, in *Property: Mainstream and Critical Positions*, ed. C.B. MacPherson (Oxford: Blackwell, 1978), pp. 42–58.

11 John Locke, *Two Treatises of Government* (1689), ed. Peter Laslett (Cambridge: Cambridge University Press, 1988), bk. 2, ch. 5; Nozick, ch. 7. There is a comprehensive discussion of this approach in Jeremy Waldron, *The Right to Private Property* (Oxford: Clarendon, 1988), chs. 6, 7.

12 Locke, *Two Treatises*, bk. 2, ch. 5, sec. 27.

13 It is not hard to see how this could be adapted to express a conclusion about the labor and the identity or personality of a whole community. A community takes possession of a resource by investing the labor of its members. The resource now contains something of the community's spirit and personality. And this is what the community is claiming back when it demands the restoration of stolen lands.

14 See Jeremy Waldron, "Two Worries about Mixing One's Labor," *Philosophical Quarterly* 33 (1983): 37–44; and Waldron, *Right to Private Property*, pp. 171–94. See also the criticisms of Locke's idea in Nozick, pp. 174–75.

15 For a full elaboration of this problem, see Waldron, *Right to Private Property*, pp. 259–62.

16 Nozick, ch. 7.

17 There were good reasons for this reticence: it was worth focusing for a while on the question of what the basic shape of a theory of justice should be. As Nozick put it, "I am as well aware as anyone of how sketchy my discussion of the entitlement theory has been. But I no more believe that we need to have formulated a complete alternative theory in order to reject Rawls's undeniably great advance over utilitarianism, than Rawls needed a complete alternative theory before he could reject utilitarianism. What more does one need or can one have, than a sketch of a plausible alternative view, which from its very different perspective highlights the inadequacies of the best existing well-worked-out theory?" (Nozick, p. 230).

18 Locke, *Two Treatises*, bk. 2, sec. 33.

19 Ibid., bk. 2, secs. 36 ff.

20 Nozick, pp. 174 ff.

21 But see the discussion in Jeremy Waldron, "Enough and as Good Left for Others," *Philosophical Quarterly* 29 (1979): 319–28.

22 The point can be borne out by comparing the following passages from Locke's *Two Treatises*. The first follows on from the statement about conditions of plenty that was quoted a page or two earlier: "He that has as good left for his Improvement, as was already taken up, needed not complain, ought not to meddle with what was already improved by another's Labour: If he did, 'tis plain he desired the benefit of another's Pains, which he had no right to, and not the Ground which God had given him in common with others to labour on, and whereof there was good left, as that already possessed." But the second passage raises the specter of scarcity: "God . . . has given no one of his Children such a Property, in his peculiar Portion of the things of this World, but that he has given his needy Brother a Right to the Surplusage of his Goods; so that it cannot justly be denied him, when his pressing Wants call for it." An action which may be condemned in one set of circumstances as the covetous meddling of someone too lazy to fend for herself, becomes in another set of circumstances the exercise of a right, which may not be resisted by the initial appropriator.

23 The example is suggested by David Lyons, "The New Indian Claims and Original Rights to Land," in *Reading Nozick*, ed. J. Paul (Oxford: Blackwell, 1982), p. 371.

24 I am grateful to Carol Sanger for this formulation of the objection.

25 The phrase is from Locke, *Two Treatises*, bk. 2, sec. 41.

26 For the assumption of "perfect compliance," see Rawls, pp. 8–9.

PART IV

Rights

18

Are There Any Natural Rights?

H. L. A. Hart

I shall advance the thesis that if there are any moral rights at all, it follows that there is at least one natural right, the equal right of all men to be free.[1] By saying that there is this right, I mean that in the absence of certain special conditions which are consistent with the right being an equal right, any adult human being capable of choice (1) has the right to forbearance on the part of all others from the use of coercion or restraint against him save to hinder coercion or restraint and (2) is at liberty to do (i.e., is under no obligation to abstain from) any action which is not one coercing or restraining or designed to injure other persons.[2]

I have two reasons for describing the equal right of all men to be free as a *natural* right; both of them were always emphasized by the classical theorists of natural rights. (1) This right is one which all men have if they are capable of choice; they have it *qua* men and not only if they are members of some society or stand in some special relation to each other. (2) This right is not created or conferred by men's voluntary action; other moral rights are.[3] Of course, it is quite obvious that my thesis is not as ambitious as the traditional theories of natural rights; for although on my view all men are *equally* entitled to be free in the sense explained, no man has an absolute or unconditional right to do or not to do any particular thing or to be treated in any particular way; coercion or restraint of any action may be justified in special conditions consistently with the general principle. So my argument will not show that men have any right (save the equal right of all to be free) which is "absolute," "indefeasible," or "imprescriptible." This may for many reduce the importance of my contention, but I think that the principle that all men have an equal right to be free, meager as it may seem, is probably all that the political philosophers of the liberal tradition need have claimed to support any program of action even if they have claimed more. But my contention that there is this one natural right may appear unsatisfying in another respect; it is only the conditional assertion that *if* there are any moral rights then there must be this one natural right. Perhaps few would now deny, as some have, that there are moral rights; for the point of that denial was usually to object to some philosophical claim as to the "ontological status" of rights, and this objection is now expressed not as a denial that there are any moral rights but as a denial of some assumed logical similarity between sentences used to assert the existence of rights and other kinds of sentences. But it is still important to remember that there may be codes of conduct quite properly termed moral moral codes (though we can of course say they are "imperfect") which do not employ the notion of *a* right, and there is nothing contradictory or otherwise absurd in a code or morality consisting wholly of prescriptions or in a code which prescribed only what should be done for the realization of happiness or some ideal of personal perfection.[4] Human actions in such systems would be evaluated or criticised as compliances with prescriptions or as *good* or *bad, right*

Originally published in *Philosophical Review* 64 (1955): 175–91.

or *wrong, wise* or *foolish, fitting* or *unfitting*, but no one in such a system would have, exercise, or claim rights, or violate or infringe them. So those who lived by such systems could not of course be committed to the recognition of the equal right of all to be free; nor, I think (and this is one respect in which the notion of a right differs from other moral notions), could any parallel argument be constructed to show that, from the bare fact that actions were recognized as ones which ought or ought not to be done, as right, wrong, good or bad, it followed that some specific kind of conduct fell under these categories.

I

(a) Lawyers have for their own purposes carried the dissection of the notion of a legal right some distance, and some of their results[5] are of value in the elucidation of statements of the form "X has a right to..." outside legal contexts. There is of course no simple identification to be made between moral and legal rights, but there is an intimate connection between the two, and this itself is one feature which distinguishes a moral right from other fundamental moral concepts. It is not merely that as a matter of fact men speak of their moral rights mainly when advocating their incorporation in a legal system, but that the concept of a right belongs to that branch of morality which is specifically concerned to determine when one person's freedom may be limited by another's[6] and so to determine what actions may appropriately be made the subject of coercive legal rules. The words "*droit*," "*diritto*," and "*Recht*," used by continental jurists, have no simple English translation and seem to English jurists to hover uncertainly between law and morals, but they do in fact mark off an area of morality (the morality of law) which has special characteristics. It is occupied by the concepts of justice, fairness, rights, and obligation (if this last is not used as it is by many moral philosophers as an obscuring general label to cover every action that morally we ought to do or forbear from doing). The most important common characteristic of this group of moral concepts is that there is no incongruity, but a special congruity in the use of force or the threat of force to secure that what is just or fair or someone's right to have done shall in fact be done; for it is in just these circumstances that coercion of another human being is legitimate. Kant, in the *Rechtslehre*, discusses the

obligations which arise in this branch of morality under the title of *officia juris*, "which do not require that respect for duty shall be of itself the determining principle of the will," and contrasts them with *officia virtutis*, which have no moral worth unless done for the sake of the moral principle. His point is, I think, that we must distinguish from the rest of morality those principles regulating the proper distribution of human freedom which alone make it morally legitimate for one human being to determine by his choice how another should act; and a certain specific moral value is secured (to be distinguished from moral virtue in which the good will is manifested) if human relationships are conducted in accordance with these principles even though coercion has to be used to secure this, for only if these principles are regarded will freedom be distributed among human beings as it should be. And it is I think a very important feature of a moral right that the possessor of it is conceived as having a moral justification for limiting the freedom of another and that he has this justification not because the action he is entitled to require of another has some moral quality but simply because in the circumstances a certain distribution of human freedom will be maintained if he by his choice is allowed to determine how that other shall act.

(b) I can best exhibit this feature of a moral right by reconsidering the question whether moral rights and "duties"[7] are correlative. The contention that they are means, presumably, that every statement of the form "X has a right to..." entails and is entailed by "Y has a duty (not) to...," and at this stage we must not assume that the values of the name-variables "X" and "Y" must be different persons. Now there is certainly one sense of "a right" (which I have already mentioned) such that it does not follow from X's having a right that X or someone else has any duty. Jurists have isolated rights in this sense and have referred to them as "liberties" just to distinguish them from rights in the centrally important sense of "right" which has "duty" as a correlative. The former sense of "right" is needed to describe those areas of social life where competition is at least morally unobjectionable. Two people walking along both see a ten-dollar bill in the road twenty yards away, and there is no clue as to the owner. Neither of the two are under a "duty" to allow the other to pick it up; each has in this sense a right to pick it up. Of course there may be many things which each has a "duty" not to do in the course of the race to the spot – neither may kill or wound the other – and corresponding to these "duties" there are rights to forbearances. The moral propriety of all economic competition implies this minimum sense of "a right" in which to say that "X has a right to" means merely that X is under no "duty" not to. Hobbes saw that the expression "a right" could have this sense but he was wrong if he thought that there is no sense in which it does follow from X's having a right that Y has a duty or at any rate an obligation.

(c) More important for our purpose is the question whether for all moral "duties" there are correlative moral rights, because those who have given an affirmative answer to this question have usually assumed without adequate scrutiny that to have a right is simply to be capable of benefiting by the performance of a "duty"; whereas in fact this is not a sufficient condition (and probably not a necessary condition) of having a right. Thus animals and babies who stand to benefit by our performance of our "duty" not to ill-treat them are said *therefore* to have rights to proper treatment. The full consequence of this reasoning is not usually followed out; most have shrunk from saying that we have rights against ourselves because we stand to benefit from our performance of our "duty" to keep ourselves alive or develop our talents. But the moral situation which arises from a promise (where the legal-sounding terminology of rights and obligations is most appropriate) illustrates most clearly that the notion of having a right and that of benefiting by the performance of a "duty" are not identical. X promises Y in return for some favor that he will look after Y's aged mother in his absence. Rights arise out of this transaction, but it is surely Y to whom the promise has been made and not his mother who *has* or *possesses* these rights. Certainly Y's mother is a person concerning whom X has an obligation and a person who will benefit by its performance, but the person *to whom* he has an obligation to look after her is Y. This is something *due to* or *owed to* Y, so it is Y, not his mother, whose right X will disregard and to whom X will have done *wrong* if he fails to keep his promise, though the mother may be physically injured. And it is Y who has a moral *claim* upon X, is *entitled* to have his mother looked after, and who can *waive* the claim and *release* Y from the obligation. Y is, in other words, morally in a position to determine by his choice how X shall act and in this way to limit X's freedom of choice; and it is this fact, not the fact that he stands to benefit, that makes it appropriate to say that he

has *a right*. Of course often the person to whom a promise has been made will be the only person who stands to benefit by its performance, but this does not justify the identification of "having a right" with "benefiting by the performance of a duty." It is important for the whole logic of rights that, while the person who stands to benefit by the performance of a duty is discovered by considering what will happen if the duty is not performed, the person who has a right (to whom performance is *owed* or *due*) is discovered by examining the transaction or antecedent situation or relations of the parties out of which the "duty" arises. These considerations should incline us not to extend to animals and babies whom it is wrong to ill-treat the notion of a right to proper treatment, for the moral situation can be simply and adequately described here by saying that it is wrong or that we ought not to ill-treat them or, in the philosopher's generalized sense of "duty," that we have a duty not to ill-treat them.[8] If common usage sanctions talk of the rights of animals or babies it makes an idle use of the expression "a right," which will confuse the situation with other different moral situations where the expression "a right" has a specific force and cannot be replaced by the other moral expressions which I have mentioned. Perhaps some clarity on this matter is to be gained by considering the force of the preposition "to" in the expression "having a duty to Y" or "being under an obligation to Y" (where "Y" is the name of a person); for it is significantly different from the meaning of "to" in "doing something to Y" or "doing harm to Y," where it indicates the person affected by some action. In the first pair of expressions, "to" obviously does not have this force, but indicates the person to whom the person morally bound is bound. This is an intelligible development of the figure of a bond (*vinculum juris: obligare*); the precise figure is not that of two persons bound by a chain, but of *one* person bound, the other end of the chain lying in the hands of another to use if he chooses.[9] So it appears absurd to speak of having "duties" or owing obligations to ourselves – of course we may have "duties" not to do harm to ourselves, but what could be meant (once the distinction between these different meanings of "to" has been grasped) by insisting that we have duties or obligations *to* ourselves not to do harm to ourselves?

(d) The essential connection between the notion of a right and the justified limitation of one person's freedom by another may be thrown into relief if we consider codes of behavior which do not purport to confer rights but only to prescribe what shall be done. Most natural law thinkers down to Hooker conceived of natural law in this way: there were natural duties compliance with which would certainly benefit man – things to be done to achieve man's natural end – but not natural rights. And there are of course many types of codes of behavior which only prescribe what is to be done, e.g., those regulating certain ceremonies. It would be absurd to regard these codes as conferring rights, but illuminating to contrast them with rules of games, which often create rights, though not, of course, moral rights. But even a code which is plainly a moral code need not establish rights; the Decalogue is perhaps the most important example. Of course, quite apart from heavenly rewards human beings stand to benefit by general obedience to the Ten Commandments: disobedience is wrong and will certainly harm individuals. But it would be a surprising interpretation of them that treated them as conferring rights. In such an interpretation obedience to the Ten Commandments would have to be conceived as due to or owed to individuals, not merely to God, and disobedience not merely as wrong but as *a wrong to* (as well as harm to) individuals. The Commandments would cease to read like penal statutes designed only to rule out certain types of behavior and would have to be thought of as rules placed at the disposal of individuals and regulating the extent to which *they* may demand certain behavior from others. Rights are typically conceived of as *possessed* or *owned by* or *belonging to* individuals, and these expressions reflect the conception of moral rules as not only prescribing conduct but as forming a kind of moral property of individuals to which they are as individuals entitled; only when rules are conceived in this way can we speak of *rights* and *wrongs* as well as right and wrong actions.[10]

II

So far I have sought to establish that to have a right entails having a moral justification for limiting the freedom of another person and for determining how he should act; it is now important to see that the moral justification must be of a special kind if it is to constitute a right, and this will emerge most clearly from an examination of the circumstances in which rights are asserted with the typical expression "I have a right to...." It is I think the case that this form of words is used in two main types of situations: (a) when the claimant has some special justification for interference with another's freedom which other persons do not have ("*I* have a right to be paid what you promised for my services"); (b) when the claimant is concerned to resist or object to some interference by another person as having no justification ("*I* have a right to say what I think").

(a)   *Special rights*

When rights arise out of special transactions between individuals or out of some special relationship in which they stand to each other, both the persons who have the right and those who have the corresponding obligation are limited to the parties to the special transaction or relationship. I call such rights special rights to distinguish them from those moral rights which are thought of as rights against (i.e., as imposing obligations upon)[11] everyone, such as those that are asserted when some unjustified interference is made or threatened as in (b) above.

(i) The most obvious cases of special rights are those that arise from promises. By promising to do or not to do something, we voluntarily incur obligations and create or confer rights on those to whom we promise; we alter the existing moral independence of the parties' freedom of choice in relation to some action and create a new moral relationship between them, so that it becomes morally legitimate for the person to whom the promise is given to determine how the promisor shall act. The promisee has a temporary authority or sovereignty in relation to some specific matter over the other's will which we express by saying that the promisor is under an obligation *to* the promisee to do what he has promised. To some philosophers the notion that moral phenomena – rights and duties or obligations – can be brought into existence by the voluntary action of individuals has appeared utterly mysterious; but this I think has been so because they have not clearly seen how special the moral notions of a right and an obligation are, nor how peculiarly they are connected with the distribution of freedom of choice; it would indeed be mysterious if we could make actions morally good or bad by voluntary choice. The simplest case of promising illustrates two points characteristic of all special rights: (1) the right and obligation arise not because the promised action has itself any particular moral quality, but just because of the voluntary transaction between the parties; (2) the identity of the parties concerned is vital – only *this* person (the promisee) has the moral justification for determining how the promisor shall act. It is *his* right; only in relation to him is the promisor's freedom of choice diminished, so that if he chooses to release the promisor no one else can complain.

(ii) But a promise is not the only kind of transaction whereby rights are conferred. They may be *accorded* by a person consenting or authorizing another to interfere in matters which but for this consent or authorization he would be free to determine for himself. If I consent to your taking precautions for my health or happiness or authorize you to look after my interests, then you have a right which others have not, and I cannot complain of your interference if it is within the sphere of your authority. This is what is meant by a person surrendering his rights to another; and again the typical characteristics of a right are present in this situation: the person authorized has the right to interfere not because of its intrinsic character but because *these* persons have stood in *this* relationship. No one else (not similarly authorized) has any *right*[12] to interfere in theory even if the person authorized does not exercise his right.

(iii) Special rights are not only those created by the deliberate choice of the party on whom the obligation falls, as they are when they are accorded or spring from promises, and not all obligations to other persons are deliberately incurred, though I think it is true of all special rights that they arise from previous voluntary actions. A third very important source of special rights and obligations which we recognize in many spheres of life is what may be termed mutuality of restrictions, and I think political obligation is intelligible only if we see what precisely this is and how it differs from the other right-creating transactions (consent, promising) to which philosophers have assimilated it. In its bare schematic outline it is this: when a number of persons conduct any joint enterprise according to rules and thus restrict their liberty, those who have submitted to these restrictions when required have a right to a similar submission from those who have benefited by their submission. The rules may provide that officials should have authority to enforce obedience and make further rules, and this will create a structure of legal rights and duties, but the moral obligation to obey the rules in such circumstances is *due to* the co-operating members of the society, and they have the correlative moral right to obedience. In social situations of this sort (of which political society is the most complex example) the obligation to obey the rules is something distinct from whatever other moral reasons there may be for obedience in terms of good consequences (e.g., the prevention of suffering); the obligation is due to the co-operating members of the society as such and not because they are human beings on whom it would be wrong to inflict suffering. The utilitarian explanation of political obligation fails to take account of this feature of the situation both in its simple version that the obligation exists because and only if the direct consequences of a particular act of disobedience are worse than obedience, and also in its more sophisticated version that the obligation exists even when this is not so, if disobedience increases the probability that the law in question or other laws will be disobeyed on other occasions when the direct consequences of obedience are better than those of disobedience.

Of course to say that there is such a moral obligation upon those who have benefited by the submission of other members of society to restrictive rules to obey these rules in their turn does not entail either that this is the only kind of moral reason for obedience or that there can be no cases where disobedience will be morally justified. There is no contradiction or other impropriety in saying "I have an obligation to do X, someone has a right to ask me to, but I now see I ought not to do it." It will in painful situations sometimes be the lesser of two moral evils to disregard what really are people's rights and not perform our obligations to them. This seems to me particularly obvious from the case of promises: I may promise to do something and thereby incur an obligation just because that is one way in which obligations (to be distinguished from other forms of moral reasons for acting) are created; reflection may show that it would in the circumstances be wrong to keep this promise because of the suffering it might cause, and we can express this by saying "*I ought not* to do it though *I have an obligation to him* to do it" just because the italicized expressions are not synonyms but come from different dimensions of morality. The attempt to explain this situation by saying that our real obligation here is to avoid the suffering and that there is only a prima facie obligation to keep the promise seems to me to confuse two quite different kinds of moral reason, and in practice such a terminology obscures the precise character of what is at stake when "for some greater good" we infringe people's rights or do not perform our obligations to them.

The social-contract theorists rightly fastened on the fact that the obligation to obey the law is not merely a special case of benevolence (direct or indirect), but something which arises between members of a particular political society out of their mutual relationship. Their mistake was to identify *this* right-creating situation of mutual restrictions with the paradigm case of promising; there are of course important similarities, and these are just the points which all special rights have in common, viz., that they arise out of special relationships between human beings and not out of the character of the action to be done or its effects.

(iv) There remains a type of situation which may be thought of as creating rights and obligations: where the parties have a special natural relationship, as in the case of parent and child. The parent's moral right to obedience from his child would I suppose now be thought to terminate when the child reaches the age "of discretion," but the case is worth mentioning because some political philosophies have had recourse to analogies with this case as an explanation of political obligation, and also because even this case has some of the features we have distinguished in special rights, viz., the right arises out of the special relationship of the parties (though it is in this case a natural relationship) and not out of the character of the actions to the performance of which there is a right.

(v) To be distinguished from special rights, of course, are special liberties, where, exceptionally, one person is *exempted* from obligations to which most are subject but does not thereby acquire a *right* to which there is a correlative obligation. If you catch me reading your brother's diary, you say, "You have no right to read it." I say, "I have a right to read it – your brother said I might unless he told me not to, and he has not told me not to." Here I have been specially *licensed* by your brother who had a right to require me not to read his diary, so I am exempted from the moral obligation not to read it, but your brother is under no obligation to let me go on reading it. Cases where *rights*, not liberties, are accorded to manage or interfere with another person's affairs are those where the license is not revocable at will by the person according the right.

(b) *General rights*

In contrast with special rights, which constitute a justification peculiar to the holder of the right for interfering with another's freedom, are general rights, which are asserted defensively, when some unjustified interference is anticipated or threatened, in order to point out that the interference is unjustified. "I have the right to say what I think."[13] "I have the right to worship as I please." Such rights share two important characteristics with special rights. (1) To have them is to have a moral justification for determining how another shall act, viz., that he shall not interfere.[14] (2) The moral justification does not arise from the character of the particular action to the performance of which the claimant has a right; what justifies the claim is simply – there being no special relation between him and those who are threatening to interfere to justify that interference – that this is a particular exemplification of the equal right to be free. But there are of course striking differences between such defensive general rights and special rights. (1) General rights do not arise out of any special relationship or transaction between men. (2) They are not rights which are peculiar to those who have them but are rights which all men capable of choice have in the absence of those special conditions which give rise to special rights. (3) General rights have as correlatives obligations not to interfere to which everyone else is subject and not merely the parties to some special relationship or transaction, though of course they will often be asserted when some particular persons threaten to interfere as a moral objection to that interference. To assert a general right is to claim in relation to some particular action the equal right of all men to be free in the absence of any of those special conditions which constitute a special right to limit another's freedom; to assert a special right is to assert in relation to some particular action a right constituted by such special conditions to limit another's freedom. The assertion of general rights directly invokes the principle that all men equally have the right to be free; the assertion of a special right (as I attempt to show in Section III) invokes it indirectly.

III

It is, I hope, clear that unless it is recognized that interference with another's freedom requires a moral justification the notion of a right could have no place in morals; for to assert a right is to assert that there is such a justification. The characteristic function in moral discourse of those sentences in which the meaning of the expression "a right" is to be found – "I have a right to . . . ," "You have no right to . . . ," "What right have you to . . . ?" – is to bring to bear on interferences with another's freedom, or on claims to interfere, a type of moral evaluation or criticism specially appropriate to interference with freedom and characteristically different from the moral criticism of actions made with the use of expressions like "right," "wrong," "good," and "bad." And this is only one of many different types of moral ground for saying "You ought . . . " or "You ought not. . . ." The use of the expression "What right have you to . . . ?" shows this more clearly, perhaps, than the others; for we use it, just at the point where interference is actual or threatened, to call for the moral *title* of the person addressed to interfere; and we do this often without any suggestion at all that what he proposes to do is otherwise wrong and sometimes with the implication that the same interference on the part of another person would be unobjectionable.

But though our use in moral discourse of "a right" does presuppose the recognition that interference with another's freedom requires a moral justification, this would not itself suffice to establish, except in a sense easily trivialized, that in the recognition of moral rights there is implied the recognition that all men have a right to equal freedom; for unless there is some restriction inherent in the meaning of "a right" on the type of moral justification for interference which can constitute a right, the principle could be made wholly vacuous. It would, for example, be possible to adopt the principle and then assert that some characteristic or behavior of some human beings (that they are improvident, or atheists, or Jews, or Negroes) constitutes a moral justification for interfering with their freedom; *any* differences between men could, so far as my argument has yet gone, be treated as a moral justification for interference and so constitute a right, so that the equal right of all men to be free would be compatible with gross inequality. It may well be that the expression "moral" itself imports some restriction on what can constitute a moral justification for interference which would avoid this consequence, but I cannot myself yet show that this is so. It is, on the other hand, clear to me that the moral justification for interference which is to constitute a *right* to interfere (as distinct from merely making it morally good or desirable to interfere) is restricted to certain special conditions and that this is inherent in the meaning of "a right" (unless this is used so loosely that it could be replaced by the other moral expressions mentioned). Claims to interfere with another's freedom based on the general character of the activities interfered with (e.g., the folly or cruelty of "native" practices) or the general character of the parties ("We are Germans; they are Jews") even when well founded are not matters of moral right or obligation. Submission in such cases even where proper is not *due to* or *owed to* the individuals who interfere; it would be equally proper whoever of the same class of persons interfered. Hence other elements in our moral vocabulary suffice to describe this case, and it is confusing here to talk of rights. We saw in Section II that the types of justification for interference involved in special rights was independent of the character of the action to the performance of which there was a right but depended upon certain previous transactions and relations between individuals (such as promises, consent, authorization, submission to mutual restrictions). Two questions here suggest themselves: (1) On what intelligible principle could these bare forms of promising, consenting, submission to mutual restrictions, be either necessary or sufficient, irrespective of their content, to justify interference with another's freedom? (2) What characteristics have these types of transaction or relationship in common? The answer to both these questions is I think this: If we justify interference on such grounds as we give when we claim a moral right, we are in fact indirectly invoking as our justification the principle that all men have an equal right to be free. For we are in fact saying in the case of promises and consents or authorizations that this claim to interfere with another's freedom is justified because he has, in exercise of his equal right to be free, freely chosen to create this claim; and in the case of mutual restrictions we are in fact saying that this claim to interfere with another's freedom is justified because it is fair; and it is fair because only so will there be an equal distribution of restrictions and so of freedom among this group of men. So in the case of special rights as well as of general rights recognition of them implies the recognition of the equal right of all men to be free.

Notes

1 I was first stimulated to think along these lines by Mr. Stuart Hampshire, and I have reached by different routes a conclusion similar to his.

2 Further explanation of the perplexing terminology of freedom is, I fear, necessary. *Coercion* includes, besides preventing a person from doing what he chooses, making his choice less eligible by threats; *restraint* includes any action designed to make the exercise of choice impossible and so includes killing or enslaving a person. But neither coercion nor restraint includes *competition*. In terms of the distinction between "having a right to" and "being at liberty to" used above and further discussed in Section I (b), all men may have, consistently with the obligation to forbear from coercion, the *liberty* to satisfy if they can such at least of their desires as are not designed to coerce or injure others, even though in fact, owing to scarcity, one man's satisfaction causes another's frustration. In conditions of extreme scarcity this distinction between competition and coercion will not be worth drawing; natural rights are only of importance "where peace is possible" (Locke). Further, freedom (the absence of coercion) can be *valueless* to those victims of unrestricted competition too poor to make use of it; so it will be pedantic to point out to them that though starving they are free. This is the truth exaggerated by the Marxists whose *identification* of poverty with lack of freedom confuses two different evils.

3 Save those general rights (cf. Section II, (b)) which are particular exemplifications of the right of all men to be free.

4 Is the notion of *a* right found in either Plato or Aristotle? There seems to be no Greek word for it as distinct from "right" or "just" (δικίον), though expressions like τὰ ἐμὰ δικαία are I believe fourth-century legal idioms. The natural expressions in Plato are τὸ ἑαὑτοῦ (ἔχειν) or τὰ τινὶ ὀφειλόμενα, but these seem confined to property or debts. There is no place for a moral right unless the moral value of individual freedom is recognized.

5 As W.D. Lamont has seen: cf. his *Principles of Moral Judgment* (Oxford, 1946); for the jurists, cf. Hohfeld's *Fundamental Legal Conceptions* (New Haven, 1923).

6 Here and subsequently I use "interfere with another's freedom," "limit another's freedom," "determine how another shall act," to mean either the use of coercion or demanding that a person shall do or not do some action. The connection between these two types of "interference" is too complex for discussion here; I think it is enough for present purposes to point out that having a justification for demanding that a person shall or shall not do some action is a necessary though not a sufficient condition for justifying coercion.

7 I write "duties" here because one factor obscuring the nature of a right is the philosophical use of "duty" and "obligation" for all cases where there are moral reasons for saying an action ought to be done or not done. In fact "duty," "obligation," "right," and "good" come from different segments of morality, concern different types of conduct, and make different types of moral criticism or evaluation. Most important are the points (1) that obligations may be voluntarily incurred or created, (2) that they are *owed to* special persons (who have rights), (3) that they do not arise out of the character of the actions which are obligatory but out of the relationship of the parties. Language roughly though not consistently confines the use of "having an obligation" to such cases.

8 The use here of the generalized "duty" is apt to prejudice the question whether animals and babies have rights.

9 Cf. A.H. Campbell, *The Structure of Stair's Institutes* (Glasgow, 1954), p. 31.

10 Continental jurists distinguish between "*subjektives*" and "*objektives Recht*," which corresponds very well to the distinction between *a* right, which an individual has, and what it is right to do.

11 Cf. Section (6).

12 Though it may be *better* (the lesser of two evils) that he should: cf. item iii below.

13 In speech the difference between general and special rights is often marked by stressing the pronoun where a special right is claimed or where the special right is denied. "You have no right to stop him reading that book" refers to the reader's general right. "*You* have no right to stop him reading that book" denies that the person addressed has a special right to interfere though others may have.

14 Strictly, in the assertion of a general right both the *right* to forbearance from coercion and the *liberty* to do the specified action are asserted, the first in the face of actual or threatened coercion, the second as an objection to an actual or anticipated demand that the action should not be done. The first has as its correlative an obligation upon everyone to forbear from coercion; the second the absence in any one of a justification for such a demand. Here, in Hohfeld's words, the correlative is not an obligation but a "no-right."

19

Taking Rights Seriously

Ronald Dworkin

I   The Rights of Citizens

The language of rights now dominates political debate in the United States. Does the Government respect the moral and political rights of its citizens? Or does the Government's war policy, or its race policy, fly in the face of these rights? Do the minorities whose rights have been violated have the right to violate the law in return? Or does the silent majority itself have rights, including the right that those who break the law be punished? It is not surprising that these questions are now prominent. The concept of rights, and particularly the concept of rights against the Government, has its most natural use when a political society is divided, and appeals to co-operation or a common goal are pointless.

The debate does not include the issue of whether citizens have *some* moral rights against their Government. It seems accepted on all sides that they do. Conventional lawyers and politicians take it as a point of pride that our legal system recognizes, for example, individual rights of free speech, equality, and due process. They base their claim that our law deserves respect, at least in part, on that fact, for they would not claim that totalitarian systems deserve the same loyalty.

Some philosophers, of course, reject the idea that citizens have rights apart from what the law happens to give them. Bentham thought that the idea of moral rights was 'nonsense on stilts'. But that view has never been part of our orthodox political theory, and politicians of both parties appeal to the rights of the people to justify a great part of what they want to do. I shall not be concerned, in this essay, to defend the thesis that citizens have moral rights against their governments; I want instead to explore the implications of that thesis for those, including the present [1970] United States Government, who profess to accept it.

It is much in dispute, of course, what *particular* rights citizens have. Does the acknowledged right to free speech, for example, include the right to participate in nuisance demonstrations? In practice the Government will have the last word on what an individual's rights are, because its police will do what its officials and courts say. But that does not mean that the Government's view is necessarily the correct view; anyone who thinks it does must believe that men and women have only such moral rights as Government chooses to grant, which means that they have no moral rights at all.

All this is sometimes obscured in the United States by the constitutional system. The American Constitution provides a set of individual *legal* rights in the First Amendment, and in the due process, equal protection, and similar clauses. Under present legal practice the Supreme Court has the power to declare an act of Congress or of a state legislature void if the Court finds that the act

Originally published in *New York Review of Books*, December 18, 1970. Published in *Oxford Essays in Jurisprudence*, 2nd Series, edited by A.W. Simpson (Oxford: Clarendon Press, 1973), pp. 202–27; reprinted in Dworkin, *Taking Rights Seriously* (London: Dutchworth, 1977), pp. 184–205. Reprinted by permission of the author.

offends these provisions. This practice has led some commentators to suppose that individual moral rights are fully protected by this system, but that is hardly so, nor could it be so.

The Constitution fuses legal and moral issues, by making the validity of a law depend on the answer to complex moral problems, like the problem of whether a particular statute respects the inherent equality of all men. This fusion has important consequences for the debates about civil disobedience; I have described these elsewhere[1] and I shall refer to them later. But it leaves open two prominent questions. It does not tell us whether the Constitution, even properly interpreted, recognizes all the moral rights that citizens have, and it does not tell us whether, as many suppose, citizens would have a duty to obey the law even if it did invade their moral rights.

Both questions become crucial when some minority claims moral rights which the law denies, like the right to run its local school system, and which lawyers agree are not protected by the Constitution. The second question becomes crucial when, as now, the majority is sufficiently aroused so that Constitutional amendments to eliminate rights, like the right against self-incrimination, are seriously proposed. It is also crucial in nations, like the United Kingdom, that have no constitution of a comparable nature.

Even if the Constitution were perfect, of course, and the majority left it alone, it would not follow that the Supreme Court could guarantee the individual rights of citizens. A Supreme Court decision is still a legal decision, and it must take into account precedent and institutional considerations like relations between the Court and Congress, as well as morality. And no judicial decision is necessarily the right decision. Judges stand for different positions on controversial issues of law and morals and, as the fights over Nixon's Supreme Court nominations showed, a President is entitled to appoint judges of his own persuasion, provided that they are honest and capable.

So, though the constitutional system adds something to the protection of moral rights against the Government, it falls far short of guaranteeing these rights, or even establishing what they are. It means that, on some occasions, a department other than the legislature has the last word on these issues, which can hardly satisfy someone who thinks such a department profoundly wrong.

It is of course inevitable that some department of government will have the final say on what law will be enforced. When men disagree about moral rights, there will be no way for either side to prove its case, and some decision must stand if there is not to be anarchy. But that piece of orthodox wisdom must be the beginning and not the end of a philosophy of legislation and enforcement. If we cannot insist that the Government reach the right answers about the rights of its citizens, we can insist at least that it try. We can insist that it take rights seriously, follow a coherent theory of what these rights are, and act consistently with its own professions. I shall try to show what that means, and how it bears on the present political debates.

II Rights and the Right to Break the Law

I shall start with the most violently argued issue. Does an American ever have the moral right to break a law? Suppose someone admits a law is valid; does he therefore have a duty to obey it? Those who try to give an answer seem to fall into two camps. The conservatives, as I shall call them, seem to disapprove of any act of disobedience; they appear satisfied when such acts are prosecuted, and disappointed when convictions are reversed. The other group, the liberals, are much more sympathetic to at least some cases of disobedience; they sometimes disapprove of prosecutions and celebrate acquittals. If we look beyond these emotional reactions, however, and pay attention to the arguments the two parties use, we discover an astounding fact. Both groups give essentially the same answer to the question of principle that supposedly divides them.

The answer that both parties give is this. In a democracy, or at least a democracy that in principle respects individual rights, each citizen has a general moral duty to obey all the laws, even though he would like some of them changed. He owes that duty to his fellow citizens, who obey laws that they do not like, to his benefit. But this general duty cannot be an absolute duty, because even a society that is in principle just may produce unjust laws and policies, and a man has duties other than his duties to the State. A man must honour his duties to his God and to his conscience, and if these conflict with his duty to the State, then he is entitled, in the end, to do what he judges to be right. If he decides that he must break the law, however, then he must submit to the judgment and punishment that the State imposes, in recognition of the fact that his duty to his fellow citizens was overwhelmed but not extinguished by his religious or moral obligation.

Of course this common answer can be elaborated in very different ways. Some would describe the duty to the State as fundamental, and picture the dissenter as a religious or moral fanatic. Others would describe the duty to the State in grudging terms, and picture those who oppose it as moral heroes. But these are differences in tone, and the position I described represents, I think, the view of most of those who find themselves arguing either for or against civil disobedience in particular cases.

I do not claim that it is everyone's view. There must be some who put the duty to the State so high that they do not grant that it can ever be overcome. There are certainly some who would deny that a man ever has a moral duty to obey the law, at least in the United States today. But these two extreme positions are the slender tails of a bell curve, and all those who fall in between hold the orthodox position I described – that men have a duty to obey the law but have the right to follow their consciences when it conflicts with that duty.

But if that is so, then we have a paradox in the fact that men who give the same answer to a question of principle should seem to disagree so much, and to divide so fiercely, in particular cases. The paradox goes even deeper, for each party, in at least some cases, takes a position that seems flatly inconsistent with the theoretical position they both accept. This position is tested, for example, when someone evades the draft on grounds of conscience, or encourages others to commit this crime. Conservatives argue that such men must be prosecuted, even though they are sincere. Why must they be prosecuted? Because society cannot tolerate the decline in respect for the law that their act constitutes and encourages. They must be prosecuted, in short, to discourage them and others like them from doing what they have done.

But there seems to be a monstrous contradiction here. If a man has a right to do what his conscience tells him he must, then how can the State be justified in discouraging him from doing it? Is it not wicked for a state to forbid and punish what it acknowledges that men have a right to do?

Moreover, it is not just conservatives who argue that those who break the law out of moral conviction should be prosecuted. The liberal is notoriously opposed to allowing Southern school officials to go slow on desegregation, even though he acknowledges that these school officials think they have a moral right to do what the law forbids. The liberal does not often argue, it is true, that the desegregation laws must be enforced to encourage general respect for law. He argues instead that the desegregation laws must be enforced because they are right. But his position also seems inconsistent: can it be right to prosecute men for doing what their conscience requires, when we acknowledge their right to follow their conscience?

We are therefore left with two puzzles. How can two parties to an issue of principle, each of which thinks it is in profound disagreement with the other, embrace the same position on that issue? How can it be that each side urges solutions to particular problems which seem flatly to contradict the position of principle that both accept? One possible answer is that some or all of those who accept the common position are hypocrites, paying lip service to rights of conscience which in fact they do not grant.

There is some plausibility in this charge. A sort of hypocrisy must be involved when public officials who claim to respect conscience deny Muhammad Ali the right to box in their states. If Ali, in spite of his religious scruples, had joined the Army, he would have been allowed to box even though, on the principles these officials say they honour, he would have been a worse human being for having done so. But there are few cases that seem so straightforward as this one, and even here the officials do not seem to recognize the contradiction between their acts and their principles. So we must search for some explanation beyond the truth that men often do not mean what they say.

The deeper explanation lies in a set of confusions that often embarrass arguments about rights. These confusions have clouded all the issues I mentioned at the outset and have crippled attempts to develop a coherent theory of how a government that respects rights must behave.

In order to explain this, I must call attention to the fact, familiar to philosophers but often ignored in political debate, that the word 'right' has different force in different contexts. In most cases when we say that someone has a 'right' to do something, we imply that it would be wrong to interfere with his doing it, or at least that some special grounds are needed for justifying any interference. I use this strong sense of right when I say that you have the right to spend your money gambling, if you wish, though you ought to spend it in a more worthwhile way. I mean that it would be wrong for anyone to interfere with you even though you propose to spend your money in a way that I think is wrong.

There is a clear difference between saying that someone has a right to do something in this sense and saying that it is the 'right' thing for him to do, or that he does no 'wrong' in doing it. Someone may have the right to do something that is the wrong thing for him to do, as might be the case with gambling. Conversely, something may be the right thing for him to do and yet he may have no right to do it, in the sense that it would not be wrong for someone to interfere with his trying. If our army captures an enemy soldier, we might say that the right thing for him to do is to try to escape, but it would not follow that it is wrong of us to try to stop him. We might admire him for trying to escape, and perhaps even think less of him if he did not. But there is no suggestion here that it is wrong of us to stand in his way; on the contrary, if we think our cause is just, we think it right for us to do all we can to stop him.

Ordinarily this distinction, between the issues of whether a man has a right to do something and whether it is the right thing for him to do, causes no trouble. But sometimes it does, because sometimes we say that a man has a right to do something when we mean only to deny that it is the wrong thing for him to do. Thus we say that the captured soldier has a "right" to try to escape when we mean, not that we do wrong to stop him, but that he has no duty not to make the attempt. We use 'right' this way when we speak of someone having the 'right' to act on his own principles, or the 'right' to follow his own conscience. We mean that he does no wrong to proceed on his honest convictions, even though we disagree with these convictions, and even though, for policy or other reasons, we must force him to act contrary to them.

Suppose a man believes that welfare payments to the poor are profoundly wrong, because they sap enterprise, and so declares his full income tax each year but declines to pay half of it. We might say that he has a right to refuse to pay, if he wishes, but that the Government has a right to proceed against him for the full tax, and to fine or jail him for late payment if that is necessary to keep the collection system working efficiently. We do not take this line in most cases; we do not say that the ordinary thief has a right to steal, if he wishes, so long as he pays the penalty. We say a man has the right to break the law, even though the State has a right to punish him, only when we think that, because of his convictions, he does no wrong in doing so.[2]

These distinctions enable us to see an ambiguity in the orthodox question: Does a man ever have a right to break the law? Does that question mean to ask whether he ever has a right to break the law in the strong sense, so that the Government would do wrong to stop him, by arresting and prosecuting him? Or does it mean to ask whether he ever does the right thing to break the law, so that we should all respect him even though the Government should jail him?

If we take the orthodox position to be an answer to the first – and most important – question, then the paradoxes I described arise. But if we take it as an answer to the second, they do not. Conservatives and liberals do agree that sometimes a man does not do the wrong thing to break a law, when his conscience so requires. They disagree, when they do, over the different issue of what the State's response should be. Both parties do think that sometimes the State should prosecute. But this is not inconsistent with the proposition that the man prosecuted did the right thing in breaking the law.

The paradoxes seem genuine because the two questions are not usually distinguished, and the orthodox position is presented as a general solution to the problem of civil disobedience. But once the distinction is made, it is apparent that the position has been so widely accepted only because, when it is applied, it is treated as an answer to the second question but not the first. The crucial distinction is obscured by the troublesome idea of a right to conscience; this idea has been at the centre of most recent discussions of political obligation, but it is a red herring drawing us away from the crucial political questions. The state of a man's conscience may be decisive, or central, when the issue is whether he does something morally wrong in breaking the law; but it need not be decisive or even central when the issue is whether he has a right, in the strong sense of that term, to do so. A man does not have the right, in that sense, to do whatever his conscience demands, but he may have the right, in that sense, to do something even though his conscience does not demand it.

If that is true, then there has been almost no serious attempt to answer the questions that almost everyone means to ask. We can make a fresh start by stating these questions more clearly. Does an American ever have the right, in a strong sense, to do something which is against the law? If so, when? In order to answer these questions put in that way, we must try to become clearer about the implications of the idea, mentioned earlier, that citizens have at least some rights against their government.

I said that in the United States citizens are supposed to have certain fundamental rights against their Government, certain moral rights made into legal rights by the Constitution. If this idea is significant, and worth bragging about, then these rights must be rights in the strong sense I just described. The claim that citizens have a right to free speech must imply that it would be wrong for the Government to stop them from speaking, even when the Government believes that what they will say will cause more harm than good. The claim cannot mean, on the prisoner-of-war analogy, only that citizens do no wrong in speaking their minds, though the Government reserves the right to prevent them from doing so.

This is a crucial point, and I want to labour it. Of course a responsible government must be ready to justify anything it does, particularly when it limits the liberty of its citizens. But normally it is a sufficient justification, even for an act that limits liberty, that the act is calculated to increase what the philosophers call general utility – that it is calculated to produce more overall benefit than harm. So, though the New York City government needs a justification for forbidding motorists to drive up Lexington Avenue, it is sufficient justification if the proper officials believe, on sound evidence, that the gain to the many will outweigh the inconvenience to the few. When individual citizens are said to have rights against the Government, however, like the right of free speech, that must mean that this sort of justification is not enough. Otherwise the claim would not argue that individuals have special protection against the law when their rights are in play, and that is just the point of the claim.

Not all legal rights, or even Constitutional rights, represent moral rights against the Government. I now have the legal right to drive either way on Fifty-seventh Street, but the Government would do no wrong to make that street one-way if it thought it in the general interest to do so. I have a Constitutional right to vote for a congressman every two years, but the national and state governments would do no wrong if, following the amendment procedure, they made a congressman's term four years instead of two, again on the basis of a judgment that this would be for the general good.

But those Constitutional rights that we call fundamental, like the right of free speech, are supposed to represent rights against the Government in the strong sense; that is the point of the boast that our legal system respects the fundamental rights of the citizen. If citizens have a moral right of free speech, then governments would do wrong to repeal the First Amendment that guarantees it, even if they were persuaded that the majority would be better off if speech were curtailed.

I must not overstate the point. Someone who claims that citizens have a right against the Government need not go so far as to say that the State is *never* justified in overriding that right. He might say, for example, that although citizens have a right to free speech, the Government may override that right when necessary to protect the rights of others, or to prevent a catastrophe, or even to obtain a clear and major public benefit (though if he acknowledged this last as a possible justification he would be treating the right in question as not among the most important or fundamental). What he cannot do is to say that the Government is justified in overriding a right on the minimal grounds that would be sufficient if no such right existed. He cannot say that the Government is entitled to act on no more than a judgment that its act is likely to produce, overall, a benefit to the community. That admission would make his claim of a right pointless, and would show him to be using some sense of 'right' other than the strong sense necessary to give his claim the political importance it is normally taken to have.

But then the answers to our two questions about disobedience seem plain, if unorthodox. In our society a man does sometimes have the right, in the strong sense, to disobey a law. He has that right whenever that law wrongly invades his rights against the Government. If he has a moral right to free speech, that is, then he has a moral right to break any law that the Government, by virtue of his right, had no right to adopt. The right to disobey the law is not a separate right, having something to do with conscience, additional to other rights against the Government. It is simply a feature of these rights against the Government, and it cannot be denied in principle without denying that any such rights exist.

These answers seem obvious once we take rights against the Government to be rights in the strong sense I described. If I have a right to speak my mind on political issues, then the Government does wrong to make it illegal for me to do so, even if it thinks this is in the general interest. If, nevertheless, the Government does make my act illegal, then it does a further wrong to enforce that law against me. My right against the Government means that it is wrong for the Government to stop me from speaking; the Government cannot make it right to stop me just by taking the first step.

This does not, of course, tell us exactly what rights men do have against the Government. It does not tell us whether the right of free speech includes the right of demonstration. But it does mean that passing a law cannot affect such rights as men do have, and that is of crucial importance, because it dictates the attitude that an individual is entitled to take toward his personal decision when civil disobedience is in question.

Both conservatives and liberals suppose that in a society which is generally decent everyone has a duty to obey the law, whatever it is. That is the source of the 'general duty' clause in the orthodox position, and though liberals believe that this duty can sometimes be 'overridden', even they suppose, as the orthodox position maintains, that the duty of obedience remains in some submerged form, so that a man does well to accept punishment in recognition of that duty. But this general duty is almost incoherent in a society that recognizes rights. If a man believes he has a right to demonstrate, then he must believe that it would be wrong for the Government to stop him, with or without benefit of a law. If he is entitled to believe that, then it is silly to speak of a duty to obey the law as such, or of a duty to accept the punishment that the State has no right to give.

Conservatives will object to the short work I have made of their point. They will argue that even if the Government was wrong to adopt some law, like a law limiting speech, there are independent reasons why the Government is justified in enforcing the law once adopted. When the law forbids demonstration, then, so they argue, some principle more important than the individual's right to speak is brought into play, namely the principle of respect for law. If a law, even a bad law, is left unenforced, then respect for law is weakened, and society as a whole suffers. So an individual loses his moral right to speak when speech is made criminal, and the Government must, for the common good and for the general benefit, enforce the law against him.

But this argument, though popular, is plausible only if we forget what it means to say that an individual has a right against the State. It is far from plain that civil disobedience lowers respect for law, but even if we suppose that it does, this fact is irrelevant. The prospect of utilitarian gains cannot justify preventing a man from doing what he has a right to do, and the supposed gains in respect for law are simply utilitarian gains. There would be no point in the boast that we respect individual rights unless that involved some sacrifice, and the sacrifice in question must be that we give up whatever marginal benefits our country would receive from overriding these rights when they prove inconvenient. So the general benefit cannot be a good ground for abridging rights, even when the benefit in question is a heightened respect for law.

But perhaps I do wrong to assume that the argument about respect for law is only an appeal to general utility. I said that a state may be justified in overriding or limiting rights on other grounds, and we must ask, before rejecting the conservative position, whether any of these apply. The most important – and least well understood – of these other grounds invokes the notion of *competing rights* that would be jeopardized if the right in question were not limited. Citizens have personal rights to the State's protection as well as personal rights to be free from the State's interference, and it may be necessary for the Government to choose between these two sorts of rights. The law of defamation, for example, limits the personal right of any man to say what he thinks, because it requires him to have good grounds for what he says. But this law is justified, even for those who think that it does invade a personal right, by the fact that it protects the right of others not to have their reputations ruined by a careless statement.

The individual rights that our society acknowledges often conflict in this way, and when they do it is the job of government to discriminate. If the Government makes the right choice, and protects the more important at the cost of the less, then it has not weakened or cheapened the notion of a right; on the contrary it would have done so had it failed to protect the more important of the two. So we must acknowledge that the Government has a reason for limiting rights if it plausibly believes that a competing right is more important.

May the conservative seize on this fact? He might argue that I did wrong to characterize his argument as one that appeals to the general benefit, because it appeals instead to competing rights, namely the moral right of the majority to have its laws enforced, or the right of society to maintain the degree of order and security it wishes. These are the rights, he would say, that must be weighed against the individual's right to do what the wrongful law prohibits.

But this new argument is confused, because it depends on yet another ambiguity in the language of rights. It is true that we speak of the 'right' of society to do what it wants, but this cannot be a 'competing right' of the sort that may justify the invasion of a right against the Government. The existence of rights against the Government would be jeopardized if the Government were able to defeat such a right by appealing to the right of a democratic majority to work its will. A right against the Government must be a right to do something even when the majority thinks it would be wrong to do it, and even when the majority would be worse off for having it done. If we now say that society has a right to do whatever is in the general benefit, or the right to preserve whatever sort of environment the majority wishes to live in, and we mean that these are the sort of rights that provide justification for overruling any rights against the Government that may conflict, then we have annihilated the latter rights.

In order to save them, we must recognize as competing rights only the rights of other members of the society as individuals. We must distinguish the 'rights' of the majority as such, which cannot count as a justification for overruling individual rights, and the personal rights of members of a majority, which might well count. The test we must use is this. Someone has a competing right to protection, which must be weighed against an individual right to act, if that person would be entitled to demand that protection from his government on his own title, as an individual, without regard to whether a majority of his fellow citizens joined in the demand.

It cannot be true, on this test, that anyone has a right to have all the laws of the nation enforced. He has a right to have enforced only those criminal laws, for example, that he would have a right to have enacted if they were not already law. The laws against personal assault may well fall into that class. If the physically vulnerable members of the community – those who need police protection against personal violence – were only a small minority, it would still seem plausible to say that they were entitled to that protection. But the laws that

provide a certain level of quiet in public places, or that authorize and finance a foreign war, cannot be thought to rest on individual rights. The timid lady on the streets of Chicago is not entitled to just the degree of quiet that now obtains, nor is she entitled to have boys drafted to fight in wars she approves. There are laws – perhaps desirable laws – that provide these advantages for her, but the justification for these laws, if they can be justified at all, is the common desire of a large majority, not her personal right. If, therefore, these laws do abridge someone else's moral right to protest, or his right to personal security, she cannot urge a competing right to justify the abridgement. She has no personal right to have such laws passed, and she has no competing right to have them enforced either.

So the conservative cannot advance his argument much on the ground of competing rights, but he may want to use another ground. A government, he may argue, may be justified in abridging the personal rights of its citizens in an emergency, or when a very great loss may be prevented, or, perhaps, when some major benefit can clearly be secured. If the nation is at war, a policy of censorship may be justified even though it invades the right to say what one thinks on matters of political controversy. But the emergency must be genuine. There must be what Oliver Wendell Holmes described as a clear and present danger, and the danger must be one of magnitude.

Can the conservative argue that when any law is passed, even a wrongful law, this sort of justification is available for enforcing it? His argument might be something of this sort. If the Government once acknowledges that it may be wrong – that the legislature might have adopted, the executive approved, and the courts left standing, a law that in fact abridges important rights – then this admission will lead not simply to a marginal decline in respect for law, but to a crisis of order. Citizens may decide to obey only those laws they personally approve, and that is anarchy. So the Government must insist that whatever a citizen's rights may be before a law is passed and upheld by the courts, his rights thereafter are determined by that law.

But this argument ignores the primitive distinction between what may happen and what will happen. If we allow speculation to support the justification of emergency or decisive benefit, then, again, we have annihilated rights. We must, as Learned Hand said, discount the gravity of the evil threatened by the likelihood of reaching that evil. I know of no genuine evidence to the effect that tolerating some civil disobedience, out of respect for the moral position of its authors, will increase such disobedience, let alone crime in general. The case that it will must be based on vague assumptions about the contagion of ordinary crimes, assumptions that are themselves unproved, and that are in any event largely irrelevant. It seems at least as plausible to argue that tolerance will increase respect for officials and for the bulk of the laws they promulgate, or at least retard the rate of growing disrespect.

If the issue were simply the question whether the community would be marginally better off under strict law enforcement, then the Government would have to decide on the evidence we have, and it might not be unreasonable to decide, on balance, that it would. But since rights are at stake, the issue is the very different one of whether tolerance would destroy the community or threaten it with great harm, and it seems to me simply mindless to suppose that the evidence makes that probable or even conceivable.

The argument from emergency is confused in another way as well. It assumes that the Government must take the position either that a man never has the right to break the law, or that he always does. I said that any society that claims to recognize rights at all must abandon the notion of a general duty to obey the law that holds in all cases. This is important, because it shows that there are no short cuts to meeting a citizen's claim of right. If a citizen argues that he has a moral right not to serve in the Army, or to protest in a way he finds effective, then an official who wants to answer him, and not simply bludgeon him into obedience, must respond to the particular point he makes, and cannot point to the draft law or a Supreme Court decision as having even special, let alone decisive, weight. Sometimes an official who considers the citizen's moral arguments in good faith will be persuaded that the citizen's claim is plausible, or even right. It does not follow, however, that he will always be persuaded or that he always should be.

I must emphasize that all these propositions concern the strong sense of right, and they therefore leave open important questions about the right thing to do. If a man believes he has the right to break the law, he must then ask whether he does the right thing to exercise that right. He must remember that reasonable men can differ about whether he has a right against the Government, and therefore the right to break the law, that he thinks he has; and therefore that reasonable men can oppose him in good faith. He must take into account the various consequences his acts will have, whether they involve violence, and such other considerations as the context makes relevant; he must not go beyond the rights he can in good faith claim, to acts that violate the rights of others.

On the other hand, if some official, like a prosecutor, believes that the citizen does *not* have the right to break the law, then *he* must ask whether he does the right thing to enforce it. In the article I mentioned earlier I argued that certain features of our legal system, and in particular the fusion of legal and moral issues in our Constitution, mean that citizens often do the right thing in exercising what they take to be moral rights to break the law, and that prosecutors often do the right thing in failing to prosecute them for it. I will not repeat those arguments here; instead I want to ask whether the requirement that Government take its citizens' rights seriously has anything to do with the crucial question of what these rights are.

III   Controversial Rights

The argument so far has been hypothetical: if a man has a particular moral right against the Government, that right survives contrary legislation or adjudication. But this does not tell us what rights he has, and it is notorious that reasonable men disagree about that. There is wide agreement on certain clear-cut cases; almost everyone who believes in rights at all would admit, for example, that a man has a moral right to speak his mind in a non-provocative way on matters of political concern, and that this is an important right that the State must go to great pains to protect. But there is great controversy as to the limits of such paradigm rights, and the so-called 'anti-riot' law involved in the Chicago Seven trial is a case in point.

The defendants were accused of conspiring to cross state lines with the intention of causing a riot. This charge is vague – perhaps unconstitutionally vague – but the law apparently defines as criminal emotional speeches which argue that violence is justified in order to secure political equality. Does the right of free speech protect this sort of speech? That, of course, is a legal issue, because it invokes the free-speech clause of the First Amendment of the Constitution. But it is also a moral issue, because, as I said, we must treat the First Amendment as an attempt to protect a moral right. It is part of the job of governing to 'define' moral rights through statutes and judicial decisions, that is, to declare officially the extent that moral rights will be taken to have in law. Congress faced this task in voting on the anti-riot bill, and the Supreme Court will face it if the Chicago Seven case goes that far. How should the different departments of government go about defining moral rights?

They should begin with a sense that whatever they decide might be wrong. History and their descendants may judge that they acted unjustly when they thought they were right. If they take their duty seriously, they must try to limit their mistakes, and they must therefore try to discover where the dangers of mistake lie.

They might choose one of two very different models for this purpose. The first model recommends striking a balance between the rights of the individual and the demands of society at large. If the Government *infringes* on a moral right (for example, by defining the right of free speech more narrowly than justice requires), then it has done the individual a wrong. On the other hand, if the Government *inflates* a right (by defining it more broadly than justice requires) then it cheats society of some general benefit, like safe streets, that it is perfectly entitled to have. So a mistake on one side is as serious as a mistake on the other. The course of government is to steer to the middle, to balance the general good and personal rights, giving to each its due.

When the Government, or any of its branches, defines a right, it must bear in mind, according to the first model, the social cost of different proposals and make the necessary adjustments. It must not grant the same freedom to noisy demonstrations as it grants to calm political discussion, for example, because the former causes much more trouble than the latter. Once it decides how much of a right to recognize, it must enforce its decision to the full. That means permitting an individual to act within his rights, as the Government has defined them, but not beyond, so that if anyone breaks the law, even on grounds of conscience, he must be punished. No doubt any government will make mistakes, and will regret decisions once taken. That is inevitable. But this middle policy will ensure that errors on one side will balance out errors on the other over the long run.

The first model, described in this way, has great plausibility, and most laymen and lawyers, I think, would respond to it warmly. The metaphor of balancing the public interest against personal claims is established in our political and judicial rhetoric, and this metaphor gives the model both familiarity and appeal. Nevertheless, the first model is a false one, certainly in the case of rights generally regarded as important, and the metaphor is the heart of its error.

The institution of rights against the Government is not a gift of God, or an ancient ritual, or a national sport. It is a complex and troublesome practice that makes the Government's job of securing the general benefit more difficult and more expensive, and it would be a frivolous and wrongful practice unless it served some point. Anyone who professes to take rights seriously, and who praises our Government for respecting them, must have some sense of what that point is. He must accept, at the minimum, one or both of two important ideas. The first is the vague but powerful idea of human dignity. This idea, associated with Kant, but defended by philosophers of different schools, supposes that there are ways of treating a man that are inconsistent with recognizing him as a full member of the human community, and holds that such treatment is profoundly unjust.

The second is the more familiar idea of political equality. This supposes that the weaker members of a political community are entitled to the same concern and respect of their government as the more powerful members have secured for themselves, so that if some men have freedom of decision whatever the effect on the general good, then all men must have the same freedom. I do not want to defend or elaborate these ideas here, but only to insist that anyone who claims that citizens have rights must accept ideas very close to these.[3]

It makes sense to say that a man has a fundamental right against the Government, in the strong sense, like free speech, if that right is necessary to protect his dignity, or his standing as equally entitled to concern and respect, or some other personal value of like consequence. It does not make sense otherwise.

So if rights make sense at all, then the invasion of a relatively important right must be a very serious matter. It means treating a man as less than a man, or as less worthy of concern than other men. The institution of rights rests on the conviction that this is a grave injustice, and that it is worth paying the incremental cost in social policy or efficiency that is necessary to prevent it. But then it must be wrong to say that inflating rights is an serious as invading them. If the Government errs on the side of the individual, then it simply pays a little more in social efficiency than it has to pay; it pays a little more, that is, of the same coin that it has already decided must be spent. But if it errs against the individual it inflicts an insult upon him that, on its own reckoning, it is worth a great deal of that coin to avoid.

So the first model is indefensible. It rests, in fact, on a mistake I discussed earlier, namely the confusion of society's rights with the rights of members of society. 'Balancing' is appropriate when the Government must choose between competing claims of right – between the Southerner's claim to freedom of association, for example, and the black man's claim to an equal education. Then the Government can do nothing but estimate the merits of the competing claims, and act on its estimate. The first model assumes that the 'right' of the majority is a competing right that must be balanced in this way; but that, as I argued before, is a confusion that threatens to destroy the concept of individual rights. It is worth noticing that the community rejects the first model in that area where the stakes for the individual are highest, the criminal process. We say that it is better that a great many guilty men go free than that one innocent man be punished, and that homily rests on the choice of the second model for government.

The second model treats abridging a right as much more serious than inflating one, and its recommendations follow from that judgment. It stipulates that once a right is recognized in clear-cut cases, then the Government should act to cut off that right only when some compelling reason is presented, some reason that is consistent with the suppositions on which the original right must be based. It cannot be an argument for curtailing a right, once granted, simply that society would pay a further price in extending it. There must be something special about that further cost, or there must be some other feature of the case, that makes it sensible to say that although great social cost is warranted to protect the original right, this particular cost is not necessary. Otherwise, the Government's failure to extend the right will show that its recognition of the right in the original case is a sham, a promise that it intends to keep only until that becomes inconvenient.

How can we show that a particular cost is not worth paying without taking back the initial rec-

ognition of a right? I can think of only three sorts of grounds that can consistently be used to limit the definition of a particular right. First, the Government might show that the values protected by the original right are not really at stake in the marginal case, or are at stake only in some attenuated form. Second, it might show that if the right is defined to include the marginal case, then some competing right, in the strong sense I described earlier, would be abridged. Third, it might show that if the right were so defined, then the cost to society would not be simply incremental, but would be of a degree far beyond the cost paid to grant the original right, a degree great enough to justify whatever assault on dignity or equality might be involved.

It is fairly easy to apply these grounds to one problem the Supreme Court has recently faced, and must face soon again. The draft law provides an exemption for conscientious objectors, but this exemption, as interpreted by the draft boards, has been limited to those who object to *all* wars on *religious* grounds. If we suppose that the exemption is justified on the ground that an individual has a moral right not to kill in violation of his own principles, then the question is raised whether it is proper to exclude those whose morality is not based on religion, or whose morality is sufficiently complex to distinguish among wars. The Court has just held that the draft boards are wrong to exclude the former, and it will soon be asked to decide whether they are wrong to exclude the latter as well.

None of the three grounds I listed can justify either of these exclusions. The invasion of personality in forcing men to kill when they believe killing immoral is just as great when these beliefs are based on secular grounds, or take account of the fact that wars differ in morally relevant ways, and there is no pertinent difference in competing rights or in national emergency. There are differences among the cases, of course, but they are insufficient to justify the distinction. A government that is secular on principle cannot prefer a religious to a non-religious morality as such. There are utilitarian arguments in favour of limiting the exception to religious or universal grounds – an exemption so limited may be less expensive to administer, and may allow easier discrimination between sincere and insincere applicants. But these utilitarian reasons are irrelevant, because they cannot count as grounds for limiting a right.

What about the anti-riot law, as applied in the Chicago trial? Does that law represent an improper limitation of the right to free speech, supposedly protected by the First Amendment? If we were to apply the first model for government to this issue, the argument for the anti-riot law would look strong. But if we set aside talk of balancing as inappropriate, and turn to the proper grounds for limiting a right, then the argument becomes a great deal weaker. The original right of free speech must suppose that it is an assault on human personality to stop a man from expressing what he honestly believes, particularly on issues affecting how he is governed. Surely the assault is greater, and not less, when he is stopped from expressing those principles of political morality that he holds most passionately, in the face of what he takes to be outrageous violations of these principles.

It may be said that the anti-riot law leaves him free to express these principles in a non-provocative way. But that misses the point of the connection between expression and dignity. A man cannot express himself freely when he cannot match his rhetoric to his outrage, or when he must trim his sails to protect values he counts as nothing next to those he is trying to vindicate. It is true that some political dissenters speak in ways that shock the majority, but it is arrogant for the majority to suppose that the orthodox methods of expression are the proper ways to speak, for this is a denial of equal concern and respect. If the point of the right is to protect the dignity of dissenters, then we must make judgments about appropriate speech with the personalities of the dissenters in mind, not the personality of the 'silent' majority for whom the anti-riot law is no restraint at all.

So the argument fails, that the personal values protected by the original right are less at stake in this marginal case. We must consider whether competing rights, or some grave threat to society, nevertheless justify the anti-riot law. We can consider these two grounds together, because the only plausible competing rights are rights to be free from violence, and violence is the only plausible threat to society that the context provides.

I have no right to burn your house, or stone you or your car, or swing a bicycle chain against your skull, even if I find these to be natural means of expression. But the defendants in the Chicago trial were not accused of direct violence; the argument runs that the acts of speech they planned made it likely that others would do acts of violence, either in support of or out of hostility to what they said. Does this provide a justification?

The question would be different if we could say with any confidence how much and what sort of violence the anti-riot law might be expected to prevent. Will it save two lives a year, or two hundred, or two thousand? Two thousand dollars of property, or two hundred thousand, or two million? No one can say, not simply because prediction is next to impossible, but because we have no firm understanding of the process by which demonstration disintegrates into riot, and in particular of the part played by inflammatory speech, as distinct from poverty, police brutality, blood lust, and all the rest of human and economic failure. The Government must try, of course, to reduce the violent waste of lives and property, but it must recognize that any attempt to locate and remove a cause of riot, short of a reorganization of society, must be an exercise in speculation, trial, and error. It must make its decisions under conditions of high uncertainty, and the institution of rights, taken seriously, limits its freedom to experiment under such conditions.

It forces the Government to bear in mind that preventing a man from speaking or demonstrating offers him a certain and profound insult, in return for a speculative benefit that may in any event be achieved in other if more expensive ways. When lawyers say that rights may be limited to protect other rights, or to prevent catastrophe, they have in mind cases in which cause and effect are relatively clear, like the familiar example of a man falsely crying 'Fire!' in a crowded theatre.

But the Chicago story shows how obscure the causal connections can become. Were the speeches of Hoffman or Rubin necessary conditions of the riot? Or had thousands of people come to Chicago for the purposes of rioting anyway, as the Government also argues? Were they in any case sufficient conditions? Or could the police have contained the violence if they had not been so busy contributing to it, as the staff of the President's Commission on Violence said they were?

These are not easy questions, but if rights mean anything, then the Government cannot simply assume answers that justify its conduct. If a man has a right to speak, if the reasons that support that right extend to provocative political speech, and if the effects of such speech on violence are unclear, then the Government is not entitled to make its first attack on that problem by denying that right. It may be that abridging the right to speak is the least expensive course, or the least damaging to police morale, or the most popular politically.

But these are utilitarian arguments in favour of starting one place rather than another, and such arguments are ruled out by the concept of rights.

This point may be obscured by the popular belief that political activists look forward to violence and 'ask for trouble' in what they say. They can hardly complain, in the general view, if they are taken to be the authors of the violence they expect, and treated accordingly. But this repeats the confusion I tried to explain earlier between having a right and doing the right thing. The speaker's motives may be relevant in deciding whether he does the right thing in speaking passionately about issues that may inflame or enrage the audience. But if he has a right to speak, because the danger in allowing him to speak is speculative, his motives cannot count as independent evidence in the argument that justifies stopping him.

But what of the individual rights of those who will be destroyed by a riot, of the passer-by who will be killed by a sniper's bullet or the shopkeeper who will be ruined by looting? To put the issue in this way, as a question of competing rights, suggests a principle that would undercut the effect of uncertainty. Shall we say that some rights to protection are so important that the Government is justified in doing all it can to maintain them? Shall we therefore say that the Government may abridge the rights of others to act when their acts might simply increase the risk, by however slight or speculative a margin, that some person's right to life or property will be violated?

Some such principle is relied on by those who oppose the Supreme Court's recent liberal rulings on police procedure. These rulings increase the chance that a guilty man will go free, and therefore marginally increase the risk that any particular member of the community will be murdered, raped, or robbed. Some critics believe that the Court's decisions must therefore be wrong.

But no society that purports to recognize a variety of rights, on the ground that a man's dignity or equality may be invaded in a variety of ways, can accept such a principle. If forcing a man to testify against himself, or forbidding him to speak, does the damage that the rights against self-incrimination and the right of free speech assume, then it would be contemptuous for the State to tell a man that he must suffer this damage against the possibility that other men's risk of loss may be marginally reduced. If rights make sense, then the degrees of their importance cannot be so different that some count not at all when others are mentioned.

Of course the Government may discriminate and may stop a man from exercising his right to speak when there is a clear and substantial risk that his speech will do great damage to the person or property of others, and no other means of preventing this are at hand, as in the case of the man shouting 'Fire!' in a theatre. But we must reject the suggested principle that the Government can simply ignore rights to speak when life and property are in question. So long as the impact of speech on these other rights remains speculative and marginal, it must look elsewhere for levers to pull.

IV Why Take Rights Seriously?

I said at the beginning of this essay that I wanted to show what a government must do that professes to recognize individual rights. It must dispense with the claim that citizens never have a right to break its law, and it must not define citizens' rights so that these are cut off for supposed reasons of the general good. The present Government's policy towards civil disobedience, and its campaign against vocal protest, may therefore be thought to count against its sincerity.

One might well ask, however, whether it is wise to take rights all that seriously after all. America's genius, at least in her own legend, lies in not taking any abstract doctrine to its logical extreme. It may be time to ignore abstractions, and concentrate instead on giving the majority of our citizens a new sense of their Government's concern for their welfare, and of their title to rule.

That, in any event, is what Vice-President Agnew seems to believe. In a recent policy statement on the issue of 'weirdos' and social misfits, he said that the liberals' concern for individual rights was a headwind blowing in the face of the ship of state. That is a poor metaphor, but the philosophical point it expresses is very well taken. He recognizes, as many liberals do not, that the majority cannot travel as fast or as far as it would like if it recognizes the rights of individuals to do what, in the majority's terms, is the wrong thing to do.

The Vice-President supposes that rights are divisive, and that national unity and a new respect for law may be developed by taking them more sceptically. But he is wrong. America will continue to be divided by its social and foreign policy, and if the economy grows weaker the divisions will become more bitter. If we want our laws and our legal institutions to provide the ground rules within which these issues will be contested, then these ground rules must not be the conqueror's law that the dominant class imposes on the weaker, as Marx supposed the law of a capitalist society must be. The bulk of the law – that part which defines and implements social, economic, and foreign policy – cannot be neutral. It must state, in its greatest part, the majority's view of the common good. The institution of rights is therefore crucial, because it represents the majority's promise to the minorities that their dignity and equality will be respected. When the divisions among the groups are most violent, then this gesture, if law is to work, must be most sincere.

The institution requires an act of faith on the part of the minorities, because the scope of their rights will be controversial whenever they are important, and because the officers of the majority will act on their own notions of what these rights really are. Of course these officials will disagree with many of the claims that a minority makes. That makes it all the more important that they take their decisions gravely. They must show that they understand what rights are, and they must not cheat on the full implications of the doctrine. The Government will not re-establish respect for law without giving the law some claim to respect. It cannot do that if it neglects the one feature that distinguishes law from ordered brutality. If the Government does not take rights seriously, then it does not take law seriously either.

Notes

1 'On Not Prosecuting Civil Disobedience', *New York Review of Books* (June 1968).
2 It is not surprising that we sometimes use the concept of having a right to say that others must not interfere with an act and sometimes to say that the act is not the wrong thing to do. Often, when someone has *no* right to do something, like attacking another man physically, it is true *both* that it is the wrong thing to do and that others are entitled to stop it, by demand, if not by force. It is therefore natural to say that someone has a right when we mean to deny *either* of these consequences, as well as when we mean to deny both.

3 He need not consider these ideas to be axiomatic. He may, that is, have reasons for insisting that dignity or equality are important values, and these reasons may be utilitarian. He may believe, for example, that the general good will be advanced, *in the long run*, only if we treat indignity or inequality as very great injustices, and never allow our *opinions* about the general good to justify them. I do not know of any good arguments for or against this sort of 'institutional' utilitarianism, but it is consistent with my point, because it argues that we must treat violations of dignity and equality as special moral crimes, beyond the reach of ordinary utilitarian justification.

20

Basic Rights

Henry Shue

"Negative" Rights and "Positive" Rights

Many Americans would probably be initially inclined to think that rights to subsistence are at least
slightly less important than rights to physical security, even though subsistence is at least as essential to survival as security is and even though
questions of security do not even arise when subsistence fails. Much official US government rhetoric routinely treats all "economic rights," among
which basic subsistence rights are buried amidst
many non-basic rights, as secondary and defer-
rable, although the fundamental enunciation of
policy concerning human rights by the then Secretary of State did appear to represent an attempt
to correct the habitual imbalance.[1] Now that the
same argument in favor of basic rights to both
aspects of personal survival, subsistence and security, is before us, we can examine critically some of
the reasons why it sometimes appears that although people have basic security rights, the
right, if any, to even the physical necessities of
existence like minimal health care, food, clothing,
shelter, unpolluted water, and unpolluted air is
somehow less urgent or less basic.

Frequently it is asserted or assumed that a
highly significant difference between rights to
physical security and rights to subsistence is that
they are respectively "negative" rights and "positive" rights.[2] This position, which I will now try to
refute, is considerably more complex than it at first

appears. I will sometimes refer to it as the position
that subsistence rights are *positive* and *therefore
secondary*. Obviously taking the position involves
holding that subsistence rights are positive in some
respect in which security rights are negative and
further claiming that this difference concerning
positive/negative is a good enough reason to assign
priority to negative rights over positive rights.
I will turn shortly to the explanation of this assumed positive/negative distinction. But first I
want to lay out all the premises actually needed
by the position that subsistence rights are positive
and therefore secondary, although I need to undercut only some – strictly speaking, only one – of
them in order to cast serious doubt upon the
position's conclusions.

The alleged lack of priority for subsistence
rights compared to security rights assumes:

1 The distinction between subsistence rights
  and security rights is (a) sharp and (b) significant.[3]
2 The distinction between positive rights and
  negative rights is (a) sharp and (b) significant.
3 Subsistence rights are positive.
4 Security rights are negative.

I am not suggesting that anyone has ever laid out
this argument in all the steps it actually needs. On
the contrary, a full statement of the argument is
the beginning of its refutation – this is an example

of the philosophical analogue of the principle that sunlight is the best antiseptic.[4]

In this chapter I will concentrate on establishing that premises 3 and 4 are both misleading. Then I will suggest a set of distinctions among duties that accurately transmits the insight distorted by 3 and 4. Insofar as 3 and 4 are inaccurate, considerable doubt is cast upon 2, although it remains possible that someone can specify some sharply contrasting pair of rights that actually are examples of 2.[5] I will not directly attack premise 1.[6]

Now the basic idea behind the general suggestion that there are positive rights and negative rights seems to have been that one kind of rights (the positive ones) require other people to act positively – to "do something" – whereas another kind of rights (the negative ones) require other people merely to refrain from acting in certain ways – to do nothing that violates the rights. For example, according to this picture, a right to subsistence would be positive because it would require other people, in the last resort, to supply food or clean air to those unable to find, produce, or buy their own; a right to security would be negative because it would require other people merely to refrain from murdering or otherwise assaulting those with the right. The underlying distinction, then, is between acting and refraining from acting; and positive rights are those with correlative duties to act in certain ways and negative rights are those with correlative duties to refrain from acting in certain ways. Therefore, the moral significance, if any, of the distinction between positive rights and negative rights depends upon the moral significance, if any, of the distinction between action and omission of action.[7]

The ordinarily implicit argument for considering rights to subsistence to be secondary would, then, appear to be basically this. Since subsistence rights are positive and require other people to do more than negative rights require – perhaps more than people can actually do – negative rights, such as those to security, should be fully guaranteed first. Then, any remaining resources could be devoted, as long as they lasted, to the positive – and perhaps impossible – task of providing for subsistence. Unfortunately for this argument, neither rights to physical security nor rights to subsistence fit neatly into their assigned sides of the simplistic positive/negative dichotomy. We must consider whether security rights are purely negative and then whether subsistence rights are purely positive. I will try to show (1) that security rights are more "positive" than they are often said to

be, (2) that subsistence rights are more "negative" than they are often said to be, and, given (1) and (2), (3) that the distinctions between security rights and subsistence rights, though not entirely illusory, are too fine to support any weighty conclusions, especially the very weighty conclusion that security rights are basic and subsistence rights are not.

In the case of rights to physical security, it may be possible *to avoid violating* someone's rights to physical security yourself by merely refraining from acting in any of the ways that would constitute violations. But it is impossible to *protect* anyone's rights to physical security without taking, or making payments toward the taking of, a wide range of positive actions. For example, at the very least the protection of rights to physical security necessitates police forces; criminal courts; penitentiaries; schools for training police, lawyers, and guards; and taxes to support an enormous system for the prevention, detection, and punishment of violations of personal security.[8] All these activities and institutions are attempts at providing social guarantees for individuals' security so that they are not left to face alone forces that they cannot handle on their own. How much more than these expenditures one thinks would be necessary in order for people actually to be reasonably secure (as distinguished from merely having the cold comfort of knowing that the occasional criminal is punished after someone's security has already been violated) depends on one's theory of violent crime, but it is not unreasonable to believe that it would involve extremely expensive, "positive" programs. Probably no one knows how much positive action would have to be taken in a contemporary society like the United States significantly to reduce the levels of muggings, rapes, murders, and other assaults that violate personal security, and in fact to make people reasonably secure.

Someone might suggest that this blurs rights to physical security with some other type of rights, which might be called rights-to-be-protected-against-assaults-upon-physical-security. According to this distinction, rights to physical security are negative, requiring others only to refrain from assaults, while rights-to-be-protected-against-assaults-upon-physical-security are positive, requiring others to take positive steps to prevent assaults.

Perhaps if one were dealing with some wilderness situation in which individuals' encounters with each other were infrequent and irregular, there might be some point in noting to someone: I am not asking you to cooperate with a system of guarantees to protect me from third parties, but only to refrain from attacking me yourself. But in an organized society, insofar as there were any such things as rights to physical security that were distinguishable from some other rights-to-be-protected-from-assaults-upon-physical-security, no one would have much interest in the bare rights to physical security. What people want and need, as even Mill partly recognized, is the protection of their rights.[9] Insofar as this frail distinction holds up, it is the rights-to-be-protected-against-assaults that any reasonable person would demand from society. A demand for physical security is not normally a demand simply to be left alone, but a demand to be protected against harm.[10] It is a demand for positive action, or, in the words of our initial account of a right, a demand for social guarantees against at least the standard threats.

So it would be very misleading to say simply that physical security is a negative matter of other people's refraining from violations. Ordinarily it is instead a matter of some people refraining from violations and of third parties being prevented from violations by the positive steps taken by first and second parties. The "negative" refraining may in a given case be less significant than the "positive" preventing – it is almost never the whole story. The end-result of the positive preventative steps taken is of course an enforced refraining from violations, not the performance of any positive action. The central core of the right is a right that others not act in certain ways. But the mere core of the right indicates little about the social institutions needed to secure it, and the core of the right does not contain its whole structure. The protection of "negative rights" requires positive measures, and therefore their actual enjoyment requires positive measures. In any imperfect society enjoyment of a right will depend to some extent upon protection against those who do not choose not to violate it.

Rights to subsistence too are in their own way considerably more complex than simply labeling them "positive" begins to indicate. In fact, their fulfillment involves at least two significantly different types of action. On the one hand, rights to subsistence sometimes do involve correlative duties on the part of others to provide the needed commodities when those in need are helpless to secure a supply for themselves, as, for example, the affluent may have a duty to finance food supplies and transportation and distribution facilities in the case of famine. Even the satisfaction of subsistence rights by such positive action, however, need not be any more expensive or involve any more complex governmental programs than the effective protection of security rights would. A food stamp program, for example, could be cheaper or more expensive than, say, an anti-drug program aimed at reducing muggings and murders by addicts. Which program was more costly or more complicated would depend upon the relative dimensions of the respective problems and would be unaffected by any respect in which security is "negative" and subsistence is "positive." Insofar as any argument for giving priority to the fulfillment of "negative rights" rests on the assumption that actually securing "negative rights" is usually cheaper or simpler than securing "positive rights," the argument rests on an empirical speculation of dubious generality.

The other type of action needed to fulfill subsistence rights is even more difficult to distinguish sharply from the action needed to fulfill security rights. Rights to physical subsistence often can be completely satisfied without the provision by others of any commodities to those whose rights are in question. All that is sometimes necessary is to protect the persons whose subsistence is threatened from the individuals and institutions that will otherwise intentionally or unintentionally harm them. A demand for the fulfillment of rights to subsistence may involve not a demand to be provided with grants of commodities but merely a demand to be provided some opportunity for supporting oneself.[11] The request is not to be supported but to be allowed to be self-supporting on the basis of one's own hard work.

What is striking is the similarity between protection against the destruction of the basis for supporting oneself and protection against assaults upon one's physical security. We can turn now to some examples that clearly illustrate that the honoring of subsistence rights sometimes involves action no more positive than the honoring of security rights does. Some cases in which all that is asked is protection from harm that would destroy the capacity to be self-supporting involve threats to subsistence of a complexity that is not usually noticed with regard to security, although the adequate protection of security would involve analyses and measures more complex than a preoccupation with police and prisons. The complexity of the circumstances of subsistence should not, however, be allowed to obscure the basic fact that essentially all that is being asked in the name of subsistence rights in these examples is protection from destructive acts by other people.

Subsistence Rights and Scarcity

The choice of examples for use in an essentially theoretical discussion that does nevertheless have implications for public policy presents an intractable dilemma. Hypothetical cases and actual cases each have advantages and disadvantages that are mirror images of each other's. A description of an actual case has the obvious advantage that it is less susceptible to being tailored to suit the theoretical point it is adduced to support, especially if the description is taken from the work of someone other than the proponent of the theoretical point. Its disadvantage is that if the description is in fact an inaccurate account of the case in question, the mistake about what is happening in that case may appear to undercut the theoretical point that is actually independent of what is happening in any single case. Thus the argument about the theoretical point may become entangled in arguments about an individual instance that was at most only one supposed illustration of the more general point.

Hypothetical cases are immune to disputes about whether they accurately depict an independent event, since, being explicitly hypothetical, they are not asserted to correspond to any one real case. But precisely because they are not constrained by the need to remain close to an independent event, they may be open to the suspicion of having been streamlined precisely in order to fit the theoretical point they illustrate and having thereby become atypical of actual cases.

The only solution I can see is to offer, when a point is crucial, an example of each kind. It is vital to the argument of this book to establish that many people's lack of the substance of their subsistence rights – of, that is, the means of subsistence like food – is a deprivation caused by standard kinds of threats that could be controlled by some combination of the mere restraint of second parties and the maintenance of protective institutions by first and third parties, just as the standard threats that deprive people of their physical security could be controlled by restraint and protection against nonrestraint. So I will start with a hypothetical case in order to clarify the theoretical point before introducing the partly extraneous complexity of actual events, and then in *Basic Rights* I go on to quote a

description of some actual current economic policies that deprive people of subsistence. The hypothetical case is at the level of a single peasant village, and the actual case concerns long-term national economic strategies. Anyone familiar with the causes of malnutrition in underdeveloped countries today will recognize that the following hypothetical case is in no way unusual.[12]

Suppose the largest tract of land in the village was the property of the descendant of a family that had held title to the land for as many generations back as anyone could remember. By absolute standards this peasant was by no means rich, but his land was the richest in the small area that constituted the universe for the inhabitants of this village. He grew, as his father and grandfather had, mainly the black beans that are the staple (and chief – and adequate – source of protein) in the regional diet. His crop usually constituted about a quarter of the black beans marketed in the village. Practically every family grew part of what they needed, and the six men he hired during the seasons requiring extra labor held the only paid jobs in the village – everyone else just worked his own little plot.

One day a man from the capital offered this peasant a contract that not only guaranteed him annual payments for a 10-year lease on his land but also guaranteed him a salary (regardless of how the weather, and therefore the crops, turned out – a great increase in his financial security) to be the foreman for a new kind of production on his land. The contract required him to grow flowers for export and also offered him the opportunity, which was highly recommended, to purchase through the company, with payments in installments, equipment that would enable him to need to hire only two men. The same contract was offered to, and accepted by, most of the other larger landowners in the general region to which the village belonged.

Soon, with the sharp reduction in supply, the price of black beans soared. Some people could grow all they needed (in years of good weather) on their own land, but the families that needed to supplement their own crop with purchases had to cut back their consumption. In particular, the children in the four families headed by the laborers who lost their seasonal employment suffered severe malnutrition, especially since the parents had originally worked as laborers only because their own land was too poor or too small to feed their families.

Now, the story contains no implication that the man from the capital or the peasants-turned-foremen were malicious or intended to do anything worse than single-mindedly pursue their own respective interests. But the outsider's offer of the contract was one causal factor, and the peasant's acceptance of the contract was another causal factor, in producing the malnutrition that would probably persist, barring protective intervention, for at least the decade the contract was to be honored. If the families in the village had rights to subsistence, their rights were being violated. Society, acting presumably by way of the government, ought to protect them from a severe type of active harm that eliminates their ability even to feed themselves.

But was anyone actually harming the villagers, or were they simply suffering a regrettable decline in their fortunes? If someone was violating their rights, who exactly was the violator? Against whom specifically should the government be protecting them? For, we normally make a distinction between violating someone's rights and allowing someone's rights to be violated while simply minding our own business. It makes a considerable difference – to take an example from another set of basic rights – whether I myself assault someone or I merely carry on with my own affairs while allowing a third person to assault someone when I could protect the victim and end the assault. Now, I may have a duty not to allow assaults that I can without great danger to myself prevent or stop, as well as a duty not to assault people myself, but there are clearly two separable issues here. And it is perfectly conceivable that I might have the one duty (to avoid harming) and not the other (to protect from harm by third parties), because they involve two different types of action.[13]

The switch in land-use within the story might then be described as follows. Even if one were willing to grant tentatively that the villagers all seemed to have rights to subsistence, some of which were violated by the malnutrition that some suffered after the switch in crops, no individual or organization can be identified as the violator: not the peasant-turned-foreman, for example, because – let us assume – he did not foresee the "systemic" effects of his individual choice; not the business representative from the capital because – let us assume – although he was knowledgeable enough to know what would probably happen, it would be unrealistically moralistic to expect him to forgo honest gains for himself and

the company he represented because the gains had undesired, even perhaps regretted, "side-effects"; not any particular member of the governmental bureaucracy because – let us assume – no one had been assigned responsibility for maintaining adequate nutrition in this particular village. The local peasant and the business representative were both minding their own business in the village, and no one in the government had any business with this village. The peasant and the representative may have attended to their own affairs while harm befell less fortunate villagers, but allowing harm to occur without preventing it is not the same as directly inflicting it yourself. The malnutrition was just, literally, unfortunate: bad luck, for which no one could fairly be blamed. The malnutrition was, in effect, a natural disaster – was, in the obnoxious language of insurance law, an act of God. Perhaps the village was, after all, becoming over-populated.[14]

But, of course, the malnutrition resulting from the new choice of crop was not a natural disaster. The comforting analogy does not hold. The malnutrition was a social disaster. The malnutrition was the product of specific human decisions permitted by the presence of specific social institutions and the absence of others, in the context of the natural circumstances, especially the scarcity of land upon which to grow food, that were already given before the decisions were made. The harm in question, the malnutrition, was not merely allowed to happen by the parties to the flower-growing contract. The harm was partly caused by the requirement in the contract for a switch away from food, by the legality of the contract, and by the performance of the required switch in crops. If there had been no contract or if the contract had not required a switch away from food for local consumption, there would have been no malnutrition as things were going.[15] In general, when persons take an action that is sufficient in some given natural and social circumstances to bring about an undesirable effect, especially one that there is no particular reason to think would otherwise have occurred, it is perfectly normal to consider their action to be one active cause of the harm. The parties to the contract partly caused the malnutrition.

But the society could have protected the villagers by countering the initiative of the contracting parties in any one of a number of ways that altered the circumstances, and the absence of the appropriate social guarantees is another cause of the malnutrition. Such contracts could, for example, have already been made illegal. Or they could have been allowed but managed or taxed in order to compensate those who would otherwise predictably be damaged by them. Exactly what was done would be, *for the most part*, an economic and political question.[16] But it is possible to have social guarantees against the malnutrition that is repeatedly caused in such standard, predictable ways.

Is a right to subsistence in such a case, then, a positive right in any important ways that a right to security is not? Do we actually find a contrast of major significance? No. As in the cases of the threats to physical security that we normally consider, the threat to subsistence is human activity with largely predictable effects.[17] Even if, as we tend to assume, the motives for deprivations of security tend to be vicious while the motives for deprivations of subsistence tend to be callous, the people affected usually need protection all the same. The design, building, and maintenance of institutions and practices that protect people's subsistence against the callous – and even the merely over-energetic – is no more and no less positive than the conception and execution of programs to control violent crimes against the person. It is not obvious which, if either, it is more realistic to hope for or more economical to pursue. It is conceivable, although I doubt if anyone really knows, that the two are more effectively and efficiently pursued together. Neither looks simple, cheap, or "negative."

This example of the flower contract is important in part because, at a very simple level, it is in fact typical of much of what is happening today among the majority of the people in the world, who are poor and rural, and are threatened by forms of "economic development" that lower their own standard of living.[18] But it is also important because, once again in a very simple way, it illustrates the single most critical fact about rights to subsistence; where subsistence depends upon tight supplies of essential commodities (like food), a change in supply can have, often by way of intermediate price effects, an indirect but predictable and devastating effect on people's ability to survive. A change in supply can transport self-supporting people into helplessness and, if no protection against the change is provided, into malnutrition or death. Severe harm to some people's ability to maintain themselves can be caused by changes in the use to which other people put vital resources (like land) they control. In such cases even someone who denied that individuals or organizations have duties to supply commodities to people who are helpless to obtain them for themselves, might grant that the government ought to execute the society's duty of protecting people from having their ability to maintain their own survival destroyed by the actions of others. If this protection is provided, there will be much less need later to provide commodities themselves to compensate for deprivations.

What transmits the effect in such cases is the local scarcity of the vital commodity. Someone might switch thousands of acres from food to flowers without having any effect on the diet of anyone else where the supply of food was adequate to prevent a significant price rise in response to the cut in supply. And it goes without saying that the price rises are vitally important only if the income and wealth of at least some people is severely limited, as of course it is in every society, often for the rural majority. It is as if an abundant supply sometimes functions as a sponge to absorb the otherwise significant effect on other people, but a tight supply (against a background of limited income and wealth) sometimes functions as a conductor to transmit effects to others, who feel them sharply.

It is extremely difficult merely to mind one's own business amidst a scarcity of vital commodities. It is illusory to think that this first commandment of liberalism can always be obeyed. The very scarcity draws people into contact with each other, destroys almost all area for individual maneuver, and forces people to elbow each other in order to move forward. The tragedy of scarcity, beyond the deprivations necessitated by the scarcity itself, is that scarcity tends to make each one's gain someone else's loss. One can act for oneself only by acting against others, since there is not enough for all. Amidst abundance of food a decision to grow flowers can be at worst a harmless act and quite likely a socially beneficial one. But amidst a scarcity of food, due partly to a scarcity of fertile land, an unmalicious decision to grow flowers can cause death – unless there are social guarantees for adequate nutrition. A call for social guarantees for subsistence in situations of scarcity is not a call for intervention in what were formerly private affairs.

Avoidance, Protection, and Aid

Still, it is true that sometimes fulfilling a right does involve transferring commodities to the person with the right and sometimes it merely involves not taking commodities away. Is there not some grain of truth obscured by the dichotomy between negative and positive rights? Are there not distinctions here that it is useful to make?

The answer, I believe, is: yes, there are distinctions, but they are not distinctions between rights. The useful distinctions are among duties, and there are no one-to-one pairings between kinds of duties and kinds of rights. The complete fulfillment of each kind of right involves the performance of multiple kinds of duties. This conceptual change has, I believe, important practical implications, although it will be only in chapter 7 [of *Basic Rights*] that the implications can begin to be illustrated. In the remainder of this chapter I would like to tender a very simple tripartite typology of duties. For all its own simplicity, it goes considerably beyond the usual assumption that for every right there is a single correlative duty, and suggests instead that for every basic right – and many other rights as well – there are three types of duties, all of which must be performed if the basic right is to be fully honored but not all of which must necessarily be performed by the same individuals or institutions. This latter point opens the possibility of distributing each of the three kinds of duty somewhat differently and perhaps confining any difficulties about the correlativity of subsistence rights and their accompanying duties to fewer than all three kinds of duties.

So I want to suggest that with every basic right, three types of duties correlate:

I. Duties to *avoid* depriving.
II. Duties to *protect* from deprivation.
III. Duties to *aid* the deprived.

This may be easier to see in the case of the more familiar basic right, the right to physical security (the right not to be tortured, executed, raped, assaulted, etc.). For every person's right to physical security, there are three correlative duties:

I. Duties not to eliminate a person's security – duties to *avoid* depriving.
II. Duties to protect people against deprivation of security by other people – duties to *protect* from deprivation.
III. Duties to provide for the security of those unable to provide for their own – duties to *aid* the deprived.

Similarly, for every right to subsistence there are:

I. Duties not to eliminate a person's only available means of subsistence – duties to *avoid* depriving.
II. Duties to protect people against deprivation of the only available means of subsistence by other people – duties to *protect* from deprivation.
III. Duties to provide for the subsistence of those unable to provide for their own – duties to *aid* the deprived.

If this suggestion is correct, the common notion that *rights* can be divided into rights to forbearance (so-called negative rights), as if some rights have correlative duties only to avoid depriving, and rights to aid (so-called positive rights), as if some rights have correlative duties only to aid, is thoroughly misguided. This misdirected simplification is virtually ubiquitous among contemporary North Atlantic theorists and is, I think, all the more pernicious for the degree of unquestioning acceptance it has now attained. It is duties, not rights, that can be divided among avoidance and aid, and protection. And – this is what matters – every basic right entails duties of all three types. Consequently the attempted division of rights, rather than duties, into forbearance and aid (and protection, which is often understandably but unhelpfully blurred into avoidance, since protection is partly, but only partly, the enforcement of avoidance) can only breed confusion.

It is impossible for any basic right – however "negative" it has come to seem – to be fully guaranteed unless all three types of duties are fulfilled. The very most "negative"-seeming right to liberty, for example, requires positive action by society to protect it and positive action by society to restore it when avoidance and protection both fail. This by no means implies, as I have already mentioned, that all three types of duties fall upon everyone else or even fall equally upon everyone upon whom they do fall. Although this tripartite analysis of duties is, I believe, perfectly general, I will focus here upon the duties correlative to subsistence rights: subsistence duties.

The Generality of the Tripartite Analysis

However, perhaps a brief word on the general issue is useful before turning to a fairly detailed analysis of the threefold duties correlative to the rights that most concern us: subsistence rights. Obviously theses of three ascending degrees of generality might be advanced:

- All subsistence rights involve threefold correlative duties.
- All basic rights involve threefold correlative duties.
- Most moral rights involve threefold correlative duties.

I subscribe to all three theses. But naturally the support will be most thorough for the first thesis and least thorough for the last. For the most part I am content to leave matters at that, because the only point that I am concerned fully to establish is the priority of subsistence rights, that is, their equal priority with all other basic rights. Consequently, the arguments need, strictly speaking, to be thorough only for subsistence rights. But a contrasting pair of observations are also in order.

On the one hand, the argument here is from the particular to the general, not the converse. It is not because I assumed that normal rights involve some, or threefold, duties that I concluded that subsistence rights involve some, and threefold, duties. I explored subsistence rights, as we are about to do, and found that they can be fully accounted for only by means of admitting three kinds of correlated duties. I looked at the same time at security rights and, in Chapter 3 of *Basic Rights*, at rights to liberty and found again that an adequate explanation involves all three kinds of multiply interrelated duties, thus coming to suspect that all basic rights, at the very least, require the same tripartite analysis of the duty side of the coin.

On the other hand, on the basis of these detailed examinations of these three rights I am indeed tempted to recommend that the most general thesis be made analytically true, that is, that any right not involving the threefold duties be acknowledged to be an exceptional case. If the account of a right given at the beginning of chapter 1 of *Basic Rights* were made a strict definition, then it would do just this. If a right provides the rational basis for a justified demand that the actual enjoyment of the substance of the right be socially guaranteed against standard threats, then a right provides the rational basis for insisting upon the performance, as needed, of duties to avoid, duties to protect, and duties to aid, as they will shortly be explained. This picture does seem to me to fit all the standard

cases of moral rights.[19] If, however, someone can give clear counter-examples to the final step of generalization (the move from duties for basic rights to duties for moral rights generally), I can see little cause for concern, provided the admission of rights that lack some kinds of correlative duties, to the realm of non-basic rights, is not allowed to devalue the coinage of rights generally.

Subsistence Duties

The first type of subsistence duty is neither a duty to provide help nor a duty to protect against harm by third parties but is the most nearly "negative" or passive kind of duty that is possible: a duty simply not to take actions that deprive others of a means that, but for one's own harmful actions, would have satisfied their subsistence rights or enabled them to satisfy their own subsistence rights, where the actions are not necessary to the satisfaction of one's own basic rights and where the threatened means is the only realistic one.[20] Duties to avoid depriving require merely that one refrain from making an unnecessary gain for oneself by a means that is destructive for others.

Part of the relation between these subsistence duties to avoid depriving (type I) and subsistence duties to protect from deprivation (type II) is quite straightforward. If everyone could be counted upon voluntarily to fulfill duties to avoid, duties to protect would be unnecessary. But since it would be naive to expect everyone to fulfill his or her duties to avoid and since other people's very survival is at stake, it is clearly necessary that some individuals or institutions have the duty of enforcing the duty to avoid. The duty to protect is, then, in part a secondary duty of enforcing the primary duty of avoiding the destruction of people's means of subsistence. In this respect it is analogous to, for example, the duty of the police to enforce the duty of parents not to starve their children.

The natural institution in many societies to have the task of enforcing those primary duties that need enforcement is the executive branch of some level of government, acting on behalf of the members of society other than the offending individuals or institutions. Which level of government takes operating responsibility is largely a practical matter and might vary among societies. Where the source of harm is, for example, a transnational corporation, protection may need to be provided by the home government or even by multilateral government action.[21] But clearly if duties to avoid depriving people of their last means of subsistence are to be taken seriously, some provision must be made for enforcing this duty on behalf of the rest of humanity upon those who would not otherwise fulfill it. Perhaps it would be worth considering non-governmental enforcement institutions as the bearers in some cases of the secondary duty to protect, but the primary institution would normally appear to be the government of the threatened person's own nation. It is normally taken to be a central function of government to prevent irreparable harm from being inflicted upon some members of society by other individual members, by institutions, or by interactions of the two. It is difficult to imagine why anyone should pay much attention to the demands of any government that failed to perform this function, if it were safe to ignore its demands.

Duties to aid (type III) are in themselves fairly complicated, and only one kind will be discussed here. At least three sub-categories of duties to aid need to be recognized. What they have in common is the requirement that resources be transferred to those who cannot provide for their own survival. First are duties to aid (III–1) that are attached to certain roles or relationships and rest therefore upon only those who are in a particular role or relationship and are borne toward only those other persons directly involved. Some central cases are the duties of parents toward their own young children and the duties of grown children toward their own aged parents. Naturally, important issues can arise even with regard to such relatively clear duties as the duty to provide food to the helplessly young and to the helplessly old, but I have nothing to add here regarding these duties, which are not universal. By their not being universal I mean that although all parents may normally have certain duties toward their own children, no child can justifiably hold that all people, or even all parents, have *this* sort of duty toward it. All people may of course have other duties toward the child, including universal ones, and possibly including one of the other two sub-categories of duties to aid that are to be mentioned next.

The only difference between the second and third sub-categories of duties to aid is the source of the deprivation because of which aid is needed. In the second case (III–2) the deprivation is the result of failures to fulfill duties to avoid depriving

and duties to protect from deprivation – some people have acted in such a way as to eliminate the last available means of subsistence for other people and the responsible government has failed to protect the victims. Thus, the need for assistance is the result of a prior twofold failure to perform duties, and the victims have been harmed by both actions and omissions of actions by other people.

In the third case (III–3) the deprivation is not the result of failures in duty and, in just this sense, the deprivation is "natural," that is, the deprivation suffered is not a case of harm primarily caused by other people. The clearest case of a natural deprivation calling for aid is a natural disaster like a hurricane or an earthquake. As always, questions arise at the borderline between cases – for example, was the death toll increased because the weather bureau or civil defense organization failed to protect with timely warnings? But uncontroversial central cases in which no human beings are much to blame are perfectly familiar, even if not so frequent as we might like to believe.

Where supplies of the necessities of life, or of the resources needed to grow or make the necessities, are scarce, duties of types I and II take on increased importance. The results of the fulfillment only of I and II would already be dramatic in the poorer areas of the world, in which most of the earth's inhabitants eke out their existences. It is easy to underestimate the importance of these two kinds of subsistence duties, which together are intended to prevent deprivation. But to eliminate the only realistic means a person has for obtaining food or other physical necessities is to cause that person, for example, the physical harm of malnutrition or of death by starvation. When physical harm but not death is caused, the effect of eliminating the only means of support can be every degree as serious as the effect of a violation of physical security by means of a bodily assault. The physical effects of malnutrition can be irreversible and far more profound than the physical effects of many an assault in fact are. And when starvation is caused, the ultimate effect of eliminating the only means of support is precisely the same as the effect of murder. Those who are helpless in the face of insuperable obstacles to their continued existence are at least one level worse off than those who are defenseless in the face of assaults upon their physical security. The defenseless will at least be able to maintain themselves if they are provided with protection against threatening assaults. If protected but otherwise left alone, they will manage. But the helpless, if simply left alone – even if they should be protected against all assaults upon their security – will die for lack of the means of subsistence. They will merely, in Coleridge's phrase, "die so slowly that none call it murder."[22]

Now of course differences between deprivations of security and deprivations of subsistence can also be noted, as already mentioned. Normally in a violation of physical security by means of assault or murder, the human agent's central intention is indeed to bring about, or at least includes bringing about, the physical harm or death that is caused for the victim, although obviously one also can injure or kill inadvertently. In the case of the elimination of the means of physical subsistence, the human agent's central intention may at least sometimes be focused on other consequences of his or her action, such as the increased security of income that would result from a multi-year salaried contract to grow flowers rather than a precarious annual attempt to grow food. The harm to the victims may be entirely unintended. Such difference in intention between the two cases is undoubtedly relevant to any assessment of the moral stature respectively of the two persons who partly cause the harm in the two cases. But for the two victims the difference between intended physical harm and unintended physical harm may matter little, since the harmfulness of the action taken may be the same in both cases and may be even greater where unintended.

Nevertheless, it may be arbitrary to assign a role of *the* perpetrator to any one person or group in a case of the deprivation of subsistence. The deprivations in question may in fact be "systemic": the product of the joint workings of individual actions and social institutions no one of which by itself caused the harm. But what follows from this is not that no one is responsible (since everyone is). What follows is that the distinction between duties to avoid (I) and duties to protect (II), which is relatively clear in the abstract, blurs considerably in concrete reality.[23] The division of labor between individual restraint and institutional protection can be worked out in any of several acceptable ways, the full details of which would go considerably beyond the scope of this book, but between the two kinds of duties, individuals ought not to be deprived by the actions (intentional or unintentional) of others of all hope of sustaining themselves.

This means, however, that duties to protect (II) are not simply secondary duties to enforce the primary duty to avoid (I). We can mark as II–1 the duties to protect that are merely secondary duties to enforce the duty to avoid. But duties to protect also encompass the design of social institutions that do not leave individuals with duties to avoid, the fulfillment of which would necessitate super-human qualities. This task of constructing institutions can be marked as II–2. In the original example of the flower contract, some would judge that the peasant receiving the offer to switch out of food production, in the circumstances stipulated, could reasonably have been expected to foresee the consequences of the switch and to refrain from making it. But it is probably more realistic neither to expect him to have the information and comprehension necessary to foresee the consequences nor to expect him to choose not to reduce his own insecurity – and certainly an example could readily be constructed in which an individual could not reasonably be expected to know in advance the probable bad consequences for others of his or her action or to give them more weight than improvements in his or her own precarious situation.[24]

For such cases, in which individual restraint would be too much to ask, the duty to protect (II–2) includes the design of laws and institutions that avoid reliance upon unreasonable levels of individual self-control. Many actions that are immoral ought nevertheless not to be made illegal. But one of the best possible reasons for making an act illegal is its contributing to harm as fundamental as the deprivation of someone's last available means of subsistence. And a number of intermediate steps between total prohibition and complete tolerance of an action are possible, such as tax laws that create disincentives of various strengths against the kind of action that would contribute to the deprivation of subsistence from others and create alternative sources of increased economic security for oneself. Social institutions must, at the very least, be designed to enable ordinary human beings, who are neither saints nor geniuses, to do each other a minimum of serious harm.

In sum, then, we find that the fulfillment of a basic right to subsistence involves at least the following kinds of duties:

I. To avoid depriving.
II. To protect from deprivation
    1. By enforcing duty (I) and

2. By designing institutions that avoid the creation of strong incentives to violate duty (I).
III. To aid the deprived
  1. Who are one's special responsibility,
  2. Who are victims of social failures in the performance of duties (I), (II–1), (II–2) and
  3. Who are victims of natural disasters.

The Systematic Interdependence of Duties

Fulfillment of a basic right (and, I think, of most other moral rights as well) requires, then, performance by some individuals or institutions of each of these three general kinds of correlative duties. Duties to avoid depriving possibly come closest to failing to be essential, because duties to protect provide for the enforcement of duties to avoid. Even if individuals, organizations, and governments were otherwise inclined to violate rights to security, for example, by failing to fulfill their respective duties to avoid, forceful fulfillment of duties to protect by whomever they fell upon – presumably a national government – could probably produce behavior in compliance with duties to avoid. But reliance on duties to protect rather than duties to avoid would constitute heavy reliance on something like national police power rather than self-restraint by individuals, corporations, and lower-level governments, and would involve obvious disadvantages even if – probably, especially if – the police power were adequate actually to enforce duties to avoid upon a generally reluctant society. Unfortunately this much power to protect would also be enormous power to deprive, which is a lesson about police that even dictators sometimes have to learn the hard way.

Since duties to avoid and duties to protect taken together have only one purpose, to prevent deprivations, the reverse of what was just described is obviously also possible: if everyone who ought to fulfill duties to avoid did so, performance of duties to protect might not be necessary. Law-enforcement agencies could perhaps be disbanded in a society of restrained organizational and individual behavior. But although reliance entirely upon duties to protect is undesirable even if possible, a safe complete reliance upon duties to avoid is most improbable in the absence of at least minimal performance of duties to protect. Organiza-

tions and individuals who will voluntarily avoid deprivation that would otherwise be advantageous to them because they know that their potential victims are protected, cannot be expected to behave in the same way when they know their potential victims are without protection.

The general conclusions about duties to avoid and duties to protect, then, are, first, that strictly speaking it is essential for the guarantee of any right only that either the one or the other be completely fulfilled, but, second, that for all practical purposes it is essential to insist upon the fulfillment of both, because complete reliance on either one alone is probably not feasible and, in the case of duties to protect, almost certainly not desirable.

What division of labor is established by one's account of duties between self-restraint and restraint by others, such as police forces, will obviously have an enormous effect upon the quality of life of those living in the social system in question. I do not want to pursue the questions involved in deciding upon the division, except to note that if either duties to avoid or duties to protect are construed too narrowly, the other duty then becomes unrealistically broad. For example, if a government, in the exercise of its duty to protect, fails to impose constraints upon agribusinesses designed to prevent them from creating malnutrition, the prevention of malnutrition will then depend upon the self-restraint of the agribusinesses. But much evidence suggests that individual agribusinesses are unwilling or unable to take into account the nutritional effect of their decisions about the use of land, local credit and capital, water, and other resources. This is especially true if the agribusiness is producing export crops and most especially if it is investing in a foreign country, the nutritional level of whose people is easily considered irrelevant.[25] If indeed a particular type of corporation has demonstrated an inability to forgo projects that produce malnutrition, given their setting, it is foolish to rely on corporate restraint, and whichever governments have responsibility to protect those who are helpless to resist the corporation's activity – host governments, home government or both – will have to fulfill their duties to protect. If, on the other hand, the corporations would restrain themselves, the governments could restrain them less. How to work this out is difficult and important. The present point is simply that between the bearers of the two duties, the job of preventing deprivation ought to get done, if there is a right not to be deprived of whatever is threatened. And the side that construes its own role too narrowly, if it actually has the power to act, may be as much at fault for contributing to the violation of rights as the side that fails to take up all the resulting slack.

However, as I have already indicated, the duty to protect ought not to be understood only in terms of the maintenance of law-enforcement, regulatory, and other closely related agencies. A major and more constructive part of the duty to protect is the duty to design social institutions that do not exceed the capacity of individuals and organizations, including private and public corporations, to restrain themselves. Not only the kinds of acute threats of deprivation that police can prevent, but the kinds of chronic threats that require imaginative legislation and, sometimes, long-term planning fall under the duty to protect.[26]

Nevertheless, it is duties to aid that often have the highest urgency, because they are often owed to persons who are suffering the consequences of failures to fulfill both duties to avoid and duties to protect, that is, they are duties of type III–2. These people will have been totally deprived of their rights to subsistence if they are then not aided either. This greater urgency does not, of course, mean that duties to aid are more compelling overall than the first two types of duty, and indeed it is specifically against duties to aid that complaints that the correlative duties accompanying subsistence rights are too burdensome may seem most plausible. It is important to notice that to the extent that duties to avoid and to protect are fulfilled, duties to assist will be less burdensome. If the fulfillment of duties to protect is sufficiently inadequate, duties to assist may be overwhelming and may seem unrealistically great, as they do today to many people. For example, because the Dutch colonial empire failed to protect the people of Java against the effects of the Dutch schemes for agricultural exports, the nutritional problems of the majority of Indonesians today strike some people as almost beyond all solution.[27] The colossal failure of the Dutch colonial government in its duties to

protect (or, even, to avoid deprivation) has created virtually Sisyphean duties to aid. These presumably fall to some degree upon the Dutch people who are today still profiting from their centuries of spoils. But whoever precisely has these duties to aid – there are plenty to go around – their magnitude has clearly been multiplied by past dereliction in the performance of the other two kinds of duties by the Dutch among others. . . .

This much, however, is already clear. The account of correlative duties is for the most part a more detailed specification of what the account of rights calls social guarantees against standard threats. Provisions for avoidance, protection, and aid are what are needed for a reasonable level of social guarantees. Making the necessary provisions for the fulfillment of subsistence rights may sometimes be burdensome, especially when the task is to recover from past neglect of basic duties. But we have no reason to believe, as proponents of the negative/positive distinction typically assert, that the performance of the duties correlative to subsistence rights would always or usually be more difficult, more expensive, less practicable, or harder to "deliver" than would the actual performance of the duties correlative to the rights that are conventionally labeled negative and that are more often announced than in fact fulfilled. And the burdens connected with subsistence rights do not fall primarily upon isolated individuals who would be expected quietly to forgo advantages to themselves for the sake of not threatening others, but primarily upon human communities that can work cooperatively to design institutions that avoid situations in which people are confronted by subsistence-threatening forces they cannot themselves handle. In spite of the sometimes useful terminology of third parties helping first parties against second parties, etc., it is worth noting, while assessing the burden of subsistence duties, that the third-party bearers of duties can also become the first-party bearers of rights when situations change. No one is assured of living permanently on one side of the rights/duties coin.

Notes

1 See introduction to Henry Shue, *Basic Rights* (Princeton: Princeton University Press, 1980).
2 For a forceful re-affirmation of this view in the current political context (and further references), see

Hugo Adam Bedau, "Human Rights and Foreign Assistance Programs," in *Human Rights and US Foreign Policy*, ed. by Peter G. Brown and Douglas MacLean (Lexington, MA: Lexington Books, 1979), pp. 29–44. Also see Charles Frankel, *Human Rights and Foreign Policy*, Headline Series No. 241 (New York: Foreign Policy Association, 1978), especially pp. 36–49, where Frankel advanced a "modest list of fundamental rights" that explicitly excluded economic rights as "dangerously utopian." A version of the general distinction has recently been re-affirmed by Thomas Nagel – see "Equality," in *Mortal Questions* (New York: Cambridge University Press, 1979), pp. 114–15. An utterly unrealistic but frequently invoked version of the distinction is in Maurice Cranston, *What Are Human Rights?* (London: The Bodley Head, 1973), chapter VIII. An interesting attempt to show that the positive/negative distinction is compatible with economic rights is John Langan, "Defining Human Rights: A Revision of the Liberal Tradition," Working Paper (Washington: Woodstock Theological Center, 1979). For a provocative and relevant discussion of "negative responsibility" (responsibility for what one fails to prevent), see Bernard Williams, "A Critique of Utilitarianism," in *Utilitarianism: For & Against* (New York: Cambridge University Press, 1973), pp. 93ff.

3 Naturally my use of the same argument for the basic status of both security and subsistence is at least an indirect challenge to (1)(b). No question is raised here, however, about (1)(a): the thesis that subsistence and security are sharply distinguishable. People who should be generally sympathetic to my fundamental thesis that subsistence rights are basic rights, do sometimes try to reach the same conclusion by the much shorter seeming route of denying that security and subsistence are importantly different from each other. For example, it is correctly observed that both security and subsistence are needed for survival and then maintained that both are included in a right to survival, or right to life. Though I am by no means hostile to this approach, it does have three difficulties that I believe can be avoided by my admittedly somewhat more circuitous path of argument. First, it is simply not correct that one cannot maintain a clear and useful distinction between security and subsistence, as, in fact, I hope to have done up to this point. Second, arguments for a general right to life that includes subsistence rights appear to need some premise to the effect that the right to life entails rights to at least some of the means of life. Thus, they face the same "weakness of too much strength" – straining credulity by implying more than most people are likely to be able to believe – that we tried to avoid at the end of chapter 1 of *Basic Rights*. A right-to-the-means-of-life argument might be able to skirt the problem equally well by using a notion of a standard threat to life, analogous to our notion of a standard threat to the enjoyment of rights, but this alternative tack seems, at best, no better off. Third, the concept of a right to life is now deeply infected with ambiguities concerning whether it is a purely negative right, a purely positive right, or, as I shall soon be maintaining with regard to both security and subsistence, an inseparable mixture of positive and negative elements. The appeal for many people of a right to life seems to depend, however, upon its being taken to be essentially negative, while it can fully include subsistence rights only if it has major positive elements.

4 I think one can often show the implausibility of an argument by an exhaustive statement of all the assumptions it needs. I have previously attempted this in the case of one of John Rawls's arguments for the priority of liberty – see "Liberty and Self-Respect," *Ethics* 85:3 (April 1975): 195–203.

5 I have given a summary of the argument against 3 and arguments against thinking that either the right to a fair trial or the right not to be tortured are negative rights in "Rights in the Light of Duties," in Brown and MacLean, pp. 65–81. I have also argued directly against what is here called 2b and briefly introduced the account of duties presented in the final sections of this chapter. My goal, which I have no illusions about having attained, has been to do as definitive a job on positive and negative rights as Gerald C. MacCallum, Jr. did on positive and negative liberty in his splendid article, "Negative and Positive Freedom," *Philosophical Review* 76:3 (July 1967): 312–34.

6 See note 3 above.

7 Elsewhere I have briefly queried the moral significance of the action/omission distinction – see the essay cited in note 5 above. For a fuller discussion, see Judith Lichtenberg, "On Being Obligated to Give Aid: Moral and Political Arguments," PhD dissertation, City University of New York, 1978.

8 In FY 1975 in the United States the cost of the "criminal justice system" was $17 billion, or $71 per capita, *New York Times*, July 21, 1977, p. A3. In several countries that year the total annual income was less than $71 per capita. Obviously such isolated statistics prove nothing, but they are suggestive. One thing they suggest is that adequate provisions for this supposedly negative right would not necessarily be less costly than adequate provisions for some rights supposed to be positive. Nor is it evident that physical security does any better on what Frankel called the test of being "realistically deliverable" (45) and Cranston called "the test of practicability" (66). On Cranston's use of the latter, see chapter 4 of *Basic Rights*.

9 "To have a right, then, is, I conceive, to have something which society ought to defend me in the possession of" – John Stuart Mill, *Utilitarianism* (Indianapolis: Bobbs-Merrill, 1957), p. 66 (chapter V, 14th paragraph from the end).

10 This is not a point about ordinary language, in which there is obviously a significant difference between "leave me alone" and "protect me against

people who will not leave me alone." My thesis is that people who are not already grinding axes for minimal government will naturally and reasonably think in terms of enjoying a considerable degree of security, will want to have done whatever within reason is necessary, and will recognize that more is necessary than refraining campaigns – campaigns urging self-restraint upon would-be murderers, muggers, rapists, et al. I am of course not assuming that existing police and penal institutions are the best forms of social guarantees for security; I am assuming only that more effective institutions would probably be at least equally complex and expensive.

11 Therefore, as we shall see below, the complete fulfillment of a subsistence right may involve not the actual provision of any aid at all but only the performance of duties to avoid depriving and to protect against deprivation.

12 The literature on underdeveloped countries in fact abounds in actual cases that have the essential features of the so-called hypothetical case, and I have simply presented a stylized sketch of a common pattern. Most anecdotes are in the form of "horror stories" about transnational corporations switching land out of the production of the food consumed by the local poor. See, for example, Robert J. Ledogar, *Hungry for Profits: US Food and Drug Multinationals in Latin America* (New York: IDOC, 1976), pp. 92–8 (Ralston Purina in Colombia) and Richard J. Barnet and Ronald E. Müller, *Global Reach: The Power of the Multinational Corporations* (New York: Simon and Schuster, 1974), p. 182 (carnations in Colombia). For a gargantuan case on a regional scale involving cattle-ranching, see Shelton H. Davis, *Victims of the Miracle: Development and the Indians of Brazil* (New York: Cambridge University Press, 1977). To a considerable extent the long-term development policy of Mexico for at least thirty of the last forty years has followed this basic pattern of depriving the rural poor of food for subsistence for the sake of greater agricultural production of other crops – see the extremely careful and balanced study by Cynthia Hewitt de Alcantara, *Modernizing Mexican Agriculture: Socioeconomic Implications of Technological Change 1940–1970*. Report No. 76.5 (Geneva: United Nations Research Institute for Social Development, 1976); and Judith Adler Hellman, *Mexico in Crisis* (New York: Holmes & Meier Publishers, 1978), chapter 3. For a sophisticated theoretical analysis of some of the underlying dynamics, see Jeffery M. Paige, *Agrarian Revolution: Social Movements and Export Agriculture in the Underdeveloped World* (New York: Free Press, 1975), which has case studies of Angola, Peru, and Vietnam.

13 That is, they are conceptually distinct; whether this distinction makes any moral difference is another matter. See above, note 7, and the distinctions at the beginning of this chapter.

14 The increasingly frequent and facile appeal to "overpopulation" as a reason not to prevent preventable starvation is considered in chapter 4 of *Basic Rights*.

15 This much of the analysis is derived from the following important article: Onora O'Neill, "Lifeboat Earth," in *World Hunger and Moral Obligation*, edited by William Aiken and Hugh La Follette (Englewood Cliffs: Prentice-Hall, 1977), pp. 140–64. I return to discussion of the causal complexity of such cases at the end of my discussion of "Subsistence Duties" below.

16 For example, land-use laws might prohibit removing prime agricultural land from food production. Alternatively, land might be allowed to be used in the manner most beneficial to the national balance of payments with tax laws designed to guarantee compensating transfers to increase the purchasing power of the villagers (e.g., food stamps), etc. I discuss the question of how to apportion the duties to prevent social disasters in chapter 5 of *Basic Rights*.

17 There are of course non-human threats to both security and subsistence, like floods, as well. And we expect a minimally adequate society also to make arrangements to prevent, to control, or to minimize the ill effects of floods and other destructive natural forces. However, for an appreciation of the extent to which supposedly natural famines are the result of inadequate social arrangements, see Richard G. Robbins, *Famine in Russia 1891–92* (New York: Columbia University Press, 1975); and Michael F. Lofchie, "Political and Economic Origins of African Hunger," *Journal of Modern African Studies*, 13:4 (December 1975): 551–67. As Lofchie says: "The point of departure for a political understanding of African hunger is so obvious it is almost always overlooked: the distinction between drought and famine.... To the extent that there is a connection between drought and famine, it is mediated by the political and economic arrangements of a society. These can either minimize the human consequences of drought or accentuate its effects" (553). For a demonstration that the weather and other natural factors actually played fairly minor roles in the Great Bengal Famine, see the analysis by Amartya Sen, *Poverty and Famines* (Oxford: Clarendon Press, 1981) and, more generally, chapter 4 of my *Basic Rights*. To treat the *absence* of adequate social arrangements as a cause of a famine precipitated by a natural event like a drought or a flood, as these writers and I do, is to assume that it is reasonable to have expected the absent arrangements to have been present.

18 See note 12 above.

19 On whether an adequate definition can be literally exceptionless, see note 2 to chapter 1 of *Basic Rights*.

20 I take the need for the qualification "not necessary to the satisfaction of one's own basic rights" to be

fairly obvious. However admirable self-sacrifice may be, it is surely not a basic duty owed to people generally, and the surrender of one's right to subsistence – or security – would in many circumstances constitute a literal sacrifice of oneself, that is, one's life. Unfortunately, the content of a duty does not dictate the identity of its bearers. Chapter 5 of *Basic Rights* discusses how to assign in a reasonable way the responsibility for fulfilling various duties.

21 How to bring transnational corporations under some constraints in order to prevent great social harms, like violations of basic rights, is one of our great political challenges. See the discussion of recommendation (4) in *Basic Rights*, chapter 7 and the relevant notes.

22 I am, of course, not proposing that we start calling it murder, but I am proposing that we acknowledge the parallels and act in appropriately parallel ways.

23 Without becoming anti-intellectual, or even atheoretical, we theorists might remember that a crystal-clear abstract distinction may not only have no positive practical value but may sometimes contribute to vice. Writing about an entirely different matter, Barrie A. Paskins has put the general point eloquently: "We can imagine and describe cases in which we would think torture justified and unjustified. We can state the grounds on which we are making the discrimination. But what we cannot do is this: *we cannot provide for ourselves, or for those who must act for us in real situations, any way of making our notional distinctions in reality.* What might be claimed about the imaginary example is not that something significantly analogous could not occur

but that in reality we cannot enable those who must act to recognize the case for what it is and other cases, by contrast, for what they are. In a real situation we can never be certain that the case in hand is of this kind rather than another. A too vivid imagination blinds us to the dust of war that drifts into the interrogation centre." Barrie A. Paskins, "What's Wrong with Torture?" *British Journal of International Studies* 2 (1976): 144. I think this is a profound methodological point with strong implications concerning the now virtually incorrigible habit among moral and political philosophers of relying upon imaginary cases and concerning the "strict compliance" situations and "ideal theory" discussed by John Rawls and Kantians generally. I am trying to develop the methodological point in an essay with the working title, "Extreme Cases."

24 On the rationality of peasants, see James C. Scott, *The Moral Economy of the Peasant: Rebellion and Subsistence in Southeast Asia* (New Haven: Yale University Press, 1976), chapters 1 and 2.

25 See note 12 above.

26 I am indebted to John Langan for having emphasized this point. For a different argument, see his paper cited in note 2 above, p. 25.

27 For the classic account, see Clifford Geertz, *Agricultural Involution: The Processes of Ecological Change in Indonesia* (Berkeley: University of California Press for the Association of Asian Studies, 1963), chapters 4 and 5. Although various aspects of Geertz's analysis are naturally no longer accepted, the main points relevant here still stand.

21

A Defense of Abortion

Judith Jarvis Thomson

Most opposition to abortion relies on the premise that the fetus is a human being, a person, from the moment of conception. The premise is argued for, but, as I think, not well. Take, for example, the most common argument. We are asked to notice that the development of a human being from conception through birth into childhood is continuous; then it is said that to draw a line, to choose a point in this development and say "before this point the thing is not a person, after this point it is a person" is to make an arbitrary choice, a choice for which in the nature of things no good reason can be given. It is concluded that the fetus is, or anyway that we had better say it is, a person from the moment of conception. But this conclusion does not follow. Similar things might be said about the development of an acorn into an oak tree, and it does not follow that acorns are oak trees, or that we had better say they are. Arguments of this form are sometimes called "slippery slope arguments" – the phrase is perhaps self-explanatory – and it is dismaying that opponents of abortion rely on them so heavily and uncritically.

I am inclined to agree, however, that the prospects for "drawing a line" in the development of the fetus look dim. I am inclined to think also that we shall probably have to agree that the fetus has already become a human person well before birth. Indeed, it comes as a surprise when one first learns how early in its life it begins to acquire human characteristics. By the tenth week, for example, it already has a face, arms and legs, fingers and toes; it has internal organs, and brain activity is detectable.[1] On the other hand, I think that the premise is false, that the fetus is not a person from the moment of conception. A newly fertilized ovum, a newly implanted clump of cells, is no more a person than an acorn is an oak tree. But I shall not discuss any of this. For it seems to me to be of great interest to ask what happens if, for the sake of argument, we allow the premise. How, precisely, are we supposed to get from there to the conclusion that abortion is morally impermissible? Opponents of abortion commonly spend most of their time establishing that the fetus is a person, and hardly any time explaining the step from there to the impermissibility of abortion. Perhaps they think the step too simple and obvious to require much comment. Or perhaps instead they are simply being economical in argument. Many of those who defend abortion rely on the premise that the fetus is not a person, but only a bit of tissue that will become a person at birth; and why pay out more arguments than you have to? Whatever the explanation, I suggest that the step they take is neither easy nor obvious, that it calls for closer examination than it is commonly given, and that when we do give it this closer examination we shall feel inclined to reject it.

I propose, then, that we grant that the fetus is a person from the moment of conception. How does the argument go from here? Something like this, I

Originally published in *Philosophy and Public Affairs* 1 (1971): 47–66. Reprinted by permission of Blackwell Publishing Ltd.

take it. Every person has a right to life. So the fetus has a right to life. No doubt the mother has a right to decide what shall happen in and to her body; everyone would grant that. But surely a person's right to life is stronger and more stringent than the mother's right to decide what happens in and to her body, and so outweighs it. So the fetus may not be killed; an abortion may not be performed.

It sounds plausible. But now let me ask you to imagine this. You wake up in the morning and find yourself back to back in bed with an unconscious violinist. A famous unconscious violinist. He has been found to have a fatal kidney ailment, and the Society of Music Lovers has canvassed all the available medical records and found that you alone have the right blood type to help. They have therefore kidnapped you, and last night the violinist's circulatory system was plugged into yours, so that your kidneys can be used to extract poisons from his blood as well as your own. The director of the hospital now tells you, "Look, we're sorry the Society of Music Lovers did this to you – we would never have permitted it if we had known. But still, they did it, and the violinist now is plugged into you. To unplug you would be to kill him. But never mind, it's only for nine months. By then he will have recovered from his ailment, and can safely be unplugged from you." Is it morally incumbent on you to accede to this situation? No doubt it would be very nice of you if you did, a great kindness. But do you *have* to accede to it? What if it were not nine months, but nine years? Or longer still? What if the director of the hospital says, "Tough luck, I agree, but you've now got to stay in bed, with the violinist plugged into you, for the rest of your life. Because remember this. All persons have a right to life, and violinists are persons. Granted you have a right to decide what happens in and to your body, but a person's right to life outweighs your right to decide what happens in and to your body. So you cannot ever be unplugged from him." I imagine you would regard this as outrageous, which suggests that something really is wrong with that plausible-sounding argument I mentioned a moment ago.

In this case, of course, you were kidnapped; you didn't volunteer for the operation that plugged the violinist into your kidneys. Can those who oppose abortion on the ground I mentioned make an exception for a pregnancy due to rape? Certainly. They can say that persons have a right to life only if they didn't come into existence because of rape; or they can say that all persons have a right to

life, but that some have less of a right to life than others, in particular, that those who came into existence because of rape have less. But these statements have a rather unpleasant sound. Surely the question of whether you have a right to life at all, or how much of it you have, shouldn't turn on the question of whether or not you are the product of a rape. And in fact the people who oppose abortion on the ground I mentioned do not make this distinction, and hence do not make an exception in case of rape.

Nor do they make an exception for a case in which the mother has to spend the nine months of her pregnancy in bed. They would agree that would be a great pity, and hard on the mother; but all the same, all persons have a right to life, the fetus is a person, and so on. I suspect, in fact, that they would not make an exception for a case in which, miraculously enough, the pregnancy went on for nine years, or even the rest of the mother's life.

Some won't even make an exception for a case in which continuation of the pregnancy is likely to shorten the mother's life; they regard abortion as impermissible even to save the mother's life. Such cases are nowadays very rare, and many opponents of abortion do not accept this extreme view. All the same, it is a good place to begin: a number of points of interest come out in respect to it.

1. Let us call the view that abortion is impermissible even to save the mother's life "the extreme view." I want to suggest first that it does not issue from the argument I mentioned earlier without the addition of some fairly powerful premises. Suppose a woman has become pregnant, and now learns that she has a cardiac condition such that she will die if she carries the baby to term. What may be done for her? The fetus, being a person, has a right to life, but as the mother is a person too, so has she a right to life. Presumably they have an equal right to life. How is it supposed to come out that an abortion may not be performed? If mother and child have an equal right to life, shouldn't we perhaps flip a coin? Or should we add to the mother's right to life her right to decide what happens in and to her body, which everybody seems to be ready to grant – the sum of her rights now outweighing the fetus' right to life?

The most familiar argument here is the following. We are told that performing the abortion would be directly killing[2] the child, whereas doing nothing would not be killing the mother, but only letting her die. Moreover, in killing the child, one would be killing an innocent person, for the child has committed no crime, and is not aiming at his mother's death. And then there are a variety of ways in which this might be continued. (1) But as directly killing an innocent person is always and absolutely impermissible, an abortion may not be performed. Or, (2) as directly killing an innocent person is murder, and murder is always and absolutely impermissible, an abortion may not be performed.[3] Or, (3) as one's duty to refrain from directly killing an innocent person is more stringent than one's duty to keep a person from dying, an abortion may not be performed. Or, (4) if one's only options are directly killing an innocent person or letting a person die, one must prefer letting the person die, and thus an abortion may not be performed.[4]

Some people seem to have thought that these are not further premises which must be added if the conclusion is to be reached, but that they follow from the very fact that an innocent person has a right to life.[5] But this seems to me to be a mistake, and perhaps the simplest way to show this is to bring out that while we must certainly grant that innocent persons have a right to life, the theses in (1) through (4) are all false. Take (2), for example. If directly killing an innocent person is murder, and thus is impermissible, then the mother's directly killing the innocent person inside her is murder, and thus is impermissible. But it cannot seriously be thought to be murder if the mother performs an abortion on herself to save her life. It cannot seriously be said that she *must* refrain, that she *must* sit passively by and wait for her death. Let us look again at the case of you and the violinist. There you are, in bed with the violinist, and the director of the hospital says to you, "It's all most distressing, and I deeply sympathize, but you see this is putting an additional strain on your kidneys, and you'll be dead within the month. But you *have* to stay where you are all the same. Because unplugging you would be directly killing an innocent violinist, and that's murder, and that's impermissible." If anything in the world is true, it is that you do not commit murder, you do not do what is impermissible, if you reach around to your back and unplug yourself from that violinist to save your life.

The main focus of attention in writings on abortion has been on what a third party may or may not do in answer to a request from a woman for an abortion. This is in a way understandable. Things being as they are, there isn't much a woman can safely do to abort herself. So the question asked is what a third party may do, and what the mother may do, if it is mentioned at all, is deduced, almost as an afterthought, from what it is concluded that third parties may do. But it seems to me that to treat the matter in this way is to refuse to grant to the mother that very status of person which is so firmly insisted on for the fetus. For we cannot simply read off what a person may do from what a third party may do. Suppose you find yourself trapped in a tiny house with a growing child. I mean a very tiny house, and a rapidly growing child – you are already up against the wall of the house and in a few minutes you'll be crushed to death. The child on the other hand won't be crushed to death; if nothing is done to stop him from growing he'll be hurt, but in the end he'll simply burst open the house and walk out a free man. Now I could well understand it if a bystander were to say, "There's nothing we can do for you. We cannot choose between your life and his, we cannot be the ones to decide who is to live, we cannot intervene." But it cannot be concluded that you too can do nothing, that you cannot attack it to save your life. However innocent the child may be, you do not have to wait passively while it crushes you to death. Perhaps a pregnant woman is vaguely felt to have the status of house, to which we don't allow the right of self-defense. But if the woman houses the child, it should be remembered that she is a person who houses it.

I should perhaps stop to say explicitly that I am not claiming that people have a right to do anything whatever to save their lives. I think, rather, that there are drastic limits to the right of self-defense. If someone threatens you with death unless you torture someone else to death, I think you have not the right, even to save your life, to do so. But the case under consideration here is very different. In our case there are only two people involved, one whose life is threatened, and one who threatens it. Both are innocent: the one who is threatened is not threatened because of any fault, the one who threatens does not threaten because of any fault. For this reason we may feel that we bystanders cannot intervene. But the person threatened can.

In sum, a woman surely can defend her life against the threat to it posed by the unborn child, even if doing so involves its death. And this shows not merely that the these in (1) through (4) are false; it shows also that the extreme view of abortion is false, and so we need not canvass any other possible ways of arriving at it from the argument I mentioned at the outset.

2. The extreme view could of course be weakened to say that while abortion is permissible to save the mother's life, it may not be performed by a third party, but only by the mother herself. But this cannot be right either. For what we have to keep in mind is that the mother and the unborn child are not like two tenants in a small house which has, by an unfortunate mistake, been rented to both: the mother *owns* the house. The fact that she does adds to the offensiveness of deducing that the mother can do nothing from the supposition that third parties can do nothing. But it does more than this: it casts a bright light on the supposition that third parties can do nothing. Certainly it lets us see that a third party who says "I cannot choose between you" is fooling himself if he thinks this is impartiality. If Jones has found and fastened on a certain coat, which he needs to keep him from freezing, but which Smith also needs to keep him from freezing, then it is not impartiality that says "I cannot choose between you" when Smith owns the coat. Women have said again and again "This body is *my* body!" and they have reason to feel angry, reason to feel that it has been like shouting into the wind. Smith, after all, is hardly likely to bless us if we say to him, "Of course it's your coat, anybody would grant that it is. But no one may choose between you and Jones who is to have it."

We should really ask what it is that says "no one may choose" in the face of the fact that the body that houses the child is the mother's body. It may be simply a failure to appreciate this fact. But it may be something more interesting, namely the sense that one has a right to refuse to lay hands on people, even where it would be just and fair to do so, even where justice seems to require that somebody do so. Thus justice might call for somebody to get Smith's coat back from Jones, and yet you have a right to refuse to be the one to lay hands on Jones, a right to refuse to do physical violence to him. This, I think, must be granted. But then what should be said is not "no one may choose," but only "*I* cannot choose," and indeed not even this, but "*I* will not *act*," leaving it open that somebody else can or should, and in particular that anyone in a position of authority, with the job of securing people's rights, both can and should. So this is no difficulty. I have not been arguing that any given third party must accede to the mother's request that he perform an abortion to save her life, but only that he may.

I suppose that in some views of human life the mother's body is only on loan to her, the loan not being one which gives her any prior claim to it. One who held this view might well think it impartiality to say "I cannot choose." But I shall simply ignore this possibility. My own view is that if a human being has any just, prior claim to anything at all, he has a just, prior claim to his own body. And perhaps this needn't be argued for here anyway, since, as I mentioned, the arguments against abortion we are looking at do grant that the woman has a right to decide what happens in and to her body.

But although they do grant it, I have tried to show that they do not take seriously what is done in granting it. I suggest the same thing will reappear even more clearly when we turn away from cases in which the mother's life is at stake, and attend, as I propose we now do, to the vastly more common cases in which a woman wants an abortion for some less weighty reason than preserving her own life.

3. Where the mother's life is not at stake, the argument I mentioned at the outset seems to have a much stronger pull. "Everyone has a right to life, so the unborn person has a right to life." And isn't the child's right to life weightier than anything other than the mother's own right to life, which she might put forward as ground for an abortion?

This argument treats the right to life as if it were unproblematic. It is not, and this seems to me to be precisely the source of the mistake.

For we should now, at long last, ask what it comes to, to have a right to life. In some views having a right to life includes having a right to be given at least the bare minimum one needs for continued life. But suppose that what in fact *is* the bare minimum a man needs for continued life is something he has no right at all to be given? If I am sick unto death, and the only thing that will save my life is the touch of Henry Fonda's cool hand on my fevered brow, then all the same, I have no right to be given the touch of Henry Fonda's cool hand on my fevered brow. It would be frightfully nice of him to fly in from the West Coast to provide it. It would be less nice, though no doubt well meant, if my friends flew out to the West Coast and carried Henry Fonda back with them. But I have no right at all against anybody that he should do this for me. Or again, to return to the story I told earlier, the fact that for continued life that violinist needs the continued use of your kidneys does not establish that he has a right to be given the continued use of your kidneys. He certainly has no right against you that *you* should give him continued use of your kidneys. For nobody has any right to use your kidneys unless you give him such a right; and nobody has the right against you that you shall give him this right – if you do allow him to go on using your kidneys, this is a kindness on your part, and not something he can claim from you as his due. Nor has he any right against anybody else that *they* should give him continued use of your kidneys. Certainly he had no right against the Society of Music Lovers that they should plug him into you in the first place. And if you now start to unplug yourself, having learned that you will otherwise have to spend nine years in bed with him, there is nobody in the world who must try to prevent you, in order to see to it that he is given something he has a right to be given.

Some people are rather stricter about the right to life. In their view, it does not include the right to be given anything, but amounts to, and only to, the right not to be killed by anybody. But here a related difficulty arises. If everybody is to refrain from killing that violinist, then everybody must refrain from doing a great many different sorts of things. Everybody must refrain from slitting his throat, everybody must refrain from shooting him – and everybody must refrain from unplugging you from him. But does he have a right against everybody that they shall refrain from unplugging you from him? To refrain from doing this is to allow him to continue to use your kidneys. It could be argued that he has a right against us that *we* should allow him to continue to use your kidneys. That is, while he had no right against us that we should give him the use of your kidneys, it might be argued that he anyway has a right against us that we shall not now intervene and deprive him of the use of your kidneys. I shall come back to third-party interventions later. But certainly the violinist has no right against you that *you* shall allow him to continue to use your kidneys. As I said, if you do allow him to use them, it is a kindness on your part, and not something you owe him.

The difficulty I point to here is not peculiar to the right to life. It reappears in connection with all the other natural rights; and it is something which an adequate account of rights must deal with. For present purposes it is enough just to draw attention to it. But I would stress that I am not arguing that people do not have a right to life – quite to the contrary, it seems to me that the primary control we must place on the acceptability of an account of rights is that it should turn out in that account to

be a truth that all persons have a right to life. I am arguing only that having a right to life does not guarantee having either a right to be given the use of or a right to be allowed continued use of another person's body – even if one needs it for life itself. So the right to life will not serve the opponents of abortion in the very simple and clear way in which they seem to have thought it would.

4. There is another way to bring out the difficulty. In the most ordinary sort of case, to deprive someone of what he has a right to is to treat him unjustly. Suppose a boy and his small brother are jointly given a box of chocolates for Christmas. If the older boy takes the box and refuses to give his brother any of the chocolates, he is unjust to him, for the brother has been given a right to half of them. But suppose that, having learned that otherwise it means nine years in bed with that violinist, you unplug yourself from him. You surely are not being unjust to him, for you gave him no right to use your kidneys, and no one else can have given him any such right. But we have to notice that in unplugging yourself, you are killing him; and violinists, like everybody else, have a right to life, and thus in the view we were considering just now, the right not to be killed. So here you do what he supposedly has a right you shall not do, but you do not act unjustly to him in doing it.

The emendation which may be made at this point is this: the right to life consists not in the right not to be killed, but rather in the right not to be killed unjustly. This runs a risk of circularity, but never mind: it would enable us to square the fact that the violinist has a right to life with the fact that you do not act unjustly toward him in unplugging yourself, thereby killing him. For if you do not kill him unjustly, you do not violate his right to life, and so it is no wonder you do him no injustice.

But if this emendation is accepted, the gap in the argument against abortion stares us plainly in the face: it is by no means enough to show that the fetus is a person, and to remind us that all persons have a right to life – we need to be shown also that killing the fetus violates its right to life, i.e., that abortion is unjust killing. And is it?

I suppose we may take it as a datum that in a case of pregnancy due to rape the mother has not given the unborn person a right to the use of her body for food and shelter. Indeed, in what pregnancy could it be supposed that the mother has given the unborn person such a right? It is not as if there were unborn persons drifting about the world, to whom a woman who wants a child says "I invite you in."

But it might be argued that there are other ways one can have acquired a right to the use of another person's body than by having been invited to use it by that person. Suppose a woman voluntarily indulges in intercourse, knowing of the chance it will issue in pregnancy, and then she does become pregnant; is she not in part responsible for the presence, in fact the very existence, of the unborn person inside her? No doubt she did not invite it in. But doesn't her partial responsibility for its being there itself give it a right to the use of her body?[6] If so, then her aborting it would be more like the boy's taking away the chocolates, and less like your unplugging yourself from the violinist – doing so would be depriving it of what it does have a right to, and thus would be doing it an injustice.

And then, too, it might be asked whether or not she can kill it even to save her own life: If she voluntarily called it into existence, how can she now kill it, even in self-defense?

The first thing to be said about this is that it is something new. Opponents of abortion have been so concerned to make out the independence of the fetus, in order to establish that it has a right to life, just as its mother does, that they have tended to overlook the possible support they might gain from making out that the fetus is *dependent* on the mother, in order to establish that she has a special kind of responsibility for it, a responsibility that gives it rights against her which are not possessed by any independent person – such as an ailing violinist who is a stranger to her.

On the other hand, this argument would give the unborn person a right to its mother's body only if her pregnancy resulted from a voluntary act, undertaken in full knowledge of the chance a pregnancy might result from it. It would leave out entirely the unborn person whose existence is due to rape. Pending the availability of some further argument, then, we would be left with the conclusion that unborn persons whose existence is due to rape have no right to the use of their mothers' bodies, and thus that aborting them is not depriving them of anything they have a right to and hence is not unjust killing.

And we should also notice that it is not at all plain that this argument really does go even as far as it purports to. For there are cases and cases, and the details make a difference. If the room is stuffy, and I therefore open a window to air it, and a burglar climbs in, it would be absurd to say:

"Ah, now he can stay, she's given him a right to the use of her house – for she is partially responsible for his presence there, having voluntarily done what enabled him to get in, in full knowledge that there are such things as burglars, and that burglars burgle." It would be still more absurd to say this if I had had bars installed outside my windows, precisely to prevent burglars from getting in, and a burglar got in only because of a defect in the bars. It remains equally absurd if we imagine it is not a burglar who climbs in, but an innocent person who blunders or falls in. Again, suppose it were like this: people-seeds drift about in the air like pollen, and if you open your windows, one may drift in and take root in your carpets or upholstery. You don't want children, so you fix up your windows with fine mesh screens, the very best you can buy. As can happen, however, and on very, very rare occasions does happen, one of the screens is defective; and a seed drifts in and takes root. Does the person-plant who now develops have a right to the use of your house? Surely not – despite the fact that you voluntarily opened your windows, you knowingly kept carpets and upholstered furniture, and you knew that screens were sometimes defective. Someone may argue that you are responsible for its rooting, that it does have a right to your house, because after all you *could* have lived out your life with bare floors and furniture, or with sealed windows and doors. But this won't do – for by the same token anyone can avoid a pregnancy due to rape by having a hysterectomy, or anyway by never leaving home without a (reliable!) army.

It seems to me that the argument we are looking at can establish at most that there are *some* cases in which the unborn person has a right to the use of its mother's body, and therefore *some* cases in which abortion is unjust killing. There is room for much discussion and argument as to precisely which, if any. But I think we should sidestep this issue and leave it open, for at any rate the argument certainly does not establish that all abortion is unjust killing.

5. There is room for yet another argument here, however. We surely must all grant that there may be cases in which it would be morally indecent to detach a person from your body at the cost of his life. Suppose you learn that what the violinist needs is not nine years of your life, but only one hour: all you need do to save his life is to spend one hour in that bed with him. Suppose also that letting him use your kidneys for that one hour

would not affect your health in the slightest. Admittedly you were kidnapped. Admittedly you did not give anyone permission to plug him into you. Nevertheless it seems to me plain you *ought* to allow him to use your kidneys for that hour – it would be indecent to refuse.

Again, suppose pregnancy lasted only an hour, and constituted no threat to life or health. And suppose that a woman becomes pregnant as a result of rape. Admittedly she did not voluntarily do anything to bring about the existence of a child. Admittedly she did nothing at all which would give the unborn person a right to the use of her body. All the same it might well be said, as in the newly emended violinist story, that she *ought* to allow it to remain for that hour – that it would be indecent in her to refuse.

Now some people are inclined to use the term "right" in such a way that it follows from the fact that you ought to allow a person to use your body for the hour he needs, that he has a right to use your body for the hour he needs, even though he has not been given that right by any person or act. They may say that it follows also that if you refuse, you act unjustly toward him. This use of the term is perhaps so common that it cannot be called wrong; nevertheless it seems to me to be an unfortunate loosening of what we would do better to keep a tight rein on. Suppose that box of chocolates I mentioned earlier had not been given to both boys jointly, but was given only to the older boy. There he sits, stolidly eating his way through the box, his small brother watching enviously. Here we are likely to say "You ought not to be so mean. You ought to give your brother some of those chocolates." My own view is that it just does not follow from the truth of this that the brother has any right to any of the chocolates. If the boy refuses to give his brother any, he is greedy, stingy, callous – but not unjust. I suppose that the people I have in mind will say it does follow that the brother has a right to some of the chocolates, and thus that the boy does act unjustly if he refuses to give his brother any. But the effect of saying this is to obscure what we should keep distinct, namely the difference between the boy's refusal in this case and the boy's refusal in the earlier case, in which the box was given to both boys jointly, and in which the small brother thus had what was from any point of view clear title to half.

A further objection to so using the term "right" that from the fact that A ought to do a thing for B, it follows that B has a right against A that A do it

for him, is that it is going to make the question of whether or not a man has a right to a thing turn on how easy it is to provide him with it; and this seems not merely unfortunate, but morally unacceptable. Take the case of Henry Fonda again. I said earlier that I had no right to the touch of his cool hand on my fevered brow, even though I needed it to save my life. I said it would be frightfully nice of him to fly in from the West Coast to provide me with it, but that I had no right against him that he should do so. But suppose he isn't on the West Coast. Suppose he has only to walk across the room, place a hand briefly on my brow – and lo, my life is saved. Then surely he ought to do it, it would be indecent to refuse. Is it to be said "Ah, well, it follows that in this case she has a right to the touch of his hand on her brow, and so it would be an injustice in him to refuse"? So that I have a right to it when it is easy for him to provide it, though no right when it's hard? It's rather a shocking idea that anyone's rights should fade away and disappear as it gets harder and harder to accord them to him.

So my own view is that even though you ought to let the violinist use your kidneys for the one hour he needs, we should not conclude that he has a right to do so – we should say that if you refuse, you are, like the boy who owns all the chocolates and will give none away, self-centered and callous, indecent in fact, but not unjust. And similarly, that even supposing a case in which a woman pregnant due to rape ought to allow the unborn person to use her body for the hour he needs, we should not conclude that he has a right to do so; we should conclude that she is self-centered, callous, indecent, but not unjust, if she refuses. The complaints are no less grave; they are just different. However, there is no need to insist on this point. If anyone does wish to deduce "he has a right" from "you ought," then all the same he must surely grant that there are cases in which it is not morally required of you that you allow that violinist to use your kidneys, and in which he does not have a right to use them, and in which you do not do him an injustice if you refuse. And so also for mother and unborn child. Except in such cases as the unborn person has a right to demand it – and we were leaving open the possibility that there may be such cases – nobody is morally *required* to make large sacrifices, of health, of all other interests and concerns, of all other duties and commitments, for nine years, or even for nine months, in order to keep another person alive.

6. We have in fact to distinguish between two kinds of Samaritan: the Good Samaritan and what we might call the Minimally Decent Samaritan. The story of the Good Samaritan, you will remember, goes like this:

A certain man went down from Jerusalem to Jericho, and fell among thieves, which stripped him of his raiment, and wounded him, and departed, leaving him half dead.

And by chance there came down a certain priest that way; and when he saw him, he passed by on the other side.

And likewise a Levite, when he was at the place, came and looked on him, and passed by on the other side.

But a certain Samaritan, as he journeyed, came where he was; and when he saw him he had compassion on him.

And went to him, and bound up his wounds, pouring in oil and wine, and set him on his own beast, and brought him to an inn, and took care of him.

And on the morrow, when he departed, he took out two pence, and gave them to the host, and said unto him, "Take care of him; and whatsoever thou spendest more, when I come again, I will repay thee." (Luke 10:30–5)

The Good Samaritan went out of his way, at some cost to himself, to help one in need of it. We are not told what the options were, that is, whether or not the priest and the Levite could have helped by doing less than the Good Samaritan did, but assuming they could have, then the fact they did nothing at all shows they were not even Minimally Decent Samaritans, not because they were not Samaritans, but because they were not even minimally decent.

These things are a matter of degree, of course, but there is a difference, and it comes out perhaps most clearly in the story of Kitty Genovese, who, as you will remember, was murdered while thirty-eight people watched or listened, and did nothing at all to help her. A Good Samaritan would have rushed out to give direct assistance against the murderer. Or perhaps we had better allow that it would have been a Splendid Samaritan who did this, on the ground that it would have involved a risk of death for himself. But the thirty-eight not only did not do this, they did not even trouble to pick up a phone to call the police. Minimally Decent Samaritanism would call for doing at least that, and their not having done it was monstrous.

After telling the story of the Good Samaritan, Jesus said "Go, and do thou likewise." Perhaps he meant that we are morally required to act as the Good Samaritan did. Perhaps he was urging people to do more than is morally required of them. At all events it seems plain that it was not morally required of any of the thirty-eight that he rush out to give direct assistance at the risk of his own life, and that it is not morally required of anyone that he give long stretches of his life – nine years or nine months – to sustaining the life of a person who has no special right (we were leaving open the possibility of this) to demand it.

Indeed, with one rather striking class of exceptions, no one in any country in the world is *legally* required to do anywhere near as much as this for anyone else. The class of exceptions is obvious. My main concern here is not the state of the law in respect to abortion, but it is worth drawing attention to the fact that in no state in this country is any man compelled by law to be even a Minimally Decent Samaritan to any person; there is no law under which charges could be brought against the thirty-eight who stood by while Kitty Genovese died. By contrast, in most states in this country women are compelled by law to be not merely Minimally Decent Samaritans, but Good Samaritans to unborn persons inside them. This doesn't by itself settle anything one way or the other, because it may well be argued that there should be laws in this country – as there are in many European countries – compelling at least Minimally Decent Samaritanism.[7] But it does show that there is a gross injustice in the existing state of the law. And it shows also that the groups currently working against liberalization of abortion laws, in fact working toward having it declared unconstitutional for a state to permit abortion, had better start working for the adoption of Good Samaritan laws generally, or earn the charge that they are acting in bad faith.

I should think, myself, that Minimally Decent Samaritan laws would be one thing, Good Samaritan laws quite another, and in fact highly improper. But we are not here concerned with the law. What we should ask is not whether anybody should be compelled by law to be a Good Samaritan, but whether we must accede to a situation in which somebody is being compelled – by nature, perhaps – to be a Good Samaritan. We have, in other words, to look now at third-party interventions. I have been arguing that no person is morally required to make large sacrifices to sustain the life of another who has no right to demand them, and this even where the sacrifices do not include life itself; we are not morally required to be Good Samaritans or anyway Very Good Samaritans to one another. But what if a man cannot extricate himself from such a situation? What if he appeals to us to extricate him? It seems to me plain that there are cases in which we can, cases in which a Good Samaritan would extricate him. There you are, you were kidnapped, and nine years in bed with that violinist lie ahead of you. You have your own life to lead. You are sorry, but you simply cannot see giving up so much of your life to the sustaining of his. You cannot extricate yourself, and ask us to do so. I should have thought that – in light of his having no right to the use of your body – it was obvious that we do not have to accede to your being forced to give up so much. We can do what you ask. There is no injustice to the violinist in our doing so.

7. Following the lead of the opponents of abortion, I have throughout been speaking of the fetus merely as a person, and what I have been asking is whether or not the argument we began with, which proceeds only from the fetus being a person, really does establish its conclusion. I have argued that it does not.

But of course there are arguments and arguments, and it may be said that I have simply fastened on the wrong one. It may be said that what is important is not merely the fact that the fetus is a person, but that it is a person for whom the woman has a special kind of responsibility issuing from the fact that she is its mother. And it might be argued that all my analogies are therefore irrelevant – for you do not have that special kind of responsibility for that violinist, Henry Fonda does not have that special kind of responsibility for me. And our attention might be drawn to the fact that men and women both *are* compelled by law to provide support for their children.

I have in effect dealt (briefly) with this argument in section 4 above; but a (still briefer) recapitulation now may be in order. Surely we do not have any such "special responsibility" for a person unless we have assumed it, explicitly or implicitly. If a set of parents do not try to prevent pregnancy, do not obtain an abortion, and then at the time of birth of the child do not put it out for adoption, but rather take it home with them, then they have assumed responsibility for it, they have given it

rights, and they cannot *now* withdraw support from it at the cost of its life because they now find it difficult to go on providing for it. But if they have taken all reasonable precautions against having a child, they do not simply by virtue of their biological relationship to the child who comes into existence have a special responsibility for it. They may wish to assume responsibility for it, or they may not wish to. And I am suggesting that if assuming responsibility for it would require large sacrifices, then they may refuse. A Good Samaritan would not refuse – or anyway, a Splendid Samaritan, if the sacrifices that had to be made were enormous. But then so would a Good Samaritan assume responsibility for that violinist; so would Henry Fonda, if he is a Good Samaritan, fly in from the West Coast and assume responsibility for me.

8. My argument will be found unsatisfactory on two counts by many of those who want to regard abortion as morally permissible. First, while I do argue that abortion is not impermissible, I do not argue that it is always permissible. There may well be cases in which carrying the child to term requires only Minimally Decent Samaritanism of the mother, and this is a standard we must not fall below. I am inclined to think it a merit of my account precisely that it does *not* give a general yes or a general no. It allows for and supports our sense that, for example, a sick and desperately frightened fourteen-year-old schoolgirl, pregnant due to rape, may *of course* choose abortion, and that any law which rules this out is an insane law. And it also allows for and supports our sense that in other cases resort to abortion is even positively indecent. It would be indecent in the woman to request an abortion, and indecent in a doctor to perform it, if she is in her seventh month, and wants the abortion just to avoid the nuisance of postponing a trip abroad. The very fact that the arguments I have been drawing attention to treat all cases of abortion, or even all cases of abortion in which the mother's life is not at stake, as morally on a par ought to have made them suspect at the outset.

Secondly, while I am arguing for the permissibility of abortion in some cases, I am not arguing for the right to secure the death of the unborn child. It is easy to confuse these two things in that up to a certain point in the life of the fetus it is not able to survive outside the mother's body; hence removing it from her body guarantees its death. But they are importantly different. I have argued that you are not morally required to spend nine months in bed, sustaining the life of that violinist; but to say this is by no means to say that if, when you unplug yourself, there is a miracle and he survives, you then have a right to turn round and slit his throat. You may detach yourself even if this costs him his life; you have no right to be guaranteed his death, by some other means, if unplugging yourself does not kill him. There are some people who will feel dissatisfied by this feature of my argument. A woman may be utterly devastated by the thought of a child, a bit of herself, put out for adoption and never seen or heard of again. She may therefore want not merely that the child be detached from her, but more, that it die. Some opponents of abortion are inclined to regard this as beneath contempt – thereby showing insensitivity to what is surely a powerful source of despair. All the same, I agree that the desire for the child's death is not one which anybody may gratify, should it turn out to be possible to detach the child alive.

At this place, however, it should be remembered that we have only been pretending throughout that the fetus is a human being from the moment of conception. A very early abortion is surely not the killing of a person, and so is not dealt with by anything I have said here.

Notes

1   Daniel Callahan, *Abortion: Law, Choice and Morality* (New York, 1970), p. 373. This book gives a fascinating survey of the available information on abortion. The Jewish tradition is surveyed in David M. Feldman, *Birth Control in Jewish Law* (New York, 1968), Part 5; the Catholic tradition in John T. Noonan, Jr., "An Almost Absolute Value in History," in *The Morality of Abortion*, ed. John T. Noonan, Jr. (Cambridge, Mass., 1970).

2   The term "direct" in the arguments I refer to is a technical one. Roughly, what is meant by "direct killing" is either killing as an end in itself, or killing as a means to some end, for example, the end of saving someone else's life. See note 6, below, for an example of its use.

3   Cf. *Encyclical Letter of Pope Pius XI on Christian Marriage*, St. Paul Editions (Boston, n.d.), p. 32: "however much we may pity the mother whose health and even life is gravely imperiled in the performance of the duty allotted to her by nature, nevertheless what could ever be a sufficient reason for excusing in any way the direct murder of the innocent? This is precisely what we are dealing with here." Noonan (*The Morality of Abortion*, p. 43) reads this as follows: "What cause can ever avail to excuse in any way the direct killing of the innocent? For it is a question of that."

4   The thesis in (4) is in an interesting way weaker than those in (1), (2), and (3): they rule out abortion even in cases in which both mother *and* child will die if the abortion is not performed. By contrast, one who held the view expressed in (4) could consistently say that one needn't prefer letting two persons die to killing one.

5   Cf. the following passage from Pius XII, *Address to the Italian Catholic Society of Midwives*: "The baby in the maternal breast has the right to life immediately from God. – Hence there is no man, no human authority, no science, no medical, eugenic, social, economic or moral "indication" which can establish or grant a valid juridical ground for a direct deliberate disposition of an innocent human life, that is a disposition which looks to its destruction either as an end or as a means to another end perhaps in itself not illicit. – The baby, still not born, is a man in the same degree and for the same reason as the mother" (quoted in Noonan, *The Morality of Abortion*, p. 45).

6   The need for a discussion of this argument was brought home to me by members of the Society for Ethical and Legal Philosophy, to whom this paper was originally presented.

7   For a discussion of the difficulties involved, and a survey of the European experience with such laws, see *The Good Samaritan and the Law*, ed. James M. Ratcliffe (New York, 1966).

22

Justice and Minority Rights

Will Kymlicka

Three Forms of Group-Differentiated Rights

Virtually all liberal democracies are either multi-national or polyethnic, or both. The 'challenge of multiculturalism' is to accommodate these national and ethnic differences in a stable and morally defensible way (Gutmann 1993). In this section, I will discuss some of the most important ways in which democracies have responded to the demands of national minorities and ethnic groups.

In all liberal democracies, one of the major mechanisms for accommodating cultural differences is the protection of the civil and political rights of individuals. It is impossible to overstate the importance of freedom of association, religion, speech, mobility, and political organization for protecting group difference. These rights enable individuals to form and maintain the various groups and associations which constitute civil society, to adapt these groups to changing circumstances, and to promote their views and interests to the wider population. The protection afforded by these common rights of citizenship is sufficient for many of the legitimate forms of diversity in society.

Various critics of liberalism – including some Marxists, communitarians, and feminists – have argued that the liberal focus on individual rights reflects an atomistic, materialistic, instrumental, or conflictual view of human relationships. I believe that this criticism is profoundly mistaken, and that individual rights can be and typically are used to sustain a wide range of social relationships. Indeed, the most basic liberal right – freedom of conscience – is primarily valuable for the protection it gives to intrinsically social (and non-instrumental) activities.[1]

However, it is increasingly accepted in many countries that some forms of cultural difference can only be accommodated through special legal or constitutional measures, above and beyond the common rights of citizenship. Some forms of group difference can only be accommodated if their members have certain group-specific rights – what Iris Young calls 'differentiated citizenship' (I. Young 1989: 258).

For example, a recent government publication in Canada noted that:

> In the Canadian experience, it has not been enough to protect only universal individual rights. Here, the Constitution and ordinary laws also protect other rights accorded to individuals as members of certain communities. This accommodation of both types of rights makes our constitution unique and reflects the Canadian value of equality that accommodates difference. The fact that community rights exist alongside individual rights goes to the very heart of what Canada is all about. (Government of Canada 1991a: 3).

Reprinted from Will Kymlicka, *Multicultural Citizenship* (Oxford: Clarendon Press, 1995), pp. 26–33, 108–30.
Copyright © 1995 by Will Kymlicka. Reprinted by permission of Oxford University Press.

It is quite misleading to say that Canada is unique in combining universal individual rights and group-specific 'community rights'. Such a combination exists in many other federal systems in Europe, Asia, and Africa. As I noted earlier, even the constitution of the United States, which is often seen as a paradigm of individualism, allows for various group-specific rights, including the special status of American Indians and Puerto Ricans.

It is these special group-specific measures for accommodating national and ethnic differences that I will focus on. There are at least three forms of group-specific rights: (1) self-government rights; (2) polyethnic rights; and (3) special representation rights. I will say a few words about each, before considering some of the issues they raise.

Self-government rights

In most multination states, the component nations are inclined to demand some form of political autonomy or territorial jurisdiction, so as to ensure the full and free development of their cultures and the best interests of their people. At the extreme, nations may wish to secede, if they think their self-determination is impossible within the larger state.

The right of national groups to self-determination is given (limited) recognition in international law. According to the United Nations' Charter, 'all peoples have the right to self-determination'. However, the UN has not defined 'peoples', and it has generally applied the principle of self-determination only to overseas colonies, not internal national minorities, even when the latter were subject to the same sort of colonization and conquest as the former. This limitation on self-determination to overseas colonies (known as the 'salt-water thesis') is widely seen as arbitrary, and many national minorities insist that they too are 'peoples' or 'nations', and, as such, have the right of self-determination. They demand certain powers of self-government which they say were not relinquished by their (often involuntary) incorporation into a larger state.[2]

One mechanism for recognizing claims to self-government is federalism, which divides powers between the central government and regional sub-units (provinces/states/cantons). Where national minorities are regionally concentrated, the boundaries of federal subunits can be drawn so that the national minority forms a majority in one of the subunits. Under these circumstances, federalism can provide extensive self-government for a national minority, guaranteeing its ability to make decisions in certain areas without being outvoted by the larger society.

For example, under the federal division of powers in Canada, the province of Quebec (which is 80 per cent francophone) has extensive jurisdiction over issues that are crucial to the survival of the French culture, including control over education, language, culture, as well as significant input into immigration policy. The other nine provinces also have these powers, but the major impetus behind the existing division of powers, and indeed behind the entire federal system, is the need to accommodate the Québécois. At the time of Confederation, most English Canadian leaders were in favour of a unitary state, like Britain, and agreed to a federal system primarily to accommodate French Canadians.

One difficulty in a federal system is maintaining the balance between centralization and decentralization. While most Quebecers want an even more decentralized division of powers, most English Canadians favour a stronger central government. One of the challenges facing Canada, therefore, is finding an acceptable form of 'asymmetrical federalism' which grants Quebec powers not given to other provinces. Other federal states face a similar problem.[3]

Federalism is often used to accommodate national diversity, and so some commentators include the rights and powers attached to federal units amongst the 'collective rights' of national minorities (e.g. F. Morton 1985: 77; Van Dyke 1982: 24–31). Of course, many federal systems arose for reasons quite unrelated to cultural diversity. Federalism is often simply a form of administrative decentralization (as in Germany), or the result of historical accidents of colonization (as in Australia). There is no inherent connection between federalism and cultural diversity. But federalism is one common strategy of accommodating national minorities. It is not surprising that countries which are 'a federation of peoples' should also form a political federation.[4]

In the United States, however, a deliberate decision was made not to use federalism to accommodate the self-government rights of national minorities. It would have been quite possible in the nineteenth century to create states dominated by the Navaho, for example, or by Chicanos, Puerto Ricans and native Hawaiians. At the time these groups were incorporated into the United

States, they formed majorities in their homelands. However, a deliberate decision was made not to accept any territory as a state unless these national groups were outnumbered. In some cases, this was achieved by drawing boundaries so that Indian tribes or Hispanic groups were outnumbered (Florida). In other cases, it was achieved by delaying statehood until anglophone settlers swamped the older inhabitants (e.g. Hawaii; the south-west). In cases where the national minority was not likely to be outnumbered, a new type of non-federal political unit was created, such as the 'commonwealth' of Puerto Rico, or the 'Protectorate' of Guam.[5]

As a result, none of the fifty states can be seen as ensuring self-government for a national minority, the way that Quebec ensures self-government for the Québécois. Self-government is instead achieved through political institutions located inside existing states (e.g. Indian reservations), or entirely outside the federal system (e.g. Puerto Rico, Guam). This has tended to make national minorities in the United States more vulnerable, since their self-government powers do not have the same constitutional protection as states' rights. On the other hand, it has provided greater flexibility in redefining those powers so as to suit the needs and interests of each minority. It is much easier to negotiate new self-government provisions for the Navaho or Puerto Ricans than to modify the powers of individual states.

Federalism can only serve as a mechanism for self-government if the national minority forms a majority in one of the federal subunits, as the Québécois do in Quebec. This is not true of most indigenous peoples in North America, who are fewer in number and whose communities are often dispersed across state/provincial lines. Moreover, with few exceptions (such as the Navaho), no redrawing of the boundaries of these federal subunits would create a state, province, or territory with an indigenous majority. It would have been possible to create a state or province dominated by an Indian tribe in the nineteenth century, but, given the massive influx of settlers since then, it is now virtually inconceivable.

One exception concerns the Inuit in the north of Canada, who wish to divide the Northwest Territories into two, so that they will form the majority in the eastern half (to be called 'Nunavut'). This redrawing of federal boundaries is seen as essential to the implementation of the Inuit's right of self-government, and has recently been approved by the federal government.

For the other indigenous peoples in North America, however, self-government has been primarily tied to the system of reserved lands (known as tribal 'reservations' in the United States, and band 'reserves' in Canada). Substantial powers have been devolved from the federal government to the tribal/band councils which govern each reserve. Indian tribes/bands have been acquiring increasing control over health, education, family law, policing, criminal justice, and resource development. They are becoming, in effect, a third order of government, with a collection of powers that is carved out of both federal and state/provincial jurisdictions.[6] However, the administrative difficulties are daunting. Indian tribes/bands differ enormously in the sorts of powers they desire. Moreover, they are territorially located within existing states/provinces, and must co-ordinate their self-government with state/provincial agencies. The exact scope and mechanisms of indigenous self-government in Canada and the United States therefore remain unclear.

Similar systems of self-government exist, or are being sought, by many other indigenous peoples. A recent international declaration regarding the rights of indigenous peoples emphasizes the importance of political self-government. In many parts of the world, however, the hope for political powers is almost utopian, and the more immediate goal is simply to secure the existing land base from further erosion by settlers and resource developers. Indeed, a recent study showed that the single largest cause of ethnic conflict in the world today is the struggle by indigenous peoples for the protection of their land rights.[7]

Self-government claims, then, typically take the form of devolving political power to a political unit substantially controlled by the members of the national minority, and substantially corresponding to their historical homeland or territory. It is important to note that these claims are not seen as a temporary measure, nor as a remedy for a form of oppression that we might (and ought) someday to eliminate. On the contrary, these rights are often described as 'inherent', and so permanent (which is one reason why national minorities seek to have them entrenched in the constitution).

Polyethnic rights

As I noted earlier, immigrant groups in the last thirty years have successfully challenged the 'Anglo-conformity' model which assumed that

Will Kymlicka

they should abandon all aspects of their ethnic heritage and assimilate to existing cultural norms and customs. At first, this challenge simply took the form of demanding the right freely to express their particularity without fear of prejudice or discrimination in the mainstream society. It was the demand, as Walzer put it, that 'politics be separated from nationality – as it was already separated from religion' (Walzer 1982: 6–11).

But the demands of ethnic groups have expanded in important directions. It became clear that positive steps were required to root out discrimination and prejudice, particularly against visible minorities.

For this reason, anti-racism policies are considered part of the 'multiculturalism' policy in Canada and Australia, as are changes to the education curriculum to recognize the history and contribution of minorities. However, these policies are primarily directed at ensuring the effective exercise of the common rights of citizenship, and so do not really qualify as group-differentiated citizenship rights.

Some ethnic groups and religious minorities have also demanded various forms of public funding of their cultural practices. This includes the funding of ethnic associations, magazines and festivals. Given that most liberal states provide funding to the arts and museums, so as to preserve the richness and diversity of our cultural resources, funding for ethnic studies and ethnic associations can be seen as falling under this heading. Indeed, some people defend this funding simply as a way of ensuring that ethnic groups are not discriminated against in state funding of art and culture. Some people believe that public funding agencies have traditionally been biased in favour of European-derived forms of cultural expression, and programmes targeted at ethnic groups remedy this bias. A related demand is for the provision of immigrant language education in schools.

Perhaps the most controversial demand of ethnic groups is for exemptions from laws and regulations that disadvantage them, given their religious practices. For example, Jews and Muslims in Britain have sought exemption from Sunday closing or animal slaughtering legislation; Sikh men in Canada have sought exemption from motorcycle helmet laws and from the official dress-codes of police forces, so that they can wear their turban; Orthodox Jews in the United States have sought the right to wear the yarmulka during military service; and Muslim girls in France have sought exemption from school dress-codes so that they can wear the *chador*.[9]

These group-specific measures – which I call 'polyethnic rights' – are intended to help ethnic groups and religious minorities express their cultural particularity and pride without it hampering their success in the economic and political institutions of the dominant society. Like self-government rights, these polyethnic rights are not seen as temporary, because the cultural differences they protect are not something we seek to eliminate. But, unlike self-government rights, polyethnic rights are usually intended to promote integration into the larger society, not self-government.

Special representation rights

While the traditional concern of national minorities and ethnic groups has been with either self-government or polyethnic rights, there has been increasing interest by these groups, as well as other non-ethnic social groups, in the idea of special representation rights.

Throughout the Western democracies, there is increasing concern that the political process is 'unrepresentative', in the sense that it fails to reflect the diversity of the population. Legislatures in most of these countries are dominated by middle-class, able-bodied, white men. A more representative process, it is said, would include members of ethnic and racial minorities, women, the poor, the disabled, etc. The under-representation of historically disadvantaged groups is a general phenomenon. In the United States and Canada, women, racial minorities, and indigenous peoples all have under one-third of the seats they would have based on their demographic weight. People with disabilities and the economically disadvantaged are also significantly under-represented.[10]

One way to reform the process is to make political parties more inclusive, by reducing the barriers which inhibit women, ethnic minorities, or the poor from becoming party candidates or party leaders; another way is to adopt some form of proportional representation, which has historically been associated with greater inclusiveness of candidates.

However, there is increasing interest in the idea that a certain number of seats in the legislature should be reserved for the members of disadvantaged or marginalized groups. During the debate in Canada over the Charlottetown Accord, for example, a number of recommendations were made for the guaranteed representation of women, ethnic minorities, official language minorities, and Aboriginals.

Group representation rights are often defended as a response to some systemic disadvantage or barrier in the political process which makes it impossible for the group's views and interests to be effectively represented. In so far as these rights are seen as a response to oppression or systemic disadvantage, they are most plausibly seen as a temporary measure on the way to a society where the need for special representation no longer exists – a form of political 'affirmative action'. Society should seek to remove the oppression and disadvantage, thereby eliminating the need for these rights.

However, the issue of special representation rights for groups is complicated, because special representation is sometimes defended, not on grounds of oppression, but as a corollary of self-government. A minority's right to self-government would be severely weakened if some external body could unilaterally revise or revoke its powers, without consulting the minority or securing its consent. Hence it would seem to be a corollary of self-government that the national minority be guaranteed representation on any body which can interpret or modify its powers of self-government (e.g. the Supreme Court). Since the claims of self-government are seen as inherent and permanent, so too are the guarantees of representation which flow from it (unlike guarantees grounded on oppression).[11]

The Equality Argument

Many defenders of group-specific rights for ethnic and national minorities insist that they are needed to ensure that all citizens are treated with genuine equality. On this view, 'the accommodation of differences is the essence of true equality',[12] and group-specific rights are needed to accommodate our differences. I think this argument is correct, within certain limits.

Proponents of 'benign neglect' will respond that individual rights already allow for the accommodation of differences, and that true equality requires equal rights for each individual regardless of race or ethnicity.[13] This assumption that liberal equality precludes group-specific rights is relatively recent, and arose in part as an (over-)gener-

alization of the racial desegregation movement in the United States. It has some superficial plausibility. In many cases, claims for group-specific rights are simply an attempt by one group to dominate and oppress another.

But some minority rights eliminate, rather than create, inequalities. Some groups are unfairly disadvantaged in the cultural market-place, and political recognition and support rectify this disadvantage. I will start with the case of national minorities. The viability of their societal cultures may be undermined by economic and political decisions made by the majority. They could be outbid or outvoted on resources and policies that are crucial to the survival of their societal cultures. The members of majority cultures do not face this problem. Given the importance of cultural membership, this is a significant inequality which, if not addressed, becomes a serious injustice.

Group-differentiated rights – such as territorial autonomy, veto powers, guaranteed representation in central institutions, land claims, and language rights – can help rectify this disadvantage, by alleviating the vulnerability of minority cultures to majority decisions. These external protections ensure that members of the minority have the same opportunity to live and work in their own culture as members of the majority.

These rights may impose restrictions on the members of the larger society, by making it more costly for them to move into the territory of the minority (e.g. longer residency requirements, fewer government services in their language), or by giving minority members priority in the use of certain land and resources (e.g. indigenous hunting and fishing rights). But the sacrifice required of non-members by the existence of these rights is far less than the sacrifice members would face in the absence of such rights.

Where these rights are recognized, members of the majority who choose to enter the minority's homeland may have to forgo certain benefits they are accustomed to. This is a burden. But without such rights, the members of many minority cultures face the loss of their culture, a loss which we cannot reasonably ask people to accept.

Any plausible theory of justice should recognize the fairness of these external protections for national minorities. They are clearly justified, I believe, within a liberal egalitarian theory, such as Rawls's and Dworkin's, which emphasizes the importance of rectifying unchosen inequalities. Indeed inequalities in cultural membership are just the sort which Rawls says we should be concerned about, since their effects are 'profound and pervasive and present from birth' (Rawls 1971: 96; cf. Dworkin 1981).[14]

This equality-based argument will only endorse special rights for national minorities if there actually is a disadvantage with respect to cultural membership, and if the rights actually serve to rectify the disadvantage. Hence the legitimate scope of these rights will vary with the circumstances. In North America, indigenous groups are more vulnerable to majority decisions than the Québécois or Puerto Ricans, and so their external protections will be more extensive. For example, restrictions on the sale of land which are necessary in the context of indigenous peoples are not necessary, and hence not justified, in the case of Quebec or Puerto Rico.[15]

At some point, demands for increased powers or resources will not be necessary to ensure the same opportunity to live and work in one's culture. Instead, they will simply be attempts to gain benefits denied to others, to have more resources to pursue one's way of life than others have. This was clearly the case with apartheid, where whites constituting under 20 per cent of the population controlled 87 per cent of the land mass of the country, and monopolized all the important levers of state power.

One could imagine a point where the amount of land reserved for indigenous peoples would not be necessary to provide reasonable external protections, but rather would simply provide unequal opportunities to them. Justice would then require that the holdings of indigenous peoples be subject to the same redistributive taxation as the wealth of other advantaged groups, so as to assist the less well off in society. In the real world, of course, most indigenous peoples are struggling to maintain the bare minimum of land needed to sustain the viability of their communities. But it is possible that their land holdings could exceed what justice allows.[16]

The legitimacy of certain measures may also depend on their timing. For example, many people have suggested that a new South African constitution should grant a veto power over certain important decisions to some or all of the major national groups. This sort of veto power is a familiar feature of various 'consociational democracies' in Europe, and, as I discuss in the next chapter, under certain circumstances it can promote justice. But it would probably be unjust to

give privileged groups a veto power before there has been a dramatic redistribution of wealth and opportunities (Adam 1979: 295). A veto power can promote justice if it helps protect a minority from unjust policies that favour the majority; but it is an obstacle to justice if it allows a privileged group the leverage to maintain its unjust advantages.

So the ideal of 'benign neglect' is not in fact benign. It ignores the fact that the members of a national minority face a disadvantage which the members of the majority do not face. In any event, the idea that the government could be neutral with respect to ethnic and national groups is patently false. One of the most important determinants of whether a culture survives is whether its language is the language of government – i.e. the language of public schooling, courts, legislatures, welfare agencies, health services, etc. When the government decides the language of public schooling, it is providing what is probably the most important form of support needed by societal cultures, since it guarantees the passing on of the language and its associated traditions and conventions to the next generation. Refusing to provide public schooling in a minority language, by contrast, is almost inevitably condemning that language to ever-increasing marginalization.

The government therefore cannot avoid deciding which societal cultures will be supported. And if it supports the majority culture, by using the majority's language in schools and public agencies, it cannot refuse official recognition to minority languages on the ground that this violates 'the separation of state and ethnicity'. This shows that the analogy between religion and culture is mistaken. As I noted earlier, many liberals say that just as the state should not recognize, endorse, or support any particular church, so it should not recognize, endorse, or support any particular cultural group or identity. But the analogy does not work. It is quite possible for a state not to have an established church. But the state cannot help but give at least partial establishment to a culture when it decides which language is to be used in public schooling, or in the provision of state services. The state can (and should) replace religious oaths in courts with secular oaths, but it cannot replace the use of English in courts with no language.

This is a significant embarrassment for the 'benign neglect' view, and it is remarkable how rarely language rights are discussed in contemporary liberal theory.[17] As Brian Weinstein put it, political theorists have had a lot to say about 'the language of politics' – that is, the symbols, metaphors, and rhetorical devices of political discourse – but have had virtually nothing to say about 'the politics of language' – that is, the decisions about which languages to use in political, legal, and educational forums (Weinstein 1983: 7–13). Yet language rights are a fundamental cause of political conflict, even violence, throughout the world, including Canada, Belgium, Spain, Sri Lanka, the Baltics, Bulgaria, Turkey, and many other countries (Horowitz 1985: 219–24).

One could argue that decisions about the language of schooling and public services should be determined, not by officially recognizing the existence of various groups, but simply by allowing each political subunit to make its own language policy on a democratic basis. If a national minority forms a majority in the relevant unit, they can decide to have their mother tongue adopted as an official language in that unit. But this is because they are a local majority, not because the state has officially recognized them as a 'nation'.

This is sometimes said to be the American approach to language rights, since there is no constitutional definition of language rights in the United States. But in fact the American government has historically tried to make sure that such 'local' decisions are always made by political units that have an anglophone majority. Decisions about state borders, or about when to admit territories as states, have been explicitly made with the aim of ensuring that there will be an anglophone majority. States in the American south-west and Hawaii were only offered statehood when the national minorities residing in those areas were outnumbered by settlers and immigrants. And some people oppose offering statehood to Puerto Rico precisely on the grounds that it will never have an anglophone majority (Rubinstein 1993; Glazer 1983: 280).

This illustrates a more general point. Leaving decisions about language to political subunits just pushes back the problem. What are the relevant political units – what level of government should make these decisions? Should each neighbourhood be able to decide on the language of public schooling and public services in that neighbourhood? Or should this decision be left to larger units, such as cities or provinces? And how do we decide on the boundaries of these subunits? If we draw municipal or provincial boundaries in one way, then a national minority will not form even a local majority. But if we draw the boundaries another way,

then the national minority will form a local majority. In a multination state, decisions on boundaries and the division of powers are inevitably decisions about which national group will have the ability to use which state powers to sustain its culture.[18]

For example, the Inuit in Canada wish to divide the Northwest Territories into two, so that they will form the majority in the eastern half. This is seen as essential to the implementation of their right of self-government. Some liberals object that this proposal violates the separation of state and ethnicity by distributing public benefits and state powers so as to make it easier for a specific group to preserve its culture. But all decisions regarding boundaries and the distribution of powers in multination states have this effect. We can draw boundaries and distribute legislative powers so that a national minority has an increased ability within a particular region to protect its social culture; or we can draw boundaries and distribute legislative powers so that the majority nation controls decisions regarding language, education, immigration, etc. on a country-wide basis.

The whole idea of 'benign neglect' is incoherent, and reflects a shallow understanding of the relationship between states and nations. In the areas of official languages, political boundaries, and the division of powers, there is no way to avoid supporting this or that societal culture, or deciding which groups will form a majority in political units that control culture-affecting decisions regarding language, education, and immigration.

So the real question is, what is a fair way to recognize languages, draw boundaries, and distribute powers? And the answer, I think, is that we should aim at ensuring that all national groups have the opportunity to maintain themselves as a distinct culture, if they so choose. This ensures that the good of cultural membership is equally protected for the members of all national groups. In a democratic society, the majority nation will always have its language and societal culture supported, and will have the legislative power to protect its interests in culture-affecting decisions. The question is whether fairness requires that the same benefits and opportunities should be given to national minorities. The answer, I think, is clearly yes.

Hence group-differentiated self-government rights compensate for unequal circumstances which put the members of minority cultures at a systemic disadvantage in the cultural market-place, regardless of their personal choices in life. This is one of many areas in which true equality requires not identical treatment, but rather differential treatment in order to accommodate differential needs.[19]

This does not mean that we should entirely reject the idea of the cultural market-place. Once the societal cultures of national groups are protected, through language rights and territorial autonomy, then the cultural market-place does have an important role to play in determining the character of the culture. Decisions about which particular aspects of one's culture are worth maintaining and developing should be left to the choices of individual members. For the state to intervene at this point to support particular options or customs within the culture, while penalizing or discouraging others, would run the risk of unfairly subsidizing some people's choices (Kymlicka 1989b). But that is not the aim or effect of many rights for national minorities, which are instead concerned with external protections.

Let me now turn to polyethnic rights for ethnic groups. I believe there is an equality-based argument for these rights as well, which also invokes the impossibility of separating state from ethnicity, but in a different way. I have argued that the context of choice for immigrants, unlike national minorities, primarily involves equal access to the mainstream culture(s). Having uprooted themselves from their old culture, they are expected to become members of the national societies which already exist in their new country. Hence promoting the good of cultural membership for immigrants is primarily a matter of enabling integration, by providing language training and fighting patterns of discrimination and prejudice. Generally speaking, this is more a matter of rigorously enforcing the common rights of citizenship than providing group-differentiated rights. In so far as common rights of citizenship in fact create equal access to mainstream culture, then equality with respect to cultural membership is achieved.

But even here equality does justify some group-specific rights. Consider the case of public holidays. Some people object to legislation that exempts Jews and Muslims from Sunday closing legislation, on the ground that this violates the separation of state and ethnicity. But almost any decision on public holidays will do so. In the major immigration countries, public holidays currently reflect the needs of Christians. Hence government offices are closed on Sunday, and on the major religious holidays (Easter, Christmas). This need not be seen as a deliberate decision to promote Christianity and discriminate against other faiths (although this was undoubtedly part of the original motivation). Decisions about government holidays were made when there was far less religious diversity, and people just took it for granted that the government work-week should accommodate Christian beliefs about days of rest and religious celebration.

But these decisions can be a significant disadvantage to the members of other religious faiths. And having established a work-week that favours Christians, one can hardly object to exemptions for Muslims or Jews on the ground that they violate the separation of state and ethnicity. These groups are simply asking that their religious needs be taken into consideration in the same way that the needs of Christians have always been taken into account. Public holidays are another significant embarrassment for the 'benign neglect' view, and it is interesting to note how rarely they are discussed in contemporary liberal theory.

Similar issues arise regarding government uniforms. Some people object to the idea that Sikhs or Orthodox Jews should be exempted from requirements regarding headgear in the police or military. But here again it is important to recognize how the existing rules about government uniforms have been adopted to suit Christians. For example, existing dress-codes do not prohibit the wearing of wedding rings, which are an important religious symbol for many Christians (and Jews). And it is virtually inconceivable that designers of government dress-codes would have ever considered designing a uniform that prevented people from wearing wedding rings, unless this was strictly necessary for the job. Again, this should not be seen as a deliberate attempt to promote Christianity. It simply would have been taken for granted that uniforms should not unnecessarily conflict with Christian religious beliefs. Having adopted dress-codes that meet Christian needs, one can hardly object to exemptions for Sikhs and Orthodox Jews on the ground that they violate 'benign neglect'.

One can multiply the examples. For example, many state symbols such as flags, anthems, and mottoes reflect a particular ethnic or religious background ('In God We Trust'). The demand by ethnic groups for some symbolic affirmation of the value of polyethnicity (e.g. in government declarations and documents) is simply a demand that their identity be given the same recognition as the original Anglo-Saxon settlers.

It may be possible to avoid some of these issues by redesigning public holidays, uniforms, and state symbols. It is relatively easy to replace religious oaths with secular ones, and so we should. It would be more difficult, but perhaps not impossible, to replace existing public holidays and work-weeks with more 'neutral' schedules for schools and government offices.[20]

But there is no way to have a complete 'separation of state and ethnicity'. In various ways, the ideal of 'benign neglect' is a myth. Government decisions on languages, internal boundaries, public holidays, and state symbols unavoidably involve recognizing, accommodating, and supporting the needs and identities of particular ethnic and national groups. Nor is there any reason to regret this fact. There is no reason to regret the existence of official languages and public holidays, and no one gains by creating unnecessary conflicts between government regulations and religious beliefs. The only question is how to ensure that these unavoidable forms of support for particular ethnic and national groups are provided fairly – that is, how to ensure that they do not privilege some groups and disadvantage others. In so far as existing policies support the language, culture, and identity of dominant nations and ethnic groups, there is an argument of equality for ensuring that some attempts are made to provide similar support for minority groups, through self-government and polyethnic rights.

The Role of Historical Agreements

A second argument in defence of group-differentiated rights for national minorities is that they are the result of historical agreements, such as the treaty rights of indigenous peoples, or the agreement by which two or more peoples agreed to federate.

There are a variety of such agreements in Western democracies, although their provisions have often been ignored or repudiated. For example, the American government has unilaterally abrogated certain treaties with Indian tribes, and the Canadian government proposed in 1969 to extinguish all of its Indian treaties. The language rights guaranteed to Chicanos in the American southwest under the 1848 Treaty of Guadelupe Hidalgo were rescinded by the anglophone settlers as soon

as they formed a majority. The language and land rights guaranteed to the Métis under the Manitoba Act of 1870 suffered the same fate in Canada. Yet many treaties and historical agreements between national groups continue to be recognized, and some have considerable legal force. For example, the 1840 Treaty of Waitangi signed by Maori chiefs and British colonists in New Zealand, declared a 'simple nullity' in 1877, has re-emerged as a central legal and political document (Sharp 1990).

The importance of honouring historical agreements is emphasized by proponents of group-differentiated rights, but has had little success convincing opponents. Those people who think that group-differentiated rights are unfair have not been appeased by pointing to agreements that were made by previous generations in different circumstances, often undemocratically and in conditions of substantial inequality in bargaining power. Surely some historical agreements are out of date, while others are patently unfair, signed under duress or ignorance. Why should governments not do what principles of equality require now, rather than what outdated and often unprincipled agreements require?[21]

One answer is to reconsider an underlying assumption of the equality argument. The equality argument assumes that the state must treat its citizens with equal respect. But there is the prior question of determining which citizens should be governed by which states. For example, how did the American government acquire the legitimate authority to govern Puerto Rico or the Navaho? And how did the Canadian government acquire legitimate authority over the Québécois and the Métis?

United Nations declarations state that all 'peoples' are entitled to 'self-determination' – i.e. an independent state. Obviously this principle is not reflected in existing boundaries, and it would be destabilizing, and indeed impossible, to fulfil. Moreover, not all peoples want their own state. Hence it is not uncommon for two or more peoples to decide to form a federation. And if the two communities are of unequal size, it is not uncommon for the smaller culture to demand various group-differentiated rights as part of the terms of federation. Forming a federation is one way of exercising a people's right of self-determination, and the historical terms of federation reflect the group's judgement about how best to exercise that right.

For example, the group-differentiated rights accorded French Canadians in the original confederation agreement in 1867, and the group-differentiated rights accorded Indians under various treaties, reflect the terms under which these communities joined Canada. It can be argued that these agreements define the terms under which the Canadian state acquired authority over these groups. These communities could have exercised their self-determination in other ways, but chose to join Canada, because they were given certain promises. If the Canadian government reneges on these promises, then it voids (morally, if not legally) the agreement which made those communities part of Canada.[22] Because these agreements define the terms under which various groups agreed to federate with Canada, the authority of the Canadian state over these groups flows from, but is also limited by, these agreements (Chartrand 1991; 1993: 240–1).

In short, the way in which a national minority was incorporated often gives rise to certain group-differentiated rights. If incorporation occurred through a voluntary federation, certain rights might be spelled out in the terms of federation (e.g. in treaties), and there are legal and moral arguments for respecting these agreements. If incorporation was involuntary (e.g. colonization), then the national minority might have a claim of self-determination under international law which can be exercised by renegotiating the terms of federation so as to make it more voluntary federation (Macklem 1993; Danley 1991).

This historical argument may justify the same rights as the equality argument. Many of the group-differentiated rights which are the result of historical agreements can be seen as providing the sort of protection required by the equality argument. For example, the right to local autonomy for Indian tribes/bands could be justified on the equality argument, if it helps the larger state show equal concern for the members of Indian communities. Autonomy is also justified on the historical argument, in so far as Indian peoples never gave the federal government jurisdiction over certain issues.

Indeed, it is likely that the equality and historical arguments will yield similar policies. If local autonomy is required to ensure that members of a minority are not disadvantaged, then it is likely that the minority would have demanded autonomy as part of the terms of federation (had the negotiations been fair).

The negotiations between English and French regarding the terms of federation in Canada provide a clear example of this. The Québécois realized that if they agreed to enter the Canadian state in 1867, they would become a permanent minority in the country, and so could be outvoted on decisions made at the federal level. They therefore faced the question whether they should remain outside Confederation, maintaining their status as a separate colony within the British Empire, and hoping one day to become a separate country with a francophone majority.

Québécois leaders agreed to join Canada, even though they would be a minority in the federal parliament. But in return they insisted that jurisdiction over language and education be guaranteed to the provinces, not the federal government. This was 'the non-negotiable condition in return for which they were prepared to concede the principle of representation by population' in the new parliament, a principle that 'would institutionalize their minority position' within the new country (J. Smith 1993: 75). In deciding whether to accept the terms of federation, therefore, Québécois leaders were explicitly concerned about equality – that is, how to ensure that they would not be disadvantaged in the new country. Since they had considerable bargaining power in the negotiations, they were able to ensure their equality in the agreement, through guarantees of language rights and provincial autonomy.

While the equality and historical arguments often lead to the same result, they are none the less quite distinct. On the historical argument, the question is not how should the state treat 'its' minorities, but rather what are the terms under which two or more peoples decided to become partners? The question is not how should the state act fairly in governing its minorities, but what are the limits to the state's right to govern them?

For example, the two arguments may generate different answers to the question of federal funding of self-government rights. Under the equality argument, fairness may require positive state support for the measures required to maintain the viability of the national group. If fairness requires recognizing self-government in certain areas of jurisdiction, then presumably fairness will also require providing the resources needed to make self-government meaningful. The historical argument, however, may only generate a negative right to non-interference from the federal state. If the members of the national minority never gave the federal government the authority to govern them in certain areas, the federal government is unlikely to accept responsibility for funding minority self-government (unless this is itself part of the historical agreement). Any federal obligation to support self-government might be seen more as a form of humanitarian foreign aid than as a matter of domestic egalitarian justice.[23]

Contemporary political philosophers have had very little to say about the moral status of such historical agreements. For example, while Rawls recognizes a moral duty to respect treaties between countries (Rawls 1971: 378), he does not say anything about treaties or other agreements between nations within a country. This is surprising, because such agreements played a vital role in the creation and expansion of many countries, including the United States and Canada.

Respect for such agreements is important, I believe, not only to respect the self-determination of the minority, but also to ensure that citizens have trust in the actions of government. Historical agreements signed in good faith give rise to legitimate expectations on the part of citizens, who come to rely on the agreements made by governments, and it is a serious breach of trust to renege on them.

One difficulty with historical agreements is that they are often hard to interpret. For example, the Canadian government claims Quebec's 'right to be different' was implicitly recognized in the original Confederation agreement (Government of Canada 1991a: p. vi). But others deny this, and insist that Confederation was a union of provinces, not a compact between two cultures. Similar disputes arise over the interpretation of some Indian treaties. Moreover, some Indian tribes did not sign treaties, or signed them under duress. It seems arbitrary and unfair that some groups signed historical agreements while others, through no fault of their own, did not.

Where historical agreements are absent or disputed, groups are likely to appeal to the equality argument. Indian tribes/bands which have clear treaty rights often rest their claim for group-differentiated status on historical agreement; groups who did not sign treaties are more likely to appeal to the equality argument. It is often quite arbitrary whether a particular group happened to sign a particular agreement. However, the equality argument can help those groups which, for whatever reason, lack historical rights.[24]

Historical agreements are much less common in the case of ethnic groups, since immigrants are rarely promised any special rights before arriving in their new country. Indeed, opponents of polyethnic rights sometimes say that ethnic groups should not expect any new group-differentiated rights, precisely because they agreed to come knowing full well that such rights did not exist. Yet there are some cases of polyethnic rights based on historical agreement. For example, the Hutterites (a Christian sect) were explicitly promised by Canadian immigration officials that they would be exempted from certain laws regarding education, land ownership, and military service if they settled in western Canada. (The Canadian government was anxious at the time to settle the newly opened up western frontier.)

This now seems like an anomalous case of an immigrant group given privileges denied to other citizens, and attempts have been made to eliminate these historical rights. On the other hand, solemn promises were given to the Hutterites, who would have emigrated elsewhere had these promises not been made. In this sense, they too can claim that the historical agreement defines the terms under which the Canadian government acquired authority over them.

In assessing group-differentiated rights claims, therefore, we need to know whether the rights being claimed are rectifying disadvantages, or recognizing historical agreements arising from the terms of federation. Both of these are legitimate grounds for group-differentiated rights, I believe, but both raise some difficult issues.

For example, how should we respond to agreements that are now unfair, due to changing conditions? The land claims recognized in various treaties may be too much, or too little, given changes in the size and lifestyle of indigenous communities. The powers given to Quebec in 1867 may no longer be appropriate in an age of telecommunications. To stick to the letter of historical agreements when they no longer meet the needs of minorities seems wrong.

Because of these changing circumstances, and because the original agreements are hard to interpret, many minority communities want to renegotiate their historical agreements. They want to make their group-differentiated rights more explicit in the constitution, and often more expansive. This is a major cause of the current constitutional crisis in Canada. For it has given those Canadians who see group-differentiated rights as unfair a chance to restrict, rather than entrench, such rights.

This suggests that, if we wish to defend group-differentiated rights, we should not rely solely on historical agreements. Since historical agreements must always be interpreted, and inevitably need to be updated and revised, we must be able to ground the historical agreements in a deeper theory of justice. The historical and equality arguments must work together.

The Value of Cultural Diversity

A third defence of group-differentiated rights for national minorities appeals to the value of cultural diversity. As I have discussed, liberals extol the virtue of having a diversity of lifestyles within a culture, so presumably they also endorse the additional diversity which comes from having two or more cultures in the same country. Surely inter-cultural diversity contributes to the richness of people's lives, as well as intracultural diversity (Schwartz 1986: ch. 1).

This argument is attractive to many people because it avoids relying solely on the interests of group members, and instead focuses on how the larger society also benefits from group-differentiated rights. As Richard Falk puts it, 'societal diversity enhances the quality of life, by enriching our experience, expanding cultural resources'. Hence protecting minority cultures 'is increasingly recognized to be an expression of overall enlightened self-interest' (Falk 1988: 23). Whereas the first two arguments appeal to the *obligations* of the majority, this third argument appeals to the *interests* of the majority, and defends rights in terms of self-interest not justice.

Cultural diversity is said to be valuable, both in the quasi-aesthetic sense that it creates a more interesting world, and because other cultures contain alternative models of social organization that may be useful in adapting to new circumstances.[25] This latter point is often made with respect to indigenous peoples, whose traditional lifestyles provide a model of a sustainable relationship to the environment. As Western attitudes towards nature are increasingly recognized to be unsustainable and self-destructive, indigenous peoples 'may provide models, inspiration, guidance in the essential work of world order redesign' (Falk 1988: 23; cf. Clay 1989: 233; O'Brien 1987: 358).

There is some truth in this argument about the value of cultural diversity. None the less, I think it is a mistake to put much weight on it as a defence of

national rights. First, one of the basic reasons for valuing intracultural diversity has less application to intercultural diversity. The value of diversity within a culture is that it creates more options for each individual, and expands her range of choices. But protecting national minorities does not expand the range of choices open to members of the majority in the same way. As I have explained before, choosing to leave one's culture is qualitatively different from choosing to move around within one's culture. The former is a difficult and painful prospect for most people, and very few people in the mainstream choose to assimilate into a minority culture. Indeed, measures to protect national minorities may actually reduce diversity within the majority culture, compared with a situation where minorities, unable to maintain their own societal culture, are forced to integrate and add their distinctive contribution to the diversity of the mainstream culture. Having two or more cultures within a state does expand choices for each individual, but only to a limited degree, and it would be implausible to make this the primary justification for minority rights.

There are other aesthetic and educational benefits from cultural diversity, apart from the value of expanding individual choice. But it is not clear that any of these values by themselves can justify minority rights. One problem is that the benefits of diversity to the majority are spread thinly and widely, whereas the costs for particular members of the majority are sometimes quite high. Everyone may benefit, in a diffuse way, from having flourishing minority cultures in Quebec and Puerto Rico. But some members of the majority culture are asked to pay a significant price so that others can gain this diffuse benefit. For example, unilingual anglophones residing in Quebec or Puerto Rico are unlikely to get government employment or publicly funded education in English – benefits which they would take for granted elsewhere. Similarly, non-Indians residing on Indian lands may be discriminated against in terms of their access to natural resources, or their right to vote in local elections. It is not clear that the diffuse benefits of diversity for society as a whole justify imposing these sorts of sacrifices on particular people. It seems to me that these sacrifices are only consistent with justice if they are needed, not to promote benefits to the members of the majority, but to prevent even greater sacrifices to the members of the national minority.

Moreover, there are many ways of promoting diversity, and it seems likely that protecting national minorities involves more cost to the majority than other possible ways. For example, a society could arguably gain more diversity at less cost by increasing immigration from a variety of countries than by protecting national minorities. The diversity argument cannot explain why we have an obligation to sustain the particular sort of diversity created by the presence of a viable, self-governing national minority.

There is one further problem with the diversity argument. Let us say that the aesthetic or educational value of diversity does justify imposing certain costs on people in the majority culture. Why then does the value of diversity not also justify imposing a duty on the members of the minority to maintain their traditional culture? If the benefits of cultural diversity to the larger society can justify restricting individual liberties or opportunities, why does it matter whether these restrictions are imposed on people inside or outside the group? I noted earlier that a liberal theory of minority rights can accept external protections, but not internal restrictions. It is difficult to see how the diversity argument can make this distinction. Because it appeals to the interests of the larger society, it cannot explain why minorities should be able to decide for themselves whether or how to maintain their culture.

So it seems to me that the diversity argument is insufficient, by itself, to justify the rights of national minorities. Protecting national minorities does provide benefits to the majority, and these are worth pointing out. But these diffuse benefits are better seen as a desirable by-product of national rights, rather than their primary justification. To date, most majority cultures have not seen it in their 'enlightened self-interest' to maintain minority cultures. No doubt this is due in part to ethnocentric prejudice, but we must recognize the powerful interests that majority nations often have in rejecting self-government rights for national minorities – e.g. increased access to the minority's land and resources, increased individual mobility, political stability, etc. It is unlikely that majorities will accept national rights solely on the basis of self-interest, without some belief that they have an obligation of justice to accept them. Conversely, it is unlikely that majorities will accept their obligations of justice towards national minorities without a belief that they gain something in the process. The diversity argument works best, therefore, when it is combined with arguments of justice.

The diversity argument is more plausible as a defence of polyethnic rights for ethnic groups.

Unlike national self-government, these rights do contribute directly to diversity within the majority culture. Moreover, they do not involve the same sort of restrictions on the mobility or economic opportunities of the majority. Indeed, certain polyethnic policies can be seen as natural extensions of state policies regarding the funding of the arts, museums, educational television, etc.[26] Yet here again the problem arises that there are many ways of promoting diversity. Teaching children to be bilingual promotes diversity, but this cannot explain why we should teach immigrant languages in particular. Hence the diversity argument supplements, but cannot replace, justice arguments based on equality or historical agreement.

The Analogy with States

So far, I have been assuming that the burden of proof lies on those who wish to find room for group-differentiated rights within the liberal tradition. But we can and should question this assumption. In many ways, it is opponents of group-differentiated rights who are proposing a revision of liberal theory and practice. Certain group-differentiated rights have been a long-established part of the liberal tradition. Moreover, such rights are logically presupposed by existing liberal practice.

For example, most liberal theorists accept without question that the world is, and will remain, composed of separate states, each of which is assumed to have the right to determine who can enter its borders and acquire citizenship. I believe that this assumption can only be justified in terms of the same sorts of values which ground group-differentiated rights within each state. I believe that the orthodox liberal view about the right of states to determine who has citizenship rests on the same principles which justify group-differentiated citizenship within states, and that accepting the former leads logically to the latter.

This point is worth exploring in some depth. The existence of states, and the right of governments to control entry across state borders, raises a deep paradox for liberals. Most liberal theorists defend their theories in terms of 'equal respect for persons', and the 'equal rights of individuals'. This suggests that all 'persons' or 'individuals' have an equal right to enter a state, participate in its political life, and share in its natural resources.

In fact, however, these rights are typically reserved for *citizens*. And not everyone can become a citizen, even if they are willing to swear allegiance to liberal principles. On the contrary, there are millions of people who want to gain citizenship in various liberal democracies, but who are refused. Even the most open Western country in terms of immigration accepts only a fraction of the number of people who would come if there were genuinely open borders. Indeed, would-be immigrants are often refused entry, turned back at the border by armed border guards. These people are refused the right to enter and participate in the state because they were not born into the right group.

Citizenship, therefore, is an inherently group-differentiated notion. Unless one is willing to accept either a single world-government or completely open borders between states – and very few liberal theorists have endorsed either of these – then distributing rights and benefits on the basis of citizenship is to treat people differentially on the basis of their group membership.[27]

This creates a profound contradiction within most liberal theories. As Samuel Black notes, liberal theorists often begin by talking about the moral equality of 'persons', but end up talking about the equality of 'citizens', without explaining or even noticing the shift (Black 1991). What can justify restricting the rights of citizenship to members of a particular group, rather than all persons who desire it?

Some critics have argued that liberals cannot justify this restriction, and that the logic of liberalism requires open borders, except perhaps for temporary restrictions in the name of public order.[28] And surely that is right if we cling to the idea that liberalism should be indifferent to people's cultural membership and national identity. Open borders would dramatically increase the mobility and opportunities of individuals, and, if liberalism requires treating people solely 'as individuals' without regard for their group membership, then open borders clearly are preferable from a liberal point of view.

I believe, however, that some limits on immigration can be justified if we recognize that liberal states exist, not only to protect standard rights and opportunities of individuals, but also to protect people's cultural membership. Liberals implicitly assume that people are members of societal cultures, that these cultures provide the context for individual choice, and that one of the functions of having separate states is to recognize the fact that people belong to separate cultures. I noted ex-

amples of this in the liberal tradition in Chapter 4 of *Multicultural Citizenship*, and with Rawls's discussion of citizenship and the bonds of culture in Chapter 5. Once we make these assumptions explicit, however, it is clear that, in multination states, some people's cultural membership can only be recognized and protected by endorsing group-differentiated rights within the state.

Liberal theorists invariably limit citizenship to the members of a particular group, rather than all persons who desire it. The most plausible reason for this – namely, to recognize and protect our membership in distinct cultures – is also a reason for allowing group-differentiated citizenship within a state. There may be other reasons for restricting citizenship to a particular group which do not make any reference to the importance of cultural groups. It is difficult to say, since few liberals actually discuss the shift from 'equality of persons' to 'equality of citizens'. But I think it is fair to say this: in so far as liberal theorists accept the principle that citizenship can be restricted to the members of a particular group, the burden of proof lies on them to explain why they are not also committed to accepting group-differentiated rights within a state.[29] So long as liberals believe in separate states with restricted citizenship, the burden of proof lies as much with opponents of group-differentiated rights as with their defenders.

Conclusion

In the last two chapters, I have tried to show that liberals can and should accept a wide range of group-differentiated rights for national minorities and ethnic groups, without sacrificing their core commitments to individual freedom and social equality.

It may be useful briefly to summarize my argument. I have tried to show how freedom of choice is dependent on social practices, cultural meanings, and a shared language. Our capacity to form and revise a conception of the good is intimately tied to our membership in a societal culture, since the context of individual choice is the range of options passed down to us by our culture. Deciding how to lead our lives is, in the first instance, a matter of exploring the possibilities made available by our culture.

However, minority cultures in multination states may need protection from the economic or political decisions of the majority culture if they are to provide this context for their members. For example, they may need self-governing powers or veto rights over certain decisions regarding language and culture, and may need to limit the mobility of migrants or immigrants into their homelands.

While these group-differentiated rights for national minorities may seem discriminatory at first glance, since they allocate individual rights and political powers differentially on the basis of group membership, they are in fact consistent with liberal principles of equality. They are indeed required by the view, defended by Rawls and Dworkin, that justice requires removing or compensating for undeserved or 'morally arbitrary' disadvantages, particularly if these are 'profound and pervasive and present from birth' (Rawls 1971: 96). Were it not for these group-differentiated rights, the members of minority cultures would not have the same ability to live and work in their own language and culture that the members of majority cultures take for granted. This, I argued, can be seen as just as profound and morally arbitrary a disadvantage as the inequalities in race and class that liberals more standardly worry about.

This equality-based argument for group-differentiated rights for national minorities is further strengthened by appeals to historical agreements and the value of cultural diversity. And it is confirmed by the way that liberals implicitly invoke cultural membership to defend existing state borders and restrictions on citizenship. I have also argued that polyethnic rights for ethnic groups can be justified in terms of promoting equality and cultural diversity within the mainstream culture.

These claims are by no means uncontroversial, and there are many places where they could be challenged. One could deny that cultural meanings are dependent on a societal culture, or that individuals are closely tied to their own particular societal culture. One could also deny that minority cultures are vulnerable to the decisions of the larger society; or that this vulnerability constitutes an injustice; or that historical agreements have any moral weight; or that cultural diversity is worth promoting.

Yet I think each of these claims is plausible. Anyone who disputes them would be required to provide some alternative account of what makes meaningful choices available to people, or what justice requires in terms of language rights, public

holidays, political boundaries, and the division of powers. Moreover, one would also have to offer an alternative account of the justification for restricting citizenship to the members of a particular group, rather than making it available to anyone who desires it. It is not enough to simply assert that a liberal state should respond to ethnic and national differences with benign neglect. That is an incoherent position that avoids addressing the inevitable connections between state and culture.

The idea that group-differentiated rights for national and ethnic groups can and should be accepted by liberals is hardly a radical suggestion. In fact, many multination liberal democracies already accept such an obligation, and provide public schooling and government services in the language of national minorities. Many have also adopted some form of federalism, so that national minorities will form a majority in one of the federal units (states, provinces, or cantons). And many polyethnic liberal states have adopted various forms of polyethnic policies and group-specific rights or exemptions for immigrant groups. Like Jay Sigler, I believe that providing a liberal defence of minority rights 'does not create a mandate for vast change. It merely ratifies and explains changes that have taken place in the absence of theory' (Sigler 1983: 196).

But if there are strong arguments in favour of group-differentiated rights, why have liberals so often rejected them? The explanation cannot be that liberalism is premised on 'abstract individualism', on a conception of the individual as a solitary atom who is independent of her cultural environment. I hope that Chapters 4 and 5 of *Multicultural Citizenship* have dispelled any perception that liberals ignore individuals' dependence on society and culture.

But this raises a puzzle. If individual autonomy and self-identity are tied to membership in one's societal culture, developing a theory of the rights of minority cultures would seem to be one of the very first tasks of any liberal theory. Why then have so few contemporary liberal theorists supported measures to protect cultural groups, such as group-specific language rights, land claims, or federal autonomy? I have explored some of the historical reasons in Chapter 4 of *Multicultural Citizenship*. Another part of the explanation, I think, is that contemporary liberal theorists implicitly assume that countries contain only one nation. They are well aware that modern states are culturally diverse – indeed, the pluralistic nature of modern liberal democracies is a pervasive theme in their writings. But they implicitly assume that this diversity is the sort that comes either from variations in people's conceptions of the good or from immigration – that is, they focus on philosophical, religious, and ethnic diversity within a single culture based on a shared language.[30] They do not recognize or discuss the existence of states that are multinational, with a diversity of societal cultures, languages and national groups.

For example, Dworkin notes that 'in the modern world of immigration and boundary shifts', citizens do not share a racial or ethnic background, and that the communal life of the political community cannot include a single 'ethnic allegiance' (1989: 497). But, as I noted earlier, he does assume a common 'cultural structure' based on a 'shared language' (1985: 230, 233; 1989: 488). Similarly, while Rawls emphasizes the 'fact of pluralism' – particularly religious pluralism – he equates the political community with a single 'complete culture', and with a single 'people' who belong to the same 'society and culture' (1978: 70 n. 8; 1993a: 18, 222, 277; 1993b: 48).

This implicit assumption that states are uninational is rarely explained or defended. It is not as if these theorists explicitly reject the possibility that national minorities have special rights, or directly criticize the arguments of equality or history in defence of these rights. On the contrary, they simply ignore the issue entirely. There is no discussion by contemporary liberal theorists of the differences between nation-states and polyethnic or multination states, or of the arguments for modifying liberal principles in countries which are a 'federation of peoples'.

This shows, I think, that it is a mistake to subsume the issue of minority rights under one of the more familiar debates in contemporary political philosophy – e.g. the debate between 'individualists' and 'communitarians', or between 'universalists' and 'contextualists', or between 'impartialists' and 'difference theorists', or between 'rationalists' and 'postmodernists'. This is a very common tendency (see e.g. I. Young 1993a; Gochnauer 1991; Galenkamp 1993; Trakman 1992; Torres 1991; Addis 1991; cf. Todorov 1993: 392–9). But it stems from an oversimplified view of the issues involved in minority rights. According to many commentators, the central question in assessing minority rights is whether one accepts in principle the idea of giving political recognition to communities or group differences. Defenders of

individualism and universalism are then said to be opposed in principle to such recognition, whereas defenders of community and difference are in principle supportive of them. But, as I have emphasized, all political theories must accord recognition to certain forms of group differences and support certain cultural communities. This is inevitable in any theory which confronts issues of language policy, public holidays, political boundaries, and immigration rules. This is as true of liberal individualists and socialist internationalists as of conservatives, communitarians and postmodernists.

So the debate over minority rights is not about whether it is ever legitimate to support 'communities' or to recognize 'difference'. Rather, the debate is whether to support the particular sort of cultural difference and community exhibited by national minorities. And, as I have noted, some liberals, despite their 'individualism' and 'universalism', recognize that justice requires extending the same support to national minorities that majority nations receive. Conversely, some communitarians and particularists, despite their commitment to 'community' and 'difference', have been reluctant to accept the demands of national minorities. They view national minorities in the same way they view ethnic groups or new social movements – that is, as forms of difference and community that can and should be accommodated by group-specific rights within the larger society. They are unwilling to accept that national minorities require recognition as separate and self-governing societies alongside the mainstream society.[31]

The history of minority rights suggests that there is little or no correlation between meta-ethical debates and support for the rights of national minorities. People's views on minority rights are shaped, not only by their foundational moral or philosophical premises, but by more concrete factors, including ethnocentric prejudice, fears about international peace and superpower relations, and concerns about the preconditions of democratic consensus and social harmony. These considerations do not correlate in any simple or consistent way with people's underlying philosophical and moral premises.

These larger philosophical debates are not irrelevant to the policy debate over minority rights. But the connection between the two debates is mediated by many additional assumptions about the nature of ethnic and national differences, and their role in domestic and international politics. It is these additional assumptions that largely account for the actual position endorsed by particular theorists, whatever their deeper philosophical premisses.

For this reason, the demands of national minorities and ethnic groups raise a deep challenge to all Western political traditions. All of these traditions have been shaped, implicitly or explicitly, by the same historical influences which have shaped liberal thinking. The task of developing a consistent and principled theory of minority rights is not one that liberals face alone.

Notes

1 On the importance of individual rights to the protection of groups, see Buchanan 1989; Walzer 1990; Macdonald 1989: 122–3; Tomasi 1991; Kymlicka 1990: chs. 4–6.

2 Some indigenous peoples have argued before the UN that they too have a right to self-determination under the UN Charter (see *Mikmaq Tribal Society v Canada* (1984) UN Doc. E/CN.4/Sub.2/204; Grand Council of the Crees 1992). For discussions of the salt-water thesis, and the right of self-determination under international law, see Pomerance 1982; Thornberry 1991: 13–21, 214–18; Crawford 1988; Makinson 1988.

3 On English Canadian opposition to nationalist demands for decentralization, see Stark 1992. A certain amount of *de facto* asymmetry in powers has been a long-standing aspect of Canadian federalism. However, many Canadians are unwilling to recognize this asymmetry formally in the constitution (see Gagnon and Garcea 1988; Taylor 1991; Cairns 1991). This is one reason why the 1992 Charlottetown Accord was defeated in the national referendum. Some people have claimed that a federal system cannot survive if it accords special status, but this is refuted by the experience of many countries. For a survey of various forms of asymmetrical federalism, see Elazar 1987: 54–7.

4 In Germany, federalism was imposed by the Allies after World War II to help prevent the rise of nationalist or authoritarian movements. For helpful discussions of the relationship between federalism and cultural diversity, see Howse and Knop 1993; Minow 1990; Majone 1990; Gagnon 1993; Long 1991; Duchacek 1977; Elkins 1992; Norman 1994.

5 Hence Nathan Glazer is quite wrong when he says that the division of the United States into federal units preceded its ethnic diversity (Glazer 1983 276–7). This is true of the original thirteen colonies, but decisions about the admission and boundaries of new states were made after the incorporation of national minorities, and these decisions were deliberately made so as to avoid creating states dominated by national minorities.

6 For a comparative review of these developments, see Fleras and Elliot 1992. A proposal to entrench Aboriginal self-government constitutionally as a third order of government in Canada was included in the 1992 Charlottetown Accord. This would have covered both the 'ethnic self-government' exercised by band councils on Indian reserves, and the 'public self-government' exercised by the Inuit majority within the new territory of Nunavut (see Asch 1984: ch. 7). For the relation of Indian self-government to federalism, see Resnik 1989; Cassidy and Bish 1989; Long 1991.

7 Gurr 1993: viii; cf. Nietschmann 1987.

8 Unless otherwise stated, all chapter cross-references in this chapter are to *Multicultural Citizenship* (Oxford: Clarendon Press, 1995).

9 For a discussion of these rights in the British context, see Parekh 1990: 705; 1991: 197–204; Modood 1992; Poulter 1987. In Canada, see E. Kallen 1987: 325–31. In the USA, see Minow 1990; Sandel 1990. For the Muslim girls in France, see Galeotti 1993. It is sometimes said that these measures are purely 'symbolic'. But measures relating to employment are very material, affecting people's 'life chances' not just their 'lifestyles'.

10 For statistics on the (under-)representation of blacks and Hispanics in the United States, see C. Davidson 1992: 46. For statistics on the representation of various social groups in Canada, see RCERPF 1991: 93–6 and 192.

11 While self-government may entail guaranteed representation on intergovernmental bodies which negotiate, interpret, and modify the division of powers, it may also entail *reduced* representation on federal bodies which legislate in areas of purely federal jurisdiction, in so far as the self-governing group is not governed by the decisions of these federal bodies. I discuss the relationship between self-government and representation in Ch. 7 of *Multicultural Citizenship*.

12 This phrase is from the judgement of the Canadian Supreme Court in explaining its interpretation of the equality guarantees under the Canadian Charter of Rights (*Andrews v. Law Society of British Columbia* 1 SCR 143; 56 DLR (4th) 1). See also Government of Canada 1991b: 10.

13 For examples of this view, see Knopff 1979; F. Morton 1985; Kukathas 1992; Hindess 1993; Maré 1992: 107–10; Rawls 1975: 88, 93, and the references cited in Ch. 1 n. 4 of *Multicultural Citizenship*.

14 I explored this relationship between national right and liberal egalitarian justice in Kymlicka 1989a: ch. 9. For what it is worth, I continue to endorse the argument in that chapter, but I should have been clearer about its scope. I would now describe the argument in that chapter as an equality-based defence of certain external protections for national minorities. I did not use those terms at the time, in part because I did not have a very clear conception of the variety of rights, groups, and moral justifications that are involved in the debate.

15 I am here disagreeing with Tamir, who argues that the larger a national minority is, the more rights it should have (1993: 75). On my view, if a binational group is large enough, it may have little need for group-differentiated rights, since it can ensure its survival and development through the usual operation of the economic market-place and democratic decision-making. (This might be true, for example, if a national state contained two nations of roughly equal size and wealth.)

16 On the role of indigenous land claims in a liberal egalitarian framework, see Kymlicka 1995; Penz 1992; 1993; Russell 1993; Tully 1994. It is important to note that the equality argument for land claims is not based on notions of compensatory justice. The compensatory argument says that because indigenous peoples were the legal owners of their traditional lands, and because their lands were taken away illegally, they should be compensated for this historical wrong. Since the debate over land claims is often couched in the language of compensatory justice, I should say a word about this. I take it as given that indigenous peoples have suffered terrible wrongs in being dispossessed of their lands, and that they should be compensated for this in some way. Moreover, I believe that indigenous peoples continue to have certain property rights under the common law (in former British colonies), wherever these have not been explicitly extinguished by legislation. (That is to say, the *terra nullius* doctrine is wrong in terms both of morality and the common law.) But it is a mistake, I think, to put too much weight on historical property rights. For one thing, these claims do not, by themselves, explain why indigenous peoples have rights of self-government. Many groups have been wrongfully dispossessed of property and other economic opportunities, including women, blacks and Japanese immigrants in the United States and Canada during World War II. Each of these groups may be entitled to certain forms of compensatory justice, but this does not by itself explain or justify granting powers of self-government (rather than compensatory programmes to promote integration and equal opportunity within the mainstream). Suffering historical injustice is neither necessary nor sufficient for claiming self-government rights.

Moreover, the idea of compensating for historical wrongs, taken to its logical conclusion, implies that all the land which was wrongly taken from indigenous peoples in the Americas or Australia or New Zealand should be returned to them. This would create massive unfairness, given that the original European settlers and later immigrants have now produced hundreds of millions of descendants, and this land is the only home they know. Changing circumstances often make it impossible and undesirable to compensate for certain historical wrongs. As Jeremy Waldron puts it, certain historical wrongs are 'superseded' (Waldron 1992). Also, the land held by some indigenous groups at the time of contact was itself the result of the conquest or coercion of other indigenous groups (Mulgan 1989: 30–1; Crowe 1974: 65–81). The compensatory argument would presumably require rectifying these pre-contact injustices as well. (For other difficulties with compensatory claims, see Brilmayer 1992.)

The equality argument does not try to turn back the historical clock, nor to restore groups to the situation they would have been in in the absence of any historical injustice. (These compensatory aims actually fit more comfortably with Nozick's libertarian theory of entitlement than with a liberal egalitarian theory of distributive justice – see Lyons 1981.) The aim of the equality argument is to provide the sort of land base needed to sustain the viability of self-governing minority communities, and hence to prevent unfair disadvantages with respect to cultural membership now and in the future. In short, the equality argument situates land claims within a theory of distributive justice, rather than compensatory justice.

Waldron assumes that indigenous land claims are all based on claims for compensatory justice (Waldron 1992). In fact, however, most indigenous groups focus, not on reclaiming all of what they had before European settlement, but on what they need now to sustain themselves as distinct societies (see the declaration of the World Council of Indigenous Peoples, quoted in Nettheim 1988: 115; Sharp 1990: 150–3). Historical factors are, of course, relevant in other ways. The 'historical agreement' argument I discuss below is very much history-based.

17 The only attempt I know of to reconcile official languages with 'benign neglect' is by Rainer Knopff. He argues that language has two functions: it can function as the vehicle for the transmission of a particular culture, but it can also function as 'a culturally neutral, or utilitarian, means of communication which allows those of different cultures to participate in the same political community' (Knopff 1979: 67). By placing the emphasis on the utilitarian function, governments 'can enact official languages without at the same time legislating offi-

cial cultures . . . in enacting 'official languages', one does not necessarily imply that the cultures which these languages transmit and represent thereby become 'official cultures' (Knopff 1979: 67). Culture, Knopff argues, 'remains a purely private affair' in Canada, for while English and French have official backing as the 'utilitarian' languages, all languages compete on equal terms for 'cultural' allegiance. It is the 'task of the individual members of a culture to show the excellence of their product on the cultural market-place, as it were. If they succeed, the language of that culture will become attractive to others . . . if [a] culture, and hence, language, cannot show itself to be worthy of choice in the light of standards of the good, then it deserves to disappear' (Knopff 1979: 70). This view of language as a 'culturally neutral medium' has been thoroughly discredited in the literature. In any event, it is simply not true that teaching in the English language in public schools is totally divorced from the teaching of the history and customs of the anglophone society.

18 Some commentators say that governments should draw boundaries and distribute powers so as to protect the viability of national minorities, but that they should not state in law that they are doing this. This enables the state to continue claiming that it treats all ethnic and national differences with 'benign neglect'. For example, van den Berghe argues that deliberately designing or revising federal units to protect minority cultures is consistent with 'benign neglect', so long as it does not involve the explicit legal recognition of groups. He thinks it is one thing to define the powers and boundaries of a political subunit so as to ensure the protection of a minority culture (what he calls 'indirect consociationalism'), but quite another for the constitution or statute law to cite the existence of that minority as the reason for those arrangements (what he calls 'group rights') (van den Berghe 1981: 348). But surely this is hypocritical. If the agreed purpose of indirect consociationalism is to protect minority cultures, then anyone who values honesty and transparency in government (as liberals claim to do) should want that justification to be clear to everyone. Van den Berghe's solution violates the 'publicity condition' which Rawls imposes on liberal theories of justice (Rawls 1971: 133). None the less, this attitude seems to be widely shared. While most Canadians accept that the powers and boundaries of Quebec were fixed to accommodate the needs of the francophone minority in Canada, many objected to the government's proposal to state in the constitution that Quebec formed a 'distinct society' as the homeland of the French Canadian nation, because they saw this as violating the principle that the constitution should not recognize particular ethnic or national groups. Quebecers, however, are no longer willing to have their special status hidden away. They view it as a matter of basic respect that their separate identity be recognized and affirmed at the level of constitutional principle (Taylor 1991: 64).

19 This is similar to the debate over affirmative action for women or people with disabilities. Like self-government rights, affirmative action programmes asymmetrically distribute rights or opportunities on the basis of group membership. Proponents argue that they are required for genuine equality. Critics respond that the economic market-place (like the cultural market-place) already respects equality, by treating job applicants without regard for their group membership. However, an equality-based argument for group-specific affirmative action can be made if the actual operation of the economic market-place works to the disadvantage of certain groups. As with self-government rights, the equality argument for affirmative action seeks to show how the structure of common individual rights is intended to treat all people equally, but in fact works to the disadvantage of the members of a particular collectivity. Many group-specific claims can be seen in this way – that is, as compensating for the disadvantages and vulnerabilities of certain groups within the structure of common individual rights.

Of course, affirmative action for women or people with disabilities differs in many ways from self-government rights for national minorities, since they are compensating for very different kinds of injustices. The former is intended to help disadvantaged groups integrate into society, by breaking down unjust barriers to full integration. The latter is intended to help cultural communities maintain their distinctiveness, by protecting against external decisions. This means that the former are (in theory) temporary, whereas the latter are permanent, barring dramatic shifts in population.

20 Imagine that schools and government offices (and presumably private businesses as well) were open seven days a week all year round, including Christmas and Easter, and that each student and employee was allowed to choose two days off per week, two weeks' vacation per year, plus, say, five additional holidays per year. This would maximize each individual's ability to adapt their schedule to their religious beliefs. But I do not know whether this is realistic or even desirable, given the extent to which social life is built around common weekends and holidays. As an atheist, I have no commitment to resting on the sabbath or celebrating religious holidays. But I do like the fact that most of my friends and family, regardless of their religion, language, and ethnicity, do not work on the weekends or on certain public holidays. Maintaining friendships and other voluntary associations would be much more difficult if society (including schools and other government institutions) were not

organized in this way. Perhaps a better solution would be to have one major holiday from each of the largest religious groups in the country. We could have one Christian holiday (say, Christmas), but replace Easter and Thanksgiving with a Muslim and Jewish holiday. This would maintain the value of common holidays, and would also encourage people of each faith to learn something about the beliefs of other faiths.

21 E.g. the Canadian government justified its proposal to eliminate the treaty rights of Indians on the grounds that 'we can only be just in our time' (Trudeau 1969: 295). Trudeau was paraphrasing John F. Kennedy's famous quote about justice for blacks in the United States.

22 Chartrand argues that this is the current situation with respect to the Métis in Canada, who agreed to join Canada on the basis of promises made to them under the Manitoba Act 1870, which have since been broken (Chartrand 1993: 241).

23 It is interesting to note that some Aboriginal groups in Canada insist that their demands for federal funding of self-government are based solely on historical compensation for the wrongful taking of land, not on appeals to distributive justice between citizens (Lyon 1984: 13–14).

24 For a subtle discussion of the complex interaction between the equality and treaty arguments in the New Zealand context, see Sharp 1990: 135–6; Mulgan 1989: ch. 4. As Sharp notes, there is a tendency to read principles of equality back into the historical treaties.

25 These arguments parallel common arguments for the protection of endangered plant and animal species, which are seen both as enriching the world aesthetically, and as providing potential sources of valuable genetic material or other substances that might be of human benefit.

26 Many liberals defend state funding of the arts or museums on the ground that the state has a responsibility to ensure an adequate range of options for future generations, which the cultural market-place may fail to protect (Dworkin 1985: ch. 11; Raz 1986: 162; Black 1992; Kymlicka 1989b: 893–5). If we accept that active measures are justified to preserve the richness and diversity of our cultural resources, then programmes such as the funding of ethnic festivals or immigrant language classes can be seen as falling under this heading. Indeed, some people defined this funding simply as a way of ensuring that ethnic groups are not discriminated against in state funding of art and culture. (I should note that other liberals view any such state funding as illegitimate (e.g. Rawls 1971: 331–2; Waldron 1989).)

27 Hence the popular contrast between 'consociational' and 'universal' modes of incorporating individuals into the state is misleading (e.g. Asch 1990). There is a distinction between models of citizenship that incorporate citizens on a uniform basis or through membership in some group. But uniform citizenship is not *universal* citizenship. No country allows for universal citizenship.

28 See the references in Ch. 5, n. 17, of *Multicultural Citizenship*.

29 One theorist who has attempted to square the circle is Michael Walzer. He argues that restricting citizenship in a state to the members of a particular group is justified in the name of protecting a distinct culture (what he calls a 'community of character'). He recognizes that this same argument can be given for group-differentiated rights *within* a state, but rejects such rights because they violate our 'shared understandings' (Walzer 1983: ch. 2). I have argued elsewhere that Walzer's argument is unsuccessful (Kymlicka 1989a: ch. 11). I should emphasize again that my defence of the legitimacy of partially closed borders is not intended to defend the right of national groups to maintain more than their fair share of resources. On the contrary, I would argue that a country forfeits its right to restrict immigration if it has failed to live up to its obligations to share its wealth with the poorer countries of the world. See Bader 1995; Ackerman 1980: 256–7.

30 On the tendency of liberals to treat diversity as a matter of variations in individual values and beliefs, see A. Phillips 1993; Galeotti 1993: 590. For an example of this 'overly cerebral' conception of diversity, see Rawls 1993a: pp. xxvii–xxix, where he treats modern conflicts of race, ethnicity, and gender as if they were analogous to conflict over religious belief during the Reformation – i.e. as conflicts over individuals' beliefs about 'the meaning, value and purposes of human life'.

31 This is true of Young's postmodernist account of minority rights. According to her view of 'relational difference', cultural groups must 'understand themselves as participating in the same society', and as 'part of a single polity', whose common decision-making procedures are seen as 'legitimately binding' on all people equally. Cultural difference within a state should be accommodated by group-differentiated rights within a single society – e.g. by group representation within the mainstream polity – rather than by establishing two or more separate and self-governing societies within a state (I. Young 1993a: 135). Like many liberals, she fears the impact of national rights on other political movements or on domestic peace.

References

Ackerman, Bruce (1980), *Social Justice in the Liberal State* (Yale University Press, New Haven, Conn.).

Adam, Heribert (1979), 'The Failure of Political Liberalism', in H. Adam and H. Giliomee (eds.), *Ethnic Power Mobilized: Can South Africa Change?* (Yale University Press, New Haven, Conn.), 258–85.

Addis, Adeno (1991), 'Individualism, Communitarianism and the Rights of Ethnic Minorities', *Notre Dame Law Review*, 67/3: 615–76.

Asch, Michael (1984), *Home and Native Land: Aboriginal Rights and the Canadian Constitution* (Methuen, Toronto).

—— (1990), 'Consociation and the Resolution of Aboriginal Political Rights', *Culture*, 10/1: 93–102.

Bader, Veit (1995), 'Citizenship and Exclusion: Radical Democracy, Community and Justice', *Political Theory*, forthcoming.

Black, Samuel (1991), 'Individualism at an Impasse', *Canadian Journal of Philosophy*, 21/3: 347–77.

—— (1992), 'Revisionist Liberalism and the Decline of Culture', *Ethics*, 102/2: 244–67.

Brilmayer, Lea (1992), 'Groups, Histories and International Law', *Cornell International Law Journal*, 25/3: 555–63.

Buchanan, Allen (1989), 'Assessing the Communitarian Critique of Liberalism', *Ethics*, 99/4: 852–82.

Cairns, Alan (1991), 'Constitutional Change and the Three Equalities', in Ronald Watts and Douglas Brown (eds.), *Options for a New Canada* (University of Toronto Press, Toronto), 77–110.

Cassidy, Frank, and Bish, Robert (1989), *Indian Government: Its Meaning in Practice* (Institute for Research on Public Policy, Halifax).

Chartrand, Paul (1991), *Manitoba's Métis Settlement Scheme of 1870* (University of Saskatchewan Native Law Centre, Saskatoon).

—— (1993), 'Aboriginal Self-Government: The Two Sides of Legitimacy', in Susan Phillips (ed.), *How Ottawa Spends: 1993–1994* (Carleton University Press, Ottawa), 231–56.

Clay, Jason (1989), 'Epilogue: The Ethnic Future of Nations', *Third World Quarterly*, 11/4: 223–33.

Crawford, James (1988), 'The Rights of Peoples', in James Crawford (ed.), *The Rights of Peoples* (Oxford University Press, Oxford), 159–75.

Crowe, Keith (1974), *A History of the Original Peoples of Northern Canada* (McGill-Queen's University Press, Montreal).

Danley, John (1991), 'Liberalism, Aboriginal Rights and Cultural Minorities', *Philosophy and Public Affairs*, 20/2: 168–85.

Davidson, Chandler (1992), 'The Voting Rights Act: A Brief History', in B. Grofman and C. Davidson (eds.), *Controversies in Minority Voting: The Voting Rights Act in Perspective* (Brookings Institute, Washington, DC), 7–51.

Duchacek, I.D. (1977), 'Federalist Responses to Ethnic Demands: An Overview', in Daniel Elazar (ed.), *Federalism and Political Integration* (Turtledove Publishing, Ramat Gan), 59–71.

Dworkin, Ronald (1981), 'What is Equality? Part II: Equality of Resources', *Philosophy and Public Affairs*, 10/4: 283–345.

—— (1985), *A Matter of Principle* (Harvard University Press, London).

—— (1989), 'Liberal Community', *California Law Review*, 77/3: 479–504.

Elazar, Daniel (1987), *Exploring Federalism* (University of Alabama, Tuscaloosa, Ala.).

Elkins, David (1992), *Where Should the Majority Rule? Reflections on Non-territorial Provinces and Other Constitutional Proposals* (Centre for Constitutional Studies, University of Alberta, Edmonton).

Falk, Richard (1988), 'The Rights of Peoples (in Particular Indigenous Peoples)', in James Crawford (ed.), *The Rights of Peoples* (Oxford University Press, Oxford), 17–37.

Fleras, Augie and Elliot, Jean Leonard (1992), *The Nations within: Aboriginal-State Relations in Canada, the United States and New Zealand* (Oxford University Press, Toronto).

Gagon, Alain-G. (1993), 'The Political Uses of Federation', in Michael Burgess and Alain-G. Gagon (eds.), *Comparative Federalism and Federation* (University of Toronto Press, Toronto), 15–44.

Gagon, Alain-G. and Garcea, Joseph (1988), 'Quebec and the Pursuit of Special Status', in R.D. Olling and M.W. Westmacott (eds.), *Perspectives on Canadian Federalism* (Prentice-Hall, Scarborough), 304–25.

Galenkamp, Marlies (1993), *Individualism and Collectivism: The Concept of Collective Rights* (Rotterdamse Filosofische Studies, Rotterdam).

Galeotti, Anna (1993), 'Citizenship and Equality: The Place for Toleration', *Political Theory*, 21/4: 585–605.

Glazer, Nathan (1983), *Ethnic Dilemmas: 1964–1982* (Harvard University Press, Cambridge, Mass.).

Gochnauer, Myron (1991), 'Philosophical Musings on Persons, Groups, and Rights', *University of New Brunswick Law Journal*, 40/1: 1–20.

Government of Canada (1991a), *Shaping Canada's Future Together: Proposals* (Supply and Services, Ottawa).

—— (1991b), *Shared Values: The Canadian Identity* (Supply and Services, Ottawa).

Gurr, Ted (1993), *Minorities at Risk: A Global View of Ethnopolitical Conflict* (Institute of Peace Press, Washington, DC).

Gutmann, Amy (1993), 'The Challenge of Multicultural-ism to Political Ethics', *Philosophy and Public Affairs*, 22/3: 171–206.

Hindess, Barry (1993), 'Multiculturalism and Citizen-ship', in Chandran Kukathas (ed.), *Multicultural Cit-izens: The Philosophy and Politics of Identity* (Centre for Independent Studies, St Leonards), 33–45.

Horowitz, D.L. (1985), *Ethnic Groups in Conflict* (Uni-versity of California Press, Berkeley, Calif.).

Howse, Robert, and Knop, Karen (1993), 'Federalism, Secession, and the Limits of Ethnic Accommodation: A Canadian Perspective', *New Europe Law Review*, 1/2: 269–320.

Kallen, Evelyn (1987), 'Ethnicity and Collective Rights in Canada', in L. Driedger (ed.), *Ethnic Canada* (Copp Clark, Toronto), 318–36.

Knopff, Rainer (1979), 'Language and Culture in the Canadian Debate: The Battle of the White Papers', *Canadian Review of Studies in Nationalism*, 6/1: 66–82.

Kukathas, Chandran (1992), 'Are There Any Cultural Rights?', *Political Theory*, 20/1: 105–39.

Kymlicka, Will (1989a), *Liberalism, Community, and Cul-ture* (Oxford University Press, Oxford).

—— (1989b), 'Liberal Individualism and Liberal Neu-trality', *Ethics*, 99/4; 883–905.

—— (1990), *Contemporary Political Philosophy: An Introduction* (Oxford University Press, Oxford).

—— (1995), 'Concepts of Community and Social Just-ice', in Fen Hampson and Judith Reppy (eds.), *Global Environmental Change and Social Justice*, forthcoming.

Long, J. A. (1991), 'Federalism and Ethnic Self-Deter-mination: Native Indians in Canada', *Journal of Com-monwealth and Comparative Politics*, 29/2: 192–211.

Lyon, Noel (1984), *Aboriginal Self-Government* (Institute of Intergovernmental Relations, Kingston).

Lyons, David (1981), 'The New Indian Claims and Ori-ginal Rights to Land', in J. Paul (ed.), *Reading Nozick* (Rowman & Littlefield, Totowa, NJ).

Macdonald, Ian (1989), 'Group Rights', *Philosophical Papers*, 28/2: 117–36.

Macklem, Patrick (1993), 'Distributing Sovereignty: In-dian Nations and Equality of Peoples', *Stanford Law Review*, 45/5: 1311–67.

Majone, Giandomenico (1990), 'Preservation of Cultural Diversity in a Federal System: The Role of the Regions', in Mark Tushnet (ed.), *Comparative Constitutional Fed-eralism* (Greenwood Press, New York), 67–76.

Makinson, David (1988), 'Rights of Peoples: Point of View of a Logician', in James Crawford (ed.), *The Rights of Peoples* (Oxford University Press, Oxford), 69–92.

Maré, Gerhard (1992), *Brothers Born of Warrior Blood: Politics and Ethnicity and South Africa* (Raven Press, Johannesburg).

Minow, Martha (1990), 'Putting up and Putting down: Tolerance Reconsidered', in Mark Tushnet (ed.), *Comparative Constitutional Federalism* (Greenwood Press, New York), 77–113.

Modood, Tariq (1992), *Not Easy Being British: Colour, Culture and Citizenship* (Trentham Books, Stoke-on-Trent).

Morton, F. L. (1985), 'Group Rights versus Individual Rights in the Charter: The Special Cases of Natives and the Québécois', in N. Nevitte and A. Kornberg (eds.), *Minorities and the Canadian State* (Mosaic Press, Oakville): 71–85.

Mulgan, Richard (1989), *Maori, Pākehā and Democracy* (Oxford University Press, Auckland).

Nettheim, Garth (1988), ' "Peoples" and "Populations": Indigenous Peoples and the Rights of Peoples', in James Crawford (ed.), *The Rights of Peoples* (Oxford University Press, Oxford), 107–26.

Nietschmann, Bernard (1987), 'The Third World War', *Cultural Survival Quarterly*, 11/3: 1–16.

Norman, W. J. (1994), 'Towards a Normative Theory of Federalism', in Judith Baker (ed.), *Group Rights* (University of Toronto Press, Toronto), 79–99.

O'Brien, Sharon (1987), 'Cultural Rights in the United States: A Conflict of Values', *Law and Inequality Jour-nal*, 5: 267–358.

Parekh, Bhikhu (1990), 'The Rushdie Affair: Research Agenda for Political Philosophy', *Political Studies*, 38: 695–709.

—— (1991), 'British Citizenship and Cultural Differ-ence', in Geoff Andrews (ed.), *Citizenship* (Lawrence & Wishart, London), 183–204.

—— (1994), 'Decolonizing Liberalism', in Aleksandras Shtromas (ed.), *The End of 'Isms'? Reflections on the Fate of Ideological Politics after Communism's Collapse* (Blackwell, Oxford), 85–103.

Penz, Peter (1992), 'Development Refugees and Dis-tributive Justice: Indigenous Peoples, Land and the Developmentalist State', *Public Affairs Quarterly*, 6/1: 105–31.

—— (1993), 'Colonization of Tribal Lands in Bangla-desh and Indonesia: State Rationales, Rights to Land, and Environmental Justice', in Michael Howard (ed.), *Asia's Environmental Crisis* (Westview Press, Boulder, Col.), 37–72.

Phillips, Anne (1993), *Democracy and Difference* (Penn-sylvania State University Press, Philadelphia).

Pomerance, Michla (1982), *Self-Determination in Law and Practice: The New Doctrine in the United Nations* (Martinus Nijhoff Publishers, The Hague).

Poulter, Sebastian (1987), 'Ethnic Minority Customs, English Law, and Human Rights', *International and Comparative Law Quarterly*, 36/3: 589–615.

Rawls, John (1971), *A Theory of Justice* (Oxford Univer-sity Press, London).

—— (1975), 'Fairness to Goodness', *Philosophical Re-view*, 84: 536–54.

—— (1978), 'The Basic Structure as Subject', in A. Goldman and J. Kim (eds.), *Values and Morals* (Reidel, Dordrecht).

—— (1993a), *Political Liberalism* (Columbia University Press, New York).

—— (1993b), 'The Law of Peoples', in S. Shute and S. Hurley (eds.), *On Human Rights: The Oxford Amnesty Lectures 1993* (Basic Books, New York), 41–82.

Raz, Joseph (1986), *The Morality of Freedom* (Oxford University Press, Oxford).

RCERPF – see Royal Commission on Electoral Reform and Party Financing.

Resnik, Judith (1989), 'Dependent Sovereigns: Indian Tribes, States, and the Federal Courts', *University of Chicago Law Review*, 56: 671–759.

Royal Commission on Electoral Reform and Party Financing (1991). *Reforming Electoral Democracy: Final Report*, vols. i and ii (Supply and Services, Ottawa).

Rubinstein, Alvin (1993), 'Is Statehood for Puerto Rico in the National Interest?', *In Depth: A Journal for Values and Public Policy*, Spring: 87–99.

Russell, John (1993), 'Nationalistic Minorities and Liberal Traditions', in Philip Bryden *et al.* (eds.), *Protecting Rights and Liberties: Essays on the Charter and Canada's Political, Legal and Intellectual Life* (University of Toronto Press, Toronto), 205–41.

Sandel, Michael (1990), 'Freedom of Conscience or Freedom of Choice', in James Hunter and O. Guinness (eds.), *Articles of Faith, Articles of Peace* (Brookings Institute, Washington, DC), 74–92.

Schwartz, Brian (1986), *First Principles, Second Thoughts: Aboriginal Peoples, Constitutional Reform and Canadian Statecraft* (Institute for Research on Public Policy, Montreal).

Sharp, Andrew (1990), *Justice and the Maori: Maori Claims in New Zealand Political Argument in the 1980s* (Oxford University Press, Auckland).

Sigler, Jay (1983), *Minority Rights: A Comparative Analysis* (Greenwood, Westport, Conn.).

Smith, Jennifer (1993), 'Canadian Confederation and the Influence of American Federalism', in Marian McKenna (ed.), *The Canadian and American Constitutions in Comparative Perspective* (University of Calgary Press, Calgary), 65–85.

Stark, Andrew (1992), 'English-Canadian Opposition to Quebec Nationalism', in R. Kent Weaver (ed.), *The Collapse of Canada?* (Brookings Institute, Washington, DC), 123–58.

Tamir, Yael (1993), *Liberal Nationalism* (Princeton University Press, Princeton, NJ).

Taylor, Charles (1991), 'Shared and Divergent Values', in Ronald Watts and D. Brown (eds.), *Options for a New Canada* (University of Toronto Press, Toronto), 53–76.

Thornberry, Patrick (1991), *International Law and the Rights of Minorities* (Oxford University Press, Oxford).

Todorov, Tzvetan (1993), *On Human Diversity: Nationalism, Racism and Exoticism in French Thought* (Harvard University Press, Cambridge, Mass.).

Tomasi, John (1991), 'Individual Rights and Community Virtues', *Ethics*, 101/3: 521–36.

Torres, Gerald (1991), 'Critical Race Theory: The Decline of the Universalist Ideal and the Hope of Plural Justice', *Minnesota Law Review*, 75: 993–1007.

Trakman, Leon (1992), 'Group Rights: A Canadian Perspective', *New York University Journal of International Law and Politics*, 24/4: 1579–650.

Trudeau, P.E. (1969), speech of 8 Aug. 1969, repr. as 'Justice in our Time', in Eldon Soifer (ed.), *Ethical Issues: Perspectives for Canadians* (Broadview Press, Peterborough, 1992), 295–7.

Tully, James (1994), 'Aboriginal Property and Western Theory: Recovering a Middle Ground', *Social Philosophy and Policy*, 11/2: 153–80.

Van den Berghe, Pierre (1981), *The Ethnic Phenomenon* (Elsevier, New York).

Van Dyke, Vernon (1982), 'Collective Entities and Moral Rights: Problems in Liberal-Democratic Thought', *Journal of Politics*, 44: 21–40.

Waldron, Jeremy (1989), 'Autonomy and Perfectionism in Raz's *Morality of Freedom*', *Southern California Law Review*, 62/3–4: 1097–152.

—— (1992), 'Superseding Historic Injustice', *Ethics*, 103/1: 4–28. [Reprinted as chapter 17 of this volume.]

Walzer, Michael (1982), 'Pluralism in Political Perspective', in M. Walzer (ed.), *The Politics of Ethnicity* (Harvard University Press, Cambridge. Mass.), 1–28.

—— (1983), *Spheres of Justice: A Defence of Pluralism and Equality* (Blackwell, Oxford).

—— (1990), 'The Communitarian Critique of Liberalism', *Political Theory*, 18/1: 6–23.

Weinstein, Brian (1983), *The Civic Tongue: Political Consequences of Language Choices* (Longman, New York).

Young, Iris Marion (1989), 'Polity and Group Difference: A Critique of the Ideal of Universal Citizenship', *Ethics*, 99/2: 250–74. [Reprinted as chapter 16 of this volume.]

—— (1990), *Justice and the Politics of Difference* (Princeton University Press, Princeton, NJ).

—— (1993a), 'Together in Difference: Transforming the Logic of Group Political Conflict', in Judith Squires (ed.), *Principled Positions: Postmodernism and the Rediscovery of Value* (Lawrence and Wishart, London), 121–50.

—— (1993b), 'Justice and Communicative Democracy', in Roger Gottlieb (ed.), *Radical Democracy: Tradition, Counter-tradition, Politics* (Temple University Press, Philadelphia), 123–43.

23

Human Rights as a Common Concern

Charles R. Beitz

More than fifty years have passed since the UN General Assembly adopted the Universal Declaration of Human Rights, and in that time the doctrine of human rights has come to play a distinctive and in some respects an unexpected role in international life. This is primarily the role of a moral touchstone – a standard of assessment and criticism for domestic institutions, a standard of aspiration for their reform, and increasingly a standard of evaluation for the policies and practices of international economic and political organizations. This role is carried out in a variety of ways. Perhaps the most visible is the increasing willingness to regard concern about human rights violations as an acceptable justification for various kinds of international intervention, ranging from diplomatic and economic sanctions to military action, in the domestic affairs of states.

But coercive intervention in any form is exceptional, and the political functions of human rights usually are considerably less dramatic. For example, a government's human rights record may determine eligibility for development assistance programs, or human rights conditions may be attached to internationally sponsored financial adjustment measures. The likely effect on satisfaction of human rights may function as a standard of evaluation for the policies of international financial and trade institutions. In the United States, legislation requires periodic reporting by the govern-

ment regarding human rights practices in other countries and makes eligibility for certain forms of preferential treatment in US foreign policy dependent on satisfaction of minimum human rights standards. In various parts of the world, most notably in Europe, regional codes have been adopted, and there is a developing capacity for adjudication and something like enforcement (even the European Court of Human Rights' capacity to hold governments accountable lacks the machinery of coercion typically associated with adjudication within the state).[1]

The public role of human rights also has been important – more so perhaps than generally recognized in the United States – beyond the sphere of intergovernmental relations. Human rights have served as bases for standard setting, monitoring, reporting, and advocacy by nongovernmental organizations at both the domestic and the international levels of world politics (Best 1995; Korey 1998). To whatever extent contemporary international political life can be said to have a "sense of justice," its language is the language of human rights.

I do not mean to overstate the case. Notwithstanding the hopes of its authors, the Universal Declaration does not function today as an "international bill of rights." The international capacity to enforce the requirements of human rights law on states is at best embryonic. Outside Europe, most individual victims of human rights abuses

Originally published in *American Political Science Review* 95 (2001): 269–82. Copyright © 2001 American Political Science Association. Published by Cambridge University Press. Reprinted by permission of Cambridge University Press.

have no effective appeal beyond their domestic courts, if there. And even in countries within the global "human rights culture" there is great variation in the degree to which internationally recognized human rights are embedded in domestic legal systems.[2] The juridical role of human rights is both limited and uneven. But none of this shows that the national foreign policy measures, international institutions, and nongovernmental organizations dedicated to the advancement of human rights are politically inconsequential. In fact, the global human rights regime is almost certainly more influential today than at any time since World War II.[3]

This fact recalls a long-standing worry about the doctrine of international human rights, expressed variously in terms of its alleged partiality or parochialism. In practice, the worry arises as an objection to external measures that are intended to induce a government to comply with the doctrine's requirements. Such measures by another government or an external organization are sometimes said to constitute the imposition of foreign values upon a culture whose history and conventional moral beliefs do not support them – in the extreme case, a kind of postcolonial imperialism.

There is a reflection of this worry at the theoretical level in a tension between two conceptions of human rights that can be found in philosophical thought. According to one conception, human rights represent the common element in a range of views about social justice or political legitimacy found among the world's cultures. A variant of this position, which is more permissive as to what might be counted as a human right but is motivated by a similar idea, regards human rights as political standards that would be reasonable to accept regardless of one's (culturally influenced) views about social justice or political legitimacy. This notion might be expressed by saying that human rights strive to be nonpartisan, nonparochial, or neutral among conflicting political cultures and ideologies.[4] I shall call this the nonpartisan or restricted conception of human rights.

The other conception regards human rights as distinctive of a particular view or family of views about social justice or political legitimacy. Although a list of human rights might not be a complete description of the requirements of social justice for a society, on this conception it would be more than the common element found among, or acceptable to, otherwise divergent views of social justice. That is, human rights identify conditions that society's institutions should meet if we are to consider them legitimate. But because there is no general reason to believe that these conditions are included in all the views about social justice or political legitimacy that exist in the world – or even among those that have achieved widespread acceptance in individual societies – there is no claim that human rights are nonpartisan. On this view, in contrast to the first, the advocate of human rights takes a stand on controverted questions of political theory. I call this the liberal or full conception of human rights.[5]

Many people will think that the restricted conception is the more plausible because it seems to embody a tolerance of culturally embedded moral differences that is missing from the liberal view. But there is something paradoxical about this thought. Once we begin to describe evaluative standards for social and political institutions, it is hard to explain why we should stop short of a full description of these requirements as we see them. Of course, any such standards should be appropriate for the empirical circumstances in which they are supposed to apply, and it is important to add that this will leave some room for variation. But the intent would still be to state conditions for the legitimacy of institutions. If this is the intent, then why should we stop short of a full, liberal conception of human rights? And what would be the principle of distinction between the full and the restricted conceptions?

My purpose here is to explore the thinking that might lead someone to advocate a nonpartisan or restricted view of human rights. More precisely, I shall take up one aspect of this subject: Does the nonpartisanship, nonparochialism, or neutrality of a set of rights, in itself, provide a reason to treat these rights, as opposed to a more extensive set like that found in international doctrine, as having a special status in international affairs? In putting the question this way, I mean to distinguish considerations of ideological and cultural pluralism from various other kinds of reasons for giving some political aims priority over others – for example, reasons of urgency, efficiency, and institutional competence. These other reasons are obviously important and may often prove decisive in establishing priorities for political action, but they are also more easily understood, so for now I lay them aside. I will conclude – tentatively, because I cannot give the view an affirmative defense here – that considerations of ideological and cultural pluralism need not, in themselves, limit the scope of a plausible doctrine of international human rights, although they may have important bearing on reasoning about the connection between human rights and political action.

International Human Rights as Partisan Standards

To place the theoretical question in its political context, I begin with some summary remarks about the history and content of the doctrine of human rights as we find it in international law and practice.

Although the contemporary international doctrine of human rights has many antecedents, both philosophical and political, it is principally a legacy of World War II. It arose, on the one hand, from the statement of allied war aims in the Atlantic Charter (1941) and, on the other, from persistent pressure brought by individuals and groups outside government for a declaration of political principles for the postwar world. The Preamble to the United Nations Charter (adopted in 1946) affirms "faith in fundamental human rights," and Article 1 commits the organization to encourage respect for "human rights and for fundamental freedoms for all." (By contrast, there was no mention of human rights or any analogous idea in the Covenant of the League of Nations [Lauren 1998: chs. 5–6].) The charter does not give content to the idea of human rights and fundamental freedoms, however. For that one must refer to the Universal Declaration (1948) and two international covenants, one on civil and political rights and the other on economic, social, and cultural rights (both 1966). It bears remembering that the declaration is just that, a declaration of the General Assembly without the force of law, whereas the covenants are treaties to which national governments have acceded. Together these documents, which often are referred to collectively (and, as I suggested earlier, misleadingly) as the International Bill of Rights, constitute an authoritative catalog of internationally recognized human rights.

There are various ways to classify the rights enumerated in these documents. For our purposes it is useful to think of internationally recognized human rights as falling roughly into five categories, although it is less important to agree about categories than to appreciate the scope and detail of the enumerated rights.

1 Rights of the person refer to life, liberty, and security of the person; privacy and freedom of movement; ownership of property; freedom of thought, conscience, and religion, including freedom of religious teaching and practice "in public and private"; and prohibition of slavery, torture, and cruel or degrading punishment.

2 Rights associated with the rule of law include equal recognition before the law and equal protection of the law; effective legal remedy for violation of legal rights; impartial hearing and trial; presumption of innocence; and prohibition of arbitrary arrest.

3 Political rights encompass freedom of expression, assembly, and association; the right to take part in government; and periodic and genuine elections by universal and equal suffrage.

4 Economic and social rights refer to an adequate standard of living; free choice of employment; protection against unemployment; "just and favorable remuneration"; the right to join trade unions; "reasonable limitation of working hours"; free elementary education; social security; and the "highest attainable standard of physical and mental health."

5 Rights of communities include self-determination and protection of minority cultures.

I note, but shall not discuss, that other international agreements have elaborated and enlarged the scope of human rights in the areas of genocide, slavery, and forced labor, racial discrimination, apartheid, discrimination against women, and the rights of children.[6]

There has been a long-standing dispute in official international discourse about human rights doctrine on two major points: whether the international community should recognize any priorities, either moral or pragmatic, among categories of rights (particularly between civil and political as against economic and social rights) and whether human rights doctrine should take note of cultural differences in a way that would make the content of a person's human rights depend upon features of that person's culture. The last major international conference on human rights, conducted in Vienna in 1993, considered these issues at length. The final act of the conference declined to set priorities among categories, holding that "all human rights are universal, indivisible and interdependent and interrelated." Although it recognized that "the significance of national and regional particularities ... must be borne in mind," it declared that "it is the duty of States, regardless of their political, economic and cultural systems, to promote and protect all human rights and fundamental freedoms" (United Nations 1993, sec. I.5).

Human rights are sometimes thought to set a minimal standard, but it is not obvious what this can mean. The rights of the declaration and the two covenants, taken in their entirety, include requirements that bear on nearly every significant dimension of a society's basic institutional structure, ranging from protections against the misuse of state power to requirements concerning the political process, welfare policy, and the organization of the economy. In scope and detail, international human rights are not more minimal than, say, the requirements of Rawls's principles of social justice. And those principles are not minimal in any very interesting sense.

Still, one can acknowledge the scope and detail of internationally recognized human rights without giving up the idea that they are or should aspire to be neutral or nonparochial standards. So it may be useful to recall, briefly and without critical comment, some recent instances in which it has been said that human rights are not neutral because they conflict with practices endorsed by one or another of the world's major conventional moralities. All of these are familiar in the human rights literature.

One example is the dispute about "Asian values." In the last decade some East Asian political leaders (e.g., Lee Kwan Yew of Singapore and Mahathir Mohamad of Malaysia) argued that some of the political and civil rights found in the international doctrine – mainly freedom of expression and political participation – are incompatible with traditional Asian political beliefs, which value social harmony over public dispute and the collective pursuit of shared interests over the individual pursuit of private interest. The civil and political rights of the declaration were distinctively "Western" values. For this reason, it was said, international pressure for domestic political reform (exerted, e.g., by means of the attachment of political conditions to international financial arrangements) was inappropriate (Kausikan 1993).

Or consider the question of the subordination of women in traditional Islamic doctrine, elements of which are carried over into some authoritative modern interpretations. There is, for example, no presumption of equal treatment or equal protection of law, no protection against forced marriage,

and either required or permitted forms of gender discrimination (e.g., mandatory veiling and sexual seclusion and segregation). To the extent that these elements are embodied in the public law and legally sanctioned practices of Islamic states, such as Iran and Pakistan (or for that matter Saudi Arabia), there is a clear conflict with the requirements of international human rights doctrine, and pressure to conform to these requirements will be regarded as partisan.[7]

Finally, there is the much discussed matter of female genital mutilation (FGM), still practiced ritualistically in Sahelian African on as many as two million girls, at or before puberty, each year. FGM, which can take several forms, is sustained by cultural acceptance rather than the force of law, so it does not obviously represent a case of a human rights violation by the state. Yet, where it occurs, FGM is not an aberration; it is entrenched in local cultures and permitted or required by local moral codes. And it is subject to intervention, if not by the state, then by nongovernmental agencies that claim to be acting to defend the human rights of the women affected. There is controversy about the seriousness of the harms brought about by FGM in comparison with various practices found in Western cultures, but whatever one's view about that, it would be hard to argue that interference to curtail FGM constitutes the application of a culturally neutral standard.[8]

In each of these cases it has been said that the local moralities that permit or require practices inconsistent with international human rights are sufficiently complex to allow for an internal critique of the offending practices.[9] This is true and important, but it does not diminish the impression that human rights operate in all three settings in a nonneutral way. Indeed, the existence of disagreements internal to a culture, combined with the fact that the weight of human rights seems usually to favor the modernizing, cosmopolitan side of the disagreement, only strengthens the view of international human rights as a partisan rather than a neutral concern. Jack Donnelly (1999: 84) has written that internationally recognized human rights "set out as a hegemonic political model something very much like the liberal democratic welfare state of western Europe." No doubt this overstates the case, at least insofar as it suggests there is an unambiguous "liberal" position about the full range of the subject matter of international human rights (there is, e.g., no single liberal view about self-determination or the rights of minority cultures). But Donnelly is correct that the declaration and covenants cannot really be regarded as setting forth a culturally or politically ecumenical or syncretistic doctrine.

Neutrality and Paternalism

The evident partisanship of international human rights doctrine has led some philosophers to suggest that we should distinguish between the full set of values recognized as human rights in international law and a restricted subset variously referred to as "basic rights" (Shue 1996)[10] or "human rights proper" (Rawls 1999a: 80, n. 23). For expository purposes I shall call the restricted subset – whatever its contents turn out to be – "genuine" human rights. The fact that the rights in the subset could be regarded as nonpartisan, or ideologically or culturally neutral, might be seen as qualifying them to play a special role in foreign policy for which international human rights generally are not suited.

Among those who believe there are grounds for restricting genuine human rights to some sort of nonparochial or neutral core, it is not always clear what these grounds are or why we should care about them. In this section and the next, I discuss these questions in connection with each of two distinct interpretations of neutrality or nonparochialism.

Consider first an approach suggested by some remarks of Michael Walzer (although he does not make the connection with human rights explicit), who distinguishes between "thin" and "thick" moralities. Walzer (1994, 9–10) speculates that a comparison of the moral codes found in various societies might produce "a set of standards to which all societies can be held – negative injunctions, most likely, rules against murder, deceit, torture, oppression, and tyranny." These standards would constitute "the moral minimum," not a complete moral code but, rather, "reiterated features of particular thick or maximal moralities." Someone influenced by such a distinction might regard human rights as part of the "minimum" or "thin" morality, nonparochial in that they are part of a core of requirements shared by all conventional or "thick" moralities – the common elements in a global moral pluralism. Thus, for example, R. J. Vincent (1986: 48–9) writes of a "core of basic rights that is common to all cultures despite their apparently divergent theories," which he describes as a "lowest common denominator."[11]

As Walzer's speculation suggests, this conception of nonparochialism, if treated as a constraint on what we should count as genuine human rights, would yield a relatively short list. Among others, rights requiring democratic political forms, religious toleration, legal equality for women, and free choice of a marriage partner would certainly be excluded. Other rights might be excluded if they were understood to generate certain kinds of duties; if, for example, the right to a high standard of physical and mental health were thought to imply that society has an obligation to ensure the accessibility of health care for all, then the existence of disagreement about distributive responsibilities outside of families or local communities would presumably exclude this right as well.[12]

The narrowness of the resulting conception might encourage us to think that this interpretation of neutrality relies excessively on the metaphor of a "core" of rights common to the world's main conventional moralities. Perhaps this is too restrictive; after all, the idea of a right is itself culturally specific. So one might shift to a more elaborate conception that sees human rights as falling within an "overlapping consensus" of political moralities.[13] On such a view, nonparochial human rights would not necessarily be part of a common core in the sense of being recognized by all conventional moralities; instead, they would be rights that could be accepted by a reasonable person consistently with acceptance of any of the main conceptions of political and economic justice in the world. The idea here is that human rights should be the objects of a possible agreement among the world's political cultures; they are norms for the conduct of governments and international organizations that anyone who belongs to one of these cultures can accept without renouncing other important political principles.[14] Such a view would be narrow in comparison with the present international doctrine, but presumably it would be broader than the "common core": A value could count as a genuine human right even if it were not explicitly present in every culture, just in case members of each culture could reasonably accept it as consistent with their culture's moral conventions.

There are other forms of this basic idea, but rather than proliferate interpretations I shall turn instead to the question why we should care about a doctrine of human rights limited to either a common core or an overlapping consensus. In answering this question, we should remember that one function of human rights in international politics is to justify external interference in a society aimed at changing some aspect of the society's internal life. Such interference might aim, for example, to stop genocide or forceful political repression, to protect the innocent against civil violence when local authorities are unwilling or unable to do so, to restore a democratic government removed by force of arms, or to deliver humanitarian assistance to those imperiled by natural disaster or political collapse.

I believe the reason many people aspire to a nonparochial or culturally neutral doctrine of human rights is connected to this interference-justifying role. Those who object to interference to protect human rights may claim that the interference is unjustifiably paternalistic. It would be paternalistic in that it limits liberty on the grounds that those whose liberty is limited (the "subjects") will be better off as a result of the interference, and it would be unjustified either because the subjects are capable of making choices for themselves or because the intervenor judges "better off" by standards the subjects have no reason to accept. A doctrine of human rights that satisfies a neutrality constraint might seem to offer the best prospect of meeting the antipaternalism objection because, if the human rights at stake are neutral in an appropriate way, then it can be replied that the aims of interference are ones that its subjects themselves would accept if they were in a position to bring their own moral beliefs to bear on the matter at hand.

The antipaternalism objection, as interpreted above, faces the following problem. When we are concerned about a violation of human rights in another society, we are usually not confronted with a situation in which people are unanimous in endorsing standards of conduct that justify the behavior of concern to us.[15] The picture of a "we" who believe in human rights and a "they" who do not is badly misleading. Among the "they" are oppressors and victims, and usually there is little reason to believe that the victims all share the values that the oppressors think justify their conduct. What this shows is that the perception of interference to defend human rights as a form of paternalism can be a misapprehension. Paternalism is an intervention in a person's self-regarding choices on the grounds that the intervention is good for that person. The individual whose liberty is interfered with is the same person as the one whose good the interference is intended to

advance. In typical cases of interference based on human rights, however, some people's liberties are infringed in order to protect the human rights of others. The justification appropriately appeals not to paternalistic considerations but to the desirability of preventing a harm or securing a benefit for someone threatened by another agent's wrongful actions or omissions. (Although not always: Interference to persuade a young girl not to undergo an FGM procedure is genuinely paternalistic, but noncoercive interference – such as providing information and so respecting the girl's capacity for choice – affords a different defense.) That this should not be immediately obvious is evidence of the continuing grip of the analogy of person and state, which tempts us to treat the state as if it had the moral attributes of an individual rather than as an aggregate of separate persons with wills and interests of their own.

In most cases, then, what I have called the antipaternalism objection, if it pertains at all, must be interpreted elliptically. It must hold that, for purposes of justifying external interference in a society, we should base our judgment of what constitutes harm or benefit to a member of that society on standards of value that belong to the conventional morality of the society, even if we have reason to believe that those on whose behalf the interference occurs would reject these values in their own cases. We might call this the principle of cultural deference.

In itself this is not necessarily a form of moral relativism, since it does not deny that sound cross-cultural moral judgments are possible. Nevertheless, taken as a general principle of practical reasoning, it is a strange, even a bizarre, view, for it allows the content of the doctrine of genuine human rights to be determined by the array of political moralities or conceptions of justice to be found in the world. Suppose a society with a racist political culture approves of the forced sterilization of a despised minority race as a means of population control. If we accept the principle of deference, we are forced to delete the right against genocide from the catalog of genuine human rights, because it is neither part of nor consistent with the racist conception. But surely we would resist doing so.

Someone might think that cases like that of a genocidal society are only theoretical possibilities, that no society would for long support such a horrible morality. Perhaps, over time, one expects a "normal distribution" of conventional moralities, each with a distinctive structure and content, but all converging on a substantial common core. This seems to me demonstrably too optimistic, but even if one regards the genocide case simply as a thought experiment, reflection about it suggests that the ground of our belief that, for example, genocide is a great wrong has to do not with the fact that other people agree it is so, but with the nature and consequences of genocide itself (compare Scanlon 1998: 337–8).[16]

Whether a standard should be accepted as a ground of action, and a fortiori as a ground of international action, does not turn on whether the standard is a part of, or implied by, existing conventional moralities. Actual agreement is too strong a condition to impose on any critical standard, and I believe it misrepresents the motivating idea of human rights. To say that human rights are "universal" is not to claim that they are necessarily either accepted by or acceptable to everyone, given their other political and ethical beliefs. Human rights are supposed to be universal in the sense that they apply to or may be claimed by everyone. To hold, also, that a substantive doctrine of human rights should be consistent with the moral beliefs and values found among the world's conventional moralities is to say something both more and different, and potentially subversive, of the doctrine's critical aims.

Decency and Minimal Legitimacy

I shall turn now to a different reason for limiting genuine human rights to a nonparochial core (and therefore a different idea of the way the core can be nonparochial). The basic idea is that we can distinguish between minimal and full legitimacy, with human rights serving as necessary conditions of minimal legitimacy. A minimally legitimate regime is one that merits respect as a cooperating member of international society, even if it falls short of being (what we would recognize as) fully legitimate or reasonably just.

Something like this distinction lies behind the conception of human rights found in Rawls's *The Law of Peoples* (1999a). It can be seen as an attempt to describe a view that is significantly nonparochial without being neutral in either of the senses I distinguished in the last section. As Rawls conceives of human rights, they are normative standards that would be satisfied by any "decent" regime, whether a liberal democracy or a (nonliberal, nondemocratic) "decent hierarchical society." For Rawls, "decency" is a term of art that serves to demarcate the boundaries of acceptable pluralism in international relations. Decent societies are those that liberal societies have reason to recognize as "equal participating members in good standing" of international society (the "Society of Peoples") (p. 59). Being so recognized, decent societies are entitled to a presumption against interference in their internal affairs; it would be wrong for foreign governments to intervene militarily, to attach political conditions to bilateral relationships and transactions, or to criticize. Rawls distinguishes decency from liberal justice: All liberal societies are decent, but not all decent societies are liberal. Human rights are common to all decent societies, whether they satisfy the requirements of liberal justice or not. So conceived, human rights "cannot be rejected as peculiarly liberal or special to the Western tradition. They are not parochial" (p. 65).

What should count as genuine human rights? Rawls believes that all decent societies would respect the rights of the person, the rights associated with the rule of law, freedom of religious belief and thought, freedom of expression (although perhaps not as extensive as justice requires in liberal societies), and certain economic (mainly subsistence) rights. Decent societies might, however, diverge beyond this area of overlap; specifically, they are not required to provide for equal freedom of public religious practice (but there must be sufficient liberty to allow the practice of minority religions "in peace and without fear" [Rawls 1999a: 74]), equal access to public office, or a right to democratic political participation. Therefore, the corresponding rights of the declaration – equal freedom of public religious practice as opposed to freedom of conscience and private religious practice, the right to vote in free and fair elections – do not count as "human rights proper"; they "seem more aptly described as stating liberal aspirations" or "appear to presuppose specific kinds of institutions" (p. 80, n. 23).[17]

Rawls's view has been criticized for being too tolerant of illiberal regimes (e.g., Buchanan 2000; Téson 1994). This may turn out to be correct, but there is a danger of overstatement: The scope of international toleration in Rawls's theory depends on the idea of "decency," which as he understands it is more restrictive than it may seem. A decent regime renounces aggressive war as an instrument of policy; follows a "common good conception of justice," in which everyone's interests are taken into account (although perhaps not on an equal basis); and respects certain basic rights, including subsistence rights, for all (so that, among other things, official discrimination against women is not permitted) (Rawls 1999a: 64–7). It is true that decency is compatible with a state religion and with undemocratic, but not nonparticipatory, political institutions: decency is, and is intended to be, a weaker requirement than liberal justice.[18] Even so, the constraints of decency are hardly undemanding and, taken seriously, probably would exclude many of the nondemocratic regimes in the world today and possibly some ostensibly democratic ones as well. In the end this may not be enough to meet the criticism, but it helps avoid a distorted picture of the theory.

It is important to see that, unlike the common core or overlapping consensus views, Rawls's view does not require the content of the human rights doctrine to be restricted by the array of political-moral conceptions in the world. The content is determined from the beginning by the normative idea of decency; human rights are said to be nonparochial in relation to all decent societies, not all societies simpliciter. This is why Rawls's view is not open to the objection that it deprives the human rights doctrine of its capacity to serve as a basis of social criticism. But there is a price to be paid. As Rawls (1999a, 80–1) observes, human rights must be considered as "binding on all peoples and societies, including outlaw states" that violate these rights. But because human rights are conceived so that they are necessarily common only to decent societies, it cannot be argued that interference to protect human rights in other societies would always be consistent with the conventional moralities of those societies.

Of course, much depends on the facts of the case, particularly on the relationship between the nature of a government and the content of its society's conventional morality. The case of a rogue tyranny oppressing a population that shares a decent political morality is different from the earlier example of a genocidal government in a racist society. But the possibility of variation does not affect the basic point that a doctrine such as Rawls's might justify interference in nondecent societies that could not easily be defended against complaints that it imposes alien values. Something more needs to be said to respond to such a complaint.

The response might have to do with the normative idea of decency itself, which serves to charac-

terize the minimum requirements of legitimacy. Where does the force of this idea come from? The answer is not clear to me. The underlying thought is that a society should not have to satisfy liberal principles of justice in order to be regarded by other societies as legitimate; a society may be deficient by liberal standards yet still embody elements that distinguish it from a band of thieves who have achieved a modus vivendi. These elements include the rule of law, an acceptance that all persons have legal personality and the capacity to participate in public life, and a "common good idea of justice" that is shared, at least, by judges and other public officials. Such a society might be said to embody a form of reciprocity even if, from a liberal perspective, it is not the preferred form.[19] Unlike liberal societies, such a society might embody and promote a single, comprehensive view of the good life; but it would do so under conditions (including respect for "human rights proper") that render the society tolerable as a cooperating partner for liberal societies in the international order.

The question, however, is not whether a society that satisfies these criteria of decency is to be preferred to one that does not; so much is clear. At issue is whether, and if so why, decent but not just societies should be regarded as legitimate and, therefore, as qualified for treatment as "members in good standing" of the international order. Why – for the (limited) purposes of international political life – should decency be regarded as on a par with liberal justice?[20]

At one point Rawls (1999a: 67) writes that the definition of decency is simply stipulated for the purposes of the theory, and the reader must judge "whether a decent people . . . is to be tolerated and accepted." But it is a serious question whether we have enough to go on intuitively to make such a judgment. Do we have a clear enough common-sense idea of decency, as a standard for institutions distinct from that of social justice, to judge other than arbitrarily? At another point he suggests that the content of the idea of decency is related to the function this idea plays in the conduct of liberal foreign policy. Liberal states should tolerate decent nonliberal states (which respect "human rights proper") because they are so structured and governed as to be peaceful, cooperating members of international society and therefore do not threaten international stability, whereas interference is permissible in "outlaw" states (which do not respect these rights) because their internal features cause them to threaten international order (p. 81). As a practical matter this may be true, but it cannot give a plausible account of the basis of human rights, because it would locate the justification in the wrong place, not in the significance of human rights for the rights holders but in the beneficial consequences for international order of reducing the number of regimes that do not respect them.[21]

Rawls's most perspicuous argument for tolerating decent but illiberal regimes appeals to the consequences of toleration for these societies themselves. Decent societies, by definition, are open to internal, nonviolent change, and Rawls (1999a, 61–2) believes that the evolution of their institutions in a liberal direction is more likely if they are treated "with due respect" as equal members of international society. This is an empirical hypothesis about political development, and I suspect that some version of it is true in a significant range of cases (although I am not sure what would count as evidence for it). Yet, although the political development hypothesis bears clearly on the question of how we should act toward a society, it does not bear so obviously on the question of the ethical significance of a society's political decency or, derivatively, of the proper scope of a doctrine of human rights. Perhaps the connection, in Rawls's view, is that human rights should be understood as a class of moral consideration whose *only* role in political discourse is to justify coercive intervention in a society's affairs. If that is correct, then the fact that a value is not sufficient to justify coercive intervention counts against identifying the value as a human right.

But whether Rawls holds this view or not, there are two reasons not to accept it. First, it is not true that the only role of human rights in international discourse is to justify coercive intervention. As I observed at the beginning, human rights are also, for example, invoked to justify noncoercive interference by outsiders (governments, international agencies, nongovernmental organizations) and to justify programs of reform by compatriots. We should conceptualize human rights in a way that is adequate to this larger role. Second, as before, the argument against interference does not easily extend to an argument for limiting the scope of human rights. Granting the political development hypothesis grants nothing about the moral standing of the values expressed as human rights; the hypothesis is about the best means of realizing these values, not about their standing as values. Indeed, the best argument against reform intervention in a decent society, assuming that the hypothesis is correct, is that intervention is more likely to retard than encourage the society's movement from decency to (liberal) justice. But such an argument depends on rather than repudiates the claim that the liberal conception is an appropriate standard for the society in question.

What is the upshot for human rights? I believe it is this. If it were possible to regard a decent society as minimally legitimate, in the sense of being, for purposes of its international relations, morally on a par with a liberally just society, then it would be possible to understand "human rights proper" as necessary conditions of minimal legitimacy. There would be a clear sense in which these human rights, as against the full catalog of internationally recognized human rights, could be defended as nonparochial. If the ethical significance of decency derives from that of liberal justice, however – for example, if its normative force depends on the hypothesis that decent societies, left to their own devices, are likely to develop into liberal ones – then the hypothesis might yield a reason not to interfere in decent societies, but there would be no deep distinction between "human rights proper" and other human rights that are part of liberal justice but not of decency. Indeed, it is hard to see any distinction of principle at all.

Purposes and Limits of International Human Rights

Notwithstanding these doubts about Rawls's interpretation of human rights, reflection about his view suggests two related precepts for any plausible conception. I shall try to formulate these precepts in a general way and then explain why they seem plausible.[22]

First, a satisfactory philosophical conception of human rights should be suited to the public role that we need human rights to play in international affairs. The doctrine of human rights is a political construction intended for certain political purposes and is to be understood against the background of a range of general assumptions about the character of the contemporary international environment.[23]

Second, the conception should interpret human rights as "common" in a special sense, not as the area of agreement among all existing political doctrines or comprehensive views, but as principles for international affairs that could be accepted by reasonable persons who hold conflicting reasonable conceptions of the good life.

Here are some points of clarification. First, to say that international human rights compose a doctrine adopted for certain political purposes is to reject some traditional views about the character of human rights, such as those that interpret human rights as a contemporary restatement of the (or a) theory of natural law or natural rights, or as a statement of a single comprehensive view about political justice or the political good that is supposed to apply to all human societies at all times and places.[24] Human rights are standards intended to play a regulative role for a range of actors in the political circumstances of the contemporary world. Yet, to describe human rights doctrine as a "political construction" is not to say that human rights are unrelated to these other kinds of views: In adhering to the doctrine or in criticizing it, one might be moved by beliefs about natural law or natural rights or by a comprehensive conception of the good. But it would be an error to identify these more fundamental moral beliefs with a political doctrine of human rights.

Second, according to these precepts, the particulars of the public political role expected of human rights are essential to a comprehension and defense of the doctrine. I shall say more about this role below. For now the essential point is that human rights are meant for certain political purposes, and we cannot think intelligently about their content and reach without taking account of these purposes. I do not mean to say that one should accept uncritically the conception of the political role of human rights prevailing in international affairs any more than one should accept the details of prevailing views of their content. But criticism must begin with some conception of the practice being examined, and the contours of this practice are to be found in the doctrine of human rights as we have it in contemporary international life.

Third, the second precept states that human rights should be acceptable to reasonable persons, not peoples. This is possibly in contrast to Rawls, who writes of peoples as corporate wholes with more or less widely shared conventional moralities. I have discussed my doubts about this elsewhere (Beitz 2000) and here simply call attention to the possible contrast and note its importance in thinking about the content of the human rights doctrine. In my view, human rights are ultimately justified by considerations about the reasonable interests of individuals, not those of whole societies conceived as corporate entities.

A view of this kind is at odds with some traditional conceptions in distinguishing between human rights as a political doctrine and various underlying views about social justice. Why should we accept the revisionist view? Part of the answer is that, as a historical matter, international human rights doctrine is not accurately interpreted as an effort to fill the same conceptual space as was filled by natural law or natural rights in the Western political tradition. Those ideas aimed to supply something different – a comprehensive conception of the good or just society, perhaps, or an account of the constraints a government should observe in the use of its monopoly of political power. By contrast, the international doctrine is a negotiated agreement (or set of agreements) that describes "a common standard of achievement for all peoples and all nations" (Universal Declaration, Preamble), and it is meant to provide guidance in the conduct of international political life by actors such as international organizations and their member states, nongovernmental organizations, and individuals.

But the argument need not rest on a historical observation. Contemporary international society needs a doctrine of the kind imagined by the framers of the Universal Declaration. One reason, which Rawls notices, arises from the developing international capacity and disposition to intervene coercively in the affairs of states to protect the interests of their own people. Standards are needed to guide the use of this coercive power. As I have been urging, however, human rights doctrine serves other purposes as well. The most general, albeit awkward, statement of these purposes might be this. The global political structure contains an array of institutions and practices, including the foreign policies of states, with the capacity to influence the conditions of life for individuals in their domestic societies. In some cases this influence comes about through intentional action, such as military intervention or the attachment of political conditions to development aid. In other cases it occurs through the normal operation of an institution, such as structural assistance provided by international financial bodies. Moreover, as I have been emphasizing, transnational action that affects human rights is not limited to the operations of governments and international organizations; it may also be carried out by nongovernmental organizations, acting in international fora or within the internal political processes of individual societies. The doctrine of human rights is a statement of standards to guide the structures and conduct of global political life insofar as these bear on the conditions of life for individuals in their societies.

To be more specific, a doctrine of human rights suited for contemporary international practice should be capable of playing at least three kinds of roles. First, it constrains the domestic constitutions of states and the fundamental rules of international organizations and regimes. (Whether this constraint should operate by means of the embodiment of these norms in constitutions, organizational charters, and so forth, I take to be another question, one not settled by theoretical considerations.) Second, it describes goals for social development applicable to all contemporary societies, to the extent that they are or can be influenced by such external forces as the foreign policies of other states and the practices of international institutions. (The degree and kinds of influence appropriate in particular cases is again another question, involving both normative and pragmatic considerations.) Third (and derivatively), the doctrine furnishes grounds of political criticism to which it would be appropriate to appeal in the setting of global politics by a range of international and transnational actors – not only governments but also officials of international institutions and nongovernmental organizations acting in their capacity as citizens of global society.

On this view the doctrine of human rights is significantly teleological. It is a statement of aspiration applicable to all contemporary societies, but all of its requirements may not be capable of being satisfied simultaneously or in the short run. Human rights may not bear on political choice as straightforwardly as they would if conceived in more traditional terms as side constraints or prohibitions. The actions required to satisfy a human right will depend on the case. This is not only because achieving a given end may require different strategies in different settings, but also because priorities will have to be set and compromises reached when, in the short term, the effort to secure one right threatens to block efforts to secure another. Joel Feinberg (1973, 95) observed long ago that some rights of the declarations seem to be more accurately conceived as rights "in an unusual new 'manifesto sense' " than on the model of legal claim-rights.[25] The view I sketch here is compatible with this observation.

A Case Study: Political Rights

According to the formula I suggest, the doctrine of human rights is "common" in the sense that, considered in light of the political purposes it is expected to serve, reasonable persons could accept it despite differences in their reasonable conceptions of the good. Because this formulation depends from the outset on judgments about which conceptions to count as reasonable, its effect is to frame the question of the justification of human rights as a substantive problem of political theory, comparable to problems such as the justification of principles of social justice for domestic society. What distinguishes the problem about human rights from the others is the special character of the international political environment in which these standards must operate. Concerns regarding cultural parochialism or political bias would arise, if at all, within the substantive argument for each of its elements.

To illustrate, let me consider whether the doctrine of human rights should recognize a right to democratic institutions. The Covenant on Civil and Political Rights is unequivocal. It holds that there are human rights to political institutions that afford every citizen an opportunity to participate in public affairs either directly or through "freely chosen representatives"; to compete for public office and to vote in "genuine periodic elections"; and to assemble peaceably without restrictions "other than those . . . which are necessary in a democratic society in the interests of national security or public safety" (Arts. 21, 25). As a purely descriptive matter, there is no question that these requirements are nonneutral in the sense that they are not endorsed by all the major political moralities in the world. What is the ethical significance of this fact? Does it mean that we should not regard democratic rights as genuine human rights, or that we should not accept the defense or promotion of democratic rights as a justification for interference in a nondemocratic society's domestic life?

These questions are worth special attention because the element of international human rights doctrine most often said to be objectionably parochial is that concerned with democratic rights. At the same time, there is a discernible trend in international law toward recognition of a universal right to democratic institutions (Franck 1995, ch. 4). So these questions mark a specific point of tension between the restricted conception of human rights prevalent in philosophical thought and the development of international law and practice.

Consider a hypothetical case. Imagine an authoritarian regime in a society in which historically the predominant political beliefs are not democratic. Citing the Covenant on Civil and Political Rights, a modernizing insurgency fighting for democratic reforms calls upon the international community for military and financial help. Given the society's cultural history, international interference, if successful, would produce a result that would be regarded as a change for the worse by a significant portion, perhaps even a majority, of the society. The question is whether this fact argues against interference to help the reformers and, if so, for what reason.

One possible reply returns to the issue of paternalism. Interference in this kind of case, perhaps in contrast to most interferences to defend human rights, would be genuinely paternalistic: It involves coercive interference in some people's liberty on the grounds that the results would be in their own interests. But it would not be justified paternalism. Normally, the justification of a paternalistic choice has at least three elements: (1) a claim that the subject is unable to choose rationally for himself owing to a failure of reason or will; (2) evidence that the choice is guided by knowledge of the subject's own interests, to the extent they can be known, or by a reasonable conception of the interests it would be rational for the subject to have; and (3) a reasonable expectation that the subject will come to agree that the agent's choices on his behalf are the best that could be made under the circumstances.[26] In my example, because a significant portion or even a majority of the population does not share democratic political values, for this portion of the population the second element (and possibly the third) of the justification would fail. The interference does not appear to take seriously the moral beliefs of those whom it coerces.

This reply seems to me to yield the most plausible account of the ethical significance of the fact that many in our hypothetical society hold moral beliefs inconsistent with democracy. Yet, it is open to certain doubts. First, it may be questioned whether what I describe as people's "moral beliefs" accurately identify their political interests. This is primarily an empirical issue, and I have not worked out the case in enough detail to resolve it one way or the other. One would want to know, for example, about the nature of the evidence that

many people reject democratic values, whether the society has any past experience with democratic forms, and whether there have been occasions for public political deliberation about forms of government.

On one set of assumptions, the very fact that political institutions lack the features characteristic of democracy – such as free expression, political competition, voting – would suggest that preferences about political forms are not either fully informed or freely arrived at. In that case the justification of paternalistic interference must fall back on a judgment about what it would be rational for people to want if they were in possession of full information and able to reason freely, and here we have no choice but to engage the substantive question of the value of democracy. Telescoping a long argument, suppose there is reason to believe that democratic institutions are instrumental to the enjoyment of certain (nonpolitical) human rights, including the rights of the person and subsistence rights. Then, assuming these other rights are not themselves culturally controversial, there is an argument that it would be rational to want democratic rights as means of ensuring the satisfaction of urgent human interests, whatever the present political values in a culture.[27] (There is also the counterargument that some other configurations of political institutions, like Rawls's "decent consultation hierarchy," would be equally effective in securing human rights. Which is correct depends on a historical and political judgment, not an ethical one.)

Second, the reply considers only the perspective of the nondemocratic portion of the population. What about the democratic insurgents who asked for outside help? Again, one needs more information, but presumably the insurgency has local causes and responds to local grievances and aspirations. From the perspective of this group, interference is not a matter of paternalism at all but of avoiding or reducing harm or protecting against injustice. It is hard to see how this issue can be addressed other than by examining the urgency of the interests at stake in relation to the costs of interference and its probability of success. Once again, it seems that the justifiability of interference to support the democratic reformers should be faced as a free-standing issue in political ethics in which the values that interference may achieve are compared with the costs and risks of making the attempt. There is no categorical conclusion possible about the sufficiency of democratic reform as a justification of intervention in a case like this.

These reflections suggest an alternative explanation of the ethical significance of local disagreement over political values. It may be that this bears on the feasibility of constructive interference, or on its prospects of success in the long run, rather than on the nature or scope of human rights themselves. If a significant portion of the population lacks democratic sympathies, then it is not likely that democratic institutions will be sustained even if a democratic insurgency attains its immediate objectives. In that case it could be true both that there is a human right to democratic institutions and that interference in support of a prodemocratic insurgency would be wrong.

Why, then, should we say there is a right at all? If the acceptability of interference to promote democratic institutions effectively depends on the extent of democratic commitment within a culture, have we not conceded that there is no universal (and hence no human) right to democracy? The answer is that we have not. The question trades on the idea that there can be no right without a remedy, or no right without some feasible strategy for its realization. But the fact that intervention is unlikely to succeed in establishing democratic institutions in a divided political culture does not imply that nothing ever will; institutional change is a complex historical process, usually accompanied by changes in political belief as well. Moreover, a human right to democracy may have practical force otherwise than by licensing coercive intervention. For example, it might call for efforts at persuasion and education or support for the development of elements of a democratic social infrastructure (associations, labor unions, and so on). Of course, to accept this as a reply to the objection, one must accept a conception of a human right as something different from a legal right or certain moral rights; for example, although it may generate duties for various agents, a human right cannot always be a ground for insisting on immediate compliance. But if human rights are regarded as political constructions in the way I have described, this is unremarkable.

Conclusion

The discourse on international human rights suffers from a strange juxtaposition. In major arenas of international politics concerns about human rights are more prominently expressed than ever before, and there is some reason to believe that these concerns increasingly motivate action. Yet, within contemporary political thought human rights are often regarded with suspicion. These suspicions are diverse. Some people think there is no such thing as *universal* human rights (i.e., rights that may be claimed by anyone). Some think there is no such thing as universal *human* rights (possessed by human beings independently of their relationships with others and their institutional memberships). Some think that "internationally recognized human rights" are not *rights* (at least not in any sense that would be familiar to someone influenced by Hohfeld). Some think the international doctrine of human rights is a good idea corrupted by overextension: Although there may be such a thing as a universal human right, some (perhaps many) of the rights specifically enumerated in the international instruments fail to qualify. And some believe the doctrine of human rights is a cloak for liberal political values, an instance of partisanship rather than a neutral basis for global agreement.

I have only addressed the last of these suspicions directly, although I have adverted to some of the others. I have observed that the doctrine of human rights, regarded for the moment as part of the positive law of international society, cannot plausibly be considered culturally or politically nonpartisan. And I have argued that this fact, in itself, does not count against the doctrine. What is distinctive about human rights as a category of normative standard is not their supposedly symmetrical relationship to the conceptions of political justice or legitimacy to be found in the world's cultures but, rather, the role they play in international relations. Human rights state conditions for political and social institutions, the systematic violation of which may justify efforts to bring about reform by agents external to the society in which the violation occurs. This interference-justifying role may limit the content of the doctrine, but there is no reason to suppose the limitations will yield a neutral or nonpartisan view. Indeed, it is hard to see how things could be otherwise. In the words of the Vienna Declaration, human rights specify conditions that institutions should satisfy in order to respect "the dignity and worth inherent in the human person" (Preamble); but the concept of a person with inherent dignity and worth is a substantive moral idea and will almost certainly be more congenial to some than to other conceptions of justice or political good.

Is this kind of partisanship problematic for the doctrine? I believe not, provided that each of its elements can be defended by an appropriately general argument, as I suggest is possible for the right to democratic institutions. Such a defense would hold that human rights are "common" in a morally significant way without being, so to speak, empirically nonparochial. This, of course, is not to say that cultural and political differences do not come into deliberation about how to act. These differences may enter in a variety of ways – for example, as factors determining the feasibility and cost of a contemplated interference or the risks of collateral harm. They may also enter at a more basic level, as factors influencing a judgment about the rightness of using coercive means of interference, particularly when the purpose of the interference is genuinely paternalistic.

This conception of human rights faces a variety of objections. Here I note three of the most prominent and simply gesture at the kind of reply that might be offered to each. First, it may seem excessively pragmatic to regard human rights as a "political conception." Whatever else they are, human rights are surely moral standards, standards whose authority rests on recognizably moral considerations. To suggest otherwise, the objection holds, fails to take seriously both the character and the history of the idea of human rights. I believe, however, that the objection starts from a faulty premise. To say that the doctrine of human rights is a political conception is not to deny that its authority rests on moral considerations; human rights are political, not in the source of their authority, but in their role in public ethical life. As I have described them, human rights are standards to which it is reasonable to hold political institutions accountable in the processes of contemporary world politics. They operate as prima facie justifications of transnational (although not only transnational) political action aimed at bringing about change in the structure and operation of domestic (and international) institutions. Any account of the authority of human rights must take note of the political contexts in which they operate, but this hardly means that the account would exclude moral considerations; in fact, it would depend upon them.

Second, in some ways a contrasting objection is that a partisan conception of human rights is insufficiently realistic. According to this objection, unless a doctrine of human rights is culturally neutral it cannot possibly play the role that we need a doctrine of human rights to play in international affairs. The reason is that if a violation of human rights is not regarded as a shared basis for political action, then the capacity to enlist international support when it is most needed will deteriorate, and the doctrine of human rights will become little more than a sectarian hope. The latter proposition seems true enough, but the point about neutrality does not obviously follow from it. It is an empirical question whether a political doctrine must be neutral in order to enlist enough international support to be influential, a claim that not only has not been proved but also is most likely false. The growth of the global human rights regime itself may be evidence to the contrary.

Third, there is a residual worry that an expansive doctrine of human rights can too easily be used as an instrument of neocolonial domination, as a way to rationalize the use of coercion by a hegemonic power to advance its own interests. Of course, there is one sense in which this is a legitimate worry if not almost a necessary truth. If an expansive doctrine of human rights embraces liberal political values, and if the hegemonic power identifies its interests with the advance of these values, then coercion that is soundly justified by human rights considerations also will advance the interests of the hegemonic power. What troubles people, however, seems to be not this kind of case but one in which human rights considerations are abused or distorted in order to make self-interested political action seem to be justified by other-regarding considerations. The fear is that an expansive doctrine will be more open to this sort of abuse than a minimalist one.

This is not an abstract fear. The history of intervention (e.g., by the United States in Central America) includes many instances of what plausibly can be seen as analogous abuses of the values of self-government and individual liberty as rationales for self-interested interference. Let us therefore concede the hypothesis that an expansive doctrine is more open to abuse by a hegemonic power than a more narrowly drawn conception. What follows? Since we are conceiving of human rights as a public, political doctrine, it cannot be replied that the possibility of abuse is irrelevant to the content of the doctrine. If this possibility were significant, and if unilateral intervention were the only mechanism realistically available to promote human rights, then a narrowing of the doctrine's content might be appropriate. But there is an alternative: It is to establish multilateral institutions to protect human rights doctrine from unilateral abuse. This is one source of the argument for a world human rights court, and it may also argue for something like the complex voting system found in the Security Council, which otherwise might be seen as objectionably constrained by its supermajority requirements and the great-power veto. If such mechanisms can be made to work, the potential for neocolonial abuse of human rights doctrine will not by itself argue for a limitation of the doctrine's substantive scope.

All of this only gestures at how one might defend a more robust theory of human rights than that presumed by those who regard neutrality as a virtue, and one more in keeping with the doctrine of human rights found in contemporary international practice. Plainly, more needs to be said to develop such a defense and to explore the objections that could be brought against it. And plainly, that would be beyond the scope of a single article.

So I will conclude with an observation on a different although related point. The question of whether an expansive conception of international human rights can be defended is different from the question of whether we ought to accord human rights a fundamental place in international political theory. As a central element in international practice, human rights are well established, and political theorists should strive for a critical understanding that takes seriously their practical role. But there are good reasons to resist thinking of human rights as the fundamental terms of international political theory. For example, rights are rarely self-evident and usually stand in need of justification, and the justification seldom terminates in another assertion of right. And because the satisfaction of a right typically imposes costs on others, we need a mechanism for assigning responsibility for bearing those costs. In itself, however, the concept of a human right is not much help in designing such a mechanism because it is concerned with the interests of the beneficiary of the right rather than with the relationship in which the right is satisfied. For both reasons it seems likely that a satisfactory theory of human rights is better conceived as an aspect of a more general theory of global justice.

Notes

1 Notwithstanding, governments seem to acknowledge the court's authority, as the decision by the British government regarding the treatment of homosexuals in the military illustrates (*Financial Times* 1999). On the variety of roles played by human rights in intergovernmental relations, see, e.g., Forsythe (2000), pt. II; Vincent (1986), esp. chs. 4–6; and the case studies in Risse, Ropp, and Sikkink (1999).

2 The idea of a human rights culture derives from the Argentinean jurist Eduardo Rabossi (Rorty 1993: 115).

3 Precisely why this should be true is an interesting question. There is a provocative discussion that focuses on the growth of the European human rights regime in Moravcsik (2000).

4 In an article whose title ("Human Rights as a Neutral Concern") inspired the title of this paper, Scanlon (1979: 83) describes human rights as "a ground for action that is neutral with respect to the main political and economic divisions in the world" and as standards that "are not controversial in the way that other political and economic issues are." He does not suggest, as do some of the writers considered below, that human rights aspire to be neutral among all conceptions of justice or legitimacy. Rawls (1999a:

65, n. 4 and accompanying text) cites the Scanlon article as a source for the conception of human rights in *The Law of Peoples*.

5 Donnelly (1999: 81) characterizes human rights as "a distinctive, historically unusual set of social values and practices." Others who have espoused a liberal view of human rights include Waldron (1993, 10–24), Nino (1991, passim), and Rorty (1993). Needless to say, agreement about the scope of human rights can coexist with disagreement in other dimensions.

6 These agreements, as well as the Universal Declaration and the two covenants, are conveniently collected in Brownlie (1992).

7 See the analysis of contemporary sources of Islamic human rights law, including the 1981 Universal Islamic Declaration of Human Rights, in Mayer (1995), 95–6 and 117–18. On the extent of officially sanctioned human rights violations in the countries mentioned, see US Department of State (1999).

8 Welch (1995), 87–97. For the criticism that concern about FGM is ethnocentric, see the discussion by Tamir (1996) and the response by Kamm (1996).

9 See Sen 1999: 231–46, on Asian values, and An-Na'im (1990, ch. 7, esp. pp. 175–7), on gender in Islamic law. In general, compare Perry (1998), 76–8.

10 Compare Miller (1995), 74–5. There is an interestingly different view in Buchanan (1999), 52–6 and 59–60.

11 Similarly, Martin (1993, 75) believes human rights are principles that "would be regarded as reasonable by persons at different times or in different cultures. And such principles, again cross-culturally, would be thought to have connection... with a fairly wide range of differing conventional moralities."

12 In Walzer's (1994: 28–31) view, distributive justice generally is part of thick but not thin morality; see his suggestive and interesting remarks on "the cure of souls and the cure of bodies in the medieval and modern West."

13 The idea of an overlapping consensus is due to Rawls, but he does not use it in the analysis of human rights. See Nussbaum (1997: 286, and 1999, 37–9) and passim, for the application of this idea to human rights.

14 I think this is consistent with Scanlon 1979, but it does not seem to be consistent with his view in *What We Owe to Each Other* (1998, 348). The position taken there allows judgments about the (un)reasonableness of culturally influenced beliefs about value to enter into bottom-line judgments about right and wrong; there is no guarantee that these judgments would satisfy the condition in the text. The latter seems to me to be closer to the truth.

15 The point has often been noted. See, e.g., Nussbaum (1999: 10–12), and Scanlon (1979: 88).

16 Brown (1999: 119) claims to the contrary that "there are no general moral standards that apply" to "Bosnian Serbs who kill Bosnian Muslims" or "Muslim extremists who think that the death penalty is an appropriate response to apostasy" because in each case the agents do not believe the conduct in question is wrong. This cannot be right. The Bosnian Serbs who killed innocent civilians were wrong to do so, whether they accept this or not.

17 Freedom of religion can be considered a human right "proper," in Rawls's sense, only if its scope is interpreted more narrowly than what some believe to be the intent of Article 18 of the Universal Declaration. The human right to freedom of religion, as Rawls understands it, forbids the persecution of minority religions, but it allows for a state religion that enjoys various political privileges, such as public offices open only to its members (1999a: 65, n. 2), and the state religion may, "on some questions, be the ultimate authority within society and may control government policy on certain important matters" (p. 74).

18 In the political sphere, for example, a decent regime need not be democratic, but it must provide regular opportunities for all citizens to communicate their views and preferences to those authorized to make political decisions. Rawls (1999a: 64) calls such an arrangement a "decent consultation hierarchy." The details are complex, and I pass over them here.

19 I am grateful to Amy Gutmann for help in clarifying this thought.

20 The restriction to international political life is important. Rawls need not (and does not) claim that decency and justice are "on a par" for any other purpose.

21 I do not mean to say that Rawls himself gives such an account of human rights.

22 Thomas Pogge's comments on an earlier draft helped me formulate these precepts.

23 Jones (1996, 183–204) emphasizes the political character of Rawls's interpretation of human rights. Note, however, that Rawls (1999a: 81, n. 25) has reservations about this interpretation.

24 For example, Finnis (1980: 198) believes human rights are "a contemporary idiom" for natural rights (see pp. 210–30 for his view of the content and limits of the doctrine of international human rights).

25 Feinberg's use of "manifesto sense" is not, as some writers have thought, derisory; he endorses and expresses sympathy for this usage. It is also worth noting that one can accept the idea that some human rights are "manifesto rights" without also accepting Feinberg's view that it is not possible to assign corresponding duties to them. That, I believe, is a mistake.

26 I rely here on the discussion in *A Theory of Justice* (Rawls 1999b: 218–20).

27 The argument is made in Shue (1996: 74–8) and Sen (1999: 178–86). I made a similar argument about the value of democracy, concentrating on the circumstances of developing societies, in Beitz (1981: 177–208).

References

An-Na'im, Abdullahi (1990) *Toward an Islamic Reformation: Civil Liberties, Human Rights, and International Law*. Syracuse, NY: Syracuse University Press.

Beitz, Charles R. (1981) "Democracy in Developing Societies." In *Boundaries: National Autonomy and its Limits*, ed. Peter G. Brown and Henry Shue. Totowa, NJ: Rowman & Littlefield, pp. 177–208.

Beitz, Charles R. (2000) "Rawls's Law of Peoples." *Ethics* 110 (July): 669–96.

Best, Geoffrey (1995) "Justice, International Relations, and Human Rights." *International Affairs* 71 (October): 775–800.

Brown, Chris (1999) "Universal Human Rights: A Critique." In *Human Rights in Global Politics*, ed. Tim

Dunne and Nicholas J. Wheeler. Cambridge: Cambridge University Press, pp. 103–27.

Brownlie, Ian, ed. (1992) *Basic Documents on Human Rights*, 3rd ed. Oxford: Clarendon.

Buchanan, Allen (1999) "Recognitional Legitimacy." *Philosophy & Public Affairs* 28 (Winter): 52–6.

Buchanan, Allen (2000) "Rawls's Law of Peoples." *Ethics* 110 (July): 697–721.

Donnelly, Jack (1999) "The Social Construction of International Human Rights." In *Human Rights in Global Politics*, eds. Tim Dunne and Nicholas J. Wheeler. Cambridge: Cambridge University Press, pp. 71–102.

Feinberg, Joel (1973) *Social Philosophy*. Englewood Cliffs, NJ: Prentice-Hall.

Financial Times (1999) "Gays Win Case against Armed Services Ban." September 28, London ed., p. 16.

Finnis, John (1980) *Natural Law and Natural Rights*. Oxford: Clarendon.

Forsythe, David P. (2000) *Human Rights in International Relations*. Cambridge: Cambridge University Press.

Franck, Thomas M. (1995) *Fairness in International Law and Institutions*. Oxford: Clarendon.

Jones, Peter (1996) "International Human Rights: Philosophical or Political?" In *National Rights, International Obligations*, eds. Simon Caney, David George, and Peter Jones. Boulder, CO: Westview. pp. 183–204.

Kamm, F. M. (1996) "Is Body Intrusion Special?" *Boston Review* 21 (October/November). http://bostonreview.mit.edu/BR21.5/Kamm. html (accessed January 30, 2001).

Kausikan, Bilahari (1993) "Asia's Different Standard." *Foreign Policy* 92 (Fall): 24–51.

Korey, William (1998) *NGOs and the Universal Declaration of Human Rights: "A Curious Grapevine."* New York: St. Martin's.

Lauren, Paul Gordon (1998) *The Evolution of International Human Rights: Visions Seen*. Philadelphia: University of Pennsylvania Press.

Martin, Rex (1993) *A System of Rights*. Oxford: Clarendon.

Mayer, Ann Elizabeth (1995) *Islam and Human Rights: Tradition and Politics*, 2nd. ed. Boulder, CO: Westview.

Miller, David (1995) *On Nationality*. Oxford: Oxford University Press.

Moravcsik, Andrew (2000) "The Origins of International Human Rights Regimes: Democratic Delegation in Postwar Europe." *International Organization* 54 (Spring): 217–52.

Nino, Carlos Santiago (1991) *The Ethics of Human Rights*. Oxford: Clarendon.

Nussbaum, Martha (1997) "Human Rights Theory: Capability and Human Rights." *Fordham Law Review* 66 (November): 273–300.

Nussbaum, Martha (1999) "In Defense of Universal Values." *The Fifth Annual Hesburgh Lectures on Ethics and Public Policy*. Notre Dame, IN: Joan B. Kroc Institute for International Peace Studies at the University of Notre Dame.

Perry, Michael J. (1998) *The Idea of Human Rights*. New York: Oxford University Press.

Rawls, John (1999a) *The Law of Peoples*. Cambridge, MA: Harvard University Press.

Rawls, John (1999b) *A Theory of Justice*, rev. ed. Cambridge, MA: Harvard University Press.

Risse, Thomas, Stephen C. Ropp, and Kathryn Sikkink, eds. (1999) *The Power of Human Rights*. Cambridge: Cambridge University Press.

Rorty, Richard (1993) "Human Rights, Rationality, and Sentimentality." In *On Human Rights: The Oxford Amnesty Lectures 1993*, eds. Stephen Shute and Susan Hurley. New York: Basic Books, pp. 111–34.

Scanlon, T. M. (1979) "Human Rights as a Neutral Concern." In *Human Rights and U.S. Foreign Policy*, ed. Peter G. Brown and Douglas MacLean. Lexington, MA: Lexington Books, pp. 83–92.

Scanlon, T. M. (1998) *What We Owe to Each Other*. Cambridge, MA: Harvard University Press.

Sen, Amartya (1999) *Development as Freedom*. New York: Alfred A. Knopf.

Shue, Henry (1996) *Basic Rights: Subsistence, Affluence, and US Foreign Policy*, 2d ed. Princeton, NJ: Princeton University Press.

Tamir, Yael (1996) "Hands Off Clitoridectomy: What Our Revulsion Reveals about Ourselves." *Boston Review* 21 (Summer). http://bostonreview.mit.edu/BR21.3/Tamir.html (accessed January 30, 2001).

Téson, Fernando (1994) "Some Observations on John Rawls's 'The Law of Peoples.' " *American Society of International Law Proceedings* 88: 18–22.

United Nations (1993) "Vienna Declaration and Programme of Action." World Conference on Human Rights. UN Doc. A/CONF.157/23 (July 12).

US Department of State (1999) *Country Reports on Human Rights Practices for 1998: Near East and North Africa*. February 29. http://www.state.gov/www/global/human_rights/1998_hrp_report/98hrp_report_-nea.html (accessed January 30, 2001).

Vincent, R. J. (1986) *Human Rights and International Relations*. Cambridge: Cambridge University Press.

Waldron, Jeremy (1993) *Liberal Rights: Collected Papers 1981–1991*. Cambridge: Cambridge University Press.

Walzer, Michael (1994) *Thick and Thin: Moral Argument at Home and Abroad*. Notre Dame, IN: University of Notre Dame Press.

Welch, Claude E. (1995) *Protecting Human Rights in Africa: Roles and Strategies of Nongovernmental Organizations*. Philadelphia: University of Pennsylvania Press.

PART V

Liberty

24

Two Concepts of Liberty

Isaiah Berlin

. . .

To coerce a man is to deprive him of freedom – freedom from what? Almost every moralist in human history has praised freedom. Like happiness and goodness, like nature and reality, the meaning of this term is so porous that there is little interpretation that it seems able to resist. I do not propose to discuss either the history or the more than two hundred senses of this protean word recorded by historians of ideas. I propose to examine no more than two of these senses – but those central ones, with a great deal of human history behind them, and, I dare say, still to come. The first of these political senses of freedom or liberty (I shall use both words to mean the same), which (following much precedent) I shall call the 'negative' sense, is involved in the answer to the question 'What is the area within which the subject – a person or group of persons – is or should be left to do or be what he is able to do or be, without interference by other persons?' The second, which I shall call the positive sense, is involved in the answer to the question 'What, or who, is the source of control or interference that can determine someone to do, or be, this rather than that?' The two questions are clearly different, even though the answers to them may overlap.

I The Notion of 'Negative' Freedom

I am normally said to be free to the degree to which no man or body of men interferes with my activity. Political liberty in this sense is simply the area within which a man can act unobstructed by others. If I am prevented by others from doing what I could otherwise do, I am to that degree unfree; and if this area is contracted by other men beyond a certain minimum, I can be described as being coerced, or, it may be, enslaved. Coercion is not, however, a term that covers every form of inability. If I say that I am unable to jump more than ten feet in the air, or cannot read because I am blind, or cannot understand the darker pages of Hegel, it would be eccentric to say that I am to that degree enslaved or coerced. Coercion implies the deliberate interference of other human beings within the area in which I could otherwise act. You lack political liberty or freedom only if you are prevented from attaining a goal by human beings.[1] Mere incapacity to attain a goal is not lack of political freedom.[2] This is brought out by the use of such modern expressions as 'economic freedom' and its counterpart, 'economic slavery'. It is argued, very plausibly, that if a man is too

Originally published in *Four Essays on Liberty* (Oxford: Clarendon Press, 1969), pp. 121–54, 169–72.

poor to afford something on which there is no legal ban – a loaf of bread, a journey round the world, recourse to the law courts – he is as little free to have it as he would be if it were forbidden him by law. If my poverty were a kind of disease, which prevented me from buying bread, or paying for the journey round the world or getting my case heard, as lameness prevents me from running, this inability would not naturally be described as a lack of freedom, least of all political freedom. It is only because I believe that my inability to get a given thing is due to the fact that other human beings have made arrangements whereby I am, whereas others are not, prevented from having enough money with which to pay for it, that I think myself a victim of coercion or slavery. In other words, this use of the term depends on a particular social and economic theory about the causes of my poverty or weakness. If my lack of material means is due to my lack of mental or physical capacity, then I begin to speak of being deprived of freedom (and not simply about poverty) only if I accept the theory[3] If, in addition, I believe that I am being kept in want by a specific arrangement which I consider unjust or unfair, I speak of economic slavery or oppression. 'The nature of things does not madden us, only ill will does', said Rousseau. The criterion of oppression is the part that I believe to be played by other human beings, directly or indirectly, with or without the intention of doing so, in frustrating my wishes. By being free in this sense I mean not being interfered with by others. The wider the area of non-interference the wider my freedom.

This is what the classical English political philosophers meant when they used this word.[4] They disagreed about how wide the area could or should be. They supposed that it could not, as things were, be unlimited, because if it were, it would entail a state in which all men could boundlessly interfere with all other men; and this kind of 'natural' freedom would lead to social chaos in which men's minimum needs would not be satisfied; or else the liberties of the weak would be suppressed by the strong. Because they perceived that human purposes and activities do not automatically harmonize with one another, and because (whatever their official doctrines) they put high value on other goals, such as justice, or happiness, or culture, or security, or varying degrees of equality, they were prepared to curtail freedom in the interests of other values and, indeed, of freedom itself. For, without this, it was impossible to create the kind of association that they thought desirable.

Consequently, it is assumed by these thinkers that the area of men's free action must be limited by law. But equally it is assumed, especially by such libertarians as Locke and Mill in England, and Constant and Tocqueville in France, that there ought to exist a certain minimum area of personal freedom which must on no account be violated; for if it is overstepped, the individual will find himself in an area too narrow for even that minimum development of his natural faculties which alone makes it possible to pursue, and even to conceive, the various ends which men hold good or right or sacred. It follows that a frontier must be drawn between the area of private life and that of public authority. Where it is to be drawn is a matter of argument, indeed of haggling. Men are largely interdependent, and no man's activity is so completely private as never to obstruct the lives of others in any way. 'Freedom for the pike is death for the minnows'; the liberty of some must depend on the restraint of others. 'Freedom for an Oxford don', others have been known to add, 'is a very different thing from freedom for an Egyptian peasant.'

This proposition derives its force from something that is both true and important, but the phrase itself remains a piece of political claptrap. It is true that to offer political rights, or safeguards against intervention by the state, to men who are half-naked, illiterate, underfed, and diseased is to mock their condition; they need medical help or education before they can understand, or make use of, an increase in their freedom. What is freedom to those who cannot make use of it? Without adequate conditions for the use of freedom, what is the value of freedom? First things come first: there are situations, as a nineteenth-century Russian radical writer declared, in which boots are superior to the works of Shakespeare; individual freedom is not everyone's primary need. For freedom is not the mere absence of frustration of whatever kind; this would inflate the meaning of the word until it meant too much or too little. The Egyptian peasant needs clothes or medicine before, and more than, personal liberty, but the minimum freedom that he needs today, and the greater degree of freedom that he may need tomorrow, is not some species of freedom peculiar to him, but identical with that of professors, artists, and millionaires.

What troubles the consciences of Western liberals is not, I think, the belief that the freedom that men seek differs according to their social or economic conditions, but that the minority who possess it have gained it by exploiting, or, at least, averting their gaze from, the vast majority who do not. They believe, with good reason, that if individual liberty is an ultimate end for human beings, none should be deprived of it by others; least of all that some should enjoy it at the expense of others. Equality of liberty; not to treat others as I should not wish them to treat me; repayment of my debt to those who alone have made possible my liberty or prosperity or enlightenment; justice, in its simplest and most universal sense – these are the foundations of liberal morality. Liberty is not the only goal of men. I can, like the Russian critic Belinsky, say that if others are to be deprived of it – if my brothers are to remain in poverty, squalor, and chains – then I do not want it for myself, I reject it with both hands and infinitely prefer to share their fate. But nothing is gained by a confusion of terms. To avoid glaring inequality or widespread misery I am ready to sacrifice some, or all, of my freedom: I may do so willingly and freely: but it is freedom that I am giving up for the sake of justice or equality or the love of my fellow men. I should be guilt-stricken, and rightly so, if I were not, in some circumstances, ready to make this sacrifice. But a sacrifice is not an increase in what is being sacrificed, namely freedom, however great the moral need or the compensation for it. Everything is what it is: liberty is liberty, not equality or fairness or justice or culture, or human happiness or a quiet conscience. If the liberty of myself or my class or nation depends on the misery of a number of other human beings, the system which promotes this is unjust and immoral. But if I curtail or lose my freedom, in order to lessen the shame of such inequality, and do not thereby materially increase the individual liberty of others, an absolute loss of liberty occurs. This may be compensated for by a gain in justice or in happiness or in peace, but the loss remains, and it is a confusion of values to say that although my 'liberal', individual freedom may go by the board, some other kind of freedom – 'social' or 'economic' – is increased. Yet it remains true that the freedom of some must at times be curtailed to secure the freedom of others. Upon what principle should this be done? If freedom is a sacred, untouchable value, there can be no such principle. One or other of these conflicting rules or principles must, at any rate in practice, yield: not always for reasons which can be clearly stated, let alone generalized into rules or universal maxims. Still, a practical compromise has to be found.

Philosophers with an optimistic view of human nature and a belief in the possibility of harmonizing human interests, such as Locke or Adam Smith and, in some moods, Mill, believed that social harmony and progress were compatible with reserving a large area for private life over which neither the state nor any other authority must be allowed to trespass. Hobbes, and those who agreed with him, especially conservative or reactionary thinkers, argued that if men were to be prevented from destroying one another and making social life a jungle or a wilderness, greater safeguards must be instituted to keep them in their places; he wished correspondingly to increase the area of centralized control and decrease that of the individual. But both sides agreed that some portion of human existence must remain independent of the sphere of social control. To invade that preserve, however small, would be despotism. The most eloquent of all defenders of freedom and privacy, Benjamin Constant, who had not forgotten the Jacobin dictatorship, declared that at the very least the liberty of religion, opinion, expression, property, must be guaranteed against arbitrary invasion. Jefferson, Burke, Paine, Mill, compiled different catalogues of individual liberties, but the argument for keeping authority at bay is always substantially the same. We must preserve a minimum area of personal freedom if we are not to 'degrade or deny our nature'. We cannot remain absolutely free, and must give up some of our liberty to preserve the rest. But total self-surrender is self-defeating. What then must the minimum be? That which a man cannot give up without offending against the essence of his human nature. What is this essence? What are the standards which it entails? This has been, and perhaps always will be, a matter of infinite debate. But whatever the principle in terms of which the area of non-interference is to be drawn, whether it is that of natural law or natural rights, or of utility or the pronouncements of a categorical imperative, or the sanctity of the social contract, or any other concept with which men have sought to clarify and justify their convictions, liberty in this sense means liberty *from*; absence of interference beyond the shifting, but always recognizable, frontier. 'The only freedom which deserves the name is that of pursuing our own good in our own way', said the most celebrated of its champions. If this is so, is compulsion ever justified? Mill had no doubt that it was. Since justice demands that all individuals be entitled to a minimum of freedom, all other individuals were of necessity to be restrained, if need be by force, from depriving anyone of it. Indeed, the whole function of law was the prevention of just such collisions: the state was reduced to what Lassalle contemptuously described as the functions of a night-watchman or traffic policeman.

What made the protection of individual liberty so sacred to Mill? In his famous essay he declares that, unless men are left to live as they wish 'in the path which merely concerns themselves', civilization cannot advance; the truth will not, for lack of a free market in ideas, come to light; there will be no scope for spontaneity, originality, genius, for mental energy, for moral courage. Society will be crushed by the weight of 'collective mediocrity'. Whatever is rich and diversified will be crushed by the weight of custom, by men's constant tendency to conformity, which breeds only 'withered capacities', 'pinched and hidebound', 'cramped and warped' human beings. 'Pagan self-assertion is as worthy as Christian self-denial.' 'All the errors which a man is likely to commit against advice and warning are far outweighed by the evil of allowing others to constrain him to what they deem is good.' The defence of liberty consists in the 'negative' goal of warding off interference. To threaten a man with persecution unless he submits to a life in which he exercises no choices of his goals; to block before him every door but one, no matter how noble the prospect upon which it opens, or how benevolent the motives of those who arrange this, is to sin against the truth that he is a man, a being with a life of his own to live. This is liberty as it has been conceived by liberals in the modern world from the days of Erasmus (some would say of Occam) to our own. Every plea for civil liberties and individual rights, every protest against exploitation and humiliation, against the encroachment of public authority, or the mass hypnosis of custom or organized propaganda, springs from this individualistic, and much disputed, conception of man.

Three facts about this position may be noted. In the first place Mill confuses two distinct notions. One is that all coercion is, in so far as it frustrates human desires, bad as such, although it may have to be applied to prevent other, greater evils; while non-interference, which is the opposite of coercion, is good as such, although it is not the only good. This is the 'negative' conception of liberty in its classical form. The other is that men should seek to discover the truth, or to develop a certain type of character of which Mill approved – critical, original, imaginative, independent, non-conforming to the point of eccentricity, and so on – and

that truth can be found, and such character can be bred, only in conditions of freedom. Both these are liberal views, but they are not identical, and the connexion between them is, at best, empirical. No one would argue that truth or freedom of self-expression could flourish where dogma crushes all thought. But the evidence of history tends to show (as, indeed, was argued by James Stephen in his formidable attack on Mill in his *Liberty, Equality, Fraternity*) that integrity, love of truth, and fiery individualism grow at least as often in severely disciplined communities among, for example, the puritan Calvinists of Scotland or New England, or under military discipline, as in more tolerant or indifferent societies; and if this is so, Mill's argument for liberty as a necessary condition for the growth of human genius falls to the ground. If his two goals proved incompatible, Mill would be faced with a cruel dilemma, quite apart from the further difficulties created by the inconsistency of his doctrines with strict utilitarianism, even in his own humane version of it.[5]

In the second place, the doctrine is comparatively modern. There seems to be scarcely any discussion of individual liberty as a conscious political ideal (as opposed to its actual existence) in the ancient world. Condorcet had already remarked that the notion of individual rights was absent from the legal conceptions of the Romans and Greeks; this seems to hold equally of the Jewish, Chinese, and all other ancient civilizations that have since come to light.[6] The domination of this ideal has been the exception rather than the rule, even in the recent history of the West. Nor has liberty in this sense often formed a rallying cry for the great masses of mankind. The desire not to be impinged upon, to be left to oneself, has been a mark of high civilization both on the part of individuals and communities. The sense of privacy itself, of the area of personal relationships as something sacred in its own right, derives from a conception of freedom which, for all its religious roots, is scarcely older, in its developed state, than the Renaissance or the Reformation.[7] Yet its decline would mark the death of a civilization, of an entire moral outlook.

The third characteristic of this notion of liberty is of greater importance. It is that liberty in this sense is not incompatible with some kinds of autocracy, or at any rate with the absence of self-government. Liberty in this sense is principally concerned with the area of control, not with its source. Just as a democracy may, in fact, deprive the individual citizen of a great many liberties which he might have in some other form of society, so it is perfectly conceivable that a liberal-minded despot would allow his subjects a large measure of personal freedom. The despot who leaves his subjects a wide area of liberty may be unjust, or encourage the wildest inequalities, care little for order, or virtue, or knowledge; but provided he does not curb their liberty, or at least curbs it less than many other régimes, he meets with Mill's specification.[8] Freedom in this sense is not, at any rate logically, connected with democracy or self-government. Self-government may, on the whole, provide a better guarantee of the preservation of civil liberties than other régimes, and has been defended as such by libertarians. But there is no necessary connexion between individual liberty and democratic rule. The answer to the question 'Who governs me?' is logically distinct from the question 'How far does government interfere with me?' It is in this difference that the great contrast between the two concepts of negative and positive liberty, in the end, consists.[9] For the 'positive' sense of liberty comes to light if we try to answer the question, not 'What am I free to do or be?', but 'By whom am I ruled?' or 'Who is to say what I am, and what I am not, to be or do?' The connexion between democracy and individual liberty is a good deal more tenuous than it seemed to many advocates of both. The desire to be governed by myself, or at any rate to participate in the process by which my life is to be controlled, may be as deep a wish as that of a free area for action, and perhaps historically older. But it is not a desire for the same thing. So different is it, indeed, as to have led in the end to the great clash of ideologies that dominates our world. For it is this – the 'positive' conception of liberty: not freedom from, but freedom to – to lead one prescribed form of life – which the adherents of the 'negative' notion represent as being, at times, no better than a specious disguise for brutal tyranny.

II   The Notion of Positive Freedom

The 'positive' sense of the word 'liberty' derives from the wish on the part of the individual to be his own master. I wish my life and decisions to depend on myself, not on external forces of whatever kind. I wish to be the instrument of my own, not of other men's, acts of will. I wish to be a subject, not an object; to be moved by reasons, by conscious purposes, which are my own, not by causes which affect me, as it were, from outside. I wish to be somebody, not nobody; a doer – deciding, not being decided for, self-directed and not acted upon by external nature or by other men as if I were a thing, or an animal, or a slave incapable of playing a human role, that is, of conceiving goals and policies of my own and realizing them. This is at least part of what I mean when I say that I am rational, and that it is my reason that distinguishes me as a human being from the rest of the world. I wish, above all, to be conscious of myself as a thinking, willing, active being, bearing responsibility for my choices and able to explain them by references to my own ideas and purposes. I feel free to the degree that I believe this to be true, and enslaved to the degree that I am made to realize that it is not.

The freedom which consists in being one's own master, and the freedom which consists in not being prevented from choosing as I do by other men, may, on the face of it, seem concepts at no great logical distance from each other – no more than negative and positive ways of saying much the same thing. Yet the 'positive' and 'negative' notions of freedom historically developed in divergent directions not always by logically reputable steps, until, in the end, they came into direct conflict with each other.

One way of making this clear is in terms of the independent momentum which the, initially perhaps quite harmless, metaphor of self-mastery acquired. 'I am my own master'; 'I am slave to no man'; but may I not (as Platonists or Hegelians tend to say) be a slave to nature? Or to my own 'unbridled' passions? Are these not so many species of the identical genus 'slave' – some political or legal, others moral or spiritual? Have not men had the experience of liberating themselves from spiritual slavery, or slavery to nature, and do they not in the course of it become aware, on the one hand, of a self which dominates, and, on the other, of something in them which is brought to heel? This dominant self is then variously identified with reason, with my 'higher nature', with the self which calculates and aims at what will satisfy it in the long run, with my 'real', or 'ideal', or 'autonomous' self, or with my self 'at its best'; which is then contrasted with irrational impulse, uncontrolled desires, my 'lower' nature, the pursuit of immediate pleasures, my 'empirical' or 'heteronomous' self, swept by every gust of desire and passion, needing to be rigidly disciplined if it is ever to rise to the full height of its 'real' nature. Presently the two selves may be represented as divided by an even larger gap: the real self may be conceived as something wider than the individual (as the term is normally understood), as a social 'whole' of which the individual is an element or aspect: a tribe, a race, a church, a state, the great society of the living and the dead and the yet unborn. This entity is then identified as being the 'true' self which, by imposing its collective, or 'organic', single will upon its recalcitrant 'members', achieves its own, and therefore their, 'higher' freedom. The perils of using organic metaphors to justify the coercion of some men by others in order to raise them to a 'higher' level of freedom have often been pointed out. But what gives such plausibility as it has to this kind of language is that we recognize that it is possible, and at times justifiable, to coerce men in the name of some goal (let us say, justice or public health) which they would, if they were more enlightened, themselves pursue, but do not, because they are blind or ignorant or corrupt. This renders it easy for me to conceive of myself as coercing others for their own sake, in their, not my, interest. I am then claiming that I know what they truly need better than they know it themselves. What, at most, this entails is that they would not resist me if they were rational and as wise as I and understood their interests as I do. But I may go on to claim a good deal more than this. I may declare that they are actually aiming at what in their benighted state they consciously resist, because there exists within them an occult entity – their latent rational will, or their 'true' purpose – and that this entity, although it is belied by all that they overtly feel and do and say, is their 'real' self, of which the poor empirical self in space and time may know nothing or little; and that this inner spirit is the only self that deserves to have its wishes taken into account.[10] Once I take this view, I am in a position to ignore the actual wishes of men or societies, to bully, oppress, torture them in the name, and on behalf, of their 'real' selves, in the secure knowledge that whatever is the true goal of man (happiness, performance of duty, wisdom, a just society, self-fulfilment) must be identical with his freedom – the free choice of his 'true', albeit often submerged and inarticulate, self.

This paradox has been often exposed. It is one thing to say that I know what is good for X, while he himself does not; and even to ignore his wishes for its – and his – sake; and a very different one to say that he has *eo ipso* chosen it, not indeed consciously, not as he seems in everyday life, but in his role as a rational self which his empirical self may not know – the 'real' self which discerns the

good, and cannot help choosing it once it is revealed. This monstrous impersonation, which consists in equating what X would choose if he were something he is not, or at least not yet, with what X actually seeks and chooses, is at the heart of all political theories of self-realization. It is one thing to say that I may be coerced for my own good which I am too blind to see: this may, on occasion, be for my benefit; indeed it may enlarge the scope of my liberty. It is another to say that if it is my good, then I am not being coerced, for I have willed it, whether I know this or not, and am free (or 'truly' free) even while my poor earthly body and foolish mind bitterly reject it, and struggle against those who seek however benevolently to impose it, with the greatest desperation.

This magical transformation, or sleight of hand (for which William James so justly mocked the Hegelians), can no doubt be perpetrated just as easily with the 'negative' concept of freedom, where the self that should not be interfered with is no longer the individual with his actual wishes and needs as they are normally conceived, but the 'real' man within, identified with the pursuit of some ideal purpose not dreamed of by his empirical self. And, as in the case of the 'positively' free self, this entity may be inflated into some superpersonal entity – a state, a class, a nation, or the march of history itself, regarded as a more 'real' subject of attributes than the empirical self. But the 'positive' conception of freedom as self-mastery, with its suggestion of a man divided against himself, has, in fact, and as a matter of history, of doctrine and of practice, lent itself more easily to this splitting of personality into two: the transcendent, dominant controller, and the empirical bundle of desires and passions to be disciplined and brought to heel. It is this historical fact that has been influential. This demonstrates (if demonstration of so obvious a truth is needed) that conceptions of freedom directly derive from views of what constitutes a self, a person, a man. Enough manipulation with the definition of man, and freedom can be made to mean whatever the manipulator wishes. Recent history has made it only too clear that the issue is not merely academic.

The consequences of distinguishing between two selves will become even clearer if one considers the two major forms which the desire to be self-directed – directed by one's 'true' self – has historically taken: the first, that of self-abnegation in order to attain independence; the second, that of self-realization, or total self-identification with a specific principle or ideal in order to attain the selfsame end.

III The Retreat to the Inner Citadel

I am the possessor of reason and will; I conceive ends and I desire to pursue them; but if I am prevented from attaining them I no longer feel master of the situation. I may be prevented by the laws of nature, or by accidents, or the activities of men, or the effect, often undesigned, of human institutions. These forces may be too much for me. What am I to do to avoid being crushed by them? I must liberate myself from desires that I know I cannot realize. I wish to be master of my kingdom, but my frontiers are long and insecure, therefore I contract them in order to reduce or eliminate the vulnerable area. I begin by desiring happiness, or power, or knowledge, or the attainment of some specific object. But I cannot command them. I choose to avoid defeat and waste, and therefore decide to strive for nothing that I cannot be sure to obtain. I determine myself not to desire what is unattainable. The tyrant threatens me with the destruction of my property, with imprisonment, with the exile or death of those I love. But if I no longer feel attached to property, no longer care whether or not I am in prison, if I have killed within myself my natural affections, then he cannot bend me to his will, for all that is left of myself is no longer subject to empirical fears or desires. It is as if I had performed a strategic retreat into an inner citadel – my reason, my soul, my 'noumenal' self – which, do what they may, neither external blind force, nor human malice, can touch. I have withdrawn into myself; there, and there alone, I am secure. It is as if I were to say: 'I have a wound in my leg. There are two methods of freeing myself from pain. One is to heal the wound. But if the cure is too difficult or uncertain, there is another method. I can get rid of the wound by cutting off my leg. If I train myself to want nothing to which the possession of my leg is indispensable, I shall not feel the lack of it.' This is the traditional self-emancipation of ascetics and quietists, of stoics or Buddhist sages, men of various religions or of none, who have fled the world, and escaped the yoke of society or public opinion, by some process of deliberate self-transformation that enables them to care no longer for any of its values, to remain, isolated and independent, on its edges, no longer vulnerable to its weapons.[11] All political isolation-

ism, all economic autarky, every form of autonomy, has in it some element of this attitude. I eliminate the obstacles in my path by abandoning the path; I retreat into my own sect, my own planned economy, my own deliberately insulated territory, where no voices from outside need be listened to, and no external forces can have effect. This is a form of the search for security; but it has also been called the search for personal or national freedom or independence.

From this doctrine, as it applies to individuals, it is no very great distance to the conceptions of those who, like Kant, identify freedom not indeed with the elimination of desires, but with resistance to them, and control over them. I identify myself with the controller and escape the slavery of the controlled. I am free because, and in so far as, I am autonomous. I obey laws, but I have imposed them on, or found them in, my own uncoerced self. Freedom is obedience, but 'obedience to a law which we prescribe to ourselves', and no man can enslave himself. Heteronomy is dependence on outside factors, liability to be a plaything of the external world that I cannot myself fully control, and which *pro tanto* controls and 'enslaves' me. I am free only to the degree to which my person is 'fettered' by nothing that obeys forces over which I have no control; I cannot control the laws of nature; my free activity must therefore, *ex hypothesi*, be lifted above the empirical world of causality. This is not the place in which to discuss the validity of this ancient and famous doctrine; I only wish to remark that the related notions of freedom as resistance to (or escape from) unrealizable desire, and as independence of the sphere of causality, have played a central role in politics no less than in ethics.

For if the essence of men is that they are autonomous beings – authors of values, of ends in themselves, the ultimate authority of which consists precisely in the fact that they are willed freely – then nothing is worse than to treat them as if they were not autonomous, but natural objects, played on by causal influences, creatures at the mercy of external stimuli, whose choices can be manipulated by their rulers, whether by threats of force or offers of rewards. To treat men in this way is to treat them as if they were not self-determined. 'Nobody may compel me to be happy in his own way', said Kant. 'Paternalism is the greatest despotism imaginable.' This is so because it is to treat men as if they were not free, but human material for me, the benevolent reformer, to mould in accordance with my own, not their, freely adopted purpose. This is, of course, precisely the policy that the early utilitarians recommended. Helvétius (and Bentham) believed not in resisting, but in using, men's tendency to be slaves to their passions; they wished to dangle rewards and punishments before men – the acutest possible form of heteronomy – if by this means the 'slaves' might be made happier.[12] But to manipulate men, to propel them towards goals which you – the social reformer – see, but they may not, is to deny their human essence, to treat them as objects without wills of their own, and therefore to degrade them. That is why to lie to men, or to deceive them, that is, to use them as means for my, not their own, independently conceived ends, even if it is for their own benefit, is, in effect, to treat them as sub-human, to behave as if their ends are less ultimate and sacred than my own. In the name of what can I ever be justified in forcing men to do what they have not willed or consented to? Only in the name of some value higher than themselves. But if, as Kant held, all values are made so by the free acts of men, and called values only so far as they are this, there is no value higher than the individual. Therefore to do this is to coerce men in the name of something less ultimate than themselves – to bend them to my will, or to someone else's particular craving for (his or their) happiness or expediency or security or convenience. I am aiming at something desired (from whatever motive, no matter how noble) by me or my group, to which I am using other men as means. But this is a contradiction of what I know men to be, namely ends in themselves. All forms of tampering with human beings, getting at them, shaping them against their will to your own pattern, all thought control and conditioning,[13] is, therefore, a denial of that in men which makes them men and their values ultimate.

Kant's free individual is a transcendent being, beyond the realm of natural causality. But in its empirical form – in which the notion of man is that of ordinary life – this doctrine was the heart of liberal humanism, both moral and political, that was deeply influenced both by Kant and by Rousseau in the eighteenth century. In its *a priori* version it is a form of secularized Protestant individualism, in which the place of God is taken by the conception of the rational life, and the place of the individual soul which strains towards union with Him is replaced by the conception of the individual, endowed with reason, straining to be governed by reason and reason alone, and to depend upon nothing that might deflect or delude him by engaging his irrational nature. Autonomy, not heteronomy: to act and not to be acted upon. The notion of slavery to the passions is – for those who think in these terms – more than a metaphor. To rid myself of fear, or love, or the desire to conform is to liberate myself from the despotism of something which I cannot control. Sophocles, whom Plato reports as saying that old age alone has liberated him from the passion of love – the yoke of a cruel master – is reporting an experience as real as that of liberation from a human tyrant or slave owner. The psychological experience of observing myself yielding to some 'lower' impulse, acting from a motive that I dislike, or of doing something which at the very moment of doing I may detest, and reflecting later that I was 'not myself', or 'not in control of myself', when I did it, belongs to this way of thinking and speaking. I identify myself with my critical and rational moments. The consequences of my acts cannot matter, for they are not in my control; only my motives are. This is the creed of the solitary thinker who has defied the world and emancipated himself from the chains of men and things. In this form, the doctrine may seem primarily an ethical creed, and scarcely political at all; nevertheless, its political implications are clear, and it enters into the tradition of liberal individualism at least as deeply as the 'negative' concept of freedom.

It is perhaps worth remarking that in its individualistic form the concept of the rational sage who has escaped into the inner fortress of his true self seems to arise when the external world has proved exceptionally arid, cruel, or unjust. 'He is truly free', said Rousseau, 'who desires what he can perform, and does what he desires.' In a world where a man seeking happiness or justice or freedom (in whatever sense) can do little, because he finds too many avenues of action blocked to him, the temptation to withdraw into himself may become irresistible. It may have been so in Greece, where the Stoic ideal cannot be wholly unconnected with the fall of the independent democracies before centralized Macedonian autocracy. It was so in Rome, for analogous reasons, after the end of the Republic.[14] It arose in Germany in the seventeenth century, during the period of the deepest national degradation of the German states that followed the Thirty Years War, when the character of public life, particularly in the small principalities, forced those who prized the dignity of human life, not for the first or last time, into a kind of inner emigration. The doctrine that maintains that what I cannot have I must teach myself not to desire; that a desire eliminated, or successfully resisted, is as good as a desire satisfied, is a sublime, but, it seems to me, unmistakable, form of the doctrine of sour grapes: what I cannot be sure of, I cannot truly want.

This makes it clear why the definition of negative liberty as the ability to do what one wishes – which is, in effect, the definition adopted by Mill – will not do. If I find that I am able to do little or nothing of what I wish, I need only contract or extinguish my wishes, and I am made free. If the tyrant (or 'hidden persuader') manages to condition his subjects (or customers) into losing their original wishes and embrace ('internalize') the form of life he has invented for them, he will, on this definition, have succeeded in liberating them. He will, no doubt, have made them *feel* free – as Epictetus feels freer than his master (and the proverbial good man is said to feel happy on the rack). But what he has created is the very antithesis of political freedom.

Ascetic self-denial may be a source of integrity or serenity and spiritual strength, but it is difficult to see how it can be called an enlargement of liberty. If I save myself from an adversary by retreating indoors and locking every entrance and exit, I may remain freer than if I had been captured by him, but am I freer than if I had defeated or captured him? If I go too far, contract myself into too small a space, I shall suffocate and die. The logical culmination of the process of destroying everything through which I can possibly be wounded is suicide. While I exist in the natural world, I can never be wholly secure. Total liberation in this sense (as Schopenhauer correctly perceived) is conferred only by death.[15]

I find myself in a world in which I meet with obstacles to my will. Those who are wedded to the 'negative' concept of freedom may perhaps be forgiven if they think that self-abnegation is not the only method of overcoming obstacles; that it is also possible to do so by removing them: in the case of non-human objects, by physical action; in the case of human resistance, by force or persuasion, as when I induce somebody to make room for me in his carriage, or conquer a country which threatens the interests of my own. Such acts may be unjust, they may involve violence, cruelty, the enslavement of others, but it can scarcely be denied that thereby the agent is able in the most literal sense to increase his own freedom. It is an irony of history that this truth is repudiated by some of those who practise it most forcibly, men who, even while they conquer power and freedom of action, reject the 'negative' concept of it in favour of its 'positive' counterpart. Their view rules over half our world; let us see upon what metaphysical foundation it rests.

IV   Self-realization

The only true method of attaining freedom, we are told, is by the use of critical reason, the understanding of what is necessary and what is contingent. If I am a schoolboy, all but the simplest truths of mathematics obtrude themselves as obstacles to the free functioning of my mind, as theorems whose necessity I do not understand; they are pronounced to be true by some external authority, and present themselves to me as foreign bodies which I am expected mechanically to absorb into my system. But when I understand the functions of the symbols, the axioms, the formation and transformation rules – the logic whereby the conclusions are obtained – and grasp that these things cannot be otherwise, because they appear to follow from the laws that govern the processes of my own reason,[16] then mathematical truths no longer obtrude themselves as external entities forced upon me which I must receive whether I want it or not, but as something which I now freely will in the course of the natural functioning of my own rational activity. For the mathematician, the proof of these theorems is part of the free exercise of his natural reasoning capacity. For the musician, after he has assimilated the pattern of the composer's score, and has made the composer's ends his own, the playing of the music is not obedience to external laws, a compulsion and a barrier to liberty, but a free, unimpeded exercise. The player is not bound to the score as an ox to the plough, or a factory worker to the machine. He has absorbed the score into his own system, has, by understanding it, identified it with himself, has changed it from an impediment to free activity into an element in that activity itself. What applies to music or mathematics must, we are told, in principle apply to all other obstacles which present themselves as so many lumps of external stuff blocking free self-development. That is the programme of enlightened rationalism from Spinoza to the latest (at times unconscious) disciples of

Hegel. *Sapere aude*. What you know, that of which you understand the necessity – the rational necessity – you cannot, while remaining rational, want to be otherwise. For to want something to be other than what it must be is, given the premises – the necessities that govern the world – to be *pro tanto* either ignorant or irrational. Passions, prejudices, fears, neuroses, spring from ignorance, and take the form of myths and illusions. To be ruled by myths, whether they spring from the vivid imaginations of unscrupulous charlatans who deceive us in order to exploit us, or from psychological or sociological causes, is a form of heteronomy, of being dominated by outside factors in a direction not necessarily willed by the agent. The scientific determinists of the eighteenth century supposed that the study of the sciences of nature, and the creation of sciences of society on the same model, would make the operation of such causes transparently clear, and thus enable individuals to recognize their own part in the working of a rational world, frustrating only when misunderstood. Knowledge liberates, as Epicurus taught long ago, by automatically eliminating irrational fears and desires.

Herder, Hegel, and Marx substituted their own vitalistic models of social life for the older, mechanical ones, but believed, no less than their opponents, that to understand the world is to be freed. They merely differed from them in stressing the part played by change and growth in what made human beings human. Social life could not be understood by an analogy drawn from mathematics or physics. One must also understand history, that is, the peculiar laws of continuous growth, whether by 'dialectical' conflict or otherwise, that govern individuals and groups, in their interplay with each other and with nature. Not to grasp this is, according to these thinkers, to fall into a particular kind of error, namely the belief that human nature is static, that its essential properties are the same everywhere and at all times, that it is governed by unvarying natural laws, whether they are conceived in theological or materialistic terms, which entails the fallacious corollary that a wise lawgiver can, in principle, create a perfectly harmonious society at any time by appropriate education and legislation, because rational men, in all ages and countries, must always demand the same unaltering satisfactions of the same unaltering basic needs. Hegel believed that his contemporaries (and indeed all his predecessors) misunderstood the nature of institutions because they did not understand the laws – the rationally intelligible laws, since they spring from the operation of reason – that create and alter institutions and transform human character and human action. Marx and his disciples maintained that the path of human beings was obstructed not only by natural forces, or the imperfections of their own character, but, even more, by the workings of their own social institutions, which they had originally created (not always consciously) for certain purposes, but whose functioning they systematically came to misconceive[17], and which thereupon became obstacles in their creators' progress. He offered social and economic hypotheses to account for the inevitability of such misunderstanding, in particular of the illusion that such man-made arrangements were independent forces, as inescapable as the laws of nature. As instances of such pseudo-objective forces, he pointed to the laws of supply and demand, or of the institution of property, or of the eternal division of society into rich and poor, or owners and workers, as so many unaltering human categories. Not until we had reached a stage at which the spells of these illusions could be broken, that is, until enough men reached a social stage that alone enabled them to understand that these laws and institutions were themselves the work of human minds and hands, historically needed in their day, and later mistaken for inexorable, objective powers, could the old world be destroyed, and more adequate and liberating social machinery substituted.

We are enslaved by despots – institutions or beliefs or neuroses – which can be removed only by being analysed and understood. We are imprisoned by evil spirits which we have ourselves – albeit not consciously – created, and can exorcize them only by becoming conscious and acting appropriately: indeed, for Marx understanding *is* appropriate action. I am free if, and only if, I plan my life in accordance with my own will; plans entail rules; a rule does not oppress me or enslave me if I impose it on myself consciously, or accept it freely, having understood it, whether it was invented by me or by others, provided that it is rational, that is to say, conforms to the necessities of things. To understand why things must be as they must be is to will them to be so. Knowledge liberates not by offering us more open possibilities amongst which we can make our choice, but by preserving us from the frustration of attempting the impossible. To want necessary laws to be other than they are is to be prey to an irrational desire – a desire that what must be X should also be not X. To go further, and believe these laws to be other than what they necessarily are, is to be insane. That is the metaphysical heart of rationalism. The notion of liberty contained in it is not the 'negative' conception of a field (ideally) without obstacles, a vacuum in which nothing obstructs me, but the notion of self-direction or self-control. I can do what I will with my own. I am a rational being; whatever I can demonstrate to myself as being necessary, as incapable of being otherwise in a rational society – that is, in a society directed by rational minds, towards goals such as a rational being would have – I cannot, being rational, wish to sweep out of my way. I assimilate it into my substance as I do the laws of logic, of mathematics, of physics, the rule of art, the principles that govern everything of which I understand, and therefore will, the rational purpose, by which I can never be thwarted, since I cannot want it to be other than it is.

This is the positive doctrine of liberation by reason. Socialized forms of it, widely disparate and opposed to each other as they are, are at the heart of many of the nationalist, communist, authoritarian, and totalitarian creeds of our day. It may, in the course of its evolution, have wandered far from its rationalist moorings. Nevertheless, it is this freedom that, in democracies and in dictatorships, is argued about, and fought for, in many parts of the earth today. Without attempting to trace the historical evolution of this idea, I should like to comment on some of its vicissitudes.

V   The Temple of Sarastro

Those who believed in freedom as rational self-direction were bound, sooner or later, to consider how this was to be applied not merely to a man's inner life, but to his relations with other members of his society. Even the most individualistic among them – and Rousseau, Kant, and Fichte certainly began as individualists – came at some point to ask themselves whether a rational life not only for the individual, but also for society, was possible, and if so, how it was to be achieved. I wish to be free to live as my rational will (my 'real self') commands, but so must others be. How am I to avoid collisions with their wills? Where is the frontier that lies between my (rationally determined) rights and the identical rights of others? For if I am rational, I cannot deny that what is right for me must, for

the same reasons, be right for others who are rational like me. A rational (or free) state would be a state governed by such laws as all rational men would freely accept; that is to say, such laws as they would themselves have enacted had they been asked what, as rational beings, they demanded; hence the frontiers would be such as all rational men would consider to be the right frontiers for rational beings. But who, in fact, was to determine what these frontiers were? Thinkers of this type argued that if moral and political problems were genuine – as surely they were – they must in principle be soluble; that is to say, there must exist one and only one true solution to any problem. All truths could in principle be discovered by any rational thinker, and demonstrated so clearly that all other rational men could not but accept them; indeed, this was already to a large extent the case in the new natural sciences. On this assumption, the problem of political liberty was soluble by establishing a just order that would give to each man all the freedom to which a rational being was entitled. My claim to unfettered freedom can prima facie at times not be reconciled with your equally unqualified claim; but the rational solution of one problem cannot collide with the equally true solution of another, for two truths cannot logically be incompatible; therefore a just order must in principle be discoverable – an order of which the rules make possible correct solutions to all possible problems that could arise in it. This ideal, harmonious state of affairs was sometimes imagined as a Garden of Eden before the Fall of Man, from which we were expelled, but for which we were still filled with longing; or as a golden age still before us, in which men, having become rational, will no longer be 'other-directed', nor 'alienate' or frustrate one another. In existing societies justice and equality are ideals which still call for some measure of coercion, because the premature lifting of social controls might lead to the oppression of the weaker and the stupider by the stronger or abler or more energetic and unscrupulous. But it is only irrationality on the part of men (according to this doctrine) that leads them to wish to oppress or exploit or humiliate one another. Rational men will respect the principle of reason in each other, and lack all desire to fight or dominate one another. The desire to dominate is itself a symptom of irrationality, and can be explained and cured by rational methods. Spinoza offers one kind of explanation and remedy, Hegel another, Marx a third. Some of these theories may perhaps, to some degree, supplement each other, others are not combinable. But they all assume that in a society of perfectly rational beings the lust for domination over men will be absent or ineffective. The existence of, or craving for, oppression will be the first symptom that the true solution to the problems of social life has not been reached.

This can be put in another way. Freedom is self-mastery, the elimination of obstacles to my will, whatever these obstacles may be – the resistance of nature, of my ungoverned passions, of irrational institutions, of the opposing wills or behaviour of others. Nature I can, at least in principle, always mould by technical means, and shape to my will. But how am I to treat recalcitrant human beings? I must, if I can, impose my will on them too, 'mould' them to my pattern, cast parts for them in my play. But will this not mean that I alone am free, while they are slaves? They will be so if my plan has nothing to do with their wishes or values, only with my own. But if my plan is fully rational, it will allow for the full development of their 'true' natures, the realization of their capacities for rational decisions 'for making the best of themselves' – as a part of the realization of my own 'true' self. All true solutions to all genuine problems must be compatible: more than this, they must fit into a single whole: for this is what is meant by calling them all rational and the universe harmonious. Each man has his specific character, abilities, aspirations, ends. If I grasp both what these ends and natures are, and how they all relate to one another, I can, at least in principle, if I have the knowledge and the strength, satisfy them all, so long as the nature and the purposes in question are rational. Rationality is knowing things and people for what they are: I must not use stones to make violins, nor try to make born violin players play flutes. If the universe is governed by reason, then there will be no need for coercion; a correctly planned life for all will coincide with full freedom – the freedom of rational self-direction – for all. This will be so if, and only if, the plan is the true plan – the one unique pattern which alone fulfils the claims of reason. Its laws will be the rules which reason prescribes: they will only seem irksome to those whose reason is dormant, who do not understand the true 'needs' of their own 'real' selves. So long as each player recognizes and plays the part set him by reason – the faculty that understands his true nature and discerns his true ends – there can be no conflict. Each man will be a liberated, self-directed actor in the cosmic drama. Thus Spinoza tells us that 'children, although they are coerced, are not slaves', because 'they obey orders given in their own interests', and that 'The subject of a true commonwealth is no slave, because the common interests must include his own.' Similarly, Locke says 'Where there is no law there is no freedom', because rational laws are directions to a man's 'proper interests' or 'general good'; and adds that since such laws are what 'hedges us from bogs and precipices' they 'ill deserve the name of confinement', and speaks of desires to escape from such laws as being irrational, forms of 'licence', as 'brutish', and so on. Montesquieu, forgetting his liberal moments, speaks of political liberty as being not permission to do what we want, or even what the law allows, but only 'the power of doing what we ought to will', which Kant virtually repeats. Burke proclaims the individual's 'right' to be restrained in his own interest, because 'the presumed consent of every rational creature is in unison with the predisposed order of things'. The common assumption of these thinkers (and of many a schoolman before them and Jacobin and Communist after them) is that the rational ends of our 'true' natures must coincide, or be made to coincide, however violently our poor, ignorant, desire-ridden, passionate, empirical selves may cry out against this process. Freedom is not freedom to do what is irrational, or stupid, or wrong. To force empirical selves into the right pattern is no tyranny, but liberation.[18] Rousseau tells me that if I freely surrender all the parts of my life to society, I create an entity which, because it has been built by an equality of sacrifice of all its members, cannot wish to hurt any one of them; in such a society, we are informed, it can be nobody's interest to damage anyone else. 'In giving myself to all, I give myself to none', and get back as much as I lose, with enough new force to preserve my new gains. Kant tells us that when 'the individual has entirely abandoned his wild, lawless freedom, to find it again, unimpaired, in a state of dependence according to law', that alone is true freedom, 'for this dependence is the work of my own will acting as a lawgiver'. Liberty, so far from being incompatible with authority, becomes virtually identical with it. This is the thought and language of all the declarations of the rights of man in the eighteenth century, and of all those who look upon society as a design constructed according to the rational laws of the wise lawgiver, or of nature, or of history, or of the Supreme

Being. Bentham, almost alone, doggedly went on repeating that the business of laws was not to liberate but to restrain: 'Every law is an infraction of liberty' – even if such 'infraction' leads to an increase of the sum of liberty.

If the underlying assumptions had been correct – if the method of solving social problems resembled the way in which solutions to the problems of the natural sciences are found, and if reason were what rationalists said that it was, all this would perhaps follow. In the ideal case, liberty coincides with law: autonomy with authority. A law which forbids me to do what I could not, as a sane being, conceivably wish to do is not a restraint of my freedom. In the ideal society, composed of wholly responsible beings, rules, because I should scarcely be conscious of them, would gradually wither away. Only one social movement was bold enough to render this assumption quite explicit and accept its consequences – that of the Anarchists. But all forms of liberalism founded on a rationalist metaphysics are less or more watered-down versions of this creed.

In due course, the thinkers who bent their energies to the solution of the problem on these lines came to be faced with the question of how in practice men were to be made rational in this way. Clearly they must be educated. For the uneducated are irrational, heteronomous, and need to be coerced, if only to make life tolerable for the rational if they are to live in the same society and not be compelled to withdraw to a desert or some Olympian height. But the uneducated cannot be expected to understand or co-operate with the purposes of their educators. Education, says Fichte, must inevitably work in such a way that 'you will later recognize the reasons for what I am doing now'. Children cannot be expected to understand why they are compelled to go to school, nor the ignorant – that is, for the moment, the majority of mankind – why they are made to obey the laws that will presently make them rational. 'Compulsion is also a kind of education.' You learn the great virtue of obedience to superior persons. If you cannot understand your own interests as a rational being, I cannot be expected to consult you, or abide by your wishes, in the course of making you rational. I must, in the end, force you to be protected against smallpox, even though you may not wish it. Even Mill is prepared to say that I may forcibly prevent a man from crossing a bridge if there is not time to warn him that it is about to collapse, for I know, or am justified in

assuming, that he cannot wish to fall into the water. Fichte knows what the uneducated German of his time wishes to be or do better than he can possibly know them for himself. The sage knows you better than you know yourself, for you are the victim of your passions, a slave living a heteronomous life, purblind, unable to understand your true goals. You want to be a human being. It is the aim of the state to satisfy your wish. 'Compulsion is justified by education for future insight.' The reason within me, if it is to triumph, must eliminate and suppress my 'lower' instincts, my passions and desires, which render me a slave; similarly (the fatal transition from individual to social concepts is almost imperceptible) the higher elements in society – the better educated, the more rational, those who 'possess the highest insight of their time and people' – may exercise compulsion to rationalize the irrational section of society. For – so Hegel, Bradley, Bosanquet have often assured us – by obeying the rational man we obey ourselves: not indeed as we are, sunk in our ignorance and our passions, weak creatures afflicted by diseases that need a healer, wards who require a guardian, but as we could be if we were rational; as we could be even now, if only we would listen to the rational element which is, *ex hypothesi*, within every human being who deserves the name.

The philosophers of 'Objective Reason', from the tough, rigidly centralized, 'organic' state of Fichte, to the mild and humane liberalism of T. H. Green, certainly supposed themselves to be fulfilling, and not resisting, the rational demands which, however inchoate, were to be found in the breast of every sentient being. But I may reject such democratic optimism, and turning away from the teleological determinism of the Hegelians towards some more voluntarist philosophy, conceive the idea of imposing on my society – for its own betterment – a plan of my own, which in my rational wisdom I have elaborated; and which, unless I act on my own, perhaps against the permanent wishes of the vast majority of my fellow citizens, may never come to fruition at all. Or, abandoning the concept of reason altogether, I may conceive myself as an inspired artist, who moulds men into patterns in the light of his unique vision, as painters combine colours or composers sounds; humanity is the raw material upon which I impose my creative will; even though men suffer and die in the process, they are lifted by it to a height to which they could never have risen without my coercive – but creative – violation of their lives. This is the argument used by every dictator, inquisitor, and bully who seeks some moral, or even aesthetic, justification for his conduct. I must do for men (or with them) what they cannot do for themselves, and I cannot ask their permission or consent, because they are in no condition to know what is best for them; indeed, what they will permit and accept may mean a life of contemptible mediocrity, or perhaps even their ruin and suicide. Let me quote from the true progenitor of the heroic doctrine, Fichte, once again: 'No one has . . . rights against reason.' 'Man is afraid of subordinating his subjectivity to the laws of reason. He prefers tradition or arbitrariness.' Nevertheless, subordinated he must be.[19] Fichte puts forward the claims of what he called reason; Napoleon, or Carlyle, or romantic authoritarians may worship other values, and see in their establishment by force the only path to 'true' freedom.

The same attitude was pointedly expressed by Auguste Comte, who asked 'If we do not allow free thinking in chemistry or biology, why should we allow it in morals or politics?' Why indeed? If it makes sense to speak of political truths – assertions of social ends which all men, because they are men, must, once they are discovered, agree to be such; and if, as Comte believed, scientific method will in due course reveal them; then what case is there for freedom of opinion or action – at least as an end in itself, and not merely as a stimulating intellectual climate, either for individuals or for groups? Why should any conduct be tolerated that is not authorized by appropriate experts? Comte put bluntly what had been implicit in the rationalist theory of politics from its ancient Greek beginnings. There can, in principle, be only one correct way of life; the wise lead it spontaneously, that is why they are called wise. The unwise must be dragged towards it by all the social means in the power of the wise; for why should demonstrable error be suffered to survive and breed? The immature and untutored must be made to say to themselves: 'Only the truth liberates, and the only way in which I can learn the truth is by doing blindly today, what you, who know it, order me, or coerce me, to do, in the certain knowledge that only thus will I arrive at your clear vision, and be free like you.'

We have wandered indeed from our liberal beginnings. This argument, employed by Fichte in his latest phase, and after him by other defenders of authority, from Victorian schoolmasters and colonial administrators to the latest nationalist or communist dictator, is precisely what the Stoic and Kantian morality protests against most bitterly in the name of the reason of the free individual following his own inner light. In this way the rationalist argument, with its assumption of the single true solution, has led by steps which, if not logically valid, are historically and psychologically intelligible, from an ethical doctrine of individual responsibility and individual self-perfection to an authoritarian state obedient to the directives of an *élite* of Platonic guardians.

What can have led to so strange a reversal – the transformation of Kant's severe individualism into something close to a pure totalitarian doctrine on the part of thinkers, some of whom claimed to be his disciples? This question is not of merely historical interest, for not a few contemporary liberals have gone through the same peculiar evolution. It is true that Kant insisted, following Rousseau, that a capacity for rational self-direction belonged to all men; that there could be no experts in moral matters, since morality was a matter not of specialized knowledge (as the utilitarians and *philosophes* had maintained), but of the correct use of a universal human faculty; and consequently that what made men free was not acting in certain self-improving ways, which they could be coerced to do, but knowing why they ought to do so, which nobody could do for, or on behalf of, anyone else. But even Kant, when he came to deal with political issues, conceded that no law, provided that it was such that I should, if I were asked, approve it as a rational being, could possibly deprive me of any portion of my rational freedom. With this the door was opened wide to the rule of experts. I cannot consult all men about all enactments all the time. The government cannot be a continuous plebiscite. Moreover, some men are not as well attuned to the voice of their own reason as others: some seem singularly deaf. If I am a legislator or a ruler, I must assume that if the law I impose is rational (and I can only consult my own reason) it will automatically be approved by all the members of my society so far as they are rational beings. For if they disapprove, they must, *pro tanto*, be irrational; then they will need to be repressed by reason: whether their own or mine cannot matter, for the pronouncements of reason must be the same in all minds. I issue my orders, and if you resist, take it upon myself to repress the irrational element in you which opposes reason. My task would be easier if you repressed it in yourself; I try to educate you to do so. But I am responsible for public welfare, I cannot wait until all men are wholly rational. Kant may protest that the essence of the subject's freedom is that he, and he alone, has given himself the order to obey. But this is a counsel of perfection. If you fail to discipline yourself, I must do so for you; and you cannot complain of lack of freedom, for the fact that Kant's rational judge has sent you to prison is evidence that you have not listened to your own inner reason, that, like a child, a savage, an idiot, you are not ripe for self-direction or permanently incapable of it.[20]

If this leads to despotism, albeit by the best or the wisest – to Sarastro's temple in the *Magic Flute* – but still despotism, which turns out to be identical with freedom, can it be that there is something amiss in the premises of the argument? that the basic assumptions are themselves somewhere at fault? Let me state them once more: first, that all men have one true purpose, and one only, that of rational self-direction; second, that the ends of all rational beings must of necessity fit into a single universal, harmonious pattern, which some men may be able to discern more clearly than others; third, that all conflict, and consequently all tragedy, is due solely to the clash of reason with the irrational or the insufficiently rational – the immature and undeveloped elements in life – whether individual or communal, and that such clashes are, in principle, avoidable, and for wholly rational beings impossible; finally, that when all men have been made rational, they will obey the rational laws of their own natures, which are one and the same in them all, and so be at once wholly law-abiding and wholly free. Can it be that Socrates and the creators of the central Western tradition in ethics and politics who followed him have been mistaken, for more than two millennia, that virtue is not knowledge, nor freedom identical with either? That despite the fact that it rules the lives of more men than ever before in its long history, not one of the basic assumptions of this famous view is demonstrable, or, perhaps, even true?

VI   The One and the Many

I do not wish to say that individual freedom is, even in the most liberal societies, the sole, or even the dominant, criterion of social action. We compel children to be educated, and we forbid public executions. These are certainly curbs to freedom. We justify them on the ground that ignorance, or a barbarian upbringing, or cruel pleasures and excitements are worse for us than the amount of restraint needed to repress them. This judgment in turn depends on how we determine good and evil, that is to say, on our moral, religious, intellectual, economic, and aesthetic values; which are, in their turn, bound up with our conception of man, and of the basic demands of his nature. In other words, our solution of such problems is based on our vision, by which we are consciously or unconsciously guided, of what constitutes a fulfilled human life, as contrasted with Mill's 'cramped and warped', 'pinched and hidebound' natures. To protest against the laws governing censorship or personal morals as intolerable infringements of personal liberty presupposes a belief that the activities which such laws forbid are fundamental needs of men as men, in a good (or, indeed, any) society. To defend such laws is to hold that these needs are not essential, or that they cannot be satisfied without sacrificing other values which come higher – satisfy deeper needs – than individual freedom, determined by some standard that is not merely subjective, a standard for which some objective status – empirical or *a priori* – is claimed.

The extent of a man's, or a people's, liberty to choose to live as they desire must be weighed against the claims of many other values, of which equality, or justice, or happiness, or security, or public order are perhaps the most obvious examples. For this reason, it cannot be unlimited. We are rightly reminded by R. H. Tawney that the liberty of the strong, whether their strength is physical or economic, must be restrained. This maxim claims respect, not as a consequence of some *a priori* rule, whereby the respect for the liberty of one man logically entails respect for the liberty of others like him; but simply because respect for the principles of justice, or shame at gross inequality of treatment, is as basic in men as the desire for liberty. That we cannot have everything is a necessary, not a contingent, truth. Burke's plea for the constant need to compensate, to reconcile, to balance; Mill's plea for novel 'experiments in living' with their permanent possibility of error, the knowledge that it is not merely in practice but in principle impossible to reach clear-cut and certain answers, even in an ideal world of wholly good and rational men and wholly clear ideas – may madden those who seek for final solutions and single, all-embracing systems, guaranteed to be eternal. Nevertheless, it is a conclusion that cannot be escaped by those who, with

Kant, have learnt the truth that out of the crooked timber of humanity no straight thing was ever made.

There is little need to stress the fact that monism, and faith in a single criterion, has always proved a deep source of satisfaction both to the intellect and to the emotions. Whether the standard of judgment derives from the vision of some future perfection, as in the minds of the *philosophes* in the eighteenth century and their technocratic successors in our own day, or is rooted in the past – *la terre et les morts* – as maintained by German historicists or French theocrats, or neo-Conservatives in English-speaking countries, it is bound, provided it is inflexible enough, to encounter some unforeseen and unforeseeable human development, which it will not fit; and will then be used to justify the *a priori* barbarities of Procrustes – the vivisection of actual human societies into some fixed pattern dictated by our fallible understanding of a largely imaginary past or a wholly imaginary future. To preserve our absolute categories or ideals at the expense of human lives offends equally against the principles of science and of history; it is an attitude found in equal measure on the right and left wings in our days, and is not reconcilable with the principles accepted by those who respect the facts.

Pluralism, with the measure of 'negative' liberty that it entails, seems to me a truer and more humane ideal than the goals of those who seek in the great, disciplined, authoritarian structures the ideal of 'positive' self-mastery by classes, or peoples, or the whole of mankind. It is truer, because it does, at least, recognize the fact that human goals are many, not all of them commensurable, and in perpetual rivalry with one another. To assume that all values can be graded on one scale, so that it is a mere matter of inspection to determine the highest, seems to me to falsify our knowledge that men are free agents, to represent moral decision as an operation which a slide-rule could, in principle, perform. To say that in some ultimate, all-reconciling, yet realizable synthesis, duty *is* interest, or individual freedom *is* pure democracy or an authoritarian state, is to throw a metaphysical blanket over either self-deceit or deliberate hypocrisy. It is more humane because it does not (as the system builders do) deprive men, in the name of some remote, or incoherent, ideal, of much that they have found to be indispensable to their life as unpredictably self-transforming human beings.[21] In the end, men choose between ultimate values; they choose as they do, because their life and thought are determined by fundamental moral categories and concepts that are, at any rate over large stretches of time and space, a part of their being and thought and sense of their own identity; part of what makes them human.

It may be that the ideal of freedom to choose ends without claiming eternal validity for them, and the pluralism of values connected with this, is only the late fruit of our declining capitalist civilization: an ideal which remote ages and primitive societies have not recognized, and one which posterity will regard with curiosity, even sympathy, but little comprehension. This may be so; but no sceptical conclusions seem to me to follow. Principles are not less sacred because their duration cannot be guaranteed. Indeed, the very desire for guarantees that our values are eternal and secure in some objective heaven is perhaps only a craving for the certainties of childhood or the absolute values of our primitive past. 'To realise the relative validity of one's convictions', said an admirable writer of our time, 'and yet stand for them unflinchingly, is what distinguishes a civilised man from a barbarian.' To demand more than this is perhaps a deep and incurable metaphysical need; but to allow it to determine one's practice is a symptom of an equally deep, and more dangerous, moral and political immaturity.

Notes

1 I do not, of course, mean to imply the truth of the converse.

2 Helvétius made this point very clearly: 'The free man is the man who is not in irons, nor imprisoned in a gaol, nor terrorized like a slave by the fear of punishment...it is not lack of freedom not to fly like an eagle or swim like a whale.'

3 The Marxist conception of social laws is, of course, the best-known version of this theory, but it forms a large element in some Christian and utilitarian, and all socialist, doctrines.

4 'A free man', said Hobbes, 'is he that...is not hindered to do what he hath the will to do.' Law is always a 'fetter', even if it protects you from being bound in chains that are heavier than those of the law, say, some more repressive law or custom, or arbitrary despotism or chaos. Bentham says much the same.

5 This is but another illustration of the natural tendency of all but a very few thinkers to believe that all the things they hold good must be intimately connected, or at least compatible, with one another. The history of thought, like the history of nations, is strewn with examples of inconsistent, or at least disparate, elements artificially yoked together in a despotic system, or held together by the danger of some common enemy. In due course the danger passes, and conflicts between the allies arise, which often disrupt the system, sometimes to the great benefit of mankind.

6 See the valuable discussion of this in Michel Villey, *Leçons d'histoire de la philosophie du droit*, who traces the embryo of the notion of subjective rights to Occam.

7 Christian (and Jewish or Moslem) belief in the absolute authority of divine or natural laws, or in the equality of all men in the sight of God, is different from belief in freedom to live as one prefers.

8 Indeed, it is arguable that in the Prussia of Frederick the Great or in the Austria of Josef II men of imagination, originality, and creative genius, and, indeed, minorities of all kinds, were less persecuted and felt the pressure, both of institutions and custom, less heavy upon them than in many an earlier or later democracy.

9 'Negative liberty' is something the extent of which, in a given case, it is difficult to estimate. It might, prima facie, seem to depend simply on the power to choose between at any rate two alternatives. Nevertheless, not all choices are equally free, or free at all. If in a totalitarian state I betray my friend under threat of torture, perhaps even if I act from fear of losing my job, I can reasonably say that I did not act freely. Nevertheless, I did, of course, make a choice, and could, at any rate in theory, have chosen to be killed or tortured or imprisoned. The mere existence of alternatives is not, therefore, enough to make my action free (although it may be voluntary) in the normal sense of the word. The extent of my freedom seems to depend on (a) how many possibilities are open to me (although the method of counting these can never be more than impressionistic. Possibilities of action are not discrete entities like apples, which can be exhaustively enumerated); (b) how easy or difficult each of these possibilities is to actualize; (c) how important in my plan of life, given my character and circumstances, these possibilities are when compared with each other; (d) how far they are closed and opened by deliberate human acts; (e) what value not merely the agent, but the general sentiment of the society in which he lives, puts on the various possibilities. All these magnitudes must be 'integrated', and a conclusion, necessarily never precise, or indisputable, drawn from this process. It may well be that there are many incommensurable kinds and degrees of freedom, and that they cannot be drawn up on any single scale of magnitude. Moreover, in the case of societies, we are faced by such (logically absurd) questions as 'Would arrangement X increase the liberty of Mr A more than it would that of Messrs. B, C, and D between them, added together?' The same difficulties arise in applying utilitarian criteria. Nevertheless, provided we do not demand precise measurement, we can give valid reasons for saying that the average subject of the King of Sweden is, on the whole, a good deal freer today than the average citizen of Spain or Albania. Total patterns of life must be compared directly as wholes, although the method by which we make the comparison, and the truth of the conclusions, are difficult or impossible to demonstrate. But the vagueness of the concepts, and the multiplicity of the criteria involved, is an attribute of the subject-matter itself, not of our imperfect methods of measurement, or incapacity for precise thought.

10 'The ideal of true freedom is the maximum of power for all the members of human society alike to make the best of themselves', said T.H. Green in 1881. Apart from the confusion of freedom with equality, this entails that if a man chose some immediate pleasure – which (in whose view?) would not enable him to make the best of himself (what self?) – what he was exercising was not 'true' freedom: and if deprived of it, would not lose anything that mattered. Green was a genuine liberal: but many a tyrant could use this formula to justify his worse acts of oppression.

11 'A wise man, though he be a slave, is at liberty, and from this it follows that though a fool rule, he is in slavery', said St. Ambrose. It might equally well have been said by Epictetus or Kant.

12 'Proletarian coercion, in all its forms, from executions to forced labour, is, paradoxical as it may sound, the method of moulding communist humanity out of the human material of the capitalist period.' These lines by the Bolshevik leader Nikolai Bukharin, in a work which appeared in 1920, especially the term 'human material', vividly convey this attitude.

13 Kant's psychology, and that of the Stoics and Christians too, assumed that some element in man – the 'inner fastness of his mind' – could be made secure against conditioning. The development of the techniques of hypnosis, 'brain washing', subliminal suggestion, and the like, has made this *a priori* assumption, at least as an empirical hypothesis, less plausible.

14 It is not perhaps far-fetched to assume that the quietism of the Eastern sages was, similarly, a response to the despotism of the great autocracies, and flourished at periods when individuals were apt to be humiliated, or at any rate ignored or ruthlessly managed, by those possessed of the instruments of physical coercion.

15 It is worth remarking that those who demanded – and fought for – liberty for the individual or for the nation in France during this period of German quietism did not fall into this attitude. Might this not be precisely because, despite the despotism of the French monarchy and the arrogance and arbitrary behaviour of privileged groups in the French state, France was a proud and powerful nation, where the reality of political power was not beyond the grasp of men of talent, so that withdrawal from battle into some untroubled heaven above it, whence it could be surveyed dispassionately by the self-sufficient philosopher, was not the only way out? The same holds for England in the nineteenth century and well after it, and for the United States today.

16 Or, as some modern theorists maintain, because I have, or could have, invented them for myself, since the rules are man-made.

17 In practice even more than in theory.

18 On this Bentham seems to me to have said the last word: 'Is not liberty to do evil, liberty? If not, what is it? Do we not say that it is necessary to take liberty from idiots and bad men, because they abuse it?' Compare with this a typical statement made by a Jacobin club of the same period: 'No man is free in doing evil. To prevent him is to set him free.' This is echoed in almost identical terms by British Idealists at the end of the following century.

19 'To compel men to adopt the right form of government, to impose Right on them by force, is not only the right, but the sacred duty of every man who has both the insight and the power to do so.'

20 Kant came nearest to asserting the 'negative' ideal of liberty when (in one of his political treatises) he declared that 'the greatest problem of the human race, to the solution of which it is compelled by nature, is the establishment of a civil society universally administering right according to law. It is only in a society which possesses the greatest liberty ... – with ... the most exact determination and guarantee of the limits of [the] liberty [of each individual] in order that it may co-exist with the liberty of others – that the highest purpose of nature, which is the development of all her capacities, can be attained in the case of mankind.' Apart from the teleological implications, this formulation does not at first appear very different from orthodox liberalism. The crucial point, however, is how to determine the criterion for 'the exact determination and guarantee of the limits' of individual liberty. Most modern liberals, at their most consistent want a situation in which as many individuals as possible can realize as many of their ends as possible, without assessment of the value of these ends as such, save in so far as they may frustrate the purposes of others. They wish the frontiers between individuals or groups of men to be drawn solely with a view to preventing collisions between human purposes, all of which must be considered to be equally ultimate, uncriticizable ends in themselves. Kant, and the rationalists of his type, do not regard all ends as of equal value. For them the limits of liberty are determined by applying the rules of 'reason', which is much more than the mere generality of rules as such, and is a faculty that creates or reveals a purpose identical in, and for, all men. In the name of reason anything that is non-rational may be condemned, so that the various personal aims which their individual imagination and idiosyncrasies lead men to pursue – for example aesthetic and other non-rational kinds of self-fulfilment – may, at least in theory, be ruthlessly suppressed to make way for the demands of reason. The authority of reason and of the duties it lays upon men is identified with individual freedom, on the assumption that only rational ends can be the 'true' objects of a 'free' man's 'real' nature.

I have never, I must own, understood what 'reason' means in this context; and here merely wish to point out that the *a priori* assumptions of this philosophical psychology are not compatible with empiricism: that is to say, with any doctrine founded on knowledge derived from experience of what men are and seek.

21 On this also Bentham seems to me to have spoken well: 'Individual interests are the only real interests ... can it be conceived that there are men so absurd as to ... prefer the man who is not to him who is; to torment the living, under pretence of promoting the happiness of them who are not born, and who may never be born?' This is one of the infrequent occasions when Burke agrees with Bentham; for this passage is at the heart of the empirical, as against the metaphysical, view of politics.

25

What's Wrong with Negative Liberty?

Charles Taylor

This is an attempt to resolve one of the issues that separate 'positive' and 'negative' theories of freedom, as these have been distinguished in Isaiah Berlin's seminal essay, 'Two Concepts of Liberty'.[1] Although one can discuss almost endlessly the detailed formulation of the distinction, I believe it is undeniable that there are two such families of conceptions of political freedom abroad in our civilisation.

Thus there clearly are theories, widely canvassed in liberal society, which want to define freedom exclusively in terms of the independence of the individual from interference by others, be these governments, corporations or private persons; and equally clearly these theories are challenged by those who believe that freedom resides at least in part in collective control over the common life. We unproblematically recognize theories descended from Rousseau and Marx as fitting in this category.

There is quite a gamut of views in each category. And this is worth bearing in mind, because it is too easy in the course of polemic to fix on the extreme, almost caricatural variants of each family. When people attack positive theories of freedom, they generally have some Left totalitarian theory in mind, according to which freedom resides exclusively in exercising collective control over one's destiny in a classless society, the kind of theory which underlies, for instance, official Communism. This view, in its caricaturally extreme form,

refuses to recognise the freedoms guaranteed in other societies as genuine. The destruction of 'bourgeois freedoms' is no real loss of freedom, and coercion can be justified in the name of freedom if it is needed to bring into existence the classless society in which alone men are properly free. Men can, in short, be forced to be free.

Even as applied to official Communism, this portrait is a little extreme, although it undoubtedly expresses the inner logic of this kind of theory. But it is an absurd caricature if applied to the whole family of positive conceptions. This includes all those views of modern political life which owe something to the ancient republican tradition, according to which men's ruling themselves is seen as an activity valuable in itself, and not only for instrumental reasons. It includes in its scope thinkers like Tocqueville, and even arguably the J.S. Mill of *On Representative Government*. It has no necessary connection with the view that freedom consists *purely and simply* in the collective control over the common life, or that there is no freedom worth the name outside a context of collective control. And it does not therefore generate necessarily a doctrine that men can be forced to be free.

On the other side, there is a corresponding caricatural version of negative freedom which tends to come to the fore. This is the tough-minded version, going back to Hobbes, or in another way to Bentham, which sees freedom simply as the absence of external physical or legal obstacles. This view will have no truck with other less immediately obvious obstacles to freedom, for instance, lack of awareness, or false consciousness, or repression, or other inner factors of this kind. It holds firmly to the view that to speak of such inner factors as relevant to the issue about freedom, to speak for instance of someone's being less free because of false consciousness, is to abuse words. The only clear meaning which can be given to freedom is that of the absence of external obstacles.

I call this view caricatural as a representative portrait of the negative view, because it rules out of court one of the most powerful motives behind the modern defence of freedom as individual independence, viz., the post-Romantic idea that each person's form of self-realisation is original to him/her, and can therefore only be worked out independently. This is one of the reasons for the defence of individual liberty by among others J.S. Mill (this time in his *On Liberty*). But if we think of freedom as including something like the freedom of self-fulfilment, or self-realisation according to our own pattern, then we plainly have something which can fail for inner reasons as well as because of external obstacles. We can fail to achieve our own self-realisation through inner fears, or false consciousness, as well as because of external coercion. Thus the modern notion of negative freedom which gives weight to the securing of each person's right to realise him/herself in his/her own way cannot make do with the Hobbes/Bentham notion of freedom. The moral psychology of these authors is too simple, or perhaps we should say too crude, for its purposes.

Now there is a strange asymmetry here. The extreme caricatural views tend to come to the fore in the polemic, as I mentioned above. But whereas the extreme 'forced-to-be-free' view is one which the opponents of positive liberty try to pin on them, as one would expect in the heat of argument, the proponents of negative liberty themselves often seem anxious to espouse their extreme, Hobbesian view. Thus even Isaiah Berlin, in his eloquent exposition of the two concepts of liberty, seems to quote Bentham[2] approvingly and Hobbes[3] as well. Why is this?

To see this we have to examine more closely what is at stake between the two views. The negative theories, as we saw, want to define freedom in terms of individual independence from others; the positive also want to identify freedom with collective self-government. But behind this lie some deeper differences of doctrines.

Isaiah Berlin points out that negative theories are concerned with the area in which the subject should be left without interference, whereas the positive doctrines are concerned with who or what controls. I should like to put the point behind this in a slightly different way. Doctrines of positive freedom are concerned with a view of freedom which involves essentially the exercising of control over one's life. On this view, one is free only to the extent that one has effectively determined oneself and the shape of one's life. The concept of freedom here is an exercise-concept.

By contrast, negative theories can rely simply on an opportunity-concept, where being free is a matter of what we can do, of what it is open to us to do, whether or not we do anything to exercise these options. This certainly is the case of the crude, original Hobbesian concept. Freedom consists just in there being no obstacle. It is a sufficient condition of one's being free that nothing stand in the way.

But we have to say that negative theories *can* rely on an opportunity-concept, rather than that they necessarily do so rely, for we have to allow for that part of the gamut of negative theories mentioned above which incorporates some notion of self-realisation. Plainly this kind of view can't rely simply on an opportunity-concept. We can't say that someone is free, on a self-realisation view, if he is totally unrealised, if for instance he is totally unaware of his potential, if fulfilling it has never even arisen as a question for him, or if he is paralysed by the fear of breaking with some norm which he has internalised but which does not authentically reflect him. Within this conceptual scheme, some degree of exercise is necessary for a man to be thought free. Or if we want to think of the internal bars to freedom as obstacles on all fours with the external ones, then being in a position to exercise freedom, having the opportunity, involves removing the internal barriers; and this is not possible without having to some extent realised myself. So that with the freedom of self-realisation, having the opportunity to be free requires that I already be exercising freedom. A pure opportunity-concept is impossible here.

But if negative theories can be grounded on either an opportunity- or an exercise-concept, the same is not true of positive theories. The view that freedom involves at least partially collective self-rule is essentially grounded on an exercise-concept. For this view (at least partly) identifies freedom with self-direction, i.e., the actual exercise of directing control over one's life.

But this already gives us a hint towards illuminating the above paradox, that while the extreme variant of positive freedom is usually pinned on its protagonists by their opponents, negative theorists seem prone to embrace the crudest versions of their theory themselves. For if an opportunity-concept is incombinable with a positive theory, but either it or its alternative can suit a negative theory, then one way of ruling out positive theories in principle is by firmly espousing an opportunity-concept. One cuts off the positive theories by the root, as it were, even though one may also pay a price in the atrophy of a wide range of negative theories as well. At least by taking one's stand firmly on the crude side of the negative range, where only opportunity concepts are recognised, one leaves no place for a positive theory to grow.

Taking one's stand here has the advantage that one is holding the line around a very simple and basic issue of principle, and one where the negative view seems to have some backing in common sense. The basic intuition here is that freedom is a matter of being able to do something or other, of not having obstacles in one's way, rather than being a capacity that we have to realise. It naturally seems more prudent to fight the Totalitarian Menace at this last-ditch position, digging in behind the natural frontier of this simple issue, rather than engaging the enemy on the open terrain of exercise-concepts, where one will have to fight to discriminate the good from the bad among such concepts; fight, for instance, for a view of individual self-realisation against various notions of collective self-realisation, of a nation, or a class. It seems easier and safer to cut all the nonsense off at the start by declaring all self-realisation views to be metaphysical hog-wash. Freedom should just be tough-mindedly defined as the absence of external obstacles.

Of course, there are independent reasons for wanting to define freedom tough-mindedly. In particular there is the immense influence of the anti-metaphysical, materialist, natural-science-oriented temper of thought in our civilisation. Something of this spirit at its inception induced Hobbes to take the line that he did, and the same spirit goes marching on today. Indeed, it is because of the prevalence of this spirit that the line is so easy to defend, forensically speaking, in our society.

Nevertheless, I think that one of the strongest motives for defending the crude Hobbes-Bentham concept, that freedom is the absence of external obstacles, physical or legal, is the strategic one above. For most of those who take this line thereby abandon many of their own intuitions, sharing as they do with the rest of us in a post-Romantic civilisation which puts great value on self-realisation, and values freedom largely because of this. It is fear of the Totalitarian Menace, I would argue, which has led them to abandon this terrain to the enemy.

I want to argue that this not only robs their eventual forensic victory of much of its value, since they become incapable of defending liberalism in the form we in fact value it, but I want to make the stronger claim that this Maginot Line mentality actually ensures defeat, as is often the case with Maginot Line mentalities. The Hobbes-Bentham view, I want to argue, is indefensible as a view of freedom.

To see this, let's examine the line more closely, and the temptation to stand on it. The advantage of the view that freedom is the absence of external obstacles is its simplicity. It allows us to say that freedom is being able to do what you want, where what you want is unproblematically understood as what the agent can identify as his desires. By contrast an exercise-concept of freedom requires that we discriminate among motivations. If we are free in the exercise of certain capacities, then we are not free, or less free, when these capacities are in some way unfulfilled or blocked. But the obstacles can be internal as well as external. And this must be so, for the capacities relevant to freedom must involve some self-awareness, self-understanding, moral discrimination and self-control, otherwise their exercise couldn't amount to freedom in the sense of self-direction; and this being so, we can fail to be free because these internal conditions are not realised. But where this happens, where, for example, we are quite self-deceived, or utterly fail to discriminate properly the ends we seek, or have lost self-control, we can quite easily be doing what we want in the sense of what we can identify as our wants, without being free; indeed, we can be further entrenching our unfreedom.

Once one adopts a self-realisation view, or indeed, any exercise-concept of freedom, then being able to do what one wants can no longer be accepted as a sufficient condition of being free. For this view puts certain conditions on one's motivation. You are not free if you are motivated, through fear, inauthentically internalised standards, or false consciousness, to thwart your self-realisation. This is sometimes put by saying that for a self-realisation view, you have to be able to do what you really want, or to follow your real will, or to fulfil the desires of your own true self. But these formulas, particularly the last, may mislead, by making us think that exercise concepts of freedom are tied to some particular metaphysic, in particular that of a higher and lower self. We shall see below that this is far from being the case, and that there is a much wider range of bases for discriminating authentic and inauthentic desires.

In any case, the point for our discussion here is that for an exercise-concept of freedom, being free can't just be a question of doing what you want in the unproblematic sense. It must also be that what you want doesn't run against the grain of your basic purposes, or your self-realisation. Or to put the issue in another way, which converges on the same point, the subject himself can't be the final authority on the question whether he is free; for he cannot be the final authority on the question whether his desires are authentic, whether they do or do not frustrate his purposes.

To put the issue in this second way is to make more palpable the temptation for defenders of the negative view to hold their Maginot Line. For once we admit that the agent himself is not the final authority on his own freedom, do we not open the way to totalitarian manipulation? Do we not legitimate others, supposedly wiser about his purposes than himself, redirecting his feet on the right path, perhaps even by force, and all this in the name of freedom?

The answer is that of course we don't. Not by this concession alone. For there may also be good reasons for holding that others are not likely to be in a better position to understand his real purposes. This indeed plausibly follows from the post-Romantic view above that each person has his/her own original form of realisation. Some others, who know us intimately, and who surpass us in wisdom, are undoubtedly in a position to advise us, but no official body can possess a doctrine or a technique whereby they could know how to put us on the rails, because such a doctrine or technique cannot in principle exist if human beings really differ in their self-realisation.

Or again, we may hold a self-realisation view of freedom, and hence believe that there are certain conditions on my motivation necessary to my being free, but also believe that there are other necessary conditions which rule out my being forcibly led towards some definition of my self-realisation by external authority. Indeed, in these last two paragraphs I have given a portrait of what I think is a very widely held view in liberal society, a view which values self-realisation, and accepts that it can fail for internal reasons, but which believes that no valid guidance can be provided in principle by social authority, because of human diversity and originality, and holds that the attempt to impose such guidance will destroy other necessary conditions of freedom.

It is however true that totalitarian theories of positive freedom do build on a conception which involves discriminating between motivations. Indeed, one can represent the path from the negative to the positive conceptions of freedom as consisting of two steps: the first moves us from a notion of freedom as doing what one wants to a notion which discriminates motivations and equates freedom with doing what we really want, or obeying our real will, or truly directing our lives. The second step introduces some doctrine purporting to show that we cannot do what we really want, or follow our real will, outside of a society of a certain canonical form, incorporating true self-government. It follows that we can only be free in such a society, and that being free *is* governing ourselves collectively according to this canonical form.

We might see an example of this second step in Rousseau's view that only a social contract society in which all give themselves totally to the whole preserves us from other-dependence and ensures that we obey only ourselves; or in Marx's doctrine of man as a species-being who realises his potential in a mode of social production, and who must thus take control of this mode collectively.

Faced with this two-step process, it seems safer and easier to stop it at the first step, to insist firmly that freedom is just a matter of the absence of external obstacles, that it therefore involves no discrimination of motivation and permits in principle no second-guessing of the subject by any one else. This is the essence of the Maginot Line strategy. It is very tempting. But I want to claim that it is wrong. I want to argue that we cannot defend a view of freedom which doesn't involve at least some qualitative discrimination as to motive, i.e., which doesn't put some restrictions on motivation among the necessary conditions of freedom, and hence which could rule out second-guessing in principle.

There are some considerations one can put forward straight off to show that the pure Hobbesian concept won't work, that there are some discriminations among motivations which are essential to the concept of freedom as we use it. Even where we think of freedom as the absence of external obstacles, it is not the absence of such obstacles *simpliciter*. For we make discriminations between obstacles as representing more or less serious infringements of freedom. And we do this, because we deploy the concept against a background understanding that certain goals and activities are more significant than others.

Thus we could say that my freedom is restricted if the local authority puts up a new traffic light at an intersection close to my home; so that where previously I could cross as I liked, consistently with avoiding collision with other cars, now I have to wait until the light is green. In a philosophical argument, we might call this a restriction of freedom, but not in a serious political debate. The reason is that it is too trivial, the activity and purposes inhibited here are not really significant. It is not just a matter of our having made a trade-off, and considered that a small loss of liberty was worth fewer traffic accidents, or less danger for the children, we are reluctant to speak here of a loss of liberty at all; what we feel we are trading off is convenience against safety.

By contrast a law which forbids me from worshipping according to the form I believe in is a serious below to liberty; even a law which tried to restrict this to certain times (as the traffic light restricts my crossing of the intersection to certain times) would be seen as a serious restriction. Why this difference between the two cases? Because we have a background understanding, too obvious to spell out, of some activities and goals as highly significant for human beings and others as less so. One's religious belief is recognised, even by atheists, as supremely important, because it is that by which the believer defines himself as a moral being. By contrast my rhythm of movement through the city traffic is trivial. We don't want to speak of these two in the same breath. We don't even readily admit that liberty is at stake in the traffic light case. For *de minimis non curat libertas.*

But this recourse to significance takes us beyond a Hobbesian scheme. Freedom is no longer just the absence of external obstacle *tout court*, but the absence of external obstacle to significant action, to what is important to man. There are discriminations to be made; some restrictions are more serious than others, some are utterly trivial. About many, there is of course controversy. But what the judgement turns on is some sense of what is significant for human life. Restricting the expression of people's religious and ethical convictions is more significant than restricting their movement around uninhabited parts of the country; and both are more significant than the trivia of traffic control.

But the Hobbesian scheme has no place for the notion of significance. It will allow only for purely quantitative judgements. On the toughest-minded version of his conception, where Hobbes seems to be about to define liberty in terms of the absence of physical obstacles, one is presented with the vertiginous prospect of human freedom being measurable in the same way as the degrees of freedom of some physical object, say a lever. Later we see that this won't do, because we have to take account of legal obstacles to my action. But in any case, such a quantitative conception of freedom is a non-starter.

Consider the following diabolical defence of Albania as a free country. We recognise that religion has been abolished in Albania, whereas it hasn't been in Britain. But on the other hand there are probably far fewer traffic lights per head in Tirana than in London. (I haven't checked for myself, but this is a very plausible assumption.) Suppose an apologist for Albanian Socialism were nevertheless to claim that this country was freer than Britain, because the number of acts restricted was far smaller. After all, only a minority of Londoners practise some religion in public places, but all have to negotiate their way through traffic. Those who do practise a religion generally do so on one day of the week, while they are held up at traffic lights every day. In sheer quantitative terms, the number of acts restricted by traffic lights must be greater than that restricted by a ban on public religious practice. So if Britain is considered a free society, why not Albania?

So the application even of our negative notion of freedom requires a background conception of what is significant, according to which some restrictions are seen to be without relevance for freedom altogether, and others are judged as being of greater and lesser importance. So some discrimination among motivations seems essential to our concept of freedom. A minute's reflection shows why this must be so. Freedom is important to us because we are purposive beings. But then there must be distinctions in the significance of different kinds of freedom based on the distinction in the significance of different purposes.

But of course, this still doesn't involve the kind of discrimination mentioned above, the kind which would allow us to say that someone who was doing what he wanted (in the unproblematic sense) wasn't really free, the kind of discrimination which allows us to put conditions on people's motivations necessary to their being free, and hence to second-guess them. All we have shown is that we make discriminations between more or less significant freedoms, based on discriminations among the purposes people have.

This creates some embarrassment for the crude negative theory, but it can cope with it by simply adding a recognition that we make judgements of significance. Its central claim that freedom just is the absence of external obstacles seems untouched, as also its view of freedom as an opportunity-concept. It is just that we now have to admit that not all opportunities are equal.

But there is more trouble in store for the crude view when we examine further what these qualitative discriminations are based on. What lies behind our judging certain purposes/feelings as more significant than others? One might think that there was room here again for another quantitative theory; that the more significant purposes are those we want more. But this account is either vacuous or false.

It is true but vacuous if we take wanting more just to mean being more significant. It is false as soon as we try to give wanting more an independent criterion, such as, for instance, the urgency or force of a desire, or the prevalence of one desire over another, because it is a matter of the most banal experience that the purposes we know to be more significant are not always those which we desire with the greatest urgency to encompass, nor the ones that actually always win out in cases of conflict of desires.

When we reflect on this kind of significance, we come up against what I have called elsewhere the fact of strong evaluation, the fact that we human subjects are not only subjects of first-order desires, but of second-order desires, desires about desires. We experience our desires and purposes as qualitatively discriminated, as higher or lower, noble or base, integrated or fragmented, significant or trivial, good and bad. This means that we experience some of our desires and goals as intrinsically more significant than others: some passing comfort is less important than the fulfilment of our lifetime

vocation, our *amour propre* less important than a love relationship; while we experience some others as bad, not just comparatively, but absolutely: we desire not to be moved by spite, or some childish desire to impress at all costs. And these judgements of significance are quite independent of the strength of the respective desires: the craving for comfort may be overwhelming at this moment, we may be obsessed with our *amour propre*, but the judgement of significance stands.

But then the question arises whether this fact of strong evaluation doesn't have other consequences for our notion of freedom, than just that it permits us to rank freedoms in importance. Is freedom not at stake when we find ourselves carried away by a less significant goal to override a highly significant one? Or when we are led to act out of a motive we consider bad or despicable?

The answer is that we sometimes do speak in this way. Suppose I have some irrational fear, which is preventing me from doing something I very much want to do. Say the fear of public speaking is preventing me from taking up a career that I should find very fulfilling, and that I should be quite good at, if I could just get over this 'hang-up'. It is clear that we experience this fear as an obstacle, and that we feel we are less than we would be if we could overcome it.

Or again, consider the case where I am very attached to comfort. To go on short rations, and to miss my creature comforts for a time, makes me very depressed. I find myself making a big thing of this. Because of this reaction I can't do certain things that I should like very much to do, such as going on an expedition over the Andes, or a canoe trip in the Yukon. Once again, it is quite understandable if I experience this attachment as an obstacle, and feel that I should be freer without it.

Or I could find that my spiteful feelings and reactions which I almost can't inhibit are undermining a relationship which is terribly important to me. At times, I feel as though I am almost assisting as a helpless witness at my own destructive behaviour, as I lash out again with my un-bridled tongue at her. I long to be able not to feel this spite. As long as I feel it, even control is not an option, because it just builds up inside until it either bursts out, or else the feeling somehow communicates itself, and queers things between us. I long to be free of this feeling.

These are quite understandable cases, where we can speak of freedom or its absence without strain. What I have called strong evaluation is essentially involved here. For these are not just cases of conflict, even cases of painful conflict. If the conflict is between two desires with which I have no trouble identifying, there can be no talk of lesser freedom, no matter how painful or fateful. Thus if what is breaking up my relationship is my finding fulfilment in a job which, say, takes me away from home a lot, I have indeed a terrible conflict, but I would have no temptation to speak of myself as less free.

Even seeing a great difference in the significance of the two terms doesn't seem to be a sufficient condition of my wanting to speak of freedom and its absence. Thus my marriage may be breaking up because I like going to the pub and playing cards on Saturday nights with the boys. I may feel quite unequivocally that my marriage is much more important than the release and comradeship of the Saturday night bash. But nevertheless I wouldn't want to talk of my being freer if I could slough off this desire.

The difference seems to be that in this case, unlike the ones above, I still identify with the less important desire, I still see it as expressive of myself, so that I couldn't lose it without altering who I am, losing something of my personality. Whereas my irrational fear, my being quite distressed by discomfort, my spite – these are all things which I can easily see myself losing without any loss whatsoever to what I am. This is why I can see them as obstacles to my purposes, and hence to my freedom, even though they are in a sense unquestionably desires and feelings of mine.

Before exploring further what's involved in this, let's go back and keep score. It would seem that these cases make a bigger breach in the crude negative theory. For they seem to be cases in which the obstacles to freedom are internal; and if this is so, then freedom can't simply be interpreted as the absence of *external* obstacles; and the fact that I'm doing what I want, in the sense of following my strongest desire, isn't sufficient to establish that I'm free. On the contrary, we have to make discriminations among motivations, and accept that acting out of some motivations, for example irrational fear or spite, or this too great need for comfort, is not freedom, is even a negation of freedom.

But although the crude negative theory can't be sustained in the face of these examples, perhaps something which springs from the same concerns can be reconstructed. For although we have to admit that there are internal, motivational, necessary conditions for freedom, we can perhaps still avoid any legitimation of what I called above the second-guessing of the subject. If our negative theory allows for strong evaluation, allows that some goals are really important to us, and that other desires are seen as not fully ours, then can it not retain the thesis that freedom is being able to do what I want, that is, what I can identify myself as wanting, where this means not just what I identify as my strongest desire, but what I identify as my true, authentic desire or purpose? The subject would still be the final arbiter of his being free/unfree, as indeed he is clearly capable of discerning this in the examples above, where I relied precisely on the subject's own experience of constraint, of motives with which he can't identify. We should have sloughed off the untenable Hobbesian reductive-materialist metaphysics, according to which only external obstacles count, as though action were just movement, and there could be no internal, motivational obstacles to our deeper purposes. But we would be retaining the basic concern of the negative theory, that the subject is still the final authority as to what his freedom consists in, and cannot be second-guessed by external authority. Freedom would be modified to read: the absence of internal or external obstacle to what I truly or authentically want. But we would still be holding the Maginot Line. Or would we?

I think not, in fact. I think that this hybrid or middle position is untenable, where we are willing to admit that we can speak of what we truly want, as against what we most strongly desire, and of some desires as obstacles to our freedom, while we still will not allow for second-guessing. For to rule this out in principle is to rule out in principle that the subject can ever be wrong about what he truly wants. And how can he never, in principle, be wrong, unless there is nothing to be right or wrong about in this matter?

That in fact is the thesis our negative theorist will have to defend. And it is a plausible one for the same intellectual (reductive-empiricist) tradition from which the crude negative theory springs. On this view, our feelings are brute facts about us; that is, it is a fact about us that we are affected in such and such a way, but our feelings can't themselves be understood as involving some perception or sense of what they relate to, and hence as potentially veridical or illusory, authentic or inauthentic. On this scheme, the fact that a certain desire represented one of our fundamental purposes, and another a mere force with which we cannot identify, would concern merely the brute quality of the affect in both cases. It would be a matter of the raw feel of these two desires that this was their respective status.

In such circumstances, the subject's own classification would be incorrigible. There is no such thing as an imperceptible raw feel. If the subject failed to experience a certain desire as fundamental, and if what we meant by 'fundamental' applied to desire was that the felt experience of it has a certain quality, then the desire couldn't be fundamental. We can see this if we look at those feelings which we can agree are brute in this sense: for instance, the stab of pain I feel when the dentist jabs into my tooth, or the crawling unease when someone runs his fingernail along the blackboard. There can be no question of misperception here. If I fail to 'perceive' the pain, I am not in pain. Might it not be so with our fundamental desires, and those which we repudiate?

The answer is clearly no. For first of all, many of our feelings and desires, including the relevant ones for these kinds of conflicts, are not brute. By contrast with pain and the fingernail-on-blackboard sensation, shame and fear, for instance, are emotions which involve our experiencing the situation as bearing a certain import for us, as being dangerous or shameful. This is why shame and fear can be inappropriate, or even irrational, where pain and a frisson cannot. Thus we can be in error in feeling shame or fear. We can even be consciously aware of the unfounded nature of our feelings, and this is when we castigate them as irrational.

Thus the notion that we can understand all our feelings and desires as brute, in the above sense, is not on. But more, the idea that we could discriminate our fundamental desires, or those which we want to repudiate, by the quality of brute affect is grotesque. When I am convinced that some career, or an expedition in the Andes, or a love relationship, is of fundamental importance to me (to recur to the above examples), it cannot be just because of the throbs, *élans* or tremors I feel; I must also have some sense that these are of great significance for me, meet important, long-lasting needs, represent a fulfilment of something central to me, will bring me closer to what I really am, or something of the sort. The whole notion of our identity, whereby we recognise that some goals, desires, allegiances are central to what we are, while others are not or are less so, can make sense only against a background of desires and feelings which are not brute, but what I shall call import-attributing, to invent a term of art for the occasion.

Thus we have to see our emotional life as made up largely of import-attributing desires and feelings, that is, desires and feelings which we can experience mistakenly. And not only can we be mistaken in this, we clearly must accept, in cases like the above where we want to repudiate certain desires, that we are mistaken.

For let us consider the distinction mentioned above between conflicts where we feel fettered by one desire, and those where we do not, where, for instance, in the example mentioned above, a man is torn between his career and his marriage. What made the difference was that in the case of genuine conflict both desires are the agent's, whereas in the cases where he feels fettered by one, this desire is one he wants to repudiate.

But what is it to feel that a desire is not truly mine? Presumably, I feel that I should be better off without it, that I don't lose anything in getting rid of it, I remain quite complete without it. What could lie behind this sense?

Well, one could imagine feeling this about a brute desire. I may feel this about my addiction to smoking, for instance – wish I could get rid of it, experience it as a fetter, and believe that I should be well rid of it. But addictions are a special case; we understand them to be unnatural, externally-induced desires. We couldn't say in general that we are ready to envisage losing our brute desires without a sense of diminution. On the contrary, to lose my desire for, and hence delectation in, oysters, mushroom pizza, or Peking duck would be a terrible deprivation. I should fight against such a change with all the strength at my disposal.

So being brute is not what makes desires repudiable. And besides, in the above examples the repudiated desires aren't brute. In the first case, I am chained by unreasoning fear, an import-attributing emotion, in which the fact of being mistaken is already recognised when I identify the fear as irrational or unreasoning. Spite, too, which moves me in the third case, is an import-attributing emotion. To feel spite is to see oneself and the target of one's resentment in a certain light; it is to feel in some way wounded, or damaged, by his success or good fortune, and the more hurt the more he is fortunate. To overcome feelings of spite, as against just holding them in, is to come to see self and other in a different light, in particular, to set aside self-pity, and the sense of being personally wounded by what the other does and is.

(I should also like to claim that the obstacle in the second example, the too great attachment to comfort, while not itself import-attributing, is also bound up with the way we see things. The problem is here not just that we dislike discomfort, but that we are too easily depressed by it; and this is something which we overcome only by sensing a different order of priorities, whereby small discomforts matter less. But if this is thought too dubious, we can concentrate on the other two examples.)

Now how can we feel that an import-attributing desire is not truly ours? We can do this only if we see it as mistaken, that is, the import or the good it supposedly gives us a sense of is not a genuine import or good. The irrational fear is a fetter, because it is irrational; spite is a fetter because it is rooted in a self-absorption which distorts our perspective on everything, and the pleasures of venting it preclude any genuine satisfaction. Losing these desires we lose nothing, because their loss deprives us of no genuine good or pleasure or satisfaction. In this they are quite different from my love of oysters, mushroom pizza and Peking duck.

It would appear from this that to see our desires as brute gives us no clue as to why some of them are repudiable. On the contrary it is precisely their not being brute which can explain this. It is because they are import-attributing desires which are mistaken that we can feel that we would lose nothing in sloughing them off. Everything which is truly important to us would be safeguarded. If they were just brute desires, we couldn't feel this unequivocally, as we certainly do not when it comes to the pleasures of the palate. True, we also feel that our desire to smoke is repudiable, but there is a special explanation here, which is not available in the case of spite.

Thus we can experience some desires as fetters, because we can experience them as not ours. And we can experience them as not ours because we see them as incorporating a quite erroneous appreciation of our situation and of what matters to us. We can see this again if we contrast the case of spite with that of another emotion which partly overlaps, and which is highly considered in some societies, the desire for revenge. In certain traditional societies this is far from being considered a despicable emotion. On the contrary, it is a duty of honour on a male relative to avenge a man's death. We might imagine that this too might give rise to conflict. It might conflict with the attempts of a new regime to bring some order to the land. The government would have to stop people taking vengeance, in the name of peace.

But short of a conversion to a new ethical outlook, this would be seen as a trade-off, the sacrifice of one legitimate goal for the sake of another. And it would seem monstrous were one to propose reconditioning people so that they no longer felt the desire to avenge their kin. This would be to unman them.[4]

Why do we feel so different about spite (and for that matter also revenge)? Because the desire for revenge for an ancient Icelander was his sense of a real obligation incumbent on him, something it would be dishonourable to repudiate; while for us, spite is the child of a distorted perspective on things.

We cannot therefore understand our desires and emotions as all brute, and in particular we cannot make sense of our discrimination of some desires as more important and fundamental, or of our repudiation of others, unless we understand our feelings to be import-attributing. This is essential to there being what we have called strong evaluation. Consequently the half-way position which admits strong evaluation, admits that our desires may frustrate our deeper purposes, admits therefore that there may be inner obstacles to freedom, and yet will not admit that the subject may be wrong or mistaken about these purposes – this position doesn't seem tenable. For the only way to make the subject's assessment incorrigible in principle would be to claim that there was nothing to be right or wrong about here; and that could only be so if experiencing a given feeling were a matter of the qualities of brute feeling. But this it cannot be if we are to make sense of the whole background of strong evaluation, more significant goals, and aims that we repudiate. This whole scheme requires that we understand the emotions concerned as import-attributing, as, indeed, it is clear that we must do on other grounds as well.

But once we admit that our feelings are import-attributing, then we admit the possibility of error, or false appreciation. And indeed, we have to admit a kind of false appreciation which the agent himself detects in order to make sense of the cases where we experience our own desires as fetters. How can we exclude in principle that there may be other false appreciations which the agent does not detect? That he may be profoundly in error, that is, have a very distorted sense of his fundamental purposes? Who can say that such people can't exist? All cases are, of course, controversial; but I should nominate Charles Manson and Andreas Baader for this category, among others. I pick them out as people with a strong sense of some purposes and goals as incomparably more fundamental than others, or at least with a propensity to act as having such a sense so as to take in even themselves a good part of the time, but whose sense of fundamental purpose was shot through with confusion and error. And once we recognise such extreme cases, how do we avoid admitting that many of the rest of mankind can suffer to a lesser degree from the same disabilities?

What has this got to do with freedom? Well, to resume what we have seen: our attributions of freedom make sense against a background sense of more and less significant purposes, for the question of freedom/unfreedom is bound up with the frustration/fulfilment of our purposes. Further, our significant purposes can be frustrated by our own desires, and where these are sufficiently based on misappreciation, we consider them as not really ours, and experience them as fetters. A man's freedom can therefore be hemmed in by internal, motivational obstacles, as well as external ones. A man who is driven by spite to jeopardise his most important relationships, in spite of himself, as it were, or who is prevented by unreasoning fear from taking up the career he truly wants, is not really made more free if one lifts the external obstacles to his venting his spite or acting on his fear. Or at best he is liberated into a very impoverished freedom.

If through linguistic/ideological purism one wants to stick to the crude definition, and insist that men are equally freed from whom the same external obstacles are lifted, regardless of their motivational state, then one will just have to introduce some other term to mark the distinction, and say that one man is capable of taking proper advantage of his freedom, and the other (the one in the grip of spite, or fear) is not. This is because in the meaningful sense of 'free', that for which we value it, in the sense of being able to act on one's important purposes, the internally fettered man is not free. If we choose to give 'free' a special (Hobbesian) sense which avoids this issue, we'll just have to introduce another term to deal with it.

Moreover since we have already seen that we are always making judgements of degrees of freedom, based on the significance of the activities or purposes which are left unfettered, how can we deny that the man, externally free but still stymied by

his repudiated desires, is less free than one who has no such inner obstacles?

But if this is so, then can we not say of the man with a highly distorted view of his fundamental purpose, the Manson or Baader of my discussion above, that he may not be significantly freer when we lift even the internal barriers to his doing what is in line with this purpose, or at best may be liberated into a very impoverished freedom? Should a Manson overcome his last remaining compunction against sending his minions to kill on caprice, so that he could act unchecked, would we consider him freer, as we should undoubtedly consider the man who had done away with spite or unreasoning fear? Hardly, and certainly not to the same degree. For what he sees as his purpose here partakes so much of the nature of spite and unreasoning fear in the other cases, that is, it is an aspiration largely shaped by confusion, illusion and distorted perspective.

Once we see that we make distinctions of degree and significance in freedoms depending on the significance of the purpose fettered/enabled, how can we deny that it makes a difference to the degree of freedom not only whether one of my basic purposes is frustrated by my own desires but also whether I have grievously misidentified this purpose? The only way to avoid this would be to hold that there is no such thing as getting it wrong, that your basic purpose is just what you feel it to be. But there is such a thing as getting it wrong, as we have seen, and the very distinctions of significance depend on this fact.

But if this is so, then the crude negative view of freedom, the Hobbesian definition, is untenable. Freedom can't just be the absence of external obstacles, for there may also be internal ones. And nor may the internal obstacles be just confined to those that the subject identifies as such, so that he is the final arbiter; for he may be profoundly mistaken about his purposes and about what he wants to repudiate. And if so, he is less capable of freedom in the meaningful sense of the word. Hence we cannot maintain the incorrigibility of the subject's judgements about his freedom, or rule out second-guessing, as we put it above. And at the same time, we are forced to abandon the pure opportunity-concept of freedom.

For freedom now involves my being able to recognise adequately my more important purposes, and my being able to overcome or at least neutralise my motivational fetters, as well as my way being free of external obstacles. But clearly the first condition (and, I would argue, also the second) require me to have become something, to have achieved a certain condition of self-clairvoyance and self-understanding. I must be actually exercising self-understanding in order to be truly or fully free. I can no longer understand freedom just as an opportunity-concept.

In all these three formulations of the issue – opportunity- versus exercise-concept; whether freedom requires that we discriminate among motivations; whether it allows of second-guessing the subject – the extreme negative view shows up as wrong. The idea of holding the Maginot Line before this Hobbesian concept is misguided not only because it involves abandoning some of the most inspiring terrain of liberalism, which is concerned with individual self-realisation, but also

because the line turns out to be untenable. The first step from the Hobbesian definition to a positive notion, to a view of freedom as the ability to fulfil my purposes, and as being greater the more significant the purposes, is one we cannot help taking. Whether we must also take the second step, to a view of freedom which sees it as realisable or fully realisable only within a certain form of society; and whether in taking a step of this kind one is necessarily committed to justifying the excesses of totalitarian oppression in the name of liberty; these are questions which must now be addressed. What is certain is that they cannot simply be evaded by a philistine definition of freedom which relegates them by fiat to the limbo of metaphysical pseudo-questions. This is altogether too quick a way with them.

Notes

1 *FEL*, pp. 118–72.
2 Ibid., p. 148, note 1.
3 Ibid., p. 164.

4 Compare the unease we feel at the reconditioning of the hero of Anthony Burgess's *A Clockwork Orange*.

26

A Third Concept of Liberty

Quentin Skinner

I

I take as my starting-point one of the claims most widely accepted in current discussions about the theory of liberty. There must be one overarching formula, we are told, under which all intelligible locutions about freedom can be subsumed.[1] The prevalence of this belief appears to be due in large part to the influence of a single classic article, Gerald MacCallum's 'Negative and Positive Freedom'.[2] Whenever the freedom of an agent is in question, MacCallum maintains, it will always be freedom from some element of constraint upon doing or becoming (or not doing or becoming) something.[3] Freedom is 'always one and the same triadic relation' between agents, constraints, and ends. To speak of the presence of freedom is always, in consequence, to speak of an absence: absence of constraint upon an agent from realising some goal or end. There is, in other words, only one concept of liberty.[4]

These observations bring me to the theorist of liberty in whose memory I have the honour to be speaking today. I did not know Sir Isaiah Berlin well, so I am not in a position to reminisce about him. But that does not seem to me a disadvantage, for Berlin was a professional thinker, and what matters about him is what he argued and thought. What he most influentially argued about – as no one here will need reminding – was the theory of freedom. It is accordingly on that topic that

I propose to concentrate. I shall focus in particular on Berlin's most celebrated contribution to the debate, his essay – just republished in a handsome new edition – entitled 'Two Concepts of Liberty'.[5]

Let me state at once what I take to be the abiding merit of Berlin's text, which has recently and I am sure rightly been characterised as the most influential single essay in contemporary political philosophy.[6] By contrast with the conventional wisdom I began by citing, Berlin succeeds in showing – beyond doubt, it seems to me – that a strong distinction needs to be marked between two rival and incommensurable concepts of liberty. He succeeds in showing, in other words, that any attempt to bring together our particular judgements about freedom under a single theory or overarching formula will be foredoomed to failure.

As all the world knows, the manner in which Berlin draws the distinction in which he is primarily interested is by speaking of negative and positive freedom or liberty.[7] When he discusses negative liberty, he gives an account closely resembling the analysis that, according to MacCallum and his numerous followers, must be given of any claim about freedom if it is to be intelligible. To see, therefore, where Berlin has something challenging to add to the argument, we need to turn to his account of what he describes as positive liberty.

Berlin's attempt to mark off this separate concept is admittedly dogged by several false starts. He begins by suggesting that, whereas negative

Originally published in *Proceedings of the British Academy* 117 (2001): 237–68. Reprinted by permission of Quentin Skinner.

liberty is freedom *from* constraint, positive liberty is freedom *to* follow a certain form of life.[8] But this distinction cannot be used to disclose two different concepts of liberty, if only because all cases of negative liberty are at once cases in which I am free from constraint and, *eo ipso*, free to act should I choose. (If I assure you that you will not be impeded *from* leaving this lecture if you don't like it, I could equally well assure you that you will be free *to* leave.)[9] Berlin next suggests that the positive sense of the word refers to the idea of being one's own master as opposed to being acted upon by external forces.[10] But this too fails to isolate a separate concept of positive liberty. For the situation in which I am free to act in virtue of not being hindered by external forces is, according to Berlin's own analysis, that of someone in possession of their liberty in the ordinary negative sense.

It soon emerges, however, that Berlin's concern is not with the idea of being your own master. Rather he is interested in the very different notion (although he sometimes runs them together) of mastering your self. When he first employs this latter formula, he uses it to refer to the familiar thought – equally familiar to students of Plato and of Freud – that the obstacles to your capacity to act freely may be internal rather than external, and that you will need to free yourself from these psychological constraints if you are to act autonomously.[11] But this too fails to capture a separate concept of positive liberty. For while the notion of an internal obstacle extends the range of things that can count as constraints, we are still speaking about the need to get rid of an element of constraint if we are to act freely, and are still speaking in consequence about the idea of negative liberty.

The principal claim, however, that Berlin wishes to make about self-mastery proves to be a different and more convincing one. According to those who have wished to give a positive content to the idea of liberty, he suggests, the freedom of an agent consists in their having managed most fully to become themselves. Freedom is thus equated not with self-mastery but rather with self-realisation, and above all with self-perfection, with the idea (as Berlin expresses it) of my self at its best.[12] The positive concept is thus that, as Berlin finally summarises, 'whatever is the true goal of man . . . must be identical with his freedom'.[13]

If there is any one philosopher whom Berlin had in mind in formulating this definition, it must I think have been Bernard Bosanquet.[14] In *The Philosophical Theory of the State*, first published

in 1899, Bosanquet speaks in so many words about the 'negative idea'[15] of being 'free from constraint'[16] and contrasts this juristic concept, as he calls it, with what he describes as the 'fuller' or 'positive' understanding of the term.[17] Furthermore, when Bosanquet proceeds to characterise the negative ideal as that of being preserved against trespass, and contrasts it with the positive view of the 'real' or 'ideal' self whose activity is identical with freedom, Berlin echoes his phraseology almost word for word.[18]

Behind Bosanquet's analysis, however, lies the overwhelming influence of T.H. Green.[19] As Bosanquet acknowledges in the chapter I have been quoting, he makes 'great use' of the analysis of freedom offered by Green in his *Principles of Political Obligation*, originally published in 1886. Green does not explicitly speak in that work (although he does elsewhere)[20] of 'positive' liberty, but he provides a subtler and more careful analysis than Bosanquet does of what might be meant by giving a positive content to the ideal. 'Real freedom,' according to Green, 'consists in the whole man having found his object.'[21] To attain freedom is thus to have attained 'harmony with the true law of one's being'.[22] To speak of the freedom of a man is to speak of 'the state in which he shall have realised his ideal of himself'.[23] Freedom is, in short, the name of an end-state; as Green concludes, it is 'in some sense the goal of moral endeavour'.[24]

It is hard nowadays to recapture how disquieting this analysis seemed to many English moral and political philosophers writing in the aftermath of World War I. L.T. Hobhouse, for example, whose critique of Hegel, Green and Bosanquet appeared in 1918, went so far as to declare that 'in the bombing of London' he had witnessed 'the visible and tangible outcome of a false and wicked doctrine'.[25] To anyone of Berlin's generation, however, these anxieties about Hegelian philosophy remained remarkably acute. One only has to think of the abusive and tendentious attack on Hegel mounted by Karl Popper in *The Open Society and its Enemies*.[26] Writing little more than a decade later, Berlin is I think registering many of the same anxieties in his analysis of positive liberty and the dangers to which it allegedly gives rise.

I do not wish, however, to press the historical point. My reason for quoting Green and Bosanquet is to lend further weight to what seems to me Berlin's most important argument. As soon as one reflects on their line of thought, one sees that

Berlin was right to insist that there is a coherent concept of liberty completely at odds with the negative idea of absence of constraint. As he rather grandly summarises, we find ourselves confronting 'not two different interpretations of a single concept, but two profoundly divergent and irreconcilable attitudes to the ends of life'.[27]

Berlin could with profit have carried this central argument of his essay much further. It seems to me a surprising fact about the Introduction to his *Four Essays on Liberty*, in which he replies to his critics, that he never refers to this neo-Hegelian understanding of freedom in responding to MacCallum's insistence that all intelligible locutions about liberty must conform to one and the same triadic scheme. To this objection Berlin merely returns the suggestion – which I have already shown to be confused – that some pleas for negative liberty must reflect a simpler dyadic structure, revealing as they do a desire to be liberated from some measure of constraint, but without any further desire to act in any particular way. What Berlin should have retorted, it seems to me, is that the positive conception of liberty he rightly isolates cannot be made to conform to the triadic structure on which MacCallum and his followers insist.[28] The crux of Bosanquet's argument – and even more clearly of Green's – is that the freedom of human agents consists in their having succeeded in realising an ideal of themselves. But this is not to speak of a condition in which someone is free to do or become something, as required by MacCallum's analysis. It is to speak of a condition in which someone has succeeded in becoming something. Freedom is not being viewed as absence of constraint on action; it is being viewed as a pattern of action of a certain kind.[29]

Berlin's argument can be carried a yet further step if we recognise that what underlies these theories of positive liberty is the belief that human nature has an essence, and that we are free if and only if we succeed in realising that essence in our lives.[30] This enables us to see that there will be as many different interpretations of positive liberty as there are different views about the moral character of humankind. Suppose, for example, you accept the Christian view that the essence of our nature is religious, and thus that we attain our highest ends if and only if we consecrate our lives to God. Then you will believe that, in the words of Thomas Cranmer, the service of God 'is perfect freedom'. Or suppose you accept

the Aristotelian argument that man is a political animal, the argument restated as a theory of freedom by Hannah Arendt in *Between Past and Future*.[31] Then you will believe that, as Arendt maintains, 'freedom ... and politics coincide' and that 'this freedom is primarily experienced in action'.[32] More specifically, you will believe that, as Charles Taylor adds, 'freedom resides at least in part in collective control over the common life', because the exercise of such control is the form of activity in which the essence of our humanity is most fully realised.[33]

Faced with these equations between freedom and certain forms of life, how can MacCallum and his followers hope to rescue their contention that all intelligible claims about liberty must be claims about absence of constraint? As far as I can see, their only recourse will be to suggest that the arguments I have cited from Green and Bosanquet are not intelligible as claims about liberty; that they must either be muddled or be talking about something else. As Berlin excellently points out, however, there is no difficulty in seeing how the neo-Hegelians took their thesis, without any incoherence, to be one about human freedom.[34] The claim they are advancing is that if and only if we actually follow the most fulfilling way of life shall we overcome the constraints and obstacles to our realisation of our full potential, and thereby realise our ideal of ourselves. The living of such a life alone frees us from such constraints and, by making us fully ourselves, makes us fully free. Liberty consists in following that way of life in which, all passion spent, we finally achieve harmony with our nature.

I am not endorsing the truth of these claims, merely their intelligibility. I happen to agree with Berlin that there are many different ends that we can equally well pursue. Perhaps he was unduly anxious about the authoritarian implications of rejecting this commitment,[35] but I also happen to agree with him that those who imagine that human nature has an essence, and thereby hold that there is just one goal to which we all ought to commit ourselves, tend to bully or at least to behave self-righteously towards those of more pluralist allegiances. However, I have no need to lapse in this way into autobiography. It is enough for me, just as it is enough for Berlin, to display the coherence of the neo-Hegelian analysis. That in itself is sufficient to dispose of the prevailing belief that there is only one concept of liberty.

II

As the title of his essay indicates, Berlin's chief concern is to contrast the positive ideal of freedom as self-perfection with what he describes, following much precedent, as negative liberty. As we have seen, by negative liberty Berlin means absence of constraint, and the specific interpretation he believes must be given to the concept of constraint is that it must consist in some act of interference, by some external agency, with the capacity of another agent to pursue 'possible choices and activities'.[36] These obstacles or hindrances need not be intentional, for Berlin allows that they may be the result of – as opposed to being deliberately caused by – the actions of others. But his fundamental contention is that the absence which marks the presence of liberty must always be absence of interference. As he puts it in his clearest summary, 'the criterion of oppression is the part that I believe to be played by other human beings, directly or indirectly, with or without the intention of doing so, in frustrating my wishes. By being free in this sense I mean not being interfered with by others. The wider the area of non-interference the wider my freedom.'[37]

While this is a familiar vision of human liberty, it is a matter of no small difficulty to state it with precision, and it is worth noting that Berlin's statement embodies a valuable qualification often omitted in more recent accounts.[38] Berlin adds that I am unfree 'if I am prevented by others from doing *what I could otherwise do*'.[39] I may be physically obstructed in such a way that an action within my powers becomes impossible to perform. Or I may be subjected to such a degree of coercion that the action is rendered, in Jeremy Bentham's phrase, ineligible. But in either case my loss of freedom stems, as Berlin puts it, from 'the deliberate interference of other human beings within the area in which I could otherwise act'.[40]

I do not wholly agree with Berlin's formulation, for I do not see why this disempowerment need be the work specifically of human agencies. If I had been prevented by a blizzard from arriving to deliver this lecture, it would make perfect sense on Berlin's own basic understanding of freedom as absence of interference to say that my freedom had been curtailed.[41] But this is a quibble. What seems to me particularly valuable about Berlin's way of stating the case is his insistence that lack of freedom must be categorically distinguished from lack of ability, and that the right way to mark this distinction is to say that we lack freedom only when an action within our powers has been rendered impossible or ineligible.

Berlin's way of articulating this distinction is strongly reminiscent of Hobbes's analysis of free action in his *Leviathan* of 1651. Hobbes compares the predicament of two men who are unable to leave a room: one possesses the power to leave, but has been 'restrained, with walls, or chayns' and thereby disempowered; the other straightforwardly lacks the ability, because he is 'fastned to his bed by sicknesse'.[42] According to Hobbes's analysis, the first man is unfree to leave, but the second is neither free nor unfree; he is simply unable. The reason, Hobbes explains, is that the idea of free action presupposes the idea of deliberating between alternatives.[43] But it makes no sense to deliberate as to whether to perform an action we already know to be beyond our powers. Hence Hobbes's definition of human freedom: 'a free man' is someone who '*in those things, which by his strength and wit he is able to do, is not hindred to doe what he has a will to*'.[44]

Contrast this understanding with the view, currently prevalent, that we need to distinguish between the formal and the effective possession of negative liberty. One of the examples Berlin gives in distinguishing lack of freedom from inability is the case of a man who cannot read because he is blind. If we apply the distinction between formal and effective freedom, we arrive at the view that the blind man is formally free to read, because no one is interfering with him in this pursuit.[45] But he is not effectively free, since he is not in a position to make use of his formal liberty.[46]

Berlin's more Hobbesian approach enables us to see that this kind of analysis results at best in confusion and at worst in a kind of mockery of freedom. There are two contrasting points to be brought out here. One is that, on Berlin's account, the blind man is neither formally nor effectively free to read. As Berlin insists, I am free only if I am capable of exercising an ability, should I choose, without interference. But the predicament of the blind man is that he is incapable of exercising the ability to read under any circumstances. The contrasting point is that, on Berlin's account, the blind man is neither formally nor effectively unfree to read. To be unfree is to have been rendered incapable of exercising an ability I possess. But the blind man has not in this way been disempowered; he is simply not in possession of the relevant ability.

Although Berlin's analysis of negative liberty is exceptionally acute and valuable, it nevertheless seems to me to suffer from a serious limitation of coverage. This weakness, moreover, is one that it shares with almost every other recent statement of the theory of negative liberty that I have come across. This being so, the nature of the weakness seems to me well worth trying to identify and remedy, and this is the task to which I shall devote myself in the rest of these remarks.

When Berlin first introduces his view of negative liberty, he rightly observes that 'this is what the classical English political philosophers meant' by freedom, and he specifically refers us to Hobbes's definition in *Leviathan*.[47] What Berlin misses, however, is the fiercely polemical character of Hobbes's analysis. When Hobbes announces, in words that Berlin echoes closely, that our liberty consists of nothing more than 'absence of externall Impediments' to the exercise of our powers,[48] he is attempting at the same time to discredit and supersede a rival and strongly contrasting understanding of negative liberty. This rival theory had risen to prominence in English public debate in the early decades of the seventeenth century, and it appeared to Hobbes to be extremely dangerous as well as hopelessly confused.

I can best bring out the significance of Hobbes's critique if I try to answer a question raised by Berlin in the Introduction to his revised edition of 'Two Concepts of Liberty'. He asks when the idea of freedom as nothing other than non-interference was first explicitly formulated, and what prompted its rise to its present hegemonal prominence.[49] I would answer that it is very hard to find an explicit statement of such a theory any earlier than Hobbes's in *Leviathan*, and that what prompted him to articulate it was his sense of the need to respond to the 'Democratical Gentlemen',[50] as he called them, who had deployed their very different theory to promote the cause of Parliament against the crown and to legitimise the execution of King Charles I.

Hobbes's counter-revolutionary challenge eventually won the day. To cite Berlin's own litany, we find his basic line of argument taken up by David Hume, Jeremy Bentham, to some degree by John Stuart Mill, and even more closely (Berlin could have added) by Henry Sidgwick.[51] This great tradition of classical utilitarianism proved impressively successful at occupying the entire conceptual space, thereby managing to dismiss any rival interpretations of liberty as either pernicious or confused. As a result of this profound and enduring ideological success, the alternative vision of negative liberty that Hobbes originally set out to discredit has virtually sunk from sight. What I now want to do is to try to lift it back to the surface.

As I have indicated, the theory in question formed part of the armoury of the Parliamentarians in their disputes with the crown in the opening decades of the seventeenth century. Critics of the royal prerogative began to argue that, to the extent that they were obliged to live in dependence on the power of the king, and obliged in consequence to rely on his goodwill for the continuation of their rights and liberties, they were living in a state of servitude. They insisted, in other words, that freedom is restricted not only by actual interference or the threat of it, but also by the mere knowledge that we are living in dependence on the goodwill of others.[52] These writers are not making the obvious point that the possibility of such arbitrary interference renders our liberty less robust or secure. They are arguing that a mere awareness of living under an arbitrary power – a power capable of interfering in our activities without having to consider our interests – serves in itself to limit our liberty.[53] Knowing that we are free to do or forbear only because someone else has chosen not to stop us is what reduces us to servitude.

The immediate inspiration for this way of thinking appears to have stemmed from a number of Medieval common-law texts, above all those of Bracton and Littleton. These were the authorities that Sir Edward Coke and his followers in the early Stuart Parliaments loved to invoke, and proceeded to quote with so much reverence that they acquired an authority they had never before enjoyed and have never subsequently lost. Henry de Bracton in his *De Legibus et Consuetudinibus Angliae* of *c.* 1260 distinguishes in his opening chapter between free persons and slaves, and proceeds to define as a slave anyone who 'lives in subjection to the dominion of someone else'.[54] Sir Thomas Littleton's fifteenth-century treatise, *Un lyver de exposicion de parcell de les tenures*,[55] draws a very similar set of distinctions between freemen, villeins, and slaves, and repeats that a slave is someone whose lack of liberty is such that his person – and not merely, as with a villein, his property – is *sub potestate*, within the power or at the mercy of someone else.

The most striking feature of these definitions (although later common lawyers did their best to ignore the fact) is that they owe their phraseology entirely to the analysis of freedom and slavery at the outset of the *Digest* of Roman law. There we are first informed that 'the fundamental division within the law of persons is that all men and women are either free or are slaves'.[56] Next we are given a formal definition of slavery. 'Slavery is an institution of the *ius gentium* by which someone is, contrary to nature, subjected to the dominion of someone else'.[57] This in turn is held to yield a definition of individual liberty. If everyone in a civil association is either bond or free, then a *civis* or free citizen must be someone who is not under the dominion of anyone else, but is *sui iuris*, capable of acting in their own right.[58] It likewise follows that what it means for someone to lack the status of a free citizen must be for that person not to be *sui iuris* but instead to be *sub potestate*, under the power or subject to the will of someone else.[59]

By the time these distinctions were summarised in Justinian's *Codex*, they had been the common coin of Roman political theory for generations. They had been popularised in particular by the great sequence of historians – Sallust, Livy, Tacitus – who had traced the subversion of the republican *civitas libera* and its collapse into the servitude of the principate.[60] This being so, it is a fact of singular importance that it was in the generation immediately prior to the disputes between crown and Parliament in the early seventeenth century that all their works were translated into English for the first time. Henry Savile's version of Tacitus's *Histories* and *Agricola* appeared in 1591, with Richard Grenewey's rendering of the *Annals* and *Germania* following in 1598.[61] Two years later Philemon Holland issued his enormous folio containing the whole of the extant sections of Livy's *History*,[62] while in 1608 Thomas Heywood published his translations of Sallust's *Bellum Catilinae* and *Bellum Iugurthinum*.[63]

If you turn to any of these authorities, you will find it argued once again that what it means to possess your liberty is, as Livy puts it, not to be subject to the power of anyone else. When, for example, Livy describes the surrender of the Collatines to the people of Rome, he stresses that they were able to take this decision because (in the words of Holland's translation) they were 'in their owne power', and hence 'at libertie to doe what they will'.[64] The same view emerges still

more clearly from the later passage in which Livy discusses the efforts of the Greek cities to restore their good relations with Rome. To enter into such negotiations, one of their spokesmen is made to say, presupposes the possession of 'true libertie', that condition in which a people 'is able to stand alone and maintain it selfe, and dependeth not upon the will and pleasure of others'.[65]

It was this understanding of political liberty that a number of spokesmen in Parliament began to deploy in criticism of the crown in the early decades of the seventeenth century. One aspect of their campaign has of course been extensively discussed, and forms the cornerstone of the traditional 'whig' explanation for the outbreak of the English Civil War in 1642. They repeatedly accused the government, most conspicuously in the Petition of Right of 1628, of forcibly interfering with a number of fundamental rights and liberties. Charles I was charged with compelling and requiring his people to make loans to him, and with imprisoning and even executing subjects without due cause being shown.[66] These actions were taken to constitute an obvious violation of rights and liberties, since they involved (in the words of the Petition) molesting large numbers of subjects contrary to the laws and franchise of the land.[67]

None of the spokesmen I am considering ever doubted that these acts of oppression undermined their freedom as subjects. As I have intimated, however, they were more concerned with a very different argument about the relations between their liberties and the royal prerogative. The further claim they advance is that such acts of violence are merely the outward manifestations of a deeper affront to liberty. The underlying principle to which they object is that, in times of necessity, the crown possesses a prerogative right, and hence a discretionary power, to imprison without trial and impose levies without parliamentary consent. The objection they develop is that, if the crown is the bearer of any such prerogatives, this is as much as to say that our property and personal liberties are held not 'of right' but merely 'of grace', since the crown is claiming that it can take them away without injustice at any time.

As these democratical gentlemen make clear, what troubles them is the view of rights implied by this understanding of the prerogative. To maintain that our basic rights and liberties are subject to being taken away with impunity is to declare that they do not have the status of rights; it is to say that they are mere licences or privileges. This is the insight that prompts them to reach for their Bracton – and indeed their Livy and Tacitus. To accept, they retort, that we hold our rights and liberties at discretion is to accept that we are living in subjection to the will of the king. But to admit that we are living in such a state of dependence is to admit that we are living not as free citizens but as slaves. The mere knowledge that the crown possesses such prerogatives serves in itself to undermine our liberty and leave us in servitude.

These arguments were vigorously deployed in the debates of 1628 about the right to imprison without cause shown. As Edward Littleton proclaimed, the effect of this prerogative is to make what he describes as 'personall libertye' dependent on the will of the king, so permitting the 'invasion' of the most fundamental freedom 'established & confirmed by the whole State'.[68] Richard Cresheld, another common lawyer, agreed that if the crown is permitted such a right, then we 'become bondage'. To which he added, referring directly to the definition of slavery in the *Digest*, that this condition 'I am sure is contrary to and against the law of nature'.[69] Later in the session Henry Sherfield, yet another lawyer, made the same point by way of distinguishing between freemen, villeins and slaves. 'If the King may imprison a freeman without a cause', then 'he is in worse case than a villein,' for a villein at least enjoys personal liberty, whereas 'to be imprisoned without cause, that is a thraldom.'[70] Speaking in support, Sir John Eliot agreed that without this 'common right of the subject' we are nothing better than bondmen.[71] Summarising at the end of the session, Sir Roger North put it to the Commons that their principal duty was to question these prerogatives: we must 'save ourselves and them that sent us from being slaves'.[72]

The belief that dependence undermines liberty was even more extensively invoked in the numerous debates about the alleged prerogative right to impose levies without consent of Parliament. The argument was first prominently deployed in the session of 1610. Thomas Wentworth opened the debate by declaring that, unless this prerogative is questioned, we might as well be sold for slaves.[73] Later he went on to add that, if we allow this prerogative 'of imposing, even upon our lands and goods', the effect will be to leave us 'at the mercy' of the king.[74] Sir Thomas Hedley in his great speech about the liberties of subjects agreed that such a prerogative places the property of free subjects 'in the absolute power and command of another'.[75] As

they both insist, however, to live at the mercy or under the absolute power of another is what it means to live in slavery. Hedley reminded the Commons that Cicero ('though an heathen yet a wise man') and Tacitus had both drawn exactly this distinction between freedom and servitude. If you 'take away the liberty of the subject in his profit or property' then 'you make a promiscuous confusion of a freeman and a bound slave'.[76]

The same issue was later to resurface with a vengeance in the Parliaments of Charles I. Sir Dudley Digges returned to the argument at the outset of the debate over the Forced Loan in 1628. We are told, he observes, that 'he is no great monarch' who cannot take 'whatsoever he will'. But any king who 'is not tied to the laws' and thereby rules by his arbitrary will is nothing better than 'a king of slaves'.[77] The same argument was restated yet again in the wake of Charles I's extension of Ship Money into a general levy in the 1630s. Perhaps the most influential attack came from Henry Parker, who emerged at this juncture as by far the most formidable and influential defender of the parliamentary cause. To coincide with the assembling of the Long Parliament. Parker published his tract entitled *The Case of Shipmony briefly discoursed* in November 1640.[78] He begins by recurring to the Roman Law view of what it means to live in servitude. 'Where the meere will of the Prince is law' we can expect 'no mediocrity or justice' and 'wee all see that the thraldome of such is most grievous, which have no bounds set to their Lord's discretion.'[79] Parker is clear that the mere existence of such powers is what reduces us to slavery. 'It is enough that we all, and all that we have, are at his discretion,' for where all law is 'subjecte to the King's meer discretion,' there 'all liberty is overthrowne.'[80] With these considerations in mind, Parker turns to the case of Ship Money. If we accept that the king has a right to impose this levy, so that 'to his sole indisputable judgement it is left to lay charges as often and as great as he pleases', this will 'leave us the most despicable slaves in the whole world'.[81] The reason is that this will leave us in a condition of total dependence on the king's goodwill. But as Parker rhetorically asks, if we have no alternative but to 'presume well of our Princes', then 'wherein doe we differ in condition from the most abject of all bondslaves?'[82]

These were serious enough assaults on the foundations of the royal prerogative, but the moment at which they finally provoked a fatal crisis came in the opening months of 1642. When the House of Commons brought forward a proposal early in February to take control of the Militia, Charles I made it clear that he would veto any such legislation by exercising his so-called prerogative of the Negative Voice. Parliament then took the revolutionary step of claiming that, at least in times of emergency, it must possess the right to legislate even in the absence of the royal assent. The reason why this must be so, a number of spokesmen now declared, is that the alternative is national servitude. If the crown can block any legislation with the Negative Voice, this will reduce Parliament – which represents the whole people of England – to a state of complete dependence on the will of the king. But if we are condemned to living under such a constitution, this will reduce the freeborn English to a nation of slaves.

Henry Parker again came to the fore at this climacteric moment, arguing exactly this case in the most important of all the defences of the Parliamentary cause, his *Observations upon some of his Majesties late Answers and Expresses* of July 1642.[83] The existence of the Negative Voice, Parker now maintains, has the effect of subjecting the whole nation 'to as unbounded a regiment of the Kings meere will, as any Nation under Heaven ever suffered under'. For 'what remains, but that all our lawes, rights, & liberties, be either no where at all determinable, or else onely in the Kings breast?'[84] With this prerogative, the king 'assumes to himselfe a share in the legislative power' so great as to open up 'a gap to as vast and arbitrary a prerogative as the Grand Seignior has' in Constantinople.[85] For he assumes to himself a power to 'take away the being of Parliament meerely by dissent'.[86] But if we permit the King 'to be the sole, supream competent Judge in this case, we resigne all into his hands, we give lifes, liberties, Laws, Parliaments, all to be held at meer discretion' and thereby consign ourselves to bondage.[87]

Charles I had complained in his *Answer to the XIX Propositions* that without the Negative Voice he would be reduced from the status of 'a King of *England*' to a mere 'Duke of *Venice*'.[88] Parker daringly picks up the objection as a means of clinching his argument about national servitude. 'Let us look upon the Venetians, and other such free Nations', he retorts, and ask ourselves why it is that they are 'so extreamly jealous over their Princes.' It is because they fear 'the sting of Monarchy', which stems (as Livy had said) from the power of monarchs to 'dote upon their owne wills,

and despise publike Councels and Laws'.[89] The jealousy of the Venetians arises, in other words, from their recognition that under a genuine monarchy they would be reduced to slavery. It is 'meerely for fear of this bondage' that they prefer their elected Dukes to the rule of hereditary kings.[90]

Parker was not the first to put forward this claim about the Negative Voice,[91] but his *Observations* offered the most confident statement of the case, and undoubtedly helped to make this neo-Roman argument pivotal to the rhetoric of the ensuing civil war. We encounter the same argument in virtually all the defences of the parliamentary decision to take up arms in the autumn of 1642.[92] They regularly insist that, if the king is permitted a Negative Voice, 'this whole Kingdome shall consist only of a King, a Parliament, and Slaves'.[93] We encounter the argument again in Parliament's own call to arms of August 1642, in which we are told that the Malignant Party advising the king now aspires 'to destroy his Parliament and good people by a Civill War; and, by that meanes to bring ruine, confusion, and perpetuall slavery upon the surviving part of a then wretched Kingdome'.[94] Finally, we encounter the same argument yet again at the conclusion of the war, when it is wheeled out once more to justify not merely the regicide but the abolition of the monarchy. The charge against Charles I at his trial was that he had sought 'to erect, and uphold in himself an unlimited and Tyrannical power to rule *according to his Will*', a course of action designed not merely 'to overthrow the Rights and Liberties of the People' but 'to take away, and make void the foundations thereof'.[95] The Act of March 1649 abolishing the office of king duly confirmed that monarchy is 'dangerous to the liberty, safety, and public interest of the people', adding that in England the effect of the prerogative has been 'to oppress and impoverish and enslave the subject'.[96] It was at this moment that an apoplectic Hobbes picked up his pen.[97]

III

It would be unfair to Berlin to imply that he fails to notice the tradition that conceptualises the idea of negative liberty not as absence of interference but as absence of dependence. It seems worth underlining this observation, if only because of how his work has been handled by those philosophers who have begun to revive this alternative way of thinking about the concept of human freedom. By far the most important of these writers has been Philip Pettit, who initially presented the argument in his *Republicanism* (1997) and has since elaborated it in *A Theory of Freedom* (2001).[98] Pettit's work is of outstanding importance, and I am deeply indebted to it, but I cannot agree with him when he contends that the effect of Berlin's argument has been to 'conceal from view' the theory that, as Pettit phrases it, negative liberty consists in non-domination, not in non-interference.[99]

It is true that Berlin fails to present the argument about non-domination with the same historical specificity as he brings to bear on the other two concepts he examines, and that he never singles out any particular theorist or movement capable of being associated with this alternative standpoint. Given, however, that he was writing at the height of the debate about decolonialisation, he could scarcely have been unaware that nations as well as individuals often claim to be unfree when they are condemned to social or political dependence. Berlin devotes considerable attention at the end of his essay to what he describes as the resulting 'search for status',[100] and he explicitly asks himself whether it might not 'be natural or desirable to call the demand for recognition and status a demand for liberty in some third sense'.[101]

Having raised the question, however, Berlin confidently answers that no such third concept of liberty can be coherently entertained. To speak of social or political dependence as lack of liberty, he writes, is to confound freedom with other concepts in a manner at once misleading and confused.[102] Stating his grounds for this conclusion, he goes on to enunciate his most general claim about the concept of liberty. He insists that it is true not merely of any coherent account of negative freedom, but of any concept of freedom whatever, that it must embody, at least as a minimum, the idea of absence of interference. If we are to speak of restrictions on liberty, we must be able to point to some intruder, some act of trespass, some actual impediment or hindrance to the exercise by an agent of their powers at will.[103] As Berlin summarises, 'the essence of the notion of liberty, in both the "positive" and the "negative" senses, is the holding off of something or someone – of others who trespass on my field'.[104]

We can perhaps bring out more clearly what is at stake here by putting the argument the other way round. We can ask, that is, what it is that we

cannot coherently claim, according to this reading, about the concept of negative liberty. We cannot claim that a mere awareness of living in a state of social or political dependence has the effect of restricting our options and thereby limiting our freedom. If we are to speak of constraints on liberty, we must be able to point to some identifiable act of hindrance, the aim or consequence of which was to impede or interfere with us in the exercise of our powers.

It is precisely this assumption, however, that the writers I am considering reject. The distinctive claim they defend is that a mere awareness of living in dependence on the goodwill of an arbitrary ruler *does* serve in itself to restrict our options and thereby limit our liberty.[105] The effect is to dispose us to make and avoid certain choices, and is thus to place clear constraints on our freedom of action, even though our ruler may never interfere with our activities or even show the least sign of threatening to interfere with them.[106]

It is of course true that the form of constraint on which these writers concentrate is self-constraint. They envisage that those living in a state of dependence will reflect on their predicament and generally decide on a course of action involving some measure of self-censorship. But the same is no less true of agents who act in the face of coercive threats. They too review their options and generally choose a course of action different from the one they would otherwise have pursued. The agent's sense of constraint is mediated in the two cases in the same way. It follows that, if we are prepared to grant that freedom can be limited by coercion,[107] we cannot exclude that it may also be limited by servitude, or at least not on the grounds that the constraint involved is merely self-constraint.

The exploration of this argument became one of the leading preoccupations of the classical writers I have singled out. If we return to Sallust, and above all to Tacitus, we find them offering an agonised analysis of the psychological impact of slipping into a state of subjection to arbitrary power. It was this analysis that in turn exercised perhaps the most formative influence on the democratical gentlemen who went on to challenge the government of Charles I and to institute the first and only English republic. So far.

As the classical writers stress, there are two contrasting ways in which you will be constrained by your awareness of living in dependence on the goodwill of an arbitrary prince. You will find in the first place that there are many things you are not free to say or do. As Sallust and Tacitus both emphasise, you will need above all to make sure that you avoid saying or doing anything that might be construed by your ruler as an act of emulation or reproach. Sallust explains the need for this caution in a passage from the *Bellum Catilinae* that the English republican writers of the seventeenth century loved to cite.[108] In the words of Heywood's translation of 1608, 'absolute Princes are alwaies more jealous of the good, then of the badde, because another mans Vertue (as they take it) is a diminution of their respectivenesse, and therefore dangerous'.[109] The moral is that, if you are a person of great talent or virtue living under such a prince, you will have no option but to keep those qualities hidden from view as much as possible. You will otherwise be only too likely to discover that, as Savile puts it in translating Tacitus's description of the reign of Nero, such qualities can be 'the readie broade way to most assured destruction'.[110]

Sallust and Tacitus are even more concerned about the long-term psychological impact of this form of self-constraint. When a whole nation is inhibited from exercising its highest talents and virtues, these qualities will begin to atrophy and the people will gradually sink into an abject condition of torpor and sluggishness. Tacitus draws the moral when speaking about the German tribe of the Tencteri and their failed uprising against Rome. In the words of Savile's translation, 'even wilde beasts shut up forget their accustomed valour and vertue'.[111] Sallust in the *Bellum Catilinae* had already drawn the corollary in another passage frequently cited by the English republican writers of the seventeenth century. If we are to enable 'everie man to estimate his owne worth, and to hammer his head on high disseigns', we must be sure to establish and uphold a 'free state', a form of government under which all forms of discretionary or arbitrary power are eliminated.[112]

The other way in which you will find yourself constrained by living under an unaccountable power is that you will lack the freedom to abstain from saying and doing certain things. When confronted by an absolute ruler and required to offer counsel and advice, you will find yourself constrained to agree with whatever he says and to endorse whatever policies he already wishes to pursue. Tacitus dramatises the predicament in his *Annals* when describing the conduct of the political classes under Tiberius, and his tone of

withering contempt is finely caught in Grenewey's translation of 1598:

> But those times were so corrupted with filthie flatterie: that not only the chiefest of the citie were forced in that servile maner to keepe their reputation; but all such as had beene Consuls; the greatest part of such as had bin Pretors; & also many pedary Senators rose up & strove, who should propound things most base and abject. It is written, that as *Tiberius* went out of the Curia, he was woont to saie in Greeke. O men ready to servitude! as though he, who could of all things least suffer publicke libertie; did yet abhorre such base and servile submission: falling by little and little from unseemely flatteries, to lewder practises.[113]

As Tacitus makes clear, the senators were in no way acting under coercion or threat. The mere recognition of their dependence was enough to make them do whatever they felt was expected of them.

It is of course true that, even in such a state of servitude, you retain some freedom of manoeuvre, at least as long as you are not directly threatened or forced. Tacitus in his account of Tiberius's descent into tyranny sardonically praises those who refused to accept that their liberty had been completely undermined. One remaining if drastic option will always be to evade the tyrant's attention altogether, as Tacitus reports of Arruntius at the end of the reign:

> I foresee (said he) a heavier servitude; and therfore I will flie as well from that which is alreadie past, as that which is at hand. Speaking these things as it had bin in the maner of a Prophesie, he cut his vaines.[114]

A further if less heroic option is to try to say as little as possible, as Tacitus reports of Piso, the high priest:

> About the same time *L. Piso* high Priest died a naturall death, which was a rare matter in those times in a man of so great nobilitie: He never of himself propounded any matter which smelled of flatterie or base minds; & if he were forced thereto, he used great moderation in doing it.[115]

As Tacitus makes vividly clear, however, the Roman senatorial class overwhelmingly took

the view that, once Augustus had established himself in absolute control, they had no option but to
submit to whatever he asked of them, as a result of
which 'the Consuls, the Senators, and Gentlemen
ranne headlong into servitude'.[116]

As before, what chiefly interests Sallust and
Tacitus are the long-term psychological consequences of enduring a life of so much anxiety
and uncertainty. The principle on which they insist is that servitude inevitably breeds servility.
Sallust in his *Bellum Iugurthinum* puts the argument into the mouth of Memmius in his denunciation of the Roman plebs for submitting to the
domination of the nobility. He mocks them for
their 'slavish patience', for allowing themselves to
live 'as a scorne to the Pride of a few' and for
remaining 'corrupted with the same sloth and
cowardice'.[117] Tacitus similarly takes a sour pleasure in describing the constantly increasing slavish-
ness of the Roman people under the principate. He
draws Book I of his *Histories* to a close with an
account of the speech in which the emperor Otho,
after the fall of Nero, announced his decision to go
to war. 'The commons after their flattering fashion
receyved the speech with cryes and acclamations
without either measure or trueth, contending to
passe one another in applause and wishes, as if it
had beene to Caesar the Dictator, or the Emperour
Augustus; neither for feare nor for love, but onely
upon a delight in servility.'[118]

These arguments were endlessly invoked by the
democratical gentlemen of seventeenth-century
England. They too were much preoccupied by
the dangerous implications of the fact that arbitrary rulers are inevitably surrounded by servile
flatterers, and have little hope of hearing frank
advice. But their main anxiety was that, under
such rulers, no one will perform any deeds requiring public spirit or courageous and great-hearted
qualities. As they liked to put it, the final effect of
living under absolutism is that everyone becomes
dispirited, discouraged, disheartened, and finally
dejected and debased.

We already find Sir Thomas Hedley speaking in
exactly these terms in his great speech to the
House of Commons in 1610:

If the liberty of the subject be in this point
impeached, that their lands and goods be any
way in the king's absolute power to be taken
from them, then they are (as hath been said)
little better than the king's bondmen, which
will so discourage them, and so abase and de-

ject their minds, that they will use little care
and industry to get that which they cannot keep
and so will grow poor and base-minded like to
the peasants in other countries.[119]

The same moral is drawn in still more minatory
tones by Henry Parker at the outset of his *Observations* in 1642:

This is therefore a great and fond errour in
some Princes to strive more to be great over
their people, then in their people, and to
ecclipse themselves by impoverishing, rather
then to magnifie themselves by infranchising
their Subjects. This we see in France at this
day, for were the Peasants there more free, they
would be more rich and magnanimous, and
were they so, their King were more puissant.[120]

From these beginnings we can date one of the most
enduring and vainglorious legacies of the classical
belief that deeds of greatness can be expected only
from those who live in so-called free states. The
proof of this, we are assured, can be seen in the
lives of the European peasantry or, still more
clearly, among the subjects of the Sultan at Constantinople. They have become so discouraged
and dispirited by the experience of living under
arbitrary power that they have become totally su-
pine and base, and nothing can now be expected of
them.

IV

You might agree with everything I have so far said
and still want to deny that I have isolated a third
concept of liberty. Whether you think I have done
so will obviously depend on your sense of what it
means to possess a concept and of how concepts
are best individuated. Berlin's response to this
question emerges only implicitly from his 'Two
Concepts of Liberty', but it seems to me that, if
I have understood his view correctly, it is one
that we have good reason to endorse. His answer
appears to be that, if a given descriptive term can
be coherently used with more than one range of
reference, so that it can be used to pick out more
than one distinct phenomenon or state of affairs,
then the term may be said to express more than
one concept.

If that is your concept of a concept, then you
will agree that I have identified a third concept of

liberty. But I have no wish to press the point. A better way of summarising my position would be to say that, while I agree with Berlin that there are two concepts of liberty, one positive and the other negative, I do not agree with his further assumption that, whenever we speak about negative liberty, we must be speaking about absence of interference. It seems to me that, as I have tried to show, we have inherited two rival and incommensurable theories of negative liberty, although in recent times we have generally contrived to ignore one of them.

It is only fair to acknowledge, however, that these conclusions have already been dismissively criticised. According to the most recent of my critics, we need to begin by recognising that, in questioning the view that negative liberty consists in non-interference, what I am claiming in effect is that it consists of 'resilient non-interference'.[121] To speak of such resilience, I am then assured, can only be to speak of certain constitutional safeguards that serve to ensure 'an especially high probability of high degrees of non-interference being maintained over time'.[122] This reading allows the inference that I am merely offering 'a useful set of empirical hypotheses' about how liberty in the ordinary sense of non-interference 'is best to be maximised'.[123] I am far from having shown that 'an *alternative conception* of liberty' is at work.[124]

If I were indeed talking about resilient non-interference (a phrase I have never used) there might be some justification for these somewhat patronising remarks. But I am not talking about resilient non-interference, nor indeed about interference or non-interference of any kind. I am talking about the predicament of those who recognise that they are living in subjection to the will of others, and I am following my classical and early-modern authorities in claiming that the mere fact of living in such a predicament has the effect of placing limits on our liberty. If freedom is construed as absence of interference, this is unquestionably to speak of an alternative theory of liberty, since it is to claim that freedom can be restricted and constrained in the absence of any element of interference or even any threat of it.[125]

This contrast can be restated in a different way, and one that perhaps serves more effectively to counter those who have insisted that, as another of my critics has recently put it, 'there is no interesting disagreement' between those who espouse the two purportedly different theories of negative

liberty.[126] One undoubted disagreement between them (although it is not for me to say whether it is 'interesting') is that they hold rival views about the underlying concept of autonomy. Those who believe that liberty is nothing other than absence of interference are committed to the view that the will is autonomous so long as it is neither threatened nor coerced.[127] By contrast, those who embrace the neo-Roman argument deny that the will can be autonomous unless it is also free from dependence on the will of anyone else.

So far I have given the impression that Berlin offers a relatively neutral appraisal of the rival merits of negative and positive liberty. But this is far from being the case. Berlin's essay represents a belated but recognisable contribution to a longstanding debate about the merits of philosophical Idealism that had continued to resonate in the Oxford of his youth. H.A. Prichard and J.P. Plamenatz had relentlessly criticised T.H. Green in the 1930s, arguing that his views of freedom, obligation and rights were all extremely dubious and confused.[128] But A.D. Lindsay had kept alive the debate by republishing Green's *Lectures* in 1941 with an admiring Introduction in which he had spoken sympathetically of Green's belief that empiricist philosophy and utilitarian psychology 'had to be fought all along the line'.[129]

As Berlin makes clear, he firmly aligned himself with those who wanted to put such figures as Lindsay in their place. Liberal political theory, Berlin insists, must be grounded after all on empiricist and utilitarian premises, not on the philosophies of Hegel and Kant.[130] As we have seen, those espousing the opposite point of view had earlier been denounced for accepting an argument that had led to World War I. By the time Berlin was writing, their successors had laid themselves open to a no less melodramatic attack. They were now assailed for adopting a concept of freedom that directly associated them, as Berlin himself declares, with the outlook of 'the latest nationalist or Communist dictator'.[131]

As this judgement suggests, Berlin's essay is strongly marked by the geopolitical and ideological divisions of the 1950s. Berlin believes that, while the positive understanding of liberty may have had lofty and even noble origins, it has wandered so far from its liberal beginnings that it has come to rest 'at the heart of many of the nationalist, Communist, authoritarian, and totalitarian creeds of our day'.[132] His essay is a warning as much as an exposition, and he finds it correspondingly important to insist that, as he proclaims at the end, the concept of negative liberty offers 'a truer and more humane ideal than the goals of those who seek in the great disciplined, authoritarian structures the ideal of "positive" self-mastery by classes, or peoples, or the whole of mankind'.[133]

What are we to make of this valedictory profession of faith? When Berlin asks himself which of the two concepts he has explicated is the 'truer' one, the question strikes me as ambiguously phrased. He may have it in mind to ask, in the manner of Habermas, which of the two concepts is truer to our deepest human interests and purposes. But if that is his question, then I cannot see that it has a determinate answer. Perhaps the idea of liberty as absence of interference was truer to the society in which he himself was writing, in which the ideal of freedom as self-perfection had come to be widely seen as a religious and collectivist nightmare from which the 'free world' had thankfully awoken. But in earlier periods the same ideal had been a dream, not a nightmare, and in many western societies of the present time there are new movements of religious faith in which the positive concept of liberty may well appear to answer to far deeper purposes than the negative idea of merely having as much elbow-room as we desire. The question of which concept best answers to our purposes will always depend on what account – if any – we believe should be given of the normative character of human nature. But this is a question that our theologians as well as philosophers have been debating for centuries, and it does not seem at all likely that they will manage in the near future to reach a final agreement.

When Berlin asks about the true concept of liberty, however, he may instead mean to ask which is the true or right way of analysing the terms by which the concept is expressed. But if this is his question, then it seems to me even clearer that it has no determinate answer. As I have tried to intimate throughout this lecture, the belief that we can somehow step outside the stream of history and furnish a neutral definition of such words as *libertas*, freedom, autonomy and liberty is an illusion well worth giving up. With terms at once so deeply normative, so highly indeterminate, and so extensively implicated in such a long history of ideological debate, the project of understanding them can only be that of trying to grasp the different roles they have played in our history and our own place in that narrative. But the more we undertake this kind of study, the more we see that there is no neutral analysis of any such keywords to be given. The history is all there is.

I must try not to end, however, by sounding as dogmatic as my critics, especially as it would be ironic to speak dogmatically about (of all things) liberty. I much prefer the tone of tolerance that Berlin, in his best moments, seems to strike so effortlessly. Speaking of our historical and philosophical debates about freedom, he brings his own analysis to a close on a deliberately anti-rhetorical note. He is content to end by observing – and here I am happy to echo him – that in thinking about the concept of liberty 'I am well aware of how much more needs to be done'.[134]

Notes

1   For different versions of this 'coherentist' approach see. for example. Rawls (1971), pp. 201–5; MacCallum (1972); Day (1983); Megone (1987); Narveson (1988), pp. 18–21; Swanton (1992); Carter (1999); Swift (2001), pp. 51–89.
2   See MacCallum (1972: originally published 1967).
3   MacCallum (1972), p. 176.
4   For this very strong way of putting the point, see for example Day (1983), p. 18; Swift (2001), p. 53.
5   See Berlin (2002). This edition incorporates Harris (2002), a valuable survey of the critical literature on Berlin's 'Two Concepts' lecture.
6   Swift (2001), p. 51.
7   Although the terms *freedom* and *liberty* are obviously not interchangeable, Berlin clearly thought of them as sufficiently synonymous for his purposes. Ignatieff (1998), p. 222, neatly captures Berlin's expression of this commitment when (speaking into a tape-recorder) he first gave a title to his lecture: 'Two Concepts of Freedom – no . . . of Liberty'. I have followed Berlin in using the terms as if they are synonyms.
8   Berlin (2002), p. 178.
9   Here I dissent from Gray (1984), p. 326 (and Gray (1995), p. 18 where the point is repeated), who sides with Berlin against MacCallum in supposing that the term 'liberty' can sometimes refer to a merely dyadic relationship.
10 Berlin (2002), p. 178.
11 Traditionally this argument has been couched in the form of the claim that our passions enslave us. On the metaphors associated with the workings of the passions see James (1997), pp. 11–14.

12 Berlin (2002), p. 179.

13 See Berlin (2002), p. 180 and cf. Berlin (2002), p. 37: 'freedom was identified . . . with the realisation of the real self'. It is thus a misunderstanding of the idea of self-mastery to assume (as does Carter (1999), p. 148) that it can be equated with the idea of internal constraints on liberty.

14 Although Berlin (2002) mentions Hegel's positive theory of freedom (p. 196), he refers more specifically to the British Idealists (p. 194n) and singles out Green (pp. 180 n, 196) as well as Bradley and Bosanquet (p. 196).

15 Bosanquet (1910), p. 124.

16 Ibid., p. 134.

17 Ibid., p. 136.

18 See ibid., pp. 125, 127, 141 and cf. Berlin (2002), pp. 179, 180, 204.

19 Nicholson (1990), p. 199 convincingly argues (against the interpretation in Hobhouse, 1918) that 'Bosanquet is repeating Green's ideas with only a little reworking and extension of them'.

20 See, for example, Green (1991), p. 21 and the discussion in Roberts (1984), pp. 251–2.

21 Green (1986), pp. 228–9.

22 Ibid., p. 240.

23 Ibid., p. 241.

24 Ibid., p. 242.

25 Hobhouse (1918), p. 6. On Hobhouse's view of Green and Bosanquet see Collini (1979), pp. 66, 142–3 and the valuable chapter in Bellamy (1992), pp. 9–57.

26 See Popper (1995), pp. 257–310. (Popper's study originally appeared in 1945.)

27 Berlin (2002), p. 212.

28 Here I am indebted to Baldwin (1984).

29 Berlin's clearest statement of this distinction occurs in the Introduction to the revised edition of his 'Two Concepts' essay. See Berlin (2002), p. 35, where he speaks of negative liberty as 'opportunity for action' by contrast with the positive idea of liberty as 'action itself'. Geuss (1995), pp. 97–8 helpfully discriminates between two different understandings of liberty as self-realisation: (1) I am free to the extent that my actions most fully realise my purposes; (2) I am free to the extent that I am able to recognise myself in the actions I perform. As Geuss observes, (2) is very hard to grasp, and Berlin confines himself to (1).

30 A point powerfully brought out in Taylor (1979), pp. 180–3.

31 For an analysis of Arendt's view of freedom as citizenship see Beiner (1984).

32 Arendt (1968); pp. 149, 151.

33 Taylor (1979), p. 175. On Taylor as a critic of Berlin see the valuable discussion in Spitz (1995), pp. 106–21.

34 Berlin (2002), pp. 178–81.

35 For convincing arguments to this effect see Macfarlane (1966), Taylor (1979), Swift (2001), pp. 77–87.

36 See Berlin (2002), pp. 32, his final and perhaps most considered definition. Gray (1995), pp. 15–16 lays particular emphasis on the fact that, according to this account, the agent who is said to be at liberty is always someone whose choice among options is unimpeded by others. This leads him to relate Berlin's analysis to that of Benn and Weinstein (1971), who likewise treat liberty as the non-restriction of options, by contrast with the narrower idea of being able to choose between alternatives.

37 Berlin (2002), p. 170.

38 For references to some of these contrasting accounts see below, nn. 45 and 46.

39 Berlin (2002), p. 169. Italics added.

40 Ibid.

41 Hobbes (1996), ch. 21, p. 146 offers a strong statement of this commitment when he claims that there is no difference between saying of the body of a man while imprisoned, and of a body of water while 'kept in by banks', that they are 'not at Liberty'. For a recent endorsement see Parent (1974), p. 149, from whom I take the example of being rendered unfree by a blizzard.

42 Hobbes (1996), ch. 21, p. 146.

43 Hobbes (1996), ch. 6, p. 44. This Hobbesian point is excellently brought out in Swanton (1992), pp. 58–60, 91–5. Benn and Weinstein (1971) defend a strong version of this commitment when they claim that it makes sense to speak of an agent as free to pursue a given option only if the option itself is a possible object of reasonable choice.

44 Hobbes (1996), ch. 21, p. 146.

45 For an analysis along exactly these lines, arguing that a person who is crippled [sic] is nevertheless free to dance, see Gert (1972) and cf. the similar analysis in Oppenheim (1981), pp. 82–8.

46 See, for example, van Parijs (1995), Swift (2001), pp. 55–9 and the discussion in Pettit (1997), p. 76 and note. It might seem that Sen, in his classic discussion of freedom and development, also agrees that to lack power is to lack liberty. See, for example, Sen (1999), pp. 15, 20, 24. But in the examples he considers Sen is always concerned with people who have in fact been disempowered by identifiable agencies, and the moral force of his argument stems from his account of how their freedom can be enlarged by empowering them. Furthermore, one of Sen's great achievements has been to show that, even where it may appear obvious that certain people simply lack power, it frequently turns out on closer analysis that they have in fact been disempowered by a failure to remedy conditions that could easily have been remedied.

47 Berlin (2002), p. 170 and note.

48 Hobbes (1996), ch. 14, p. 91 and ch. 21, p. 145. I have further discussed Hobbes's theory of liberty in Skinner (2002b), pp. 209–37.

49 Berlin (2002), pp. 32–3.

50 Hobbes (1969), p. 26.
51 Sidgwick (1897). pp. 45–7 refers to Hobbes and follows his argument with particular closeness. It goes without saying, however, that a full exploration of this tradition of thought would need to take account of the fact that these thinkers likewise make use of the neo-Hobbesian theory for their own polemical purposes.
52 Special thanks to Ingmar Persson for pressing me to emphasise that it is not the mere fact of our dependence, but this fact combined with our awareness of it, that has the effect of restricting our liberty.
53 Note the implicit definition here of arbitrariness. A power is arbitrary if the person wielding it is capable of interfering with others, with impunity, solely on the basis of his or her own *arbitrium* or will, and hence with no obligation to take into account the interests of those subject to the interference.
54 Bracton (1968–77), vol. 2, p. 30: '*Quid est servitus. Est quidem servitus . . . qua quis dominio alieno . . . subicitur.*'
55 This is the title found in the earliest extant manuscript. See Cambridge University Library MS Mm. v. 2, fos. 2–77, at fo. 2^r.
56 Mommsen and Krueger (eds.) (1985), I. V. 3. 35: 'Summa itaque de iure personarum divisio haec est, quod omnes homines aut liberi sunt aut servi'. (Note that, in this and subsequent quotations from the *Digest*, I have made my own translations.)
57 Ibid., I. V. 4. 35: 'Servitus est constitutio iuris gentium, qua quis dominio alieno contra naturam subicitur'.
58 Ibid., I. VI. 1. 36: 'Some persons are in their own power, some are subject to the power of others, such as slaves, who are in the power of their masters'. ['quaedam personae sui iuris sunt, quaedam alieno iuri subiectae sunt . . . in potestate sunt servi dominorum . . .']
59 Berlin (2002), p. 33 maintains that we find no clear formulation of the concept of negative liberty in the ancient world. Perhaps there was no concept of liberty as non-interference, and perhaps there was no concept of a right. As my quotations show, however, there was undoubtedly a clear (and immensely influential) concept of negative liberty as absence of dependence.
60 See Wirszubski 1968, pp. 1–30.
61 See Tacitus (1591) and Tacitus (1598) and cf. Peltonen (1995), pp. 124–35 on these translations and their influence.
62 See Livy (1600) and on Holland's translation see Peltonen (1995), pp. 135–6.
63 Sallust (1608).
64 Livy (1600), p. 28.
65 Livy (1600), p. 907.
66 Gardiner (1906), pp. 66, 67.
67 Ibid., p. 69.
68 Cambridge University Library MS Ii. 5. 32, fos. 218^r–221^v: 'Mr Littletons Argument concerning the personall libertye of the Subject', a speech delivered on 4 April 1628. Quotations from fos. 218^{r-v} and 221^v.
69 Johnson et al. (eds.) (1977a), p. 149.
70 Ibid., pp. 189, 208.
71 Ibid., (1977b), p. 6.
72 Ibid., p. 269.
73 Foster (1966), II, p. 83; cf. Sommerville (1999), p. 97.
74 Ibid., II, p. 108.
75 Foster (1966), II. p. 196. For an analysis of Hedley's speech see Peltonen (1995), pp. 220–8.
76 Ibid., II, p. 192.
77 Johnson et al., (eds.) (1977a), p. 66.
78 For the attribution, and an account of the context in which this tract appeared, see Mendle (1995), pp. 32–50.
79 [Parker] (1999), vol. 1, p. 98.
80 Ibid., pp. 110, 112.
81 Ibid., p. 108.
82 Ibid., p. 109.
83 For the attribution, and an account of the context in which this tract appeared, see Mendle (1995), pp. 70–89.
84 [Parker] (1933), pp. 175–6.
85 Ibid., pp. 182–3.
86 Ibid., p. 187.
87 [Parker] (1933), pp. 209–10.
88 Charles I (1999), p. 167.
89 [Parker] (1933), p. 192.
90 Ibid., p. 192.
91 It is already adumbrated, for example, in the parliamentary Remonstrance of 26 May 1642. See Husbands et al. (1643); pp. 263–4.
92 On the repeated contrast in these tracts between freedom and national servitude see Skinner (2002a); pp. 338–42.
93 *Reasons* (1642), p. 14.
94 Husbands et al. (1643), p. 509.
95 *Charge* (1649), pp. 3–4.
96 Gardiner (ed.) (1906), p. 385.
97 For the detailed evidence suggesting that Hobbes began writing *Leviathan* only in the course of 1649 see Skinner (2002b), pp. 15–20.
98 See Pettit (1997) and Pettit (2001). While Pettit (1997) was his first full-scale presentation of the case, it had been preceded by numerous important articles. For a list see Pettit (1997), pp. 315–16.
99 See Pettit (1997), pp. 19, 41. A further question is whether the idea of freedom as non-domination (which I assume to be more or less equivalent to absence of dependence) is a strictly negative concept of liberty. Pettit (1997), p. 51 suggests that it may embody positive as well as negative elements. But this commitment appears to depend on treating positive liberty as an ideal of autonomy rather than

self-perfection. As I have already tried to make clear in Skinner (1998), my own conviction is that the concept is a wholly negative one. But for further doubts see Woolcock (1998), p. 47 and Brown (2001).

100 Berlin (2002), p. 200.

101 Ibid., p. 204.

102 Ibid., pp. 200, 204.

103 Ibid., p. 204.

104 Ibid., p. 204. The formulation in Berlin (1969), p. 158 is slightly different.

105 If we are to speak of dependence as a source or form of constraint, it cannot be the case that we *know* that our absolute ruler will never in fact interfere. For in that case we are not under any constraint. This is not to say, however, that the probability of interference must rise above a certain level for liberty to be constrained. If there is the slightest probability of interference, we are under some corresponding pressure and our liberty will to that degree be constrained. For those who like formulae, it could perhaps be said that the pressure equals the probability of interference multiplied by its anticipated degree of harmfulness.

106 Gray (1984). p. 327 rightly stresses Berlin's interest in 'the conception of social freedom as possessing a certain social status', but adds that this conception 'seems hard, if not impossible, to accommodate within MacCallum's triadic analysis'. It is perhaps worth underlining that, as my own account makes clear, there is no difficulty about this accommodation. The liberty enjoyed by citizens of free states, by contrast with slaves, is that citizens are free *from* the constraint of dependence *to* pursue their own chosen ends.

107 It is important to register, however, that by no means all contemporary theorists of liberty have been willing to grant that coercion limits liberty. The contention in Hobbes (1996), p. 146 to the effect that 'Feare, and Liberty are consistent' has been echoed and developed by a number of recent writers. See, for example, Parent (1974). Steiner (1974–5), Taylor (1982), pp. 142–8 and the discussion in Swanton (1992), pp. 67–9.

108 John Milton, for example, closely paraphrases it in Milton (1991), p. 3, puts it on the title-page of Milton (1962) and quotes it in Milton (1962), p. 501.

109 See also Tacitus (1591), p. 256: 'the manhood and fierce courage of the subject pleaseth not much the jelous Soverayne'.

110 Tacitus (1591), p. 2.

111 Tacitus (1598), p. 217.

112 Sallust (1608), p. 17 [*recte* p. 7].

113 Tacitus (1598), p. 84.

114 Ibid., p. 139.

115 Ibid., p. 125.

116 Tacitus (1598), p. 3.

117 Sallust (1608), p. 29.

118 Tacitus (1591), p. 51.

119 Foster (ed.) (1966), pp. 194–5.

120 [Parker] (1933), p. 168.

121 Carter (1999), p. 237 claims that this phrase, which he takes from Pettit (1993), offers 'an interesting conceptual clarification' of my own view of negative liberty. As I argue above, however, it appears to go with the very theory of negative liberty I reject. It needs to be stressed, moreover, that Pettit himself has abandoned this formula in his recent work. He now prefers to contrast liberty as non-interference with liberty as non-domination. See Pettit (1997), pp. 21, 41 and Pettit (2001), pp. 132–44. I have been much influenced by this shift in his thinking, which aligns his theory closely with my own account (and that of my ancient and early-modern authorities) of the predicament of living in dependence on the power of another.

122 Carter (1999), p. 239.

123 Ibid., pp. 238–9. For the same contention see Patten (1996), p. 29. Patten's article offers some helpful criticisms of my earlier work on this issue. As I note in Skinner (1998), p. 70 n., however, I have since changed my mind. I am no longer arguing simply about the conditions necessary for maximising negative liberty, but about how to construe the concept itself.

124 Carter (1999), p. 239. See also Ferejohn (2001), esp. pp. 85–6 for the related objection, interestingly developed as a critique of Pettit's analysis of non-domination, that this account produces an analysis not of liberty but merely of security, a distinct and more equivocal value.

125 I deliberately speak of a rival theory of liberty here, rather than following Carter in speaking of a rival conception. It has become usual to follow John Rawls (as Carter is here doing) in distinguishing between different *concepts* and different *conceptions* (of liberty, justice, and so forth). I am not wholly clear, however, what difference this distinction is supposed to mark, and for me it is in any case enough to say that I have isolated a theory of negative liberty at once different from – and indeed a rival to – the theory that liberty consists in absence of interference.

126 Patten (1996), pp. 27, 36.

127 See, for example, Swanton (1992), p. 124, denying that autonomy is limited by lack of independence.

128 See Plamenatz (1938), pp. 62–81, 89–97 and Prichard (1949) (reprinting work done in the 1930s), pp. 54–86, 120–8.

129 Lindsay (1941), p. ix.

130 Berlin (2002), pp. 178–81, 191–200.

131 Ibid., p. 198.

132 Ibid., pp. 190, 198.

133 Ibid., p. 216.

134 Ibid., p. 54.

References

Arendt, Hannah (1968) 'What is Freedom?' in *Between Past and Future: Eight Exercises in Political Thought*, New York, pp. 143–71.

Baldwin, Tom (1984) 'MacCallum and the Two Concepts of Freedom', *Ratio* 26: 125–42.

Beiner, Ronald (1984) 'Action, Natality and Citizenship: Hannah Arendt's Concept of Freedom' in *Conceptions of Liberty in Political Philosophy*, ed. Zbigniew Pelczynski and John Gray, pp. 349–75.

Bellamy, Richard (1992) *Liberalism and Modern Society: A Historical Argument*, Philadelphia, Penn.

Benn, Stanley I. and Weinstein, W. L. (1971) 'Being Free to Act and Being a Free Man', *Mind* 80, pp. 194–211.

Berlin, Isaiah (1969) *Four Essays on Liberty*.

—— (2002) 'Two Concepts of Liberty' in *Liberty*, ed. Henry Hardy, Oxford, pp. 166–217. [Reprinted in part in chapter 24 of this volume.]

Bosanquet, Bernard (1910) *The Philosophical Theory of the State*, 2nd edn.

Bracton, Henry de (1968–77) *De Legibus et Consuetudinibus Angliae*, trans. and ed. Samuel E. Thorne, 4 vols., Cambridge, Mass.

Brown, Vivienne (2001) 'Self-government: The Master Trope of Republican Liberty', *The Monist* 84: 60–76.

Carter, Ian (1999) *A Measure of Freedom*, Oxford.

Charge of the Commons of England, Against Charls Stuart, King of England, The (1649).

Charles I (1999) *XIX. Propositions Made By both Houses of Parliament . . . With his Majesties Answer thereunto* in *The Struggle for Sovereignty: Seventeenth-Century English Political Tracts*, ed. Joyce Lee Malcolm, 2 vols., Indianapolis, Ind., vol. 1, pp. 145–78.

Collini, Stefan (1979) *Liberalism and Sociology: L. T. Hobhouse and Political Argument in England 1880–1914*, Cambridge.

Day, J. P. (1983) 'Individual Liberty' in *Of Liberty*, ed. A. Phillips Griffith, Cambridge, pp. 17–29.

Ferejohn, John (2001) 'Pettit's Republic', *The Monist* 84: 77–97.

Fleischacker, Samuel (1999) *A Third Concept of Liberty: Judgment and Freedom in Kant and Adam Smith*, Princeton, NJ.

Foster, Elizabeth Read (ed.) (1966) *Proceedings in Parliament 1610*, 2 vols., New Haven, Conn.

Gardiner, S. R. (ed.) (1906) *The Constitutional Documents of the Puritan Revolution 1625–1660*, 3rd edn., Oxford.

Gert, Bernard (1972) 'Coercion and Freedom' in *Coercion*, ed. Roland J. Pennock and John W. Chapman, Chicago, pp. 30–48.

Geuss, Raymond (1995) 'Freedom as an Ideal', *Proceedings of the Aristotelian Society*, Supplementary vol. 69: 87–100.

Gray, John (1984) 'On Negative and Positive Liberty' in *Conceptions of Liberty in Political Philosophy*, ed. Zbigniew Pelczynski and John Gray, pp. 321–48.

—— (1995). *Isaiah Berlin*.

Green, T. H. (1986) 'On the Different Senses of "Freedom" as Applied to Will and to the Moral Progress of Man' in *Lectures on the Principles of Political Obligation and Other Writings*, ed. Paul Harris and John Morrow, pp. 228–49.

—— (1991) 'Liberal Legislation and Freedom of Contract' in *Liberty*, ed. David Miller, Oxford, pp. 21–32.

Harris, Ian (2002) 'Berlin and his Critics' in *Liberty*, ed. Henry Hardy, Oxford, pp. 349–66.

Hobbes, Thomas (1969) *Behemoth or The Long Parliament*, ed. Ferdinand Tönnies, 2nd edn., introd. M. M. Goldsmith.

—— (1996) *Leviathan, Or The Matter, Forme, & Power of a Common-Wealth Ecclesiasticall and Civill*, ed. Richard Tuck, Cambridge.

Hobhouse, L. T. (1918) *The Metaphysical Theory of the State: A Criticism*.

Husbands, Edward, Warren, T. and Best, R. (eds.) (1643) *An Exact Collection Of all Remonstrances, Declarations, Votes, Orders, Ordinances, Proclamations, Petitions, Messages, Answers, and other Remarkable Passages between . . . December 1641, and continued untill March the 21, 1643*.

Ignatieff, Michael (1998) *Isaiah Berlin: A Life*.

James, Susan (1997) *Passion and Action: The Emotions in Seventeenth-Century Philosophy*, Oxford.

Johnson, Robert C. and Cole, Maija Jansson (eds.) (1977a) *Commons Debates 1628, volume 2: 17 March–19 April 1628*, New Haven, Conn.

Johnson, Robert C., Keeler, Mary Frear, Cole, Maija Jansson, and Bidwell, William B. (eds.) (1977b) *Commons Debates 1628*, volume 3: *21 April–27 May 1628*, New Haven, Conn.

Lindsay, A. D. (1941) Introduction to T. H. Green, *Lectures on the Principles of Political Obligation*, pp. vii–xix.

Livy (1600) *The Romane Historie*, trans. Philemon Holland.

MacCallum, Gerald (1972) 'Negative and Positive Freedom', in *Philosophy, Politics and Society*, Fourth Series, ed. Peter Laslett, W. G. Runciman, and Quentin Skinner, Oxford, pp. 174–93.

Macfarlane, L. J. (1966) 'On Two Concepts of Liberty', *Political Studies* 14: 77–81.

Megone, Christopher (1987) 'One Concept of Liberty', *Political Studies* 35: 611–22.

Mendle, Michael (1995) *Henry Parker and the English Civil War: The Political Thought of the Public's 'Privado'*, Cambridge.

Milton, John (1962) *Eikonoklastes* in *Complete Prose Works*, vol. 3: *1648–1649*, ed. Merritt Y. Hughes, New Haven, Conn., pp. 337–601.

—— (1991) *The Tenure of Kings and Magistrates* in *John Milton: Political Writings*, ed. Martin Dzelzainis, Cambridge, pp. 1–48.

Mommsen, Theodor and Krueger, Paul (eds.) (1985) *The Digest of Justinian*, translation ed. Alan Watson, 4 vols., Philadelphia, Penn.

Narveson, Jan (1988) *The Libertarian Ideal*, Philadelphia, Penn.

Nicholson, Peter P. (1990) *The Political Philosophy of the British Idealists: Selected Studies*, Cambridge.

Oppenheim, Felix (1981) *Political Concepts: a Reconstruction*, Oxford.

Parent, William A. (1974) 'Some Recent Work on the Concept of Liberty', *American Philosophical Quarterly* 11, 149–67.

[Parker, Henry] (1933) *Observations upon some of his Majesties late Answers and Expresses in Tracts on Liberty in the Puritan Revolution 1638–1647*, ed. William Haller, New York, vol. 2, pp. 167–213.

[Parker, Henry] (1999) *The Case of Shipmony briefly discoursed in The Struggle for Sovereignty: Seventeenth-Century English Political Tracts*, ed. Joyce Lee Malcolm, 2 vols., Indianapolis, Ind., vol. 1, pp. 93–125.

Patten, Alan (1996) 'The Republican Critique of Liberalism', *British Journal of Political Science* 26: 25–44.

Peltonen, Markku (1995) *Classical Humanism and Republicanism in English Political Thought 1570–1640*, Cambridge.

Pettit, Philip (1993) 'Negative Liberty, Liberal and Republican', *European Journal of Philosophy* 1:15–38.

—— (1997) *Republicanism: A Theory of Freedom and Government*, Oxford.

—— (2001) *A Theory of Freedom: From the Psychology to the Politics of Agency*, Cambridge.

Plamenatz, J. P. (1938) *Consent, Freedom and Political Obligation*, Oxford.

Popper, Karl (1995) *The Open Society and its Enemies*.

Prichard, H. A. (1949) *Moral Obligation: Essays and Lectures*, Oxford.

Rawls, John (1971) *A Theory of Justice*, Cambridge, Mass.

Reasons why this kingdome ought to adhere to the Parliament (1642).

Roberts, John (1984) 'T. H. Green' in *Conceptions of Liberty in Political Philosophy*, ed. Zbigniew Pelczynski and John Gray, pp. 243–62.

Sallust (1608) *The Two most worthy and Notable Histories which remaine unmaimed to Posterity: (viz:) The Conspiracie of Cateline . . . and The Warre which Iugurth for many years maintained against the same State*, trans. Thomas Heywood.

Sen, Amartya (1999) *Development as Freedom*, Oxford.

Sidgwick, Henry (1897) *The Elements of Politics*, 2nd edn.

Skinner, Quentin (1998) *Liberty Before Liberalism*, Cambridge.

—— (2002a) *Visions of Politics*, vol. 2: *Renaissance Virtues*, Cambridge.

—— (2002b) *Visions of Politics*, vol. 3: *Hobbes and Civil Science*, Cambridge.

Sommerville, Johann P. (1999) *Royalists and Patriots: Politics and Ideology in England 1603–1640*.

Spitz, Jean-Fabien (1995) *La liberté politique: Essai de généalogie conceptuelle*, Paris.

Steiner, Hillel (1974–5) 'Individual Liberty', *Proceedings of the Aristotelian Society* 75: 33–50.

Swanton, Christine (1992) *Freedom: A Coherence Theory*, Indianapolis, Ind.

Swift, Adam (2001) *Political Philosophy*, Cambridge.

Tacitus (1591) *The Ende of Nero and Beginning of Galba. Fower Bookes of the Histories Of Cornelius Tacitus. The Life of Agricola*, trans. Henry Savile, Oxford.

—— (1598) *The Annales of Cornelius Tacitus. The Description of Germanie*, trans. Richard Grenewey.

Taylor, Charles (1979) 'What's Wrong with Negative Liberty' in *The Idea of Freedom: Essays in Honour of Isaiah Berlin*, ed. Alan Ryan, Oxford, pp. 175–93. [Reprinted as chapter 25 of this volume.]

Taylor, Michael (1982) *Community, Anarchy and Liberty*, Cambridge.

Van Parijs, Philippe (1995) *Real Freedom for All*, Oxford.

Wirszubski, Ch. (1968) *Libertas as a Political Idea at Rome During the Late Republic and Early Principate*, Cambridge.

Woolcock, Peter G. (1998) *Power, Impartiality and Justice*, Aldershot.

27

Are Freedom and Equality Compatible?

G. A. Cohen

I   Self-ownership, World Ownership and Equality

Most right-wing philosophers believe that freedom and equality are conflicting ideals, so that if you have one of them, you cannot have the other too. And they also believe that, when freedom and equality conflict, freedom should be preferred and equality should be rejected. Some of them regret that, as they suppose, equality has to be rejected, whereas others see no harm in that.

Most leftists reply either that there is no real conflict between equality and freedom, when both are properly conceived, or that, to the extent that there indeed is one, freedom should give way to equality, since justice demands equality, and justice comes before all other political values.

This chapter is about equality and freedom, and its author is one kind of leftist. But I shall not try to show that there is no conflict between freedom and equality for leftists to worry about. What I shall show, instead, is that there is no conflict between what the Right *calls* freedom and equality. The difficulty for socialists is not that we cannot preserve the freedom that the Right offers and also promote equality. The difficulty is that real freedom, which the Right cannot offer, may well re-quire some revision of the traditional Left egalitarian prospectus.

The right-wing conception of freedom is, I think, founded on the idea that each person is, as one might put it, the *morally* rightful owner of himself, even if existing legal systems do not fully acknowledge that moral fact.[1] Let us call that the self-ownership thesis. The most impressive contemporary proponent of the self-ownership thesis is the Harvard philosopher Robert Nozick. He holds that each person possesses over himself, as a matter of moral right, all those rights that a slaveholder has over a complete chattel slave as a matter of legal right; and that each person is entitled, morally speaking, to dispose over himself in the way that such a slaveholder is entitled, legally speaking, to dispose over his slave. Such a slaveholder may not direct his slave to harm other people, but he is not legally obliged to place him at their disposal to the slightest degree: He owes none of his slave's service to anyone else. Analogously, if I am the moral owner of myself and, therefore, of my right arm, then, although others are entitled, because of *their* self-ownership, to prevent it from hitting them, no one is entitled, without my consent, to press it into their own or anyone else's service, even where my failure to

Originally published as two articles: "Self-ownership, World Ownership and Equality," from *Justice and Equality Here and Now*, edited by Frank S. Lucash (Ithaca, NY: Cornell University Press, 1986), pp. 108–35. Copyright © 1986 by Cornell University. Reprinted by permission of Cornell University Press; and "Self-ownership, World Ownership and Equality: Part II" from *Marxism and Liberalism*, edited by Ellen Frankel Paul, Fred D. Miller Jr, Jeffrey Paul, and John Ahrens (Oxford: Basil Blackwell, 1986), pp. 77–96. Reprinted by permission of Blackwell Publishing Ltd.

lend it voluntarily to others would be morally wrong.

My failure to help someone could indeed, according to Nozick, be morally wrong, but he denies that anyone, be it a private person or the state, would then be justified in *forcing* me to help him. Notice, then, that Nozick does not encourage people not to help one another. Nor does he think that they should not be blamed if they never do so. What he forbids is *constrained* helping, such as is involved, or so he would claim, in redistributive taxation. No one, he thinks, enjoys an enforceable non-contractual claim on anyone else's service. The state must therefore refrain, for example, from taxing the rich person to pay for the poor person's medical care: such taxation is a monstrous violation of the rich person's rights. But Nozick might nevertheless tell the rich person that it would be a jolly good thing if he contributed voluntarily to medical charity, and he might even say that a rich person who contributes nothing to charity is not at all nice. Nozick believes that people should be free to live their lives as they wish, but he does not believe that how they choose to live them is beyond criticism.

Nozick thinks not only that people own themselves, but also that they can become, with equally strong moral right, sovereign owners of the potentially indefinitely unequal amounts of worldly resources that they can gather to themselves as a result of proper exercises of their own and/or others' self-owned personal powers. When, moreover, private property in natural resources has been rightly generated, its morally privileged origin insulates it against expropriation of limitation.

Now a union of self-ownership and unequal distribution of worldly resources readily leads to indefinitely great inequality of private property in external goods of all kinds and, hence, to inequality of condition, on any view of what would constitute equality of condition. It follows that inequality of condition is, when properly generated, morally protected, and that the attempt to promote equality of condition at the expense of private property is an unacceptable violation of people's rights. Removing someone's legitimately acquired private property may not be as outrageous as removing his arm, but it is an outrage of the same kind. It is wrong for substantially the same reason.

A common left-wing response to Nozick is to recoil from the inequality his view allows, to affirm some sort of equality of condition as a fundamental principle, and to reject self-ownership because of the inequality of condition it supposedly generates. The left-wing conclusion is then that people lack the exclusive right to their own powers that goes with self-ownership, and that force may be applied against naturally well endowed people not only to prevent them from harming others but also to ensure that they help them, so that equality of condition (or not too much inequality of condition) will be secured.

But this line of response to Nozick, in which some sort of equality of condition is affirmed at the outset and a denial of self-ownership is derived from it, suffers from two related disadvantages. It has, first, the polemical disadvantage that the response is powerless against those who occupy Nozick's position, since they have not failed to notice that their view contradicts the fundamentalist egalitarianism that is here pressed against it. The other disadvantage of this response to Nozick is that the thesis of self-ownership has, after all, plenty of appeal on its own account, quite apart from anything Nozick says on its behalf. The antecedent appeal of the self-ownership principle rivals that of the egalitarian principles it is thought to contradict, even for many committed defenders of such principles: that, indeed, is why Nozick's book, *Anarchy, State and Utopia*, unsettles so many of its left liberal and socialist readers.[2]

In my experience, leftists who disparage Nozick's forthright affirmation of each person's rights over himself lose confidence in their unqualified denial of the thesis of self-ownership when they are asked to consider who has the right to decide what should happen to, for example, their own eyes. They do not immediately agree that, were eye transplants easy to achieve, it would then be acceptable for the state to conscribe potential eye donors into a lottery whose losers must yield an eye to beneficiaries who would otherwise be not one-eyed but blind. The fact that they do not deserve their good eyes, that they do not need two good eyes more than blind people need one and so forth – the fact, in a word, that they are merely lucky to have good eyes – does not always convince even left-wing people that their claim on their own eyes is no stronger that that of some unlucky blind person. But if standard leftist objections to inequality of resources, private property and ultimate condition are taken quite literally, then the fact that it is sheer luck that these (relatively) good eyes are mine should deprive me of special privileges in them.

Now one might infer, not that the usual objections to considerable inequality of private property in external things are without force, but that their force is due to the comparative antecedent weakness of the case for exclusive rights in *external* things. It is an intelligible presumption that I alone am entitled to decide about the use of this arm, and to benefit from its dexterity, simply because it is my arm. It seems not only as a mere matter of *fact* attached to me, but also something that, as a matter of *norm*, I *ought* to decide about the use of, and the same goes for these legs, this brain and all the other parts and faculties that are liable to be pressed into someone else's service. But there is no comparable presumptive normative tie between a person and any part or portion of the external world. Hence one may plausibly say of external things, or at any rate of external things in their initial state, of raw land and natural resources (out of which all unraw external things are, be it noted, made), that no person has, at least to begin with, a greater right in them than any other does; whereas the same thought is less compelling when it is applied to human parts and powers. Jean-Jacques Rousseau described the original formation of private property as a usurpation of what rightly should be held in common, and many have found that thesis persuasive. But few have discerned a comparable injustice in a person's insistence on sovereignty over his own being.

These reflections suggest that those who stand to the left of Nozick might consider a different reaction to him than from the one I described earlier. Instead of premissing that equality of condition is morally mandatory and rejecting self-ownership on that basis, they might relax their opposition to the idea of self-ownership but resist its use as the foundation of an argument that proceeds, via a legitimation of inequality in ownership of external resources, to defend the inequality of condition they oppose.

They might try to see whether, or to what extent, they can achieve the equality of condition they prize by adopting an egalitarian approach to worldly resources while accepting, or at any rate not rejecting, the thesis of self-ownership.

In the third section of this chapter I offer a critical assessment of one attempt to unite self-ownership with equality of worldly resources and preserve, thereby, equality of condition. But before embarking on that project, I shall show in the second section that, whatever may be said about the principle of self-ownership in its own right, and whether or not it can indeed by combined with equality of worldly resources, affirm-ation of it does not warrant the strongly inegalitarian distribution of worldly resources with which Nozick associates it.

II Nozick on Appropriation

Even now not everything around us is privately owned, and most people would think that what remains privately unowned, such as the air we breathe and the sidewalks we tread, should not be available for privatisation. But most of what we need to live by is, by now, private property. Why was its original privatisation not a theft of what rightly should be held in common?

Notice that the question applies not only to raw natural resources, but in fact to all private property in external things. For since people create nothing ex nihilo, all external private property either is, or was made of, something that was once no one's private property, either in fact or morally (or was made of something that was made of something that was once not private property, or was made of something that was made of something that was made of something that was once not private property, and so on). In the prehistory of anything that is now private property there was at least one moment at which something privately un-owned was taken into private ownership. If, then, someone claims a Nozick-like right to something he legally owns, we may ask, apart from how he in particular came to own it, with what right it came to be *anyone's* private property in the first place.

Now it is easy to doubt that much actually existing private property was formed in what any-one could think was a legitimating way. Take for example, the shirt I am wearing. Superior force, nothing more, is the likely means whereby who-ever first privatised the land from which came the cotton out of which it is made secured his title to it. But let us here set aside questions about actual history. Let us ask, instead, how, if at all, private property *could* legitimately be formed.

Nozick's answer to that question is that one may acquire 'a permanent bequeathable property right in a previously unowned thing' as long as 'the position of others no longer at liberty to use the thing is [not] thereby worsened'.[3] That is the condition he lays down for permissible initial appropriation. And it seems, on the face of it, a sufficiently stringent condition, which is to say stringent enough to ensure that, when the condition really is satisfied, no one can properly complain about the appropriation it endorses.

In a moment I shall show that that is an illusion, that Nozick's condition is in truth woefully lax. But first let me explain what the condition says. It requires of an appropriation of an object O, which was unowned and available to all, that its withdrawal from general use not make anyone's prospects worse than they would have been *had O remained in general use*. If no one's position is in any way made worse than it would have been had O remained unowned, then, of course, the condition is satisfied. But it is also satisfied when someone's position is in some relevant way worsened, as long as his position is in other ways sufficiently improved to counterbalance that worsening. Hence I appropriate something legitimately if and only if no one has any reason to prefer its remaining in general use, or whoever does have some reason to prefer that it remain gets something in the new situation that he did not have before and that is worth at least as much to him as what I have caused him to lose. To illustrate: I enclose the beach, which has been common land, declare it my own and announce a price of one dollar per person per day for the use of it (or, if you think that there could not be dollars in what sounds like a state-of-nature situation, imagine that my price is a certain amount of massage of my bad back). But I so enhance the recreational value of the beach (perhaps by dyeing the sand different attractive colours, or just by picking up the litter every night) that all would-be users of it regard a dollar (or a massage) for a day's use of it as a dollar well spent: they prefer a day at the beach as it now is in exchange for a dollar to a free day at the beach as it was and as it would have remained had no one appropriated it. Hence my appropriation of the beach satisfies Nozick's condition.

Now it might seem that appropriations satisfying Nozick's condition could not conceivably generate a grievance. But that, as I promised to show, is an illusion. It is possible for people to be made seriously worse off than they would have become, even when Nozick's condition on appropriation is fulfilled. For Nozick has arbitrarily narrowed the class of alternatives with which we are to compare what happens when an appropriation occurs with a view to determining whether anyone is harmed by it. One might agree with Nozick that the way to determine the legitimacy of an appropriation is by looking at what would otherwise have happened to the people concerned, but Nozick does not consider enough alternative possibilities.

To see this, imagine a world with two people, whom I shall call, for mnemonic reasons only, Grabber and Johnny-Come-Lately, or Johnny, for short. (Some people think it is unrealistic to draw morals from worlds with only two people in them, but everything I shall say about this small world can be applied to more realistic big ones.) Initially nothing is privately owned, and each lives on milk, which he gets by temporarily arresting lactating female wild moose and drawing it from them. Each spends an average of six hours per day doing that. Each thereby obtains a certain number of gallons of milk per year, a number that reflects the quality of his own moose-trapping and moose-milking powers, and who gets more milk is not here relevant. Now suppose that Grabber seizes all the land, and all the moose with it, and designs a division of labour under which he himself traps, for an hour each day, and Johnny milks, for six hours each day. What is more, Grabber offers Johnny a salary consisting of the same amount of milk per year as Johnny was able to get on his own. Grabber himself gets not only five extra hours of leisure but also much more milk from the new arrangement.

Then Johnny is not worse off than he was before Grabber's grab and, let us assume, than he would have become had the land and the moose *remained* unprivately owned. And this means that Grabber's appropriation is, by Nozick's condition, legitimate. He gains enormously in comparison with the state of nature, and Johnny gains nothing, but Johnny does not lose, so the privatisation is immune to Nozickian criticism.

Now to see that Grabber's appropriation is, though clearly legitimate according to Nozick, not clearly legitimate on a more searching view of the matter, consider these further possibilities.

1 Suppose Johnny is just as good an organiser as Grabber is. He could have done exactly what Grabber did, but he did not because he thought doing so would be too grasping. Then, although Grabber's appropriation satisfies Nozick's condition, it does not seem that Grabber has, what Nozick's condition gives him, the right to force Johnny to respect it.

2 That is more evident still if we now suppose that Johnny could have designed an even better division of labour than the one Grabber imposes under which *both* he *and* Grabber would

have fared better than they do following Grabber's appropriation. Yet even under that supposition, Grabber's appropriation is, for Nozick, justified. It follows that Nozick's condition licenses, and protects, appropriations with upshots that make everyone worse off than he needs to be.

3   There is a third alternative with which to compare Grabber's appropriation, beyond the single alternative with which Nozick compares it, which is the persistence of unstructured common ownership, and the further alternative I complain he neglects, which is an appropriation by Johnny. That third alternative, also unjustifiably neglected by Nozick, is that it might be the case that Johnny and Grabber would have agreed to a division of labour without either of them privately appropriating the land. Such an agreement would, in effect, institute a form of socialism, and whether or not such a socialism would be productively superior to the dispensation following on one or other of the two private appropriations, it would certainly be productively superior to the initial no-ownership situation, and it is arbitrary to ignore how Johnny would have fared under the socialist alternative when considering whether Grabber's appropriation is justified.

Suppose, however, that Johnny lacks Grabber's organisational skills, that Grabber's appropriation actually makes Johnny better off than he was before and that socialism would, for some reason, benefit neither party by comparison with the initial no-ownership dispensation. Is not Grabber's appropriation, at least under those maximally favourable assumptions, as legitimate as Nozick thinks it is?

Note that, even if we say that it is legitimate, it is legitimate only by virtue of satisfying conditions far stronger than those Nozick lays down. And my own view is that its legitimacy is even then contestable. For to suppose otherwise is to take for granted that the land is not, from the start, collectively owned by Grabber and Johnny, so that the proper way to decide its fate would be by the socialist device of consensual agreement, instead of unilaterally. Why should we not regard the land, before Grabber's appropriation, as collectively owned rather than, as Nozick takes for granted, owned by no one?

Now the real-world equivalents of Johnny are those billions, a majority of humankind, who are born into the world substantially propertyless and who therefore depend for their survival on someone wanting to buy their labour power. What would Nozick say about them? He would say, of those propertyless persons who do manage to sell their labour power, that they will get at least as much and probably more in exchange for it than they could have hoped to get by applying it in an unregulated state of nature; and of those propertyless persons whose labour power is not worth buying that, though, in Nozick's non-welfare state, they might therefore die, they would have died in the state of nature anyway.

But we can now make two replies to that tough and complacent talk about the lot of the dispossessed. The first is that, even if we concede that the world is originally, morally speaking, unowned, the fact that those now without worldly resources would have been no better off had the world remained unowned and not been privately appropriated in the particular way it was does not legitimate their condition, since it might be true that they would have been better off still if those private appropriations had not occurred. And the second reply is to withdraw the concession offered in the first one, by objecting that Nozick has not shown that the world's initial normative state *is* one of not being owned by anyone. What prevents us from regarding it as jointly owned to begin with, even if we also regard each of its inhabitants as a sovereign self-owner?

I conclude that we may dispatch Nozick's inegalitarianism without raising any challenge against the thesis of self-ownership.

III   Two Concepts of Liberty

What we may challenge is the blithe assumption that 'virgin' things are quite unowned and therefore up for grabs: one scarcely need share that assumption *even* if one accepts that people are full owners of themselves. Now one alternative to the view that things are, in their native state, quite unowned is, as we saw, to regard them as jointly or collectively owned by all persons, and I shall now present and discuss an attempt to combine that different conception of the original moral relationship between people and things with the principle of self-ownership, with a view to shedding some light on the distributive effect of self-ownership in a world whose parts are not open to unilateral privatisation. What follows is one attempt to realise the project described at the end of Section 1, the project of respecting self-ownership and subjecting worldly resources to an egalitarian dispensation, in the hope of securing equality of resultant condition without rejecting self-ownership.

Once again we imagine a two-person world, but once again the results will apply, mutatis mutandis, to a world teeming with people. This time our individuals are called Able and Infirm, after their respective natural endowments. Each owns himself and both jointly own everything else. With suitable external resources Able can produce life-sustaining and life-enhancing goods, but Infirm has no productive power at all. We suppose that each is rational and exclusively self-interested, and we ask what scheme of production and distribution they will agree on. We thereby investigate the reward that self-owned ability would command in one kind of world without private property.

Now what Able and Infirm get depends not only on their own powers and decisions but also on what the world is like, materially speaking. Five mutually exclusive and jointly exhaustive possible material situations, not all of which are interesting, may readily be distinguished:

1 Able cannot produce per day what is needed for one person for a day, so Able and Infirm both die.
2 Able can produce enough or more than enough for one person, but not enough for two. Infirm lets Able produce what he can, since only spite or envy would lead him not to. Able lives and Infirm dies.
3 Able can produce just enough to sustain both himself and Infirm. So Infirm forbids him to produce unless he produces that much. Able consequently does, and both live at subsistence.
4 If Able produces at all, the amount he produces is determined independently of his choice, and it exceeds what is needed to sustain both Able and Infirm. They therefore bargain over the distribution of a fixed surplus. The price of failure to agree (what theorists of bargaining call the 'threat point') is no production, and therefore death for both.
5 Again Able can produce a surplus, but now, more realistically, he can vary its size, so that Able and Infirm will bargain not only, as in situation 4, over who gets how much, but over how much will be produced.

The interesting cases are 4 and 5, in which bargains will be struck. It is a controversial question, in the relevant philosophical and technical literature, what one should expect the outcome of such bargaining to be. But it seems clear that the inputs to the bargaining process will be what are called the utility functions of Able and Infirm, including the disutility of labour for Able and the disutility of infirmity for Infirm. What will matter, in other and less technical words, is their preferences, what they like and dislike, and how much. And the crucial point is that Able's talent will not, just as such, affect how much he gets. If the exercise of his talent is irksome to him, then he will indeed get additional compensation, but only because he is irked, not because it is his labour that irks him. In short, he gets nothing extra just because it is he, and not Infirm, who does the producing. Infirm controls one necessary condition of production (relaxing his veto over use of the land), and Able controls two, but that gives Able no bargaining advantage. If a good costs 101 dollars and you have 100 of the needed dollars and I only one of them, then, if we are both rational and self-interested, you will not get a greater share of the good if we buy it jointly just because you supply so much more of what is required to obtain it.

Here, then, joint world ownership prevents self-ownership from generating an inequality to which egalitarians would object, and although the Able and Infirm story is an extremely special one in several respects, the particular point that talent as such yields no extra reward even under self-ownership, where there is also joint ownership of external resources, is, I believe, generalisable. (I do not say that no inequality repugnant to egalitarians can arise in the Able and Infirm situation, but only that either there will be no such inequality or its foundation will not be Able's ownership of his own powers but the parties' utility functions as they operate in the bargaining process. One cannot guarantee that no inequality repugnant to egalitarians will arise, since different egalitarians believe in different equalities, and not all of them are likely to emerge from the bargaining process.)

But we must now consider a seemingly fatal objection to the lesson just drawn from the Able and Infirm story. The lesson is that, without denying self-ownership and without affirming equality of condition as an underived principle, one may move towards a form of equality of condition by insisting on joint ownership of the external world. And the seemingly fatal objection is that to affirm joint ownership of the world is, as the story of Able and Infirm might be thought to show, inconsistent with achieving the purpose and expected effect of self-ownership. What is the point of my owning myself if I may do nothing without the agreement of others? Do not Able and Infirm jointly own not only the world but also, in effect, each other? Would they not bargain exactly as they do if we supposed that, instead of being self-owning, they jointly owned one another? It looks, then, as though the suggested form of external resource equality, namely, joint world ownership, renders nugatory the self-ownership with which we have sought to combine it. Self-ownership is not eliminated, but it is made useless, rather as it is useless to own a corkscrew when you are forbidden access to bottles of wine.

But the objection just stated can, for the present polemical purposes, be set aside. Joint world ownership indeed renders self-ownership merely formal, but, as we shall see, that is not an objection that defenders of capitalism are entitled to press.

The polemical task of the present chapter is to respond to Robert Nozick's contention that honouring people's self-ownership requires extending to them a freedom to live their own lives that is incompatible with the equality of condition prized by socialists. Our response to that contention was that self-ownership is, contrary to what Nozick says, compatible with equality of condition, since the inequality that Nozick defends depends on adjoining to self-ownership an inegalitarian principle of external resource distribution, which need not be accepted. When, instead, self-ownership is combined with joint ownership of the world, its tendency to generate inequality is removed.

The objection to that response was that the resource distribution under joint world ownership renders the self-ownership with which it is officially combined merely formal. *But that objection would, for immediate polemical purposes, be laid to rest if it could be shown that the self-ownership defended by Nozick is itself merely formal*, for he could not then maintain that what he defends generates inequality of condition.

To be sure, Nozick would like us to think, what he evidently himself thinks, that the self-ownership he favours is more than merely formal. In Chapter 3 of *Anarchy, State and Utopia* he pleads that each person should be free to live his own life, a *desideratum* that is supposed to be secured by the rights constituting Nozickian self-ownership. But Nozick also thinks that the most abject proletarian, who must either sell his labour power to a capitalist or die, enjoys the relevant rights. And if that is so, then Nozick could not complain that Able's self-ownership is merely formal, since, whether or not it is indeed merely formal, it is not less consequential than the proletarian's.

If Able and the proletarian lack substantive self-ownership, that is because neither can do anything without the agreement of Infirm and the capitalist, respectively. But they are, nevertheless, different from chattel slaves; for while each can do nothing without another's agreement, it is also true that there is nothing that either need do without his own agreement: neither Infirm nor the capitalist has rights of sheer command that are not grounded in a prior contract to obey. By contrast, the slave's master may determine unilaterally what the slave must do.

The resulting dilemma for Nozick is severe. Either capitalism does not confer consequential self-ownership, since the worker's self-ownership is not robust enough to qualify as such, or, if it does so qualify, consequential self-ownership is at least as robust as the worker's, and no inequality follows from self-ownership in the world of Able and Infirm.

Let me describe Nozick's dilemma in a different way. He says that a propensity to inequality is unavoidable when people are allowed to live their own lives. Yet he must hold that, despite the constraints on his life choices, the proletarian leads his own life. But it then follows that he is wrong that, when people lead their own lives, equality of condition cannot be guaranteed, since Able and Infirm lead their own lives as much as the proletarian does, and the constitution under which they live guarantees a certain equality of condition.

We can now draw three conclusions. First, the tale of Able and Infirm shows that strict socialist equality is compatible with the freedom that defenders of capitalism boast everyone has in capitalist society, since that freedom is nothing more than formal self-ownership, and formal self-ownership obtains in the world of Able and Infirm.

Second, although it indeed turns out that the freedom of which Nozick speaks can be reconciled with equality, that is only because it is a very confined freedom, and it remains to be shown that equality can be reconciled with a freedom more worthy of the name.

Such freedom – and this is the third conclusion – is not self-ownership, but autonomy, the circumstance of genuine control over one's own life. Universal self-ownership fails to ensure autonomy, since it tends to produce proletarians, who lack it. Universal self-ownership does not produce proletarians when it is conjoined with appropriate rules about external resources, but such rules, to preserve self-ownership while securing everyone against proletarianhood, must breach autonomy in a different way. The indicated conclusion is that, for real freedom, or autonomy, to prevail, there have to be restrictions on self-ownership. That is ironical, since it is autonomy that attracts us to self-ownership, through a disastrous misidentification. The very thing that makes the self-ownership thesis attractive should actually make us reject self-ownership.

The natural next step is to ask what kind and degree of control over external things a person must have to enjoy autonomy, and then to ask whether such control is compatible with socialist equality. Those questions compose a real challenge to contemporary Left political philosophy, even after Nozick has been set aside. Nozick's freedom is consistent with equality, but the same may not be true of a freedom whose claims are less illusory. But I have to add, at the cost of ending on a pedantic instead of a rhetorical note, that I do mean just that there *may* be incompatibility between socialist equality and freedom. Whether there actually *is* that incompatibility is a matter for further investigation and debate.

Notes

1 In so designating what is foundational and what is derivative in right-wing thought, I am suggesting that the right-wing idea is not that freedom comes first and, in order to be free, people should be self-owning. For the Right gives us no independent purchase on the concept of freedom that would enable us to tie freedom and self-ownership that way around. It is rather that the scope and nature of the freedom we must enjoy reflects the self-ownership conception. That is why the apparent unfreedom of the proletar-

ian is not treated as a counterexample to the right-wing belief that freedom prevails in capitalist society. For the proletarian forced daily to sell his labour power is nevertheless a self-owner, indeed must be one in order to sell it, and is therefore nevertheless free in the relevant sense.

2 Robert Nozick, *Anarchy, State and Utopia* (New York: Basic Books, 1974).

3 Ibid., p. 178

28

Liberal Pluralism and Constitutional Democracy: The Case of Freedom of Conscience

William A. Galston

Introduction

It is said that during medieval times, Bulan, king of the Khazers, summoned four wise men to his kingdom – a secular philosopher, a Muslim scholar, a Christian scholar, and a rabbi. After interrogating them on the content and basis of their beliefs, Bulan called his people together in an assembly, declared that he accepted Judaism, and decreed that all Khazers would thenceforth be instructed in and practice Judaism as their communal faith.

I suspect that this chain of events strikes most modern readers as strange. Would it seem less strange if – rather than one man deciding for all – the people had assembled themselves and, after the most scrupulous democratic deliberation, settled on Judaism as the official national religion? I think not.

There is a threshold question, which I take to be the defining question for theoretical liberalism: does the state possess the legitimate power to make collectively binding decisions on this matter? If not, the question of *how* such decisions should be made is never reached. From this liberal pluralist perspective, the content of religious faith is a clear example of a matter that is not rightfully subject to plenipotentiary state power.

It is not hard to forge a theoretical link between liberalism and political pluralism. (In my recent book I call this complex of ideas "liberal pluralism.") The more difficult question is whether

liberalism, so understood, makes a compelling claim to truth. Why should we treat non-state authority as anything other than the creature of (perhaps tacit) political decisions? Is liberty, however understood, anything more than a political construction, subject to alteration through normal political processes? I doubt that theoretical argumentation can decisively adjudicate such questions. So I want to take a different tack – an appeal to moral intuitions and experiences encoded in our tradition of constitutional adjudication. Specifically, I want to ask how claims based on freedom of conscience are most plausibly understood.

Freedom of Conscience: Two Cases

To frame this inquiry, I begin by recalling an important but largely forgotten episode in US constitutional history: the rapid and almost unprecedented turnabout by the Supreme Court on a matter of fundamental importance.

Acting under the authority of the state government, the school board of Minersville, Pennsylvania had required both students and teachers to participate in a daily pledge of allegiance to the flag. In the 1940 case of *Minersville v. Gobitis*, the Supreme Court decided against a handful of Jehovah's Witnesses who sought to have their children exempted on the grounds that this exercise amounted to a form of idolatry strictly forbidden

Originally published in *Philosophy and Public Policy Quarterly* 24, no. 3 (Summer 2004): 21–7. Reprinted by the kind permission of the author.

by their faith. With but a single dissenting vote, the Court ruled that it was permissible for a school board to make participation in saluting the American flag a condition for attending public school, regardless of the conscientious objections of parents and students.

Relying on this holding and quoting liberally from the majority's decision, the West Virginia State Board of Education issued a regulation making the flag statute mandatory statewide. When a challenge to this decision arose barely three years later, the Court in *West Virginia v. Barnette* reversed itself by a vote of six to three. To be sure, during the brief interval separating these cases, the lone dissenter in *Gobitis* had been elevated to Chief Justice and two new voices, both favoring reversal, had joined the Court, while two supporters of the original decision had departed. But of the seven justices who heard both cases, three saw fit to reverse themselves and to set forth their reasons for the change.

This kind of abrupt, explicit reversal is very rare in the annals of the Court, and it calls for some explanation. A clue is to be found in the deservedly well-known peroration of Justice Jackson's majority decision overturning compulsory flag salutes:

If there is any fixed star in our constitutional constellation, it is that no official, high or petty, can prescribe what shall be orthodox in politics, nationalism, religion, or other matters of opinion or force citizens to confess by word or act their faith therein. If there are any circumstances which permit an exception, they do not now occur to us. We think the action of the local authorities in compelling the flag salute and pledge transcends constitutional limitation on their power and invades the sphere of intellect and spirit which it is the purpose of the First Amendment to our Constitution to reserve from all official control.

I want to suggest that the protected "sphere of intellect and spirit" and the antipathy to forced professions of faith to which Jackson refers enjoy a central place in the development of American political thought and in liberal political theory more generally. Expounded under the rubric of "conscience," not least by James Madison, it provides one of the clearest examples of inherent limits to legitimate state power.

In his famous "Memorial and Remonstrance" of 1785, coauthored with Thomas Jefferson and directed against the Virginia proposal to publicly fund teachers of Christianity, Madison insisted that the religion of every man "must be left to the conviction and conscience of every man; and it is the right of every man to exercise it as these may dictate." He described this right as "unalienable", indeed, two of the amendments that Madison drafted for inclusion in the *Bill of Rights* made explicit reference to "right of conscience":

The civil rights of none shall be abridged on account of religious belief or worship, nor shall any national religion be established; nor shall the full and equal rights of conscience be in any manner, or in any pretext, infringed.

And:

No state shall violate the equal rights of conscience, or the freedom of the press, or the trial by jury in criminal cases.

In the subsequent floor debate on the draft *Bill of Rights* (August 17, 1789), Madison characterized the proposed restriction on the states as "the most valuable amendment in the whole list." Although the House of Representatives accepted Madison's proposal to make guarantees of basic rights binding on the states, the Senate refused to go along. (It took nearly 150 years for the Supreme Court to decide that the Fourteenth Amendment had provided the vehicle for enforcing these rights vis-à-vis state governments as well as the federal government.)

Substantive Due Process, Fundamental Liberties, and Freedom of Conscience

Over the next century, the Supreme Court played at most a minor role in protecting what we now understand as the basic civil rights of individuals. During the decades after the Civil War, the Court increasingly deployed a broad construction of individual property rights against states while typically leaving political and civil liberties under the aegis of state power. In 1920, for example, the case of *Gilbert v. Minnesota* came before the Supreme Court. Gilbert, a pacifist, had criticized American participation in World War I. He was convicted under a state statute prohibiting advocacy of teaching that interfered with or discouraged enlistment in the military. While the Court's majority declined to extend Fourteenth Amendment liberty guarantees to Gilbert, Justice Brandeis dissented, writing:

> I have difficulty believing that the liberty guaranteed by the Constitution, which has been held to protect [a wide property rights], does not include liberty to teach, either in the privacy of the home or publicly, the doctrine of pacifism... I cannot believe that the liberty guaranteed by the 14th Amendment includes only liberty to acquire and to enjoy property.

Over time, the Court's unwillingness to abandon its doctrine of broad economic rights helped create the basis for a broader understanding of constitutionally protected and enforceable liberties. Two important cases decided in the 1920s spearheaded this expansion and helped lay the foundation for nationally recognized rights of conscience. The first stemmed from a Nebraska law which, reflecting the nativist passions stirred by World War I, prohibited instruction in any modern language other than English. Acting under statute, a trial court convicted a teacher in a Lutheran parochial school for teaching a Bible class in German. In *Meyer v. Nebraska*, the Supreme Court struck down this law as a violation of the Fourteenth Amendment's liberty guarantee. Writing for a seven-member majority, Justice McReynolds declared that while the state

> May do much, go very far indeed, in order to improve the quality of its citizens, physically, mentally, and morally... but the individual has certain fundamental rights which must be respected. A desirable end cannot be promoted by prohibited means.

Two years later, the Supreme Court handed down a second key ruling. Through a ballot initiative, the people of Oregon enacted a law requiring all parents and legal guardians to send children between the ages of eight and sixteen to public schools. This amounted to outlawing most nonpublic schools. The Society of Sisters, an Oregon corporation that maintained a system of Catholic schools, sued on the grounds that this law was inconsistent with the Fourteenth Amendment. In *Pierce v. Society of Sisters*, decided in 1925, the Court agreed. Justice McReynolds, this time writing for a unanimous court, declared that

> The fundamental theory of liberty upon which all governments in the Union repose excludes any general power of the State to standardize its children by forcing them to accept instruction from public teachers only. The child is not the mere creature of the State...

Six years later, in 1931, the Supreme Court handed down its decision in the case of *US v. Macintosh*. Douglas Clyde Macintosh was born in Canada, came to the US as a graduate student at the University of Chicago, was ordained as a Baptist minister in 1907, and became Chaplain of the Yale Graduate School. When World War I broke out, he returned to his native Canada to volunteer for service as a military chaplain. He reentered the US in 1916 and applied for naturalization in 1925. When asked whether he would bear arms on behalf of his country, he responded that he could not accept an undertaking without knowing the cause for which his country was asking him to fight or believing the war was just, and he declared that his "first allegiance was to the will of God." After he was denied naturalization, he went to court.

The government argued that naturalization was a privilege, not a right; that the government has the right to impose any conditions it sees fit on that privilege; that the exemption of native-born citizens from military service on grounds of conscience was a statutory grant, not a Constitutional belief; and that Congress had not provided such statutory exemption for individuals seeking naturalization. The lawyers for Macintosh argued that our history makes it clear that conscientious exemption from military service was an integral element of the rights of conscience, guaranteed by the First and Ninth Amendments.

By a vote of five to four, a deeply divided Court decided in favor of the government. The case turned on matters of statutory construction and on broader considerations. Writing for the majority, Justice Sutherland insisted that

> When [Macintosh] speaks of putting his allegiance to the will of God above his allegiance to the government, it is evident, in light of his entire statement, that he means to make *his own interpretation* of the will of God the decisive test... We are a Christian people... but, also, we are a Nation with a duty to survive.... Submission and obedience to the laws of the land, as well as those made for war... are not inconsistent with the will of God.

Writing for the four dissenters, Chief Justice Hughes began by offering an argument based on statutory construction, but like Sutherland, he did not end there. Hughes framed the broader argument this way:

> When one's belief collides with the power of the State, the latter is supreme within its sphere and submission or punishment follows. But, in the forum of conscience, duty to a moral power higher than the State has always been maintained . . . The essence of religion is belief in a relation to God involving duties superior to those arising from any human relation . . . There is abundant room for enforcing the requisite authority of law as it is enacted and requires obedience, and for maintaining the conception of the supremacy of law as essential to orderly government, without demanding that either citizens or applicants for citizenship shall assume by oath an obligation to regard allegiance to God as subordinate to allegiance to civil power.

From Gobitis to Barnette: The Rise and Fall of Felix Frankfurter

This brings me back to the dueling Court decision with which I began. As I will show, *Gobitis* and *Barnette* bring into play a number of issues much debated among students of jurisprudence and political theory during the past decade: the clash between history-based and principle-based interpretations of constitutional norms; the roles of courts and legislatures in a constitutional democracy; the competition between parents and the state for control of education; the appropriate contents and limits of civic education. The deepest issue is the relative weight to be given to claims based upon individual liberties and those based upon social order and cohesion.

In writing for the majority in the *Gobitis* case, Justice Frankfurter offered an argument in favor of a democratic state whose legitimate powers include the power to prescribe civic exercises such as the flag salute. He located the controversy in a complex field of plural and competing claims: liberty of individual conscience versus the state's authority to safeguard the nation's civic unity. The task is to "reconcile" these competing claims, which means "prevent[ing] either from destroying the other." Because liberty of conscience is so funda-

mental, "every possible leeway" should be given to the claims of religious faith; however, the "very plurality of principles" prevents us from establishing the "freedom to *follow* conscience" as absolute.

In considering the judicial enforcement of religious freedom, Frankfurter contended that we are dealing with a "*historic* concept." That is, we should not look at its underlying logic or principles, but rather and only at the way this concept has been applied in the past. Further, Frankfurter insisted that "the mere possession of religious convictions which contradict the relevant concerns of a political society does not relieve the citizen from the discharge of political responsibilities." On its face, this premise is fair enough; but it raises the question of what must be added to "mere possession" to create a valid claim against the state. When (if ever) does the Constitution require some individuals to be exempted from doing what society thinks is necessary to promote the common good? Conversely, what are the kinds of collective claims that rightly trump individual reservations?

Frankfurter offers a specific answer to the latter, insisting that social order and tranquility provide the basis for enjoying all civil rights – including rights of conscience and exercise. Indeed, all specific activities and advantages of government "presuppose the existence of an organized political society." National unity is the basis of national security – a highest-order public value (as we would now say, a "compelling state interest"). National unity is secured by the "binding tie of cohesive sentiment," which is the "ultimate foundation of a free society."

Toward the conclusion of his opinion, Frankfurter touched on an issue that figures centrally in our current debates – the right of public authorities "to awaken in the child's mind considerations . . . contrary to those implanted by the parent." He is right to suggest that the bare fact of a clash with parents does not suffice to render a state's action illegitimate. But who seriously thinks that parental claims are always trumps? The thesis is rather that there are certain classes of claims that parents can interpose against state authority – especially when the state employs particularly intrusive means in pursuit of public purposes. Recall that what was at stake in *Gobitis* was not just the right of the state to require civic education; it was the state's power to compel students to engage in affirmations contrary to conscientious belief.

427

Frankfurter insisted that the state "may in self-protection utilize the educational process for inculcating those almost unconscious feelings which bind men together." And if the state gets it wrong? Frankfurter concluded his opinion with a profession of faith in the democratic process: It is better to use legislative processes to protect liberty and rectify error, rather than transferring the contest to the judicial arena. So long as the political liberties needed for effective political contestations are left unaffected, "education in the abandonment of foolish legislation is itself a training in liberty [and] serves to vindicate the self-confidence of a free people." There is clearly some wisdom in this position, which is enjoying a modest resurgence today. What it overlooks is the cost – especially to the most affected individuals and groups – of waiting for a democratic majority to recognize its mistake.

However, Justice (soon to be Chief Justice) Stone had forcefully dissented, arguing that the law in dispute did more than suppress and prohibit the free exercise of religion: it sought to coerce individuals to perform acts to which they are conscientiously opposed. Further, a valid end does not imply that all means in its pursuit are permitted. Even if national unity is an important interest of the state, Stone argued, "there are other ways to teach loyalty and patriotism which are the sources of national unity, than by compelling the pupil to affirm that which he does not believe and by commanding a form of affirmance which violates his religious convictions."

Despite his eloquence, Stone persuaded none of his brethren to follow him. But Frankfurter's argument raised a storm of controversy the moment it was handed down, and many of those criticisms anticipated the kind of jurisprudence that emerged only a few years later and flowered in the following decades.

Among many critics, William Fennell, a prominent member of the New York Bar, argued against Frankfurter's endorsement of the liberal democratic position, asking his readers to consider the consequences for previous decisions, such as *Pierce v. Society of Sisters*: wouldn't Frankfurter's jurisprudence have left every Catholic in the state of Oregon vulnerable to the anti-Catholic majority's repressive folly? Another critic, William F. Anderson, writing in the *Michigan Law Review*, contended that "if individual liberties are something more than the by-product of a democratic process, if in fact they have an intrinsic value

worthy of protection, it is difficult to justify a decision which subordinates a fundamental liberty to a legislative program of questionable worth."

What may well be regarded as the *coup de grace* was delivered by Thomas Reed Powell, Joseph Story Professor of Law at Harvard, a pioneering legal realist, and no softy. His article addressing conscience and the Constitution drips with scorn for Jehovah's Witnesses. Powell termed them "ignorant," "unreflecting, dogmatic, indoctrinated," and "simple-minded and unintelligent." He even compared them to "mental defectives" and spoke approvingly of an education that weans children away from the "nonsense of their parents."

Yet Powell could not bring himself to accept Frankfurter's opinion. Three stumbling blocks proved insurmountable. First, as a matter of legal fact, he could not agree with Frankfurter's assertion that freedom of religion cannot be deployed against general legislation not specifically directed against religion. Second, as a practical matter, the effort to coerce children to salute the flag insincerely and contrary to conscience "seems . . . likely to be self-defeating" when measured against its goal of fostering patriotism and national unity. But finally, the issue of religious liberty was squarely on the table, in tension with the inculcation of national unity. By the logic of Frankfurter's own argument, if important constitutional values are in competition, then they must be weighed against one another. This the majority failed to do. Powell insisted that the Court must address quantitative as well as qualitative issues: How "important" is it to the nation to compel children to join in a patriotic ceremony which for them is idolatry? To what "extent" would exempting them impair the power of the state to preserve itself? Is the public interest "slight" or "major"?

The effects of these criticisms became apparent by 1942, when the Court decided the case of *Jones v. Opelika*. The facts were these: Jehovah's Witnesses had been going door-to-door selling religious books. Various municipalities enacted statutes requiring all booksellers to take out licenses and pay substantial fees in order to distribute books legally. The Jehovah's Witnesses refused to do so, citing free exercise claims as well as other arguments.

Writing for the five-man majority, Justice Reed argued that, granting the presumption in favor of First Amendment freedoms, public determinations of time, place, and manner were rightly viewed as consistent with those freedoms. Indeed:

We see nothing in the collection of a non-discriminatory licensing fee . . . from those selling books or papers, which abridges the freedoms of worship, speech, or press.

Led by Chief Justice Stone, four members of the Court dissented. In his opinion, Stone argued that it is essential to examine the extent for the burden the law places on religious free exercise, which the majority blithely refused to do. The power to tax may well amount to the power to censor or suppress. Further, it does not suffice to say that the tax on speech and religion is "non-discriminatory."

Justice Murphy's dissent addressed Stone's questions and amplified his argument. The burden, Murphy insisted, was significant, and that fact was significant in resolving the case. To be sure, it was necessary to distinguish between burdens on thought and those on action. Moreover, the defendants had failed to specify the harms to be avoided through the licensing system or to show that the statutes were drawn narrowly and precisely to address those evils.

Even more significant than these two individual dissents was a brief dissenting statement jointly authored by three justices (Murphy, Black, and Douglas) who had formed part of the *Gobitis* majority:

The opinion of the Court sanctions a device which in our opinion suppresses or tends to suppress the free exercise of a religion practiced by a minority group. This is but another step in the direction which *Minersville School District v. Gobitis* took against the same religious minority and is a logical extension of the principles upon which that decision rested. Since we joined in the opinion in the *Gobitis* case, we think this is an appropriate decision to state that we now believe that it was also wrongly decided.

In the course of a comprehensive survey of the development of liberties protected under the Fourteenth Amendment, John Raeburn Green commented that while there was nothing good to be said about the majority decision, *Jones v. Opelika* "in the long run will mark an advance for [religious] liberty, because of the dissenting opinions." He was right, and sooner than he thought. In the very next year (1943), the replacement of Justice Byrnes, one of the *Opelika* majority, led to

its reversal by a vote of five to four in the case of *Murdock v. Pennsylvania*. More remarkably, *Gobitis* was overruled by a stunning six to three, in *West Virginia v. Barnette*.

In his majority decision, Justice Jackson did not question that state's right to educate for patriotism and civic unity. But in his view, what was at stake was not education, rightly understood, but something quite different: "a compulsion of students to declare a belief." Jackson insisted that assuring individual rights strengthens government by bolstering support for it. In the long run, individual freedom of mind is more sustainable and powerful than is "officially disciplined uniformity." Indeed, "to believe that patriotism will not flourish if patriotic ceremonies are voluntary and spontaneous instead of a compulsory routine is to make an unflattering estimate of the appeal of our institutions to free minds."

There is no question that government officials and institutions may seek to promote national unity through persuasion and example, but the question is whether under the Constitution compulsion is a permissible means for its achievement. It is in this context that Jackson penned his famous words about the fixed star in our constitutional constellation.

The three repentant justices who had issued promissory notes in the *Opelika* dissent redeemed them by joining the *Barnette* majority. Black and Douglas began their concurrence by noting the appropriateness of explaining the reasons for their change of view. They insisted that, as a constitutional matter, while the state can impose reasonable regulations on time, place, or manner of religious activity, it can suppress religious liberty only to ward off "grave and pressingly immediate dangers." But in this case the danger was remote at best, and the policy only speculatively connected to its professed end. Further, the state's burden is especially heavy because the nature of the means employed – the statutory exaction of specific words – constitutes a form of "test oath" that has always been especially "abhorrent" in the United States. And even if this policy were constitutionally acceptable, it would be self-defeating: "Words uttered under coercion are proof of nothing but loyalty to self-interest. Love of country must spring from willing hearts and free minds . . ."

The third penitent, Justice Murphy, also concurred. Freedom of thought and religion, he contended, implies the right both to speak and to remain silent, except when compulsion is required for the preservation of an ordered society – as in the case of compulsion to testify in court. The compelled flag salute did not come close to meeting that test: its benefits were too indefinite and intangible to justify the restriction on freedom and invasion of privacy.

Justice Frankfurter, the author of the majority opinion in *Gobitis*, penned a lengthy dissent, with a personal *apologia* whose tone of injured dignity was set by its opening sentence: "one who belongs to the most vilified and persecuted minority in history is not likely to be insensible to the freedoms guaranteed by our Constitution." But he declared that what was at stake was not a constitutional question but rather a policy judgment. In this arena, the courts should override legislatures only if reasonable legislators could not have chosen to employ the contested means in furtherance of legitimate ends. As a general proposition, there is a presumption in favor of legislatures, and legislation must be considered valid if there exists some rational basis for connecting it to a valid public purpose.

Frankfurter contended that liberal democracy is more a matter of active, self-governing citizens than of protective or tutelary courts:

Of course patriotism cannot be enforced by the flag salute...Only a persistent positive translation of the faith of a free society into the convictions and habits and actions of a community is the ultimate reliance against unabated temptations to fetter the human spirit.

Conclusion: Jurisprudence, Moral Intuition, and Political Theory

I am not a legal historian, and it must be obvious that I have told this tale not for its own sake, but with moral intent. I want to use these materials as a basis for testing our judgments about two questions. First: looking at the judicial bottom-line – the "holding" – are we more inclined to favor the outcome in *Gobitis* or in *Barnette*? Second: what kinds of broader principles underlie our judgment concerning these specific cases?

I have discussed the dueling cases with a number of scholars and friends (some are both). The consensus runs roughly as follows. It is easy to sympathize with Frankfurter's dismay at the deployment of judicial review to immunize concentrated economic power against public scrutiny;

with his belief that democratic majorities should enjoy wide latitude to pursue the common good as they see it; with his belief that the requirements of social order and unity may sometimes override the claims, however worthy, of individuals, parents, civil associations, and religious faith; and with his conviction that the systematic substitution of judicial review of democratic self-correction can end by weakening citizenship itself. Nonetheless, say my interlocutors, Frankfurter's reasoning in *Gobitis* was unsound, and his holding unacceptable. There are certain goods and liberties that enjoy a preferred position in our order and are supposed to be lifted above everyday policy debate. If liberty of conscience is a fundamental good, as Frankfurter acknowledges, then it follows that state action interfering with it bears a substantial burden of proof. A distant harm, loosely linked to the contested policy, is not enough to meet that burden. The harm must be a real threat; it must be causally linked to the policy in question; and the proposed remedy must do the least possible damage to the fundamental liberty, consistent with the abatement of the threat. The state's mandatory pledge of allegiance failed all three of these tests. *Gobitis* was wrongly decided; the ensuing uproar was a public indication that the Court had gone astray; and the quick reversal in *Barnette*, with fully half the justices in the new six-member majority switching sides, was a clear indication of the moral force of the objections. This is my position as well, and I would be happy to test it against those whose conscientious judgments differ.

We now reach my second question: is our judgment on these cases a particularized moral intuition, or does it reflect some broader principles? The latter, I think. What Justice Jackson termed the "sphere of intellect and spirit" is at or near the heart of what makes us human. The protection of that sphere against unwarranted intrusion represents the most fundamental of all human liberties. There is a strong presumption against state policies that prevent individuals from the free exercise of intellect and spirit. There is an even stronger presumption against compelling individuals to make affirmations contrary to their convictions. (These presumptions drive Madison's understanding of freedom of conscience, discussed earlier in this essay.) This does not mean that compulsory speech is always wrong; courts and legislatures may rightly compel unwilling witnesses to give testimony and may rightly punish any failure to do so that does not invoke a well-established principle of immunity, such as the bar against coerced self-incrimination. Even here, the point of the compulsion is to induce individuals to tell the truth as they see it, not to betray their innermost convictions in the name of a state-administered orthodoxy.

It is easy for politics – even stable constitutional democracies – to violate these principles. In that obvious empirical sense, fundamental liberties are political constructions. But that democratic majorities can deprive minorities of liberty, often with impunity, does not make it right. Like all politics, democratic politics is legitimate to the extent that it recognizes and observes the principle limits to the exercise of democratic power. The liberties that individuals and the associations they constitute should enjoy in all but the most desperate circumstances go well beyond the political rights that democratic politics requires. We cannot rightly assess the importance of politics without acknowledging the limits of politics. The claims that political institutions can make in the name of the common good coexist with claims of at least equal importance that individuals and civil associations make, based on particular visions of the good for themselves or for human kind. This "political pluralism" may be messy; it may lead to confrontations not conducive to maximizing public unity and order. But if political pluralism, thus understood, reflects the complex truth of the human condition, then the practice of politics must do its best to honor the principles that limit the scope of politics.

Sources

Bulan is discussed in Jehuda Halevy, *The Book of Proof and Argument*, edited with an introduction and commentary by Isaak Heinemann (Oxford: East and West Library, 1947); William A. Galston, *Liberal Pluralism: The Implications of Value Pluralism for Political Theory and Practice* (Cambridge UP, 2002); *Minersville v. Gobitis*, 310 US 586 (1940); *West Virginia v. Barnette*, 319 US 624 (1943); James Madison and Thomas Jefferson, "Memorial and Remonstrance" (1785); James Madison, Amendment to the Constitution for inclusion in the *Bill of Rights* (June 8, 1789); *Gilbert v. Minnesota*, 254 US 325 (1920); Justice Brandeis' dissent is found at 254 US 343; *Meyer v. Nebraska*, 262 US 390 (1923); Justice McReynold's decision can be found at 262 US 401; *Pierce v. Society of Sisters*, 268 US 510 (1925); Justice McReynold's opinion is found at 268 US 535; *US v. Macintosh*, 283 US 605 (1931); Justice Sutherland's majority opinion is found at 283 US 625 and Chief Justice Hughes' dissent is found at 633–4; Justice Frankfurter's remarks are found at 301 US 591–600 (italics are mine); Justice Stone's remark can be found at 301 US 601; William G. Fennell, "The 'Reconstructed Court' and Religious Freedom: The *Gobitis* Case in Retrospect," *New York University Law Quarterly Review* 31; William F. Anderson, *Michigan Law Review* 39 (1940); Thomas Reed Powell, "Conscience and the Constitution," in *Democracy and National Unity*, edited by William T. Hutchinson (Chicago: University of Chicago Press, 1941); *Jones v. Opelika*, 316 US 584 (1942); Justice Reed's remark can be found at 316 US 598; Justice Murphy's dissent can be found at 316 US 618–20; the dissent of Murphy, Black and Douglas can be found at 316 US 623–4; John Raeburn Green, "Liberty under the Fourteenth Amendment," *Washington University Law Quarterly*, 27 (1942); *Murdock v. Pennsylvania*, 319 US 105; Justice Jackson's decision in *West Virginia v. Barnette* can be found at 319 US 630–7; Black and Douglas's decision can be found at 319 US 643–4; Justice Murphy's decision can be found at 319 US 644–6; Justice Jackson's dissent can be found at 319 US 646–6.

29

Homelessness and the Issue of Freedom

Jeremy Waldron

Introduction

There are many facets to the nightmare of homelessness. In this essay, I want to explore just one of them: the relation between homelessness, the rules of public and private property, and the underlying freedom of those who are condemned by poverty to walk the streets and sleep in the open. Unlike some recent discussions, my concern is not with the constitutionality of various restrictions on the homeless (though that, of course, is important).[1] I want to address a prior question – a more fundamental question – of legal and moral philosophy: how should we think about homelessness, how should we conceive of it, in relation to a value like freedom?

The discussion that follows is, in some ways, an abstract one. This is intentional. The aim is to refute the view that, on abstract liberal principles, there is no reason to be troubled by the plight of the homeless, and that one has to come down to the more concrete principles of a communitarian ethic in order to find a focus for that concern. Against this view, I shall argue that homelessness is a matter of the utmost concern in relation to some of the most fundamental and abstract principles of liberal value. That an argument is abstract should not make us think of it as thin or watery. If homelessness raises questions even in regard to the most basic principles of liberty, it is an issue that ought to preoccupy liberal theorists every bit as much as more familiar worries about torture, the suppression of dissent, and other violations of human rights. That the partisans of liberty in our legal and philosophical culture have not always been willing to see this (or say it) should be taken as an indication of the consistency and good faith with which they espouse and proclaim their principles.

I Location and Property

Some truisms to begin with. Everything that is done has to be done somewhere. No one is free to perform an action unless there is somewhere he is free to perform it. Since we are embodied beings, we always have a location. Moreover, though everyone has to be somewhere, a person cannot always choose any location he likes. Some locations are physically inaccessible. And, physical inaccessibility aside, there are some places one is simply not allowed to be.

One of the functions of property rules, particularly as far as land is concerned, is to provide a basis for determining who is allowed to be where. For the purposes of these rules, a country is divided up into spatially defined regions or, as we usually say, places. The rules of property give us a way of determining, in the case of each place, who is allowed to be in that place and who is not. For example, if a place is governed by a private property rule, then there is a way of identifying an individual whose determination is final on the

Originally published in *UCLA Law Review* 39 (1991): 295–324. Reprinted by permission of the author.

question of who is and who is not allowed to be in that place. Sometimes that individual is the owner of the land in question, and sometimes (as in a landlord-tenant relationship) the owner gives another person the power to make that determination (indeed to make it, for the time being, even as against the owner). Either way, it is characteristic of a private ownership arrangement that some individual (or some other particular legal person) has this power to determine who is allowed to be on the property.

The actual rules of private property are, of course, much more complicated than this and they involve much besides this elementary power of decision.[2] However, to get the discussion going, it is enough to recognize that there is something like this individual power of decision in most systems of private ownership. Private ownership of land exists when an individual person may determine who is, and who is not, allowed to be in a certain place, without answering to anyone else for that decision. I say who is allowed to be in my house. He says who is to be allowed in his restaurant. And so on.

The concept of *being allowed* to be in a place is fairly straightforward. We can define it negatively. An individual who is in a place where he is not allowed to be may be removed, and he may be subject to civil or criminal sanctions for trespass or some other similar offense. No doubt people are sometimes physically removed from places where they *are* allowed to be. But if a person is in a place where he is not allowed to be, not only may he be physically removed, but there is a social rule to the effect that his removal may be facilitated and aided by the forces of the state. In short, the police may be called and he may be dragged away.

I said that one function of property rules is to indicate procedures for determining who is allowed and not allowed (in this sense) to be in a given place, and I gave the example of a private property rule. However, not all rules of property are like private property rules in this regard. We may use a familiar classification and say that, though many places in this country are governed by private property rules, some are governed by rules of collective property, which divide further into rules of state property and rules of common property (though neither the labels nor the exact details of this second distinction matter much for the points I am going to make).[3]

If a place is governed by a *collective* property rule, then there is no private person in the position of owner. Instead, the use of collective property is determined by people, usually officials, acting in the name of the whole community.

Common property may be regarded as a subclass of collective property. A place is common property if part of the point of putting it under collective control is to allow anyone in the society to make use of it without having to secure the permission of anybody else. Not all collective property is like this: places like military firing ranges, nationalized factories, and government offices are off-limits to members of the general public unless they have special permission or a legitimate purpose for being there. They are held as collective property for purposes other than making them available for public use. However, examples of common property spring fairly readily to mind: they include streets, sidewalks, subways, city parks, national parks, and wilderness areas. These places are held in the name of the whole society in order to make them fairly accessible to everyone. As we shall see, they are by no means unregulated as to the nature or time of their use. Still, they are relatively open at most times to a fairly indeterminate range of uses by anyone. In the broadest terms, they are places where anyone may be.

Sometimes the state may insist that certain places owned by private individuals or corporations should be treated rather like common property if they fulfill the function of public places. For example, shopping malls in the United States are usually on privately owned land. However, because of the functions such places serve, the state imposes considerable restrictions on the owners' powers of exclusion (people may not be excluded from a shopping mall on racial grounds, for example) and on their power to limit the activities (such as political pamphleteering) that may take place there.[4] Though this is an important development, it does not alter the analysis I am developing in this Essay, and for simplicity I shall ignore it in what follows.

Property rules differ from society to society. Though we describe some societies (like the United States) as having systems of private property, and others (like the USSR – at least until recently) as having collectivist systems, clearly all societies have some places governed by private property rules, some places governed by state property rules, and some places governed by common property rules. Every society has private houses, military bases, and public parks. So if we want to categorize whole societies along these lines, we have to say it is a matter of balance and emphasis. For example, we say the USSR is (or used to be) a collectivist society and that the USA is not, not because there was no private property in the USSR, but because most industrial and agricultural land there was held collectively whereas most industrial and agricultural land in the United States is privately owned. The distinction is one of degree. Even as between two countries that pride themselves on having basically capitalist economies, for example, New Zealand and Britain, we may say that the former is "communist" to a greater extent (i.e. is more a system of common property) than the latter because more places (for example, all river banks) are held as common property in New Zealand than are held as common property in Britain. Of course, these propositions are as vague as they are useful. If we are measuring the "extent" to which a country is collectivist, that measure is ambiguous as between the quantitative proportion of land that is governed by rules of collective property and some more qualitative assessment of the importance of the places that are governed in this way.[5]

II Homelessness

Estimates of the number of homeless people in the United States range from 250,000 to three million.[6] A person who is homeless is, obviously enough, a person who has no home. One way of describing the plight of a homeless individual might be to say that there is no place governed by a private property rule where he is allowed to be.

In fact, that is not quite correct. Any private proprietor may invite a homeless person into his house or onto his land, and if he does there *will* be some private place where the homeless person is allowed to be. A technically more accurate description of his plight is that there is no place governed by a private property rule where he is allowed to be whenever *he* chooses, no place governed by a private property rule from which he may not at any time be excluded as a result of someone else's say-so. As far as being on private property is concerned – in people's houses or gardens, on farms or in hotels, in offices or restaurants – the homeless person is utterly and at all times at the mercy of others. And we know enough about how this mercy is generally exercised to figure that the

description in the previous paragraph is more or less accurate as a matter of fact, even if it is not strictly accurate as a matter of law.[7]

For the most part the homeless are excluded from *all* of the places governed by private property rules, whereas the rest of us are, in the same sense, excluded from *all but one* (or maybe all but a few) of those places. That is another way of saying that each of us has at least one place to be in a country composed of private places, whereas the homeless person has none.

Some libertarians fantasize about the possibility that *all* the land in a society might be held as private property ("Sell the streets!").[8] This would be catastrophic for the homeless. Since most private proprietors are already disposed to exclude him from their property, the homeless person might discover in such a libertarian paradise that there was literally *nowhere* he was allowed to be. Wherever he went he would be liable to penalties for trespass and he would be liable to eviction, to being thrown out by an owner or dragged away by the police. Moving from one place to another would involve nothing more liberating than moving from one trespass liability to another. Since land is finite in any society, there is only a limited number of places where a person can (physically) be, and such a person would find that he was legally excluded from all of them. (It would not be entirely mischievous to add that since, in order to exist, a person has to be *somewhere*, such a person would not be permitted to exist.)

Our society saves the homeless from this catastrophe only by virtue of the fact that some of its territory is held as collective property and made available for common use. The homeless are allowed to *be* – provided they are on the streets, in the parks, or under the bridges. Some of them are allowed to crowd together into publicly provided "shelters" after dark (though these are dangerous places and there are not nearly enough shelters for all of them). But in the daytime and, for many of them, all through the night, wandering in public places is their only option. When all else is privately owned, the sidewalks are their salvation. They are allowed to *be* in our society only to the extent that our society is communist.

This is one of the reasons why most defenders of private property are uncomfortable with the libertarian proposal, and why that proposal remains sheer fantasy.[9] But there is a modified form of the libertarian catastrophe in prospect with which moderate and even liberal defenders of ownership seem much more comfortable. This is the increasing regulation of the streets, subways, parks, and other public places to restrict the activities that can be performed there. What is emerging – and it is not just a matter of fantasy – is a state of affairs in which a million or more citizens have no place to perform elementary human activities like urinating, washing, sleeping, cooking, eating, and standing around. Legislators voted for by people who own private places in which they can do all these things are increasingly deciding to make public places available only for activities other than these primal human tasks. The streets and subways, they say, are for commuting from home to office. They are not for sleeping; sleeping is something one does at home. The parks are for recreations like walking and informal ball-games, things for which one's own yard is a little too confined. Parks are not for cooking or urinating; again, these are things one does at home. Since the public and the private are complementary, the activities performed in public are to be the complement of those appropriately performed in private. This complementarity works fine for those who have the benefit of both sorts of places. However, it is disastrous for those who must live their whole lives on common land. If I am right about this, it is one of the most callous and tyrannical exercises of power in modern times by a (comparatively) rich and complacent majority against a minority of their less fortunate fellow human beings.

III   Locations, Actions and Freedom

The points made so far can be restated in terms of freedom. Someone who is allowed to be in a place is, in a fairly straightforward sense, free to be there. A person who is not allowed to be in a place is unfree to be there. However, the concept of freedom usually applies to actions rather than locations: one is free or unfree to do X or to do Y. What is the connection, then, between freedom to be somewhere and freedom to do something?

At the outset I recited the truism that anything a person does has to be done somewhere. To that extent, all actions involve a spatial component (just as many actions involve, in addition, a material component like the use of tools, implements, or raw materials). It should be fairly obvious that, if one is not free to be in a certain place, one is not free to do anything at that place. If I am not allowed to be in your garden (because you have forbidden me) then I am not allowed to eat my lunch, make a speech, or turn a somersault in your garden. Though I may be free to do these things somewhere else, I am not free to do them there. It follows, strikingly, that a person who is not free to be in any place is not free to do anything; such a person is comprehensively unfree. In the libertarian paradise we imagined in the previous section, this would be the plight of the homeless. They would be simply without freedom (or, more accurately, any freedom they had would depend utterly on the forbearance of those who owned the places that made up the territory of the society in question).

Fortunately, our society is not such a libertarian paradise. There are places where the homeless may be and, by virtue of that, there are actions they may perform; they are free to perform actions on the streets, in the parks, and under the bridges. Their freedom depends on common property in a way that ours does not. Once again, the homeless have freedom in our society only to the extent that our society is communist.

That conclusion may sound glib and provocative. But it is meant as a reflection on the cold and awful reality of the experience of men, women, and children who are homeless in America. For them the rules of private property are a series of fences that stand between them and somewhere to be, somewhere to act. The only hope they have so far as freedom is concerned lies in the streets, parks, and public shelters, and in the fact that those are collectivized resources made available openly to all.

It is sometimes said that freedom means little or nothing to a cold and hungry person. We should focus on the material predicament of the homeless, it is said, not on this abstract liberal concern about freedom. That may be an appropriate response to someone who is talking high-mindedly and fatuously about securing freedom of speech or freedom of religion for people who lack the elementary necessities of human life.[10] But the contrast between liberty and the satisfaction of material needs must not be drawn too sharply, as though the latter had no relation at all to what one is free or unfree to do. I am focusing on freedoms that are intimately connected with food, shelter, clothing, and the satisfaction of basic needs. When a person is needy, he does not cease to be preoccupied with freedom; rather, his preoccupation tends to focus on freedom to perform certain actions in particular. The freedom that means most to a person who is cold and wet is the freedom that consists in staying under whatever shelter he has found. The freedom that means most to someone who is exhausted is the freedom not to be prodded with a nightstick as he tries to catch a few hours sleep on a subway bench.

There is a general point here about the rather *passive* image of the poor held by those who say we should concern ourselves with their needs, not their freedom.[11] People remain agents, with ideas and initiatives of their own, even when they are poor. Indeed, since they are on their own, in a situation of danger, without any place of safety, they must often be more resourceful, spend more time working out how to live, thinking things through much more carefully, taking much less for granted, than the comfortable autonomous agent that we imagine in a family with a house and a job in an office or university. And – when they are allowed to – the poor do find ways of using their initiative to rise to these challenges. They have to; if they do not, they die.

Even the most desperately needy are not always paralyzed by want. There are certain things they are physically capable of doing for themselves. Sometimes they find shelter by occupying an empty house or sleeping in a sheltered spot. They gather food from various places, they light a fire to cook it, and they sit down in a park to eat. They may urinate behind bushes, and wash their clothes in a fountain. Their physical condition is certainly not comfortable, but they are *capable* of acting in ways that make things a little more bearable for themselves. Now one question we face as a society – a broad question of justice and social policy – is whether we are willing to tolerate an economic system in which large numbers of people are homeless. Since the answer is evidently, "Yes," the question that remains is whether we are willing to allow those who are in this predicament to act as free agents, looking after their own needs, in public places – the only space available to them. It is a deeply frightening fact about the modern United States that those who *have* homes and jobs are willing to answer "Yes" to the first question and "No" to the second.

Negative freedom

Before going on, I want to say something about the conception of freedom I am using in this essay. Those who argue that the homeless (or the poor

generally) have less freedom than the rest of us are often accused of appealing to a controversial, dangerous, and question-begging conception of "positive" freedom.[12] It is commonly thought that one has to step outside the traditional liberal idea of "negative" freedom in order to make these points.

However, there is no need to argue about that here. The definition of freedom with which I have been working so far is as "negative" as can be. There is nothing unfamiliar about it (except perhaps the consistency with which it is being deployed). I am saying that a person is free to be someplace just in case he is not legally liable to be physically removed from that place or penalized for being there. At the very least, negative freedom is freedom from obstructions such as someone else's forceful effort to prevent one from doing something.[13] In exactly this negative sense (absence of forcible interference), the homeless person is unfree to be in any place governed by a private property rule (unless the owner for some reason elects to give him his permission to be there). The familiar claim that, in the negative sense of "freedom," the poor are as free as the rest of us – and that you have to move to a positive definition in order to dispute that – is simply false.[14]

That private property limits freedom seems obvious.[15] If I own a piece of land, others have a duty not to use it (without my consent) and there is a battery of legal remedies which I can use to enforce this duty as I please. The right correlative to this duty is an essential incident of ownership, and any enforcement of the duty necessarily amounts to a deliberate interference with someone else's action. It is true that the connection between property and the restriction of liberty is in some ways a contingent one: as Andrew Reeve notes, "even if I am entitled to use my property to prevent you from taking some action, I will not necessarily do so."[16] But there is a similar contingency in any juridical restriction. A repressive state may have laws entitling officials to crush dissent. In theory, they might choose to refrain from doing so on certain occasions; but we would still describe the law as a restriction on freedom if dissidents had to take into account the likelihood of its being used against them. Indeed we often say that the unpredictable element of official discretion "chills" whatever freedom remains in the interstices of its enforcement. Thus, in exactly the way in which we call repressive political laws restrictions on freedom, we can call property rights restrictions on freedom. We do not need any special definition of freedom over and above the negative one used by liberals in contexts that are more ideologically congenial.

The definitional objection is sometimes based on a distinction between freedom and ability.[17] The homeless, it is said, are in the relevant sense *free* to perform the same activities as the rest of us; but the sad fact is that they do not have the *means* or the *power* or the *ability* to exercise these freedoms. This claim is almost always false. With the exception of a few who are so weakened by their plight that they are incapable of anything, the homeless are not *unable* to enter the privately owned places from which they are banned. They can climb walls, open doors, cross thresholds, break windows, and so on, to gain entry to the premises from which the laws of property exclude them. What stands in their way is simply what stands in the way of anyone who is negatively unfree: the likelihood that someone else will forcibly prevent their action. Of course, the rich do try to make it impossible as well as illegal for the homeless to enter their gardens: they build their walls as high as possible and top them with broken glass. But that this does not constitute mere inability as opposed to unfreedom is indicated by the fact that the homeless are not permitted even to *try* to overcome these physical obstacles. They may be dragged away and penalized for attempting to scale the walls.

A second line that is sometimes taken is this: one should regard the homeless as less free than the rest of us only if one believes that some human agency (other than their own) is responsible for their plight.[18] However, the idea of someone else's being responsible for the plight of the homeless is an ambiguous one. It may well be the case that people are homeless as a result of earlier deliberate and heartless actions by landlords, employers, or officials, or as a result of a deliberate capitalist strategy to create and sustain a vast reserve industrial army of the unemployed.[19] That *may* be the case. But even if it is not, even if their being homeless cannot be laid at anyone's door or attributed to anything over and above their own choices or the impersonal workings of the market, my point remains. Their homelessness *consists* in unfreedom. Though it may not be anyone's fault that there is no place they can go without being dragged away, still their being removed from the places they are not allowed to be is itself a derogation from their freedom, a derogation constituted

by the deliberate human action of property-owners, security guards, and police officers. To repeat, their having nowhere to go *is* their being unfree (in a negative sense) to be anywhere; it is identical with the fact that others are authorized deliberately to drag them away from wherever they choose to be. We do not need any further account of the *cause* of this state of affairs to describe it as, in itself, a situation of unfreedom.

Thirdly, someone may object that a person is not made unfree if he is prevented from doing something wrong – something he has a duty not to do. Since entering others' property and abusing common property are wrong, it is not really a derogation from freedom to enforce a person's duties in these respects. Ironically, this "moralization" of the concept of freedom certainly *would* amount to a shift in the direction of a positive definition.[20] It was precisely the identification of freedom with virtue (and the inference that a restriction on vice was no restriction at all) that most troubled liberals about theories of positive liberty.[21]

In any case, the "moralization" of freedom is confusing and question-begging in the present context. It elides the notions of a restriction on freedom and an unjustified restriction on freedom, closing off certain questions that common sense regards as open. It seems to rest on a sense – elsewhere repudiated by many liberals – that all our moral and political concerns fit together in a tidy package, so that we need not ever worry about trade-offs between freedom (properly understood) and other values, such as property and justice.[22]

To say – as I have insisted we should say – that property rules limit freedom, is not to say they are *eo ipso* wrong.[23] It is simply to say that they engage a concern about liberty, and that anyone who values liberty should put himself on alert when questions of property are being discussed. (The argument I have made about the homeless is a striking illustration of the importance of our not losing sight of that.)

Above all, by building the morality of a given property system (rights, duties, and the current distribution) into the concept of freedom, the moralizing approach precludes the use of that concept as a basis for arguing about property. If when we use the words "free" and "unfree," we are already assuming that it is wrong for A to use something that belongs to B, we cannot appeal to "freedom" to explain why B's ownership of the resource is justified. We cannot even extol our property system as the basis of a "free" society, for such a boast would be nothing more than tautological. It is true that if we have independent grounds of justification for our private property system, then we *can* say that interfering with property rights is wrong without appealing to the idea of freedom. In that case, there is nothing question-begging about the claim that preventing someone from violating property rights does not count as a restriction on his freedom. But the price of this strategy is high. It not only transforms our conception of freedom into a moralized definition of positive liberty (so that the only freedom that is relevant is the freedom to do what is right), but it also excludes the concept of freedom altogether from the debate about the justification of property rights. Since most theorists of property do not want to deprive themselves of the concept of freedom as a resource in that argument, the insistence that the enforcement of property rules should not count as a restriction on freedom is, at the very least, a serious strategic mistake.

General prohibitions and particular freedoms

I think the account I have given is faithful to the tradition of negative liberty. One is free to do something only if one is not liable to be forcibly prevented from or penalized for doing it. However, the way I have applied this account may seem a little disconcerting. The issue has to do with the level of generality at which actions are described.

The laws we have usually mention general *types* of actions, rather than particular actions done by particular people at specific times and places. Statutes do not say, "Jane Smith is not to assault Sarah Jones on Friday, November 24, on the corner of College Avenue and Bancroft." They say, "Assault is prohibited," or some equivalent, and it is understood that the prohibition applies to all such actions performed by anyone anywhere. A prohibition on a general type of action is understood to be a prohibition on all tokens of that type. Jurists say we ought to value this generality in our laws; it is part of what is involved in the complex ideal of "The Rule of Law." It makes the laws more predictable and more learnable. It makes them a better guide for the ordinary citizen who needs to have a rough and ready understanding (rather than a copious technical knowledge) of what he is and is not allowed to do as he goes about his business. A quick checklist of prohibited acts, formulated in general terms, serves that purpose

admirably.[24] It also serves moral ideals of universalizability and rationality: a reason for restraining any particular act ought to be a reason for restraining any other act of the same type, unless there is a relevant difference between them (which can be formulated also in general terms).[25]

All that is important. However, there is another aspect of "The Rule of Law" ideal that can lead one into difficulties if it is combined with this insistence on generality. Legal systems of the kind we have pride themselves on the following feature: "Everything which is not explicitly prohibited is permitted." If the law does not formulate any prohibition on singing or jogging, for example, that is an indication to the citizen that singing and jogging are permitted, that he is free to perform them. To gauge the extent of his freedom, all he needs to know are the prohibitions imposed by the law. His freedom is simply the complement of that.[26]

The difficulty arises if it is inferred from this that a person's freedom is the complement of the *general* prohibitions that apply to him. For although it is possible to infer particular prohibitions from prohibitions formulated at a general level ("All murder is wrong" implies "This murder by me today is wrong"), it is not possible to infer particular permissions from the absence of any general prohibition. In our society, there is no general prohibition on cycling, but one cannot infer from this that any particular act of riding a bicycle is permitted. It depends (among other things) on whether the person involved has the right to use the particular bicycle he is proposing to ride.

This does not affect the basic point about complementarity. Our freedoms *are* the complement of the prohibitions that apply to us. The mistake arises from thinking that the only prohibitions that apply to us are general prohibitions. For, in addition to the general prohibitions laid down (say) in the criminal law, there are also the prohibitions on using particular objects and places that are generated by the laws of property. Until we know how these latter laws apply, we do not know whether we are free to perform a particular action.

It is *not* a telling response to this point to say that the effect of the laws of property can be stated in terms of a general principle – "No one is to use the property of another without his permission." They *can* be so stated; but in order to apply that principle, we need particular knowledge, not just general knowledge.[27] A person needs to know that *this* bicycle belongs to him, whereas *those* bicycles belong to other people. He needs that particular knowledge about specific objects as well as his general knowledge about the types of actions that are and are not permitted.

At any rate, the conclusions about freedom that I have reached depend on taking the prohibitions relating to particular objects generated by property laws as seriously as we take the more general prohibitions imposed by the criminal law. No doubt these different types of prohibition are imposed for different reasons. But if freedom means simply the absence of deliberate interference with one's actions, we will not be in a position to say how free a person is until we know everything about the universe of legal restraints that may be applied to him. After all, it is not freedom in the abstract that people value, but freedom to perform particular actions. If the absence of a general prohibition tells us nothing about anyone's concrete freedom, then we should be wary of using only the checklist of general prohibitions to tell us how free or unfree a person or a society really is.

These points can readily be applied to the homeless. There are no general prohibitions in our society on actions like sleeping or washing. However, we cannot infer from this that anyone may sleep or wash wherever he chooses. In order to work out whether a particular person is free to sleep or wash, we must also ask whether there are any prohibitions *of place* that apply to his performance of actions of this type. As a matter of fact, all of us face a formidable battery of such prohibitions. Most private places, for example, are off-limits to us for these (or any other) activities. Though I am a well-paid professor, there are only a couple of private places where I am allowed to sleep or wash (without having someone's specific permission): my home, my office, and whatever restaurant I am patronizing. Most homeless people do not have jobs and few of them are allowed inside restaurants. ("Bathrooms for the use of customers only.") Above all, they have no homes. So there is literally no private place where they are free to sleep or wash.

For them, that is a desperately important fact about their freedom, one that must preoccupy much of every day. Unlike us, they have no private place where they can take it for granted that they will be allowed to sleep or wash. Since everyone needs to sleep and wash regularly, homeless people have to spend time searching for non-private places – like public restrooms (of which there are precious few in America, by the standards of most civilized countries) and shelters (available, if at all, only at night) – where these actions may be performed without fear of interference. If we regard freedom as simply the complement of the general prohibitions imposed by law, we are in danger of overlooking this fact about the freedom of the homeless. Most of us can afford to overlook it, because we have homes to go to. But without a home, a person's freedom is his freedom to act in public, in places governed by common property rules. That is the difference between our freedom and the freedom of the homeless.

Public places

What then are we to say about public places? If there is anywhere the homeless are free to act, it is in the streets, the subways and the parks. These regions are governed by common property rules. Since these are the only places they are allowed to be, these are the only places they are free to act.

However, a person is not allowed to do just whatever he likes in a public place. There are at least three types of prohibition that one faces in a place governed by rules of common property.

(1) If there are any general prohibitions on types of action in a society, like the prohibition on murder or the prohibition on selling narcotics, then they apply to all tokens of those types performed anywhere, public or private. And these prohibitions apply to everyone: though it is only the homeless who have no choice but to be in public places, the law forbids the rich as well as the poor from selling narcotics, and *a fortiori* from selling narcotics on the streets and in the parks.

(2) Typically, there are also prohibitions that are specific to public places and provide the basis of their commonality. Parks have curfews; streets and sidewalks have rules that govern the extent to which one person's use of these places may interfere with another's; there are rules about obstruction, jaywalking, and so on. Many of these rules can be characterized and justified as rules of fairness. If public places are to be available for everyone's use, then we must make sure that their use by some people does not preclude or obstruct their use by others.

(3) However, some of the rules that govern behavior in public places are more substantive than that: they concern particular forms of behavior

that are not to be performed in public whether there is an issue of fairness involved or not. For example, many states and municipalities forbid the use of parks for making love. It is not that there is any general constraint on lovemaking as a type of action (though some states still have laws against fornication). Although sexual intercourse between a husband and wife is permitted and even encouraged by the law, it is usually forbidden in public places. The place for that sort of activity, we say, is the privacy of the home.

Other examples spring to mind. There is no law against urinating – it is a necessary and desirable human activity. However, there is a law against urinating in public, except in the specially designated premises of public restrooms. In general, it is an activity which, if we are free to do it, we are free to do it mainly at home or in some other private place (a bathroom in a restaurant) where we have an independent right to be. There is also no law against sleeping – again a necessary and desirable human activity. To maintain their physical and mental health, people need to sleep for a substantial period every day. However, states and municipalities are increasingly passing ordinances to prohibit sleeping in public places like streets and parks.[28] The decision of the Transit Authority in New York to enforce prohibitions on sleeping in the subways attracted national attention a year or two ago.[29]

Such ordinances have and are known and even intended to have a specific effect on the homeless which is different from the effect they have on the rest of us. We are all familiar with the dictum of Anatole France: "[L]a majestueuse égalité des lois . . . interdit au riche comme au pauvre de coucher sous les ponts. . . . "[30] We might adapt it to the present point, noting that the new rules in the subway will prohibit anyone from sleeping or lying down in the cars and stations, whether they are rich or poor, homeless or housed. They will be phrased with majestic impartiality, and indeed their drafters know that they would be struck down immediately by the courts if they were formulated specifically to target those who have no homes. Still everyone is perfectly well aware of the point of passing these ordinances, and any attempt to defend them on the basis of their generality is quite disingenuous. Their point is to make sleeping in the subways off limits to those who have nowhere else to sleep.[31]

Four facts are telling in this regard. First, it is well known among those who press for these laws that the subway is such an unpleasant place to sleep that almost no one would do it if they had anywhere else to go. Secondly, the pressure for these laws comes as a response to what is well known to be "the problem of homelessness." It is not as though people suddenly became concerned about *sleeping* in the subway as such (as though that were a particularly dangerous activity to perform there, like smoking or jumping onto a moving train). When people write to the Transit Authority and say, "Just get them out. I don't care. Just get them out any way you can," we all know who the word "them" refers to.[32] People do not want to be confronted with the sight of the homeless – it is uncomfortable for the well-off to be reminded of the human price that is paid for a social structure like theirs – and they are willing to deprive those people of their last opportunity to sleep in order to protect themselves from this discomfort. Thirdly, the legislation is called for and promoted by people who are secure in the knowledge that they themselves have some place where they are permitted to sleep. Because *they* have some place to sleep which is not the subway, they infer that the subway is not a place for sleeping. The subway is a place where those who have some other place to sleep may do things besides sleeping.

Finally, and most strikingly, those who push for these laws will try to amend them or reformulate them if they turn out to have an unwelcome impact on people who are not homeless. For example, a city ordinance in Clearwater, Florida, prohibiting sleeping in public, was struck down as too broad because it would have applied even to a person sleeping in his car.[33] Most people who have cars also have homes, and we would not want a statute aimed at the homeless to prevent car owners from sleeping in public.

Though we all know what the real object of these ordinances is, we may not have thought very hard about their cumulative effect. That effect is as follows.

For a person who has no home, and has no expectation of being allowed into something like a private office building or a restaurant, prohibitions on things like sleeping that apply particularly to public places pose a special problem. For although there is no *general* prohibition on acts of these types, still they are effectively ruled out altogether for anyone who is homeless and who has no shelter to go to. The prohibition is comprehensive in effect because of the cumulation, in the case of the homeless, of a number of different bans, differently imposed. The rules of property prohibit the homeless person from doing any of these acts in private, since there is no private place that he has a right to be. And the rules governing public places prohibit him from doing any of these acts in public, since that is how we have decided to regulate the use of public places. So what is the result? Since private places and public places between them exhaust all the places that there are, there is nowhere that these actions may be performed by the homeless person. And since freedom to perform a concrete action requires freedom to perform it at some place, it follows that the homeless person does not have the freedom to perform them. If sleeping is prohibited in public places, then sleeping is comprehensively prohibited to the homeless. If urinating is prohibited in public places (and if there are no public lavatories) then the homeless are simply unfree to urinate. These are not altogether comfortable conclusions, and they are certainly not comfortable for those who have to live with them.

IV Intention, Responsibility and Blame

I said the predicament is cumulative. I argued that if an action X is prohibited (to everyone) in public places *and* if a person A has no access to a private place wherein to perform it, then action X is effectively prohibited to A *everywhere*, and so A is comprehensively unfree to do X.

However, people may balk at this point. They may argue:

> Surely prohibition is an intentional notion, and nobody is intending that A not be permitted to do X. We do intend that he should be prohibited from X-ing in public, but we don't intend that he should be prohibited from X-ing in private. That's just the way the distribution of property turns out. We don't intend as a society – and certainly the state does not intend – that there should be *no* place where A is permitted to do X. It just happens that way.[34]

We have already seen that this point about intention cannot be sustained at the level of individual acts. If a homeless tramp tries to urinate in a rich person's yard, the rich person may try to prevent that, and he is authorized to do so. There is no doubt about the intentionality of this particular restraint on this particular violation of property rules. However, the point of the present objection

is that the rich person does not intend that there should be nowhere the tramp is allowed to urinate (indeed, he probably hopes that there is somewhere – provided it is not in his back yard). And similarly for each proprietor in turn. None of them intends that the tramp should never be allowed to urinate. That just happens, in an invisible hand sort of way, as a result of each proprietor saying, in effect, "Anywhere but here." Though each particular unfreedom involves an intentional restraint, their cumulation is not in itself the product of anyone's intention.

The objection can be conceded. We can tie judgments about freedom and unfreedom this closely to intentionality if we like. On that approach, all we can say about the homeless person's freedom is that he is unfree to urinate in place X *and* he is unfree to urinate in place Y *and* he is unfree to urinate in place Z *and* ... so on, for each place that there is. We refrain from the inference: "So he is unfree to urinate (anywhere)." However, even if we are scrupulous about not making that generalization, still there is *something* we can say at a general level about his predicament. We can say, for example, "There is no place where he is free to urinate." The logic of such a quantified sentence (i.e. "There is no place p such that he is free to urinate at p") does not commit us to any cumulation of unfreedoms, and it is an accurate statement of his position. Anyway, even if no one has intended that there be no place this person is free to urinate, it cannot be said that his predicament, so described, is a matter of no concern. It is hard to imagine how anyone could think freedom important in relation to each particular restraint, but yet have no concern about the cumulative effect of such restraints. Moreover, even if our concern about the cumulation is not directly expressed in terms of freedom because freedom is taken to be an intentional notion, still it is at least in part freedom *related*. If we value freedom in each particular case because of the importance of choice and of not being constrained in the choices one makes, then that value ought to lead us to pay some attention to how many choices a person has left after each constraint has been exercised. From any point of view that values choice and freedom of action, it ought to be a matter of concern that the choices left open to a person are being progressively closed off, one by one, and that he is nearing a situation where there is literally nowhere he can turn.

The fact that no one intended his overall predicament may mean that there is no one to *blame* for it. However, for one thing, each private proprietor will have a pretty good idea about how others may be expected to exercise their rights in this regard. It would be quite disingenuous for any of them to say. "I thought some of the other owners would let him use their property." Moral philosophers have developed interesting models of joint and collective responsibility for outcomes like these, and those models seem quite applicable here.[35] For another thing, those who impose a ban on these activities in public places certainly do know very well what the result of *that* will be: that the homeless will have almost nowhere to go, in the territory subject to their jurisdiction. Indeed the aim – again, as we all know – is often to drive them out of the jurisdiction so that some other city or state has to take care of the problem. Even where this is not intentional, still the intentional infliction of harm is not the only thing we blame people for. "I didn't mean to," is not the all-purpose excuse it is often taken to be. We blame people for recklessness and negligence, and certainly the promoters of these ordinances are quite reckless whether they leave the homeless anywhere to go or not. ("Just get them out. I do not care. Just get them out any way you can.")[36]

In any case, our concern about freedom and unfreedom is not principally a concern to find someone to blame. An intentional attack on freedom is blameworthy in part because the freedom of those who are attacked matters. If freedom is sufficiently important to sustain moral blame for those who attack it, it ought to matter also in other cases where blame is not the issue. Sometimes we can promote freedom, or make people more free, or organize our institutions so that there are fewer ways in which their freedom is restricted, and we may want to do this even in cases where we are not responding with outrage to the moral culpability of an attack on freedom. Freedom is a multifaceted concern in our political morality. Sure, we blame those who attack it deliberately or recklessly. But we are also solicitous for it and do our best to make it flourish, even when there is no evil freedom-hater obstructing our efforts. Blame, and the intentionality that blame is sometimes thought to presuppose, are not the only important things in the world.

V   Freedom and Important Freedoms

I have argued that a rule against performing an act in a public place amounts *in effect* to a *comprehen-* sive ban on that action so far as the homeless are concerned. If that argument is accepted, our next question should be: "How serious is this limitation on freedom?" Freedom in any society is limited in all sorts of ways: I have no freedom to pass through a red light nor to drive east on Bancroft Avenue. Any society involves a complicated array of freedoms and unfreedoms, and our assessment of *how free* a given society is (our assessment, for example, that the United States is a freer society than Albania) involves some assessment of the balance in that array.

Such assessments are characteristically qualitative as well as quantitative. We do not simply ask, "How many actions are people free or unfree to perform?" Indeed, such questions are very difficult to answer or even to formulate coherently.[37] Instead we often ask qualitative questions: "How important are the actions that people are prohibited from performing?" One of the tasks of a theory of human rights is to pick out a set of actions that it is thought particularly important from a moral point of view that people should have the freedom to perform, choices that it is thought particularly important that they should have the freedom to make, whatever other restrictions there are on their conduct.[38] For example, the Bill of Rights picks out things like religious worship, political speech, and the possession of firearms as actions or choices whose restriction we should be specially concerned about. A society that places restrictions on activities of these types is held to be worse, in point of freedom, than a society that merely restricts activities like drinking, smoking, or driving.

The reason for the concern has in part to do with the special significance of these actions. Religious worship is where we disclose and practice our deepest beliefs. Political speech is where we communicate with one another as citizens of a republic. Even bearing arms is held, by those who defend its status as a right, to be a special assertion of dignity, mature responsibility, civic participation, and freedom from the prospect of tyranny. And people occasionally disagree about the contents of these lists of important freedoms. Is it really important to have the right to bear arms, in a modern democratic society? Is commercial advertising as important as individual political discourse? These are disputes about which choices have this high ethical import, analogous to that attributed, say, to religious worship. They are disputes about which liberties should be given special protection in the name of human dignity or autonomy, and which attacks on freedom should be viewed as particularly inimical to the identity of a person as a citizen and as a moral agent.

On the whole, the actions specified by Bills of Rights are not what are at stake in the issue of homelessness. Certainly there would be an uproar if an ordinance was passed making it an offense to pray in the subway or to pass one's time there in political debate.[39] There has been some concern in America about the restriction of free speech in public and quasi-public places[40] (since it is arguable that the whole point of free speech is that it take place in the public realm). However, the actions that are being closed off to the homeless are, for the most part, not significant in this high-minded sense. They are significant in another way: they are actions basic to the sustenance of a decent or healthy life, in some cases basic to the sustenance of life itself. There may not seem anything particularly autonomous or self-assertive or civically republican or ethically ennobling about sleeping or cooking or urinating. You will not find them listed in any Charter. However, that does not mean it is a matter of slight concern when people are prohibited from performing such actions, a concern analogous to that aroused by a traffic regulation or the introduction of a commercial standard.

For one thing, the regular performance of such actions is a precondition for all other aspects of life and activity. It is a precondition for the sort of autonomous life that is celebrated and affirmed when Bills of Rights are proclaimed. I am not making the crude mistake of saying that if we value autonomy, we must value its preconditions in exactly the same way. But if we value autonomy we should regard the satisfaction of its preconditions as a matter of importance; otherwise, our values simply ring hollow so far as real people are concerned.

Moreover, though we say there is nothing particularly dignified about sleeping or urinating, there is certainly something deeply and inherently *un*dignified about being prevented from doing so. Every torturer knows this: to break the human spirit, focus the mind of the victim through petty restrictions pitilessly imposed on the banal necessities of human life. We should be ashamed that we have allowed our laws of public and private property to reduce a million or more citizens to something approaching this level of degradation.

Increasingly, in the way we organize common property, we have done all we can to prevent people from taking care of these elementary needs themselves, quietly, with dignity, as ordinary human beings. If someone needs to urinate, what he needs above all as a dignified person is the *freedom* to do so in privacy and relative independence of the arbitrary will of anyone else. But we have set things up so that either the street person must *beg* for this opportunity, several times every day, as a favor from people who recoil from him in horror, or, if he wants to act independently on his own initiative, he must break the law and risk arrest. The generous provision of public lavatories would make an immense difference in this regard – and it would be a difference to freedom and dignity, not just a matter of welfare.

Finally we need to understand that any restriction on the performance of these basic acts has the feature of being not only uncomfortable and degrading, but more or less literally *unbearable* for the people concerned. People need sleep, for example, not just in the sense that sleep is necessary for health, but also in the sense that they will eventually fall asleep or drop from exhaustion if it is denied them. People simply cannot bear a lack of sleep, and they will do themselves a great deal of damage trying to bear it. The same, obviously, is true of bodily functions like urinating and defecating. These are things that people simply have to do; any attempt voluntarily to refrain from doing them is at once painful, dangerous, and finally impossible. That our social system right in effect deny them the right to do these things, by prohibiting their being done in each and every place, ought to be a matter of the gravest concern.[41]

It may seem sordid or in bad taste to make such a lot of these elementary physical points in a philosophical discussion of freedom. But if freedom is important, it is as freedom for human beings, that is, for the embodied and needy organisms that we are. The point about the activities I have mentioned is that they are both urgent and quotidian. They are urgent because they are basic to all other functions. They are actions that have to be performed, if one is to be free to do anything else without distraction and distress. And they are quotidian in the sense that they are actions that have to be done every day. They are not actions that a person can *wait* to perform until he acquires a home. Every day, he must eat and excrete and sleep. Every day, if he is homeless, he will face the overwhelming task of trying to find somewhere where he is allowed to do this.

VI Homes and Opportunities

That last point is particularly important as an answer to a final objection that may be made. Someone might object that I have so far said nothing at all about the fact that our society gives everyone the *opportunity* to acquire a home, and that we are all – the homeless and the housed – equal in *this* regard even if we are unequal in our actual ownership of real estate.

There is something to this objection, but not much. Certainly a society that denied a caste of persons the right (or juridical power) to own or lease property would be even worse than ours. The opportunity to acquire a home (even if it is just the juridical power) is surely worth having. But, to put it crudely, one cannot pee in an opportunity. Since the homeless, like us, are real people, they need some real place to be, not just the notional reflex of an Hohfeldian power.[42]

We also know enough about how the world works to see that one's need for somewhere to sleep and wash is, if anything, greatest during the time that one is trying to consummate this opportunity to find a home. The lack of liberty that homelessness involves makes it harder to impress, appeal to, or deal with the people who might eventually provide one with a job and with the money to afford housing. The irony of opportunity, in other words, is that the longer it remains unconsummated, for whatever reason, the more difficult it is to exploit.

In the final analysis, whether or not a person really has the *opportunity* to obtain somewhere to live is a matter of his position in a society; it is a matter of his ability to deal with the people around him and of there being an opening in social and economic structures so that his wants and abilities can be brought into relation with others.[43] That position, that ability, and that opening do not exist magically as a result of legal status. The juridical fact that a person is not legally barred from becoming a tenant or a proprietor does not mean that there is any realistic prospect of that happening. Whether it happens depends, among other things, on how he can present himself, how reliable and respectable he appears, what skills and abilities he can deploy, how much time, effort, and mobility he can invest in a search for housing, assistance, and employment, and so on.

Those are abstract formulations. We could say equally that it is hard to get a job when one appears filthy, that many of the benefits of social and economic interaction cannot be obtained without an address or without a way of receiving telephone calls, that a person cannot take *all* his possessions with him in a shopping cart when he goes for an interview but he may have nowhere to leave them, that those who have become homeless become so because they have run out of cash altogether and so of course do not have available the up-front fees and deposits that landlords require from potential tenants, and so on.

Everything we call a social or economic opportunity depends cruelly on a person's being able to *do* certain things – for example, his being able to wash, to sleep, and to base himself somewhere. When someone is homeless he is, as we have seen, effectively *banned* from doing these things; these are things he is *not allowed* to do. So long as that is the case, it is a contemptible mockery to reassure the victims of such coercion that they have the *opportunity* to play a full part in social and economic life, for the rules of property are such that they are *prohibited* from doing the minimum that would be necessary to take advantage of that opportunity.[44]

Conclusion

Lack of freedom is not all there is to the nightmare of homelessness. There is also the cold, the hunger, the disease and lack of medical treatment, the danger, the beatings, the loneliness, and the shame and despair that may come from being unable to care for oneself, one's child, or a friend. By focusing on freedom in this essay, I have not wanted to detract from any of that.

But there are good reasons to pay attention to the issue of freedom. They are not merely strategic, though in a society that prides itself as "the land of the free," this may be one way of shaming a people into action and concern. Homelessness is partly about property and law, and freedom provides the connecting term that makes those categories relevant. By considering not only what a person is allowed to do, but where he is allowed to do it, we can see a system of property for what it is: rules that provide freedom and prosperity for some by imposing restrictions on others. So long as everyone enjoys some of the benefits as well as some of the restrictions, that correlativity is bearable. It ceases to be so when there is a class of persons who bear *all* of the restrictions and nothing else, a class of persons for whom property is nothing but a way of limiting their freedom.

Perhaps the strongest argument for thinking about homelessness as an issue of freedom is that it forces us to see people in need as *agents*. Destitution is not necessarily passive; and public provision is not always a way of compounding passivity. By focusing on what we allow people to do to satisfy their own basic needs on their own initiative, and by scrutinizing the legal obstacles that we place in their way (the doors we lock, the ordinances we enforce, and the night-sticks we raise), we get a better sense that what we are dealing with here is not just "the problem of homelessness," but a million or more *persons* whose activity and dignity and freedom are at stake.

Notes

1 See, e.g., Siebert, *Homeless People: Establishing Rights to Shelter*, 4 Law & Inequality 393 (1986) (no constitutional guarantee of adequate housing): Comment, *The Unconstitutionality of "Anti-homeless" Laws: Ordinances Prohibiting Sleeping in Outdoor Public Areas as a Violation of the Right to Travel*, 77 Calif. L. Rev. 595 (1989) (authored by Ades) (arguing that laws that proscribe sleeping in outdoor public areas violate the right to travel).

2 The best discussion remains Honoré, *Ownership*, in Oxford Essays in Jurisprudence 107 (A.G. Guest ed. 1961); see also S. Munzer, *A Theory of Property* 21–61 (1990); J. Waldron, *The Right to Private Property* 15–36 (1988).

3 See J. Waldron, note 2 (above), at 40–42; Macpherson, *The Meaning of Property*, in *Property: Mainstream and Critical Positions* 1, 4–6 (C. Macpherson ed. 1978).

4 In Pruneyard Shopping Center v: Robins, 447 US 74 (1980), the United States Supreme Court held that the California courts may reasonably require the owners of a shopping mall to allow persons to exercise rights of free speech on their premises under the California Constitution, and that such a requirement does not constitute a taking for the purposes of the Fifth Amendment to the Constitution of the United States.

5 For a more complete discussion, see J. Waldron, note 2 (above), at 42–6.

6 Diluliu, *There But For Fortune*, New Republic, June 24, 1991, at 27, 28.

7 But this ignores the fact that a large number of people with no home of their own are kept from having to wander the streets only by virtue of the fact that friends and relatives are willing to let them share their homes, couches, and floors. If this generosity were less forthcoming, the number of "street people" would be much greater. Still, this generosity is contingent and precarious: those who offer it are often under great strain themselves. So the situation affords precious little security: at the first family crisis, the friend or relative may have to move out.

8 See, e.g., M. Rothbard, *For a New Liberty*, 201–2 (1973) (emphasis in original):

> The ultimate libertarian program may be summed up in one phrase: the *abolition* of the public sector, the conversion of all operations and services performed by the government into activities performed voluntarily by the private enterprise economy.... Abolition of the public sector means, of course, that *all* pieces of land, all land areas, including streets and roads, would be owned privately, by individuals, corporations, cooperatives, or any other voluntary groupings of individuals and capital.... What we need to do is to reorient our thinking to consider a world in which all land areas are privately owned.

9 Herbert Spencer was so disconcerted by the possibility that he thought it a good reason to prohibit the private ownership of land altogether.

> For if *one* portion of the earth's surface may justly become the possession of an individual, and may be held by him for his sole use and benefit, as a thing to which he has an exclusive right, then *other* portions of the earth's surface may be so held; and eventually the *whole* of the earth's surface may be so held; and our planet may thus lapse altogether into private hands.... Supposing the entire habitable globe be so enclosed, it follows that if the landowners have a valid right to its surface, all who are not landowners, have no right at all to its surface. Hence, such can exist on the earth by sufferance only. They are all trespassers. Save by permission of the lords of the soil, they can have no room for the soles of their feet. Nay, should others think fit to deny them a resting-place, these landless men might equitably be expelled from the planet altogether.
>
> A. Reeve, Property 85 (1986) (quoting H. Spencer, Social Statics 114–15 (1851)).

10 For a useful discussion, see I. Berlin, *Introduction*, in Four Essays on Liberty i, xlv–lv (1969).

11 See also Waldron, *Welfare and the Images of Charity*, 36 Phil. Q. 463 (1986)

12 For the contrast between "positive" and "negative" conceptions of freedom, see I. Berlin, *Two Concepts of Liberty*, in Four Essays on Liberty 118 (1969).

13 The *locus classicus* of negative liberty, defined in this way, is T. Hobbes, Leviathan 261–74 (C.B. Macpherson ed. 1968).

14 The claim that the poor are as free as the rest of us is sometimes associated with the view that they have the same *opportunity* as the rest of us to acquire property and become, if not rich, then at least well-off. This line of argument is discussed in Part VI. For the moment, it does not affect the point that *being* poor amounts to being unfree, even if there are ways of extricating oneself from that predicament. (An analogy may help here: a prisoner who has the opportunity to obtain parole and fails to take advantage of that opportunity still remains unfree inasmuch as he remains imprisoned.)

15 For a particularly clear statement, see Cohen, *Capitalism, Freedom and the Proletariat*, in *The Idea of Freedom 9*, 11–14 (A. Ryan ed. 1979).

16 A. Reeve, note 9 (above), at 107.

17 This distinction is found in Hobbes's discussion: he defines liberty as the absence of "external impediments." and adds that "when the impediment of motion, is in the constitution of the thing it selfe, we use not to say, it wants the Liberty; but the Power to move; as when a stone lyeth still, or a man is fastned to his bed by sicknesse." T. Hobbes, note 13 (above), at 262. It is found also in Berlin's account: "If I say that I am unable to jump more than ten feet in the air, or cannot read because I am blind, or cannot understand the darker pages of Hegel, it would be eccentric to say that I am to that degree enslaved or coerced." I. Berlin, note 12 (above), at 122.

18 Cf. I. Berlin, note 12 (above), at 123:

> It is only because I believe that my inability to get a given thing is due to the fact that other human beings have made arrangements whereby I am, whereas others are not, prevented from having enough money with which to pay for it, that I think myself a victim of coercion or slavery. In other words, this use of the term depends on a particular social and economic theory about the causes of my poverty or weakness.

19 See 1 K. Marx, *Capital*, 781–802 (B. Fowkes trans. 1976).

20 For the idea of a "moralized" definition of freedom, see Cohen, note 15 (above), at 12–14.

21 Cf. I. Berlin, note 12 (above), at 133:

> Once I take this view, I am in a position to ignore the actual wishes of men or societies, to bully, oppress, torture them in the name, and on behalf, of their "real" selves, in the secure knowledge that whatever is the true goal of man (happiness, performance of duty, wisdom, a just society, self-fulfilment) must be identical with his freedom . . .

22 The whole burden of Isaiah Berlin's work has been that such tidy packaging is not to be expected.

23 It is not even to deny that they may enlarge the amount of freedom overall. Isaiah Berlin put the point precisely: "Every law seems to me to curtail *some* liberty, although it may be a means to increasing another. Whether it increases the total sum of attainable liberty will of course depend on the particular situation." I. Berlin, note 10 (above), at xlix n. 1 (emphasis in original).

24 For the connection between generality, predictability, and the rule of law, see F. Hayek, *The Constitution of Liberty*, 148–61 (1960).

25 See R. Hare, Freedom and Reason 10–21 (1963).

26 For example, Dicey puts forward the following as the first principle of "the rule of law": "no man is punishable or can be lawfully made to suffer in body or goods except for a distinct breach of law established in the ordinary legal manner before the ordinary courts of the land." A. Dicey, *Introduction to the Study of the Law of the Constitution 188* (10th ed. 1959). Hobbes stated the same doctrine more succinctly: "As for other Lyberties, they depend on the silence of the Law. In cases where the Soveraign has prescribed no rule, there the Subject hath the liberty to do, or forbeare, according to his own discretion." T. Hobbes, note 13 (above), at 271.

27 For a discussion of how a lay person applies the rules of property, see B. Ackerman, *Private Property and the Constitution*, 116–18 (1977).

28 Here are some examples. The City Code of Phoenix, Arizona provides: "It shall be unlawful for any person to use a public street, highway, alley, lane, parkway, [or] sidewalk . . . for lying [or] sleeping . . . except in the case of a physical emergency or the administration of medical assistance." A St. Petersburg, Florida ordinance similarly provides that: "No person shall sleep upon or in any street, park, wharf or other public place." I am indebted to Paul Ades for these examples. Comment, note 1 (above), at 595 n. 5, 596 n. 7 (quoting Phoenix, Ariz., City Code § 23–48.01 (1981); St. Petersburg, Fla., Ordinance 25.57 (1973)).

29 And New Yorkers have grown tired of confronting homeless people every day on the subway, at the train station and at the entrances to supermarkets and apartment buildings.

> "People are tired of stepping over bodies," the advocacy director for the Coalition for the Homeless, Keith Summa, said.

> Lynette Thompson, a Transit Authority official who oversees the outreach program for the homeless in the subway, said there had been a marked change this year in letters from riders.

"At the beginning of last year, the tenor of those letters was, 'Please do something to help the homeless,' " Ms. Thompson said. "But since August and September, they've been saying: 'Just get them out. I don't care. Just get them out any way you can.' It got worse and people got fed up."

. . .

For the homeless, the new restrictions mean it is more difficult than ever to find a place to rest. Charles Lark, 29 years old, who said he had spent the last three years sleeping on subway trains and platforms, left New York on the day the subway-enforcement program began: "This is a cold-hearted city," he said. "I'm going to Washington. I hope it'll be better there."

Doors Closing as Mood on the Homeless Sours, N.Y. Times, Nov. 18, 1989; at 1, col. 2, 32, col. 1, col. 2.

30 A. France, *Le Lys Rouge* 117–18 (rev. ed. 1923) ("The law in its majestic equality forbids the rich as well as the poor to sleep under the bridges.").

31 See M. Davis, *City of Quartz: Excavating the Future in Los Angeles,* 232–36 (1990) for an excellent account of similar devices designed to render public spaces in downtown Los Angeles "off-limits" to the homeless, as well as Davis's *Afterword – A Logic Like Hell's: Being Homeless in Los Angeles,* 39 UCLA L. Rev. 325 (1991).

32 See note 29 (above).

33 Bracing for the annual influx of homeless people fleeing the Northern cold, the police here [in Miami, Florida] have proposed an emergency ordinance that would allow them to arrest some street people as a way of keeping them on the move.

. . .

The new measure would replace a century-old law against sleeping in public that was abandoned after a similar statute in Clearwater, Fla., was struck down by Federal courts in January. The courts said the statute was too broad and would have applied even to a person sleeping in his car.

The new proposal seeks to get around the court's objection by being more specific. But it would also be more far-reaching than the original law, applying to such activities as cooking and the building of temporary shelters.

Terry Cunningham, a 23-year-old who lives on the steps of the Federal Courthouse, asked of the police, "Where do they expect me to sleep?"

City and county officials had no answer. "That's a good question," Sergeant Rivero of the Police Department said, "No one is willing to address the problem."

Miami Police Want to Control Homeless by Arresting Them, N.Y. Times, Nov. 4, 1988, at A1, col. 1. A16, col. 4.

34 Cf. 2 F. Hayek, *Law, Legislation and Liberty: The Mirage of Social Justice,* 64 (1976):

It has of course to be admitted that the manner in which the benefits and burdens are apportioned by the market mechanism would in many instances have to be regarded as very unjust *if* it were the result of a deliberate allocation to particular people. But this is not the case. Those shares are the outcome of a process the effect of which on particular people was neither intended nor foreseen by anyone . . .

35 See D. Parfit, *Reasons and Persons,* 67–86 (1984); D. Regan, *Utilitarianism and Cooperation* (1980). The tenor of these works is that each person should pay attention, not only to the immediate consequences of her individual actions, but also to the consequences of a certain set of actions (which includes actions by her and actions by others). As Parfit puts it:

It is not enough to ask. "Will my act harm other people?" Even if the answer is No, my act may still be wrong, *because* of its effects on other people. I should ask. "Will my act be one of a set of acts that will *together* harm other people?" The answer may be Yes. And the harm to others may be great.

D. Parfit at 86 (above), (emphasis in original).

36 See note 29 (above).

37 For a critique of the purely quantitative approach, see Taylor, *What's Wrong with Negative Liberty?* in *The Idea of Freedom,* note 15 (above), at 183. [Reprinted as chapter 25 of this volume.]

38 Cf. R. Dworkin, *Taking Rights Seriously* 270–2 (rev. ed. 1978) (discussion of the theory that a right to certain liberties can be derived from the "special character" of the liberties).

39 The failure of First Amendment challenges to restrictions on panhandling does not bode well for the survival of even these protections. *See* Young v. New York City Transit Auth., 903 F.2d 146 (2d Cir.), *cert. denied,* 111 S. Ct. 516 (1990). But see Hershkoff and Cohen, *Begging to Differ: The First Amendment and the Right to Beg,* 104 Harv. L. Rev. 896 (1991) (arguing that begging is protected speech).

40 See note 4 (above).

41 I hope it will not be regarded as an attempt at humor if I suggest that the Rawlsian doctrine of "the strains of commitment" is directly relevant here. J. Rawls, *A Theory of Justice,* 175–6 (1971). If the effect of a principle would be literally unbearable to some of those to whom it applies, it must be rejected by the parties in Rawls's contractarian thought-experiment, known as the "original position": "They cannot enter into agreements that may have

consequences they cannot accept. They will avoid those that they can adhere to only with great difficulty." *Id.* at 176. As Rawls emphasizes, this is a matter of the *bona fides* of bargaining, not of any particular psychology of risk-aversion.

42 See also the discussion in J. Waldron, note 2 (above), at 390–422.

43 This idea is sometimes expressed in terms of "social citizenship." See King & Waldron, *Citizenship, Social Citizenship, and the Defense of Welfare Provision*, 18 Brit. J. Pol. Sci. 415 (1988); see also R. Dahren-dorf, *The Modern Social Conflict: An Essay on the Politics of Liberty*, 29–47 (1988).

44 And this is to say nothing about the appalling deprivation of ordinary opportunity that will be experienced by those tens of thousands of *children* growing up homeless in America. To suggest that a child sleeping on the streets or in a dangerous, crowded shelter, with no place to store toys or books, and no sense of hope or security, has an opportunity equal to that of anyone in our society is simply a mockery.

PART VI

Equality

30

The Idea of Equality

Bernard Williams

The idea of equality is used in political discussion both in statements of fact, or what purport to be statements of fact – that men *are* equal – and in statements of political principles or aims – that men *should be* equal, as at present they are not. The two can be, and often are, combined: the aim is then described as that of securing a state of affairs in which men are treated as the equal beings which they in fact already are, but are not already treated as being. In both these uses, the idea of equality notoriously encounters the same difficulty: that on one kind of interpretation the statements in which it figures are much too strong, and on another kind much too weak, and it is hard to find a satisfactory interpretation that lies between the two.[1]

To take first the supposed statement of fact: it has only too often been pointed out that to say that all men are equal in all those characteristics in respect of which it makes sense to say that men are equal or unequal, is a patent falsehood; and even if some more restricted selection is made of these characteristics, the statement does not look much better. Faced with this obvious objection, the defender of the claim that all men are equal is likely to offer a weaker interpretation. It is not, he may say, in their skill, intelligence, strength or virtue that men are equal, but merely in their being men: it is their common humanity that constitutes their equality. On this interpretation, we should not seek for some special characteristics in respect of which men are equal, but merely remind ourselves that they are all men. Now to this it might be objected that being men is not a respect in which men can strictly speaking be said to be *equal*; but, leaving that aside, there is the more immediate objection that if all that the statement does is to remind us that men are men, it does not do very much, and in particular does less than its proponents in political argument have wanted it to do. What looked like a paradox has turned into a platitude.

I shall suggest in a moment that even in this weak form the statement is not so vacuous as this objection makes it seem; but it must be admitted that when the statement of equality ceases to claim more than is warranted, it rather rapidly reaches the point where it claims less than is interesting. A similar discomfiture tends to overcome the practical maxim of equality. It cannot be the aim of this maxim that all men should be treated alike in all circumstances, or even that they should be treated alike as much as possible. Granted that, however, there is no obvious stopping point before the interpretation which makes the maxim claim only that men should be treated alike in similar circumstances; and since 'circumstances' here must clearly include reference to what a man is, as well as to his purely external situation, this comes very much to saying that for every difference in the way men are treated, some general reason or principle of differentiation must be given. This may well be

Originally published in *Philosophy, Politics and Society*, Series 2, edited by Peter Laslett and W. G. Runciman (Oxford: Blackwell, 1979), pp. 110–31. Reprinted by permission of Blackwell Publishing Ltd.

an important principle; some indeed have seen in it, or in something very like it, an essential element of morality itself.[2] But it can hardly be enough to constitute the principle that was advanced in the name of *equality*. It would be in accordance with this principle, for example, to treat black men differently from others just because they were black, or poor men differently just because they were poor, and this cannot accord with anyone's idea of equality.

In what follows I shall try to advance a number of considerations that can help to save the political notion of equality from these extremes of absurdity and of triviality. These considerations are in fact often employed in political argument, but are usually bundled together into an unanalysed notion of equality in a manner confusing to the advocates, and encouraging to the enemies, of that ideal. These considerations will not enable us to define a distinct third interpretation of the statements which use the notion of equality; it is rather that they enable us, starting with the weak interpretations, to build up something that in practice can have something of the solidity aspired to by the strong interpretations. In this discussion, it will not be necessary all the time to treat separately the supposedly factual application of the notion of equality, and its application in the maxim of action. Though it is sometimes important to distinguish them, and there are clear grounds for doing so, similar considerations often apply to both. The two go significantly together: on the one hand, the point of the supposedly factual assertion is to back up social ideals and programmes of political action; on the other hand – a rather less obvious point, perhaps – those political proposals have their force because they are regarded not as gratuitously egalitarian, aiming at equal treatment for reasons, for instance, of simplicity or tidiness, but as affirming an equality which is believed in some sense already to exist, and to be obscured or neglected by actual social arrangements.

I Common Humanity

The factual statement of men's equality was seen, when pressed, to retreat in the direction of merely asserting the equality of men as men; and this was thought to be trivial. It is certainly insufficient, but not, after all, trivial. That all men are human is, if a tautology, a useful one, serving as a reminder that

those who belong anatomically to the species *homo sapiens*, and can speak a language, use tools, live in societies, can interbreed despite racial differences, etc., are also alike in certain other respects more likely to be forgotten. These respects are notably the capacity to feel pain, both from immediate physical causes and from various situations represented in perception and in thought; and the capacity to feel affection for others, and the consequences of this, connected with the frustration of this affection, loss of its objects, etc. The assertion that men are alike in the possession of these characteristics is, while indisputable and (it may be) even necessarily true, not trivial. For it is certain that there are political and social arrangements that systematically neglect these characteristics in the case of some groups of men, while being fully aware of them in the case of others; that is to say, they treat certain men as though they did not possess these characteristics, and neglect moral claims that arise from these characteristics and which would be admitted to arise from them.

Here it may be objected that the mere fact that ruling groups in certain societies treat other groups in this way does not mean that they neglect or overlook the characteristics in question. For, it may be suggested, they may well recognize the presence of these characteristics in the worse-treated group, but claim that in the case of that group, the characteristics do not give rise to any moral claim; the group being distinguished from other members of society in virtue of some further characteristic (for instance, by being black), this may be cited as the ground of treating them differently, whether they feel pain, affection, etc., or not.

This objection rests on the assumption, common to much moral philosophy that makes a sharp distinction between fact and value, that the question whether a certain consideration is *relevant* to a moral issue is an evaluative question: to state that a consideration is relevant or irrelevant to a certain moral question is, on this view, itself to commit oneself to a certain kind of moral principle or outlook. Thus, in the case under discussion, to say (as one would naturally say) that the fact that a man is black is, by itself, quite irrelevant to the issue of how he should be treated in respect of welfare, etc., would, on this view, be to commit oneself to a certain sort of moral principle. This view, taken generally, seems to me quite certainly false. The principle that men should be differentially treated in respect of welfare merely on grounds of their colour is not a special sort of moral principle, but (if anything) a purely arbitrary assertion of will, like that of some Caligulan ruler who decided to execute everyone whose name contained three 'R's.

This point is in fact conceded by those who practise such things as colour discrimination. Few can be found who will explain their practice merely by saying, 'But they're black: and it is my moral principle to treat black men differently from others'. If any reasons are given at all, they will be reasons that seek to correlate the fact of blackness with certain other considerations which are at least candidates for relevance to the question of how a man should be treated: such as insensitivity, brute stupidity, ineducable irresponsibility, etc. Now these reasons are very often rationalizations, and the correlations claimed are either not really believed, or quite irrationally believed, by those who claim them. But this is a different point; the argument concerns what counts as a moral reason, and the rationalizer broadly agrees with others about what counts as such – the trouble with him is that his reasons are dictated by his policies, and not conversely. The Nazis' 'anthropologists' who tried to construct theories of Aryanism were paying, in very poor coin, the homage of irrationality to reason.

The question of relevance in moral reasons will arise again, in a different connexion, in this paper. For the moment its importance is that it gives a force to saying that those who neglect the moral claims of certain men that arise from their human capacity to feel pain, etc., are *overlooking* or *disregarding* those capacities; and are not just operating with a special moral principle, conceding the capacities to these men, but denying the moral claim. Very often, indeed, they have just persuaded themselves that the men in question have those capacities in a lesser degree. Here it is certainly to the point to assert the apparent platitude that these men are also human.

I have discussed this point in connexion with very obvious human characteristics of feeling pain and desiring affection. There are, however, other and less easily definable characteristics universal to humanity, which may all the more be neglected in political and social arrangements. For instance, there seems to be a characteristic which might be called 'a desire for self-respect'; this phrase is perhaps not too happy, in suggesting a particular culturally limited, bourgeois value, but I mean by it a certain human desire to be identified with what one is doing, to be able to realize purposes of one's own, and not to be the instrument of another's will unless one has willingly accepted such a role. This is a very inadequate and in some ways rather empty specification of a human desire; to a better specification, both philosophical reflection and the evidences of psychology and anthropology would be relevant. Such investigations enable us to understand more deeply, in respect of the desire I have gestured towards and of similar characteristics, what it is to be human; and of what it is to be human, the apparently trivial statement of men's equality as men can serve as a reminder.

II Moral Capacities

So far we have considered respects in which men can be counted as all alike, which respects are, in a sense, negative: they concern the capacity to suffer, and certain needs that men have, and these involve men in moral relations as the recipients of certain kinds of treatment. It has certainly been a part, however, of the thought of those who asserted that men were equal, that there were more positive respects in which men were alike: that they were equal in certain things that they could do or achieve, as well as in things that they needed and could suffer. In respect of a whole range of abilities, from weight-lifting to the calculus, the assertion is, as was noted at the beginning, not plausible, and has not often been supposed to be. It has been held, however, that there are certain other abilities, both less open to empirical test and more essential in moral connexions, for which it is true that men are equal. These are certain sorts of moral ability or capacity, the capacity for virtue or achievement of the highest kind of moral worth.

The difficulty with this notion is that of identifying any purely moral capacities. Some human capacities are more relevant to the achievement of a virtuous life than others: intelligence, a capacity for sympathetic understanding, and a measure of resoluteness would generally be agreed to be so. But these capacities can all be displayed in non-moral connexions as well, and in such connexions would naturally be thought to differ from man to man like other natural capacities. That this is the fact of the matter has been accepted by many thinkers, notably, for instance, by Aristotle. But against this acceptance, there is a powerful strain of thought that centres on a feeling of ultimate and outrageous absurdity in the idea that the achievement of the highest kind of moral worth should depend on natural capacities, unequally and fortuitously distributed as they are; and this feeling is backed up by the observation that these natural capacities are not themselves the bearers of the moral worth, since those that have them are as gifted for vice as for virtue.

This strain of thought has found many types of religious expression; but in philosophy it is to be found in its purest form in Kant. Kant's view not only carries to the limit the notion that moral worth cannot depend on contingencies, but also emphasizes, in its picture of the Kingdom of Ends, the idea of *respect* which is owed to each man as a rational moral agent – and, since men are equally such agents, is owed equally to all, unlike admiration and similar attitudes, which are commanded unequally by men in proportion to their unequal possession of different kinds of natural excellence. These ideas are intimately connected in Kant, and it is not possible to understand his moral theory unless as much weight is given to what he says about the Kingdom of Ends as is always given to what he says about duty.

The very considerable consistency of Kant's view is bought at what would generally be agreed to be a very high price. The detachment of moral worth from all contingencies is achieved only by making man's characteristic as a moral or rational agent a transcendental characteristic; man's capacity to will freely as a rational agent is not dependent on any empirical capacities he may have – and, in particular, is not dependent on empirical capacities which men may possess unequally – because, in the Kantian view, the capacity to be a rational agent is not itself an empirical capacity at all. Accordingly, the respect owed equally to each man as a member of the Kingdom of Ends is not owed to him in respect of any empirical characteristics that he may possess, but solely in respect of the transcendental characteristic of being a free and rational will. The ground of the respect owed to each man thus emerges in the Kantian theory as a kind of secular analogue of the Christian conception of the respect owed to all men as equally children of God. Though secular, it is equally metaphysical: in neither case is it anything empirical *about* men that constitutes the ground of equal respect.

This transcendental, Kantian conception cannot provide any solid foundation for the notions of equality among men, or of equality of respect owed to them. Apart from the general difficulties

of such transcendental conceptions, there is the obstinate fact that the concept of 'moral agent', and the concepts allied to it such as that of responsibility, do and must have an empirical basis. It seems empty to say that all men are equal as moral agents, when the question, for instance, of men's responsibility for their actions is one to which empirical considerations are clearly relevant, and one which moreover receives answers in terms of different degrees of responsibility and different degrees of rational control over action. To hold a man responsible for his actions is presumably the central case of treating him as a moral agent, and if men are not treated as equally responsible, there is not much left to their equality as moral agents.

If, without its transcendental basis, there is not much left to men's equality as moral agents, is there anything left to the notion of the *respect* owed to all men? This notion of 'respect' is both complex and unclear, and I think it needs, and would repay, a good deal of investigation. Some content can, however, be attached to it; even if it is some way away from the ideas of moral agency. There certainly is a distinction, for instance, between regarding a man's life, actions or character from an aesthetic or technical point of view, and regarding them from a point of view which is concerned primarily with what it is *for him* to live that life and do those actions in that character. Thus from the technological point of view, a man who has spent his life in trying to make a certain machine which could not possibly work is merely a failed inventor, and in compiling a catalogue of those whose efforts have contributed to the sum of technical achievement, one must 'write him off': the fact that he devoted himself to this useless task with constant effort and so on, is merely irrelevant. But from a human point of view, it is clearly not irrelevant: we are concerned with him, not merely as 'a failed inventor', but as a man who wanted to be a successful inventor. Again, in professional relations and the world of work, a man operates, and his activities come up for criticism, under a variety of professional or technical titles, such as 'miner' or 'agricultural labourer' or 'junior executive'. The technical or professional attitude is that which regards the man solely under that title, the human approach that which regards him as *a man who has* that title (among others), willingly, unwillingly, through lack of alternatives, with pride, etc.

That men should be regarded from the human point of view, and not merely under these sorts of titles, is part of the content that might be attached to Kant's celebrated injunction 'treat each man as an end in himself, and never as a means only'. But I do not think that this is all that should be seen in this injunction, or all that is concerned in the notion of 'respect'. What is involved in the examples just given could be explained by saying that each man is owed an effort at identification: that he should not be regarded as the surface to which a certain label can be applied, but one should try to see the world (including the label) from his point of view. This injunction will be based on, though not of course fully explained by, the notion that men are conscious beings who necessarily have intentions and purposes and see what they are doing in a certain light. But there seem to be further injunctions connected with the Kantian maxim, and with the notion of 'respect', that go beyond these considerations. There are forms of exploiting men or degrading them which would be thought to be excluded by these notions, but which cannot be excluded merely by considering how the exploited or degraded men see the situation. For it is precisely a mark of extreme exploitation or degradation that those who suffer it do *not* see themselves differently from the way they are seen by the exploiters; either they do not see themselves as anything at all, or they acquiesce passively in the role for which they have been cast. Here we evidently need something more than the precept that one should respect and try to understand another man's consciousness of his own activities; it is also that one may not suppress or destroy that consciousness.

All these I must confess to be vague and inconclusive considerations, but we are dealing with a vague notion: one, however, that we possess, and attach value to. To try to put these matters properly in order would be itself to try to reach conclusions about several fundamental questions of moral philosophy. What we must ask here is what these ideas have to do with equality. We started with the notion of men's equality as moral agents. This notion appeared unsatisfactory, for different reasons, in both an empirical and a transcendental interpretation. We then moved, *via* the idea of 'respect', to the different notion of regarding men not merely under professional, social or technical titles, but with consideration of their own views and purposes. This notion has at least this much to do with equality: that the titles which it urges us to look behind are the conspicuous bearers of social, political and technical *inequality*, whether they refer to achievement (as in the example of the inventor), or to social roles (as in the example of work titles). It enjoins us not to let our fundamental attitudes to men be dictated by the criteria of technical success or social position, and not to take them at the value carried by these titles and by the structures in which these titles place them. This does not mean, of course, that the more fundamental view that should be taken of men is in the case of every man the same: on the contrary. But it does mean that each man is owed the effort of understanding, and that in achieving it, each man is to be (as it were) abstracted from certain conspicuous structures of inequality in which we find him.

These injunctions are based on the proposition that men are beings who are necessarily to some extent conscious of themselves and of the world they live in. (I omit here, as throughout the discussion, the clinical cases of people who are mad or mentally defective, who always constitute special exceptions to what is in general true of men.) This proposition does not assert that men are equally conscious of themselves and of their situation. It was precisely one element in the notion of exploitation considered above that such consciousness can be decreased by social action and the environment; we may add that it can similarly be increased. But men are at least potentially conscious, to an indeterminate degree, of their situation and of what I have called their 'titles', are capable of reflectively standing back from the roles and positions in which they are cast; and this reflective consciousness may be enhanced or diminished by their social condition.

It is this last point that gives these considerations a particular relevance to the political aims of egalitarianism. The mere idea of regarding men from 'the human point of view', while it has a good deal to do with politics, and a certain amount to do with equality, has nothing specially to do with political equality. One could, I think, accept this as an ideal, and yet favour, for instance, some kind of hierarchical society, so long as the hierarchy maintained itself without compulsion, and there was human understanding between the orders. In such a society, each man would indeed have a very conspicuous title which related him to the social structure; but it might be that most people were aware of the human beings behind the titles, and found each other for the most part content, or even proud, to have the titles that they had. I do not know whether anything like this has been true of historical hierarchical societies; but I can see no inconsistency in some-one's espousing it as an ideal, as some (influenced in many cases by a sentimental picture of the Middle Ages) have done. Such a person would be one who accepted the notion of 'the human view', the view of each man as something more than his title, as a valuable ideal, but rejected the ideals of political equality.

Once, however, one accepts the further notion that the degree of man's consciousness about such things as his role in society is itself in some part the product of social arrangements, and that it can be increased, this ideal of a stable hierarchy must, I think, disappear. For what keeps stable hierarch-ies together is the idea of necessity, that it is somehow foreordained or inevitable that there should be these orders; and this idea of necessity must be eventually undermined by the growth of people's reflective consciousness about their role, still more when it is combined with the thought that what they and the others have always thought about their roles in the social system was the product of the social system itself.

It might be suggested that a certain man who admitted that people's consciousness of their roles was conditioned in this way might nevertheless believe in the hierarchical ideal: but that in order to preserve the society of his ideal, he would have to make sure that the idea of the conditioning of consciousness did not get around to too many people, and that their consciousness about their roles did not increase too much. But such a view is really a very different thing from its naïve pre-decessor. Such a man, no longer himself 'im-mersed' in the system, is beginning to think in terms of compulsion, the deliberate *prevention* of the growth of consciousness, which is a poisonous element absent from the original ideal. Moreover, his attitude (or that of rulers similar to himself) towards the other people in the ideal society must now contain an element of condescension or contempt, since he will be aware that their accept-ance of what they suppose to be necessity is a delusion. This is alien to the spirit of human understanding on which the original ideal was based. The hierarchical idealist cannot escape the fact that certain things which can be done decently without self-consciousness can, with self-con-sciousness, be done only hypocritically. This is why even the rather hazy and very general notions that I have tried to bring together in this section contain some of the grounds of the ideal of polit-ical equality.

III Equality in Unequal Circumstances

The notion of equality is invoked not only in connexions where men are claimed in some sense all to be equal, but in connexions where they are agreed to be unequal, and the question arises of the distribution of, or access to, certain goods to which their inequalities are relevant. It may be objected that the notion of equality is in fact misapplied in these connexions, and that the appropriate ideas are those of fairness or justice, in the sense of what Aristotle called 'distributive justice', where (as Aristotle argued) there is no question of regarding or treating everyone as equal, but solely a question of distributing certain goods in proportion to men's recognized inequalities.

I think it is reasonable to say against this objec-tion that there is some foothold for the notion of equality even in these cases. It is useful here to make a rough distinction between two different types of inequality, inequality of *need* and inequal-ity of *merit*, with a corresponding distinction be-tween goods – on the one hand, goods demanded by the need, and on the other, goods that can be earned by the merit. In the case of needs, such as the need for medical treatment in case of illness, it can be presumed for practical purposes that the persons who have the need actually desire the goods in question, and so the question can indeed be regarded as one of distribution in a simple sense, the satisfaction of an existing desire. In the case of merit, such as for instance the possession of abilities to profit from a university education, there is not the same presumption that everyone who has the merit has the desire for the goods in question, though it may, of course, be the case. Moreover, the good of a university education may be legitimately, even if hopelessly, desired by those who do not possess the merit; while medical treatment or unemployment benefit are either not desired, or not legitimately desired, by those who are not ill or unemployed, i.e. do not have the appropriate need. Hence the distri-bution of goods in accordance with merit has a competitive aspect lacking in the case of distribu-tion according to need. For these reasons, it is appropriate to speak, in the case of merit, not only of the distribution of the good, but of the distribution of the opportunity of achieving the good. But this, unlike the good itself, can be said to be distributed equally to everybody, and so one does encounter a notion of *general* equality, much vaunted in our society today, the notion of equality of opportunity.

Before considering this notion further, it is worth noticing certain resemblances and differences between the cases of need and of merit. In both cases, we encounter the matter (mentioned before in this paper) of the relevance of reasons. Leaving aside preventive medicine, the proper ground of distribution of medical care is ill health: this is a necessary truth. Now in very many societies, while ill health may work as a necessary condition of receiving treatment, it does not work as a sufficient condition, since such treatment costs money, and not all who are ill have the money; hence the possession of sufficient money becomes in fact an additional necessary condition of actually receiving treatment. Yet more extravagantly, money may work as a sufficient condition by itself, without any medical need, in which case the reasons that actually operate for the receipt of this good are just totally irrelevant to its nature; however, since only a few hypochondriacs desire treatment when they do not need it, this is, in this case, a marginal phenomenon.

When we have the situation in which, for instance, wealth is a further necessary condition of the receipt of medical treatment, we can once more apply the notions of equality and inequality: not now in connexion with the inequality between the well and the ill, but in connexion with the inequality between the rich ill and the poor ill, since we have straightforwardly the situation of those whose needs are the same not receiving the same treatment, though the needs are the ground of the treatment. This is an irrational state of affairs.

It may be objected that I have neglected an important distinction here. For, it may be said, I have treated the ill health and the possession of money as though they were regarded on the same level, as 'reasons for receiving medical treatment', and this is a muddle. The ill health is, at most, a ground of the *right* to receive medical treatment; whereas the money is, in certain circumstances, the causally necessary condition of securing the right, which is a different thing. There is something in the distinction that this objection suggests: there is a distinction between a man's rights, the reasons why he should be treated in a certain way, and his power to secure those rights, the reasons why he can in fact get what he deserves. But this objection does not make it inappropriate to call the situation of inequality an 'irrational' situation: it just makes it clearer what is

meant by so calling it. What is meant is that it is a situation in which reasons are insufficiently *operative*; it is a situation insufficiently controlled by reasons – and hence by reason itself. The same point arises with another form of equality and equal rights, equality before the law. It may be said that in a certain society, men have equal rights to a fair trial, to seek redress from the law for wrongs committed against them, etc. But if a fair trial or redress from the law can be secured in that society only by moneyed and educated persons, to insist that everyone *has* this right, though only these particular persons can *secure* it, rings hollow to the point of cynicism: we are concerned not with the abstract existence of rights, but with the extent to which those rights govern what actually happens.

Thus when we combine the notions of the *relevance* of reasons, and the *operativeness* of reasons, we have a genuine moral weapon, which can be applied in cases of what is appropriately called unequal treatment, even where one is not concerned with the equality of people as a whole. This represents a strengthening of the very weak principle mentioned at the beginning of this paper, that for every difference in the way men are treated, a reason should be given: when one requires further that the reasons should be relevant, and that they should be socially operative, this really says something.

Similar considerations will apply to cases of merit. There is, however, an important difference between the cases of need and merit, in respect of the relevance of reasons. It is a matter of logic that particular sorts of needs constitute a reason for receiving particular sorts of good. It is, however, in general a much more disputable question whether certain sorts of merit constitute a reason for receiving certain sorts of good. For instance, let it be agreed, for the sake of argument, that the public school system provides a superior type of education, which it is a good thing to receive. It is then objected that access to this type of education is unequally distributed, because of its cost: among boys of equal promise or intelligence, only those from wealthy homes will receive it, and, indeed, boys of little promise or intelligence will receive it, if from wealthy homes; and this, the objection continues, is irrational.

The defender of the public school system might give two quite different sorts of answer to this objection; besides, that is, the obvious type of answer which merely disputes the facts alleged by the objector. One is the sort of answer already discussed in the case of need: that we may agree, perhaps, that boys of promise and intelligence have a right to a superior education, but in actual economic circumstances, this right cannot always be secured, etc. The other is more radical: this would dispute the premise of the objection that intelligence and promise are, at least by themselves, the grounds for receiving this superior type of education. While perhaps not asserting that wealth itself constitutes the ground, the defender of the system may claim that other characteristics significantly correlated with wealth are such grounds; or, again, that it is the purpose of this sort of school to maintain a tradition of leadership, and the best sort of people to maintain this will be people whose fathers were at such schools. We need not try to pursue such arguments here. The important point is that, while there can indeed be genuine disagreements about what constitutes the relevant sort of merit in such cases, such disagreements must also be disagreements about the nature of the good to be distributed. As such, the disagreements do not occur in a vacuum, nor are they logically free from restrictions. There is only a limited number of reasons for which education could be regarded as a good, and a limited number of purposes which education could rationally be said to serve; and to the limitations on this question, there correspond limitations on the sorts of merit or personal characteristic which could be rationally cited as grounds of access to this good. Here again we encounter a genuine strengthening of the very weak principle that, for differences in the way that people are treated, reasons should be given.

We may return now to the notion of equality of opportunity; understanding this in the normal political sense of equality of opportunity for *everyone in society* to secure certain goods. This notion is introduced into political discussion when there is question of the access to certain goods which, first, even if they are not desired by everyone in society, are desired by large numbers of people in all sections of society (either for themselves, or, as in the case of education, for their children), or would be desired by people in all sections of society if they knew about the goods in question and thought it possible for them to attain them; second, are goods which people may be said to earn or achieve; and third, are goods which not all the people who desire them can have. This third condition covers at least three different cases, however, which it is

worth distinguishing. Some desired goods, like positions of prestige, management, etc., are *by their very nature* limited: whenever there are some people who are in command or prestigious positions, there are necessarily others who are not. Other goods are *contingently* limited, in the sense that there are certain conditions of access to them which in fact not everyone satisfies, but there is no intrinsic limit to the numbers who might gain access to it by satisfying the conditions: university education is usually regarded in this light nowadays, as something which requires certain conditions of admission to it which in fact not everyone satisfies, but which an indefinite proportion of people might satisfy. Third, there are goods which are *fortuitously* limited, in the sense that although everyone or large numbers of people satisfy the conditions of access to them, there is just not enough of them to go round; so some more stringent conditions or system of rationing have to be imposed, to govern access in an imperfect situation. A good can, of course, be both contingently and fortuitously limited at once: when, due to shortage of supply, not even the people who are qualified to have it, limited in numbers though they are, can in every case have it. It is particularly worth distinguishing those kinds of limitation, as there can be significant differences of view about the way in which a certain good is limited. While most would now agree that high education is contingently limited, a Platonic view would regard it as necessarily limited.

Now the notion of equality of opportunity might be said to be the notion that a limited good shall in fact be allocated on grounds which do not *a priori* exclude any section of those that desire it. But this formulation is not really very clear. For suppose grammar school education (a good perhaps contingently, and certainly fortuitously, limited) is allocated on grounds of ability as tested at the age of 11; this would normally be advanced as an example of equality of opportunity, as opposed to a system of allocation on grounds of parents' wealth. But does not the criterion of ability exclude *a priori* a certain section of people, viz. those that are not able – just as the other excludes *a priori* those who are not wealthy? Here it will obviously be said that this was not what was meant by *a priori* exclusion: the present argument just equates this with exclusion of anybody, i.e. with the mere existence of some condition that has to be satisfied. What then is *a priori* exclusion? It must mean exclusion on grounds *other* than those appropriate or rational for the good in question. But this still will not do as it stands. For it would follow from this that so long as those allocating grammar school education on grounds of wealth thought that such grounds were appropriate or rational (as they might in one of the ways discussed above in connexion with public schools), they could sincerely describe their system as one of equality of opportunity – which is absurd.

Hence it seems that the notion of equality of opportunity is more complex than it first appeared. It requires not merely that there should be no exclusion from access on grounds other than those appropriate or rational for the good in question, but that the grounds considered appropriate for the good should themselves be such that people from all sections of society have an equal chance of satisfying them. What now is a 'section of society'? Clearly we cannot include under this term sections of the populace identified just by the characteristics with figure in the grounds for allocating the good – since, once more, any grounds at all must exclude some section of the populace. But what about sections identified by characteristics which are *correlated* with the grounds of exclusion? There are important difficulties here: to illustrate this, it may help first to take an imaginary example.

Suppose that in a certain society great prestige is attached to membership of a warrior class, the duties of which require great physical strength. This class has in the past been recruited from certain wealthy families only; but egalitarian reformers achieve a change in the rules, by which warriors are recruited from all sections of the society, on the results of a suitable competition. The effect of this, however, is that the wealthy families still provide virtually all the warriors, because the rest of the populace is so undernourished by reason of poverty that their physical strength is inferior to that of the wealthy and well nourished. The reformers protest that equality of opportunity has not really been achieved; the wealthy reply that in fact it has, and that the poor now have the opportunity of becoming warriors – it is just bad luck that their characteristics are such that they do not pass the test. 'We are not,' they might say, 'excluding anyone *for* being poor; we exclude people for being weak, and it is unfortunate that those who are poor are also weak.'

This answer would seem to most people feeble, and even cynical. This is for reasons similar to those discussed before in connexion with equality before the law; that the supposed equality of op-portunity is quite empty – indeed, one may say that it does not really exist – unless it is made more effective than this. For one knows that it could be made more effective; one knows that there is a causal connexion between being poor and being undernourished, and between being undernour-ished and being physically weak. One supposes further that something could be done – subject to whatever economic conditions obtain in the imagined society – to alter the distribution of wealth. All this being so, the appeal by the wealthy to the 'bad luck' of the poor must appear as disingenuous.

It seems then that a system of allocation will fall short of equality of opportunity if the allocation of the good in question in fact works out unequally or disproportionately between different sections of society, if the unsuccessful sections are under a disadvantage which could be removed by further reform or social action. This was very clear in the imaginary example that was given, because the causal connexions involved are simple and well known. In actual fact, however, the situations of this type that arise are more complicated, and it is easier to overlook the causal connexions involved. This is particularly so in the case of educational selection, where such slippery concepts as 'intel-lectual ability' are involved. It is a known fact that the system of selection for grammar schools by the '11+' examination favours children in direct pro-portion to their social class, the children of profes-sional homes having proportionately greater success than those from working class homes. We have every reason to suppose that these results are the product, in good part, of environmental fac-tors; and we further know that imaginative social reform, both of the primary educational system and of living conditions, would favourably effect those environmental factors. In these circumstan-ces, this system of educational selection falls short of equality of opportunity.[3]

This line of thought points to a connexion be-tween the idea of equality of opportunity, and the idea of equality of persons, which is stronger than might at first be suspected. We have seen that one is not really offering equality of opportunity to Smith and Jones if one contents oneself with ap-plying the same criteria to Smith and Jones at, say, the age of 11; what one is doing there is to apply the same criteria to Smith as affected by favourable conditions and to Jones as affected by unfavour-able but curable conditions. Here there is a neces-sary pressure to equal up the conditions: to give

Smith and *Jones* equality of opportunity involves regarding their conditions, where curable, as themselves part of what is done to Smith and Jones, and not part of Smith and Jones themselves. Their identity, for these purposes, does not include their curable environment, which is itself unequal and a contributor of inequality. This abstraction of persons in themselves from unequal environments is a way, if not of regarding them as equal, at least of moving recognizably in that direction; and is itself involved in equality of opportunity.

One might speculate about how far this movement of thought might go. The most conservative user of the notion of equality of opportunity is, if sincere, prepared to abstract the individual from some effects of his environment. We have seen that there is good reason to press this further, and to allow that the individuals whose opportunities are to be equal should be abstracted from more features of social and family background. Where should this stop? Should it even stop at the boundaries of heredity? Suppose it were discovered that when all curable environmental disadvantages had been dealt with, there was a residual genetic difference in brain constitution, for instance, which was correlated with differences in desired types of ability; but that the brain constitution could in fact be changed by an operation.[4] Suppose further that the wealthier classes could afford such an operation for their children, so that they always came out top of the educational system; would we then think that poorer children did not have equality of opportunity, because they had no opportunity to get rid of their genetic disadvantages?

Here we might think that our notion of personal identity itself was beginning to give way; we might well wonder *who were* the people whose advantages and disadvantages were being discussed in this way. But it would be wrong, I think, to try to solve this problem simply by saying that in the supposed circumstances our notion of personal identity would have collapsed in such a way that we could no longer speak of the individuals involved – in the end, we could still pick out the individuals by spatio-temporal criteria, if no more. Our objections against the system suggested in this fantasy must, I think, be moral rather than metaphysical. They need not concern us here. What is interesting about the fantasy, perhaps, is that if one reached this state of affairs, the individuals would be regarded as in all respects equal in themselves – for in themselves they would be, as it were, pure subjects or bearers of predicates, everything else about them, including their genetic inheritance, being regarded as a fortuitous and changeable characteristic. In these circumstances, where everything about a person is controllable, equality of opportunity and absolute equality seem to coincide; and this itself illustrates something about the notion of equality of opportunity.

I said that we need not discuss here the moral objections to the kind of world suggested in this fantasy. There is, however, one such point that is relevant to the different aspects of equality that have been discussed in this paper as a whole. One objection that we should instinctively feel about the fantasy world is that far too much emphasis was being placed on achieving high ability; that the children were just being regarded as locations of abilities. I think we should still feel this even if everybody (with results hard to imagine) was treated in this way; when not everybody was so treated, the able would also be more successful than others, and those very concerned with producing the ability would probably also be over-concerned with success. The moral objections to the excessive concern with such aims are, interestingly, not unconnected with the ideal of equality itself; they are connected with equality in the sense discussed in the earlier sections of this paper, the equality of human beings despite their differences, and in particular with the complex of notions considered in the second section under the heading of 'respect'.

This conflict within the ideals of equality arises even without resort to the fantasy world. It exists today in the feeling that a thorough-going emphasis on equality of opportunity must destroy a certain sense of common humanity which is itself an ideal of equality.[5] The ideals that are felt to be in conflict with equality of opportunity are not necessarily other ideals of equality – there may be an independent appeal to the values of community life, or to the moral worth of a more integrated and less competitive society. Nevertheless, the idea of equality itself is often invoked in this connexion, and not, I think, inappropriately.

If the idea of equality ranges as widely as I have suggested, this type of conflict is bound to arise with it. It is an idea which, on the one hand, is invoked in connexion with the distribution of certain goods, some at least of which are bound to confer on their possessors some preferred status or prestige. On the other hand, the idea of equality of respect is one which urges us to give less consideration to those structures in which people enjoy status or prestige, and to consider people independently of those goods, on the distribution of which equality of opportunity precisely focuses our, and their, attention. There is perhaps nothing formally incompatible in these two applications of the idea of equality: one might hope for a society in which there existed both a fair, rational and appropriate distribution of these goods, and no contempt, condescension or lack of human communication between persons who were more and less successful recipients of the distribution. Yet in actual fact, there are deep psychological and social obstacles to the realization of this hope; as things are, the competitiveness and considerations of prestige that surround the first application of equality certainly militate against the second. How far this situation is inevitable, and how far in an economically developed and dynamic society, in which certain skills and talents are necessarily at a premium, the obstacles to a wider realization of equality might be overcome, I do not think that we know: these are in good part questions of psychology and sociology, to which we do not have the answers.

When one is faced with the spectacle of the various elements of the idea of equality pulling in these different directions, there is a strong temptation, if one does not abandon the idea altogether, to abandon some of its elements: to claim, for instance, that equality of opportunity is the only

ideal that is at all practicable, and equality of respect a vague and perhaps nostalgic illusion; or, alternatively, that equality of respect is genuine equality, and equality of opportunity an inegalitarian betrayal of the ideal – all the more so if it were thoroughly pursued, as now it is not. To succumb to either of these simplifying formulae would, I think, be a mistake. Certainly, a highly rational and efficient application of the ideas of equal opportunity, unmitigated by the other considerations, could lead to a quite inhuman society (if it worked – which, granted a well-known desire of parents to secure a position for their children at least as good as their own, is unlikely). On the other hand, an ideal of equality of respect that made no contact with such things as the economic needs of society for certain skills, and human desire for some sorts of prestige, would be condemned to a futile Utopianism, and to having no rational effect on the distribution of goods, position and power that would inevitably proceed. If, moreover, as I have suggested, it is not really known how far, by new forms of social structure and of education, these conflicting claims might be reconciled, it is all the more obvious that we should not throw one set of claims out of the window; but should rather seek, in each situation, the best way of eating and having as much cake as possible. It is an uncomfortable situation, but the discomfort is just that of genuine political thought. It is no greater with equality than it is with liberty, or any other noble and substantial political ideal.

Notes

1 For an illuminating discussion of this and related questions, see R. Wollheim and I. Berlin, *Equality*, *Proceedings of the Aristotelian Society*, vol. LVI (1955–6), p. 281 seq.
2 For instance, R. M. Hare: see his *Language of Morals*, Oxford: Clarendon Press, 1952.
3 See on this C. A. R. Crosland, *Public Schools and English Education, Encounter*, July 1961.

4 A yet more radical situation – but one more likely to come about – would be that in which an individual's characteristics could be *pre-arranged* by interference with the genetic material. The dizzying consequences of this I shall not try to explore.
5 See, for example, Michael Young, *The Rise of the Meritocracy*, London: Thames & Hudson, 1958.

31

Equality and Priority

Derek Parfit

In his article 'Equality', Nagel imagines that he has two children, one healthy and happy, the other suffering from some painful handicap. Nagel's family could either move to a city where the second child could receive special treatment, or move to a suburb where the first child would flourish. Nagel writes:

> This is a difficult choice on any view. To make it a test for the value of equality, I want to suppose that the case has the following feature: the gain to the first child of moving to the suburb is substantially greater than the gain to the second child of moving to the city.

He then comments:

> If one chose to move to the city, it would be an egalitarian decision. It is more urgent to benefit the second child, even though the benefit we can give him is less than the benefit we can give to the first child.[1]

My aim, in this paper, is to discuss this kind of reasoning.

I

Nagel's decision turns on the relative importance of two facts: he could give one child a greater benefit, but the other child is worse off. There are countless cases of this kind. In these cases, when we are choosing between two acts or policies, one relevant fact is how great the resulting benefits would be. For Utilitarians, that is all that matters. On their view, we should always aim for the greatest sum of benefits. But, for egalitarians, it also matters how well off the beneficiaries would be. We should sometimes choose a smaller sum of benefits, for the sake of a better distribution.

Should we aim for a better distribution? If so, when and how? These are difficult questions, but their subject matter is, in a way, simple. It is enough to consider different possible states of affairs, or outcomes, each involving the same set of people. We imagine knowing how well off, in these outcomes, these people would be. We then ask whether either outcome would be better, or would be the outcome that we ought to bring about.

Some writers reject these questions. Nozick objects, for example, that these questions wrongly assume that there is something to be distributed. Most goods, he argues, are not up for distribution, or redistribution.[2] They are goods to which particular people already have entitlements, or special claims. Others make similar claims about desert.

These objections we can set aside. We can assume that, in the cases we are considering, no one

Originally published in *Ratio* 10 (1997): 202–21; reprinted in Andrew Mason (ed.), *Ideals of Equality* (Oxford: Blackwell Publishers, 1998), pp. 1–20. Reprinted by permission of Blackwell Publishing Ltd. An expanded version of this chapter appears in *The Ideal of Equality*, edited by Matthew Clayton and Andrew Williams (London: Macmillan, 2000), pp. 81–125.

deserves to be better off than anyone else; nor does anyone have special claims to whatever we are distributing. Since there are *some* cases of this kind, we have a subject. If we can reach conclusions, we can then consider how widely these apply. Like Rawls and others, I believe that, at the fundamental level, most cases are of this kind.

To ask my questions, we need only two assumptions. First, some people can be worse off than others, in ways that are morally relevant. Second, these differences can be matters of degree. To describe my imagined cases, I shall use figures. Nagel's choice, for example, can be shown as follows:

	The first child	The second child
Move to the city:	20	10
Move to the suburb:	25	9

Such figures misleadingly suggest precision. Even in principle, I believe, there could not be precise differences between how well off different people are. I intend these figures to show only that the choice between these outcomes makes much more difference to Nagel's first child, but that, in both outcomes, the second child would be much worse off.

One point about my figures is important. Each unit is a roughly equal benefit, however well off the person is who receives it. If someone rises from 99 to 100, this person benefits as much as someone else who rises from 9 to 10. Without this assumption we cannot ask some of our questions. Thus we cannot ask whether some benefit would matter more if it came to someone who was worse off.

Since each extra unit is an equal benefit, however well off the recipient is, these units should not be thought of as equal quantities of resources. The same increase in resources usually brings greater benefits to those who are worse off. But these benefits need not be thought of in Utilitarian terms, as involving greater happiness, or desire-fulfilment. They might be improvements in health, or length of life, or education, or range of opportunities, or involve any other goods that we take to be morally important.[3]

II

Most of us believe in some kind of equality. We believe in political equality, or equality before the law, or we believe that everyone has equal rights, or that everyone's interests should be given equal weight. Though these kinds of equality are of great importance, they are not my subject here. I am concerned with people's being *equally well off*. To be egalitarians, in my sense, this is the kind of equality in which we must believe.

Some egalitarians believe that, if people were equally well off, that would be a better state of affairs. If we hold this view, we can be called *Teleological* – or, for short, *Telic* – Egalitarians. We accept

> *The Principle of Equality*: It is in itself bad if some people are worse off than others.[4]

Suppose that the people in some community could all be either equally well off, or equally badly off. The Principle of Equality does not tell us that the second would be worse. To explain that obvious truth, we might appeal to

> *The Principle of Utility*: It is in itself better if people are better off.

When people would be on average better off, or would receive a greater sum of benefits, we can say, for brevity, that there would be more *utility*.

If we cared only about equality, we would be *Pure* Egalitarians. If we cared only about utility, we would be Utilitarians. Most of us accept a *pluralist* view: one that appeals to more than one principle or value. According to *Pluralist Egalitarians*, it would be better both if there was more equality, and if there was more utility. In deciding which of two outcomes would be better, we give weight to both these values.

These values may conflict. One of two outcomes may be in one way worse, because there would be more inequality, but in another way better, because there would be more utility. We must then decide which of these two facts would be more important. Consider, for example, the following possibilities:

(1) Everyone at 150
(2) Half at 199 Half at 200
(3) Half at 101 Half at 200

For Pure Egalitarians, (1) is the best outcome, since it contains the least inequality. For Utilitarians, (1) is the worst outcome, since it contains the least utility. For most Pluralist Egalitarians,

(1) would be neither the best nor the worst of these outcomes. (1) would be, on balance, worse than (2), since it would be *much* worse in terms of utility, and only *slightly* better in terms of equality. Similarly, (1) would be better than (3), since it would be much better in terms of equality, and only slightly worse in terms of utility.

In many cases the Pluralist View is harder to apply. Compare

(1)   Everyone at 150

with

(4)   Half at N Half at 200.

If we are Pluralist Egalitarians, for which values of N would we believe (1) to be worse than (4)? For some range of values – such as 120 to 150 – we may find this question hard to answer. And it may not have an answer. The relative importance of equality and utility may be, even in principle, imprecise.

We should next distinguish two kinds of value. If we claim that equality is good, we may mean only that it has good effects. If people are unequal, for example, that can produce conflict, or damage the self-respect of those who are worst off, or put some people in the power of others. If we care about equality because we are concerned with such effects, we believe that equality has *instrumental* value, or is good as a means. But I am concerned with a different idea. For true Egalitarians, equality has *intrinsic* value, or is in itself good.

This distinction is important. If we believe that, besides having bad effects, inequality is in itself bad, we shall think it to be worse. And we shall think it bad even when it has no bad effects.

To illustrate this second point, consider what I shall call *the Divided World*. The two halves of the world's population are, we can suppose, unaware of each other's existence. Perhaps the Atlantic has not yet been crossed. Consider next two possible states of affairs:

(1)   Half at 100 Half at 200
(2)   Everyone at 145

Of these two states, (1) is in one way better than (2), since people are on average better off. But we may believe that, all things considered, (1) is worse than (2). How could we explain this view?

If we are Telic Egalitarians, our explanation would be this. While it is good that, in (1), people are on average better off, it is bad that some people are worse off than others. The badness of this inequality morally outweighs the extra benefits.

In making such a claim, we could not appeal to inequality's bad effects. Since the two halves of the world's population are quite unconnected, this inequality has no effects. If we are to claim that (1) is worse because of its inequality, we must claim that this inequality is in itself bad.[5]

III

We can now turn to a different kind of egalitarian view. According to *Deontic Egalitarians*, though we should sometimes aim for equality, that is *not* because we would thereby make the outcome better. On this view, it is not in itself bad if some people are worse off than others. When we ought to aim for equality, that is always for some other moral reason.

Such a view typically appeals to claims about *comparative* justice. Whether people are unjustly treated, in this comparative sense, depends on whether they are treated *differently* from other people. Thus it may be unfair if, in a distribution of resources, some people are denied their share. Fairness may require that, if certain goods are given to some, they should be given to all.

Another kind of justice is *non-comparative*. Whether people are unjustly treated, in this other sense, depends only on facts about them. It is irrelevant whether others are treated differently. Thus, if we treated no one as they deserved, this treatment would be unjust in the non-comparative sense. But, if we treated everyone equally unjustly, there would be no comparative injustice.[6]

It can be hard to distinguish these two kinds of justice, and there are difficult questions about the relation between them.[7] One point should be mentioned here. Non-comparative justice may require us to produce equality. Perhaps, if everyone were equally deserving, we should make everyone equally well off. But such equality would be merely the effect of giving people what they deserved. Only comparative justice makes equality our aim.

When I said that, in my examples, no one deserves to be better off than others, I did not mean that everyone is equally deserving. I meant that, in these cases, questions of desert do not arise. It is only comparative justice with which we are here concerned.

There is another relevant distinction. In some cases, justice is *purely procedural*. It requires only that we act in a certain way. For example, when some good cannot be divided, we may be required to conduct a lottery, which gives everyone an equal chance to receive this good. In other cases, justice is in part *substantive*. Here too, justice may require a certain kind of procedure; but there is a separate criterion of what the outcome ought to be. One example would be the claim that people should be given equal shares.[8]

We can now redescribe our two kinds of Egalitarianism. On the Telic View, inequality is bad; on the Deontic View, it is unjust.

It may be objected that, when inequality is unjust, it is, for that reason, bad. But this does not undermine this way of drawing our distinction. On the Deontic View, injustice is a special kind of badness, one that necessarily involves wrong-doing. What is unjust, and therefore bad, is not strictly the state of affairs, but the way in which it was produced.

There is one kind of case which most clearly separates these two views: those in which some inequality cannot be avoided. For Deontic Egalitarians, if nothing can be done, there can be no injustice. In Rawls's words, if some situation 'is unalterable . . . the question of justice does not arise'.[9]

Consider, for example, the inequality in our natural endowments. Some of us are born more talented or healthier than others, or are more fortunate in other ways. If we are Deontic Egalitarians, we shall not believe that such inequality is in itself bad. We might agree that, if we *could* distribute talents, it would be unjust or unfair to distribute them unequally. But, except when there are bad effects, we shall see nothing to regret in the inequalities produced by the random shuffling of our genes. Many Telic Egalitarians take a different view. They believe that, even when such inequality is unavoidable, it is in itself bad.[10]

These views differ in several other ways. The Telic View, for example, is likely to have wider scope. If we believe that inequality is in itself bad, we may think it bad whoever the people are between whom it holds. It may seem to make no difference whether these people are in the same or different communities. We may also think it irrelevant what the respects are in which some people are worse off than others: whether they have less income, or worse health, or are less fortunate in other ways. *Any* inequality, if undeserved and unchosen, we may think bad. Nor,

third, will it seem to make a difference how such inequality arose. That is implied by the very notion of intrinsic badness. When we ask whether some state is in itself bad, it is irrelevant how it came about.

If we are Deontic Egalitarians, our view may have none of these features. Though there are many versions of the Deontic View, one large group are broadly contractarian. Such views often appeal to the idea of reciprocity, or mutual benefit. On some views of this kind, when goods are co-operatively produced, and no one has special claims, all the contributors should get equal shares. There are here two restrictions. First, what is shared are only the fruits of co-operation. Nothing is said about other goods, such as those that come from nature. Second, the distribution covers only those who produce these goods. Those who cannot contribute, such as the handicapped, or children, or future generations, have no claims.[11]

Other views of this kind are less restrictive. They may cover all the members of the same community, and all kinds of good. But they still exclude outsiders. It is irrelevant that, in other communities, there are people who are much worse off. On such views, if there is inequality between people in different communities, this need not be anyone's concern. Since the greatest inequalities are on this global scale, this restriction has immense importance.

Consider next the question of causation. The Telic View naturally applies to all cases. On this view, we always have a reason to prevent or reduce inequality, if we can. If we are Deontic Egalitarians, we might think the same; but that is less likely. Since our view is not about the goodness of outcomes, it may cover only inequalities that result from acts, or only those that are intentionally produced. And it may tell us to be concerned only with the inequalities that we ourselves produce. On such a view, when we are responsible for some distribution, we ought to distribute equally. But, when no one is responsible, inequality is not unjust. In such cases, there is nothing morally amiss. We have no reason to remove such inequality, by redistribution. Here again, since this view has narrower scope, this can make a great practical difference.

IV

Let us now consider two objections to the Telic View.

On the widest version of this view, *any* inequality is bad. It is bad, for example, that some people are sighted and others are blind. We would therefore have a moral reason to take single eyes from the sighted and give them to the blind. That conclusion may seem horrific.

Such a reaction is, I believe, mistaken. To set aside some irrelevant complications, we can imagine a simplified example. Suppose that, after some genetic change, children are henceforth born as twins, one of whom is always blind. And suppose that, as a universal policy, operations are performed after every birth, in which one eye from the sighted twin is transplanted into its blind sibling. That would be non-voluntary redistribution, since newborn babies cannot give consent. But I am inclined to believe that such a policy would be justified.

Some people would reject this policy, believing that it violates the rights of the sighted twins. But that belief provides no ground for rejecting the Telic View. As pluralists, Telic Egalitarians could agree that the State should not redistribute organs. Since they do not believe equality to be the only value, they could agree that, in this example, some other principle has greater weight, or is overriding. Their belief is only that, if we all had one eye, this would be *in one way* better than if half of us had two eyes and the other half had none. Far from being horrific, that belief is clearly true. If we all had one eye, that would be much better for all of the people who would otherwise be blind.[12]

A second objection is more serious. If inequality is bad, its disappearance must be in one way a change for the better, however this change occurs. Suppose that, in some natural disaster, those who are better off lose all their extra resources, and become as badly off as everyone else. Since this change would remove the inequality, it must be in one way welcome, on the Telic View. Though this disaster would be worse for some people, and better for no one, it must be, in one way, a change for the better. Similarly, it would be in one way an improvement if we destroyed the eyes of the sighted, not to benefit the blind, but only to make the sighted blind. These implications can be more plausibly regarded as monstrous, or absurd. The appeal to such examples we can call *the Levelling Down Objection*.[13]

It is worth repeating that, to criticize Egalitarians by appealing to this objection, it is not enough to claim that it would be *wrong* to produce equality by levelling down. Since they are pluralists, who do not care only about equality, Egalitarians could

accept that claim. Our objection must be that, if we achieve equality by levelling down, there is *nothing* good about what we have done. Similarly, if some natural disaster makes everyone equally badly off, that is not in any way good news. These claims do contradict the Telic Egalitarian View.

I shall return to the Levelling Down Objection. The point to notice now is that, on a Deontic view, we avoid this objection. If we are Deontic Egalitarians, we do not believe that inequality is bad, so we are not forced to admit that, on our view, it would be in one way better if inequality were removed by levelling down. We may believe that we have a reason to remove inequality only *when*, and only *because*, our way of doing so benefits the people who are worse off. Or we may believe that, when some people are worse off than others, through no fault or choice of theirs, they have a special claim to be raised up to the level of the others, but they have no claim that others be brought down to their level.

Given these differences between the Telic and Deontic Views, it is important to decide which view, if either, we should accept. If we are impressed by the Levelling Down Objection, we may be tempted by the Deontic View. But, if we give up the Telic View, we may find it harder to justify some of our beliefs. If inequality is not in itself bad, we may find it harder to defend our view that we should often redistribute resources. And some of our beliefs might have to go. Reconsider the Divided World, in which the two possible states are these:

(1) Half at 100   Half at 200
(2) Everyone at 145

In outcome (1) there is inequality. But, since the two groups are unaware of each other's existence, this inequality was not deliberately produced, or maintained. Since this inequality does not involve wrong-doing, there is no injustice. On the Deontic View, there is nothing more to say. If we believe that (1) is worse, and because of the inequality, we must accept the Telic form of the Egalitarian View. We must claim that the inequality in (1) is in itself bad.

We might, however, give a different explanation. Rather than believing in equality, we might be especially concerned about those people who are worse off. That could be our reason for preferring (2).

Let us now consider this alternative.

V

In discussing his imagined case, Nagel writes:

> If one chose to move to the city, it would be an egalitarian decision. It is more urgent to benefit the second child . . . This urgency is not necessarily decisive. It may be outweighed by other considerations, for equality is not the only value. But it is a factor, and it depends on the worse off position of the second child. An improvement in his situation is more important than an equal or somewhat greater improvement in the situation of the first child.[14]

This passage contains the idea that equality has value. But it gives more prominence to another idea. It is more important, Nagel claims, to benefit the child who is worse off. That idea can lead us to a quite different view.

Consider first those people who are badly off: those who are suffering, or those whose basic needs have not been met. It is widely believed that we should give priority to helping such people. This would be claimed even by Utilitarians, since, if people are badly off, they are likely to be easier to help.

Nagel, and others, make a stronger claim. On their view, it is more urgent to help these people even if they are *harder* to help. While Utilitarians claim that we should give these people priority when, and because, we can help them *more*, this view claims that we should give them priority, even when we can help them *less*.

Some people apply this view only to the two groups of the well off and the badly off.[15] But I shall consider a broader view, which applies to everyone. On what I shall call

The Priority View. Benefiting people matters more the worse off these people are.

For Utilitarians, the moral importance of each benefit depends only on how great this benefit would be. For *Prioritarians*, it also depends on how well off the person is to whom this benefit comes. We should not give equal weight to equal benefits, whoever receives them. Benefits to the worse off should be given more weight.[16] This priority is not, however, absolute. On this view, benefits to the worse off could be morally outweighed by sufficiently great benefits to the better off. If we ask what would be sufficient, there may not always be a precise answer. But there would be many cases in which the answer would be clear.[17]

On the Priority View, I have said, it is more important to benefit those who are worse off. But this claim does not, by itself, amount to a different view, since it would be made by all Egalitarians. If we believe that we should aim for equality, we shall think it more important to benefit those who are worse off, since such benefits reduce inequality. If *this* is why we give such benefits priority, we do not hold the Priority View. On this view, as I define it here, we do *not* believe in equality. We do not think it in itself bad, or unjust, that some people are worse off than others. That is what makes this a distinctive view.

The Priority View can be easily misunderstood. On this view, if I am worse off than you, benefits to me matter more. Is this *because* I am worse off than you? In one sense, yes. But this has nothing to do with my relation to you.

It may help to use this analogy. People at higher altitudes find it harder to breathe. Is this because they are higher up than other people? In one sense, yes. But they would find it just as hard to breathe even if there were no other people who were lower down. In the same way, on the Priority View, benefits to the worse off matter more, but that is only because these people are at a lower *absolute* level. It is irrelevant that these people are worse off *than others*. Benefits to them would matter just as much even if there *were* no others who were better off.

The chief difference is, then, this. Egalitarians are concerned with *relativities*: with how each person's level compares with the level of other people. On the Priority View, we are concerned only with people's absolute levels. This is a fundamental structural difference. Because of this difference, there are several ways in which these views have different implications.

One example concerns scope. Telic Egalitarians may, I have said, give their view wide scope. They may believe that inequality is bad even when it holds between people who have no connections with each other. This may seem dubious. Why would it matter if, in some far off land, and quite unknown to me, there are other people who are better off than me?

On the Priority View, there is no ground for such doubts. This view naturally has universal scope. If it is more important to benefit one of two people, because this person is worse off, it is irrelevant whether these people are in the same community, or are aware of each other's existence. The greater urgency of benefiting this person does not depend on her relation to the other person, but only on her lower absolute level.

These views differ in other ways, which I have no space to discuss here. But I have described the kind of case in which these views most deeply disagree. These are the cases which raise the Levelling Down Objection. Egalitarians face this objection because they believe that inequality is in itself bad. If we accept the Priority View, we avoid this objection. On this view, except when it is bad for people, inequality does not matter.

VI

Though equality and priority are different ideas, this distinction has been often overlooked.

One reason is that, especially in earlier centuries, Egalitarians have often fought battles in which this distinction did not arise. They were demanding legal or political equality, or attacking arbitrary privileges, or differences in status. These are not the kinds of good to which our distinction applies. And it is here that the demand for equality is most plausible.

Second, when Egalitarians considered other kinds of good, they often assumed that, if equality were achieved, this would either increase the sum of these goods, or would at least not reduce this sum. In either of these cases, equality and priority cannot conflict.

Third, even when a move to equality would reduce the total sum of benefits, Egalitarians often assumed that such a move would at least bring *some* benefits to the people who were worse off. In such cases, equality and priority could not deeply conflict. Egalitarians ignored the cases in which equality could not be achieved except by levelling down.

Since this distinction has been overlooked, some writers have made claims that are not really about equality, and would be better stated as claims about priority. For example, Nagel writes:

> To defend equality as a good in itself, one would have to argue that improvements in the lot of people lower on the scale of well-being took priority over greater improvements to those higher on the scale.[18]

In the example with which we began, Nagel similarly claims that it would be 'more urgent' to benefit the handicapped child. He then writes:

> This urgency is not necessarily decisive. It may be outweighed by other considerations, for equality is not the only value.[19]

These remarks suggest that, to the question 'Why is it more urgent to benefit this child?', Nagel would answer, 'Because this would reduce the inequality between these two children'. But I doubt that this is really Nagel's view. Would it be just as urgent to benefit the handicapped child, even if he had no sibling who was better off? I suspect that, on Nagel's view, it would. Nagel would then, though using the language of equality, really be appealing to the Priority View.[20]

Consider next the idea of distribution according to need. Several writers argue that, when we are moved by this idea, our aim is to achieve equality. Thus Raphael writes:

> If the man with greater needs is given more than the man with lesser needs, the intended result is that each of them should have (or at least approach) the same level of satisfaction; the inequality of nature is corrected.[21]

When discussing the giving of extra resources to meet the needs of the ill, or handicapped, Norman similarly writes:

> the underlying idea is one of equality. The aim is that everybody should, as far as possible, have an equally worthwhile life.[22]

As before, if that were the aim, it could be as well achieved by levelling down. This cannot be what Norman means. He could avoid this implication by omitting the word 'equally', so that his claim became: 'the aim is that everybody should, as far as possible, have a worthwhile life.' With this revision, Norman could not claim that equality is the underlying idea. But that, I believe, would strengthen his position. Distribution according to need is better regarded as a form of the Priority View.[23]

What these writers claim about need, some have claimed about all kinds of distributive principle. For example, Ake writes:

> Justice in a society as a whole ought to be understood as a complete equality of the overall

level of benefits and burdens of each member of that society.

The various principles of distributive justice, Ake claims, can all be interpreted as having as their aim 'to restore a situation of complete equality to the greatest degree possible'.[24] Some writers even make such claims about retributive justice. They argue that, by committing crimes, criminals make themselves better off than those who keep the law. The aim of punishment is to restore them to their previous level.

These writers, I believe, claim too much for equality. But there are some plausible views which are rightly expressed in egalitarian terms. For example, Cohen suggests that 'the right reading of egalitarianism' is that 'its purpose is to eliminate involuntary disadvantage'.[25] He means by this *comparative* disadvantage: being worse off than others. This is an essentially relational idea. Only equality could eliminate such disadvantage. Cohen's view could not be re-expressed in the language of priority. Similar assumptions underlie Rawls's view, whose complexity leads me to ignore it here.

Some Egalitarians are not moved by the Levelling Down Objection. For example, Ake writes

What about the case of someone who suddenly comes into good fortune, perhaps entirely by his or her own efforts? Should additional burdens . . . be imposed on that person in order to restore equality and safeguard justice? . . . Why wouldn't it be just to impose any kind of additional burden whatsoever on him in order to restore the equality? The answer is that, strictly speaking, it would be . . . [26]

Ake admits that, on his view, it *would* be just to level down, by imposing burdens on this person. What he concedes is only that the claim of justice would here be overridden. Levelling down would be in one way good, or be something that we would have a moral reason to do. Similarly, Temkin writes:

I, for one, believe that inequality is bad. But do I *really* think that there is some respect in which a world where only some are blind is worse than one where all are? Yes. Does this mean I think it would be better if we blinded everybody? No. Equality is not all that matters.[27]

Several other writers make such claims.[28]

VII

Since some writers are unmoved by the Levelling Down Objection, let us now reconsider that objection. Consider these alternatives:

(1) Everyone at some level
(2) Some at this level   Others better off

In outcome (1) everyone is equally well off. In outcome (2), some people are better off, but in a way that is worse for no one. For Telic Egalitarians, the inequality in (2) is in itself bad. Could this make (2), all things considered, a worse outcome than (1)?

Some Egalitarians answer Yes. These people do not believe that the avoidance of inequality always matters most. But they regard inequality as a great evil. On their view, a move to inequality *can* make an outcome worse, even when this outcome would be better for everyone. Those who hold this view we can call *Strong Egalitarians*.

Others hold a different view. Since they believe that inequality is bad, they agree that outcome (2) is *in one way* worse than outcome (1). But they do not believe that (2) is worse all things considered. In a move from (1) to (2), some people would become better off. According to these Egalitarians, the loss of equality would be morally outweighed by the benefits to these people. (2) would be, on balance, better than (1). Those who hold this view we can call *Moderates*.

This version of Egalitarianism is often overlooked, or dismissed. People assume that, if we are Egalitarians, we must be against a move to inequality, even when this move would be bad for no one. If we regard such inequality as outweighed by the extra benefits, our view must, they assume, be trivial.[29]

That assumption is mistaken. If some change would increase inequality, but in a way that is worse for no one, the inequality must come from benefits to certain people. And there cannot be a *great* loss of equality unless these benefits are also great. Since these gains and losses would roughly march in step, there is room for Moderates to hold a significant position. They believe that, in all such cases, the gain in utility would outweigh the loss in equality. That is consistent with the claim that, in many other cases, that would not be so. Moderates can claim that *some* gains in utility, even if *great*, would *not* outweigh some losses in equality. Consider, for example, these alternatives:

(1) All at 100
(4) Half at 100   Half at 200
(5) Half at 70   Half at 200.

Moderates believe that, compared with (1), (4) is better. But they might claim that (5) is worse. Since (5) would involve a much greater sum of benefits, that is not a trivial claim.

Return now to the Levelling Down Objection. Strong Egalitarians believe that, in some cases, a move towards inequality, even though it would be worse for no one, would make the outcome worse.[30] This view may seem incredible. One of two outcomes *cannot* be worse, we may claim, if it would be worse for no one. To challenge Strong Egalitarians, it would be enough to defend this claim. To challenge Moderates, we must defend the stronger claim that, when inequality is worse for no one, it is not in any way bad.

Many of us would make this stronger claim. It is widely assumed that nothing can be bad if it is bad for no one. This we can call the *Person-affecting View*.

This view might be defended by an appeal to some account of the nature of morality, or moral reasoning. According to some writers, for example, to explain the impersonal sense in which one of two outcomes can be *worse* – or worse, period – we must appeal to claims about what would be worse *for* particular people. The Person-affecting View can also be supported by various kinds of contractualism.[31]

Egalitarians might reply by defending a different meta-ethical view. Or they might argue that, when the Person-affecting View is applied to certain other questions, it has unacceptable implications, since it conflicts too sharply with some of our beliefs.[32] Since I have no space to discuss these questions here, I shall merely express an opinion. The Person-affecting View has, I believe, less plausibility than, and cannot be used to strengthen, the Levelling Down Objection.

VIII

I shall now summarize what I have claimed. According to Telic Egalitarians, it is in itself bad, or unfair, if some people are worse off than others

through no fault or choice of theirs. Though this view is widely held, and can seem very plausible, it faces the Levelling Down Objection. This objection seems to me to have great force, but is not, I think, decisive.

Suppose that we began by being Telic Egalitarians, but we are convinced by this objection. We cannot believe that, if the removal of inequality would be bad for some people, and better for no one, this change would be in any way good. If we are to salvage something of our view, we then have two alternatives.

We might become Deontic Egalitarians. We might come to believe that, though we should sometimes aim for equality, that is not because we would thereby make the outcome better. We must then explain and defend our beliefs in some other way. And the resulting view may have narrower scope. For example, it may apply only to goods of certain kinds, such as those that are co-operatively produced, and it may apply only to inequality between members of the same community.

We may also have to abandon some of our beliefs. Reconsider the Divided World:

(1) Half at 100   Half at 200
(2) Everyone at 145

On the Deontic View, we cannot claim that it would be better if the situation changed from (1) to (2). This view is only about what people ought to do, and makes no comparisons between states of affairs.

Our alternative is to move to the Priority View. We could then keep our belief about the Divided World. It is true that, in a change from (1) to (2), the better off would lose more than the worse off would gain. That is why, in utilitarian terms, (2) is worse than (1). But, on the Priority View, though the better off would lose more, the gains to the worse off count for more. Benefits to the worse off do more to make the outcome better. That could be why (1) is worse than (2).

The views that I have been discussing often coincide. But, as I have tried to show, they are quite different. They can support different beliefs, and policies, and they can be challenged and defended in different ways. Taxonomy, though unexciting, needs to be done. Until we have a clearer view of the alternatives, we cannot hope to decide which view is true, or is the best view.

Notes

1 Thomas Nagel, *Mortal Question* (Cambridge: Cambridge University Press, 1979), pp. 123–4. See also Nagel's *Equality and Partiality* (New York: Oxford University Press, 1991).

2 Robert Nozick, *Anarchy, State, and Utopia* (New York: Basic Books, 1974), pp. 149–50.

3 For two such broader accounts of well-being, see Amartya Sen, 'Capability and Well-Being', in *The Quality of Life*, edited by Martha Nussbaum and Amartya Sen (Oxford: Oxford University Press, 1993), Amartya Sen, *Inequality Reexamined* (Oxford: Oxford University Press, 1992), ch. 3; and Thomas Scanlon, 'Value, Desire, and the Quality of Life', in Nussbaum and Sen, op. cit.

4 We might add, 'through no fault or choice of theirs'. In a fuller statement of this principle, we would need to assess the relative badness of different patterns of inequality. But we can here ignore these complications. They are well discussed in Larry Temkin's *Inequality* (New York: Oxford University Press, 1993).

5 In his paper in this volume, which I cannot properly discuss here, Richard Norman writes: '[Parfit] asks us whether (1) is worse that (2). I have to confess that I do not know how to answer that question, and I do not think that this is simply a personal confession on my part…I want to say of Parfit's Divided world example that when you abstract the question from the social context in which we make judgements about equality and inequality, it is no longer clear how to answer it'. It is, I agree, not obvious whether the inequality in (1) is bad. But that it is not because we cannot make value judgments about such examples. It is clear that (1) would be better than

    (3)   Half at 100, Half at 50,

but worse than

    (4)   Everyone at 200.

6 Cf. Joel Feinberg, 'Noncomparative Justice', *Philosophical Review* 83 (1974).

7 Cf. Philip Montague, 'Comparative and Non-comparative Justice', *Philosophical Quarterly* 30 (1980).

8 There is an intermediate case. Justice may require a certain outcome, but only because this avoids a procedural flaw. One such flaw is partiality. Suppose that we have to distribute certain publicly-owned goods. If we could easily divide these goods, others might be rightly suspicious if we gave to different people unequal shares. That might involve favouritism, or wrongful discrimination. We may thus believe that, to avoid these flaws, we should distribute these goods equally.

    How does this view differ from a view that requires equality for substantive reasons? One difference is this. Suppose that we have manifestly tried to distribute equally, but our procedure has innocently failed. If we aimed for equality only to avoid the taint of partiality or discrimination, there would be no case for correcting the result. (For discussions of these points, see Robert Goodin, 'Egalitarianism, Fetishistic and Otherwise', *Ethics* 98 (1987); and Lawrence Sager and Lewis Kornhauser, 'Just Lotteries', *Social Science Information* (Sage, London, Newbury Park and New Delhi, vol. 27, 1988).)

9 John Rawls, *A Theory of Justice*, (Cambridge: Harvard University Press, 1971), p. 291.

10 There is now a complication. Those who hold this second view do not merely think that such inequality is bad. They often speak of natural injustice. On their view, it is unjust or unfair that some people are born less able, or less healthy, than others. Similarly, it is unfair if nature bestows on some richer resources. Talk of unfairness here is sometimes claimed to make no sense. I believe that it does make sense. But, even on this view, our distinction stands. According to Telic Egalitarians, it is the state of affairs which is bad, or unjust; but Deontic Egalitarians are concerned only with what we ought to do.

11 See, for example, David Gauthier, *Morals by Agreement* (Oxford: Oxford University Press, 1980), pp. 18 and 268.

12 Cf. Nozick, op. cit., p. 206 (though Nozick's target here is not the Principle of Equality but Rawls's Difference Principle).

13 Such an objection is suggested, for example, in Joseph Raz, *The Morality of Freedom* (Oxford: Oxford University Press, 1986), ch. 9, and Larry Temkin, op. cit. pp. 247–8.

14 Nagel, op. cit., p. 124.

15 Cf. H. Frankfurt, *The Importance of What We Care About* (Cambridge: Cambridge University Press, 1988), ch. 11, and Joseph Raz, op. cit., ch. 9.

16 Several other writers have suggested such a view. See, for example, Thomas Scalon, 'Nozick on Rights, Liberty, and Property', *Philosophy & Public Affairs* 6 (1976), pp. 6 to 10, Joseph Raz, op. cit. Harry Frankfurt, 'Equality as a Moral Ideal', in *The Importance of What We Care About* (Cambridge: Cambridge University Press, 1988), David Wiggins, 'Claims of Need', in his *Needs, Values, Truth* (Oxford: Blackwell, 1987), Dennis McKerlie, 'Egalitarianism', *Dialogue* 23 (1984), and 'Equality and Priority', *Utilitas* 6 (1994).

17 Like the belief in equality, the Priority View can take either Telic or Deontic forms. It can be a view about which outcomes would be better, or a view that is only about what we ought to do. But, for our purposes here, this difference does not matter.

18 *Reading Nozick*, edited by Jeffrey Paul (Oxford: Blackwell, 1981) p. 203.

19 Op. cit., p. 124.

20 Similar remarks apply to section 117 of my *Reasons and Persons* (Oxford: Oxford University Press, 1984). For a later discussion of the choice between these views, see Nagel's *Equality and Partiality*, op. cit., chs. 7 and 8.

21 D. D. Raphael, *Justice and Liberty* (London: Athlone Press, 1980), p. 10. Cf. p. 49.

22 Richard Norman, *Free and Equal* (Oxford: Oxford University Press, 1987), p. 80

23 See, however, the excellent discussion in David Miller, 'Social Justice and the Principle of Need', in *The Frontiers of Political Theory*, ed. Michael Freeman and David Robertson (Brighton: Harvester Press, 1980).

24 Christopher Ake, 'Justice as Equality', *Philosophy & Public Affairs* 5 (1975), pp. 71 and 77.

25 G. A. Cohen, 'On the Currency of Egalitarian Justice', *Ethics* 99 (1989).

26 Op cit., p. 73.

27 *Inequality*, p. 282.

28 See for example Amartya Sen, *Inequality Reexamined* (Oxford: Oxford University Press, 1992), pp. 92–3.

29 See, for example, Antony Flew, *The Politics of Procrustes* (Buffalo, New York: Prometheus, 1981), p. 26, McKerlie, 'Egalitarianism', op. cit., p. 232. See also Nozick, op. cit., p. 211.

30 I am assuming here that inequality is not in itself bad for people. It is not bad for me if, unknown to me and without affecting me, there exist some other people who are better off than me. That assumption is implied, not only by hedonistic theories about well-being, but also by plausible versions both of desire-fulfilment theories, and of theories that appeal to what Scanlon calls *substantive goods*. For a contrary view, however, which would need a further discussion, see John Broome, *Weighing Goods* (Oxford: Blackwell, 1991), ch. 9.

31 Such as the view advanced in Thomas Scanlon's 'Contractualism and Utilitarianism', in ed. Amartya Sen and Bernard Williams, *Utilitarianism and Beyond* (Cambridge: Cambridge University Press, 1982).

32 See Temkin, op. cit., ch. 9. Another objection to the Person-affecting View comes from what I have called *the Non–Identity Problem* (in my *Reasons and Persons*), ch. 16).

32

Equality of What?

Amartya Sen

Discussions in moral philosophy have offered us a wide menu in answer to the question: equality of what? In this lecture I shall concentrate on three particular types of equality, viz., (i) utilitarian equality, (ii) total utility equality, and (iii) Rawlsian equality. I shall argue that all three have serious limitations, and that while they fail in rather different and contrasting ways, an adequate theory cannot be constructed even on the *combined* grounds of the three. Towards the end I shall try to present an alternative formulation of equality which seems to me to deserve a good deal more attention than it has received, and I shall not desist from doing some propaganda on its behalf.

First a methodological question. When it is claimed that a certain moral principle has shortcomings, what can be the basis of such an allegation? There seem to be at least two different ways of grounding such a criticism, aside from just checking its *direct* appeal to moral intuition. One is to check the *implications* of the principle by taking up particular cases in which the results of employing that principle can be seen in a rather stark way, and then to examine these implications against our intuition. I shall call such a critique a *case-implication critique*. The other is to move not from the general to the particular, but from the general to the *more* general. One can examine the consistency of the principle with another principle that is acknowledged to be more fundamental.

Such prior principles are usually formulated at a rather abstract level, and frequently take the form of congruence with some very general procedures. For example, what could be reasonably assumed to have been chosen under the *as if* ignorance of the Rawlsian "original position," a hypothetical primordial state in which people decide on what rules to adopt without knowing who they are going to be – as if they could end up being any one of the persons in the community.[1] Or what rules would satisfy Richard Hare's requirement of "universalizability" and be consistent with "giving equal weights to the equal interests of the occupants of all the roles."[2] I shall call a critique based on such an approach a *prior-principle critique*. Both approaches can be used in assessing the moral claims of each type of equality, and will indeed be used here.

I Utilitarian Equality

Utilitarian equality is the equality that can be derived from the utilitarian concept of goodness applied to problems of distribution. Perhaps the simplest case is the "pure distribution problem": the problem of dividing a given homogeneous cake among a group of persons.[3] Each person gets more utility the larger his share of the cake, and gets utility *only* from his share of the cake; his utility increases at a diminishing rate as the amount of his

Originally published in *The Tanner Lectures on Human Values*, edited by S. M. McMurrin, 1 (Cambridge: Cambridge University Press, 1980), pp. 195–220. Reprinted by permission of Utah Press and the Trustees of the Tanner Lectures on Human Values.

share goes up. The utilitarian objective is to maximize the sum-total of utility irrespective of distribution, but that requires the *equality* of the *marginal* utility of everyone – marginal utility being the incremental utility each person would get from an additional unit of cake.[4] According to one interpretation, this equality of marginal utility embodies equal treatment of everyone's interests.[5]

The position is a bit more complicated when the total size of the cake is not independent of its distribution. But even then maximization of the total utility sum requires that transfers be carried to the point at which the marginal utility gain of the gainers equals the marginal utility loss of the losers, after taking into account the effect of the transfer on the size and distribution of the cake.[6] It is in this wider context that the special type of equality insisted upon by utilitarianism becomes assertively distinguished. Richard Hare has claimed that "giving equal weight to the equal interests of all the parties" would "lead to utilitarianism" – thus satisfying the prior-principle requirement of universalizability.[7] Similarly, John Harsanyi shoots down the non-utilitarians (including this lecturer, I hasten to add), by claiming for utilitarianism an exclusive ability to avoid "unfair discrimination" between 'one person's and another person's equally urgent human needs.'[8]

The moral importance of needs, on this interpretation, is based exclusively on the notion of utility. This is disputable, and having had several occasions to dispute it in the past,[9] I shall not shy away from disputing it in this particular context. But while I will get on to this issue later, I want first to examine the nature of utilitarian equality without – for the time being – questioning the grounding of moral importance entirely on utility. Even when utility is the sole basis of importance there is still the question as to whether the size of *marginal* utility, irrespective of *total* utility enjoyed by the person, is an adequate index of moral importance. It is, of course, possible to define a metric on utility characteristics such that each person's utility scale is coordinated with everyone else's in a way that equal social importance is simply "scaled" as equal marginal utility. If interpersonal comparisons of utility are taken to have no descriptive content, then this can indeed be thought to be a natural approach. No matter how the relative social importances are arrived at, the marginal utilities attributed to each person would then simply reflect these values. This can be done explicitly by appropriate interpersonal scaling,[10] or

implicitly through making the utility numbering reflect choices in situations of *as if* uncertainty associated with the "original position" under the additional assumption that ignorance be interpreted as equal probability of being anyone.[11] This is not the occasion to go into the technical details of this type of exercise, but the essence of it consists in using a scaling procedure such that marginal utility measures are automatically identified as indicators of social importance.

This route to utilitarianism may meet with little resistance, but it is non-controversial mainly because it says so little. A problem arises the moment utilities and interpersonal comparisons thereof are taken to have some independent descriptive content, as utilitarians have traditionally insisted that they do. There could then be conflicts between these descriptive utilities and the appropriately scaled, essentially normative, utilities in terms of which one is "forced" to be a utilitarian. In what follows I shall have nothing more to say on utilitarianism through appropriate interpersonal scaling, and return to examining the traditional utilitarian position, which takes utilities to have interpersonally comparable descriptive content. How moral importance should relate to these descriptive features must, then, be explicitly faced.

The position can be examined from the prior-principle perspective as well as from the case-implication angle. John Rawls's criticism as a preliminary to presenting his own alternative conception of justice took mostly the prior-principle form. This was chiefly in terms of acceptability in the "original position," arguing that in the postulated situation of *as if* ignorance people would not choose to maximize the utility sum. But Rawls also discussed the violence that utilitarianism does to our notions of liberty and equality. Some replies to Rawls's arguments have reasserted the necessity to be a utilitarian by taking the "scaling" route, which was discussed earlier, and which – I think – is inappropriate in meeting Rawls's critique. But I must confess that I find the lure of the "original position" distinctly resistible since it seems very unclear what precisely would be chosen in such a situation. It is also far from obvious that prudential choice under *as if* uncertainty provides an adequate basis for moral judgment in *un*original, i.e., real-life, positions.[12] But I believe Rawls's more direct critiques in terms of liberty and equality do remain powerful.

Insofar as one is concerned with the *distribution* of utilities, it follows immediately that utilitarianism would in general give one little comfort. Even the minutest gain in total utility *sum* would be taken to outweigh distributional inequalities of the most blatant kind. This problem would be avoidable under certain assumptions, notably the case in which everyone has the *same* utility function. In the pure distribution problem, with this assumption the utilitarian best would require absolute equality of everyone's total utilities.[13] This is because when the marginal utilities are equated, so would be the total utilities if everyone has the same utility function. This is, however, egalitarianism by serendipity: just the accidental result of the marginal tail wagging the total dog. More importantly, the assumption would be very frequently violated, since there are obvious and well-discussed variations between human beings. John may be easy to please, but Jeremy not. If it is taken to be an acceptable prior-principle that the equality of the distribution of total utilities has some value, then the utilitarian conception of equality – marginal as it is – must stand condemned.

The recognition of the fundamental diversity of human beings does, in fact, have very deep consequences, affecting not merely the utilitarian conception of social good, but others as well, including (as I shall argue presently) even the Rawlsian conception of equality. If human beings are identical, then the application of the prior-principle of universalizability in the form of "giving equal weight to the equal interest of all parties" simplifies enormously. Equal marginal utilities of all – reflecting one interpretation of the equal treatment of needs – coincides with equal total utilities – reflecting one interpretation of serving their overall interests equally well. With diversity, the two can pull in opposite directions, and it is far from clear that "giving equal weight to the equal interest of all parties" would require us to concentrate only on one of the two parameters – taking no note of the other.

The case-implication perspective can also be used to develop a related critique, and I have tried to present such a critique elsewhere.[14] For example, if person A as a cripple gets half the utility that the pleasure-wizard person B does from any given level of income, then in the pure distribution problem between A and B the utilitarian would end up giving the pleasure-wizard B more income than the cripple A. The cripple would then be doubly worse off: both since he gets less utility from the same level of income,

and since he will also get less income. Utilitarianism must lead to this thanks to its single-minded concern with maximizing the utility sum. The pleasure-wizard's superior efficiency in producing utility would pull income away from the less efficient cripple.

Since this example has been discussed a certain amount,[15] I should perhaps explain what is being asserted and what is not. First, it is *not* being claimed that anyone who has lower total utility (e.g., the cripple) at any given level of income must of necessity have lower marginal utility also. This must be true for some levels of income, but need not be true everywhere. Indeed, the opposite could be the case when incomes are equally distributed. If that were so, then of course even utilitarianism would give the cripple more income than the non-cripple, since at that point the cripple would be the more efficient producer of utility. My point is that there is no guarantee that this will be the case, and more particularly, if it were the case that the cripple were not only worse off in terms of total utility but could convert income into utility less efficiently everywhere (or even just at the point of equal income division), then utilitarianism would compound his disadvantage by settling him with less income on top of lower efficiency in making utility out of income. The point, of course, is not about cripples in general, nor about all people with total utility disadvantage, but concerns people – including cripples – with disadvantage in terms of both total *and* marginal utility at the relevant points.

Second, the descriptive content of utility is rather important in this context. Obviously, if utilities were scaled to reflect moral importance, then wishing to give priority to income for the cripple would simply amount to attributing a higher "marginal utility" to the cripple's income; but this – as we have already discussed – is a very special sense of utility – quite devoid of descriptive content. In terms of descriptive features, what is being assumed in our example is that the cripple can be helped by giving him income, but the increase in his utility as a consequence of a marginal increase in income is less – in terms of the accepted descriptive criteria – than giving that unit of income to the pleasure-wizard, when both have initially the same income.

Finally, the problem for utilitarianism in this case-implication argument is not dependent on an implicit assumption that the claim to more income arising from disadvantage must dominate over the claim arising from high marginal utility.[16] A system that gives some weight to both claims would still fail to meet the utilitarian formula of social good, which demands an exclusive concern with the latter claim. It is this narrowness that makes the utilitarian conception of equality such a limited one. Even when utility is accepted as the only basis of moral importance, utilitarianism fails to capture the relevance of overall advantage for the requirements of equality. The prior-principle critiques can be supplemented by case-implication critiques using this utilitarian lack of concern with distributional questions except at the entirely marginal level.

II   Total Utility Equality

Welfarism is the view that the goodness of a state of affairs can be judged entirely by the goodness of the utilities in that state.[17] This is a less demanding view than utilitarianism in that it does not demand – in addition – that the goodness of the utilities must be judged by their sum-total. Utilitarianism is, in this sense, a special case of welfarism, and provides one illustration of it. Another distinguished case is the criterion of judging the goodness of a state by the utility level of the worst-off person in that state – a criterion often attributed to John Rawls. (*Except* by John Rawls! He uses social primary goods rather than utility as the index of advantage, as we shall presently discuss.) One can also take some other function of the utilities – other than the sum-total or the minimal element.

Utilitarian equality is one type of welfarist equality. There are others, notably the equality of total utility. It is tempting to think of this as some kind of an analogue of utilitarianism shifting the focus from marginal utility to total utility. This correspondence is, however, rather less close than it might first appear. First of all, while we economists often tend to treat the marginal and the total as belonging to the same plane of discourse, there is an important difference between them. Marginal is an essentially *counter-factual* notion: marginal utility is the additional utility that *would be* generated if the person had one more unit of income. It contrasts what is observed with what allegedly would be observed if something else were different: in this case if the income had been one unit greater. Total is not, however, an inherently counter-factual concept; whether it is or is not would

depend on the variable that is being totalled. In case of utilities, if they are taken to be observed facts, total utility will not be counter-factual. Thus total utility equality is a matter for direct observation, whereas utilitarian equality is not so, since the latter requires hypotheses as to what things would have been under different postulated circumstances. The contrast can be easily traced to the fact that utilitarian equality is essentially a consequence of sum *maximization*, which is itself a counter-factual notion, whereas total utility equality is an equality of some directly observed magnitudes.

Second, utilitarianism provides a complete ordering of all utility distributions – the ranking reflecting the order of the sums of individual utilities – but as specified so far, total utility equality does not do more than just point to the case of absolute equality. In dealing with two cases of non-equal distributions, something more has to be said so that they could be ranked. The ranking can be completed in many different ways.

One way to such a complete ranking is provided by the lexicographic version of the maximin rule, which is associated with the Rawlsian Difference Principle, but interpreted in terms of utilities as opposed to primary goods. Here the goodness of the state of affairs is judged by the level of utility of the worst-off person in that state; but if the worst-off persons in two states respectively have the same level of utility, then the states are ranked according to the utility levels of the second worst-off. If they too tie, then by the utility levels of the third worst-off, and so on. And if two utility distributions are matched at each rank all the way from the worst off to the best off, then the two distributions are equally good. Following a convention established in social choice theory, I shall call this *leximin*.

In what way does total utility equality lead to the leximin? It does this when combined with some other axioms, and in fact the analysis closely parallels the recent axiomatic derivations of the Difference Principle by several authors.[18] Consider four utility levels *a, b, c, d*, in decreasing order of magnitude. One can argue that in an obvious sense the pair of extreme points (*a, d*) displays greater inequality than the pair of intermediate points (*b, c*). Note that this is a purely *ordinal* comparison based on ranking only, and the exact magnitudes of *a, b, c,* and *d* make no difference to the comparison in question. If one were *solely* concerned with equality, then it could be argued that (b, c) is superior – or at least non-inferior – to (a, d). This requirement may be seen as a strong version of preferring equality of utility distributions, and may be called "utility equality preference." It is possible to combine this with an axiom due to Patrick Suppes which captures the notion of *dominance* of one utility distribution over another, in the sense of each element of one distribution being at least as large as the corresponding element in the other distribution.[19] In the two-person case this requires that state x must be regarded as at least as good as y, *either* if each person in state x has at least as much utility as himself in state y, *or* if each person in state x has at least as much utility as the *other* person in state y. If, in addition, at least one of them has strictly more, then of course x could be declared to be strictly better (and not merely at least as good). If this Suppes principle and the "utility equality preference" are combined, then we are pushed in the direction of leximin. Indeed, leximin can be fully derived from these two principles by requiring that the approach must provide a complete ordering of all possible states no matter what the interpersonally comparable individual utilities happen to be (called "unrestricted domain"), and that the ranking of any two states must depend on utility information concerning *those* states only (called "independence").

Insofar as the requirements other than utility equality preference (i.e., the Suppes principle, unrestricted domain, and independence) are regarded as acceptable – and they have indeed been widely used in the social choice literature – leximin can be seen as the natural concomitant of giving priority to the conception of equality focussing on total utility.

It should be obvious, however, that leximin can be fairly easily criticised from the prior-principle perspective as well as the case-implication perspective. Just as utilitarianism pays no attention to the force of one's claim arising from one's disadvantage, leximin ignores claims arising from the *intensity* of one's needs. The *ordinal* characteristic that was pointed out while presenting the axiom of utility equality preference makes the approach insensitive to the magnitudes of potential utility gains and losses. While in the critique of utilitarianism that was presented earlier I argued against treating these potential gains and losses as the only basis of moral judgment, it was *not* of course alleged that these have no moral relevance at all. Take the comparison of (a, d) vis-à-vis (b, c),

discussed earlier, and let (b, c) stand for $(3, 2)$. Utility equality preference would assert the superiority of $(3, 2)$ over $(10, 1)$ as well as $(4, 1)$. Indeed, it would not distinguish between the two cases at all. It is this lack of concern with "how much" questions that makes leximin rather easy to criticise *either* by showing its failure to comply with such prior-principles as "giving equal weight to the equal interest of all parties," *or* by spelling out its rather austere implications in specific cases.

Aside from its indifference to "how much" questions, leximin also has little interest in "how many" questions – paying no attention at all to the number of people whose interests are overridden in the pursuit of the interests of the worst off. The worst-off position rules the roost, and it does not matter whether this goes against the interests of one other person, or against those of a million or a billion other persons. It is sometimes claimed that leximin would not be such an extreme criterion if it could be modified so that this innumeracy were avoided, and if the interests of *one* worse-off position were given priority over the interests of exactly *one* better-off position, but not necessarily against the interests of *more than one* better-off position. In fact, one can define a less demanding version of leximin, which can be called leximin-2, which takes the form of applying the leximin principle *if* all persons other than two are indifferent between the alternatives, but not necessarily otherwise. Leximin-2, as a compromise, will be still unconcerned with "how much" questions on the magnitudes of utilities of the two non-indifferent persons, but need not be blinkered about "how many" questions dealing with numbers of people: the priority applies to one person over exactly one other.[20]

Interestingly enough, a consistency problem intervenes here. It can be proved that given the regularity conditions, viz., unrestricted domain and independence, leximin-2 logically entails leximin in general.[21] That is, given these regularity conditions, there is no way of retaining moral sensitivity to the number of people on each side by choosing the limited requirement of leximin-2 without going all the way to leximin itself. It appears that indifference to *how much* questions concerning utilities implies indifference to *how many* questions concerning the number of people on different sides. One innumeracy begets another.

Given the nature of these critiques of utilitarian equality and total utility equality respectively, it is natural to ask whether some *combination* of the two should not meet both sets of objections. If utilitarianism is attacked for its unconcern with inequalities of the utility distribution, and leximin is criticised for its lack of interest in the magnitudes of utility gains and losses, and even in the numbers involved, then isn't the right solution to choose some mixture of the two? It is at this point that the long-postponed question of the relation between utility and moral worth becomes crucial. While utilitarianism and leximin differ sharply from each other in the use that they respectively make of the utility information, both share an exclusive concern with utility data. If non-utility considerations have any role in either approach, this arises from the part they play in the determination of utilities, or possibly as surrogates for utility information in the absence of adequate utility data. A combination of utilitarianism and leximin would still be confined to the box of welfarism, and it remains to be examined whether welfarism as a general approach is *itself* adequate.

One aspect of the obtuseness of welfarism was discussed clearly by John Rawls.

> In calculating the greatest balance of satisfaction it does not matter, except indirectly, what the desires are for. We are to arrange institutions so as to obtain the greatest sum of satisfactions; we ask no questions about their source or quality but only how their satisfaction would affect the total of well-being.... Thus if men take a certain pleasure in discriminating against one another, in subjecting others to a lesser liberty as a means of enhancing their self-respect, then the satisfaction of these desires must be weighed in our deliberations according to their intensity, or whatever, along with other desires.... In justice as fairness, on the other hand, persons accept in advance a principle of equal liberty and they do this without a knowledge of their more particular ends.... An individual who finds that he enjoys seeing others in positions of lesser liberty understands that he has no claim whatever to this enjoyment. The pleasure he takes in other's deprivation is wrong in itself: it is a satisfaction which requires the violation of a principle to which he would agree in the original position.[22]

It is easily seen that this is an argument not merely against utilitarianism, but against the adequacy of utility information for moral judgments

of states of affairs, and is, thus, an attack on welfarism in general. Second, it is clear that as a criticism of welfarism – and *a fortiori* as a critique of utilitarianism – the argument uses a principle that is unnecessarily strong. If it were the case that pleasures taken "in other's deprivation" were not taken to be wrong in itself, but simply *disregarded*, even then the rejection of welfarism would stand. Furthermore, even if such pleasures were regarded as valuable, but *less* valuable than pleasures arising from other sources (e.g., enjoying food, work, or leisure), welfarism would still stand rejected. The issue – as John Stuart Mill had noted – is the lack of "parity" between one source of utility and another.[23] Welfarism requires the endorsement not merely of the widely shared intuition that any pleasure has some value – and one would have to be a bit of a kill-joy to dissent from this – but also the much more dubious proposition that pleasures must be relatively weighed *only* according to their respective intensities, irrespective of the source of the pleasure and the nature of the activity that goes with it. Finally, Rawls's argument takes the form of an appeal to the prior-principle of equating moral rightness with prudential acceptability in the original position. Even those who do not accept that prior principle could reject the welfarist no-nonsense counting of utility irrespective of all other information by reference to other prior principles, e.g., the irreducible value of liberty.

The relevance of non-utility information to moral judgments is the central issue involved in disputing welfarism. Libertarian considerations point towards a particular class of non-utility information, and I have argued elsewhere that this may require even the rejection of the so-called Pareto principle based on utility dominance.[24] But there are also other types of non-utility information which have been thought to be intrinsically important. Tim Scanlon has recently discussed the contrast between "urgency" and utility (or intensity of preference). He has also argued that "the criteria of well-being that we actually employ in making moral judgments are objective," and a person's level of well-being is taken to be "independent of that person's tastes and interests."[25] These moral judgments could thus conflict with utilitarian – and more generally (Scanlon could have argued) with welfarist – moralities, no matter whether utility is interpreted as pleasure, or – as is increasingly common recently – as desire-fulfilment.

However, acknowledging the relevance of objective factors does not require that well-being be taken to be independent of tastres, and Scanlon's categories are *too* pure. For example, a lack of "parity" between utility from self-regarding actions and that from other-regarding actions will go beyond utility as an index of well-being and will be fatal to welfarism, but the contrast is not, of course, independent of tastes and subjective features. "Objective" considerations can count along with a person's tastes. What is required is the denial that a person's well-being be judged *exclusively* in terms of his or her utilities. If such judgments take into account a person's pleasures and desire-fulfilments, but also certain objective factors, e.g., whether he or she is hungry, cold, or oppressed, the resulting calculus would still be non-welfarist. Welfarism is an extremist position, and its denial can take many different forms – pure and mixed – so long as totally ignoring non-utility information is avoided.

Second, it is also clear that the notion of urgency need not work only *through* the determinants of personal well-being – however broadly conceived. For example, the claim that one should not be *exploited* at work is not based on making exploitation an additional parameter in the specification of well-being on top of such factors as income and effort, but on the moral view that a person deserves to get what he – according to one way of characterizing production – has produced. Similarly, the urgency deriving from principles such as "equal pay for equal work" hits directly at discrimination without having to redefine the notion of personal well-being to take note of such discriminations. One could, for example, say: "She must be paid just as much as the men working in that job, not primarily because she would otherwise have a lower level of well-being than the others, but simply because she is doing the *same* work as the men there, and why should she be paid less?" These moral claims, based on non-welfarist conceptions of equality, have played important parts in social movements, and it seems difficult to sustain the hypothesis that they are purely "instrumental" claims – ultimately justified by their indirect impact on the fulfilment of welfarist, or other well-being-based, objectives.

Thus the dissociation of urgency from utility can arise from two different sources. One disentangles the notion of personal well-being from utility, and the other makes urgency not a function only of well-being. But, at the same time, the former does not require that well-being be independent of utility, and the latter does not necessitate a notion of urgency that is independent of personal well-being. Welfarism is a purist position and must avoid any contamination from either of these sources.

III   Rawlsian Equality

Rawls's "two principles of justice" characterize the need for equality in terms of – what he has called – "primary social goods."[26] These are "things that every rational man is presumed to want," including "rights, liberties and opportunities, income and wealth, and the social bases of self-respect." Basic liberties are separated out as having priority over other primary goods, and thus priority is given to the principle of liberty which demands that "each person is to have an equal right to the most extensive basic liberty compatible with a similar liberty for others." The second principle supplements this, demanding efficiency and equality, judging advantage in terms of an index of primary goods. Inequalities are condemned unless they work out to everyone's advantage. This incorporates the "Difference Principle" in which priority is given to furthering the interests of the worst-off. And that leads to maximin, or to leximin, defined not on individual utilities but on the index of primary goods. But given the priority of the liberty principle, no trade-offs are permitted between basic liberties and economic and social gain.

Herbert Hart has persuasively disputed Rawls's arguments for the priority of liberty,[27] but with that question I shall not be concerned here. What is crucial for the problem under discussion is the concentration on bundles of primary social goods. Some of the difficulties with welfarism that I tried to discuss will not apply to the pursuit of Rawlsian equality. Objective criteria of well-being can be directly accommodated within the index of primary goods. So can be Mill's denial of the parity between pleasures from different sources, since the sources can be discriminated on the basis of the nature of the goods. Furthermore, while the Difference Principle is egalitarian in a way similar to leximin, it avoids the much-criticized feature of leximin of giving more income to people who are hard to please and who have to be deluged in champagne and buried in caviar to bring them to a normal level of utility, which you and I get from a sandwich and beer. Since advantage is judged not in terms of utilities at all, but through the index of primary goods, expensive tastes cease to provide a ground for getting more income. Rawls justifies this in terms of a person's responsibility for his own ends.

But what about the cripple with utility disadvantage, whom we discussed earlier? Leximin will give him more income in a pure distribution problem. Utilitarianism, I had complained, will give him *less*. The Difference Principle will give him neither more nor less on grounds of his being a cripple. His utility disadvantage will be irrelevant to the Difference Principle. This may seem hard, and I think it is. Rawls justifies this by pointing out that "hard cases" can "distract our moral perception by leading us to think of people distant from us whose fate arouses pity and anxiety."[28] This can be so, but hard cases do exist, and to take disabilities, or special health needs, or physical or mental defects, as morally irrelevant, or to leave them out for fear of making a mistake, may guarantee that the *opposite* mistake will be made.

And the problem does not end with hard cases. The primary goods approach seems to take little note of the diversity of human beings. In the context of assessing utilitarian equality, it was argued that if people were fundamentally similar in terms of utility functions, then the utilitarian concern with maximizing the sum-total of utilities would push us simultaneously also in the direction of equality of utility levels. Thus utilitarianism could be rendered vastly more attractive if people really were similar. A corresponding remark can be made about the Rawlsian Difference Principle. If people were basically very similar, then an index of primary goods might be quite a good way of judging advantage. But, in fact, people seem to have very different needs varying with health, longevity, climatic conditions, location, work conditions, temperament, and even body size (affecting food and clothing requirements). So what is involved is not merely ignoring a few hard cases, but overlooking very widespread and real differences. Judging advantage purely in terms of primary goods leads to a partially blind morality.

Indeed, it can be argued that there is, in fact, an element of "fetishism" in the Rawlsian framework. Rawls takes primary goods as the embodiment of advantage, rather than taking advantage to be a *relationship* between persons and goods. Utilitarianism, or leximin, or – more generally – welfarism does not have this fetishism, since utilities are reflections of one type of relation between persons and goods. For example, income and wealth are

not valued under utilitarianism as physical units, but in terms of their capacity to create human happiness or to satisfy human desires. Even if utility is not thought to be the right focus for the person-good relationship, to have an entirely good-oriented framework provides a peculiar way of judging advantage.

It can also be argued that while utility in the form of happiness or desire-fulfilment may be an *inadequate* guide to urgency, the Rawlsian framework asserts it to be *irrelevant* to urgency, which is, of course, a much stronger claim. The distinction was discussed earlier in the context of assessing welfarism, and it was pointed out that a rejection of welfarism need not take us to the point in which utility is given no role whatsoever. That a person's interest should have nothing directly to do with his happiness or desire-fulfilment seems difficult to justify. Even in terms of the prior-principle of prudential acceptability in the "original position," it is not at all clear why people in that primordial state should be taken to be so indifferent to the joys and sufferings in occupying particular positions, or if they are not, why their concern about these joys and sufferings should be taken to be morally irrelevant.

IV Basic Capability Equality

This leads to the further question: Can we not construct an adequate theory of equality on the *combined* grounds of Rawlsian equality and equality under the two welfarist conceptions, with some trade-offs among them? I would now like to argue briefly why I believe this too may prove to be informationally short. This can, of course, easily be asserted *if* claims arising from considerations other than well-being were acknowledged to be legitimate. Non-exploitation, or non-discrimination, requires the use of information not fully captured either by utility or by primary goods. Other conceptions of entitlements can also be brought in going beyond concern with personal well-being only. But in what follows I shall not introduce these concepts. My contention is that *even* the concept of *needs* does not get adequate coverage through the information on primary goods and utility.

I shall use a case-implication argument. Take the cripple again with marginal utility disadvantage. We saw that utilitarianism would do nothing for him; in fact it will give him *less* income than to the physically fit. Nor would the Difference Principle help him; it will leave his physical disadvantage severely alone. He did, however, get preferential treatment under leximin, and more generally, under criteria fostering total equality. His low level of total utility was the basis of his claim. But now suppose that he is no worse off than others in utility terms despite his physical handicap because of certain other utility features. This could be because he has a jolly disposition. Or because he has a low aspiration level and his heart leaps up whenever he sees a rainbow in the sky. Or because he is religious and feels that he will be rewarded in after-life, or cheerfully accepts what he takes to be just penalty for misdeeds in a past incarnation. The important point is that despite his marginal utility disadvantage, he has no longer a total utility deprivation. Now not even leximin – or any other notion of equality focussing on total utility – will do much for him. If we still think that he has needs as a cripple that should be catered to, then the basis of that claim clearly rests neither in high marginal utility, nor in low total utility, nor – of course – in deprivation in terms of primary goods.

It is arguable that what is missing in all this framework is some notion of "basic capabilities": a person being able to do certain basic things. The ability to move about is the relevant one here, but one can consider others, e.g., the ability to meet one's nutritional requirements, the wherewithal to be clothed and sheltered, the power to participate in the social life of the community. The notion of urgency related to this is not fully captured by either utility or primary goods, or any combination of the two. Primary goods suffers from fetishist handicap in being concerned with goods, and even though the list of goods is specified in a broad and inclusive way, encompassing rights, liberties, opportunities, income, wealth, and the social basis of self-respect, it still is concerned with good things rather than with what these good things *do* to human beings. Utility, on the other hand, *is* concerned with what these things do to human beings, but uses a metric that focusses not on the person's capabilities but on his mental reaction. There is something still missing in the combined list of primary goods and utilities. If it is argued that resources should be devoted to remove or substantially reduce the handicap of the cripple despite there being no marginal utility argument (because it is expensive), despite there being no total utility argument (because he is so contented), and despite there being no primary goods deprivation (because

he has the goods that others have), the case must rest on something else. I believe what is at issue is the interpretation of needs in the form of basic capabilities. This interpretation of needs and interests is often implicit in the demand for equality. This type of equality I shall call "basic capability equality."

The focus on basic capabilities can be seen as a natural extension of Rawls's concern with primary goods, shifting attention from goods to what goods do to human beings. Rawls himself motivates judging advantage in terms of primary goods by referring to capabilities, even though his criteria end up focussing on goods as such: on income rather than on what income does, on the "social bases of self-respect" rather than on self-respect itself, and so on. If human beings were very like each other, this would not have mattered a great deal, but there is evidence that the conversion of goods to capabilities varies from person to person substantially, and the equality of the former may still be far from the equality of the latter.

There are, of course, many difficulties with the notion of "basic capability equality." In particular, the problem of indexing the basic capability bundles is a serious one. It is, in many ways, a problem comparable with the indexing of primary good bundles in the context of Rawlsian equality. This is not the occasion to go into the technical issues involved in such an indexing, but it is clear that whatever partial ordering can be done on the basis of broad uniformity of personal preferences must be supplemented by certain established conventions of relative importance.

The ideas of relative importance are, of course, conditional on the nature of the society. The notion of the equality of basic capabilities is a very general one, but any application of it must be rather culture-dependent, especially in the weighting of different capabilities. While Rawlsian equality has the characteristic of being both culture-dependent and fetishist, basic capability equality avoids fetishism, but remains culture-dependent. Indeed, basic capability equality can be seen as essentially an extension of the Rawlsian approach in a non-fetishist direction.

V   Concluding Remarks

I end with three final remarks. First, it is not my contention that basic capability equality can be the sole guide to the moral good. For one thing morality is not concerned only with equality. For another, while it is my contention that basic capability equality has certain clear advantages over other types of equality, I did not argue that the others were morally irrelevant. Basic capability equality is a partial guide to the part of moral goodness that is associated with the idea of equality. I have tried to argue that as a partial guide it has virtues that the other characterizations of equality do not possess.

Second, the index of basic capabilities, like utility, can be used in many different ways. Basic capability equality corresponds to total utility equality, and it can be extended in different directions, e.g., to leximin of basic capabilities.

On the other hand, the index can be used also in a way similar to utilitarianism, judging the strength of a claim in terms of incremental contribution to *enhancing* the index value. The main departure is in focussing on a *magnitude* different

from utility as well as the primary goods index. The new dimension can be utilized in different ways, of which basic capability equality is only one.

Last, the bulk of this lecture has been concerned with rejecting the claims of utilitarian equality, total utility equality, and Rawlsian equality to provide a sufficient basis for the equality-aspect of morality – indeed, even for that part of it which is concerned with needs rather than deserts. I have argued that none of these three is sufficient, nor is any combination of the three.

This is my main thesis. I have also made the constructive claim that this gap can be narrowed by the idea of basic capability equality, and more generally by the use of basic capability as a morally relevant dimension taking us beyond utility and primary goods. I should end by pointing out that the validity of the main thesis is not conditional on the acceptance of this constructive claim.

Notes

1   Rawls, *A Theory of Justice* (Cambridge: Harvard University Press, 1971), pp. 17–22. See also W. Vickrey, "Measuring Marginal Utility by Reactions to Risk," *Econometrica* 13 (1945), and J.C. Harsanyi, "Cardinal Welfare, Individualistic Ethics, and Interpersonal Comparisons of Utility," *Journal of Political Economy* 63 (1955).

2   R.M. Hare, *The Language of Morals* (Oxford: Clarendon Press, 1952); "Ethical Theory and Utilitarianism," in H.D. Lewis, ed., *Contemporary British Philosophy* (London: Allen and Unwin, 1976), pp. 116–17.

3   I have tried to use this format for an axiomatic contrast of the Rawlsian and utilitarian criteria in "Rawls versus Bentham: An Axiomatic Examination of the Pure Distribution Problem," in *Theory and Decision* 4 (1974); reprinted in N. Daniels, ed., *Reading Rawls* (Oxford: Blackwell, 1975). See also L. Kern, "Comparative Distributive Ethics: An Extension of Sen's Examination of the Pure Distribution Problem," in H.W. Gottinger and W. Leinfellner, eds., *Decision Theory and Social Ethics* (Dordrecht: Reidel, 1978), and J.P. Griffin, "Equality: On Sen's Equality Axiom," Keble College, Oxford, 1978, mimeographed.

4   The equality condition would have to be replaced by a corresponding combination of inequality requirements when the appropriate "continuity" properties do not hold. Deeper difficulties are raised by "non-convexities" (e.g., increasing marginal utility).

5   J. Harsanyi, "Can the Maximin Principle Serve as a Basis for Morality? A Critique of John Rawls' Theory," *American Political Science Review* 64 (1975).

6   As mentioned in note 4, the equality conditions would require modification in the absence of continuity of the appropriate type. Transfers must be carried to the point at which the marginal utility gain of the gainers from any further transfer is *no more than* the marginal utility loss of the losers.

7   Hare (1976), pp. 116–17.

8   John Harsanyi, "Non-linear Social Welfare Functions: A Rejoinder to Professor Sen," in R.E. Butts and J. Hintikka, eds., *Foundational Problems in the Special Sciences* (Dordrecht: Reidel, 1977), pp. 294–5.

9   *Collective Choice and Social Welfare* (San Francisco: Holden-Day, 1970), chapter 6 and section 11.4; "On Weights and Measures: Informational Constraints in Social Welfare Analysis," *Econometrica* 45 (1977). See also T.M. Scanlon's arguments against identifying utility with "urgency" in his "Preference and Urgency," *Journal of Philosophy* 72 (1975).

10 For two highly ingenious examples of such an exercise, see Peter Hammond, "Dual Interpersonal Comparisons of Utility and the Welfare Economics of Income Distribution," *Journal of Public Economics* 6 (1977): 51–7; and Menahem Yaari, "Rawls, Edgeworth, Shapley and Nash: Theories of Distributive Justice Re-examined," Research Memorandum No. 33, Center for Research in Mathematical Economics and Game Theory, Hebrew University, Jerusalem, 1978.

11 See Harsanyi (1955, 1975, 1977).

12 On this, see Thomas Nagel, "Rawls on Justice," *Philosophical Review* 83 (1973), and "Equality" in his *Mortal Questions* (Cambridge: Cambridge University Press, 1979).

13 The problem is much more complex when the total cake is not fixed, and where the maximization of utility sum need not lead to the equality of total utilities unless some additional assumptions are made, e.g., the absence of incentive arguments for inequality.

14 *On Economic Inequality* (Oxford: Clarendon Press, 1973), pp. 16–20.

15 See John Harsanyi, "Non-linear Social Welfare Functions," *Theory and Decision* 6 (1976): 311–12; Harsanyi (1977); Kern (1978); Griffin (1978); Richard B. Brandt, *A Theory of the Good and the Right* (Oxford: Clarendon Press, 1979), chapter 16.

16 Such an assumption is made in my Weak Equity Axiom, proposed in Sen (1973), but it is unnecessarily demanding for rejecting utilitarianism. See Griffin (1978) for a telling critique of the Weak Equity Axiom, in this exacting form.

17 See Sen (1977), and also my "Welfarism and Utilitarianism," *Journal of Philosophy* 76 (1979).

18 See P.J. Hammond, "Equity, Arrow's Conditions and Rawls' Difference Principle," *Econometrica* 44 (1976); S. Strasnick, "Social Choice Theory and the Derivation of Rawls' Difference Principle," *Journal of Philosophy* 73 (1976); C. d'Aspremont and L. Gevers, "Equity and Informational Basis of Collective Choice," *Review of Economic Studies* 44 (1977); K.J. Arrow, "Extended Sympathy and the Possibility of Social Choice," *American Economic Review* 67 (1977); A.K. Sen, "On Weights and Measures: Informational Constraints in Social Welfare Analysis," *Econometrica* 45 (1977); R. Deschamps and L. Gevers, "Leximin and Utilitarian Rules: A Joint Characterization," *Journal of Economic Theory* 17 (1978); K.W.S. Roberts, "Possibility Theorems with Interpersonally Comparable Welfare Levels," *Review of Economic Studies* 47 (1980); P.J. Hammond, "Two Person Equity," *Econometrica* 47 (1979).

19 P. Suppes, "Some Formal Models of Grading Principles," *Synthese* 6 (1966).

20 Leximin – and maximin – are concerned with conflicts between positional priorities, i.e., between ranks (such as the "worst-off position," "second worst-off position," etc.), and not with interpersonal priorities. When positions coincide with persons (e.g., the *same* person being the worst off in each state), then positional conflicts translate directly into personal conflicts.

21 Theorem 8, Sen (1977). See also Hammond (1979) for extensions of this result.

22 Rawls (1971), pp. 30–1.

23 John Stuart Mill, *On Liberty* (1859), p. 140.

24 Sen (1970), especially chapter 6. Also Sen (1979).

25 T.M. Scanlon (1975), pp. 658–9.

26 Rawls (1971), pp. 60–5.

27 H.L.A. Hart, "Rawls on Liberty and Its Priority," *University of Chicago Law Review* 40 (1973); reprinted in N. Daniels, ed., *Reading Rawls* (Oxford: Blackwell, 1975).

28 John Rawls, "A Kantian Concept of Equality," *Cambridge Review* (February 1975), p. 96.

33

Complex Equality

Michael Walzer

Pluralism

Distributive justice is a large idea. It draws the entire world of goods within the reach of philosophical reflection. Nothing can be omitted; no feature of our common life can escape scrutiny. Human society is a distributive community. That's not all it is, but it is importantly that: we come together to share, divide, and exchange. We also come together to make the things that are shared, divided, and exchanged; but that very making – work itself – is distributed among us in a division of labor. My place in the economy, my standing in the political order, my reputation among my fellows, my material holdings: all these come to me from other men and women. It can be said that I have what I have rightly or wrongly, justly or unjustly; but given the range of distributions and the number of participants, such judgments are never easy.

The idea of distributive justice has as much to do with being and doing as with having, as much to do with production as with consumption, as much to do with identity and status as with land, capital, or personal possessions. Different political arrangements enforce, and different ideologies justify, different distributions of membership, power, honor, ritual eminence, divine grace, kinship and love, knowledge, wealth, physical security, work and leisure, rewards and punishments, and a host of goods more narrowly and materially conceived – food, shelter, clothing, transportation, medical care, commodities of every sort, and all the odd things (paintings, rare books, postage stamps) that human beings collect. And this multiplicity of goods is matched by a multiplicity of distributive procedures, agents, and criteria. There are such things as simple distributive systems – slave galleys, monasteries, insane asylums, kindergartens (though each of these, looked at closely, might show unexpected complexities); but no full-fledged human society has ever avoided the multiplicity. We must study it all, the goods and the distributions, in many different times and places.

There is, however, no single point of access to this world of distributive arrangements and ideologies. There has never been a universal medium of exchange. Since the decline of the barter economy, money has been the most common medium. But the old maxim according to which there are some things that money can't buy is not only normatively but also factually true. What should and should not be up for sale is something men and women always have to decide and have decided in many different ways. Throughout history, the market has been one of the most important mechanisms for the distribution of social goods; but it has never been, it nowhere is today, a complete distributive system.

Similarly, there has never been either a single decision point from which all distributions are controlled or a single set of agents making decisions. No

Originally published in *Spheres of Justice: A Defense of Pluralism and Equality* (Oxford: Martin Robertson, 1983), pp. 3–30. Reprinted by permission of Blackwell Publishing Ltd.

state power has ever been so pervasive as to regulate all the patterns of sharing, dividing, and exchanging out of which a society takes shape. Things slip away from the state's grasp; new patterns are worked out – familial networks, black markets, bureaucratic alliances, clandestine political and religious organizations. State officials can tax, conscript, allocate, regulate, appoint, reward, punish, but they cannot capture the full range of goods or substitute themselves for every other agent of distribution. Nor can anyone else do that: there are market coups and cornerings, but there has never been a fully successful distributive conspiracy.

And finally, there has never been a single criterion, or a single set of interconnected criteria, for all distributions. Desert, qualification, birth and blood, friendship, need, free exchange, political loyalty, democratic decision: each has had its place, along with many others, uneasily coexisting, invoked by competing groups, confused with one another.

In the matter of distributive justice, history displays a great variety of arrangements and ideologies. But the first impulse of the philosopher is to resist the displays of history, the world of appearances, and to search for some underlying unity: a short list of basic goods, quickly abstracted to a single good; a single distributive criterion or an interconnected set; and the philosopher himself standing, symbolically at least, at a single decision point. I shall argue that to search for unity is to misunderstand the subject matter of distributive justice. Nevertheless, in some sense the philosophical impulse is unavoidable. Even if we choose pluralism, as I shall do, that choice still requires a coherent defense. There must be principles that justify the choice and set limits to it, for pluralism does not require us to endorse every proposed distributive criteria or to accept every would-be agent. Conceivably, there is a single principle and a single legitimate kind of pluralism. But this would still be a pluralism that encompassed a wide range of distributions. By contrast, the deepest assumption of most of the philosophers who have written about justice, from Plato onward, is that there is one, and only one, distributive system that philosophy can rightly encompass.

Today this system is commonly described as the one that ideally rational men and women would choose if they were forced to choose impartially, knowing nothing of their own situation, barred from making particularist claims, confronting an abstract set of goods.[1] If these constraints on knowing and claiming are suitably shaped, and if the goods are suitably defined, it is probably true that a singular conclusion can be produced. Rational men and women, constrained this way or that, will choose one, and only one, distributive system. But the force of that singular conclusion is not easy to measure. It is surely doubtful that those same men and women, if they were transformed into ordinary people, with a firm sense of their own identity, with their own goods in their hands, caught up in everyday troubles, would reiterate their hypothetical choice or even recognize it as their own. The problem is not, most importantly, with the particularism of interest, which philosophers have always assumed they could safely – that is, uncontroversially – set aside. Ordinary people can do that too, for the sake, say, of the public interest. The greater problem is with the particularism of history, culture, and membership. Even if they are committed to impartiality, the question most likely to arise in the minds of the members of a political community is not, What would rational individuals choose under universalizing conditions of such-and-such a sort? But rather, What would individuals like us choose, who are situated as we are, who share a culture and are determined to go on sharing it? And this is a question that is readily transformed into, What choices have we already made in the course of our common life? What understandings do we (really) share?

Justice is a human construction, and it is doubtful that it can be made in only one way. At any rate, I shall begin by doubting, and more than doubting, this standard philosophical assumption. The questions posed by the theory of distributive justice admit of a range of answers, and there is room within the range for cultural diversity and political choice. It's not only a matter of implementing some singular principle or set of principles in different historical settings. No one would deny that there is a range of morally permissible implementations. I want to argue for more than this: that the principles of justice are themselves pluralistic in form; that different social goods ought to be distributed for different reasons, in accordance with different procedures, by different agents; and that all these differences derive from different understandings of the social goods themselves – the inevitable product of historical and cultural particularism.

Michael Walzer

A Theory of Goods

Theories of distributive justice focus on a social process commonly described as if it had this form:

People distribute goods to (other) people.

Here, "distribute" means give, allocate, exchange, and so on, and the focus is on the individuals who stand at either end of these actions: not on producers and consumers, but on distributive agents and recipients of goods. We are as always interested in ourselves, but, in this case, in a special and limited version of ourselves, as people who give and take. What is our nature? What are our rights? What do we need, want, deserve? What are we entitled to? What would we accept under ideal conditions? Answers to these questions are turned into distributive principles, which are supposed to control the movement of goods. The goods, defined by abstraction, are taken to be movable in any direction.

But this is too simple an understanding of what actually happens, and it forces us too quickly to make large assertions about human nature and moral agency – assertions unlikely, ever, to command general agreement. I want to propose a more precise and complex description of the central process:

People conceive and create goods, which they then distribute among themselves.

Here, the conception and creation precede and control the distribution. Goods don't just appear in the hands of distributive agents who do with them as they like or give them out in accordance with some general principle.[2] Rather, goods with their meanings – because of their meanings – are the crucial medium of social relations; they come into people's minds before they come into their hands; distributions are patterned in accordance with shared conceptions of what the goods are and what they are for. Distributive agents are constrained by the goods they hold; one might almost say that goods distribute themselves among people.

> Things are in the saddle
> And ride mankind.[3]

But these are always particular things and particular groups of men and women. And, of course, we make the things – even the saddle. I don't want

to deny the importance of human agency, only to shift our attention from distribution itself to conception and creation: the naming of the goods, and the giving of meaning, and the collective making. What we need to explain and limit the pluralism of distributive possibilities is a theory of goods. For our immediate purposes, that theory can be summed up in six propositions.

1. All the goods with which distributive justice is concerned are social goods. They are not and they cannot be idiosyncratically valued. I am not sure that there are any other kinds of goods; I mean to leave the question open. Some domestic objects are cherished for private and sentimental reasons, but only in cultures where sentiment regularly attaches to such objects. A beautiful sunset, the smell of new-mown hay, the excitement of an urban vista: these perhaps are privately valued goods, though they are also, and more obviously, the objects of cultural assessment. Even new inventions are not valued in accordance with the ideas of their inventors; they are subject to a wider process of conception and creation. God's goods, to be sure, are exempt from this rule – as in the first chapter of Genesis: "and God saw every thing that He had made, and, behold, it was very good" (1:31). That evaluation doesn't require the agreement of mankind (who might be doubtful), or of a majority of men and women, or of any group of men and women meeting under ideal conditions (though Adam and Eve in Eden would probably endorse it). But I can't think of any other exemptions. Goods in the world have shared meanings because conception and creation are social processes. For the same reason, goods have different meanings in different societies. The same "thing" is valued for different reasons, or it is valued here and disvalued there. John Stuart Mill once complained that "people like in crowds," but I know of no other way to like or to dislike social goods.[4] A solitary person could hardly understand the meaning of the goods or figure out the reasons for taking them as likable or dislikable. Once people like in crowds, it becomes possible for individuals to break away, pointing to latent or subversive meanings, aiming at alternative values – including the values, for example, of notoriety and eccentricity. An easy eccentricity has sometimes been one of the privileges of the aristocracy: it is a social good like any other.

2. Men and women take on concrete identities because of the way they conceive and create, and then possess and employ social goods. "The line

between what is me and mine," wrote William James, "is very hard to draw."[5] Distributions cannot be understood as the acts of men and women who do not yet have particular goods in their minds or in their hands. In fact, people already stand in a relation to a set of goods; they have a history of transactions, not only with one another but also with the moral and material world in which they live. Without such a history, which begins at birth, they wouldn't be men and women in any recognizable sense, and they wouldn't have the first notion of how to go about the business of giving, allocating, and exchanging goods.

3. There is no single set of primary or basic goods conceivable across all moral and material worlds – or, any such set would have to be conceived in terms so abstract that they would be of little use in thinking about particular distributions. Even the range of necessities, if we take into account moral as well as physical necessities, is very wide, and the rank orderings are very different. A single necessary good, and one that is always necessary – food, for example – carries different meanings in different places. Bread is the staff of life, the body of Christ, the symbol of the Sabbath, the means of hospitality, and so on. Conceivably, there is a limited sense in which the first of these is primary, so that if there were twenty people in the world and just enough bread to feed the twenty, the primacy of bread-as-staff-of-life would yield a sufficient distributive principle. But that is the only circumstance in which it would do so; and even there, we can't be sure. If the religious uses of bread were to conflict with its nutritional uses – if the gods demanded that bread be baked and burned rather than eaten – it is by no means clear which use would be primary. How, then, is bread to be incorporated into the universal list? The question is even harder to answer, the conventional answers less plausible, as we pass from necessities to opportunities, powers, reputations, and so on. These can be incorporated only if they are abstracted from every particular meaning – hence, for all practical purposes, rendered meaningless.

4. But it is the meaning of goods that determines their movement. Distributive criteria and arrangements are intrinsic not to the good-in-itself but to the social good. If we understand what it is, what it means to those for whom it is a good, we understand how, by whom, and for what reasons it ought to be distributed. All distributions are just or unjust relative to the social meanings of the goods at stake. This is in obvious ways a principle of legitimation, but it is also a critical principle.[6] When medieval Christians, for example, condemned the sin of simony, they were claiming that the meaning of a particular social good, ecclesiastical office, excluded its sale and purchase. Given the Christian understanding of office, it followed – I am inclined to say, it necessarily followed – that office holders should be chosen for their knowledge and piety and not for their wealth. There are presumably things that money can buy, but not this thing. Similarly, the words *prostitution* and *bribery*, like *simony*, describe the sale and purchase of goods that, given certain understandings of their meaning, ought never to be sold or purchased.

5. Social meanings are historical in character; and so distributions, and just and unjust distributions, change over time. To be sure, certain key goods have what we might think of as characteristic normative structures, reiterated across the lines (but not all the lines) of time and space. It is because of this reiteration that the British philosopher Bernard Williams is able to argue that goods should always be distributed for "relevant reasons" – where relevance seems to connect to essential rather than to social meanings.[7] The idea that offices, for example, should go to qualified candidates – though not the only idea that has been held about offices – is plainly visible in very different societies where simony and nepotism, under different names, have similarly been thought sinful or unjust. (But there has been a wide divergence of views about what sorts of position and place are properly called "offices.") Again, punishment has been widely understood as a negative good that ought to go to people who are judged to deserve it on the basis of a verdict, not of a political decision. (But what constitutes a verdict? Who is to deliver it? How, in short, is justice to be done to accused men and women? About these questions there has been significant disagreement.) These examples invite empirical investigation. There is no merely intuitive or speculative procedure for seizing upon relevant reasons.

6. When meanings are distinct, distributions must be autonomous. Every social good or set of goods constitutes, as it were, a distributive sphere within which only certain criteria and arrangements are appropriate. Money is inappropriate in the sphere of ecclesiastical office; it is an intrusion from another sphere. And piety should make for

no advantage in the marketplace, as the marketplace has commonly been understood. Whatever can rightly be sold ought to be sold to pious men and women and also to profane, heretical, and sinful men and women (else no one would do much business). The market is open to all comers; the church is not. In no society, of course, are social meanings entirely distinct. What happens in one distributive sphere affects what happens in the others; we can look, at most, for relative autonomy. But relative autonomy, like social meaning, is a critical principle – indeed, as I shall be arguing throughout this book, a radical principle. It is radical even though it doesn't point to a single standard against which all distributions are to be measured. There is no single standard. But there are standards (roughly knowable even when they are also controversial) for every social good and every distributive sphere in every particular society; and these standards are often violated, the goods usurped, the spheres invaded, by powerful men and women.

Dominance and Monopoly

In fact, the violations are systematic. Autonomy is a matter of social meaning and shared values, but it is more likely to make for occasional reformation and rebellion than for everyday enforcement. For all the complexity of their distributive arrangements, most societies are organized on what we might think of as a social version of the gold standard: one good or one set of goods is dominant and determinative of value in all the spheres of distribution. And that good or set of goods is commonly monopolized, its value upheld by the strength and cohesion of its owners. I call a good dominant if the individuals who have it, because they have it, can command a wide range of other goods. It is monopolized whenever a single man or woman, a monarch in the world of value – or a group of men and women, oligarchs – successfully hold it against all rivals. Dominance describes a way of using social goods that isn't limited by their intrinsic meanings or that shapes those meanings in its own image. Monopoly describes a way of owning or controlling social goods in order to exploit their dominance. When goods are scarce and widely needed, like water in the desert, monopoly itself will make them dominant. Mostly, however, dominance is a more elaborate social creation, the work of many hands, mixing reality

and symbol. Physical strength, familial reputation, religious or political office, landed wealth, capital, technical knowledge: each of these, in different historical periods, has been dominant; and each of them has been monopolized by some group of men and women. And then all good things come to those who have the one best thing. Possess that one, and the others come in train. Or, to change the metaphor, a dominant good is converted into another good, into many others, in accordance with what often appears to be a natural process but is in fact magical, a kind of social alchemy.

No social good ever entirely dominates the range of goods; no monopoly is ever perfect. I mean to describe tendencies only, but crucial tendencies. For we can characterize whole societies in terms of the patterns of conversion that are established within them. Some characterizations are simple: in a capitalist society, capital is dominant and readily converted into prestige and power; in a technocracy, technical knowledge plays the same part. But it isn't difficult to imagine, or to find, more complex social arrangements. Indeed, capitalism and technocracy are more complex than their names imply, even if the names do convey real information about the most important forms of sharing, dividing, and exchanging. Monopolistic control of a dominant good makes a ruling class, whose members stand atop the distributive system – much as philosophers, claiming to have the wisdom they love, might like to do. But since dominance is always incomplete and monopoly imperfect, the rule of every ruling class is unstable. It is continually challenged by other groups in the name of alternative patterns of conversion.

Distribution is what social conflict is all about. Marx's heavy emphasis on productive processes should not conceal from us the simple truth that the struggle for control of the means of production is a distributive struggle. Land and capital are at stake, and these are goods that can be shared, divided, exchanged, and endlessly converted. But land and capital are not the only dominant goods; it is possible (it has historically been possible) to come to them by way of other goods – military or political power, religious office and charisma, and so on. History reveals no single dominant good and no naturally dominant good, but only different kinds of magic and competing bands of magicians.

The claim to monopolize a dominant good – when worked up for public purposes – constitutes an ideology. Its standard form is to connect legitimate possession with some set of personal qualities through the medium of a philosophical principle. So aristocracy, or the rule of the best, is the principle of those who lay claim to breeding and intelligence: they are commonly the monopolists of landed wealth and familial reputation. Divine supremacy is the principle of those who claim to know the word of God: they are the monopolists of grace and office. Meritocracy, or the career open to talents, is the principle of those who claim to be talented: they are most often the monopolists of education. Free exchange is the principle of those who are ready, or who tell us they are ready, to put their money at risk: they are the monopolists of movable wealth. These groups – and others, too, similarly marked off by their principles and possessions – compete with one another, struggling for supremacy. One group wins, and then a different one; or coalitions are worked out, and supremacy is uneasily shared. There is no final victory, nor should there be. But that is not to say that the claims of the different groups are necessarily wrong, or that the principles they invoke are of no value as distributive criteria; the principles are often exactly right within the limits of a particular sphere. Ideologies are readily corrupted, but their corruption is not the most interesting thing about them.

It is in the study of these struggles that I have sought the guiding thread of my own argument. The struggles have, I think, a paradigmatic form. Some group of men and women – class, caste, strata, estate, alliance, or social formation – comes to enjoy a monopoly or a near monopoly of some dominant good; or, a coalition of groups comes to enjoy, and so on. This dominant good is more or less systematically converted into all sorts of other things – opportunities, powers, and reputations. So wealth is seized by the strong, honor by the well-born, office by the well educated. Perhaps the ideology that justifies the seizure is widely believed to be true. But resentment and resistance are (almost) as pervasive as belief. There are always some people, and after a time there are a great many, who think the seizure is not justice but usurpation. The ruling group does not possess, or does not uniquely possess, the qualities it claims; the conversion process violates the common understanding of the goods at stake. Social conflict is intermittent, or it is endemic; at some point, counterclaims are put forward. Though these are of many different sorts, three general sorts are especially important:

1 The claim that the dominant good, whatever it is, should be redistributed so that it can be equally or at least more widely shared: this amounts to saying that monopoly is unjust.

2 The claim that the way should be opened for the autonomous distribution of all social goods: this amounts to saying that dominance is unjust.

3 The claim that some new good, monopolized by some new group, should replace the currently dominant good: this amounts to saying that the existing pattern of dominance and monopoly is unjust.

The third claim is, in Marx's view, the model of every revolutionary ideology – except, perhaps, the proletarian or last ideology. Thus, the French Revolution in Marxist theory: the dominance of noble birth and blood and of feudal landholding is ended, and bourgeois wealth is established in its stead. The original situation is reproduced with different subjects and objects (this is never unimportant), and then the class war is immediately renewed. It is not my purpose here to endorse or to criticize Marx's view. I suspect, in fact, that there is something of all three claims in every revolutionary ideology, but that, too, is not a position that I shall try to defend here. Whatever its sociological significance, the third claim is not philosophically interesting – unless one believes that there is a naturally dominant good, such that its possessors could legitimately claim to rule the rest of us. In a sense, Marx believed exactly that. The means of production is the dominant good throughout history, and Marxism is a historicist doctrine insofar as it suggests that whoever controls the prevailing means legitimately rules.[8] After the communist revolution, we shall all control the means of production: at that point, the third claim collapses into the first. Meanwhile, Marx's model is a program for ongoing distributive struggle. It will matter, of course, who wins at this or that moment, but we won't know why or how it matters if we attend only to the successive assertions of dominance and monopoly.

Simple Equality

It is with the first two claims that I shall be concerned, and ultimately with the second alone, for that one seems to me to capture best the plurality of social meanings and the real complexity of distributive systems. But the first is the more common among philosophers; it matches their own search for unity and singularity; and I shall need to explain its difficulties at some length.

Men and women who make the first claim challenge the monopoly but not the dominance of a particular social good. This is also a challenge to monopoly in general; for if wealth, for example, is dominant and widely shared, no other good can possibly be monopolized. Imagine a society in which everything is up for sale and every citizen has as much money as every other. I shall call this the "regime of simple equality." Equality is multiplied through the conversion process, until it extends across the full range of social goods. The regime of simple equality won't last for long, because the further progress of conversion, free exchange in the market, is certain to bring inequalities in its train. If one wanted to sustain simple equality over time, one would require a "monetary law" like the agrarian laws of ancient times or the Hebrew sabbatical, providing for a periodic return to the original condition. Only a centralized and activist state would be strong enough to force such a return; and it isn't clear the state officials would actually be able or willing to do that, if money were the dominant good. In any case, the original condition is unstable in another way. It's not only that monopoly will reappear, but also that dominance will disappear.

In practice, breaking the monopoly of money neutralizes its dominance. Other goods come into play, and inequality takes on new forms. Consider again the regime of simple equality. Everything is up for sale, and everyone has the same amount of money. So everyone has, say, an equal ability to buy an education for his children. Some do that, and others don't. It turns out to be a good investment: other social goods are, increasingly, offered for sale only to people with educational certificates. Soon everyone invests in education; or, more likely, the purchase is universalized through the tax system. But then the school is turned into a competitive world within which money is no longer dominant. Natural talent or family upbringing or skill in writing examinations is dominant instead, and educational success and certification are monopolized by some new group. Let's call them (what they call themselves) the "group of the talented." Eventually the members of this group claim that the good they control should be dominant outside the school: offices, titles, prerogatives, wealth too, should all be possessed by

themselves. This is the career open to talents, equal opportunity, and so on. This is what fairness requires; talent will out; and in any case, talented men and women will enlarge the resources available to everyone else. So Michael Young's meritocracy is born, with all its attendant inequalities.[9]

What should we do now? It is possible to set limits to the new conversion patterns, to recognize but constrain the monopoly power of the talented. I take this to be the purpose of John Rawls's difference principle, according to which inequalities are justified only if they are designed to bring, and actually do bring, the greatest possible benefit to the least advantaged social class.[10] More specifically, the difference principle is a constraint imposed on talented men and women, once the monopoly of wealth has been broken. It works in this way: Imagine a surgeon who claims more than his equal share of wealth on the basis of the skills he has learned and the certificates he has won in the harsh competitive struggles of college and medical school. We will grant the claim if, and only if, granting it is beneficial in the stipulated ways. At the same time, we will act to limit and regulate the sale of surgery – that is, the direct conversion of surgical skill into wealth.

This regulation will necessarily be the work of the state, just as monetary laws and agrarian laws are the work of the state. Simple equality would require continual state intervention to break up or constrain incipient monopolies and to repress new forms of dominance. But then state power itself will become the central object of competitive struggles. Groups of men and women will seek to monopolize and then to use the state in order to consolidate their control of other social goods. Or, the state will be monopolized by its own agents in accordance with the iron law of oligarchy. Politics is always the most direct path to dominance, and political power (rather than the means of production) is probably the most important, and certainly the most dangerous, good in human history.[11] Hence the need to constrain the agents of constraint, to establish constitutional checks and balances. These are limits imposed on political monopoly, and they are all the more important once the various social and economic monopolies have been broken.

One way of limiting political power is to distribute it widely. This may not work, given the well-canvassed dangers of majority tyranny; but these dangers are probably less acute than they are often made out to be. The greater danger of democratic government is that it will be weak to cope with re-emerging monopolies in society at large, with the social strength of plutocrats, bureaucrats, technocrats, meritocrats, and so on. In theory, political power is the dominant good in a democracy, and it is convertible in any way the citizens choose. But in practice, again, breaking the monopoly of power neutralizes its dominance. Political power cannot be widely shared without being subjected to the pull of all the other goods that the citizens already have or hope to have. Hence democracy is, as Marx recognized, essentially a reflective system, mirroring the prevailing and emerging distribution of social goods.[12] Democratic decision making will be shaped by the cultural conceptions that determine or underwrite the new monopolies. To prevail against these monopolies, power will have to be centralized, perhaps itself monopolized. Once again, the state must be very powerful if it is to fulfill the purposes assigned to it by the difference principle or by any similarly interventionist rule.

Still, the regime of simple equality might work. One can imagine a more or less stable tension between emerging monopolies and political constraints, between the claim to privilege put forward by the talented, say, and the enforcement of the difference principle, and then between the agents of enforcement and the democratic constitution. But I suspect that difficulties will recur, and that at many points in time the only remedy for private privilege will be statism, and the only escape from statism will be private privilege. We will mobilize power to check monopoly, then look for some way of checking the power we have mobilized. But there is no way that doesn't open opportunities for strategically placed men and women to seize and exploit important social goods.

These problems derive from treating monopoly, and not dominance, as the central issue in distributive justice. It is not difficult, of course, to understand why philosophers (and political activists, too) have focused on monopoly. The distributive struggles of the modern age begin with a war against the aristocracy's singular hold on land, office, and honor. This seems an especially pernicious monopoly because it rests upon birth and blood, with which the individual has nothing to do, rather than upon wealth, or power, or education, all of which – at least in principle – can be earned. And when every man and woman becomes, as it were, a smallholder in the sphere of birth and blood, an important victory is indeed

won. Birthright ceases to be a dominant good; henceforth, it purchases very little; wealth, power, and education come to the force. With regard to these latter goods, however, simple equality cannot be sustained at all, or it can only be sustained subject to the vicissitudes I have just described. Within their own spheres, as they are currently understood, these three tend to generate natural monopolies that can be repressed only if state power is itself dominant and if it is monopolized by officials committed to the repression. But there is, I think, another path to another kind of equality.

Tyranny and Complex Equality

I want to argue that we should focus on the reduction of dominance – not, or not primarily, on the break-up or the constraint of monopoly. We should consider what it might mean to narrow the range within which particular goods are convertible and to vindicate the autonomy of distributive spheres. But this line of argument, though it is not uncommon historically, has never fully emerged in philosophical writing. Philosophers have tended to criticize (or to justify) existing or emerging monopolies of wealth, power, and education. Or, they have criticized (or justified) particular conversions – of wealth into education or of office into wealth. And all this, most often, in the name of some radically simplified distributive system. The critique of dominance will suggest instead a way of reshaping and then living with the actual complexity of distributions.

Imagine now a society in which different social goods are monopolistically held – as they are in fact and always will be, barring continual state intervention – but in which no particular good is generally convertible. As I go along, I shall try to define the precise limits on convertibility, but for now the general description will suffice. This is a complex egalitarian society. Though there will be many small inequalities, inequality will not be multiplied through the conversion process. Nor will it be summed across different goods, because the autonomy of distributions will tend to produce a variety of local monopolies, held by different groups of men and women. I don't want to claim that complex equality would necessarily be more stable than simple equality, but I am inclined to think that it would open the way for more diffused and particularized forms of social conflict. And the resistance to convertibility would be maintained, in large degree, by ordinary men and women within their own spheres of competence and control, without large-scale state action.

This is, I think, an attractive picture, but I have not yet explained just why it is attractive. The argument for complex equality begins from our understanding – I mean, our actual, concrete, positive, and particular understanding – of the various social goods. And then it moves on to an account of the way we relate to one another through those goods. Simple equality is a simple distributive condition, so that if I have fourteen hats and you have fourteen hats, we are equal. And it is all to the good if hats are dominant, for then our equality is extended through all the spheres of social life. On the view that I shall take here, however, we simply have the same number of hats, and it is unlikely that hats will be dominant for long. Equality is a complex relation of persons, mediated by the goods we make, share, and divide among ourselves; it is not an identity of possessions. It requires then, a diversity of distributive criteria that mirrors the diversity of social goods.

The argument for complex equality has been beautifully put by Pascal in one of his *Pensées*.

> The nature of tyranny is to desire power over the whole world and outside its own sphere.
>
> There are different companies – the strong, the handsome, the intelligent, the devout – and each man reigns in his own, not elsewhere. But sometimes they meet, and the strong and the handsome fight for mastery – foolishly, for their mastery is of different kinds. They misunderstand one another, and make the mistake of each aiming at universal dominion. Nothing can win this, not even strength, for it is powerless in the kingdom of the wise. . . .
>
> *Tyranny.* The following statements, therefore, are false and tyrannical: "Because I am handsome, so I should command respect." "I am strong, therefore men should love me. . . ." "I am . . . et cetera."
>
> Tyranny is the wish to obtain by one means what can only be had by another. We owe different duties to different qualities: love is the proper response to charm, fear to strength, and belief to learning.[13]

Marx made a similar argument in his early manuscripts; perhaps he had this *pensée* in mind:

> Let us assume man to be man, and his relation to the world to be a human one. Then love can only be exchanged for love, trust for trust, etc. If you wish to enjoy art you must be an artistically cultivated person; if you wish to influence other people, you must be a person who really has a stimulating and encouraging effect upon others. . . . If you love without evoking love in return, i.e., if you are not able, by the manifestation of yourself as a loving person, to make yourself a beloved person – then your love is impotent and a misfortune.[14]

These are not easy arguments, and most of my book is simply an exposition of their meaning. But here I shall attempt something more simple and schematic: a translation of the arguments into the terms I have already been using.

The first claim of Pascal and Marx is that personal qualities and social goods have their own spheres of operation, where they work their effects freely, spontaneously, and legitimately. There are ready or natural conversions that follow from, and are intuitively plausible because of, the social meaning of particular goods. The appeal is to our ordinary understanding and, at the same time, against our common acquiescence in illegitimate conversion patterns. Or, it is an appeal from our acquiescence to our resentment. There is something wrong, Pascal suggests, with the conversion of strength into belief. In political terms, Pascal means that no ruler can rightly command my opinions merely because of the power he wields. Nor can he, Marx adds, rightly claim to influence my actions: if a ruler wants to do that, he must be persuasive, helpful, encouraging, and so on. These arguments depend for their force on some shared understanding of knowledge, influence, and power. Social goods have social meanings, and we find our way to distributive justice through an interpretation of those meanings. We search for principles internal to each distributive sphere.

The second claim is that the disregard of these principles is tyranny. To convert one good into another, when there is no intrinsic connection between the two, is to invade the sphere where another company of men and women properly rules. Monopoly is not inappropriate within the spheres. There is nothing wrong, for example, with the grip that persuasive and helpful men and women (politicians) establish on political power. But the use of political power to gain access to other goods is a tyrannical use. Thus, an old description of tyranny is generalized: princes become tyrants, according to medieval writers, when they seize the property or invade the family of their subjects.[15] In political life – but more widely, too – the dominance of goods makes for the domination of people.

The regime of complex equality is the opposite of tyranny. It establishes a set of relationships such that domination is impossible. In formal terms, complex equality means that no citizen's standing in one sphere or with regard to one social good can be undercut by his standing in some other sphere, with regard to some other good. Thus, citizen X may be chosen over citizen Y for political office, and then the two of them will be unequal in the sphere of politics. But they will not be unequal generally so long as X's office gives him no advantages over Y in any other sphere – superior medical care, access to better schools for his children, entrepreneurial opportunities, and so on. So long as office is not a dominant good, is not generally convertible, office holders will stand, or at least can stand, in a relation of equality to the men and women they govern.

But what if dominance were eliminated, the autonomy of the spheres established – and the same people were successful in one sphere after another, triumphant in every company, piling up goods without the need for illegitimate conversions? This would certainly make for an inegalitarian society, but it would also suggest in the strongest way that a society of equals was not a lively possibility. I doubt that any egalitarian argument could survive in the face of such evidence. Here is a person whom we have freely chosen (without reference to his family ties or personal wealth) as our political representative. He is also a bold and inventive entrepreneur. When he was younger, he studied science, scored amazingly high grades in every exam, and made important discoveries. In war, he is surpassingly brave and wins the highest honors. Himself compassionate and compelling, he is loved by all who know him. Are there such people? Maybe so, but I have my doubts. We tell stories like the one I have just told, but the stories are fictions, the conversion of power or money or academic talent into legendary fame. In any case, there aren't enough such people to constitute a ruling class and dominate the rest of us. Nor can they be successful in every distributive sphere, for there are some spheres to which the idea of success doesn't pertain. Nor are their chil-

dren likely, under conditions of complex equality, to inherit their success. By and large, the most accomplished politicians, entrepreneurs, scientists, soldiers, and lovers will be different people; and so long as the goods they possess don't bring other goods in train, we have no reason to fear their accomplishments.

The critique of dominance and domination points toward an open-ended distributive principle. *No social good x should be distributed to men and women who possess some other good y merely because they possess y and without regard to the meaning of x*. This is a principle that has probably been reiterated, at one time or another, for every *y* that has ever been dominant. But it has not often been stated in general terms. Pascal and Marx have suggested the application of the principle against all possible *y*'s, and I shall attempt to work out that application. I shall be looking, then, not at the members of Pascal's companies – the strong or the weak, the handsome or the plain – but at the goods they share and divide. The purpose of the principle is to focus our attention; it doesn't determine the shares or the division. The principle directs us to study the meaning of social goods, to examine the different distributive spheres from the inside.

Three Distributive Principles

The theory that results is unlikely to be elegant. No account of the meaning of a social good, or of the boundaries of the sphere within which it legitimately operates, will be uncontroversial. Nor is there any neat procedure for generating or testing different accounts. At best, the arguments will be rough, reflecting the diverse and conflict-ridden character of the social life that we seek simultaneously to understand and to regulate – but not to regulate until we understand. I shall set aside, then, all claims made on behalf of any single distributive criterion, for no such criterion can possibly match the diversity of social goods. Three criteria, however, appear to meet the requirements of the open-ended principle and have often been defended as the beginning and end of distributive justice, so I must say something about each of them. Free exchange, desert, and need: all three have real force, but none of them has force across the range of distributions. They are part of the story, not the whole of it.

Free exchange

Free exchange is obviously open-ended; it guarantees no particular distributive outcome. At no point in any exchange process plausibly called "free" will it be possible to predict the particular division of social goods that will obtain at some later point.[16] (It may be possible, however, to predict the general structure of the division.) In theory at least, free exchange creates a market within which all goods are convertible into all other goods through the neutral medium of money. There are no dominant goods and no monopolies. Hence the successive divisions that obtain will directly reflect the social meanings of the goods that are divided. For each bargain, trade, sale, and purchase will have been agreed to voluntarily by men and women who know what that meaning is, who are indeed its makers. Every exchange is a revelation of social meaning. By definition, then, no x will ever fall into the hands of someone who possesses y, merely because he possesses y and without regard to what x actually means to some other member of society. The market is radically pluralistic in its operations and its outcomes, infinitely sensitive to the meanings that individuals attach to goods. What possible restraints can be imposed on free exchange, then, in the name of pluralism?

But everyday life in the market, the actual experience of free exchange, is very different from what the theory suggests. Money, supposedly the neutral medium, is in practice a dominant good, and it is monopolized by people who possess a special talent for bargaining and trading – the green thumb of bourgeois society. Then other people demand a redistribution of money and the establishment of the regime of simple equality, and the search begins for some way to sustain that regime. But even if we focus on the first untroubled moment of simple equality – free exchange on the basis of equal shares – we will still need to set limits on what can be exchanged for what. For free exchange leaves distributions entirely in the hands of individuals, and social meanings are not subject, or are not always subject, to the interpretive decisions of individual men and women.

Consider an easy example, the case of political power. We can conceive of political power as a set of goods of varying value, votes, influence, offices, and so on. Any of these can be traded on the market and accumulated by individuals willing to sacrifice other goods. Even if the sacrifices are real, however, the result is a form of tyranny – petty tyranny, given the conditions of simple equality. Because I am willing to do without my hat, I shall vote twice; and you who value the vote less than you value my hat, will not vote at all. I suspect that the result is tyrannical even with regard to the two of us, who have reached a voluntary agreement. It is certainly tyrannical with regard to all the other citizens who must now submit to my disproportionate power. It is not the case that votes can't be bargained for; on one interpretation, that's what democratic politics is all about. And democratic politicians have certainly been known to buy votes, or to try to buy them, by promising public expenditures that benefit particular groups of voters. But this is done in public, with public funds, and subject to public approval. Private trading is ruled out by virtue of what politics, or democratic politics, is – that is, by virtue of what we did when we constituted the political community and of what we still think about what we did.

Free exchange is not a general criterion, but we will be able to specify the boundaries within which it operates only through a careful analysis of particular social goods. And having worked through such an analysis, we will come up at best with a philosophically authoritative set of boundaries and not necessarily with the set that ought to be politically authoritative. For money seeps across all boundaries – this is the primary form of illegal immigration; and just where one ought to try to stop it is a question of expediency as well as of principle. Failure to stop it at some reasonable point has consequences throughout the range of distributions, but consideration of these belongs in a later chapter.

Desert

Like free exchange, desert seems both open-ended and pluralistic. One might imagine a single neutral agency dispensing rewards and punishments, infinitely sensitive to all the forms of individual desert. Then the distributive process would indeed be centralized, but the results would still be unpredictable and various. There would be no dominant good. No x would ever be distributed without regard to its social meaning; for, without attention to what x is, it is conceptually impossible to say that x is deserved. All the different companies of men and women would receive their appropriate reward. How this would work in practice, however, is not easy to figure out. It might make sense to say of this charming man, for example, that he deserves to be loved. It makes no sense to say that he deserves to be loved by this (or any) particular woman. If he loves her while she remains impervious to his (real) charms, that is his misfortune. I doubt that we would want the situation corrected by some outside agency. The love of particular men and women, on our understanding of it, can only be distributed by themselves, and they are rarely guided in these matters by considerations of desert.

The case is exactly the same with influence. Here, let's say, is a woman widely thought to be stimulating and encouraging to others. Perhaps she deserves to be an influential member of our community. But she doesn't deserve that I be influenced by her or that I follow her lead. Nor would we want my followership, as it were, assigned to her by any agency capable of making such assignments. She may go to great lengths to stimulate and encourage me, and do all the things that are commonly called stimulating or encouraging. But if I (perversely) refuse to be stimulated or encouraged, I am not denying her anything that she deserves. The same argument holds by extension for politicians and ordinary citizens. Citizens can't trade their votes for hats; they can't individually decide to cross the boundary that separates the sphere of politics from the market-place. But within the sphere of politics, they do make individual decisions; and they are rarely guided, again, by considerations of desert. It's not clear that offices can be deserved – another issue that I must postpone; but even if they can be, it would violate our understanding of democratic politics were they simply distributed to deserving men and women by some central agency.

Similarly, however we draw the boundaries of the sphere within which free exchange operates, desert will play no role within those boundaries. I am skillful at bargaining and trading, let's say, and so accumulate a large number of beautiful pictures. If we assume, as painters mostly do, that pictures are appropriately traded in the market, then there is nothing wrong with my having the pictures. My title is legitimate. But it would be odd to say that I deserve to have them simply because I am good at bargaining and trading. Desert seems to require an especially close connection between particular goods and particular persons, whereas justice only sometimes requires a connec-

tion of that sort. Still, we might insist that only artistically cultivated people, who deserve to have pictures, should actually have them. It's not difficult to imagine a distributive mechanism. The state could buy all the pictures that were offered for sale (but artists would have to be licensed, so that there wouldn't be an endless number of pictures), evaluate them, and then distribute them to artistically cultivated men and women, the better pictures to the more cultivated. The state does something like this, sometimes, with regard to things that people need – medical care, for example – but not with regard to things that people deserve. There are practical difficulties here, but I suspect a deeper reason for this difference. Desert does not have the urgency of need, and it does not involve having (owning and consuming) in the same way. Hence, we are willing to tolerate the separation of owners of paintings and artistically cultivated people, or we are unwilling to require the kinds of interference in the market that would be necessary to end the separation. Of course, public provision is always possible alongside the market, and so we might argue that artistically cultivated people deserve not pictures but museums. Perhaps they do, but they don't deserve that the rest of us contribute money or appropriate public funds for the purchase of pictures and the construction of buildings. They will have to persuade us that art is worth the money; they will have to stimulate and encourage our own artistic cultivation. And if they fail to do that, their own love of art may well turn out to be "impotent and a misfortune."

Even if we were to assign the distribution of love, influence, offices, works of art, and so on, to some omnipotent arbiters of desert, how would we select them? How could anyone deserve such a position? Only God, who knows what secrets lurk in the hearts of men, would be able to make the necessary distributions. If human beings had to do the work, the distributive mechanism would be seized early on by some band of aristocrats (so they would call themselves) with a fixed conception of what is best and most deserving, and insensitive to the diverse excellences of their fellow citizens. And then desert would cease to be a pluralist criterion; we would find ourselves face to face with a new set (of an old sort) of tyrants. We do, of course, choose people as arbiters of desert – to serve on juries, for example, or to award prizes; it will be worth considering later what the prerogatives of a juror are. But it is important to stress here that he operates within a narrow range. Desert is a strong claim, but it calls for difficult judgments; and only under very special conditions does it yield specific distributions.

Need

Finally, the criterion of need. "To each according to his needs" is generally taken as the distributive half of Marx's famous maxim: we are to distribute the wealth of the community so as to meet the necessities of its members.[17] A plausible proposal, but a radically incomplete one. In fact, the first half of the maxim is also a distributive proposal, and it doesn't fit the rule of the second half. "From each according to his ability" suggests that jobs should be distributed (or that men and women should be conscripted to work) on the basis of individual qualifications. But individuals don't in any obvious sense need the jobs for which they are qualified. Perhaps such jobs are scarce, and there are a large number of qualified candidates: which candidates need them most? If their material needs are already taken care of, perhaps they don't need to work at all. Or if, in some non-material sense, they all need to work, then that need won't distinguish among them, at least not to the naked eye. It would in any case be odd to ask a search committee looking, say, for a hospital director to make its choice on the basis of the needs of the candidates rather than on those of the staff and the patients of the hospital. But the latter set of needs, even if it isn't the subject of political disagreement, won't yield a single distributive decision.

Nor will need work for many other goods. Marx's maxim doesn't help at all with regard to the distribution of political power, honor and fame, sailboats, rare books, beautiful objects of every sort. These are not things that anyone, strictly speaking, needs. Even if we take a loose view and define the verb *to need* the way children do, as the strongest form of the verb *to want*, we still won't have an adequate distributive criterion. The sorts of things that I have listed cannot be distributed equally to those with equal wants because some of them are generally, and some of them are necessarily, scarce, and some of them can't be possessed at all unless other people, for reasons of their own, agree on who is to possess them.

Need generates a particular distributive sphere, within which it is itself the appropriate distributive principle. In a poor society, a high proportion of social wealth will be drawn into this sphere. But given the great variety of goods that arises out of any common life, even when it is lived at a very low material level, other distributive criteria will always be operating alongside of need, and it will always be necessary to worry about the boundaries that mark them off from one another. Within its sphere, certainly, need meets the general distributive rule about x and y. Needed goods distributed to needy people in proportion to their neediness are obviously not dominated by any other goods. It's not having y, but only lacking x that is relevant. But we can now see, I think, that every criterion that has any force at all meets the general rule within its own sphere, and not elsewhere. This is the effect of the rule: different goods to different companies of men and women for different reasons and in accordance with different procedures. And to get all this right, or to get it roughly right, is to map out the entire social world.

Hierarchies and Caste Societies

Or, rather, it is to map out a particular social world. For the analysis that I propose is imminent and phenomenological in character. It will yield not an ideal map or a master plan but, rather, a map and a plan appropriate to the people for whom it is drawn, whose common life it reflects. The goal, of course, is a reflection of a special kind, which picks up those deeper understandings of social goods which are not necessarily mirrored in the everyday practice of dominance and monopoly. But what if there are no such understandings? I have been assuming all along that social meanings call for the autonomy, or the relative autonomy, of distributive spheres; and so they do much of the time. But it's not impossible to imagine a society where dominance and monopoly are not violations but enactments of meaning, where social goods are conceived in hierarchical terms. In feudal Europe, for example, clothing was not a commodity (as it is today) but a badge of rank. Rank dominated dress. The meaning of clothing was shaped in the image of the feudal order. Dressing in finery to which one wasn't entitled was a kind of lie; it made a false statement about who one was. When a king or a prime minister dressed as a commoner in order to learn something about the opinions of his subjects, this was a kind of politic deceit. On the other hand, the difficulties of enforcing the clothing code (the sumptuary laws) suggests that there was all along an alternative sense of what clothing meant. At some point, at least, one can begin to recognize the boundaries of a distinct sphere within which people dress in accordance with what they can afford or what they are willing to spend or how they want to look. The sumptuary laws may still be enforced, but now one can make – and ordinary men and women do, in fact, make – egalitarian arguments against them.

Can we imagine a society in which all goods are hierarchically conceived? Perhaps the caste system of ancient India had this form (though that is a far-reaching claim, and it would be prudent to doubt its truth: for one thing, political power seems always to have escaped the laws of caste). We think of castes as rigidly segregated groups, of the caste system as a "plural society," a world of boundaries.[18] But the system is constituted by an extraordinary integration of meanings. Prestige, wealth, knowledge, office, occupation, food, clothing, even the social good of conversation: all are subject to the intellectual as well as to the physical discipline of hierarchy. And the hierarchy is itself determined by the single value of ritual purity. A certain kind of collective mobility is possible, for castes or subcastes can cultivate the outward marks of purity and (within severe limits) raise their position in the social scale. And the system as a whole rests upon a religious doctrine that promises equality of opportunity, not in this life but across the lives of the soul. The individual's status here and now "is the result of his conduct in his last incarnation . . . and if unsatisfactory can be remedied by acquiring merit in his present life which will raise his status in the next."[19] We should not assume that men and women are ever entirely content with radical inequality. Nevertheless, distributions here and now are part of a single system, largely unchallenged, in which purity is dominant over other goods – and birth and blood are dominant over purity. Social meanings overlap and cohere.

The more perfect the coherence, the less possible it is even to think about complex equality. All goods are like crowns and thrones in a hereditary monarchy. There is no room, and there are no criteria, for autonomous distributions. In fact, however, even hereditary monarchies are rarely so simply constructed. The social understanding of royal power commonly involves some notion of divine grace, or magical gift, or human insight; and these criteria for office holding are potentially independent of birth and blood. So it is for most social goods: they are only imperfectly integrated

into larger systems; they are understood, at least sometimes, in their own terms. The theory of goods explicates understandings of this sort (where they exist), and the theory of complex equality exploits them. We say, for example, that it is tyrannical for a man without grace or gift or insight to sit upon the throne. And this is only the first and most obvious kind of tyranny. We can search for many other kinds.

Tyranny is always specific in character: a particular boundary crossing, a particular violation of social meaning. Complex equality requires the defense of boundaries; it works by differentiating goods just as hierarchy works by differentiating people. But we can only talk of a *regime* of complex equality when there are many boundaries to defend; and what the right number is cannot be specified. There is no right number. Simple equality is easier: one dominant good widely distributed makes an egalitarian society. But complexity is hard: how many goods must be autonomously conceived before the relations they mediate can become the relations of equal men and women? There is no certain answer and hence no ideal regime. But as soon as we start to distinguish meanings and mark out distributive spheres, we are launched on an egalitarian enterprise.

The Setting of the Argument

The political community is the appropriate setting for this enterprise. It is not, to be sure, a self-contained distributive world: only the world is a self-contained distributive world, and contemporary science fiction invites us to speculate about a time when even that won't be true. Social goods are shared, divided, and exchanged across political frontiers. Monopoly and dominance operate almost as easily beyond the frontiers as within them. Things are moved, and people move themselves, back and forth across the lines. Nevertheless, the political community is probably the closest we can come to a world of common meanings. Language, history, and culture come together (come more closely together here than anywhere else) to produce a collective consciousness. National character, conceived as a fixed and permanent mental set, is obviously a myth; but the sharing of sensibilities and intuitions among the members of a historical community is a fact of life. Sometimes political and historical communities don't coincide, and there may well be a growing number of states in the world today where sensibilities and intuitions aren't readily shared; the sharing takes place in smaller units. And then, perhaps, we should look for some way to adjust distributive decisions to the requirements of those units. But this adjustment must itself be worked out politically, and its precise character will depend upon understandings shared among the citizens about the value of cultural diversity, local autonomy, and so on. It is to these understandings that we must appeal when we make our arguments – all of us, not philosophers alone; for in matters of morality, argument simply is the appeal to common meanings.

Politics, moreover, establishes its own bonds of commonality. In a world of independent states, political power is a local monopoly. These men and women, we can say, under whatever constraints, shape their own destiny. Or they struggle as best they can to shape their own destiny. And if their destiny is only partially in their own hands, the struggle is entirely so. They are the ones whose decision it is to tighten or loosen distributive criteria, to centralize or decentralize procedures, to intervene or refuse to intervene in this or that distributive sphere. Probably, some set of leaders make the actual decisions, but the citizens should be able to recognize the leaders as their own. If the leaders are cruel or stupid or endlessly venal, as they often are, the citizens or some of the citizens will try to replace them, fighting over the distribution of political power. The fight will be shaped by the institutional structures of the community – that is, by the outcomes of previous fights. Politics present is the product of politics past. It establishes an unavoidable setting for the consideration of distributive justice.

There is one last reason for adopting the view of the political community as setting, a reason that I shall elaborate on at some length in the next chapter. The community is itself a good – conceivably the most important good – that gets distributed. But it is a good that can only be distributed by taking people in, where all the senses of that latter phrase are relevant: they must be physically admitted and politically received. Hence membership cannot be handed out by some external agency; its value depends upon an internal decision. Were there no communities capable of making such decisions, there would in this case be no good worth distributing.

The only plausible alternative to the political community is humanity itself, the society of na-

tions, the entire globe. But were we to take the globe as our setting, we would have to imagine what does not yet exist: a community that included all men and women everywhere. We would have to invent a set of common meanings for these people, avoiding if we could the stipulation of our own values. And we would have to ask the members of this hypothetical community (or their hypothetical representatives) to agree among themselves on what distributive arrangements and patterns of conversion are to count as just. Ideal contractualism or undistorted communication, which represents one approach – not my own – to justice in particular communities, may well be the only approach for the globe as a whole.[20] But whatever the hypothetical agreement, it could not be enforced without breaking the political monopolies of existing states and centralizing power at the global level. Hence the agreement (or the enforcement) would make not for complex but for simple equality – if power was dominant and widely shared – or simply for tyranny – if power was seized, as it probably would be, by a set of international bureaucrats. In the first case, the people of the world would have to live with the difficulties I have described: the continual reappearance of local privilege, the continual reassertion of global statism. In the second case, they would have to live with difficulties that are considerably worse. I will have a little more to say about these difficulties later. For now I take them to be reasons enough to limit myself to cities, countries, and states that have, over long periods of time, shaped their own internal life.

With regard to membership, however, important questions arise between and among such communities, and I shall try to focus on them and to draw into the light all those occasions when ordinary citizens focus on them. In a limited way, the theory of complex equality can be extended from particular communities to the society of nations, and the extension has this advantage: it will not run roughshod over local understandings and decisions. Just for that reason, it also will not yield a uniform system of distributions across the globe, and it will only begin to address the problems raised by mass poverty in many parts of the globe. I don't think the beginning unimportant; in any case, I can't move beyond it. To do that would require a different theory, which would take as its subject not the common life of citizens but the more distanced relations of states: a different theory, a different book, another time.

Notes

1 See John Rawls, *A Theory of Justice* (Cambridge, Mass., 1971); Jürgen Habermas, *Legitimation Crisis*, trans. Thomas McCarthy (Boston, 1975), esp. p. 113; Bruce Ackerman, *Social Justice in the Liberal State* (New Haven, 1980).

2 Robert Nozick makes a similar argument in *Anarchy, State, and Utopia* (New York, 1974), pp. 149–50, but with radically individualistic conclusions that seem to me to miss the social character of production.

3 Ralph Waldo Emerson, "Ode," in *The Complete Essays and Other Writings*, ed. Brooks Atkinson (New York, 1940), p. 770.

4 John Stuart Mill, *On Liberty*, in *The Philosophy of John Stuart Mill*, ed. Marshall Cohen (New York, 1961), p. 255. For an anthropological account of liking and not liking social goods, see Mary Douglas and Baron Isherwood, *The World of Goods* (New York, 1979).

5 William James, quoted in C.R. Snyder and Howard Fromkin, *Uniqueness: The Human Pursuit of Difference* (New York, 1980), p. 108.

6 Aren't social meanings, as Marx said, nothing other than "the ideas of the ruling class," "the dominant material relationships grasped as ideas"? (Karl Marx, *The German Ideology*, ed. R. Pascal (New York, 1947), p. 89). I don't think that they are ever only that or simply that, though the members of the ruling class and the intellectuals they patronize may well be in a position to exploit and distort social meanings in their own interests. When they do that, however, they are likely to encounter resistance, rooted (intellectually) in those same meanings. A people's culture is always a joint, even if it isn't an entirely cooperative, production; and it is always a complex production. The common understanding of particular goods incorporates principles, procedures, conceptions of agency, that the rulers would not choose if they were choosing *right now* – and so provides the terms of social criticism. The appeal to what I shall call "internal" principles against the usurpations of powerful men and women is the ordinary form of critical discourse.

7 Bernard Williams, *Problems of the Self: Philosophical Papers, 1956–1972* (Cambridge, England, 1973), pp. 230–49 ("The Idea of Equality"). This essay is one of the starting points of my own thinking about distributive justice. See also the critique of Williams's argument (and of an earlier essay of my own) in Amy Gutmann, *Liberal Equality* (Cambridge, England, 1980), chap. 4.

8 See Alan W. Wood, "The Marxian Critique of Justice," *Philosophy and Public Affairs* 1 (1972): 244–82.

9 Michael Young, *The Rise of the Meritocracy, 1870–2033* (Harmondsworth, England, 1961) – a brilliant piece of social science fiction.

10 Rawls, *Theory of Justice*, pp. 75ff.

11 I should note here what will become more clear as I go along, that political power is a special sort of good. It has a twofold character. First, it is like the other things that men and women make, value, exchange, and share: sometimes dominant, sometimes not; sometimes widely held, sometimes the possession of a very few. And, second, it is unlike all the other things because, however it is had and whoever has it, political power is the regulative agency for social goods generally. It is used to defend the boundaries of all the distributive spheres, including its own, and to enforce the common understandings of what goods are and what they are for. (But it can also be used, obviously, to invade the different spheres and to override those understandings.) In this second sense, we might say, indeed, that political power is always dominant – at the boundaries, but not within them. The central problem of political life is to maintain that crucial distinction between "at" and "in." But this is a problem that cannot be solved given the imperatives of simple equality.

12 See Marx's comment, in his "Critique of the Gotha Program," that the democratic republic is the "form of state" within which the class struggle will be fought to a conclusion: the struggle is immediately and without distortion reflected in political life (Marx and Engels, *Selected Works* [Moscow, 1951], vol. II, p. 31).

13 Blaise Pascal, *The Pensées*, trans. J.M. Cohen (Harmondsworth, England, 1961), p. 96 (no. 244).

14 Karl Marx, *Economic and Philosophical Manuscripts*, in *Early Writings*, ed. T.B. Bottomore (London, 1963), pp. 193–94. It is interesting to note an earlier echo of Pascal's argument in Adam Smith's *Theory of Moral Sentiments* (Edinburgh, 1813), vol. I, pp. 378–9; but Smith seems to have believed that distributions in his own society actually conformed to this view of appropriateness – a mistake neither Pascal nor Marx ever made.

15 See the summary account in Jean Bodin, *Six Books of a Commonweale*, ed. Kenneth Douglas McRae (Cambridge, Mass., 1962), pp. 210–18.

16 Cf. Nozick on "patterning," *Anarchy, State, and Utopia* [2], pp. 155ff.

17 Marx, "Gotha Program", (above) p. 23.

18 J.H. Hutton, *Caste in India: Its Nature, Function, and Origins* (4th ed., Bombay, 1963), pp. 127–8.

I have also drawn on Célestin Bouglé, *Essays on the Caste System*, trans. D.F. Pocock (Cambridge, England, 1971), esp. Part III, chaps. 3 and 4; and Louis Dumont, *Homo Hierarchus: The Caste System and Its Implications* (revised English ed., Chicago, 1980).

19 Hutton, *Caste in India*, (above) p. 125.
20 See Charles Beitz, *Political Theory and International Relations* (Princeton, 1979), part III, for an effort to apply Rawlsian ideal contractualism to international society.

34

Justice Engendered

Martha Minow

I Introduction

(a) *What's the difference?*

The use of anesthesia in surgery spread quickly once discovered. Yet the nineteenth-century doctors who adopted anesthesia selected which patients needed it and which deserved it. Both the medical literature and actual medical practices distinguished people's need for painkillers based on race, gender, ethnicity, age, temperament, personal habits, and economic class. Some people's pain was thought more serious than others; some people were thought to be hardy enough to withstand pain. Doctors believed that women, for example, needed painkillers more than men and that the rich and educated needed painkillers more than the poor and uneducated. How might we, today, evaluate these examples of discrimination? What differences between people should matter, and for what purposes?

The endless variety of our individualism means that we suffer different kinds of pain and may well experience pain differently. But when professionals use categories like gender, race, ethnicity, and class to presume real differences in people's pain and entitlement to help, I worry. I worry that unfairness will result under the guise of objectivity and neutrality. I worry that a difference assigned by someone with power over a more vulnerable person will become endowed with an apparent reality, despite powerful competing views. If no one can really know another's pain, who shall decide how to treat pain, and along what calculus? These are questions of justice, not science. These are questions of complexity, not justifications for passivity, because failing to notice another's pain is an act with significance.

(b) *The problem and the argument*

Each term, the Supreme Court and the nation confront problems of difference in this heterogeneous society. The cases that present these problems attract heightened media attention and reenact continuing struggles over the meanings of subgroup identity in a nation committed to an idea called equality. The drama of these cases reveals the enduring grip of "difference" in the public imagination, and the genuine social and economic conflicts over what particular difference come to mean over time. During the 1986 term, litigators framed for the Court issues about the permissible legal meanings of difference in the lives of individuals, minority groups, and majority groups in cases involving gender, race, ethnicity, religion, and handicap.

Uniting these questions is the dilemma of difference. The dilemma of difference has three versions. The first version is the dilemma that we may recreate difference either by noticing it or by

Originally published in *Harvard Law Review* 101 (1987): 10–95; reprinted in part in Patricia Smith (ed.), *Feminist Jurisprudence* (New York: Oxford University Press, 1993), pp. 217–43. Copyright © 1987 by Harvard Law Review Association. Reprinted by permission of Harvard Law Review and the author.

ignoring it. Decisions about employment, benefits, and treatment in society should not turn on an individual's race, gender, religion, or membership in any other group about which some have deprecating or hostile attitudes. Yet refusing to acknowledge these differences may make them continue to matter in a world constructed with some groups, but not others, in mind. If women's biological differences from men justify special benefits for women in the workplace, are women thereby helped or hurt? Are negative active stereotypes reinforced, and does that matter? Focusing on differences poses the risk of recreating them. Especially when used by decision makers who award benefits and distribute burdens, traits of difference can carry meanings uncontrolled and unwelcomed by those to whom they are assigned. Yet denying those differences undermines the value they may have to those who cherish them as part of their own identity.

The second version of the dilemma is the riddle of neutrality. If the public schools must remain neutral toward religion, do they do so by balancing the teaching of evolution with the teaching of scientific arguments about divine creation – or does this accommodation of a religious view depart from the requisite neutrality? Governmental neutrality may freeze in place the past consequences of differences. Yet any departure from neutrality in governmental standards uses governmental power to make those differences matter and thus symbolically reinforces them.

The third version of the dilemma is the choice between broad discretion, which permits individualized decisions, and formal rules that specify categorical decisions for the dispensing of public – or private – power. If the criminal justice system must not take the race of defendants or victims into account, is this goal achieved by granting discretion to prosecutors and jurors, who can then make individualized decisions but may also introduce racial concerns, or should judges impose formal rules specifying conditions under which racial concerns must be made explicit to guard against them? By granting discretion to officials or to private decision makers, legislators and judges disengage themselves from directly endorsing the use of differences in decisions; yet this grant of discretion also allows those decision makers to give significance to differences. Formal rules constrain public or private discretion, but their very specificity may make differences significant.

I believe these dilemmas arise out of powerful unstated assumptions about whose point of view matters and about what is given and what is mutable in the world. "Difference" is only meaningful as a comparison. I am no more different from you than you are from me. A short person is different only in relation to a tall one. Legal treatment of difference tends to take for granted an assumed point of comparison: Women are compared to the unstated norm of men, "minority" races to whites, handicapped persons to the ablebodied, and "minority" religions to "majorities." Such assumptions work in part through the very structure of our language, which embeds the unstated points of comparison inside categories that bury their perspective and wrongly imply a natural fit with the world. The term *working mother* modifies the general category *mother*, revealing that the general term carries some unstated common meanings (that is, a woman who cares for her children full time without pay), which, even if unintended, must expressly be modified. Legal treatment of difference thus tends to treat as unproblematic the point of view from which difference is seen, assigned, or ignored, rather than acknowledging that the problem of difference can be described and understood from multiple points of view.

Noticing the unstated point of comparison and point of view used in assessments of difference does not eliminate the dilemma of difference; instead, more importantly, it links problems of difference to questions of vantage point. I will argue that what initially may seem to be an objective stance may appear partial from another point of view. Furthermore, what initially appears to be a fixed and objective difference may seem from another viewpoint like the subordination or exclusion of some people by others. Regardless of which perspective ultimately seems persuasive, the possibility of multiple viewpoints challenges the assumption of objectivity and shows how claims to knowledge bear the imprint of those making the claims.

Difference may seem salient not because of a trait intrinsic to the person but instead because the dominant institutional arrangements were designed without that trait in mind. Consider the difference between buildings built without considering the needs of people in wheelchairs and buildings that are accessible to people in wheelchairs. Institutional arrangements define whose reality is to be the norm and make what is known as different seem natural. By asking how power influences knowledge, we can address the question of whether difference was assigned as an expression of domination or as a remedy for past domination. In so doing, we can determine the risks of creating a new pattern of domination while remedying unequal power relationships.

The commitment to seek out and to appreciate a perspective other than one's own animates the reasoning of some Supreme Court justices, some of the time. It is a difficult commitment to make and to fulfill. Aspects of language, social structure, and political culture steer in the opposite direction: toward assertions of absolute categories transcending human choice or perspective. It is not only that justice is created by, and defeated by, people who have genders, races, ethnicities, religions – people who are themselves situated in relation to the differences they discuss. It is also the case that justice is made by people who live in a world already made. Existing institutions and language already carve the world and already express and recreate attitudes about what counts as a difference and who or what is the relevant point of comparison. Once we see that any point of view, including one's own, *is* a point of view, we will realize that every difference we see is seen in relation to something already assumed as the starting point. Then we can expose for debate what the starting points should be. The task for judges is to identify vantage points, to learn how to adopt contrasting vantage points, and to decide which vantage points to embrace in given circumstances.

A difficulty here, as always, is who is "we." Writing not just for judges, but for all who judge, I mean to invoke a broad array of people in the exploration of justice. Yet the perspective I advance cannot escape my own critique of the partiality of every perspective. The very focus on the "difference" problem selects that problem rather than others (for example, the loss of coherence and tradition in society) as the point of discussion. My use of "we," then, represents an invitation to the reader to assent, to disagree, but above all, to engage with this focus. I use "we," moreover, to emphasize the human authorship of the problems and solutions at hand, and to avoid locutions that eliminate human pronouns.

In Part II, I explore three versions of the dilemma of difference, illustrating how they arose in the contexts of religion, ethnicity, race, gender, and handicapping conditions in cases before the Supreme Court during the 1986 term. Next, in Part III, I turn to the influence in these cases of unstated assumptions about points of reference and starting points for analysis, assumptions that are continually reinforced by established modes of thought, language, and patterns of legal reasoning.

In Part IV, I first identify how members of the Court periodically challenge these assumptions by seeking the perspective of individuals and groups unlike themselves. Unfortunately, the justices are not always successful in their efforts. Feminist scholars have done much to reveal the persistence of these assumptions, particularly the assumption that men – their needs and experiences – are the standard for individual rights, and in Part IV I go on to develop and pursue this basic feminist insight. In so doing, I also explore ways in which some feminist analyses have recreated the problems they sought to address, elaborating the idea of "woman's experience," leaving unstated the race, ethnicity, religion, and bodily condition presumed in the identification of woman's point of view.

What, then, is to be done? In Part V, I urge the judiciary to make a perpetual commitment to approach questions of difference by seeking out unstated assumptions about difference and typically unheard points of view. There will not be a rule, a concept, a norm, or a test to apply to these problems. The very yearning for simple and clear solutions is part of the difference problem. The allure of this simplicity reflects our dangerous tendency to assign differences, to pretend that they are natural, and to use categorical solutions to cut off rather than to promote understanding. Instead of a new solution, I urge struggles over descriptions of reality. Litigation in the Supreme Court should be an opportunity to endow rival vantage points with the reality that power enables, to redescribe and remake the meanings of difference in a world that has treated only some vantage points on difference as legitimate.

Far from being unmanageable, this approach describes what happens already in the best practices of justice. Justice, in this view, is not abstract, universal, or neutral. Instead, justice is the quality of human engagement with multiple perspectives framed by, but not limited to, the relationships of power in which they are formed. Decisions, then, can and must be made. Despite the distortions sometimes injected by a language of objectivity and neutrality, the Supreme Court has "engendered" justice in many cases. These cases show the commitment in contemporary statutory and constitutional law to give equality meaning for people once thought to be "different" from those in charge. From the work of this term, which is the last for Justice Powell, the first for Justice Scalia, and the first for Chief Justice Rehnquist as head of the Court, I hope to demonstrate how our common humanity wins when the Court struggles with our differences.

II   A Case of Differences

Arguments before the Supreme Court engage all three versions of the difference dilemma and cut across cases otherwise differentiated by doctrine and contexts. The dilemma arises in both equality and religion cases, and in statutory and constitutional contexts. This section explicitly draws connections across these seemingly disparate cases and explores the dilemma in cases decided in the 1986 term.

(a)   *The dilemma of recreating difference both by ignoring it and by noticing it*

California Federal Savings & Loan Association v. Guerra (Cal Fed)[1] presented in classic form the dilemma of recreating difference through both noticing and ignoring it. Petitioners, a collection of employers, argued that a California statute[2] mandating a qualified right to reinstatement following an unpaid pregnancy disability leave amounted to special preferential treatment, in violation of Title VII's prohibition of discrimination on the basis of pregnancy.[3] Writing an opinion announcing the judgment for the Court, Justice Marshall transformed the question presented by the plaintiffs: Instead of asking whether the federal ban against discrimination on the basis of pregnancy precluded a state's decision to require special treatment for pregnancy, the majority asked whether the state could adopt a minimum protection for pregnant workers while still permitting employers to avoid treating pregnant workers differently by extending similar benefits to nonpregnant workers. Framing the problem this way, the majority ruled that "Congress intended the PDA to be 'a floor beneath which pregnancy disability benefits may not drop – not a ceiling above which they may not rise.' "[4] The majority acknowledged the risk that recognizing the difference of pregnancy could recreate its stigmatizing effects, but noted that "a State could not mandate special treatment of pregnant workers based on stereotypes or generalizations about their needs and

abilities."[5] Thus, despite the federal antidiscrimination requirement, the majority found that states could direct employers to take the sheer physical disability of the pregnancy difference into account, but not any stereotyped views associated with that difference. The majority gave two responses to the problem of difference: First, accommodating pregnant workers would secure a workplace that would equally enable both female and male employees to work and have a family; second, the federal and state statutes should be construed as inviting employers to provide the same benefits to men and women in comparable situations of disability.[6]

Writing for the dissenters, Justice White maintained that the California statute required disability leave policies for pregnant workers even in the absence of similar policies for men. It thus violated the PDA, which "leaves no room for preferential treatment of pregnant workers."[7] In the face of this conflict, the federal statute must pre-empt the state law. The commands of nondiscrimination prohibit taking differences into account, Justice White argued, regardless of the impact of this neglect on people with the difference. Justice White acknowledged the majority's argument that preferential treatment would revive nineteenth-century protective legislation, perpetuating sex role stereotypes and "imped[ing] women in their efforts to take their rightful place in the workplace."[8] For Justice White, however, such arguments were irrelevant, because the Court's role was restricted to interpreting congressional intent and thus would not permit consideration of the arguments about stereotyping. Yet to some extent, the issue of stereotypes was unavoidable: The dilemma in the case, from one point of view, was whether women could secure a benefit that would eliminate a burden connected with their gender, without at the same time reactivating negative meanings about their gender.

In two other cases in the 1986 term, the Court confronted the dilemma of recreating difference in situations in which individuals claimed to be members of minority races in order to obtain special legal protections. By claiming an identity in order to secure some benefit from it, the individuals faced the dilemma that they might fuel negative meanings of that identity, meanings beyond their control. Although racial identification under federal civil rights statutes provides a means of legal redress, it also runs the risk of recreating stigmatizing associations, thereby stimulating prejudice.

In *Saint Francis College v. Al-Khazraji,*[9] a man from Iraq who had failed to secure tenure from his employer, a private college, brought a claim of racial discrimination under 42 U.S.C. section 1981. His case foundered, however, when the lower courts rejected his claim that his Arab identity constituted racial membership of the sort protected by the federal statute.

In *Shaare Tefila Congregation v. Cobb,*[10] members of a Jewish congregation whose synagogue was defaced by private individuals alleged violations of the federal guarantee against interference with property rights on racial grounds. The difference dilemma appeared on the face of the complaint: The petitioners argued that Jews are not a racially distinct group, and yet they claimed that Jews should be entitled to protection against racial discrimination because others treat them as though they were distinct. The petitioners thus demonstrated their reluctance to have a difference identified in a way that they themselves could not control, while simultaneously expressing their desire for protection against having that difference assigned to them by others. To gain this protection, the petitioners had to identify themselves through the very category they rejected as a definition of themselves. Both the district court and the court of appeals refused to allow the petitioners to be included in the protected group on the basis of the attitudes of others, without some proof of well-established traits internal to the group. The court of appeals reasoned:

Although we sympathize with appellant's position, we conclude that it cannot support a claim of racial discrimination solely on the basis of defendants' perception of Jews as being members of a racially distinct group. To allow otherwise would permit charges of racial discrimination to arise out of nothing more than the subjective, irrational perceptions of defendants.[11]

In contrast, one member of the appeals panel, dissenting on this point, argued: "Misperception lies at the heart of prejudice, and the animus formed of such ignorance sows malice and hatred wherever it operates without restriction."[12]

Is the cause of individualized treatment advanced by allowing groups to claim legal protections by dint of group membership, however erroneously assigned by others? Conversely, may denying these claims of legal protection against

assigned difference allow the Supreme Court to avoid addressing the dilemma and thereby reenact it? In both *Shaare Tefila* and *Saint Francis*, the Court asked only whether the legislators adopting the antidiscrimination legislation shortly after the Civil War viewed Jews and Arabs as distinct races. The Court answered the question affirmatively in both cases but based its conclusion on a review of the legislative histories and contemporaneous dictionaries and encyclopedias instead of tackling the difference dilemma directly.

The Court's historical test for membership in a minority race effectively revitalized not just categorical thinking in general, but the specific categorical thinking about race prevailing in the 1860s, despite considerable changes in scientific and moral understandings of the use of abstract categories to label people and solve problems. Whether the issue is gender, religion, or race, reviving old sources for defining group difference may reinvigorate older attitudes about the meanings of group traits. Denying the presence of those traits, however, and their significance in society, deprives individuals of protection against discrimination due to outmoded or unsubstantiated conceptions of group difference.

(b) *Neutrality and nonneutrality: the dilemma of government embroilment in difference*

The dilemma of difference appears especially acute for a government committed to acting neutrally. Neutral means might not produce neutral results, given historic practices and social arrangements that have not been neutral. For example, securing neutrality toward religious differences is the explicit goal of both the First Amendment's ban against the establishment of religion and its protection of the free exercise of religion. Thus to be truly neutral, the government must walk a narrow path between promoting or endorsing religion and failing to make room for religious exercise. Accommodation of religious practices may look nonneutral, but failure to accommodate may also seem nonneutral by burdening the religious minority whose needs were not built into the structure of mainstream institutions.

The "creation science" case, *Edwards v. Aguillard,*[13] raised the question of how the government, in the form of public schools, can respect religious differences while remaining neutral toward them. In *Edwards*, parents and students claimed that a

Louisiana statute requiring public schools to teach creation science whenever they taught the theory of evolution violated the establishment clause. Community members subscribing to fundamentalist religious beliefs, however, have argued that public school instruction in evolution alone is not neutral, because it gives a persuasive advantage to views that undermine their own religious beliefs. Relying on similar arguments, the state avowed a neutral, nonreligious purpose for its statute.[14]

The majority, in an opinion by Justice Brennan, concluded that the legislation was actually intended to "provide persuasive advantage to a particular religious doctrine that rejects the factual basis of evolution in its entirety."[15] By contrast, the dissenting opinion by Justice Scalia, which was joined by Chief Justice Rehnquist, expressly tangled with the neutrality problem, noting the difficult tensions between antiestablishment and free exercise concerns and between neutrality through indifference and neutrality through accommodation. In the end, the dissent was moved by the state's attempt to avoid undermining the different views of fundamentalist Christian students, while the majority was persuaded that the statute gave an illegal preference to a particular religious view. For both sides, however, the central difficulty was how to find a neutral position between these two risks.

In a second case, *Hobbie v. Unemployment Appeals Commission*,[16] the neutrality problem arose when the Court reviewed a state's decision to deny unemployment benefits to a woman under an apparently neutral scheme. Hobbie was discharged from her job when she refused to work during her religious Sabbath. The state argued that Hobbie's refusal to work amounted to misconduct related to her work and rendered her ineligible for unemployment benefits under a statute limiting compensation to persons who become "unemployed through no fault of their own."[17] The Court rejected this emphasis on the cause of the conflict, because the "salient inquiry" was whether the denial of unemployment benefits unlawfully burdened Hobbie's free exercise right. The Court also rejected the state's claim that making unemployment benefits available to Hobbie would unconstitutionally establish religion by easing eligibility requirements for religious adherents.[18] By requiring accommodation for free exercise, despite charges of establishing religion, the Court's solution thus framed a dilemma of neutrality: How can the government's means be neutral in a world that is not itself neutral?

A facially neutral state policy on unemployment compensation also figured in *Wimberly v. Labor & Industrial Relations Commission*.[19] Wimberly had taken a pregnancy leave from her job with no guarantee of reinstatement, and upon her return the employer told her that there were no positions available. Her application for unemployment benefits was denied under a state law disqualifying applicants unless their reasons for leaving were directly attributable to the work or to the employer. Wimberly argued that a federal statute forbidding discrimination in unemployment compensation "solely on the basis of pregnancy or termination of pregnancy"[20] required accommodation for women who leave work because of pregnancy.

The Supreme Court unanimously rejected Wimberly's claim that this denial of benefits contravened the federal statute. The Court found that the state had not singled out pregnancy as the reason for withholding unemployment benefits; instead, pregnancy fell within a broad class of reasons for unemployment unrelated to work or to the employer. The Court interpreted the federal statute to forbid discrimination but not to mandate preferential treatment. In the Court's eyes, then, it was neutral to have a general rule denying unemployment benefits to anyone unemployed for reasons unrelated to the workplace or the employer.[21]

In essence, the Court interpreted the federal statutory scheme as granting discretion to state legislatures to define their own terms for disqualification from eligibility for benefits. Although many states provide unemployment benefits for women who leave their jobs because of pregnancy, subsuming it under terms like "good cause," along with other compelling personal reasons, injury, illness, or the federal ban against refusing benefits "solely on the basis of pregnancy" does not, according to the Court, compel such coverage. A state choosing to define its unemployment eligibility narrowly enough to disqualify not just those who leave work due to pregnancy but also those who leave work for good cause, illness, or compelling personal reasons may thus do so without violating federal law.

The Court in *Wimberly* rejected the argument that ignoring the difference of pregnancy produces illicit discrimination under an apparently neutral unemployment benefits rule. In *Hobbie*, on the other hand, the Court embraced the view that ignoring a religious difference produces illicit discrimination under an apparently neutral unemployment benefits rule. In both cases, the Court grappled with the dilemma of whether to give meaning to neutrality by recognizing or not recognizing difference.

(c) *Discretion and formality: the dilemma of using power to differentiate*

The Court's commitment to the rule of law often leads it to specify, in formal terms, the rules that govern the decisions of others. This practice can secure adherence to the goals of equality and neutrality by ensuring that differences are not taken into account except in the manner explicitly specified by the Court. Although likely to promote accountability, this solution of formal rules has drawbacks. Making and enforcing specific rules engages the Court in the problem of reinvesting differences with significance by noticing them. Specifically requiring the Court to articulate permissible and impermissible uses of difference may enshrine categorical analysis and move further away from the ideal of treating persons as individuals. One way for the Court to resolve the difference dilemma is to grant or cede discretion to other decision makers. Then the problems from both noticing and ignoring difference, and from risking nonneutrality in means and results, are no longer problems for the Court but, instead, matters within the discretion of other private or public decision makers. This approach simply moves the problem to another forum, allowing the decision maker with the discretion to take difference into account in an impermissible manner. The tension between formal, predictable rules and individualized judgments under discretionary standards thus assumes heightened significance in dilemmas of difference.

This dilemma of discretion and formality most vividly occupied the Court in *McCleskey v. Kemp*,[22] in which the Court evaluated charges of racial discrimination in the administration of the death penalty in Georgia's criminal justice system. A statistical study of over two thousand murder cases in Georgia during the 1970s, submitted by the defendant and assumed by the Court to be valid, demonstrated that the likelihood of a defendant's receiving the death sentence was correlated with the victim's race and, to a lesser extent, the defendant's race. According to the study, black defendants convicted of killing white victims "have the greatest likelihood of receiving the death penalty." Should the Court treat a sentencing "discrepancy that appears to correlate with race" as a defect requiring judicial constraints on prosecutorial and jury discretion, or as an unavoidable consequence of such discretion? In making this choice, the majority and the dissenters each latched onto opposing sides of the dilemma about discretion and formality.

Justice Powell, for the majority, began by asserting that the discretion of the jury is critical to the criminal justice system and operates to the advantage of criminal defendants because it permits individualized treatment rather than arbitrary application of rules. Because of the importance of discretion, unexplained racial discrepancies in the sentencing process should not be assumed to be invidious or unconstitutional. In the majority's view, recognizing claims such as McCleskey's would open the door "to claims based on unexplained discrepancies that correlate to membership in other minority groups, and even to gender" or physical appearance. This argument, perhaps meant in part to trivialize the dissent's objections by linking physical appearance with race, sex, and ethnicity, implied that discrepancies in criminal sentences are random and too numerous to control. Furthermore, in the majority's view, any attempt to channel discretion runs the risk of undermining it altogether: "It is difficult to imagine guidelines that would produce the predictability sought by the dissent without sacrificing the discretion essential to a humane and fair system of criminal justice."[23]

Justice Brennan, in dissent, approached the problem of discretion and formality from the other direction. Like the majority, Justice Brennan asserted that imposition of the death penalty must be based on an "individualized moral inquiry." To Justice Brennan, however, the statistical correlation between death sentences and the race of defendants and victims showed that participants in the state criminal justice system had, in fact, considered race and produced judgments "completely at odds with [the] concern that an individual be evaluated as a unique human being." Justice Brennan argued that "discretion is a means, not an end" and that, under the circumstances, the Court must monitor the discretion of others. Justice Brennan also responded to the majority's fear of widespread challenges to all aspects of criminal sentencing: "Taken on its face, such a statement seems to suggest a fear of too much justice.... The prospect that there may be more widespread abuse than McCleskey documents may be dismaying, but it does not justify complete abdication of our judicial role."[24]

Justice Stevens, also in dissent, argued that there remains a middle road between forbidding the death penalty and ignoring, in the name of prosecutorial and jury discretion, the correlation between the death penalty and the defendant's and victim's races. He urged a specific rule: The class of defendants eligible for the death penalty should be narrowed to the category of cases, identified by the study, in which "prosecutors consistently seek, and juries consistently impose, the death penalty without regard to the race of the victim or the race of the offender."[25]

For the majority in *McCleskey*, constricting prosecutorial and jury discretion would push toward so regulated a world that the criminal justice system would no longer produce particularized, individualized decisions about defendants. For the dissenters, the Court's acquiescence in unmonitored prosecutorial and jury discretion, in the face of sentencing disparities correlated with race, condoned and perpetuated racial discrimination and thereby allowed racial stereotyping to be substituted for individualized justice.

Debate among the justices last term in an entirely different context exposed a similar tension between rules and discretion. In *Corporation of the Presiding Bishop of the Church of Jesus Christ of Latter-Day Saints v. Amos (Presiding Bishop)*,[26] the Court considered whether the federal statute exempting religious organizations from nondiscrimination requirements in their employment decisions arising out of nonprofit activities violated the establishment clause. The Court's majority endorsed the legislative grant of discretion to religious organizations while rejecting the discharged engineer's claims that such state accommodation unconstitutionally promotes religion.

The opinions in the case clearly illustrate the dilemma of discretion. The majority reasoned that under the exemption the preference for religion was not exercised by the government but, rather, by the church. Justice O'Connor, however, pointed out in her concurring opinion that allowing discretion to the private decision maker to use religion in his decisions inevitably engaged the government in that differentiation. The Court could not, simply by protecting the discretion of religious organizations, escape consideration of the tension between the constitutional command against promoting religion and the constitu-

tional demand for free exercise of religion. Instead, Justice O'Connor argued, in distinguishing constitutional accommodation of religion from unconstitutional assistance to religious organizations, the Court must evaluate the message of the government's policy as perceived by an "objective observer."[27]

Justice Brennan's separate opinion also treated this tension as unavoidable. Yet Justice Brennan focused on the risk that case-by-case review by the Court would chill the very freedom assured to religious organizations. He therefore endorsed a categorical exemption from the ban against religious discrimination in employment for the nonprofit activities of religious organizations but argued for reserving judgment as to profit-making activities. Like Justice Stevens in *McCleskey*, Justice Brennan searched for a formal rule that could preserve discretion for other decision makers while also implementing the Court's special commitment to protect individuals from categorical, discriminatory treatment.

(d)   *The dilemmas in sum*

Other cases before the Court have raised one or more aspects of the difference dilemma. The Court's voluntary affirmative action cases, during the 1986 term and earlier, directly present dilemmas about recreating difference, risking nonneutral means to transform nonneutral ends, and choosing between rules and discretion in an effort to avoid categorical decisions. Decisions about handicapped persons also raise perplexing issues about when the Court should permit public and private decision makers to make the difference of handicap matter. The Court comes down one way or another in each case, but the splits between majority and minority views persist and recreate the dilemmas. The next section argues that assumptions buried within the dilemmas make them seem more difficult than they need be. The task, then, is to articulate those assumptions and to evaluate the choices that remain for decision makers.

III   Behind and Beyond the Dilemma

The dilemma of difference appears unresolvable. The risk of nonneutrality – the risk of discrimination – accompanies efforts both to ignore and to recognize difference in equal treatment and special treatment; in color blindness or gender blindness and in affirmative action; in governmental neutrality and in governmental preferences; and in decision makers' discretion and in formal constraints on discretion. Yet the dilemma is not as intractable as it seems. What makes it seem so difficult are unstated assumptions about the nature of difference. Once articulated and examined, these assumptions can take their proper place among other choices about how to treat difference. I will explore here the assumptions underlying the dilemma of difference, assumptions that usually go without saying.

(a) The five unstated assumptions

Assumption 1: difference is intrinsic, not relational

> [M]any of us have never conceived of ourselves only as somebody's other. (Barbara Christian)[28]

Can and should the questions about who is different be resolved by a process of discovering intrinsic differences? Is difference an objective, verifiable matter rather than something constructed by social attitudes? By posing legal claims through the difference dilemma, litigants and judges treat the problem of difference as what society or a given decision maker should do about the "different person" – a formulation that implicitly assigns the label of difference to that person.

The difference inquiry functions by pigeonholing people into sharply distinguished categories based on selected facts and features. Categorization helps people cope with complexity and understand each other. The legal analyst tends to treat the difference question as one of discovery rather than of choice. The judge asks: "Into what category does a given person or feature belong?" The categories then determine the significance of the persons or features situated within them. The distinguishing features behind critical perceptions and behind the categories themselves appear natural rather than chosen. It is hard, if not impossible, to find commonalities across differences and to argue for the same treatment across difference. Responsibility for the consequences of identifying difference, then, is dispersed through the process of perception and categorization, even as the process of categorization itself can create new perceptions and realities.

Assumption 2: the unstated norm

> Anyone who deviates from the official norm, whatever that is, anyone who fails to bear a likeness to the Standard Product, is simply not viewed as fully human, and then becomes at best invisible, at worst a threat to the national security. (Giles Gunn)[29]

To treat someone as different means to accord them treatment that is different from treatment of someone else; to describe someone as "the same" implies "the same as" someone else. When differences are discussed without explicit reference to the person or trait on the other side of the comparison, an unstated norm remains. Usually, this default reference point is so powerful and well established that it need not be specified.

Some remedial statutes explicitly state the norm: In 42 U.S.C. section 1981, the norm is "white citizens" – with an emphasis on both terms, implicitly establishing the terms of sameness and difference in this very statement of the norm. Claimants invoking the statute must show themselves to be relatively similar to "white citizens." Hence, these cases focus on whether the claimant is a member of a race.

When women argue for rights, the implicit reference point used in discussions of sameness and difference is the privilege accorded some males. This reference point can present powerful arguments for overcoming the exclusion of women from activities and opportunities available to men. For example, reform efforts on behalf of women during both the nineteenth and the twentieth centuries asserted women's fundamental similarities to privileged, white men as a tactic for securing equal treatment. Unfortunately for the reformers, embracing the theory of 'sameness' meant that any sign of difference between women and men could be used to justify treating women differently from men. Men remained the unstated norm.

Jerome Bruner wrote, "There is no seeing without looking, no hearing without listening, and both looking and listening are shaped by expectancy, stance, and intention."[30] Unstated reference points lie hidden in legal discourse, which is full of the language of abstract universalism. Legal language seeks universal applicability, regardless of the particular traits of an individual. Yet abstract universalism often "takes the part for the whole, the particular for the universal and essential, the present for the eternal."[31] Making explicit the unstated points of reference is the first step in addressing this problem; the next is challenging the presumed neutrality of the observer who in fact sees from an unacknowledged perspective.

Assumption 3: the observer can see without a perspective

> Inevitably, "seeing" entails a form of subjectivity, an act of imagination, a way of looking that is necessarily in part determined by some private perspective. Its results are never simple "facts," amenable to "objective" judgments, but facts or pictures that are dependent on the internal visions that generate them. (Evelyn Fox Keller)[32]

If differences are intrinsic, then anyone can see them; if there is an objective reality, then any impartial observer can make judgments unaffected and untainted by his or her own perspective or experience. Once rules are selected, regardless of disputes over the rules themselves, a distinct aspiration is that they will be applied evenhandedly. This aspiration to impartiality, however, is just that – an aspiration rather than a description – because it may suppress the inevitability of the existence of a perspective and thus make it harder for the observer, or anyone else, to challenge the absence of objectivity.

What interests us, given who we are and where we stand, affects our ability to perceive. Philosophers such as A.J. Ayer and W.V. Quine note that although we can alter the theory we use to frame our perceptions of the world, we cannot see the world unclouded by preconceptions. The impact of the observer's perspective may be crudely oppressive. Yet we continue to believe in neutrality.

Judges often see difference in relation to some unstated norm or point of comparison and fail to acknowledge their own perspective and its influence on the assignment of difference. This failure prevents us from discovering who is doing the labeling, but it does not negate the effect of the labeling of difference itself. Veiling the standpoint of the observer conceals its impact on our perception of the world. This leads to the next unstated assumption: that all other perspectives are either presumptively identical to the observer's own or are irrelevant.

Assumption 4: the irrelevance of other perspectives

> We have seen the blindness and deadness to each other which are our natural inheritance. (William James)[33]

Glimpsing contrasting perspectives helps resolve problems of difference. Several of the justices have tried, on different occasions, to glimpse the point of view of a minority group or a person quite different from themselves; some have articulated eloquently the difficulty or even impossibility of knowing another's perspective and have developed legal positions that take into account this difficulty. Others have rejected as irrelevant or relatively unimportant the experience of "different" people and have denied their own partiality, often by using stereotypes as though they were real.

Thus, some justices, on some occasions, have tried to see beyond the dominant perspective and reach an alternative construction of reality. In many other instances, however, the justices presume that the perspective they adopt is either universal or superior to others. A perspective may go unstated because it is so powerful and pervasive that it may be presumed without defense; it may also go unstated because it is so unknown to those in charge that they do not recognize it as a perspective. Presumptions about whose perspective matters ultimately may be embedded in the final, typically unstated assumption: When in doubt, the status quo is preferred and is indeed presumed natural and free from coercion.

Assumption 5: the status quo is natural, uncoerced, and good

> To settle for the constitutionalization of the status quo is to bequeath a petrified forest. (Aviam Soifer)[34]

Connected with many of the other assumptions is the idea that critical features of the status quo – general social and economic arrangements – are natural and desirable. From this assumption follow three propositions: First, the goal of governmental neutrality demands the status quo because existing societal arrangements are assumed to be neutral. Second, governmental actions that change the status quo have a different status than omissions, or failures to act, that maintain the status quo. Third, prevailing social and political arrangements are not forced on anyone. Individuals are free to make choices and to assume responsibility for those choices. These propositions are rarely stated, both because they are deeply entrenched and because they view the status quo as good, natural, and freely chosen. At times, however, the justices have engaged in debate that exposes the status quo assumption.

For the most part, unstated assumptions work in subtle and complex ways. Assumptions fill the basic human need to simplify and to make our world familiar and unsurprising. Yet, by their very simplification, assumptions exclude contrasting views. Moreover, they contribute to the dilemma of difference by frustrating legislative and constitutional commitments to change the treatment of differences in race, gender, ethnicity, religion, and handicap. Before justice can be done, judges need to hear and understand contrasting points of view about the treatment of difference.

IV Perspectives on Perspectives

The difference dilemma seems paralyzing if framed by the unstated assumptions described in Part 3. Those assumptions so entrench one point of view as natural and orderly that any conscious decision to notice or to ignore difference breaks the illusion of a legal world free of perspective. The assumptions make it seem that departures from unstated norms violate commitments to neutrality. Yet adhering to the unstated norms undermines commitments to neutrality – and to equality. Is it possible to proceed differently, putting these assumptions into question?

I will suggest that it is possible, even if difficult, to move beyond the constricting assumptions. At times in the past term, members of the Court have employed the most powerful device to expose and challenge the unstated assumptions: looking at an issue from another point of view. By asking how a member of a religious group might experience a seemingly neutral rule or how a nonmember might experience the discretion of a religious group, Justices O'Connor, Brennan, and White made an effort in several cases to understand a different perspective.[35] Justice Marshall and the majority in *Cal Fed* tried to assume the perspective of pregnant women by considering how treatment of pregnancy affects women's abilities to work outside the home while having a family. The dissenting justices in *McCleskey* asked how defend-

ants would react to the statistical disparity in capital sentencing by race, breaking out of the tendency to see the challenge only as a threat to the discretion and manageability of the criminal justice system. In *Saint Francis College, Shaare Tefila*, and *Arline*, members of the Court struggled over whose perspective should count for purposes of defining a race and a handicap, reaching conclusions that refused to take the usual answers for granted.

Efforts to adopt or imagine alternate perspectives are also reflected in opinions from previous terms. For example, Justice Stevens assessed an equal protection challenge to a zoning restriction burdening mentally retarded people by expressing sensitivity to a point of view other than his own: "I cannot believe that a rational member of this disadvantaged class could ever approve of the discriminatory application of the city's ordinance in this case."[36] Still earlier, Justice Douglas invited inquiry into the experience of non-English-speaking students sitting in a public school classroom conducted entirely in English.[37] Similarly, litigants have sometimes tried to convince the Court to adopt their perspective, Justice Harlan's dissent in *Plessy v. Ferguson*[38] may have been assisted by Homer Plessy's attorney, who had urged the justices to imagine themselves in the shoes of a black person:

> Suppose a member of this court, nay, suppose every member of it, by some mysterious dispensation of providence should wake tomorrow with a black skin and curly hair . . . and in traveling through that portion of the country where the "Jim Crow Car" abounds, should be ordered into it by the conductor. It is easy to imagine what would be the result . . . What humiliation, what rage would then fill the judicial mind![39]

It may be ultimately impossible to take the perspective of another completely, but the effort to do so may help us recognize that our perspective is partial and that the status quo is not inevitable or ideal. After shaking free of these unstated assumptions and developing a sense of alternative perspectives, judges must then choose. The process of looking through other perspectives does not itself yield an answer, but it may lead to an answer different from the one that the judge would otherwise have reached. Seen in this light, the difference dilemma is hard but not impossible.

Historians have described how a conception of reality, when it triumphs, convinces even those injured by it of its actuality. Accordingly, political and cultural success itself submerges the fact that conceptions of reality represent a perspective of some groups, not a picture of reality free from any perspective. At the turn of the century, for example, a new middle class justified industrialism and the control of immigrants by spreading understandings of science, technology, and bureaucracy as neutral and progressive.[40] Similarly, studies have shown how groups with relatively little social and economic power internalize the views of those with more power – often at the cost of personal conflict and damaged self-respect.[41] Taking minority perspectives seriously calls for a process of dialogue in which the listener actually tries to reach beyond the assumption of one reality, one version of the truth. There is no neutrality, no escape from choice. But it is possible to develop better abilities to name and grasp competing perspectives and to make more knowing choices thereafter. In the next section, I suggest that efforts along these lines are central to the challenge of engendering justice.

V Engendering Justice

The problem of freedom is the problem of how to divest our categories of their halo of external truth. (Mary Douglas)[42]

The truth is that we are all responsible, even if we are not to blame. (Sarah Burns)[43]

The nineteenth-century American legal system recognized only three races: "white," "Negro," and "Indian." Californian authorities faced an influx of Chinese and Mexicans and were forced to confront the now complicated question of racial categorization. They solved the problem of categorizing Mexicans by defining them as "whites" and by according them the rights of free white persons. Chinese, however, were labeled "Indian" and denied the political and legal rights of white persons. Similarly, in 1922, a unanimous Supreme Court concluded that Japanese persons were not covered by a federal naturalization statute applicable to "free white persons," "aliens of African nativity," and "persons of African descent."[44]

In retrospect, these results seem arbitrary. The legal authorities betrayed a striking inability to reshape their own categories for people who did not fit. Of course, it is impossible to know what might have happened if some piece of history had been otherwise. Still, it is tempting to wonder: What if the California legal authorities had changed their racial scheme, rather than forcing the Chinese and Mexican applicants into it? The officials then might have noticed that nationality, not race, distinguished these groups. What if these officials and the justices in 1922 had tried to take the point of view of the people they were labeling? Perhaps, from this vantage point, the justices would have realized the need for reasons – beyond racial classification – for granting or withholding legal rights and privileges.

In this chapter, I have argued that trying to take seriously the point of view of people labeled *different* is a way to move beyond current difficulties in the treatment of differences in our society. This last statement, like much of the chapter, is addressed to people in positions of sufficient power to label others *different* and to make choices about how to treat difference. If you have such power, you may realize the dilemma of difference: By taking another person's difference into account in awarding goods or distributing burdens, you risk reiterating the significance of that difference and, potentially, its stigma and stereotyping consequences. But if you do not take another person's difference into account – in a world that has made that difference matter – you may also recreate and reestablish both the difference and its negative implications. If you draft or enforce laws, you may worry that the effects of the laws will not be neutral whether you take difference into account or you ignore it. If you employ people, judge guilt or innocence, or make other decisions affecting lives, you may want and need the discretion to make an individualized assessment, free from any focus on categorical differences. But if that discretion is exercised without constraint, difference may be taken into account in a way that does not treat that person as an individual – and in a way that disguises this fact from view.

These dilemmas, I have argued, become less paralyzing if you try to break out of unstated assumptions and take the perspective of the person you have called *different*. Once you do that, you may glimpse that your patterns for organizing the world are both arbitrary and foreclose their own reconsideration. You may find that the categories you take for granted do not well serve features you had not focused upon in the past. You may see an injury that you had not noticed or take more seriously a harm that you had otherwise discounted. If you try to take the view of the other person, you will find that the "difference" you notice is part of the relationship or comparison you draw between that person and someone else, with reference to a norm, and you will then get the chance to examine the reference point you usually take for granted. Maybe you will conclude that the reference point itself should change. Employers do not have to treat pregnancy and parenthood as a disability, but instead as a part of the lives of valued workers. You may find that you had so much ignored the point of view of others that you did not realize that you were mistaking your point of view for reality. Perhaps you will find that the way things are is not the only way things could be – that changing the way you classify, evaluate, reward, and punish may make the differences you had noticed less significant, or even irrelevant, to the way you run your life.

I have also argued, however, that we often forget how to take the perspective of another. We forget even that our point of view is not reality and that our conceptual schemes are simplifications, serving some interests and uses rather than others. We forget because our minds – and probably our hearts – cannot contain the whole world, and so we reduce the world to shorthand that we can handle. Our shorthand – because it is our shorthand – reflects what we thought we needed, where we stood, and who we are. We treat our divisions of the world as though they were real and universal. We do not see that they embody our early experiences of discovering how we are both the same as and different from our parents. We forget how we learned from them to encode the world into the same classifications they used to serve their own needs. We forget that things may appear frightful only because they are unfamiliar. We look at people we do not know and think they are different from us in important ways. We forget that even if they are different, in a way that matters to them, too, they also have a view of reality, and ours is as different from theirs as theirs is from ours.

We think we know what is real, what differences are real, and what really matters, even though sometimes we realize that our perceptions and desires are influenced by others. Sometimes we realize that television, radio, classes we had in school, or the attitudes of people who matter to us, affect our inclinations. Every time we wear an item of clothing that we now think is fashionable but used to think was ugly, we brush up against the outside influences on what we think inside. Yet we think that we think independently. We forget that widely held beliefs may be the ones most influenced from the outside.

The more powerful we are, the less we may be able to see that the world coincides with our view precisely because we shaped it in accordance with those views. That is just one of our privileges. Another is that we are able to put and hear questions in ways that do not question ourselves. In contrast, the more marginal we feel from the world, from the groups we know, the more likely we are to glimpse a contrast between some people's perceptions of reality and our own. Yet we still may slip into the world view of the more powerful, because it is more likely to be validated. We prefer to have our perceptions validated; we need to feel acknowledged and confirmed. But when we fail to take the perspective of another, we deny that very acknowledgment and confirmation in return.

If we want to preserve justice, we need to develop a practice for more knowing judgments about problems of difference. We must stop seeking to get close to the "truth" and instead seek to get close to other people's truths. The question is, how do we do this? In this section, I argue that we must persuade others as much as they must persuade us about the reality we should construct. Justice can be impartial only if judges acknowledge their own partiality. Justice depends on the possibility of conflicts among the values and perspectives that justice pursues. Courts, and especially the Supreme Court, provide a place for the contest over realities that govern us – if we open ourselves to the chance that a reality other than our own may matter. Justice can be engendered when we overcome our pretended indifference to difference and instead people our world with individuals who surprise one another about difference.

(a) *Impartiality and partial truths*

It is a paradox. Only by admitting our partiality can we strive for impartiality. Impartiality is the guise partiality takes to seal bias against exposure. It looks neutral to apply a rule denying unemployment benefits to anyone who cannot fulfill the work schedule, but it is not neutral if the work schedule was devised with one religious Sabbath, and not another, in mind. The idea of impartiality implies human access to a view beyond human experience, a "God's eye" point of view. Not only do humans lack this inhuman perspective, but humans who claim it are untruthful, trying to exercise power to cut off conversation and debate. Doris Lessing argues that a single absolute truth would mean the end of human discourse but that we are happily saved from that end because any truth, once uttered, becomes immediately one truth among many, subject to more discourse and dispute. If we treat other points of view as irritants in the way of our own vision, we are still hanging on to faulty certainty. Even if we admit the limits of our view, while treating those limits as gaps and leaving the rest in place, we preserve the pretense that our view is sufficiently rooted in reality to resist any real change prompted by another.

Acknowledging partiality may cure the pretense of impartiality. But unless we have less capacity to step outside our own skins than I think we do, we then have a choice of which partial view to advance or accept. Whose partial view should resolve conflicts over how to treat assertions of difference, whether assigned or claimed? Preferring the standpoint of an historically denigrated group can reveal truths obscured by the dominant view, but it can also reconfirm the underlying conceptual scheme of the dominant view by focusing on it. Similarly, the perspective of those who are labeled *different* may offer an important challenge to the view of those who imposed the label, but it is a corrective lens, another partial view, not absolute truth.[45] We then fight over whether to prefer it. "Standpoint theories" may also deny the multiple experiences of members of the denigrated group and create a new claim of essentialism.

Instead of an impartial view, we should strive for the standpoint of someone who is committed to the moral relevance of contingent particulars.[46] Put in personal terms, if I pretend to be impartial, I hide my partiality; however, if I embrace partiality, I risk ignoring you, your needs, and your alternative reality – or, conversely, embracing and appropriating your view into yet another rigid, partial view. I conclude that I must acknowledge and struggle against my partiality by making an effort to understand your reality and what it means for my own. I need to stop seeking certainty and acknowledge the complexity of our shared and colliding realities, as well as the tragic impossibility of all prevailing at once. It is this complexity that constitutes our reciprocal realities, and it is the conflict between our realities that constitutes us, whether we engage in it overtly or submerge it under a dominant view.

Moral action, then, takes place in a field of complexity, and we act ethically when we recognize what we give up as well as what we embrace. The solution is not to adopt and cling to some new standpoint but, instead, to strive to become and remain open to perspectives and claims that challenge our own. Justice, like philosophy, ought

> to trust rather to the multitude and variety of its arguments than to the conclusiveness of any one. Its reasoning should not form a chain which is no stronger than its weakest link, but a cable whose fibers may be ever so slender, provided they are sufficiently numerous and intimately connected.[47]

We who judge should remove the removal of ourselves when we either ignore or notice a difference. We can and should confront our involvement in and responsibility for what happens when we act in a reality we did not invent but still have latitude to discredit or affirm. We should have the humility and the courage to act in each situation anew, rather than applying what we presume to know already, as though each case were merely a repetition of an episode from the past.

Two exercises can help those who judge to glimpse the perspectives of others and to avoid a false impartiality. The first is to explore our own stereotypes, our own attitudes toward people we treat as different – and, indeed, our own categories for organizing the world. Audre Lorde put it powerfully: "I urge each one of us here to reach down into that deep place of knowledge inside herself and touch that terror and loathing of any difference that lives there. See whose face it wears. Then the personal as the political can begin to illuminate all our choices."[48] This is a call for applying "strict scrutiny" not just to a defendant's reasons for burdening a protected minority group but also to ourselves when we judge those reasons. It is a process that even we who see ourselves as victims of oppression need to undertake, for devices of oppression are buried within us. We must also examine and retool our methods of classification and consider how they save us from questioning our instincts, ourselves, and our existing social arrangements. Putting ourselves in the place of those who look different can push us to challenge our ignorance and fear and to investigate our usual categories for making sense of the world. This is an opportunity to enlarge judges' understanding and abilities to become better practitioners in the business of solving problems.

The second exercise is to search out differences and celebrate them by constructing new bases for connection. We can pursue the possibilities of difference behind seeming commonalities and seek out commonalities across difference, thereby confronting the ready association of sameness with equality and difference with inferiority. One route is to emphasize our common humanity, despite our different traits. Another tack is to disentangle difference from the allocation of benefits and burdens in society – a tack that may well require looking at difference to alter how people use it. The Court's effort to ensure equality for women and men in the conjunction of work and family life in *Cal Fed* represents such an effort to disentangle institutional arrangements from the difference they create. A third approach is to cherish difference and welcome anomaly. Still another is to understand that which initially seems strange and to learn about sense and reason from this exercise – just as philosophers, anthropologists and psychologists have urged us to take seriously the self-conceptions and perceptions of others. In the process of trying to understand how another person understands, we may even remake our categories of understanding. Other persons may not even define "self" the same way we do, and glimpsing their "self-concepts" thus challenges us to step beyond our operating assumptions. A further skill to practice is to recognize commonality in difference itself: in the relationships within which we construct difference and connect and distinguish ourselves from one another.

These exercises in taking the perspective of the other will deepen and broaden anyone's perspective. For judges, who debate the use of the coercive forces of the law in relation to issues of difference, these exercises are critical. Judges can and should act as representatives, standing in for others and symbolizing society itself. Judicial acts of representation must also be responsive to the demands of the people they govern, in order to secure apparent legitimacy and, ultimately, to remain effective. One judge explained that law's coercive power must be applied to ensure "the viability of a pluralistic democracy," which "depends upon the willingness to accept all of the 'thems' as 'us' " Whether the motives of the framers be considered moralistic or pragmatic, the structure of the Constitution rests on the foundational principle that successful self-governance can be achieved only through public institutions following egalitarian policies.[49]

This exhortation – that we must take the perspective of another while remembering that we cannot really know what another sees and must put our own categories up for challenge, without ceding the definition of reality over the others – sounds quite complicated. What do we do with the sense of complexity?

(b) *Complexity, passivity, and the status quo: the problem of deference*

We are mistaken when we hold onto simple certainties. Yet complexity seems both overwhelming and incapacitating. By bearing into complexity rather than turning away from it, by listening to the variety of voices implicated in our problems, we may lose a sense of ready solutions and steady certainties. But clear answers have been false gods, paid homage to in the coinage of other people's opportunities, and also at cost to our own character. We harden ourselves when we treat our categories as though they were real, closing off responses to new facts and to challenges to how we live and think. Our certainties also leave unresolved conflicts among incompatible but deeply held values. In the face of complexity, "the politics of difference can all too easily degenerate into the politics of 'mutual indifference' "[50] If we care about justice, the biggest mistake would be to respond to complexity with passivity. That response is not impartial; it favors the status quo, those benefited by it, and the conception of reality it fosters.

1. Forms of passivity. Four forms of judicial passivity may be tempting in the face of complexity: deference, intent requirements, reliance on apparent choices or concessions of the parties, and reliance on doctrine. I will consider each in turn.

Respect for other institutions and persons is a critical part of judging, but there are particular risks when the Court, while acknowledging the complexity of a problem of difference, defers to other branches or levels of government, to private actors, or even to the parties before the Court. One risk is that the Court will pretend that it has no power over or responsibility for what results. When the Court defers to Congress, the executive, a state government, or a private actor, the justices are saying, Let's not make a decision, let's leave it to others, or let's endorse the freedom or respect the power of others. It is surely important for the justices to understand their relationship with other people or institutions with interests in a matter, but such understanding is quite different from ceding responsibility for what ensues. This principle is important for everybody, but especially for a judicial body, which has parties with genuine conflicts before it. As Frank Michelman put it, "Attention [to other branches of government] cannot mean deference, or talismanic invocation of authority. The norm of justice to parties itself commands that no other norm should ever take a form that preempts questions or exempts from reason-giving."[51]

Problems also arise when the Court takes on the second form of passivity: focusing on the intentions of the parties before it. When the Court demands evidence of intentional discrimination before upholding a plaintiff's charges, the justices are deferring to and thereby entrenching the perspective of the defendant, thus rejecting the perspective of the plaintiff-victim. Asking only about the sincerity of the motive behind a statute whose effect is challenged is also an act that takes sides, defines which reality will govern, and avoids the real challenge of responding to the perspective of the plaintiff.

It is equally problematic for the Court, in a third form of passivity, to point to apparent choices made by plaintiffs, victims, or members of minority groups, as Justice Scalia did in *Johnson*[52] as a justification for holding against them. The Court may presume incorrectly that the choices are free and uncoerced, or the Court may wrongly attribute certain meanings to a choice. Similarly, judicial references to litigants' concessions during litigation, including during oral argument, are not without risk. Although the Court may be trying to take the perspective of others seriously, its reliance on litigants' concessions as the peg for a judicial decision may also be the Court's way of reducing the task of deciding on its own. Reliance on concessions of the lawyer may be especially troubling in cases involving the rights of minorities, because it is unclear for whom the lawyer speaks at that moment: the client, the cause, or others unrepresented there who will be affected in the future by the Court's ruling.

The fourth form of passivity is perhaps one of the most effective circumventions of responsibility: the Court's reliance on its own doctrinal boundaries and categories to resolve the cases before it. This chapter has demonstrated that the difference dilemma poses similar problems in a wide variety of contexts, including cases involving religion, gender, race, and sexual preference. Yet when the Court takes the boundaries between doctrines as given, filling the doctrines with operative tests and lines of precedent, it obscures these potential similarities across contexts. By the time a case reaches an appellate court, the adversary process has so focused on specific issues of doctrinal disagreement that the competing arguments have come under one framework, not under competing theories. Legal analogy is typically inseparable from precedential reasoning, telescoping the creative potential of a search for surprising similarities into a narrow focus on prior rulings that could "control" the instant case. The Court's practice vividly demonstrates how fabricated categories can assume the status of immutable reality. Of course, law would be overwhelming without doctrinal categories and separate lines of precedent. Yet by holding to rigid categories, the Court denies the existence of tensions and portrays a false simplicity amid a rabbit warren of complexity. The Court's strict segregation of doctrine also cloisters lines of thought and insights, thereby restricting the Court's ability to use larger frames of judgment.

2. Avoiding passivity. Besides resisting tempting forms of passivity – which do not lessen judicial responsibility – the Court can and should challenge rigid patterns of thought. What if litigants argued more emphatically across contexts and reminded members of the Court, "You have seen something like this before?" Litigants can help the Court to avoid the dangers of complacency and complexity by searching out analogies and developing unfamiliar perspectives. At the same time, litigants may gain a tactical advantage, because they may persuade a member of the Court of their point of view by analogizing to something the justice has glimpsed elsewhere. This practice also has some support in epistemology. The difficulties each of us has in seeing around the bend of our own thought can be eased with the help of insights from others who are positioned differently. Given the relationship between knowledge and power, those with less privilege may well see better than those with more.

Surprisingly, traditional legal techniques actually provide fruitful starting points for avoiding passivity. One noted feature of the legal system that can be used to mount this challenge is analogical reasoning.[53] The existence of encrusted practices and categories however, frustrates the full use of these tools. Litigants and judges should search out unexpected analogies to scrape off barnacles of thought and to challenge views so settled that they are not thought to be views. This process may persuade particular judges, in particular cases, to see a different angle on a problem. It also holds promise as a method for finding surprising commonalities that can nudge us all to reassess well-established categories of thought.

The promise of reasoning by analogy is lost if it becomes an arid conceptualist enterprise. Yet when immersed in the particulars of a problem, we sometimes are able to think up analogies that break out of ill-fitting conceptual schemes. As one observer of creative processes in art, science, and philosophy has commented, "In the history of human thinking the most fruitful developments frequently take place at those points where two different lines of thought meet."[54] By seeing something in a new light, seeing its similarity to something else once thought quite different, we are able to attribute different meanings and consequences to what we see. A glimpse of difference in one context may enable litigants and judges better to appreciate it in another context.

The adversarial process is another feature of the legal system that, with some modification, can be used to challenge judicial complacency. In fact, the values of thinking through analogies bear a striking similarity to the virtues of reasoning in dialogue. The dialogue form puts the student in a position to follow the connections and divergences in argument and invent for herself ways to think anew, rather than simply internalizing the monologue of inherited knowledge. Barbara Johnson notes that "learning seems to take place most rapidly when the student must respond to the contradiction between *two* teachers. And what the student learns in the process is both the power of ambiguity and the non-innocence of ignorance."[55] Similarly, dialogue in legal briefs and courtroom arguments can stretch the minds of listeners, especially if they are actively forming their own position and not simply picking between the ones before them.

The introduction of additional voices may enable adversary dialogue to expand beyond a stylized, either/or mode, prompting new and creative insights. Consequently, the Court can, and should seek out alternative views in *amicus* briefs. Inventive approaches can bring the voices of those who are not present before the Court, as in the recent brief filed with the Court that collected the autobiographical accounts of men and women who believed their lives had been changed by the availability of legalized abortion.[56] Similarly, the famous "Brandeis brief" in *Muller v. Oregon*[57] marked a creative shift for the Court, introducing the use of vivid, factual detail as a way to break out of the formalist categories dominating the analysis. Seeking unusual perspectives enables justices to avail themselves of the "partial superiority" of other people's views and to reach for what is unfamiliar and perhaps suppressed under the dominant ways of seeing. Bringing in a wider variety of views can also make the so-called countermajoritarian Court more "democratic."

Besides seeking out unfamiliar perspectives and analogies new to the law, all judges should also consider the human consequences of their decisions in difference cases, rather than insulating themselves in abstractions. Such engagement encourages the judge to fill in textual gaps based on his or her own experiences. It may seem paradoxical to urge those who judge to bring their own experiences to the problems before them, after identifying the dangerous ways in which we all confuse our own perceptions and interests for reality. In the process of personal reflection, however, the judge may stretch faculties for connection while engaging in dialogue with the parties over their legal arguments and analogies. I petition all judges to open up to the chance that someone may move them – the experience will not tell them what to do, but it may give them a way outside routinized categories to forge new approaches to the problem at hand.

This call to be open, to canvas personal experience, applies to all legal controversies, but it is especially important in the context of cases that present the dilemma of difference. Here the judicial mainstays of neutrality and distance prove most risky, for they blind judges to their own involvement in recreating the negative meanings of difference. Yet the dangers of making differences matter also argue against categorical solutions. By struggling to respond humanly to the dilemma in each particular context, the judge can supply the possibility of connection otherwise missing in the categorical treatments of difference.

(c)   *Choosing among divergent demands*

Urging judges to allow themselves to be moved by the arguments may seem misguided. A judge who identifies with every perspective may simply feel indecisive and overburdened. Would feeling the tugs in all directions render us powerless to choose? It may be just this fear that explains our attachment to simplifying categories, stereotypes, and fixed ways of thought. Some of us may fear being overwhelmed by the world, others fear being too moved by it, others fear being powerless before it. Challenging familiar categories and styles of reasoning may threaten the search for order, decisiveness, and manageability that maintain the predictability in our lives. But there are other ways to hold things together than the methods we have used in the past.

Some may aspire to a jurisprudence of individualism, never treating any individual as a member of a group. Yet, resonant as it is with many American traditions, individualization is a myth: Because our language is shared and our categories communally invented, any word I use to describe your uniqueness draws you into the classes of people sharing your traits. Even if ultimately I produce enough words so that the intersection of all classes you belong in contains only one member – you – we understand this through a language of comparison with others. This language, however, seems to embroil us in the dilemma of difference.

What could we do instead? I believe we should welcome complexity and challenge complacency – and stop fearing that we will be unable to make judgments. We can and do make judgments all the time, in a way committed to making meaning, rather than recreating or ignoring difference. We make commitments when we make decisions; we reconfirm or remake current understandings by reflecting so deeply and particularly about a new situation that we challenge presumptive solutions. Instead of trying continually to fit people into categories, and to enforce or deny rights on that basis, we can and do make decisions by immersing in particulars to renew commitments to a fair world.

Thus, one reason we can still decide, amid powerfully competing claims, is that immersion in particulars does not require the relinquishment of general commitments. The struggle is not over the validity of principles and generalizations – it is over which ones should prevail in a given context. The choice from among principles, in turn, implicates choices about which differences, and which similarities, should matter. These are moral choices, choices about which voices should persuade those who judge.

Even when we understand them, some voices will lose. The fundamentalist Christians who supported the Balanced Treatment Act in Louisiana deserve respect and understanding: Their view of the world may well be threatened by the curriculum taught to their children in the public schools. However, this is what the fight is about. Whose view of reality should prevail in public institutions? This deep conundrum involves the conflicts between the worldview animating any rule for the entire society, and the worldviews of subgroups who will never share the dominant views. I am tempted to propose a seemingly "neutral" rule, such as a rule that judges interpreting the commitment to respect difference should make the choice that allows difference to flourish without imposing it on others. If exclusion of their worldview from the biology curriculum creates an intolerable choice for the fundamentalists, they do and they must have the choice to establish their own educational institutions, and their own separate community. Yet this seemingly "neutral" position is a comfortable view for a nonfundamentalist like myself, who cannot appreciate the full impact of the evolution science curriculum as experienced by at least some fundamentalists. Rather than pretending to secure a permanent solution through a "neutral" rule, I must acknowledge the tragedy of nonneutrality – and admit that our very commitment to tolerance yields intolerance toward some views. If the fundamentalists lose in this case, they can continue to struggle to challenge the meaning of the commitment to separate church and state, and they may convince the rest of us in the next round. Although it may be little solace for the minority group, its challenge achieves something even when it loses, by reminding the nation of our commitment to diversity, and our inability, thus far, to achieve it fully.

Thus, choices from among competing commitments do not end after the Court announces its judgment. Continuing skepticism about the reality endorsed by the Court – or any source of governmental power – is the only guard against tyranny.

The continuing process of debate over deeply held but conflicting commitments is both the mechanism and the promise of our governmental system. Within that system, the Supreme Court's power depends upon persuasion. As Hannah Arendt wrote: "The thinking process which is active in judging something is not, like the thought process of pure reasoning, a dialogue between me and myself, but finds itself always and primarily, even if I am quite alone in making up my mind, in an anticipated communication with others with whom I know I must finally come to some agreement."[58] The important question is, with whom must you come to agreement? In a society of diversity with legacies of discrimination, within a polity committed to self-governance, the judiciary becomes a critical arena for demands of inclusion. I see the judicial arena as a forum for contests over competing realities. The question remains, however, whose definitions of realities will govern in a given case and over time.

Court judgments endow some perspectives, rather than others, with power. Judicial power is least accountable when judges leave unstated – and treat as a given – the perspective they select. Litigation before the Supreme Court sometimes highlights individuals who otherwise seldom imprint their perspective on the polity. In eliciting these perspectives and accepting their challenge to the version of reality the justices otherwise would take for granted, the Court advances the fundamental constitutional commitment to require reasons before exercises of power, whether public or private. Growing from our history, wrought from many struggles, is the tradition we have invented, and it is a tradition that declares that the status quo cannot be immune from demands for justification. Litigation over the meanings of difference represents demands for such accountability. By asking how power influences knowledge, the Court can address whether a "difference" has been assigned through past domination or as a remedy for past domination. In this way, the Court can solicit information about contrasting views of reality without casting off the moorings of historical experience, and in this inquiry, the Court can assess the risk of creating new patterns of domination while remedying inequalities of the past. As we compete for power to give reality to our visions, we confront tragic limits in our abilities to make meaning together. Yet we must continue to seek a language to speak across conflicting affiliations.

We need settings in which to engage in the clash of realities that breaks us out of settled and complacent meanings and creates opportunities for insight and growth. This is the special burden and opportunity for the Court: to enact and preside over the dialogue through which we remake the normative endowment that shapes current understandings.

When the Court performs these roles, it engenders justice. Justice is engendered when judges admit the limitations of their own viewpoints, when judges reach beyond those limits by trying to see from contrasting perspectives, and when people seek to exercise power to nurture differences, not to assign and control them. Rather than securing an illusory universality and objectivity, law is a medium through which particular people can engage in the continuous work of making justice. The law "is part of a distinctive manner of imagining the real."[59] Legal decisions engrave upon our culture the stories we tell to and about ourselves, the meanings that constitute the traditions we invent. Searching for words to describe realities too multiple and complex to be contained by their language, litigants and judges struggle over what will be revealed and what will be concealed in the inevitable partiality of human judgment. Through deliberate attention to our own partiality, we can begin to acknowledge the dangers of pretended impartiality. By taking difference into account, we can overcome our pretended indifference to difference, and people our worlds with those who can surprise and enrich one another. As we make audible, in official arenas, the struggles over which version of reality will secure power, we disrupt the silence of one perspective, imposed as if universal. Admitting the partiality of the perspective that temporarily gains official endorsement may embolden resistance to announced rules. But only by admitting that rules are resistible – and by justifying to the governed their calls for adherence – can justice be done in a democracy. "It is only through the variety of relations constructed by the plurality of beings that truth can be known and community constructed."[60] Then we constitute ourselves as members of conflicting communities with enough reciprocal regard to talk across differences. We engender mutual regard for pain we know and pain we do not understand.

Notes

1   107 S. Ct. 683 (1987).

2   California Fair Employment and Housing Act, Cal. Gov't Code Ann. § 12945(b)(2) (West 1980).

3   See 107 S. Ct. at 691. In the Pregnancy Discrimination Act of 1978 (PDA), Pub. L. No. 95–555, 92 Stat. 2076 (1978) (codified at 42 U.S.C. § 2000e(k)

(1978)), Congress amended Title VII to include discrimination on the basis of pregnancy, rejecting the Supreme Court's contrary ruling in General Electric Co. v. Gilbert. 429 U.S. 125 (1976).

4   107 S. Ct. at 692 (quoting *Cal Fed*, 758 F.2d 390, 396 (9th Cir. 1985)).

5   *Id*. at 691, n. 17. In *Cal Fed*, the Court tried to avoid the problems of stereotyping by characterizing pregnancy solely as a physical disability – ignoring alternative characterizations that analogize women's role in pregnancy to veterans' role in national defense – a role justifying preferential treatment in employment. See Littleton, *Reconstructing Sexual Equality*, 75 Calif. L. Rev. 201 (forthcoming 1987).

6   See 107 S. Ct. at 694.

7   107 S. Ct. at 698 (White, J., dissenting). The dissent rejected the claim that employers could comply with both statutes by providing benefits to both women and men in comparable situations, because that approach would extend the scope of the state statute beyond its express language and because the federal statute did not require programs where none currently existed. See *id*. at 701.

8   *Id*. at 700. See 107 S. Ct. at 694 (opinion of the Court).

9   107 S. Ct. 2022 (1987).

10 107 S. Ct. 2019 (1987).

11 785 F.2d 523, 527 (4th Cir. 1986).

12 *Id*. at 529 (Wilkinson, J., concurring in part and dissenting in part). Judge Wilkinson explained: "It is an understatement to note that attempts to place individuals in distinct racial groups frequently serve only to facilitate continued discrimination and postpone the day when all individuals will be addressed as such" (*id*. at 533).

13 107 S. Ct. 2573 (1987).

14 See 107 S. Ct. at 2576; *id*. at 2600–5 (Scalia, J., dissenting).

15 *Id*. at 2582; *accord id*. at 2587 (Powell, J., concurring).

16 107 S. Ct. 1046 (1987).

17 *Id*. at 1048 (quoting Fla. Stat. § 443.021 (1985)).

18 See 107 S. Ct. at 1051 and n. 11.

19 107 S. Ct. 821 (1987).

20 26 U.S.C. § 3304(a)(12)(1982).

21 107 S. Ct. at 825.

22 107 S. Ct. 1756 (1987).

23 107 S. Ct. at 1778, n. 37.

24 *Id*. at 1791; *accord id*. at 1806 (Stevens, J., dissenting); *id*. at 1805 (Blackmun, J., dissenting) ("If a grant of relief to [McCleskey] were to lead to a closer examination of the effects of racial considerations throughout the criminal-justice system, the system, and hence society, might benefit.").

25 *Id*. at 1806 (Stevens, J., dissenting).

26 107 S. Ct. 2862 (1987).

27 107 S. Ct. at 2874 (O'Connor, J., concurring in the judgment).

28 Christian, *The Race for Theory*, Cultural Critique, Spring 1987, at 51, 54.

29 G. Gunn, *The Interpretation of Otherness: Literature, Religion, and the American Imagination* 177 (1979).

30 J. Bruner, *Actual Minds, Possible Worlds* 110 (1986) (paraphrasing Robert Woodworth). Similarly, Albert Einstein said. "It is the theory which decides what we can observe." D. Bell, *The Coming of Post-Industrial Society* 9 (1973) (quoting Einstein).

31 Gould, *The Woman Question: Philosophy of Liberation and the Liberation of Philosophy*, in Women and Philosophy: Toward a Theory of Liberation 21 (C. Gould and M. Wartofsky eds. 1976).

32 E. Keller, *A Feeling for the Organism: The Life and Work of Barbara McClintock* 150 (1983).

33 W. James, *What Makes a Life Significant*, in *On Some of Life's Ideals*, at 49, 81.

34 Soifer, at 409.

35 It is not clear whether Justice Scalia looked at the Balanced Treatment Act in *Edwards* from the vantage point of fundamentalist parents, or instead from the vantage point of state legislators.

36 City of Cleburne v. Cleburne Living Center, 473 U.S. 432, 455 (1985) (Stevens, J., concurring).

37 See Lau v. Nichols, 414 U.S. 563, 566 (1974).

38 163 U.S. 537, 552 (1896) (Harlan, J., dissenting).

39 Brief for the Plaintiff, *Plessy v. Ferguson*, reprinted in Civil Rights and the American Negro 298, 303–4 (A. Blaustein and R. Zangrando eds. 1968).

40 See R. Wiebe, *The Search for Order, 1877–1920*, at 111–13 (1967).

41 See, e.g., Castaneda v. Partida, 430 U.S. 482, 503 (1977) (Marshall, J., concurring).

42 M. Douglas, *Implicit Meanings: Essays in Anthropology* 224 (1975).

43 Burns, *Apologia for the Status Quo* (Book Review), 74 Geo. L.J. 1791, 1819 (1986).

44 See Ozawa v. United States, 260 U.S. 178 (1922).

45 See, e.g., C. Gilligan, *In a Different Voice* (1982), at 151–74 (linking a vision of maturity to a complementary and productive tension between (feminine) ethos of care and a (masculine) ethic of rights).

46 See M. Nussbaum, *The Fragility of Goodness* (1986), at 314. Nussbaum adds that the someone should be committed to "the value of the passions, and the incommensurability of the values that will tend to approve of this particular sort of judge as a guide" (*id*. at 311). The point is that a judge must have a plurality of attachments and do justice in the tension among them (*id*. at 314).

47 C.S. Peirce, *Some Consequences of Four Incapacities*, in 5 Collected Papers at 157 (C. Hartshorne and P. Weiss eds. 1931).

48 Lorde, *The Master's Tools Will Never Dismantle the Master's House*, in *This Bridge Called My Back: Writings by Radical Women of Color* 98 (C. Moraga and G. Anzaldua eds. 1981). This is not sympathy, tolerance,

or even compassion, each of which leaves the viewer's understanding fundamentally unchanged.

49 Keyes v. School Dist. No. 1, 576 F. Supp. 1503, 1520 (D. Colo. 1983) (Matsch. J.).

50 Cornell, *The Poststructuralist Challenge to the Ideal of Community*, 8 Cardozo L.R. 989–90 (1987).

51 Michelman, *The Supreme Court, 1985 Term – Forward*, 100 Harv. L.R. 1, at 76 (1986).

52 Johnson v. Transportation Agency 107 S. Ct. 1442 (1987). In Hobbie v. Unemployment Appeals Commission, 107 S. Ct. 1046, 1051 (1987), however, the Court's majority was sympathetic about constraints on choice, arguing that it is unlawful coercion to force an employee to choose between fidelity to religious beliefs and continued employment.

53 See E. Levi, An Introduction to Legal Reasoning (1972), at 8.

54 F. Capra, *The Tao of Physics* xii (1984) (quoting Werner Weisenberg); *cf.* S. Harding, at 235: "Analogies are not aids to the establishment of theories; they are an utterly essential part of theories, without which theories, without which theories would be completely valueless and unworthy of the name" (quoting N. Campbell, *Physics, the Elements* (1920)).

55 B. Johnson, *A World of Difference* (1987) at 83 (emphasis in original).

56 See Brief Amici Curiae, of National Abortion Rights Action League et al., Thornburgh v. American College of Obstetricians & Gynecologists, 476 U.S. 747 (1986) (no. 84–495 and 84–1379).

57 208 U.S. 412 (1908).

58 H. Arendt, *Between Past and Future* 220 (1961).

59 C. Geertz, *Local Knowledge* (1983), at 184.

60 N. Hartsock, at 254 (describing the view of Hannah Arendt), *Money, Sex, & Power: Toward a Feminist Historical Materialism* (1983).

35

Egalitarianism and the Undeserving Poor

Richard J. Arneson

Recently in the US a near-consensus has formed around the idea that it would be desirable to "end welfare as we know it," in the words of President Bill Clinton.[1] In this context, the term "welfare" does not refer to the entire panoply of welfare state provision including government-sponsored old age pensions, government-provided medical care for the elderly, unemployment benefits for workers who have lost their jobs without being fired for cause, or aid to the disabled. "Welfare" in contemporary debates means "cash, food, or housing assistance to healthy non-aged persons with low incomes."[2] In the US, the main policy that qualifies as welfare in this sense is Aid to Families with Dependent Children.[3] Although contemporary attacks on welfare are identified with conservative policy analysts such as Charles Murray, in fact dissatisfaction with the policies Murray targets for criticism is widespread among liberal intellectuals. For example, in a sharply critical review essay on Murray's book *Losing Ground*, Christopher Jencks worries that "the social policies that prevailed from 1964 to 1980 often seemed to reward vice" instead of rewarding virtuous conduct by the poor. The problem as Jencks, following Murray, views it is not easy to repair, because "if you set out to help people who are in trouble, you almost always find that most of them are to some extent responsible for their present troubles. Few victims are completely innocent. Helping those who are not doing their best to help themselves

poses extraordinarily difficult moral and political problems."[4] David T. Ellwood writes that Murray "is almost certainly correct in stating that welfare does not reflect or reinforce our most basic values. He is also correct in stating that no amount of tinkering with benefit levels or work rules will change that."[5]

An especially interesting feature of these contemporary debates about the welfare state and how it might be reformed is the emergence of conservative cultural themes in the writings of liberal policy intellectuals. The new consensus proclaims that our policies should be designed to reward the deserving and punish the undeserving. This sort of rhetoric is reminiscent of what liberals formerly were wont to call "blaming the victim." The question arises whether this switch in the tone of liberal rhetoric is theoretically well motivated. Do plausible theories of distributive justice provide a significant role for notions of individual responsibility and deservingness? In a recent essay Samuel Scheffler has speculated that the theories of justice of John Rawls and Ronald Dworkin – flagships in the fleet of philosophical liberalism – might be politically vulnerable insofar as neither theory includes as a fundamental norm of justice the principle that individuals ought to get what they deserve (according to some intuitively plausible conception of desert).[6] Scheffler's suggestion is that these liberal theories of justice, lacking any commitment to desert as morally important in its

Originally published in *Journal of Political Philosophy* 5 (December 1997): 327–50. Reprinted by permission of Blackwell Publishing Ltd.

own right rather than just as a possible means to the achievement of other moral goals, thereby render themselves unattractive to the commonsense of ordinary citizens and unlikely to gain their allegiance. If Scheffler is right, the philosophical liberalism of Rawls and Dworkin is deeply at odds with the contemporary efforts by policy advisors to rethink the line between individual and social responsibility in the area of poverty policy.

The message of this essay is that any plausible theory of justice should be hospitable to norms of individual responsibility and deservingness. To claim that "it is economic circumstances rather than individual failure which explains the difficulty citizens encounter in finding employment" perpetuates an unrealistic dichotomy.[7] If there is a conflict between philosophical liberalism and current efforts to improve welfare state policies, this conflict only afflicts versions of philosophical liberalism that have not properly come to grips with this issue.[8]

Moreover, when we think carefully about individual responsibility, we see that the incorporation of this norm into a theory of justice need have no tendency to cause the theory to generate stingy policy prescriptions. This essay concentrates on normative political theory and does not address any issues of policy in detail, but even at this level of abstraction it will become manifest that egalitarianism and responsibility are comrades, not adversaries. Three considerations drive this result: (1) morality and prudence do not dictate that all able-bodied persons should strive to be economically self-supporting, (2) since we are only responsible for doing as well as can reasonably be expected given circumstances beyond our control, even if morality and prudence do dictate that we should strive to be self-supporting, those who fail to satisfy this norm are not likely to be, on average, less deserving than anyone else, and (3) the information available to policy planners precludes tailoring policy to fine-grained assessments of individual deservingness. This essay also discusses whether the rebuttal of the deservingness objection to redistributive transfers provides a paternalistic case for providing transfers in the form of employment opportunities rather than cash.

I The Deservingness Objection to Transfers

Consider a stylized decision problem. An individual is badly off, and could be helped by redistributive transfer organized coercively by the state. The state could tax better off individuals and redistribute the money to the badly off individual in some form. Aid would help the individual and might affect his behavior in the future for better or worse. The form in which the aid is given may affect the extent to which the individual is aided now and the impact of the aid on his incentives to behave in the future in ways society deems appropriate. Finally, we may imagine that the individual may have become badly off either due to circumstances beyond his power to control or due to contingencies that were influenceable by choices he could have made. To simplify, suppose that the individual might have engaged in an imprudent act in the past, and if he did engage in this act, he suffered a risk of misfortune that reasonably prudent choice on his part could have avoided. (Notice that such imprudent conduct might be either virtuous or nonvirtuous. Virtuous imprudence would consist of imprudent actions reasonably undertaken from moral motives, including altruism, devotion to a worthy cause, or scrupulous unwillingness to violate one's moral principles.)

Many theories of justice would converge on the judgment that in the generic situation just described, there is good reason, though not necessarily conclusive reason, to favor a policy that calls for a redistributive transfer of resources from better off individuals to the worse off. This will be true of utilitarianism, close relatives of utilitarianism such as weighted utilitarian theories that give priority to achieving gains and avoiding losses of utility for those who are badly off in this respect, resourcist doctrines such as Rawls's injunction to maximin the level of primary social goods, egalitarian theories that hold that it is morally desirable that individuals be equally well off, and others. Details aside, many conceptions of justice will agree that an important aim of justice is to improve the condition of the needy simply in virtue of their neediness.

The contrary response is that being in need does not suffice to render it morally obligatory that your fellow community members should lend you a helping hand.

Here is Thomas Malthus on the personal responsibilities of the indigent:

> When the wages of labour are hardly sufficient to maintain two children, a man marries and has five or six; he of course finds himself miserably distressed. He accuses the insufficiency

of the price of labour to maintain a family. He accuses his parish for their tardy and sparing fulfillment of their obligation to assist him. He accuses the avarice of the rich, who suffer him to want what they can so well spare. He accuses the partial and unjust institutions of society, which have awarded him an inadequate share of the produce of the earth. He accuses perhaps the dispensations of providence, which have assigned him a place in society so beset with unavoidable distress and dependence. In searching for objects of accusation, he never adverts to the quarter from which his misfortunes originate. The last person that he would think of accusing is himself, on whom in fact the principal blame lies, except so far as he has been deceived by the higher classes of society.[9]

Malthus observes that individuals who are badly off may have become so through their own undeserving conduct. That an individual is blameworthy for his plight does not foreclose the possibility that society is under a duty of humanity to alleviate his condition. But the issue is at least open; some argument is needed. A distributive justice argument for an enforced transfer of resources can be countered by the assertion that the proposed beneficiary of the transfer is at fault.

This appeal to undeservingness can be purely instrumental in character or it can invoke a moral ideal deemed to be valuable for its own sake. For example, in a utilitarian framework, undeserving conduct is understood as conduct whose nature is such that blaming its perpetrator maximizes utility and declining to compensate individuals for the bad consequences that this conduct brings upon themselves maximizes utility. On this view, the notions of deserving and undeserving and the practices of holding (1) individuals to be blameworthy or not for their conduct, and (2) the condition that results from their conduct to be compensable or not are instruments to be manipulated so as to maximize utility.

In contrast, deservingness matters for its own sake if helping the undeserving (and failing to help the deserving) is deemed intrinsically unfair quite apart from its further consequences.

Murray explicitly appeals to deservingness for its own sake, not merely as a tool to achieve other ends. He imagines a choice between two healthy non-aged individuals who might be candidates for transfer aid. One is a worker who has been working steadily for many years and is now out of work on account of a plant closing. He is unlucky, we might say, to explain our sympathy for the plight of this laid-off worker and our willingness to help him out via a mechanism such as unemployment benefits. In contrast, "a second man, healthy and in the prime of life, refuses to work. I offer him a job, and he still refuses to work."[10] Of the choice to aid the drone (Murray's term) or the laid-off worker, Murray observes that even if funds were available to aid both, it would be wrong to confer a similar level of benefits on the less deserving and on the more deserving individuals. Indeed, even if lavishing benefits on the less deserving individual somehow does not lessen the amount that can be made available to the more deserving even in the long run, still, fair is fair. Murray offers the opinion that "it is not humane to the laid-off worker to treat him the same as the drone. It is not just to accord the drone the respect the laid-off worker has earned."[11]

II Fine-grained Deservingness

Murray is making up an example to illustrate a point, so he is free to stipulate that the person he calls the "drone" is less deserving than the laid-off worker. But it should be noted that the information he gives is insufficient for this judgment. Any theory of deservingness includes two aspects. One is a standard of conduct, an account of what we morally and prudently ought to do. The second aspect is an account of responsibility. This account specifies to what extent one is properly subject to praise or blame, reward or punishment, for conforming to the given standard or failing to do so. Taking it as given that Murray's laid-off worker fulfills the relevant standard of conduct and the drone does not, we do not yet know enough to know who is more deserving. For all that we have been told, the laid-off worker might be blessed by circumstances that make it easy for him to conform to the norm, whereas the drone's circumstances make conformity difficult. We might on balance judge that Murray's drone is the more deserving of the pair, even if we were to agree with Murray that being self-supporting is a paramount moral requirement.[12]

The degree to which one can reasonably hold someone truly responsible for conforming to a given standard of conduct depends on the difficulty and personal cost of conformity. We reasonably hold people responsible at most for doing the best they can with the cards that fate has dealt them. I say "at most" because the circumstances of an individual's life that are set beyond her power to control may be so discouraging as to render failure to make a steady good effort excusable.

Favorable or unfavorable genetic inheritance and early childhood socialization experiences crucially affect any adult individual's ability to make sensible choices and implement them. But these matters of genetic and social inheritance are entirely beyond one's power to control, and hence not matters for which one could be held personally responsible. This means that responsibility for voluntary choices and actions and individual values and goals is problematic. Even if we have freedom of the will, empirical helps and hindrances to exercising it virtuously fall randomly in different amounts on different persons. Discovering good values, making sensible choices, and putting one's choices into action will be variably easy and costly for individuals depending on their choice-making and choice-following abilities as fixed by genetic and social inheritance. Given a valid standard of conduct that applies to a group of persons, the degree to which each should be held accountable for failure to comply and given credit for successful conformity to the standard varies from person to person.

Let us say that a coarse-grained measure of deservingness posits a standard of conduct for everyone and rates each person as more or less deserving depending on the degree to which each conforms to the standard. A fine-grained measure of deservingness adjusts individual's performance scores according to the circumstances and abilities of each individual that render it more or less difficult and costly to perform well. But once the distinction between fine-grained and coarse-grained measures is before the mind, it is clear that the coarse-grained account cannot be the proper measure of the true deservingness of an individual that is invoked when it is proposed that proportioning good fortune to deservingness would be morally desirable for its own sake, not just as a means to some further morally desirable goals.

Moreover, even though many factors determine the distribution of poverty, on the average we would expect that impoverished members of society tend to be cursed with choice-making and choice-following deficits, so even if their degree of conformity to accepted standards of conduct is less than average, one cannot infer that their de-servingness, all things considered, is less than average.

The proponent and the critic of redistribution may disagree about the empirical issue to what extent individuals should register as deserving or undeserving on a fine-grained approach, and these empirical issues may for practical purposes be intractable, given the difficulty of disentangling the factors in the causation of the pertinent behavior. Disagreement about what are the standards of conduct, conformity to which renders persons variously deserving, is ubiquitous, but for the most part unlikely to be a significant element in disagreements concerning the morality of redistribution. This is so because in the context of proposals to aid the needy, all sides to controversies about redistribution tend to agree that the relevant standard of conduct that is in question is prudence (within the limits of the law). An important exception is the idea that there is a moral obligation to be self-supporting if one can, which the poor are alleged to violate. If this particular moralism can be rebutted, it turns out that controversy about deservingness and responsibility becomes peripheral to debates about redistribution. After all, if the disagreement comes down to disagreement over facts, and available evidence does not enable us to settle these issues, then we should all become agnostic about these factual matters, which is to say, we should all agree. Of course fundamental normative principles may lead to conflicting conclusions about redistribution. Conservatives may embrace libertarian theories of rights and entitlements which liberals and radicals reject. But these issues are not properly posed as a debate about the role of conceptions of individual responsibility and deservingness within conflicting theories of justice. The moral differences lie elsewhere.[13]

III   Fair Welfare Maximizing

To focus discussion I will set forth a plain and simple set of principles of distributive justice that would tend to favor redistributive transfers in the generic situation and that are also responsive to considerations of deservingness. These principles assess policies and actions according to their consequences. The consequentialism I shall assume is welfarist, egalitarian, and responsive to deservingness. Welfarist consequentialism holds that the goal that morality bids us to pursue is the maximization of some function of individual human welfare or well-being. Individual human well-being is the good, and the aim set by morality is the maximization of some function of human good. Egalitarianism holds that the moral value of achieving a one-unit gain of well-being for an individual is greater, the lower the individual's well-being level is prior to gaining this increment.[14] Desert responsiveness holds that the moral value of achieving a one-unit gain of well-being is greater, the greater the individual's level of deservingness.[15] This version of consequentialism then instructs us to maximize a function of human welfare that gives priority to well-being gains for the badly off and the deserving. We are to maximize human well-being weighted by consideration for egalitarianism and deservingness. (Prior to the assignment of precise weights, only a family of views, not a determinate principle, has been specified.) Identifying these as fairness norms, I call this version of consequentialism Fair Welfare Maximizing.

The statement of Fair Welfare Maximizing assumes that, in principle, one can make cardinal interpersonal comparisons of well-being and deservingness. Even if this assumption is granted, in practice the information required for well-being and deservingness measurement will often be unavailable, or obtainable only at excessive cost in terms of Fair Welfare Maximizing values. The policies we ought to choose will usually be designed to achieve increases in some measureable proxies for the goals, progress towards which we cannot directly measure. If the best proxy measures are too unreliable and uncertain, their use can become counterproductive, and what morality requires is uncertain. Deservingness may be especially liable to shift to an epistemic status that renders it irrelevant to policy formation. If we cannot know whether people are deserving we cannot reasonably reward them for it.

"Well-being" and "deservingness" are placeholders for whatever conceptions of these values prove most acceptable. Regarding well-being, few would disagree that the question which of the available means to one's goals would most effectively advance their fulfillment has a correct answer which is independent of people's opinions on this matter. I shall take it for granted that an individual's choice of basic goals can also be correct or incorrect. Theories of well-being give various accounts of how this is so.[16] My own inclination is toward a mixed view, according to which a person's life goes better the more her important basic

preferences are satisfied, the value of the satisfaction of a preference varying with the extent to which it could withstand ideally extended rational deliberation with full information. A preference for a thing is basic when it is preferred for its own sake, rather than as a means to further goals. To say that an individual prefers X over Y is to say that she desires X over Y when confronted with a choice between them and that she judges X to be more valuable for her than Y. The view is mixed in that the notion of a preference combines desire and judgment. In what follows I make use only of the idea that in the domain of well-being, thinking does not make it so: An individual's judgment, even her considered judgment, of her own good might be incorrect.

IV   Reagan and Mill on Perverse Incentives

A popular suspicion is that to help the needy by institutional measures on which the needy can rely is counterproductive, because in the long run the assurance of aid will cause the numbers of the needy to increase. President Ronald Reagan gave voice to this concern in his characteristically simple and persuasive style: "In 1964 the famous War on Poverty was declared and a funny thing happened. Poverty, as measured by dependency, stopped shrinking and then actually began to grow worse. I guess you could say poverty won the war."[17] Writing a century and a half ago, J. S. Mill worries in a similar spirit about "cases in which the tender of help perpetuates the state of things which renders help necessary." Mill continues: "[I]n all cases of helping, there are two sets of consequences to be considered; the consequences of the assistance, and the consequences of relying on the assistance. The former are generally beneficial, but the latter, for the most part, injurious; so much so, in many cases, as greatly to outweigh the value of the benefit."[18] If Smith lacks the means of subsistence, providing them helps Smith now, which is good, but may encourage Smith to be imprudent in the future, in the confident expectation that his subsistence is secure in any case. Moreover, helping Smith in this way may encourage other observing individuals to take less prudent care for their future well-being than they would otherwise take if the state did not supply a guarantee of subsistence to the destitute. In fact, the standing offer of aid by the state should affect individuals' calculations as to what level of risk it is prudent to bear, and may increase the incidence of prudent conduct that leads to a condition of poverty and a reliance by the individual on state-supplied subsistence. The considerations that Mill is raising are relevant to other areas of state policy besides welfare provision – for example, bankruptcy law. As Mill recognizes, whether or not the relationship that troubles him actually holds is an empirical question. It could after all be the case that the state provision of a generous safety net encourages economic agents to be bolder and more adventurous in their economic plans, and to make career and investment decisions that on the average improve the productivity of the economy and the flourishing of the individuals within it, even though some agents fall into the safety net.[19] For example, individuals might be more willing to move to a distant region of the country where their skills are reported to be in demand, if they know that if the expected jobs fail to materialize, they will not become destitute. In this case the general reliance by economic agents on the security net would be socially advantageous, all things considered. Mill's empirical hunch is that a generous safety net will act as a magnet, drawing too many agents to itself over time. Hence he proposes this norm: "if assistance is given in such a manner that the condition of the person helped is as desirable as that of the person who succeeds in doing the same thing without help, the assistance, if capable of being previously counted on, is mischievous: but if, while available to everybody, it leaves to every one a strong motive to do without it if he can, it is then for the most part beneficial."[20]

Let us call this norm the Lesser Eligibility Principle. It holds that welfare provision should be set so that for each person, the condition she reaches when taking state relief is less attractive to her than the least attractive paid employment or self-employment opportunity that is available to her, so that she has no incentive to choose a condition of dependency on state aid over a condition of self-sufficiency. Mill supposes that this principle is that of the Poor Law of 1834, which was deliberately punitive and stingy in the provision of aid to the needy able-bodied. But in fact Mill's Lesser Eligibility is compatible with a generous provision of cash to the able-bodied working-aged unemployed impoverished members of society. To satisfy Lesser Eligibility when welfare relief is generous and the least attractive private sector jobs pay little and offer bleak working conditions, what is required is that the cash subsidy given to the unemployed should be supplemented by cash subsidies to the working poor, the system of subsidies being set so that the state aid gradually tapers off as the individual's income from wages increases. On its face, then, the Lesser Eligibility Principle proposed by Mill does not set an obvious upper bound on aid to the unemployed able-bodied poor.

Like Reagan, Mill supposes that self-sufficiency is desirable and being dependent on the help of others for one's well-being should be avoided. What ethical judgments and empirical hunches underlie this assumption?

V The Alleged Moral Obligation to be Self-supporting

Why might spurning paid activity be immoral or render one undeserving? Perhaps the simplest answer would be that each able-bodied non-aged adult is morally obligated to be economically self-supporting (without violating the law). If one lacks the ability or opportunity to fulfill this obligation, one's nonfulfillment is excused. If such an obligation can be shown to exist, this immediately would explain why assistance to the able-bodied non-aged poor should be offered only in the form of opportunities to work (or engage in paying self-employment) and never in the form of cash income supplements or the equivalent. The explanation would be that if each is obligated to be self-supporting (provided that she can be), the society should adapt its aid to helping the poor individual to satisfy this obligation. Or at least, this would be so if one holds that if one is under an obligation he is unable to meet, it is better to help the individual to fulfill the obligation rather than merely to provide the individual a good excuse for nonfulfillment. (Another way to make this point would be to say that if individuals lack opportunities to work and the government gives them an income instead of providing opportunities to work, some of those aided by cash might be disposed not to take work opportunities if they were offered. But if there is an obligation to earn one's livelihood if one can, this disposition to spurn work would render these individuals morally undeserving of aid. The quality of their will as imagined is deficient.) At the same time, if one accepts that each individual is under an obligation to be self-supporting, then if individuals are able to support themselves but choose not to do so, society's obligation to fill in the breach by providing support may diminish or disappear altogether.

The moral norm that one should be self-supporting can be interpreted in two quite different ways. To see the two interpretations, consider a person who never works but gains his livelihood from interest payments generated by his inherited wealth or a person who never works but gets his livelihood in the form of steady cash gifts from his generous and affluent grandmother. Does the coupon-clipper or the sponger violate the norm of self-sufficiency? One might interpret the norm as the injunction against gaining one's livelihood by becoming impoverished and begging from strangers or private associations or by accepting transfers from the state. According to the alternative construal, the norm requires that one must earn one's own livelihood by paid labor or active self-employment. (John Stuart Mill accepts the primacy of labor version of the norm of economic self-sufficiency when he writes, "I do not accept as either just or salutary, a state of society in which there is any 'class' which is not labouring.")[21] Once the two versions of self-sufficiency are distinguished, it seems to me that neither version sounds very plausible, not at least if construed as a fundamental moral principle.

One possible argument in favor of self-sufficiency construed as the obligation not to become destitute and throw oneself on the mercy of strangers is that willfully becoming destitute harms the strangers, at least if they will be bound by morality or by law to make sacrifices so as to eliminate the destitution. If a social safety net is in place, and one either willfully throws oneself on the net or negligently or recklessly engages in conduct that unreasonably risks a fall into the net, one is thereby wrongfully harming the taxpayers who pay for the maintenance of the net.

But an individual who chooses unemployment may be making the best of a set of bad options in a situation in which society has the obligation to improve his option set, his set of life prospects. If the individual's labor market options are sufficiently bleak, and the person's unemployment options include any that are by comparison attractive, a prudent choice of unemployment would not gainsay the obligation of society to ease the individual's plight. (To anticipate the terminology of a later section of this essay, the willfully unemployed person might be a needy bohemian.)

According to an egalitarian doctrine such as Fair Welfare Maximizing, if all of the able-bodied are among the better off members of society, then they might well have obligations to aid the less well off, all of whom would be non-able-bodied. Failure to support oneself by work when one can would appear to be a gross violation of one's duty to help the worse off non-able-bodied. But if the non-able-bodied are few in number, as seems likely, then some able-bodied persons will fall within the class of badly off persons who will constitute the appropriate beneficiaries of transfer policies. To make further progress with this issue, it would be necessary to clarify this notion of the "able-bodied." So long as the able-bodied include some of the badly off members of society, the self-sufficiency norm appears to be unacceptable.

The norm of self-sufficiency in its primacy of labor version might still be morally acceptable, so far as my arguments are concerned, provided the norm is restricted in its application to the class of better off individuals.[22] It is not to my purpose to try to settle this issue. But in its application to badly off individuals, the injunction that one is morally obligated to others to make good-faith efforts to earn one's livelihood by paid work seems perverse. If some individuals face grim life prospects, and would be even worse off if they remained steadfastly attached to the labor market, why should any liberal egalitarian doctrine require this attachment? What obligation to the better off would spurning work in these circumstances plausibly be thought to violate? (Here I am assuming that the badly off are in this condition by unchosen circumstances, not by their own voluntary choice.)

VI Reciprocity

Perhaps the basic moral intuition that underlies Murray's revulsion against a system of welfare-state transfers is that those who benefit as members of society but decline to make good-faith efforts to be self-supporting violate a basic norm of reciprocity. Society has lavished benefits on each individual who survives to adulthood, after all, only because older members of society have cooperated to make this possible. To work is to reciprocate the benefit. Or if one is poor and society offers some form of aid, willingness to work at paid labor in order to eliminate or reduce one's needy condition is appropriate reciprocity.

The norm of reciprocity in its simplest form holds that one should return good for good and evil for evil. One interpretation of the norm is that favors should be repaid in the same currency, at the same level of value, so if I invite you to dinner, you reciprocate by inviting me to dinner, and if I serve you fish, you serve me fish or an "equivalent." Leaving aside the problem of how to determine what counts as equivalent value in acts of reciprocity, I note that in this guise the norm of reciprocity would seem incompatible with the transfers of benefit that are at the heart of egalitarian principle. If I am badly off and society, committed to egalitarianism, offers me benefits, the thought that I must reciprocate and pay back society for these benefits would seem to defeat the point of the transfer. The point is to make me better off, and if I reciprocate, then I am no better off (in the currency in which reciprocity duties are calculated) than I was before the transfer.

The norm "Do unto others as they do unto you" might be interpreted as requiring that one should repay individuals according to the actual effects (or perhaps the reasonably expectable effects) of their behavior on one's well-being. This would mean that if each of several individuals intends to benefit one and works equally hard to this end, one should repay each individual according to the actual pay-off one gets from her behavior that impinges on one's prospects. This would imply that, other things being equal, one owes more according to the reciprocity norm to those who are talented and produce more benefit to oneself per unit of expended effort, and also more to those who are lucky and produce much benefit with little effort. This also implies that one who intends injury but generates benefit for others by mistake is owed reciprocating benefits by those others.

Clearly the requirement that the benefit one gives back is equivalent to the benefit one gets is too strong as it stands. If Smith at small cost confers a large benefit on me, and the only way I can pay Smith back is by incurring a very large cost, reciprocity plausibly construed does not demand the repayment. Perhaps the requirement is that if Smith confers a benefit on me, incurring a certain cost in doing so, my reciprocity obligation is to confer a similar amount of benefit on Smith when I can do so at a cost to myself similar to the level of Smith's cost. But this seems implausible. Someone who confers slight benefit on me at huge cost to himself does not plausibly trigger an obligation on my part to pay him back a comparable benefit at comparable huge cost.

Perhaps a looser interpretation of reciprocity would render the norm more plausible. Perhaps I am to reciprocate favors received by returning the favor by an act that involves just as much sacrifice on my part as the sacrifice that the initial favor cost its giver. But is effortless reciprocity that is not experienced as a sacrifice nonreciprocity or rather gracious and cheerful reciprocity? Another thought is that reciprocity might be general: a passing motorist stops to help me when my car is broken down on a deserted roadway late at night; I reciprocate not by doing a favor for that Good Samaritan but by being a Good Samaritan myself when an occasion arises to benefit some other stranger in need. But suppose such occasions do not arise? A weaker notion would be dispositional reciprocity: If you do me a favor in certain circumstances, I reciprocate by disposing myself to return the favor (to you or to a generalized substitute for you) should the tables be turned and I find myself in relevantly similar circumstances in the position of the potential aid-giver. This seems to me the most appropriate form of reciprocity: In a just society we are all disposed to act in conformity to the same principles, which might imply that you should aid me continuously, or that I should aid you continuously, but no matter. We are all disposed to behave in conformity with the same appropriate principles.

But in this weak dispositional sense of reciprocity I, as able-bodied recipient of aid to the needy even though I am willfully unemployed, might be fully disposed to act in conformity with these principles of justice that determined that I should get this dole. My conformity to the reciprocity norm is determined not by what actually happens, for the norms of justice we all subscribe to might never demand my sacrificing for others, but by what I would have done in counterfactual scenarios in which I were better off and you were the needy willfully unemployed person.

This line of thought leads to the conclusion that one cannot show that principles of justice do not dictate obligations on the part of advantaged members of society to give aid to disadvantaged members of society who happen to be willfully unemployed by invoking an ideal of reciprocity which the willfully unemployed are flouting. Reciprocity is in a sense a formal notion. It does not determine what the principles of justice are, to which aid-givers and aid-recipients alike should be loyal. If justice demands no aid to the disadvantaged willfully unemployed, then it would violate reciprocity for me to demand a handout in violation of what justice demands. But this does not advance the discussion of what justice demands. The appeal to reciprocity therefore seems to me to be a red herring.

VII   Work and Status Inequalities

One important and obvious determinant of the quality of a job is how it compares with other jobs. A "good" job is one that offers a more attractive sum of benefits and burdens than most other jobs, or than most other jobs in some salient comparison class. Part of the benefit a jobholder derives from a good job is the awareness that most others (in a salient comparison class) have worse jobs. If our economy were transformed so that Ivy League professors, lawyers at fancy Wall Street firms, heart surgeons and nuclear scientists became those with the least attractive and interesting jobs, their jobs would thereby become much worse, even though their work activities, pay, conditions of work and other benefits remained exactly as they are now.[23] As matters stand, these jobs confer high status and satisfy the preference to do better than others. To a large extent the status hierarchies of work are local, but local hierarchies are also connected and nested; the man who has a "good job" working the cash register at a gas station knows full well that scare quotes are needed to describe the job as "good."

This means that those who fill the bottom rungs in status hierarchies are performing a service for the benefit of those who occupy the top rungs. Higher rungs require lower rungs; if there is a top, there is a bottom. This is not a service that those whose skills and habits place them as the least qualified members of the work force perform gladly, and for some the status inequalities of work are more galling than for others. The individual who performs a menial job may be a college student on her way to bigger and better things, or a hard-working immigrant confident that she will be able to use this job to advance in the world. To others, the menial job registers the considered judgment of the labor market on the value and promise of their labor. The job is a badge of inferiority.

Writing in the 1960s about the streetcorner society of African American males, Elliot Liebow observes that "the streetcorner man puts no lower value on the job than does the larger society around him." He continues: The jobs available to the streetcorner man "are at the bottom of the employment ladder in every respect... The rest of society (whatever its ideal values regarding the dignity of labor) holds the job of the dishwasher or janitor or unskilled laborer in low esteem if not outright contempt. So does the streetcorner man. He cannot do otherwise. He cannot draw from a job those social values which other people do not put into it."[24] Individuals differ in their willingness to wear the badge of inferiority that is associated with employment in a dead-end job.

Not surprisingly, aversion to bottom-of-the-barrel-employment has been interpreted in a positive light, as a mark of good character, an aversion to meritocratic status hierarchy. Michael Walzer has suggested the view that it is a sign of the success of a contemporary welfare state that its beneficiaries develop increased self-respect and are unwilling to take available menial jobs that are below some minimal level of dignity.[25] At the very least we might say that individuals with a poor endowment of job skills and traits will vary in the extent to which they experience workplace status inequality as a source of distress, and that it is excusable that individuals who are especially sensitive on this score may shun paid employment of the type they reasonably believe they can find.

The distribution of status from work is a factor that partly determines both the "work ethic" standard of conduct that should apply to badly off individuals and also any given individual's degree of responsibility for meeting or failing to meet the standard.

VIII   From the Generic Case to Welfare

To this point this essay has defended the generic case for transfers against the objection from deservingness. The pieces of this argument may appear not to fit together smoothly, so a summary is in order. I argue:

1   An account of what people deserve includes two components, a standard of conduct and a norm that determines to what extent any given individual is rightly held responsible for meeting or failing to meet the standard.

2   In the context of considering the justification of government programs that transfer re-

sources to the needy, the pertinent standard of conduct is prudence within the limits of the law and ordinary moral constraints. The standard of conduct in its application to the needy does not include fulfillment of the alleged moral obligation to make good-faith efforts to be economically self-supporting. There is no such obligation. In particular, no plausible norm of reciprocity entails such an obligation.

3 Although prudent conduct for most persons in market economies requires that one make good-faith efforts to be economically self-supporting, this requirement may not apply to all untalented and poor individuals whose access to paid employment is limited to extremely low-wage, low-skill jobs that confer low social status.

4 Even on the assumption that each able-bodied person is morally obligated to make good-faith efforts to be economically self-supporting, and given that some able-bodied poor persons fail to fulfill this obligation, such failure may not render them undeserving of aid in the form of government transfer programs. The issue of responsibility remains open. The same is true if it is assumed that individuals should be prudent, that it is prudent to make good-faith efforts to be economically self-supporting, and that some able-bodied poor persons fail to meet this requirement of prudence.

5 The extent to which one is reasonably held responsible (liable to praise or blame, reward or punishment) for conforming or failing to conform to moral and prudential requirements depends on how difficult and costly it is to conform.

6 Individuals vary in their abilities to engage in complex reasoning that has a bearing on what it is most reasonable to choose and to carry through the choices that they make. Making sensible choices and putting them into action is easy for some, difficult for others, and pleasant for some, painful for others. Favorable and unfavorable external circumstances can also conspire to render making and implementing good choices easy and pleasant for some, difficult and painful for others. The extent to which it is reasonable to hold people responsible for their moral and prudential failures varies with the degree to which it would have been difficult and painful or easy and pleasant to have avoided these failures. On the whole and on the average, individuals with poor prospects for well-being over the course of their lives (the truly disadvantaged, we might say) have lesser choice-making and choice-following abilities than others. And on the whole and on the average, impoverished people have poor prospects for well-being.

7 The rebuttal of the deservingness objection against transfers boils down to these claims: The net benefits from steady efforts to seek and hold paid employment are uncertain and questionable for untalented able-bodied individuals, so the prudential case for putting forth such steady efforts is not compelling for some members of this class. Moreover, if prudence does not require such people to seek employment, morality does not require this course either. Even if prudence or morality does require efforts to be self-supporting, the extent to which one is blameworthy for failing to make the efforts depends on the difficulty and cost of doing so, and the difficulty and cost tend to be greater for impoverished and untalented persons. In short, even if some of these people are failing to conform to reasonable standards, it may well be unreasonable to blame them for failure to comply.[26]

This line of argument does not deny that able-bodied individuals with low stocks of personal and material resources have capacities of rational agency. The argument claims that these people labor under special obstacles that render it more difficult for them to meet reasonable standards. These obstacles give rise to a general excusing condition, not a denial that the conditions necessary for responsible agency are in place. If I am severely demented, I lack the capacity to "own" my actions, so cannot be given credit for nice behavior any more than I can be blamed for nasty behavior. In contrast, if I am impoverished and untalented, these conditions are hurdles rendering good conduct harder, so if I fail to behave badly I am less to blame than someone who behaves similarly badly without facing similar hurdles and if I behave well I deserve more credit than someone who behaves the same but did not need to overcome comparable hurdles.

The situation is complicated by a pervasive and unavoidable paucity of information about who faces exactly what obstacles and hurdles. Among the class of able-bodied impoverished persons with weak labor force attachment, some are obligated by morality or prudence to make good-faith efforts to be self-supporting, and some comply with these norms and some do not, and of those that do not, some are genuinely blameworthy and the lapses of some are excusable or even, given their circumstances, constitute admirable conduct. But the subgroups are not readily distinguishable, even to close observers such as work-mates, family and friends – even the individuals themselves. Needless to say, the information that sorts individuals into these subgroups, if not available to intimate observers, is not available to bureaucrats administering state policies.

The rebuttal of the deservingness objection against transfers does not unequivocally support transfers. Suppose you say that Arneson is not to be blamed for his failure to make good-faith efforts to be self-supporting because, even though this course of action is required by prudence and morality, Arneson lacks the personal traits that make it sufficiently easy to do the right thing that doing the wrong thing reasonably elicits a blaming response. The excuse you are offering to rebut the claim that Arneson does not deserve aid because he is undeserving simultaneously undermines the positive case for aid. If Arneson lacks the skills and character traits needed for prudent conduct, why suppose that bestowing resources on him will make his life better as opposed to giving him the opportunity to be imprudent on a grander scale? If Arneson is going to spend his welfare check on beer and cigarettes, he might be better off with less money. The rebuttal of the conservatism of stinginess raises the spectre of the conservatism of paternalism. The former would deny resources to the poor because they are blameworthy and deserve a miserable life. The latter would deny resources to the poor for their own good.

The Reagan-Mill argument previously mentioned proposes that even though getting transfer aid is beneficial to the poor person, coming to rely on the aid may be disadvantageous to her, and this disadvantage may outweigh the benefit. (This argument does not rely on any claim to the effect that the poor are undeserving, so it obviously is untouched by the defeat of that claim.) The twist just added is that perhaps getting transfer aid is itself disadvantageous to some poor people who predictably will not use the aid wisely. But this paternalist argument is unconvincing on its face, because in dealing with poverty a society is not confined to the choice of providing unrestricted resources to individuals or doing nothing for them.

A third alternative is the provision of resources in a restricted form, which makes unwise use of the transfer aid more difficult and less likely. Under the section below on "Job Opportunities and Quasipaternalism" this alternative is further explored.

The Reagan-Mill concern about perverse incentives challenges the advocate of transfers to design policies that achieve long-run benefits to the poor – for example, by meeting the Lesser Eligibility standard. Notice also that the extent to which this concern tells against welfare-state policies depends on the specific egalitarian goals that are being pursued and, in particular, the degree to which one believes that it is more important to achieve gains for those whose condition is extremely bad than for those whose condition is less bad. If one eliminates benefits in the hope of encouraging individuals to put forth self-supporting behavior, predictably people's abilities to put forth effective coping behavior will vary with their condition, so that a "get-tough" policy might help the moderately disadvantaged but be disastrous for the most destitute.

The heterogeneity of the class of individuals affected by welfare state policies has further consequences. It also defeats any simple inference from the generic case for transfers to specific welfare state redistributive policies. Since policies cannot be tailored to individual characteristics, the class of people singled out for aid by a given policy will not be exactly the set of people who would most benefit from that type of aid, and may include some individuals whom we would not wish to benefit at all.

IX The Non-needy Bohemian Argument

A small cash income is not a perfectly reliable indicator that one's life is not going well. A talented mendicant friar may report a small income, but be leading exactly the life that he most wishes to lead, one that involves the satisfaction of his most important preferences, where his preferences seem to be reasonable ones that would withstand critical scrutiny with full information. If well-being to a first approximation is flourishing in a way of life that is choiceworthy in the sense that it could withstand informed deliberative scrutiny, then income is at best only a very rough proxy indicator of well-being. Some persons with low incomes will be talented individuals leading rich and satisfying lives, who happen to have aims and values such that they need a lot of leisure and very little cash income to fulfill their most important aims. These persons are advantaged if their condition is evaluated by a sensitive measure of well-being, but they look disadvantaged according to the measure of yearly income. Call these low-income individuals, who are well off in well-being and have a strong preference for leisure over work, non-needy bohemians.

A disadvantage, from a Fair Welfare Maximizing standpoint, of a redistributive transfer program that offers cash income supplements to low-income individuals is that the recipients of these transfers will include advantaged persons – the non-needy bohemians, who should be helping the needy rather than benefiting from state policies ostensibly designed to alleviate their plight. In contrast, offering assistance to those who are identified as needy by the rough proxy of low income in the form of opportunities for low-skill decent employment will screen the non-needy bohemians from receipt of benefits. The non-needy bohemians may not be acting badly in shunning work, but they are not genuinely poor persons, so they do not deserve the aid that should be targeted to the genuinely poor. In ideal theory, one could design transfer policies that would be sensitive to relevant personal characteristics of individuals besides lack of cash income, but in a world in which policies must be coarse-grained, and cannot discriminate finely in determining to whom benefits should be allocated, the problem of the non-needy bohemians provides a reason to favor transfer policies that offer opportunities for work rather than cash assistance.

This argument for offering aid to the able-bodied only in the form of paid employment opportunities rather than in the form of cash assistance is not exactly watertight.[27] After all, one must also consider the likelihood that the group of low-income persons contains some persons we might call needy bohemians – individuals who lack personal resources and talents and are leading lives of substandard quality but who nonetheless have strong preferences for leisure over work and strong aversion to paid employment. A flaw in the proposal to supply aid to the cash-poor only in the form of decent low-skill job opportunities is that needy bohemians, genuinely disadvantaged persons with strong preferences for leisure, would find this form of aid unattractive, either worth nothing to

them or worth little. From this point of view, the issue becomes the likely ratio of needy to non-needy bohemians in the class of low-income unemployed persons. The more the non-needy predominate, the less desirable is the policy of cash aid to the low-income unemployed. To this extent at least one version of a liberal egalitarian theory of distributive justice can support the currently fashionable cry that we should "end welfare as we know it."

In the abstract, one can think of reasons for either the conjecture that the numbers of needy bohemians will exceed the numbers of the non-needy or the reverse. On the one side, one might note that personal talent can complement the good of leisure even with little income to give an individual the means to achieve her personal goals, but the leisure that accrues with unemployment for a person of little personal talent tends not to be worth much. Sociological studies of the long-term unemployed report that they experience filling up time as difficult. On the other side, some of the goods that steady employment brings include goods of steady association with work-mates and praise for valued work that is well done, and these goods may be less than normally available for individuals who lack marketable personal talents from the types of employment they can secure. Dropping out of the rat-race may make more sense for individuals who see themselves as likely to be vying for last place.

Hypothetical conjectures aside, we note that from an egalitarian standpoint it would seem that getting aid to each badly off person will have higher priority than setting transfer policy with the goal of excluding all persons who are not truly badly off from receiving aid. If the moral priority of the egalitarian is to help those who are badly off, then a failure of targeting that includes the non-needy seems likely to be more acceptable, other things equal, than a failure that excludes some of the needy. Only if the indirect effects of defining the class of recipients of aid too broadly bring it about that the most needy as a group are less well served than they would be if the class of recipients were set too narrowly would erring on the overinclusive side be worse. My own sense then is that the "quasi-paternalism" considerations raised in the next section must be crucial if it is to be shown that aid only in the form of provision of work opportunities is superior from an egalitarian standpoint.

X   Job Opportunities and Quasi-Paternalism

Any liberal egalitarian theory of justice will surely be predisposed to favor redistributive transfers that aid the needy by way of cash transfers rather than any type of aid in kind. Cash is a maximally flexible asset that limits least the uses to which a recipient can put the aid she is allotted. Other things being equal, cash transfers should do better than in kind aid both on the score of providing greater freedom to beneficiaries and providing greater increases to their well-being. These considerations should powerfully recommend cash transfers over in-kind benefits. The case for cash transfers over provision of aid in the form of employment opportunities is merely a special case of this general liberal predisposition.

However, what holds in general may not hold for the tricky policy issues involving employment and the poor. One simple consideration is that a recipient of a cash transfer cannot use that extra income to purchase a job as one can purchase consumer goods. If the labor market functioned in a simple textbook fashion, then a poor person who desired employment and could count on some cash income assistance from the state could bid down the price of a desired job, and secure employment by undercutting the current price of that labor. More realistic models of the labor market suggest that labor markets do not always clear – that at equilibrium some individuals may be qualified to perform certain jobs and willing to perform those jobs at going rates of pay or slightly less but are unable to secure employment on those terms. Jobs may be a special benefit, such that cash transfers to the unemployed do not necessarily augment the access of these unemployed persons to employment opportunities.

Let us confine our attention to truly disadvantaged persons who are averse to paid employment and would prefer cash income assistance to comparable employment opportunities if given the choice. Why should we override the considered choice of the person we are trying to aid as to what form of benefit that we could offer her would be most beneficial?

Stated baldly, the answer that would support the policy of offering aid to the able-bodied only in the form of paid employment opportunities is that, on the average, the disadvantaged person who shuns work is making a costly mistake that lowers her prospects of well-being, and that government transfer policy should be set to encourage labor force attachment even by the able-bodied poor person who would stay detached from the labor force if her own preferences in this matter were respected. The basis of the "paid employment only" transfer policy is the judgment that for most poor people, having a job is good for you whether you think so or not.

The policy I am recommending would be quasi-paternalistic in that policy designed to benefit an adult individual who is neither feeble-minded nor crazy would not be guided by that individual's judgment of where her good lies. A policy that overrides the judgment of the individual about her own good when benefit to her is the aim of the policy is, let us say, quasi-paternalistic. It is not fully paternalistic in that the element of coercion with respect to the person we are trying to aid is not present. I suppose without any argument that rounding up the unemployed and forcing them to take paid employment under threat would be an unlikely means to benefit them. The policy that is envisaged is offering aid in a form that the individual would not prefer on a take it or leave it basis.

There is some reason to believe that the conditions that produce destitution and long-range prospects of low well-being also erode individuals' sense of judgment about what is best for themselves, what life strategies make sense. There are also culture of poverty considerations. Those with weak labor force attachment tend not to keep company with those with strong labor force attachment. The marginally employable individuals of society, buffeted about by the labor market, tend to seek solace and consolation in attitudes that are adaptive for a life that does not revolve around work but nonadaptive for taking best advantage of employment opportunities.[28] There are also non-negligible arguments to the conclusion that assiduously seeking paid employment, taking it when it is available, and standing fast by the best job one can get even if it is from the dregs of labor market opportunities are in the self-interest of almost any individual in the long run. Paid employment gives structure to one's life, provides opportunities for earned respect, and tends to provide opportunities for solidarity and social contact with work-mates. To be decisive, these considerations need not stretch so far as to show that every poor person who shuns work is making a mistake about how to make her life go best. Even if some able-bodied individuals would be better off with a decent income offered without a work requirement, the question is what holds true on the average for the class of potential beneficiaries of transfer policies. Finally, note that even if in some future more humane and just and tolerant society, freedom from the obligation to work at paid employment (or comparable self-employment) would be desirable, it may yet be the case that in societies that are as strongly wedded to the work ethic as ours is, abiding by it rather than violating it is for most disadvantaged persons a prudent life strategy. Since many people in our society hold Charles Murrayish beliefs about the moral obligation to be self-supporting, working to earn one's livelihood is in practice needed for now in order to earn the respect of one's fellow citizens.

Although some conservatives entertain the fantasy that eliminating welfare benefits by itself suffices to offer jobs to all, on the theory that the labor market will absorb all who seek work, a more sensible policy of providing welfare benefits in the form of employment opportunities provides state sector employment. To be a benefit to their low-skill takers, state sector jobs should have low skill requirements, include opportunities for training, be decently and demandingly supervised, and involve tasks that are genuinely socially beneficial rather than makework.[29]

Given the weakness of the other arguments against cash assistance to the able-bodied that I have surveyed, the quasi-paternalism issue becomes crucial. Even a strong "libertarian" tilt in liberal egalitarianism might well be overridden in this or that policy context by motivated worries about the quality of choices we humans are likely to make on matters that are important for our individual well-being but hard to survey and assess in a clear-headed way from the standpoint of our own best interests.

XI Conclusion

The factors that make it easy or difficult, and more or less costly, for an individual to behave as she ought are densely intertwined with aspects of her circumstances for which it is sensible to hold her accountable. Sorting out these factors and deciding to what degree an individual is truly deserving can be hard, even intractable, even in a small-scale and local context that does not stretch out over time. "Judge not," says the Bible.

A society might care a great deal about bringing it about that to the greatest extent possible the good fortune that each individual enjoys is proportional to her true deservingness. Such a society could set its institutions and practices giving top priority to this aim. But this is very definitely not the society we inhabit. The major institutions that distribute good fortune are the family and the market. Neither of these institutions is responsive to individual deservingness. Market prices are determined by supply and demand. The family distributes care and concern according to ties of blood and marriage; as a parent I do not try to determine which children are more deserving and help them – I try to give my own children every advantage. We could try to institute very different institutions that would attempt to establish a republic of virtue, a moralized meritocracy, in which people receive benefits according to their fine-grained deservingness. This would not be a crazy project, but it is hard to conceive what shape institutions must assume in order to make progress towards achieving it, and it is clear that any attempt to reform society in this way would leave us all far worse off in material terms than we are under current institutions.

The question then arises, given that we do not in fact care enough about deservingness to scrap the market and reshape the family in order to try to tailor individual good fortune to individual deservingness, why does this issue suddenly loom in importance when we are discussing social welfare policies that address the alleviation of poverty? We blandly tolerate such facts as that Japanese language teachers earn more than Spanish language teachers even if both are equally deserving, because there is greater demand for instruction in Japanese. If social values comparable in importance to market efficiency are at stake in choices about social welfare policy for the poor, why not forgo the attempt to create a republic of virtue in this one domain? A pincer movement is formed by two considerations: (1) the massive actual irrelevance of fine-grained desert to the working of major institutions of our society, and (2) the massive difficulty of monitoring individuals' fine-grained deservingness scores even on the assumption that we could coherently and nonarbitrarily assign weights to the various dimensions of deservingness so as to generate a single interpersonally comparable measure of individuals' overall desert. The pincers exerts pressure to forgo the attempt to make the treatment of individuals responsive to desert a major consideration in social welfare policy directed toward poverty relief. This decision to downplay deservingness results from

thinking through its nature and implications rather than from ignoring it.

Notes

1 This near-consensus includes two ideas: (1) Income assistance to able-bodied adults should be short-term. No able-bodied person should gain subsistence from welfare for a long duration, and no one should gain subsistence from welfare at intervals that over the course of one's life amount to considerable dependency. (2) Aid to the able-bodied should be given only in exchange for work, for sincere efforts to secure paid employment, or for training efforts that are set so as to promote the self-sufficiency of the recipient. For skeptical observations on the feasibility of centering antipoverty policy on the attempt to increase employment among low-income individuals, see Rebecca Blank, "The employment strategy: public policies to increase work and earnings," *Confronting Poverty: Prescriptions for Change*, ed. Sheldon Danziger, Gary Sandefur and Daniel Weinberg (Cambridge, Mass.: Harvard University Press, 1994), pp. 168–204.

2 David Ellwood, *Poor Support: Poverty in the American Family* (New York: Basic Books, 1988), p. 5.

3 One might suppose that the primary aim of AFDC is to help children. But we could, if we chose, give a lot of aid to children in ways that would not aid their parents (except in so far as parents have a strong interest in their children's well-being).

4 Christopher Jencks, *Rethinking Social Policy: Race, Poverty, and the Underclass* (Cambridge, Mass.: Harvard University Press, 1992), p. 88. In the passage quoted Jencks is summarizing Charles Murray's argument rather than speaking in his own voice. But Jencks makes it plain that he thinks that Murray's moral critique of welfare raises the right issue in the right terms; at most, Jencks quibbles that Murray and other conservative critics exaggerate the character-sapping causal effects of the welfare policies they hate. In the final sentence of his review, Jencks asserts accusingly that the liberal coalition that controlled US social policy from 1964 to 1980 "often rewarded folly and vice, and it never had enough confidence in its own norms of behavior to assert that those who violated these norms deserved whatever sorrows followed." In this same connection see chapter 6 of *Rethinking Social Policy*. For the locus classicus of contemporary conservative thinking on welfare, see Charles Murray, *Losing Ground: American Social Policy 1950–1980* (New York: Basic Books, 1984). See also Lawrence Mead, *Beyond Entitlement: The Social Obligations of Citizenship* (New York: Free Press, 1995); also Mead, *The New Politics of Poverty* (New York: Basic Books, 1992).

5 Ellwood, *Poor Support: Poverty in the American Family*, p. 6. See also Mary Jo Bane and David Ellwood, *Welfare Realities: From Rhetoric to Reform* (Cambridge, Mass.: Harvard University Press, 1994); see esp. ch. 5, "Reducing poverty by replacing welfare."

6 Samuel Scheffler, "Responsibility, reactive attitudes, and liberalism in philosophy and politics," *Philosophy and Public Affairs*, 21 (1992), 299–323. On John Rawls, see *A Theory of Justice* (Cambridge, Mass.: Harvard University Press, 1971), ch. 5. On Ronald Dworkin, see "What is equality? Part 2: equality of resources," *Philosophy and Public Affairs*, 10 (1981), 283–345.

7 Desmond King, *Actively Seeking Work? The Politics of Unemployment and Welfare Policy in the United States and Great Britain* (Chicago: University of Chicago Press, 1995). King is paraphrasing an op-ed piece by M. Abramovitz and F. Piven.

8 This is also the message of John Roemer, *Theories of Distributive Justice* (Cambridge: Harvard University Press, 1996).

9 Thomas Malthus, *An Essay on Population*, as cited in Theodore Marmor, Jerry Mashaw and Philip Harvey, *America's Misunderstood Welfare State: Persistent Myths, Enduring Realities* (New York: Basic Books, 1990), p. 24.

10 Murray, *Losing Ground*, p. 197.

11 Ibid., p. 198. Murray acknowledges that at the level of policy formation, it may be unfeasible to devise practices that will discriminate the truly deserving from the nondeserving among those who are potential recipients of government transfers. But, in principle, Murray supposes we can all agree, we ought to vary our treatment of people according to what they deserve.

12 Rawls makes a similar observation in *A Theory of Justice*, p. 312.

13 A qualification must be added. Murray's position might be construed as holding not merely that it is better, other things being equal, to gain benefits for the more rather than the less deserving, but that it is bad to gain benefits for people above the level that they deserve. The Fair Welfare Maximizing norm described below does not support the latter, non-comparative principle of rewarding the deserving.

14 Nothing in Fair Welfare Maximizing limits the scope of morally desirable redistribution within national boundaries. This means that strictly speaking, in a world in which poor people in rich societies are

not poor relative to the entire population of the earth, the focus on the moral merits of redistribution within a single rich nation is misplaced. When policy choices pose conflicts of interest among various levels of better and worse off individuals across the globe, egalitarian theories of justice will tilt in favor of the globally worse off.

15 The desert responsiveness view stated in the text is too crude. If Smith is more deserving than Jones, but the ratio of Smith's deservingness level to her well-being (good fortune) level is higher than Jones's, it will be more urgent on grounds of deservingness to achieve gains of welfare for Jones than for Smith. I will not try to state a more accurate view here; this is a topic for another occasion.

16 For an "Objective List" account of human welfare, see Thomas Hurka, *Perfectionism* (Oxford: Oxford University Press, 1993); and for a rational informed desire account, see Richard Brandt, *The Theory of the Right and the Good* (Oxford: Oxford University Press, 1979); also Peter Railton, "Facts and values," *Philosophical Topics*, 14 (1986), 5–31.

17 A 1986 radio address by President Ronald Reagan, cited in King, *Actively Seeking Work*, p. 183. By "dependency" Reagan appears to be referring to the number of people who fall below the poverty line if the calculation subtracts government transfers from their income.

18 John Stuart Mill, *Principles of Political Economy* (Toronto: University of Toronto Press, 1965), bk V, ch. 11, sec. 13, at p. 960.

19 A.B. Atkinson, *The Economics of the Welfare State* (Memphis: P.K. Seidman Foundation, 1995), p. 3.

20 Mill, *Principles of Political Economy*, p. 961.

21 Ibid., bk IV, ch. 7, sec. 1, p. 758.

22 Reference to the "better off" and "worse off" in this context is loose talk. For Fair Welfare Maximizing, the moral urgency of obtaining a benefit for a person does not directly depend on how well off she is as compared with others, but on how well off or badly off she is in absolute terms. For a maximin principle such as Rawls's difference principle, the badly off are those individuals who are worst off in terms of their shares of primary social goods other than basic liberties. I count as "egalitarian" any principles of distributive justice that directly or indirectly give priority to helping those – among those who are below the average level of advantage (however "advantage" is defined by the principle under review) – who are worse off than others.

23 See Robert Frank, *Choosing the Right Pond* (New York: Basic Books, 1986).

24 Elliot Liebow, *Tally's Corner: A Study of Negro Streetcorner Men* (Boston: Little, Brown, 1967), pp. 57 and 58–9 respectively.

25 Michael Walzer, *Spheres of Justice: A Defense of Pluralism and Equality* (New York: Basic Books, 1983), at pp. 166–7.

26 These claims echo the two-pronged argument that Kristin Luker advances to mitigate adverse judgment on poor teenaged women who have children. She argues, on the one hand, that these women may well be behaving reasonably and prudently, making the best of their grim circumstances, and on the other hand, that even if these women are to some extent behaving badly, their conduct is revealed to be excusable when one attends carefully to the obstacles that hinder them from behaving well. See Luker, *Dubious Conceptions: The Politics of Teenage Pregnancy* (Cambridge, Mass.: Harvard University Press, 1996, chs. 5–6).

27 See Richard Arneson, "Is work special? Justice and the distribution of employment," *American Political Science Review* 10 (1990), 1127–47. The following paragraph partially withdraws the conclusion I tried to draw in this essay from the existence of needy and non-needy bohemians.

28 Despite all the literature that has been produced lately about the "underclass," I find Liebow's *Tally's Corner* still the best account of cultural norms in grim circumstances impinging on individual lives among one segment of the persistently poor. Liebow highlights men's stories. To gain a sense of poverty and welfare as experienced by poor women, see Jill Berrick, *Faces of Poverty: Portraits of Women and Children on Welfare* (Oxford and New York: Oxford University Press, 1995).

29 For some elaboration of this idea, see Arneson, "Is work special?," pp. 1145–6.

PART VII

Oppression

36

Power, Right, Truth

Michel Foucault

The course of study that I have been following until now – roughly since 1970/71 – has been concerned with the *how* of power. I have tried, that is, to relate its mechanisms to two points of reference, two limits: on the one hand, to the rules of right that provide a formal delimitation of power; on the other, to the effects of truth that this power produces and transmits, and which in their turn reproduce this power. Hence we have a triangle: power, right, truth.

Schematically, we can formulate the traditional question of political philosophy in the following terms: how is the discourse of truth, or quite simply, philosophy as that discourse which *par excellence* is concerned with truth, able to fix limits to the rights of power? That is the traditional question. The one I would prefer to pose is rather different. Compared to the traditional, noble and philosophic question it is much more down to earth and concrete. My problem is rather this: what rules of right are implemented by the relations of power in the production of discourses of truth? Or alternatively, what type of power is susceptible of producing discourses of truth that in a society such as ours are endowed with such potent effects? What I mean is this: in a society such as ours, but basically in any society, there are manifold relations of power which permeate, characterise and constitute the social body, and these relations of power cannot themselves be established, consolidated nor implemented without the production, accumulation, circulation and functioning of a discourse. There can be no possible exercise of power without a certain economy of discourses of truth which operates through and on the basis of this association. We are subjected to the production of truth through power and we cannot exercise power except through the production of truth. This is the case for every society, but I believe that in ours the relationship between power, right and truth is organised in a highly specific fashion. If I were to characterise, not its mechanism itself, but its intensity and constancy, I would say that we are forced to produce the truth of power that our society demands, of which it has need, in order to function: we *must* speak the truth; we are constrained or condemned to confess or to discover the truth. Power never ceases its interrogation, its inquisition, its registration of truth: it institutionalises, professionalises and rewards its pursuit. In the last analysis, we must produce truth as we must produce wealth, indeed we must produce truth in order to produce wealth in the first place. In another way, we are also subjected to truth in the sense in which it is truth that makes the laws, that produces the true discourse which, at least partially, decides, transmits and itself extends upon the effects of power. In the end, we are judged, condemned, classified, determined in our undertakings, destined to a certain mode of living or dying, as a function of the true discourses which are the bearers of the specific effects of power.

Originally published in *Power/Knowledge*, edited by Colin Gordon (Brighton: Harvester, 1980), pp. 92–108.

So, it is the rules of right, the mechanisms of power, the effects of truth or if you like, the rules of power and the powers of true discourses, that can be said more or less to have formed the general terrain of my concern, even if, as I know full well, I have traversed it only partially and in a very zig-zag fashion. I should like to speak briefly about this course of research, about what I have considered as being its guiding principle and about the methodological imperatives and precautions which I have sought to adopt. As regards the general principle involved in a study of the relations between right and power, it seems to me that in Western societies since medieval times it has been royal power that has provided the essential focus around which legal thought has been elaborated. It is in reponse to the demands of royal power, for its profit and to serve as its instrument or justification, that the juridical edifice of our own society has been developed. Right in the West is the King's right. Naturally everyone is familiar with the famous, celebrated, repeatedly emphasised role of the jurists in the organiation of royal power. We must not forget that the re-vitalisation of Roman Law in the twelfth century was the major event around which, and on whose basis, the juridical edifice which had collapsed after the fall of the Roman Empire was reconstructed. This resurrection of Roman Law had in effect a technical and constitutive role to play in the establishment of the authoritarian, administrative, and, in the final analysis, absolute power of the monarchy. And when this legal edifice escapes in later centuries from the control of the monarch, when, more accurately, it is turned against that control, it is always the limits of this sovereign power that are put in question, its prerogatives that are challenged. In other words, I believe that the King remains the central personage in the whole legal edifice of the West. When it comes to the general organisation of the legal system in the West, it is essentially with the King, his rights, his power and its eventual limitations, that one is dealing. Whether the jurists were the King's henchmen or his adversaries, it is of royal power that we are speaking in every case when we speak of these grandiose edifices of legal thought and knowledge.

There are two ways in which we do so speak. Either we do so in order to show the nature of the juridical armoury that invested royal power, to reveal the monarch as the effective embodiment of sovereignty, to demonstrate that his power, for all that it was absolute, was exactly that which befitted his fundamental right. Or, by contrast, we do so in order to show the necessity of imposing limits upon this sovereign power, of submitting it to certain rules of right, within whose confines it had to be exercised in order for it to remain legitimate. The essential role of the theory of right, from medieval times onwards, was to fix the legitimacy of power; that is the major problem around which the whole theory of right and sovereignty is organised.

When we say that sovereignty is the central problem of right in Western societies, what we mean basically is that the essential function of the discourse and techniques of right has been to efface the domination intrinsic to power in order to present the latter at the level of appearance under two different aspects: on the one hand, as the legitimate rights of sovereignty, and on the other, as the legal obligation to obey it. The system of right is centred entirely upon the King, and it is therefore designed to eliminate the fact of domination and its consequences.

My general project over the past few years has been, in essence, to reverse the mode of analysis followed by the entire discourse of right from the time of the Middle Ages. My aim, therefore, was to invert it, to give due weight, that is, to the fact of domination, to expose both its latent nature and its brutality. I then wanted to show not only how right is, in a general way, the instrument of this domination – which scarcely needs saying – but also to show the extent to which, and the forms in which, right (not simply the laws but the whole complex of apparatuses, institutions and regulations responsible for their application) transmits and puts in motion relations that are not relations of sovereignty, but of domination. Moreover, in speaking of domination I do not have in mind that solid and global kind of domination that one person exercises over others, or one group over another, but the manifold forms of domination that can be exercised within society. Not the domination of the King in his central position, therefore, but that of his subjects in their mutual relations: not the uniform edifice of sovereignty, but the multiple forms of subjugation that have a place and function within the social organism.

The system of right, the domain of the law, are permanent agents of these relations of domination, these polymorphous techniques of subjugation. Right should be viewed, I believe, not in terms of a legitimacy to be established, but in terms of the methods of subjugation that it instigates.

The problem for me is how to avoid this question, central to the theme of right, regarding sovereignty and the obedience of individual subjects in order that I may substitute the problem of domination and subjugation for that of sovereignty and obedience. Given that this was to be the general line of my analysis, there were a certain number of methodological precautions that seemed requisite to its pursuit. In the very first place, it seemed important to accept that the analysis in question should not concern itself with the regulated and legitimate forms of power in their central locations, with the general mechanisms through which they operate, and the continual effects of these. On the contrary, it should be concerned with power at its extremities, in its ultimate destinations, with those points where it becomes capillary, that is, in its more regional and local forms and institutions. Its paramount concern, in fact, should be with the point where power surmounts the rules of right which organise and delimit it and extends itself beyond them, invests itself in institutions, becomes embodied in techniques, and equips itself with instruments and eventually even violent means of material intervention. To give an example: rather than try to discover where and how the right of punishment is founded on sovereignty, how it is presented in the theory of monarchical right or in that of democratic right, I have tried to see in what ways punishment and the power of punishment are effectively embodied in a certain number of local, regional, material institutions, which are concerned with torture or imprisonment, and to place these in the climate – at once institutional and physical, regulated and violent – of the effective apparatuses of punishment. In other words, one should try to locate power at the extreme points of its exercise, where it is always less legal in character.

A second methodological precaution urged that the analysis should not concern itself with power at the level of conscious intention or decision; that it should not attempt to consider power from its internal point of view and that it should refrain from posing the labyrinthine and unanswerable question: 'Who then has power and what has he in mind? What is the aim of someone who possesses power?' Instead, it is a case of studying power at the point where its intention, if it has one, is completely invested in its real and effective practices. What is needed is a study of power in its external visage, at the point where it is in direct and immediate relationship with that which we can provisionally call its object, its target, its field of application, there – that is to say – where it installs itself and produces its real effects.

Let us not, therefore, ask why certain people want to dominate, what they seek, what is their overall strategy. Let us ask, instead, how things work at the level of on-going subjugation, at the level of those continuous and uninterrupted processes which subject our bodies, govern our gestures, dictate our behaviours etc. In other words, rather than ask ourselves how the sovereign appears to us in his lofty isolation, we should try to discover how it is that subjects are gradually, progressively, really and materially constituted through a multiplicity of organisms, forces, energies, materials, desires, thoughts etc. We should try to grasp subjection in its material instance as a constitution of subjects. This would be the exact opposite of Hobbes' project in *Leviathan*, and of that, I believe, of all jurists for whom the problem is the distillation of a single will – or rather, the constitution of a unitary, singular body animated by the spirit of sovereignty – from the particular wills of a multiplicity of individuals. Think of the scheme of Leviathan: insofar as he is a fabricated man, Leviathan is no other than the amalgamation of a certain number of separate individualities, who find themselves reunited by the complex of elements that go to compose the State; but at the heart of the State, or rather, at its head, there exists something which constitutes it as such, and this is sovereignty, which Hobbes says is precisely the spirit of Leviathan. Well, rather than worry about the problem of the central spirit, I believe that we must attempt to study the myriad of bodies which are constituted as peripheral *subjects* as a result of the effects of power.

A third methodological precaution relates to the fact that power is not to be taken to be a phenomenon of one individual's consolidated and homogeneous domination over others, or that of one group or class over others. What, by contrast, should always be kept in mind is that power, if we do not take too distant a view of it, is not that which makes the difference between those who exclusively possess and retain it, and those who do not have it and submit to it. Power must be analysed as something which circulates, or rather as something which only functions in the form of a chain. It is never localised here or there, never in anybody's hands, never appropriated as a commodity or piecc of wealth. Power is employed and exercised through a net-like organisation. And not only do individuals circulate between its threads; they are always in the position of simultaneously undergoing and exercising this power. They are not only its inert or consenting target; they are always also the elements of its articulation. In other words, individuals are the vehicles of power, not its points of application.

The individual is not to be conceived as a sort of elementary nucleus, a primitive atom, a multiple and inert material on which power comes to fasten or against which it happens to strike, and in so doing subdues or crushes individuals. In fact, it is already one of the prime effects of power that certain bodies, certain gestures, certain discourses, certain desires, come to be identified and constituted as individuals. The individual, that is, is not the *vis-à-vis* of power; it is, I believe, one of its prime effects. The individual is an effect of power, and at the same time, or precisely to the extent to which it is that effect, it is the element of its articulation. The individual which power has constituted is at the same time its vehicle.

There is a fourth methodological precaution that follows from this: when I say that power establishes a network through which it freely circulates, this is true only up to a certain point. In much the same fashion we could say that therefore we all have a fascism in our heads, or, more profoundly, that we all have a power in our bodies. But I do not believe that one should conclude from that that power is the best distributed thing in the world, although in some sense that is indeed so. We are not dealing with a sort of democratic or anarchic distribution of power through bodies. That is to say, it seems to me – and this then would be the fourth methodological precaution – that the important thing is not to attempt some kind of deduction of power starting from its centre and aimed at the discovery of the extent to which it permeates into the base, of the degree to which it reproduces itself down to and including the most molecular elements of society. One must rather conduct an *ascending* analysis of power, starting, that is, from its infinitesimal mechanisms, which each have their own history, their own trajectory, their own techniques and tactics, and then see how these mechanisms of power have been – and continue to be – invested, colonised, utilised, involuted, transformed, displaced, extended etc., by ever more general mechanisms and by forms of global domination. It is not that this global domination extends itself right to the base in a plurality of repercussions: I believe that the manner in which the phenomena, the techniques and the procedures of power enter into play at the most basic levels must be analysed, that the way in which these procedures are displaced, extended and altered must certainly be demonstrated; but above all what must be shown is the manner in which they are invested and annexed by more global phenomena and the subtle fashion in which more general powers or economic interests are able to engage with these technologies that are at once both relatively autonomous of power and act as its infinitesimal elements. In order to make this clearer, one might cite the example of madness. The descending type of analysis, the one of which I believe one ought to be wary, will say that the bourgeoisie has, since the sixteenth or seventeenth century, been the dominant class; from this premise, it will then set out to deduce the internment of the insane. One can always make this deduction, it is always easily done and that is precisely what I would hold against it. It is in fact a simple matter to show that since lunatics are precisely those persons who are useless to industrial production, one is obliged to dispense with them. One could argue similarly in regard to infantile sexuality – and several thinkers, including Wilhelm Reich have indeed sought to do so up to a certain point. Given the domination of the bourgeois class, how can one understand the repression of infantile sexuality? Well, very simply – given that the human body had become essentially a force of production from the time of the seventeenth and eighteenth century, all the forms of its expenditure which did not lend themselves to the constitution of the productive forces – and were therefore exposed as redundant – were banned, excluded and repressed. These kinds of deduction are always possible. They are simultaneously correct and false. Above all they are too glib, because one can always do exactly the opposite and show, precisely by appeal to the principle of the dominance of the bourgeois class, that the forms of control of infantile sexuality could in no way have been predicted. On the contrary, it is equally plausible to suggest that what was needed was sexual training, the encouragement of a sexual precociousness, given that what was fundamentally at stake was the constitution of a labour force whose optimal state, as we well know, at least at the beginning of the nineteenth century, was to be infinite: the greater the labour force, the better able would the system of capitalist production have been to fulfil and improve its functions.

I believe that anything can be deduced from the general phenomenon of the domination of the bourgeois class. What needs to be done is something quite different. One needs to investigate historically, and beginning from the lowest level, how mechanisms of power have been able to function. In regard to the confinement of the insane, for example, or the repression and interdiction of sexuality, we need to see the manner in which, at the effective level of the family, of the immediate environment, of the cells and most basic units of society, these phenomena of repression or exclusion possessed their instruments and their logic, in response to a certain number of needs. We need to identify the agents responsible for them, their real agents (those which constituted the immediate social *entourage*, the family, parents, doctors etc.), and not be content to lump them under the formula of a generalised bourgeoisie. We need to see how these mechanisms of power, at a given moment, in a precise conjuncture and by means of a certain number of transformations, have begun to become economically advantageous and politically useful. I think that in this way one could easily manage to demonstrate that what the bourgeoisie needed, or that in which its system discovered its real interests, was not the exclusion of the mad or the surveillance and prohibition of infantile masturbation (for, to repeat, such a system can perfectly well tolerate quite opposite practices), but rather, the techniques and procedures themselves of such an exclusion. It is the mechanisms of that exclusion that are necessary, the apparatuses of surveillance, the medicalisation of sexuality, of madness, of delinquency, all the micro-mechanisms of power, that came, from a certain moment in time, to represent the interests of the bourgeoisie. Or even better, we could say that to the extent to which this view of the bourgeoisie and of its interests appears to lack content, at least in regard to the problems with which we are here concerned, it reflects the fact that it was not the bourgeoisie itself which thought that madness had to be excluded or infantile sexuality repressed. What in fact happened instead was that the mechanisms of the exclusion of madness, and of the surveillance of infantile sexuality, began from a particular point in time, and for reasons which need to be studied, to reveal their political usefulness and to lend themselves to economic profit, and that as a natural consequence, all of a sudden, they came to be colonised and maintained by global mechanisms and the entire State system. It

is only if we grasp these techniques of power and demonstrate the economic advantages or political utility that derives from them in a given context for specific reasons, that we can understand how these mechanisms come to be effectively incorporated into the social whole.

To put this somewhat differently: the bourgeoisie has never had any use for the insane; but the procedures it has employed to exclude them have revealed and realised – from the nineteenth century onwards, and again on the basis of certain transformations – a political advantage, on occasion even a certain economic utility, which have consolidated the system and contributed to its overall functioning. The bourgeoisie is interested in power, not in madness, in the system of control of infantile sexuality, not in that phenomenon itself. The bourgeoisie could not care less about delinquents, about their punishment and rehabilitation, which economically have little importance, but it is concerned about the complex of mechanisms with which delinquency is controlled, pursued, punished and reformed etc.

As for our fifth methodological precaution: it is quite possible that the major mechanisms of power have been accompanied by ideological productions. There has, for example, probably been an ideology of education, an ideology of the monarchy, an ideology of parliamentary democracy etc.; but basically I do not believe that what has taken place can be said to be ideological. It is both much more an much less than ideology. It is the production of effective instruments for the formation and accumulation of knowledge – methods of observation, techniques of registration, procedures for investigation and research, apparatuses of control. All this means that power, when it is exercised through these subtle mechanisms, cannot but evolve, organise and put into circulation a knowledge, or rather apparatuses of knowledge, which are not ideological constructs.

By way of summarising these five methodological precautions, I would say that we should direct our researches on the nature of power not towards the juridical edifice of sovereignty, the State apparatuses and the ideologies which accompany them, but towards domination and the material operators of power, towards forms of subjection and the inflections and utilisations of their localised systems, and towards strategic apparatuses. We must eschew the model of Leviathan in the study of power. We must escape from the limited field of juridical sovereignty and State institutions, and instead base our analysis of power on the study of the techniques and tactics of domination.

This, in its general outline, is the methodological course that I believe must be followed, and which I have tried to pursue in the various researches that we have conducted over recent years on psychiatric power, on infantile sexuality, on political systems, etc. Now as one explores these fields of investigation, observing the methodological precautions I have mentioned, I believe that what then comes into view is a solid body of historical fact, which will ultimately bring us into confrontation with the problems of which I want to speak this year.

This solid, historical body of fact is the juridical-political theory of sovereignty of which I spoke a moment ago, a theory which has had four roles to play. In the first place, it has been used to refer to a mechanism of power that was effective under the feudal monarchy. In the second place, it has served as instrument and even as justification for the construction of the large scale administrative monarchies. Again, from the time of the sixteenth century and more than ever from the seventeenth century onwards, but already at the time of the wars of religion, the theory of sovereignty has been a weapon which has circulated from one camp to another, which has been utilised in one sense or another, either to limit or else to reinforce royal power: we find it among Catholic monarchists and Protestant anti-monarchists, among Protestant and more-or-less liberal monarchists, but also among Catholic partisans of regicide or dynastic transformation. It functions both in the hands of aristocrats and in the hands of parliamentarians. It is found among the representatives of royal power and among the last feudatories. In short, it was the major instrument of political and theoretical struggle around systems of power of the sixteenth and seventeenth centuries. Finally, in the eighteenth century, it is again this same theory of sovereignty, re-activated through the doctrine of Roman Law, that we find in its essentials in Rousseau and his contemporaries, but now with a fourth role to play: now it is concerned with the construction, in opposition to the administrative, authoritarian and absolutist monarchies, of an alternative model, that of parliamentary democracy. And it is still this role that it plays at the moment of the Revolution.

Well, it seems to me that if we investigate these four roles there is a definite conclusion to be drawn: as long as a feudal type of society survived, the problems to which the theory of sovereignty was addressed were in effect confined to the general mechanisms of power, to the way in which its forms of existence at the higher level of society influenced its exercise at the lowest levels. In other words, the relationship of sovereignty, whether interpreted in a wider or a narrower sense, encompasses the totality of the social body. In effect, the mode in which power was exercised could be defined in its essentials in terms of the relationship sovereign – subject. But in the seventeenth and eighteenth centuries, we have the production of an important phenomenon, the emergence, or rather the invention, of a new mechanism of power possessed of highly specific procedural techniques, completely novel instruments, quite different apparatuses, and which is also, I believe, absolutely incompatible with the relations of sovereignty.

This new mechanism of power is more dependent upon bodies and what they do than upon the Earth and its products. It is a mechanism of power which permits time and labour, rather than wealth and commodities, to be extracted from bodies. It is a type of power which is constantly exercised by means of surveillance rather than in a discontinuous manner by means of a system of levies or obligations distributed over time. It presupposes a tightly knit grid of material coercions rather than the physical existence of a sovereign. It is ultimately dependent upon the principle, which introduces a genuinely new economy of power, that one must be able simultaneously both to increase the subjected forces and to improve the force and efficacy of that which subjects them.

This type of power is in every aspect the antithesis of that mechanism of power which the theory of sovereignty described or sought to transcribe. The latter is linked to a form of power that is exercised over the Earth and its products, much more than over human bodies and their operations. The theory of sovereignty is something which refers to the displacement and appropriation on the part of power, not of time and labour, but of goods and wealth. It allows discontinuous obligations distributed over time to be given legal expression but it does not allow for the codification of a continuous surveillance. It enables power to be founded in the physical existence of the sovereign, but not in continuous and permanent systems of surveillance. The theory of sovereignty permits the foundation of an absolute power in the absolute expenditure of power. It does not allow for a calculation of power in terms of the minimum expenditure for the maximum return.

This new type of power, which can no longer be formulated in terms of sovereignty, is, I believe, one of the great inventions of bourgeois society. It has been a fundamental instrument in the constitution of industrial capitalism and of the type of society that is its accompaniment. This non-sovereign power, which lies outside the form of sovereignty, is disciplinary power. Impossible to describe in the terminology of the theory of sovereignty from which it differs so radically, this disciplinary power ought by rights to have led to the disappearance of the grand juridical edifice created by that theory. But in reality, the theory of sovereignty has continued not only to exist as an ideology of right, but also to provide the organising principle of the legal codes which Europe acquired in the nineteenth century, beginning with the Napoleonic Code.

Why has the theory of sovereignty persisted in this fashion as an ideology and an organising principle of these major legal codes? For two reasons, I believe. On the one hand, it has been, in the eighteenth and again in the nineteenth century, a permanent instrument of criticism of the monarchy and of all the obstacles that can thwart the development of disciplinary society. But at the same time, the theory of sovereignty, and the organisation of a legal code centred upon it, have allowed a system of right to be superimposed upon the mechanisms of discipline in such a way as to conceal its actual procedures, the element of domination inherent in its techniques, and to guarantee to everyone, by virtue of the sovereignty of the State, the exercise of his proper sovereign rights. The juridical systems – and this applies both to their codification and to their theorisation – have enabled sovereignty to be democratised through the constitution of a public right articulated upon collective sovereignty, while at the same time this democratisation of sovereignty was fundamentally determined by and grounded in mechanisms of disciplinary coercion.

To put this in more rigorous terms, one might say that once it became necessary for disciplinary constraints to be exercised through mechanisms of domination and yet at the same time for their effective exercise of power to be disguised, a theory of sovereignty was required to make an appearance at the level of the legal apparatus, and to re-emerge in its codes. Modern society, then, from the nineteenth century up to our own day, has been characterised on the one hand, by a legislation, a discourse, an organisation based on public right, whose principle of articulation is the social body and the delegative status of each citizen; and, on the other hand, by a closely linked grid of disciplinary coercions whose purpose is in fact to assure the cohesion of this same social body. Though a theory of right is a necessary companion to this grid, it cannot in any event provide the terms of its endorsement. Hence these two limits, a right of sovereignty and a mechanism of discipline, which define, I believe, the arena in which power is exercised. But these two limits are so heterogeneous that they cannot possibly be reduced to each other. The powers of modern society are exercised through, on the basis of, and by virtue of, this very heterogeneity between a public right of sovereignty and a polymorphous disciplinary mechanism. This is not to suggest that there is on the one hand an explicit and scholarly system of right which is that of sovereignty, and, on the other hand, obscure and unspoken disciplines which carry out their shadowy operations in the depths, and thus constitute the bedrock of the great mechanism of power. In reality, the disciplines have their own discourse. They engender, for the reasons of which we spoke earlier, apparatuses of knowledge (*savoir*) and a multiplicity of new domains of understanding. They are extraordinarily inventive participants in the order of these knowledge-producing apparatuses. Disciplines are the bearers of a discourse, but this cannot be the discourse of right. The discourse of discipline has nothing in common with that of law, rule, or sovereign will. The disciplines may well be the carriers of a discourse that speaks of a rule, but this is not the juridical rule deriving from sovereignty, but a natural rule, a norm. The code they come to define is not that of law but that of normalisation. Their reference is to a theoretical horizon which of necessity has nothing in common with the edifice of right. It is human science which constitutes their domain, and clinical knowledge their jurisprudence.

In short, what I have wanted to demonstrate in the course of the last few years is not the manner in which at the advance front of the exact sciences the uncertain, recalcitrant, confused dominion of human behaviour has little by little been annexed to science: it is not through some advancement in the rationality of the exact sciences that the human sciences are gradually constituted. I believe that the process which has really rendered the discourse of the human sciences possible is the juxtaposition, the encounter between two lines of approach, two mechanisms, two absolutely heterogeneous types of discourse: on the one hand there is the re-organisation of right that invests sovereignty, and on the other, the mechanics of the coercive forces whose exercise takes a disciplinary form. And I believe that in our own times power is exercised simultaneously through this right and these techniques and that these techniques and these discourses, to which the disciplines give rise invade the area of right so that the procedures of normalisation come to be ever more constantly engaged in the colonisation of those of law. I believe that all this can explain the global functioning of what I would call a *society of normalisation*. I mean, more precisely, that disciplinary normalisations come into ever greater conflict with the juridical systems of sovereignty: their incompatibility with each other is ever more acutely felt and apparent; some kind of arbitrating discourse is made ever more necessary, a type of power and of knowledge that the sanctity of science would render neutral. It is precisely in the extension of medicine that we see, in some sense, not so much the linking as the perpetual exchange or encounter of mechanisms of discipline with the principle of right. The developments of medicine, the general medicalisation of behaviours, conducts, discourses, desires etc., take place at the point of intersection between the two heterogeneous levels of discipline and sovereignty. For this reason, against these usurpations by the disciplinary mechanisms, against this ascent of a power that is tied to scientific knowledge, we find that there is no solid recourse available to us today, such being our situation, except that which lies precisely in the return to a theory of right organised around sovereignty and articulated upon its ancient principle. When today one wants to object in some way to the disciplines and all the effects of power and knowledge that are linked to them, what is it that one does, concretely, in real life, what do the Magistrates Union[1] or other similar institutions do, if not precisely appeal to this canon of right, this famous, formal right, that is said to be bourgeois, and which in reality is the right of sovereignty? But I believe that we find ourselves here in a kind of blind alley: it is not through recourse to sovereignty against discipline that the effects of disciplinary power can be limited, because sovereignty and disciplinary mechanisms are two absolutely integral constituents of the general mechanism of power in our society.

If one wants to look for a non-disciplinary form of power, or rather, to struggle against disciplines and disciplinary power, it is not towards the ancient right of sovereignty that one should turn, but towards the possibility of a new form of right, one which must indeed be anti-disciplinarian, but at the same time liberated from the principle of sovereignty. It is at this point that we once more come up against the notion of repression, whose use in this context I believe to be doubly unfortunate. On the one hand, it contains an obscure reference to a certain theory of sovereignty, the sovereignty of the sovereign rights of the individual, and on the other hand, its usage introduces a system of psychological reference points borrowed from the human sciences, that is to say, from discourses and practices that belong to the disciplinary realm. I believe that the notion of repression remains a juridical-disciplinary notion whatever the critical use one would make of it. To this extent the critical application of the notion of repression is found to be vitiated and nullified from the outset by the two-fold juridical and disciplinary reference it contains to sovereignty on the one hand and to normalisation on the other.

Note

1 This Union, established after 1968, has adopted a radical line on civil rights, the law and the prisons.

37

Racism, Sexism, and Preferential Treatment: An Approach to the Topics

Richard A. Wasserstrom

Introduction

Racism and sexism are two central issues that engage the attention of many persons living within the United States today. But while there is relatively little disagreement about their importance as topics, there is substantial, vehement, and apparently intractable disagreement about what individuals, practices, ideas, and institutions are either racist or sexist – and for what reasons. In dispute are a number of related questions concerning how individuals and institutions ought to regard and respond to matters relating to race or sex.

One particularly contemporary example concerns those programs variously called programs of "affirmative action," "preferential treatment," or "reverse discrimination" that are a feature of much of our institutional life. Attitudes and beliefs about these programs are diverse. Some persons are convinced that all such programs in virtually all of their forms are themselves racist and sexist and are for these among other reasons indefensible.[1] The programs are causally explicable, perhaps, but morally reprehensible. Other persons – a majority, I suspect – are sorely troubled by these programs. They are convinced that some features of some programs, e.g., quotas, are indefensible and wrong. Other features and programs are tolerated, but not with fervor or enthusiasm. They are seen as a kind of moral compromise, as, perhaps, a lesser evil among a set of unappealing options.[2] They are reluctantly perceived and implemented as a covert, euphemistic way to do what would clearly be wrong – even racist or sexist – to do overtly and with candor. And still a third group has a very different view. They think these programs are important and appropriate. They do not see these programs, quotas included, as racist or sexist, and they see much about the dominant societal institutions that is.[3] They regard the racism and sexism of the society as accounting in substantial measure for the failure or refusal to adopt such programs willingly and to press vigorously for their full implementation.

I think that much of the confusion in thinking and arguing about racism, sexism and affirmative action results from a failure to see that there are three different perspectives within which the topics of racism, sexism and affirmative action can most usefully be examined. The first of these perspectives concentrates on what in fact is true of the culture, on what can be called the social realities. Here the fundamental question concerns the way the culture is: What are its institutions, attitudes and ideologies in respect to matters of race and sex?[4]

The second perspective is concerned with the way things ought to be. From this perspective, analysis focuses very largely on possible, desirable states of affairs. Here the fundamental question concerns ideals: What would the good society – in terms of its institutions, its attitudes, and its values – look like in respect to matters involving race and sex?[5]

Originally published in *UCLA Law Review* 24 (1977): 581–622. Copyright © 1977 by Richard A. Wasserstrom. Reprinted by permission of the author.

The third perspective looks forward to the means by which the ideal may be achieved. Its focus is on the question: What is the best or most appropriate way to move from the existing social realities, whatever they happen to be, to a closer approximation of the ideal society? This perspective is concerned with instrumentalities.[6]

Many of the debates over affirmative action and over what things are racist and sexist are unilluminating because they neglect to take into account these three perspectives, which are important and must be considered separately. While I do not claim that all the significant normative and conceptual questions concerning race, sex, or affirmative action can be made to disappear, I do believe that an awareness and use of these perspectives can produce valuable insights that contribute to their resolution. In particular, it can almost immediately be seen that the question of whether something is racist or sexist is not as straightforward or unambiguous as may appear at first. The question may be about social realities, about how the categories of race or sex in fact function in the culture and to what effect. Or the question may be about ideals, about what the good society would make of race or sex. Or the question may be about instrumentalities, about how, given the social realities as to race and sex, to achieve a closer approximation of the ideal. It can also be seen, therefore, that what might be an impermissible way to take race or sex into account in the ideal society, may also be a desirable and appropriate way to take race or sex into account, given the social realities.

It is these three different perspectives and these underlying issues that I am interested in exploring. This framework is used to clarify a number of the central matters that are involved in thinking clearly about the topics of racism, sexism and affirmative action. Within this framework, some of the analogies and disanalogies between racism and sexism are explored – the ways they are and are not analytically interchangeable phenomena. I also provide an analytic scheme for distinguishing different respects in which a complex institution such as the legal system might plausibly be seen to be racist or sexist. And I examine some of the key arguments that most often arise whenever these topics are considered. In respect to programs of affirmative action, or preferential treatment, I argue specifically that much of the opposition to such programs is not justifiable. It rests upon confusion in thinking about the relevant issues and upon a failure to perceive and appreciate some of the ways in which our society is racist and sexist. I argue that there is much to be said for the view that such programs, even when they include quotas, are defensible and right. My central focus is not, however, on affirmative action per se, but rather on how a consideration of affirmative action is linked to a deepened understanding of these larger, related issues.

I Social Realities

One way to think and talk about racism and sexism is to concentrate upon the perspective of the social realities. Here one must begin by insisting that to talk about either is to talk about a particular social and cultural context. In this section I concentrate upon two questions that can be asked about the social realities of our culture. First, I consider the position of blacks and females in the culture vis-à-vis the position of those who are white, and those who are male. And second, I provide an analysis of the different ways in which a complex institution, such as our legal system, can be seen to be racist or sexist. The analysis is offered as a schematic account of the possible types of racism or sexism.

(a) *The position of blacks and women*

In our own culture the first thing to observe is that race and sex are socially important categories. They are so in virtue of the fact that we live in a culture which has, throughout its existence, made race and sex extremely important characteristics of and for all the people living in the culture.[7]

It is surely possible to imagine a culture in which race would be an unimportant, insignificant characteristic of individuals. In such a culture race would be largely if not exclusively a matter of superficial physiology; a matter, we might say, simply of the way one looked. And if it were, then any analysis of race and racism would necessarily assume very different dimensions from what they do in our society. In such a culture, the meaning of the term "race" would itself have to change substantially. This can be seen by the fact that in such a culture it would literally make no sense to say of a person that he or she was "passing."[8] This is something that can be said and understood in our own culture and it shows at least that to talk of race is to talk of more than the way one looks.[9]

Sometimes when people talk about what is wrong with affirmative action programs, or programs of preferential hiring, they say that what is wrong with such programs is that they take a thing as superficial as an individual's race and turn it into something important.[10] They say that a person's race doesn't matter; other things do, such as qualifications. Whatever else may be said of statements such as these, as descriptions of the social realities they seem to be simply false. One complex but true empirical fact about our society is that the race of an individual is much more than a fact of superficial physiology. It is, instead, one of the dominant characteristics that affects both the way the individual looks at the world and the way the world looks at the individual. As I have said, that need not be the case. It may in fact be very important that we work toward a society in which that would not be the case, but it is the case now and it must be understood in any adequate and complete discussion of racism. That is why, too, it does not make much sense when people sometimes say, in talking about the fact that they are not racists, that they would not care if an individual were green and came from Mars, they would treat that individual the same way they treat people exactly like themselves. For part of *our* social and cultural history is to treat people of certain races in a certain way, and we do not have a social or cultural history of treating green people from Mars in any particular way. To put it simply, it is to misunderstand the social realities of race and racism to think of them simply as questions of how some people respond to other people whose skins are of different hues, irrespective of the social context.

I can put the point another way: Race does not function in our culture as does eye color. Eye color is an irrelevant category; nobody cares what color people's eyes are; it is not an important cultural fact; nothing turns on what eye color you have. It is important to see that race is not like that at all. And this truth affects what will and will not count as cases of racism. In our culture to be nonwhite – and especially to be black[11] – is to be treated and seen to be a member of a group that is different from and inferior to the group of standard, fully developed persons, the adult white males. To be black is to be a member of what was a despised minority and what is still a disliked and oppressed one.[12] That is simply part of the awful truth of our cultural and social history, and a significant feature of the social reality of our culture today.

We can see fairly easily that the two sexual categories, like the racial ones, are themselves in important respects products of the society. Like one's race, one's sex is not merely or even primarily a matter of physiology. To see this we need only realize that we can understand the idea of a transsexual. A transsexual is someone who would describe himself or herself either as a person who is essentially a female but through some accident of nature is trapped in a male body, or a person who is essentially a male but through some accident of nature is trapped in the body of a female. His (or her) description is some kind of a shorthand way of saying that he (or she) is more comfortable with the role allocated by the culture to people who are physiologically of the opposite sex. The fact that we regard this assertion of the transsexual as intelligible seems to me to show how deep the notion of sexual identity is in our culture and how little it has to do with physiological differences between males and females. Because people do pass in the context of race and because we can understand what passing means; because people are transsexuals and because we can understand what transsexuality means, we can see that the existing social categories of both race and sex are in this sense creations of the culture.

It is even clearer in the case of sex than in the case of race that one's sexual identity is a centrally important, crucially relevant category within our culture. I think, in fact, that it is more important and more fundamental than one's race. It is evident that there are substantially different role expectations and role assignments to persons in accordance with their sexual physiology, and that the positions of the two sexes in the culture are distinct. We do have a patriarchal society in which it matters enormously whether one is a male or a female.[13] By almost all important measures it is more advantageous to be a male rather than a female.

Women and men are socialized differently. We learn very early and forcefully that we are either males or females and that much turns upon which sex we are. The evidence seems to be overwhelming and well-documented that sex roles play a fundamental role in the way persons think of themselves and the world – to say nothing of the way the world thinks of them.[14] Men and women are taught to see men as independent, capable, and powerful; men and women are taught to see women as dependent, limited in abilities, and passive. A woman's success or failure in life is defined largely in terms of her activities within the family. It is important for her that she marry, and when she does she is expected to take responsibility for the wifely tasks: the housework, the child care, and the general emotional welfare of the husband and children.[15] Her status in society is determined in substantial measure by the vocation and success of her husband.[16] Economically, women are substantially worse off than men. They do not receive any pay for the work that is done in the home. As members of the labor force their wages are significantly lower than those paid to men, even when they are engaged in similar work and have similar educational backgrounds.[17] The higher the prestige or the salary of the job, the less present women are in the labor force. And, of course, women are conspicuously absent from most positions of authority and power in the major economic and political institutions of our society.

As is true for race, it is also a significant social fact that to be a female is to be an entity or creature viewed as different from the standard, fully developed person who is male as well as white. But to be female, as opposed to being black, is not to be conceived of as simply a creature of less worth. That is one important thing that differentiates sexism from racism: The ideology of sex, as opposed to the ideology of race, is a good deal more complex and confusing. Women are both put on a pedestal and deemed not fully developed persons. They are idealized; their approval and admiration is sought; and they are at the same time regarded as less competent than men and less able to live fully developed, fully human lives – for that is what men do.[18] At best, they are viewed and treated as having properties and attributes that are valuable and admirable for humans of this type. For example, they may be viewed as especially empathetic, intuitive, loving, and nurturing. At best, these qualities are viewed as good properties for women to have, and, provided they are properly muted, are sometimes valued within the more well-rounded male. Because the sexual ideology is complex, confusing, and variable, it does not unambiguously proclaim the lesser value attached to being female rather than being male, nor does it unambiguously correspond to the existing social realities. For these, among other reasons, sexism could plausibly be regarded as a deeper phenomenon than racism. It is more deeply embedded in the culture, and thus less visible. Being harder to detect, it is harder to eradicate. Moreover, it is less unequivocally regarded as unjust and unjustifiable.

That is to say, there is less agreement within the dominant ideology that sexism even implies an unjustifiable practice or attitude. Hence, many persons announce, without regret or embarrassment, that they are sexists or male chauvinists; very few announce openly that they are racists.[19] For all of these reasons sexism may be a more insidious evil than racism, but there is little merit in trying to decide between two seriously objectionable practices which one is worse.

While I do not think that I have made very controversial claims about either our cultural history or our present-day culture, I am aware of the fact that they have been stated very imprecisely and that I have offered little evidence to substantiate them. In a crude way we ought to be able both to understand the claims and to see that they are correct if we reflect seriously and critically upon our own cultural institutions, attitudes, and practices. But in a more refined, theoretical way, I am imagining that a more precise and correct description of the social reality in respect to race and sex would be derivable from a composite, descriptive account of our society which utilized the relevant social sciences to examine such things as the society's institutions, practices, attitudes and ideology[20] – if the social sciences could be value-free and unaffected in outlook or approach by the fact that they, themselves, are largely composed of persons who are white and male.[21]

Viewed from the perspective of social reality it should be clear, too, that racism and sexism should not be thought of as phenomena that consist simply in taking a person's race or sex into account, or even simply in taking a person's race or sex into account in an arbitrary way. Instead, racism and sexism consist in taking race and sex into account in a certain way, in the context of a specific set of institutional arrangements and a specific ideology which together create and maintain a *system* of unjust institutions and unwarranted beliefs and attitudes. That system is and has been one in which political, economic, and social power and advantage are concentrated in the hands of those who are white and male.

One way to bring this out, as well as to show another respect in which racism and sexism are different, concerns segregated bathrooms – a topic that may seem silly and trivial but which is certainly illuminating and probably important. We know, for instance, that it is wrong, clearly racist, to have racially segregated bathrooms. There is, however, no common conception that it is wrong, clearly sexist, to have sexually segregated ones. How is this to be accounted for? The answer to the question of why it was and is racist to have racially segregated bathrooms can be discovered through a consideration of the role that this practice played in that system of racial segregation we had in the United States – from, in other words, an examination of the social realities. For racially segregated bathrooms were an important part of that system. And that system had an ideology; it was complex and perhaps not even wholly internally consistent. A significant feature of the ideology was that blacks were not only less than fully developed humans, but that they were also dirty and impure. They were the sorts of creatures who could and would contaminate white persons if they came into certain kinds of contact with them – in the bathroom, at the dinner table, or in bed, although it was appropriate for blacks to prepare and handle food, and even to nurse white infants. This ideology was intimately related to a set of institutional arrangements and power relationships in which whites were politically, economically, and socially dominant. The ideology supported the institutional arrangements, and the institutional arrangements reinforced the ideology. The net effect was that racially segregated bathrooms were both a part of the institutional mechanism of oppression and an instantiation of this ideology of racial taint. The point of maintaining racially segregated bathrooms was not in any simple or direct sense to keep both whites and blacks from using each other's bathrooms; it was to make sure that blacks would not contaminate bathrooms used by whites. The practice also taught both whites and blacks that certain kinds of contacts were forbidden because whites would be degraded by the contact with the blacks.

The failure to understand the character of these institutions of racial oppression is what makes some of the judicial reasoning about racial discrimination against blacks so confusing and unsatisfactory. At times when the courts have tried to explain what is constitutionally wrong with racial segregation, they have said that the problem is that race is an inherently suspect category. What they have meant by this, or have been thought to mean, is that any differentiation among human beings on the basis of racial identity is inherently unjust, because arbitrary, and therefore any particular case of racial differentiation must be shown to be fully rational and justifiable.[22] But the primary evil of the various schemes of racial segregation against

blacks that the courts were being called upon to assess was not that such schemes were a capricious and irrational way of allocating public benefits and burdens. That might well be the primary wrong with racial segregation if we lived in a society very different from the one we have. The primary evil of these schemes was instead that they designedly and effectively marked off all black persons as degraded, dirty, less than fully developed persons who were unfit for full membership in the political, social, and moral community.[23]

It is worth observing that the social reality of sexually segregated bathrooms appears to be different. The idea behind such sexual segregation seems to have more to do with the mutual undesirability of the use by both sexes of the same bathroom at the same time. There is no notion of the possibility of contamination; or even directly of inferiority and superiority. What seems to be involved – at least in part – is the importance of inculcating and preserving a sense of secrecy concerning the genitalia of the opposite sex. What seems to be at stake is the maintenance of that same sense of mystery or forbiddenness about the other sex's sexuality which is fostered by the general prohibition upon public nudity and the unashamed viewing of genitalia.

Sexually segregated bathrooms simply play a different role in our culture than did racially segregated ones. But that is not to say that the role they play is either benign or unobjectionable – only that it is different. Sexually segregated bathrooms may well be objectionable, but here too, the objection is not on the ground that they are prima facie capricious or arbitrary. Rather, the case against them now would rest on the ground that they are, perhaps, one small part of that scheme of sex-role differentiation which uses the mystery of sexual anatomy, among other things, to maintain the primacy of heterosexual sexual attraction central to that version of the patriarchal system of power relationships we have today.[24] Whether sexually segregated bathrooms would be objectionable, because irrational, in the good society depends once again upon what the good society would look like in respect to sexual differentiation.

(b) *Types of racism or sexism*

Another recurring question that can profitably be examined within the perspective of social realities is whether the legal system is racist or sexist. Indeed, it seems to me essential that the social realities of the relationships and ideologies concerning race and sex be kept in mind whenever one is trying to assess claims that are made about the racism or sexism of important institutions such as the legal system. It is also of considerable importance in assessing such claims to understand that even within the perspective of social reality, racism or sexism can manifest itself, or be understood, in different ways. That these are both important points can be seen through a brief examination of the different, distinctive ways in which our own legal system might plausibly be understood to be racist. The mode of analysis I propose serves as well, I believe, for an analogous analysis of the sexism of the legal system, although I do not undertake the latter analysis in this paper.

The first type of racism is the simplest and the least controversial. It is the case of overt racism, in which a law or a legal institution expressly takes into account the race of individuals in order to assign benefits and burdens in such a way as to bestow an unjustified benefit upon a member or members of the racially dominant group or an unjustified burden upon members of the racial groups that are oppressed. We no longer have many, if any, cases of overt racism in our legal system today, although we certainly had a number in the past. Indeed, the historical system of formal, racial segregation was both buttressed by, and constituted of, a number of overtly racist laws and practices. At different times in our history, racism included laws and practices which dealt with such things as the exclusion of nonwhites from the franchise, from decent primary and secondary schools and most professional schools, and the prohibition against interracial marriages.

The second type of racism is very similar to overt racism. It is covert, but intentional, racism, in which a law or a legal institution has as its purpose the allocation of benefits and burdens in order to support the power of the dominant race, but does not use race specifically as a basis for allocating these benefits and burdens. One particularly good historical example involves the use of grandfather clauses which were inserted in statutes governing voter registration in a number of states after passage of the fifteenth amendment.[25]

Covert racism within the law is not entirely a thing of the past. Many instances of de facto school segregation in the North and West are cases of covert racism. At times certain school boards – virtually all of which are overwhelmingly white in composition – quite consciously try to maintain exclusively or predominantly white schools within a school district. The classifications such school boards use are not ostensibly racial, but are based upon the places of residence of the affected students. These categories provide the opportunity for covert racism in engineering the racial composition of individual schools within the board's jurisdiction.[26]

What has been said so far is surely neither novel nor controversial. What is interesting, however, is that a number of persons appear to believe that as long as the legal system is not overtly or covertly racist, there is nothing to the charge that it is racist. So, for example, Mr. Justice Powell said in a speech a few years ago:

> It is of course true that we have witnessed racial injustice in the past, as has every other country with significant racial diversity. But no one can fairly question the present national commitment to full equality and justice. Racial discrimination, by state action, is now proscribed by laws and court decisions which protect civil liberties more broadly than in any other country. But laws alone are not enough. Racial prejudice in the hearts of men cannot be legislated out of existence; it will pass only in time, and as human beings of all races learn in humility to respect each other – a process not furthered by recrimination or undue self-accusation.[27]

I believe it is a mistake to think about the problem of racism in terms of overt or covert racial discrimination by state action, which is now banished, and racial prejudice, which still lingers, but only in the hearts of persons. For there is another, more subtle kind of racism – unintentional, perhaps, but effective – which is as much a part of the legal system as are overt and covert racist laws and practices. It is what some critics of the legal system probably mean when they talk about the "institutional racism" of the legal system.[28]

There are at least two kinds of institutional racism. The first is the racism of sub-institutions within the legal system such as the jury, or the racism of practices built upon or countenanced by the law. These institutions and practices very often, if not always, reflect in important and serious ways a variety of dominant values in the operation of what is apparently a neutral legal mechanism. The result is the maintenance and reenforcement of a system in which whites dominate over nonwhites. One relatively uninteresting (because familiar) example is the case of de facto school segregation. As observed above, some cases of de facto segregation are examples of covert racism. But even in school districts where there is no intention to divide pupils on grounds of race so as to maintain existing power relationships along racial lines, school attendance zones are utilized which are based on the geographical location of the pupil. Because it is a fact in our culture that there is racial discrimination against black people in respect to housing, it is also a fact that any geographical allocation of pupils – unless one pays a lot of attention to housing patterns – will have the effect of continuing to segregate minority pupils very largely on grounds of race. It is perfectly appropriate to regard this effect as a case of racism in public education.[29]

A less familiar, and hence perhaps more instructive, example concerns the question of the importance of having blacks on juries, especially in cases in which blacks are criminal defendants. The orthodox view within the law is that it is unfair to try a black defendant before an all-white jury if blacks were overtly or covertly excluded from the jury rolls used to provide the jury panel, but not otherwise.[30] One reason that is often given is that the systematic exclusion of blacks increases too greatly the chance of racial prejudice operating against the black defendant.[31] The problem with this way of thinking about things is that it does not make much sense. If whites are apt to be prejudiced against blacks, then an all-white jury is just as apt to be prejudiced against a black defendant, irrespective of whether blacks were systematically excluded from the jury rolls. I suspect that the rule has developed in the way it has because the courts think that many, if not most, whites are not prejudiced against blacks, unless, perhaps, they happen to live in an area where there is systematic exclusion of blacks from the jury rolls. Hence prejudice is the chief worry, and a sectional, if not historical, one at that.

White prejudice against blacks is, I think, a problem, and not just a sectional one. However, the existence or nonexistence of prejudice against blacks does not go to the heart of the matter. It is a worry, but it is not the chief worry. A black person may not be able to get a fair trial from an all-white jury even though the jurors are disposed to be fair and impartial, because the whites may unknowingly bring into the jury box a view about a variety of matters which affects in very fundamental re-

spects the way they will look at and assess the facts. Thus, for example, it is not, I suspect, part of the experience of most white persons who serve on juries that police often lie in their dealings with people and the courts. Indeed, it is probably not part of their experience that persons lie about serious matters except on rare occasions. And they themselves tend to take truth telling very seriously. As a result, white persons for whom these facts about police and lying are a part of their social reality will have very great difficulty taking seriously the possibility that the inculpatory testimony of a police witness is a deliberate untruth. However, it may also be a part of the social reality that many black persons, just because they are black, have had encounters with the police in which the police were at best indifferent to whether they, the police, were speaking the truth. And even more black persons may have known a friend or a relative who has had such an experience. As a result, a black juror would be more likely than his or her white counterpart to approach skeptically the testimony of ostensibly neutral, reliable witnesses such as police officers. The point is not that all police officers lie; nor is the point that all whites always believe everything police say, and blacks never do. The point is that because the world we live in is the way it is, it is likely that whites and blacks will on the whole be disposed to view the credibility of police officers very differently. If so, the legal system's election to ignore this reality, and to regard as fair and above reproach the common occurrence of all-white juries (and white judges) passing on the guilt or innocence of black defendants is a decision in fact to permit and to perpetuate a kind of institutional racism within the law.[32]

The second type of institutional racism is what I will call "conceptual" institutional racism. We have a variety of ways of thinking about the legal system, and we have a variety of ways of thinking within the legal system about certain problems. We use concepts. Quite often without realizing it, the concepts used take for granted certain objectionable aspects of racist ideology without our being aware of it. The second *Brown* case (*Brown II*) provides an example.[33] There was a second *Brown* case because, having decided that the existing system of racially segregated public education was unconstitutional (*Brown I*),[34] the Supreme Court gave legitimacy to a second issue – the nature of the relief to be granted – by treating it as a distinct question to be considered and decided

Richard A. Wasserstrom

separately. That in itself was striking because in most cases, once the Supreme Court has found unconstitutionality, there has been no problem about relief (apart from questions of retroactivity): The unconstitutional practices and acts are to cease. As is well known, the Court in *Brown II* concluded that the desegregation of public education had to proceed "with all deliberate speed."[35] The Court said that there were "complexities arising from the transition to a system of public education freed from racial discrimination."[36] More specifically, time might be necessary to carry out the ruling because of

> problems related to administration, arising from the physical condition of the school plant, the school transportation system personnel, revision of school districts and attendance areas into compact units to achieve a system of determining admission to the public school on a non-racial basis, and revision of local laws and regulations which may be necessary in solving the foregoing problems.[37]

Now, I do not know whether the Court believed what it said in this passage, but it is a fantastic bit of nonsense that is, for my purposes, most instructive. Why? Because there was nothing complicated about most of the dual school systems of the southern states. Many counties, especially the rural ones, had one high school, typically called either "Booker T. Washington High School" or "George Washington Carver High School," where all the black children in the county went; another school, often called "Sidney Lanier High School" or "Robert E. Lee High School," was attended by all the white children in the country. There was nothing difficult about deciding that – as of the day after the decision – half of the children in the country, say all those who lived in the southern part of the county, would go to Robert E. Lee High School, and all those who lived in the northern half would go to Booker T. Washington High School. *Brown I* could have been implemented the day after the Court reached its decision. But it was also true that the black schools throughout the South were utterly wretched when compared to the white schools. There never had been any system of separate but equal education. In almost every measurable respect, the black schools were inferior. One possibility is that, without being explicitly aware of it, the members of the Supreme Court made use of some assumptions that were a

significant feature of the dominant racist ideology. If the assumptions had been made explicit, the reasoning would have gone something like this: Those black schools are wretched. We cannot order white children to go to those schools, especially when they have gone to better schools in the past. So while it is unfair to deprive blacks, to make them go to these awful, segregated schools, they will have to wait until the black schools either are eliminated or are sufficiently improved so that there are good schools for everybody to attend.

What seems to me to be most objectionable, and racist, about *Brown II* is the uncritical acceptance of the idea that during this process of change, black schoolchildren would have to suffer by continuing to attend inadequate schools. The Supreme Court's solution assumed that the correct way to deal with this problem was to continue to have the black children go to their schools until the black schools were brought up to par or eliminated. That is a kind of conceptual racism in which the legal system accepts the dominant racist ideology, which holds that the claims of black children are worth less than the claims of white children in those cases in which conflict is inevitable.[38] It seems to me that any minimally fair solution would have required that during the interim process, if anybody had to go to an inadequate school, it would have been the white children, since they were the ones who had previously had the benefit of the good schools. But this is simply not the way racial matters are thought about within the dominant ideology.

A study of *Brown II* is instructive because it is a good illustration of conceptual racism within the legal system. It also reflects another kind of conceptual racism – conceptual racism about the system. *Brown I* and *II* typically are thought of by our culture, and especially by our educational institutions, as representing one of the high points in the legal system's fight against racism. The dominant way of thinking about the desegregation cases is that the legal system was functioning at its very best. Yet, as I have indicated, there are important respects in which the legal system's response to the then existing system of racially segregated education was defective and hence should hardly be taken as a model of the just, institutional way of dealing with this problem of racial oppression. But the fact that we have, as well as inculcate, these attitudes of effusive praise toward *Brown I* and *II* and its progeny reveals a kind of persistent conceptual racism in talk about the character of the legal system, and what constitutes the right way to have dealt with the social reality of American racial oppression of black people.[39]

In theory, the foregoing analytic scheme can be applied as readily to the social realities of sexual oppression as to racism. Given an understanding of the social realities in respect to sex – the ways in which the system of patriarchy inequitably distributes important benefits and burdens for the benefit of males, and the ideology which is a part of that patriarchal system and supportive of it – one can examine the different types of sexism that exist within the legal system. In practice the task is more difficult because we are inclined to take as appropriate even overt instances of sexist laws, e.g., that it is appropriately a part of the definition of rape that a man cannot rape his wife.[40] The task is also more difficult because sexism is, as I have suggested, a "deeper" phenomenon than racism.[41] As a result, there is less awareness of the significance of much of the social reality, e.g., that the language we use to talk about the world and ourselves has embedded within it ideological assumptions and preferences that support the existing patriarchal system.[42] Cases of institutional sexism will therefore be systematically harder to detect. But these difficulties to one side, the mode of analysis seems to me to be in principle equally applicable to sexism, although, as I indicate in the next section on ideals, a complete account of the sexism of the legal system necessarily awaits a determination of what is the correct picture of the good society in respect to sexual differences.

II Ideals

A second perspective is also important for an understanding and analysis of racism and sexism. It is the perspective of the ideal. Just as we can and must ask what is involved today in our culture in being of one race or of one sex rather than the other, and how individuals are in fact viewed and treated, we can also ask different questions: What would the good or just society make of race and sex, and to what degree, if at all, would racial and sexual distinctions ever be taken into account? Indeed, it could plausibly be argued that we could not have an adequate idea of whether a society was racist or sexist unless we had some conception of what a thoroughly nonracist or nonsexist society would look like. This perspective is an extremely instructive as well as an often

neglected one. Comparatively little theoretical literature dealing with either racism or sexism has concerned itself in a systematic way with this perspective.[43] Moreover, as I shall try to demonstrate, it is on occasion introduced in an inappropriate context, e.g., in discussions of the relevance of the biological differences between males and females.

To understand more precisely what some of the possible ideals are in respect to racial or sexual differentiation, it is necessary to distinguish in a crude way among three levels or areas of social and political arrangements and activities.[44] First, there is the area of basic political rights and obligations, including the right to vote and to travel and the obligation to pay taxes. Second, there is the area of important, nongovernmental institutional benefits and burdens. Examples are access to and employment in the significant economic markets, the opportunity to acquire and enjoy housing in the setting of one's choice, the right of persons who want to marry each other to do so, and the duties (nonlegal as well as legal) that persons acquire in getting married. Third, there is the area of individual, social interaction, including such matters as whom one will have as friends, and what aesthetic preferences one will cultivate and enjoy.

As to each of these three areas we can ask whether in a nonracist society it would be thought appropriate ever to take the race of the individuals into account. Thus, one picture of a nonracist society is that which is captured by what I call the assimilationist ideal: A nonracist society would be one in which the race of an individual would be the functional equivalent of the eye color of individuals in our society today.[45] In our society no basic political rights and obligations are determined on the basis of eye color. No important institutional benefits and burdens are connected with eye color. Indeed, except for the mildest sort of aesthetic preferences, a person would be thought odd who even made private, social decisions by taking eye color into account. And for reasons that we could fairly readily state, we could explain why it would be wrong to permit anything but the mildest, most trivial aesthetic preference to turn on eye color. The reasons would concern the irrelevance of eye color for any political or social institution, practice or arrangement. It would, of course, be equally odd for a person to say that while he or she looked blue-eyed, he or she regarded himself or herself as really a brown-eyed person. That is, because eye color functions differently in our culture than does race or sex, there is no analogue in respect to eye color to passing or transsexuality. According to the assimilationist ideal, a nonracist society would be one in which an individual's race was of no more significance in any of these three areas than is eye color today.

The assimilationist ideal is not, however, the only possible plausible ideal. There are two others that are closely related, but distinguishable. One is the ideal of diversity; the other, the ideal of tolerance. Both can be understood by considering how religion, rather than eye color, tends to be thought about in our culture. According to the ideal of diversity, heterodoxy in respect to religious belief and practice is regarded as a positive good. In this view there would be a loss – it would be a worse society – were everyone to be a member of the same religion. According to the other view, the ideal of tolerance, heterodoxy in respect to religious belief and practice would be seen more as a necessary, lesser evil. In this view there is nothing intrinsically better about diversity in respect to religion, but the evils of achieving anything like homogeneity far outweigh the possible benefits.

Now, whatever differences there might be between the ideals of diversity and tolerance, the similarities are more striking. Under neither ideal would it be thought that the allocation of basic political rights and duties should take an individual's religion into account. We would want equalitarianism or nondiscrimination even in respect to most important institutional benefits and burdens – for example, access to employment in the desirable vocations. Nonetheless, on both views it would be deemed appropriate to have some institutions (typically those which are connected in an intimate way with these religions) which do in a variety of ways take the religion of members of the society into account. For example, it might be thought permissible and appropriate for members of a religious group to join together in collective associations which have religious, educational and social dimensions. And on the individual, interpersonal level, it might be thought unobjectionable, or on the diversity view, even admirable, were persons to select their associates, friends, and mates on the basis of their religious orientation. So there are two possible and plausible ideals of what the good society would look like in respect to religion in which religious differences would be to some degree maintained because the variety of religions was seen either as a valuable feature of the society, or as one to be tolerated. The picture is a more complex, less easily describable one than that of the assimilationist ideal.

The point of all this is its relevance to the case of sexism. One central and difficult question is what the ideal society would look like in respect to sex. The assimilationist ideal does not seem to be as readily plausible and obviously attractive here as it is in the case of race. Many persons invoke the possible realization of the assimilationist ideal as a reason for rejecting the equal rights amendment and indeed the idea of women's liberation itself. My view is that the assimilationist ideal may be just as good and just as important an ideal in respect to sex as it is in respect to race.[46] But many persons think there are good reasons why an assimilationist society in respect to sex would not be desirable. One reason for their view might be that to make the assimilationist ideal a reality in respect to sex would involve more profound and fundamental revisions of our institutions and our attitudes than would be the case in respect to race. It is certainly true that on the institutional level we would have to alter radically our practices concerning the family and marriage. If a nonsexist society is a society in which one's sex is no more significant than eye color in our society today, then laws which require the persons who are being married to be of different sexes would clearly be sexist laws. Insofar as they are based upon the desirability of unifying the distinctive features of one male and one female, laws and institutions which conceive of the nuclear family as ideally composed of two and only two adults should also be thought of as anachronistic as well as sexist laws and institutions.

On the attitudinal and conceptual level, the assimilationist ideal would require the eradication of all sex-role differentiation. It would never teach about the inevitable or essential attributes of masculinity or femininity; it would never encourage or discourage the ideas of sisterhood or brotherhood; and it would be unintelligible to talk about the virtues as well as disabilities of being a woman or a man. Were sex like eye color, these things would make no sense. A nonsexist world might conceivably tolerate both homosexuality and heterosexuality (as peculiar kinds of personal erotic preference), but any kind of sexually *exclusive* preference would be either as anomalous or as statistically fortuitous as is a sexual preference connected with eye color in our society today. Just as the normal, typical adult is virtually oblivious to the eye color of other persons for all major interpersonal relationships, so the normal, typical adult in this kind of nonsexist society would be indifferent to the sexual, physiological differences of other persons for all interpersonal relationships. Bisexuality, not heterosexuality or homosexuality, would be the norm for intimate, sexual relationships in the ideal society that was assimilationist in respect to sex.

All of this seems to me to be worth talking about because unless and until we are clear about issues such as these we cannot be wholly certain about whether, from the perspective of the ideal, some of the institutions in our own culture are or are not sexist. We know that racially segregated bathrooms are racist. We know that laws that prohibit persons of different races from marrying are racist. But throughout our society we have sexually segregated bathrooms, and we have laws which prohibit individuals of the same sex from marrying. As I have argued above,[47] from the perspective of the existing social reality there are important ways to distinguish the racial from the sexual cases and to criticize both practices. But that still leaves open the question of whether in the good society these sexual distinctions, or others, would be thought worth preserving either because they were meritorious, or at least to be tolerated because they were necessary.

As I have indicated, it may be that the problem is with the assimilationist ideal. It may be that in respect to sex (and conceivably, even in respect to race) something more like either of the ideals in respect to religion – pluralistic ideals founded on diversity or tolerance – is the right one. But the problem then – and it is a very substantial one – is to specify with a good deal of precision and care what that ideal really comes to. Which legal, institutional and personal differentiations are permissible and which are not? Which attitudes and beliefs concerning sexual identification and difference are properly introduced and maintained and which are not? Part, but by no means all, of the attractiveness of the assimilationist ideal is its clarity and simplicity. In the good society of the assimilationist sort we would be able to tell easily and unequivocally whether any law, practice or attitude was in any respect either racist or sexist. Part, but by no means all, of the unattractiveness of any pluralistic ideal is that it makes the question of what is racist or sexist a much more difficult and complicated one to answer. But although simplicity and lack of ambiguity may be virtues, they are

not the only virtues to be taken into account in deciding among competing ideals. We quite appropriately take other considerations to be relevant to an assessment of the value and worth of alternative nonracist and nonsexist societies.

Nor do I even mean to suggest that all persons who reject the assimilationist ideal in respect to sex would necessarily embrace either something like the ideal of tolerance or the ideal of diversity. Some persons might think the right ideal was one in which substantially greater sexual differentiation and sex-role identification was retained than would be the case under either of these conceptions. Thus, someone might believe that the good society was, perhaps, essentially like the one they think we now have in respect to sex: equality of political rights, such as the right to vote, but all of the sexual differentiation in both legal and nonlegal institutions that is characteristic of the way in which our society has been and still is ordered. And someone might also believe that the usual ideological justifications for these arrangements are the correct and appropriate ones.[48] This could, of course, be regarded as a version of the ideal of diversity, with the emphasis upon the extensive character of the institutional and personal difference connected with sexual identity. Whether it is a kind of ideal of diversity or a different ideal altogether turns, I think, upon two things: first, how pervasive the sexual differentiation is; second, whether the ideal contains a conception of the appropriateness of significant institutional and interpersonal inequality, e.g., that the woman's job is in large measure to serve and be dominated by the male. The more this latter feature is present, the clearer the case for regarding this as a distinctively different ideal.

The question of whether something is a plausible and attractive ideal turns in part on the nature of the empirical world. If it is true, for example, that race is not only a socially significant category in our culture but also largely a socially created one, then many ostensible objections to the assimilationist ideal appear to disappear immediately. What I mean is this: It is obvious that we could formulate and use some sort of a crude, incredibly imprecise physiological concept of race. In this sense we could even say that race is a naturally occurring rather than a socially created feature of the world. There are diverse skin colors and related physiological characteristics distributed among human beings. But the fact is that except for skin hue and the related physiological characteristics, race is a socially created category. And skin hue, as I have shown, is neither a necessary nor a sufficient condition for being classified as black in our culture.[49] Race as a naturally occurring characteristic is also a socially irrelevant category. There do not in fact appear to be any characteristics that are part of this natural concept of race and that are in any plausible way even relevant to the appropriate distribution of any political, institutional, or interpersonal concerns in the good society. Because in this sense race is like eye color, there is no plausible case to be made on this ground against the assimilationist ideal.[50]

There is, of course, the social reality of race. In creating and tolerating a society in which race matters, we must recognize that we have created a vastly more complex concept of race which includes what might be called the idea of ethnicity as well – a set of attitudes, traditions, beliefs, etc., which the society has made part of what it means to be of a race. It may be, therefore, that one could argue that a form of the pluralist ideal ought to be preserved in respect to race, in the socially created sense, for reasons similar to those that might be offered in support of the desirability of some version of the pluralist ideal in respect to religion. As I have indicated, I am skeptical, but for the purposes of this essay it can well be left an open question.

Despite appearances, the case of sex is more like that of race than is often thought. What opponents of assimilationism seize upon is that sexual difference appears to be a naturally occurring category of obvious and inevitable social relevance in a way, or to a degree, which race is not. The problems with this way of thinking are twofold. To begin with, an analysis of the social realities reveals that it is the socially created sexual differences which tend in fact to matter the most. It is sex-role differentiation, not gender per se,[51] that makes men and women as different as they are from each other, and it is sex-role differences which are invoked to justify most sexual differentiation at any of the levels of society.[52]

More importantly, even if naturally occurring sexual differences were of such a nature that they were of obvious prima facie social relevance, this would by no means settle the question of whether in the good society sex should or should not be as minimally significant as eye color. Even though there are biological differences between men and women in nature, this fact does not determine the question of what the good society can and should

make of these differences. I have difficulty understanding why so many persons seem to think that it does settle the question adversely to anything like the assimilationist ideal. They might think it does settle the question for two different reasons. In the first place, they might think the differences are of such a character that they substantially affect what would be possible within a good society of human persons. Just as the fact that humans are mortal necessarily limits the features of any possible good society, so, they might argue, the fact that males and females are physiologically different limits the features of any possible good society.

In the second place, they might think the differences are of such a character that they are relevant to the question of what would be desirable in the good society. That is to say, they might not think that the differences *determine* to a substantial degree what is possible, but that the differences ought to be taken into account in any rational construction of an ideal social existence.

The second reason seems to me to be a good deal more plausible than the first. For there appear to be very few, if any, respects in which the ineradicable, naturally occurring differences between males and females *must* be taken into account. The industrial revolution has certainly made any of the general differences in strength between the sexes capable of being ignored by the good society in virtually all activities.[53] And it is sex-role acculturation, not biology, that mistakenly leads many persons to the view that women are both naturally and necessarily better suited than men to be assigned the primary responsibilities of child rearing. Indeed, the only fact that seems required to be taken into account is the fact that reproduction of the human species requires that the fetus develop *in utero* for a period of months. Sexual intercourse is not necessary, for artificial insemination is available. Neither marriage nor the family is required for conception or child rearing. Given the present state of medical knowledge and the natural realities of female pregnancy, it is difficult to see why any important institutional or interpersonal arrangements *must* take the existing gender difference of *in utero* pregnancy into account.

But, as I have said, this is still to leave it a wholly open question to what degree the good society *ought* to build upon any ineradicable gender differences to construct institutions which would maintain a substantial degree of sexual differentiation. The arguments are typically far less persuasive for doing so than appears upon the initial statement of this possibility. Someone might argue that the fact of menstruation, for instance, could be used as a premise upon which to predicate different social roles for females than for males. But this could only plausibly be proposed if two things were true: first, that menstruation would be debilitating to women and hence relevant to social role even in a culture which did not teach women to view menstruation as a sign of uncleanliness or as a curse,[54] and second, that the way in which menstruation necessarily affected some or all women was in fact related in an important way to the role in question. But even if both of these were true, it would still be an open question whether any sexual differentiation ought to be built upon these facts. The society could still elect to develop institutions that would nullify the effect of the natural differences. And suppose, for example, what seems implausible – that some or all women will not be able to perform a particular task while menstruating, e.g., guard a border. It would be easy enough, if the society wanted to, to arrange for substitute guards for the women who were incapacitated. We know that persons are not good guards when they are sleepy, and we make arrangements so that persons alternate guard duty to avoid fatigue. The same could be done for menstruating women, even given these implausibly strong assumptions about menstruation. At the risk of belaboring the obvious, what I think it important to see is that the case against the assimilationist ideal – if it is to be a good one – must rest on arguments concerned to show why some other ideal would be preferable; it cannot plausibly rest on the claim that it is either necessary or inevitable.

There is, however, at least one more argument based upon nature, or at least the "natural," that is worth mentioning. Someone might argue that significant sex-role differentiation is natural not in the sense that it is biologically determined but only in the sense that it is a virtually universal phenomenon in human culture. By itself, this claim of virtual universality, even if accurate, does not directly establish anything about the desirability or undesirability of any particular ideal. But it can be made into an argument by the addition of the proposition that where there is a virtually universal social practice, there is probably some good or important purpose served by the practice. Hence, given the fact of sex-role differentiation in all, or almost all, cultures, we have

some reason to think that substantial sex-role differentiation serves some important purpose for and in human society.

This is an argument, but I see no reason to be impressed by it. The premise which turns the fact of sex-role differentiation into any kind of a strong reason for sex-role differentiation is the premise of conservatism. And it is no more convincing here than elsewhere. There are any number of practices that are typical and yet upon reflection seem without significant social purpose. Slavery was once such a practice; war perhaps still is.

More to the point, perhaps, the concept of "purpose" is ambiguous. It can mean in a descriptive sense "plays some role" or "is causally relevant." Or it can mean in a prescriptive sense "does something desirable" or "has some useful function." If "purpose" is used prescriptively in the conservative premise, then there is no reason to think that premise is true.

To put it another way, the question is whether it is desirable to have a society in which sex-role differences are to be retained at all. The straightforward way to think about that question is to ask what would be good and what would be bad about a society in which sex functioned like eye color does in our society. We can imagine what such a society would look like and how it would work. It is hard to see how our thinking is substantially advanced by reference to what has typically or always been the case. If it is true, as I think it is, that the sex-role differentiated societies we have had so far have tended to concentrate power in the hands of males, have developed institutions and ideologies that have perpetuated that concentration and have restricted and prevented women from living the kinds of lives that persons ought to be able to live for themselves, then this says far more about what may be wrong with any nonassimilationist ideal than does the conservative premise say what may be right about any nonassimilationist ideal.

Nor is this all that can be said in favor of the assimilationist ideal. For it seems to me that the strongest affirmative moral argument on its behalf is that it provides for a kind of individual autonomy that a nonassimilationist society cannot attain. Any nonassimilationist society will have sex roles. Any nonassimilationist society will have some institutions that distinguish between individuals by virtue of their gender, and any such society will necessarily teach the desirability of doing so. Any substantially nonassimilationist society will make one's sexual identity an important characteristic, so that there are substantial psychological, role, and status differences between persons who are males and those who are females. Even if these could be attained without systemic dominance of one sex over the other, they would, I think, be objectionable on the ground that they necessarily impaired an individual's ability to develop his or her own characteristics, talents and capacities to the fullest extent to which he or she might desire. Sex roles, and all that accompany them, necessarily impose limits – restrictions on what one can do, be or become. As such, they are, I think, at least prima facie wrong.

To some degree, all role-differentiated living is restrictive in this sense. Perhaps, therefore, all role-differentiation in society is to some degree troublesome, and perhaps all strongly role-differentiated societies are objectionable. But the case against sexual differentiation need not rest upon this more controversial point. For one thing that distinguishes sex roles from many other roles is that they are wholly involuntarily assumed. One has no choice whatsoever about whether one shall be born a male or female. And if it is a consequence of one's being born a male or a female that one's subsequent emotional, intellectual, and material development will be substantially controlled by this fact, then substantial, permanent, and involuntarily assumed restraints have been imposed on the most central factors concerning the way one will shape and live one's life.[55] The point to be emphasized is that this would necessarily be the case, even in the unlikely event that substantial sexual differentiation could be maintained without one sex or the other becoming dominant and developing institutions and an ideology to support that dominance.

I do not believe that all I have said in this section shows in any conclusive fashion the desirability of the assimilationist ideal in respect to sex. I have tried to show why some typical arguments against the assimilationist ideal are not persuasive,[56] and why some of the central ones in support of that ideal are persuasive. But I have not provided a complete account, or a complete analysis. At a minimum, what I have shown is how thinking about this topic ought to proceed, and what kinds of arguments need to be marshalled and considered before a serious and informed discussion of alternative conceptions of a nonsexist society can even take place. Once assembled, these arguments need to be individually and carefully assessed before any final, reflective choice among

the competing ideals can be made. There does, however, seem to me to be a strong presumptive case for something very close to, if not identical with, the assimilationist ideal.

III Instrumentalities

The instrumental perspective does not require much theoretical attention beyond what has already been said. It is concerned with the question of what would be the best way to move from the social realities to the ideal. The most salient considerations are, therefore, empirical ones – although of a complex sort.

Affirmative action programs, even those which require explicit racial and sexual minimum quotas, are most plausibly assessed from within this perspective.[57] If the social reality is one of racial and sexual oppression – as I think it is – and if, for example, the most defensible picture of a nonracist, nonsexist society is the one captured by the assimilationist ideal, then the chief and perhaps only question to be asked of such programs is whether they are well suited to bring about movement from the existing state of affairs to a closer approximation of the assimilationist ideal.[58] If it turns out, for example, that explicit racial quotas will in fact exacerbate racial prejudice and hostility,[59] thereby making it harder rather than easier to achieve an assimilationist society, that is a reason which counts against the instrumental desirability of racial quotas. This would not settle the matter, of course, for there might also be respects in which racial quotas would advance the coming of the assimilationist society, e.g., by redistributing wealth and positions of power and authority to blacks, thereby creating previously unavailable role models, and by putting persons with different perspectives and interests in a position more directly to influence the course of social change.

But persons might be unhappy with this way of thinking about affirmative action – and especially about quotas. They might have three different but related objections. The first objection would be that there are more questions to be asked about means or instruments than whether they will work to bring about a certain end. In particular, there is also the question of the *way* they will work as means to bring about the end. Some means may be morally objectionable as means, no matter how noble or desirable the end. That is the good sense in the slogan: The ends do not justify the means.

I certainly agree with this general point. It is the application to particular cases, for example this one, that vitiates the force of the objection. Indeed, given the way I have formulated the instrumental perspective, I have left a good deal of room for the moral assessment of means to be built in. That is to say, I have described the question as one of the instrumental "desirability," not just the "efficaciousness" in any narrow sense, of the means that are selected.

The second objection is rather more sophisticated. Someone might say something like this: it is just wrong in principle ever to take an individual's race or sex into account.[60] Persons just have a right never to have race or sex considered. No reasons need be given; we just know they have that right. This is a common way of talking today in moral philosophy,[61] but I find nothing persuasive or attractive about it. I do not know that persons have such a right. I do not "see" it. Instead, I think I can give and have given reasons in my discussion of the social realities as well as my discussion of ideals for why they might be said to have rights not to be treated in certain ways. That is to say, I have tried to show something of what was wrong about the way blacks and women were and are treated in our culture.[62] I have not simply proclaimed the existence of a right.

Another form of this objection is more convincing. The opponent of quotas and affirmative action programs might argue that any proponent of them is guilty of intellectual inconsistency, if not racism or sexism. At times past, employers, universities, and many social institutions did have racial or sexual quotas, when they did not practice overt racial or sexual exclusion, and it was clear that these quotas were pernicious. What is more, many of those who were most concerned to bring about the eradication of those racial quotas are now untroubled by the new programs which reinstitute them. And this is just a terrible sort of intellectual inconsistency which at worst panders to the fashion of the present moment and at best replaces intellectual honesty and integrity with understandable but misguided sympathy. The assimilationist ideal requires ignoring race and sex as distinguishing features of people.

Such an argument is a useful means by which to bring out the way in which the analysis I am proposing can respond. The racial quotas and practices of racial exclusion that were an integral part of the fabric of our culture, and which are still to some degree a part of it, were pernicious. They were a grievous wrong and it was and is important that all morally concerned individuals work for their eradication from our social universe. The racial quotas that are a part of contemporary affirmative action programs are, I think, commendable and right. But even if I am mistaken about the latter, the point is that there is no inconsistency involved in holding both views. For even if contemporary schemes of racial quotas are wrong, they are wrong for reasons very different from those that made quotas against blacks wrong.

As I have argued,[63] the fundamental evil of programs that discriminated against blacks or women was that these programs were a part of a larger social universe which systematically maintained an unwarranted and unjust scheme which concentrated power, authority, and goods in the hands of white males. Programs which excluded or limited the access of blacks and women into these institutions were wrong both because of the direct consequences of these programs on the individuals most affected and because the system of racial and sexual superiority of which they were constituents was an immoral one in that it severely and without any adequate justification restricted the capacities, autonomy, and happiness of those who were members of the less favored categories.

Whatever may be wrong with today's affirmative action programs and quota systems, it should be clear that the evil, if any, is not the same. Racial and sexual minorities do not constitute the dominant social group. Nor is the conception of who is a fully developed member of the moral and social community one of an individual who is either female or black. Quotas which prefer women or blacks do not add to the already relatively overabundant supply of resources and opportunities at the disposal of white males. If racial quotas are to be condemned or if affirmative action programs are to be abandoned, it should be because they will not work well to achieve the desired result. It is not because they seek either to perpetuate an unjust society or to realize a corrupt ideal.

Still a third version of this objection might be that when used in affirmative action programs, race and sex are categories that are too broad in scope. They include some persons who do not have the appropriate characteristics and exclude some persons who do. If affirmative action programs made race and sex the sole criteria of selection, this would certainly be a plausible objection, although even here it is very important to see that the objection is no different in kind from that which applies to all legislation and rules. For example, in restricting the franchise to those who are eighteen and older, we exclude some who have all the relevant qualifications for voting and we include some who lack them. The fit can never be precise. Affirmative action programs almost always make race or sex a *relevant* condition, not a conclusive one. As such, they function the way all other classificatory schemes do. The defect, if there is one, is generic, and not peculiar to programs such as these.

There is finally the third objection: that affirmative action programs are wrong because they take race and sex into account rather than the only thing that matters – an individual's qualifications. Someone might argue that what is wrong with these programs is that they deprive persons who are more qualifed by bestowing benefits on those who are less qualified in virtue of their being either black or female.

There are many things wrong with the objection based on qualifications. Not the least of them is that we do not live in a society in which there is even the serious pretense of a qualification requirement for many jobs of substantial power and authority. Would anyone claim that the persons who comprise the judiciary are there because they are the most qualified lawyers or the most qualified persons to be judges? Would anyone claim that Henry Ford II was the head of the Ford Motor Company because he was the most qualified person for the job? Or that the one hundred men who are Senators are the most qualified persons to be Senators? Part of what is wrong with even talking about qualifications and merit is that the argument derives some of its force from the erroneous notion that we would have a meritocracy were it not for affirmative action.[64]

But there is a theoretical difficulty as well, which cuts much more deeply into the argument about qualifications. The argument cannot be that the most qualified ought to be selected because the most qualified will perform most efficiently, for this instrumental approach was what the opponent of affirmative action thought was wrong with taking the instrumental perspective in the first place. To be at all persuasive, the argument must be that those who are the most qualified *deserve* to receive the benefits (the job, the place in law school, etc.) because they are the most qualified. And there is just no reason to think that this is a correct premise. There is a logical gap in the inference that the person who is most qualified to perform a task,

e.g., be a good student, deserves to be admitted as a student. Of course, those who deserve to be admitted should be admitted. But why do the most qualified deserve anything? There is just no necessary connection between academic merit (in the sense of qualification) and deserving to be a member of a student body. Suppose, for instance, that there is only one tennis court in the community. Is it clear that the two best tennis players ought to be the ones permitted to use it? Why not those who were there first? Or those who will enjoy playing the most? Or those who are the worst and therefore need the greatest opportunity to practice? Or those who have the chance to play least frequently?

We might, of course, have a rule that says that the best tennis players get to use the court before the others. Under such a rule, the best players would deserve the court more than the poorer ones. But that is just to push the inquiry back one stage. Is there any reason to think that good tennis players are entitled to such a rule? Indeed, the arguments that might be given for or against such a rule are many and varied. And few if any of the arguments that might support the rule would depend upon a connection between ability and desert.

Someone might reply that the most able students deserve to be admitted to the university because all of their earlier schooling was a kind of competition, with university admission being the prize awarded to the winners. They deserve to be admitted because that is what the rule of the competition provides. In addition, it would be unfair now to exclude them in favor of others, given the reasonable expectations they developed about the way in which their industry and performance would be rewarded. Minority admission programs, which inevitably prefer some who are less qualified over some who are more qualified, all possess this flaw.

There are several problems with this argument. The most substantial of them is that it is an empirically implausible picture of our social world. Most of what are regarded as the decisive characteristics for higher education have a great deal to do with things over which the individual has neither control nor responsibility: such things as home environment, socioeconomic class of parents, and, of course, the quality of the primary and secondary schools attended. Since individuals do not deserve having had any of these things vis-à-vis other individuals, they do not, for the most part, deserve their qualifications. And since they do not deserve their abilities they do not in any strong sense deserve to be admitted because of their abilities.

To be sure, if there is a rule which connects, say, performance at high school with admission to college, then there is a weak sense in which those who do well at high school deserve, for that reason alone, to be admitted to college. But then, as I have said, the merits of this rule need to be explored and defended. In addition, if persons have built up or relied upon their reasonable expectations concerning performance and admission, they have a claim to be admitted on this ground as well. But it is certainly not obvious that these claims of desert are any stronger or more compelling than competing claims based upon the needs of or advantages to women or blacks.[65]

Qualifications are also potentially relevant in at least three other respects. In the first place, there is some minimal set of qualifications without which the benefits of participation in higher education cannot be obtained by the individuals involved. In the second place, the qualifications of the students within the university will affect to some degree or other the benefits obtainable to anyone within it. And finally, the qualifications of students within the university may also affect the way the university functions vis-à-vis the rest of the world. The university will do some things better and some things worse, depending upon the qualifications of those who make it up. If the students are "less qualified," teachers may have to spend more time with them and less time on research. Some teachers may find teaching now more interesting. Others may find it less so. But all these considerations only establish that qualifications, in this sense, are relevant, not that they are decisive. This is wholly consistent with the claim that minority group membership is also a relevant but not a decisive consideration when it comes to matters of admission.[66] And that is all that virtually any preferential treatment program – even one with quotas – has ever tried to claim.

I do not think I have shown programs of preferential treatment to be right and desirable, because I have not sought to answer all of the empirical questions that may be relevant. But I have, I hope, shown that it is wrong to think that contemporary affirmative action programs are racist or sexist in the centrally important sense in which many past and present features of our society have been and are racist and sexist. The social realities do make a fundamental difference. It is also wrong to think that these programs are in any strong sense either unjust or unprincipled. The case for programs of preferential treatment can plausibly rest on the view that the programs are not unfair (except in the weak sense described above) to white males, and on the view that it is unfair to continue the present set of unjust – often racist and sexist – institutions that comprise the social reality. The case for these programs also rests on the thesis that it is fair, given the distribution of power and influence in the United States, to redistribute in this way, and that such programs may reasonably be viewed as useful means by which to achieve very significant social ideals.

Conclusion

I do not think that the topics of racism, sexism, and preferential treatment are easily penetrable. Indeed, I have tried to show that they contain complicated issues which must be carefully distinguished and discussed. But I also believe, and have tried to show, that the topics are susceptible to rational analysis. There is a difference between problems that are difficult because confusion is present, and problems that are difficult because a number of distinct ideas and arguments must be considered. It is my ambition to have moved thinking about the topics and issues in question some distance from the first to the second of these categories.

Notes

1 Such a view appears to be held in, e.g., Brief for the Anti-Defamation League of the B'nai B'rith as Amicus Curiae on Appeal, DeFunis v. Odegaard, 416 U.S. 312 (1974): "Discrimination on the basis of race is illegal, immoral, unconstitutional, and inher-

ently wrong." *Id.* at 16–17; Mr Justice Douglas' dissent in *DeFunis* (above): "There is no superior person by constitutional standards. A DeFunis who is white is entitled to no advantage by reason of that fact; nor is he subject to any disability, no matter what his race or color. Whatever his race, he has a constitutional right to have his application considered on its individual merits in a racially neutral manner," *id.* at 337; Anderson v. San Francisco Unified School Dist., 357 F. Supp. 248 (N.D. Cal. 1972): Preferential treatment "under the guise of 'affirmative action' is the imposition of . . . racial discrimination," *id.* at 249; Bakke v. Regents of the Univ. of Cal., 18 Cal. 3d 34, 553 P. 2d 1152, 132 Cal. Rptr. 680 (1976), *cert. granted*, L.A. Daily Jour., Feb. 23, 1977, at 1. col. 2 (No. 76–811): "We cannot agree with the proposition that deprivation based on race is subject to a less demanding standard of review under the Fourteenth Amendment if the race discriminated against is the majority rather than a minority. We have found no case so holding, and we do not hesitate to reject the notion that racial discrimination may be more easily justified against one race rather than another," *id.* at 50, 553 P. 2d at 1163, 132, Cal. Rptr. at 691 (footnotes omitted); Graglia, *Special Admission of the "Culturally Deprived" to Law School*, 119 U. Pa. L. Rev. 351 (1970); Lavinsky, DeFunis v. Odegaard: *The Non-Decision with a Message*, 75 Colum. L. Rev. 520 (1975).

I say such a view "appears to be held" because it is never wholly clear within the context of constitutional adjudication and commentary whether the claim is that it is wrong to take race into account in these ways or that it is forbidden by the Constitution so to take race into account. The two claims are intimately related. What one thinks about the rightness or wrongness of a practice or program will, appropriately, influence the way in which a constitutional provision – particularly one as general as the equal protection clause of the 14th amendment – is interpreted. And, in fact, it does appear that those who think these programs are unconstitutional also believe that it is good that the Constitution prohibits such programs, because they independently believe that it is wrong to have programs such as these that take race into account. But the two claims are also distinguishable. Legislative history, prior judicial decisions, and various doctrinal considerations, such as standing and state action, are also appropriately taken into account in interpreting and applying the Constitution to particular cases and practices.

The inquiry I conduct in this paper is not directed to the constitutional question, but to broader questions concerning a number of moral, conceptual and methodological issues involving race and sex. Since the two kinds of questions are related, my comments have relevance, I believe, within and for the constitutional context. The focus of my inquiry is not the constitutional question, however. I therefore do not seek to elucidate doctrine or even to discuss cases and commentaries dealing with these matters in the way or to the degree one might otherwise expect.

2   See, e.g., Nagel, *Equal Treatment and Compensatory Discrimination*, 2 Phil. & Pub. Aff. 348, 362 (1973).

3   Among those who have defended such programs, in one form or another, are Askin, *The Case for Compensatory Treatment*, 24 Rut. L. Rev. 65 (1964); Bell, *In Defense of Minority Admissions Programs: A Reply to Professor Graglia*, 119 U. Pa. L. Rev. 364 (1970); Ely, *The Constitutionality of Reverse Discrimination*, 41 U. Chi. L. Rev. 723 (1974); Hughes, *Reparations for Blacks*, 43 N.Y.U. L. Rev. 1063 (1968). The precise programs defended vary greatly, as do the reasons offered to justify them.

4   This perspective is discussed in Part I.

5   This perspective is discussed in Part II.

6   This perspective is discussed in Part III.

7   In asserting the importance of one's race and sex in our culture I do not mean to deny the importance of other characteristics – in particular, socioeconomic class. I do think that in our culture race and sex are two very important facts about a person, and I am skeptical of theories which "reduce" the importance of these features to a single, more basic one, e.g., class. But apart from this one bit of skepticism I think that all of what I have to say is compatible with several different theories concerning why race and sex are so important – including, for instance, most versions of Marxism. See, e.g., the account provided in J. Mitchell, Woman's Estate (1971). The correct causal explanation for the social realities I describe is certainly an important question, both in its own right and for some of the issues I address. It is particularly significant for the issue of how to alter the social realities to bring them closer to the ideal. See Part III. Nonetheless, I have limited the scope of my inquiry to exclude a consideration of this large, difficult topic.

8   Passing is the phenomenon in which a person who in some sense knows himself or herself to be black "passes" as white because he or she looks white. A version of this is described in Sinclair Lewis' novel Kingsblood Royal (1947), where the protagonist discovers when he is an adult that he, his father, and his father's mother are black (or, in the idiom of the late 1940s, Negro) in virtue of the fact that his great grandfather was black. His grandmother knew this and was consciously passing. When he learns about his ancestry, one decision he has to make is whether to continue to pass, or to acknowledge to the world that he is in fact "Negro."

9   That looking black is not in our culture a necessary condition for being black can be seen from the phenomenon of passing. That it is not a sufficient condition can be seen from the book Black Like Me (1960), by John Howard Griffin, where "looking black" is easily understood by the reader to be different from being black. I suspect that the concept of being black is, in our culture, one which combines both physiological and ancestral criteria in some moderately complex fashion.

10 Mr. Justice Douglas suggests something like this in his dissent in *DeFunis*: "The consideration of race as

a measure of an applicant's qualification normally introduces a capricious and irrelevant factor working an invidious discrimination." DeFunis v. Odegaard, 416 U.S. 312, 333 (1974).

11 There are significant respects in which the important racial distinction is between being white and being nonwhite, and there are other significant respects in which the fact of being black has its own special meaning and importance. My analysis is conducted largely in terms of what is involved in being black. To a considerable extent, however, what I say directly applies to the more inclusive category of being nonwhite. To the extent to which what I say does not apply to the other nonwhite racial distinctions, the analysis of those distinctions should, of course, be undertaken separately.

12 See, e.g., J. Baldwin, The Fire Next Time (1963); W.E.B. DuBois, The Souls of Black Folks (1903); R. Ellison, Invisible Man (1952); J. Franklin, From Slavery to Freedom (3rd ed. 1968); C. Hamilton and S. Carmichael, Black Power (1967); Report of the US Commission on Civil Disorders (1968); Kilson, *Whither Integration?*, 45 Am. Scholar 360 (1976); and hundreds, if not thousands of other books and articles, both literary and empirical. These sources describe a great variety of features of the black experience in America: such things as the historical as well as the present day material realities, and the historical as well as present day ideological realities, the way black people have been and are thought about within the culture. In Kingsblood Royal (above) note 8, Lewis provides a powerful account of what he calls the "American Credo" about the Negro, circa 1946. *Id.* at 194–97.

13 The best general account I have read of the structure of patriarchy and of its major dimensions and attributes is that found in Sexual Politics in the chapter, "Theory of Sexual Politics." K. Millett, Sexual Politics 23–58 (1970). The essay seems to me to be truly a major contribution to an understanding of the subject. Something of the essence of the thesis is contained in the following:

[A] disinterested examination of our system of sexual relationship must point out that the situation between the sexes now, and throughout history, is a case of that phenomenon Max Weber defined as *herrschaft*, a relationship of dominance and subordinance. What goes largely unexamined, often even unacknowledged (yet is institutionalized nonetheless) in our social order, is the birthright priority whereby males rule females. Through this system a most ingenious form of "interior colonization" has been achieved. It is one which tends moreover to be sturdier than any form of segregation and more rigorous than class stratification, more uniform,

certainly more enduring. However muted its present appearance may be, sexual dominion obtains nevertheless as perhaps the most pervasive ideology of our culture and provides its most fundamental concept of power.

This is so because our society, like all other historical civilizations, is a patriarchy. The fact is evident at once if one recalls that the military, industry, technology, universities, science, political office, and finance – in short, every avenue of power within the society, including the coercive force of the police, is entirely in male hands....

Sexual politics obtains consent through the "socialization" of both sexes to basic patriarchal politics with regard to temperament, role, and status. As to status, a pervasive assent to the prejudice of male superiority guarantees superior status in the male, inferior in the female. The first item, temperament, involves the formation of human personality along stereotyped lines of sex category ("masculine" and "feminine"), based on the needs and values of the dominant group and dictated by what its members cherish in themselves and find convenient in subordinates: aggression, intelligence, force and efficacy in the male; passivity, ignorance, docility, "virtue," and ineffectuality in the female. This is complemented by a second factor, sex role, which decrees a consonant and highly elaborate code of conduct, gesture and attitude for each sex. In terms of activity, sex role assigns domestic service and attendance upon infants to the female, the rest of human achievement, interest and ambition to the male.... Were one to analyze the three categories one might designate status as the political component, role as the sociological, and temperament as the psychological – yet their interdependence is unquestionable and they form a chain.

Id. at 24–26 (footnotes omitted).

14 See, e.g., Hochschild, *A Review of Sex Role Research*, 78 Am. J. Soc. 1011 (1973), which reviews and very usefully categorizes the enormous volume of literature on this topic. See also Stewart, *Social Influences on Sex Differences in Behavior*, in Sex Differences 138 (M. Teitelbaum ed. 1976); Weitzman, *Sex-Role Socialization*, in Women: A Feminist Perspective 105 (J. Freeman ed. 1975). A number of the other pieces in Women: A Feminist Perspective also describe and analyze the role of women in the culture, including the way they are thought of by the culture. I return to consider further the question of what accounts for the existing psychological and sociological sex differences in section II below.

15 For the married woman, her husband and children must always come first; her own needs and desires, last. When the children reach school age,

they no longer require constant attention. The emotional-expressive function assigned to the woman is still required of her. Called the "stroking function" by sociologist Jessie Bernard, it consists of showing solidarity, raising the status of others, giving help, rewarding, agreeing, concurring, complying, understanding, and passively accepting. The woman is expected to give emotional support and comfort to other family members, to make them feel like good and worthwhile human beings.

B. Deckard, The Women's Movement 59 (1975), *citing* J. Bernard, Women and the Public Interest 88 (1971).

Patriarchy's chief institution is the family. It is both a mirror of and a connection with the larger society; a patriarchal unit within a patriarchal whole. Mediating between the individual and the social structure, the family effects control and conformity where political and other authorities are insufficient.

K. Millett, note 13 (above), at 33.

16 Even if the couple consciously try to attain an egalitarian marriage, so long as the traditional division of labor is maintained, the husband will be "more equal." He is the provider not only of money but of status. Especially if he is successful, society values what he does; she is just a housewife. Their friends are likely to be his friends and co-workers; in their company, she is just his wife. Because his provider function is essential for the family's survival, major family decisions are made in terms of how they affect his career. He need not and usually does not act like the authoritarian paterfamilias [*sic*] of the Victorian age. His power and status are derived from his function in the family and are secure so long as the traditional division of labor is maintained.

B. Deckard, note 15 (above), at 62.

17 In 1970, women workers were, on the average, paid only 59 percent of men's wages. And when wages of persons with similar educational levels are compared, women still were paid over 40 percent less than men. *Id*. at 79–81.

18 It is generally accepted that Western patriarchy has been much softened by the concepts of courtly and romantic love. While this is certainly true, such influence has also been vastly overestimated. In comparison with the candor of "machismo" or oriental behavior, one realizes how much of a concession traditional chivalrous behavior represents – a sporting kind of reparation to allow the subordinate female certain means of saving face. While a palliative to the injustice of woman's social position, chivalry is also a technique for disguising it. One must acknowledge that the chivalrous stance is a game the master group plays in elevating its subject to pedestal level. Historians of courtly love stress the fact that the raptures of the poets had no effect upon the legal or economic standing of women, and very little upon their social status. As the sociologist Hugo Beigel has observed, both the courtly and the romantic versions of love are "grants" which the male concedes out of his total powers. Both have the effect of obscuring the patriarchal character of Western culture and in their general tendency to attribute impossible virtues to women, have ended by confining them in a narrow and often remarkably conscribing sphere of behavior. It was a Victorian habit, for example, to insist the female assume the function of serving as the male's conscience and living the life of goodness he found tedious but felt someone ought to do anyway.

K. Millett, note 13 (above), at 36–37.

19 Thus, even after his "joke" about black persons became known to the public, the former Secretary of Agriculture, Earl Butz, took great pains to insist that this in no way showed that he was a racist. This is understandable, given the strongly condemnatory feature of being described as a racist.

Equally illuminating was the behavior of Butz's associates and superiors. Then-President Ford, for example, criticized Butz for the joke, but did not demand Butz's removal until there was a strong public outcry. It was as though Butz's problem was that he had been indiscreet; he had done something rude like belching in public. What Ford, Butz, and others apparently failed to grasp is that it is just as wrong to tell these jokes in private because to tell a joke of this sort is to have a view about what black people are like: that they can appropriately be ridiculed as being creatures who care only about intercourse, shoes, and defecation. What these persons also failed to grasp is how implausible it is to believe that one can hold these views about black people and at the same time deal with them in a nonracist fashion.

20 At a minimum, this account would include: (1) a description of the economic, political, and social positions of blacks and whites, males and females in the culture; (2) a description of the sexual and racial roles, i.e., the rules, conventions and expectations concerning how males and females, blacks and whites, should behave, and the attitudes and responses produced by these roles; and (3) a description of the de facto ideology of racial and sexual differences. This would include popular beliefs about how males and females, blacks and whites, differ, as well as the beliefs as to what accounts for these differences, roles, and economic, political and social realities.

21 The problem of empirical objectivity is compounded by the fact that part of the dominant, white male ideology is that white males are the one group in society whose members are able to be genuinely detached and objective when it comes to things like an understanding of the place of race and sex in the culture. Thus, for example, when a sex-discrimination suit was brought against a law firm and the case was assigned to Judge Constance Motley, the defendant filed a motion that she be disqualified partly because, as a woman judge, she would be biased in favor of the plaintiff. Judge Motley denied the motion. Bank v. Sullivan & Cromwell, 418 F. Supp. 1 (S.D.N.Y. 1975), *writ of mandamus denied sub nom.* Sullivan & Cromwell v. Motley, No. 75–3045 (2d Cir. Aug. 26, 1975). Explaining her decision, Judge Motley stated: "[I]f background or sex or race of each judge were, *by definition*, sufficient grounds for removal, no judge on this court could hear this case, or many others, by virtue of the fact that all of them were attorneys, of a sex, often with distinguished law firm or public service backgrounds." 418 F. Supp. at 4 (emphasis added).

22 Thus, in Bolling v. Sharpe, 347 U.S. 497 (1953), the Supreme Court said that what was wrong with preventing black children from attending the all white schools of the District of Columbia was that

> [s]egregation in public education is not reasonably related to any proper governmental objective, and thus it imposes on Negro children of the District of Columbia a burden that constitutes an arbitrary deprivation of their liberty in violation of the Due Process Clause.

Id. at 500. I ignore those cases in which the courts decline to formulate a view about racial differentiation because the behavior involved is not the sort that the law thinks it appropriate to deal with, e.g., "private" racial discrimination.

23 Others have made this general point about the nature of the evil of racial segregation in the United States. See, e.g., Ely, note 3 (above); Fiss, *Groups and Equal Protection*, 5 Phil. & Pub. Aff. 107 (1976); Thalberg, *Reverse Discrimination and the Future*, 5 Phil. F. 268 (1973).

The failure fully to understand this general point seems to me to be one of the things wrong with Weschler's famous article, *Toward Neutral Principles of Constitutional Interpretation*, 73 Harv. L. Rev. 1 (1959). Near the very end of the piece Weschler reports, "In the days when I joined with Charles H. Houston [a well-known black lawyer] in a litigation in the Supreme Court, before the present building was constructed, he did not suffer more than I in knowing that we had to go to Union Station to lunch together during the recess." *Id.* at 34. If the stress in that sentence is wholly on the fact of *knowing*, no one can say for certain that Weschler is wrong. But what is certain is that Charles H. Houston suffered more than Weschler from *living* in a system in which he could only lunch at Union Station.

24 This conjecture about the role of sexually segregated bathrooms may well be inaccurate or incomplete. The sexual segregation of bathrooms may have more to do with privacy than with patriarchy. However, if so, it is at least odd that what the institution makes relevant is sex rather than merely the ability to perform the eliminatory acts in private.

25 See, e.g., Guinn v. United States, 238 U.S. 347 (1915). Such statutes provided that the grandchild of someone who had been registered to vote in the state was permitted to vote in that state; but the grandchild of somebody who had never been registered to vote in the state had to take a special test in order to become qualified to vote. It does not take much knowledge of history to know that in most of the southern states few if any black people had grandparents who before the Civil War were registered to vote. And the persons who enacted these laws knew it too. So even though race was not made a category by the described laws, they effectively divided people on grounds of race into those who were qualified to vote without more, and those who had to submit to substantially more rigorous tests before they could exercise the franchise. All of this was done, as is well known, so as to perpetuate the control of the franchise by whites.

26 See, e.g., Crawford v. Board of Educ., 17 Cal. 3d 280 (1976); Jackson v. Pasadena City School Dist., 59 Cal. 2d 876, 382 P.2d 878, 31 Cal. Rptr. 606 (1963).

27 N.Y. Times, Aug. 31, 1972, §1, at 33, col. 3.

28 All of the laws, institutional arrangements, etc., that I analyze are, I think, cases of racism and not, for example, cases of prejudice. The latter concept I take to refer more specifically to the defective, incomplete or objectionable beliefs and attitudes of individuals. Prejudiced individuals often engage in racist acts, enact racist laws and participate in racist institutions. But they need not. Nor is it true that the only persons connected with racist acts, laws, or institutions need be prejudiced individuals.

A perceptive account of the differences between prejudice and racism, and of the different kinds of racism, including institutional racism of the sorts I discuss below, can be found in M. Jones, Prejudice and Racism (1972). See especially *id.* at 60–115 (ch. 4, "Perspectives on Prejudice"); *id.* at 116–67 (ch. 5, "Realities of Racism"). A somewhat analogous set of distinctions concerning sexism is made in Jaggar, *On Sexual Equality*, 84 Ethics 275, 276–77 (1974).

29 One example of what may have been an instance of genuine de facto racism in a noneducational setting is found in Gregory v. Litton Systems, Inc., 316 F. Supp. 401 (C.D. Cal. 1970), *modified*, 472 F.2d 631 (9th Cir. 1972). Litton Systems had a policy of refusing to employ persons who had been frequently arrested. The court found this to violate Title VII of the Civil Rights Act of 1964, 42 U.S.C. § 2000e (1970):

> Negroes are arrested substantially more frequently than whites in proportion to their numbers. The evidence on this question was overwhelming and utterly convincing. For example, negroes nationally comprise some 11% of the population and account for 27% of reported arrests and 45% of arrests reported as "suspicious arrests". Thus, any policy that disqualifies prospective employees because of having been arrested once, or more than once, discriminates in fact against negro applicants. This discrimination exists even though such a policy is objectively and fairly applied as between applicants of various races. A substantial and disproportionately large number of negroes are excluded from employment opportunities by Defendant's policy.
> 316 F. Supp. at 403.

30 Whitus v. Georgia, 385 U.S. 545 (1967), Avery v. Georgia, 345 U.S. 559 (1953), and Strauder v. West Virginia, 100 U.S. 303 (1880), are three of the many cases declaring it unconstitutional to exclude blacks systematically from the jury rolls when the defendant is black. Swain v. Alabama, 380 U.S. 202 (1965), is one of the many cases declaring that it is not unconstitutional that no blacks were in fact on the jury that tried the defendant.

31 See, e.g., Peters v. Kiff, 407 U.S. 493, 508–09 (Burger, C.J., dissenting).

32 I discuss this particular situation in somewhat more detail in Wasserstrom, *The University and the Case for Preferential Treatment*, 13 Am. Phil. Q. 165, 169–70 (1976). Mr. Justice Marshall expresses a view that I take to be reasonably close to mine in Peters v. Kiff, 407 U.S. 493 (1972). The case involved the question whether a white defendant could challenge the systematic exclusion of blacks from the jury rolls. Mr. Justice Marshall held that he could:

> [W]e are unwilling to make the assumption that the exclusion of Negroes has relevance only for issues involving race. When any large and identifiable segment of the community is excluded from jury service, the effect is to remove from the jury room qualities of human nature and varieties of human experience, the range of which is unknown and perhaps unknowable. It

is not necessary to assume that the excluded group will consistently vote as a class in order to conclude, as we do, that its exclusion deprives the jury of a perspective on human events that may have unsuspected importance in any case that may be presented.
Id. at 503–04 (footnote omitted).

Given my analysis, I think any defendant is disadvantaged by the absence of blacks from the jury, where, for instance, the testimony of a police officer is a significant part of the prosecution case. Because police are more apt to lie about black defendants, and because black jurors are more apt to be sensitive to this possibility, black defendants are, I think, especially likely to be tried unfairly by many all-white juries. What matters in terms of fairness is that blacks be represented on particular juries; non-exclusion from the jury rolls is certainly not obviously sufficient.

33 Brown v. Board of Educ., 349 U.S. 294 (1955).

34 Brown v. Board of Educ., 347 U.S. 483 (1954).

35 349 U.S. at 301.

36 *Id.* at 299.

37 *Id.* at 300–01.

38 The unusual character of *Brown II* was recognized by Mr. Justice Goldberg in Watson v. City of Memphis, 373 U.S. 526 (1963):

> Most importantly, of course, it must be recognized that even the delay countenanced by *Brown* was a necessary, albeit significant, adaptation of the usual principle that any deprivation of constitutional rights calls for prompt rectification. The rights here asserted are, like all such rights, *present* rights; they are not merely hopes to some *future* enjoyment of some formalistic constitutional promise. The basic guarantees of our Constitution are warrants for the here and now and, unless there is an overwhelmingly compelling reason, they are to be promptly fulfilled. The second *Brown* decision is but a narrowly drawn, and carefully limited, qualification upon usual precepts of constitutional adjudication. . . .

Id. at 532–33 (emphasis in original; footnote omitted). As I have indicated, the problem with Brown II is that there was no "overwhelmingly compelling reason" to delay. It might be argued though, that the Court deliberately opted for "all deliberate speed" and all that meant about the dreary pace of desegregation because it believed the country would not accept full, immediate implementation of Brown I. If this was the reasoning, it is equally pernicious. It is sound, only if the country is identified with white people; blacks were surely willing to accept the immediate elimination of the system of racial segregation.

But someone might still say that the Court was just dealing sensibly with the political realities. The white power structure would not have accepted anything more drastic. Arguments such as these are developed at considerable length by A. Bickel, The Least Dangerous Branch 247–54 (1962). The problem with this is twofold. First, what is deemed a drastic solution has a lot to do with whether whites or blacks are being affected, and how. It was and is thought to be drastic for force and the criminal law to be used against whites to secure compliance with laws relating to segregation. It was and is thought to be much less drastic to use force and the criminal law against blacks who object vigorously and sometimes violently to the system of racial oppression. The simple truth is that when the executive branch, as well as the judiciary, thought about these issues it typically weighed the claims of whites very differently from the claims of blacks. The history of the enforcement of civil rights by the federal government in the 1950s and early 1960s is largely a history of the consistent overvaluation of the claims and concerns of whites vis-à-vis blacks. I have suggested some of the ways this was true of the Civil Rights Division of the Department of Justice. See Wasserstrom, Book Review, 33 U. Chi. L. Rev. 406, 409–13 (1966); Wasserstrom, Postscript: Lawyers and Revolution, 30 U. Pitt. L. Rev. 125, 131 (1968).

Second, whether the decision would have been "accepted" is in large measure a function of what the United States government would have been prepared to do to get the decision implemented. During this same era things that were viewed as absolutely unacceptable or as not feasible suddenly became acceptable and feasible without any substantial change in material circumstances, e.g., the passage of the 1965 Voting Rights Act, 42 U.S.C. §§ 1973 et seq. (1970). It mysteriously became acceptable to the Congress, enforceable by the government and accepted by the South when Reverend Reeb and Mrs. Liuzzo were murdered during the time of the Selma march, and former President Johnson declared his determination to see the law enacted and enforced.

39   A discussion of some of these same kinds of issues concerning ideology can be found in Thalberg, *Justifications for Institutional Racism*, 5 Phil. F. 243 (1973).

40   In California, rape was traditionally defined as "an act of sexual intercourse, accomplished with a female *not the wife of the perpetrator*, under either of the following circumstances. . . . " Cal. Penal Code § 261 (West Supp. 1976) (emphasis added).

41   For an example of a kind of analysis that is beginning to show some of the ways in which the law builds upon and supports the patriarchal system of marriage, see Johnston, *Sex and Property: The Common Law Tradition, The Law School Curriculum, and Developments Toward Equality*, 47 N.Y.U. L. Rev. 1033,

1071–89 (1972). Another very rich source is the recent casebook on sex discrimination by B. Babcock, A. Freedman, E. Norton and S. Ross, Sex Discrimination and the Law – Causes and Remedies (1975).

42   See, e.g., R. Lakoff, Language and Woman's Place (1975); Baker, *"Pricks" and "Chicks": A Plea for "Persons"*, in Philosophy and Sex 45 (R. Baker and F. Elliston eds. 1975); Moulton, *Sex and Reference* in *id.* at 34.

43   One thorough and very valuable exploration of this and a number of the other topics discussed in this section is Alison Jaggar's *On Sexual Equality*, note 28. The article also contains a very useful analysis of the views of a number of other feminists who have dealt with this issue.

44   An analysis of the social realities of an existing society can also divide things up into these three areas.

45   There is a danger in calling this ideal the "assimilationist" ideal. That term suggests the idea of incorporating oneself, one's values, and the like into the dominant group and its practices and values. I want to make it clear that no part of that idea is meant to be captured by my use of this term. Mine is a stipulative definition.

46   Jaggar describes something fairly close to the assimilationist view in this way:

> The traditional feminist answer to this question [of what the features of a nonsexist society would be] has been that a sexually egalitarian society is one in which virtually no public recognition is given to the fact that there is a physiological sex difference between persons. This is not to say that the different reproductive function of each sex should be unacknowledged in such a society nor that there should be no physicians specializing in female and male complaints, etc. But it is to say that, except in this sort of context, the question whether someone is female or male should have no significance.
>
> . . .
>
> . . . In the mainstream tradition, the non-sexist society is one which is totally integrated sexually, one in which sexual differences have ceased to be a matter of public concern.
>
> Jaggar, note 28 (above), at 276–77.

47   See section 1. A above.

48   Thus, for example, a column appeared a few years ago in the *Washington Star* concerning the decision of the Cosmos Club to continue to refuse to permit women to be members. The author of the column (and a member of the club) defended the decision on the ground that women appropriately had a different status in the society. Their true distinction was to be achieved by being faithful spouses and devoted mothers. The column closed with this paragraph:

In these days of broken homes, derision of marriage, reluctance to bear children, contempt for the institution of the family – a phase in our national life when it seems more honorable to be a policewoman, or a model, or an accountant than to be a wife or mother – there is a need to reassert a traditional scale of values in which the vocation of homemaker is as honorable and distinguished as any in political or professional life. Such women, as wives and widows of members, now enjoy in the club the privileges of their status, which includes [sic] their own drawing rooms, and it is of interest that they have been among the most outspoken opponents of the proposed changes in club structure.
Groseclose, *Now – Shall We Join the Ladies?*, Washington Star, Mar. 13, 1975.

The same view may be held by Senator Daniel Moynihan. It is his view, apparently, that the United States government ought to work primarily to strengthen the institution of the family. Moynihan is quoted as saying:

If the family is strong, the economy will be productive. If the family is strong, law will be respected and crime will decrease. If the family is strong, the welfare rolls will shrink . . . All this is true, and its truth has been confirmed and reconfirmed by the evidence of history, of social science, of direct observation, and of simple common sense.
Buckley, *The Main Event East*, N.Y. Times, Oct. 31, 1976, § 6 (Magazine), at 16, 57.

For the reasons that I give in the remainder of section II, I think any version of this ideal is seriously flawed. But it is one that is certainly much more widely held in respect to sex than is a comparable one held today in respect to race.

49 See note 9 (above).

50 This is not to deny that certain people believe that race is linked with characteristics that prima facie are relevant. Such beliefs persist. They are, however, unjustified by the evidence. See, e.g., Block and Dworkin, *IQ Heritability and Inequality* (pts. 1–2), 3 Phil. & Pub. Aff. 331, 4 *id.* 40 (1974). More to the point, even if it were true that such a linkage existed, none of the characteristics suggested would require that political or social institutions, or inter-personal relationships, would have to be structured in a certain way.

51 The term "gender" may be used in a number of different senses. I use it to refer to those anatomical, physiological, and other differences (if any) that are naturally occurring in the sense described above. Some persons refer to these differences as "sex differences," but that seems to me confusing. In

any event, I am giving a stipulative definition to "gender."

52 See, e.g., authorities cited in note 14 (above); M. Mead, Sex and Temperament in Three Primitive Societies (1935):

These three situations [the cultures of the Anapesh, the Mundugumor, and the Tchambuli] suggest, then, a very definite conclusion. If those temperamental attitudes which we have traditionally regarded as feminine – such as passivity, responsiveness, and a willingness to cherish children – can so easily be set up as the masculine pattern in one tribe, and in another to be outlawed for the majority of women as well as for the majority of men, we no longer have any basis for regarding such aspects of behaviour as sex-linked . . .
. . . We are forced to conclude that human nature is almost unbelievably malleable, responding accurately and contrastingly to contrasting cultural conditions . . . Standardized personality differences between the sexes are of this order, cultural creations to which each generation, male and female is trained to conform. *Id.* at 190–91.

A somewhat different view is expressed in J. Sherman, On the Psychology of Women (1971). There, the author suggests that there are "natural" differences of a psychological sort between men and women, the chief ones being aggressiveness and strength of sex drive. See *id.* at 238. However, even if she is correct as to these biologically based differences, this does little to establish what the good society should look like, as argued in the remainder of section II.

Almost certainly the most complete discussion of this topic is E. Macoby and C. Jacklin, The Psychology of Sex Differences (1974). The authors conclude that the sex differences which are, in their words, "fairly well established," are: (1) that girls have greater verbal ability than boys; (2) that boys excel in visual-spatial ability; (3) that boys excel in mathematical ability; and (4) that males are aggressive. *Id.* at 351–52. They conclude, in respect to the etiology of these psychological sex differences, that there appears to be a biological component to the greater visual-spatial ability of males and to their greater aggressiveness. *Id.* at 360.

53 As Sherman observes,

Each sex has its own special physical assets and liabilities. The principal female liability of less muscular strength is not ordinarily a handicap in a civilized, mechanized, society . . . There is nothing in the biological evidence to prevent women from taking a role of equality in a civilized society.
J. Sherman note 52 (above), at 11.

There are, of course, some activities that would be sexually differentiated in the assimilationist society; namely, those that were specifically directed toward, say, measuring unaided physical strength. Thus, I think it likely that even in this ideal society, weight-lifting contests and boxing matches would in fact be dominated, perhaps exclusively so, by men. But it is hard to find any significant activities or institutions that are analogous. And it is not clear that such insignificant activities would be thought worth continuing, especially since sports function in existing patriarchal societies to help maintain the dominance of males. See K. Millett, note 13 (above), at 48–49.

It is possible that there are some nontrivial activities or occupations that depend sufficiently directly upon unaided physical strength that most if not all women would be excluded. Perhaps being a lifeguard at the ocean is an example. Even here, though, it would be important to see whether the way lifeguarding had traditionally been done could be changed to render such physical strength unimportant. If it could be changed, then the question would simply be one of whether the increased cost (or loss of efficiency) was worth the gain in terms of equality and the avoidance of sex-role differentiation. In a nonpatriarchal society very different from ours, where sex was not a dominant social category, the argument from efficiency might well prevail. What is important, once again, is to see how infrequent and peripheral such occupational cases are.

54 See, e.g., Paige, *Women Learn to Sing the Menstrual Blues*, in The Female Experience 17 (C. Tavis ed. 1973).

I have come to believe that the "raging hormones" theory of menstrual distress simply isn't adequate. All women have the raging hormones, but not all women have menstrual symptoms, nor do they have the same symptoms for the same reasons. Nor do I agree with the "raging neurosis" theory, which argues that women who have menstrual symptoms are merely whining neurotics, who need only a kind pat on the head to cure their problems.

We must instead consider the problem from the perspective of women's subordinate social position, and of the cultural ideology that so narrowly defines the behaviors and emotions that are appropriately "feminine." Women have perfectly good reasons to react emotionally to reproductive events. Menstruation, pregnancy and childbirth – so sacred, yet so unclean – are the woman's primary avenues of achievement and self-expression. Her reproductive abilities define her femininity; other routes to success are only second-best in this society ...

. . .

...My current research on a sample of 114 societies around the world indicates that ritual observances and taboos about menstruation are a method of controlling women and their fertility. Men apparently use such rituals, along with those surrounding pregnancy and childbirth, to assert their claims to women and their children.... The hormone theory isn't giving us much mileage, and it's time to turn it in for a better model, one that looks to our beliefs about menstruation and women. It is no mere coincidence that women get the blue meanies along with an event they consider embarrassing, unclean – and a curse.

Id. at 21.

55 One article that explores this point in some detail is Hill, *Self-Determination and Autonomy*, in Today's Moral Problems 171 (Wasserstrom ed. 1975). See also Jaggar note 28 (above), at 289–91.

56 Still other arguments against something like the assimilationist ideal and in favor of something like the idea of diversity are considered by Jaggar and shown by her to be unpersuasive. See Jaggar note 28 (above), at 281–91.

57 Although ostensibly empirical, the question of whether and to what extent affirmative action programs "work" has a substantial nonempirical component. There are many variables that can plausibly be taken into account, and many differing weights to be assigned to these variables. Consequently, how one marshalls and assesses the "evidence" concerning which programs "work" and which do not, has at least as much to do with whether one believes that the programs are or are not justifiable on other grounds as it does with a disinterested marshalling of the "facts." See, e.g., T. Sowell, Affirmative Action Reconsidered 34–40 (1975); N. Glazer, Affirmative Discrimination: Ethnic Inequality and Public Policy (1975). This also is a feature of Mr. Justice Mosk's analysis where he asserts, for example, that "[t]he overemphasis upon race as a criterion will *undoubtedly* be counterproductive." Bakke v. Regents of the Univ. of Cal., 18 Cal. 3d 34, 62, 553 P.2d 1152, 1171, 132 Cal. Rptr. 680, 699 (1976) (emphasis added), *cert. granted*, L.A. Daily Jour., Feb. 23, 1977, at 1, col. 2 (No. 76–811).

The general point is related to my discussion of *Brown II*, note 39 (above) A tremendous amount does turn in this area on who defines the nature of the problem and how the problem gets defined. My own analysis, to the degree to which it has endeavored to be empirical is, of course, subject to this same potential distortion.

58 It is here that an understanding of the *causes* of the position of blacks and women is most important. Such an understanding is crucial to an ability to make the kinds of changes and interventions that

will successfully make real and lasting differences in the status quo. See note 7 and accompanying text (above).

59 *See* Bakke v. Regents of the Univ. of Cal., 18 Cal. 3d 34, 62, 553 P.2d 1152, 1171, 132 Cal. Rptr. 680, 699 (1976), *cert. granted*, 45 U.S.L.W. 3437 (U.S. Dec. 14, 1976) (No. 76–811).

60 See, e.g., the sources cited in note 1 (above).

61 For example, such an approach seems, at least at times, to underlie the writings of R. Nozick, Anarchy, State and Utopia (1974).

62 I have also tried to discuss some of these matters, although not with anything like complete success, in Wasserstrom, *Rights, Human Rights, and Racial Discrimination*, 61 J. Phil. 628 (1964).

63 *See* Part I.

64 The point is a more general one than the few random examples suggest. The more prestige, power, wealth or influence is attached to the job, the less likely it is that there are specifiable qualifications that make it easy to determine who in fact is the most qualified. There are, to be sure, minimum qualifications. But these are satisfied by a large number of individuals. Moreover, for most of these positions the notion simply does not exist that the most qualified individuals from among this large class are the ones who deserve to be selected, e.g., the dean of a college or the head of a federal agency.

65 I prefer to focus on these aspects of desert and considerations of fairness rather than principles of compensation and reparation because I can thereby bypass the claim that compensation or reparation is being exacted from the wrong individuals, because they are innocent of any wrongdoing, and causally unconnected with the injuries suffered. I do think the causal link is often present and the claim of innocence often suspect. But my analysis puts these issues to one side. For a discussion of some of the literature that discusses the issues of compensation and reparation, see, e.g., Boxill, *The Morality of Reparation*, 2 Soc. Theory & Prac. 113 (1972).

66 The preceding six paragraphs appear in substantially the same form in Wasserstrom, note 32 (above), at 166–67.

38

"Mistresses of Their Own Destiny": Group Rights, Gender, and Realistic Rights of Exit*

Susan Moller Okin

Many recent arguments for rights or exemptions for religious or other cultural groups that may not themselves be liberal are based on liberal premises – whether the central liberal value be individual autonomy or tolerance for diversity of ways of life.[1] Any consistent defense of group rights or exemptions that is based on liberal premises has to ensure that at least one individual right – the right to exit one's group of origin – trumps any group right. What this entails will be explored later, but for several reasons, the claim itself seems prima facie incontrovertible. Not to be able to leave the group in which one has been raised for an alternative mode of life is a serious violation of the kind of freedom that is basic to liberalism. Indeed, advocates of the rights of groups that do not espouse or practice liberal principles with regard to their own members frequently justify these rights provisionally: any group to which such rights are accorded must (at least) allow its members the right of exit. It seems, moreover, that any liberal defender of the rights of groups should recognize that individuals must be

not only formally free but substantively and more or less equally free to leave their religions or cultures of origin; they must have realistic rights of exit.

Given this, it is surprising that so little attention has been paid in the literature about multicultural group rights to the fact that persons in different subgroups within most cultural and religious groups have very different chances of being able to exit from them successfully. As I shall argue here, in many cultural or religious groups on whose behalf liberal theorists have argued for special rights or exemptions, women are far less likely than men to be able to exercise the right of exit. They need not even be formally discriminated against in the public sphere, though they often are, for this to be so. For sex discrimination of various kinds is more likely than other forms of discrimination to occur out of public view, within the domestic sphere. Wherever it occurs, the unequal treatment of girls and women can mean, as I shall show, that by the time they reach young

Originally published in *Ethics* 112 (2002): 205–30. Reprinted by permission of the University of Chicago Press.

*Justice William Douglas wrote: "If a parent keeps his child out of school beyond the grade school, then the child will be forever barred from entry into the new and amazing world of diversity that we have today. The child may decide that that is the preferred course, or he may rebel. It is the student's judgment, not his parents', that is to be essential if we are to give full meaning to the Bill of Rights and of the right of students to be masters of their own destiny. If he is harnessed to the Amish way of life by those in authority over him and if his education is truncated, his entire life may be stunted and deformed" (Wisconsin v. Yoder, 406 U.S. 205, 245–46 [1972], Justice Douglas dissenting). Converting the phrase into "mistresses of their own destiny" has an unavoidable irony, since there is no apparent way of making it apply specifically to young women without using a word that both has sexual connotations and makes reference to them in relation to men.

adulthood in many cultures and religions, they are effectively far less able to exit their respective groups of origin than are men. Any liberal group rights theorist – especially any who is concerned to defend the claims of illiberal groups to rights or exemptions – should be concerned about this inequality. For some individuals not to be able to choose an alternative mode of life, when others in the group are far more likely to be able to do so, is a serious violation of the equality of persons that is basic to liberalism.

My argument has three main parts. First, I show, looking at three examples, that liberal defenders of group rights tend not to take gender inequality as seriously as other forms of morally arbitrary inequality (such as that of race or caste, for example) when considering group rights and the limitations that should be placed on them by anyone starting from liberal premises. Second, I specify and discuss a number of reasons that contribute to women's being, in many cultural contexts, significantly less able than men to chart their own courses of life – outside of their community of origin if they should so choose. I then return to the three theorists discussed earlier, looking at their arguments for why religious or cultural groups – whether liberal or illiberal in their internal practices – must permit their members the right to exit the group. Each of the three calls on the right of exit at least in part to lessen the effect of illiberal or oppressive internal group practices. I show, drawing on the second section, that the option of exit is, in the great majority of cases concerning group rights, considerably less likely to be available to female than to male members of the group.

I conclude that the theories I examine thus contain several problematic elements. If girls and women are treated unequally in various important ways within their cultural groups, it cannot but affect their capacities to exercise the right of exit that is of crucial importance to each theory. Moreover, women's having an unequal capacity to exit leads to another significant inequality, for it cannot but affect their potential to influence the directions taken by the group. Thus they have less chance of being able to change the group's norms and practices – including being able to remedy their status and to achieve gender equality within the group. To call on the right of exit as a palliative for oppression is unsatisfactory for another reason, too, for in many circumstances, oppressed persons, in particular women, are not only less able to exit but have many reasons not to *want* to exit their

culture of origin; the very idea of doing so may be unthinkable. Rather, they want, and should have the right, to be treated fairly within it. Thus, I conclude, the right of exit, while no doubt important, does not have the clout it is often thought to have in arguments defending the rights of illiberal groups within liberal contexts. Instead, it is inherently problematic. Those most likely to need it are those least likely to be able to employ it. Neither may they see it as a desirable or even an imaginable option.

Gender and Other Forms of Inequality in Group Rights Theories

As I have argued elsewhere, tensions exist between the feminist project of achieving equality between the sexes and the multicultural project of recognizing minority religious or other cultural groups by granting them special group rights.[2] Both the neglect of significant groups, whose interests may differ, within groups and the lack of attention to the private sphere have resulted in a widespread failure to recognize that, in cases where groups with more patriarchal beliefs and practices exist as minorities within contexts that are generally less patriarchal, women may well be harmed rather than benefited by special group rights. But until recently, inequalities between the sexes within groups received scant attention from those arguing for group rights. Even those – such as Will Kymlicka – who explicitly deny rights to cultural or religious groups that overtly discriminate against women are insufficiently attentive to private sphere discrimination, which often has serious impacts on women's well-being and life opportunities.[3] Not surprisingly, though, liberals who defend the right of illiberal, overtly discriminatory groups to regulate the lives of their members pose greater problems from a feminist point of view.

Ayelet Shachar has recently published very important work addressing these problems.[4] She has critiqued accommodations of cultural or religious groups that include differential membership status for women or give them unequal rights in marriage and divorce. In doing so, she has shed considerable light, as almost no other theorist has, on "the troubling fact that some categories of 'at-risk' group members are being asked to shoulder a disproportionate share of the costs of multiculturalism."[5] Shachar's and my diagnoses of the problem overlap, although her treatment of many of the cases and issues is both more detailed and more comprehensive. We also arrive at similar conclusions about how to address the tension between women's equality and multicultural group rights; in particular, we both insist that any legitimate liberal model of multiculturalism "take into account ... the voices of less powerful group members" – notably, women.[6] Somewhat unaccountably, then, Shachar distances herself from my position, which she labels the "re-universalized citizenship" response and presents as "requir[ing] that women make a choice of penalties between their rights as citizens and their group identities."[7]

Notwithstanding this misconception, Shachar's feminist analysis of the issues is excellent, and it is no coincidence that she is one of the very few theorists concerned with group rights who takes exception to the exit solution – addressing in particular the problem of women being offered exit rights as a response if and when they object to their treatment within their cultural group. As she says, the "troubling doctrine of 'implied consent' assumes that those who have not used the exit option have implicitly agreed to their own subordination."[8]

More generally, in the context of arguments for group rights, as I have suggested, the right of exit is cited as helping to legitimate the illiberal treatment of some or all group members. More generally, discrimination against women and girls is, at best, overlooked or mentioned briefly, only to be passed over. Not infrequently, it is given special status in a negative sense – by being perceived as somehow not really discrimination or at least absolved from the scrutiny that is given to other types of discrimination. It is, of course, in one sense not surprising that gender inequality is less or differently scrutinized, even often ignored, by liberals arguing for group rights. For, as I have argued, since virtually all cultures are to some degree patriarchal, it is exceedingly difficult to reconcile the claim that women be treated equally with the practices of many religions and other cultural groups, including many of those claiming special rights. But gender inequality is nonetheless a problem that any liberal theorist needs to understand and address since, despite the common tendency to forget the fact, women are more than half of those individuals who constitute the world's population, and any theory based on the liberty or well-being of individuals cannot afford to ignore them or to pay relatively little attention to discrimination against them. First, then, let us look at three examples in which discrimination between the sexes is treated less seriously than other forms of discrimination.

The first is Joseph Raz's essay, "Multiculturalism: A Liberal Perspective." Raz argues for the recognition of multicultural group rights, though he does not specify clearly just which rights he would defend. He claims generally that "multiculturalism requires a political society to recognize the equal standing of all the stable and viable cultural communities existing in that society."[9] His argument is based on the fact of "value pluralism" in contemporary societies and, in line with his general emphasis on autonomy, on the rights of individuals to freedom and well-being or prosperity – for which he claims that "full and unimpeded membership in a respected and flourishing cultural group" is a prerequisite.[10] While arguing for such rights, Raz does not think that all cultural groups merit them. One dimension on which cultures can be judged for this purpose is "obvious," he says. "Some cultures repress groups of either their own members or of outsiders. Slave cultures, racially discriminatory cultures, and homophobic cultures are obvious examples." He states: "Such cultures may be supported only to the degree that it is possible to neutralize their oppressive aspects, or compensate for them" (e.g., by permitting exit, which I shall discuss below).[11]

It is striking that Raz does not include sexist or patriarchal cultures in his list. Rather, he discusses them separately. Having already mentioned the "treatment of women" as one of those reasons, along with "decadence, ... vulgarity, [and] lack of sense of humour," that make cultures in general tend to disapprove of each other, he seems already to have given it a different, less serious, valance.[12] He reintroduces it in order to illustrate the point that what is not oppressive in one context may become oppressive in another – more multicultural – one. He first says: "Set aside the various cultures which repressed women." (A feminist reader may wonder why he uses the past tense here and may also wonder how many, and which, cultures this set-aside retains.) He continues: "Probably all cultures known to us, even those which did not repress women, distinguished between men and women in that a large array of social relationships, occupations, leisure activities, educational and cultural opportunities, and the like were gender-specific." But provided such separation "does not carry with it the implication of an inferior status" and neither men's nor women's "full development and self-expression" are stunted, "there is nothing wrong with such gender-sensitive cultures so long as they succeed in socializing the young to a willing acceptance of their ways." (Again, given the first two conditions, and that gender specificity and separation are typically coupled with claims of female inferiority, one wonders which cultures he has in mind.) However, Raz goes on to say that, if transplanted to a different cultural context in which "gender determination of opportunities" is a rarity, "the transplanted group is transformed into an oppressive one." What results in this transformation? Precisely, he says, the culture's failure to continue to be able to socialize "all its young to accept its ways and reject the ideas prevalent in the general culture." The latter's "prevailing notions of gender non-discrimination and the debate about feminism is [sic] bound to filter across the cultural barriers," affecting the minority culture's members' perceptions of their own practices, which many will come to understand "as consigning women to an inferior status." The new setting can not only, according to Raz, "lead to a change in the meaning of some of its practices"; it can "make them oppressive."[13]

This is a strange and unconvincing story, not only because the pervasively "gender-sensitive" but acceptably egalitarian societies Raz invents bear little relation to the real world. If the practices of such hypothetical cultures did not imply female inferiority, and if indeed, as he specifies, they "provided the opportunities available to either men or women . . . adequate for their full development and self-expression," then why and how would the feminism and the prevailing nondiscrimination of the new context cause them to be understood so differently? If they were not previously oppressive, how could the move to a new cultural context "make them oppressive"?[14] Raz's own definition of 'oppression' is an objective one: he says that it is "a result of a structural feature of [a] culture which systematically frustrates the ability of people, or groups of people, to fulfill or give expression to an important aspect of their nature within that society."[15] But according to the story he tells about gender and culture, the key to what makes the previously nonoppressive practices oppressive depends on the subjective perceptions of its members: the young women are now unable to be successfully socialized to accept them. Would it not be truer to Raz's own definition to acknowledge that so long as the culture existed in relative isolation, its socializing techniques prevented its

people – most importantly, its young women – from perceiving the oppressiveness of oppressive practices? For if such practices come to be seen as systematically frustrating the fulfillment of an important aspect of their nature in the new setting, how could it be that they did not do so in the old? Perhaps Raz might respond that the women's "nature" has been significantly changed by their move to a new cultural setting. If so, however, Raz gives no account of why we should expect greater human plasticity in the case of gender than in other, seemingly similar, cases. As we saw, he is unwilling to extend the advantages of group recognition to slave cultures, racially discriminatory cultures, and homophobic cultures. Yet such cultures, too, not infrequently succeed in successfully socializing their oppressed members into not recognizing their oppression.[16] But Raz does not even raise the possibility that slave-holding, racist, and homophobic cultures are not oppressive until they come to be perceived as such by their oppressed members. Women and their treatment, it seems, are different. The fact that women are successfully socialized into their various degrees of inferior status in virtually all of the world's cultures means, Raz implies, that they are less oppressed.

The second example I shall discuss of lesser scrutiny's being given to sex discrimination than to another form of discrimination (racial) occurs at a fairly pivotal point in William Galston's defense of group rights in "Two Concepts of Liberalism." Galston tests his theory of "the Diversity State" which, as he has argued, should cede considerable liberty to minority cultural groups, including religious groups, that do not respect the value of individual autonomy, though they must meet certain other conditions. He tests it by considering two cases.[17] While I think the two cases are extremely similar, Galston does not. In the first, Bob Jones University sought to keep its tax-exempt status while forbidding its students, on religious grounds, from dating interracially. Galston thinks, as I do, that the Supreme Court decided correctly in denying this request. His reasoning is that the free exercise of religion protected by the First Amendment – though it may in many conflictual cases require the nonprohibition of "conduct judged obnoxious by public principles" – does not properly extend to "associations conducting their internal affairs in a manner contrary to core public purposes," which include the government's "fundamental, overriding interest in eradicating racial discrimination."[18] In the second case, a fundamentalist religious school in Dayton, Ohio, terminated the employment of a (married) pregnant teacher because of its religious belief that mothers with young children should not engage in paid work outside their homes. The Ohio Civil Rights Commission ordered full reinstatement with back pay, but its decision was reversed by a court. The Supreme Court, which Galston says "ducked the issue" of religious freedom, heard the case and reversed again, stating that "we have no doubt that the elimination of prohibited sex discrimination is a sufficiently important state interest to bring the case within the ambit of the cited authorities" and that "even religious schools cannot claim to be wholly free from some state regulation."[19] However, Galston voices disagreement with the Court in this case, unlike the other, saying: "I believe a reasonable case can be made in this instance for giving priority to free exercise claims."[20] Strangely, while he acknowledges that "the teacher unquestionably experienced serious injury through loss of employment on religious grounds,"[21] Galston does not even mention sex discrimination in the context of this case. He presents the Civil Rights Commission's finding that the school had impermissibly "discriminated on the basis of religion," without mentioning the Supreme Court's reference to sex discrimination.[22]

But surely the Dayton case is no less an example of sex discrimination than the Bob Jones case is one of racial discrimination. After all, if the young teacher involved had been a man about to become a father, the school would have had no objection to his continued employment. Moreover, its policy in the actual case seems unrelated to the expected child's well-being, since leaving the mother unemployed could have undermined an intention on the part of the parents-to-be to have the father take care of the baby. As Galston says, the reason for the school's ending her contract was so that it could not only preach but also practice its "distinctive religious views" (by which he means, but does not say, its sex-discriminatory views about the roles of parents), and to disallow this would have "forced [the religious community] to conform to majoritarian beliefs and practices concerning gender."[23]

How and why is this different from the Bob Jones University case? There, the religious institution was not, and should not have been, according to Galston, permitted to enforce racial discrimination. Here, the religious institution was not, but should have been, according to Galston,

allowed to practice sex discrimination. Implicit in his analysis, clearly, is the belief that it is less offensive for a religion to enforce its views about sex roles than its views about race relations on its dissenting members, but he does not explain what justifies this belief. His stated reasoning on the matter is unconvincing. He argues that since the religious community was not coextensive with the political community, the Dayton teacher had the secure and available right of exit, since she had outside of the religious community "a wide array of other employment options."[24] There are two major problems with this reasoning. First, the Bob Jones students who wanted to date interracially also had plenty of exit options if they were prepared to go outside of the particular religious community. They could have opted for a nonracist religious college, of which there were surely many, or for a secular one. Yet Galston does not apply this reasoning to their case. Second, by forcing exit in the one case and not the other, he radically reduces the opportunities for change within the religion in the one case and not the other. Let us speculate that both the students at Bob Jones who wanted to date interracially and the teacher in Dayton who wanted to share the care of their baby with her husband, though in general religious fundamentalists, objected, respectively, to the racism and the sexism of their religion. Perhaps both aimed, by their choices, to try to initiate change within it. Galston's analysis and solution would give only the former any chance of effecting change from within.

Here, we are reminded that important aspects of exit rights reach far beyond the interests of the particular individuals involved. If the existence of such rights is held to justify oppression or the silencing of dissent within a group, on the ground that dissenters or those who consider themselves oppressed can leave, this is likely to reinforce conservative tendencies within the group. For it clearly tends to disempower potential reformers and thus to empower those who are likely to want to preserve the group's hierarchy and prevent its beliefs and practices from changing. On the one hand, as Albert Hirschman famously argued, having the meaningful and substantive opportunity of exit is likely to enhance one's ability to exert influence on both the general direction and specific decisions taken by one's group, since one – and those like oneself – can, whether overtly or, more often, implicitly, plausibly threaten to leave.[25] On the other hand, having only the purely formal right of exit, without any real capacity to exercise it, tends to eviscerate such capacity for influence. But being subject to *involuntary* exit, in order to practice one's dissent, as the Dayton teacher was, is even worse than merely having the formal right of exit, since it utterly eliminates one's potential influence. These aspects of exit rights are clearly relevant in any analysis of group rights that is concerned with the kinds of intragroup inequalities often faced by women.

My final example of gender inequality's being taken less than fully seriously comes from Chandran Kukathas's arguments that any truly tolerant liberal society should leave alone religious or cultural groups to live by their own ways. (He argues that even worse forms of treatment of children than of women should be permitted, as I shall also discuss.) Though not an advocate of positive groups rights, Kukathas is the most extreme defender of tolerance for the internal practices – even extremely coercive and harmful ones – of diverse groups within liberal contexts. His position seems to have hardened over time, so that by 1997, he claimed that the tolerant liberal state was justified in interfering with almost no illiberal practices of groups within it. However, since he does not retract the positions somewhat more restrictive of group practices that he took in a 1992 article, it seems reasonable to consider them alongside his more recent statements. In the earlier article, Kukathas set certain limits on the practices of cultural or religious groups that should be protected against interference by the wider society. He writes: "In recognizing the right of exit, they would also have to abide by liberal norms forbidding slavery [including 'voluntary slavery'] and physical coercion. More generally, they would be bound by liberal prohibitions on 'cruel, inhuman or degrading treatment.' "[26] It is unclear just how Kukathas thinks such norms can justifiably be enforced. Does he mean, given his initial reference to the right of exit, simply that members who object to such treatment must have the right to leave the group? Or does he mean that the liberal state can intervene so as to curtail any such group practices? He seems to mean the former only, since the passage concludes with the statement that "cultural groups that persisted in violating such norms would therefore disappear as their dissident members exercised their enforceable claims against the community."[27] However, this is often neither a viable nor a desired option for persons treated badly by their groups; it is a particularly unfeasible

route to offer to dissenting (but helpless) children; and it is, as we shall see, an option often far less available to a group's female than to its male members.

Moreover, in his more recent article, Kukathas takes a more extreme position, arguing that a whole range of practices that "could count as intolerable" by liberal standards should be tolerated by liberal states. Some of the most extreme such practices affect children of both sexes, whose parents or group Kukathas thinks should be permitted to limit their socialization so as to restrict their opportunities to prepare for life outside their group of origin, to subject them to high-risk initiation rites, and even to deny them conventional medical care in life-threatening situations. A number of the other practices he argues groups should be allowed to practice seriously affect girls and women. They include "denying them the right to hold property, or limiting their access to education, or 'forcing' them into unequal marriages," as well as mandatory "operations (performed with or without the fully informed consent of the subject) which are physically harmful . . . [including] clitoridectomy."[28] It is not at all easy to reconcile Kukathas's position regarding these to-be-tolerated, though seemingly intolerable, practices with the minimal restrictions he argued in his earlier article could rightly be placed on groups. If slavery – even voluntary slavery – and physical coercion are beyond the pale, then how can forcing women into unequal marriages (in which they can become quasi slaves, including sexual slaves, of their husbands) be sanctioned? If physical coercion and cruel, inhuman, or degrading treatment are ruled out, then how can clitoridectomy (which Kukathas agrees with Amy Gutmann in calling a form of torture) be tolerated?[29] Again, a double standard seems to be operating, as with the other theorists I have discussed, though here it is even more anti-feminist as well as dismissive of the rights of children in some cultural groups to life and physical integrity.

Cultural Factors Affecting Women's Realistic Rights of Exit

Clearly, defenders of cultural group rights or exemptions are often relatively insensitive to issues of gender and sometimes explicitly differentiate sex inequality from other forms of morally arbitrary inequality such as racial discrimination. Not surprisingly, as we shall see, this tendency to neglect issues of gender or treat them less than seriously continues into their discussions relevant to, or their conclusions about, the issue of exit rights. However, because of the general tendency of most cultures to try to control the lives of girls and women more than those of boys and men, women's capacities to exit their cultures of origin are usually considerably more restricted than men's.[30] There are at least three major reasons this is so, which are often closely linked. I shall focus on education, practices concerning marriage and divorce, and socialization for gender roles and gender hierarchy.

In many of the world's cultures, girls receive far less education than boys. This is especially likely to be so in poorer countries, where education is not freely provided and many families cannot afford much education, and in cultural contexts where girls, but not boys, are expected to play a major role in taking care of younger siblings and performing other domestic work.[31] However, it is also the case in a few much more affluent societies, mostly Muslim ones. Factors affecting girls' educational deprivation include specific religious or other cultural beliefs that women's only significant role in life is to bear and rear children and marital practices in which girls are married very young and/or become part of their husbands' families once married. The education of daughters, in such cases, may be considered a luxury, or even a waste of their parents' money. When only some children can stay in school, often boys are given preference. The World Bank's figures on adult illiteracy by sex and by country reveal some of the results of such practices. Illiteracy rates are much higher for women in many countries, especially poorer countries.[32] The rates of female to male illiteracy in the world's two most populous countries, China and India, in which the prevalent culture or cultures are still in their various ways highly patriarchal, are 27 percent: 10 percent and 62 percent: 35 percent, respectively. Clearly, many factors, including poverty, affect women's lesser chances of becoming educated. However, cultural factors are clearly significant, since among both the poorest and the richest countries, those with highly patriarchal traditions and cultural heritages have some of the highest discrepancies between female and male literacy.

It is not only the *lack* of education that can disproportionately affect girls' future potential to exit their cultural groups of origin; what is imparted to them in the course of their education can also have far-ranging effects.[33] In the United States, fundamentalist Christians, as in the case of *Mozert v. Hawkins*, have claimed the right, even in the public schools, to shelter their children from any alternatives but enculturation into strict gender roles, claiming this as in accordance with religious truth.[34] But for the exceptional case of *Wisconsin v. Yoder*, the courts have not allowed religious exemptions within public schooling. However, according to James Dwyer, approximately 1.5 million children in the United States are in private fundamentalist Christian schools and about 2.6 million are in Catholic schools. In both cases, but especially in the former (since there is great variation among Catholic schools, though all are ultimately accountable to a male-only hierarchy), the message often given to girls is that they are less than fully equal to boys and that their proper role in life is to care for their families and to obey their husbands. Dwyer relates that teachers in some fundamentalist schools ''openly tell their students that a woman must submit to a subordinate, obedient role in the home; if she does not, 'the doors are wide open to Satan.' ''[35] That the belief in hierarchical marriage extends further than fundamentalist fringes was confirmed in June of 1998 by a vote of the leadership of the largest Protestant denomination in the United States, the Southern Baptist Convention, that wives should ''graciously submit to the servant leadership of their husbands.'' Dwyer argues strongly and persuasively that it is a violation of children's rights to subject them to this and other forms of indoctrination. But a number of liberal defenders of group rights, even though they claim that illiberal groups should be required to allow their members to exit, think that parents should be free to thus define and restrict their children's education.

Other cultural practices that can radically affect a woman's capacity to exit her culture of origin are early or involuntarily arranged marriage and other practices that result in significant inequalities in marriage, including lesser rights to exit from a bad marriage. In many cultural groups, girls are married early (sometimes even as children, though cohabitation does not usually begin until after puberty), and marriages are often arranged for them, regardless of their preferences about either the timing or the husband.[36] Commonly cited reasons for these practices are to ensure the wife's virginity at the time of marriage, to accustom her to her husband's family while she is still malleable, and, of course, to enable parents to have a very large say, if not the only say, in whom their children can marry. The frequent results of early marriage for girls include interruption of their education, very long years of childbearing with accompanying depletion of their health, and age differences between themselves and their husbands that augment the latter's already often significant power over them.[37] But in addition to this, of course, arranged and early marriages preempt young women's choices about the kinds of lives they might want to lead, including the choice to exit their cultural group. Once married within it, especially since such marriages are unequal in many ways, a woman is far more encumbered by its requirements of her than a man is, has far less power than her husband (and often his family, especially his mother) to make decisions about her life, and, in most cases, has little room to maneuver her destiny.[38] Uma Narayan's moving essay "Contesting Cultures" and the powerful short stories of Chitra Banerjee Divakaruni pay testimony to the burdens often borne by women expected to submit to arranged marriages and, once within them, to their husbands and their husbands' families.[39] In many of the cultures with these marriage customs, divorce is also much more difficult for a woman to attain than for her husband, and she often has far less chance of gaining custody of their children, though she has usually altered her life far more than he has for the sake of the marriage. These factors, too, of course, restrain her options of exiting an unhappy or abusive relationship, let alone changing the course of her life or her cultural membership.

The overall socialization that girls undergo and the expectations placed on them in many cultures also tend to undermine their self-esteem – a necessary quality for persons to plan their own lives and pursue such plans, including, if they wish, choosing a different mode of life from that into which they were born. Even in our prevalent North American culture, where most young women's opportunities are relatively expansive, eating disorders show up in far more women than men as a symptom of self-esteem problems in a society obsessed with female beauty that is focused on thinness. In many other cultures, the more extreme and pervasive inequality between the sexes surely cannot fail to damage many women's self-esteem. One of the young Indian brides interviewed in a recent *New York Times* article explained that no woman in her family

had ever called her husband by his first name, since "for a wife, your husband is God."[40] And Martha Nussbaum has recently spoken and written of women in South Asia's SEWA (Self-Employed Women's Association) who are so accustomed to modesty and humility that their first training in the program consists of learning to stand up, look someone in the eye, and say their names. Without a cultural context that allows one to develop a sound sense of self, it is difficult to imagine a woman being able even to conceive of exit as an option.[41]

Such cultural practices concerning girls and women affect the relationship between gender, group rights, and the realistic capacity for exit in the context of a number of liberal states. In multicultural liberal states where group rights exist, sexist biases within the various cultures can seriously affect girls' and young women's access to education, choices about and status within marriage, and socialization for subordinate status. In the case of India, the existence of "communalism," in particular, the rights of the country's various religious groups to rule their members entirely in the realm of personal law – which regulates such crucial matters as marriage, divorce, child custody, and inheritance – is clearly detrimental to women's status, including their opportunities to be educated.[42] Many aspects of the religious-group rights system in India, and the custom of arranged marriage, certainly make it even more difficult for women than it is for men to exercise the right to exit the religious group into which they were born, should they want to do so or even be able to conceive of doing so.

In the context of liberal states whose majority cultures are less patriarchal than those of most immigrant groups and other indigenous ethnic or religious groups that are actual or potential claimants of group rights, such rights would be likely to affect adversely the education and the marriages of girls, as well as other important aspects of their lives relevant to this discussion. In many of the cultural groups that now form significant minorities in the United States, Canada, and Europe, families place their daughters under significantly greater constraints than their sons. A recent study by Laurie Olsen of first-generation immigrant adolescents in an urban California high school focuses particularly on the experiences of the young women. Olsen shows that, even in the absence of group rights, tight controls are often exerted on them. The young women are expected, far more than the young men, to perpetuate their parents' cultures; they are expected to negotiate their way between these cultures and that of the surrounding United States, often at considerable cost to themselves. Like the boys, they go through the traumas of being different and of having to learn English as fast as possible. Like the boys, too, they often experience racism and exclusionary treatment from the majority culture. But unlike the boys, they carry the added burdens of both the patriarchal attitudes of their own cultures and the expectation that they are responsible for the preservation of these cultures. As Olsen writes, though the girls from the various cultures "handle the dilemmas differently ... each hears the clock ticking in terms of cultural expectations about marriage, having children, and assuming female roles." The young women with whom she spoke were unsure if or when their parents would expect or arrange their marriages, require their help in assuming responsibility for siblings or other family members, or send them back to their homelands to begin a process of traditional marriage.[43] But clearly, the girls – unlike their brothers – are very rarely allowed to decide how to combine the surrounding majority culture with their own culture of origin or to choose between the two. They are expected to maintain and to reproduce in their own marriages and children their original cultural identity. To this end, their parents frequently restrict or dictate their mode of dress, their participation in extracurricular and social activities, and their choices of further education, future employment, time of marriage and, in some cultural groups, not only the ethnicity of their husband but their actual husband. Many spoke of marriage within their cultures as "a state of isolation and constriction," and they feared they might be assigned to husbands who would control them strictly or even abuse them.[44] Olsen found that it was largely in order to prevent such power imbalances in marriage that the young women wanted to further their educations and gain employment skills, though they often had few realistic plans for accomplishing these goals.

For those who want to become "American," the constraints can be harsh, and Olsen was told by some that they often lie to their parents, risking severe penalties if found out. But many, not surprisingly, are extremely attached to their cultures and religions, as well as to their families. They chafe against and are sometimes severely distressed by the restrictions placed on their lives but are very far from considering the option of leaving their cultural or religious group. The words of a seventeen-and-a-half-year-old Indian student from Fiji capture the dilemma such young women face. Suddenly faced with a coerced marriage that would not allow her to graduate from high school, she said: "I don't know what to do now. My dreams and plans are all messed up. ... I am tormented." But when a teacher suggested that she need not, perhaps, go through with the marriage, she responded indignantly: "In our religion, we have to think of our parents first. It would kill them if I ran away or disobeyed them. ... For me, I couldn't marry someone who wasn't a Muslim. I will do it the Muslim way. And I would never go against my parents!"[45] A young woman like this has a formal right of exit, since as a resident of the United States, she could legally change her religion. So also could she appeal to the law against her parents in order to prevent the unwanted marriage. But clearly neither of these options is thinkable to her, for, given the manner in which she has been raised, by doing either, she would lose much of what she most values in life. As we shall see, theorists who look to exit rights in order to counterbalance or mitigate discrimination or oppression within groups do not often seem to consider the depth of acquired cultural attachments, which can render the exit option not merely undesirable but unthinkable.[46] As Ayelet Shachar writes, in the context of women oppressed within groups whose traditions are "accommodated" by multicultural states, the "right of exit 'solution' ... throws on the already beleaguered individual the responsibility to either miraculously transform the legal-institutional conditions that keep her vulnerable or find the resources to leave her whole world behind."[47]

Rights of Exit and Realistic Rights of Exit for Women

All liberal defenders of group rights, as I have mentioned, insist that such rights cannot be justified unless individuals have the right to exit their cultures or religions of origin. Those who reject the centrality of individual freedom or autonomy in favor of toleration and who are more concerned that the state not interfere with the internal lives of groups than that groups not restrict their own members' beliefs or behavior nevertheless express the view that individuals must have the right of exit.[48] Disagreement does not begin until the question arises as to what such a right requires, and here, as we shall see, views diverge widely. Let us now turn back to the theorists discussed above – Raz, Galston, and Kukathas – in order to examine what they say about the right of exit in light of their own treatment of gender inequality and the points I have just made about its strong links with many cultures and religions. Specifically, I shall bring to bear on their arguments both the fact that various cultural practices concerning women are liable to effectively nullify or severely restrict their rights of exit and the point that even a realistic right of exit is by no means always a satisfactory solution to the forms of culturally reinforced discrimination women often experience.

Raz raises the issue of the individual's right of exit from his or her cultural group explicitly in the context of groups that oppress at least some of their own members. "Such cultures," he says, "may be supported only to the degree that it is possible to neutralize their oppressive aspects, or compensate for them (for example, by providing convenient exit from the oppressive community to members of the discriminated-against group)."[49] Later, he reinforces this connection between the likelihood of repression and the individual's right of exit:

> Moreover, the opportunity to exit from a group is a vital protection for those members of it who are repressed by its culture. Given that most cultures known to us are repressive to a lesser or greater degree, the opportunity of exit is of vital importance as a counter to the worry that multiculturalism encourages repressive cultures to perpetuate their ways. . . . [While] groups should be encouraged to change their repressive practices . . . this is a very slow process. Opportunities of exit should be encouraged as a safeguard, however imperfect, for members who cannot develop and find adequate avenues for self-expression within their native culture.[50]

While Raz is clearly aware of some of the difficulties of leaving one's cultural group, he does not specify what conditions he thinks must obtain to ensure that opportunities of exit as a "viable option" are available.[51] As we have seen, however, for girls and women especially, formal rights of exit are a less than satisfactory palliative for oppression for several reasons. First, as I pointed out

above and as Raz himself implies in his example, girls are often successfully socialized into the acceptance of practices that they would be likely to come to regard as oppressive if they were living in a less sexist cultural context. Second, as we have seen, many cultures are far more inclined to short-change girls than boys educationally. But having an education that prepares one for alternative modes of life is surely an essential prerequisite for a realistic or substantive right of exit. Third, in many cultural or religious groups, families control their daughters' times of marriage and choices of husbands far more than they do their sons'. Once a young woman is married within a culture, especially if she bears children early (as is often expected of her to prove her fertility and ensure the continuation of the male line) and especially if the terms of marriage and divorce are biased against her (as is also often the case), her capacity to exit even her marriage, let alone her cultural group, is severely restricted. Further, the right of exit from one's cultural group is, surely, often not at all desired as the sole option to such modes of female deprivation or oppression. As accounts such as Olsen's make clear, young women, not surprisingly, often value their cultural and familial ties extremely highly, even though they suffer from and chafe against their oppressive aspects. An adolescent girl faced with the choice of either giving up her education and marrying against her will or leaving her family and her culture of origin may find this choice very far from a convenient opportunity to exit. It may well be such an unbearable choice as to be, in practice, no choice at all.

Galston raises issues pertinent to exit early in his discussion of group rights, in the context of Justice Douglas's dissent in *Yoder*. He quotes Douglas on the right of students to be "masters of their own destiny" and also his ensuing statement that "if a child is harnessed to the Amish way of life by those in authority over him and if his education is truncated, his entire life may be stunted and deformed."[52] While Galston disagrees with Douglas's position, he acknowledges that there is "obviously something to Douglas's distinction between the interests and standing of parents and those of their children." He continues by arguing that anyone who wishes (as Galston does) to deny Jehovah's Witnesses or Christian Scientists the right to let their children die for lack of conventional medical treatment yet allow the Amish to deny their children an education adequate for other ways of life "must either find some principled basis for distinguishing these cases or treat them similarly."[53] While distinguishing himself from liberals primarily focused on individual autonomy, and claiming that "properly understood, liberalism is about the protection of diversity, not the valorization of choice," he aims to show that "respect for diversity, and especially group diversity, does not improperly disregard individual autonomy claims."[54] As we saw earlier, however, Galston recognizes that there can be significant tension between individual autonomy and commitment to a wide diversity of ways of life. Since "many cultures or groups do not place a high value on choice and (to say the least) do not encourage their members to exercise it" and since membership in such a group may be among "the deepest sources of . . . identity," throwing state power behind the promotion of individual autonomy can "weaken or undermine" such groups.[55]

Given this, however, Galston is adamant that individuals should retain the right of exit: the liberal state "must defend . . . the personal liberty not to be coerced into, or trapped within, ways of life" and "accordingly, . . . must safeguard the ability of individuals to shift allegiances and cross boundaries."[56] As well as ensuring that groups protect human life, protect and promote the "normal development of basic capacities," and develop "social rationality (the kind of understanding needed to participate in the society, economy, and polity)" in their members, the liberal "Diversity State" Galston favors must "enforce strong prohibitions" against coerced entrance into and exit from such groups.[57] He concludes that "in circumstances of genuine pluralism, individual freedom is adequately protected by secure rights of exit coupled with the existence of a wider society open to individuals wishing to leave their groups of origin."[58]

However, Galston's defense of illiberal groups that do not value autonomy, and his position on the Dayton case in particular, are incompatible with any kind of realistic or meaningful right of exit, especially for women. Neither is the right of exit sufficient to justify the kinds of restrictions on individuals that his theory permits. He himself acknowledges that his position is "hardly unproblematic." On the one hand, there are "entrance problems," since people are born into groups that they do not choose for themselves. On the other hand, there are "exit problems, especially if 'exit'

is understood substantively as well as formally." And thus Galston acknowledges, in conclusion, that a "meaningful" right of exit seems to require a number of conditions: the awareness of alternatives to one's current way of life, the ability to assess these alternatives if one wishes, freedom from brainwashing and from other forms of coercion, and the ability to participate effectively in at least some other ways of life. As he says, this protection of a meaningful right of exit "brings us back some distance toward policies more typically associated with autonomy concerns."[59]

Undoubtedly, Galston's conditions for the existence of a meaningful right of exit bring us back very far toward autonomy-based policies.[60] Moreover, the issue of sex-role indoctrination can illustrate well just how far. If parents are permitted to educate their children in sheltered settings in which they are taught, by example, doctrine, and the content of their curriculum, that it is the will of an omnipotent and punitive God that women's proper role in life is to be an obedient wife and a full-time mother, how can the girls be said to be "aware of . . . alternatives" in any meaningful way, to be able to "assess these alternatives" (or even to think it desirable to do so), or to be able to "participate effectively" in other roles or ways of life? As I briefly indicated above, many fundamentalist religious schools and other institutions of cultural groups do socialize their children into the inevitability of sex roles and sex hierarchy and the godlessness of any departure from them. By thus limiting their autonomy, most especially in the case of girls, they clearly do not meet the specific requirements Galston sets out for meaningful exit, without which his argument loses its claim to being liberal. Also, as I pointed out earlier, the right of exit is insufficient to justify illiberal practices, especially if it is the kind of involuntary exit to which Galston does not object in the case of the Dayton woman who wanted to continue teaching after the birth of her child. For this kind of forced exit especially prevents those within the group who might want to liberalize it from the inside from having any chance of doing so. Even the bare availability of exit for such practical dissenters, though, is insufficient to gain them what others may take for granted: the choice between exerting a fair share of influence within their cultural group and exiting from it if they should find any of its beliefs or practices unduly constraining. Rights of exit provide no help to women or members of other oppressed groups who are deeply attached to their cultures but not to their oppressive aspects. It is likely to be far preferable, from their point of view, to have the wider society address the discrimination they suffer from, just as it would for its other citizens.

Kukathas, who, as we saw earlier, defends the right of religious or cultural groups to be left alone even to the point of allowing children to die preventable deaths, paradoxically also claims that the members of such groups have "the inalienable right to leave – to renounce membership of – the community."[61] Later, in the context of addressing the problem of various injustices that might occur within groups, he adds: "What is crucially important here . . . is the extent to which the individual does enjoy a *substantial* freedom to leave."[62] The right of exit is of considerable importance in Kukathas's argument for three reasons. First, an important basis for his argument against positive group rights is his liberal attachment to individual rights, and not being captive in a group one wishes to leave seems fundamental among such rights. Second, like both Raz and Galston, he thinks that the right of exit mitigates the harm of group injustice or oppression. Third, unlike these other theorists, he notes that "the nature of his community is transformed" by the individual's freedom to leave, "particularly if the formal right comes with substantive opportunities."[63] Thus, implicitly, at least, he acknowledges the important relationship between exit and voice.

In several ways, however, Kukathas both recognizes the limitations of and significantly dilutes the exit rights on which he insists. First, he acknowledges (but fails to respond to) the point that the exit option is "insufficient to ensure any kind of freedom from oppression since it is precisely the most vulnerable members of such communities who would find exit most difficult and costly."[64] This is a valid and important point, which, as we have seen, is particularly pertinent to women and children in many cultural contexts. It badly needs a response. But instead, apparently discounting this point, he claims that if persons or subgroups who seem to be being treated unjustly by their group do not leave it, this mitigates the injustice: "If an individual continues to live in a community and according to ways that (in the judgment of the wider society) treat her unjustly, even though she is free to leave, then our concern about the injustice diminishes."[65] This, however, is one of the passages in which he stresses that the freedom to leave must be "substantial" – must have "consid-

erable substantive bite" – and that certain conditions must hold for this to be so. However, the only condition he mentions, which he regards as the most important, is the existence of a wider liberal society that is open to those wishing to leave their groups. For freedom of exit to be "credible," he says, there must exist in such a society "a considerable degree of individual independence."[66] But while Kukathas is clearly aware that substantial freedom to leave depends in part in having somewhere to go, he largely ignores another important prerequisite: that one must have the capacity to get there. Given many of the group practices Kukathas claims must be permitted by a tolerant society, it is impossible to see how some members – a child who has been allowed to die, for example – could leave; and it is hard to see how others could leave without enormous difficulty, including persons of both sexes deprived of the education required for alternative modes of life and girls and women who had, in addition, no access to property, had undergone clitoridectomy, or had been forced into unequal marriages (especially if at an early age, without access to contraception, or with little or no possibility of initiating divorce). It is perhaps not surprising that Kukathas does not elaborate what capacities individuals must have in order to have a "substantial" right of exit, since such requirements would run into serious conflict with many of the group practices he thinks should be permitted.

Conclusion

As I have argued elsewhere, in the case of groups that have emigrated from cultures which are more patriarchal to a more liberal majority culture, as well as in other multicultural states, rights to maintain cultural practices that discriminate against women are frequently among those sought after by group leaders.[67] Raz, Galston, and Kukathas seem prepared to concede such rights to minority groups, whether immigrant or not. Each tries to mitigate the rights or exemptions by specifying that individuals must have the right of exit, but in no case is the argument convincing. Raz, to be sure, would rather the wider society successfully discourage the repressive practices of groups but sees the right of exit as a safeguard while this lengthy process takes place. However, he neither specifies what having a realistic right of exit would entail nor considers the substantial obstacles that are likely to impede women's exit from such groups. Galston clearly does not put overt sex discrimination in the same serious category as overt racial discrimination, the elimination of which he does think overrides group rights. It is fine with him, apparently, if girls in Christian schools learn from who is and who is not allowed to teach them, as well as from what they are directly taught in class, that it is divinely ordained that the mothers of young children should not be employed outside of the home. But this runs directly contrary to his stated requirements for a person's having a "meaningful right of exit." And Kukathas thinks that groups should be allowed, within tolerant liberal states, to continue even practices that harm or restrict women (as well as children) seriously, as he has recently made clear. He, too, states that persons must have "substantial" rights of exit from such groups, but the only condition he specifies is the existence of a wider liberal society that is willing to take them in. He takes no account of the extent to which many of the practices he advocates permitting groups to practice would make some of their members' exercise of their exit options extremely difficult or even impossible.

In proposing that the right to exit one's cultural or religious group of origin somehow makes the repressive practices of some such groups more tolerable to liberals, the three theorists whose arguments I have discussed seem insufficiently aware of the impossible position in which this is bound to put some persons. To be sure, Kukathas

mentions, though he does not respond to, the objection that often the most repressed are the least able to exit. Neither Raz nor Galston even mentions this relevant fact. And none of the three takes seriously enough the problem that, even if it were feasible or even possible in a practical sense, exit may not be an option at all desirable, or even thinkable, to those most in need of it. But this is not infrequently the case, which partly explains why women put up with some of the practices they do. Only by neglecting such pertinent facts could one argue, in the name of tolerance or in the name of individual freedom and well-being, for group rights that might give no recourse at all to a seventeen-year-old girl forced to choose between not finishing high school in order to marry a virtual stranger and losing her ties with not only her family but also her religion. What kind of a choice is one between total submission and total alienation from the person she understands herself to be? Is this a choice that a group within a liberal state should place some of its members in the position of having to make? The liberal state, I conclude, should not only not give special rights or exemptions to cultural and religious groups that discriminate against or oppress women. It should also enforce individual rights against such groups when the opportunity arises and encourage all groups within its borders to cease such practices.[68] Not to do so, from the point of view of a liberal who takes women's, children's, and other potentially vulnerable persons' rights seriously, is to let toleration for diversity run amok.

Notes

1 The autonomy-based argument I focus on here is that of Joseph Raz in "Multiculturalism: A Liberal Perspective," in *Ethics in the Public Domain* (Oxford: Clarendon, 1994), pp. 170–91; those based on tolerance for diversity are that of William Galston in "Two Concepts of Liberalism," *Ethics* 105 (April 1995): 516–34; and that of Chandran Kukathas in "Are There Any Cultural Rights?" *Political Theory* 20 (February 1992): 105–39, and "Cultural Toleration," in *Nomos XXXIX: Ethnicity and Group Rights*, ed. Ian Shapiro and Will Kymlicka (New York: New York University Press, 1997), pp. 69–104.

2 Susan Moller Okin, "Is Multiculturalism Bad for Women?" *Boston Review* 22 (1997): 25–8, and "Feminism and Multiculturalism: Some Tensions," *Ethics* 108 (1998): 661–84. The former, with comments by twelve scholars and a response by me, was subsequently published as Joshua Cohen, Martha Nussbaum, and Matthew Howard, eds., *Is Multiculturalism Bad for Women?* (Princeton, N.J.: Princeton University Press, 1999).

3 Will Kymlicka, *Liberalism, Community, and Culture* (Oxford: Clarendon, 1989), and *Multicultural Citizenship: A Liberal Theory of Minority Rights* (Oxford: Oxford University Press, 1995).

4 Ayelet Shachar, "Group Identity and Women's Rights in Family Law; The Perils of Multicultural Accommodation," *Journal of Political Philosophy* 6 (1998): 285–305, "The Paradox of Multicultural Vulnerability: Identity Groups, the State and Individual Rights," in *Multicultural Questions*, ed. Christian Joppke and Steven Lukes (Oxford: Oxford University

Press, 1999), and "On Citizenship and Multicultural Vulnerability," *Political Theory* 28 (February 2000): 64–89.

5 Shachar, "On Citizenship and Multicultural Vulnerability," p. 65.

6 Ibid., p. 81; cf. Okin, "Feminism and Multiculturalism: Some Tensions," pp. 683–4.

7 Shachar, "On Citizenship and Multicultural Vulnerability," p. 86, n. 48.

8 Ibid., pp. 79–80, quotation from p. 80. See also Shachar, "The Paradox of Multicultural Vulnerability," p. 100.

9 Raz, "Multiculuralism: A Liberal Perspective," p. 174. This requirement is rather vague. What would it mean, e.g., to give a group whose membership numbered in the hundreds "equal standing" with one whose membership numbered in the tens of millions?

10 For his arguments about autonomy, see Joseph Raz, *The Morality of Freedom* (Oxford: Clarendon, 1986), esp. ch. 14. The quotations are from Raz, "Multiculturalism: A Liberal Perspective," pp. 171, 174.

11 Raz, "Multiculturalism: A Liberal Perspective," p. 184.

12 Ibid., p. 179.

13 Ibid., p. 186.

14 I do not mean here to deny that a new social context cannot make some of a cultural group's practices worse for women. This has clearly been the case for immigrant women in polygynous marriages now living in France. As some said when interviewed, what was a barely tolerable institution in their North African countries of origin is an unbearable imposition in the French context. However, the main reason for this was clearly the change in living conditions: whereas in Africa, each wife had her own hut and some privacy, living in a French apartment designed for a nuclear family made polygynous marriage in practice much worse. It was clearly by no means principally a change in the women's perception of the practice. "News Section," *International Herald Tribune* (February 2, 1996).

15 Raz, "Multiculturalism: A Liberal Perspective," p. 184.

16 See, e.g., Elinor Burkett, "God Created Me to Be a Slave," *New York Times Magazine* (October 12, 1997): 56–60.

17 Galston also mentions the Civil War Amendments and Brown v. Board of Education of Topeka, 347 U.S. 483 (1954). He says of the amendments and the earlier race cases, but not of the more recent gender case, that they "have significantly reshaped our understanding" (p. 531).

18 Galston, p. 532. The second quotation is from Bob Jones University v. United States, 461 U.S. 574, 604 (1983).

19 Galston, p. 533. The other quotations are from Ohio Civil Rights Commission v. Dayton Schools, 477 U.S. 619, 628 (1986).

20 Galston, p. 533.

21 Ibid., p. 532.

22 Ibid.

23 Ibid., p. 533.

24 Ibid.

25 See Albert O. Hirschman, *Exit, Voice, and Loyalty: Responses to Declines in Firms, Organizations, and States* (Cambridge, Mass: Harvard University Press, 1970).

26 Kukathas, "Are There Any Cultural Rights?" p. 128.

27 Ibid.

28 Kukathas, "Cultural Toleration," p. 70.

29 Ibid., p. 88, citing Amy Gutmann, "The Challenge of Multiculturalism in Political Ethics," *Philosophy & Public Affairs* (1993): 171–206, p. 116.

30 For more detail on cultural controls on women, see Okin, "Feminism and Multiculturalism: Some Tensions," esp. pp. 667–70, and references, esp. n. 17; also see Cohen, Nussbaum, and Howard, eds., passim.

31 In many cases, the costs and unavailability of education have risen due to the structural adjustment policies enforced on indebted countries since the 1970s by the World Bank and the International Monetary Fund. It is well documented that this and other cuts in social spending have had considerably worse impacts on women and girls in these countries than on men and boys. See, e.g., Haleh Afshar and Carolynne Dennis, eds., *Women and Adjustment Policies in the Third World* (New York: St. Martin's, 1992); Mariarosa Dalla Costa and Giovanna F. Dalla Costa, eds., *Paying the Price: Women and the Politics of International Economic Strategy* (London: Zed, 1995).

32 Of the forty poorest countries for which data are available for 1995, the illiteracy rates for women are nontrivially higher – in most cases much higher – than those of men in all but three. In eighteen cases – India, Pakistan, and sixteen African countries – the illiteracy rates for women are between 150 percent and 200 percent of men's, and in four others – Tanzania, Zambia, Cambodia, and China – they are more than twice as high. In the lower-middle- and middle-income economies, the discrepancies between the sexes are still high. In only seven out of the twenty-six such countries with data available are the figures equal or almost so. In ten, the rate of women's illiteracy is between 150 percent and 200 percent of men's; in four, it is between twice and three times as high; and in another three, it is three times as high or more. Of the last seven countries, four are predominantly Muslim. In the upper-middle- and high-income countries, where illiteracy

is in general much lower, for obvious reasons, there are still wide discrepancies between the sexes in a few countries where it is high, most notably Saudi Arabia, Malaysia, and Gabon, but much less discrepancy in others where it is also quite high, including the most affluent Muslim countries, Kuwait and United Arab Emirates. *Human Development Report* (Oxford: Oxford University Press, for the World Bank, 1997), pp. 220–1.

33 For a more general discussion of the importance of education for substantive rights of exit, see Rob Reich, *Bridging Liberalism and Multiculturalism in American Education* (Chicago: University of Chicago Press, 2002).

34 Mozert v. Hawkins County Bd. of Education, 827 F.2d 1058 (6th Cir. 1987).

35 James G. Dwyer, *Religious Schools v. Children's Rights* (Ithaca, N.Y.: Cornell University Press, 1998), p. 26.

36 In a recent *New York Times* story about Indians in the United States who practice arranged marriage, it was fairly evident that the men involved had more choice about the marriages being arranged for them, about the marital partners, and about the timing. One twenty-year-old woman, a student at Barnard – who had obviously put much effort into her education – clearly did not want to terminate her education as she was being required to do by her parents, but she saw herself as having no choice. She said: "I wish it didn't have to be this way, but I can't really do anything about it" (Celia Dugger, "In India, an Arranged Marriage of Two Worlds," *New York Times* (July 20, 1998).)

37 Neera Kuckreja Sohoni, *The Burden of Girlhood: A Global Inquiry into the Status of Girls* (Oakland, Calif.: Third Party, 1995), ch. 3.

38 Another anecdote in Dugger's *New York Times* story is about a young, though fully adult, married woman who has to wear what her mother-in-law decrees, even while at home, and to await her mother-in-law's permission to resume her education. See Shachar, "On Citizenship and Multicultural Vulnerability," pp. 73–77, for discussion of how and why women are often given the role of bearers of their cultures.

39 Uma Narayan, "Contesting Cultures," in her *Dislocating Cultures: Identities, Traditions, and Third World Feminisms* (New York: Routledge, 1997), pp. 3–39; Chitra Banerjee Divakaruni, *Arranged Marriage* (New York: Doubleday, 1995). See also Chitra Banerjee Divakaruni, *The Mistress of Spices* (New York: Doubleday, 1997).

40 Dugger.

41 Martha Nussbaum, *Women and Human Development: The Capabilities Approach* (Cambridge: Cambridge University Press, 2000), p. 268.

42 Obviously, communalism in India – given the country's history of violent religious conflict, has important virtues, but these do not include the promotion of women's equality in most Indian states, with a few exceptions, such as Kerala, where women's status is notably higher than average. On the effects of religious group rights on women, see Kirti Singh, "Obstacles to Women's Rights in India," in *Human Rights of Women: National and International Perspectives*, ed. Rebecca J. Cook (Philadelphia: University of Pennsylvania Press, 1994), pp. 375–96, esp. pp. 378–89.

43 Laurie Olsen, *Made in America: Immigrant Students in Our Public Schools* (New York: New Press, 1997), p. 124.

44 Ibid., p. 134.

45 Ibid., pp. 136, 138.

46 Jeffrey Spinner-Halev points out that Olsen's respondents almost all say that they will raise their own daughters less restrictively, concluding that "their experiences and views [are] testimony to the tremendous power of liberal public culture" ("Feminism, Multiculturalism, Oppression, and the State," *Ethics* 112 [October 2001]: 84–113, p. 90). However, in saying that this proves "liberalism . . . victorious" (p. 90), he does not take sufficient account of the troublesome fact that, to the extent that multiculturalism helps these young women's parents and their traditional culture to prevail over their own preferences now, they themselves will lead radically unfree lives (they are, as he acknowledges, "caught in lives that they will not like" [p. 89]) although they are residents or citizens of a liberal state.

47 Shachar, "On Citizenship and Multicultural Vulnerability," p. 80.

48 See, e.g., Galston, pp. 553–4.

49 Raz, "Multiculturalism: A Liberal Perspective," p. 184.

50 Ibid., p. 187.

51 Ibid., p. 190.

52 Wisconsin v. Yoder, 406 U.S. 205, 245–6 (1972), quoted in Galston, p. 517.

53 Galston, pp. 517–18.

54 Ibid., pp. 523, 518.

55 Ibid., pp. 521–2.

56 Ibid., p. 522.

57 Ibid., pp. 525, 528.

58 Ibid., p. 533.

59 Ibid., p. 534.

60 See Kimberly A. Yuracko, "Enforcing Liberalism: Liberal Responses to Illiberal Groups," in *Handbook of Global Legal Policy*, ed. Stuart S. Nagel (New York: Dekker, 2000), pp. 485–509, for an insightful discussion of the relationship between toleration-based and autonomy-based arguments for group rights.

61 Kukathas, "Are There Any Cultural Rights?"
    p. 117.
62 Ibid., p. 133.
63 Ibid., p. 128.
64 Kukathas, "Cultural Toleration," p. 87. He responds to the charge that the extent of tolerance of group practices he advocates would make society into a "mosaic of tyrannies" by citing examples of the persecution of groups by the wider society and claiming that "islands of tyranny in a sea of indifference" are to be preferred to more centralized tyranny. Most of his examples, however, have little or nothing to do with the control of groups in order to protect their members; one such example is the twentieth-century persecution of Jews.
65 Kukathas, "Are There Any Cultural Rights?"
    p. 133.
66 Ibid., p. 134
67 Okin, *Is Multiculturalism Bad for Women?* passim; Bhikhu Parekh, "Minority Practices and Principles of Toleration," *International Migration Review* 30 (April 1996): 251–84.
68 These guidelines should, of course, apply equally to old groups as to newly arrived ones. For example, religious groups such as the Catholic Church and Orthodox Judaism should be denied tax-exempt status as long as they discriminate against women.

39

"Dependency" Demystified: Inscriptions of Power in a Keyword of the Welfare State

Nancy Fraser and Linda Gordon

"Dependency" is the single most crucial term in the current US debate about welfare reform. "Welfare dependent" in the United States means someone who relies on one of the stigmatized programs of public assistance, as distinguished from honorable programs such as old age insurance, which are not called "welfare." The paradigmatic "dependent" is the poor solo mother who collects benefits from the stingy and politically unpopular program, Aid to Families with Dependent Children (AFDC). "Welfare reform" today means reducing "dependency" by getting claimants off the rolls.

Few concepts in US social policy discussions do as much ideological work as "dependency." The term leaks a profusion of stigmatizing connotations – racial, sexual, misogynist, and more. It alludes implicitly to a normative state of "independence," which will itself not withstand critical scrutiny. Naming the problems of poor solo mothers and their children "dependency," moreover, tends to make them appear to be individual rather than social problems, as much moral or psychological as economic. The word carries strong emotive and visual associations and a powerful pejorative charge. The most common image is a "welfare mother," typically figured as a young unmarried black woman of uncontrolled sexuality and fertility. This stereotype haunts even the most neutral-sounding talk about dependency in discussions of welfare reform.

Why does the word "dependency" carry so much ideological weight? Part of the reason, we suggest, is historical. The term carries the debris of several centuries of poor relief policies that relieved hunger while stigmatizing recipients, often actually impeding their escape from the dole into wage labor. Branding welfare recipients as "dependents" continues a long tradition of opposing dependence to independence. Both terms were redefined in the last few centuries in ways that helped adapt old traditions of gender, race, and class domination to new social and economic conditions. But the fundamental opposition remains: "independence" is strong, virtuous, white, and male, while "dependence" is weak, disreputable, colored, and/or female. In the last half-century, as "dependency" became associated particularly with AFDC, it has intensified disrespect for women's unpaid labor.

Tracing the historical career of "dependency," then, can illuminate contemporary social policy debates.[1] In this article we analyze the term as a keyword of the US welfare state and we reconstruct its genealogy.[2] We excavate broad historical shifts in the term's usage, and in the assumptions undergirding its usage, in order to advance a critique of the present. By historicizing "dependency," we aim to defamiliarize it, to render explicit assumptions and connotations that usually go without saying (e.g., assumptions about human nature, gender roles, the causes of poverty, the sources of entitlement, and what counts as work and as a contribution to society).

This article is a critique of US welfare ideology in the form of a critical political semantics. The project of analyzing "dependency" as a "keyword of the welfare state" owes much to Raymond Williams's *Keywords: A Vocabulary of Culture and Society* (1976), which mapped some major currents of modern English culture by studying shifts in the usage, and in the assumptions and experiences undergirding usage, of some salient cultural terms. We share with Williams the premise that the terms used to describe social life are also active forces shaping it. These terms contain sedimented traces of past usages and function as vehicles through which the past influences the present. Some words become sites at which the meaning of social experience is negotiated and contested. Studies of their shifting usages in the past, then, can illuminate social conflict in the present.

The aim of our genealogy is activist. When ideological assumptions are tacitly inscribed in social policy discourse, they are difficult to challenge. Policy discourse then becomes a medium through which political hegemony is reproduced. To render explicit such assumptions, in contrast, is to render them contestable and to challenge their power. Thus, by constructing a genealogy of "dependency" we provide a challenge to ideology. We show how unreflective mainstream uses of this keyword serve to enshrine certain interpretations of social life as authoritative and to delegitimate or obscure others, usually to the advantage of dominant groups in society and the disadvantage of subordinates.

Such a critique is not merely negative. By questioning the terms in which social problems are named, we expand the collective capacity to imagine solutions. A genealogy of "dependency" should encourage rethinking welfare from a feminist and democratic perspective.

Reviling welfare recipients serves not only to dishonor those individuals, but also to mystify and legitimate inequalities that affect us all. Giving and receiving welfare will remain a necessary aspect of citizenship for a long time. To prevent welfare programs from being used by conservatives to promote hostility to feminism, single mothers, minorities, and poor people, we must imbue our public language with different meanings and associations. We will need to develop alternative meanings for "welfare," "dependence," and "independence." It is in this spirit that we offer a genealogy of "dependency." After charting the term's history and current uses, we sketch the beginnings of an alter-

native semantics premised on the inescapable fact of human interdependence.

Registers of Meaning

In its root meaning, the verb "to depend" refers to a physical relationship in which one thing hangs from another. The more abstract meanings – social, economic, psychological, and political – were originally metaphorical. In current usage, we find four registers in which the meanings of dependency reverberate. The first is an economic register, in which one depends on some other person(s) or institution for subsistence. In a second register, the term denotes a socio-legal status, the lack of a separate legal or public identity, as in the status of married women created by coverture. The third register is political: dependency means subjection to an external ruling power and may be predicated of a colony or subject caste of noncitizen residents. The fourth register we call the moral/psychological; dependency in this sense is an individual character trait similar to lack of will power or excessive emotional neediness.

To be sure, not every use of "dependency" fits neatly into one and only one of these registers. By distinguishing them analytically, however, we present a matrix on which to plot the historical adventures of the term. In what follows, we shall trace the shift from a patriarchal preindustrial usage in which women, however subordinate, shared a condition of dependency with many men to a modern, industrial, male-supremacist usage that constructed a specifically feminine sense of dependency. That usage is now giving way, we contend, to a postindustrial usage in which growing numbers of relatively prosperous women claim the same kind of independence that men do while a more stigmatized but still feminized sense of dependency attaches to groups considered deviant and superfluous. Not just gender but also racializing practices play a major role in these shifts, as do changes in the organization and meaning of labor.

Preindustrial "Dependency"

In preindustrial English usage, the most common meaning of "dependency" was subordination. The economic, socio-legal, and political registers were relatively undifferentiated, reflecting the fusion of various forms of hierarchy in state and society.

Further, the moral/psychological use of the term barely existed. The earliest social definition of the verb "to depend (on)" in the *Oxford English Dictionary (OED)* is "to be connected within a relation of subordination." A "dependent," from at least 1588, was one "who depends on another for support, position, etc.; a retainer, attendant, subordinate, servant." A "dependency" was either a retinue or body of servants or a foreign territorial possession or colony. This family of terms applied widely in a hierarchical social context in which nearly everyone was subordinate to someone else but did not incur individual stigma thereby (Gundersen 1987).

We can appreciate just how common dependency was in preindustrial society by examining its opposite. The term "independence" at first applied primarily to aggregate entities, not to individuals; thus in the seventeenth century a nation or a church congregation could be independent. By the eighteenth century, however, an individual could be said to have an "independency," meaning an ownership of property, a fortune that made it possible to live without laboring. (This sense of the term, which we would today call economic, survives in our expressions "to be independently wealthy" and "a person of independent means.") To be independent, in contrast, was to gain one's livelihood by working for someone else. This of course was the condition of most people, of wage laborers as well as serfs and slaves, of most men as well as most women.[3]

Dependency, therefore, was a normal, as opposed to a deviant, condition; a social relation, as opposed to an individual trait. Thus, it did not carry any moral opprobrium.[4] Yet it did mean status inferiority and legal coverture, being a part of a unit headed by someone else who had legal standing. In a world of status hierarchies dominated by great landowners and their retainers, all members of a household other than its "head" were dependents, as were peasants, free or bound. They were, as Peter Laslett wrote, "caught up, so to speak, 'subsumed'...into the personalities of their fathers and masters" (1971, 21).

Dependency also had what today we would call political consequences. While the term did not mean precisely "unfree," its context was a social order in which subjection, not citizenship, was the norm. Throughout most of the European development of representative government, independence in the sense of property ownership was a prerequisite for political rights. When dependents began to claim rights and liberty, they perforce became revolutionaries.

"Dependency" was not then applied uniquely to characterize the relation of a wife to her husband. Women's dependency, like children's, meant being on a lower rung in a long social ladder; their husbands and fathers were above them but below others. For the agrarian majority, moreover, there was no implication of unilateral economic dependency, because women's and children's labor was recognized as essential to the family economy. Women's dependency in preindustrial society was similar in kind to that of subordinate men, only multiplied. But so too were the lives of children, servants, and the elderly overlaid with multiple layers of dependency.[5]

Nevertheless, dependency was not universally approved or uncontested. It was subject, rather, to principled challenges since at least the seventeenth century, when liberal-individualist political arguments became common. The terms "dependence" and "independence" often figured centrally in political debates in this period.[6] Sometimes they even became key signifiers of social crisis, as in the seventeenth-century English controversy about "out-of-doors" servants, hired help who did not reside in the homes of their masters and who were not bound by indentures or similar legal understandings. In the discourse of the time, the anomalous "independence" of these men served as a general symbol for social disorder, a lightning rod focusing diffuse cultural anxieties – much as the anomalous "dependence" of "welfare mothers" does today.

Industrial "Dependency": The Worker and his Negatives

With the rise of industrial capitalism, the semantic geography of dependency shifted significantly. What in preindustrial society had been a normal and unstigmatized condition became deviant and stigmatized. More precisely, certain dependencies became shameful while others were deemed natural and proper. In particular, as eighteenth- and nineteenth-century political culture intensified gender difference, new, specifically gendered uses of dependency appeared – considered proper for women, but degrading for men. Likewise, emergent racial constructions made some forms of dependency appropriate for the "dark races," but intolerable for "whites." Such differentiated valuations became possible as the term's preindustrial usage fractured. No longer designating only generalized subordination, "dependency" in the industrial era could be socio-legal, political, or economic. With these distinctions came another major semantic shift: "dependency" need not always refer to a social relation; it could also designate an individual character trait. Thus, the moral/psychological register was born.

These redefinitions were greatly influenced by Radical Protestantism, which elaborated a new positive image of individual independence and a critique of socio-legal and political dependency. From this perspective, status hierarchies no longer appeared natural or just, and subjection and subsumption were increasingly objectionable. These beliefs informed a variety of radical movements throughout the industrial era, including abolition of slavery, feminism, and labor organizing, with substantial successes. In the nineteenth century these movements abolished slavery and some of the legal disabilities of women. More thoroughgoing victories were won in the United States by white male workers who, in the eighteenth and nineteenth centuries, threw off their socio-legal and political dependency and won civil and electoral rights. In the age of democratic revolutions, the newly developing concept of citizenship rested on independence; dependency was deemed antithetical to citizenship.

Changes in the civil and political landscape of dependence and independence were accompanied by even more dramatic changes in the economic register. When white workingmen demanded civil and electoral rights, they claimed to be independent. This entailed reinterpreting the meaning of wage labor so as to divest it of the association with dependency. That in turn required a shift in focus – from the experience or means of labor (e.g., ownership of tools or land, control of skills, and the organization of work) to its remuneration and how that was spent. As a result of the struggles of radical workingmen, economic independence came eventually to encompass the ideal of earning a family wage, a wage sufficient to maintain a household and support a dependent wife and children. Thus, workingmen expanded the meaning of economic independence to include wage labor in addition to property ownership and self-employment.[7]

This shift in the meaning of independence also transformed the meanings of dependency. As wage labor became increasingly normative – and increasingly associated with independence – it

was precisely those excluded from wage labor who appeared to personify dependency. In the new industrial semantics, three principal icons of dependency emerged, all effectively negatives of the dominant image of "the worker," and each embodying a different aspect of nonindependence.

The first icon of industrial dependency was "the pauper," who lived not on wages but on poor relief.[8] In the strenuous new culture of emergent capitalism, the figure of the pauper was like a bad double of the upstanding workingman, threatening the worker should he lag. The image of the pauper was elaborated largely in an emerging new register of dependency discourse – the moral/psychological register. Paupers were not simply poor but degraded, their character corrupted and their will sapped through reliance on charity. Toward the end of the nineteenth century, as hereditarian (eugenic) thought caught on, the pauper's character defects were given a basis in biology. The pauper's dependency was figured as unlike the serf's in that it was unilateral, not reciprocal. To be a pauper was not to be subordinate within a system of productive labor; it was to be outside such a system altogether.

A second icon of industrial dependency was embodied alternately in the figures of the "colonial native" and the "slave." They, of course, were very much inside the economic system; their labor was often fundamental to the development of capital and industry. Whereas the pauper personified economic dependency, natives and slaves personified political subjection.[9] Their images as "savage," "childlike," and "submissive" became salient as the old, territorial sense of dependency as a colony was intertwined with a new, racist discourse developed to justify colonialism and slavery.[10] There emerged a drift from an older sense of dependency as a relation of subjection imposed by an imperial power on an indigenous population to a newer sense of dependency as an inherent property or character trait of the people so subjected. In earlier usage, colonials were dependent because they had been conquered; in nineteenth-century imperialist culture, they were conquered because they were dependent. In this new conception, the intrinsic, essential dependency of natives and slaves justified their colonization and enslavement. Racialist thought was the linchpin for this reasoning.

Like paupers, natives and slaves were excluded from wage labor and thus were negatives of the image of the "worker." They shared that characteristic, if little else, with the third major icon of dependency in the industrial era: the newly invented figure of "the housewife." As we saw, the independence of white workingmen presupposed the ideal of the family wage, a wage sufficient to maintain a household and support a (nonemployed) wife and children. Thus, for wage labor to create (white male) independence, (white) female economic dependence was required. Women were thus transformed "from partners to parasites" (Land 1980, 57; Boydston 1991). This transformation was by no means universal; since few husbands actually were able to support a family single-handedly, most families continued to depend on the labor of women and children.[11]

Several different registers of dependency converged in the figure of the housewife. This figure melded woman's traditional socio-legal and political dependency with her more recent economic dependency in the industrial order.[12] In addition, the connotations of female dependency were altered. Although erstwhile dependent white men gained political rights, most white women remained legally and politically dependent. The result was to feminize – and stigmatize – socio-legal and political dependency.

Together, then, a series of new personifications of dependency combined to constitute the underside of the workingman's independence. Henceforth, those who aspired to full membership in society would have to distinguish themselves from the pauper, native, slave, and housewife in order to construct their independence. In a social order in which wage labor was becoming hegemonic, all of these distinctions could be encapsulated simultaneously in the ideal of the family wage. On the one hand, and most overtly, that ideal premised the white workingman's independence on his wife's subordination and economic dependence. On the other hand, it simultaneously contrasted with counterimages of dependent men – first with degraded male paupers on poor relief and later with racist stereotypes of black men unable to dominate black women. The family wage, therefore, was a vehicle for elaborating meanings of dependence and independence that were deeply inflected by gender, race, and class.

In this new industrial semantics, white workingmen appeared to be economically independent, but their independence was largely illusory and ideological. Since few actually earned enough to single-handedly support a family, most depended in fact – if not in word – on their wives' and children's contributions. Equally important, dominant understandings of wage labor in capitalism denied workers' dependence on their employers, thereby veiling their status as subordinates in a unit headed by someone else. Thus, the hierarchy that had been relatively explicit and visible in the peasant-landlord relation was mystified in the relationship of factory operative to factory owner. There was a sense, then, in which the economic dependency of white workingmen was spirited away through linguistic sleight of hand – somewhat like reducing the number of poor people by lowering the official poverty demarcating line.

By definition, then, economic inequality among white men no longer created dependency. But noneconomic hierarchy among white men was considered unacceptable in the United States. Thus, "dependency" was redefined to refer exclusively to those noneconomic relations of subordination deemed suitable only for people of color and white women. Whereas all relations of subordination had previously counted as dependency relations, now capital-labor relations were exempted. Socio-legal and political hierarchy appeared to diverge from economic hierarchy, and only the first two seemed incompatible with hegemonic views of society. It seemed to follow, moreover, that were socio-legal dependency and political dependency ever to be formally abolished, no social-structural dependency would remain. Any dependency that did persist could only be moral or psychological.

The Rise of American "Welfare Dependency": 1890–1945

Informed by these general features of industrial-era semantics, a distinctive welfare-related use of "dependency" developed in the United States. Originating in the late nineteenth-century discourse of pauperism, modified in the Progressive Era, and stabilized in the period of the New Deal, this use of the term was fundamentally ambiguous, slipping easily and repeatedly from an economic meaning to a moral/psychological meaning.

As we saw, the most general definition of economic dependency in this era was simply nonwage-earning. By the end of the nineteenth century, however, that definition had divided into a "good" household dependency, predicated on children's and wives' relation to the male bread-winner, and an increasingly "bad" (or at least dubious) charity dependency, predicated on recipients of relief.

Both definitions used as their reference point the ideal of the family wage, and both were eventually incorporated into the discourse of the national state. The good, household definition was elaborated by the census (Folbre 1991) and Internal Revenue Service, which installed the category of dependent as the norm for wives. Meanwhile, the stigma of dependence on charity or public assistance continued and was often intensified by "scientific charity" late in the nineteenth century.

Ironically, reformers in the 1890s introduced the word "dependent" into relief discourse as a substitute for the older pejorative "pauper" precisely in order to destigmatize the receipt of help. They first applied the new word to children, the paradigmatic "innocent" victims of poverty (Warner 1894–1930; Abbott and Breckinridge 1921, 7; National Conference of Charities and Correction 1890s–1920s). Then, in the early twentieth century, Progressive Era reformers began to apply the term to adults, again to rid them of stigma. Only after World War II did "dependent" become the hegemonic word for a recipient of aid (Brown 1940; Bruno 1948; Howard 1943).

The attempt to get rid of stigma by replacing "pauperism" with "dependency" failed. Discourse about economic dependency repeatedly slid into condemnation of moral/psychological dependency. Even during the depression of the 1930s, experts worried that receipt of relief would create "habits of dependence," or "a belligerent dependency, an attitude of having a right and title to relief" (Brandt 1932, 23–24; Vaile 1934, 26; Gibbons 1933). Many needy people accepted public aid only after much hesitation and with great shame, so strong was the stigma of dependency (Bakke 1940a; Bakke 1940b).

Most important, the New Deal intensified the dishonor of receiving help by consolidating a two-track welfare system. First-track social insurance programs such as unemployment and old age insurance offered aid as an entitlement, without stigma or supervision and hence without dependency. Such programs were deliberately designed to create the appearance that beneficiaries merely got back what they put in. They constructed an honorable status for recipients; today no one calls these programs "welfare." Intended to replace temporarily the family wage, first-track programs excluded most women and minorities. In contrast, second-track public assistance programs (among which Aid to Dependent Children [ADC], later Aid to Families with Dependent Children

[AFDC], became the biggest and most well-known) continued the private charity tradition of searching out the deserving among the chiselers. Funded from general tax revenues instead of earmarked wage deductions, these programs created the appearance that claimants were getting something for nothing (Fraser and Gordon 1992). They established entirely different conditions for receiving aid: means-testing, morals-testing, moral and household supervision, home visits, extremely low stipends – in short, they humiliated, infantilized, and thus created the "welfare dependency" they feared (Fraser 1987; Gordon 1990b; Nelson 1990).

The racial and sexual exclusions of the first-track programs were not accidental. They were designed to win the support of southern legislators who wanted to keep blacks dependent in another sense – on low wages or sharecropping (Quadagno 1988). Equally deliberate was the construction of the differential in legitimacy between the two tracks of the welfare system.[13] Most Americans today still distinguish between "welfare" and "non-welfare" forms of public provision and view only the former as creating dependency. The assumptions underlying these distinctions, however, had to be constructed politically. Older people became privileged (non-welfare) recipients only through decades of militant organization and lobbying. All programs of public provision, whether they are called welfare or not, shore up some dependencies and discourage others. Social Security subverted adults' sense of responsibility for their parents, for example. Public assistance programs, by contrast, aimed to buttress the dependence of the poor on low-wage labor, wives on husbands, and children on their parents.

The conditions of second-track assistance made recipients view their dependence on public assistance as inferior to the supposed independence of wage labor (Pope 1989, 73, 144; West 1981; Milwaukee County Welfare Rights Organization 1972). But the designers of ADC did not initially intend to drive white solo mothers into paid employment. Rather, they wanted to protect the norm of the family wage by making dependence on a male breadwinner continue to seem preferable to dependence on the state (Gordon 1992). ADC occupied the strategic semantic space where the good, household sense of dependency and the bad, relief sense of dependency intersected. It enforced at the same time the positive connotations of the first and the negative connotations of the second.

Thus, the poor solo mother was enshrined as the quintessential "welfare dependent."[14] That designation has become significant not only for what it includes, but also for what it excludes and occludes. Although it appears to mean relying on the government for economic support, not all recipients of public funds are equally considered dependent. Hardly anyone today calls recipients of Social Security retirement insurance "dependents." Similarly, persons receiving unemployment insurance, agricultural loans, and home mortgage assistance are excluded from that categorization, as indeed are defense contractors and the beneficiaries of corporate bail-outs and regressive taxation.

Postindustrial Society and the Disappearance of "Good" Dependency

With the transition to a postindustrial phase of capitalism, the semantic map of dependency is being redrawn yet again. Whereas industrial usage had cast some forms of dependency as natural and proper, postindustrial usage casts all forms as avoidable and blameworthy; and it focuses even more intensely on the traits of individuals. One major influence is the formal abolition of much of the gender- and race-based legal and political dependency that was endemic to industrial society. Housewives, paupers, natives, and the descendants of slaves are no longer formally excluded from most civil and political rights; neither their subsumption nor their subjection is viewed as legitimate. Thus, major forms of dependency deemed proper in industrial usage are now considered objectionable, and postindustrial uses of the term carry a stronger negative charge.

A second major shift in the geography of postindustrial dependency is affecting the economic register. This is the decentering of the ideal of the family wage, which had been the gravitational center of industrial usage. The relative deindustrialization of the United States is restructuring the political economy, making the single-earner family even more mythical. The loss of higher paid "male" manufacturing jobs and the massive entry of women into low-wage service work is meanwhile altering the gender composition of employment (Smith 1984). At the same time, divorce is common and, thanks in large part to the feminist and gay and lesbian liberation movements, changing gender norms are helping to proliferate new family forms, making the male breadwinner/ female homemaker model less attractive to many (Stacey 1987; Stacey 1990; Weston 1991). It no longer goes without saying that a woman should rely on a man for economic support, nor that mothers should not also be "workers." Thus, another major form of dependency that was positively inflected in industrial semantics has become contested if not simply negative.

The combined result of these developments is to increase the stigma of dependency. With all legal and political dependency now illegitimate, and with wives' economic dependency now contested, there is no longer any self-evidently "good" adult dependency in postindustrial society. Rather, all dependency is suspect, and independence is enjoined upon everyone. Independence, however, remains identified with wage labor. Everyone is expected to "work" and be "self-supporting." Any adult not perceived as a worker shoulders a heavier burden of self-justification.

With the formal dismantling of coverture and Jim Crow, it has become possible to claim that equality of opportunity exists and that individual merit determines outcomes. With capitalist economic dependency already abolished by definition, and with legal and political dependency now abolished by law, postindustrial society appears to some conservatives and liberals to have eliminated every social-structural basis of dependency. Whatever dependency remains, therefore, can be interpreted as the fault of individuals.

Welfare Dependency as Postindustrial Pathology

The worsening connotations of "welfare dependency" have been nourished by several streams from outside the field of welfare. New postindustrial medical and psychological discourses have associated dependency with pathology. Social scientists began in the 1980s to write about "chemical," "alcohol," and "drug dependency," euphemisms for addiction (e.g., Haynes 1988). Because welfare claimants are often – falsely – assumed to be addicts, the pathological connotations of "drug dependency" tend also to infect "welfare dependency," increasing stigmatization.

A second important postindustrial current is the rise of new psychological meanings of dependency, which have very strong feminine associations. In the 1950s, social workers influenced by psychiatry began to diagnose dependence as a form of immaturity common among women, particularly among solo mothers (who were often, of course, welfare claimants). The problem was that women were supposed to be just dependent enough, and it was easy to tip over into excess in either direction.[15]

Psychologized dependency became the target of some of the earliest second-wave feminism. Betty Friedan's 1963 classic, *The Feminine Mystique*, provided a phenomenological account of the housewife's psychological dependency and drew from it a political critique of her social subordination. More recently, however, a burgeoning cultural-feminist, postfeminist, and antifeminist self-help and pop-psychology literature has obfuscated the link between the psychological and the political. In Colette Dowling's 1981 book, *The Cinderella Complex*, women's dependency was hypostatized as a depth-psychological gender structure: "women's hidden fear of independence" or the "wish to be saved." The late 1980s saw a spate of books about "co-dependency," a supposedly prototypically female syndrome of supporting or "enabling" the dependency of someone else. In a metaphor that reflects the drug hysteria of the period, dependency in this case, too, is an addiction. Apparently, even if a woman manages to escape her gender's predilection to dependency, she is still liable to incur the blame for facilitating the dependency of her husband or children. This completes the vicious circle: the increased stigmatizing of dependency in the culture at large has also deepened contempt for those who care for dependents (Sapiro 1990).

The 1980s saw a cultural panic about dependency. In 1980, the American Psychiatric Association codified "Dependent Personality Disorder" (DPD) as an official psychopathology. According to the 1987 edition of the *Diagnostic and Statistical Manual of Mental Disorders (DSM-III-R)*, "the essential feature of this disorder is a pervasive pattern of dependent and submissive behavior beginning by early childhood...People with this disorder are unable to make everyday decisions without an excessive amount of advice and reassurance from others, and will even allow others to make most of their important decisions.... The disorder is apparently common and is diagnosed more frequently in females" (American Psychiatric Association 1987, 353–54).

The codification of DPD as an official psychopathology represents a new stage in the history of the moral/psychological register. Here the social relations of dependency disappear entirely into the (individual) personality of the dependent. Overt moralism also disappears in the apparently neutral, scientific, medicalized formulation. Thus, although the defining traits of the dependent personality match point for point the traits traditionally ascribed to housewives, paupers, natives, and slaves, all links to subordination have vanished. The only remaining trace of those themes is the flat, categorical, and uninterpreted observation that DPD is "diagnosed more frequently in females."

If psychological discourse has further feminized and individualized dependency, other postindustrial developments have further racialized it. The increased stigmatization of welfare dependency followed a general increase in public provision in the United States, the removal of some discriminatory practices that had previously excluded minority women from participation in AFDC, especially in the South, and the transfer of many white women to first-track programs as social insurance coverage expanded. By the 1970s the figure of the black solo mother had come to epitomize welfare dependency. As a result, the new discourse about welfare draws on older symbolic currents that linked dependency with racist ideologies.

The ground was laid by a long, somewhat contradictory stream of discourses about "the black family," in which African American gender and kinship relations were measured against white middle-class norms and deemed pathological. One supposedly pathological element was "the excessive independence" of black women, an ideologically distorted allusion to long traditions of wage work, educational achievement, and community activism. The 1960s and 1970s discourse about poverty recapitulated traditions of misogyny toward African American women; in Daniel Moynihan's diagnosis, for example, "matriarchal" families had "emasculated" black men and created a "culture of poverty" based on a "tangle of [family] pathology" (Rainwater and Yancey 1967). This discourse placed black AFDC claimants in a double bind: they were pathologically independent with respect to men and pathologically dependent with respect to government.

By the 1980s, however, the racial imagery of dependency had shifted. The black welfare mother that haunted the white imagination ceased to be the powerful matriarch. Now the preeminent stereotype is the unmarried teenage mother caught in the "welfare trap" and rendered drone-like and passive. This new icon of welfare dependency is younger and weaker than the matriarch. She is often evoked in the phrase "children having children," which can express feminist sympathy or antifeminist contempt, black appeals for parental control or white racist eugenic anxieties.

Many of these postindustrial discourses coalesced in the early 1990s. Then Vice President Dan Quayle brought together the pathologized, feminized, and racialized currents in his comment on the May 1992 Los Angeles riot: "Our inner cities are filled with children having children... with people who are dependent on drugs and on the narcotic of welfare" (Quayle 1992).

Thus postindustrial culture has called up a new personification of dependency: the black, unmarried, teenaged, welfare dependent mother. This image has usurped the symbolic space previously occupied by the housewife, pauper, native, and slave, while absorbing and condensing their connotations. Black, female, a pauper, not a worker, a housewife and mother, yet practically a child herself – this new stereotype partakes of virtually every quality that has been coded historically as antithetical to independence. Condensing multiple, often contradictory meanings of dependency, it is a powerful ideological trope that simultaneously organizes diffuse cultural anxieties and dissimulates their social bases.

Postindustrial Policy and the Politics of Dependency

Contemporary policy discourse about welfare dependency is thoroughly inflected by these assumptions. It divides into two major streams. The first continues the rhetoric of pauperism and the culture of poverty. It is used in both conservative and liberal, victim-blaming or non-victim-blaming ways, depending on the causal structure of the argument. The contention is that poor, dependent people have something more than lack of money wrong with them. Conservatives, such as George Gilder (1981) and Lawrence Mead (1986), argue that welfare causes moral/psychological dependency. Some liberals, such as William Julius Wilson (1987) and Christopher Jencks (1992), blame social and economic influences but agree that claimants' culture and behavior are problematic.

A second stream of thought draws on neoclassical economic premises. It assumes a "rational man" facing choices in which welfare and work are both options. For these policy analysts, the moral/psychological meanings of dependency are accepted, not interrogated, assumed to be undesirable. Liberals of this school grant that welfare inevitably has some bad, dependency-creating effects, but claim that these are outweighed by other, good effects such as improved conditions for children, increased societal stability, and relief of suffering (Pearce 1990). Conservatives of this school, such as Charles Murray (1984), believe the negative effects of welfare outweigh the positive. The two camps argue above all about the question of incentives. Do AFDC stipends encourage women to have out-of-wedlock children? Do they discourage them from accepting jobs? Can reducing or withholding stipends serve as a stick to encourage recipients to stay in school, keep their children in school, get married?

Certainly, there are real and significant differences here, but there are also important similarities. Liberals and conservatives of both schools rarely situate the notion of dependency in its historical or economic context; nor do they interrogate its presuppositions. Neither group questions the assumption that independence is an unmitigated good nor its identification with wage labor. Many poverty and welfare analysts equivocate between an official position that "dependency" is a value-neutral term for receipt of (or need for) welfare and a usage that makes it a synonym for "pauperism."

These assumptions permeate the public sphere. In the current discussion of welfare dependency, it is increasingly claimed that "welfare mothers ought to work," a usage that tacitly defines work as wage-earning and child-raising as nonwork. Here we run up against a contradiction in the discourse of dependency: when the subject under consideration is teenage pregnancy, these mothers are cast as children; when the subject is welfare, they become adults who should be self-supporting.

None of the negative imagery about welfare dependency has gone uncontested, of course. Much of it was directly challenged in the mid-1960s by an organization of women welfare claimants, the National Welfare Rights Organization. NWRO women cast their relation with the welfare system as active rather than passive, a matter of claiming rights rather than receiving charity. They also insisted that their domestic labor was socially necessary and praiseworthy. Their perspective helped reconstruct the arguments for welfare, spurring poverty lawyers and radical intellectuals to develop a legal and political-theoretical basis for welfare as an entitlement and right. Edward

Sparer, a legal strategist for the welfare rights movement, challenged the dominant understanding of dependency: "The charge of antiwelfare politicians is that welfare makes the recipient 'dependent.' What this means is that the recipient depends on the welfare check for his [*sic*] material subsistence rather than upon some other source.... Whether that is good or bad depends on whether a better source of income is available.... The real problem ... is something entirely different. The recipient and the applicant traditionally have been dependent on the whim of the caseworker" (Sparer 1970–71; 71). The cure for welfare dependency, then, was welfare rights (Goodin 1988). Had the NWRO not been greatly weakened in the late 1970s, the revived discourse of pauperism in the 1980s could not have become hegemonic.

Even in the absence of a powerful National Welfare Rights Organization, many AFDC recipients maintained their own oppositional interpretation of welfare dependency. In their view, it is a social condition, not a psychological state or what a left-wing English dictionary of social welfare calls "enforced dependency," "the creation of a dependent class" as a result of "enforced reliance ... for necessary psychological or material resources" (Timms and Timms 1982, 55–56).

Meanwhile, during the period in which NWRO activism was at its height, New Left revisionist historians developed an interpretation of the welfare state as an apparatus of social control. They argued that what apologists portrayed as helping practices were actually modes of domination that created enforced dependency.[16] Another challenge to mainstream uses of "dependency" arose from a New Left school of international political economy. The context was the realization, after the first heady days of postwar decolonization, that politically independent former colonies remained economically dependent. In "dependency theory," radical theorists of "underdevelopment" used the concept of dependency to analyze the global neocolonial economic order from an antiracist and anti-imperialist perspective. In so doing, they resurrected the old preindustrial meaning of dependency as a subjected territory, seeking thereby to divest the term of its newer moral/psychological accretions and to retrieve the occluded dimensions of subjection and subordination.

What all these oppositional discourses share is a rejection of the dominant emphasis on dependency as an individual trait: they seek to shift the focus back to the social relations of subordination. But they no longer have much impact on mainstream discussion about welfare in the United States. On the contrary, with economic dependency now a synonym for poverty, and moral/psychological dependency now a personality disorder, talk of dependency as a social relation of subordination has become increasingly rare. Power and domination tend to disappear.[17]

Recapitulation

"Dependency," once a general term for all social relations of subordination, is now differentiated into several analytically distinct registers. In the economic register, its meaning has shifted from gaining one's livelihood by working for someone else to relying on charity or welfare for support; wage labor now confers independence. In the socio-legal register, the meaning of dependency as subsumption is unchanged, but its scope of reference and connotations have altered: once a socially approved majority condition, it became first a group-based status deemed proper for some classes of persons but not others and then shifted to designate (except in the case of children) an anomalous, highly stigmatized status of deviant and incompetent individuals. In the political register, dependency's meaning as subjection to an external governing power has remained relatively constant, but its evaluative connotations worsened as individual political rights and national sovereignty became normative. Meanwhile, with the emergence of a newer moral/psychological register, properties once ascribed to social relations were posited instead as inherent character traits of individuals or groups, and the connotations here, too, have worsened. This last register now claims an increasingly large proportion of the discourse, as if the social relations of dependency were being absorbed into personality. Symptomatically, erstwhile relational understandings have been hypostatized in a veritable portrait gallery of dependent personalities: first, housewives, paupers, natives, and slaves; then poor black teenage solo mothers.

These shifts in the semantics of dependency reflect some major socio-historical developments. One is the progressive differentiation of the official economy – that which is counted in the gross domestic product (GDP) – as a seemingly autonomous system that dominates social life. Before the rise of capitalism, any particular dependency was part of a net of dependencies, a single, continuous fabric of social hierarchies. Although women were subordinated and their labor often controlled by others, their labor was more visible, understood, and formally valued. With the emergence of religious and secular individualism, on the one hand, and industrial capitalism, on the other, a sharp, new dichotomy was constructed in which economic dependency and economic independence were opposed to one another. A crucial corollary of this dichotomy, and of the hegemony of wage labor in general, was the occlusion and devaluation of women's unpaid domestic and parenting labor.

The genealogy of dependency also expresses the modern emphasis on individual personality. Fear of dependency, both explicit and implicit, posits an ideal, independent personality in contrast to which those considered dependent are deviant. This contrast bears traces of a sexual division of labor that assigns men primary responsibility as providers or breadwinners and women primary responsibility as caretakers and nurturers and then treats the derivative personality patterns as fundamental. It is as if male breadwinners absorbed into their personalities the independence associated with their ideologically interpreted economic role, whereas the persons of female nurturers became saturated with the dependency of those for whom they care. The opposition between the independent and dependent personalities maps onto a whole series of hierarchical oppositions and dichotomies that are central in modern culture: masculine/feminine, public/private, work/care-giving, success/love, individual/community, economy/family, and competitive/self-sacrificing.

Toward Interdependence

Often, though not always, the various registers of dependency discourse are associated with political positions. Today the moral/psychological critique is associated with neoconservatism, the focus on the economic with liberalism. The Left is more likely to deny the existence of dependency as a problem and to presume that, given economic justice and freedom from domination, poor women would assume their "independent" potential. Feminists are just beginning to generate what we might call a transvaluative critique, influenced primarily by the welfare rights movement, which questions the opposition between dependence

and independence. We conclude with some modest efforts at developing that feminist vision.

A genealogy of dependency, obviously, does not automatically produce a political strategy. But it does suggest the limits of a response that presupposes, rather than challenges, the definition of the problem implicit in the expression "welfare dependency." An adequate response would need to question our received valuations and definitions of "dependency" and "independence" in order to allow new, emancipatory social visions to emerge.

We might start from the insight that all versions of the opposition between dependence and independence are ideological; these versions simultaneously reflect and dissimulate male-supremacist social organization. The feminist activist and scholar Diana Pearce formulates this point:

> The campaign against women's poverty should not be premised, implicitly or explicitly, on a false distinction between those who are economically "independent" and those who are "dependent." Frequently this contrast is drawn between women whose work is in the home, either unpaid or poorly paid (such as housekeepers and child-care workers), versus those whose work is in the marketplace, including some women as well as most men. Those in paid employment outside the home environment could not be "independent" without the support system provided by the home or its surrogates, such as "housewives" and day care centers. Such workers' "independence" could not occur without the hidden and unrecognized dependence the workers have on others. At the heart of this false dichotomy, of course, is the devaluation of the work that women perform, as those who take care of "dependents" as well as "independents." (Pearce 1990, 275)

Pearce's formulation suggests that one crucial element of a feminist response is to revalue the devalued side of the dichotomy (i.e., to rehabilitate dependency as a normal, even valuable, human quality). This sort of approach has been articulated relatively widely in the moral/psychological register, in feminist work that reconsiders the moral and social value of personality traits such as interpersonal sensitivity. We have been reminded that every pejoratively coded feminine trait can be positively recoded (e.g., worrying about the opinion of others is also sensitivity; being "other-directed" is also being good at building relationships; gossip is also the nurturing of social networks). Conversely, the canonical masculine-coded characteristics of independence, such as ambition and bravery, can be recoded perjoratively as ruthlessness, insensitivity, and inability to build intimate relationships. Dependency, thus, can be re-described as a virtue.

We must do this re-describing cautiously. We are reminded, often by welfare recipients themselves, that the existing conditions of claiming AFDC are wretched and damaging. "Welfare" in the United States – as opposed to dignified ways of getting help from the state – really does reduce self-esteem and autonomy. Re-describing the program will not change that.

Moreover, the contemporary feminist debate about the work of Carol Gilligan (1982), and particularly her suggestion that women have different moral approaches and ego development, reminds us of how easy it is to romanticize women's adaptations to powerlessness (Kittay and Meyers 1987; Kerber et al. 1986; Flanagan and Jackson 1987). It will not do to argue, as the Sears Corporation did several years ago in a much publicized sex discrimination case, that women were stuck in low-paying jobs because they did not aspire to more competitive, higher-paying jobs. Not only have such gender differences evidently been primarily conditioned by women's subordination, but it is dubious that they have rendered women morally superior, as our Victorian ancestors claimed. In addition, when women have developed their own ambitiousness, that very quality is likely to be perceived more negatively, as abrasiveness, than when it is displayed in men. All of this suggests that a simple revaluative strategy will not suffice.

To avoid these distortions, we might borrow a conceptual strategy from Herbert Marcuse. In *Eros and Civilization* (1955), he distinguished between "socially necessary repression" and "surplus repression". "Necessary repression" was defined as the quantity and quality of repression that any society – however libertarian, egalitarian, and democratic – would have to impose on unsocialized infants in the process of socialization. "Surplus repression," in contrast, was repression in excess – quantitative and qualitative – of the inevitable minimum, hence repression rooted in unjust and potentially remediable social institutions. Likewise, feminists interested in developing a transvaluative critique of dependence might distinguish socially necessary dependence from sur-

plus dependence. Socially necessary dependence would be the sort of dependence, or need for others' care, that is an inescapable feature of the human condition, experienced particularly intensely in the beginning and end of the life cycle, as well as frequently in between. Surplus dependence, in contrast, would be dependence that is rooted in unjust and potentially remediable social institutions.

On the basis of this distinction, feminists could safely argue to revalue socially necessary dependence. This means challenging the hyperbolic masculinist-capitalist view that the normal human condition is independence and that dependence is deviant. It entails building and institutionalizing respect for the activity of caring for those who are necessarily dependent (i.e., children, older persons, the sick, the troubled). Then, what is now the unpaid and unrecognized care-giving work of women would be revealed as crucial to society, and the surplus dependence that currently adheres to those who perform this work would be eliminated. The utopian end would be abolition of the current link between caring for dependents and thereby being rendered dependent oneself (Kittay 1993; Sapiro 1990).

A second, more far-reaching task is overcoming the dependence/independence dichotomy altogether. This dichotomy is negated by the most essential characteristics of the modern world, which create ever higher relations of interdependence, based on an ever increasing division of labor, from the global to the neighborhood level. Yet many existing welfare programs replicate or reinforce the dichotomy even in their administration. For example, AFDC rules prohibit sharing, insisting on dyadic relations between identified recipients and the bureaucracy; and many welfare systems ideologically identify some people as 100 percent dependent and others as 100 percent independent. It is in our broad social interest to do the opposite: to spread responsibility and the freedom to take help from others. We know, for example, that children are less likely to be abused or neglected when more than one adult contributes to their welfare; that women with large circles of friends and acquaintances are much less vulnerable to abuse. Moreover, only by challenging this fundamental dichotomy can we appreciate giving and taking help without losing that which is valuable in the work ethic. "Dependency" cannot be redefined without also redefining "work," for otherwise welfare programs meet strenuous political opposition from those who are aware that they work hard and earn little while others seem to them lazy and irresponsible. We need, in fact, to historicize work and redefine it so that it is understood to include non-wage-earning labor; to elaborate historical change in what has counted as work, reconsidering a variety of labor such as housework and child care, children's activity in attending school, the labor of artists, and the effort that goes into nurturance of friends and maintenance of social networks. This means overcoming not only arbitrary divisions of labor but also arbitrary divisions of labor's meanings.

Some contemporary US welfare rights activists have adopted this strategy, continuing the NWRO tradition. Pat Gowens, for example, expresses such a feminist reinterpretation of "dependency": "The vast majority of mothers of *all classes and all educational levels* 'depends' on another income. It may come from child support... or from a husband who earns $20,000 while she averages $7,000. But 'dependence' more accurately defines dads who count on women's unwaged labor to raise children and care for the home. Surely, 'dependence' doesn't define the single mom who does it all: child-rearing, home-making, and bring in the money (one way or another). When caregiving is valued and paid, when dependence is not a dirty word, and interdependence is the norm – only then will we make a dent in poverty" (Gowens 1991, 90–91).

Notes

1 Another part of the story, of course, concerns the word "welfare." In this article, our focus is US political culture and thus US English usage. Our findings should be of more general interest, however, as some other languages have similar meanings embedded in analogous words. In this article we have of necessity used British sources for the early stages of our genealogy, which spans the sixteenth and seventeenth centuries. We assume that these meanings of "dependency" were brought to the "New World" and were formative for the early stages of US political culture.

2 The term "genealogy" is today associated with Michel Foucault (1984). Our approach differs from Foucault's, however, in two crucial respects: we seek to contextualize discursive shifts in relation to broad institutional and socio-structural shifts, and we welcome normative political reflection (Fraser 1989).

3 In preindustrial society, moreover, the reverse dependence of the master upon his men was widely recognized. The historian Christopher Hill evoked that understanding when he characterized the "essence" of feudal society as "the bond of loyalty and dependence between lord and man" (1972, 32). Here "dependence" means interdependence.

4 Neither English nor US dictionaries report any pejorative uses of the term before the early twentieth century. In fact, some leading preindustrial definitions were explicitly positive, implying trusting, relying, or counting on another, the predecessors of today's "dependable."

5 In practice, of course, these preindustrial arrangements did not always provide satisfactorily for the poor. In the fourteenth century, new, stronger states began to limit the freedom of movement of the destitute and codify older informal distinctions between those worthy and unworthy of assistance. When the English Poor Law of 1601 confirmed this latter distinction, it was already considered shameful to ask for public help. But the culture neither disapproved of dependency nor valorized individual independence. Rather, the aim of the statutes was to return the mobile, uprooted, and excessively "independent" poor to their local parishes or communities, and hence to enforce their traditional dependencies.

6 For example, they were central to the Putney Debates of the English Civil War.

7 One might say that this redefinition foregrounded wage labor as a new form of property, namely property in one's own labor power. This conception was premised on what C.B. Macpherson called "possessive individualism," the assumption of an individual's property in his [*sic*] own person (1962). Leading to the construction of wages as an entitlement, this approach was overwhelmingly male. It represented a loss of systemic critique, a sense of independence gained by narrowing the focus to the individual worker and leaving behind aspirations for collective independence from capital.

8 In the sixteenth century the term "pauper" had meant simply a poor person and, in law, one who was allowed to sue or defend in court without paying costs (*OED*). Two centuries later, it took on a more restricted definition, denoting a new class of persons who subsisted on poor relief instead of wages and who were held to be deviant and blameworthy.

9 Actually, there are many variants within the family of images that personify subjection in the industrial era. Among these are related but not identical stereotypes of the Russian serf, the Caribbean slave, the slave in the United States, and Native Americans. Moreover, there are distinct male and female stereotypes within

each of those categories. We simplify here in order to highlight the features that are common to all these images, notably the idea of natural subjection rooted in race. We focus especially on stereotypes that portray African Americans as personifications of dependency because of their historic importance and contemporary resonance in the US language of social welfare.

10 The evolution of the term "native" neatly encapsulates this process. Its original meaning in English, dating from about 1450, was tied to dependency: "one born in bondage; a born thrall," but without racial meaning. Two centuries later it carried the additional meaning of colored or black (*OED*).

11 In the United States, the family wage ideal held greater sway among whites than among blacks, and was at variance with actual practice for all of the poor and working classes. Moreover, both employed and non-employed wives continued to perform work once considered crucial to a family economy.

12 Continuing from preindustrial usage was the assumption that fathers headed households and that other household members were represented by them, as codified in the legal doctrine of coverture. The socio-legal and political dependency of wives enforced their new economic dependency, since under coverture even married women who were wage workers could not legally control their wages.

13 The Social Security Board propagandized for Social Security Old Age Insurance (the program today called "Social Security") precisely because, at first, it did not seem more earned or dignified than public assistance. To make Social Security more acceptable, the Board worked to stigmatize public assistance, even pressuring states to keep stipends low (Cates 1983).

14 Men on "general relief" are sometimes also included in that designation; their treatment by the welfare system is usually as bad or worse.

15 The norm, moreover, was racially marked, as white women were usually portrayed as erring on the side of excessive dependence, while black women were typically charged with excessive independence.

16 The New Left critique bore some resemblance to the NWRO critique, but the overlap was only partial. The historians of social control told their story mainly from the perspective of the "helpers" and cast recipients as almost entirely passive. They thereby occluded the agency of actual or potential welfare claimants in articulating needs, demanding rights, and making claims. For a fuller discussion of the social control critique, see Gordon (1990b). On needs claims, see Fraser (1990) and Nelson (1990).

17 For an argument that President Clinton's recent neo-liberal discourse continues to individualize dependency, see Fraser (1993).

References

Abbott, Edith, and Sophonisba P. Breckinridge. 1921. *The Administration of the Aid-to-Mothers Law in Illinois*. Publication no. 82. Washington, D.C.: U.S. Children's Bureau.

American Psychiatric Association. 1987. *Diagnostic and Statistical Manual of Mental Disorders*, 3rd ed. Washington, D.C.: American Psychiatric Association.

Bakke, E. Wight. 1940a. *Citizens without Work: A Study of the Effects of Unemployment upon Workers' Social Relations and Practices*. New Haven: Yale University Press.

—— 1940b. *The Unemployed Worker: A Study of the Task of Making a Living without a Job*. New Haven: Yale University Press.

Boydston, Jeanne. 1991. *Home and Work: Housework, Wages, and the Ideology of Labor in the Early Republic*. New York: Oxford.

Brandt, Lilian. 1932. *An Impressionistic View of the Winter of 1930–31 in New York City*. New York: Welfare Council of New York City.

Brown, Josephine Chapin. 1940. *Public Relief, 1929–1939*. New York: Henry Holt.

Bruno, Frank J. 1948. *Trends in Social Work*. New York: Columbia University Press.

Cates, Jerry R. 1983. *Insuring Inequality: Administrative Leadership in Social Security, 1935–54*. Ann Arbor: University of Michigan Press.

Dowling, Colette. 1981. *The Cinderella Complex: Women's Hidden Fear of Independence*. New York: Summit Books.

Flanagan, Owen, and Kathryn Jackson. 1987. "Justice, Care, and Gender: The Kohlberg–Gilligan Debate Revisited." *Ethics* 97: 622–37.

Folbre, Nancy. 1991. "The Unproductive Housewife: Her Evolution in Nineteenth-Century Economic Thought." *Signs: Journal of Women in Culture and Society* 16, no. 3: 463–84.

Foucault, Michel. 1984. "Nietzsche, Genealogy, History." Pp. 76–100 in *The Foucault Reader*, ed. Paul Rabinow. New York: Pantheon.

Fraser, Nancy. 1987. "Women, Welfare, and the Politics of Need Interpretation." *Hypatia: A Journal of Feminist Philosophy* 2, no. 1: 103–21.

—— 1989. *Unruly Practices: Power, Discourse, and Gender in Contemporary Social Theory*. Minneapolis: University of Minnesota Press.

—— 1990. "Struggle over Needs: Outline of a Socialist-Feminist Critical Theory of Late-Capitalist

Political Culture." Pp. 199–225 in *Women*, ed. Gordon.

—— 1993. "Clintonism, Welfare, and the Antisocial Wage: The Emergence of a Neoliberal Political Imaginary." *Rethinking Marxism* 6, no. 1: 9–23.

Fraser, Nancy, and Linda Gordon. 1992. "Contract versus Charity: Why Is There No Social Citizenship in the United States?" *Socialist Review* 22, no. 3: 45–68.

Friedan, Betty. 1963. *The Feminine Mystique*. New York: Norton.

Gibbons, Mary L. 1933. "Family Life Today and Tomorrow." *Proceedings* (National Conference of Catholic Charities) 19:133–68.

Gilder, George. 1981. *Wealth and Poverty*. New York: Basic Books.

Gilligan, Carol. 1982. *In a Different Voice: Psychological Theory and Women's Development*. Cambridge, Mass.: Harvard University Press.

Goodin, Robert E. 1988. *Reasons for Welfare: The Political Theory of the Welfare State*. Princeton, N.J.: Princeton University Press.

Gordon, Linda, ed. 1990a. *Women, the State, and Welfare*. Madison: University of Wisconsin Press.

—— 1990b. "The New Feminist Scholarship on the Welfare State." Pp. 9–35 in *Women*, ed. Gordon.

—— 1992. "Social Insurance and Public Assistance: The Influence of Gender in Welfare Thought in the United States, 1890–1935." *American Historical Review* 97, no. 1: 19–54.

Gowens, Pat. 1991. "Welfare, Learnfare – Unfair! A Letter to My Governor." *Ms.* (Sept.–Oct.), 90–91.

Gundersen, Joan R. 1987. "Independence, Citizenship, and the American Revolution." *Signs: Journal of Women in Culture and Society* 13, no. 1: 59–77.

Haynes, M. 1988. "Pharmacist Involvement in a Chemical-Dependency Rehabilitation Program." *American Journal of Hospital Pharmacy* 45, no. 10: 2099–101.

Hill, Christopher. 1972. *The World Turned Upside Down: Radical Ideas during the English Revolution*. New York: Viking.

Howard, Donald S. 1943. *The WPA and Federal Relief Policy*. New York: Russell Sage.

Jencks, Christopher. 1992. *Rethinking Social Policy: Race, Poverty, and the Underclass*. Cambridge, Mass.: Harvard University Press.

Kerber, Linda K., Catherine G. Green, Eleanor E. Maccoby, Zella Luria, Carol B. Stack, and Carol Gilligan. 1986. "On *In a Different Voice*: An Interdisciplinary Forum." *Signs: Journal of Women in Culture and Society* 11, no. 2: 304–33.

Kittay, Eva. 1993. We Are All Some Mother's Child: Vulnerability, Equality, and the Dependency Worker. Unpublished manuscript.

Kittay, Eva, and Diana T. Meyers, eds. 1987. *Women and Moral Theory*. Totowa, N.J.: Rowman and Littlefield.

Land, Hilary. 1980. "The Family Wage." *Feminist Review* 6:55–77.

Laslett, Peter. 1971. *The World We Have Lost: England before the Industrial Age*. New York: Charles Scribner.

Macpherson, C.B. 1962. *The Political Theory of Possessive Individualism: Hobbes to Locke*. Oxford: Oxford University Press.

Marcuse, Herbert. 1955. *Eros and Civilization: A Philosophical Inquiry into Freud*. Boston: Beacon Press.

Mead, Lawrence. 1986. *Beyond Entitlement: The Social Obligations of Citizenship*. New York: Free Press.

Milwaukee County Welfare Rights Organization. 1972. *Welfare Mothers Speak Out*. New York: Norton.

Murray, Charles. 1984. *Losing Ground: American Social Policy, 1950–1980*. New York: Basic Books.

National Conference of Charities and Correction. 1890s–1920s. *Proceedings*.

Nelson, Barbara J. 1990. "The Origins of the Two-Channel Welfare State: Workmen's Compensation and Mothers' Aid." Pp. 123–51 in *Women*, ed. Gordon.

Pearce, Diana. 1990. "Welfare Is Not *for* Women: Why the War on Poverty Cannot Conquer the Feminization of Poverty." Pp. 265–79 in *Women*, ed. Gordon.

Pope, Jacqueline. 1989. *Biting the Hand That Feeds Them: Organizing Women on Welfare at the Grass Roots Level*. New York: Praeger.

Quadagno, Jill. 1988. "From Old-Age Assistance to Supplemental Social Security Income: The Political Economy of Relief in the South, 1935–1972." Pp. 235–63 in *The Politics of Social Policy in the United States*, ed. Margaret Weir, Ann Shola Orloff, and Theda Skocpol. Princeton, N.J.: Princeton University Press.

Quayle, Dan. 1992. "Excerpts from Vice President's Speech on Cities and Poverty." *New York Times*, May 20.

Rainwater, Lee, and William L. Yancey. 1967. *The Moynihan Report and the Politics of Controversy*. Cambridge, Mass.: MIT Press.

Sapiro, Virginia. 1990. "The Gender Basis of American Social Policy." Pp. 36–54 in *Women*, ed. Gordon.

Smith, Joan. 1984. "The Paradox of Women's Poverty: Wage-Earning Women and Economic Transformation." *Signs: Journal of Women in Culture and Society* 10, no. 2: 291–310.

Sparer, Edward V. 1970–71. "The Right to Welfare." Pp. 65–93 in *The Rights of Americans: What They Are – What They Should Be*, ed. Norman Dorsen. New York: Pantheon.

Stacey, Judith. 1987. "Sexism by a Subtler Name? Postindustrial Conditions and Postfeminist Consciousness in the Silicon Valley." *Socialist Review* 96:7–28.

—— 1990. *Brave New Families: Stories of Domestic Upheaval in Late Twentieth Century America*. New York: Basic Books.

Timms, Noel, and Rita Timms. 1982. *Dictionary of Social Welfare*. London: Routledge and Kegan Paul.

Vaile, Gertrude. 1934. "Public Relief." Pp. 19–40 in *College Women and the Social Sciences*, ed. Herbert Elmer Mills. New York: John Day.

Warner, Amos Griswold. 1894–1930 editions. *American Charities and Social Work*. New York: Thomas Y. Crowell.

West, Guida. 1981. *The National Welfare Rights Movement: The Social Protest of Poor Women*. New York: Praeger.

Weston, Kath. 1991. *Families We Choose: Lesbians, Gays, Kinship*. New York: Columbia University Press.

Williams, Raymond. 1976. *Keywords: A Vocabulary of Culture and Society*. Oxford: Oxford University Press.

Wilson, William Julius. 1987. *The Truly Disadvantaged: The Inner City, the Underclass, and Public Policy*. Chicago: University of Chicago Press.

40

Bearing the Consequences of Belief

Peter Jones

I The Issue

Should people suffer social disadvantage because of their beliefs? There is a strong element in the liberal tradition which holds that they should not. According to that tradition, people should be free to adopt and to live in accordance with whatever beliefs they find persuasive. People can be considered 'free' to adopt and to live in accordance with a set of beliefs only if they are not subject to persecution and harassment for holding those beliefs. If there are any 'settled convictions' of liberalism, this commitment to freedom of belief is surely one of them. One offshoot of that conviction is an antipathy to discrimination against people on grounds of religious faith in matters such as employment and education. In some societies discrimination against people on grounds of religious faith is legally prohibited along with discrimination on other grounds such as race and sex. In other societies, religious discrimination remains legally unproscribed but is still frowned upon in their official and unofficial cultures and may well become the subject of legislative action in the near future. Yet just what ought to count as 'discrimination' in relation to religious belief and just what 'toleration' requires of us are often far from clear. Consider the following celebrated case.[1]

Mr Ahmad, a devout Muslim, was employed as a full-time school teacher by the Inner London Education Authority (ILEA). His faith required that, if possible, he should attend a mosque for prayers on Friday afternoons. At first Mr Ahmad taught in a district too far from a mosque to enable him to fulfil this injunction. But when he was transferred by ILEA to a district within reasonable distance of a mosque, he insisted that, thenceforth, he should attend the mosque each Friday afternoon. His doing so meant that he was absent for the first three-quarters of an hour of teaching time on Friday afternoons and his absence had to be covered by other teachers. ILEA advised the head-teachers of the schools at which Mr Ahmad taught that he should not be given permission to absent himself in this way. However, Mr Ahmad continued to attend the mosque.[2] Eventually ILEA informed Mr Ahmad that, if he insisted on absenting himself on Friday afternoons, he would have to relinquish his appointment as a full-time teacher. The Authority offered to re-employ him as a part-time teacher for $4\frac{1}{2}$ days a week though, of course, that would have meant a commensurate reduction in his salary. Mr Ahmad found the offer of part-time employment unacceptable and resigned from his full-time post.

Mr Ahmad contended that his treatment by ILEA amounted to unfair dismissal and appealed to an industrial tribunal. The tribunal dismissed his appeal, a decision that was subsequently upheld by the Employment Appeal Tribunal. Mr Ahmad then took his case to the Court of Appeal where, by a majority decision, his appeal was again rejected, the dissenting judgment in his favour coming from Scarman L.J. Finally Mr Ahmad

Originally published in *Journal of Political Philosophy* 2 (1994): 24–43. Reprinted by permission of Blackwell Publishing Ltd.

petitioned the European Court of Human Rights but still without success; his application was found by the European Commission to be manifestly ill-founded and declared inadmissible.[3]

Was Mr Ahmad treated fairly? My concern here is not with the legal niceties of his case which turned, in large part, upon the precise interpretation that should be placed upon section 30 of the British 1944 Education Act and section 9 of ILEA's staff code, both of which made provision for the religious convictions of teachers. Rather I want to focus on the general point of principle underlying the case. In part, this was a question of what constituted equitable treatment of different faiths. This was a worry expressed by Scarman L.J. in the Court of Appeal who pointed out that the established five-day working week created no problem for Jewish teachers in relation to Saturday or for Christian teachers in relation to Sundays. But a rigid adherence to the five-day working week would mean that a devout Muslim, who took seriously his duty to attend Friday prayers, could never become a full-time teacher.[4]

However, beneath this question of equity lay a more fundamental issue. On whom should the 'costs' of belief fall? Who should bear the consequences of belief? Should the inconvenience and the loss of working time involved in a teacher's attending an act of worship during the working day be borne by the education authority? Or should the costs consequent upon belief fall upon the believer himself? In the Court of Appeal, Lord Denning M.R. and Scarman L.J. differed not only in their interpretation of the legal details that bore upon the case but also in their general approach to this question. Lord Denning, while 'upholding religious freedom to the full', clearly regarded the demands of Mr Ahmad's beliefs as a burden that Mr Ahmad should bear and construed his claim that he should be able to attend the mosque, on full pay, as a demand that the Muslim community be given 'preferential treatment over the great majority of the people'.[5] By contrast, Scarman L.J. argued that the educational system should be sufficiently flexible to accommodate the beliefs and observances of all religions and held that, if it did not accommodate a demand like Mr Ahmad's, Muslims could properly complain of 'discrimination'.[6]

In Mr Ahmad's case, then, it is not enough to be told that we should not engage in religious discrimination for it is not clear what should count as 'discrimination' in a case like his. Nor is anything

settled by insisting that all religious beliefs should be 'tolerated', for the issue here is not so much whether or why we should tolerate Mr Ahmad's beliefs, but rather of 'how' his beliefs should be tolerated, of what toleration itself requires. Is it enough that we simply leave Mr Ahmad to pursue his faith and to bear whatever burdens that brings his way? Or should a society arrange things so that believers are spared the incidental but adverse effects that might otherwise be consequent upon their beliefs?

The general issue underlying Mr Ahmad's case arises in many other forms in the contemporary world. For example, is it acceptable that orthodox Jews should find their employment opportunities curtailed because they refuse to work on Saturdays? Should Christian Sabbatarian traders have to suffer commercial disadvantage, relative to their non-Sabbatarian competitors, because they refuse to trade on Sundays or should law prohibit all commercial activity on Sundays so that Sabbatarians and non-Sabbatarians enjoy 'equal terms of trade'?[7] Should churches be taxed like other organisations or should they receive tax concessions so that their members do not incur financial burdens because they possess religious beliefs? Should people be safeguarded from conduct which they find offensive because of their religious beliefs, or should their offended condition be regarded as a consequence of their beliefs which they should therefore have to endure? Should religious groups who want their children to be separately educated be required to meet the additional expense that that involves, or should their separate education be financed entirely from the public purse?

In contemporary western societies these issues are likely to arise most frequently in relation to minorities, several of whom will be ethnic as well as religious minorities. It is worth noting therefore that the question of beliefs and their consequences is not inherently one about the status of minorities. In principle, it could be a majority that is required to suffer disadvantages consequent upon its beliefs. For example, in a society in which the majority were Sabbatarians and in which people were required to bear the consequences of their beliefs, it would be the majority that would find itself commercially disadvantaged relative to the minority.

Nor is this issue limited to religious belief. In this article, I shall confine myself to the case of religious belief since the issue of consequences arises particularly obviously and acutely in relation to that form of belief. But the question of who should bear the consequences can arise in relation to any sort of belief that is treated as a matter of private conviction. 'Private' here obviously does not mean 'behind closed doors'; people can and do make public expressions of the beliefs with which I am concerned. Nor does 'private' necessarily mean 'individual'. We might treat groups rather than individuals as the bearers of beliefs; that would make no material difference to the issue of consequences. Rather, these beliefs are appropriately described as 'private' only because and in so far as a society treats them as outside the proper realm of public decision.

A society cannot remove all matters of belief from the public domain. Some matters have to be the subject of public decision and the outcomes of those decisions must be regarded as matters of public responsibility. Suppose, for example, that the majority of a society believes that, for reasons of social justice, taxation should be increased while the minority strongly opposes any such increase. If taxation is then increased, it will hardly do for the minority to argue that, since the increase in taxation is a consequence of the beliefs of the majority, only the majority should have to pay that increase. That would not do because taxation is properly a matter of public decision and public decisions properly apply to all members of the public. Henceforth, when I use the term 'belief' I shall use it to refer only to those beliefs that a society treats as matters of private conviction. I shall pass over the question of why we should not treat all matters of belief as properly the subjects of public decision.

Generally the liberal tradition has held, or perhaps taken for granted, that people should bear the consequences of their beliefs. John Rawls will serve as an example.[8] Indeed, Rawls is a particularly apt example since he is willing to go a considerable way in requiring the members of a society to take responsibility for one another's well-being. He regards the distribution of natural abilities amongst people as morally arbitrary; no one has a claim to a better lot in life merely because he or she has been favoured by nature. Thus, a just society would distribute its resources so that those of its members who had been least favoured by nature were not materially disadvantaged because of that fact about themselves. In particular, Rawls's difference principle allows inequality in the distribution of income and wealth only in so far as that inequality works to the advantage of the least

well-off group in society. So Rawls does not allow that individuals should have simply to endure whatever consequences happen to follow upon their possessing or not possessing natural abilities.

However, he handles people's beliefs quite differently from their natural abilities. He places individuals' beliefs, including their religious beliefs, within what he calls their 'conceptions of the good'. In Rawls's scheme of things, the basic rules of a society are set without reference to the different content of people's conceptions of the good. Subject to the difference principle, liberties and resources are apportioned to people equally. People are then at liberty, within the structure established by that just distribution, to pursue whatever conception of the good they choose. That may mean, of course, that some conceptions of the good – those demanding more resources or more than one's allotted portion of liberty – are more difficult to fulfil than others. But individuals must take responsibility for their conceptions of the good and there can be no complaint of 'injustice' merely because a more demanding conception is harder to realise than a less demanding conception.[9] Thus, if some beliefs turn out to be more demanding than others, and therefore less easy to fulfil, that is an outcome that the believers have to endure. By the same token, individuals have to look to themselves and to other like-minded individuals to cope with the consequences of their beliefs. They cannot, in fairness, impose those consequences upon others.

Why should that be? Why should people bear the consequences of their beliefs? Why does justice not require us to even out those consequences so that no body of believers is more or less well placed than any other?

II Foundations

Belief and choice

One consideration which may be invoked to justify our making people bear the consequences of their beliefs is choice. People do not choose their race or their sex and it is unfair that their opportunities in life should be prejudiced by these unchosen features of themselves. Similarly people do not choose their abilities and talents – in so far as those abilities and talents are determined by each individual's genetic endowment rather than by the subsequent development of that endowment. We might argue therefore, like Rawls, that a society should try to arrange things so that those who have not been favoured in the genetic lottery do not suffer economic and social disadvantage as a consequence of their having been disadvantaged by nature. By contrast, people's beliefs are not a given part of themselves like their race or sex or genetic make-up. People choose what they believe and they can therefore be held responsible for what they believe and, by extension, for the consequences of what they believe. The consequences of people's beliefs are the consequences of their choices; they must therefore shoulder the burden of those consequences themselves rather than expect that burden to be shouldered by others.[10]

In some ways the language of choice goes quite naturally with that of belief. For example, we might casually remark to someone, 'if that is what you choose to believe, that is up to you'. But there is also reason to question whether people can really be said to 'choose' what they believe.

Firstly, people are greatly influenced in what they believe by the social context in which they develop. In reality, it might be said, people do not adopt beliefs via a process of autonomous, critical reflection. They simply imbibe beliefs from the social and cultural context in which they find themselves. Thus, although people do not come into the world already possessed of beliefs, the process of socialisation ensures that their beliefs are just as 'unchosen' as their race or their sex.[11]

This is a large and complicated matter. In so far as the link between socialisation and belief is an empirical matter, different things are likely to be true of different circumstances and different individuals and, perhaps also, different beliefs. There is reason to resist the claim that, in Richard Rorty's phrase, socialisation 'goes all the way down' for everyone, everywhere.[12] Clearly many people can and do shed beliefs which were part of their upbringing, and they can and do adopt beliefs that were not a part of their upbringing. This fluidity is more likely to characterise the sort of society with which we are concerned here: a plural society which, just because it is plural, causes its members to be aware of beliefs other than those which form their immediate context. However I can do little to settle this issue here and I do not wish to deny the tremendous importance of socialisation in the formation of beliefs. I suggest only that there is reason to hesitate before accepting that people are the entirely helpless victims of inherited systems of belief.

How we regard this issue is likely to be biased by how we conceptualise it. I have characterised it in terms of beliefs, but nowadays it is also likely to be characterised by reference to 'cultures'. It is part of the idea of a 'culture' that it is something which envelops those who belong to it. Individuals do not make their own cultures, nor do they choose a culture. Their culture is something that they find themselves within and the culture to which they belong constitutes part of their given identity. The idea of 'choosing' a culture has the same absurdity about it as the idea of deciding to start a tradition. Cultures and traditions do not work like that. Thus, in so far as we treat people's beliefs as ingredients of their culture, we will be predisposed to treat those beliefs as part of their given identity rather than features of their lives over which they have control.

However, we should not allow our thought to be tyrannised by concepts like 'culture'. That term takes in a large array of very different aspects of people's lives – their language, diet, manners, mores, dress, and so on. Some of these, such as language and dress, would not normally be objects of critical reflection. But beliefs have epistemic content. They make claims about the way the world is and about how we should behave in it. They can be assessed as true or false, more or less supported by evidence, more or less plausible, and so on. Beliefs are therefore open to critical appraisal in a way that is quite irrelevant to many of the other ingredients of culture. Anyone who takes his beliefs seriously must be concerned about the truth or merit of their content. He cannot regard his own beliefs as a mere quirk of culture. A person's culture may be invoked in a *causal* explanation of his beliefs, but it cannot be offered by the believer himself as a *reason* for his believing what he does. In addition, the notion, which has been voiced in some quarters recently, that it is somehow disloyal and traitorous to do other than accept the truth or the rightness of the beliefs that form a part of one's inherited culture is both silly and sinister.[13]

Once again, I do not mean to be dismissive of the significance of culture. I mean only to question whether societies and cultures imprison their members in systems of belief from which there is no escape. At the very least, the appeals to socialisation and culture would seem insufficiently conclusive to remove all reason for holding people responsible for their beliefs.

However, there is a second and less contingent way in which the idea of 'choosing beliefs' may be questioned. Do I 'choose' what to believe? Do I not simply believe? I do not choose to believe Pythagoras's theorem; I simply believe it. I do not choose to believe that New York is in the United States; I just believe that that is where it is. The use of 'choice' in conjunction with 'belief' implies an act of choosing which is separate from that of believing: we choose what to believe and then we believe it. But that is not how belief works. I can choose to go to France for a holiday and that act of choosing can be distinguished from my subsequently going to France. I can decide to buy a car and that act of deciding can be distinguished from my actually buying the car. But there is not a similar act of choosing or deciding to believe which is distinguishable from a subsequent and separate act of believing. There is just believing. I may, of course, gradually come to believe something and my beliefs may be the outcome of a long process of deliberation. But 'coming to believe' is not the same as choosing to believe something and then going on to believe it.

In addition, 'choosing to believe' implies an optionality of a sort that is not normally a part of the believing process. I choose to go to France for a holiday when I might have chosen to go to Spain or Italy. Similarly I choose to buy a car when I might have chosen to buy a yacht or to have spent my money on something else. But it is not similarly open to me to choose to believe that the square on the hypotenuse is not equal to the sum of the squares of the two other sides of a right-angled triangle. Nor can I simply opt to believe that New York is in Canada or Mexico rather than in the USA. Thus, when people are told that their beliefs are the offspring of their choices, they may reasonably object that, on the contrary, they have no choice about what they believe. They cannot but believe what seems to them to be the case. Their beliefs are no more at their disposal than their physical make-up.

At this point, it may be that we should begin to distinguish between different sorts of belief. What is morally right or what is religiously true are not, it might be said, matters on which people find themselves confronted with indisputable states of affairs which they cannot but recognise. Thus, in these areas, there remains a significant element of choice. Even if there is no scope for people to choose what to believe about Pythagoras's theorem or about the location of New York, there is scope for them to choose which God or gods to believe in. However, even that is disputable. Some be-

lievers would protest that their religious beliefs are so manifestly true to themselves, even if not to others, that they have no choice but to believe. Those who accept that there is scope for different people to arrive intelligibly at different beliefs in religious matters might still object that the language of choice misdescribes the process by which particular individuals come to hold particular beliefs.[14] Since the role of choice, or of processes akin to choice, in believing is likely to remain controversial, let me add one further comment on the alleged centrality of choice to the issue of consequences.

Even if some feature of a person is a product of that person's choice, it does not follow that others are justified in treating that person any old how in respect of that choice. Suppose we accept that I have the right to adopt any religion that I 'choose'; it does not follow that others are free to persecute me for my religious beliefs just because those beliefs are 'chosen'. On the contrary, it is implicit in my having a *right* to adopt the religion I choose that others are duty-bound not to persecute me in that way. If we move from outright persecution to discrimination, we may still say that my having chosen a particular religion does not justify others' discriminating against me in matters such as employment and education. If I have the right to adopt whatever religion I choose, my choice ought to be respected and others ought not to deprive me of opportunities because they dislike the particular choice I have made.

Of course, much depends on how we define the right at issue here. Assuming that the right to adopt and to pursue a religion is, in jurisprudential terminology, a claim as well as a liberty, the scope of that claim can be drawn more or less generously. Libertarians, for example, would normally accept that the right to religious liberty constitutes a claim upon others to refrain from religious persecution, but not a claim which properly limits the freedom of employers to hire and fire whomsoever they choose, for whatever reason they choose. We should note, however, that the libertarian's objection centres on the right of private employers to determine the make-up of their own workforce. It is not therefore special to laws prohibiting religious discrimination and counts equally against the legal prohibition of racial and sexual discrimination.[15] But, if we do not share this general aversion to antidiscrimination measures, it does not seem extravagant to hold that, if the freedom to adopt and to pursue a religion has the status of a

fundamental right, people should not have to suffer unfavourable treatment because of the use they
make of that fundamental right. But that, in turn,
simply takes us back to the question of what is to
count as 'suffering unfavourable treatment'. If
people have a right to hold the beliefs they do –
whether or not those beliefs are 'chosen' – does
requiring them to bear the consequences of their
beliefs amount to a violation of that right? We may
find a clearer answer to that question if we shift
our focus from the idea of choice to that of freedom of belief.

Freedom of belief

I shall simply take for granted that people should
be accorded freedom of belief and leave unstated
the many cogent arguments that may be urged in
favour of that freedom. That people should possess freedom of belief is not an extravagant assumption in this context for, in the absence of
that freedom, the issue of who should bear the
diverse consequences of diverse beliefs could
hardly arise. By 'freedom of belief' I understand
not only the liberty to believe but also the liberty
to act upon one's beliefs. Limits may have to be
imposed upon that freedom and, in a plural society, just where those limits should fall, and why,
are likely to be controversial matters. Again, I shall
not pursue those matters here. Rather, I want to
suggest that, if we accord people freedom of belief,
it is reasonable to require them to bear the consequences of what they believe.

Freedom of belief, I have said, includes not just
the freedom to believe but also the freedom to
shape one's life in accordance with one's belief.
Indeed, it is the latter freedom that has been the
more significant in that it has been the more vulnerable. It is, of course, possible to control what
people believe – sadly, more so in this century than
in any other. But, for the most part, what goes on
in the recesses of people's minds has been of less
concern to others and less vulnerable to interference and suppression than the external manifestations of belief. In particular, given that our
concern is with the consequences of belief, it is
not merely believing but 'practising' one's belief
that is more pertinent.

Now as long as my beliefs shape only my life,
I can reasonably keep others at bay. My beliefs,
I can protest, are properly no one's concern but my
own. In particular, as long as I bear the consequences of my belief, I can maintain that my

beliefs remain purely my affair. However, if I
expect others to bear those consequences, that
ceases to be true. What I believe then affects
lives other than my own. The more burdensome
the consequences of my beliefs, the more those
beliefs will burden the lives of others. That provides reason for others having some control over
what I believe. Of course, they may be unable to
alter what I believe and it may be highly undesirable that they should if they could. But they are
capable of controlling how far I *act* on my beliefs
and, if they are going to have to meet the costs of
my actions, why should they not spare themselves
that expense by preventing my acting in costly
ways? In other words, why should they not be
entitled to limit my freedom rather than bear its
consequences? If my acting on my beliefs significantly affects the lives of others, it becomes implausible for me to claim an inviolable and
exclusive right to determine how I should behave
in matters of religious faith. The force of this line
of argument is all the greater for its arising in a
context of conflicting beliefs. It is bad enough
that others should have to bear the costs of my
freely chosen actions. How much worse that they
should have to bear the consequences of my beliefs, which beliefs they may reckon (perhaps with
good reason) to be false, wrong or evil. How
much stronger the case for protecting people
from becoming the unwilling 'victims' of another's
freedom.

It will not do to reply that any such pre-emptive
strategy should be vetoed in the name of 'freedom', for it is not just my freedom that is at
stake. If others have to bear the consequences of
my beliefs, my use of my freedom can unilaterally
diminish the freedom of others. We should be
concerned not only with freedom but also with
its equitable distribution and it is difficult to see
how an arrangement which places the freedom
of some at the mercy of the freedom of others
can be consistent with any standard of equitable
distribution.

Thus, I suggest, the reason why people should
bear the consequences of their beliefs is that
that is a natural concomitant of their enjoying freedom of belief. Those who claim that freedom must
accept responsibility for the use they make of it. We
could, of course, turn this around and argue that
people have to bear the consequence of one
another's beliefs and that freedom of belief should
be curtailed accordingly. But that, I suspect, is an
option which will appeal to no one.[16]

Promoting diversity

The argument I have developed here may be regarded as altogether too negative in spirit. Is not the diversity of a plural society something that we should cherish and celebrate rather than merely tolerate? It is enough merely to refrain from persecuting or impeding ways of life other than our own? Should we not take positive steps to see that all ways of life flourish? This more positive, promotive approach to diversity might be used to argue that the consequences of belief should be treated as a burden to be borne by society as a whole. By taking collective responsibility for those consequences, we will ensure that no system of belief labours under any special disadvantage and that a hundred flowers can bloom.

There are many forms of human diversity and many of those forms are quite intelligibly cherished and fostered. A society may be said to be richer for having a diversity of forms of literature, of music, of food, and so on. It may therefore be in the interests of all of us that we should ensure that that diversity should continue and develop; if that requires a sharing of costs, so be it. But what are we to say to a diversity of beliefs about the true, the right and the good? Can we similarly celebrate the propagation and proliferation of beliefs which we ourselves believe to be erroneous, evil, and wrong? It is one thing to refrain from preventing people holding and acting upon beliefs which we ourselves believe to be false. It is quite another positively to contribute towards the maintenance and promotion of those erroneous beliefs. It borders on absurdity to suppose that a group of people with a system of belief about the true and the right should welcome and feel duty-bound to support a rival system of belief which they hold to be false and wrong.

This objection is likely to be felt particularly keenly by those who possess a religious faith. Atheists, of course, can regard religious beliefs as pernicious as well as false. But the non-believer might also take a more relaxed and benign view of religion. He might regard it as a relatively harmless delusion which adds to the range of human experience and which has some fortunate social and cultural side-effects. He might therefore be relatively undisturbed by having to play some small part in its continuance. But it is hard to see how the religious adherent could be similarly relaxed about his having to sustain a rival system of belief – unless he subscribes to the rather odd belief that all religions, without distinction, are equally valid and valuable paths to God (or the gods?). Imagine how Muslims and Hindus in contemporary India would respond to the suggestion that they should help to maintain and promote one another's beliefs. At a minimum they would be likely to react with indignation and incredulity and I, for my part, could not fault those reactions.

However, there is another sort of argument that might be used to justify our adopting a more positive attitude and assisting with the consequences of others' beliefs. Instead of appealing to an alleged collective interest that we all have in the maintenance of a diversity of beliefs, we might focus upon each person's 'good' and how that good is related to that person's beliefs. People, it might be argued, should be able to flourish in whatever lives they lead and a society ought to ensure that all of its members have genuinely equal opportunities to lead equally fulfilled lives. What constitutes 'flourishing' and 'fulfilment' for individuals or groups must be tied to their fundamental beliefs. That is, they can flourish and find fulfilment only in forms of life to which they themselves are committed. We have to accept that people believe what they believe and work from there. Thus a society ought to do its utmost to assist its members to maintain and promote their beliefs, not because that society has a collective interest in the continuance of all of those beliefs, but because its members ought to flourish equally in whatever lives they themselves believe to be right.[17]

This argument raises large and fundamental issues about the character of a just society and here I can do no more than point to various reasons for rejecting it. Notice that it is an argument which demands far more than that we should cancel out whatever material inequalities happen to be consequent upon differences in belief. It shifts the focus of justice from the distribution of resources to the relative levels of individuals' fulfilment. A just society ceases to be one which distributes resources fairly amongst people and then leaves them to use those resources in the pursuit of whatever goals they think good, right or desirable. Instead it becomes one in which a society is made responsible for ensuring that people attain equal levels of fulfilment in whatever forms of life they commit themselves to.

There would clearly be massive practical problems in implementing this principle of equal fulfilment. Large philosophical doubts must also hang over the intelligibility of 'equal fulfilment' in the context of radically different forms of life. The most obvious candidate for reducing different forms of life to commensurability would be some form of utilitarianism, but a utilitarian measure would be both inappropriate and improper in the context of forms of life which were non-utilitarian in character.[18] Even if equal fulfilment were feasible, we might still question whether it would be just. If people are left free to pursue any form of life, should some have to suffer because of the extravagant, eccentric or ill-judged use that others make of that freedom? As I argued earlier, if some have to pay the price for the use that others make of their freedom, including their freedom of belief, the legitimacy of that freedom is very much in doubt. In addition, the view that people's 'good' consists in fulfilment in *whatever* form of life they pursue is obviously a highly contestable form of perfectionism and is a conception of the good which is most unlikely to be shared by the members of a religiously plural society.[19]

There is much more to be said on the ideal of equal fulfilment, but I hope that these brief remarks are sufficient to intimate why a society should not assume collective responsibility for securing equal levels of 'belief fulfilment' for each of its members.

III Identifying Consequences

Even if we accept that, in principle, people should bear the consequences of their beliefs, we are not yet out of the woods. We have still to establish what *are*, or what are to *count as*, the consequences of belief. That is far from straightforward.

Consider Mr Ahmad's position. His predicament arose not merely from his duty (as he understood it) to attend a mosque on Friday afternoons. It arose because Friday afternoon forms part of the normal working week in Britain. If the working week had run from Sundays to Thursdays, with Fridays and Saturdays counting as the 'week-end', Mr Ahmad's beliefs would not have had problematic consequences. It would then have been Christian Sabbatarians who would have been in trouble. So was Mr Ahmad's inability to perform his teaching duties to the full a consequence of his beliefs? Might he not claim that it was rather a consequence of the particular set of days that children were required to attend school in Britain?

In some cases we may be able to say that an outcome is a 'natural' consequence of a belief such

that no-one but the believer can be held responsible for that outcome. For example, if a Jehovah's Witness contracts an illness which can be cured only by a blood transfusion and if he refuses to receive a transfusion, his death can be characterised as a natural consequence of his belief.[20] But most controversial cases will not be like that. They will result not from a conjunction of beliefs and 'nature' but from a confluence of beliefs and humanly established circumstances.

Here it may help to distinguish between two different ways in which systems of belief can make demands upon their adherents. Demands which are intrinsic to a system of belief I shall call *burdens* of belief. Those which are extrinsic to the system of belief I shall call *consequences* of belief. The 'burden' of a belief is intrinsic to the belief in that it is imposed by the belief itself. Thus it is part of the burden of Islamic belief that one must pray five times a day. It is part of the burden of Catholic belief that one should attend Mass on Sundays. It is part of the burden of orthodox Judaism that one should not work between nightfall on Friday and nightfall on Saturday. (What I describe as a 'burden' of belief may, of course, be experienced as joyous rather than onerous by the believer.) By contrast what I label the 'consequences' of belief are distinct from the belief itself in that they are not essential requirements of the belief even though that belief is essential to their occurrence. If, for the sake of argument, we accept Mr Ahmad's own interpretation of the demands of his faith, it is part of the 'burden' of his belief that he should attend a mosque on Friday afternoons, but it is not a part of that burden that he should refrain from performing the duties of a full-time teacher. That is simply a 'consequence' of his belief which arises in the context of the British educational system. Similarly, refraining from working on the Lord's Day is part of the 'burden' of Sabbatarian belief, but suffering commercial disadvantage is not; that may be a 'consequence' of Sabbatarian belief but 'suffering commercial disadvantage' is not something enjoined by Sabbatarianism itself.

Given all that I have argued up to now and, in particular, assuming that we reject the equal fulfilment principle, we should require people to bear the 'burdens' of their beliefs for those burdens are imposed only by their beliefs. But assigning responsibility for what I have distinguished as the 'consequences' of belief is altogether more complicated since those consequences are not uniquely determined by belief. Let me identify two fundamentally different approaches to this issue.

The first possibility is that we establish a set of social arrangements independently of people's religious beliefs. Those arrangements would be set according to certain standards of fairness or rightfulness and would constitute a 'fixed background'. People would then be free to live according to their beliefs within the constraints set by that background. Whatever consequences, advantageous or disadvantageous, arose from the conjunction of a particular set of beliefs with those background arrangements would have to be borne by believers themselves. This approach is implicit in the work of liberal theorists such as Rawls and Ackerman.[21]

The second possibility is more even-handed in character. If an outcome is the result of two (or more) factors, it would hold both (or all) factors responsible for the outcome and proceed accordingly. Believers should be held jointly rather than solely responsible for the consequences which emanate from the conjunction of their beliefs and social circumstances. That points to a policy of compromise, mutual accommodation or cost-sharing or, where no such middle way is possible, a decision which is reached only after due weight has been given to all of the interests involved, including those of religious believers.

For the sake of clarity it might help to mention a third approach which would be the obverse of the first: beliefs should be treated as fixed features of the social landscape and believers should bear no responsibility at all for consequences which emanate from the interaction of those beliefs with social circumstances. The purpose of the second part of this article was to rule out this third approach. But how should we decide between the first and second?

That question is not easy to answer within the limits of this article, or indeed outside of them, since it turns not on the status to be given to beliefs and to the demands of belief, but on the status to be given to the circumstances and arrangements which combine with beliefs to yield consequences. Thus where one stands on this issue will depend upon where one stands on some of the most fundamental questions of political philosophy. People of significantly different political persuasions will give significantly different answers not because they give different values to belief and to the demands of belief, but because of their different evaluations of the social and political contexts in which beliefs are held and acted

upon. It is not therefore easy to make progress in this area. Here I shall confine myself to pointing out that the two approaches I have described need not be thought of as mutually exclusive and that some mix of the two has considerable appeal.

Suppose a religion requires that a temple be constructed for the glory and worship of God. According to the distinction I made a moment ago, it will be part of the 'burden' of belief of that religion that a temple should be constructed. Constructing the temple will take time, effort and money. But the expenditure of that time, effort and money is not itself part of the 'burden' of belief. It is a 'consequence' of the belief. The belief requires only that there be a temple; it does not prescribe that its adherents, and its adherents alone, must sacrifice specific amounts of time, effort and money to construct the temple. Those costs arise for the believers only because non-believers will not share in financing the temple and/or because, and to the extent that, people charge for the expenditure of labour and for materials in the society concerned. Now we have shown that believers should not be entirely absolved of responsibility for the consequences of their beliefs. The temple should not, therefore, be financed wholly out of general taxation. But might we argue that, since the costs of constructing the temple arise only in part because the faithful believe it ought to be constructed, and since they arise also because people are unwilling to provide labour and materials at less than the going rates, those costs are jointly brought about by believers and non-believers and therefore should be met jointly by the two groups? The temple might then be financed partly from the private funds of believers and partly from general taxation.

That proposal would not, I suspect, win much approval – from either believers or non-believers. The reason is not that current rates for labour and materials (whether fixed by the market or by the state) contribute nothing causally to the costs incurred in building the temple. Clearly they do. Rather it is because material and labour costs set a 'background' against which people are to make decisions about their lives and against which, in the ordinary course of things, they are required to take responsibility for the costs of their own projects. Of course, what that 'background' should be is open to disputes of a familiar sort – a range of possibilities is on offer from the libertarian to the liberal socialist. But, given that those background arrangements are 'just', believers should have to bear the financial consequences of having to construct temples, to go on pilgrimages, to stage festivals, and the like. For moral and political purposes, those consequences are to be deemed exclusively consequences of belief.

I myself would respond to Sabbatarianism in this way. Other things being equal,[22] people should be free to enter into whatever voluntary arrangements they choose, with whom they choose, when they choose. If some people possess beliefs according to which it is wrong to trade or work on Saturdays or Sundays, they should be free to abstain from trading and working on those days. But any commercial disadvantage they suffer as a consequence should be regarded as a consequence of their beliefs and not as a consequence of others not sharing those beliefs. That disadvantage should not therefore rank as a reason for removing or limiting the freedom of non-Sabbatarians to trade and work as they see fit and it would be quite wrong to deal with this issue in a utilitarian, or quasi-utilitarian, fashion by simply weighing up the competing interests involved.

But, however one sets those background constraints, there may also be cases which arise *within* them, cases in which private or public projects are at odds with, or in competition with, the demands of religious belief and which are properly dealt with by weighing and, if possible, accommodating the competing interests involved. Consider the once contentious issue of Sikhs and motor-cycle crash helmets. In 1972 the British Parliament passed a law empowering the Minister of Transport to require all motor-cyclists to wear crash helmets, which he duly did. That caused problems for biking Sikhs who would not remove their turbans. In 1976 the law was amended to exempt Sikhs from this requirement. Should Sikhs have been accommodated in that way?

In a case that went to trial before the law was amended, a Sikh claimed that his religious beliefs provided adequate excuse for his not wearing a crash helmet. In response a judge presiding at the trial commented that no one was bound to ride a motor-cycle and the law prescribed simply that, if you rode a motor-cycle, you had to wear a crash helmet; members of the Sikh community might find themselves unable to ride motor-cycles but they were prevented 'not because of the English law but by the requirements of their religion'.[23] In other words, a Sikh's inability to ride a motor-cycle was to be deemed a consequence not of the law but of his beliefs. But that construction

seems much less plausible in this case. Why? In part, no doubt, the answer is that compelling people to wear crash helmets is a largely paternalistic measure and Sikhs have a reason, special to themselves, for taking a different view of what is for their good. However, that is not the only consideration. Other-regarding interests are also at stake in this issue but those interests do not seem sufficiently special to trump all competing considerations.[24] Consequently, in this sort of case, it seems appropriate that interests should be weighed and the law adjusted accordingly.

One further comment on this alternative. An argument commonly used in relation to religiously plural societies is that their constitutions and policies should not be grounded upon religious principles. The justification usually given is that public rules and public policies should be based upon reasons of a kind that are accessible to, and that can be acknowledged by, all members of the public; in a religiously diverse society, religious doctrine cannot provide that shared form of reason.[25] But that argument does not require that public decisions should ignore the interests that people have as holders of religious beliefs, nor does it require that any non-religious concern should routinely trump any interest that has its foundation in a religious belief. It does not therefore require us to adopt the 'background' approach to the complete exclusion of the approach that I have just described.

However, as I have already indicated, I cannot settle the question of how beliefs should rank alongside other factors which contribute to consequences. All I have sought to establish is that a society does not have a *general* duty to relieve people of the consequences of their beliefs. If, in a particular instance, there is a case for relief, that case must be grounded not in any such general duty but in a claim that, morally as well as empirically, the relevant consequence is not to be considered a consequence of belief alone.

Since I began with the case of Mr Ahmad, perhaps I should conclude with it. Applied to that case, the thrust of my argument is that Mr Ahmad had no general claim, *qua* believer, that others should bear the consequences of his not being available for teaching on Friday afternoons. However, there is obviously more to be said. Mr Ahmad's beliefs caused difficulty only in the context of the working week in Britain. The pattern of that week cannot pretend to be a fact of nature nor can the use of Sunday as a day of rest pretend to be religiously neutral either in effect or, more importantly, in intention. For those who take the view that Britain and other western societies are, or ought to be, 'Christian societies' there is nothing untoward in that; those societies' arrangements are rightly Christian in character and other religions have to take their chances against that background. In so far as Saturdays are also non-working days for many people in Christian societies, that is simply fortunate for members of the Jewish faith; in so far as Fridays are working days for almost everyone in Christian societies, that is simply unfortunate for members of the Islamic faith. (*Mutatis mutandis*, the same might be said of Islamic or Jewish societies.) But for those who hold that, in its laws and its public policy, a society should aspire to be neutral be-

tween religions, the 'inequitable' character of the British week must be a source of concern. It would of course be possible to make the non-working day neutral between religions by shifting it to, say, Tuesday or Wednesday, or by altering its frequency, so that it would be equally inconvenient for all religions. But to invert the Pareto principle in that way ('make some people worse off while making no one better off') would seem entirely without merit. As long as Sundays retain their traditional status in societies like Britain, Mr Ahmad and Muslims like him have some claim to be accommodated.[26] Whether, all things considered, they should be accommodated must depend upon the feasibility and the costs of that accommodation.

Notes

1 *Ahmad v. Inner London Education Authority*. Employment Appeal Tribunal: [1976] I.C.R. 461. Court of Appeal: [1978] 1 Q.B. 36; [1977] 3 W.L.R. 396. The case is described in detail in Sebastian Poulter, *English Law and Ethnic Minority Customs* (London: Butterworths, 1986), pp. 247–52. See also St John A. Robilliard, *Religion and the Law* (Manchester: Manchester University Press, 1984).

2 Whether the demands of employment provide sufficient reason for not attending Friday prayers seems to be disputed within the Muslim community. ILEA pointed out that it employed hundreds of Muslim teachers none of whom had made the same request as Mr Ahmad; [1978] 1 Q.B. 39, 40–1, 43–4.

3 *X v. United Kingdom*, (1981) 22 Decisions and Reports of the European Commission 27.

4 [1978] 1 Q.B. 47, 50.

5 [1978] 1 Q.B. 41.

6 [1978] 1 Q.B. 48, 50. See also Lord Scarman, 'Toleration and the law', *On Toleration*, ed. S. Mendus and D. Edwards (Oxford: Clarendon Press, 1987), pp. 49–62.

Mr Ahmad's case is not unique in English law. For another case arising from a conflict between patterns of work and Muslim religious obligations, see *Hussain v. London Country Bus Services Ltd*, Incomes Data Services (IDS) Brief 283 (Aug 1984) p. 5. For similar cases, concerning other faiths, see *London Borough of Tower Hamlets v. Rabin*, IDS Brief 406 (Oct 1989) p. 12, and *Fluss v. Grant Thornton Chartered Accountants*, IDS Brief 360 (1987) p. 6 (both concerning Jews); *Esson v. London Transport Executive*, [1975] I.R.L.R. 48 (concerning a Seventh Day Adventist); *Post Office v. Mayers*, IDS Brief 397 (May 1989) p. 4

(concerning a member of the World Wide Church of God). There have also been a number of notable cases concerning specific religious festivals; see *Ostreicher v. Secretary of State for the Environment*, [1978] 1 All ER 591, [1978] 3 All ER 82 (C.A.); *Prais v. EC Council*, [1977] ICR 284; *Naiz v. Ryman Ltd*, IDS Brief 376 (July 1988) p. 6.

Currently law in the United Kingdom prohibits direct and indirect discrimination on grounds of race and sex but, with the exception of Northern Ireland, not on grounds of religious faith. However, in the case of groups such as Jews and Sikhs, a high degree of coincidence between ethnic identity and religious belief means that, under the 1976 Race Relations Act, those groups do receive a measure of legal protection against adverse treatment related to their religious beliefs. The House of Lords ruled that Sikhs were a racial group (by reference to their 'ethnic origins') within the meaning of the Race Relations Act 1976, in *Mandla v. Dowell Lee*; [1983] 2 A.C. 548. Lord Fraser gave 'a common religion' as one of several characteristics that might contribute to the identification of a community as an 'ethnic group' (562). In the same case, the Court of Appeal had previously ruled that Sikhs were a religious rather than a racial group who therefore, *qua* Sikhs, fell outside the protection afforded by the Race Relations Act; [1982] W.L.R. 932. In a recent unreported case, *Dawkins v. The Crown Suppliers (P.S.A.)*, a tribunal decided that Rastafarians were an ethnic group, rather than merely a religious group, and therefore came within the provisions of the Act; see Dave Marrington, 'Legal decisions', *New Community*, 16 (1990) 296–8. However, that decision was subsequently overturned; [1991] I.R.L.R. 327; [1993] I.R.L.R. 284.

If British law had provided against religious discrimination on the model of current British laws prohibiting racial and sexual discrimination, Mr Ahmad could not have complained of direct discrimination since he did not lose his full-time post because he was a Muslim. Rather he lost his post because he failed to comply fully with ILEA's requirement to teach on Friday afternoons. But he might well have complained of indirect discrimination in respect of that requirement since he, and Muslims like him, were prevented by their religious beliefs from complying fully with that requirement and suffered disadvantage as a consequence. It would then have been open to ILEA to have shown that that requirement was 'justifiable' in spite of its disadvantageous effect for devout Muslims.

For two significant American cases, raising issues similar in character to the case of Mr Ahmad, see *T.W.A. v. Hardison*, 432 U.S. 63 (1977), and *Ansonia Board of Education v. Philbrook*, 55 USLW 4019 (1986). For investigations of these issues in the context of American law, see David E. Retter, 'The rise and fall of Title VII's requirement of reasonable accommodation for religious employees', *Columbia Human Rights Law Review* 11 (1979), 63–86; Michael W. McConnell, 'Accommodation of Religion', *The Supreme Court Review*, ed. P. Kurland, G. Casper, D.J. Hutchinson (Chicago: University of Chicago Press, 1986), pp. 1–59; William L. Kandel, 'Current developments in EEO: religious accommodation after *Philbrook*', *Employee Relations Law Journal* 12 (1987), 690–7; and Gloria T. Beckley and Paul Burstein, 'Religious pluralism, equal opportunity, and the state', *Western Political Quarterly* 44 (1991), 185–208.

7   Cf. Albert Weale, 'Toleration, individual differences and respect for persons', *Aspects of Toleration*, ed. J. Horton and S. Mendus (London: Methuen, 1985), pp. 16–35 at p. 27; and Susan Mendus, *Toleration and the Limits of Liberalism* (Basingstoke: Macmillan, 1989), p. 84. There are, of course, many arguments for and against keeping Sundays 'special' which do not turn on the issue that I am concerned with here.

8   John Rawls, *A Theory of Justice* (Oxford: Oxford University Press, 1972).

9   Rawls has underlined this feature of his theory in articles that he has written since the publication of *A Theory of Justice*. See especially, 'Fairness to goodness', *Philosophical Review* 84 (1975), 536–54; 'Justice as fairness: political not metaphysical', *Philosophy and Public Affairs* 14 (1985), 223–51; 'The priority of right and ideas of the good', *Philosophy and Public Affairs* 17 (1988), 251–76.

10 That religious faith, unlike race, is a 'chosen' rather than an 'unalterable' feature of people was a consideration that weighed with the English Court of Appeal in reaching its decision, in *Mandla v. Dowell Lee*, that Sikhs did not constitute an 'ethnic group'.

In particular, Oliver L.J. thought the expression 'ethnic group' was 'entirely inappropriate to describe a group into and out of which anyone may travel as a matter of free choice; and freedom of choice – to join, to remain or to leave – is inherent in the whole philosophy of Sikhism'; [1982] W.L.R. 932 at 941–2; see also the similar views of Kerr L.J. at 945–9. The House of Lords recognised that people may convert into and out of Sikhism but held that that did not preclude Sikhs being an ethnic group; [1983] 2 A.C, 548 at 562–3, 569.

11 Cf. Susan Mendus, 'The tigers of wrath and the horses of instruction', *Free Speech*, ed. B. Parekh (London: Commission for Racial Equality, 1990), pp. 3–17.

12 Richard Rorty, *Contingency, Irony and Solidarity* (Cambridge: Cambridge University Press, 1989), p. xiii.

13 Cf. Ali A. Mazrui, 'The Satanic Verses or a satanic novel? Moral dilemmas of the Rushdie affair', *Free Speech*, ed. B. Parekh (London: Commission for Racial Equality, 1990), pp. 79–103 at pp. 80–1, 101.

14 Cf. Mendus, *Toleration and the Limits of Liberalism*, pp. 32–5.

15 Even the libertarian need not be wholly indifferent to discrimination. Firstly, to say that employers have an unlimited right to decide whom they employ is not to say that they cannot be criticised for the use they make of that right. Secondly, even in the minimal state there will be a public sector and the libertarian's claim that anti-discrimination measures violate the rights of private employers has no obvious equivalent in that sector.

16 For a British case which comes close to this alternative, see *Singh v. British Rail Engineering Ltd*, [1986] I.C.R. 22. Singh was not allowed to continue with his job because he refused to remove his turban so that he could wear a hard hat. Part of the justification offered by the employer was that, if Singh continued with the job wearing only his turban and then incurred injury, the fact that the injury was a consequence of Singh's beliefs would not absolve the employer of legal liability for that injury. In other words, that the employer would have to bear the financial consequences of Singh's acting on his beliefs – that is, the costs that would be consequent upon Singh's sustaining injury through wearing a turban rather than a hard hat – became a reason for depriving Singh of the freedom to continue with his job while wearing a turban.

17 Cf. Charles Taylor, 'Atomism', in his *Philosophy and the Human Sciences*, vol. 2 (Cambridge: Cambridge University Press, 1985), pp. 187–210.

18 For a close examination of the idea of equal fulfilment, see Ronald Dworkin, 'What is equality? Part I: equality of welfare', *Philosophy and Public Affairs*, 10 (1981), 185–246. See also my 'The Ideal of the Neutral State', *Liberal Neutrality*, ed. R.E. Goodin

and A. Reeve, pp. 9–38 at pp. 14–17. For a defence of a utilitarian form of 'equal fulfilment', but one cast only in terms of 'preferences', see Richard J. Arneson, 'Liberalism, distributive subjectivism, and equal opportunity for welfare', *Philosophy and Public Affairs*, 19 (1990), 158–94; see also his 'Neutrality and utility', *Canadian Journal of Philosophy* 20 (1990), 215–40.

19 See further my 'Liberalism, belief and doubt', *Liberalism and Recent Social and Political Philosophy*, ed. R. Bellamy, ARSP, Beiheft 36 (Stuttgart: Steiner, 1989), pp. 51–69 at pp. 63–8. I use the term 'perfectionism' in the special sense given to it by Rawls, *Theory of Justice*, pp. 25, 325–32.

20 One could resist that only by claiming that others were duty-bound to override the Jehovah's Witness's freedom of belief and to force a blood transfusion upon him; his death could then be characterised as a consequence of their failure to perform that duty.

21 Bruce A. Ackerman, *Social Justice in the Liberal State* (New Haven: Yale University Press, 1980).

22 I include this phrase only to provide for restrictions upon freedom of contract other than those at issue here.

23 *R v. Aylesbury Crown Court ex parte Chahal*, [1976] R.T.R. 489 at 492.

24 I have in mind here the distress caused to those involved in accidents causing serious injury to others. Hospital treatment and other supportive public expenditure following injury are also at issue, although those are not always straightforwardly unpaternalistic in character; see my 'Toleration, harm, and moral effect', *Aspects of Toleration*, ed. Horton and Mendus, pp. 136–57.

25 The exclusion of religious reasons from public policy is implicit in the approaches of Rawls and Ackerman. See also Jeremy Waldron, 'Theoretical foundations of liberalism', *Philosophical Quarterly* 37 (1987), 127–50, and Thomas Nagel, 'Moral conflict and political legitimacy', *Philosophy and Public Affairs* 16 (1987), 215–40. For critical examinations of this approach, see Kent Greenawalt, *Religious Convictions and Political Choice* (New York: Oxford University Press, 1988), and Joseph Raz, 'Facing diversity: the case of epistemic abstinence', *Philosophy and Public Affairs* 19 (1990), 3–46.

26 The number of those within a religious group making demands like Mr Ahmad's has implications which point in opposite directions. The smaller the number, the more easily they can be accommodated. But, the smaller the number, the greater must also be doubts about whether they *rightly* make that demand. Suppose Mr Ahmad were *mistaken* in believing that, within Islam, the exigencies of employment did not provide adequate reason for not attending a mosque (on which see note 2 above). Should that make a difference? In principle, surely it should, since Mr Ahmad's claims about what his own religion required of him would be false. In practice, public bodies would probably be reluctant to become embroiled in questions of correct doctrine. This is one respect in which a 'group' approach might yield a different answer from an 'individual' approach, i.e. an approach which identifies beliefs and the demands of belief by reference to groups rather than individuals. This issue arose in Britain in *Saggers v. British Railways Board*, a case concerning exemption from a trade union closed shop on grounds of religious belief; [1977] I.R.L.R. 266. Saggers, a Jehovah's Witness, believed that his religion was incompatible with his membership of a trade union even though membership of trade unions was not proscribed by the doctrine of Jehovah's Witnesses. The Employment Appeal Tribunal ruled that (as far as the law relevant to that case was concerned) 'belief' referred to the belief of the relevant individual and not to the established creed or dogma of the religious body of which that individual was a member.

PART VIII

International Affairs

41

Just War: The Case of World War II

G. E. M. Anscombe

I The Justice of the Present War Examined (1939)

(a) *Introductory*

In these days the authorities claim the right to control not only the policy of the nation but also the actions of every individual within it; and their claim has the support of a large section of the people of the country, and of a peculiar force of emotion. This support is gained, and this emotion caused by the fact that they are 'evil things' that we are fighting against. That they are evil we need have no doubt; yet many of us still feel distrust of these claims and these emotions lest they blind men to their duty of considering carefully, before they act, the justice of the things they propose to do. Men can be moved to fight by being made to hate the deeds of their enemies; but a war is not made just by the fact that one's enemies' deeds are hateful. Therefore it is our duty to resist passion and to consider carefully whether all the conditions of a just war are satisfied in this present war, lest we sin against the natural law by participating in it.

(b) *The natural moral law*

This idea of natural moral law is one which modern men have lost; but without it they cannot live in peace within themselves, or socially or internationally. For the natural law is the law of man's own nature, showing how he must choose to act in matters where his will is free, if his nature is to be properly fulfilled. It is the proper use of his functions; their misuse or perversion is sin. So, lying is the misuse of speech, and is therefore wicked. So, justice is the proper working out of relations between man and man, and between societies, each having his due.

To those who believe in God it will rightly appear that His law, the eternal law, has its reflection in the ordered activity of Creation, that 'law of nature' which is the truth of things. In man, this activity is not wholly determined, but there is an element of choice. Thus far, 'to him the law is proposed; it is not imposed upon him'.[1] But it is not less law for that; it binds because it is the law of his nature. And in what it consists he can discover by reason, checked and guaranteed by the divine revelation of Scripture. Aquinas called it 'the participation in the eternal law of the rational creature' (Thomas Aquinas, *Summa Theologica*, 1a 2ae. 91, art. 2 ad 3); the law in him from his creation, which he, making use of the gifts of reason and revelation, will find for his salvation. Thus will he proceed to his eternal destiny in God; but the condition of the love of God is the observance of the natural law; if man does not live according to his proper nature he will not attain his proper end.[2]

With this in mind, let us proceed to consider what is justice in the matter of war, remembering that whatever human hopes for the happiness of

Originally published in her collected papers, *Ethics, Religion and Politics* (Minneapolis: University of Minnesota Press, 1981), pp. 72–81 and 62–71, respectively. Reprinted by permission of Mary Gormally.

mankind may be, the only way to that happiness is an observance of the law of God without any deviation.

(c)   The conditions of the just war

There are seven conditions which must be all fulfilled for a war to be just:

1   There must be a just occasion: that is, there must be violation of, or attack upon, strict rights.
2   The war must be made by a lawful authority: that is, when there is no higher authority, a sovereign state.
3   The warring state must have an upright intention in making war: it must not declare war in order to obtain, or inflict anything unjust.
4   Only right means must be used in the conduct of the war.
5   War must be the only possible means of righting the wrong done.
6   There must be a reasonable hope of victory.
7   The probable good must outweigh the probable evil effects of the war.[3]

For this present war there is a just occasion; the rights of Poland have been infringed. The war was declared by a lawful authority. There is, so far as we can tell, a reasonable hope of victory. And though we may suspect that war could have been averted by a more intelligent policy up to a very short time before war broke out, yet at the time when war was declared it is possible that the wrong done could not have been righted by peaceful means. But there remain three conditions to be fulfilled: the intentions of our government must be upright, both (i) as to means, and (ii) as to ends, and (iii) the probable good effects of the war must outweigh the probable evil. If these conditions are not fulfilled, *this* war is rendered wrong, however just the occasion, however desirable that we should fight *a* war. Nor, if we know that a war is wrong, may we take part in it without sin, however grievous it may seem to stand apart from our fellow countrymen.

We must note that, if we fight a war, it is the government's war, since, as we have seen, wars can only be made by sovereign states. Therefore we cannot say: 'The government's intentions are *vicious*; but the things *I* am fighting for are just,' or 'The government intends to use evil means, but *I* shall do nothing unjust.' A private person may not make war; and if he joins in a war, he joins in it as justified or vitiated by the just or unjust intentions of the government under which he fights. By 'government' we mean the persons holding power in a sovereign state. Another point to note is that a government may succumb to temptation in the course of the war; if this involved departure from any of the seven conditions the justice of the war would be vitiated. But isolated pieces of wickedness, though participation in them would be wrong, would not themselves vitiate the whole war on grounds of intention; the probability of such would simply contribute to the balance of evil effects which must be considered.

(d)   *On Aims*

If a war is to be just, the warring state must intend only what is just, and the aim of the war must be to set right certain specific injustices. That is, the righting of wrong done must be a sufficient condition on which peace will be made.

In the present war, we may have grave doubts about our government's sincerity. It may seem that we never cared about Poland, but made the Polish treaty as a pretext for seizing the next opportunity to oppose the German government. Our government was badly frightened; it had been weak; it wanted to take a strong line lest it be utterly discredited; and hence the Polish pact. These beginnings are dubious enough; partly because the injustice done to Poland seems our pretext, not our cause, for entering the war; partly because our government appears to have acted from fear and pride, rather than from a desire for justice. Nevertheless it is not wrong to be afraid of Germany's unjust encroachments and to make war in order to stop them, so long as we feared them because they attacked a just settlement and endangered our just interests. But what is the evidence? After the last war, we made the treaty of Versailles, now condemned by every one. But we have made no attempt to rectify it, even when it became urgently necessary that we should do so. We have not tried to make a just and reasonable settlement with Germany; we have merely allowed Germany to set aside portions of the treaty by force, and with grave injustice. Finally, we have clamoured to negotiate at the last moment, when otherwise Germany would take by force; and our offers have been rejected. Unjustly, it may be; but the evil done by our enemies does not affect our own condemnation.

Our policy, it might be said, is incomprehensible, except as a policy, not of opposing German injustice, but of trying to preserve the status quo and that an unjust one. Some of us may think the case clear enough; yet such argument is likely to lead us into endless controversy. It may be that we could not prove irrefutably that our government's aims are positively vicious. Some might say that the government is not clear enough about its aims for them to be vicious. Yet if this is so, the government's intention in fighting the war must still be condemned. For it is a condition of a just war that it *should* be fought with a *just* intention; not that it should *not* be fought with an *unjust* intention. If the government's intentions cannot be known to be unjust because they are vague, that vagueness itself vitiates them. But the case is even clearer than this. For the truth is that the government's professed intentions are not merely vague, but unlimited. They have not said: 'When justice is done on points A, B and C, then we will stop fighting.' They have talked about 'sweeping away everything that Hitlerism stands for' and about 'building a new order in Europe'. What does this mean but that our intentions are so unlimited that there is no point at which we or the Germans could say to our government: 'Stop fighting; for your conditions are satisfied.' It is true that our government has said that it will not consider peace negotiations until certain injustices are set right. But it has made this only a necessary and not a sufficient condition; therefore it is nothing against our argument.

There results a tendency to interpret our government's phrases according to various predilections. A socialist will tell you that he is fighting for social justice and free speech, a Catholic that he is fighting for the Church. We should forget our own desires and consider narrowly what can be deduced from our government's actions, coupled with these vague and inevitable catchwords. There can be only one conclusion: we are fighting against an unjust cause, indeed; but not for a just one.

(e) *On the morality of means*

Before considering whether or not there are any persons who may not be attacked in war, we must try to elucidate, in however crude a fashion, the doctrine of intention in human acts. For in all actions of rational beings we can distinguish three ends of action: there is the motive or motives of the agent, the proper effect of the act as such, and the completed act itself. These are not always distinct in fact, but they can be; if they do coincide this does not make them less distinct in nature, though the distinction is sometimes subtle. For example, take the action of a carpenter in the stroke of a chisel. His motive may be the glory of God, or the obtaining of wages, or the satisfaction of a completed job, or several or all of these, and more besides. The proper effect of the act as such is the removal of a shaving of wood, and this may also be considered as one of the ends of the agent as well as of the action. The completed act itself is simply the completed successful stroke. Let us apply this analysis to military attack. The motive may be to win the war, or medals, or simply to attack successfully and destroy the enemy who receives the impact of the attack. The proper effect is the weakening, disabling or destruction of those who receive that impact. The completed act itself is the completed attack, or, in the case, let us say, of bombing, the dropping and explosion in the right place of the bomb.

Now as to morals. If an act is to be lawful, it is not sufficient that the motives of the agent should be good, though this is necessary. First, the act itself must not be intrinsically wrong; it must not be such an act as is wrong under any circumstance. Second, the proper effects of the act must be permissible. And unless these conditions are present, the act is wrong. To apply these principles once more in the case of military attack: an attack on men is not intrinsically vicious: is not, that is, a perverted act; it is circumstances that make it right or wrong. The motive of the attackers belongs to a consideration of aims rather than of means; or, if we are considering individual soldiers, it is matter for God at the Last Judgement, not for us here. But what of the proper effects of the completed action? These, as we have seen, consist in the destruction of the persons attacked. If, therefore, the attack is to be lawful, the persons attacked must be persons whom the attackers may legitimately destroy. Our object is to consider whether in warfare these persons include civilians.

(f) *on means*

(i) The prospect of attack on civilians. It is generally recognized that, in certain circumstances, we shall attack civilians from the air; we are already attacking them by blockade. We have no space to prove these facts in detail: for the first, it suffices

to recall the answer made by our government to President Roosevelt, when he asked for a promise not to attack civilians. We said that we should adhere to international law on the matter, but that we reserved the right 'to adopt appropriate measures' if the Germans should break it. If the right to adopt appropriate measures is a reservation to a promise not to attack civilians, then it can only mean that, given certain circumstances, we should attack civilians. The language is veiled, but it can hardly be interpreted in any other way.

(ii) On blockade. As for blockade: it has been pretended, in justification, that the blockade is not a blockade; or that it does not attack civilians. But some people, when they are arguing on another subject, when they are assuring us of victory, *then* they tell us that we cannot but win because the Germans cannot survive the blockade, since it prevents things essential to their national life from reaching them. Others, at this point, say that we could not really be responsible for starving the German people, because they divert the supplies to the fighting forces, and therefore are responsible themselves. But this argument admits that civilians do suffer attack and therefore can be dealt with under that head.

(iii) The 'indivisibility' of modern war and the justification of killing enemies in war. It is argued that it is just to attack civilians in war because war is now 'indivisible'. The civilian population is really as much combatant as the fighting forces, for it is their essential backing. The military strength of a country is its whole economic and social strength. Therefore civilians may be attacked as combatants.

Here we must ask two questions: first, what is the justification of killing in war? And, second, in what does the indivisibility of war consist? It is no sin to kill a man in self-defence or in defence of rights, if there is no possibility of appeal to a higher authority. A private person can appeal to the authority of the state, and therefore has no right to choose the death of a man in order to defend his rights; though he commits no sin if his action in resisting attack, at the time of attack, results in the death of the attacker; for such death is accidental. But where there is no higher authority to which to appeal, as in the case of a sovereign state at war, men who are wrongfully attacking rights may be killed in order to defend those rights if they cannot be defended in any other way.

We must notice two things about this doctrine: first that those who are killed are killed as *wrongfully* attacking rights, in virtue of the fact that it is not possible to appeal to any higher authority than the parties in the dispute. In this sense, the justly warring state is 'in the stead of a judge', having chosen to inflict death on men for the general good. Those men *must* be *wrongfully attacking* rights, or retaining what they have *wrongfully* gained; for it is wrong to slay the innocent for the good of the people. But second, though it proceeds from this quasi-judicial position of the justly warring state, that it can give its ministers authority deliberately to kill its enemies, *yet* they may only kill as a means of self-defence or the defence of rights; the judicial power does not permit them to kill purely punitively; for it is not lawful to kill men simply punitively, except after trial. The justly warring state has to judge of the right or wrong done; but it has no power of judgement on personal guilt or innocence. These two points must therefore be maintained: to quote St Thomas Aquinas,

> it is unlawful for a man to intend to kill any one in order to defend himself, except for one with public authority; and he, intending to kill a man for his own defence, refers this to the general good, as is plain in the case of a soldier fighting enemies, and the minister of a judge fighting against robbers. (2a 2ae. 64, art. 7.)

We have it, then, that no one may be deliberately attacked in war, unless his actions constitute an attack on the rights which are being defended or restored. To deny this will be to assert that we may attack any one anywhere, whose life in any way hinders the prosecution of the war, or in any way assists our enemies; and such a conclusion is as immoral as to be a *reductio ad absurdum* in itself.

Now in what does the 'indivisibility' of war consist? It consists in this, that it would be impossible for the combatant forces to fight, unless they were backed by the economic and social strength of the nation behind them. Therefore, it is argued, the civil population is a military target. To this there is only one reply. The civilian population behind an army does not fulfil the conditions which make it right to kill a man in war. Civilians are not committing wrong acts against those who are defending or restoring rights. They are maintaining the economic and social strength of a nation, and that is not wrong, even though that strength is being used by their government as the essential backing of an army unjustly fighting in the field.

It has been argued that, as accessories to a murder are by law punished equally with the murderer, so the citizens of an enemy country may be killed equally with the fighting forces. But the analogy is false. An accessory is punished as morally guilty of murder. But we have seen that it is not right to kill merely punitively in war; so whatever the guilt of the enemy nation, we cannot arrogate to ourselves the position of a judge, and execute them. A man cannot be judge in his own suit; and we are one of the parties in the quarrel. In default of a higher authority, we may kill those whose actions are an attack on our rights, in order to defend those rights: but the actions must themselves be wrong. The actions of a great mass of the civilian population are not in themselves wrongful attacks on us. Therefore they may not be killed by us, simply as deserving to die, nor yet because their death would be useful to us.

(iv) A note on reprisals.   It follows from this analysis that no warring state may claim the right to reprisals as such, because the other side deserves them. It is not right to inflict a certain harm on the enemy simply because he has inflicted it on you.[4] The morality of the action itself must be considered before it can be justified.

(v)   On double effect.   It has been argued that it is justifiable to attack civilians because their death is an example of 'double effect'. But this is no example of double effect, which is exemplified when an action designed to produce one effect produces another as well by accident. If, for example, a military target is being attacked and in the course of the attack civilians are also destroyed, then their destruction is not wicked, for it is accidental. Obviously before their destruction can be passed over on these grounds, it must also be shown that the action is of sufficient importance to allow such grave incidental effects. No action can be excused whose consequences involve a greater evil than the good of the action itself, whether these consequences are accidental or not.[5] Double effect therefore only excuses a grave incidental consequence where the balance of the total effects of an action is on the side of the good.

There is a great distinction between attacking a group of persons directly, and killing them accidentally in the course of attack on others. But yet another distinction must be made. It is a different thing, while making one group of persons a target, to kill others by accident, and to make a group of persons a target, in order – by attacking them all – to attack some members of the group who are persons who may legitimately be attacked. The first case involves no sin; the second involves murder and is not an example of double effect. It has been claimed as such by some who, defending blockade, allow that civilians are not a proper military target, but who argue that attack may be made on a whole group of persons which includes both civilians and combatants. This claim cannot be allowed.

Again, we cannot say with regard to blockade that the starvation of a civilian population by the diversion of supplies to its army is an incidental and unintentional effect of an action intended to demoralize the army. For to do so it would be necessary not only to prove that such an evil effect would in fact be outweighed by the good effects expected, but also that there would be no causal relation between the preceding starvation of a civilian population and the demoralization of an army.[6] This aspect of the problem of double effect is distinct from that treated immediately above. There we were considering whether it is an example of double effect to attack one group of persons as a means of destroying a part of the same group; here, whether an alleged example of double effect is not rather an attack on one group of persons as a means to attacking another and distinct group. Both cases are immoral if a group of, or including, civilians, is made a military target; and neither is a case of double effect.

(vi)   On the balance of good and evil.   It is said that war admittedly produces a number of evil effects, including attacks on civilians, but that these must be balanced against the probable good effects of the war, and if they are outweighed by good, then they can be discounted. It is indeed true that such a balance must be made; but we cannot propose to sin, because that evil will be outweighed by the good effects of the war. That would be to commit sin that good might come; and we may not commit any sin, however small, for the sake of any good, however great, and if the choice lies between our total destruction and the commission of sin, then we must choose to be destroyed.

There is a sense in which it is true to say that the sinful means chosen by the government would not vitiate the whole of a war, on account of the smallness of the sin. Though we could not join in committing the sin, however small, yet if it were very small, it would not, on account of the 'parvity of matter' render the whole war wrong. But unjust deliberate killing is murder and this is a great sin which 'cries to heaven for vengeance'; if, therefore, the warring state intends, under any circumstances, to commit it as a means of prosecuting the war, then the war is made wicked. As we have seen, our government does intend to do that which is unlawful, and it is already blockading Germany with intent to starve the national life. The present war is therefore wrong on account of means.

(vii) On propaganda. Europe since the outbreak of war has been comparatively quiet, and in consequence indiscriminate hatred has been far less noticeable than it was during the last war. But as the conflict grows more serious, we cannot expect this state of things to last; already there is less moderation in public speeches and private conversation than at the outset. Worse, there is already suppression and distortion of truth 'in the interests of the state'; and news has become propaganda and advocacy of a case. One man's lies are not justified because they contradict another's. We assert that, on the contrary, to fight for, while not observing, truth, is the same contradiction, madness and unreason which we condemn among the Nazis.

(g) On the probable evil effects of the war

Finally it remains to consider the last condition. The probable good effects of a war must outweigh its probable evil ones. We hold to the contrary that in this present struggle this condition is not satisfied. We have seen that our government's aims are suspect at the outset; that it is fighting with no desire for justice, so far as we can see, and that it is either ignorant of morals or malicious as far as means are concerned. What is likely to be the end, if we win, if this is what we are like at the beginning? To quote Pope Pius XII in his first encyclical:

> Let us leave the past and turn our eyes to the future which according to those who control the fate and fortune of the peoples, is to consist, once the bloody conflicts have ceased, in a new order, founded on justice and prosperity. Will that future really be different: above all,

will it really be better? Will the treaties of peace, will the new international order at the end of the war be animated by justice and equity towards all, by that spirit which frees and pacifies? Or will there be a lamentable repetition of the ancient and recent errors? To hope for a decisive change exclusively from the shock of war and its final issue is idle, as experience shows. The hour of victory is the hour of external triumph for the party to whom the victory falls, but it is, in equal measure, the hour of temptation. In this hour the angel of justice strives with the demon of violence ...the excited passions of the people, often inflamed by the sacrifices and sufferings they have borne, obscure the vision, even of responsible persons, and make them inattentive to the warning voice of humanity and equity which is overwhelmed and drowned in the inhuman cry 'woe to the conquered'. There is danger lest settlements and decisions born under such conditions be nothing else than injustice under the cloak of justice.[7]

If, therefore, there is little chance of a just and lasting peace, of a 'new order in Europe', do not all the inevitable evils which accompany war also condemn this one?

It has been said that the victory of the Allies would at least be better than that of their enemies; for there would be a certain fluidity in the situation which we could scarcely expect if the Germans won. We must repeat that this in itself would supply no justification for the war. And the argument is fallacious. On the one hand no situation is purely static; on the other, a repeated Versailles would determine the future as inevitably and as evilly as the first. The 'preservation of democracy', the possibility of free speech and the other such ideals which are valuable only as means, cannot weigh against considerations which belong to the essence of the moral law. The death of men, the curtailment of liberty, the destruction of property, the diminution of culture, the obscuring of judgement by passion and interest, the neglect of truth and charity, the decrease in belief and in the practice of religion – all these are the normal accompaniments of a war. We have, as we have seen, little enough hope of a just settlement to set against such prospects. And finally, there is a widespread tendency to make what our country chooses to do the criterion of what may be done, and to call this patriotism. So a war against totalitarianism produces a totalitarian tendency; not only are morals lowered, but the very theory of morals is corrupted. If a war lasts a short while, the evils may be slight; but if the war should be engaged in for a long time with a bloody seriousness, then those evil effects will be enormous. Already men are talking of Germany as a pariah nation; they are already saying that she must henceforward be kept down and never allowed to become powerful again. And if they speak thus in England, is it not obvious that our French allies will be even fiercer in this insane determination, which is as foolish as it is immoral? Then after the war, what prospects have we, but of greater poverty, greater difficulties, greater misery than ever, for a space; until just another such war will break out.

Such are the probable evil effects; and they greatly outweigh the good effects of putting an end to the injustices of Germany at the present day, since we have so little hope of substituting anything for them but other injustices.

II Mr Truman's Degree (1957)

(a)

In 1939, on the outbreak of war, the President of the United States asked for assurances from the belligerent nations that civil populations would not be attacked.

In 1945, when the Japanese enemy was known by him to have made two attempts towards a negotiated peace, the President of the United States gave the order for dropping an atom bomb on a Japanese city; three days later a second bomb, of a different type, was dropped on another city. No ultimatum was delivered before the second bomb was dropped.

Set side by side, these events provide enough of a contrast to provoke enquiry. Evidently development has taken place; one would like to see its course plotted. It is not, I think, difficult to give an intelligible account:

1. The British Government gave President Roosevelt the required assurance with a reservation which meant 'If the Germans do it we shall do it too.' You don't promise to abide by the Queensberry Rules even if your opponent abandons them.

2. The only condition for ending the war was announced to be unconditional surrender. Apart from the 'liberation of the subject peoples', the

objectives were vague in character. Now the demand for unconditional surrender was mixed up with a determination to make no peace with Hitler's government. In view of the character of Hitler's regime that attitude was very intelligible. Nevertheless some people have doubts about it now. It is suggested that defeat of itself would have resulted in the rapid discredit and downfall of that government. On this I can form no strong opinion. The important question to my mind is whether the intention of making no peace with Hitler's government necessarily entailed the objective of unconditional surrender. If, as may not be impossible, we could have formulated a pretty definite objective, a rough outline of the terms which we were willing to make with Germany, while at the same time indicating that we would not make terms with Hitler's government, then the question of the wisdom of this latter demand seems to me a minor one; but if not, then that settles it. It was the insistence on unconditional surrender that was the root of all evil. The connection between such a demand and the need to use the most ferocious methods of warfare will be obvious. And in itself the proposal of an unlimited objective in war is stupid and barbarous.

3. The Germans did a good deal of indiscriminate bombing in this country. It is impossible for an uninformed person to know how much, in its first beginnings, was due to indifference on the part of pilots to using their loads only on military targets, and how much to actual policy on the part of those who sent them. Nor do I know what we were doing in the same line at the time. But certainly anyone would have been stupid who had thought in 1939 that there would not be such bombing, developing into definite raids on cities.

4. For some time before war broke out, and more intensely afterwards, there was propaganda in this country on the subject of the 'indivisibility' of modern war. The civilian population, we were told, is really as much combatant as the fighting forces. The military strength of a nation includes its whole economic and social strength. Therefore the distinction between the people engaged in prosecuting the war and the population at large is unreal. There is no such thing as a non-participator; you cannot buy a postage stamp or any taxed article, or grow a potato or cook a meal, without contributing to the 'war effort'. War indeed is a 'ghastly evil', but once it has broken out no one can 'contract out' of it. 'Wrong' indeed must be being done if war is waged, but you

cannot help being involved in it. There was a doctrine of 'collective responsibility' with a lugubriously elevated moral tone about it. The upshot was that it was senseless to draw any line between legitimate and illegitimate objects of attack. Thus the court chaplains of the democracy. I am not sure how children and the aged fitted into this story: probably they cheered the soldiers and munitions workers up.

5. The Japanese attacked Pearl Harbor and there was war between America and Japan. Some American (Republican) historians now claim that the acknowledged fact that the American Government knew an attack was impending some hours before it occurred, but did not alert the people in local command, can only be explained by a purpose of arousing the passions of American people. However that may be, those passions were suitably aroused and the war was entered on with the same vague and hence limitless objectives; and once more unconditional surrender was the only condition on which the war was going to end.

6. Then came the great change: we adopted the system of 'area bombing' as opposed to 'target bombing'. This differed from even big raids on cities, such as had previously taken place in the course of the war, by being far more extensive and devastating and much less random; the whole of a city area would be systematically plotted out and dotted with bombs. 'Attila was a Sissy', as the *Chicago Tribune* headed an article on this subject.

7. In 1945, at the Potsdam conference in July, Stalin informed the American and British statesmen that he had received two requests from the Japanese to act as a mediator with a view to ending the war. He had refused. The Allies agreed on the 'general principle' – marvellous phrase! – of using the new type of weapon that America now possessed. The Japanese were given a chance in the form of the Potsdam Declaration, calling for unconditional surrender in face of overwhelming force soon to be arrayed against them. The historian of the Survey of International Affairs considers that this phrase was rendered meaningless by the statement of a series of terms; but of these the ones incorporating the Allies' demands were mostly of so vague and sweeping a nature as to be rather a declaration of what unconditional surrender would be like than to constitute conditions. It seems to be generally agreed that the Japanese were desperate enough to have accepted the Declaration but for their loyalty to their Emperor: the 'terms' would certainly have permitted the Allies to get rid of

him if they chose. The Japanese refused the Declaration. In consequence, the bombs were dropped on Hiroshima and Nagasaki. The decision to use them on people was Mr Truman's.

For men to choose to kill the innocent as a means to their ends is always murder, and murder is one of the worst of human actions. So the prohibition on deliberately killing prisoners of war or the civilian population is not like the Queensberry Rules: its force does not depend on its promulgation as part of positive law, written down, agreed upon, and adhered to by the parties concerned.

When I say that to choose to kill the innocent as a means to one's ends is murder, I am saying what would generally be accepted as correct. But I shall be asked for my definition of 'the innocent'. I will give it, but later. Here, it is not necessary; for with Hiroshima and Nagasaki we are not confronted with a borderline case. In the bombing of these cities it was certainly decided to kill the innocent as a means to an end. And a very large number of them, all at once, without warning, without the interstices of escape or the chance to take shelter, which existed even in the 'area bombings' of the German cities.

I have long been puzzled by the common cant about President Truman's courage in making this decision. Of course, I know that you can be cowardly without having reason to think you are in danger. But how can you be courageous? Light has come to me lately: the term is an acknowledgement of the truth. Mr Truman was brave because, and only because, what he did was so bad. But I think the judgement unsound. Given the right circumstances (for example that no one whose opinion matters will disapprove), a quite mediocre person can do spectacularly wicked things without thereby becoming impressive.

I determined to oppose the proposal to give Mr Truman an honorary degree here at Oxford. Now, an honorary degree is not a reward of merit: it is, as it were, a reward for being a very distinguished person, and it would be foolish to enquire whether a candidate deserves to be as distinguished as he is. That is why, in general, the question whether so-and-so should have an honorary degree is devoid of interest. A very distinguished person will hardly be also a notorious criminal, and if he should chance to be a non-notorious criminal it would, in my opinion, be improper to bring the matter up. It is only in the rather rare case in which a man is known everywhere for an action, in face of which it is sycophancy to honour him, that the question can be of the slightest interest.

I have been accused of being 'high-minded'. I must be saying 'You may not do evil that good may come', which is a disagreeably high-minded doctrine. The action was necessary, or at any rate it was thought by competent, expert military opinion to be necessary; it probably saved more lives than it sacrificed; it had a good result, it ended the war. Come now: if you had to choose between boiling one baby and letting some frightful disaster befall a thousand people – or a million people, if a thousand is not enough – what would you do? Are you going to strike an attitude and say 'You may not do evil that good may come'? (People who never hear such arguments will hardly believe they take place, and will pass this rapidly by.)

'It pretty certainly saved a huge number of lives'. Given the conditions, I agree. That is to say, if those bombs had not been dropped the Allies would have had to invade Japan to achieve their aim, and they would have done so. Very many soldiers on both sides would have been killed; the Japanese, it is said – and it may well be true – would have massacred the prisoners of war; and large numbers of their civilian population would have been killed by 'ordinary' bombing.

I do not dispute it. Given the conditions, that was probably what was averted by that action. But what were the conditions? The unlimited objective, the fixation on unconditional surrender. The disregard of the fact that the Japanese were desirous of negotiating peace. The character of the Potsdam Declaration – their 'chance'. I will not suggest, as some would like to do, that there was an exultant itch to use the new weapons, but it seems plausible to think that the consciousness of the possession of such instruments had its effect on the manner in which the Japanese were offered their 'chance'.

We can now reformulate the principle of doing evil that good may come: every fool can be as much of a knave as suits him.

I recommend this history to undergraduates reading Greats as throwing a glaring light on Aristotle's thesis that you cannot be or do any good where you are stupid.

I informed the Senior Proctor of my intention to oppose Mr Truman's degree. He consulted the Registrar to get me informed on procedure. The Vice-Chancellor was informed; I was cautiously asked if I had got up a party. I had not; but a fine House was whipped up to vote for the honour.

The dons at St John's were simply told 'The women are up to something in Convocation; we have to go and vote them down'. In Worcester, in All Souls, in New College, however, consciences were greatly exercised, as I have heard. A reason was found to satisfy them: *It would be wrong to try to PUNISH Mr Truman!* I must say I rather like St John's.

The Censor of St Catherine's had an odious task. He must make a speech which should pretend to show that a couple of massacres to a man's credit are not exactly a reason for not showing him honour. He had, however, one great advantage: he did not have to persuade his audience, who were already perfectly convinced of that proposition. But at any rate he had to make a show.

The defence, I think, would not have been well received at Nuremberg.

We do not approve the action; no, we think it was a *mistake*. (That is how communists now talk about Stalin's more murderous proceedings.) Further, Mr Truman did not make the bombs by himself, and decide to drop them without consulting anybody; no, he was only responsible for the decision. Hang it all, you can't make a man responsible just because 'his is the signature at the foot of the order'. Or was he not even responsible for the decision? It was not quite clear whether Mr Bullock was saying that or not; but I never heard anyone else seem to give the lie to Mr Truman's boasts. Finally, an action of this sort is, after all, only one episode: an incidental, as it were, in a career. Mr Truman has done some good.

I know that in one way such a speech does not deserve scrutiny; after all, it was just something to say on its occasion. And he had to say something. One must not suppose that one can glean anything a man actually thinks from what he says in such circumstances. Professor Stebbing exposing the logical fallacies in politicians' speeches is a comic spectacle.

(b)

Choosing to kill the innocent as a means to your ends is always murder. Naturally, killing the innocent as an end in itself is murder too; but that is no more than a possible future development for us:[8] in our part of the globe it is a practice that has so far been confined to the Nazis. I intend my formulation to be taken strictly; each term in it is necessary. For killing the innocent, even if you know as a matter of statistical certainty that the things you do involve it, is not necessarily murder. I mean that if you attack a lot of military targets, such as munitions factories and naval dockyards, as carefully as you can, you will be certain to kill a number of innocent people; but that is not murder. On the other hand, unscrupulousness in considering the possibilities turns it into murder. I here print as a case in point a letter which I received lately from Holland:

> We read in our paper about your opposition to Truman. I do not like him either, but do you know that in the war the English bombed the dykes of our province Zeeland, an island where nobody could escape anywhere to. Where the whole population was drowned, children, women, farmers working in the field, all the cattle, everything, hundreds and hundreds, and we were your allies! Nobody ever speaks about that. Perhaps it were well to know this. Or, to remember.

That was to trap some fleeing German military. I think my correspondent has something.

It may be impossible to take the thing (or people) you want to destroy as your target; it may be possible to attack it only by taking as the object of your attack what includes large numbers of innocent people. Then you cannot very well say they died by accident. Here your action is murder.

'But where will you draw the line? It is impossible to draw an exact line.' This is a common and absurd argument against drawing any line; it may be very difficult, and there are obviously borderline cases. But we have fallen into the way of drawing no line, and offering as justifications what an uncaptive mind will find only a bad joke. Wherever the line is, certain things are certainly well to one side or the other of it.

Now who are 'the innocent' in war? They are all those who are not fighting and not engaged in supplying those who are with the means of fighting. A farmer growing wheat which may be eaten by the troops is not 'supplying them with the means of fighting'. Over this, too, the line may be difficult to draw. But that does not mean that no line should be drawn, or that, even if one is in doubt just where to draw the line, one cannot be crystal clear that this or that is well over the line.

'But the people fighting are probably conscripts! In that case they are just as innocent as anyone else.' 'Innocent' here is not a term referring to personal responsibility at all. It means rather 'not harming'. But the people fighting are 'harming', so they can be attacked; but if they surrender they become in this sense innocent and so may not be maltreated or killed. Nor is there ground for trying them on a criminal charge; not, indeed, because a man has no personal responsibility for fighting, but because they were not the subjects of the state whose prisoners they are.

There is an argument which I know from experience it is necessary to forestall at this point, though I think it is visibly captious. It is this: on my theory, would it not follow that a soldier can only be killed when he is actually attacking? Then, for example, it would be impossible to attack a sleeping camp. The answer is that 'what someone is doing' can refer either to what he is doing at the moment or to his role in a situation. A soldier under arms is 'harming' in the latter sense even if he is asleep. But it is true that the enemy should not be attacked more ferociously than is necessary to put them *hors de combat*.

These conceptions are distinct and intelligible ones; they would formerly have been said to belong to the Law of Nations. Anyone can see that they are good, and we pay tribute to them by our moral indignation when our enemies violate them. But in fact they are going, and only fragments of them are left. General Eisenhower, for example, is reported to have spoken slightingly once of the notion of chivalry towards prisoners – as if that were based on respect for their virtue or for the nation from which they come, and not on the fact that they are now defenceless.

It is characteristic of nowadays to talk with horror of killing rather than of murder, and hence, since in war you have committed yourself to killing – for example 'accepted an evil' – not to mind whom you kill. This seems largely to be the work of the devil; but I also suspect that it is in part an effect of the existence of pacifism, as a doctrine which many people respect though they would not adopt it. This effect would not exist if people had a distinct notion of what makes pacifism a false doctrine.

It therefore seems to me important to show that for one human being deliberately to kill another is not inevitably wrong. I may seem to be wasting my time, as most people do reject pacifism. But it is nevertheless important to argue the point because if one does so one sees that there are pretty severe restrictions on legitimate killing. Of course, people accept this within the state, but when it comes to war they have the idea that any restrictions are something like the Queensberry Rules – instead of making the difference between being guilty and not guilty of murder.

I will not discuss the self-defence of a private person. If he kills the man who attacks him or someone else, it ought to be accidental. To aim at killing, even when one is defending oneself, is murderous. (I fear even this idea is going. A man was acquitted recently who had successfully set a lethal booby trap to kill a thief in his absence.)

But the state actually has the authority to order deliberate killing in order to protect its people or to put frightful injustices right. (For example, the plight of the Jews under Hitler would have been a reasonable cause of war.) The reason for this is pretty simple: it stands out most clearly if we first consider the state's right to order such killing within its confines. I am not referring to the death penalty, but to what happens when there is rioting or when violent malefactors have to be caught. Rioters can sometimes only be restrained, or malefactors seized, by force. Law without force is ineffectual, and human beings without laws miserable (though we, who have too many and too changeable laws, may easily not feel this very distinctly). So much is indeed fairly obvious, though the more peaceful the society the less obvious it is that the force in the hands of the servants of the law has to be force up to the point of killing. It would become perfectly obvious any time there was rioting or gangsterism which had to be dealt with by the servants of the law fighting.

The death penalty itself is a completely different matter. The state is not fighting the criminal who is condemned to death. That is why the death penalty is not indispensable. People keep on discussing whether the point of it is deterrence or vengeance; it is neither. Not deterrence, because nobody has proved anything about that, and people think what they think in accordance with their prejudices. And not vengeance, because that is nobody's business. Confusion arises on this subject because the state is said, and correctly said, to *punish* the criminal, and 'punishment' suggests 'vengeance'. Therefore many humane people dislike the idea and prefer such notions as 'correction' and 'rehabilitation'. But the action of the state in depriving a man of his rights, up to his very life, has to be considered from two sides. First, from that of the man himself. If he could justly say 'Why have you done this to me? I have not deserved it', then the state would be acting with injustice. Therefore he must be proved guilty,

and only as punishment has the state the right to inflict anything on him. The concept of punishment is our one safeguard against being done 'good' to, in ways involving a deprivation of rights, by impudent powerful people. Second, from the side of the state, divine retributive justice is not its affair: it only has to protect its people and restrain malefactors. The ground of its right to deprive of liberty and even life is only that the malefactor is a nuisance, like a gangrenous limb. Therefore it can cut him off entirely, if his crime is so bad that he could not justly protest 'I have not deserved *this*.' But when I say that the sole ground of the state's right to kill him is that he is a nuisance, I only mean that he is a nuisance *qua* malefactor. The lives of the innocent are the actual point of society, so the fact that in some other way they may be a nuisance (troublesome to look after, for example) does not justify the state in getting rid of them. Though that is another thing we may yet come to. But the blood of the innocent cries to heaven for vengeance.

Thus the malefactor who has been found guilty is the only defenceless person whom the state may put to death. It need not; it can choose more merciful laws. (I have no prejudice in favour of the death penalty.) Any other defenceless person is as such innocent, in the sense 'not harming'. And so the state can only order to kill others of its subjects besides convicted criminals if they are rioting or doing something that has to be stopped, and can only be stopped by the servants of the law fighting them.

Now, this is also the ground of the state's right to order people to fight external enemies who are unjustly attacking them or something of theirs. The right to order to fight for the sake of other people's wrongs, to put right something affecting people who are not actually under the protection of the state, is a rather more dubious thing obviously, but it exists because of the common sympathy of human beings whereby one feels for one's neighbour if he is attacked. So in an attenuated sense it can be said that something that belongs to, or concerns, one is attacked if anybody is unjustly attacked or maltreated.

Pacifism, then, is a false doctrine. Now, no doubt, it is bad just for that reason, because it is always bad to have a false conscience. In this way the doctrine that it is a bad act to lay a bet is bad: it is all right to bet what it is all right to risk or drop in the sea. But I want to maintain that pacifism is a harmful doctrine in a far stronger sense than this.

Even the prevalence of the idea that it was wrong to bet would have no particularly bad consequences; a false doctrine which merely forbids what is not actually bad need not encourage people in anything bad. But with pacifism it is quite otherwise. It is a factor in that loss of the conception of murder which is my chief interest in this pamphlet.

I have very often heard people say something like this: 'It is all very well to say "Don't do evil that good may come." But *war* is evil. We all know that. Now, of course, it is possible to be an Absolute Pacifist. I can respect that, but I can't be one myself, and most other people won't be either. So we have to accept the evil. It is not that we do not see the evil. And once you are in for it, you have to go the whole hog.'

This is much as if I were defrauding someone, and when someone tried to stop me I said: 'Absolute honesty! I respect that. But of course absolute honesty really means having no property at all . . .' Having offered the sacrifice of a few sighs and tears to absolute honesty, I go on as before.

The correct answer to the statement that 'war is evil' is that it is bad – for example a misfortune – to be at war. And no doubt if two nations are at war at least one is unjust. But that does not show that it is wrong to fight or that if one does fight one can also commit murder.

Naturally my claim that pacifism is a very harmful doctrine is contingent on its being a false one. If it were a true doctrine, its encouragement of this nonsensical 'hypocrisy of the ideal standard' would not count against it. But given that it is false, I am inclined to think it is also very bad, unusually so for an idea which seems as it were to err on the noble side.

When I consider the history of events from 1939 to 1945, I am not surprised that Mr Truman is made the recipient of honours. But when I consider his actions by themselves, I am surprised again.

Some people actually praise the bombings and commend the stockpiling of atomic weapons on the ground that they are so horrible that nations will be afraid ever again to make war. 'We have made a covenant with death, and with hell we are at an agreement.' There does not seem to be good ground for such a hope for any long period of time.

Pacifists have for long made it a point in their propaganda that men must grow more murderous as their techniques of destruction improve, and those who defend murder eagerly seize on this point, so that I imagine by now it is pretty well accepted by the whole world. Of course, it is not true. In Napoleon's time, for example, the means of destruction had much improved since the time of Henry V; but Henry, not Napoleon, was a great massacrer of civilians, saying when he did particularly atrocious things that the French were a sinful nation and that he had a mission from God to punish them. And, of course, really large scale massacre up to now has belonged to times with completely primitive methods of killing. Weapons are now manufactured whose sole point is to be used in massacre of cities. But the people responsible are not murderous because they have these weapons; they have them because they are murderous. Deprived of atomic bombs, they would commit massacres by means of other bombs.

Protests by people who have not power are a waste of time. I was not seizing an opportunity to make a 'gesture of protest' at atomic bombs; I vehemently object to *our* action in offering Mr Truman honours, because one can share in the guilt of a bad action by praise and flattery, as also by defending it. When I puzzle myself over the attitude of the Vice-Chancellor and the Hebdomadal Council, I look round to see if any explanation is available why so many Oxford people should be willing to flatter such a man.

I get some small light on the subject when I consider the productions of Oxford moral philosophy since the First World War, which I have lately had occasion to read. Its character can easily be briefly demonstrated. Up to the Second World War the prevailing moral philosophy in Oxford taught that an action can be 'morally good' no matter how objectionable the thing done may be. An instance would be Himmler's efforts at exterminating the Jews: he did it from the 'motive of duty' which has 'supreme value'. In the same philosophy – which has much pretence of moral seriousness, claiming that 'rightness' is an objective character in acts, that can be discerned by a moral sense – it is also held that it might be right to kill the innocent for the good of the people, since the 'prima facie duty' of securing some advantage might outweigh the 'prima facie duty' of not killing the innocent. This sort of philosophy is less prevalent now, and in its place I find another, whose cardinal principle is that 'good' is not a 'descriptive' term, but one expressive of a favourable attitude on the part of the speaker. Hand in hand with this, though I do not know if there is any logical connection, goes a doctrine that it is impossible to have any quite general moral laws; such laws as 'It is wrong to lie' or 'Never commit sodomy' are rules of thumb which an experienced person knows when to break. Further, both his selection of these as the rules on which to proceed, and his tactful adjustments of them in particular cases, are based on their fitting together with the 'way of life' which is his preference. Both these philosophies, then, contain a repudiation of the idea that any class of actions, such as murder, may be absolutely excluded. I do not know how

influential they may have been or be; they are perhaps rather symptomatic. Whether influential or symptomatic, they throw some light on the situation.

It is possible still to withdraw from this shameful business in some slight degree; it is possible not to go to Encaenia; if it should be embarrassing to someone who would normally go to plead other business, he could take to his bed. I, indeed, should fear to go, in case God's patience suddenly ends.

Notes

1 Sertillanges, quoted 'Moral Principles and Practice', Cambridge Summer School (1932), p. 74.

2 For a fuller discussion of the natural law, see Thomas Aquinas, 1a 2ae, 91, 1a 2ae, 94, or any textbook of moral theology.

3 For sources concerning the conditions of the just war, see J. Eppstein, *Catholic Tradition and the Law of Nations* (London, 1935), and, more fully, Regaut, *La Doctrine de la Guerre Juste*.

4 This, of course, does not apply to denunciation of those parts of international law not affected by the natural law.

5 Ctr. Thomas Aquinas, *Summa Theologica* 2a 2ae. 64, *De Homicidio*, on the example of killing in self-de-

fence. 'The force used must be proportioned to the necessity.'

6 See any textbook of moral theology.

7 *Summi Pontificatus*, pp. 29–30, in the Vatican Latin edition. When quoting from this encyclical we have sometimes made use of the Vatican official English translation, sometimes of the English version of Mgr Knox; but comparing these with the Latin original we have often found cause to alter the translation ourselves.

8 This will seem a preposterous assertion; but we are certainly on the way, and I can think of no reasons for confidence that it will not happen.

42

National Self-determination

Avishai Margalit and Joseph Raz

In the controversy-ridden fields of international law and international relations, the widespread recognition of the existence of national rights to self-determination provides a welcome point of agreement. Needless to say, the core consensus is but the eye of a raging storm concerning the precise definition of the right, its content, its bearers, and the proper means for its implementation. This chapter will not address such questions, though indirectly it may help with their investigation. Its concern is with the moral justification of the case for national self-determination. Its purpose is critical and evaluative, its subject lies within the morality of international relations rather than within international law and international relations proper.

It is assumed throughout that states and international law should recognize such a right only if there is a sound moral case for it. This does not mean that international law should mirror morality. Its concern is with setting standards that enjoy the sort of clarity required to make them the foundations of international relations between states and fit for recognition and enforcement through international organs. These concerns give rise to special considerations that should be fully recognized in the subtle process of applying moral principles to the law. The derivation of legal principles from moral premises is never a matter of copying morality into law. Still, the justification of the law rests ultimately on moral considerations, and therefore those considerations should also help shape the contours of legal principles. That is why

the conclusions of this article bear on controversies concerning the proper way in which the law on this subject should develop, even though such issues are not here discussed directly.

Moral inquiry is sometimes understood in a utopian manner, i.e., as an inquiry into the principles that should prevail in an ideal world. It is doubtful whether this is a meaningful enterprise, but it is certainly not the one we are engaged in here. We assume that things are roughly as they are, especially that our world is a world of states and of a variety of ethnic, national, tribal, and other groups.[1] We do not question the justification for this state of affairs. Rather, we ask whether, given that this is how things are and for as long as they remain the same, a moral case can be made in support of national self-determination.

I Isolating the Issue

The core content of the claim to be examined is that there is a right to determine whether a certain territory shall become, or remain, a separate state (and possibly also whether it should enjoy autonomy within a larger state). The idea of national self-determination or (as we shall refer to it in order to avoid confusion) the idea of self-government encompasses much more. The value of national self-government is the value of entrusting the general political power over a group and its members to the group. If self-government is valu-

Originally published in *Journal of Philosophy* LXXXVII (1990): 439–61. Reprinted by permission of the authors.

able then it is valuable that whatever is a proper matter for political decision should be subject to the political decision of the group in all matters concerning the group and its members. The idea of national self-government, in other words, speaks of groups determining the character of their social and economic environment, their fortunes, the course of their development, and the fortunes of their members by their own actions, i.e., by the action of those groups, in as much as these are matters which are properly within the realm of political action.[2] Given the current international state system, in which political power rests, in the main, with sovereign states,[3] the right to determine whether a territory should be an independent state is quite naturally regarded as the main instrument for realizing the ideal of self-determination. Consideration of this right usually dominates all discussions of national self-determination. To examine the justification of the right is the ultimate purpose of this article. But we shall continuously draw attention to the fact that, as we shall try to show, the right of self-determination so understood is not ultimate, but is grounded in the wider value of national self-government, which is itself to be only instrumentally justified.

The next section deals with the nature of the groups that might be the subject of such a right. Section III considers what value, if any, is served by the enjoyment of political independence by such groups. Section IV examines the case for conceding that there is a moral right to self-determination. This examination may lead to revising our understanding of the content of the right. It may reveal that moral considerations justify only a narrower right, or that the argument that justifies the right warrants giving it a wider scope. But the core as identified here will provide the working base from which to launch the inquiry.

Before we start, a few words about this way of identifying the problem may be in place. In two ways the chosen focus of our examination is narrower than many discussions of self-determination in international relations. First, we disregard the claims made, typically by third-world countries, in the name of self-determination, against the economic domination of multinational companies, the World Bank, or against powerful regional or world powers. The considerations canvassed in this paper are relevant to such issues, but fall short of directly tackling them. To be complete, a discussion of a right must examine both its grounds and its consequences. This paper is concerned mostly

with the grounds for the right of self-determination. It asks the question: Who has the right and under what conditions is it to be exercised? It does not go into the question of the consequences of the right beyond the assumption, already stated, that it is a right that a territory be a self-governing state. A good deal of the current turmoil in international law, and international relations, has to do with the exploration of that last notion. What is entailed by the fact that a state is a sovereign, self-governing, entity? The claims that economic domination violate the right to self-determination belong to that discussion. The conclusions of this paper provide part of the grounds by which such claims are to be settled. But we do not propose to pursue this question here.

Second, claims of self-determination are invariably raised whenever one state invades and occupies another, or a territory belonging to another. Yet it is important to distinguish between the wrongness of military invasion or occupation, and the rights available against it, and the right (whatever it may turn one to be) to self-determination. In a word, the latter is a source of title, whereas the former is a possessory right based largely on public-order considerations. Any legal system, international law not excluded, recognizes certain ways as legitimate ways of solving disputes, and outlaws others. Subject to the exceptions of legitimate self-defense and self-help, the use of violence is forbidden. Violation of that prohibition gives rise to a right to have the *status quo ante* restored, before the deeper sources of the dispute between the parties are examined; that is, regardless of the soundness of one's title to a territory, one may not use force to occupy it. This is why the right to recover a territory lost by force is a possessory right. It does not depend on the ultimate soundness of one's title, and that is why it was said to be based on public-order considerations. A large part of its justification is in the need to establish that the proper means of dispute resolution be the only ones resorted to.

Not surprisingly, invocation of this possessory right is, however, accompanied by a claim of good title (the merits of which are not immediately relevant). The underlying title is often the right to self-determination. Hence the temptation to confuse the two. But notice that, apart from the different justificatory foundations, the two are far from identical in consequence. They merely overlap. The claims of a people who have been for many years ruled by another cannot be based on the possessory right that applies only against a recent occupier. On the other hand, the occupation of portions of Antarctica, or of some uninhabited island, do violate the possessory right, but not the right of self-determination. The latter is that of the inhabitants, and does not apply when there are no inhabitants.[4]

II Groups

Assuming that self-determination is enjoyed by groups, what groups qualify? Given that the right is normally attributed to peoples or nations, it is tempting to give that as the answer and concentrate on characterizing "peoples" or "nations." The drawbacks of this approach are two: it assumes too much and it poses problems that may not require a solution.

It is far from clear that peoples or nations rather than tribes, ethnic groups, linguistic, religious, or geographical groups are the relevant reference group. What is it that makes peoples particularly suited to self-determination? The right concerns determination whether a certain territory shall be self-governing or not. It appears to affect most directly the residents of a territory, and their neighbors. If anyone, then residents of geographical regions seem intuitively to be the proper bearers of the right. Saying this does not get us very far. It does not help in identifying the residents of which regions should qualify. To be sure, this is the crucial question. But even posing it in this way shows that the answer, "the largest regions inhabited by one people or nation," is far from being the obvious answer.

We have some understanding of the benefits self-government might bring. We need to rely on this in looking for the characteristics that make groups suitable recipients of those benefits. We want, in other words, to identify groups by those characteristics which are relevant to the justification of the right. If it turns out that those do not apply to peoples or nations, we shall have shown that the right to self-determination is misconceived and, as recognized in international law, unjustified. Alternatively, the groups identified may encompass peoples (or some peoples) as well as other groups. This will provide a powerful case for redrawing the boundaries of the right. Either way we shall be saved much argument concerning the characterization of nations which, interesting as it is in itself, is irrelevant to our purpose.

Having said that, it may be useful to take nations and peoples as the obvious candidates for the right. We need not worry about their defining characteristics. But we may gain insight by comparing them with groups, e.g., the fiction-reading public, or Tottenham Football Club supporters, which obviously do not enjoy such a right. Reflection on such examples suggests six characteristics that in combination are relevant to a case for self-determination.

1. The group has a common character and a common culture that encompass many, varied and important aspects of life, a culture that defines or marks a variety of forms or styles of life, types of activities, occupations, pursuits, and relationships. With national groups we expect to find national cuisines, distinctive architectural styles, a common language, distinctive literary and artistic traditions, national music, customs, dress, ceremonies and holidays, etc. None of these is necessary. They are but typical examples of the features that characterize peoples and other groups that are serious candidates for the right to self-determination. They have pervasive cultures, and their identity is determined at least in part by their culture. They possess cultural traditions that penetrate beyond a single or a few areas of human life, and display themselves in a whole range of areas, including many which are of great importance for the well-being of individuals.

2. The correlative of the first feature is that people growing up among members of the group will acquire the group culture, will be marked by its character. Their tastes and their options will be affected by that culture to a significant degree. The types of careers open to one, the leisure activities one learned to appreciate and is therefore able to choose from, the customs and habits that define and color relations with strangers and with friends, patterns of expectations and attitudes between spouses and among other members of the family, features of lifestyles with which one is capable of empathizing and for which one may therefore develop a taste – all these will be marked by the group culture.

They need not be indelibly marked. People may migrate to other environments, shed their previous culture, and acquire a new one. It is a painful and slow process, success in which is rarely complete. But it is possible, just as it is possible that socialization will fail and one will fail to be marked by the culture of one's environment, except negatively, to reject it. The point made is merely the modest one that, given the pervasive nature of the culture of the groups we are seeking to identify, their influence on individuals who grow up in their midst is profound and far-reaching. The point needs to be made in order to connect concern with the prosperity of the group with concern for the well-being of individuals. This tie between the individual and the collective is at the heart of the case for self-determination.

As one would expect, the tie does not necessarily extend to all members of the group, and failure of socialization is not the only reason. The group culture affects those who grow up among its members, be they members or not. But to say this is no more than to point to various anomalies and dilemmas that may arise. Most people live in groups of these kinds, so that those who belong to none are denied full access to the opportunities that are shaped in part by the group's culture. They are made to feel estranged and their chances to have a rewarding life are seriously damaged. The same is true of people who grow up among members of a group so that they absorb its culture, but are then denied access to it because they are denied full membership of the group.

Nothing in the above presupposes that groups of the kind we are exploring are geographically concentrated, let alone that their members are the only inhabitants of any region. Rather, by drawing on the transmission of the group culture through the socialization of the young, these comments emphasize the historical nature of the groups with which we are concerned. Given that they are identified by a common culture, at least in part, they also share a history, for it is through a shared history that cultures develop and are transmitted.

3. Membership in the group is, in part, a matter of mutual recognition. Typically, one belongs to such groups if, among other conditions, one is recognized by other members of the group as belonging to it. The other conditions (which may be the accident of birth or the sharing of the group culture, etc.) are normally the grounds cited as reasons for such recognition. But those who meet those other conditions and are yet rejected by the group are at best marginal or problematic members of it. The groups concerned are not formal institutionalized groups, with formal procedures of admission. Membership in them is a matter of informal acknowledgment of belonging by others generally, and by other members specifically. The fiction-reading public fails our previous tests. It is not identified by its sharing a wide-ranging pervasive culture. It also fails the third test. To belong to the fiction-reading public all we have to do is to read fiction. It does not matter whether others recognize us as fiction-reading.[5]

4. The third feature prepares the way for, and usually goes hand in hand with, the importance of membership for one's self-identification. Consider the fiction-reading public again. It is a historically significant group. Historians may study the evolution of the fiction-reading public, how it spread from women to men, from one class to others, from reading aloud in small groups to silent reading, from reliance on libraries to book buying, etc.; how it is regarded as important to one's qualification as a cultured person in one country, but not in another; how it furnishes a common topic of conversation in some classes but not in others; how belonging to the group is a mark of political awareness in some countries, while being a sign of escapist retreat from social concerns in another.

Such studies will show, however, that it is only in some societies that the existence of these features of the fiction-reading public is widely known. For the most part, one can belong to the group without being aware that one is a typical reader, that one's profile is that of most readers. Sometimes this is a result of a mistaken group image's being current in that society. Our concern is rather with those cases where the society lacks any very distinct image of that group. This indicates that, in such societies, membership of that group does not have a highly visible social profile. It is not one of the facts by which people pigeonhole each other. One need not be aware who, among people one knows, friends, acquaintances, shopkeepers one patronizes, one's doctor, etc., shares the habit. In such societies, membership of the fiction-reading public is not highly visible, that is, it is not one of the things one will normally know about people one has contact with, one of the things that identify "who they are." But it happens in some countries that membership of the reading public becomes a highly visible mark of belonging to a social group, to the intelligentsia, etc. In such countries, talk of the recently published novel becomes a means of mutual recognition.

One of the most significant facts differentiating various football cultures is whether they are cultures of self-recognition: whether identification as a fan or supporter of this club or that is one of the features that are among the main markers of people in the society. The same is true of occupational groups. In some countries, membership is highly visible and is among the primary means of pigeonholing people, of establishing "who they are"; in others, it is not.

Our concern is with groups, membership of which has a high social profile, that is, groups, membership of which is one of the primary facts by which people are identified, and which form expectations as to what they are like, groups membership of which is one of the primary clues for people generally in interpreting the conduct of others. Since our perceptions of ourselves are in large measure determined by how we expect others to perceive us, it follows that membership of such groups is an important identifying feature for each about himself. These are groups, members of which are aware of their membership and typically regard it as an important clue in understanding who they are, in interpreting their actions and reactions, in understanding their tastes and their manner.

5. Membership is a matter of belonging, not of achievement. One does not have to prove oneself, or to excel in anything, in order to belong and to be accepted as a full member. To the extent that membership normally involves recognition by others as a member, that recognition is not conditional on meeting qualifications that indicate any accomplishment. To be a good Irishman, it is true, is an achievement. But to be an Irishman is not. Qualification for membership is usually determined by nonvoluntary criteria. One cannot choose to belong. One belongs because of who one is. One can come to belong to such groups, but only by changing, e.g., by adopting their culture, changing one's tastes and habits accordingly – a very slow process indeed. The fact that these are groups, membership of which is a matter of belonging and not of accomplishment, makes them suitable for their role as primary foci of identification. Identification is more secure, less liable to be threatened, if it does not depend on accomplishment. Although accomplishments play their role in people's sense of their own identity, it would seem that at the most fundamental level our sense of our own identity depends on criteria of belonging rather than on those of accomplishment. Secure identification at that level is particularly important to one's well-being.

6. The groups concerned are not small face-to-face groups, members of which are generally known to all other members. They are anonymous groups where mutual recognition is secured by the possession of general characteristics. The exclusion of small groups from consideration is not merely ad hoc. Small groups that are based on personal familiarity of all with all are markedly different in the character of their relationships and interactions from anonymous groups. For example, given the importance of mutual recognition to members of these groups, they tend to develop conventional means of identification, such as the use of symbolic objects, participation in group ceremonies, special group manners, or special vocabulary, which help quickly to identify who is "one of us" and who is not.

The various features we listed do not entail each other but they tend to go together. It is not surprising that groups with pervasive cultures will be important in determining the main options and opportunities of their members, or that they will become focal points of identification, etc. The way things are in our world, just about everyone belongs to such a group, and not necessarily to one only. Membership is not exclusive and many people belong to several groups that answer to our description. Some of them are rather like national groups, e.g., tribes or ethnic groups. Others are very different. Some religious groups meet our conditions, as do social classes, and some racial groups. Not all religions or racial groups did develop rich and pervasive cultures. But some did and those qualify.

III The Value of Self-government

(a) *The value of encompassing groups*

The description of the relevant groups in the preceding section may well disappoint the reader. Some will be disappointed by the imprecise nature of the criteria provided. This would be unjustified. The criteria are not meant to provide operational legal definitions. As such they clearly would not do. Their purpose is to pick on the features of groups which may explain the value of self-determination. As already mentioned, the key to the explanation is in the importance of these groups to the well-being of their members. This thought guided the selection of the features. They are meant to assist in identifying that link. It is not really surprising that they are all vague matters of degree, admitting of many variants and many nuances. One is tempted to say "that's life." It does not come in neatly parceled parts. While striving to identify the features that matter, we have to recognize that they come in many shapes, in many shades, and in many degrees rife with impurities in their concrete mixing.

A more justified source of disappointment is the suspicion that we have cast the net too wide. Social classes clearly do not have a right to self-determination. If they meet the above conditions then those conditions are at best incomplete. Here we can only crave the reader's patience. We tried to identify the features of groups which help explain the value of self-determination. These may apply not only beyond the sphere in which the right is commonly recognized. They may apply to groups that really should not possess it for other reasons yet to be explored.

The defining properties of the groups we identified are of two kinds. On the one hand, they pick out groups with pervasive cultures; on the other, they focus on groups, membership of which is important to one's self-identity. This combination makes such groups suitable candidates for self-rule. Let us call groups manifesting the six features *encompassing groups*. Individuals find in them a culture which shapes to a large degree their tastes and opportunities, and which provides an anchor for their self-identification and the safety of effortless secure belonging.

Individual well-being depends on the successful pursuit of worthwhile goals and relationships. Goals and relationships are culturally determined. Being social animals means not merely that the means for the satisfaction of people's goals are more readily available within society. More crucially it means that those goals themselves are (when one reaches beyond what is strictly necessary for biological survival) the creatures of society, the products of culture. Family relations, all other social relations between people, careers, leisure activities, the arts, sciences, and other obvious products of "high culture" are the fruits of society. They all depend for their existence on the sharing of patterns of expectations, on traditions preserving implicit knowledge of how to do what, of tacit conventions regarding what is part of this or that enterprise and what is not, what is appropriate and what is not, what is valuable and what is not. Familiarity with a culture determines the boundaries of the imaginable. Sharing in a culture, being part of it, determines the limits of the feasible.

It may be no more than a brute fact that our world is organized in a large measure around groups with pervasive cultures. But it is a fact with far-reaching consequences. It means, in the first place, that membership of such groups is of great importance to individual well-being, for it greatly affects one's opportunities, one's ability to engage in the relationships and pursuits marked by the culture. Secondly, it means that the prosperity of the culture is important to the well-being of its members. If the culture is decaying, or if it is persecuted or discriminated against, the options and opportunities open to its members will shrink, become less attractive, and their pursuit less likely to be successful.

It may be no more than a brute fact that people's sense of their own identity is bound up with their sense of belonging to encompassing groups and that their self-respect is affected by the esteem in which these groups are held. But these facts, too, have important consequences. They mean that individual dignity and self-respect require that the groups, membership of which contributes to one's sense of identity, be generally respected and not be made a subject of ridicule, hatred, discrimination, or persecution.

All this is mere common sense, and is meant to be hedged and qualified in the way our common understanding of these matters is. Of course, strangers can participate in activities marked by a culture. They are handicapped, but not always very seriously. Of course, there are other determinants of one's opportunities, and of one's sense of self-respect. Membership of an encompassing group is but one factor. Finally, one should mention that groups and their culture may be pernicious, based on exploitation of people, be they their members or not, or on the denigration and persecution of other groups. If so, then the case for their protection and flourishing is weakened, and may disappear altogether.

Having regard for this reservation, the case for holding the prosperity of encompassing groups as vital for the prosperity of their members is a powerful one. Group interests cannot be reduced to individual interests. It makes sense to talk of a group's prospering or declining, of actions and policies as serving the group's interest or of harming it, without having to cash this in terms of individual interests. The group may flourish if its culture prospers, but this need not mean that the lot of its members or of anyone else has improved. It is in the interest of the group to be held in high regard by others, but it does not follow that, if an American moon landing increases the world's admiration for the United States, Americans necessarily benefit from this. Group interests are conceptually connected to the interests of their members but such connections are nonreductive and generally indirect. For example, it is possible that what enhances the interest of the group provides opportunities for improvement for its members, or that it increases the chance that they will benefit.

This relative independence of group interest is compatible with the view that informs this article: that the moral importance of the group's interest depends on its value to individuals. A large decline in the fortunes of the group may, e.g., be of little consequence to its members. There is no a priori way of correlating group interest with that of its members or of other individuals. It depends on the circumstances of different groups at different times. One clear consequence of the fact that the moral significance of a group's interest is in its service to individuals is the fact that it will depend, in part, on the size of the group. The fortunes of a larger group may be material to the well-being of a larger number of people. Other things being equal, numbers matter.

(b) *The instrumental case*

Does the interest of members in the prosperity of the group establish a right to self-determination? Certainly not, at least not yet, not without further argument. For one thing we have yet to see any connection between the prosperity of encompassing groups and their political independence. The easiest connection to establish under certain conditions is an instrumental one. Sometimes the prosperity of the group and its self-respect are aided by, sometimes they may be impossible to secure without, the group's enjoying political sovereignty over its own affairs. Sovereignty enables the group to conduct its own affairs in a way conducive to its prosperity.[6] There is no need to elaborate the point. It depends on historical conditions. Hence the prominence of a history of persecution in most debates concerning self-determination. But a history of persecution is neither a necessary nor a sufficient condition for the instrumental case for self-government. It is not a necessary condition, because persecution is not the only reason why the groups may suffer without independence. Suffering can be the result of neglect or ignorance of or indifference to the prosperity of a minority group by the majority. Such attitudes

may be so well entrenched that there is no realistic prospect of changing them.

Persecution is not a sufficient condition, for there may be other ways to fight and overcome persecution and because whatever the advantages of independence it may, in the circumstances, lead to economic decline, cultural decay, or social disorder, which only make their members worse off. Besides, as mentioned above, pernicious groups may not deserve protection, especially if it will help them to pursue repressive practices with impunity. Finally, there are the interests of nonmembers to be considered. In short, the instrumental argument (as well as others) for self-government is sensitive to counterarguments pointing to its drawbacks, its cost in terms of human well-being, possible violations of human rights, etc.

We shall return to these issues below. First, let us consider the claim that the instrumental argument trivializes the case for self-government by overlooking its intrinsic value. Of the various arguments for the intrinsic value of self-government which have been and can be advanced, we examine one which seems the most promising.

(c) *An argument for the intrinsic value of self-government*

The argument is based on an extension of individual autonomy or of self-expression (if that is regarded as independently valuable). The argument unravels in stages: (1) people's membership of encompassing groups is an important aspect of their personality, and their well-being depends on giving it full expression; (2) expression of membership essentially includes manifestation of membership in the open, public life of the community; (3) this requires expressing one's membership in political activities within the community. The political is an essential arena of community life, and consequently of individual well-being; (4) therefore, self-government is inherently valuable, it is required to provide the group with a political dimension.

The first premise is unexceptionable. So is the second, though an ambiguity might be detected in the way it is often understood. Two elements need separating. First, given the importance of membership to one's well-being, it is vital that the dignity of the group be preserved. This depends, in part, on public manifestations of respect for the group and its culture, and on the absence of ridicule of the group, etc., from the public life of the society of which one is a member. One should not have to identify with or feel loyalty to a group that denigrates an encompassing group to which one belongs. Indeed, one should not have to live in an environment in which such attitudes are part of the common culture. Second, an aspect of well-being is an ability to express publicly one's identification with the group and to participate openly in its public culture. An encompassing group is centered on mutual recognition and is inevitably a group with a public culture. One cannot enjoy the benefits of membership without participation in its public culture, without public participation in its culture.

Both elements are of great importance. Both indicate the vital role played by public manifestations of group culture and group membership among the conditions of individual well-being. To the extent that a person's well-being is bound up with his identity as a member of an encompassing group it has an important public dimension. But that dimension is not necessarily political in the conventional narrow sense of the term. Even where it is, its political expression does not require a political organization whose boundaries coincide with those of the group. One may be politically active in a multinational, multicultural polity.

Here supporters of the argument for the intrinsic value of self-government may protest. The expression of membership in the political life of the community, they will say, involves more than its public expression. It involves the possibility of members of an encompassing group participating in the political life of their state, and fighting in the name of group interests in the political arena. Such actions, they will insist, may be not only instrumentally valuable to the group, but intrinsically important to its politically active members. They are valuable avenues of self-fullfilment. These points, too, have to be readily admitted. There is no reason to think that everyone must take part in politics, or else his or her development is stunted and personality or life are deficient. In normal times, politics is but an option that people may choose to take or to leave alone. Although its availability is important, for its absence deprives people of valuable opportunities, its use is strictly optional. Even if it is possible to argue that one's personal well-being requires some involvement with larger groups, and the avoidance of exclusive preoccupation with one's own affairs and those of one's close relations or friends, that involvement can take nonpolitical forms, such as activity in a

social club, interest in the fortunes of the arts in one's region, etc.

Politics is no more than an option, though this is true in normal times only. In times of political crises that have moral dimensions, it may well be the duty of everyone to stand up and be counted. In Weimar, Germans had a moral duty to become politically involved to oppose Nazism. There are many other situations where an apolitical attitude is not morally acceptable. But all of them are marked by moral crises. In the absence of crisis there is nothing wrong in being nonpolitical.

Having said this, we must repeat that the option of politics must remain open, and with it the option of fighting politically for causes to do with the interests of one's encompassing groups. But there is nothing here to suggest that this should be done in a political framework exclusive to one's group or dominated by it. There is nothing wrong with multinational states, in which members of the different communities compete in the political arena for public resources for their communities. Admittedly, prejudice, national fanaticism, etc., sometimes make such peaceful and equitable sharing of the political arena impossible. They may lead to friction and persecution. This may constitute a good argument for the value of self-government, but it is an instrumental argument of the kind canvassed above. There is nothing in the need for a public or even a political expression of one's membership of an encompassing group which points to an intrinsic value of self-government.

(d) *The subjective element*

In an indirect way, the attempt to argue for the intrinsic value of self-government does point to the danger of misinterpreting the instrumental approach to the question. First, the argument does not deny the intrinsic value of the existence of the political option as a venue for activity and self-expression to all (adult) members of society. We are not advocating a purely instrumentalist view of politics generally. The intrinsic value to individuals of the political option does not require expression in polities whose boundaries coincide with those of encompassing groups. That is the only point argued for above.

Second, the pragmatic, instrumentalist character of the approach advocated here should not be identified with an aggregating impersonal consequentialism. Some people tend to associate any instrumentalist approach with images of a bureaucracy trading off the interest of one person against that of another on the basis of some cost-benefit analysis designed to maximize overall satisfaction; a bureaucracy, moreover, in charge of determining for people what is really good for them, regardless of their own views of the matter. Nothing of the kind should be countenanced. Of course, conflicts among people's interests do arise, and call for rational resolution that is likely to involve sacrificing some interests of some people for the sake of others. Such conflicts, however, admit of a large degree of indeterminacy, and many alternative resolutions may be plausible or rational. In such contexts, talking of maximization, with its connotations of comparability of all options, is entirely out of place.

Furthermore, nothing in the instrumentalist and pragmatic nature of our approach should be allowed to disguise its sensitivity to subjective elements, its responsiveness to the perceptions and sensibilities of the people concerned. To a considerable extent, what matters is how well people feel in their environment: Do they feel at home in it or are they alienated from it? Do they feel respected or humiliated? etc. This leads to a delicate balance between "objective" factors and subjective perceptions. On the one hand, when prospects for the future are concerned, subjective perceptions of danger and likely persecution, etc., are not necessarily to be trusted. These are objective issues on which the opinion of independent spectators may be more reliable than that of those directly involved. On the other hand, the factual issue facing the independent spectators is how people will respond to their conditions, what will be their perceptions, their attitudes to their environment, to their neighbors, etc. Even a group that is not persecuted may suffer many of the ills of real persecution if it feels persecuted. That its perceptions are mistaken or exaggerated is important in pointing to the possibility of a different cure: removing the mistaken perception. But that is not always possible, and up to a point in matters of respect, identification, and dignity, subjective responses, justified or not, are the ultimate reality so far as the well-being of those who have them is concerned.

IV   A Right to Self-determination

It may seem that the case for self-government establishes a right to self-determination. That is, it establishes the reasons for the right sort of

group, an encompassing group, to determine that a territory shall be self-governing. But things are not that simple. The case for self-government shows that sometimes, under certain conditions, it is best that the political unit be roughly an encompassing group. A group's right to self-determination is its right to determine that a territory be self-governing, regardless of whether the case for self-government, based on its benefits, is established or not. In other words, the right to self-determination answers the question "who is to decide?", not "what is the best decision?". In exercising the right, the group should act responsibly in light of all the considerations we mentioned so far. It should, in particular, consider not only the interests of its members but those of others who may be affected by its decision. But if it has the right to decide, its decision is binding even if it is wrong, even if the case for self-government is not made.[7]

The problem in conceding the existence of such a right is, of course, not the possibility that a group that would best be self-governing does not wish to be so. Given the strong subjectivist element in the instrumentalist argument, such reluctance to assume independence would suggest that the case for its being self-governing is much weakened. The problem is that the case for self-government is hedged by considerations of the interest of people other than members of the groups, and by the other interests of members of the groups, i.e., other than their interests as members of the groups. These include their fundamental individual interests which should be respected, e.g., by a group whose culture oppresses women or racial minorities. These considerations raise the question whether encompassing groups are the most suitable bodies to decide about the case for self-government. Can they be entrusted with the decision in a matter in which their group interests are in conflict with other interests of members of the group as well as with the interests of other people? At the very least this suggests that the right must be qualified and hedged to protect other interests.

More fundamental still is the question of how the right of self-determination fits within our general conception of democratic decision making. We are used to a two-level structure of argument concerning social issues, such as just taxation, the provision of public education, etc. First, we explore the principles that should govern the matter at issue. Second, we devise a form of democratic procedure for determining what shall be done.

The first level answers the question "what should be done?". The second responds to the question "who should decide?".

On a simple majoritarian view, the issue of self-government seems to defy a democratic decision procedure. The question is "what is the relevant democratic unit?" and that question cannot be democratically decided, at least not entirely so. In fact, of course, we are not simple majoritarians. We adopt a whole range of democratic procedures such as constitution-making privileged majorities, ordinary legislative processes, plebiscites, administrative processes, and decisions by special agencies under conditions of public accountability and indirect democratic control. We match various democratic processes with various social and political problems. This means that there is no universal democratic formula serving as the universal answer to "who decides?" questions. Rather, we operate a mixed principled-democratic system in which principles, whose credentials do not derive entirely from their democratic backing, determine what form of a democratic procedure is suited for what problem. Within this mixed principled-democratic framework, the right to self-determination fits as just another qualified democratic process suited to its object.

What are the principles involved? It is tempting to see here a principle giving the part veto over the issue of membership in a larger whole. To form a new political unit, or to remain part of an existing one, all component parts should agree. To break up a political unit, or to foil the creation of a new one, all that is required is the will of the group that wants to secede or to stay out. This principle derives its appeal from its voluntaristic aura. It seems to regard the justification of all political units as based on consent. But this is an undesirable illusion. It is undesirable since, as was explained above regarding encompassing groups, the more important human groupings need to be based on shared history, and on criteria of non-voluntaristic (or at least not wholly contractarian) membership to have the value that they have. The principle presents no more than an illusion of a contractarian principle since it refers to groups, not to individuals. But the whole contractarian ethos derives its appeal from the claim that each individual's consent is a condition of the legitimacy of political units. Beyond all that, the principle simply begs the question that it is meant to answer, namely, what are the parts? Which groupings have the veto and which do not? Can the group of all the

people whose surnames begin with a "g" and end with an "e" count for these purposes? Do they have the veto on membership in a larger political unit?

The right to self-determination derives from the value of membership in encompassing groups. It is a group right, deriving from the value of a collective good, and as such opposed in spirit to contractarian-individualistic[8] approaches to politics or to individual well-being. It rests on an appreciation of the great importance that membership in and identification with encompassing groups has in the life of individuals, and the importance of the prosperity and self-respect of such groups to the well-being of their members. That importance makes it reasonable to let the encompassing group that forms a substantial majority in a territory have the right to determine whether that territory shall form an independent state in order to protect the culture and self-respect of the group, provided that the new state is likely to respect the fundamental interests of its inhabitants, and provided that measures are adopted to prevent its creation from gravely damaging the just interests of other countries. This statement of the argument for the right requires elaboration.

1. The argument is an instrumental one. It says, essentially, that members of a group are best placed to judge whether their group's prosperity will be jeopardized if it does not enjoy political independence. It is in keeping with the view that, even though participation in politics may have intrinsic value to individuals, the shape and boundaries of political units are to be determined by their service to individual well-being, i.e., by their instrumental value. In our world, encompassing groups that do not enjoy self-government are not infrequently persecuted, despised, or neglected. Given the importance of their prosperity and self-respect to the well-being of their members, it seems reasonable to entrust their members with the right to determine whether the groups should be self-governing. They may sacrifice their economic or other interests for the sake of group self-respect and prosperity. But such a sacrifice is, given the circumstances of this world, often not unreasonable.

One may ask why should such matters not be entrusted to international adjudication by an international court, or some other international agency. Instead of groups having a right to self-determination which makes them judges in their own cause, the case for a group's becoming self-governing should be entrusted to the judgment of an impartial tribunal. This would have been a far superior solution to the question 'who is to decide?'. Unfortunately, there simply does not exist any international machinery of enforcement that can be relied upon in preference to a right of self-determination as the right of self-help, nor is there any prospect of one coming into existence in the near future. In the present structure of international relations, the most promising arrangement is one that recognizes group rights to self-determination and entrusts international bodies with the duty to help bring about its realization, and to see to it that the limits and preconditions of the right are observed (these are enumerated in the points two to five below).

2. The right belongs to the group. But how should it be exercised? Not necessarily by a simple majority vote. Given the long-term and irreversible nature of the decision (remember that while independence is up to the group, merger or union is not), the wish for a state must be shared by an overwhelming majority, reflecting deep-seated beliefs and feelings of an enduring nature, and not mere temporary popularity. The precise institutional requirements for the exercise of the right are issues that transcend the topic of this paper. They are liable to vary with the circumstances of different national and ethnic groups. Whatever they are they should reflect the above principle.

3. The right is over a territory. This simply reflects the territorial organization of our political world. The requirement that the group be a substantial majority of the territory stems from further considerations aimed at balancing the interest in self-government against the interests of non-members. First, it is designed to ensure that self-government for a territory does not generate a problem as great as it is meant to solve, by ensuring that the independence will not generate a large-scale new minority problem. That risk cannot be altogether avoided. As was remarked before, numbers count in the end.

A further factual assumption underlying this condition is that people are, even today, most directly affected by the goings-on in their region. It is true that one's economic conditions are affected by the economic activities in faraway places. This, however, is more and more true of the international system generally. The ideal of economic autarchy died a natural death. (Correspondingly, the condition of economic viability which used to figure in theories of the states in international relations has little role in the modern world.) What can be secured and protected, and what vitally matters to the quality of life, is its texture as determined by the local culture and custom, the nature of the physical environment, etc. Hence the right is given only to a group that is the majority in a territory. The case for self-government applies to groups that are not in the majority anywhere, but they do not have the right to self-determination anywhere. Their members, like other people, may have a right to immigration on an individual basis to a territory of their choice. But their case is governed by general principles of freedom of movement and the sovereign rights of existing states. This means that their communal interests remain an important consideration to be born in mind by the decision makers, but they have no right, i.e., the decision is not up to them.

Do historical ties make a difference? Not to the right if voluntarily abandoned. Suppose that the group was unjustly removed from the country. In that case, the general principle of restitution applies, and the group has a right to self-determination and control over the territory it was expelled from, subject to the general principle of prescription. Prescription protects the interests of the current inhabitants. It is based on several deep-seated concerns. It is meant to prevent the revival of abandoned claims, and to protect those who are not personally to blame from having their life unsettled by claims of ancient wrongs, on the ground that their case now is as good as that of the wronged people or their descendants. Prescription, therefore, may lose the expelled group the right even though its members continue to suffer the effects of the past wrong. Their interest is a consideration to be borne in mind in decisions concerning immigration policies, and the like, but because of prescription they lost the right to self-determination. The outcome is not up to them to decide.

4. The right is conditional on its being exercised for the right reasons, i.e., to secure conditions necessary for the prosperity and self-respect of the group. This is a major protection against abuse. Katanga cannot claim a right to self-determination as a way of securing its exclusive control over uranium mines within its territory. This condition does not negate the nature of a right. The group is still entrusted with the right to decide, and its decision is binding even if wrong, even if the case for self-government does not obtain, provided the reasons that motivate the group's decision are of the right kind.

5. Finally, there are the two broad safeguards on which the exercise of the right is conditional. First, that the group is likely to respect the basic rights of its inhabitants, so that its establishment will do good rather than add to the ills of this world. Secondly, since the establishment of the new state may fundamentally endanger the interests of inhabitants of other countries, its exercise is conditional on measures being taken to prevent or minimize the occurrence of substantial damage of this kind. Such measures, which will vary greatly from case to case, include free-trade agreements, port facilities, granting of air routes, demilitarization of certain regions, etc.

Two kinds of interests do not call for special protection. One is the interest of a people to regard themselves as part of a larger rather than a smaller grouping or country. The English may have an interest in being part of Great Britain, rather than mere Englanders. But that interest can be justly satisfied only with the willing co-operation of, e.g., the Scots. If the other conditions for Scottish independence are met, this interest of the English should not stand in its way. Secondly, unjust economic gains, the product of colonial or other form of exploitation of one group by another, may be denied to the exploiting group without hesitation or compensation (barring arrangements for a transitory period). But where secession and independence will gravely affect other and legitimate interests of other countries, such interests should be protected by creating free-trade zones, demilitarized areas, etc.

6. A right in one person is sufficient ground to hold some other person(s) to be under a duty.[9] What duties arise out of the right to self-determination? How is this matter to be settled? As the previous discussion makes clear, the right of self-determination is instrumentally justified, as the method of implementing the case for self-government, which itself is based on the fact that in many circumstances self-government is necessary for the prosperity and dignity of encompassing groups. Hence, in fixing the limits of the right, one has to bear in mind the existing system of international politics, and show that, given other elements in that system, certain duties can be derived from the right to self-determination, whereas others cannot. The first and most important duty arising out of the right is the duty not to impede the exercise of the right, i.e., not to impede groups in their attempts to decide whether appropriate territories should be independent, so long as they do so within the limits of the right. This duty affects in practice first and foremost the state that governs the territory concerned and its inhabitants.

There may be other duties following from the right of self-determination. In particular, there may be a duty on the state governing the territory to provide aid in exercising the right, and a duty on other states to aid the relevant group in realizing its right, and thus to oppose the state governing the territory if it impedes its implementation. But the extent of these duties must be subject to the general principles of international morality, which indicate what methods may and may not be used in pursuit of worthwhile goals and in preventing the violation of rights. As indicated at the outset, the examination of the details of such implications of the right is beyond the scope of this article.

This brings to an end our consideration of the outlines of the case for a right to self-determination and its limits. It is an argument that proceeds in several stages from fundamental moral concerns to the ways in which they can be best implemented, given the way our world is organized. The argument is meant to present the normal justification for the right. It does not claim that there could not be alternative justifications. But it does claim to be the central case, which alternatives presuppose or of which they are variations.[10]

Two conclusions emerge from this discussion. On the one hand, the right to self-determination is neither absolute nor unconditional. It affects important and diverse interests of many people, from those who will be citizens of the new state, if it comes into being, to others far away from it. Those who may benefit from self-government cannot insist on it at all costs. Their interests have to be considered along those of others. On the other hand, the interests of members of an encompassing group in the self-respect and prosperity of the group are among the most vital human interests. Given their importance, their satisfaction is justified even at a considerable cost to other interests. Furthermore, given the absence of effective enforcement machinery in the international arena, the interest in group prosperity justifies entrusting the decision concerning self-government to the hands of an encompassing group that constitutes the vast majority of the population in the relevant territory, provided other vital interests are protected.

Notes

1 This fact is doubly relevant. It is a natural fact about our world that it is a populated world with no unappropriated lands. It is a social and a moral fact that it is a world of nations, tribes, peoples, etc., that is, that people's perception of themselves and of others and their judgments of the opportunities and the responsibilities of life are shaped, to an extent, by the existence of such groups and their membership of them. It may be meaningful to claim that our views regarding national self-determination apply only to a populated world like ours. One may point to different principles that would prevail in a world with vast unoccupied fertile lands. Such speculation is utopian but it may serve to highlight some of the reasons for the principles that apply in our condition. To speculate concerning a reality different from ours in its basic social and moral constitution is pointless in a deeper way. Such social facts are constitutive of morality. Their absence undercuts morality's very foundations. We could say that under such changed conditions people will have normative beliefs and will be guided by some values. But they are not ones for which we can claim any validity.

2 This qualification is to take account of the fact that, according to doctrines of limited government, certain matters are outside the realm of politics, and no political action regarding them may be undertaken.

3 Among the exceptions to this rule are the slowly growing importance of supernational, especially regional, associations, such as the European Community, the growth of a doctrine of sovereignty limited by respect for fundamental human rights, and the continuing (usually thinly veiled) claims of some states that they are not bound by the international law regarding the sovereignty of states.

4 The substantive right protected indirectly by the possessory right in cases of this kind is one of the other rights providing a title in a territory. The right to self-determination is only one of the possible sources of title.

5 The fiction-reading public can take the character of a literary elite with mutual recognition as part of its identity. The importance of "acceptability" in such groups has often been noted and analyzed.

6 This is not meant to suggest that there are not often drawbacks to self-rule. They will be considered below.

7 It should be made clear that these observations relate to the right to self-determination as it is commonly understood in the discourse of international relations and international morality. In principle, there could be a different right of self-determination, i.e., a right that, when the case for self-government is established, self-government should be granted, i.e., that all the international agents have a duty to take what action is necessary to grant self-government to the encompassing group regarding which the case for self-government has been established. That is, there could in principle have been a substantive right to have self-government when it is right that one should have it, rather than a "who is to decide" right, that an encompassing group should be entitled to decide whether it should be self-governing. Below we touch briefly on the reasons that explain why the right of self-determination as we know it today is not of this kind.

8 The reference is to moral individualism, or value individualism, not to methodological individualism. It is impossible here to deal with the matter adequately. Let us simply indicate our position briefly. There is no accepted characterization of the term. In *The Morality of Freedom* [(New York: Oxford, 1986), p. 198], Raz identified moral individualism with the view that only individual goods, and no collective goods, have intrinsic values. According to individualism so understood, membership of encompassing groups, and the prosperity of such groups, cannot be of intrinsic value. But we believe that it is intrinsically valuable. Hence, on this definition our approach is not individualistic. In "Three Grades of Social Involvement" [*Philosophy and Public Affairs*, XVIII (1989), p. 133], George Sher characterizes moral individualism as the belief that moral justification proceeds through premises relating to individuals and their preferences. His characterization is too vague to be conclusively disputed (e.g., all holistic justifications will include premises relating to preferences as well as to everything else – does that make them individualistic?). But if Sher has in mind the standard type of (actual or hypothetical) contractarian justifications, then our approach is not individualistic. Because actual individual preferences heavily depend on social practices, there is no reason to give them justificatory primacy. The content of hypothetical preferences is either too indefinite to yield any results or is made definite by assuming a certain social context to give them meaning. Either way it cannot be endowed with justificatory primacy, though of course people's capacity to respond to various conditions, and to form various goals and attachments, is central to any moral justification.

9 See Raz, *The Morality of Freedom*, ch. 7: The Nature of Rights. On the relations of moral and legal rights, see also Raz, "Legal Rights," *Oxford Journal of Legal Studies*, IV (1984), p. 1. Raz has applied this analysis to the case of constitutional rights in general in ch. 10 of *The Morality of Freedom*.

10 On the notion of a "normal justification," and the reasons why it cannot be analyzed as either a necessary or a sufficient condition, see Raz, *The Morality of Freedom*, ch. 3.

43

The Law of Peoples

John Rawls

One aim of this lecture is to sketch – in a short space, I can do no more than that – how the law of peoples[1] may be developed out of liberal ideas of justice similar to but more general than the idea I called justice as fairness and presented in my book *A Theory of Justice* (1971). By the law of peoples I mean a political conception of right and justice[2] that applies to the principles and norms of international law and practice. In section 58 of the above work I indicated how from justice as fairness the law of peoples might be developed for the limited purpose of addressing several questions of just war. In this lecture my sketch of that law covers more ground and includes an account of the role of human rights. Even though the idea of justice I use to do this is more general than justice as fairness, it is still connected with the idea of the social contract: the procedure of construction, and the various steps gone through, are much the same in both cases.

A further aim is to set out the bearing of political liberalism once a liberal political conception of justice is extended to the law of peoples. In particular, we ask: What form does the toleration of nonliberal societies take in this case? Surely tyrannical and dictatorial regimes cannot be accepted as members in good standing of a reasonable society of peoples. But equally not all regimes can reasonably be required to be liberal, otherwise the law of peoples itself would not express liberalism's own principle of toleration for other reasonable ways of ordering society nor further its attempt to find a shared basis of agreement among reasonable peoples. Just as a citizen in a liberal society must respect other persons' comprehensive religious, philosophical, and moral doctrines provided they are pursued in accordance with a reasonable political conception of justice, so a liberal society must respect other societies organized by comprehensive doctrines, provided their political and social institutions meet certain conditions that lead the society to adhere to a reasonable law of peoples.

More specifically, we ask: Where are the reasonable limits of toleration to be drawn? It turns out that a well-ordered nonliberal society will accept the same law of peoples that well-ordered liberal societies accept. Here I understand a well-ordered society as being peaceful and not expansionist; its legal system satisfies certain requisite conditions of legitimacy in the eyes of its own people; and, as a consequence of this, it honors basic human rights (part IV). One kind of nonliberal society satisfying these conditions is illustrated by what I call, for lack of a better term, a well-ordered hierarchical society. This example makes the point, central for this argument, that although any society must honor basic human rights, it need not be liberal. It also indicates the role of human rights as part of a reasonable law of peoples.

I   How a Social Contract Doctrine is Universal in its Reach

I begin by explaining the way in which a social contract doctrine with its procedure of construction is universal in its reach.

Every society must have a conception of how it is related to other societies and of how it is to conduct itself toward them. It lives with them in the same world and except for the very special case of isolation of a society from all the rest – long in the past now – it must formulate certain ideals and principles for guiding its policies toward other peoples. Like justice as fairness, the more general liberal conception I have in mind – as specified in Part III – begins with the case of a hypothetically closed and self-sufficient liberal democratic society and covers only political values and not all of life. The question now arises as to how that conception can be extended in a convincing way to cover a society's relations with other societies to yield a reasonable law of peoples. In the absence of this extension to the law of peoples, a liberal conception of political justice would appear to be historicist and to apply only to societies whose political institutions and culture are liberal. In making the case for justice as fairness, and for similar more general liberal conceptions, it is essential to show that this is not so.

The problem of the law of peoples is only one of several problems of extension for these ideas of justice. There is the additional problem of extending these ideas to future generations, under which falls the problem of just savings. Also, since the ideas of justice regard persons as normal and fully cooperating members of society over a complete life, and having the requisite capacities to do this, there arises the problem of what is owed to those who fail to meet this condition, either temporarily or permanently, which gives rise to several problems of justice in health care. Finally, there is the problem of what is owed to animals and the rest of nature.

We would eventually like an answer to all these questions, but I doubt that we can find one within the scope of these ideas of justice understood as political conceptions. At best they may yield reasonable answers to the first three problems of extension: to other societies, to future generations, and to certain cases of health care. With regard to the problems which these liberal ideas of justice fail to address, there are several things we might say. One is that the idea of political justice does not cover everything and we should not expect it to. Or the problem may indeed be one of political justice but none of these ideas is correct for the question at hand, however well they may do for other questions. How deep a fault this shows must wait until the question itself can be examined, but we should not expect these ideas, or I think any account of political justice, to handle all these matters.

Let's return to our problem of extending liberal ideas of justice similar to but more general than justice as fairness to the law of peoples. There is a clear contrast between these and other familiar views in the way they are universal in reach. Take, for example, Leibniz's or Locke's doctrines: These are universal both in their source of authority and in their formulation. By that I mean that their source is God's authority or the divine reason, as the case may be; and they are universal in that their principles are stated so as to apply to all reasonable beings everywhere. Leibniz's doctrine is an ethics of creation. It contains the idea of morals as the *imitatio Dei* and applies straightway to us as God's creatures endowed with reason. In Locke's doctrine, God having legitimate authority over all creation, the natural law – that part of God's law that can be know by our natural powers of reason – everywhere has authority and binds us and all peoples.

Most familiar philosophical views – such as rational intuitionism, (classical) utilitarianism, and perfectionism – are also formulated in a general way to apply to us directly in all cases. Although they are not theologically grounded, let's say their source of authority is (human) reason, or an independent realm of moral values, or some other proposed basis of universal validity. In all these views the universality of the doctrine is the direct consequence of its source of authority and of how it is formulated.

By contrast, a constructivist view such as justice as fairness, and more general liberal ideas, do not begin from universal first principles having authority in all cases.[3] In justice as fairness the principles of justice for the basic structure of society are not suitable as fully general principles: They do not apply to all subjects, not to churches and universities, or to the basic structures of all societies, or to the law of peoples. Rather, they are constructed by way of a reasonable procedure in which rational parties adopt principles of justice for each kind of subject as it arises. Typically, a constructivist doctrine proceeds by taking up a series of subjects, starting, say, with principles of political justice for the basic structure of a closed and self-contained democratic society. That done, it then works forward to principles for the claims of future generations, outward to principles for the law of peoples, and inward to principles for special social questions. Each time the constructivist procedure is modified to fit the subject in question. In due course all the main principles are on hand, including those needed for the various political duties and obligations of individuals and associations.[4] Thus, a constructivist liberal doctrine is universal in its reach once it is extended to give principles for all politically relevant subjects, including a law of peoples for the most comprehensive subject, the political society of peoples. Its authority rests on the principles and conceptions of practical reason, but always on these as suitably adjusted to apply to different subjects as they arise in sequence; and always assuming as well that these principles are endorsed on due reflection by the reasonable agents to whom the corresponding principles apply.

At first sight, a constructivist doctrine of this kind appears hopelessly unsystematic. For how are the principles that apply to different cases tied together? And why do we proceed through the series of cases in one order rather than another? Constructivism assumes, however, that there are other forms of unity than that defined by completely general first principles forming a consistent scheme. Unity may also be given by an appropriate sequence of cases and by supposing that the parties in an original position (as I have called it) are to proceed through the sequence with the understanding that the principles for the subject of each later agreement are to be subordinate to those of subjects of all earlier agreements, or else coordinated with and adjusted to them by certain priority rules. I shall try out a particular sequence and point out its merits as we proceed. There is in advance no guarantee that it is the most appropriate sequence and much trial and error may be needed.

In developing a conception of justice for the basic structure or for the law of peoples, or indeed for any subject, constructivism does not view the variation in numbers of people alone as accounting for the appropriateness of different principles in different cases. That families are smaller than constitutional democracies does not explain why different principles apply to them. Rather, it is the distinct structure of the social framework, and the purpose and role of its various parts and how they fit together, that explain why there are different principles for different kinds of subjects. Thus, it is characteristic of a constructivist idea of justice to regard the distinctive nature and purpose of the elements of society, and of the society of peoples, as requiring persons, within a domain where other principles leave them free, to act from principles designed to fit their peculiar roles. As we shall see as we work out the law of peoples, these principles are identified in each case by rational agents fairly, or reasonably, situated given the case at hand. They are not derived from completely general principles such as the principle of utility or the principle of perfectionism.

II Three Preliminary Questions

Before showing how the extension to the law of peoples can be carried out, I go over three preliminary matters. First, let's distinguish between two parts of justice as fairness, or of any other similar liberal and constructivist conception of justice. One part is worked up to apply to the domestic institutions of democratic societies, their regime and basic structure, and to the duties and obligations of citizens. The other part is worked up to apply to the society of political societies and thus to the political relations between peoples.[5] After the principles of justice have been adopted for domestic justice, the idea of the original position is used again at the next higher level.[6] As before, the parties are representatives, but now they are representatives of peoples whose basic institutions satisfy the principles of justice selected at the first level. We start with the family of societies, each well-ordered by some liberal view meeting certain conditions (justice as fairness is an example), and then work out principles to govern their relations with one another. Here I mention only the first stage of working out the law of peoples. As we shall see in part IV, we must also develop principles which govern the relations between liberal and what I shall call hierarchical societies. It turns out that liberal and hierarchical societies can agree on the same law of peoples and thus this law does not depend on aspects peculiar to the Western tradition.

It may be objected that to proceed in this way is to accept the state as traditionally conceived, with all its familiar powers of sovereignty. These powers include first, the right to go to war in pursuit of state policies – Clausewitz's pursuit of politics by other means – with the aims of politics given by a state's rational prudential interests.[7] They include second, the state's right to do as it likes with people within its own borders. The objection is misapplied for this reason. In the first use of the original position domestic society is seen as closed, since we abstract from relations with other societies. There is no need for armed forces and the question of the government's right to be prepared militarily does not arise, and would be denied if it did. The principles of domestic justice allow a police force to keep domestic order but that is another matter, and although those domestic principles are consistent with a qualified right of war in a society of peoples, they do not of themselves support that right. That is up to the law of peoples itself, still to be constructed. And, as we shall see, this law will also restrict a state's internal sovereignty, its right to do as it likes to people within its borders.

Thus, it is important to see that in this working out of the law of peoples, a government as the political organization of its people is not, as it were, the author of its own power. The war powers of governments, whatever they should be, are only those acceptable within a reasonable law of peoples. Presuming the existence of a government whereby a people is domestically organized with institutions of background justice does not prejudge these questions. We must reformulate the powers of sovereignty in light of a reasonable law of peoples and get rid of the right to war and the right to internal autonomy, which have been part of the (positive) international law for the two and a half centuries following the Thirty Years War, as part of the classical states system.[8]

Moreover, these ideas accord with a dramatic shift in how international law is now understood. Since World War II international law has become far more demanding than in the past. It tends to restrict a state's right to wage war to cases of self-defense (this allows collective security), and it also tends to limit a state's right of internal sovereignty.[9] The role of human rights connects most obviously with the latter change as part of the effort to provide a suitable definition of, and limits on, a government's internal sovereignty, though it is not unconnected with the first. At this point I leave aside the many difficulties of interpreting these rights and limits, and take their general meaning and tendency as clear enough.

What is essential is that our elaboration of the law of peoples should fit – as it turns out to do – these two basic changes, and give them a suitable rationale.

The second preliminary matter concerns the question: In working out the law of peoples, why do we start (as I said above) with those societies well-ordered by liberal views somewhat more general than justice as fairness? Wouldn't it be better to start with the world as a whole, with a global original position, so to speak, and discuss the question whether, and in what form, there should be states, or peoples, at all? Some writers (I mention them later) have thought that a social contract constructivist view should proceed in this manner, that it gives an appropriate universality from the start.

I think there is no clear initial answer to this question. We should try various alternatives and weigh their pluses and minuses. Since in working out justice as fairness I begin with domestic society, I shall continue from there as if what has been done so far is more or less sound. Thus I build on the steps taken until now, as this seems to provide a suitable starting point for the extension to the law of peoples. A further reason for proceeding thus is that peoples as corporate bodies organized by their governments now exist in some form all over the world. Historically speaking, all principles and standards proposed for the law of peoples must, to be feasible, prove acceptable to the considered and reflective public opinion of peoples and their governments.

Suppose, then, that we are (even though we are not) members of a well-ordered society. Our convictions about justice are roughly the same as those of citizens (if there are any) in the family of societies well-ordered by liberal conceptions of justice and whose social and historical conditions are similar to ours. They have the same kinds of reasons for affirming their mode of government as we do for affirming ours. This common understanding of liberal societies provides an apt starting point for the extension to the law of peoples.

Finally, I note the distinction between the law of peoples and the law of nations, or international law. The latter is an existing, or positive, legal order, however incomplete it may be in some ways, lacking, for example, an effective scheme of sanctions such as normally characterizes domestic law. The law of peoples, by contrast, is a family of political concepts with principles of right, justice, and the common good, that specify the content of a liberal conception of justice worked up to extend to and to apply to international law. It provides the concepts and principles by which that law is to be judged.

This distinction between the law of peoples and the law of nations should be straightforward. It is no more obscure than the distinction between the principles of justice that apply to the basic structure of domestic society and the existing political, social, and legal institutions that actually realize that structure.

III The Extension to Liberal Societies

The three preliminary matters settled, I turn to the extension of liberal ideas of justice to the law of peoples. I understand these ideas of justice to contain three main elements: (i) a list of certain basic rights and liberties and opportunities (familiar from constitutional democratic regimes); (ii) a high priority for these fundamental freedoms, especially with respect to claims of the general good and of perfectionist values; and (iii) measures assuring for all citizens adequate all-purpose means to make effective use of their freedoms. Justice as fairness is typical of these conceptions except that its egalitarian features are stronger. To some degree the more general liberal ideas lack the three egalitarian features of the fair value of the political liberties, of fair equality of opportunity, and of the difference principle. These features are not needed for the construction of a reasonable law of peoples and by not assuming them our account has greater generality.

There are two main stages to the extension to the law of peoples and each stage has two steps. The first stage of the extension I call the ideal, or strict compliance, theory, and unless otherwise stated, we work entirely in this theory. This means that the relevant concepts and principles are strictly complied with by all parties to the agreements made and that the requisite favorable conditions for liberal or hierarchical institutions are on hand. Our first aim is to see what a reasonable law of peoples, fully honored, would require and establish in this case.

To make the account manageable, we suppose there are only two kinds of well-ordered domestic societies, liberal societies and hierarchical societies. I discuss at the first step the case of well-ordered liberal democratic societies. This leads to the idea of a well-ordered political society of societies of

democratic peoples. After this I turn to societies that are well-ordered and just, often religious in nature and not characterized by the separation of church and state. Their political institutions specify a just consultation hierarchy, as I shall say, while their basic social institutions satisfy a conception of justice expressing an appropriate conception of the common good. Fundamental for our rendering of the law of peoples is that both liberal and hierarchical societies accept it. Together they are members in good standing of a well-ordered society of the just peoples of the world.

The second stage in working out the law of peoples is that of nonideal theory, and it also includes two steps. The first step is that of noncompliance theory. Here we have the predicament of just societies, both democratic and hierarchical, as they confront states that refuse to comply with a reasonable law of peoples. The second step of this second stage is that of unfavorable conditions. It poses the different problem of how the poorer and less technologically advanced societies of the world can attain historical and social conditions that allow them to establish just and workable institutions, either liberal or hierarchical. In actual affairs, nonideal theory is of first practical importance and deals with problems we face every day. Yet, for reasons of space, I shall say very little about it (Parts VI and VII).

Before beginning the extension we need to be sure that the original position with the veil of ignorance is a device of representation for the case of liberal societies. In the first use of the original position, its function as a device of representation means that it models what we regard – you and I, and here and now[10] – as fair conditions for the parties, as representatives of free and equal citizens, to specify the terms of cooperation regulating the basic structure of their society. Since that position includes the veil of ignorance, it also models what we regard as acceptable restrictions on reasons for adopting a political conception of justice. Therefore, the conception the parties would adopt identifies the conception of justice that we regard – you and I, here and now – as fair and supported by the best reasons.

Three conditions are essential: First, the original position represents the parties (or citizens) fairly, or reasonably; second, it represents them as rational; and third, it represents them as deciding between available principles for appropriate reasons. We check that these three conditions are satisfied by observing that citizens are indeed represented fairly, or reasonably, in virtue of the symmetry and equality of their representatives' situation in the original position. Next, citizens are represented as rational in virtue of the aim of their representatives to do the best they can for their essential interests as persons. Finally, they are represented as deciding for appropriate reasons: The veil of ignorance prevents their representatives from invoking reasons deemed unsuitable, given the aim of representing citizens as free and equal persons.

At the next level, when the original position is used to extend a liberal conception to the law of peoples, it is a device of representation because it models what we would regard – you and I, here and now[11] – as fair conditions under which the parties, this time as representatives of societies well-ordered by liberal conceptions of justice, are to specify the law of peoples and the fair terms of their cooperation.

The original position is a device of representation because, as before, free and equal peoples are represented as both reasonably situated and rational, and as deciding in accordance with appropriate reasons. The parties as representatives of democratic peoples are symmetrically situated, and so the peoples they represent are represented reasonably. Moreover, the parties deliberate among available principles for the law of peoples by reference to the fundamental interests of democratic societies in accordance with, or as presupposed by, the liberal principles of domestic justice. And finally, the parties are subject to a veil of ignorance: They do not know, for example, the size of the territory, or the population, or the relative strength of the people whose fundamental interests they represent. Although they know that reasonably favorable conditions obtain that make democracy possible, they do not know the extent of their natural resources, or level of their economic development, or any such related information. These conditions model what we, as members of societies well-ordered by liberal conceptions of justice, would accept as fair – here and now – in specifying the basic terms of cooperation between peoples who, as peoples, regard themselves as free and equal. We use the original position at the second level as a device of representation as we did at the first.

I assume that working out the law of peoples for liberal democratic societies only will result in the adoption of certain familiar principles of justice, and will also allow for various forms of cooperative association among democratic peoples and not for a world state. Here I follow Kant's lead in *Perpetual Peace* (1795) in thinking that a world government – by which I mean a unified political regime with the legal powers normally exercised by central governments – would be either a global despotism or else a fragile empire torn by frequent civil strife as various regions and peoples try to gain political autonomy.[12] On the other hand, it may turn out, as I sketch below, that there will be many different kinds of organizations subject to the judgment of the law of democratic peoples, charged with regulating cooperation between them, and having certain recognized duties. Some of these organizations (like the United Nations) may have the authority to condemn domestic institutions that violate human rights, and in certain severe cases to punish them by imposing economic sanctions, or even by military intervention. The scope of these powers is all peoples' and covers their domestic affairs.

If all this is sound, I believe the principles of justice between free and democratic peoples will include certain familiar principles long recognized as belonging to the law of peoples, among them the following:

1 Peoples (as organized by their governments) are free and independent and their freedom and independence is to be respected by other peoples.
2 Peoples are equal and parties to their own agreements.
3 Peoples have the right of self-defense but no right to war.
4 Peoples are to observe a duty of nonintervention.
5 Peoples are to observe treaties and undertakings.
6 Peoples are to observe certain specified restrictions on the conduct of war (assumed to be in self-defense).
7 Peoples are to honor human rights.

This statement of principles is of course incomplete; other principles would need to be added. Further, they require much explanation and interpretation, and some of them are superfluous in a society of well-ordered democratic peoples, for instance, the sixth regarding the conduct of war and the seventh regarding human rights. The main point is that given the idea of a society of free and independent democratic peoples, who are ready to recognize certain basic principles of political justice governing their conduct, principles of this kind constitute the charter of their association.[13] Obviously, a principle such as the fourth – that of nonintervention – will have to be qualified in the general case. Although suitable for a society of well-ordered democratic peoples who respect human rights, it fails in the case of disordered societies in which wars and serious violations of human rights are endemic. Also, the right to independence, and equally the right to self-determination, hold only within certain limits, to be specified by the law of peoples for the general case. Thus, no people has the right to self-determination, or a right to secession, at the expense of the subjugation of another people;[14] nor can a people protest their condemnation by the world society when their domestic institutions violate the human rights of certain minorities living among them. Their right to independence is no shield from that condemnation, or even from coercive intervention by other peoples in grave cases.

There will also be principles for forming and regulating federations (associations) of peoples, and standards of fairness for trade and other cooperative arrangements. There should be certain provisions for mutual assistance between peoples in times of famine and drought, and were it feasible, as it should be, provisions for ensuring that in all reasonably developed liberal societies people's basic needs are met.[15] These provisions will specify duties of assistance in certain situations, and they will vary in stringency depending on the severity of the case.

An important role of a people's government, however arbitrary a society's boundaries may appear from a historical point of view,[16] is to be the representative and effective agent of a people as they take responsibility for their territory and the size of their population, as well as for maintaining its environmental integrity and its capacity to sustain them. The idea here appeals to the point of the institution of property: Unless a definite agent is given responsibility for maintaining an asset and bears the loss for not doing so, that asset tends to deteriorate. In this case the asset is the people's territory and its capacity to sustain them in perpetuity; the agent is the people themselves as politically organized. They must recognize that they cannot make up for irresponsibility in caring for their land and conserving their natural resources by conquest in war or by migrating into other people's territory without their consent.[17]

These remarks belong to ideal theory and indicate some of the responsibilities of peoples in a just society of well-ordered liberal societies. Since the boundaries of peoples are often historically the outcome of violence and aggression, and some peoples are wrongly subjected to others, the law of peoples in its nonideal part should, as far as possible, contain principles and standards – or at least some guidelines – for coping with these matters.

To complete this sketch of the law of peoples for well-ordered liberal societies only, let's consider under what conditions we can reasonably accept this part of the law of peoples and regard it as justified.

There are two conditions beyond the three requirements earlier noted in discussing the original position as a device of representation. These requirements were: that the parties (as representatives of free and equal peoples) be represented as reasonably situated, as rational, and as deciding in accordance with appropriate reasons. One of the two further conditions is that the political society of well-ordered democratic peoples should itself be stable in the right way.[18] Given the existence of a political society of such peoples, its members will tend increasingly over time to accept its principles and judgments as they come to understand the ideas of justice expressed in the law among them and appreciate its benefits for all liberal peoples.

To say that the society of democratic peoples is stable in the right way is to say that it is stable with respect to justice, that is, that the institutions and practices among peoples always more or less satisfy the relevant principles of justice, although social conditions are presumably always changing. It is further to say that the law of peoples is honored not simply because of a fortunate balance of power – it being in no people's interest to upset it – but because, despite the possibly shifting fortunes of different peoples, all are moved to adhere to their common law accepting it as just and beneficial for all. This means that the justice of the society of democratic peoples is stable with respect to the distribution of fortune among them. Here fortune refers not to a society's military success or the lack of it, but to other kinds of success: its achievement of political and social freedom, the fullness and expressiveness of its culture, the economic well-being of all its citizens.

The historical record suggests that, at least so far as the principle against war is concerned, this condition of stability would be satisfied in a society of just democratic peoples. Although democratic societies have been as often involved in war as nondemocratic states[19] and have often vigorously defended their institutions, since 1800, as Michael Doyle points out, firmly established liberal societies have not gone to war with one another.[20] And in wars in which a number of major powers were engaged, such as the two World Wars, democratic states have fought as allies on the same side. Indeed, the absence of war between democracies is as close as anything we know to an empirical law in relations between societies.[21] This being so, I shall suppose that a society of democratic peoples, all of whose basic institutions are well ordered by liberal conceptions of justice (though not necessarily by the same conception) will be stable in the right way as above specified. The sketch of the law of such peoples therefore seems to meet the condition of political realism given by that of stability for the right reasons.

Observe that I state what I call Doyle's law as holding between well-established and well-ordered liberal democracies that are significant if not major powers. The reasons for this law's holding (supposing it does) are quite compatible with actual democracies, marked as they are by considerable injustice and oligarchic tendencies, intervening, often covertly, in smaller countries whose democracies are less well established and secure. Witness the United States' overturning the democracies of Allende in Chile, Arbenz in Guatemala, Mossadegh in Iran, and, some would add, the Sandinistas in Nicaragua. Whatever the merits of these regimes, covert operations against them can be carried out by a government bureaucracy at the urging of oligarchic interests without the knowledge or criticism of the public, and presenting it with a fait accompli. All this is made easier by the handy appeal to national security given the situation of superpower rivalry in the Cold War, which allowed those democracies, however implausibly, to be cast as a danger. While democratic peoples are not expansionist, they do defend their security interest, and this an oligarchic government can easily manipulate in a time of superpower rivalry to support covert interventions once they are found out.[22]

The last condition for us to accept this sketch of the law of democratic peoples as sound is that we can, as citizens of liberal societies, endorse the principles and judgments of this law on due reflection. We must be able to say that the doctrine of the law of peoples for such societies, more than any other doctrine, ties together our considered political convictions and moral judgments at all levels of generality, from the most general to the more particular, into one coherent view.

IV Extension to Hierarchical Societies

Recall from Part III that the extension of liberal ideas of justice to the law of peoples proceeds in two stages, each stage having two steps. The first stage is that of ideal theory and we have just completed the first step of that: the extension of the law of peoples to well-ordered liberal societies only. The second step of ideal theory is more difficult: It requires us to specify a second kind of society – a hierarchical society, as I shall say – and then to state when such a society is well ordered. Our aim is to extend the law of peoples to these well-ordered hierarchical societies and to show that they accept the same law of peoples as liberal societies do. Thus, this shared law of well-ordered peoples, both liberal and hierarchical, specifies the content of ideal theory. It specifies the kind of society of well-ordered peoples all people should want and it sets the regulative end of their foreign policy. Important for us, it has the obvious corollary that nonliberal societies also honor human rights.

To show all this we proceed thus. First, we state three requirements for any well-ordered hierarchical regime. It will be clear that satisfying these requirements does not entail that a regime be liberal. Next, we confirm that, in an original position with a veil of ignorance, the representatives of well-ordered hierarchical regimes are reasonably situated as well as rational, and are moved by appropriate reasons. In this case also, the original position is a device of representation for the adoption of law among hierarchical peoples. Finally, we show that in the original position the representatives of well-ordered hierarchical societies would adopt the same law of peoples that the representatives of liberal societies do. That law thus serves as a common law of a just political society of well-ordered peoples.

The first of the three requirements for a hierarchical society to be well ordered is that it must be peaceful and gain its legitimate aims through diplomacy and trade, and other ways of peace. It follows that its religious doctrine, assumed to be comprehensive and influential in government policy, is not expansionist in the sense that it fully respects the civic order and integrity of other societies. If it seeks wider influence, it does so in ways compatible with the independence of, and the liberties within, other societies. This feature of its religion supports the institutional basis of its peaceful conduct and distinguishes it from leading European states during the religious wars of the sixteenth and seventeenth centuries.

A second fundamental requirement uses an idea of Philip Soper. It has several parts. It requires first, that a hierarchical society's system of law be such as to impose moral duties and obligations on all persons within its territory.[23] It requires further that its system of law be guided by a common good conception of justice, meaning by this a conception that takes impartially into account what it sees not unreasonably as the fundamental interests of all members of society. It is not the case that the interests of some are arbitrarily privileged, while the interests of others go for naught. Finally, there must be sincere and not unreasonable belief on the part of judges and other officials who administer the legal order that the law is indeed guided by a common good conception of justice. This belief must be demonstrated by a willingness to defend publicly the state's injunctions as justified by law. Courts are an efficient way of doing this.[24] These aspects of a legal order are necessary to establish a regime's legitimacy in the eyes of its own people. To sum up the second requirement we say: The system of law is sincerely and not unreasonably believed to be guided by a common good conception of justice. It takes into account people's essential interests and imposes moral duties and obligations on all members of society.

This second requirement can be spelled out further by adding that the political institutions of a well-ordered hierarchical society constitute a reasonable consultation hierarchy. They include a family of representative bodies, or other assemblies, whose task is to look after the important interests of all elements of society. Although in hierarchical societies persons are not regarded as free and equal citizens, as they are in liberal societies, they are seen as responsible members of society who can recognize their moral duties and obligations and play their part in social life.

With a consultation hierarchy there is an opportunity for different voices to be heard, not, to be sure, in a way allowed by democratic institutions, but appropriately in view of the religious and philosophical values of the society in question. Thus, individuals do not have the right of free speech as in a liberal society; but as members of associations and corporate bodies they have the right at some point in the process of consultation to express political dissent and the government has an obligation to take their dissent seriously and to give a conscientious reply. That different voices can be heard is necessary because the sincere belief of judges and other officials has two components: honest belief and respect for the possibility of dissent.[25] Judges and officials must be willing to address objections. They cannot refuse to listen to them on the grounds that they think those expressing them are incompetent and cannot understand. Then we would not have a consultation hierarchy but a purely paternalistic regime.

In view of this account of the institutional basis of a hierarchical society, we can say that its conception of the common good of justice secures for all persons at least certain minimum rights to means of subsistence and security (the right to life),[26] to liberty (freedom from slavery, serfdom, and forced occupations) and (personal) property, as well as to formal equality as expressed by the rules of natural justice[27] (for example, that similar cases be treated similarly). This shows that a well-ordered hierarchical society also meets a third requirement: it respects basic human rights.

The argument for this conclusion is that the second requirement rules out violations of these rights. For to satisfy it, a society's legal order must impose moral duties and obligations on all persons in its territory and it must embody a reasonable consultation hierarchy which will protect human rights. A sincere and reasonable belief on the part of judges and other officials that the system of law is guided by a common good conception of justice has the same result. Such a belief is simply unreasonable, if not irrational, when those rights are infringed.

There is a question about religious toleration that calls for explicit mention. Whereas in hierarchical societies a state religion may be on some questions the ultimate authority within society and control government policy on certain important matters, that authority is not (as I have said) extended politically to other societies. Further, their (comprehensive) religious or philosophical doctrines are not unreasonable: They admit a measure of liberty of conscience and freedom of thought, even if these freedoms are not in general equal for all members of society as they are in liberal regimes.[28] A hierarchical society may have an established religion with certain privileges.

Still, it is essential to its being well-ordered that no religions are persecuted, or denied civic and social conditions that permit their practice in peace and without fear.[29] Also essential, and this because of the inequality of religious freedom, if for no other reason, is that a hierarchical society must allow for the right of emigration.[30] The rights noted here are counted as human rights. In Part V we return to the role and status of these rights.

An institutional basis that realizes the three requirements can take many forms. This deserves emphasis, as I have indicated only the religious case. We are not trying to describe all possible forms of social order consistent with membership in good standing of a reasonable society of peoples. Rather, we have specified three necessary conditions for membership of a reasonable society of peoples and then shown by example that these conditions do not require a society to be liberal.

This completes the account of the requirements imposed on the basic institutions of a well-ordered hierarchical society. My aim has been to outline a conception of justice that, although distant from liberal conceptions, still has features that give to societies regulated accordingly the moral status required to be members in good standing in a reasonable society of well-ordered peoples. It is important to see, as I have noted, that an agreement on a law of peoples ensuring human rights is not an agreement only liberal societies can make. We must now confirm this.

Hierarchical societies are well ordered in terms of their own conceptions of justice.[31] This being so, their representatives in an appropriate original position would adopt the same principles as those sketched above that would be adopted by the representatives of liberal societies. Each hierarchical society's interests are understood by its representatives in accordance with or as presupposed by its conception of justice. This enables us to say in this case also that the original position is a device of representation.

Two considerations confirm this. The first is that, in view of the common good conception of justice held in a hierarchical society, the parties care about the good of the society they represent, and so about its security as assured by the laws against war and aggression. They also care about the benefits of trade and assistance between peoples in time of need. All these help protect human rights. In view of this, we can say that the representatives of hierarchical societies are rational. The second consideration is that they do not try to extend their religious and philosophical doctrines to other peoples by war or aggression, and they respect the civic order and integrity of other societies. Hence, they accept – as you and I would accept[32] – the original position as fair between peoples and would endorse the law of peoples adopted by their representatives as specifying fair terms of political cooperation between them and other societies. Thus, the representatives are reasonably situated and this suffices for the use of the original position as a device of representation in extending the law of peoples to hierarchical societies.[33]

Note that I have supposed that the parties as representatives of peoples are to be situated equally, even though the conception of justice of the hierarchical society they represent allows basic inequalities between its members. For example, some of its members are not granted equal liberty of conscience. There is, however, no inconsistency in this: A people sincerely affirming a nonliberal conception of justice may still think their society should be treated equally in a just law of peoples, even though its members accept basic inequalities among themselves. Though a society lacks basic equality, it is not unreasonable for that society to insist on equality in making claims against other societies.

About this last point, two observations. One is that although the original position at the first level, that of domestic justice, incorporates a political conception of the person rooted in the public culture of a liberal society, the original position at the second level, that of the law of peoples, does not. I emphasize this fact, since it enables a liberal conception of justice to be extended to yield a more general law of peoples without prejudging the case against nonliberal societies.

This leads to a second observation. As mentioned earlier, the law of peoples might have been worked out by starting with an all-inclusive original position with representatives of all the individual persons of the world.[34] In this case the question of whether there are to be separate societies, and of the relations between them, will be settled by the parties behind a veil of ignorance. Offhand it is not clear why proceeding this way should lead to different results than, as I have done, proceeding from separate societies outward. All things considered, one might reach the same law of peoples in either case. The difficulty with an all-inclusive, or global, original position is that its use of liberal ideas is much more troublesome, for in this case we are treating all persons, regardless of their society and culture, as individuals who are free and equal, and as reasonable and rational, and so according to liberal conceptions. This makes the basis of the law of peoples too narrow.

Hence I think it best to follow the two-level[35] bottom-up procedure, beginning first with the principles of justice for the basic structure of domestic society and then moving upward and outward to the law of peoples. In so doing our knowledge of how peoples and their governments have acted historically gives us guidance in how to proceed and suggests questions and possibilities we might not otherwise have thought of. But this is simply a point of method and settles no questions of substance. These depend on what can actually be worked out.

One might well be skeptical that a liberal social contract and constructivist[36] idea of justice can be worked out to give a conception of the law of peoples universal in its reach and also applying to nonliberal societies. Our discussion of hierarchical societies should put these doubts to rest. I have noted the conditions under which we could accept the law of liberal peoples we had sketched as sound and justified. In this connection we considered whether that law was stable with respect to justice, and whether, on due reflection, we could accept the judgments that its principles and precepts led us to make. If both these things hold, we said, the law of liberal peoples as laid out could, by the criteria we can now apply, be accepted as justified.

Parallel remarks hold for the wider law of peoples including well-ordered hierarchical societies. Here I simply add, without argument or evidence, but hoping it seems plausible, that these societies will honor a just law of peoples for much the same reasons liberal peoples will do so, and that both we and they will find the judgments to which it leads acceptable to our convictions, all things considered. I believe it is of importance here that well-ordered hierarchical societies are not expansionist and their legal order is guided by a common good conception of justice ensuring that it honors human rights. These societies also affirm a peaceful society of peoples and benefit therefrom as liberal societies do. All have a common interest in changing the way in which politics among peoples – war and threats of war – has hitherto been carried on.

We may therefore view this wider law of peoples as sound and justified. This fundamental point deserves emphasis: There is nothing relevantly different between how, say, justice as fairness is worked out for the domestic case in *A Theory of Justice*, and how the law of peoples is worked out from more general liberal ideas of justice. In both cases we use the same fundamental idea of a reasonable procedure of construction in which rational agents fairly situated (the parties as representatives of citizens in one case and of peoples or societies in the other) select principles of justice for the relevant subject, either their separate domestic institutions or the shared law of peoples. As always, the parties are guided by the appropriate reasons as specified by a veil of ignorance. Thus, obligations and duties are not imposed by one society on another; instead, reasonable societies agree on what the bonds will be. Once we confirm that a domestic society, or a society of peoples, when regulated by the corresponding principles of justice, is stable with respect to justice (as previously defined), and once we have checked that we can endorse those principles on due reflection, then in both domains the ideals, laws, and principles of justice are justified in the same way.[37]

V Human Rights

A few of the features of human rights as we have described them are these. First, these rights do not depend on any particular comprehensive moral doctrine or philosophical conception of human nature, such as, for example, that human beings are moral persons and have equal worth, or that they have certain particular moral and intellectual powers that entitle them to these rights. This would require a quite deep philosophical theory that many if not most hierarchical societies might reject as liberal or democratic, or in some way distinctive of the Western political tradition and prejudicial to other cultures.

We therefore take a different tack and say that basic human rights express a minimum standard of well-ordered political institutions for all peoples who belong, as members in good standing, to a just political society of peoples.[38] Any systematic violation of these rights is a serious matter and troubling to the society of peoples as a whole, both liberal and hierarchical. Since they must express a minimum standard, the requirements that yield these rights should be quite weak.

Recall that we postulated that a society's system of law must be such as to impose moral duties and obligations on all its members and be regulated by what judges and other officials reasonably and sincerely believe is a common good conception of justice. For this condition to hold, the law must at least uphold such basic rights as the right to life and security, to personal property, and the elements of the rule of law, as well as the right to a certain liberty of conscience and freedom of association, and the right to emigration. These rights we refer to as human rights.

Next we consider what the imposition of these duties and obligations implies, including (i) a common good conception of justice and (ii) good faith on the part of officials to explain and justify the legal order to those bound by it. For these things to hold does not require the liberal idea that persons are first citizens and as such free and equal members of society who hold those basic rights as the rights of citizens. It requires only that persons be responsible and cooperating members of society who can recognize and act in accordance with their moral duties and obligations. It would be hard to reject these requirements (a common good conception of justice and a good faith official justification of the law) as too strong for a minimally decent regime. Human rights, understood as resulting from these requirements, could not be rejected as peculiarly liberal or special to our Western tradition. In that sense, they are politically neutral.[39]

To confirm this last point, I consider an alleged difficulty. Many societies have political traditions that are different from Western individualism in its many forms. In considering persons from a political point of view, these traditions are said to regard persons not as citizens first with the rights of citizens but rather as first being members of groups: communities, associations, or corporations.[40] On this alternative, let's say associationist, view, whatever rights persons have arise from this prior membership and are normally enabling rights, that is, rights that enable persons to perform their duties in the groups to which they belong. To illustrate with respect to political rights: Hegel rejects the idea of one person one vote on the grounds that it expresses the democratic and individualistic idea that each person, as an atomic unit, has the basic right to participate equally in political deliberation.[41] By contrast, in the well-ordered rational state, as Hegel presents it in *The Philosophy of Right*, persons belong first to estates, corporations, and associations. Since these social forms represent the rational[42] interests of their members in what Hegel views as a just con-

sultation hierarchy, some persons will take part in politically representing these interests in the consultation process, but they do so as members of estates and corporations and not as individuals, and not all individuals are involved.

The essential point here is that the basic human rights as we have described them can be protected in a well-ordered hierarchical state with its consultation hierarchy; what holds in Hegel's scheme of political rights holds for all rights.[43] Its system of law can fulfill the conditions laid down and ensure the right to life and security, to personal property and the elements of the rule of law, as well as the right to a certain freedom of conscience and freedom of association. Admittedly it ensures these rights to persons as members of estates and corporations and not as citizens. But that does not matter. The rights are guaranteed and the requirement that a system of law must be such as to impose moral rights and duties is met. Human rights understood in the light of that condition cannot be rejected as peculiar to our Western tradition.

Human rights are a special class of rights designed to play a special role in a reasonable law of peoples for the present age. Recall that the accepted ideas about international law changed in two basic ways following World War II, and this change in basic moral beliefs is comparable to other profound historical changes.[44] War is no longer an admissible means of state policy. It is only justified in self-defense and a state's internal sovereignty is now limited. One role of human rights is precisely to specify limits to that sovereignty.

Human rights are thus distinct from, say, constitutional rights, or the rights of democratic citizenship,[45] or from other kinds of rights that belong to certain kinds of political institutions, both individualist and associationist. They are a special class of rights of universal application and hardly controversial in their general intention. They are part of a reasonable law of peoples and specify limits on the domestic institutions required of all peoples by that law. In this sense they specify the outer boundary of admissible domestic law of societies in good standing in a just society of peoples.[46]

Human rights have these three roles:

1 They are a necessary condition of a regime's legitimacy and of the decency of its legal order.

2 By being in place, they are also sufficient to exclude justified and forceful intervention by other peoples, say by economic sanctions, or in grave cases, by military force.

3 They set a limit on pluralism among peoples.[47]

VI Nonideal Theory: Noncompliance

So far we have been concerned solely with ideal theory. By developing a liberal conception of justice we have reviewed the philosophical and moral grounds of an ideal conception of a society of well-ordered peoples and of the principles that apply to its law and practices. That conception is to guide the conduct of peoples toward one another and the design of common institutions for their mutual benefit.

Before our sketch of the law of peoples is complete, however, we must take note of, even though we cannot properly discuss, the questions arising from the highly nonideal conditions of our world with its great injustices and widespread social evils. Nonideal theory asks how the ideal conception of the society of well-ordered peoples might be achieved, or at least worked toward, generally in gradual steps. It looks for policies and courses of action likely to be effective and politically possible as well as morally permissible for that purpose. So conceived, nonideal theory presupposes that ideal theory is already on hand for, until the ideal is identified, at least in outline, nonideal theory lacks an objective by reference to which its questions can be answered. And although the specific conditions of our world at any given time – the status quo – do not determine the ideal conception of the society of well-ordered peoples, those conditions do affect answers to the questions of nonideal theory. They are questions of transition: In any given case, they start from where a society is and seek effective ways permitted by the law of peoples to move the society some distance toward the goal.

We may distinguish two kinds of nonideal theory. One kind deals with conditions of noncompliance, that is, with conditions in which certain regimes refuse to acknowledge a reasonable law of peoples. These we may call outlaw regimes. The other kind of nonideal theory deals with unfavorable conditions, that is, with the conditions of peoples whose historical, social, and economic circumstances make their achieving a well-ordered regime, whether liberal or hierarchical, difficult if not impossible.

I begin with noncompliance theory. As we have said, a reasonable law of peoples guides the well-ordered regimes in facing outlaw regimes by specifying the goal they should always have in mind and indicating the means they may use or must avoid in pursuing that goal.

Outlaw regimes are a varied lot. Some are headed by governments that seem to recognize no conception of right and justice at all; often their legal order is at bottom a system of coercion and terror. The Nazi regime is a demonic example of this. A more common case, philosophically more interesting and historically more respectable, are those societies – they would scoff at being referred to as outlaw regimes – whose rulers affirm comprehensive doctrines that recognize no geographic limits to the legitimate authority of their established religious or philosophical views. Spain, France, and the Hapsburgs all tried at some time to subject much of Europe and the world to their will.[48] They hoped to spread true religion and culture, sought dominion and glory, not to mention wealth and territory. Such societies are checked only by a balance of power, but as this is changing and unstable, the hegemonic theory of war, so-called, fits nicely.[49]

The law-abiding societies – both liberal and hierarchical – can at best establish a modus vivendi with the outlaw expansionist regimes and defend the integrity of their societies as the law of peoples allows. In this situation the law-abiding societies exist in a state of nature with the outlaw regimes, and they have a duty to their own and to one another's societies and well-being, as well as a duty to the well-being of peoples subjected to outlaw regimes, though not to their rulers and elites. These several duties are not all equally strong, but there is always a duty to consider the more extensive long-run aims and to affirm them as overall guides of foreign policy. Thus, the only legitimate grounds of the right to war against outlaw regimes is defense of the society of well-ordered peoples and, in grave cases, of innocent persons subject to outlaw regimes and the protection of their human rights. This accords with Kant's idea that our first political duty is to leave the state of nature and submit ourselves along with others to the rule of a reasonable and just law.[50]

The defense of well-ordered peoples is only the first and most urgent task. Another long-run aim, as specified by the law of peoples, is to bring all societies eventually to honor that law and to be full and self-standing members of the society of well-ordered peoples, and so secure human rights everywhere. How to do this is a question of foreign policy; these things call for political wisdom, and success depends in part on luck. They are not matters to which political philosophy has much to add. I venture several familiar points.

For well-ordered peoples to achieve this long-run aim they should establish among themselves new institutions and practices to serve as a kind of federative center and public forum of their common opinion and policy toward the other regimes. This can either be done separately or within institutions such as the United Nations by forming an alliance of well-ordered peoples on certain issues. This federative center may be used both to formulate and to express the opinion of the well-ordered societies. There they may expose to public view the unjust and cruel institutions of oppressive and expansionist regimes and their violations of human rights.

Even these regimes are not altogether indifferent to this kind of criticism, especially when the basis of it is a reasonable and well-founded law of peoples that cannot be easily dismissed as simply liberal or Western. Gradually over time the well-ordered peoples may pressure the outlaw regimes to change their ways; but by itself this pressure is unlikely to be effective. It must be backed up by the firm denial of all military aid, or economic and other assistance; nor should outlaw regimes be admitted by well-ordered peoples as members in good standing into their mutually beneficial cooperative practices.

VII Nonideal Theory: Unfavorable Conditions

A few words about the second kind of nonideal theory, that of unfavorable conditions. By these I mean the conditions of societies that lack the political and cultural traditions, the human capital and know-how, and the resources, material and technological, that make well-ordered societies possible. In noncompliance theory we saw that the goal of well-ordered societies is somehow to bring the outlaw states into the society of well-ordered peoples. The outlaw societies in the historical cases we mentioned above were not societies burdened by unfavorable resources, material and technological, or lacking in human capital

and know-how; on the contrary, they were among the most politically and socially advanced and economically developed societies of their day. The fault in those societies lay in their political traditions and the background institutions of law, property, and class structure, with their sustaining beliefs and culture. These things must be changed before a reasonable law of peoples can be accepted and supported.

We must ask the parallel question: What is the goal specified by nonideal theory for the case of unfavorable conditions? The answer is clear. Eventually each society now burdened by unfavorable conditions should be raised to, or assisted toward, conditions that make a well-ordered society possible.

Some writers have proposed that the difference principle, or some other liberal principle of distributive justice, be adopted to deal with this problem and to regulate accordingly the economic inequalities in the society of peoples.[51] Although I think the difference principle is reasonable for domestic justice in a democratic society, it is not feasible as a way to deal with the general problem of unfavorable conditions among societies. For one thing, it belongs to the ideal theory for a democratic society and is not framed for our present case. More serious, there are various kinds of societies in the society of peoples and not all of them can reasonably be expected to accept any particular liberal principle of distributive justice; and even different liberal societies adopt different principles for their domestic institutions. For their part, the hierarchical societies reject all liberal principles of domestic justice. We cannot suppose that they will find such principles acceptable in dealing with other peoples. In our construction of the liberal law of peoples, therefore, liberal principles of domestic distributive justice are not generalized to answer questions about unfavorable conditions.

Confirming this is the fact that in a constructivist conception there is no reason to think that the principles that apply to domestic justice are also appropriate for regulating inequalities in a society of peoples. As we saw at the outset, each kind of subject – whether an institution or an individual, whether a political society or a society of political societies – may be governed by its own characteristic principles. What these principles are must be worked out by a suitable procedure beginning from a correct starting point. We ask how rational representatives suitably motivated, and reasonably situated with respect to one another, would be most strongly moved to select among the feasible ideals and principles to apply to the subject in question. Since the problem and subject are different in each case, the ideals and principles adopted may also be different. As always, the whole procedure and the principles it yields must be acceptable on due reflection.

Although no liberal principle of distributive justice would be adopted for dealing with unfavorable conditions, that certainly does not mean that the well-ordered and wealthier societies have no duties and obligations to societies burdened by such conditions. For the ideal conception of the society of peoples that well-ordered societies affirm directs that in due course all societies must reach, or be assisted to, the conditions that make a well-ordered society possible. This implies that human rights are to be recognized and secured everywhere, and that basic human needs are to be met. Thus, the basis of the duty of assistance is not some liberal principle of distributive justice. Rather, it is the ideal conception of the society of peoples itself as consisting of well-ordered societies, with each people, as I have said, a full and self-standing member of the society of peoples, and capable of taking charge of their political life and maintaining decent political and social institutions as specified by the three requirements earlier surveyed.[52]

I shall not attempt to discuss here how this might be done, as the problem of giving economic and technological aid so that it makes a sustained contribution is highly complicated and varies from country to country. Moreover the problem is often not the lack of natural resources. Many societies with unfavorable conditions don't lack for resources. Well-ordered societies can get on with very little; their wealth lies elsewhere: in their political and cultural traditions, in their human capital and knowledge, and in their capacity for political and economic organization. Rather, the problem is commonly the nature of the public political culture and the religious and philosophical traditions that underlie its institutions. The great social evils in poorer societies are likely to be oppressive government and corrupt elites; the subjection of women abetted by unreasonable religion, with the resulting overpopulation relative to what the economy of the society can decently sustain. Perhaps there is no society anywhere in the world whose people, were they reasonably and rationally governed, and their numbers sensibly adjusted to

their economy and resources, could not have a decent and worthwhile life.

These general remarks indicate what is so often the source of the problem: the public political culture and its roots in the background social structure. The obligation of wealthier societies to assist in trying to rectify matters is in no way diminished, only made more difficult. Here, too, in ways I need not describe, an emphasis on human rights may work, when backed by other kinds of assistance, to moderate, albeit slowly, oppressive government, the corruption of elites, and the subjection of women.[53]

VIII   Concluding Reflections

I have not said much about what might be called the philosophical basis of human rights. That is because, despite their name, human rights are a special class of rights explained by their role in a liberal conception of the law of peoples acceptable to both well-ordered liberal and hierarchical societies. I have therefore sketched how such a law of peoples might be worked out on the basis of a liberal conception of justice.[54] Within this framework I have indicated how respect for human rights is one of the conditions imposed on any political regime to be admissible as a member in good standing into a just political society of peoples. Once we understand this, and once we understand how a reasonable law of peoples is developed out of the liberal conception of justice and how this conception can be universal in its reach, it is perfectly clear why those rights hold across cultural and economic boundaries, as well as the boundaries between nation states, or other political units. With our two other conditions, these rights determine the limits of toleration in a reasonable society of peoples.

About these limits, the following observation: If we start with a well-ordered liberal society that realizes an egalitarian conception of justice such as justice as fairness,[55] the members of that society will nevertheless accept into the society of peoples other liberal societies whose institutions are considerably less egalitarian. This is implicit in our beginning with liberal conceptions more general than justice as fairness as defined in Part III. But citizens in a well-ordered egalitarian society will still view the domestic regimes of those societies as less congenial to them than the regime of their own society.

This illustrates what happens whenever the scope of toleration is extended: The criteria of reasonableness are relaxed.[56] In the case we have considered, we seek to include other than liberal societies as members in good standing of a reasonable society of peoples. Hence when we move to these societies, their domestic regimes are less, often much less, congenial to us. This poses the problem of the limits of toleration. Where are these limits to be drawn? Clearly, tyrannical and dictatorial regimes must be outlawed, and also, for basic liberal reasons, expansionist states like those of the Wars of Religion. The three necessary conditions for a well-ordered regime – that it respect the principles of peace and not be expansionist, that its system of law meet the essentials of legitimacy in the eyes of its own people, and that it honor basic human rights – are proposed as an answer as to where those limits lie. These conditions indicate the bedrock beyond which we cannot go.

We have discussed how far many societies of the world have always been, and are today, from meeting these three conditions for being a member in good standing of a reasonable society of peoples. The law of peoples provides the basis for judging the conduct of any existing regime, liberal as well as nonliberal. And since our account of the law of peoples was developed out of a liberal conception of justice, we must address the question whether the liberal law of peoples is ethnocentric and merely Western.

To address this question, recall that in working out the law of peoples we assumed that liberal societies conduct themselves toward other societies from the point of view of their own liberal political conception. Regarding this conception as sound, and as meeting all the criteria they are now able to apply, how else are they to proceed? To the objection that to proceed thus is ethnocentric or merely Western, the reply is: no, not necessarily. Whether it is so turns on the content of the political conception that liberal societies embrace once it is worked up to provide at least an outline of the law of peoples.

Looking at the outline of that law, we should note the difference between it and the law of peoples as it might be understood by religious and expansionist states that reject the liberal conception. The liberal conception asks of other societies only what they can reasonably grant without submitting to a position of inferiority, much less to domination. It is crucial that a liberal conception of the law of peoples not ask well-ordered hierarchical societies to abandon their religious institutions and adopt liberal ones. True, in our sketch we supposed that traditional societies would affirm the law of peoples that would hold among just liberal societies. That law is therefore universal in its reach: It asks of other societies only what they can accept once they are prepared to stand in a relation of equality with all other societies and once their regimes accept the criterion of legitimacy in the eyes of their own people. In what other relations can a society and its regime reasonably expect to stand?

Moreover, the liberal law of peoples does not justify economic sanctions or military pressure on well-ordered hierarchical societies to change their ways, provided they respect the rules of peace and their political institutions satisfy the essential conditions we have reviewed. If, however, these conditions are violated, external pressure of one kind or another may be justified depending on the severity and the circumstances of the case. A concern for human rights should be a fixed part of the foreign policy of liberal and hierarchical societies.

Looking back at our discussion, let's recall that besides sketching how the law of peoples might be developed from liberal conceptions of right and justice, a further aim was to set out the bearing of political liberalism for a wider world society once a liberal political conception of justice is extended to the law of peoples. In particular, we asked: What form does the toleration of nonliberal societies take in this case? Although tyrannical and dictatorial regimes cannot be accepted as members in good standing of a reasonable society of peoples, not all regimes can reasonably be required to be liberal. If so, the law of peoples would not express liberalism's own principle of toleration for other reasonable ways of ordering society. A liberal society must respect other societies organized by comprehensive doctrines, provided their political and social institutions meet certain conditions that lead the society to adhere to a reasonable law of peoples.

I did not try to present an argument to this conclusion. I took it as clear that if other nonliberal societies honored certain conditions, such as the three requirements discussed in Part IV, they would be accepted by liberal societies as members in good standing of a society of peoples. There would be no political case to attack these nonliberal societies militarily, or to bring economic or other sanctions against them to revise their institutions.

Critical commentary in liberal societies would be fully consistent with the civic liberties and integrity of those societies.

What conception of toleration of other societies does the law of peoples express? How is it connected with political liberalism? If it should be asked whether liberal societies are, morally speaking, better than hierarchical societies, and therefore whether the world would be a better place if all societies were liberal, those holding a comprehensive liberal view could think it would be. But that opinion would not support a claim to rid the world of nonliberal regimes. It could have no operative force in what, as a matter of right, they could do politically. The situation is parallel to the toleration of other conceptions of the good in the domestic case. Someone holding a comprehensive liberal view can say that their society would be a better place if every one held such a view. They might be wrong in this judgment even by their own lights, as other doctrines may play a moderating and balancing role given the larger background of belief and conviction, and give society's culture a certain depth and richness. The point is that to affirm the superiority of a particular comprehensive view is fully compatible with affirming a political conception of justice that does not impose it, and thus with political liberalism itself.

Political liberalism holds that comprehensive doctrines have but a restricted place in liberal democratic politics in this sense: Fundamental constitutional questions and matters concerning basic rights and liberties are to be settled by a public political conception of justice, exemplified by the liberal political conceptions, and not by those wider doctrines. For given the pluralism of democratic societies – a pluralism best seen as the outcome of the exercise of human reason under free institutions, and which can only be undone by the oppressive use of state power – affirming such a public conception and the basic political institutions that realize it, is the most reasonable basis of social unity available to us.

The law of peoples, as I have sketched it, is simply the extension of these same ideas to the political society of well-ordered peoples. That law, which settles fundamental constitutional questions and matters of basic justice as they arise for the society of peoples, must also be based on a public political conception of justice and not on a comprehensive religious, philosophical, or moral doctrine. I have sketched the content of such a political conception and tried to explain how it could be endorsed by well-ordered societies, both liberal and hierarchical. Except as a basis of a modus vivendi, expansionist societies of whatever kind could not endorse it; but in principle there is no peaceful solution in their case except the domination of one side or the peace of exhaustion.

Notes

1 The name "law of peoples" derives from the traditional *ius gentium*, and the way I use it is closest to its meaning in the phrase "ius gentium intra se" (laws of peoples among themselves). In this meaning it refers to what the laws of all peoples had in common. See R. J. Vincent, *Human Rights and International Relations* (Cambridge: Cambridge University Press, 1986), p. 27. Taking these laws to be a core paired with principles of justice applying to the laws of peoples everywhere gives a meaning related to my use of the law of peoples.

2 A political conception of justice has the following three features: (1) it is framed to apply to basic political, economic, and social institutions; in the case of domestic society, to its basic structure, in the present case to the law and practices of the society of political peoples; (2) it is presented independently of any particular comprehensive religious, philosophical, or moral doctrine, and though it may be derived from or related to several such doctrines, it is not worked out in that way; (3) its content is expressed in terms of certain fundamental ideas seen as implicit in the public political culture of a liberal society. See my *Political Liberalism* (New York: Columbia University Press, 1993), pp. 11–15.

3 In this and the next two paragraphs I draw on the first section of "Basic Structure as Subject" (1978), reprinted in *Political Liberalism*.

4 For a detailed example of how this is done in the case of the four-stage sequence of original position, constitutional convention, the legislature, and the courts, see *A Theory of Justice* (Cambridge, MA: Harvard University Press, 1971), pp. 195–201. A briefer statement is found in "Basic Liberties and Their Priority" (1982), reprinted in *Political Liberalism*.

5 By peoples I mean persons and their dependents seen as a corporate body and as organized by their political institutions, which establish the powers of government. In democratic societies persons will be citizens, while in hierarchical and other societies they will be members.

6 See *Theory of Justice* p. 378ff., where this process is very briefly described.

7 It would be unfair to Clausewitz not to add that for him the state's interests can include regulative moral aims of whatever kind, and thus the aims of war may be to defend democratic societies against tyrannical regimes, somewhat as in World War II. For him the aims of politics are not part of the theory of war, although they are ever present and may properly affect the conduct of war. On this, see the instructive remarks of Peter Paret, "Clausewitz," in Peter Paret, ed., *The Makers of Modern Strategy* (Princeton, NJ: Princeton University Press, 1986), pp. 209–13. The view in my text characterizes the *raison d'état* as pursued by Frederick the Great. Or so Gerhard Ritter says in *Frederick the Great*, trans. Peter Paret (Berkeley: California University Press, 1968). See chapter 10, and the statement on p. 197.

8 These powers Charles Beitz characterizes as belonging to what he calls the morality of states in part II of his *Political Theory and International Relations* (Princeton, NJ: Princeton University Press, 1980). They depend, he argues, on a mistaken analogy between individuals and states.

9 Stanley Hoffman, *Janus and Minerva* (Boulder, CO: Westview Press, 1987), p. 374.

10 Note: "You and I" are "here and now" citizens of the same liberal democratic society and we are working out the liberal conception of justice in question.

11 In this case "you and I" are citizens of liberal democratic societies but not of the same one.

12 Kant says at Ak: VIII: 367: "The idea of international law presupposes the separate existence of independent neighboring states. Although this condition is itself a state of war (unless federative union prevents the outbreak of hostilities), this is rationally preferable to the amalgamation of states under one superior power, as this would end in one universal monarchy, and laws always lose in vigor what government gains in extent; hence a condition of soulless despotism falls into anarchy after stifling seeds of good." This attitude to universal monarchy was shared by other writers of the eighteenth century. See, for example, Hume's "Of the Balance of Power" (1752). F. H. Hinsley, *Power and the Pursuit of Peace* (Cambridge: Cambridge University Press, 1966), pp. 162ff., also mentions Montesquieu, Voltaire, and Gibbon. Hinsley also has an instructive discussion of Kant's ideas in chapter 4. See also Patrick Riley, *Kant's Political Philosophy* (Towanda, PA: Rowman and Littlefield, 1983), chapters 5 and 6. Thomas Nagel, in his *Equality and Partiality* (New York: Oxford University Press, 1991), pp. 169ff., 174, gives strong reasons supporting the same conclusion.

13 See Terry Nardin, *Law, Morality and the Relations of States* (Princeton, NJ: Princeton University Press, 1983), pp. 269 ff., who stresses this point.

14 A clear example regarding secession is whether the South had a right to secede from 1860 to 1861. By this test it had no such right, since it seceded to perpetuate its domestic institution of slavery. This is as severe a violation of human rights as any, and it extended to nearly half the population.

15 By basic needs I mean roughly those that must be met if citizens are to be in a position to take advantage of the rights, liberties, and opportunities of their society. They include economic means as well as institutional rights and freedoms.

16 From the fact that boundaries are historically arbitrary it does not follow that their role in the law of peoples cannot be justified. To wit: that the boundaries between the several states of the United States are historically arbitrary does not argue for the elimination of our federal system, one way or the other. To fix on their arbitrariness is to fix on the wrong thing. The right question concerns the political values served by the several states in a federal system as compared with the values served by a central system. The answer is given by states' function and role: by the political values they serve as subunits, and whether their boundaries can be, or need to be, redrawn, and much else.

17 This remark implies that a people has at least a qualified right to limit immigration. I leave aside here what these qualifications might be.

18 See "The Domain of the Political and Overlapping Consensus," *New York University Law School Review* 64 (1989): 245, Section VII.

19 See Jack S. Levy, "Domestic Politics and War," an essay in Robert Rotberg and Theodore Rabb, eds., *The Origin and Prevention of Major Wars* (Cambridge: Cambridge University Press, 1989), p. 87. Levy refers to several historical studies that have confirmed the finding of Small and Singer in the *Jerusalem Journal of International Relations*, vol. 1, (1976), mentioned in note 21 below.

20 See Doyle's two-part article, "Kant, Liberal Legacies, and Foreign Affairs," *Philosophy and Public Affairs* 12 (1983): 205, 323. A survey of the evidence is in the first part, pp. 206–32. Doyle says: "These conventions [those based on the international implications of liberal principles and institutions] of mutual respect have formed a cooperative foundation for relations among liberal democracies of a remarkably effective kind. *Even though liberal states have become involved in numerous wars with nonliberal states, constitutionally secure liberal states have yet to engage in war with one another.* [Italicized in the original.] No one should argue that such wars are impossible; but preliminary evidence does appear to indicate . . . a significant predisposition against warfare between liberal states" (p. 213).

21 See Levy, "Domestic Politics," p. 88. In these studies most definitions of democracy are comparable to that of Small and Singer as listed by Levy in a

footnote: (1) regular elections and the participation of opposition parties, (2) at least 10 percent of the adult population being able to vote for a (3) parliament that either controlled or shared parity with the executive branch (ibid., p. 88). Our definition of a liberal democratic regime goes well beyond this definition.

22   On this see Alan Gilbert, "Power-Rivalry Motivated Democracy," *Political Theory* 20 (1992): p. 681, and esp. pp. 684 ff.

23   Here I draw upon Philip Soper's *A Theory of Law* (Cambridge, MA: Harvard University Press, 1984), esp. pp. 125–47. Soper holds that a system of law, as distinct from a system of mere commands coercively enforced, must be such as to give rise, as I have indicated, to moral duties and obligations on all members of society, and judges and other officials must sincerely and reasonably believe that the law is guided by a common good conception of justice. The content of a common good conception of justice is such as to impose morally binding obligations on all members of society. I mention some of the details of Soper's view here, but I do so rather freely and not with the intent of explaining his thought. As the text shows, my aim is to indicate a conception of justice that, while not a liberal conception, still has features that give to societies regulated accordingly the moral standing required to be members of a political society adhering to a reasonable law of peoples. However, we must be careful in understanding this second requirement. For Soper it is part of the definition of a system of law. It is a requirement which a scheme of rules must satisfy to be a system of law properly thus called. See chapter 4, pp. 91–100. I don't follow Soper in this respect; nor do I reject this idea either, as Soper makes a strong case for it. Rather, it is put aside and the requirement is adopted as a substantive moral principle explicable as part of the law of peoples worked up from a liberal conception of justice. The reason for doing this is to avoid the long debated jurisprudential problem of the definition of law. Also, I don't want to have to argue that the antebellum South, say, didn't have a system of law. I am indebted to Samuel Freeman for valuable discussion of these points.

24   Soper, *A Theory of Law*, pp. 112, 118.

25   Ibid., p. 141.

26   Henry Shue, *Basic Rights: Substance, Affluence, and US Foreign Policy* (Princeton, NJ: Princeton University Press, 1980). Shue (p. 23) and Vincent (*Human Rights*) interpret subsistence as including certain minimum economic security, and both hold that subsistence rights are basic. One must agree with this since the reasonable and rational exercise of all liberties, of whatever kind, as well as the intelligent use of property, always implies having certain general all-purpose economic means.

27   On the rules of natural justice, see H. L. A. Hart, *The Concept of Law* (Oxford: Clarendon Press), pp. 156ff.

28   One might raise the question here as to why religious or philosophical doctrines that deny full and equal liberty of conscience are not unreasonable. I did not say, however, that they are reasonable, but rather that they are not unreasonable. One should allow, I think, a space between the reasonable or the fully reasonable, which requires full and equal liberty of conscience, and the unreasonable, which denies it entirely. Traditional doctrines that allow a measure of liberty of conscience but do not allow it fully are views that lie in that space and are not unreasonable. On this see my *Political Liberalism*, Lecture II, section 3.

29   On the importance of this, see Judith Shklar's *Ordinary Vices* (Cambridge, MA: Harvard University Press, 1984), in which she presents what she calls the "liberalism of fear." See especially the introduction and chapters 1 and 6. She once called this kind of liberalism that of "permanent minorities." See her *Legalism* (Cambridge, MA: Harvard University Press, 1963), p. 224.

30   Subject to certain qualifications, liberal societies must also allow for this right.

31   These are not political conceptions of justice in my sense; see note 2 above.

32   Here "you and I" are members of hierarchical societies but again not the same one.

33   Here I am indebted to Lea Brilmayer of New York University for pointing out to me that in my sketch of the law of peoples (October 1990) I failed to state these conditions satisfactorily.

34   Brian Barry, in his splendid *Theories of Justice* (Berkeley: University of California Press, 1989), discusses the merits of doing this. See pp. 183–89 ff. Along the way he raises serious objections to what he takes to be my view of the principles of distributive justice for the law of peoples. I do not discuss these important criticisms here, but I do mention questions related to them hereafter.

35   We can go on to third and later stages once we think of groups of societies joining together into regional associations or federations of some kind, such as the European Community, or a commonwealth of the republics in the former Soviet Union. It is natural to envisage future world society as in good part composed of such federations together with certain institutions, such as the United Nations, capable of speaking for all the societies of the world.

36   Justice as fairness is such an idea. For our purposes other more general liberal ideas of justice fit the same description. Their lacking the three egalitarian elements of justice as fairness noted in the first paragraph of part 3 does not affect this.

37   There are, however, some differences. The three requirements of legitimacy discussed in this section

are to be seen as necessary conditions for a society to be a member in good standing of a reasonable society of peoples; and many religious and philosophical doctrines with their different conceptions of justice may lead to institutions satisfying these conditions. In specifying a reasonable law of peoples, societies with such institutions are viewed as well ordered. However, those requirements do not specify a political conception of justice in my sense (see note 2 above). For one thing, I suppose that a society's common good conception of justice is understood as part of its comprehensive religious or philosophical doctrine. Nor have I suggested that such a conception of justice is constructivist, and I assume it is not. Whether the three requirements for legitimacy can themselves be constructed within a social contract view is another question. I leave it open here. The point, though, is that none of these differences affect the claim in the text that in both domains the ideals and principles of justice are justified in the same way.

38 Here I draw upon T. M. Scanlon's instructive discussion in "Human Rights as a Neutral Concern," in P. Brown and D. MacLean, eds., *Human Rights and US Foreign Policy* (Lexington, MA: Lexington Books, 1979).

39 Scanlon emphasizes this point in "Human Rights," pp. 83, 89–92. It is relevant when we note later in parts 6 and 7 that support for human rights should be part of the foreign policy of well-ordered societies.

40 See R. J. Vincent, "The Idea of Rights in International Ethics," in Terry Nardin, ed. with David Mapel, *Traditions of International Ethics* (Cambridge: Cambridge University Press, 1992), 262–65.

41 Hegel, *The Philosophy of Right* (1821), section 308.

42 The meaning of *rational* here is closer to *reasonable* than to *rational* as I have used these terms. The German is *vernünftig*, and this has the full force of reason in the German philosophical tradition. It is far from the economist's meaning of *rational*, given by *zweckmässig* or *rationell*.

43 There is a complication about Hegel's view in that some rights are indeed rights of individuals. For him the rights to life, security, and (personal) property are grounded in personhood; and liberty of conscience follows from being a moral subject with the freedom of subjectivity. I am indebted to Frederick Neuhouser for discussion of these points.

44 See Keith Thomas, *Man and the Natural World* (New York: Pantheon Books, 1983) for an account of the historical change in attitudes toward animals and nature.

45 See Judith Shklar's illuminating discussion of these in her *American Citizenship* (Cambridge, MA: Harvard University Press, 1991), with her emphasis on the historical significance of slavery.

46 This fact about human rights can be clarified by distinguishing among the rights that have been listed as human rights in various international declarations. Consider the Universal Declaration of Human Rights of 1948. First, there are human rights proper, illustrated by Article 3: "Everyone has a right to life, liberty and security of person"; and by Article 5: "No one shall be subjected to torture or to cruel, degrading treatment or punishment." Articles 3 to 18 may fall under this heading of human rights proper, pending certain questions of interpretation. Then there are human rights that are obvious implications of these rights. These are the extreme cases described by the special conventions on genocide (1948) and on apartheid (1973). These two classes comprise the human rights.

Of the other declarations, some seem more aptly described as stating liberal aspirations, such as Article 1 of the Universal Declaration of Human Rights of 1948: "All human beings are born free and equal in dignity and rights. They are endowed with reason and conscience and should act towards one another in a spirit of brotherhood." Others appear to presuppose specific kinds of institutions, such as the right to social security, in Article 22, and the right to equal pay for equal work, in Article 23.

47 Nardin, *Law, Morality and the Relations of States*, p. 240, citing Luban's "The Romance of the Nation-State," p. 396.

48 On this, see Ludwig Dehio, *The Precarious Balance* (New York: Knopf, 1962).

49 Robert Gilpin, "The Theory of Hegemonic War," in Rotberg and Rabb, eds., *The Origin and Prevention of Major Wars*.

50 See Kant, *Rechtslehre*, sections 44 and 61.

51 Beitz, *Political Theory and International Relations*, part III gives a sustained discussion. This principle is defined in my *A Theory of Justice*, section 13. I do not review the principle here because, as my text says, I believe all liberal distributive principles are unsuitable for the case we are considering.

52 With much of Beitz's view the law of peoples agrees. Thus it seems that he thinks of the difference principle between societies as "a resource redistribution principle that would give each society a fair chance to develop just political institutions and an economy capable of satisfying its members' basic needs" (p. 141). And "It [the resource distribution principle] provides assurance to persons in resource-poor societies that their adverse fate will not prevent them from realizing economic conditions sufficient to support just social institutions and to protect human rights" (p. 142). The law of peoples accepts Beitz's goals for just institutions, securing human rights, and meeting basic needs. But, as I suggest in the next paragraph, persons' adverse fate is more often to be born into a distorted and corrupt political culture than into a country lacking resources.

The only principle that does away with that misfortune is to make the political traditions and culture of all peoples reasonable and able to sustain just political and social institutions that secure human rights. It is this principle that gives rise to the duties and obligations of assistance. We do not need a liberal principle of distributive justice for this purpose.

53 That the insistence on human rights may help here is suggested by Amartya Sen's work on famines. He has shown in *Poverty and Famines* (Oxford: Clarendon Press, 1981), by an empirical study of four well-known historical cases (Bengal, 1943; Ethiopia, 1972–74; Sahel, 1972–73; and Bangladesh, 1974), that food decline need not be the main cause of famine, or even a cause, nor even present. But sometimes it can be an important cause of famine, for example, in Ireland in the 1840s and in China from 1959 to 1961. In the cases Sen studies, while a drop in food production may have been present, it was not great enough to lead to famine given a decent government that cares for the well-being of all of its people and has in place a reasonable scheme of backup entitlements provided through public institutions. For Sen "famines are economic disasters, not just food crises" (p. 162). In the well-known historical cases they revealed faults of the political and social structure and its failure to institute appropriate policies to remedy the effects of shortfalls in food production. After all, there would be massive starvation in any modern Western democracy were there not schemes in place to remedy the losses in income of the unemployed. Since a government's allowing people to starve when this is preventable is a violation of their human rights, and if well-ordered regimes as we have described them will not allow this to happen, then insisting on human rights is exerting pressure in the direction of decent governments and a decent society of peoples. Sen's book with Jean Drèze, *Hunger and Public Action* (Oxford: Clarendon Press, 1989) confirms these points and stresses the success of democratic regimes in coping with these problems. See their summary statement in chapter 13: 257–79. See also the important work of Partha Dasgupta, *An Inquiry into Well-Being and Destitution* (Oxford: Clarendon Press, 1993), chapters 1–2, 5, and passim.

54 It might be asked why the law of peoples as here constructed is said to be liberal when it is also accepted by well-ordered hierarchical societies. I have called it liberal because the law of peoples is presented as an extension from liberal conceptions of domestic justice. I do not mean to deny, however, that a well-ordered hierarchical society may have conceptions of justice that can be extended to the law of peoples and that its content would be the same as that of liberal conceptions. For the present I leave this question open. I would hope that there are such conceptions in all well-ordered hierarchical societies, as this would widen and strengthen the support for the law of peoples.

55 Three egalitarian elements are the fair value of equal political rights and liberties, fair equality of opportunity, and the difference principle, all to be understood as specified in my *A Theory of Justice*.

56 In the domestic case we are led in parallel fashion to count many comprehensive doctrines reasonable that we would not, in our own case, regard as worthy of serious consideration. See my *Political Liberalism*, Lecture II, Section 3.1 and the footnote.

44

The Romance of the Nation-State

David Luban

The theory I espoused in "Just War and Human Rights" entitles nations to wage war to enforce basic human rights.[1] This entitlement stems from the cosmopolitan nature of human rights. The rights of security and subsistence, with which I was concerned, are necessary for the enjoyment of any other rights at all; no one can do without them. Basic rights, therefore, are universal. They are no respecters of political boundaries, and require a universalist politics to implement them, even when this means breaching the wall of state sovereignty.

Since the time of the French Revolution, which linked the Rights of Man with the demand for national sovereignty, cosmopolitan theories have been criticized by appealing to the ideology of nationalism. National sovereignty, it was thought, gives people their most important entitlement: a state that expresses their traditions, history and unity – their "national soul."[2] Attack the state, and you attack the soul of its people. The cosmopolitan vision of humanity is really a flattening universalism, a philosopher's conceit. As Herder says, "Every nation has its own core of happiness just as every sphere has its center of gravity!... Philosopher in a northern valley, with the infant's scales of your century in your hand, do you know better than Providence?"[3]

Nationalism may have originated as an ideology of liberation and tolerance; in our century it is drenched in blood. What Mazzini began, Il Duce

ended; other examples are equally obvious and equally painful. The violence of modern nationalism and its indifference to basic human rights arises, I believe, from the conviction that the only right which matters politically is the right to a unified nation-state. Its picture of the nation-state, however, is a myth. It emphasizes a nation's commonality, affinity, shared language and traditions and history, what Mazzini called "unanimity of mind."[4] The picture glosses over intramural class conflict, turmoil, violence, and repression; these it represents as the reflection of inscrutable processes akin to national destiny.[5] This view I shall call the Romance of the Nation-State. In place of respect for people it sets respect for peoples, in place of universalism, relativism.

What disturbs me about Walzer's essay is its acceptance of the premises of nationalism.[6] Walzer embodies his anti-cosmopolitanism in five theses: (i) that nations are comparatively self-enclosed (p. 227); (ii) that "the state is constituted by the union of people and government" (p. 212); (iii) that the political and moral status of a nation is aptly characterized by the metaphor of the social contract; (iv) that "the only global community is...a community of nations, not of humanity" (p. 226); and (v) that the main moral principle of international politics is "pluralism": respect for the integrity of nations and their states; in particular, respect for their right to choose political forms which from our point of view are morally deficient.

Originally published in *Philosophy and Public Affairs* 9, no. 2 (1980): 160–81. Reprinted by permission of Blackwell Publishing Ltd.

This is a molecular theory of world politics, in which self-contained nation-states are the units of moral regard: molecular, because each is bound together from within and presents itself as a unit from without. The fourth and fifth theses yield the anti-cosmopolitan international morality that underlies Walzer's theory of *jus ad bellum*; these theses depend, however, on the first three, which represent the Romance of the Nation-State.

The social contract metaphor is central to this myth. It suggests reciprocity, coincident interests, mutual obligation, formal equality of the parties. But the presence of these features is not a conceptual truth about the nation-state, nor, I think, a factual one. The metaphor and the myth, I shall argue, lead Walzer to a deficient account of human rights and a blindness to the threat physical repression poses to political processes.

The controversial thesis of Walzer's essay is this: he believes that states which oppress their people may, nevertheless, be considered legitimate in international society, as long as they do not fall under what he calls the "rules of disregard." Intervention is allowable in a nation when a national minority is seceding from it; when a foreign power has intervened in a civil war it is fighting; or when it is massacring, enslaving, or expelling large numbers of people. In these instances, Walzer argues, "the absence of 'fit' between the government and community is radically apparent" (p. 214). The rest of the time we are obliged to act *as if* states are legitimate. Walzer calls this "the politics of *as if*" (p. 216); its leading principle is "a morally necessary presumption: that there exists a certain 'fit' between the community and its government and that the state is 'legitimate' " (p. 212). Hard as it is for liberal democrats to believe, foreigners may want their tyranny – there may be a "fit" between government and people.

What supports this presumption? According to Walzer, foreigners just can't judge an alien culture's fit with its government. "They don't know enough about its history, and they have no direct experience, and can form no concrete judgments of the conflicts and harmonies, the historical choices and cultural affinities, the loyalties and resentments, that underlie it" (p. 212).

I find no plausibility in this. True, *if* we don't know enough about a foreign culture to judge its "fit" with its government, we should give it the benefit of the doubt and presume the fit is there. But why presume we are ignorant? We aren't, usually. There are, after all, experts, experienced

travelers, expatriates, scholars, and spies; libraries have been written about the most remote cultures. Bafflingly, Walzer does not mention the obvious sources of information even to dismiss them. He seems to take as an a priori truth – it is part of the Romance of the Nation-State – that without "direct experience" a member of one culture cannot, ultimately, know what it's really like to be a member of another. But this is of a piece with "no man can really know what it's like to be a woman" or "you can't know what it's really like to be me": even granting their validity, we don't assume that such considerations preclude making true judgments about other people. That is more like solipsism than pluralism, and if it were true it would spell the end, not the principle, of politics.

Of course Walzer is right that the lack of fit between government and people should be "radically apparent" to justify intervening, because intervention based on a misperception is horribly wrong. But what does it take to make things radically apparent? In my view, Walzer's rules of disregard set the threshold too high; what he calls "ordinary oppression" can make the lack of fit apparent enough. Let us look at ordinary oppression in a medium-size dictatorship. Each year there are a few score executions, a few hundred tortures, a few thousand political imprisonments, a few million people behaving cautiously because they know that a single slip will bring the police. The police and army believe that if the government falls they are dead men; it is the bargain they accepted to escape the poverty of their villages. They take their foreign-made fighters, small arms, and pepper gas and hope for the best.

If this is a "union of people and government," why are the jails so full? Surely all those strapped to the torture table are not misfits in their own culture. I think we should aim at a more commonsense explanation than Walzer's of why people put up with the regime, such as the idea that they are afraid of being "disappeared" (to use a phrase current in Argentina and the Philippines). The government fits the people the way the sole of a boot fits a human face: after a while the patterns of indentation match with uncanny precision.

It was central to my argument in "Just War and Human Rights" that under ordinary oppression peoples' socially basic human rights are violated – not, to be sure, on the scale envisioned in Walzer's third rule of disregard, which refers to what the Nuremberg court called "crimes against humanity," but systematically enough to define the state's political physiognomy and justify intervention. Walzer's theory of intervention as aggression is also based on individual rights, but those that control are the rights emphasized by nationalism: to fight for the homeland and to live under institutions formed by one's fellow nationals. They are rights to a nation-state, not claims against it.

This difference is illustrated by Walzer's analysis of the recent Nicaraguan revolution. He emphasizes the fact that in the wake of their initial defeat the *Sandinistas* were forced to clarify their program and solidify their political base. This is indeed an instance of self-determination, and if Walzer's position is that, other things being equal, it is better that it should happen than not, he is undoubtedly right. Let us not forget, though, that other things were not equal. Fifty thousand people were killed in the second round of revolution, Nicaragua's productive capacity was ravaged, and Somoza's followers had an additional year to strip the country of everything they could crate. Because of this, the new government has been forced to make a number of deals that have weakened its political base. Neither should we dismiss as unimportant the fact that Nicaraguans had to live under an oppressive regime one year longer. We cannot ignore, as Walzer's theory does, the cost in blood, the bottom line in an account that makes socially basic human rights its guiding concept.

The problem with Walzer's argument is this. Human rights accrue to people no matter what country they live in and regardless of history and traditions. If human rights exist at all, they set a moral limit to pluralism. For this reason Walzer's appeal to pluralism begs the question, for making pluralism the overriding value is incompatible from the outset with a theory that grants universal human rights.

Rights, moreover, are crucial values for us – as Walzer points out, they are deeply connected with our notions of personality and moral agency. Thus, when murders, tortures, imprisonments go unchecked, more so when their perpetrators (the worst people in the world) are treated *as if* they are legitimate, the common humanity of all of us is stained. In this way, the politics of *as if*, in which we acknowledge rights but turn our backs on their enforcement (p. 226), fails to take our values seriously. It raises politics above moral theory.

Walzer sees it differently. He claims that he is defending politics while his critics are expressing "the traditional philosophical dislike for politics." This, he says, is because we are unwilling to tolerate unwanted outcomes of "the political process itself, with all its messiness and uncertainty, its inevitable compromises, and its frequent brutality"; we would restrict the outcomes by force of arms (p. 31).

But why is this less political than standing by while an uprising against a repressive regime is crushed by force of arms? Repression is itself an attempt to restrict, or rather, to eliminate the political process. It subjects politics to the essentially apolitical technology of violence, the "great unequalizer." Intervention, when it is just, should restore self-determination, not deny it. In this respect it is similar to counter-intervention of the sort countenanced by Walzer's second rule of disregard – an analogy which is particularly apposite in view of the fact that military technology is usually provided to repressive regimes by foreign powers.

Walzer dismisses the ability of sheer force to stifle the political process because force cannot prevail against the united community, while if the community is not united intervention would be wrong. But a united community is a rare political achievement, particularly under conditions of class oppression and terror, and I think it is wrong to make it the yardstick of politics – doing so is another metamorphosis of the Romance of the Nation-State. One might doubt whether in a civil war an intervener can know which side to support. But the entitlement to intervene derives from the cosmopolitan character of human rights; one intervenes, then, on behalf of socially basic human rights, for it is these which enable people to enjoy their political rights. Walzer's hands-off approach, on the other hand, waiting for the day when the nation unites, simply yields to guns and tanks.

Notes

1 See *Philosophy and Public Affairs* 9, no. 2 (Winter 1980): 160–81.
2 See Hannah Arendt, *The Origins of Totalitarianism*, rev. ed. (New York: Meridian, 1958), pp. 230–1.

3 "Auch eine Philosophie der Geschichte zur Bildung der Menschheit," *Werke*, ed. Suphan, vol. 5, pp. 501 ff.; quoted in Ernst Cassirer, *The Philosophy of the Enlightenment*, trans. Koelln and Pettegrove (Prince-

ton: Princeton University Press, 1951), pp. 232–3. See also Cassirer, *The Myth of the State* (New Haven: Yale University Press, 1946), pp. 176–86; Isaiah Berlin, *Against the Current* (New York: Viking, 1979), chs. 1, 13; and Berlin, *Vico and Herder* (New York: Viking, 1976).

4 For this citation, together with a short survey of nineteenth-century nationalist ideology, see Victor Alba, *Nationalists Without Nations* (New York: Praeger, 1968), pp. 5–17.

5 Even Mill seems to subscribe to this, for according to Walzer it is his idea "that citizens get the government they deserve, or, at least, the government for which they are 'fit,' " *Just and Unjust Wars* (New York: Basic Books, 1977), p. 88.

6 Parenthetical references in the text are to Walzer, "The Moral Standing of States: A Response to Four Critics," *Philosophy & Public Affairs* 9, no. 3 (Spring 1980).

45

Democracy: From City-states to a Cosmopolitan Order?

David Held

Democracy seems to have scored an historic victory over alternative forms of governance.[1] Nearly everyone today professes to be a democrat. Political regimes of all kinds throughout the world claim to be democracies. Yet what these regimes say and do is often substantially different from one to another. Democracy bestows an aura of legitimacy on modern political life: laws, rules and policies appear justified when they are 'democratic'. But it was not always so. The great majority of political thinkers from ancient Greece to the present day have been highly critical of the theory and practice of democracy. A uniform commitment to democracy is a very recent phenomenon. Moreover, democracy is a remarkably difficult form of government to create and sustain. The history of twentieth-century Europe alone makes this clear: fascism, Nazism and Stalinism came very close to obliterating democracy altogether.

Against this background, it is unsettling that some recent political commentators have proclaimed (by means of a phrase borrowed most notably from Hegel) the 'end of history' – the triumph of the west over all political and economic alternatives. The revolutions which swept across Central and Eastern Europe at the end of 1989 and the beginning of 1990 stimulated an atmosphere of celebration. Liberal democracy was championed as the agent of progress and capitalism as the only viable economic system: ideological conflict, it was said, is being steadily displaced by universal democratic reason and market-orientated thinking.[2] But such a view is quite inadequate in a number of respects.

In the first instance, the 'liberal' component of liberal democracy cannot be treated simply as a unity. There are distinctive liberal traditions which embody quite different conceptions from each other of the individual agent, of autonomy, of the rights and duties of subjects, and of the proper nature and form of community. In addition, the 'celebratory' view of liberal democracy neglects to explore whether there are any tensions, or even perhaps contradictions, between the 'liberal' and 'democratic' components of liberal democracy; for example, between the liberal preoccupation with individual rights or 'frontiers of freedom' which 'nobody should be permitted to cross', and the democratic concern for the regulation of individual and collective action, that is, for public accountability.[3] Those who have written at length on this question have frequently resolved it in quite different directions. Furthermore, there is not simply one institutional form of liberal democracy. Contemporary democracies have crystallized into a number of different types, which makes any appeal to a liberal position vague at best.[4] An uncritical affirmation of liberal democracy essentially leaves unanalysed the whole meaning of democracy and its possible variants.

This essay seeks to address this lacuna, first, by examining the development of different models of

Originally published in *Political Studies* 40, Special Issue (1992): 10–39. Copyright © 1992 by Political Studies Association. Reprinted by permission of Blackwell Publishing Ltd.

democracy; secondly, by considering the conditions of application of these models; thirdly, by exploring the meaning of democracy in the context of the progressive enmeshment today of states and societies in regional and global networks; and finally, by assessing the proper form and scope of democracy in relation to systems of international governance. The first two sets of issues will be examined in the next section, and the second two sets in the subsequent one. It will be argued, ultimately, that democracy can result from, and only from, a nucleus, or federation, of democratic states and societies. Or, to put the point differently, national democracies require international democracy if they are to be sustained and developed in the contemporary era. Paradoxically, perhaps, democracy has to be extended and deepened within and between countries for it to retain its relevance in the twenty-first century.

If the case for rethinking democracy in relation to the interconnectedness of states and societies is established successfully, a new agenda will have been created for democratic theory and practice. It is important to be clear about the meaning of 'new' in this context. The agenda will not be new in the sense of being without precedent; others before have sought to understand the impact of the international order on the form and operation of domestic politics within democratic states. Others before have also sought to set out the normative implications of changes in the international order for the role and nature of democratic government. Nor will the agenda be new in the sense that traditional questions of democratic theory will be wholly displaced. On the contrary, questions will remain about the proper form of citizenship, the nature of individual rights and duties and the extent of participation and representation, for instance. But the agenda will be new to the extent that the case is made that a theory of democracy (whether focusing on philosophical or empirical-analytic concerns) requires a theory of the interlocking processes and structures of the global system. For a theory of democracy must offer, it will be maintained, an account both of the changing meaning of democracy within the global order and of the impact of the global order on the development of democratic associations. Democratic institutions and practices have to be articulated with the complex arena of national and international politics, and the mutual interpenetration of the national and international must be mapped. Political understanding, and the successful pursuit

of democratic political theory, is dependent on the outcome of these tasks.[5] Before pursuing them, however, the concept of democracy itself requires some clarification.

Models of Democracy

Within the history of democratic theory lies a deeply rooted conflict about whether democracy should mean some kind of popular power (a form of politics in which citizens are engaged in self-government and self-regulation) or an aid to decision-making (a means of conferring authority on those periodically voted into office). This conflict has given rise to three basic variants or models of democracy, which it is as well to bear in mind. First, there is direct or participatory democracy, a system of decision-making about public affairs in which citizens are directly involved. This was the 'original' type of democracy found in ancient Athens, among other places. Secondly, there is liberal or representative democracy, a system of rule embracing elected 'officers' who undertake to 'represent' the interests or views of citizens within the framework of the 'rule of law'. Thirdly, there is a variant of democracy based on a one-party model (although some may doubt whether this is a form of democracy at all). Until recently, the Soviet Union, East European societies and many third world countries have been dominated by this conception. The following discussion deals briefly with each of these models in turn, developing concepts and issues which will be drawn upon in later argument.

The active citizen and republican government

Athenian democracy has long been taken as a fundamental source of inspiration for modern western political thought. This is not to say that the west has been right to trace many elements of its democratic heritage exclusively to Athens; for, as recent historical and archaeological research has shown, some of the key political innovations, both conceptual and institutional, of the nominally western political tradition can be traced to older civilizations in the east. The city-state or *polis* society, for example, existed in Mesopotamia long before it emerged in the west.[6] Nonetheless, the political ideals of Athens – equality among citizens, liberty, respect for the law and justice – have been taken as integral to western political thinking, and it is for this reason that Athens constitutes a useful starting point.

The Athenian city-state, ruled as it was by citizen-governors, did not differentiate between state and society. In ancient Athens, citizens were at one and the same time subjects of political authority and the creators of public rules and regulations. The people (*demos*) engaged in legislative and judicial functions, for the Athenian concept of citizenship entailed their taking a share in these functions, participating *directly* in the affairs of 'the state.'[7] Athenian democracy required a general commitment to the principle of civic virtue: dedication to the republican city-state and the subordination of private life to public affairs and the common good. 'The public' and 'the private' were intertwined. Citizens could properly fulfil themselves and live honourably only in and through the *polis*. Of course, who was to count as a citizen was a tightly restricted matter; among the excluded were women and a substantial slave population.

The Athenian city-state – eclipsed ultimately by the rise of empires, stronger states and military regimes – shared features with republican Rome. Both were predominantly face-to-face societies and oral cultures; both had elements of popular participation in governmental affairs, and both had little, if any, centralized bureaucratic control. Furthermore, both sought to foster a deep sense of public duty, a tradition of civic virtue or responsibility to 'the republic' – to the distinctive matters of the public realm. And in both polities, the claims of the state were given a unique priority over those of the individual citizen. But if Athens was a democratic republic, contemporary scholarship generally affirms that Rome was, by comparison, an essentially oligarchical system.[8] Nevertheless, from antiquity, it was Rome which was to prove the most durable influence on the dissemination of republican ideas.

Classical republicanism received its most robust restatement in the early Renaissance, especially in the city-states of Italy. The meaning of the concept of 'active citizenship in a republic' became a leading concern. Political thinkers of this period were critical of the Athenian formulation of this notion; shaped as their views were by Aristotle, one of the most notable critics of Greek democracy, and by the centuries-long impact of republican Rome, they recast the republican tradition. While the concept of the *polis* remained central to the political theory of Italian cities, most notably in Florence, it was no longer regarded as a means to self-fulfilment.[9] Emphasis continued to be placed on the importance of civic virtue but the latter was understood as highly fragile, subject particularly to corruption if dependent solely upon the political involvement of any one major grouping: the people, the aristocracy or the monarchy. A constitution which could reflect and balance the interests of all leading political factions became an aspiration. Niccolò Machiavelli thus argued that all singular constitutional forms (monarchy, aristocracy and democracy) were unstable, and only a governmental system combining elements of each could promote the kind of political culture on which civic virtue depends.[10] The best example of such a government was, he proclaimed, Rome: Rome's mixed government (with its system of consuls, Senate and tribunes of the people) was directly linked to its sustained achievements.

The core of the Renaissance republican case was that the freedom of a political community rested upon its accountability to no authority other than that of the community itself. Self-government is the basis of liberty, together with the right of citizens to participate – within a constitutional framework which creates distinct roles for leading social forces – in the government of their own common business.[11] As one commentator put it, 'the community as a whole must retain the ultimate sovereign authority', assigning its various rulers or chief magistrates 'a status no higher than that of elected officials'.[12] Such 'rulers' must ensure the effective enforcement of the laws created by the community for the promotion of its own good; for they are not rulers in a traditional sense, but 'agents of *ministri* of justice'.

In Renaissance republicanism, as well as in Greek democratic thought, a citizen was someone who participated in 'giving judgement and holding office'.[13] Citizenship meant participation in public affairs. This definition is noteworthy because it suggests that theorists within these traditions would have found it hard to locate citizens in modern democracies, except perhaps as representatives or office holders. The limited scope in contemporary politics for the active involvement of citizens would have been regarded as most undemocratic.[14] Yet the idea that human beings should be active citizens of a political order – citizens of their states – and not merely dutiful subjects of a ruler has had few advocates from the earliest human associations to the early Renaissance.[15]

The demise in the west of the idea of the active citizen, one whose very being is affirmed in and through political action, is hard to explain fully. But it is clear enough that the antithesis of *Homo politicus* is the *Homo credens* of the Christian faith: the citizen whose active judgement is essential is displaced by the true believer.[16] Although it would be quite misleading to suggest that the rise of Christianity effectively banished secular considerations from the lives of rulers and ruled, it unquestionably shifted the source of authority and wisdom from this-worldly to other-worldly representatives. During the Middle Ages, the integration of Christian Europe came to depend above all on two theocratic authorities: the Roman Catholic Church and the Holy Roman Empire. There was no theoretical alternative to their account of the nature of power and rule.[17] Not until the end of the sixteenth century, when it became apparent that religion had become a highly divisive force and that the powers of the state would have to be separated from the duty of rulers to uphold any particular faith, did the nature and limits of political authority, law, rights and obedience become a preoccupation of European political thought from Italy to England.[18]

Liberal representative democracy

Modern liberal and liberal democratic theories have constantly sought to justify the sovereign power of the state while at the same time justifying limits on that power.[19] The history of this attempt since Thomas Hobbes is the history of arguments to balance might and right, power and law, duties and rights. On the one hand, states must have a monopoly of coercive power in order to provide a secure basis on which trade, commerce, religion and family life can prosper. On the other hand, by granting the state a regulatory and coercive capability, political theorists were aware that they had accepted a force that could, and frequently did, deprive citizens of political and social freedoms.

Liberal democrats provided the key institutional innovation to try to overcome this dilemma: representative democracy. The liberal concern with reason, law and freedom of choice could only be upheld properly by recognizing the political equality of all mature individuals. Such equality would ensure not only a secure social environment in which people would be free to pursue their private activities and interests, but also a state which, under the watchful eye of the electorate, would do what was best in the general or public interest. Thus, liberal democrats argued, the democratic

constitutional state, linked to other key institutional mechanisms, particularly the free market, would resolve the problems of ensuring both authority and liberty.

Two classic statements of the new position can be found in the philosophy of James Madison and in the work of one of the key figures of nineteenth-century English liberalism: Jeremy Bentham. In Madison's account, 'pure democracies' (by which he means societies 'consisting of a small number of citizens, who assemble and administer the government in person') have always been intolerant, unjust and unstable.[20] By contrast, representative government overcomes the excesses of 'pure democracy' because regular elections force a clarification of public issues, and the elected few, able to withstand the political process, are likely to be competent and capable of 'discerning the true interest of their country'.

The central concern of Madison's argument is not the rightful place of the active citizen in the life of the political community but, instead, the legitimate pursuit by individuals of their interests, and government as a means for the enhancement of these interests. Although Madison himself sought clear ways of reconciling particular interests with what he called modern 'extended republics', his position signals a clear shift from the classical ideals of civic virtue and the public realm to liberal preoccupations.[21] He conceived the representative state as the chief mechanism to aggregate individuals' interests and to protect their rights. In such a state, he believed, security of person and property would be sustained and politics could be made compatible with the demands of large nation-states, with their complex patterns of trade, commerce and international relations.[22]

In parallel with this view, Bentham held that representative democracy 'has for its characteristic object and effect... securing its members against oppression and depredation at the hands of those functionaries which it employs for its defence'.[23] Democratic government is required to protect citizens from the despotic use of political power, whether it be by a monarch, the aristocracy or other groups. The representative state thus becomes an umpire or referee while individuals pursue in civil society, according to the rules of economic competition and free exchange, their own interests. The free vote and the free market are both essential, for a key presupposition is that the collective good can be properly realized in most domains of life only if individuals interact in competitive exchanges, pursuing their utility with minimal state interference. Significantly, however, this argument has another side. Tied to the advocacy of a 'minimal state', whose scope and power need to be strictly limited, there is a strong commitment to certain types of state intervention: for instance, to regulate the behaviour of the disobedient, and to reshape social relations and institutions if, in the event of the failure of *laissez-faire*, the greatest happiness of the greatest number is not achieved – the only scientifically defensible criterion, Bentham held, of the public good.

From classical antiquity to the seventeenth century, democracy was largely associated with the gathering of citizens in assemblies and public meeting places. By the early nineteenth century it was beginning to be thought of as the right of citizens to participate in the determination of the collective will through the medium of elected representatives.[24] The theory of representative democracy fundamentally shifted the terms of reference of democratic thought: the practical limits that a sizeable citizenry imposes on democracy, and which had been the focus of so much critical (anti-democratic) attention, were practically eliminated. Representative democracy could now be celebrated as both accountable and feasible government, potentially stable over great territories and time spans.[25] It could even be heralded, as James Mill put it, as 'the grand discovery of modern times' in which 'the solution of all difficulties, both speculative and practical, will be found'.[26] Accordingly, the theory and practice of popular government shook off its traditional association with small states and cities, opening itself to become the legitimating creed of the emerging world of nation-states. But who exactly was to count as a legitimate participant, or a 'citizen' or 'individual', and what his or her exact role was to be in this new order, remained either unclear or unsettled. Even in the work of the enlightened John Stuart Mill ambiguities remained: the idea that all citizens should have equal political weight in the polity remained outside his actual doctrine, along with that of most of his contemporaries.[27]

It was left by and large to the extensive and often violently suppressed struggles of working-class and feminist activists in the nineteenth and twentieth centuries to accomplish a genuinely universal suffrage in some countries. Their achievement was to remain fragile in places such as Germany, Italy and Spain, and was in practice denied to some groups; for instance, many African-Americans in the US before the civil rights movement in the 1950s and 1960s. However, through these struggles the idea that the rights of citizenship should apply equally to all adults became slowly established; many of the arguments of the liberal democrats could be turned against existing institutions to reveal the extent to which the principles and aspirations of equal political participation and equal human development remained unfulfilled. It was only with the actual achievement of citizenship for all adult men and women that liberal democracy took on its distinctively contemporary form: a cluster of rules and institutions permitting the broadest participation of the majority of citizens in the selection of representatives who alone can make political decisions (that is, decisions affecting the whole community).

This cluster includes elected government; free and fair elections in which every citizen's vote has an equal weight; a suffrage which embraces all citizens irrespective of distinctions of race, religion, class, sex and so on; freedom of conscience, information and expression on all public matters broadly defined; the right of all adults to oppose their government and stand for office; and associational autonomy – the right to form independent associations including social movements, interest groups and political parties.[28] The consolidation of representative democracy, thus understood, has been a twentieth-century phenomenon; perhaps one should even say a late twentieth-century phenomenon. For it is only in the closing decades of this century that democracy has been securely established in the west and widely adopted in principle as a suitable model of government beyond the west.

Marxism and one-party democracy

The struggle of liberalism against tyranny, and the struggle by liberal democrats for political equality, represented a major step forward in the history of human emancipation, as Karl Marx and Friedrich Engels readily acknowledged. But for them, and for the Marxist tradition more broadly, the great universal ideals of 'liberty, equality and justice' cannot be realized simply by the 'free' struggle for votes in the political system together with the 'free' struggle for profit in the market-place. Advocates of the democratic state and the market economy present these institutions as the only ones under which liberty can be sustained and inequalities minimized. However, according to the Marxist critique, the capitalist economy, by virtue of its internal dynamics, inevitably produces systematic inequality and massive restrictions on real freedom. The formal existence of certain liberties is of little value if they cannot be exercised in practice. Therefore, although each step towards formal political equality is an advance, its liberating potential is severely curtailed by inequalities of class.

In class societies the state cannot become the vehicle for the pursuit of the common good or public interest. Far from playing the role of emancipator, protective knight, umpire, or judge in the face of disorder, the agencies of the liberal representative state are enmeshed in the struggles of civil society. Marxists conceive the state as an extension of civil society, reinforcing the social order for the enhancement of particular interests. Their argument is that political emancipation is only a step towards human emancipation: that is, the complete democratization of both society and the state. In their view, liberal democratic society fails when judged by its own promises.

Among these promises are, first, political participation, or general involvement mediated by representatives in decisions affecting the whole community; secondly, accountable government; and thirdly, freedom to protest and reform.[29] But 'really existing liberal democracy', as one Marxist recently put it, fails to deliver on any of these promises. For it is distinguished by the existence of a largely passive citizenry (significant numbers of eligible citizens do not vote in elections, for example); the erosion and displacement of parliamentary institutions by unelected centres of power (typified by the expansion of bureaucratic authority and of the role of functional representatives); and substantial structural constraints on state action and, in particular, on the possibility of the piecemeal reform of capitalism (the flight of capital, for example, is a constant threat to elected governments with strong programmes of social reform).[30]

Marx himself envisaged the replacement of the liberal democratic state by a 'commune structure': the smallest communities, which were to administer their own affairs, would elect delegates to larger administrative units (districts, towns); these in turn would elect candidates to still larger areas of administration (the national delegation).[31] This arrangement is known as the 'pyramid' structure of 'delegative democracy': all delegates are revocable, bound by the instructions of their constituency, and organized into a 'pyramid' of directly elected committees. The post-capitalist state would not, therefore, bear any resemblance to a liberal, parliamentary regime. All state agencies would be brought within the sphere of a single set of directly accountable institutions. Only when this happens will 'that self-reliance, that freedom, which disappeared from earth with the Greeks, and vanished into the blue haze of heaven with Christianity', as the young Marx put it, gradually be restored.[32]

In the Marxist-Leninist account, the system of delegative democracy is to be complemented, in principle, by a separate but somewhat similar system at the level of the Communist Party. The transition to socialism and communism necessitates the 'professional' leadership of a disciplined cadre of revolutionaries.[33] Only such a leadership has the capacity to organize the defence of the revolution against counter-revolutionary forces, to plan the expansion of the forces of production, and to supervise the reconstruction of society. Since all fundamental differences of interest are class interests, since the working-class interest (or standpoint) is the progressive interest in society, and since during and after the revolution it has to be articulated clearly and decisively, a revolutionary party is essential. The party is the instrument which can create the framework for socialism and communism. In practice, the party has to rule; and it was only in the 'Gorbachev era' in the Soviet Union (from 1984 to August 1991) that a pyramid of councils, or 'Soviets', from the central authority to those at local village and neighbourhood level, was given anything more than a symbolic or ritualistic role in the post-revolutionary period.

Democracy, the state, and civil society

What should be made of these various models of democracy in contemporary circumstances? The classical participatory model cannot easily be adapted to stretch across space and time. Its emergence in the context of city-states, and under conditions of 'social exclusivity', was an integral part of its successful development. In complex industrial societies, marked by a high degree of social, economic and political differentiation, it is very hard to envisage how a democracy of this kind could succeed on a large scale.

The significance of these reflections is reinforced by examining the fate of the conception of democracy advocated by Marx and Engels, and their followers. In the first instance, the 'deep structure' of Marxist categories – with its emphasis on the centrality of class, the universal standpoint of the proletariat, and a conception of politics which is rooted squarely in production – ignores or severely underestimates the contributions to politics of other forms of social structure, collectivity, agency, identity, interest and knowledge. Secondly, as an institutional arrangement that allows for mediation, negotiation and compromise among struggling factions, groups or movements, the Marxist model does not stand up well under scrutiny, especially in its Marxist-Leninist form. A system of institutions to promote discussion, debate and competition among divergent views – a system encompassing the formation of movements, pressure groups and/or political parties with independent leaderships to help press their cases – appears both necessary and desirable. Further, the changes in Central and Eastern Europe after 1989 seem to provide remarkable confirmatory evidence of this, with their emphasis on the importance of political and civil rights, a competitive party system, and the 'rolling back of the state', that is, the freeing of civil society from state domination.

One cannot escape the necessity, therefore, of recognizing the importance of a number of fundamental liberal tenets, concerning the centrality, in principle, of an 'impersonal' structure of public power, of a constitution to help guarantee and protect rights, of a diversity of power centres within and outside the state, and of mechanisms to promote competition and debate among alternative political platforms. What this amounts to, among other things, is confirmation of the fundamental liberal notion that the 'separation' of state from civil society must be an essential element of any democratic political order. Conceptions of democracy that depend on the assumption that the state could ever replace civil society, or vice versa, must be treated with caution.

To make these points is not, however, to affirm any one liberal democratic model as it stands, although many advocates of democracy appear to take this view. It is one thing to accept the arguments concerning the necessary protective, conflict-mediating and redistributive functions of the democratic state, quite another to accept these as prescribed in existing accounts of liberal democracy. Advocates of liberal democracy have tended to be concerned, above all else, with the proper principles and procedures of democratic govern-ment. But by focusing on 'government', they have drawn attention away from a thorough examination of the relation between formal rights and actual rights; between commitments to treat citizens as free and equal and practices which do neither sufficiently; between concepts of the state as, in principle, an independent authority, and state involvement in the reproduction of the inequalities of everyday life; between notions of political parties as appropriate structures for bridging the gap between state and society, and the array of power centres which such parties and their leaders cannot reach. To ignore these questions is to risk the establishment of 'democracy' in the context of a sea of political, economic and social inequality. And it is to risk the creation of, at best, a very partial form of democratic politics – a form of politics in which the involvement of some bears a direct relation to the limited or non-participation of others.

The implications of these points are, I believe, of considerable significance. For democracy to flourish it has to be reconceived as a double-sided phenomenon: concerned, on the one hand, with the reform of state power and, on the other hand, with the restructuring of civil society. This entails recognizing the indispensability of a process of what I have elsewhere called 'double democratization': the interdependent transformation of both state and civil society.[34] Such a process must be premised on the principles that the division between state and civil society must be a central aspect of democratic life, and that the power to make decisions must be free of the inequalities and constraints which can be imposed by an unregulated system of private capital, as Marx foresaw. But, of course, to recognize the importance of both these points is to recognize the necessity of recasting substantially their traditional connotations.[35]

In short, if democratic life involves no more than a periodic vote, citizens' activities will be largely confined to the 'private' realm of civil society and the scope of their actions will depend largely on the resources they can command. Few opportunities will exist for citizens to act as citizens; that is, as participants in public life. But if democracy is understood as a double-sided process, this state of affairs might be redressed by creating opportunities for people to establish themselves 'in their capacity of being citizens'.[36] The 'active citizen' could once again return to the centre of public life, involving him- or herself in the realms of both state and civil society.

Of course, the nature of this involvement would differ in each of these realms, according to their organizational and institutional features. But opportunities will at least have been created for all those affected by the decision-making structures of their communities to participate in the latters' regulation – or so the story of democracy has so far suggested. However, democracy has another side.

Democracy, Globalization and International Governance

Throughout the nineteenth and twentieth centuries democratic theory has tended to assume a 'symmetrical' and 'congruent' relationship between political decision-makers and the recipients of political decisions.[37] In fact, symmetry and congruence have often been taken for granted at two crucial points: first, between citizen-voters and the decision-makers whom they are, in principle, able to hold to account; and secondly, between the 'output' (decisions, policies, and so on) of decision-makers and their constituents – ultimately, 'the people' in a delimited territory.

Even the critics of modern democracies have tended to share this assumption; following the narrative of democracy as conventionally told, they have thought of the problem of political accountability as, above all, a national problem. Contemporary representative structures are, they hold, insufficiently responsive to their citizens; and, in discussing various forms of participatory democracy, or contemporary interpretations of the relevance of republicanism, they place emphasis on making the political process more transparent and intelligible, more open to, and reflective of, the heterogeneous wants and needs of 'the people'.[38]

But the problem, for defenders and critics alike of modern democratic systems, is that regional and global interconnectedness contests the traditional national resolutions of the key questions of democratic theory and practice. The very process of governance can escape the reach of the nation-state. National communities by no means exclusively make and determine decisions and policies for themselves, and governments by no means determine what is right or appropriate exclusively for their own citizens.[39] To take some topical examples: a decision to increase interest rates in an attempt to stem inflation or exchange-rate instability is most often taken as a 'national' decision, although it may well stimulate economic changes in other countries. Similarly, a decision to permit the 'harvesting' of the rainforests may contribute to ecological damage far beyond the borders which formally limit the responsibility of a given set of political decision-makers. These decisions, along with policies on issues as diverse as investment, arms procurement and AIDS, are typically regarded as falling within the legitimate domain of authority of a sovereign nation-state. Yet, in a world of regional and global interconnectedness, there are major questions to be put about the coherence, viability and accountability of national decision-making entities themselves.

Further, decisions made by quasi-regional or quasi-supranational organizations such as the European Community, the North Atlantic Treaty Organization, or the International Monetary Fund diminish the range of decisions open to given national 'majorities'. The idea of a community which rightly governs itself and determines its own future – an idea at the very heart of the democratic polity itself – is, accordingly, today deeply problematic. Any simple assumption in democratic theory that political relations are, or could be, 'symmetrical' or 'congruent' appears unjustified.

If the inadequacy of this assumption can be fully shown, issues are raised which go to the heart of democratic thought. The idea that *consent* legitimates government and the state system more generally has been central to nineteenth- and twentieth-century liberal democrats.[40] The latter have focused on the ballot box as the mechanism whereby the individual citizen expresses political preferences and citizens as a whole periodically confer authority on government to enact laws and regulate economic and social life. The principle of 'majority rule', or the principle that decisions which accrue the largest number of votes should prevail, is at the root of the claim of political decisions to be regarded as worthy or legitimate.[41] But the very idea of consent through elections, and the particular notion that the relevant constituencies of voluntary agreement are the communities of a bounded territory or a state, becomes problematic as soon as the issue of national, regional and global interconnectedness is considered and the nature of a so-called 'relevant community' is contested. Whose consent is necessary and whose participation is justified in decisions concerning, for instance, AIDS, or acid rain, or the use of nonrenewable resources? What is the relevant constituency: national, regional or international? To whom do decision-makers have to justify their decisions? To whom should they be accountable? Further, what are the implications for the idea of legitimate rule of decisions taken in polities, with potentially life-and-death consequences for large numbers of people, many of whom might have no democratic stake in the decision-making process?

Territorial boundaries demarcate the basis on which individuals are included and excluded from participation in decisions affecting their lives (however limited the participation might be), but the outcomes of these decisions most often 'stretch' beyond national frontiers. The implications of this are considerable, not only for the categories of consent and legitimacy, but for all the key ideas of democracy: the nature of a constituency, the meaning of representation, the proper form and scope of political participation, and the relevance of the democratic nation-state, faced with unsettling patterns of relations and constraints in the international order, as the guarantor of the rights, duties and welfare of subjects. Of course, these considerations would probably come as little surprise to those nations and countries whose independence and identity have been deeply affected by the hegemonic reach of empires, old and new, but they do come as a surprise to many in the west.

In order to explore the significance of these matters further, it is necessary to examine why for most of the nineteenth and twentieth centuries democracy *in* nation-states has not been accompanied by democratic relations *among* states; why the inter-state system is now coming under pressure in a way which makes the relation between democracy within borders and democracy across borders a more urgent concern; why contemporary circumstances are creating the possibility of re-thinking democracy at regional and global levels; and why democracy at such levels is an important condition for the development of democracy within local and national communities. I shall endeavour to show that democracy within a nation-state or region requires democracy within a network of interwoven international forces and relations; and that such a requirement is thwarted by the 'deep structure' of the sovereign state order and the grafting on to this structure of the United Nations system in the immediate aftermath of the Second World War. Nonetheless, one can glimpse the possibility, I shall also seek to show, of an alternative to this state of affairs.

Sovereignty and the Westphalian order

The history of the modern inter-state system, and of international relations more generally, has borne little relation to any democratic principle of organization. In the arena of world politics, Hobbes's way of thinking about power and power relations has often been regarded as the most insightful account of the meaning of the state at the global level.[42] Hobbes drew a comparison between international relations and the state of nature, describing the international system of states as being in a continuous 'posture of war'.[43] A war of 'all against all' is a constant threat, since each state is at liberty to act to secure its own interests unimpeded by any higher religious or moral strictures.

In the study of international affairs, Hobbes's account has become associated with the 'realist' theory of international politics.[44] Realism posits, in the spirit of Hobbes's work, that the system of sovereign states is inescapably anarchic in character; and that this anarchy forces all states, in the inevitable absence of any supreme arbiter to enforce moral behaviour and agreed international codes, to pursue power politics in order to attain their vital interests. This *realpolitik* view of states has had a significant influence on both the analysis and practice of international relations in recent times as it offers a convincing *prima facie* explanation of the chaos and disorder of world affairs. In this account, the modern system of nation-states is a 'limiting factor' which will always thwart any attempt to conduct international relations in a manner which transcends the politics of the sovereign state.

A concomitant of each and every modern state's claim to supreme authority is a recognition that such a claim gives other states an equal entitlement to autonomy and respect within their own borders. In the context of the rapid erosion of 'Christian society' from the late sixteenth century, the development of sovereignty can be interpreted as part of a process of mutual recognition whereby states granted each other rights of jurisdiction in their respective territories and communities. Accordingly, sovereignty involved the assertion by the modern state of independence; that is, of its possession of sole rights to jurisdiction over a particular people and territory. And in the world of relations among states, the principle of the sovereign equality of all states gradually became adopted as the paramount principle governing the formal conduct of states towards one another, however representative or unrepresentative were their particular regimes.

The conception of international order which emerged to clarify and formalize the inter-state system has been referred to as the 'Westphalian' model (after the Peace of Westphalia of 1648 which brought to an end the German phase of the thirty years war).[45] The model covers a period from 1648 to 1945 (although some would argue it still holds today).[46] It depicts the emergence of a world community consisting of sovereign states which settle their differences privately and often by force; which engage in diplomatic relations but otherwise minimal cooperation; which seek to place their own national interest above all others; and which accept the logic of the principle of effectiveness, that is, the principle that might eventually makes right in the international world – appropriation becomes legitimation.[47] The model of Westphalia is summarized in Table 1.[48]

This framework of international affairs had a lasting and paradoxical quality rich in implications: an increasingly developed and interlinked states system simultaneously endorsed the right of each state to autonomous and independent action. As one commentator has aptly noted, the upshot of this was that states were 'not subject to

international moral requirements because they represent separate and discrete political orders with no common authority among them'.[49] In this situation, the world consists of separate political powers, pursuing their own interests, backed ultimately by their organization of coercive power.[50]

The consolidation of the modern states system resulted from the expansion of Europe across the globe. If the Iberian monarchies led the early wave of 'European globalization', their position was eroded in the seventeenth century by the Dutch, and subsequently by the English. Key features of the modern states system – the centralization of political power, the expansion of administrative rule, the legitimation of power through claims to representation, the emergence of massed armies – which existed in Europe in embryo in the sixteenth century, were to become prevalent features of the entire global system.[51]

While the diffusion of European power mainly occurred through the medium of sea-going military and commercial endeavours, Europe became connected to a global system of trade and production relationships. At the centre of the latter were new and expanding capitalistic economic mechanisms which had their origins in the sixteenth century, or in what is sometimes called the 'long sixteenth century', running from about 1450 to 1640.[52] Capitalism was from the beginning an international affair:[53] capital never allowed its aspirations to be determined by national boundaries alone. Consequently, the emergence of capitalism ushered in a fundamental change in the world order: it made possible, for the first time, genuinely global interconnections among states and societies; it penetrated the distant corners of the world and brought far-reaching changes to the dynamics and nature of political rule.

The development of the world capitalist economy initially took the form of the expansion of market relations, driven by a growing need for raw materials and other factors of production. Capitalism stimulated this drive and was, in turn, stimulated by it. It is useful to make a distinction between the expansion of capitalist market relations based on the desire to buy, sell and accumulate mobile resources (capital), and the formation of industrial capitalism involving highly distinctive class relations – based initially on those who own and control the means of production and those who have only their labouring capacity to sell. It is only with the development of capitalism in

Table 1 The model of Westphalia

1 The world consists of, and is divided by, sovereign states which recognize no superior authority.

2 The processes of law-making, the settlement of disputes and law-enforcement are largely in the hands of individual states subject to the logic of 'the competitive struggle for power'.

3 Differences among states are often settled by force: the principle of effective power holds sway. Virtually no legal fetters exist to curb the resort to force; international legal standards afford minimal protection.

4 Responsibility for cross-border wrongful acts are a 'private matter' concerning only those affected; no collective interest in compliance with international law is recognized.

5 All states are regarded as equal before the law: legal rules do not take account of asymmetries of power.

6 International law is orientated to the establishment of minimal rules of coexistence; the creation of enduring relationships among states and peoples is an aim, but only to the extent that it allows national political objectives to be met.

7 The minimization of impediments on state freedom is the 'collective' priority.

Europe after 1500, and in particular with the formation of the capitalist organization of production from the middle of the eighteenth century, that the activities of capitalists and the capitalist system began to converge.[54] From this period, the objectives of war became linked to economic objectives: military endeavour and conquest became more directly connected with the pursuit of economic advantage than they had been in earlier periods.[55]

The globalization of economic life – broadly, the growth of complex economic interconnections among states and societies – has not by any means been, of course, a uniform process, affecting each region and country in a similar way. From the outset, this process has involved great costs for the autonomy and independence of many: for example, the progressive collapse of non-European civilizations, among them the Moslem, Indian and Chinese; the disorganizing effects of western rule on a large number of small societies; and the interlinked degradation of the non-European and European worlds caused by the slave trade. In fact, globalization has been characterized both by 'hierarchy' and 'unevenness'.[56] Hierarchy denotes the structure of economic globalization: its domination by those constellations of economic power concentrated in the west and north. With the decline of Europe's empires in the twentieth century, and the end of the cold war, economic globalization has arguably become more significant than ever as the determinant of hierarchy, and the front line of geopolitics. It is likely that the economic summits of the leading industrial countries will supplant superpower summits as the primary arena within which to discern new contours of hierarchy and power. While there may be uncertainty about the precise distribution of influence at the centre of the advanced industrial countries, the hierarchical structure of the economic processes of globalization firmly places the leading economic powers of the west or north in central positions.

The other side of hierarchy is unevenness. This refers to the asymmetrical effects of economic globalization upon the life-chances and well-being of peoples, classes, ethnic groupings, movements and the sexes. The contours of these processes of 'unevenness' are not difficult to discern, although they will not be documented here. They are broadly correlated with geography, race and gender and, accordingly, with the clusters of poverty and deprivation found among the countries of the south, among non-Whites and among women. However, the existence of significant poverty in the north (in Europe and the US), the persistence of unemployment in the most advanced industrial countries (even during periods of marked growth), and the fate of many indigenous peoples, indicates the approximate nature of conceiving unevenness in these terms alone. Unevenness is a phenomenon of both international and national development. The categories of social and political stratification must, therefore, be thought of as denoting systematic divisions within and across territories.[57]

The effective power which sovereignty bestows is, to a significant degree, connected to the economic resources at the disposal of a state or people. Clearly, the resources a polity can mobilize will vary according to its position in the global structure of economic relations, its place in the international division of labour, and the support it can muster from regional economic networks.[58] The growing awareness in many western countries that their sovereignty is under pressure from a variety of sources and forces places before them (often for the first time) issues that have been apparent to many countries for a long time. The struggle for sovereignty and autonomy in many third world countries was closely related to the struggle for freedom from colonial domination. *De jure* sovereignty has been of the utmost importance to those countries that had previously been denied it; but *de jure* sovereignty is not, of course, the same thing as *de facto* or practical sovereignty. The often weak and debt-ridden economies of many third world countries leave them vulnerable and dependent on economic forces and relations over which they have little, if any, control. Although the internationalization of production and finance places many instruments of economic control beyond even the most powerful countries, the position of those at the lower end of the globalization hierarchy, experiencing the worst effects of unevenness, is substantially worse.

Political independence often provides at best only a brief respite from the processes of marginalization in the world economy. In countries such as those of the Sub-Sahara, where the boundaries of the state (with two small exceptions) do not correspond to the boundaries of any that existed before colonization, where there has been no 'established habit' of exercising central authority and accepting its role, and where some of the most elementary human securities have often been absent, independence has been fraught with many types of difficulty.[59] Against this background, the achievement of any form of democracy is significant. Nevertheless, the achievement is handicapped by vulnerability to the international economy, by a fragile resource base which is threatening to the autonomy of political organizations, and by social groups often deeply divided by extreme poverty, hardship and ill-health as well as by ethnic, cultural and other considerations. In addition, it is handicapped by the very *structure* of the international political system which leaves individual states, locked into the competitive pursuit of their own security and interests, without systematic means to pursue the accountability and regulation of some of the most powerful forces ordering national and international affairs. It is political and economic might which ultimately determines the effective deployment of rules and resources within and beyond borders in the Westphalian world.

The international order and the United Nations Charter

The titanic struggles of the first and second world wars led to a growing acknowledgement that the nature and process of international governance would have to change if the most extreme forms of violence against humanity were to be outlawed, and the growing interconnectedness and interdependence of nations recognized. Slowly, the subject, scope and very sources of the Westphalian conception of international regulation, particularly its conception of international law, were all called into question.[60]

First and foremost, opinion moved against the doctrine that international law, as Oppenheim put it, is a 'law between states only and exclusively'.[61] Single persons and groups became recognized as subjects of international law. It is generally accepted, for example, that persons as individuals are subjects of international law on the basis of such documents as the Charters of the Nuremberg and Tokyo War Crimes Tribunals, the Universal Declaration of Human Rights of 1948, the Covenants on Civil and Political Rights of 1966, and the European Convention on Human Rights of 1950.

Opinion has also moved against the doctrine that international law is primarily about political and strategic (state) affairs. According to this position, international law is concerned progressively with orchestrating and regulating economic, social and environmental matters. Linked to substantial increases in the numbers of 'actors' in world politics – for example, the UN, the UN Economic and Social Council, UNCTAD, the World Bank, the International Monetary Fund, the Food and Agricultural Organization and the World Health Organization – there have been many pressures to increase the scope of international law. Faced with this development, there are those who characterize the changing reach of international law as being ever less concerned with the freedom or liberty of states, and ever more with the general welfare of all those in the global system who are able to make their voices count.[62]

Finally, the influential legal doctrine that the only true source of international law is the consent of states – either their expressed consent, or their implied consent – has been fundamentally challenged. Today, a number of sources of international law jostle for recognition. These include the traditional sources such as international conventions or treaties (general or particular) which are recognized by states; international custom or practice which provides evidence of an accepted rule or set of rules; and the underlying principles of law recognized by 'civilized nations'. They also include the 'will of the international community', which can assume the 'status of law' or the 'basis of international legal obligation' under certain circumstances.[63] The latter represents a break in principle with the requirement of individual state consent in the making of international rules and responsibilities.[64]

Although the Westphalian model of international law had its critics throughout the modern era, particularly during the ill-fated efforts of the League of Nations, it was not until after the Second World War that a new model of international law and accountability was widely advocated and accepted, culminating in the adoption of the UN Charter. The image of international regulation projected by the Charter (and related documents) was one of 'states still jealously "sovereign" ', but linked together in a 'myriad of relations'; under pressure to resolve disagreements by peaceful means and according to legal criteria; subject in principle to tight restrictions on the resort to force; and constrained to observe 'certain standards' with regard to the treatment of all persons on their territory, including their own citizens.[65] Of course, how restrictive the provisions of the Charter have been to states, and to what extent they have been actually operationalized, are important questions. Before addressing them, however, leading elements of the Charter model should be sketched (see Table 2).[66]

Table 2 The UN Charter Model

1   The world community consists of sovereign states, connected through a dense network of relations, both *ad hoc* and institutionalized. Single persons and groups are regarded as legitimate actors in international relations (albeit with limited roles).
2   Certain peoples oppressed by colonial powers, racist regimes or foreign occupants are assigned rights of recognition and a determinate role in articulating their future and interests.
3   Gradual acceptance of standards and values which call into question the principle of effective power; accordingly, major violations of given international rules are not in theory to be regarded as legitimate. Restrictions are placed on the resort to force, including the unwarranted use of economic force.
4   The creation of new rules, procedures and institutions designed to aid law-making and law-enforcement in international affairs.
5   The adoption of legal principles delimiting the form and scope of the conduct of all members of the international community, and providing a set of guidelines for the structuring of international rules.
6   Fundamental concern expressed for the rights of individuals, and the creation of a corpus of international rules seeking to constrain states to observe certain standards in the treatment of all, including their own citizens.
7   The preservation of peace, the advancement of human rights and the establishment of greater social justice are the stated collective priorities; 'public affairs' include the whole of the international community. With respect to certain values – peace, the prohibition of genocide – international rules now provide in principle for the personal responsibility of state officials and the attribution of criminal acts to states.
8   The recognition of systematic inequalities among peoples and states and the establishment of new rules – including the concept of 'the common heritage of mankind'[67] – to create ways of governing the distribution, appropriation and exploitation of territory, property and natural resources.

The shift in the structure of international regulation from the Westphalian to the UN Charter model raised fundamental questions about the nature and form of international law – questions which point to the possibility of a significant disjuncture between the law of nation-states, of the states system, and of the wider international community. At the heart of this shift lies a conflict between claims made on behalf of individual states and those made on behalf of an alternative organizing principle of world affairs: ultimately, a demo-cratic community of states, with equal voting rights in the General Assembly of nation-states, openly and collectively regulating international life while constrained to observe the UN Charter and a battery of human rights conventions. However, this conflict has not been settled, and it would be quite misleading to conclude that the era of the UN Charter model simply displaced the Westphalian logic of international governance. The essential reason for this is that the Charter framework represents, in many respects, an extension of the interstate system.

The organizations and procedures of the UN were designed partly to overcome weaknesses in the League of Nations. Its 'architecture', therefore, was drawn up to accommodate the international power structure as it was understood in 1945. The division of the globe into powerful nation-states, with distinctive sets of geopolitical interests, was built into the Charter conception. As a result, the UN was virtually immobilized as an autonomous actor on many pressing issues.[68] One of the most obvious manifestations of this was the special veto power accorded to the five Permanent Members of the UN Security Council. This privileged political status added authority and legitimacy to the position of each of the major powers; for although they were barred in principle from the use of force on terms contrary to the Charter, they were protected against censure and sanctions in the event of unilateral action in the form of their veto. Moreover, the Charter gave renewed credence (through Article 51) to unilateral strategic state initiatives if they were necessary in 'self-defence', since there was no clear delimitation of the meaning of this phrase. In addition, while the Charter placed new obligations on states to settle disputes peacefully, and laid down certain procedures for passing judgement on alleged acts of self-defence, these procedures have rarely been used and there has been no insistence on compliance with them. The possibility of mobilizing the collective coercive measures envisaged in the Charter itself against illegitimate state action has, furthermore, never materialized, and even the UN's peacekeeping missions have been restricted generally to areas in which the consent of the territorial state in question has first been given.

The UN's susceptibility to the agendas of the most powerful states has been reinforced by its dependence on finance provided by its members. This position of vulnerability to state politics is underscored by the absence of any mechanism to confer some kind of direct UN status on regional and transnational functional or cultural forces (agencies, groups or movements) who often might have a significant perspective on international questions. In sum, the UN Charter model, despite its good intentions, failed effectively to generate a new principle of organization in the international order – a principle which might break fundamentally with the logic of Westphalia and generate new democratic mechanisms of political coordination and change.

Nonetheless, it would be wrong simply to leave the argument here. The UN Charter system has been distinctively innovative and influential in a number of respects. It has provided an international forum in which all states are in certain respects equal, a forum of particular value to third world countries and to those seeking a basis for 'consensus' solutions to international problems. It has provided a framework for decolonization, and for the pursuit of the reform of international economic institutions. Moreover, it has provided a vision, valuable in spite of all its limitations, of a new world order based upon a meeting of governments and, under appropriate circumstances, of a supranational presence in world affairs championing human rights.[69] Further, some of the deficiencies attributed to the UN can be better placed at the door of the states system itself, with its deep structural embeddedness in the global capitalist economy.

It might, accordingly, be a considerable step forward in the cross-border regulation of world affairs if the UN system were to live up to its Charter. Among other things, this would involve pursuing measures to implement key elements of the rights Conventions, enforcing the prohibition on the discretionary right to use force, activating the collective security system envisaged in the Charter itself and, more generally, ensuring compliance with the Charter's main articles.[70] In addition, if the Charter model were extended – for example, by adding the requirement of compulsory jurisdiction in the case of disputes falling under the UN rubric, or by providing means of redress in the case of human rights violations through a new international human rights court, or by making a (near) consensus vote in the General Assembly a legitimate source of international law, or by modifying the veto arrangement in the Security Council and rethinking representation on it to allow for an adequate regional presence – a basis might be established for the Charter model to generate political resources of its own, and to act as an autonomous decision-making centre.

While each move in this direction would be significant, particularly in enhancing the prospects of world peace, it would still represent, at best, a movement towards a very partial or 'thin' form of democracy in international affairs. Certainly, each state would enjoy formal equality in the UN system, and regional interests would be better represented. But it would still be possible for a plethora of different kinds of political regimes to participate on an equal footing in the Charter framework; the dynamics and logic of the inter-state system would still represent an immensely powerful principle of organization in global affairs, especially with its military machinery largely intact; the massive disparities of power and asymmetries of resources in the hierarchical and uneven global political economy would be left virtually unaddressed; the changing structure of the global order reflected in discussion about the proper subject, scope and sources of international law would remain marginal to the model; and transnational actors, civil associations, non-governmental organizations and social movements might still have a minimal role in this governance system. It would remain, then, a state-centred or sovereignty-centred model of international politics, and would lie at some considerable distance from what might be called a 'thicker' democratic ordering of international affairs. Furthermore, it would lie at some distance from an adequate recognition of the transformations being wrought in the wake of globalization – transformations which are placing increasing strain on both the Westphalian and Charter conceptions of international governance.

Cosmopolitan democracy and the new international order

There is a striking paradox to note about the contemporary era: from Africa to Eastern Europe, Asia to Latin America, more and more nations and groups are championing the idea of 'the rule of the people'; but they are doing so at just that moment when the very efficacy of democracy as a national form of political organization appears open to question. As substantial areas of human activity are progressively organized on a global level, the fate of democracy, and of the independent democratic nation-state in particular, is fraught with difficulty.

It could be objected that there is nothing particularly new about global interconnections, and that the significance of global interconnections for politics has, in principle, been plain for people to see for a long time. Such an objection could be elaborated by emphasizing, as I have done, that a dense pattern of global interconnections began to emerge with the initial expansion of the world economy and the rise of the modern state from the late sixteenth century. Further, it could be suggested that domestic and international politics have been interwoven throughout the modern era: domestic politics has always to be understood against the background of international politics, and the former is often the source of the latter.[71] However, it is one thing to claim that there are elements of continuity in the formation and structure of modern states, economies and societies, quite another to claim that there is nothing new about aspects of their form and dynamics. For there is a fundamental difference between, on the one hand, the development of particular trade routes, or select military and naval operations which have an impact on certain towns, rural centres and territories, and, on the other hand, an international order involving the emergence of a global economic system which stretches beyond the control of any single state (even of dominant states); the expansion of networks of transnational relations and communications over which particular states have limited influence; the enormous growth in international organizations and regimes which can limit the scope for action of the most powerful states; the development of a global military order, and the build-up of the means of 'total' warfare as an enduring feature of the contemporary world, which can reduce the range of policies available to governments and their citizens. While trade routes and military expeditions can link distant populations together in long loops of cause and effect, contemporary developments in the international order link peoples through multiple networks of transaction and coordination, reordering the very notion of distance itself.[72]

It needs to be emphasized that processes of globalization do not necessarily lead to growing global integration; that is, to a world order marked by the progressive development of a homogenous or unified society and politics. For globalization can generate forces of both fragmentation and unification. Fragmentation or disintegrative trends are possible for several reasons. The growth of dense patterns of interconnectedness among states and societies can increase the range of developments affecting people in particular locations. By

creating new patterns of transformation and change, globalization can weaken old political and economic structures without necessarily leading to the establishment of new systems of regulation. Further, the impact of global and regional processes is likely to vary under different international and national conditions – for instance, a nation's location in the international economy, its place in particular power blocs, its position with respect to the international legal system. In addition, globalization can engender an awareness of political difference as much as an awareness of common identity; enhanced international communications can highlight conflicts of interest and ideology, and not merely remove obstacles to mutual understanding.

In positive terms, globalization implies at least two distinct phenomena. First, it suggests that political, economic and social activity is becoming worldwide in scope. And, secondly, it suggests that there has been an intensification of levels of interaction and interconnectedness within and among states and societies.[73] What is new about the modern global system is the spread of globalization through new dimensions of activity – technological, organizational, administrative and legal, among others – each with their own logic and dynamics of change; and the chronic intensification of patterns of interconnectedness mediated by such phenomena as the modern communications industry and new information technology. Politics unfolds today, with all its customary uncertainty and indeterminateness, against the background of a world shaped and permeated by the movement of goods and capital, the flow of communication, the interchange of cultures and the passage of people.[74]

In this context, the meaning and place of democratic politics, and of the contending models of democracy, have to be rethought in relation to a series of overlapping local, regional and global processes and structures.[75] It is essential to recognize at least three elements of globalization: first, the way processes of economic, political, legal and military interconnectedness are changing the nature, scope and capacity of the sovereign state from above, as its 'regulatory' ability is challenged and reduced in some spheres; secondly, the way in which local groups, movements and nationalisms are questioning the nation-state from below as a representative and accountable power system; and, thirdly, the way global interconnectedness creates chains of interlocking political decisions and outcomes among states and their citizens, altering the nature and dynamics of national political systems themselves. Democracy has to come to terms with all three of these developments and their implications for national and international power centres. If it fails to do so, it is likely to become ever less effective in determining the shape and limits of political activity. The international form and structure of politics and civil society has, accordingly, to be built into the foundations of democratic thought and practice.

Three distinct requirements arise: first, that the territorial boundaries of systems of accountability be recast so that those issues which escape the control of a nation-state – aspects of monetary management, environmental questions, elements of security, new forms of communication – can be brought under better democratic control. Secondly, that the role and place of regional and global regulatory and functional agencies be rethought so that they might provide a more coherent and useful focal point in public affairs. Thirdly, that the articulation of political institutions with the key groups, agencies, associations and organizations of international civil society be reconsidered to allow the latter to become part of a democratic process – adopting, within their very *modus operandi*, a structure of rules and principles compatible with those of democracy.

How might this approach to democracy be developed? What are its essential characteristics? Addressing these questions requires recalling earlier arguments about the need to conceive democracy as a double-sided process, while reappraising the proper domain for the application of this process.[76] For if the above arguments are correct, democracy has to become a transnational affair if it is to be possible both within a restricted geographic domain and within the wider international community. The possibility of democracy today must, in short, be linked to an expanding framework of democratic institutions and agencies. I refer to such a framework as 'the cosmopolitan model of democracy'.[77] The framework can be elaborated by focusing initially on some of its institutional requirements.

In the first instance, the 'cosmopolitan model of democracy' presupposes the creation of regional parliaments (for example, in Latin America and Africa) and the enhancement of the role of such bodies where they already exist (the European Parliament) in order that their decisions become recognized, in principle, as legitimate independent sources of regional and international law. Alongside such developments, the model anticipates the possibility of general referendums, cutting across nations and nation-states, with constituencies defined according to the nature and scope of controversial transnational issues. In addition, the opening of international governmental organizations to public scrutiny and the democratization of international 'functional' bodies (on the basis perhaps of the creation of elected supervisory boards which are in part statistically representative of their constituencies) would be significant.

Hand in hand with these changes the cosmopolitan model of democracy assumes the entrenchment of a cluster of rights, including civil, political, economic and social rights, in order to provide shape and limits to democratic decision-making.[78] This requires that they be enshrined within the constitutions of parliaments and assemblies (at the national and international level); and that the influence of international courts is extended so that groups and individuals have an effective means of suing political authorities for the enactment and enforcement of key rights, both within and beyond political associations.

In the final analysis, the formation of an authoritative assembly of all democratic states and societies – a re-formed UN, or a complement to it – would be an objective. The UN, as previously noted, combines two contradictory principles of representation: the equality of all countries (one country, one vote in the General Assembly) and deference to geopolitical strength (special veto power in the Security Council to those with current or former superpower status). An authoritative assembly of all democratic states and societies would seek unreservedly to place principles of democratic representation above those of superpower politics. Moreover, unlike the UN General Assembly, it would not, to begin with at least, be an assembly of all nations; for it would be an assembly of democratic nations which would draw in others over time, perhaps by the sheer necessity of being a member if their systems of governance are to enjoy legitimacy in the eyes of their own populations. As such, the new Assembly in its early stages can best be thought of as a complement to the UN, which it would either replace over time or accept in a modified form as a 'second chamber' – a necessary meeting place for all states irrespective of the nature of their regimes.

Of course, the idea of a new democratic international Assembly is open to a battery of objections commonly put to similar schemes. Would it have any teeth to implement decisions? How would democratic international law be enforced? Would there be a centralized police and military force?[79] And so forth. These concerns are significant, but many of them can be met and countered. For instance, it needs to be stressed that any global legislative institution should be conceived above all as a 'standard-setting' institution. Although a distinction ought to be made between legal instruments which would have the status of law independently of any further negotiation or action on the part of a region or state or local government, and instruments which would require further discussion with them, implementation of the detail of a broad range of recommendations would be a matter for non-global levels of governance.[80] In addition, the question of law enforcement at a regional and global level is not beyond resolution in principle: a proportion of a nation-state's police and military (perhaps a growing proportion over time) could be 'seconded' to the new international authorities and placed at their disposal on a routine basis. To this end, avenues could be established to meet the concern that 'covenants, without the sword, are but words'.[81]

Equally, only to the extent that the new forms of 'policing' are locked into an international democratic framework would there be good grounds for thinking that a new settlement could be created between coercive power and accountability. If such a settlement seems like a fantasy, it should be emphasized that it is a fantasy to imagine that one can advocate democracy today without confronting the range of issues elaborated here. If the emerging international order is to be democratic, these issues have to be considered, even though their details are, of course, open to further specification.

The implications for international civil society of all this are in part clear. A democratic network of states and civil societies is incompatible with the existence of powerful sets of social relations and organizations which can, by virtue of the very bases of their operations, systematically distort democratic conditions and processes. At stake are, among other things, the curtailment of the power of corporations to constrain and influence the *political* agenda (through such diverse measures as the public funding of elections, the use of 'golden shares' and citizen directors), and the restriction of the activities of powerful transnational interest groups to pursue their interests unchecked

(through, for example, the regulation of bargaining procedures to minimize the use of 'coercive tactics' within and between public and private associations, and the enactment of rules limiting the sponsorship of political representatives by sectional interests, whether these be particular industries or trade unions).

If individuals and peoples are to be free and equal in determining the conditions of their own existence there must be an array of social spheres – for instance, privately and cooperatively owned enterprises, independent communications media, and autonomously run cultural centres – which allow their members control of the resources at their disposal without direct interference from political agencies or other third parties.[82] At issue here is a civil society that is neither simply planned nor merely market orientated but, rather, open to organizations, associations and agencies pursuing their own projects, subject to the constraints of democratic processes and a common structure of action.[83]

The key features of this model are set out in Table 3. The cosmopolitan model of democracy presents a programme of possible transformations with short- and long-term political implications. It does not present an all-or-nothing choice, but rather lays down a direction of possible change with clear points of orientation (see Appendix I).

Would a cosmopolitan framework of democracy, assuming its details could be adequately fleshed out, have the organizational resources – procedural, legal, institutional and military – to alter the dynamics of resource production and distribution, and of rule creation and enforcement, in the contemporary era? It would be deeply misleading to suggest that it would initially have these capabilities. Nevertheless, its commitment to the extension and deepening of mechanisms of democratic accountability across major regions and international structures would help to regulate resources and forces which are already beyond the reach of national democratic mechanisms and movements. Moreover, its commitment to the protection and strengthening of human rights, and to the further development of a regional and international court system, would aid the process whereby individuals and groups could sue their governments for the enactment of key human rights.

In addition, the establishment of regional authorities as major independent voices in world politics might contribute further to the erosion of

Table 3 The Cosmopolitan Model of Democracy

1   The global order consists of multiple and overlapping networks of power including the political, social and economic.

2   All groups and associations are attributed rights of self-determination specified by a commitment to individual autonomy and a specific cluster of rights. The cluster is composed of rights within and across each network of power. Together, these rights constitute the basis of an empowering legal order – a 'democratic international law'.

3   Law-making and law-enforcement can be developed within this framework at a variety of locations and levels, along with an expansion of the influence of regional and international courts to monitor and check political and social authority.

4   Legal principles are adopted which delimit the form and scope of individual and collective action within the organizations and associations of state *and* civil society. Certain standards are specified for the treatment of all, which no political regime or civil association can legitimately violate.

5   As a consequence, the principle of non-coercive relations governs the settlement of disputes, though the use of force remains a collective option in the last resort in the face of tyrannical attacks to eradicate democratic international law.

6   The defence of self-determination, the creation of a common structure of action and the preservation of the democratic good are the overall collective priorities.

7   Determinate principles of social justice follow: the *modus operandi* of the production, distribution and the exploitation of resources must be compatible with the democratic process and a common framework of action.

the old division of the world by the US and the former USSR. Likewise, the new institutional focus at the global level on major transnational issues would go some way towards eradicating sectarian approaches to these questions, and to countering 'hierarchy' and some of the major asymmetries in life chances. Finally, new sets of regional and global rules and procedures might help prevent public affairs from becoming a quagmire of infighting among nations wholly unable to settle pressing collective issues.

Of course, there would be new possible dangers – no political scheme is free from such risks. But what would be at issue would be the beginning of the creation of a new international democratic culture and spirit – one set off from the partisan claims of the nation-state. Such developments might take years, if not decades, to become entrenched. But 1989–91 has shown that political change can take place at an extraordinary speed, itself no doubt partially a result of the process of globalization.

Conclusion

In order to avoid possible misunderstandings about the arguments offered above, it might be useful, by way of a conclusion, to emphasize the terrain they occupy and the ground they reject. This can be done by assessing critically a number of conceptual polarities frequently found in political discourse: globalism versus cultural diversity; constitutionalism versus politics; political ambition versus political feasibility; participatory or direct democracy versus liberal representative democracy and global governance from above versus the extension of grassroots associations from below. Although these polarities provide much of the tension which charges the debate about the possibility of democracy beyond borders, there are good reasons for doubting their coherence.

To begin with, globalism and cultural diversity are not simply opposites. For global interconnectedness is already forming a dense web of relations linking cultures one to another. The issue is how and in what way cultures are linked and interrelated, not how a sealed cultural diversity can persist in the face of globalization.

Secondly, the juxtaposition of constitutionalism – or the elaboration of theoretical models of principles of political organization – with politics as a practical activity sets up another false polarity. Politics typically operates within a framework – albeit a shifting framework – of rules. Politics is rarely without some pattern, and is most often about the nature of the rules which will shape and delimit political activity. For politics is at root about the ways in which rules and resources are distributed, produced and legitimated. The question is whether politics will be shaped by an explicit, formal constitution or model which might, in principle, be open and contestable, or whether politics will be subject to an unwritten constitution, which is altogether more difficult to invoke as a defence in the face of unaccountable systems of power.

Thirdly, the question of feasibility cannot simply be set up in opposition to the question of political ambition. For what is ambitious today might be feasible tomorrow. Who anticipated the remarkable changes of 1989–90 in Eastern Europe? Who foresaw the fall of communism in the Soviet Union? The growing interconnectedness between states and societies is generating consequences, intended and unintended, for the stability of regimes, governments and states. While the question of political feasibility is of the utmost significance, it would be naive to juxtapose it simply with programmes of political ambition.

Fourthly, versions of participatory democracy cannot simply be opposed to liberal representative democracy. Programmes of participatory or direct democracy are fraught with complexities and questions. Likewise, liberal representative democracy does not simply mean one set of possible institutions or forms. The nature of liberal democracy is itself an intensely contested issue. So while there seem to be good grounds for accepting the liberal distinction between state and civil society, there are not equally good grounds for uncritically accepting either of these in their liberal form. The juxtaposition of participation with liberal representative democracy leaves most of political analysis to one side.

Fifthly, the problems of global governance from above cannot be solved through the extension of grassroots democracy alone. For the questions have to be posed: which grassroots, and which democracy? There are many social movements – for instance, right-wing nationalist movements or the Eugenics movement – which highlight how the very nature of a grassroots movement can be contested and fought over. Grassroots movements are by no means merely noble or wise. Like most social, economic or political forms, they can appear in a variety of shapes, with a variety of patterns of internal organization. Appeal to the nature of in-

Appendix I: Objectives of the Cosmopolitan Model of Democracy: Illustrative Issues

Polity/governance	
Short-term	Long-term
1 Reform of UN Security Council (to give the third world a significant voice)	1 Global Parliament (with limited revenue-raising capacity) connected to regions, nations and localities
2 Creation of a UN second chamber (on the model of the EC?)	2 New Charter of Rights and Duties locked into different domains of power
3 Enhanced political regionalization (EC and beyond)	3 Separation of political and economic interests; public funding of electoral processes
4 Compulsory jurisdiction before the International Court. New International Criminal Court and New Human Rights Court for the pursuit of rights	4 Interconnected global legal system
5 Establishment of a small but effective, accountable, international, military force	5 Permanent 'secondment' of a growing proportion of a nation-state's coercive capability to regional and global institutions. Aim: demilitarization and transcendence of war system
Civil society	
1 Enhancement of non-state, non-market solutions in the organization of civil society	1 Creation of a diversity of self-regulating associations and groups in civil society
2 Introduction of limits to private ownership of key 'public-shaping' institutions: media, information, etc.	2 Systematic experimentation with different democratic organizational forms in civil society
3 Provision of resources to those in the most vulnerable social positions to defend and articulate their interests	3 Multi-sectoral economy and pluralization of patterns of ownership and possession

herent goodness of grassroots associations and movements bypasses the necessary work of theoretical analysis.

Today, any attempt to set out a position of what could be called 'embedded utopianism' must begin both from where we are – the existing pattern of political relations and processes – and from an analysis of what might be: desirable political forms and principles.[84] If utopia is to be embedded it must be linked into patterns and movements as they are. But if this context of embeddedness is not simply to be affirmed in the shape and patterns generated by past groups and movements, it has to be assessed according to standards, criteria and principles. These, in my view, follow from a theory of democracy.

Finally, if the history and practice of democracy has until now been centred on the idea of locality (the city-state, the community, the nation), it is likely that in the future it will be centred on the international or global domain. It would be immensely naive to claim that there are any straightforward solutions to the problems posed by global interconnectedness, with its complex and often profoundly uneven effects; but there is, without doubt, an inescapably important set of questions to be addressed. Certainly, one can find many good reasons for being optimistic about finding a path forward, and many good reasons for thinking that at this juncture democracy will face another critical test.

Notes

1 The essay seeks to draw together and expand upon a number of themes discussed in my recent writings, particularly in *Models of Democracy* (Cambridge, Polity Press, 1987), ch. 9; 'Democracy, the nation-state and the global system', in D. Held (ed.), *Political Theory Today* (Cambridge, Polity Press, 1991); and 'Democracy and globalization', *Alternatives*, 16: 2 (1991).

2 See F. Fukuyama, 'The end of History', *The National Interest*, 16 (1989) and 'A reply to my critics', *The National Interest*, 18 (1989/90). For a more detailed commentary on these texts, cf. D. Held, 'Liberalism, Marxism and democracy', *Theory and Society* (forthcoming).

3 I. Berlin, *Four Essays on Liberty* (Oxford, Oxford University Press, 1969), pp. 164ff.

4 See, for example, A. Lijphart, *Democracies* (New Haven, CT, Yale University Press, 1984) and R. Dahl, *Democracy and Its Critics* (New Haven, CT, Yale University Press, 1989).

5 A fuller account of the nature and scope of political theory as outlined here can be found in the 'Introduction' to Held, *Political Theory Today*, pp. 1–21.

6 See M. Bernal, *Black Athena* (London, Free Association Books, 1987), vol. I and P. Springborg, *Western Republicanism and the Oriental Prince* (Cambridge, Polity Press, 1992).

7 When referring to the Greek *polis*, some scholars prefer to use the term 'city-republic' on the grounds that the concept of the state was an early modern formulation. For some of the issues underpinning this preference see Held, *Models of Democracy*, ch. 2.

8 M. Finley, *Politics in the Ancient World* (Cambridge, Cambridge University Press, 1983). pp. 84ff.

9 See J.G.A. Pocock, *The Machiavellian Moment: Florentine Political Thought and the Atlantic Repub-lican Tradition* (Princeton, NJ, Princeton University Press, 1975), pp. 64–80.

10 See N. Machiavelli, *The Discourses* (Harmondsworth, Penguin, 1983), pp. 104–11.

11 The republican view emphasizes, in short, that the freedom of citizens consists above all in their unhindered pursuit of their self-chosen ends. The highest political ideal is the civic freedom of an independent, self-governing republic.

12 Q. Skinner, 'The state', in T. Ball, J. Farr and R. Hanson (eds), *Political Innovation and Conceptual Change* (Cambridge, Cambridge University Press, 1989), p. 105.

13 Aristotle, *The Politics* (Harmondsworth, Penguin, 1981), p. 169.

14 See M. Finley, *Democracy Ancient and Modern* (London, Chatto and Windus, 1973).

15 The concern with aspects of 'self-government' in Renaissance Italy had a significant influence in seventeenth- and eighteenth-century England, France and America. The problem of how civic life was to be constructed, and public life sustained, was faced by diverse thinkers. While the meaning of the ideal of active citizenship was progressively altered – and denuded of many of its most challenging implications – threads of this ideal remained and continued to have an impact. It is possible to trace 'radical' and 'conservative' strains of republicanism throughout the early modern period. Cf. Pocock, *The Machiavellian Moment* and G.S. Wood, *The Creation of the American Republic: 1776–1787* (Chapel Hill, University of North Carolina Press, 1969).

16 Pocock, *The Machiavellian Moment*, p. 550.

17 H. Bull, *The Anarchical Society* (London, Macmillan, 1977), p. 27.

18 Q. Skinner, *The Foundations of Political Thought*, vol. 1 (Cambridge, Cambridge University Press, 1978), p. 352.

19 See D. Held, 'The development of the modern state', in S. Hall and B. Gieben (eds), *Formations of Modernity* (Cambridge, Polity Press, 1992).

20 J. Madison, *The Federalist Papers*, edited by R. Fairfield (New York, Doubleday, 1966), No. 10, p. 20.

21 Madison, *The Federalist Papers*, No. 10, pp. 21–2.

22 See R. W. Krouse, 'Classical images of democracy in America: Madison and Tocqueville', in G. Duncan (ed.), *Democratic Theory and Practice* (Cambridge, Cambridge University Press, 1983), pp. 58–78.

23 J. Bentham, *Constitutional Code, Book 1*, in *The Works of Jeremy Bentham*, vol. IX (Edinburgh, W. Tait, 1843), p. 47.

24 N. Bobbio, *Democracy and Dictatorship* (Cambridge, Polity Press, 1989), p. 144.

25 See Dahl, *Democracy and Its Critics*, pp. 28–30.

26 Quoted in G.H. Sabine, *A History of Political Theory* (London, George G. Harrap, 3rd edn, 1963), p. 695.

27 See Held, *Models of Democracy*, ch. 3.

28 See N. Bobbio, *Which Socialism?* (Cambridge, Polity Press, 1987), p. 66 and Dahl, *Democracy and Its Critics*, pp. 221 and 233.

29 Bobbio, *Which Socialism?*, pp. 42–4.

30 A. Callinicos, *The Revenge of History: Marxism and the East European Revolutions* (Cambridge, Polity Press, 1991), pp. 108–9.

31 K. Marx, *The Civil War in France* (Peking, Foreign Languages Press, 1970), pp. 67–70.

32 Marx, Letter 2, from the *Deutsch-Französische Jahrbücher* (Paris, 1844).

33 See, for example, V. I. Lenin, *What Is To Be Done?* (Moscow, Progress Publishers, 1947).

34 Held, *Models of Democracy*, ch. 9.

35 For texts which seek to do this, see Held, *Models of Democracy*, chs 8 and 9; Held, 'Democracy, the nation-state and the global system', pp. 227–35; and J. Keane, *Democracy and Civil Society* (London, Verso, 1988). See also Keane's essay in *Political Studies*, 40, Special Issue (1992), 116–29.

36 H. Arendt, *On Revolution* (New York, Viking Press, 1963), p. 256.

37 Held, 'Democracy, the nation–state and the global system', p. 198. Some of the material in the following paragraphs is adapted from pp. 201–5 of that essay.

38 Cf., for example, C.B. Macpherson, *The Life and Times of Liberal Democracy* (Oxford, Oxford University Press, 1977); C. Pateman, *The Problem of Political Obligation* (Cambridge, Polity Press, 2nd edn, 1985); and B. Barber, *Strong Democracy* (Berkeley, University of California Press, 1984).

39 C. Offe, *Disorganized Capitalism* (Cambridge, Polity Press, 1985), pp. 286ff.

40 R. Hanson, 'Democracy', in T. Ball, J. Farr and R. Hanson (eds), *Political Innovation and Conceptual Change* (Cambridge, Cambridge University Press, 1989), pp. 68–9.

41 Cf. Dahl, *Democracy and Its Critics*, chs 10 and 11.

42 See, for example, R. Aron, *Peace and War: A Theory of International Relations* (New York, Doubleday, 1966).

43 T. Hobbes, *Leviathan* (Harmondsworth, Penguin, 1968), pp. 187–8.

44 Cf. H.J. Morgenthau, *Politics Among Nations* (New York, Knopf, 1948); M. Wight, *Power Politics* (Harmondsworth, Penguin, 1986); and S. Smith, 'Reasons of state', in D. Held and C. Pollitt (eds), *New Forms of Democracy* (London, Sage, 1987).

45 See R. Falk, 'The interplay of Westphalia and Charter conceptions of the international legal order', in R. Falk and C. Black (eds), *The Future of the International Legal Order*, vol. 1 (Princeton, NJ, Princeton University Press, 1969); R. Falk, *A Study of Future Worlds* (New York, The Free Press, 1975), ch. 2; and A. Cassese, *International Law in a Divided World* (Oxford, Clarendon Press, 1986), especially pp. 393ff. While the emergence of this model can be linked directly to the Peace of Westphalia, important qualifications ought also to be noted. First, the basic conception of territorial sovereignty was outlined well before this settlement (although not generally assented to). Secondly, there were few, if any, references in the classic texts of early modern political theory to an intrinsically territorial state; as T. Baldwin put it, 'political theory had still to catch up with practice'. On both these points see T. Baldwin, 'The territorial state', in H. Gross and T.R. Harrison, (eds), *Cambridge Essays in Jurisprudence* (Oxford, Clarendon Press, 1992).

46 By a 'model' I mean a theoretical construction designed to reveal and explain the main elements of a political form or order and its underlying structure of relations. Models in this context are 'networks' of concepts and generalizations about aspects of the political, economic and social spheres.

47 A. Cassese, 'Violence, war and the rule of law in the International Community', in D. Held (ed.), *Political Theory Today* (Cambridge, Polity Press, 1991), p. 256.

48 These points are adapted from Falk, 'The interplay of Westphalia and Charter conceptions of the international legal order', and Cassese, *International Law in a Divided World*, pp. 396–9.

49 C. Beitz, *Political Theory and International Relations* (Princeton, NJ, Princeton University Press, 1979), p. 25.

50 The resort to coercion or armed force by non-state actors is also, arguably, an almost inevitable outcome in such a world. For communities contesting established territorial boundaries have, as Baldwin succinctly wrote, 'little alternative but to resort to arms in order to establish "effective control" over

the area they seek as their territory, and in that way make their case for international recognition (cf. Eritrea, East Timor, Kurdistan...)'. See Baldwin 'The territorial state'.

51 See G. Modelski, *Principles of World Politics* (New York, Free Press, 1972).

52 See F. Braudel, *Capitalism and Material Life* (London, Weidenfeld & Nicolson, 1973).

53 I. Wallerstein, *The Capitalist Economy* (Cambridge, Cambridge University Press, 1979), p. 19.

54 C. Tilly, *Coercion, Capital and European States, AD 990–1990* (Oxford, Blackwell, 1990), pp. 17 and 189.

55 See M. Mann, *The Sources of Social Power*, vol. 1 (Cambridge, Cambridge University Press, 1986), pp. 510–16.

56 The following analysis is indebted to R. Falk, 'Economic dimensions of global civilization: a preliminary perspective' (working paper prepared for the Cairo meeting of the Global Civilization Project, Oct. 1990), pp. 2–12.

57 See R. W. Cox, *Production, Power, and World Order: Social Forces in the Making of History* (New York, Columbia University Press, 1987), ch. 9.

58 I do not mean this to be an 'economistic' point. There are obviously other important factors involved in determining a state's effective power. See D. Held, *Political Theory and the Modern State* (Cambridge, Polity Press, 1989), ch. 8.

59 See G. Hawthorn, 'Sub-Saharan Africa', in D. Held (ed.), *Prospects for Democracy: North, South, East, West* (Cambridge, Polity Press, forthcoming, 1993). Cf. R.H. Jackson and C.G. Rosberg, 'Why Africa's weak states persist: the empirical and the juridical in statehood', *World Politics*, 17 (1982), 1–24.

60 For an overview see Bull, *The Anarchical Society*, Ch. 6.

61 See L. Oppenheim, *International Law*, vol. 1 (London, Longman, 1905), ch. 1.

62 Cf., for example, B. Röling, *International Law in an Expanded World* (Amsterdam, Djambatan, 1960); W. Friedmann, *The Changing Structure of International Law* (London, Stevens and Son, 1964); and Cassese, *International Law in a Divided World*, especially chs 7–9.

63 Cf. Bull, *The Anarchical Society*, pp. 147–58; C. Jenks, *Law, Freedom and Welfare* (London, Stevens and Son, 1963), ch. 5; and R. Falk, *The Status of Law in International Society* (Princeton, NJ. Princeton University Press, 1970), ch. 5.

64 It is interesting to note that the tradition of natural law thinking, which informed early modern international law in particular, recognized a certain tension between the requirement of governmental consent and the existence of international rights and duties.

65 Cassese, 'Violence, war and the rule of law', p. 256.

66 I have drawn these points from Cassese, *International Law in a Divided World*, pp. 398–400.

67 First propounded in the late 1960s, the concept of 'the common heritage of mankind' has been enshrined in two notable treaties: the Convention on the Moon and Other Celestial Bodies (1979) and the Convention on the Law of the Sea (1982). The concept has been proposed as a device to exclude a state or private right of appropriation over certain resources and to permit the development of these resources, where appropriate, for the benefit of all, with due regard paid to environmental protection.

68 See Falk, *A Study of Future Worlds*, pp. 69–72; R. Falk, *A Global Approach to National Policy* (Cambridge, MA, Harvard University Press, 1975), pp. 169–96; Cassese, *International Law in a Divided World*, pp. 142–3, 200–1, 213–14 and 246–50.

69 Cf. R. Falk, 'Reflections on democracy and the Gulf War', *Alternatives*, 16: 2 (1991), p. 272.

70 In making these proposals I do not wish to imply that the UN Charter itself is a fully coherent document. It includes some contradictory stipulations and procedures; some of its clauses are vague at best; and some of its recommendations can generate conflicting priorities. It is, in short, open to conflicts of interpretation which would have to be addressed thoroughly if it were to take on a more robust role.

71 P. Gourevitch, 'The second image reversed: the international sources of domestic politics', *International Organization*, 32 (1978).

72 Or, as Anthony Giddens usefully put it, globalization can be defined as 'the intensification of worldwide social relations which link distant localities in such a way that local happenings are shaped by events occurring many miles away and vice versa', in *Consequences of Modernity* (Cambridge, Polity Press, 1990), p. 64.

73 See A. McGrew, 'Conceptualizing global politics', in A. McGrew, P. Lewis et al., *Global Politics* (Cambridge, Polity Press, 1992), pp. 1–28.

74 C.W. Kegley and E.R. Wittkopf, *World Politics* (Basingstoke, Macmillan, 1989), p. 511.

75 I have discussed these processes and structures in 'Democracy, the nation–state and the global system', pp. 207–27 and at greater length in *Foundations of Democracy: the Principle of Autonomy and the Global Order* (Cambridge, Polity Press, 1993).

76 See above pp. 84–5.

77 In previous publications I have referred to this as 'the federal model', but given the current controversy about 'federalism' in Europe the term has become unhelpful in conveying my intentions. I would like to thank Daniele Archibugi for pressing this point. A central theme of my forthcoming work, *Foundations of Democracy*, is what I now prefer to call 'the cosmopolitan model of democracy' or, better still, of 'democratic autonomy'. Of course, anyone who seeks to use the term 'cosmopolitan' needs to clarify its meaning, especially in relation to Kant's thought. I seek to do this in *Foundations*.

78 It is beyond the scope of this essay to set out my particular conception of rights which I link to the notion of a 'common structure of action': the necessary conditions for people in principle to enjoy free and equal political participation. See Held, 'Democracy, the nation-state and global system', pp. 227–35, and, particularly, Held, *Foundations of Democracy*.

79 Among other difficulties to be faced would be the rules determining the Assembly's representative base. One country, one vote? Representatives allocated according to population size? Would major international functional organizations be represented? Cf. I. McLean, 'Forms of representation and systems of voting', in D. Held (ed.), *Political Theory Today* (Cambridge, Polity Press, 1991), pp. 190–96 and J. Burnheim, *Is Democracy Possible?* (Cambridge, Polity Press, 1985), pp. 82–124.

80 European Community law embodies a range of relevant distinctions among legal instruments and types of implementation which are helpful to reflect on in this context. However, I leave open these complex issues in this essay.

81 Hobbes, *Leviathan*, p. 223.

82 The models for the organization of such spheres are, it must be readily acknowledged, far from settled. See D. Held and C. Pollitt (eds), *New Forms of Democracy* (London, Sage, 1986).

83 The proposed European Social Charter embodies principles and rules which are compatible with the idea of generating elements of a common structure of action. If operationalized it would, in principle, alter the structure and functioning of market processes in a number of ways. While the Charter falls considerably short of what I have in mind by a common structure of action, and its details require extensive consideration which I shall not offer here, it is a useful illustration of the possibility of legislation to alter the background conditions and operations of the economic organizations of civil society.

84 Cf. R. Falk, *Positive Prescriptions for the Near Future* (Princeton, NJ, Princeton University, Center for International Studies, World Order Studies Program Occasional Paper, No. 20, 1991), pp. 8–10.

46

Global Governance and Democratic Accountability

Robert O. Keohane

Globalization in the contemporary world means that transnational relationships are both extensive and intensive.[1] States and other organizations exert effects over great distances; people's lives can be fundamentally changed, or ended, as a result of decisions made only days or moments earlier, thousands of miles away. In other words, interdependence is high.

States remain the most powerful actors in world politics, but it is no longer even a reasonable simplification to think of world politics simply as politics among states. A larger variety of other organizations, from multinational corporations to non-governmental organizations, exercise authority and engage in political action across state boundaries. Increasingly extensive networks of communication and affiliation link people in different societies, even when they do not belong to the same formal organization. Some of these networks are benign; others are designed to achieve nefarious purposes such as drug smuggling and money laundering, while members of still other seek to destroy societies or groups of people whom they fear or hate.

Interdependence without any organized government would lead actors to seek to solve their own problems by imposing costs on others. In response, those of their targets who could rationally retaliate – and perhaps some for whom retaliation would be less rational – would do so. The result, familiar in times of war or severe economic strife, would be conflict.

Seeking to ameliorate such conflict, states have for over a century sought to construct international institutions to enable them to cooperate when they have common or complementary interests.[2] That is, they have established rudimentary institutions of governance, bilaterally, regionally, or globally. These attempts at governance, including global governance, are a natural result of increasing interdependence. They also help to create the conditions for further development of the networks of interdependence that are commonly referred to as globalization.[3]

Since states do not monopolize channels of contact among societies, they cannot hope to monopolize institutions of global governance, even those that they have formally established, such as the World Bank, International Monetary Fund and World Trade Organization. States have a privileged position in these organizations, since they founded them, constitute their membership, monopolize voting rights, and provide continuing financial support. Except in the European Union, states also retain the legal authority to implement the decisions of international organizations in domestic law. Yet the entities whose activities are regulated include firms as well as states; and non-governmental organizations play an active role in lobbying governments and international institutions, and in generating publicity for the causes they espouse. NGOs are typically more single-minded and agile than states, which gives

Originally published in *Taming Globalization*, edited by David Held and Mathias Koenig-Archibugi (Cambridge: Polity Press, 2003), pp. 130–59. Reprinted by permission of Polity Press.

them advantages in media struggles. Equally important, religious organizations and movements command the allegiance of billions of people.

The complexity of these patterns of politics makes it very difficult to trace causal relationships and determine patterns of influence. This complexity also makes normative analysis difficult. Emerging patterns of governance are new, and operate at multiple levels. Globalization makes some degree of global-level regulation essential, but both institutions and loyalties are much deeper at local and national levels. Hence it is not clear what principles and practices that are justified domestically would be appropriate at a world scale. Governance can be defined as the making and implementation of rules, and the exercise of power, within a given domain of activity. "Global governance" refers to rule making and power exercise at a global scale, but not necessarily by entities authorized by general agreement to act. Global governance can be exercised by states, religious organizations, and business corporations, as well as by intergovernmental and non-governmental organizations. Since there is no global government, global governance involves strategic interactions among entities that are not arranged in formal hierarchies. Since there is no global constitution, the entities that wield power and make rules are often not authorized to do so by general agreement. Therefore their actions are often not regarded as legitimate by those who are affected by them.

We live in a democratic era, and I share the widespread belief that rules are only legitimate if they conform to broadly democratic principles, appropriately adapted for the context. In democratic theory, individuals are regarded as inherently equal in fundamental rights, and political power is granted to officials by the people, who can withdraw that authority in accordance with constitutional arrangements. The legitimacy of an official action in a democracy depends in part on whether the official is accountable. Hence a key question of global governance involves the types and practices of accountability that are appropriate at this scale. The key question addressed in this article is: what do democratic principles, properly adapted, imply about desirable patterns of accountability in world politics? Which entities should be held accountable, to whom, in what ways? And from a policy standpoint, what do these normative judgments imply about "accountability gaps" – situations in which actual practice differs greatly from a desirable state of affairs?

Part II of this chapter discusses the concept of accountability, as related to global governance. Part III discusses the various entities that we might want to hold accountable, and how to do this. Contrary to what one might believe on the basis of much writing on the subject, intergovernmental organizations, along with weak states, seem among the most accountable entities in world politics. Corporations, transgovernmental networks, religious organizations and movements, terrorist networks, and powerful states are much less accountable. If we believe in accountability, as I do, we need especially to pay attention to states. How can powerful states be held more accountable in world politics?

Before getting to these arguments, which constitute the heart of this chapter, it seems important to put the issue of accountability into the context of an interpretation of global society and the global system. It would otherwise be too easy to sketch a highly idealized view of the world. Such a conception is very helpful in thinking about fundamental normative principles, as in the profoundly important work of John Rawls,[4] but it is not adequate if one's purpose is to critique actual situations in world politics. To make such a critique, one needs to sketch out institutional arrangements that satisfy our normative criteria to the extent feasible given the realities of world politics. Although these institutions may be normatively much superior to the actual state of affairs, they may nevertheless fall well short of the arrangements that would fully satisfy abstract normative demands.[5] I therefore begin in Part I by contrasting the concept of a "universal global society" with the reality: that world politics as a whole lacks universally accepted values and institutions. In reality, many people and groups in the contemporary world not only hold values that are antithetical to those of others, but seek forcibly to make others' practices conform to their own preferences. Attempts to increase accountability in world politics must take account of the airplane assassins of 9/11, their confederates, and their supporters. Political theory will not be credible if it demands that good people enter into what is in effect a suicide pact.[6]

I Non-universal Global Society within a Global System

David Held has recently outlined in a very sophisticated way a vision of three models of sovereignty:

classic, liberal, cosmopolitan. For Held, there has been movement over the past century from classic to liberal sovereignty. In liberal conceptions of sovereignty, legitimacy is not conferred automatically by control. Indeed, institutions that limit state authority have been developed. Moving beyond liberal sovereignty, Held envisages a prospective movement to cosmopolitan law and governance. Multilevel governance, including governance at the global level, will be "shaped and formed by an overarching cosmopolitan legal framework."[7]

This is an attractive vision, somewhat more ambitious than my own call two years ago to create "working institutions for a [global] polity of unprecedented size and diversity."[8] Both visions, however, would be much more attainable if global society were universal. Twenty-five years ago, Hedley Bull drew an important conceptual distinction between society and system. The states in an international society, for Bull, are "conscious of certain common interests and common values." They "conceive themselves to be bound by a common set of rules in their relations with one another, and share in the working of common institutions."[9] States in an international system that is not an international society do not share common values or work together in international institutions. "When Cortes and Pizarro parleyed with the Aztec and Inca kings [and] when George III sent Lord Macartney to Peking...this was outside the framework of any shared conception of an international society of which the parties on both sides were members with like rights and duties."[10] However, Bull believed that the European states system had become, by the 1970s, an international society.

Since in the contemporary world entities other than states help to compose society, it seems more appropriate to speak now of global rather than international society. But 9/11 should make us be cautious about believing that global society is becoming universalized. Terrorists have brought sudden external violence and the fear of such violence back into our lives with a vengeance, and the security-seeking, force-wielding state has not been far behind. We therefore need to remind ourselves that a universal global society remains a dream, and one that may be receding from view rather than becoming closer. An increasingly globalized world society has indeed been developing, but it exists within a violence-prone system, both international and transnational. The world is not neatly divided into "zones of peace" and "zones of turmoil,"[11] or areas of "complex interdependence" and "realism."[12] Relationships of peaceful exchange among societies, and violent conflict involving non-state actors, can occur in the same physical spaces.

Human rights advocates have long been aware that a universal global society is more aspiration than reality. The torturers and mass murderers of the world do not share fundamental values with committed and humane democrats. In the wake of 9/11 we have become acutely aware of terrorists' attempts to kill other people, personally unknown to them, who merely stand for hated values or live in states whose policies the terrorists oppose. Perhaps even more soberly, we realize that millions of people cheered or at least sought to justify the evil deeds of 9/11.

On a global scale, common values are lacking. The Taliban did not try to emulate the social organization of Western society, and in fact rejected much of it, such as the practice of enabling women to live public lives. Many fundamentalist religious people do not share – indeed, reject – secular ideals such as those of pluralist democracy. Indeed, one reason that democratic values are not spreading universally is that dogmatic religions claiming exclusive access to comprehensive ultimate truth contain fundamentally anti-democratic elements. Their claim of comprehensiveness means that they assert authority over issues involving the governance of human affairs. Their claim of exclusive access to ultimate truth means that they appeal for authority not to human experience, science or public opinion but to established authority or privileged knowledge of the divine, and they reject accountability to publics and human institutions. Insofar as people believe that power is legitimated by divine authority, they will not be drawn toward liberal democracy.

We must unfortunately conclude that the vision of a universal global society is a mirage. There is indeed a global society: common values and common institutions are not geographically bounded. But the global society in which we live is not universal: it does not include members of al-Qaeda, suicide bombers, or substantial elements of the populations of US allies such as Saudi Arabia and Pakistan. It also excludes other fundamentalists who believe that as the "chosen people" they have special rights and privileges. People with these beliefs may belong to global societies of their own, but they do not belong to the same global society as do those of us who believe in liberal and democratic values. To genuinely belong to an open global society, one must accept others, with very different beliefs about ultimate truth and the good life, as participants, as long as they follow principles of reciprocity in accordance with fair procedural rules.[13]

Even a universal global society would propose a challenge to global governance under the best of circumstances, and it would be difficult to implement a cosmopolitan vision. If globalization of public authority occurred, individual citizens would have few incentives to try to monitor governments' behavior. Indeed, the larger the polity, the more individuals can rationally be ignorant, since each person's actions would have so little effect on policies. That is, the very size of a global polity would create immense incentive problems for voters – in mass election campaigns it would seem pointless to most voters to invest in acquiring information when one's own vote would count, relatively speaking, for so little. It would also be hard, without political parties that operated on a global scale, or a coherent civil society, to aggregate interests and coherently articulate claims. Even a universal global society would lack a strong civil society with robust communication patterns and strong feelings of solidarity with others in the society.

We see these difficulties in the European Union, which is a highly favorable situation, with common democratic values and democratic institutions such as the European Parliament. But the European Union remains largely a set of intergovernmental and supranational institutions supported by a pact among elites, without deep loyalty from the publics of member countries. Even after 45 years of the European Community, it lacks a broad sense of collective identity and mutual support.

Recognizing these realities, sophisticated proponents of greater global governance understand that cosmopolitan democracy cannot be based on a strict analogy with domestic democratic politics, and they do not rely exclusively on electoral accountability. They recognize that even in constitutional democracies, many other kinds of accountability exist, including hierarchical and supervisory accountability, legal accountability (interpreted by courts), and peer accountability among government agencies that compete with one another. Even in the absence of institutionalized accountability mechanisms, reputational accountability can also play a role.[14]

Reliance on diversified types of accountability is supported by the experience of the EU. There is significant accountability in the EU, but electoral accountability, involving the European Parliament, is only part of the picture. EU institutions are accountable to governments; agencies within governments are held accountable to one another through the process of "comitology"; a considerable degree of transparency holds participants, much of the time, accountable to the public through the media. In the EU, political authority and forms of government have become "diffused."[15] As Anne-Marie Slaughter puts it, "disaggregating the State makes it possible to disaggregate sovereignty as well."[16]

In the absence of a universal global society, cosmopolitan democracy is very unlikely on a global scale. Disaggregating the state seems like a recipe for self-destruction when faced with al-Qaeda. Indeed, the strong tendency in the United States since 9/11 has been to consolidate and centralize authority. Transgovernmental networks of cooperation against terrorism will play a role, but they will be accompanied by stronger, more aggregated states. Powerful states will seek to link the various levels of governance more coherently rather than to differentiate them or to allow themselves only to serve as elements of a broader structure of cosmopolitan governance. They will tighten control of their borders and surveillance of people within those borders.

The overall result will be a *system* in Bull's sense. Globalization, implying a high level of interdependence, will continue. At a superficial level, most states may remain in a universal international society, accepting common institutions and rules. They can hardly do otherwise if they are to receive political recognition, be allowed freely to trade, and attract investment, much less to be recipients of aid. But acceptance of common global values within societies will be more uneven. No set of common values and institutions will be universally accepted. Global society will therefore be not universal but rather partial. It will exist within the context of a broader international and transnational system, in which both states and non-state actors will play crucial roles.

What will this society-within-system look like? Of course, we don't know – anything said on this subject is speculation. However, five features of this society-within-system can very tentatively be suggested:

1 Large parts of the world will remain in the imagined global society of pre-9/11 times. Indeed, some parts of the world formerly outside this society – such as China and Russia – may well move into it, even at an accelerated rate in response to terrorist threats. Within this sphere, "complex interdependence"[17] and 'soft power'[18] will remain important.

2 The fundamental values of substantial populations will be antithetical to one another – especially wherever fundamentalist versions of exclusivist, messianic religions, claiming that their doctrines are comprehensive, prevail in one society. Judaism, Christianity and Islam are all subject to such interpretations. People who believe that their doctrines alone represent revealed truth have often in history been ill-disposed toward people with different beliefs, and the present seems no exception. Relatively few societies now are dominated by people professing such beliefs, but there is a danger that the number of such societies will increase. Between societies dominated by such people and democratic societies there will not be a common global society – only a system of interactions.[19]

3 Force will continue to be fragmented, controlled mostly by states, but sometimes in the hands of small groups that need not control large amounts of contiguous territory.

4 Within the open global society – the world of complex interdependence – progress toward the cosmopolitan ideal may well occur. Common rules and practices will develop on the basis of procedural agreement, as suggested by the work of Jürgen Habermas or John Rawls.[20]

5 But in the wider system, the cosmopolitan ideal will be unrealistic even as an ideal. Coercion and bargaining will be the chief means of influence, not persuasion and emulation. Hence the state will remain a central actor. Power will not be diffused. Furthermore, territoriality may well be strengthened. For instance, we are now seeing strong pressures to re-establish controls over national borders in the US and in Europe.

II Governance and the Accountability Gap

An accountability relationship is one in which an individual, group or other entity makes demands on an agent to report on his or her activities, and has the ability to impose costs on the agent. We can speak of an authorized or institutionalized accountability relationship when the requirement to report, and the right to sanction, are mutually understood and accepted. Other accountability relationships are more contested. In such situations, certain individuals, groups, or entities claim the right to hold agents accountable, but the agents do not recognize a corresponding obligation. I refer to the actor holding an agent accountable as a "principal" when the accountability relationship is institutionalized. When the relationship is not institutionalized, I refer to the actor seeking to hold an agent accountable as a "would-be principal." Much of the politics of accountability involves struggles over who should be accepted as a principal.[21]

Democratic accountability within a constitutional system is a relationship in which power wielders are accountable to broad publics. Democratic accountability in world politics could be conceptualized as a hypothetical system in which agents whose actions made a sufficiently great impact on the lives of people in other societies would have to report to those people and be subject to sanctions from them.[22] But accountability need not be democratic. Indeed, it can also be hierarchical (in which subordinates are accountable to superiors) or pluralistic (as in Madisonian constitutionalism, in which different branches of government are accountable to one another). Actual systems of accountability in constitutional democracies combine all three syndromes of accountability: democratic, hierarchic, and pluralistic. As noted above, they rely on a number of different mechanisms, not just on hierarchy and elections. They also rely on horizontal supervision (checks and balances), fiscal and legal controls, peer review, markets, and general concerns about reputation.

Normatively, from the perspective of democratic theory, what justifies demands that an agent be held accountable by some person or group? Three different sets of justifications are commonly enunciated:

(a) *Authorization* Hobbes, and many others, have emphasized that the process by which one entity authorizes another to act may confer rights on the authorizer and obligations on the agent.[23]

(b) *Support* Those who provide financial or political support to a ruler have a claim to hold the ruler accountable. As in the American Revolution, a basic democratic claim is "no taxation without representation."

(c) *Impact* It is often argued, as David Held has said, that "those who are 'choice-determining' for some people [should be] fully accountable for their actions."[24]

Authorization and support are the basis for what I will call internal accountability. They create capabilities to hold entities accountable because the principal is providing legitimacy or financial resources to the agent. This is "internal" accountability since the principal and agent are institutionally linked to one another. Since providing authorization and support creates means of influence, such influence can be used to close any "accountability gap" that may open up between valid normative arguments for internal accountability and actual practice. Nevertheless, much of the literature on accountability, and much anti-globalization talk from Right and Left, focuses exclusively on internal accountability. Globalization, and international institutions, are said to threaten democracy.[25]

In my view, however, the most serious normative problems arise with respect to what I call external accountability: accountability to people outside the acting entity, whose lives are affected by it. African farmers may suffer or prosper as a result of World Bank policies; economic opportunities of people in the India area are affected by the strategies of IBM and Microsoft; Afghans are liberated, displaced, or destroyed by United States military action. The normative question arises in these situations: should the acting entity be accountable to the set of people it affects? This is a very difficult normative question. Merely being affected cannot be sufficient to create a valid claim. If it were, virtually nothing could ever be done, since there would be so many requirements for consultation, and even veto points. I do not seek to resolve this issue here, but I note it as a problem that political philosophers should address. Perhaps the law of torts will be useful here. "In every instance, before negligence can be predicated of a given act, back of the act must be sought and found a duty to the individual complaining."[26] To develop a theory of external accountability, it may be necessary to construct a theory of the duties that parties owe to one another in a poorly institutionalized but increasingly globalized world.

If we determine that a group affected by some set of actions has a valid claim on the acting entity, we can ask the empirical question: in practice, can it effectively demand the accountability that it deserves? If not, there is an accountability gap. In the rest of this article, I am concerned principally with external accountability gaps and how they might be closed.[27]

In general, rulers dislike being held accountable. To be sure, they may often have reasons to submit to accountability mechanisms. In a democratic or pluralistic system, accountability may be essential to maintain the confidence of the public; and in any system, some degree of accountability may be necessary to maintain the credibility of the agent. That is, other dimensions of power may be more important to the ruler than lack of accountability.[28] Furthermore, constitutional systems may be designed to limit abuses of power without reducing the amount of influence the leaders have when action is necessary. But we can expect power-holders to seek to avoid accountability when they can do so without jeopardizing other goals. And in the absence of a constitutional system, *the ability to avoid being held externally accountable can be viewed as one dimension of power*. Discussing accountability without focusing on issues of power would be like discussing motivations of corporate leaders without mentioning money.

III Accountability in System and Society

The mixed society-within-system that I am projecting yields mixed implications for accountability. Internal accountability will be strong, but external accountability will be weak. It almost goes without saying that where conflicts of interest are pronounced, powerful states will not let themselves be held accountable to their adversaries. The United States is not going to be held accountable for its anti-terrorism tactics to al-Qaeda. It is also true that asymmetries of power attenuate accountability. Europe is not going to be held accountable for its immigration policies to the countries of origin of would-be immigrants. Only when they have interests in holding others accountable – as on trade policies in the WTO – are powerful states disposed to let themselves be held accountable.

Yet demands for external accountability will continue to be made against states, intergovernmental organizations, corporations, and other entities viewed as powerful. These demands will largely be made by non-state actors and advocacy networks – hence I speak of "transnational accountability." Meeting these demands, to some extent, will be essential to the legitimacy of institutional arrangements within global society, since many of these claims for accountability will be widely viewed as having some elements of validity.

With respect to transnational accountability, two sets of questions then arise: (i) With respect to which entities are there significant accountability gaps? (ii) What types of external accountability could be applicable to these entities?

Transnational accountability: entities

Consider the entities conventionally held accountable on a transnational basis. The most prominent, judging from demonstrations, press coverage, and even scholarly articles, are major intergovernmental organizations concerned with economic globalization: the European Union, World Bank, International Monetary Fund, and the World Trade Organization. These organizations are major targets of demands for accountability. They certainly have deficiencies in accountability. They do not meet democratic standards of accountability as applied in the best-functioning democracies of our era. But ironically, these entities seem to me to be relatively accountable compared to other important global actors.

The European Union is *sui generis*, since it is so much stronger and more elaborately institutionalized than traditional international organizations. Its members have pooled their sovereignty, giving up both a veto over many decisions and the right to decide whether an EU decision will become part of their own domestic law. The EU may or may not evolve into a sovereign state, but in its current condition it lies somewhere between an international organization and a state. As noted above, the EU combines traditional accountability of the bureaucracy to governments with a variety of other forms of accountability, including elections to the European Parliament and multiple forums in which governmental departments can query their counterparts on issues ranging from agriculture to finance.

Traditional international organizations are internally accountable to states on the basis of authorization and support. They have to be created by states and they require continuing financial support from states. Externally, there are significant accountability gaps. Indeed, many poor people affected by the policies of the IMF, World Bank and the WTO have no direct ability to hold these organizations accountable. Nevertheless, there is a vaguely held notion that these people should have some say in what these organizations do – that the "voices of the poor," in the World Bank's phrase, should be heard. That is, many people feel that these organizations should be externally as well as internally accountable.

Various NGOs purporting to speak for affected people, and principles that would help these people, gain legitimacy on the basis of this widespread belief. One result of their endeavors is that the decision-making processes of multilateral organizations have become remarkably more transparent. The World Bank in particular has done a great deal to incorporate NGOs into its decision-making processes.[29] Indeed, in transparency multilateral organizations now compare well to the decision-making processes of most governments, even some democratic governments. When their processes are not transparent, the chief source of non-transparency is governmental pressure for confidentiality. But the decentralization and discord characteristic of world politics mean that these organizations cannot keep secrets very well. Important negotiations, such as those about the Multilateral Agreement on Investment several years ago, are almost bound to "leak." And their leaders spend much of their time trying to answer charges against their organizations, seeking to persuade constituencies that the organizations are actually both constructive and responsive.

Multilateral organizations are therefore anything but "out of control bureaucracies," accountable to nobody.[30] Indeed, the real problem seems to me quite the opposite. These organizations are subject to accountability claims from almost everybody, but in the last analysis they are in fact accountable, through internal processes, only to a few powerful states and the European Union. NGOs and other would-be principals demand accountability. But these NGOs are weak compared to governments, to which the multilateral organizations are chiefly accountable. When these would-be principals lose the battle due to their institutionally weak positions, they condemn the multilateral organizations as "unaccountable." Their real targets are powerful governments of rich countries, perhaps multinational corporations, or even global capitalism – but it is the multilateral organizations that are damaged by the NGO attacks.

What the controversies indicate is not that the intergovernmental organizations are unaccountable, but that accountability is a distributional issue. The issue is not so much: are these organizations accountable? The answer to that question is yes. They are internally accountable to the states that authorized their creation and that provide financial support, and to a lesser extent they are accountable to NGOs and the media. The real issues are whether the balance of internal and external accountability is justifiable, and whether multilateral organizations are accountable to the right groups. NGOs make a normative claim for accountability to groups that are affected, or for accountability to principles such as "sustainable development" or "human rights." In other words, external accountability claims based on the impact of these organizations compete with internal accountability claims, largely by governments, based on authorization and support. These are serious issues, but they are not issues of "lack of accountability" as much as issues of "accountability to whom?" Different types of accountability favor different accountability holders. Once again, accountability is largely a matter of power.

Ironically, intergovernmental organizations have been the principal targets of people demanding external accountability because they are weak and visible. They are good targets because they do not have strong constituencies, and it is much easier to see how they could be reformed than to reform more powerful entities such as multinational corporations or states.

It seems to me that the external accountability gaps are greatest with respect to entities that are not conventionally held accountable on a transnational basis. Six sets of such entities can be mentioned:

1   *Multinational corporations* Multinational corporations are held internally accountable, with more or less success, to their shareholders, who authorize action and provide support. But their actions also have enormous effects on other people. The "anti-globalization movement" is right to be concerned about corporate power, even if its proposed remedies seem incoherent. If we are concerned about the effects of powerful entities on powerless people, we scholars should be asking how to hold corporations accountable – as national

governments in capitalist societies have sought to hold corporations accountable for over a century. The effects are particularly pronounced for media conglomerates, but we have not focused on them. Globalization means that it is more difficult for national governments to hold corporations accountable than in the past. Why isn't our field paying more attention?[31]

2   *Transgovernmental and private sector networks*[32] Anne-Marie Slaughter has argued that these networks – such as those linking securities regulators or central bankers – lead to "disaggregated sovereignty" and that, on the whole, this is a benign development.[33] I am much less sanguine than she is about disaggregated sovereignty being compatible with meaningful accountability. Disaggregating sovereignty makes it much more difficult to identify the locus of decisions. Since these networks are often informal, they are not very transparent. Institutionalized arrangements that would structure internal accountability are lacking, and it is often hard for groups that are affected to identify those effects and demand external accountability.

3   *The Roman Catholic Church* The Vatican has a secretive, authoritarian structure, and is not very accountable to any human institutions or groups. The Church in a democratic society, such as the United States, has to be much more accountable if it is to retain the active allegiance of its members. In the pedophilia scandal in the United States in 2002, accountability was the central issue.

4   *Mass religious movements* without hierarchical organizations. Fundamentalist Islamic movements fall into this category. Unlike the situation of the Roman Catholic Church, there is no hierarchical organization to hold accountable. Who holds imams who preach support for terrorism accountable?

5   *Covert terrorist networks* such as al-Qaeda. These networks are almost by definition not externally accountable. They do not accept the responsibility of identifying themselves, much less responding to questions or accepting others' right to sanction them. They cannot be "held accountable," although they can be punished.

6   *Powerful states* The doctrine of sovereignty has traditionally served to protect states from external accountability, although it has not necessarily protected weak states from accountability to the strong.[34] Multilateral institutions

are designed to make states accountable to each other, if not to outsiders. Even moderately powerful states, however, can resist external accountability on many issues. It has been notably difficult for the United Nations to hold Israel accountable for its military actions on the West Bank. Egypt and Saudi Arabia have not been held accountable to the victims of the terrorists whose supporters they have often encouraged. And most of all, extremely powerful states seem virtually immune from accountability if they refuse to accept it. The United States is of course the chief case in point.[35]

Non-governmental organizations pose a more difficult issue. In an earlier version of this chapter I listed NGOs as a seventh type of entity operating in world politics that should be held more accountable. Indeed, they are often not very transparent. Perhaps more seriously, their legitimacy and their accountability are disconnected. Their claims to a legitimate voice over policy are based on the disadvantaged people for whom they claim to speak, and on the abstract principles that they espouse. But they are internally accountable to wealthy, relatively public-spirited people in the United States and other rich countries, who do not experience the results of their actions. Hence there is a danger that they will engage in symbolic politics, satisfying to their internal constituencies but unresponsive to the real needs of the people whom they claim to serve.

On the other hand, NGOs, on the whole, only wield influence through persuasion and lobbying: they do not directly control resources. Apart from their moral claims and media presence, they are relatively weak. They are highly vulnerable to threats to their reputations. Weakness, as we have seen, ameliorates problems of accountability. My ironic conclusion is that we should not demand strong internal accountability of relatively weak NGOs – the proverbial "two kooks, a letterhead, and a fax machine." But as a particular NGO gains influence, it can exert effects, for good or ill, on people not its members. At this point, it can be as legitimately held externally accountable as other powerful entities that operate in world politics.[36]

The external accountability of states

States are powerful and are often not externally accountable. But institutions of multilateralism

exist that hold them accountable on some issues. If we care about accountability, we should inquire as to how such institutions could be extended, and made more effective.

We should begin by recognizing, as Rousseau did, that internal democracy will not assure accountability to outsiders whom the powerful democracy affects.[37] The United States, Israel, and other democracies are internally accountable but on key issues are not externally accountable. David Held has astutely pointed out that the external accountability problem may even be greater as a result of democracy: "arrogance has been reinforced by the claim of the political elites to derive their support from that most virtuous source of power – the demos."[38]

Yet three mechanisms of external accountability apply to states. First, weak countries that depend economically on the decisions of richer countries are subject to demands for fiscal accountability. Albert Hirschman pointed out over 50 years ago that foreign trade, when it produces benefits, generates an "influence effect."[39] As I have repeatedly emphasized, accountability is a power-laden concept. Power comes from asymmetrical interdependence in favor of the power wielder.[40]

The implication of the influence effect is that if rich countries are genuinely interested in holding poor countries accountable, they will give more aid. Dramatically increased efforts to increase the benefits that poor countries receive from globalization would create an influence effect, making it easier to hold these countries accountable for their actions. Of course, for the poor countries such generosity would be problematic, precisely because it would make them more dependent on the rich.

A second mechanism of external accountability relies on the pockets of institutionalized accountability that currently exist in world politics. States that are members of regional organizations such as the European Union are subject to demands for accountability from their peers. And states that have joined organizations such as the WTO or the new International Criminal Court are subject to legal accountability with respect to specified activities. Europe, the United States, Japan and other rich countries are targets of demands for accountability in trade, with their agricultural subsidies and protection of old industries such as steel serving as prominent examples. The extension of some degree of accountability to powerful states, through multilateral institutions, offers a glimmer of hope. But we should remember that these powerful states do not accept accountability for its own sake, but chiefly because they gain benefits themselves from these institutions. And as recent US policies on steel and agriculture remind us, powerful democratic states are subject to much more internal than external accountability.

Finally, the most general form of accountability in world politics is reputational. States and other organizations with strong sources of internal loyalty probably rely on external reputation less than organizations, such as most NGOs, that lack broad bases of loyal members. Nevertheless, reputation is the only form of external accountability that appears to constrain the United States with respect to its political-military activities. Reputation is double-edged, since states may seek reputations for being tough bullies as well as for being reliable partners. And the lack of institutionalization of reputational concerns makes reputation a relatively unreliable source of constraint. Yet reputational accountability has some potential significance because reputations of states matter for their other activities. To be effective, states have to be included in the relevant networks.[41] Hence, reputational accountability, weak though it is, is significant.

On any given issue, the United States can typically act unilaterally, dismissing demands for external accountability. Indeed, one of my themes is the weakness of external as opposed to internal accountability, as far as powerful states are concerned. However, the US has many objectives in the world, some of which require voluntary cooperation from others. It would be impossible for the United States to coerce other states on all issues of concern for it. Failing to cooperate with others leads them to retaliate in one form or another, following practices of reciprocity. More diffusely, damage to the reputation of the United States as a potential cooperator reduces the incentives for others to cooperate with the United States in anticipation of cooperation on some other issues in the future. Most generally, any country playing a long-term leadership role in global governance has a long-term interest in the legitimacy of global governance, as well as in its status as leader. To any sensible US Administration, such concern for leadership would be a constraint – and a reason to let itself be held accountable, to some extent, on other issues.[42]

I have pointed to three sources of external accountability – the need of poor countries for aid, institutionalization in international organizations, and reputational concerns arising from multiple issues for powerful states such as the United States. None is very strong. But we should note that all three sources of accountability are augmented by the political institutions that are part of globalization. Globalization is not a single phenomenon. Some aspects of globalization reflect economic and technological facts that cannot be affected by political action. Action at a distance, and harm at a distance, are more feasible, and frequent, now than ever before. Other aspects of globalization, such as the construction of multilateral institutions and policy networks, and efforts to create public spaces in which persuasion based on reason can occur, require political action: Max Weber's "strong and slow boring of hard boards."[43] It would be tragic if the "anti-globalization" movement succeeded in demolishing or diminishing the institutions and networks developed to cope with globalization, without putting comparable institutions in their place. Since technologically driven globalization will not disappear, such dismantling would reduce accountability and create more opportunities for the irresponsible use of power. Globalization may weaken internal accountability within democracies, but its political institutionalization is a condition for external accountability.

Here is another irony. Opponents of globalization often raise the issue of accountability as an argument against globalization. But they are thinking of a largely imaginary bygone world in which states really controlled their borders and in which democratic governments regulated domestic activities through democratic means. Their imaginary world is the United States during the New Deal, as they would have liked it to evolve – without Nazism, fascism, Communism and World War II. In fact, the choice is not globalization or not, but relatively legitimate globalization with a measure of democratic and pluralistic external accountability over powerful entities, versus illegitimate globalization without such accountability.

Having said all of this, it would nevertheless be naive to believe that the United States will be easy to hold externally accountable. Indeed, for the United States to be held accountable, internal accountability will have to supplement external accountability rather than substituting for it. Those of its own people who are sensitive to world politics will have to demand it, both on the grounds of self-interest and with respect to American values.

In view of contemporary American public attitudes, this hortatory comment does not necessarily offer much hope, at least in the short run. Indeed, my ironic conclusion is that with respect to accountability, the two sworn enemies – al-Qaeda and the United States – have in common their relative lack of accountability, compared to other actors in world politics.

Conclusions

Those of us who would like to see greater democratic and pluralistic accountability in world politics must recognize that global society, while real, will not become universal in the foreseeable future. Too many people believe in the superiority of their own worldviews and deny the obligation to tolerate the views of others. The resulting threats, along with traditional security concerns, help to ensure that powerful states seeking to control territory will continue to assert themselves. Cosmopolitan democracy is a distant ideal, not a feasible option for our time.

We should demand more external accountability of powerful entities engaged in various forms of global governance. Intergovernmental organizations and weak, dependent states are most easily held accountable. We cannot expect to hold shadowy terrorist movements accountable. But we should pay more attention to the accountability of corporations, transgovernmental networks, religious organizations and movements, and powerful states.

The United States especially needs to be held accountable, because its internal democracy cannot be counted on to defend the interests of weak peoples whom American action may harm. Yet it is very difficult to hold the United States accountable, since one dimension of power is that it protects the power-holder from accountability. 9/11 implies more concentration of power and more state action. As a result, the world is further from the ideal of transnational accountability now than most of us recognized before 9/11.

If we recognize that powerful states pose the most serious threats to accountability in world politics, we will see that well-meaning efforts to demand "more accountability" from international organizations can be problematic. As I have argued, "more accountable" often means "accountable to NGOs and advocacy networks," rather than just to governments. Certainly some real benefits could result from making the WTO and the IMF more accountable to a wider range of interests and values. But we should be alert to the prospect that the political result of such a shift would be a reduction of states' interests in such organizations. If states get less benefit from international institutions, they will be less willing to provide resources and to accept demands on them, through these institutions, for accountability. The ultimate result of such well-meaning moves, therefore, could be a weakening of the accountability, limited as it is, that multilateralism imposes on powerful states.

In the long run global governance will only be legitimate if there is a substantial measure of external accountability. Global governance can impose limits on powerful states and other powerful organizations, but it also helps the powerful, because they shape the terms of governance. In their own long-run self-interest, therefore, powerful states such as the United States should accept a measure of accountability – despite their inclinations to the contrary. As in 1776, Americans should display "a decent respect for the opinions of mankind."

How, then, can we hope to hold powerful entities accountable in world politics? The first point is that to hold powerful states accountable, the world needs more multilateral governance, not less. Indeed, one of my concerns about claims that multilateral organizations are "not accountable" is that weakening these organizations will give powerful governments more ability simply to act as they please. Holding states accountable depends on certain aspects of globalization: those that derive from the existence of significant political institutions with global scope. If leaders of the anti-globalization movement believe that they are fostering equality and progressive policies in world politics by attacking multilateral institutions, they are sadly mistaken.

More fundamentally, holding powerful organizations accountable will require meshing together more effectively mechanisms of internal and external accountability. Global institutions are not strong enough to impose a fully satisfactory measure of external accountability on powerful states, corporations, or religious organizations. Multilateralism is not sufficient to control, in Benjamin Barber's phrase, either Jihad or McWorld.[44] For such control to be exercised, states themselves will have to take action, but in concert with one another.

Only democratic states can be counted on, more or less, to exercise such control on behalf of broad publics. But as we have seen, if those publics are encapsulated within state boundaries, leaders of states will tend to ignore the costs that their policies impose on outsiders. External accountability will be minimal. In the long term, the only remedy for this situation is that networks of connection, and empathy, develop on a global basis so that democratic publics in powerful states demand that the interests of people in weaker states be taken into account. That is, people need to adopt a moral concept of reciprocity as described above, and as articulated by Rawls. To do so they need to renounce doctrines, religious or otherwise, that deny the moral equality of other people, who hold different beliefs. In light of 9/11 it seems utopian to expect people everywhere to accept this moral concept of reciprocity. Yet such a conception is widely shared with successful national states, even within large ones. There is no doubt that the people of the United States as a whole empathized with the people of Oklahoma City in 1995 and of New York City in 2001. At a global level the bonds of connection are much too weak now, even where common societies are well established, to support the level of empathy that we observe within nation-states. But our best hope for cosmopolitan governance in the long run is the construction and strengthening of these personal and social ties.

Our principal task as scholars and citizens who believe in more accountability is to build support within our powerful, rich countries for acceptance of more effective and legitimate multilateral governance to achieve human purposes, for stronger transnational bonds of empathy, and for the increased external accountability that is likely to follow.

Notes

1 David Held, Anthony McGrew, David Goldblatt, and Jonathan Perraton, *Global Transformations: Politics, Economics and Culture* (Cambridge: Polity, 1999).

2 Robert O. Keohane, *After Hegemony: Cooperation and Discord in the World Political Economy* (Princeton: Princeton University Press, 1984).

3 Robert O. Keohane and Joseph S. Nye Jr, *Power and Interdependence*, 3rd edn (New York: Addison-Wesley Longman, 2001), ch. 10.

4 John Rawls, *A Theory of Justice* (Cambridge, Mass.: Belknap Press of Harvard University Press, 1971) and *Political Liberalism* (New York: Columbia University Press, 1993).

5 In *The Law of Peoples* Rawls has sought to move in the direction of sketching what he calls a "realistic utopia." He has, of course, not escaped criticism for allegedly relaxing his principles too much, in order to develop an international law that could be accepted by "decent hierarchical peoples" as well as by liberal democracies. Yet the level of specificity of *The Law of Peoples* is not sufficient to make judgments about which entities in world politics are subject to appropriate procedures for accountability. See John Rawls, *The Law of Peoples* (Cambridge, Mass.: Harvard University Press, 1999).

6 Justice Robert H. Jackson is quoted as having said that the Bill of Rights should not be made into a suicide pact. See, for instance, Richard A. Posner, "Civil Liberties and the Law," *The Atlantic*, Dec. 2001.

7 David Held, "Law of States, Law of Peoples: Three Models of Sovereignty," *Legal Theory*, 8 (2002), p. 33.

8 Robert O. Keohane, "Governance in a Partially Globalized World," *American Political Science Review*, 95 (2001), p. 12.

9 Hedley Bull, *The Anarchical Society: A Study of Order in World Politics* (New York: Columbia University Press, 1977), p. 13.

10 Ibid., p. 15.

11 Max Singer and Aaron Wildavsky, *The Real World Order: Zones of Peace, Zones of Turmoil* (Chatham, N.J.: Chatham House Publishers, 1993).

12 Keohane and Nye, *Power and Interdependence*.

13 Rawls, *Political Liberalism*.

14 For a detailed discussion of types of accountability, see Robert O. Keohane and Joseph S. Nye Jr, "Redefining Accountability for Global Governance," in Miles Kahler and David A. Lake (eds.), *Globalizing Authority* (Princeton: Princeton University Press, 2003).

15 David Held, "Law of States, Law of Peoples," p. 38.

16 Anne-Marie Slaughter, "Governing the Economy through Government Networks," in Michael Byers (ed.), *The Role of Law in International Politics* (Oxford: Oxford University Press, 2000), p. 203.

17 Keohane and Nye, *Power and Interdependence*.

18 Joseph S. Nye Jr, *The Paradox of American Power* (New York: Oxford University Press, 2002).

19 In my view, Samuel Huntington overgeneralized his insights about a "clash of civilizations," but he was right to call attention to the importance of the different values to which people from different cultures are committed. Samuel P. Huntington, *The Clash of Civilizations and the Remaking of World Order* (New York: Simon and Schuster, 1996).

20 Jürgen Habermas, *Between Facts and Norms: Contributions to a Discourse Theory of Law and Democracy* (Cambridge, Mass.: MIT Press, 1996); Rawls, *The Law of Peoples.*

21 Robert D. Behn, *Rethinking Democratic Accountability* (Washington DC: Brookings Institution, 2001).

22 Held, "Law of States, Law of Peoples," p. 27.

23 Hannah Pitkin, *The Concept of Representation* (Berkeley: University of California Press, 1972).

24 Held, "Law of States, Law of Peoples," p. 26.

25 Robert A. Dahl, "Can International Organizations be Democratic? A Skeptic's View," in Ian Shapiro and Casiano Hacker-Cordon (eds.), *Democracy's Edges* (Cambridge: Cambridge University Press, 1999).

26 Chief Justice McSherry in *W. Va. Central R. Co. v State*, 96 Md. 652, 666; quoted in Chief Justice Benjamin Cardozo's majority opinion in *Palsgraf v Long Island Railroad Company*, 248 NY. 339, 162 N.E. 99 (1928).

27 My normative perspective is founded on the impartialist views that stem from Kant, as enunciated recently by such thinkers as Rawls and Habermas. See Rawls, *A Theory of Justice*, and Habermas, *Between Facts and Norms*. It is also cosmopolitan, broadly consistent with arguments made by David Held, "Globalization, Corporate Practice and Cosmopolitan Social Standards," *Contemporary Political Theory*, 1 (2002), pp. 58–78.

28 Hannah Arendt defined power as "the human ability to act in concert"; Hannah Arendt, *Crises of the Republic* (New York: Harcourt Brace Jovanovich, 1969), p. 143. In democratic, pluralistic societies, the ability to act in concert may require accountability of rulers.

29 I am grateful to Kathryn Sikkink for this point.

30 The reference is to Arendt, *Crises of the Republic*, p. 137, who described bureaucracy as "rule by Nobody."

31 I am not including labor unions, since I do not regard them as powerful transnational actors. They are heavily rooted in domestic society and despite their activity at Seattle and elsewhere in protesting globalization, they have difficulty coordinating their actions on a transnational basis.

32 Robert O. Keohane and Joseph Nye Jr, "Transgovernmental Relations and World Politics," *World Politics*, 27 (1974), pp. 39–62.

33 Slaughter, "Governing the Economy through Government Networks."

34 Stephen D. Krasner, *Sovereignty: Organized Hypocrisy* (Princeton: Princeton University Press, 1999).

35 This is not to say that the United States is immune from influence by other states. It moderated its stance on the Geneva Conventions for prisoners from Afghanistan, and it followed established treaty practice in notifying foreign governments of the incarceration of their nationals in the wake of 9/11. But the ability of outsiders to hold the United States accountable in a meaningful sense is small.

36 For a thoughtful set of discussions of the accountability of NGOs, see *Chicago Journal of International Law* (2002).

37 Stanley Hoffmann, *Janus and Minerva: Essays in the Theory and Practice of International Politics* (Boulder, Colo.: Westview, 1987), p. 43.

38 Held, "Law of States, Law of Peoples," p. 21.

39 Albert Hirschman, *National Power and the Structure of Foreign Trade* (Berkeley: University of California Press, 1945).

40 Keohane and Nye, *Power and Interdependence.*

41 Abram Chayes and Antonia Handler Chayes, *The New Sovereignty: Compliance with International Regulatory Agreements* (Cambridge, Mass.: Harvard University Press, 1995).

42 For a fine discussion of these and related issues, see Nye, *The Paradox of American Power.*

43 Max Weber, *Politics as a Vocation* (1919; Philadelphia: Fortress Press, 1965), p. 55.

44 Benjamin Barber, *Jihad vs. McWorld* (New York: Times Books, 1995).

47

Migration and Poverty

Thomas Pogge

Many privileged and influential persons and governments hold that they have no weighty moral responsibility toward foreigners in desperate need. I have attacked this view elsewhere, arguing that we do have such a responsibility.[1] Of those who accept a weighty responsibility toward needy foreigners, most advocate that more such persons be admitted into the richer states and that more be done to ensure that those already here gain equal citizenship with ourselves in the fullest sense. I will argue here that such advocacy is not a good way of discharging our responsibility.

This argument may be a little hard to understand, because I agree with what I say we should not advocate. I agree that the richer states ought to admit more needy persons and ought to give equal citizenship to foreigners already here. But I question whether we should expend our scarce political energy and resources on these issues. Rather than try to get our compatriots to support admitting more needy foreigners and to support equal citizenship for foreigners already here, we should instead try to enlist them for other moral projects with regard to which our mobilizing efforts can be much more effective. What these other moral projects are will become clear in due course.

For purposes of the present argument, I can take for granted a moral concern for needy foreigners, many of whom would like to be admitted into the rich countries. To get a sense of the real-life dimensions of this issue, we must ask: who are the persons

seeking admission? Why do they want to come? And what moral claims do they have on us?

The answers to the first two questions are familiar. Very large numbers of persons live under truly terrible conditions: desperately poor and without effective rights of any sort. Every now and then, one can learn about some such lives through the media.[2] One can learn, for example, about the other side of the sex tourism advertisements – about the young girls and boys who, after being kidnapped, or sold by their parents, spend their teenage years enslaved in brothels in Bangkok or in Bombay or in any one of hundreds of cities in the so-called Third World. One can learn about the other side of those beautiful oriental rugs by reading about that little boy who was relinquished by his parents to settle a debt of $15 and who was then chained to a loom and forced to make carpets during every waking hour of his life. He escaped and tried to mobilize world public opinion in order to rescue other children forced into a similar fate. But his campaign did not last long: he was shot and killed in his native Pakistan still only twelve years old. One can read, finally, the latest Amnesty International annual report, detailing how some 150 national governments imprison and torture their political opponents.

We know at least vaguely that such things are going on, and this knowledge lends moral urgency to our conviction that the rich states have a moral obligation to take such people in, to rescue them

Originally published in *Citizenship and Exclusion*, edited by Veit Bader (London: Macmillan, 1997), pp. 12–27. Reprinted by permission of Palgrave Macmillan from their dreadful situation. But before we act on this conviction, before we publicize it and try to win the support of our compatriots and governments, we should reflect upon two further facts.

The first further fact is the sheer extent of desperate need, which can be grasped by looking merely at the problem of global poverty. Some 20 million deaths per year – mostly female and mostly children[3] – are attributed to poverty: "Nearly 800 million people do not get enough food, and about 500 million people are chronically malnourished" and about 1300 million people (24 percent of humankind) live below the international poverty line[4] – which is defined as "that income or expenditure level below which a minimum, nutritionally adequate diet plus essential non-food requirements are not affordable"[5] and currently corresponds to an annual *per capita* income of ca. $75. With hundreds of millions falling significantly below this line, we can assume that the income of the poorest fifth (1100 million) of humankind is about one-quarter percent of world income, or $50 *per capita* annually – while the richest fifth has over 90 percent of world income, or $19000 *per capita* annually, nearly 400 times more than the poorest fifth.[6] With regard to wealth, the disparity is even greater, because the poor tend to have much less wealth than annual income, while the rich tend to have much more wealth than annual income. The wealth of the richest five persons suffices to match the combined annual income of the poorest fifth, and the wealth of the richest 358 (the dollar billionaires) suffices to match the combined annual income of the poorest 45 percent.[7]

Two important lessons may be drawn from these amazing statistics – one piece of bad news and one piece of good news. The bad news is that the number of desperate foreigners whom the rich countries now admit every year, and also the larger number of desperate foreigners they might conceivably come to admit under the best of circumstances – these numbers are ridiculously small in comparison to the number of those who are in desperate need and would like to come. The good news is that, despite the huge number of the global poor, it would be quite possible to improve their conditions decisively, if the rich countries were willing to make a concerted effort. Remember: just one percent of the income of the richest fifth is nearly *four times* the income of the poorest fifth of humankind.

I will now discuss each of these two points, before drawing the obvious conclusion from

them, which is: other things being equal, those who accept a weighty moral responsibility toward needy foreigners should devote their time, energy, and resources *not* to the struggle to get more of them admitted into the rich countries, but *rather* to the struggle to institute an effective program of global poverty eradication. The rider "other things being equal" is meant to exclude those whose jobs or expertise give them special opportunities to support needy foreigners who are seeking or have gained admission into one of the rich countries. My argument may not apply to them.

The first point – the bad news – was that the admission of needy foreigners into the rich countries cannot possibly protect all who now live under dreadful conditions and would want to come. One reason for this is that the number of needy persons in the world – including at least those 1300 million who cannot afford "a minimum, nutritionally adequate diet plus essential non-food requirements" – is simply out of all proportion to the number of needy foreigners which the rich countries admit or could admit. To see this, compare the 1300-million figure to two other numbers:

(a) The number of refugees legally admitted in 1995 by all the countries of the European Union combined: ca. 25,000;

(b) The number of legal aliens from all outside countries estimated to be now living in the European Union: ca. 10 million.[8]

For every person we can persuade some rich country to admit, there will be hundreds, if not thousands, left in desperate need.

There is another reason why the admission of needy foreigners will not solve the problem. This is the second further fact I had wanted to mention, namely: not many of those whom the rich countries admit are really among the worst-off. It is quite obvious, on reflection, why this should be so: it helps a very great deal, in the scramble to gain admission, to have money for bribing officials, for paying smugglers, and for hiring a lawyer; to have some education, professional skills, and language training; to have some relative who has already succeeded in gaining admission; and also to be well endowed: bright, tall, healthy, and good looking. But persons with these advantages will rarely be among the neediest. In whatever way the rules for admitting needy foreigners may be designed – in this or that rich country, now or in the future –

the truly worst-off always compete at a great disadvantage against more privileged persons from the poor countries who will often be able to elbow them aside.

This important second fact also helps to put into perspective an argument often made in favor of admitting needy foreigners. When admitted and allowed to work in one of the rich countries, so it is said, they are likely to send money back home to their families. This is true. But the families to whom this money is being sent are often among the more privileged in the poor country in question. Of course, some of these funds may "trickle down" to the poorest. But some will also be used to cement and entrench the oppression of the poorest by Third-World "elites". In any case, these funds are far more likely to increase than to reduce domestic inequality in the poor countries and therefore are a mixed blessing at best.

I must respond at least briefly to one prominent objection against my claim that the task of persuading our compatriots and governments to admit more needy foreigners has less moral urgency than we tend to suppose. The objection is this: there is a small class of needy foreigners whose admission is of much greater moral importance than that of the desperately poor. These are *political refugees*, fleeing persecution for their expressed beliefs or peaceful political activity. In response: I cannot see why the moral importance of admitting political refugees should be any greater than that of admitting so-called economic migrants. For one thing, the politically persecuted are not, in general, worse off than the desperately poor. Being imprisoned for one's beliefs is not, in general, worse than working 16-hour days while being permanently hungry. Being beaten to death for participating in a demonstration is not, in general, worse than dying of diarrhoea or simple starvation. Second, the politically persecuted are generally better educated and more resourceful, hence better able to protect themselves. Third, the desperately poor are *also* the victims of political oppression, for they are excluded from all better economic opportunities through the coercive power of governments. Their plight is produced by the present national and international economic order which is coercively upheld by their governments and ours.[9] And fourth, even if this third reason did not hold and desperate poverty were not then imposed upon the global poor by others, there would still be no moral reason to discriminate. For protecting one person from being killed by an attacker is not,

in general, morally more important than protecting another from drowning. There may be special circumstances, of course, as when our own government has played a role in the attack – for example, by delivering arms to a government that now uses them to oppress its opponents. But such special circumstances often obtain also in regard to desperate poverty, as when our market demand for coffee and flowers causes land use in some poor country to be converted toward these export crops, thereby driving the prices of rice and beans beyond the means of the local poor.

So much in support of the first point. There are hundreds of millions of needy people in this world. Helping to protect them is of great moral importance. Getting such persons admitted into one of the rich countries does indeed protect them. But by this method only a ridiculously small fraction of those in desperate need can be protected, even under the most optimistic assumptions about what we can get our governments and compatriots to accept.

Let us now attend to the second point, the *good* news, which is that it is quite possible to protect most of those in desperate need by other means. You may remember my estimate that the annual *per capita* income of the poorest fifth of humankind is around $50. You may have thought this estimate misleading because, as is well known, one dollar buys much more in a poor country than it would buy in a developed country. Economists take account of this fact by converting annual income figures in terms of "purchasing power parities" (PPP). Instead of saying of some poor textile worker in India that she is earning one dollar a week, they say that she is earning, say, five dollars PPP per week. Behind this lies the following thought. While the 36 rupees this woman earns weekly are equivalent to one dollar at the market exchange rate, these 36 rupees can buy much more in India than one dollar can buy in the developed countries. So the translation of 36 rupees into five dollars PPP means that this woman can buy with her 36 rupees about as much as we can buy with five dollars.[10]

I mention purchasing power parities for two reasons. First, to respond to the suspicion that I have shamelessly overstated the severity of global poverty. I plead guilty. So instead of saying that the annual income of the global poor is around $50, let us instead say that it is around $250 PPP.[11] But this surely does not invalidate what I have said about the severity of global poverty. Having on average as much purchasing power as $250 annually would supply in the developed countries, the poorest fifth are still desperately poor. They can perhaps, in normal times, afford just enough basic foodstuffs to survive – but virtually nothing else by way of vacations, education or medicines, presents for the children, or savings. Any small mishap – such as an illness or a rice shortage with increase in price – can spell disaster.

My second reason for getting into purchasing power parities is to reinforce my plea for the alternative strategy toward protecting the global poor. The fact that 36 rupees buys much more in India than one dollar buys in the developed world presents a golden opportunity. This is so, because in the currency market one can actually receive 36 rupees for a dollar and thus multiply the purchasing power of one's funds. It is therefore much cheaper than one might think to reduce global poverty despite the huge number of persons affected by it. Ironically, those who like to claim that eradicating world poverty would impoverish the developed countries do not know how incredibly poor the global poor really are. Thus Rorty, for example, doubts that we are able to "help" the global poor by appealing to the claim that "a politically feasible project of egalitarian redistribution of wealth, requires there to be enough money around to insure that, after the redistribution, the rich will still be able to recognize themselves – will still think their lives worth living."[12] Rorty can rest assured; the total amount of money that the poorest 1300 million persons are lacking toward being able to satisfy their basic needs is exceedingly small. For them $75 billion a year would make a phenomenal difference – it could *double* their current income – while for us it is just 0.4 percent of the GDP of the developed countries (or one-seventh of the value of annual crude oil production or one-third of US military expenditure).

Of course, in the real world things are not so simple. Even if $75 billion could be raised in or from the rich countries, there would be no possible way of spending this money, in a concentrated way, toward the emancipation of the global poor. This is so for at least three reasons. First, there will be transaction costs, as the disbursement of the funds in dozens of countries must be planned and organized. Hundreds of people would need to be hired, including economists and accountants, and the money would have to be exchanged and transported to where it is needed, generally by hand. Second, there will be targeting costs, as

some of the funds will inevitably benefit persons not in desperate need. And, third, there will be corruption costs as well: members of the local "elites" will try very hard to divert some of the funds into their own pockets, for instance by demanding payment for all sorts of bureaucratic licences and authorizations; and some of the persons involved in the distribution will inevitably be tempted to engage in extortion, passive bribery, or theft.

Because of these costs, considerably more than $75 billion per year would be needed to double the income of the global poor. Nevertheless, getting the rich countries and their citizens to support such a project is still vastly more effective than getting them to support the admission of more needy foreigners – effective, that is, toward the purpose of protecting those in desperate need. And the same holds on a smaller scale as well: with the political effort it would take to pressure some Western government to admit an extra hundred needy foreigners, we could alternatively pressure this same government to allocate a few extra million dollars to global poverty eradication. And these few extra million dollars, if effectively spent, could protect not a hundred, but thousands or even tens of thousands of desperately poor persons.

Let me be clear about the conclusion I want to draw from the two points I have developed thus far. My conclusion is *not* that we should oppose the admission of needy foreigners into our richer countries. *Not at all.* Nor am I denying that persuading our governments and compatriots to accept more needy foreigners is a worthy cause. But if this *is* a worthy cause, it is so in virtue of the protection it affords to persons who are very badly off. Protecting such persons from the oppressive conditions imposed upon them by current institutional arrangements is indeed a principal moral priority. I have argued, however, that we can do much more in respect to this priority by attempting to promote better living conditions in the poorer countries than by attempting to promote the admission of needy foreigners. Through efforts of the first kind we can protect many more, and more needy, people than through efforts of the second kind.

What then should we try to persuade our compatriots and governments to do? First, we should probably not spend our time and resources on advocating more governmental development aid. It is now abundantly clear to those who care to know that such aid is generally ineffective in protecting the global poor and is rarely even intended to do so.[13] This should not be surprising. Our government officials have some public-relations reasons to care about our country's overall foreign aid allocation as a percentage of national income. Charts with these percentages are compiled and circulated widely in the media. But why should they be concerned whether foreign aid projects they are funding now will help alleviate severe poverty in the long run? Who will evaluate those projects, keep track of who authorized them, and hold these officials accountable for their decisions in two or five or ten years' time? The only incentives our officials have toward spending foreign-aid funds well are *moral* incentives, and among politicians these are, alas, somewhat of a rarity. Moreover, these moral incentives are opposed by powerful prudential incentives. When a rich country's government has at its disposal funds targeted for foreign aid, it has opportunities to spend them so as to promote its own interests and perhaps those of its country. Such a government can, for example, use its foreign aid funds to buy political support from domestic creditor banks and exporters, or from "elites" in strategically important Third-World countries. Moreover, such a government is likely to gain more recognition and prestige from large, high-visibility projects, which tend to benefit the poorest segments of the recipient country's population only very indirectly, if at all. A large new power plant affords nice photo opportunities, and it may also provide lots of cheap electricity. But the poorest of the poor have no electric outlets or appliances and need safe drinking water much more urgently in any case. Pressing for additional governmental development aid is not, then, the most promising idea. The rich countries are already spending some $60 billion under this rubric,[14] but the effect of this spending on the global poor is rather slight.

It is a much better idea, secondly, to persuade our compatriots to support the more efficient anti-poverty organizations such as UNICEF and Oxfam. At very low cost, these organizations provide what the poorest really need – for example, oral rehydration therapy to combat diarrhoea, wells for safe drinking water, elementary education so people can read and write and understand their rights, micro-loans to break the dependence on local landlords and loan sharks, quality seeds to increase crop yields and to reduce the need for fertilizers, stoves for fuel-efficient cooking, med-ical and family-planning services. The proven effectiveness of these organizations entails, on a small scale, that we as individuals have strong moral reasons to support them: we can help protect many more persons by collecting a few thousand dollars for UNICEF or Oxfam than by getting a few additional needy foreigners admitted into our country; and we are also far more likely to succeed with the first project than with the second. The proven effectiveness of these organizations entails, on a larger scale, that severe global poverty could be largely eradicated in a matter of years, if such organizations had anything like the money now available for official development aid.

This suggests a third idea about what we might persuade our compatriots and governments to do with respect to global poverty. This idea would seek to combine the best of what we already have. Official development aid is mostly inefficient, but it does provide an amount of money – about $60 billion per year – that is at least in the right ballpark. The better anti-poverty organizations are quite effective, but they do not have anything like the funds they would need to succeed on a large scale.[15] The third idea is then to create by treaty suitable global institutional mechanisms for raising a stable flow of international financing for global poverty eradication. The funds to be raised should initially be between $65 and $200 billion a year (or between one-third and one percent of the combined GNP of 25 OECD countries).

Let me indicate, just very briefly, how these funds might be raised and spent. The simplest way of raising the funds would be to oblige the governments of the rich countries to pay them out of general tax revenues. But other ways of raising the funds are better by being morally more compelling and/or by having positive collateral effects. One such idea has been floated for many years by the Nobel laureate James Tobin. He proposes a half-percent tax on currency transactions in order to discourage currency speculation. The specific intent of this tax is to reduce speculation-induced exchange rate fluctuations and thereby to enable national governments and central banks better to adapt their monetary policy to domestic economic conditions. But the tax would also raise revenues, which Tobin proposes to use for global poverty eradication.[16] Presently the volume of currency transactions is an incredible $1.5 *trillion per day*. Even if the tax achieved its purpose by reducing this volume dramatically, by a factor of 25, say, down to $60 billion a day, this tax would still raise

$300 million per day or $110 billion annually – enough to eradicate malnutrition, trivial diseases, and severe poverty in a matter of years.

Another, quite plausible idea almost became reality. It was the basic principle of Part XI of the 1982 *United Nations Convention on the Law of the Sea* that natural resources on the ocean floors beneath international waters "are the common heritage of mankind" (Article 136), to be used "for the benefit of mankind as a whole . . . taking into particular consideration the interests and needs of developing States [through an] equitable sharing of financial and economic benefits" (Article 140), which was to have been effected by sharing of seabed mining technologies and profits (Annex III, Articles 5 and 13) under the auspices of the International Seabed Authority, or ISA (Annexes III and IV). How could anyone have wanted to oppose this idea, to exclude the global poor, who are literally starving, from the value of seabed resource? Three successive US administrations have tried quite hard to secure the great benefits of the treaty in "protecting and promoting the wide range of U.S. ocean interests"[17] without the sharing regime. Shortly before the Convention was to come into force (November 28, 1996), the Clinton Administration succeeded in having the sharing provisions replaced by a superseding *Agreement*.[18] This *Agreement* endorses the US view that the common-heritage principle really means that the oceans and their resources "are open to use by all in accordance with commonly accepted rules."[19] Accordingly, it frees mining companies from having to share seabed mining technologies[20] and greatly reduces the sharing of profits.[21] The *Agreement* further accommodates US demands by "1) guaranteeing a U.S. seat in the Council [the executive organ of the ISA]; 2) allowing ourselves and a few other industrialized nations acting in concert to block decisions in the Council . . ."[22] In managing to renegotiate the *Law of the Sea Convention* – by pressing the Reagan era threat of founding a competing seabed resources regime with a few like-minded countries[23] – the Clinton Administration won a great victory for the US and any other countries that will have the capital and technologies for profitable seabed mining. The reaction in these wealthy countries was quiet relief: their governments raised no objections and their media largely ignored the event. The governments of the poorer countries went along as well in the interest of making the treaty universal. It is the poor persons, in any case, who can

least afford being shut out from this common heritage of humankind. And so, for rather trivial gains,[24] one viable and morally plausible opportunity of raising funds for poverty eradication through the sale of seabed mining rights has been lost.[25] A mobilization in defense of the common-heritage idea could have achieved much more for foreigners in desperate need than any comparable mobilization for the sake of having more of them admitted into the rich countries.

A Global Resources Dividend or GRD offers yet another alternative for raising the requisite funds.[26] Here states, while retaining full control over the natural resources in their territories, would be required to pay a dividend proportional to the value of any of these resources they decide to use or sell. The word "dividend" is meant to suggest that all human beings, including those now excluded, are viewed as owning an inalienable stake in all limited natural resources. As with preferred stock, this stake confers no control over whether or how natural resources are to be used, but merely a claim to share in their economic benefits. Take crude oil for example. Every state extracting crude oil might be required to pay a $2 dividend per barrel ($0.0125 per liters) extracted, which would be, for the most part, passed along to the end users of petroleum products. The current global crude oil production is about 4 trillion liters (or four cubic kilometers) per year. From just the consumption of this single resource, the GRD scheme could therefore raise $50 billion annually – or somewhat less if, as is desirable, crude oil demand would decline as a consequence of its slightly increased price. The GRD could be extended to other nonrenewable resources and also, importantly, to the use of air, water and soil for the discharging of pollutants. It would then not only raise the needed revenues, but would also tend to slow down the depletion of natural resources and the pollution of our environment.

I can speak only briefly about how the funds raised for global poverty eradication should be spent. Here the most obvious idea – transferring the funds to the governments of the poorest countries – is clearly problematic: many Third-World governments and officials are even less interested in effective poverty eradication than most rich-country politicians in charge of foreign aid funds. Making them the recipients of funds raised from seabed mining, or through a Tobin tax or GRD, would greatly dilute, if not erase, their intended benefits.

To make development funds effective, the full spectrum of possible channels must be explored and exploited in a competitive way. The most important possibilities are to give funds directly to the poor themselves or to their local organizations, to spend funds through specialized organizations such as UNICEF and Oxfam, and to transfer funds to poor-country governments. The idea of competitive allocation provides that fund flows be directed and redirected to where they have the greatest effect in enabling the global poor to fulfill their needs and to defend their basic interests on their own. The effects of fund flows in terms of poverty eradication are to be closely monitored and the allocation of funds is to be adjusted accordingly, pursuant to clear rules announced in advance, so that funds flow through *those* channels and to *those* countries which lead them to their most effective use. By formulating the allocation rules in this way, incentive effects are created and mobilized. Thus, the political and economic elite of any poor country has an interest in attracting funds to its country because it, too, will benefit from these funds in various ways. The rules governing fund disbursement should be designed to take full advantage of this interest – making it clear to such elites that, if they want to benefit from their society's receipt of funds, they must cooperate in making these funds effective toward improving the conditions and opportunities of the domestic poor. In general terms, the rules for the disbursement of funds must be designed so as to stimulate a worldwide peaceful competition in poverty eradication.[27]

It is time to take stock. We have organized our social world – and, in particular, our world economy – so that it produces and reproduces truly monstrous poverty and inequality. Over 20 million persons die each year from poverty-related causes, hundreds of millions are in desperate need. It is quite understandable, and noble actually, that our first reaction to this suffering should be to insist that we must take these people in.

> Give me your tired, your poor,
> your huddled masses yearning to breathe free
> the wretched refuse of your teeming shore . . .

I have argued that this first reaction is nevertheless mistaken. If there were no political resistance to open or fairly open borders, if our compatriots and governments were quite ready to receive the moral

argument for them and to act on it, then things might be different. But as things stand, the needy foreigners we manage to get admitted are very costly indeed in terms of the political effort necessary to get them in and in terms also of the hostility and anger they generate among our compatriots, which makes it ever harder to enlist their support for *any* initiatives on behalf of the global poor. We can be vastly more effective in protecting those we are concerned to protect by adopting a different strategy.

Having presented the argument that this is so, it strikes me that this argument is not particularly difficult or unobvious. This raises the question why people do not generally see things my way. Why do most of those who care about needy foreigners at all think in terms of taking people in, rather than in terms of alleviating the terrible conditions that make them want to come here in the first place? To make my argument complete, I should be able to explain why this is so and also to show that any reasons others might have for thinking as they do are not good reasons.

One possible explanation is patriotism. Here I have in mind not the silly view that our country is so wonderful that no one can be happy outside of it – though I must say that this view does have its adherents, e.g. in France and the US. Nor do I have in mind the chauvinist view that only Europeans with their rich history and political traditions can govern a country well, though this view, too, seems to have some adherents, albeit a dying breed. What I mean by patriotism, rather, is the idea that we have more moral reason to promote the justice and moral perfection of our own country than those of the rest of the world. The idea is that the hostility many of our compatriots harbor against the admission of foreigners is a flaw in them that we ought to correct quite independently of the effects this correction would have on the fate of needy foreigners. We have a special responsibility, as it were, for the sentiments and prejudices of our compatriots which can seem to trump the more general responsibility we feel for global poverty.

I can surely feel the emotional force of this idea. I certainly share the moral preference for living in a country where needy foreigners are welcomed. But reversing the moral priority I have been arguing for on this ground is nevertheless, I believe, a gross mistake – for two reasons: First, it is true that our countries are often actively involved in turning away needy foreigners. But it is just as true, if much less obvious, that our countries are also actively involved in upholding the prevailing world order and, in particular, the present structure of the world economy which, quite regularly and predictably, produces and reproduces severe global poverty and inequality. In the latter case, the active involvement of the officials who purport to act in our name is so much less obvious, because the present global economic order is already in place and appears to reproduce itself without any human agency, and also because we and our officials are no more involved in its reproduction than millions of persons from the other rich countries. You feel awful, if one desperate asylum seeker is turned away by a consular official purporting to act in your name. But you feel much less awful if your government, like all the others, shows no interest in supporting or defending global economic reforms and thereby collaborates in continuing Third-World starvation and disease at current levels. The economic exclusion of 1300 million persons is brought about by the citizens and governments of the rich countries, together with corrupt Third-World elites, and, though we clearly are collectively responsible for it, we have a tendency not to feel particularly responsible, because no one is really in a position to alter this exclusion, to change the world economy. The fact that so many are maintaining this exclusion together creates the illusion that no one is really doing it, that it just happens, naturally, as it were.

A second explanation of the widespread mistaken priority is somewhat related to the first. We tend to think of refugees and asylum seekers as particular individuals, as persons with a face. We think of them as having stepped forward and knocked on our door and told us their story. How can we slam the door in their face? Of course, no one will deny that the 1300 million global poor are also persons with faces. But we think of them as an anonymous, amorphous mass. Since they have not stepped forward, they can become persons with faces only if *we* reach out to *them*, selecting them from the crowd. This requires an initiative that few of us ever take. Fundraisers, by the way, know about this quirk in our psychology and, instead of requesting a donation for poverty-stricken children in the Third World, often ask us to sponsor some *particular* child, picture enclosed. With such an appeal, the project of protecting needy children can gain some of the psychological urgency that we tend to attach to not turning back needy foreigners asking for admission.

Two other sample contrasts display the same psychological propensity of ours. Think back to World War II, of those forced to live under the terror of German occupation. Imagine what it was like to know Jews threatened by deportation while also knowing about some reasonably safe places to hide or routes of escape. It is *much* easier, psychologically, merely to fail to approach any of the Jews one knows with the offer to help than to turn away a Jewish family standing on one's doorstep. Or think of a person trapped in a cave or in a well. In such a case, we are willing to move heaven and earth, to spend millions of dollars and thousands of hours to save a human life. Do we feel the same moral urgency about installing a guard rail on a busy highway which we know would save two or three lives a year? Or about reducing emissions from a plant which we know would prevent several cancer deaths? No, we do not. We have a tendency to accept much greater costs for the sake of protecting someone we think of as a determinate individual – though on reflection this seems quite irrational, especially in a case like global poverty, where the only distinction of the determinate individuals is that they have asked for admission or have somehow managed to come here – which, if anything, tends to show that they are *less* in need than many others.

A third explanation why people might think it morally more important to work for the admission of more needy foreigners than for global poverty eradication projects is that they take the former itself to be the most effective means for promoting the latter. Once persons from the poor countries are living among us, so one might reason, they can influence those around them to be more sympathetic to the plight of Third-World populations and they can also work through our political process to initiate the kind of global poverty eradication mechanisms I have proposed. While some may accept this line of thought, I do not think there is much evidence for it. In Europe's recent experience, the influx of poor foreigners has made the population in general *less* sympathetic to suffering in foreign lands. And in the US, which has a much longer history of significant Third-World immigration, there is little indication of such immigrants even *attempting* to influence government policy in favor of their former compatriots (in contrast to Polish-, Irish-, and Jewish-Americans, for example, who make considerable political efforts on behalf of, respectively, Polish, Irish, and Israeli causes).

I have taken a position that goes against the moral beliefs, sentiments, and conduct of many persons I respect. I have tried to show, in a rudimentary way, that their contrasting view can be explained in a way that does not provide reasons against mine. For the moment, then, I believe that my view is correct. Let me say clearly, one last time, what my view is and what it is not. I have *not* argued against the admission of needy foreigners into the rich countries, nor against equal citizenship for those already here. I have *not* denied that it is wrong to refuse admission to truly needy foreigners. What I have argued is, *first*, that awful living conditions abroad are due, for the most part, to the economic exclusion of the global poor as practiced by the citizens and governments of the rich countries; and, *second*, that there are much more effective ways of protecting these poor persons from the deprivations they now suffer than by trying to get them admitted into the rich countries. Given that we – those who recognize a weighty moral responsibility toward foreigners in desperate need – have only limited resources at our disposal and cannot possibly devote ourselves to every worthy political goal, we should focus our efforts to where we can achieve the most toward overcoming the greatest injustice of our time: the impoverishment and starvation of hundreds of millions of people. We should stop attempting to get more needy foreigners admitted into the rich countries and instead concentrate on improving the local living conditions of the global poor through international institutional reforms, like the Tobin Tax or the GRD, and through effective international aid organizations, like UNICEF and Oxfam.

Notes

1 Pogge 1989, Ch. 6, Pogge 1992, Pogge 1994, Pogge 1995; Pogge 1997a; Pogge 1997b.
2 For example: 'Asia's Plantations of the '90s', *International Herald Tribune*, April 15, 1996, p. 2; 'The Flourishing Business of Slavery', *The Economist*, September 21, 1996, pp. 43–4.
3 Some 3 million children annually die of simple diarrhoea because their parents cannot obtain a 15-cent oral rehydration pack. Lack of vitamins and antibiotics leads to another 3.5 million deaths from pneumonia, one million deaths from measles, and so on. See Grant 1993.
4 UNDP 1996, p. 20.
5 Ibid., p. 222.
6 What I say here may seem to conflict with a prominent statement in the Report: "The poorest 20% of the world's people saw their share of global income decline from 2.3% to 1.4% in the past 30 years. Meanwhile, the share of the richest 20% rose from 70% to 85%. That doubled the ratio of the shares of the richest and the poorest – from 30:1 to 61:1" (ibid, p. 2). These ratios were, however, calculated from country aggregates. The two relevant fifths were formed by simply taking the populations of the richest and poorest *countries*, with each set of countries selected so that it represents one fifth of world population (according to the written explanation I received from Mr. Selim Jahan, Deputy Director of the UNDP Human Development Report Office, New York City). But this yields the ratio between the average income in the richest countries and the average income in the poorest countries, not the income ratio between the richest and poorest fifths of "the world's people." The former ratio is obviously a very

bad estimate of the latter: the income of the richest fifth is underestimated, as many poor in the richest countries are much poorer than many rich in non-rich countries (so the latter, not the former, should be included in the top fifth). And the income of the poorest fifth is hugely inflated as the poorest in middle-income countries such as Brazil are excluded in favor of more affluent persons in the poorest countries (among them, for instance, President Mobutu Sese Seko, whose income is a rather considerable part of the Zairian national income).
7 Ibid, p. 13.
8 These two figures are from the *International Herald Tribune*, March 5, 1996, p. 5.
9 See Pogge 1997b.
10 The 5:1 ratio is realistic, in that India's 1993 GDP *per capita* is $250 (calculated from GDP and population; UNDP 1996, pp. 179, 185) and its real GDP (PPP) *per capita* is given as $1240 (*ibid*, p. 136). The weighted average ratio for all poor countries is close to 5:1, though the ratios given for individual poor countries differ significantly – ranging from 2:1 (Mali) to 8:1 (Tanzania).
11 Similarly, the international poverty line should then be expressed not as annual *per capita* income of $75 (20 cents a day), but as annual *per capita* purchasing power of $375. Being poor means having less purchasing power than $1 a day affords in the developed countries. 1300 million persons, 24 percent of humankind, are poor in this sense (UNDP 1996, 27). (Mr Selim Jahan, Deputy Director of the UNDP Human Development Report Office, has confirmed orally that the $1-per-day figure printed in the Report represents purchasing power, not

income. This squares with figures given in Dasgupta 1993, pp. 79–80.)

12 Rorty 1996, pp. 14–15. Rorty's essays are, of course, to be taken as "narratives".

13 There are important exceptions, notably the Scandinavian countries and the Netherlands. The present paragraph does not apply to them.

14 Official development assistance by the rich countries was $59 billion, or 0.3 percent of their combined GNP, in 1994. Of this, less than one quarter went to the least developed countries. Norway was the most generous country, allocating 1.05 percent of its GNP (0.44 percent for the least developed countries). The US was the least generous, allocating 0.15 percent of its GNP (0.04 percent for the least developed countries). Though Norway, Sweden, Denmark and the Netherlands together have only 13 percent of the US population and 12 percent of US GNP, they spend more than the US on aid for the least developed countries. For all these 1994 data, see UNDP 1996, pp. 199, 203, 208. In 1995, the US reduced its official development aid by more than one quarter, from $9.927 billion to $7.367 billion (written communication from Sigismund Niebel, OECD, Paris).

15 The entire United Nations Organization with its dozens of agencies has an annual budget of $1.3 billion and is undergoing drastic cut-backs this year [1997] as a result of unpaid membership dues. The UN is owed some $3 billion in back dues, about half of this by the US.

16 For a brief statement of the idea, see Tobin 1994, where he acknowledges that "raising revenues for international purposes was not a primary motivation of my proposal."

17 Ambassador David A. Colson, Deputy Assistant Secretary of State for Oceans, in testimony before the Subcommittee on Oceanography of the Merchant Marine and Fisheries Committee of the US House of Representatives (April 26, 1994).

18 *Agreement Relating to the Implementation of Part XI of the United Nations Convention on the Law of the Sea of 10 December 1982.* Its Article 2(1) says: "In the event of an inconsistency between this agreement and Part XI, the provisions of this agreement shall prevail."

19 US Department of State: *Commentary on the Law of the Sea Convention including the 1994 Amendments* p. 3. "The Agreement fully meets the objections of the United States and other industrialized states to

Part XI" (ibid, p.2), which were that: "it established a structure for administering the seabed mining regime that does not accord the industrialized States influence in the regime commensurate with their interests; it incorporated economic principles inconsistent with free market philosophy; and its specific provisions created numerous problems from an economic and commercial policy perspective that would have impeded access by the United States and other industrialized countries to the resources of the deep seabed beyond national jurisdiction" (ibid, pp. 2–3).

20 The provisions of Annex III, article 5, of the Convention shall not apply." Section 5(2) of the Annex to the *Agreement* (cited in note 18).

21 Section 7(1) of the Annex to the *Agreement* (cited in note 18) limits the sharing of profits to "economic assistance" to "developing countries which suffer serious adverse effects on their export earnings or economies resulting from a reduction in the price of an affected mineral or in the volume of exports of that mineral, to the extent that such reduction is caused by [seabed mining]." Section 8(3) halves the application fee for exploration and exploitation of sites to $250,000 and Section 8(2) eliminates the $1,000,000 annual production fee as well as the profit-related financial contributions (all of which were mandated in the *Convention*'s Annex III, Article 13).

22 Colson *op.cit.* (note 17).

23 Germany and Great Britain were especially willing to go along with such a move.

24 At current metals prices, seabed mining is not expected to become commercially worthwhile for quite some time.

25 One may object that any funds Part XI of the *Convention* might have raised for the least developed countries would – like so much official development aid – have ended up in the pockets of corrupt Third-World politicians and bureaucrats. But, surely, the choice of throwing money at corrupt Third-World elites versus ignoring global poverty does not exhaust the available options. Clinton might well have pressed for terms that ensure that the funds raised are spent on effective poverty eradication.

26 For an elaborate statement of this proposal, see Pogge 1995c.

27 Pogge 1995c, section 3, develops these points in more detail.

References

Dasgupta, P. S., *An Inquiry into Well-being and Destitution* (Oxford: Oxford University Press, 1993).

Grant, J. P., *The State of the World's Children* (New York: Oxford University Press, 1993).

Pogge, T. W., *Realizing Rawls* (Ithaca, NY: Cornell University Press, 1989).

Pogge, T. W., "Cosmopolitanism and sovereignty," *Ethics*, 103 (1992), 79–98.

Pogge, T. W., "An egalitarian law of peoples," *Philosophy and Public Affairs*, 23 (1994), 195–224.

Pogge, T. W., "Eine globale Rohstoffdividende," *Analyse und Kritik*, 17 (1995), 183–208.

Pogge, T. W., "Menschenrechte als moralische Ansprüche an globale Institutionen," *Die Philosophie der Menschenrechte*, ed. Stefan Gosepath and Georg Lohmann (Frankfurt: Schurkamp, 1997a).

Pogge, T. W., "The bounds of nationalism," *Canadian Journal of Philosophy*, supplementary volume (1997b).

Rorty, R., "Who are we? Moral universalism and economic triage," *Diogenes*, 173 (1996), 14–15.

Tobin, J. (1994), "A tax on international currency transactions," in UNDP *Human Development Report* (New York: Oxford University Press, 1994), p. 70.

UNDP (United Nations Development Program), *Human Development Report* (New York: Oxford University Press, 1996).

48

Humanity and Justice in Global Perspective

Brian Barry

This chapter has three sections. The first argues that considerations of humanity require that rich countries give aid to poor ones. The second argues that considerations of justice also require transfers from rich countries to poor ones. The third picks up the distinction between aid and transfer and argues that, when we get into detail, the obligations imposed by humanity and justice are different, although not incompatible.

I Humanity

Introduction

What is it to act in a way called for by humanity? A humane act is a beneficent act, but not every beneficent act is a humane one. To do something that helps to make someone who is already very happy even happier is certainly beneficent, but it would not naturally be described as an act called for by considerations of humanity.

The *Oxford English Dictionary* defines humanity as "Disposition to treat human beings and animals with consideration and compassion, and to relieve their distresses; kindness, benevolence."[1] In this essay I shall understand by "humanity" the relief of distress. As a matter of usage, it seems to me that the *OED* is right to put this before the more extended sense of kindness or benevolence in general. In any case, it is this notion that I want to

discuss, and the word "humanity" is the closest representation of it in common use.

There are three questions to be dealt with. First, is it morally obligatory to behave humanely, or is it simply laudable but not morally delinquent to fail so to act? Second, if it is morally obligatory, what implications does it have, if any, for the obligations of rich countries to aid poor ones? Third, if (as I shall suggest) rich countries have a humanitarian obligation to aid poor ones, on what criterion can we determine how much sacrifice the rich countries should be prepared to make?

The obligation of humanity

I shall begin my discussion by taking up and considering the argument put forward by Peter Singer in his article "Famine, Affluence and Morality."[2] Singer puts forward a simple, clear, and forceful case for a humanitarian obligation for those in rich countries to give economic aid to those in poor countries. The premises of his argument are as follows. The first is "that suffering and death from lack of food, shelter, and medical care are bad."[3] The second is given in two alternative forms. One is that "if it is in our power to prevent something bad from happening, without thereby sacrificing anything of comparable moral importance, we ought, morally, to do it."[4] The other, and weaker, form is that "if it is in our power to prevent something very bad from happening,

Originally published in *Nomos XXIV: Ethics, Economics and the Law*, edited by J. R. Pennock and J. W. Chapman (New York: New York University Press, 1982), pp. 219–52. Reprinted by permission of New York University Press.

without sacrificing anything morally significant, we ought, morally, to do it."[5] He goes on to say that "an application of this principle [i.e., the second version] would be as follows: if I am walking past a shallow pond and see a child drowning in it, I ought to wade in and pull the child out. This will mean getting my clothes muddy, but this is insignificant, while the death of the child would presumably be a very bad thing."[6] All that has to be added is that the application of the second premise is unaffected by proximity or distance and "makes no distinction between cases in which I am the only person who could possibly do anything and cases in which I am just one among millions in the same position."[7] If we accept these premises, we are committed, Singer claims, to the conclusion that people in the rich countries have a moral obligation to help those in the poor countries.

For the purpose of this chapter, I am going to take it as common ground that one would indeed be doing wrong to walk past Peter Singer's drowning child and do nothing to save it. This of course entails that, at least in the most favorable cases, duties of humanity must exist. In the space available, it hardly makes sense to try to argue for a complete theory of morality from which this can be deduced, and in any case I myself am more sure of the conclusion than of any of the alternative premises from which it would follow. Anyone who disagrees with the claim that there is an obligation to rescue the child in the case as stated will not find what follows persuasive, since I certainly do not think that the case for international aid on humanitarian grounds is *stronger* than the case for rescuing the drowning child.

Does the drowning child case extend to international aid?

The extension of the drowning child case may be challenged along several lines. Here I can only state them and say briefly why I do not think they undercut the basic idea that the case for an obligation to save the drowning child applies also to giving international aid. The appearance of dogmatism is purely a result of compression.

The first argument is that the child may be supposed not to be responsible for his plight (or at any rate it may be on that supposition that the example gets to us) but that countries are responsible for their economic problems. My comments here are two. First, even if it were true that the death by disease and or starvation of somebody in a

poor country were to some degree the result of past acts or omissions by the entire population, that scarcely makes it morally decent to hold the individual responsible for his plight; nor, similarly, if his predicament could have been avoided had the policies of his government been different.

Let us move on to consider another way in which a challenge may be mounted to Singer's extension of the argument for a duty to aid from the case of the drowning child to that of famine relief. It may be recalled that Singer explicitly made the shift from one case to the other via the statement that neither proximity nor the one-to-one relation between the victim and the potential rescuer makes any moral difference. Clearly, if this claim is denied, we can again agree on the duty to rescue the drowning child but deny that this is an appropriate analogue to the putative duty of people in rich countries to aid those in poor ones. A number of philosophers have tried to drive a wedge between the cases in this way, but I have to say that I am not very impressed by their efforts. The argument for proximity as a relevant factor is that, if we posit a duty to rescue those near at hand, we keep the duty within narrow bounds and thus do not let it interfere with people's life plans; but, if we allow the duty to range over the whole of mankind, it becomes too demanding. Although some people see merit in this, it appears to me that it is invoked simply because it provides a way of arbitrarily truncating the application of the principle so as to arrive at a convenient answer. I shall go on later to agree that there are limits to what people can be required to sacrifice. But I see no ethically defensible reason for saying that, if we can't (or can't be required to) do anything we might, we should simply contract the sphere of operation of the principle that we are obliged to relieve suffering. Perhaps we should channel our limited humanitarian efforts to where they are most needed, which, if we live in a relatively rich country, is likely to be outside its boundaries.

Singer also made it explicit that, if the case of the drowning child were to be extended to international aid, one would have to rule out the one-to-one relation between the rescuer and the potential rescuee as a morally relevant factor. Attempts have been made to do so, but they likewise seem to me to lack merit. If there are several people who could save the drowning child, it is sometimes said that none of them is particularly responsible for saving it. But if the child drowns because none of them saves it, they are all, I would suggest, morally responsible for its death. Conversely, suppose that several people are drowning at some distance from one another and there is only one person around to save them. It has been argued that since that person cannot do his duty, if that is defined as saving all those whom he might save (assuming that he could save any one of them but cannot save more than one), no such duty exists. The obvious reply to this is that the duty has been incorrectly defined: the duty in this case is to save one, and his duty is not affected by the fact that there are others who cannot be saved.

Finally, it might be accepted that the case of the drowning child would extend to international aid if the aid would do any good, but then denied that it will. The main lines of this argument are two. The first is the one from waste and inefficiency: aid does not get to the right people; development projects are a disaster; and so on. But I would claim that even if waste is endemic in aid to poor (and probably ill-organized) countries, the difference it makes to health and nutrition is sufficient to make it worth giving if only part of it gets to the people it is supposed to get to. And if, as is all too true, aid in the past has often been inappropriate, the answer is not to withhold aid but to make it more appropriate: no more massive dams, electricity-generating stations, or steel mills, but cheaper, less complex, and more decentralized technology.

The second line of argument is the neo-Malthusian: that the only effect of aid in the long run is to lead to population increase and thus to even more suffering. I agree that if this is the only effect of aid, the humanitarian case for it falls to the ground. But it is clear that economic development combined with appropriate social policies and the widespread availability of contraception can actually reduce the rate of population growth. The implication is thus that aid should be given in large amounts where the social and political conditions are right, so as to get countries through the demographic transition from high birthrate and high death rate to low birthrate and low death rate as rapidly as possible.

Where ideological or religious dogmas result in pronatalist government policies or rejection of contraception by the population, one might conclude that aid would be better withheld, since the only foreseeable effect of economic improvement will be to increase numbers. But can we really be so sure that attitudes will not change? The election of a relatively young and doctrinally reactionary pope does not encourage hopes of any early change in official doctrine. But even without any change at that level, it is striking how, in the developed countries, the practices of Roman Catholics have altered dramatically in just a couple of decades. For example, in the Province of Quebec, which had for more than two centuries a birthrate close to the physical maximum, with families of more than 10 children quite common, has now one of the lowest birthrates in North America.

How far does the obligation extend?

If we accept the conclusion that the rich have some obligation on humanitarian grounds to provide economic aid to the poor, the next question is, How much sacrifice is required? In my view, no simple and determinate criterion is available. This is a problem of the obligation of humanity in general, not a peculiarity of the international context. In the standard case of rescuing someone in danger of drowning, the usual guidance one gets from moral philosophers is that the obligation does not extend to risking one's life, though it does require that one suffer a fair amount of inconvenience. However, the decision in such cases, like that of Singer's drowning child, characteristically has clear and finite limits to its implications. But, given the failure of most people or governments in rich countries to give much aid, it would clearly be possible for individuals to give up a high proportion of their incomes without risking their lives and still leave millions of savable lives in poor countries unsaved. Thus, the question of limits is pressing.

There is an answer that is, in principle, straightforward. It is the one embodied in Singer's claim that one is obliged to help up to the point at which one is sacrificing something of "comparable moral importance." This is, of course, a maximizing form of consequentialism. If you say that pains and pleasures are what is of moral importance, you get Benthamite utilitarianism (in the traditional interpretation, anyway); if you say it is the enjoyment of beauty and personal relationships, you get G.E. Moore's ideal consequentialism; and so on. The trouble with this is, needless to say, that most of us do not see any reason for accepting an obligation to maximize the total amount of good in the universe.

Singer's weaker principle that we should give aid up to the point at which we are sacrificing anything of moral importance seems to me useless:

for a Benthamite utilitarian, for example, even getting one's trousers muddy would be in itself an evil – not one comparable to the death of a child, but an evil none the less. Even Singer's chosen case would therefore be eliminated on this criterion, let alone any more strenuous sacrifices.

Conclusion

I conclude, provisionally and in the absence of any plausible alternative, that there is no firm criterion for the amount of sacrifice required to relieve distress. This does not mean that nothing can be said. I think it is fairly clear that there is a greater obligation the more severe the distress, the better off the potential helper would still be after helping, and the higher the ratio of benefit to cost. What is indefinite is where the line is to be drawn. In the words of C.D. Broad, in what may be the best single article in philosophical ethics ever written, "it is no objection to say that it is totally impossible to determine exactly where this point comes in any particular case. This is quite true, but it is too common a difficulty in ethics to worry us, and we know that we are lucky in ethical questions if we can state upper and lower limits that are not too ridiculously far apart."[8]

What, in any case, are we talking about here as the range? We could perhaps wonder whether the level of aid from a country like the United States should be 3 percent of GNP (the level of Marshall aid) or 10 or 25 percent. But, unless we reject the idea of an obligation to aid those in distress altogether, we can hardly doubt that one quarter of 1 percent is grotesquely too little.

II   Justice

The concept of justice

'Are we not trying to pack too much into the concept of justice and the correlative concept of rights? The question whether it is *wrong* to act in certain ways is not the same question as whether it is *unjust* so to act.'[9] I think the answer to Passmore's rhetorical question is in the affirmative. We should not expect to get out of "justice" a blueprint for the good society – nor should we wish to, since that degree of specificity would inevitably limit potential applicability. Surely it ought to be possible for a just society to be rich or poor, cultivated or philistine, religious or secular and

(within limits that are inherent in justice itself) to have more or less of liberty, equality, and fraternity.

Up to this point, I have studiously avoided any reference to justice. I have been talking about the obligation to relieve suffering as a matter of humanity. The fact that the obligation is not derived from justice does not make it a matter of generosity, nor does it entail that it should be left to voluntary action to adhere to it. It is an obligation that it would be wrong not to carry out and that could quite properly be enforced upon rich countries if the world political system made this feasible. And the core of the discussion has been the claim that the obligation to help (and a fortiori the obligation not to harm) is not limited in its application to those who form a single political community.

It is of course open to anyone who wishes to do so to argue that, if the rich have a properly enforceable obligation to give, this is all we need in order to be able to say that the rich must give to the poor as a matter of justice. I have no way of proving that it is a mistake to use the term "just" to mark out the line between, on the one hand, what is morally required and, on the other, what is praiseworthy to do but not wrong to omit doing. All I can say is that such a way of talking seems to me to result in the blunting of our moral vocabulary and therefore to a loss of precision in our moral thinking. Justice, I wish to maintain, is not merely one end of a monochromatic scale that has at the other end sacrifice of self-interest for the good of others to a heroic or saintly degree. Rather, it points to a particular set of reasons why people (or societies) may have duties to one another and to particular features of institutions that make them morally condemnable.[10]

I shall return to the distinction between humanity and justice in Section 3, where I shall be able to refer to the results of my discussions of each of them. My plan is to analyze justice under two heads. The first is justice as reciprocity; the second, justice as equal rights. These are both familiar ideas though I shall give the second a slightly unfamiliar twist. Justice as reciprocity I will discuss in three aspects: justice as fidelity, justice as requital, and justice as fair play.

Justice as fidelity

The notion of justice as fidelity is that of keeping faith. In addition to covering contract and promises, it extends, in a rather indefinite way, to meeting legitimate expectations not derived from explicit voluntary agreement. Clearly it is an essentially conservative principle and tends if anything to operate contrary to the interests of poor countries, insofar as they often find themselves in the position of seeking to renegotiate disadvantageous deals with transnational corporations within their territories.

Justice as requital

Justice as requital is also a basically conservative principle but can, on occasion, have revisionist implications vis-à-vis justice as fidelity. No simple rule governs what happens when they conflict. Henry Sidgwick, with characteristic caution, said that we have two standards of justice, as the customary distribution and as the ideal distribution, and added that "it is the reconciliation between these two views which is the problem of political justice."[11] I shall not take up that challenge here, but explore the possible implications of justice as requital for international distribution.

The idea of justice as requital is that of a fair return: a fair exchange, a fair share of benefits from some common endeavor, and so on. The most obvious application in the relations between rich and poor countries is whether poor countries are getting fair prices for their exports and paying fair prices for their imports. This, of course, raises the obvious question of what the criterion of a "fair price" is. Suppose, however, that we say, minimally, that it is the prevailing world price. Then it seems clear that, even on this criterion, many poor countries have legitimate complaints about the transfer pricing of transnational corporations. For example, when in the late 1960s the Andean Pact countries (Bolivia, Colombia, Ecuador, and Peru) started taking a serious interest in the pricing policies of transnational corporations operating within their territories, they found overpricing of imports to be the norm, sometimes by factors of hundreds of percent, and, less spectacularly, underpricing of the value of exports.[12] This enabled the companies to attain rates of return on capital of often more than 100 percent while at the same time evading government limits on repatriation of profits. Since the Andean Pact countries have been politically independent for a century and a half and have relatively sophisticated bureaucracies compared with most countries in the Third World, it is inconceivable that similar practices do not obtain in other, more vulnerable countries.

When we turn to the structure of world prices itself, the criterion of justice as requital becomes less helpful. The countries of the Third World, as part of their demands for a "New International Economic Order" have demanded an "Integrated Program" of commodity management that would be designed to push up the prices of raw materials in relation to manufactured products.

The success of the Organization of Petroleum Exporting Countries (OPEC) is, of course, significant here in providing a dazzling example of the effectiveness of a producer cartel. Oil, however, seems to be unique in that it is so cheap to extract and worth so much to consumers. This means that it has always, since the days of the Pennsylvania oilfields, yielded enormous economic rents. The only question has been who captured them. And clearly, until 1973, the Middle Eastern oil producers were getting only a small proportion of the economic rent.

Other commodities are not like oil. It may indeed be possible to push up the prices by restricting supply, but substitution or recycling is likely to set in. From the long-run point of view of the world, this pressure toward conservation would be desirable, no doubt, but the point is that it does not spell a bonanza for the raw material producers.

Clearly, this is only scratching the surface, but I think that it is, at any rate, important to keep in mind that, even if commodity prices could be raised substantially across the board, this would not make most poor countries *appreciably* better off; and it would make some, including the important cases of India and Bangladesh, worse off. Whatever conclusion one wishes to draw, therefore, about the applicability to world prices of justice as requital, the implications are not going to be such as to solve the problem of poor countries that are also resource poor.

Justice as fair play

We still have to see if any redistributive implications flow from the third branch of justice as reciprocity: justice as fair play. The idea here is that if one benefits (or stands to benefit) from some cooperative practice, one should not be a "free rider" by taking the benefits (or being ready to take them if the occasion arises) while failing to do one's part in sustaining the practice when it is one's turn to do so. Thus, if others burn smokeless fuel in their fireplaces, pack their litter out of the backcountry, or clean up after their dogs, it is unfair for you to refuse to do the same.

The principle of fair play has a potentiality for underwriting a certain amount of redistribution from rich to poor insofar as one practice that might be regarded as prospectively beneficial to all concerned would be the practice of helping those in need. If such a practice existed, it would operate analogously to insurance, which is a contractual way of transferring money from those who have not suffered from certain specified calamities to those who have. The principle of fair play would then hold that it would be unfair to be a free rider on a scheme of helping those in need by refusing to do your part when called upon.

The invocation of this notion of what the sociobiologists call "reciprocal altruism" may appear to provide a new way of distinguishing the drowning child case from that of international aid. Perhaps what motivates us in agreeing that there is an obligation to rescue the child is an unarticulated contextual assumption that the child belongs to our community (however widely we may conceive that "community") and that there are norms within that community calling for low-cost rescue from which we stand to gain if ever we find ourselves in need of rescue. Such feelings of obligation as we have in this case can therefore be adequately explained by supposing that they arise from the application of the principle of fair play. It was, thus, an error to have taken it for granted that an acknowledgment of an obligation to help in the drowning child case must show that we accepted a general principle of an obligation to aid those in distress.

I believe that the objection is formally valid. That is to say, it is possible by invoking the principle of fair play to underwrite the obligation to rescue the drowning child without committing oneself to a universal obligation to rescue. One could respond to this by arguing that the conclusions in Section I of this essay can be reinstated by deriving universal obligations from the existence of world community. I shall consider this argument below. But before doing so, I should like to follow an alternative and more aggressive line.

The point to observe is that, although we may indeed be motivated to agree that we ought to rescue the drowning child by considerations of justice as reciprocity, it does not follow that we are motivated solely by those considerations. Sup-

pose that you are briefly visiting a foreign country, with an entirely alien culture, and have no idea about the local norms of rescue. Would you, if you came across Singer's drowning child, have an obligation to wade in and rescue it? I think that most people would say yes in answer to that question. And, clearly, those who do are acknowledging obligations of humanity as distinct from obligations of justice.

None of this, of course, is intended to suggest that the difficulties in moving from a general obligation of humanity to an obligation on the part of rich countries to give economic aid to poor ones is any less problematic than it appeared earlier. But it does fend off a possible challenge to the move from the drowning child case to the universal obligation to aid. The view I want to maintain is that the answer in the drowning child case is overdetermined where the duty of fair play also underwrites rescue. The strength of the obligation depends upon the circumstances, but it never disappears. Both psychologically and morally, the obligation to aid would be strongest if there were an explicit and generally observed agreement among a group of parents to keep an eye on one another's children: humanity, fidelity, and fair play would then coincide and reinforce each other. The obligation would be perhaps a little less strong but still very strong in a small, stable, and close-knit community with a well-developed tradition of "neighborliness," since the obligation of fair play would here have maximum force. It would be less strong if the norm of rescue were more widely diffused over a whole society, and would of course vary according to the society. (New Zealand would rate much higher than the United States on the strength of the norm of helping strangers within the society, for example.) And, finally, in the absence of any established practice of aiding strangers that would give rise to obligations of fair play, there is still, I am suggesting, an obligation of humanity that does not in any way depend upon considerations of reciprocity.[13]

I have been taking for granted that the existence of a practice of rescue does give rise to an obligation to play one's part. This can be questioned. Somebody might say: "Why should I cooperate with the scheme if I'm willing to renounce any benefits that might be due to me under it?[14] But the cogency of the objection depends upon the existence of stringent conditions of publicity: it must be possible to make this known to all those in the scheme, and it must be remembered perhaps for decades. (This is essential, since many transfers to those in need are going to be predominantly from the young and middle-aged to the old, so it would undermine the integrity of any such co-operative scheme if people could change their minds about its value as they got older.) Neither condition is generally met. Consider a practice of rescuing the victims of accidents – drowning swimmers are the usually cited case. If this practice exists in a whole society, it is not feasible for those who wish to opt out to notify everybody else in advance. And how many could be counted on to be strong-minded enough to wave away a would-be rescuer when they were in need of help themselves? Even if they could, in many cases the rescuer has to incur the trouble and risk in order to get there (as with rescuing a swimmer) or the victim may be unconscious and thus incapable of spurning help.

It is crucially important to notice, however, that the principle of fair play is conditional; that is to say, it stipulates that it is unfair to be a free rider on an actually existing cooperative practice, and that it *would* be unfair to free ride on other mutually beneficial practices if they did exist. But it does not say that it is unfair for a practice that would, if it existed, be mutually beneficial, not to exist.

As anyone familiar with Rawls's theory of justice will have been aware for some time, we are here on the edge of deep waters. For one strand of Rawls's theory is precisely the notion of justice as reciprocity that is embodied in the principle of fair play. According to Rawls, a society is a scheme of social cooperation, and from this fact we can generate, via the notion of fair play, principles of justice. But, clearly, any actual society simply generates whatever is generated by its actual cooperative practice. If it provides retirement pensions out of social security taxes, it is unfair to be a free rider on the scheme by dodging your share of the cost. And so on. But if I am right about the applicability of the principle of fair play, the most Rawls can say about a society that does not have such a scheme is that it suffers from collective irrationality in that it is passing up a chance to do itself some good. He cannot, I suggest, employ the principle as a step in an argument that such a society is unjust.

I make this point because Charles Beitz, in the last part of his admirable book, *Political Philosophy and International Relations*,[15] has argued, within a Rawlsian framework, for a global difference principle. That is to say, income should be redistrib-uted internationally so that the worst-off representative individual in the world is as well off as possible. Beitz acknowledges that he is taking for granted the general validity of Rawls's theory and is simply arguing from within its basic premises for the dropping of Rawls's restriction on the application of the two principles of justice to societies. I have been suggesting that, even within a society, one cannot use the fact that it is a cooperative scheme to argue that it is unfair not to have more extensive cooperation, though not to do so may be collectively irrational. But the international scene presents two further difficulties. First, I think that Rawls is broadly right in (implicitly) denying that the whole world constitutes a single cooperative partnership in the required sense. Second, I do not think that international redistribution can plausibly be said to be advantageous to rich as well as poor countries. Rawls is therefore probably correct in deducing from his system only nonaggression, diplomatic immunity, and the like as mutually advantageous to countries and thus, on his side of the principle of fair play, just. If I am right, however, they are simply collectively rational and give rise to duties of fair play only to the extent that they are instantiated in actual practice.

Beitz's argument for extending the Rawlsian difference principle is in essence that the network of international trade is sufficiently extensive to draw all countries together in a single cooperative scheme. But it seems to be that trade, however multilateral, does not constitute a cooperative scheme of the relevant kind. Trade, if freely undertaken, is (presumably) beneficial to the exchanging parties, but it is not, it seems to me, the kind of relationship that gives rise to duties of fair play. To the extent that justice is involved it is, I would say, justice as requital, that is, giving a fair return. Justice as fair play arises not from simple exchange but from either the provision of public goods that are collectively enjoyed (parks; defense; a litter-free, or unpolluted, environment; and so on) or from quasi-insurance schemes for mutual aid of the kind just discussed. Trade in pottery, ornamentation, and weapons can be traced back to prehistoric times, but we would hardly feel inclined to think of, say, the Beaker Folk as forming a single cooperative enterprise with their trading partners. No more did the spice trade unite East and West.

To the extent that we are inclined to think of the world as more of a cooperative enterprise now, this is, in my judgment, not because trade is more extensive or multilateral, but because there really are rudimentary organs of international cooperation in the form of United Nations agencies and such entities as the International Monetary Fund (IMF) and the World Bank. But the resulting relationships clearly fall short of those of mutual dependence found within societies. And my second point comes in here to draw attention to the fact that the extent of increased cooperation that would really be mutually beneficial is probably quite limited. In particular, redistribution on the insurance principle seems to have little appeal to rich countries. In the foreseeable future, aid to the needy is going to flow from, say, the United States to Bangladesh rather than vice versa. The conditions for reciprocity – that all the parties stand prospectively to benefit from the scheme – simply do not exist. One could, of course, again retreat behind the "veil of ignorance" and argue that, if people did not know to which society they belonged, they would surely choose something like a global difference principle – or at any rate a floor below which nobody should be allowed to fall. And this seems plausible enough. (I have argued it myself in an earlier work.[16]) But this move clearly points up even more sharply than in the case of a single society the degree to which inserting the "veil of ignorance" takes us away from the sphere of the principle of fair play.

Justice as equal rights

In his well-known article, "Are There Any Natural Rights?"[17] H.L.A. Hart argued that special rights must presuppose general rights. Before people can act in ways that modify their, and others', rights (paradigmatically by promising), they must, as a matter of elementary logic, have rights that do not stem from such modifications. Putting this in terms of the present discussion, we can say that justice as reciprocity needs a prior assignment of rights before it can get off the ground.

Now we might try to solve the problem of sanctifying the status quo. We could, in other words, simply declare that we are going to push the principle of justice as the fulfillment of reasonable expectations to the limit and say that whatever rights somebody now has are to be taken as the baseline in relation to which all future developments must satisfy the requirements of fidelity, requital, and fair play. If we note that the conser-

vation of value is akin to the Pareto principle, we may observe that this would give us the Virginia school of political economy, especially associated with James Buchanan.

I have criticized his approach elsewhere,[18] and I shall not repeat my criticisms here. But it is surely enough for the present purpose to draw attention to the fact that on the principle of the unquestioned justice of the status quo, the most grotesque features of the existing allocation of rights would be frozen in place forever unless those who suffered from them could find some quid pro quo that would make it worth the while of, say, a shah of Iran or a General Somoza to accept change. But that would be, if it could be found, an improvement in efficiency arising from the reallocation of the existing rights. It would not face the real problem, which was, of course, the injustice of the initial allocation of rights.

Hart's answer to his own question is that the general right that is presupposed by any special rights is an equal right to liberty. He does not give any explicit argument, as far as I can see, for its being equal. But I take it the point is that since a general right is something that is necessarily anterior to any act giving rise to a special right, there is simply no basis for discriminating among people in respect of general rights. In order to discriminate, one would either have to do so on the basis of some quality that is obviously irrelevant to the assignment of rights (e.g., skin color) or on the basis of something the person has done (e.g., made a promise) that provides a reason for attributing different rights to him. But then we get back to the original point, namely that such a differentiation in rights entails that we have an idea of the proper distribution of rights without the special factor adduced. And that must, it seems, be an equal distribution.

In this essay I want to take this idea and apply it to the case of natural resources. I shall suggest that they fit all the requirements for being the subjects of a general right and that therefore everyone has an equal right to enjoy their benefits.

As Hillel Steiner has remarked, "Nozick rightly insists that our commonsense view of what is just – of what is owed to individuals by right – is inextricably bound up with what they *have done* . . . [but] unlike other objects, the objects of appropriative rights . . . are *not* the results of individuals' past actions. . . . Appropriative claims, and the rules governing them, can have nothing to do with desert."[19] Consider, for example, Bruce

Ackerman's fable of the spaceship and the manna. One of the claimants, "Rusher," says: "I say that the first person who grabs a piece of manna should be recognized as its true owner" and, when asked for a reason, says, "Because people who grab first are better than people who grab second."[20] That, I think, illustrates my point. What exactly is supposed to be the virtue of getting there first, or even worse, in merely having some ancestor who got there first?

The position with regard to countries is parallel to that of individuals. Today the basis of state sovereignty over natural resources is convention reinforced by international declarations such as votes of the United Nations General Assembly in 1970, 1972, and 1974 to the effect that each country has "permanent sovereignty over natural resources" within its territory.[21] It is easy enough to see the basis of the convention. It has a transcendent simplicity and definiteness that must recommend it in international relations. For, in the absence of a "common power," stability depends heavily on conventions that leave the minimum amount of room for interpretation. Within a municipal legal system, by contrast, it is possible to introduce and enforce complex rules limiting the rights of individual appropriation (e.g., restricting the amount of water that can be drawn off from a river) and transferring a portion of the economic rent from the property owner to the state. Moreover, in the absence of a "common power" it is a convention that is relatively easy to enforce – at any rate easier than any alternative. For a state may be presumed, other things being equal, to be in a better position to control the appropriation of the natural resources of its own territory than to control those of some other country.

In practice, of course, things are not always equal, and many Third World countries have found that controlling foreign companies that own their natural resources is no easy matter: an unholy alliance of multinational corporations and their patron governments (for most, this is the United States) stand ready to organize international boycotts, to manipulate institutions such as the World Bank and the IMF against them; and, if all else fails, go in for "destabilization" on the Chilean model. The problem is exacerbated when a country seeks to gain control of the exploitation of its own natural resources by expropriating the foreign-based companies that have been there, often long before the country became independent. For the issue of compensation then arises, and

this is likely to be contentious, not only because of the possibility of dispute about the current value of the investment, but also because the country may claim compensation for inadequate (or no) royalties paid on extraction in the past, a claim that (as we noted above) falls under the head of justice as requital.

However, as far as I am aware, no body of opinion in either the North or the South is averse to the principle that each country is entitled to benefit exclusively from its own natural resources, and to decide whether they should be exploited and, if so, at what rate and in what order. And even the practice has come a long way in the last twenty years. The OPEC is of course the outstanding illustration, but the same pattern of improved royalties and more control over the amount extracted and the way in which it is done obtains also in other countries and other commodities.

It would hardly be surprising if, when the principle of national sovereignty over natural resources has been so recently and precariously established, Third World countries should be highly suspicious of any suggestion that natural resources should in future be treated as collective international property. They may well wonder whether this is anything more than a cover for the reintroduction of colonialism. I do not see how such doubts can be allayed by mere assertion. Clearly, everything would depend on the principle's being applied across the board rather than in a one-sided way that lets the industrialized countries act on the maxim "What's yours is mine and what's mine is my own." So far, that is precisely how it has been used, as in the proposals of American chauvinists such as Robert Tucker that the United States should be prepared to occupy the Saudi Arabian oilfields by military force in order to maintain the flow of oil at a "reasonable" price, so that Americans can continue to use up a grossly disproportionate share of the world's oil. Since the United States, if it used only domestically produced oil, would still have one of the world's highest per capita levels of consumption, the effrontery of this proposal for the international control of other countries' oil would be hard to beat.

If the Third World countries were too weak to do anything more than hang on to the present position of national sovereignty over natural resources, we would, it seems to me, have to regard that as the best outcome that can be obtained. It is clearly preferable to the earlier setup, in which countries with the power to do so controlled the natural resources of others. For, although the distribution of natural resources is entirely arbitrary from a moral point of view, it has at any rate the kind of fairness displayed by a lottery. That is presumably better than a situation in which the weak are despoiled of their prizes by force and fraud.

In spite of these forebodings about the potential misuse of the principle that natural resources are the joint possession of the human race as a whole, I think it is worth pursuing. For it is scarcely possible to be satisfied with the present situation from any angle except that of extreme pessimism about the chances of changing it for the better rather than for the worse. The overwhelming fact about the existing system is, obviously, that it makes the economic prospects of a country depend, to a significant degree, on something for which its inhabitants (present or past) can take absolutely no credit and lay no just claim to its exclusive benefits, namely its natural resources – including in this land, water, minerals, sunlight, and so on. The claims of collectivities to appropriate natural resources rest, as do those of individuals, on convention or on law (in this case, such quasi-law as the United Nations resolutions cited above). No doubt, the point has been impressed on people in the West by examples such as Kuwait, the United Arab Emirates, or Saudi Arabia, and it may be that such small numbers of people have never before become so rich without any effort on their own part, simply as a result of sitting on top of rich deposits. But I see no coherent way of saying why there is anything grotesque about, say, the case of Kuwait, without acknowledging that the fault lies in the whole principle of national sovereignty over natural resources. If it were simply a matter of a few million people hitting the jackpot, things would not be bad, but of course the obverse of that is countries that have poor land, or little land per head, and few mineral resources or other sources of energy such as hydroelectric power.

Obviously, some countries are richer than others for many reasons, and some, like Japan, are among the more affluent in spite of having to import almost all their oil and the greatest part of many other natural resources. What, then, about the other advantages that the people in the rich countries inherit – productive capital, good systems of communications, orderly administration, well-developed systems of education and training, and so on? If the point about special rights is that someone must have done something to acquire a special right, what have the fortunate inheritors of all the advantages done to give them an exclusive claim to the benefits flowing from them?

The answer that the defenders of property rights normally give at this point is that, although the inheritors have done nothing to establish any special rights, those who left it to them did do something (namely, help to create the advantages) and had a right to dispose of it to some rather than to others. The special rights of those in the present generation thus derive from the use made by those in the previous generation of *their* special rights.

I cannot, in this already long chapter, undertake here to ask how far this answer takes us. We would have to get into questions that seem to me very difficult, such as the extent to which the fact that people who are no longer alive wanted something to happen, and perhaps even made sacrifices in order to insure that it could happen, provides any basis in justice for determining what those now alive now should do. I shall simply say here that I regard any claims that those now alive can make to special advantages derived from the efforts of their ancestors as quite limited. First, the inheritance must itself have been justly acquired in the first place, and that cannot be said of any country that violated the equal claims of all on natural resources – which means almost all industrial countries. Second, the claims to inheritance seem to me to attenuate with time, so that, although the present generation might legitimately derive some special advantages from the efforts of the preceding one, and perhaps the one before that, the part of what they passed on that was in turn inherited from their predecessors should, I think, be regarded as by now forming part of the common heritage.

Obviously, making this case out would require elaboration beyond the space available. But I do want to emphasize that what follows constitutes, in my view, a minimalist strategy. That is to say, whatever obligations of justice follow from it represent the absolutely rock-bottom requirements of justice in international affairs. To the extent that other advantages can be brought within the net of the principle of equal rights, the obligations of rich countries go beyond what is argued for here.

International institutions

It would be ridiculous to spend time here on a blueprint for a scheme to put into effect the principle that I have been advancing. Its implementation on a worldwide scale, if it happens at all, is going to occur over a period measured in decades and, indeed, centuries. It will depend on both fundamental changes in outlook and on the development of international organs capable of taking decisions and carrying them out with reasonable efficiency and honesty.

The history of domestic redistribution is, I think, very much to the point here in suggesting that there is a virtuous circle in which the existence of redistributive institutions and beliefs in the legitimacy of redistribution are mutually reinforcing and have a strong tendency to become more extensive together over time. When Hume discussed redistribution in the *Enquiry*, the only form of it that he considered was "perfect equality of possessions."[22] The notion of continuous redistribution of income through a system of progressive taxation does not seem to have occurred to him. The Poor Law did, of course, provide a minimum of relief to the indigent, but it was organized by parishes and it is doubtful that the amateurish and nepotistic central administration of the eighteenth century could have handled a national scheme. The introduction of unemployment and sickness benefits and old age pensions in one Western European country after another in the late nineteenth century and early twentieth century was made possible by the development of competent national administrations.

At the same time, these programs constituted a political response to the extension of the suffrage, or perhaps one might more precisely say a response to conditions that, among other things, made the extension of the suffrage necessary for the continued legitimacy of the state. A certain measure of redistribution was the price the privileged were prepared to pay for mass acceptance of their remaining advantages. Once in place, however, such programs have shown a universal tendency to take on a life of their own and to grow incrementally as gaps in the original coverage are filled in and the whole level of benefits is gradually raised. Indeed, it has been found in cross-national studies that the best predictor of the relative size of a given program (say, aid to the blind) within the whole welfare system is the amount of time the program has been running compared with others. In the long run, the programs seem to generate supporting sentiments, so that even Margaret Thatcher and Ronald Reagan proposed only reductions of a few percentage points in programs that even thirty years previously would have seemed quite ambitious.

I do not want to drive the comparison with the international arena into the ground, but I think that, if nothing else, reflecting on domestic experience ought to lead us to look at international transfers from an appropriate time perspective. The United Nations Organization obviously has a lot wrong with it, for example, but its administration is probably less corrupt, self-serving, and inefficient than that which served Sir Robert Walpole. If one takes a time span of thirty years, it is, I suggest, more remarkable that the network of international cooperation has developed as far as it has than that it has not gone further. And in the realm of ideas the notion that poor countries have claims of one sort or another to aid from rich ones has moved from being quite exotic to one that is widely accepted in principle. At any rate in public, the representatives of the rich countries on international bodies no longer deny such a responsibility. They merely seek to evade any binding commitment based on it. But in the long run what is professed in public makes a difference to what gets done because it sets the terms of the discussion.

International taxation

It is not at all difficult to come up with proposals for a system by which revenues would be raised on a regular basis from the rich countries and transferred to the poor ones. Accordingly, no elaborate discussion is needed here. If any such scheme ever gained enough momentum to be a serious international issue, economists and accountants would no doubt have a field day arguing about the details. There is no point in anticipating such arguments, even in outline here. However, the relative brevity of treatment here should not lead to any underestimation of its importance. It is in fact the centerpiece of what is being put forward in this essay.

Now, broadly speaking, two alternative approaches are possible. One would be to take up each of the aspects of international justice that have been discussed – and whatever others might be raised – and to base a system of taxes and receipts upon each. This would be messy and endlessly contentious. The alternative, which is, I predict, the only way in which any systematic redistribution will ever take place, if it ever does, is to have one or two comprehensive taxes and distribute the proceeds according to some relatively simple formula among the poor countries.

The most obvious, and in my view the best, would be a tax on the governments of rich countries, assessed as a proportion of gross national product that increases with per capita income, the proceeds to be distributed to poor countries on a parallel basis of negative income tax. Gross national product reflects, roughly, the use of irreplaceable natural resources, the burden on the ecosphere, and advantages derived from the efforts of past generations, and past exploitation of other countries. Ideally, this tax would be supplemented by a severance tax on the extraction of mineral resources and a shadow tax on the value of land and similar resources. (States could be left to collect the money by any means they chose. But their aggregate liability would be assessed by valuing the taxable base and applying the set rate.) This would certainly be required to take care of some glaring inequities that would still otherwise remain. But the simple system of transfer based on gross national product would be such an advance over the status quo that it would be a mistake to miss any chance to implement it by pursuing further refinements.

I believe that any other kinds of general tax, that is to say, taxes not related specifically to some aspect of justice, should be rejected. For example, a tax on foreign trade, or on foreign trade in fossil fuels has been proposed.[23] This is so obviously arbitrary that it is hard to see how anyone can have considered it worth mooting. It has the manifest effect of penalizing small countries and countries that export (or import, if one believes that the tax on exports of fossil fuel would be shifted forward) coal and oil. It conversely has an absurdly favorable effect on very large countries that import and export little in relation to the size of the GNPs and are relatively self-sufficient in energy derived from fossil fuels. No doubt the State Department loves it, but why anyone else should be imposed on is a mystery to me.

I have assumed without discussion that resources transferred to satisfy the requirements of justice should go straight to poor countries rather than being channeled through international agencies and dispensed in the form of aid for specific projects. I shall spell out the rationale for this in the next section. But I will simply remark here that nothing I have said about justice rules out additional humanitarian transfers. And these would appropriately be administered by international organizations. The basis for raising such revenues for humanitarian aid would very reasonably be a progressive international shadow income tax, since this would perfectly reflect ability to pay. We might thus envisage a dual system of international taxation – one part, corresponding to the requirements of justice, going directly to poor countries to be spent at their own discretion; the other going to the World Bank or some successor organization less dominated by the donor countries.

III The Relations between Humanity and Justice

Introduction

I have been arguing that both humanity and justice require a substantial expansion in the scale of economic transfers from rich countries to poor ones. I should now like to show that, as the two rationales are very different, so are their practical implications. This point is, I think, worth emphasizing because those who pride themselves on the possession of sturdy Anglo-Saxon "common sense" tend to conclude that, if we agree on the humanitarian obligation, we are wasting our breath in arguing about claims of injustice – claims for the rectification of alleged unrequited transfers from poor to rich countries in the past that are hard to assess and impossible to quantify or involving more or less abstruse doctrines about the nature of justice in the contemporary world. If we recognize the case for action on simple and straightforward humanitarian grounds, the idea goes, shouldn't we concentrate on putting into place the appropriate aid policies, rather than allow ourselves to get sidetracked into fruitless wrangles about justice? In this context it is often said that the demands made by the countries of the South are "symbolic" or "ideological" and have the effect only of making more difficult the real, practical task of negotiating actual concessions by the countries of the North. The question that seems to me of more import is the following: If an obligation of humanity is accepted, under whatever name, how much difference does it make whether or not the kinds of claims I have been discussing under the heading of "justice" are also conceded?

Rights and goals

The answer is, I believe, that it makes a great deal of difference. Putting it in the most abstract terms, the obligations of humanity are goal-based, whereas those of justice are rights-based.[24] I would once have expressed the distinction between humanity and justice as one between an aggregative principle and a distributive principle.[25] I now, however, regard that distinction as less fundamental than the one I wish to mark by talking of goal-based and rights-based obligations. The point is that humanity and justice are not simply alternative prescriptions with respect to the same thing. Rather, they have different subject matters.

Humanity, understood as a principle that directs us not to cause suffering and to relieve it where it occurs, is a leading member of a family of principles concerned with what happens to people (and other sentient creatures) – with what I shall call their well-being, intending to include in this such notions as welfare, happiness, self-fulfillment, freedom from malnutrition and disease, and satisfaction of basic needs. Justice, by contrast, is not directly concerned with such matters at all. As well as principles that tell us what are good and bad states of affairs and what responsibilities we have to foster the one and to avert the other, we also have principles that tell us how control over resources should be allocated. If we understand "resources" in a very wide sense, so that it includes all kinds of rights to act without interference from others, to constrain the actions of others, and to bring about changes in the nonhuman environment, then we can say that the subject matter of justice (at any rate, in modern usage) is the distribution of control over material resources. At this high level of generality, it is complemented by the principle of equal liberty, which is concerned with the control over nonmaterial resources. To put it in a slogan, which has the advantages as well as the disadvantages of any slogan, humanity is a question of doing good; justice is a question of power.

When the contrast is stated in those terms, it might seem that bothering about justice is indeed a waste of time and that the bluff Anglo-Saxon advocates of commonsensical utilitarianism have the best of it after all. Why, it may naturally be asked, should we care about the distribution of *stuff* as against the distribution of *welfare*? Isn't this simply commodity fetishism in a new guise?

The easy but inadequate answer is that the concept of justice is, of course, concerned not only with old stuff but the kind of stuff that has the capacity to provide those who use it with the material means of well-being: food, housing, clothing, medical care, and so on. This is correct as far as it goes and shows that being concerned with

justice is not irrational. But it is inadequate because it leaves the supporter of justice open to an obvious flanking movement. His opponent may reply: "You say that the only reason for concern about the distribution of the things whose proper allocation constitutes the subject matter of justice is that they are the means to well-being. Very well. But are you not then in effect conceding that your 'deep theory' is goal-based? For what you are saying is that we really are ultimately concerned with the distribution of well-being. We simply take an interest in the distribution of the means of well-being because they are what we can actually allocate. But this means that justice is a derivative principle."

There are two lines of response open at this point. One is to concede that criteria for the distribution of resources are ultimately to be referred to the goal of well-being, but at the same time to deny that it follows from that concession that we can cut out the middleman (or put in the Michelman) and set out our principles for the allocation of resources with an eye directly on the well-being they are likely to produce. Or, more precisely, we may say that among the constituents of well-being is autonomy, and autonomy includes the power to choose frivolously or imprudently. Thus, on one (admittedly controversial) interpretation, Mill's talk of justice in Book V of *Utilitarianism* and his presentation of the "simple principle" of *On Liberty* in terms of rights is all consistent with an underlying utilitarian commitment if we allow for the importance to people of being able to plan their own lives and make their own decisions.

I think that this is by no means an unreasonable view and has more to be said for it than is, perhaps, fashionable to admit. Anyone who wishes at all costs to hold up a monistic ethical position is, I suspect, almost bound to finish up by trying to make some such argument as this. But I think that it is, nevertheless, in the last analysis a heroic attempt to fudge the issue by using the concept of autonomy to smuggle a basically foreign idea into the goal-based notion of advancing well-being.

The alternative is to deny that, in conceding that control over resources is important only because of the connection between resources and well-being, one is thereby committed to the view that principles for the distribution of resources are derivative. According to this view, there simply are two separate kinds of question. One concerns the deployment of resources to promote happiness and reduce misery. The other concerns the ethically defensible basis for allocating control over resources. Neither is reducible, even circuitously, to the other. When they conflict, we get hard questions, such as those involved in the whole issue of paternalism. But there is no overarching criterion within which such conflicts can be solved, as is offered (at least in principle) by the idea that autonomy is an important, but not the only, ingredient in well-being.

As may be gathered, this is the position that I hold. In what follows, I want to show what difference it makes to employ an independent principle of justice in considering issues of international distribution. To make the discussion as clear as possible, I shall draw my contrast with a principle of humanity understood in the kind of pretty straightforward way exemplified in Section 1 of this chapter. The contrast would be softened the more weight we were to give to autonomy as a component in well-being. Note, however, that even those who might wish to emphasize the importance of individual autonomy are likely to doubt the value to individual well-being of autonomy for states; yet it is precisely the question of autonomy for states that is going to turn out to be the main dividing line between humanity and justice at the international level.

International applications

The point is one of control. The rich countries already mostly concede, at least in verbal declarations, that they have a humanitarian obligation to assist the poor countries economically. The importance to the future of the world of their beginning to live up to those declarations can scarcely be overestimated. I trust that nothing in this chapter will be taken as disparaging humanitarian aid. To the extent that it does in fact relieve problems of poverty, disease, malnutrition, and population growth it is, obviously, of enormous value.

But to see its limitations, let us be really utopian about humanitarian aid. Let us imagine that it is collected on a regular and automatic basis from rich countries according to some formula that more or less reflects ability to pay; for example, a shadow tax on GNP graduated by the level of GNP per capita. And suppose that the proceeds were pooled and dispersed through agencies of the United Nations, according to general criteria for entitlement to assistance.

Now, undoubtedly such a world would be an immense improvement over the present one, just as the modern welfare state has transformed, say, Henry Mayhew's London. But it would still have the division between the donor countries, free to spend "their" incomes as they pleased and the recipient countries, which would have to spend their incomes "responsibly." No doubt, this would be less objectionable if the criteria were drawn up in partnership between donor and recipient countries rather than, as now, being laid down by bodies such as the IMF and the World Bank in whose governing councils the rich countries have a preponderant voice. But funds earmarked and conditional upon approved use would still be basically different from income of the usual kind.

In contrast, transfers that were consequential upon considerations of justice would simply reduce the resources of one set of countries and augment those of another set. The distribution of control of resources would actually be shifted. It is therefore easy to see that the question of justice in the relations between rich and poor countries is by no means a purely "symbolic" one. Real issues are at stake, and it is no self-delusion that leads the poor countries to press for a recognition of the claims of justice and the rich countries to resist.

The conclusion we have reached, then, is that the crucial characteristic of justice is that the obligation to make the transfers required by it does not depend upon the use made of them by the recipient. At this point, I find that the following kinds of objection are usually made: What if the recipient country wastes the resources transferred to it? What if it is going to spend the money on armaments? What if it has a very unequal distribution of income and the additional income will be divided in the same unequal way? Such objections illustrate how difficult it is to get across the idea that if some share of resources is justly owed to a country, then it is (even before it has been actually transferred) as much that country's as it is now normally thought that what a country produces belongs to that country.

The answer that I give is that there are extreme circumstances in which the international community or some particular donor country would be justified in withholding resources owed as a matter of justice to some country. But these are exactly the same extreme conditions under which it would also be justifiable to refuse to pay debts to it or to freeze its assets overseas.

One could envisage a world in which there were indeed an international authority that allowed countries to keep only that income that would be justly distributed internally and used in approved, nonwasteful ways. Such a world would not be at all like ours, since it would accept no principle of national autonomy. It would be a world in which a presently nonexisting world society had inscribed on its banner: "From each according to his ability, to each according to his needs."

The alternative is a world in which the general presumption is of national autonomy, with countries being treated as units capable of determining the use of those resources to which they were justly entitled. This is the world that we now have, and the only modification in the status quo I am arguing for is a redefinition of what justly belongs to a country. It inevitably, as the price of autonomy, permits countries to use their resources in wasteful ways ("theirs," on my interpretation, being of course those in their own territories plus or minus transfers required by justice) and does not insist that a country that allows some to live in luxury while others have basic needs unfulfilled should lose income to which it is entitled as a matter of justice.

My point is that both of the models I have sketched are internally consistent. We could have a system in which there are no entitlements based on justice and in which, assuming that states are still the administrative intermediaries, funds are allocated for worthy purposes and cut off if they are misspent, just as in the United States the federal government cuts off funds to state and local governments that do not comply with various guidelines. Or we could have a world in which, once the demands of just distribution between countries are satisfied, we say that we have justice at the world level, and the question of domestic distribution and national priorities then becomes one for each country to decide for itself.

What is not consistent is to have a world in which those countries that are required by international justice to be donors live under the second system while those that are recipients live under the stern dispensation of the first. If the idea is going to be that countries should have their entitlements reduced if they are wasteful and fail in internal equity, then the obvious place to start is not with some poor country in sub-Saharan Africa or South Asia but with, say, a country that burns one ninth of the world's daily oil consumption on its roads alone and that, in spite of having a quarter of the world's GNP, is unable to provide for much of its population decent medical care, while a substantial proportion live in material conditions of abject squalor that (except for being more dirty and dangerous) recall the cities of Germany and Britain in the aftermath of World War II.

None of this, of course, denies the independent significance of humanity as a criterion in international morality. But we cannot sensibly talk about humanity unless we have a baseline set by justice. To talk about what I ought, as a matter of humanity, to do with what is mine makes no sense until we have established what is mine in the first place. If I have stolen what is rightfully somebody else's property, or if I have borrowed from him and refuse to repay the debt when it is due, and as a result he is destitute, it would be unbecoming on my part to dole out some part of the money that should belong to him, with various strings attached as to the way in which he should spend it, and then go around posing as a great humanitarian. That is, in my judgment, an exact description of the position in which the rich countries have currently placed themselves.

The need for humanitarian aid would be reduced in a world that had a basically just international distribution. It would be required still to meet special problems caused by crop failure owing to drought, destruction owing to floods and earthquakes, and similar losses resulting from other natural disasters. It would also, unhappily, continue to be required to cope with the massive refugee problems that periodically arise from political upheavals.

Beyond that, humanitarian aid in the form of food, technical assistance, or plain money is always a good thing, of course. How much the rich countries would be obliged to give depends first on the extent of redistribution we hold to be required by justice and, second, on the stringency that we assign to the obligation of humanity – how much sacrifice can be demanded to deal with what level of need.

As will be clear, this chapter is concerned only with a preliminary investigation of the principles relevant to an ethical appraisal of international distribution and redistribution. I must therefore leave any more precise statement of implications for future discussions – and not necessarily by me. Ultimately, if anything is to be done, it will require a widespread shift in ideas. Greater precision can be expected to develop *pari passu* with such a shift. I very much doubt the value of single-handed attempts to produce a blueprint in advance of that.

Notes

1   *Oxford English Dictionary*, sub. Humanity, 3b. In the light of the central example to be discussed below, it is interesting to note that the title of a society founded in England for the rescuing of drowning persons in 1774 was the Humane Society (*OED*, sub. Humane, 1c).

2   1 *Philosophy & Public Affairs*, 229–43 (1972). See, for a briefer and more recent statement of the same basic case, Peter Singer, *Practical Ethics* (Cambridge: Cambridge University Press, 1979), ch. 8, pp. 158–81.

3   Ibid., p. 231.

4   Ibid.

5   Ibid.

6   Ibid.

7   Ibid.

8   C.D. Broad, "On the Function of False Hypotheses in Ethics," 26 *International Journal of Ethics* 377–97, at 389–90 (1916).

9   John Passmore, "Civil Justice and Its Rivals," in Eugene Kamenka and Alice Erh-Soon Tay, *Justice* (London: Edward Arnold, 1979) pp. 25–49, at 47 [italics in original].

10 For a sustained argument along these lines, see T.D. Campbell, "Humanity before Justice," 4 *British Journal of Political Science* 1–16 (1974).

11 Henry Sidgwick, *The Methods of Ethics* (London: Macmillan, 1907), p. 273.

12 Constantine V. Vaitsos, *Intercountry Income Distribution and Transnational Enterprises* (Oxford: Clarendon Press, 1974), esp. ch. 4.

13 See for an elaboration of these remarks "And Who Is My Neighbor?" 88 *Yale L. J.* 629–58 (1979).

14 Adam Smith expressed this view: "As a man doth, so it shall be done to him, and retaliation seems to be the great law which is dictated to us by nature. Beneficence and generosity we think due to the generous and beneficent. Those whose hearts never open to the feelings of humanity should, we think, be shut out in the same manner, from the affections of all their fellow-creatures, and be allowed to live in the midst of society, as in a great desert, where there is nobody to care for them, or to enquire after them." Adam Smith, *The Theory of Moral Sentiments* (Indianapolis: Liberty Classics, n.d.), p. 160.

15 Princeton, N.J.: Princeton University Press, 1979. The part of the book in question was first published in substantially the same form as "Justice and International Relations," 4 *Philosophy & Public Affairs* 360–89 (1975).

16 *The Liberal Theory of Justice* (Oxford: Clarendon Press, 1973), ch. 12.

17 H.L.A. Hart, "Are There Any Natural Rights?" 64 *Philosophical Review* 175–91 (1955). [Reprinted as chapter 18 of this volume.]

18 See my extended review in 12 *Theory and Decision*, 95–106 (1980).

19 Hillel Steiner, "The Natural Right to the Means of Production," 27 *The Philosophical Quarterly* 41–49, at 44–45 (1977). The reference to Nozick is to *Anarchy, State, and Utopia* (New York: Basic Books, 1974), p. 154.

20 Bruce A. Ackerman, *Social Justice in the Liberal State* (New Haven: Yale University Press, 1980), p. 38.

21 Oscar Schachter, *Sharing the World's Resources* (New York: Columbia University Press, 1977), p. 124, references n, 52, p. 159.

22 David Hume, *An Enquiry Concerning the Principles of Morals*, 3rd ed. (Oxford: Clarendon Press, 1975), pp. 193–4.

23 Eleanor B. Steinberg and Joseph Y. Yager, eds., *New Means of Financing International Needs* (Washington, D.C.: The Brookings Institution, 1978), ch. 3.

24 For a distinction stated in these terms see Ronald Dworkin, "The Original Position," 4 *Chi. L. Rev.*, 500–33 (1973), reprinted in Norman Daniels, ed., *Reading Rawls* (Oxford: Basil Blackwell, 1975) pp. 16–53. The relevant discussion is on pp. 38–40 of this reprint.

25 *Political Argument* (London: Routledge & Kegan Paul, 1965), pp. 43–4.

Index

Note: Numbers in **bold** refer to chapters written by named author

Index